## CONTENTS

## ACKNOWLEDGMENTS

Deepest gratitude is expressed for the assistance of my friend, the late Caroline Underwood, for her insistent and thorough research in London, and to those offices and individuals who aided her efforts, especially the British Film Institute. Also to Richard Trupp for his hours in the library, as well as those successful efforts to track down elusive issues in New York offices.

Cooperation through correspondence and provision of important material helped fill many research source gaps. With gratitude those contributors are acknowledged: After Dark, Afterimage, American Film Institute, Black Oracle, Brighton Film Review, Castle of Frankenstein, Cinema (BH), Cinema Journal, Contempora, CTVD, Film Comment, Film Fan Monthly, Film Heritage, The Film Journal, Film Library Quarterly, Filmmaker's Newsletter, Filmograph, Films and Filming, Films In Review, For Monsters Only, Funnyworld, Gallery, Game, Gore Creatures, Interview, Oui, Making Films in New York, MS, Penthouse, People, Playgirl, Show, Sightlines, Take One, Today's Filmmaker, TV Guide and Viva. A special note of thanks for the unusual generosity of Jon Tuska, Editor of Views and Reviews (recently changed to Close-Up, views and reviews of the popular arts), and P. M. Evanchuck, Editor/Publisher of Motion.

The run of Classic Film Collector (including 8mm Collector) was effected through the above-and-beyond efforts of Robert F. Gray whose private collection was supplemented by the publication's office.

Ernest D. Burns, proprietor of Cinemabilia, made some material available which might otherwise have been improbable.

A warm thank you to friends Ralph Gutman, Bob Lehrer, Richard Jackson and Don Madison who each contributed in a unique way to an atmosphere of ease and encouragement during the course of this work.

And finally, a usual, but no less enthusiastic thanks to the staffs of both the research and circulation departments at the Lincoln Center Library in New York City, for their patience and helpfulness. Of particular assistance on this project were David Bartholomew, Rod Bladel and Monty Arnold, but it is reassuring to a New York researcher to know that any of the staff would have been equally willing. A special note of gratitude is reserved for all those pages who uncomplainingly search, deliver and refile all those obscure and delinquent issues.

Mel Schuster
New York City
January 16, 1975

# INTRODUCTION

The basic volume of this bibliography, published in 1971, examined material on 2,900 performers appearing in selected periodicals from 1900 through 1969. This First Supplement deepens the scope of the basic work in the following ways:

1. All research sources consulted in the first volume are updated through 1974; research sources were applied to all performers appearing in the basic volume.

2. Material on 2,600 additional performers is now represented, bringing the total to 5,500. Because of the vastness of the project, the original volume was limited to a selected performer list. Response pointed out inevitable omissions, as well as some minor misunderstandings of the scope; e.g., "If you went through (TV Guide) (Photoplay), why did you find nothing on (Carol Burnett) (Jackie Gleason) (Irene Ryan)?" Such questions resulted in another trip through a number of publications, with doors thrown open to all comers. Motion Picture Performers thus becomes somewhat a misnomer in that a guide is now offered to material on many performers whose involvement with the motion picture medium is very limited or even nonexistent.

In addition to expanding in this less-structured direction because of user request, it also was invited by the fact that many performers who were intentionally omitted on the grounds of other-medium primacy are now enjoying a film career. The quickness with which performers change and interchange media results in immediate out-datedness if they are not included.

A third and obvious reason for new subject entries is new performers. This is no small consideration since the independent-oriented industry frequently results in a quick rise (and sometimes fall) of performers.

3.  Complete runs of many additional magazines are included. These new sources include:

  a.  Film and general magazines started since completion of the first volume.

  b.  Film magazines unavailable for inclusion in the first volume.

  c.  Several publications not documented in major bibliographies (Readers' Guide, Biography Index) but which offer feature interviews and profiles. These include such publications as MS, People, New York, Cue, Show, After Dark, as well as the voluptuous offerings of Playboy, Playgirl, Penthouse, Viva, Gallery, Game, etc.

4.  A major bibliographic source has been incorporated into this work: Cumulated Dramatic Index 1909-1949: a cumulation of the F. W. Faxon Company's Dramatic Index, published in 1965 by G. K. Hall & Co. of Boston, Mass.

This vast 2,000+ page publication is not readily available in most libraries and is out of financial reach of most individuals. Thus, pertinent data has been abstracted for convenience and accessibility to users of this Supplement. Much of the Dramatic Index is coverage of fan magazines, but it should again be stated that (roughly) pre-1930 magazines did not devote much space to cinema. The fan magazines were thus the most important, and frequently only, sources of information about film people.

The inclusion of pertinent material from the Dramatic Index counteracts the strong emphasis on the sound-to-current period of cinema history in the first volume of this work.

5.  A large number of missing issues of runs of magazines have been located and are herein documented. The effort entailed much correspondence, trips to publishers' offices and a week's research in London.

6.  The original decision to downgrade fan magazines was applauded and criticized. In an effort to find a middle road, one major fan magazine has been added in this Supplement: Silver Screen. It should be noted, however, that only the collection at

New York's Lincoln Center Library was consulted. Barring a few missing issues, they own the run of Silver Screen from its inception through 1956. In this isolated case, no further effort was made to go beyond the scope offered by the Lincoln Center Library.

Since this work is intended to be used in conjunction with the basic volume, it is not necessary to restate structure and aims. Nevertheless, a few observations should be made concerning slight differences in this volume:

a. Concentrated effort was made to obviate any repeat of citations. It is highly probable there are some repeats, nevertheless.

b. Runs of some magazines covered in the first volume suffered missing issues here and there. Efforts to locate those missing issues have been largely successful and are herein documented. However, completeness of coverage is still not 100 per cent in every case, but most magazines covered in the two volumes are totally represented.

c. Although newspapers remain outside the scope of this work, personal reading and a "clipping service" provided by friends have resulted in frequent citations to newspaper articles.

d. Performers equally well known in other areas (e.g., politics, sports, music) frequently have much written about their "other careers." Many of these "other career" citations are omitted, and are so noted throughout the book.

It is important to note that this volume goes far beyond the boundaries of the original volume. Although the first volume was closely aligned to the availability of material in the New York libraries, New York researchers should be warned that much of the material referred to in this volume is not available in those vast deposits of words. A cinema-oriented shop, a magazine publisher, or perhaps a library in another city may have to be consulted.

# A QUICK GUIDE TO USING THIS VOLUME

1. Entries are arranged alphabetically.
2. Citations within entries are arranged by date.
3. Information given in the citations varies, but is as thorough as possible:
   a. Author's name.
   b. Article title.
   c. Publication.
   d. Volume Number.
   e. Issue Number.
   f. Page Number.
   g. Date.
4. Cross references are minimal, but do occur when adjudged helpful or necessary.
5. A key to abbreviations used frequently is found in Appendix I.
6. Abbreviations for publications are assumed self-explanatory by consulting the list of publications researched--Appendix II.

## SPECIAL NOTE

In abstracting citations from other bibliographies, it is always possible to continue an error as well as add new ones. Readers are invited to make known any incorrect citations, allowing for correction in future supplements. Advice as to omissions, oversights, constructive criticism and suggestions for future improvement are invited.

# BIBLIOGRAPHY OF PERFORMERS

AAKER, LEE
   Readin' ritin' and rehearsal.   TV Guide 4-38:20 S 22 '56

ABASCAL, NATIVIDAD
   O'Brien, G.   Interview.   Interview 2-5:13 Ag '71

ABBE, JOHN, PATIENCE & RICHARD
   How we feel about becoming movie stars.   Photop 50:32 O '36
   Seeing Hollywood with the Abbes.   Cosmop 103:48 O '37

ABBOTT, BUD
   Reid, J.   Still up to their old tricks.   Silver S. 12-2:34 D '41
   I'm Abbott.   Lions R. 1-8:no p# D '44
   Eddy, D.   Story of.   Am Mag 135:42 Ja '43
   Wilson, E.   Meet the box-office champs.   Silver S. 13-6:34 Ap
      '43
   He's a b-a-a-d boy!   Lions R 3-5:no p# D '44
   Comedians.   Screen Greats 1-2:62 Sum '71
   Peary, D.   Top comics of the forties.   Velvet Light 5:30 Sum
      '72
   Obit.   Classic Film Collect 43:X6 Sum '74
      N.Y. Times Bio Ed p467 Ap '74
      N.Y. Post p3 Ap 24 '74

ABBOTT, DOROTHY
   She goes for cops.   TV Guide 2-36:20 S 4 '54

ABEL, WALTER
   Spensley, D.   Interview.   Motion Pic 52:43 D '36
   Hoaglin, J.   Down memory lane.   Hollywood Stu 7-7:19 N '72

ABERG, SIVI
   Raddatz, L.   They always cast her as a pretty girl.   TV Guide
      17-39:29 S 27 '69

ABSHIRE, THOMAS
   Playwrights in residence.   Time 98:43 Jl 26 '71

ACKER, SHARON
   Whitney, D.   The senator needed a wife.   TV Guide 19-18:40
      My 1 '71

ACORD, ART
   Ashburn, S.   Sketch.   Motion Pic Classic 33:36 Jl '31
   Phillips, A. Western real-life tragedian.   8mm Collect 14:11
      Spg '66
   Everett, E. K.   The tragic cowpuncher.   Classic Film Collect
      44:43 Fall '74

ACQUANETTA, BURNU
   Venezuelan volcano.   Life 13:57 Ag 24 '42

ACTMAN, JANE
   Adler, D.   She awoke one day to find herself famous.   TV Guide
      21-18:16 My 5 '73

ADAM, NOËLLE
   La belle mademoiselle Noelle.   Life 44:87 Je 9 '58
   A flash on...   Unifrance 48:10 O '58
   No skirt.   Time 79:61 Mr. 30 '62

ADAMS, CLAIRE
   Goldberg, W.   Interview.   Motion Pic Classic 11:26 D '20
   Lake, J. M.   Interview.   Motion Pic Classic 14:50 My '22

ADAMS, DON
   On the scene.   Playboy 12-9:187 S '65
   A secret agent should be stupid and funny.   TV Guide 13-40:14
      O 2 '65
   Smith, G.   Would you believe Don Adams?   Sat Eve Post 239:32
      Je 4 '66
   Hobson, D.   The one-and-a-half-sewer man grows up.   TV
      Guide 15-25:20 Je 24 '67
   Hano, A.   Comic with a killer instinct.   TV Guide 19-46:32 N
      13 '71

ADAMS, EDIE
   Minoff, P.   Edie's quite a lady.   Cue 22-14:14 Ap 4 '53

ADAMS, JOEY
   Salute of the week.   Cue 39-48:1 N 28 '70

ADAMS, JULIE
   Kasindorf, J.   It took 19 years to get to the altar.   TV Guide
      20-14:16 Ap 1 '72

ADAMS, KATHRYN
   Obit.   Screen World 11:215 '60

ADAMS, NEILE
   Manila, Hong Kong and Wall Street.   TV Guide 8-19:21 My 7 '60
   Romance.   Photop 82-6:41 D '72

ADAMS, NICK
   Obit.   N. Y. Times p49 F 8 '68

Newsweek 71:81 F 19 '68
Hair-raising stories from the stars.    Photop 78-1:62 Jl '70
Pitts, M.   The rebel; filmog.   Classic Film Collect 38:26 Spg
  '73

ADAMS, STANLEY
  A breed apart.   TV Guide 11-26:19 Je 29 '63

ADLER, LUTHER
  Luther Adler talks of common ground.   Cue 14-17:9 Ap 28 '45

ADOREE, RENEE
  Dilke, E.   Recollection of.   Fortnightly R 108:165 Jl '20
  Goldbeck, W.   Sketch.   Motion Pic Classic 12:56 My '21
  Sketch.   Photop 19:60 My '21
  Carr, H.   Sketch.   Classic 18:39 S '23
  Donnell, D.   Interview.   Motion Pic Classic 22:32 O '25
  White, C.   Sketch.   Motion Pic Classic 23:38 Ap '26
  Wilson, H.   Sketch.   Photop 30:62 Je '26
  Stare, R.   Sketch.   Motion Pic 32:53 Ag '26
  York, C.   Sketch.   Photop 30:84 N '26
  Paton, C.   Sketch.   Motion Pic Classic 24:58 D '26
  Moak, B.   The girl who loved laughter.   Silver S. 1-7:19 My '31
  Dibble, S.   Will resume her career.   Movie Classic 2:29 Je '32
  Albert, K.   Her story.   Cosmop 94:54 Je '33

ADRIAN, IRIS
  Maltin, L.   Iris Adrian; filmog.   Film Fan Mo. 131:11 My '72
  Crivello, K.   Adrian and Martin...best of the tough dames.
    Film Collect Reg 4-3:5 My/Je '72

ADRIAN, MAX
  Bio. note.   Ill Lon N 211:524 N 8 '47
  GBS; one man show.   Newsweek 70:115 O 23 '67
  TRW dishes up a bit of GBS.   Bsns W p.36 N 2 '68
  TRW sponsors free performances at colleges.   Newsweek 72:99 N
    18 '68
  Obit.   N.Y. Times p61 Ja 21 '73
    Same.   N.Y. Times Bio Ed pl Ja '73
    Screen World p231 '74
  In memory of...   Show 3-2:66 Ap '73

AEMS, AGATHE
  They didn't plan to be movie stars.   Unifrance 56: no p# Spg '62

AGAR, JOHN
  Parsons, L.   Cosmopolitan's citation for best supporting actor.
    Cosmop 124:13 Ap '48
  Maddox, B.   His plans for a new future.   Silver S. 21-8:44 Je
    '51

AGUTTER, JENNY
  Jenny.   Films Illus 1-4:11 O '71

Filmog.   Films Illus 1-4:26 O '71
Miller, E.   Interview.   Seventeen 30:62 N '71
Filmog.   Film Dope 1:6 D '72

AHEARNE, TOM
Obit.   Screen World 21:233 '70

AHERNE, BRIAN
Vandour, C.   Interview.   Motion Pic 54:46 N '37
His wedding.   Life 7:78 S 11 '39
Bio note; filmog.   Movies & People 2:3 '40
Sketch.   Photop 22:67 Mr '43
What a man.   Cue 12-52:10 D 25 '43
Kaufman, S.   Brian is back.   Silver S 15-10:44 Ag '45

AHERNE, PATRICK
Obit.   Screen World 22:235 '71

AHN, PHILIP
Raddatz, L.   No. 1 son is now Master Po.   TV Guide 21-25:27
Je 23 '73

AIMÉE, ANOUK
Bio note.   Unifrance 45:9 D '57
Sketch.   Take One 1-1:28 S/O '66
Durham, M.   ... it means to be loved.   Life 62:85 My 19 '67
Fellini talks about the face of...   Vogue 150:160 O 1 '67
West, A.   Grande amourence.   Vogue 152:174 O 1 '68
African idyll.   Harp Baz 102:184 Ap '69
Filmog.   Film Dope 1:7 D '72

AITKEN, SPOTTISWOODE
Delvigne, D.   Interview.   Motion Pic 19:64 Ap/My '20

AKIN, MARY
Sursa, H.   Interview.   Motion Pic 31:121 Mr '27

AKINS, CLAUDE
Edelman, R.   What gear am I in?   TV Guide 22-50:9 D 14 '74

ALBERGHETTI, ANNA MARIA
Rising stars.   Film R p113 '53/54
Happy in the rain.   Life 37:65 Ag 30 '54

ALBERONI, SHERRY
Versatile Sherry Alberoni.   TV Guide 12-50:26 D 12 '64

ALBERS, HANS
Lundquist, G.   Hans Albers; filmog.   Films In R 16-3:150 Mr
'65
Letters.   Films In R 16-4:260 Ap '65

ALBERT, EDDIE
  Sketch.   Photop 53:68 Mr '39
  Love, E.   Absent minded Eddie.   Silver S 10-10:38 Ag '40
  Lindsay, M.   Sketch.   Photop 18:30 Ja '41
  Minoff, P.   Notes on TV.   Cue 22-31:15 Ag 1 '53
  Minoff, P.   A talk with...   Cue 23-24:15 Je 12 '54
  Whitney, D.   Green acres are a matter of life and death.   TV
    Guide 18-35:16 Ag 29 '70

ALBERT, EDWARD
  Manners, D.   I nominate for stardom.   Mod Screen 66-6:18 Je
    '72
  Miller, E.   Masculine mystique.   Seventeen 31:88 Jl '72
  Ronan, M.   ... in his own right.   Sr Schol 101:28 N 27 '72
  Strout, D.   Interview.   Mod Screen 66-11:28 N '72
  Sketch.   Movie Dig 1-6:32 N '72
  Flatley, G.   Eddie Albert's boy and how he grew.   N. Y. Times
    sec 2:11 D 3 '72
    Same.   N. Y. Times Bio Ed p2094 D '72
  Sketch.   Films Illus 3-28:154 O '73
  My father gave me freedom, and I took it.   Photop 84-5:39 N '73

ALBERTSON, ARTHUR
  Courtlandt, R.   Sketch.   Motion Pic 11:36 Jl '16

ALBERTSON, FRANK
  Sketch.   Photop 37:52 Mr '30
  York, C.   Sketch.   Photop 38:69 N '30
  Fender, R.   Sketch.   Motion Pic Classic 33:73 My '31
  Gray, B.   Character actor.   Films In R 15-4:254 Ap '64

ALBERTSON, JACK
  Gussow, M.   Stars share espirit of Sunshine boys.   N. Y. Times
    Bio Ed p2096 D '72
  Berkvist, R.   Jack spreads a little sunshine.   N. Y. Times sec
    2:1 Ja 7 '73
    Same.   N. Y. Times Bio Ed pl Ja '73
  Eyles, A.   Bio sketch; filmog.   Focus On Film 8:10 n. d.
  Barber, R.   The happy hoofer.   TV Guide 22-42:24 O 19 '74

ALBERTSON, MABEL
  Raker, A.   Letter; filmog.   Films In R 19-8:521 O '68

ALBRIGHT, HARDIE
  Sketch.   Photop 40:80 N '31

ALBRIGHT, LOLA
  Silke, J. R.   Interview.   Cinema(BH) 1-3:16 '63
  Filmog.   Film Dope 1:8 D '72

ALDA, ALAN
  Lochte, D.   He falls down a lot.   TV Guide 21-8:20 F 24 '73
  Berkvist, R.   *M*A*S*H is his P*A*S*S*I*O*N.   N. Y. Times

sec 2:19 My 19 '74
Same.  N. Y. Times Bio Ed p637 My '74
Last season's Emmy-winning actor is writing for TV, too.  Cue
  43-32:4 Ag 19 '74

ALDA, ROBERT
  Lane, L.  The great unknown.  Silver S 17-3:53 Ja '47
  Minoff, P.  Alda plays it straight.  Cue 20-14:14 Ap 7 '51

ALDEN, MARY
  Sketch.  Motion Pic 10:116 N '15
  Art for art's sake didn't appeal to her.  Photop 11-6:49 My '17
  St. John, A. R.  The ages of Mary.  Photop 16-2:89 Jl '19
  Notice of.  Motion Pic Classic 8:36 Ag '19
  Shelby, H.  Interview.  Motion Pic Classic 13:46 D '21
  Her darkest hour.  Classic 15:58 Ja '23
  Service, F.  Sketch.  Classic 16:40 Ag '23
  Franchey, J. R.  She stooped to conquer.  Silver S 14-1:40 N
    '43
  Holland, J.  How to catch a man.  Silver S 16-2:24 D '45

ALDRIDGE, KATHARINE
  Crichton, K.  Story of.  Colliers 110:13 O 24 '42
  The perils of...  Cue 12-27:10 Jl 3 '43
  Queen of the daredevils.  Scholastic 43:31 N 15 '43
  Sheridan, A.  Story of.  Cosmop 115:6 N '43
  Vallee, W. L.  New queen of the serials.  Silver S 14-3:42 Ja
    '44

ALEXANDER, BEN
  St. Johns, I.  Interview.  Photop 26:76 Ag '24
  Home of.  Motion Pic Classic 21:34 Ap '25
  Hall, G.  Sketch.  Motion Pic Classic 32:33 S '30
  Friday's man Friday.  TV Guide 2-18:5 Ap 30 '54
  Obit.  British Book Yr 1970:578 '70
    Classic Film Collect 24:14 Sum '69
    Screen World 21:233 '70

ALEXANDER, DENISE
  Raddatz, L.  She prescribes for six million housewives.  TV
    Guide 21-30:16 Jl 28 '73

ALEXANDER, JANE
  Childs, C.  Jane Alexander.  Show 1-8:29 Jl 9 '70
  Berg, B.  Mischief becomes her, too.  N. Y. Times Bio Ed Jl
    25 '71

ALEXANDER, JOAN
  In the cast.  TV Guide 1-1:22 Ap 3 '53

ALEXANDER, MILLETTE
  Jobin, J.  This lady has a 17-room house, 4 children, 6 dogs, 7
    cats and a soap-opera career too.  TV Guide 17-41:18 O 11 '69

ALEXANDER, NICHOLAS BENTON III
  Notice.  Motion Pic Classic 8:34 Ag '19

ALEXANDER, ROSS
  Sketch.  Photop 47:104 F '35
  Spensley, D.  Sketch.  Motion Pic 53:38 F '37

ALLAN, ELIZABETH
  Hall, G.  Interview.  Movie Classic 8:40 Mr '35
  Sketch.  Photop 49:82 My '36
  Roberts, F.  Interview.  Theatre World 28:86 Ag '37

ALLBRITTON, LOUISE
  Franchey, J. R.  She stooped to conquer.  Silver S 14-1:40 N
    '43
  Holland, J.  How to catch a man.  Silver S 16-2:24 D '45
  About sociability.  Photop 28:62 Mr '46

ALLEN, ALTA
  Goldbeck, W.  Interview.  Motion Pic Classic 12:63 My '21

ALLEN, BARBARA JO
  (see: VAGUE, VERA)

ALLEN, DIANA
  Paul, S.  Interview.  Motion Pic Classic 14:36 Ap '22

ALLEN, ELIZABETH
  And away she went.  TV Guide 13-5:10 Ja 30 '65

ALLEN, FRED
  How I got that way.  Theatre 50:31 Jl '29
  Kennedy, J. B.  Wisecracker.  Colliers 85:19 Je 7 '30
  Apology.  Time 35:44 F 5 '40
  Three decades.  Newsweek 15:42 Ap 29 '40
  Mason, A.  A friendship built on gags and insults.  Silver S 10-
    10:24 Jl '40
  Perennial comic.  Time 36:42 O 7 '40
  Mason, A.  The sentimental grouch.  Silver S 11-2:26 D '40
  Bryan, J. III.  Eighty hours for a laugh.  Sat Eve Post 214:22
    O 4 '41
  Biography.  Cur Bio '41
  Fred Allen cuts a slice of old vaudeville ham.  Life 12:28 Je 8
    '42
  Hutchens, J. K.  Comedians' comedian.  Theatre Arts 26:307
    My '42
  Mighty Allen no player.  Newsweek 22:66 D 27 '43
  The mighty Allen's airlane art.  Cue 13-18:11 Ap 29 '44
  Hirschfeld, A.  A grim success story.  N. Y. Times Mag p18
    Jl 2 '44
  Speaking of pictures.  Life 17:8 D 18 '44
  Hollywood is okay with...  Cue 14-1:10 Ja 6 '45
  Back in Allen's alley.  Newsweek 26:99 O 15 '45

Smith, B.  Want a job at a million a year?  Am Mag 140:24 D
    '45
    Same abbreviated with title Fred Allen marches on.  Read Dig
    48:35 Ja '46
Gargantua has the last laugh.  N. Y. Times Mag p14 Ap 1 '46
The age of Allen.  Cue 15-21:42 My 25 '46
Bah!  Time 48:66 O 21 '46
Perry, G. S.  Backstage in Allen's alley.  Sat Eve Post 219:14
    Ja 4 '47
World's worst juggler.  Time 49:71 Ap 7 '47
Curious Fred Allen affair.  Nation 164:503 My 3 '47
Little men who were there.  Newsweek 29:63 My 5 '47
Mr. Allen, Mr. Allen.  Newsweek 30:56 S 22 '47
Foal the drab.  Time 52:75 S 6 '48
Forever Allen.  Newsweek 32:46 S 6 '48
Mr. Allen regrets.  Time 52:51 D 13 '48
Juggler.  Colliers 123:58 Ja 29 '49
McCarthy, J.  What do you think of television, Mr. Allen?  Life
    27:69 Jl 4 '49
Minoff, P.  It's no joke.  Cue 19-37:16 S 16 '50
Back to the movies.  Time 56:48 O 2 '50
Perelman, S. J.  Great sourpuss.  Holiday 12:95 D '52
Ace, G.  New program titled Judge for yourself.  Sat R 36:26
    Ag 1 '53
It isn't Tonto, kiddies.  TV Guide 1-21:5 Ag 21 '53
Oh, Mr. Allen.  Newsweek 42:58 Ag 31 '53
Oldtimer.  Time 62:60 Ag 31 '53
Hamburger, P.  Judge for yourself.  New Yorker 29:74 S 5 '53
Minoff, P.  Notes on TV.  Cue 22-37:7 S 12 '53
Judge for yourself.  TV Guide 1-28:13 O 9 '53
Moderate life of a moderator.  Theatre Arts 37:24 O '53
Sniping in Allen's alley.  Newsweek 44:62 O 25 '54
Kalb, B.  Twin cornucopias of yak.  Sat R 37:32 N 6 '54
Cerf, B.  Trade winds.  Sat R 37:7 N 13 '54
Fadiman, C.  Party of one.  Holiday 16:6 D '54
Debus, A. G.  Current collectors' recordings; saxophone solo.
    Hobbies 60:24 S '55
Comedians' comedian.  Newsweek 47:62 Mr 26 '56
Obit.  Time 67:102 Mr 26 '56
    Wilson Lib Bull 30:669 My '56
Sad farewell to a very funny man.  Life 40:98 Ap 2 '56
Seldes, G.  Envying the dead.  Sat R 39:24 Ap 7 '56
Fred Allen's last interview.  TV Guide 4-16:5 Ap 21 '56
Excerpt from Much ado about me.  Life 41:72 N 12 '56
Cerf, B.  Trade winds.  Sat R 39:10 N 17 '56
Levin, M.  Juggler's progress.  Sat R 39:22 N 24 '56
Funny man's legacy.  Newsweek 48:103 D 3 '56
Sullivan's travels.  Time 68:63 D 31 '56
Getlein, F.  True comic insight into life.  Commonweal 65:364
    Ja 4 '57
Harkins, J.  Most unforgettable character I've met.  Read Dig
    75:129 N '59
Excerpts from his letters.  Esquire 63:64 Mr '65
Wallace, I.  Never without a gag.  Liberty 1-7:77 Win '72

ALLEN, GRACIE
    Hall, G.  Interview.  Movie Classic 6:56 My '34
    Hamilton, S.  Story of.  Photop 52:27 Ap '38
    Best, K.  Story of.  Stage 16:35 My 1 '39
    Allen, G.  Being Mrs. North is more exciting.  Lions R 1-5:no
        p# Ja '44
    One finger virtuoso.  Lions R 3-3(sup):no p# Ap '44
    Holiday in Hawaii.  TV Guide 1-26:10 S 25 '53
    Davies, D.  Filmog.  Films In R 16-1:57 Ja '65
    Letters; additional filmog.  Films In R 16-2:124 F '65


ALLEN, HUGH
    Pryor, N.  Sketch.  Motion Pic Classic 27:26 Je '28


ALLEN, JONELLE
    Interview.  New Yorker 47:28 F 12 '72
    Klemesrud, J.  Jonelle Allen is spelled s-e-x.  N. Y. Times Bio
        Ed F 27 '72
    Miller, E.  Interview.  Seventeen 31:36 Jl '72
    Sketch.  Movie Dig 1-6:27 N '72


ALLEN, JUDITH
    Sharon, M.  The girl who fooled the great De Mille.  Silver S
        4-2:25 D '33


ALLEN, LESTER
    Obit.  Screen World 1:233 '49


ALLEN, RAE
    Appelbaum, N.  Here's to the ladies who lunch.  After Dark 4-2:
        18 Je '71


ALLEN, SIAN BARBARA
    Richard Thomas is so easy to love.  Photop 83-6:72 Je '72
    Sex, drugs and God in our lives.  Photop 84-5:51 N '73


ALLEN, STEVE
    Big switch.  Newsweek 35:55 Je 12 '50
    Leisurely style.  Time 58:52 Jl 30 '51
    Biography.  Cur Bio Jl '51
    Allen, S.  Notes on TV.  Cue 20-31:20 Ag 4 '51
    Minoff, P.  Mirth before midnight.  Cue 22-38:14 S 19 '53
    Later than funnier.  Newsweek 42:64 O 12 '53
    In the cast.  TV Guide 1-29:12 O 16 '53
    No laughter please.  Time 62:83 N 23 '53
    The Steve Allen you don't know.  TV Guide 2-5:A-2 Ja 29 '54
    Frazier, G.  Intellectual night owl.  Cosmop 136:124 Ap '54
    Minoff, P.  Jester before midnight.  Cue 23-20:12 My 15 '54
    This is our line.  Theatre Arts 38:94 My '54
    Two heads are better than one.  TV Guide 2-34:15 Ag 21 '54
    Hamburger, P.  Television; tonight.  New Yorker 30:90 O 9 '54
    A third titan?  Newsweek 44:66 O 11 '54
    Shayon, R. L.  Reflections in the eighty-eight.  Sat R 37:40 N
        6 '54

Clown with a conscience.   Look 18:65 N 16 '54
Clock stopper.   Newsweek 44:60 N 29 '54
Millstein, G.   Portrait of an m.a.l.   N.Y. Times Mag p17 Ja
    9 '55
Hefner, K.   TV's ad glibber.   Playboy 2:11 My '55
Ten things that make my heart beat faster.   Good House 141:109
    S '55
Bergquist, L.   All about Steve.   Look 19:120 N 29 '55
Here's the real Goodman.   Colliers 137:29 Ja 20 '56
Benny is heard but not seen.   Life 40:56 F 13 '56
Down Allen's way.   Coronet 39:10 F '56
Seldes, G.   Envying the dead.   Sat R 39:24 Ap 7 '56
Minoff, P.   New mission for Steve.   Cue 25-24:17 Je 16 '56
Egomaniacs.   Time 67:84 Je 18 '56
The challenger!   TV Guide 4-25:17 Je 23 '56
Bester, A.   Backstage with...   Holiday 19:79 Je '56
Allen, S.   Sounding off against awards.   TV Guide 5-27:20 Jl 6
    '57
Week in review.   Time 68:40 Jl 9 '56
Allen, S.   On being a woman.   Cue 25-32:12 Ag 11 '56
Shayon, R. L.   Late and soon.   Sat R 39:42 O 6 '56
Jousting and jitters.   Newsweek 48:87 O 15 '56
Allen, S.   My wife Jayne.   TV Guide 4-48:28 D 1 '56
Author in the news.   Sat R 39:17 D 29 '56
Steve Allen's almanac.   Cosmop 140:18 My; 6 Je; 141:14 Jl; 10
    Ag; 8 S; 8 O; 8 N; 6 D '56; 142:12 Ja; 12 F '57
Philosophic lunacy.   Sat R 40:16 F 2 '57
TV's biggest battle.   Newsweek 49:71 Mr 18 '57
Steve Allen's almanac.   Cosmop 142:12 Mr '57
What dance means to me.   Dance 31:22 Je '57
Vanishing comedian.   Atlantic 200:115 D '57
High wind in Havana.   Time 71:64 F 3 '58
Meadows, J.   Seven men in my life.   Look 22:26 Mr 4 '58
Counterattack.   Time 71:42 Mr 31 '58
State of the nation's humor.   N.Y. Times Mag p27 D 7 '58
Most unusual autobiography.   Look 23:32 Mr 17; 52 Mr 31; 57
    Ap 14 '59
Shayon, R. L.   Serious side of...   Sat R 43:26 Ja 30 '60
Comedian with convictions.   TV Guide 8-19:17 My 7 '60
Excerpt from Mark it and strike it.   Sat R 43:14 Ag 20 '60
Brown, H.   Proteus in Hollywood.   Sat R 43:15 Ag 20 '60
How will it work?   America 104:756 Mr 11 '61
Hip comics and the new humor; discussion.   Playboy 8:35 Mr '61
Overlooked weapon.   America 105:148 Ap 15 '61
Steve's family frolic.   Life 50:65 Ap 28 '61
Allen a la carte.   Newsweek 58:46 Jl 24 '61
People on the way up.   Sat Eve Post 234:30 O 28 '61
Smith for Allen.   New Rep 146:8 Ja 29 '62
Liston, J.   Interview.   Am Home 65:6 Ap '62
Redbook dialogue.   Redbook 119:15 Je '62
Steverino.   Newsweek 60:70 Jl 9 '62
Interview.   New Yorker 38:45 N 10 '62
How to attack a liberal.   Nat R 14:149 F 26 '63

Amory, C.  Celebrity register.  McCalls 90:182 My '63
Gehman, R.  Summing up Steverino.  TV Guide 12-23:26 Je 6
    '64
Uses and abuses of the new leisure; discussion.  Playboy 12:51
    Mr '65
Hobson, D.  I am worried about mankind's rating.  TV Guide
    15-30:10 Jl 29 '67
Letters.  Esquire 73:73 Ja '69
Renz, M.  Interview.  Writers Dig 52:32 D '72

ALLEN, VALERIE
    A tempting dish.  TV Guide 9-6:29 F 11 '61

ALLEN, WOODY
    Pushing back.  Newsweek 60:87 Ag 20 '62
    His own Boswell.  Time 81:78 F 15 '63
    Mee, C. L.  On stage.  Horizon 5:46 My '63
    Zinsser, W. K.  Bright new comic clowns toward success.  Sat
        Eve Post 236:26 S 21 '63
    Stang, J.  Verbal cartoons.  N. Y. Times Mag p120 N 3 '63
    Kolowrat, E.  Loser on top.  Sr Schol 83:23 N 22 '63
    Six quitters.  Esquire 62:102 S '64
    Miller, E.  Tallest dwarf in the world.  Seventeen 25:159 My '66
    Biography.  Cur Bio 27:3 D '66
        Same.  Cur Bio Yrbk 1966:3 '67
    Woody, Woody, everywhere.  Time 89:90 Ap 14 '67
    Interview.  Playboy 14-5:63 My '67
    Reddy, J.  Woody Allen's bed of neuroses.  Read Dig 91:113 Jl
        '67
    Allen, W.  Woody Allen talks to Woody Allen.  New York 1-22:
        50 S 2 '68
    Higgins, R.  He has more hangups than a pop-poster joint.  TV
        Guide 16-47:43 N 23 '68
    Hellman, P.  Is Woody Allen really Charlie Brown?  New York
        2-7:44 F 17 '69
    Allen, W.  How Bogart made me the superb lover I am today.
        Life 66:64 Mr 21 '69
    Bester, A.  Conversation with...  Holiday 45:71 My '69
    Tornabene, L.  Walking with...  McCalls 96:44 Je '69
    Salute of the week.  Cue 38-37:1 S 13 '69
    What directors are saying.  Action 6-4:20 Jl/Ag '71
    The professional director speaks.  Making Films 5-4:40 Ag '71
    Weiner, B.  The wooden acting of...  Take One 3-7:17 S/O '71
    Wolf, W.  The intellectual schnook makes good.  Cue 41-21:2
        May 20 '72
    Miller, E.  Lines from the face of a funny man.  Seventeen 31:
        144 My '72
    Allen, W.  Everything you've always wanted to know about sex
        you'll find in my new movie.  Playboy 19-9:115 S '72
    Bisken, S.  Inside his looking-glass.  Movie Dig 1-6:46 N '72
    Filmog.  Film Dope 1:21 D '72
    Match wits with Inspector Ford; parody.  Playboy 19-12:232 D
        '72

Eyles, A.   Bio note; filmog.   Focus On F 12:6 Win '72
Wasserman, H.   Stumbling through the looking glass.   Velvet
    Light 7:37 Win '72/73
Mundy, R. & Mamber, S.   Interview; filmog.   Cinema(BH) 7-3:
    6 Win '72/73
Schickel, R.   The basic Woody Allen joke.   N. Y. Times Mag
    p10 Ja 7 '73
    Same.   N. Y. Times Bio Ed p4 Ja '73
Socrates of Brooklyn.   Films Illus 2-19:14 Ja '73
Mundy, R.   Woody Allen (reprint Cinema(Lon) Spring '73)
    AFI Report 4-3:6 Jl '73
Lax, E.   What's Woody Allen doing on the music page?   N. Y.
    Times sec 2:17 D 2 '73
Maltin, L.   Take Woody Allen--please!   Film Comment 10-2:42
    Mr/Ap '74
Trotsky, J.   Woody Allen and Sleeper.   Filmmakers Newsletter
    9/10:20 Sum '74


ALLGOOD, SARA
    Work with Irish players.   Theatre 14:157 N '11
    Stearns, H. E.   Interview.   N. Y. Drama 69:3 F 26 '13
    Sketch.   Theatre 17:108 Ap '13
    Mulvey, K.   Sketch.   Womans Home C 69:46 Je '42
    Obit.   Screen World 2:233 '51
    Slide, T.   Sara Allgood; filmog.   Film Fan Mo 108:15 Je '70


ALLISON, MAY
    Patterson, A.   Sketch.   Theatre 20:106 S '14
    Sketch.   Strand (NY) 48:404 O '14
    Willis, R.   The American beauty.   Film Players Herald 2-7:19
        F '16
    Courtlandt, R.   Sketch.   Motion Pic 11:117 My '16
    Courtlandt, R.   Sketch.   Motion Pic Classic 4:34 My '17
    Gaddis, P.   Interview.   Motion Pic 14:65 D '17
    Naylor, H. S.   Sketch.   Motion Pic Classic 7:22 D '18
    Interview.   Dramatic Mirror D 11 '20
    Cheatham, M.   Interview.   Motion Pic 21:38 Ap '21
    Adams, E.   Her horoscope.   Photop 26:34 N '24
    Sketch.   Motion Pic Classic 20:63 Ja '25
    Sketch.   Photop 27:66 Ap '25
    Edmonton, S.   Her many personalities.   Motion Pic Classic 21:
        58 Ag '25
    Bodeen, D.   Lockwood and Allison; filmog.   Films In R 22-5:275
        My '71


ALLISTER, CLAUD
    Belfrage, C.   Is Hollywood going old-English?   Motion Pic Clas-
        sic 32:56 S '30
    Obit.   Film R p13 '71/72
        Screen World 22:235 '71


ALLYSON, JUNE
    Stars of tomorrow.   Lions R 1-11/12:no p# Jl/Ag '42

Actress by choice.  Lions R 3-3(sup):no p# Ap '44
My teen-age mistake.  Photop 25:58 Jl '44
Hamilton, S.  Sketch.  Photop 25:55 Ag '44
Sketch.  Photop 25:53 N '44
Wilson, E.  The people's choice.  Silver Screen 15-2:52 D '44
You can't hide talent.  Lions R 4-1:no p# F '45
Marsh, P.  Still newlyweds.  Silver S 16-8:37 Je '46
Graham, S.  The Allyson-Powell puzzle.  Photop 34:46 D '48
Allyson, J.  Don'ts for brides.  Silver S 19-6:24 Ap '49
Autobiographical.  Photop 36:46 Je '49
Sketch.  Photop 36:21 Je '49
Powell, D.  I never had so much fun.  Silver S 20-8:30 Je '50
MacDonald, E.  A letter to a star.  Silver S 21-9:38 Jl '51
Stevens, B.  Hold on to your dreams.  Silver S 24-1:38 N '53
Sheridan, M.  Junie fooled 'em all.  Silver S 24-6:42 Ap '54
Zunser, J.  Never a bridesmaid.  Cue 26-11:11 My 16 '57
Good girl, bad girl.  Screen Greats 1-2:65 Sum '71
Kendall, R.  Joyous June.  Hollywood Stu 6-8:11 D '71
Balling, F. D.  June Allyson picks 'the musical I liked best--
    The gay divorcee.'  Movie Dig 2-1:46 Ja '73
June the first.  Films Illus 3-25:25 Jl '73

ALVARADO, DON
Calhoun, D.  Interview.  Motion Pic 38:64 D '29

ALYN, KIRK
Stephens, W.  Film 'Superman' flies on wings of nostalgia.  (Re-
    print from Los Angeles Times) Classic Film Collect 36:extra
    3 Fall '72
Filmog.  Films & Filming 19-5:58 F '73

AMECHE, DON
Sketch.  Motion Pic 52:15 S '36
French, W. R.  Interview.  Motion Pic 52:52 O '36
Zeitlin, I.  Story of.  Movie Classic 11:32 N '36
Sketch.  Photop 51:4 Jl '37
Decker, M.  Story of.  Motion Pic 54:24 Ag '37
Gillespie-Hayck, A.  Oh what a dummy!  Silver S 7-12:18 O '37
Smith, M.  Mi amigo Ameche.  Screen Book 19-4:14 N '37
Wilson, E.  Projection.  Silver S 8-7:22 My '38
Maddox, B.  The star who has everything.  Screen Book 21-2:
    31 S '38
Story of.  Photop 53:13 F '39
Pine, D.  Hollywood holiday.  Screen Book 21-10:40 My '39
Maddox, B.  The private lives of the Don Ameches.  Silver S
    10-11:42 S '40
Biographical note; filmog.  Movies & People 2:3 '40
The Don Ameche Hollywood knows.  Silver S 11-10:36 Ag '41
From beans to eggs benedict.  Lions R 1-2:no p# O '41
Hopper, H.  His married life.  Photop 22:27 My '43
The amazing Ameches.  Photop 23:96 N '43
The role I liked best.  Sat Eve Post 218:50 F 9 '46
Corneau, E. N.  I remember Don Ameche.  Classic Film Collect

29:37 Win '70
Madden, J. C.   Don Ameche; filmog.   Films In R 23-1:8 Ja '72

AMES, ADRIENNE
    Dust off four pedestals in the hall of fame.   Silver S 2-3:36 Ja
        '32
    Benham, L.   Life is so wonderful.   Silver S 2-11:25 S '32
    Spensley, D.   Sketch.   Movie Classic 5:38 O '33
    Perry, E.   Her story.   Movie Classic 5:38 D '33
    Schallert, E.   Interview.   Motion Pic 47:60 F '34
    Home of.   Motion Pic 51:18 F '38
    Invisible beauty.   Cue 12-36:10 S 4 '43

AMES, ALLYSON
    Cinderella made the slipper fit.   TV Guide 12-31:27 Ag 1 '64

AMES, ED
    Ugh!   TV Guide 14-34:20 Ag 20 '66
    Diehl, D.   He's finally combing those feathers out of his hair.
        TV Guide 16-13:28 Mr 30 '68
    The dangers of galloping inflation.   TV Guide 16-14:14 Ap 6 '68
    Wittgens, C.   A view of working in Canada.   Motion p66 N/D
        '73

AMES, JEAN
    Sketch.   Photop 20:50 Mr '42

AMES, LEON
    Ames, L.   You can have 'em.   Lions R 4-1:no p# F '45

AMES, MICHAEL
    (See: ANDREWS, TOD)

AMOS, JOHN
    Berkow, I.   Even the Norfolk Neptunes cut him.   TV Guide 22-
        33:15 Ag 17 '74

AMSTERDAM, MOREY
    Morey the merrier hits big time.   Cue 17-24:15 Je 12 '48
    Amsterdam plays Europe--for 'high stakes. "   TV Guide 2-48:A-2
        N 27 '54
    Adams, C.   Morey.   TV Guide 11-31:15 Ag 3 '63
    The fastest joke in the west.   TV Guide 19-3:34 Ja 16 '71

ANDERS, LAURIE
    In the cast.   TV Guide 1-8:15 My 22 '53

ANDERS, MERRY
    Queen of the pilots.   TV Guide 8-28:23 Jl 9 '60

ANDERSON, BARBARA
    Raddatz, L.   Girl on the run.   TV Guide 16-14:25 Ap 6 '68
    Opinions on liberation; my man and me.   Photop 78-3:78 S '70

I need a husband.  Photop 79-3:75 Mr '71
Barbara the secret bride.  Photop 79-5:82 My '71
I know how to be his mistress but not his wife.  Photop 79-6:89
    Je '71

ANDERSON, CARL
    Vallely, J.  People you should know.  Viva 1-2:101 N '73

ANDERSON, DONNA
    Rising stars.  Film R p22 '60/61

ANDERSON, EDDIE (ROCHESTER)
    Rhea, M.  Sketch.  Photop 53:67 S '39
    This is Rochester.  Lions R 2-4:no p# Ap '43
    Talent in triplicate.  Lions R 3-3:no p# Ap '44

ANDERSON, GILBERT MAXWELL (BRONCHO BILLY)
    Courtlandt, R.  Interview.  Motion Pic 8:99 Ja '15
    Sketch.  Motion Pic Classic 2:33 Mr '16
    Gaddis, I.  As Broncho Billy.  Motion Pic 11:98 Mr '16
    LaBadie, D. W.  The last roundup.  Show 2-9:74 S '62
    Estes, O. Jr.  The reel pioneer!  8mm Collect 8:19 My '64
    Bosquet, J.  Broncho Billy--the first star.  (Reprint from Los
        Angeles Herald-Examiner) 8mm Collect 8:19 My '64
    Obit.  Classic Film Collect 30:extra 2 Spg '71
        Film R p38 Ja 21 '71
        N. Y. Times p38 Ja 21 '71
        Same.  N. Y. Times Bio Ed Ja 21 '71
        Newsweek 77:61 F 1 '71
        Screen World 23:235 '72
        Time 97:67 F 1 '71
    Shootin' mad:  from 100 finest westerns.  Views & Rs 4-1:38
        Fall '72
    Bell, G.  Making films in the old west.  AFI Report 3:4 N '72

ANDERSON, HELEN
    Sketch.  Motion Pic 11:66 Ap '16

ANDERSON, JUDITH
    A stage vamp on women.  Theatre 39:22 O '24
    Fields, W.  Miss Anderson and Miss Menken...two who share
        the same spotlight.  Cue 3-41:3 Ag 10 '35
    Hamilton, S.  Sketch.  Photop 54:18 F '40
    Sketch.  Harp Baz 76:50 F '42
    Triumphs as Medea.  Life 23:112 N 17 '47
    People.  Time 93:32 Ja 3 '69
    Young, C.  Judith Anderson; filmog.  Films In R 21-4:193 Ap
        '70
    Kernan, M.  The Dame as Dane.  Show 1-11:12 Ag 20 '70
    Filmog.  Film Dope 1:29 D '72

ANDERSON, MARY
    Sketch.  Blue Book 19:689 Ag '14

How she got into motion pictures.  Motion Pic 14:78 D '17
Andre, R.  Sketch.  Motion Pic 15:63 N '18
Interview.  Motion Pic 20:74 S '20
Story of.  Life 12:55 Ap 27 '42
Davis, L. & Cleveland, J.  Story of.  Colliers 109:17 Je 20 '42
Should a girl propose?  Photop 24:43 F '44

ANDERSON, MIGNON
Sketch.  Motion Pic Supp 1:61 O '15
Thayer, J. E.  Mignon and Thanhouser.  Classic Film Collect
40:7 Fall '73
Biographical and autobiographical notes.  Filmograph 4-1:40 '73

ANDERSON, ROBERT
What is to become of the theater?  Illus World 24:660 Ja '16
Meet "M'sieu Cuckoo!"  Photop 15-1:41 D '18

ANDERSON, WARNER
Minoff, P.  Notes on TV.  Cue 21-38:6 S 20 '52
On the trail of a rusty anvil.  TV Guide 5-8:22 F 23 '57
Inspector Damon and Lieutenant Pythias.  TV Guide 6-46:20 N
15 '58

ANDERSSON, BIBI
Filmog.  Film Dope 1:33 D '72

ANDERSSON, HARRIET
Filmog.  Film Dope 1:34 D '72

ANDRE, GWILI
Appreciation.  Colliers 90:11 Jl 2 '32
Sketch.  Motion Pic 43:42 Jl '32
Manners, D.  Sketch.  Motion Pic 44:48 Ag '32
Lee, S.  Her love affairs.  Movie Classic 4:32 Mr '33
Obit.  Screen World 11:215 '60

ANDRE, LONA
Uselton, R. A.  The Wampus baby stars.  Films In R 21-2:73
F '70

ANDRESON, CAROL
Imagine coming out of ether and...  TV Guide 10-13:19 Mr 31
'62

ANDRESS, URSULA
Silke, J. R.  She said yes to Dr. No.  Cinema (BH) 1-4:21 Je/
Jl '62
She is Ursula Andress (with photos by John Derek).  Playboy 12-
6:130 Je '65
Ursula.  (Photos by John Derek)  Playboy 13-7:104 Jl '66
Seven year love scandal ends.  Mod Screen 66-9:42 S '72
Filmog.  Film Dope 1:36 D '72
Enchore; photos.  Playboy 20-11:103 N '73
Getting it on with Ursula; photos.  Oui 3-4:34 Ap '74

ANDREWS, DANA
  Hamilton, S.   Sketch.   Photop 21:47 Jl '42
  Watkins, W.   Remarkable Andrews.   Silver S 13-4:36 F '43
  I learned about money.   Photop 23:59 S '43
  Home life.   Photop 26:52 D '44
  Hall, G.   Mistakes I have made.   Silver S 15-3:42 Ja '45
  What he and his wife argue about.   Photop 27:61 Jl '45
  Tips on how to play.   Photop 27:50 Ag '45
  Latest bobby-sox bait.   Cue 15-4:13 Ja 26 '46
  Johaneson, B.   Patience, my friends.   Silver S 16-10:40 Ag '46
  My luckiest day.   Cosmop 121:182 N '46
  Parsons, L.   Cosmop's citation for one of the best performances
      of the month.   Cosmop 122:99 Ja 4 '47
  Andrews, Mrs. D.   The man I married.   Silver S 17-12:42 O '47
  Sails the coast of Mexico to film a travelogue.   Photop 33:62 Ag
      '48
  Sheridan, M.   He lives as he pleases.   Silver S 24-7:26 My '54
  McAsh, I.   Filmog. and biography.   Films Illus 1-12:22 Je '72
  Filmog.   Film Dope 1:37 D '72

ANDREWS, EDWARD
  Filmog.   Films & Filming 19-4:58 Ja '73
  Eyles, A.   Edward Andrews; filmog.   Focus On F 15:16 Sum '73

ANDREWS, HARRY
  Sketch.   N.Y. Drama 71:12 Ja 28 '14
  Johns, E.   Discusses the benefits derived from playing under the
      Old Vic banner.   Theatre World 43:31 D '47
  Tierney, M.   ...plays the king.   Plays & Players 19-2:18 N '71
  McGillivray, D.   Bio note; filmog.   Focus On F 10:9 Sum '72

ANDREWS, JULIE
  Lewis, E.   Valentines from Britain.   Cue 24-6:12 F 12 '55
  Wolf, W.   Hollywood's wanted woman.   Cue 34-3:9 Ja 16 '65
  Julie plays Gertie.   Look 31:63 S 19 '67
  Wells, T.   My daughter.   Good House 166:98 Mr '68
  Lawrenson, H.   Sweet Julie.   Esquire 71:62 Ja '69
  Christy, G.   New life of...   Good House 170:90 My '70
  Nine minds in trouble.   Photop 78-3:56 S '70
  Davidson, B.   As if someone had turned up the bright yellow
      lights.   TV Guide 19-49:14 D 4 '71
  Bell, J. N.   My friend, Carol Burnett.   Good House 174:57 Ja
      '72
  Righter, C.   Star of the month; horoscope.   Mod Screen 66-11:
      62 O '72
  Upton, F.   The transition from theater to film to television.
      Show 2-7:24 O '72
  Whitney, D.   Miss Andrews' appointment with television.   TV
      Guide 20-50:24 D 9 '72
  Filmog.   Film Dope 1:38 D '72
  Blake Edwards talks to Iain McAsh.   Films Illus 3-28:144 O '73
  Canby, V.   Two formidable female stars.   N.Y. Times sec 2:1
      Jl 21 '74
  Omar and Julie.   Films Illus 3-35:445 Jl '74

ANDREWS, LaVERNE
    The Andrews Sisters.   Cue 12-29:10 Jl 17 '43
    We won the war while they won our hearts.   Photop 86-1:44 Jl
        '74

ANDREWS, LOIS
    Obit.   N. Y.  Times p40 Ap 6 '68
    Crivello, K.   Whatever happened to the most beautiful girl in the
        world?   Film Fan Mo 109/110:38 Jl/Ag '70

ANDREWS, MAXENE
    The Andrews Sisters.   Cue 12-29:10 Jl 17 '43
    Wilson, J. S.   Bei him they're still schon.   N. Y.  Times sec
        2:1 Ap 28 '74
        Same.   N. Y.  Times Bio Ed p470 Ap '74
    We won the war while they won our hearts.   Photop 86-1:44 Jl
        '74
    Hagen, R.   Interview; filmog.   Film Fan Mo 157-8:10 Jl/Ag '74
    Glassner, L.   Interview.   Interview 4-10:25 O '74

ANDREWS, PATTY
    The Andrews Sisters.   Cue 12-29:10 Jl 17 '43
    Wilson, J. S.   Bei him they're still schon.   N. Y.  Times sec
        2:1 Ap 28 '74
        Same.   N. Y.  Times Bio Ed p470 Ap '74
    We won the war while they won our hearts.   Photop 86-1:44 Jl
        '74
    Hagen, R.   Interview with Maxene Andrews; filmog.   Film Fan
        Mo 157-8:10 Jl/Ag '74
    Glassner, L.   Interview.   Interview 4-10:25 O '74

ANDREWS, STANLEY
    Obit.   N. Y.  Times p41 Je 26 '69
    Screen World 21:233 '70

ANDREWS, TIGE
    His face spells c-o-p.   TV Guide 18-47:37 N 21 '70
    Ecology note.   TV Guide 20-42:18 O 14 '72

ANDREWS, TOD
    (Formerly known as Michael Ames)
    The rebel's from New York.   TV Guide 6-35:28 Ag 30 '58
    Obit.   N. Y.  Times Bio Ed N '72

ANGEL, HEATHER
    Miller, L.   Sketch.   Movie Classic 4:43 Jl '33
    Standish, J.   Her marriage.   Movie Classic 7:40 N '34
    Meet the cover(all) girls.   Lions R 3-2:no p#.  Ja '44
    Hoaglin, J.   Down memory lane.   Hollywood Stu 7-7:19 N '72

ANGELI, PIER
    Rising stars.   Film R p40 '51/52
    Holland, J.   Is too much freedom bad?   Silver S 22-7:44 My '52

Holland, J.   Pier angel.   Silver S 23-2:38 D '52
Kaufman, H.   Love has changed me.   Silver S 23-12:35 O '53
Morris, G.   Watch out, Pier!   Silver S 24-1:26 N '53
Obit.   N. Y.   Times Bio Ed S 11 '71
   Newsweek 78:71 S 20 '71
   Screen World 23:235 '72
Pier Angeli at peace at last.   Mod Screen 65-12:51 D '71

ANGELUS, MURIEL
   Vallee, W. L.   The truth about "Mrs. McGinty. "   Silver S 10-
   11:36 S '40

ANGOLD, EDIT
   Obit.   N. Y.   Times p50 O 7 '71
   Screen World 23:235 '72

ANKA, PAUL
   The baby-faced Midas of rock 'n' roll.   TV Guide 10-24:19 Je
   16 '62
   Windeler, R.   Once-a-year millionaire.   People 2-11:50 S 9 '74

ANKERS, EVELYN
   McClelland, D.   Queen of horrors; filmog.   Film Fan Mo 88:3
   O '68
   Ankers, E.   Recollections of filming The wolf man.   Filmograph
   3-2:6 '72
   Piper, B. M.   Letter; filmog.   Films In R 24-6:383 Je/Jl '73

ANNABELLA
   Annabella.   Visages 7:(entire issue) D '36
   Rhea, M.   Story of.   Motion Pic 54:43 S '37
   Bio note; filmog.   Movies & People 2:3 '40
   Wilson, E.   Annabella comes back.   Silver S 13-4:48 F '43
   Her ideas about love.   Photop 23:40 N '43
   Reid, L.   No tears, please.   Silver S 17-6:37 Ap '47

ANNA-LISA
   She'd trade her six-gun for a sword.   TV Guide 7-51:20 D 19 '59

ANN-MARGRET
   Barber, R.   New star in the West.   Show 2-9:68 S '62
   Leppard, S.   Cinderella lets her hair down.   Sound Stage 1-4:19
   Je '65
   Ducette, V.   Sex legend on a tight-rope; filmog.   Screen Legends
   1-3:39 O '65
   Ann-Margret as art (pictorial).   Playboy 13-10:86 O '66
   Opinions on liberation.   Photop 78-3:78 S '70
   Ehrlich, H.   The prude and the passion.   Look 35:49 Je 15 '71
   Darrach, B.   Ordeal of Ann-Margret.   Time 98:57 Jl 19 '71
   Mouse that roared.   Newsweek 78:78 Jl 19 '71
   Flatley, G.   But a girl you can't forget.   N. Y. Times Bio Ed
   Ag 1 '71
   Suddenly blooming.   Life 71:31 Ag 6 '71

Macdonough, S. At 30, suddenly she's in. Show 2-8:18 O '71
The man I loved died. Photop 80-5:45 N '71
Was Mike Nichols the Svengali who changed her life? Mod
    Screen 65-12:26 D '71
I'm afraid I'll die in childbirth. Mod Screen 66-1:32 Ja '72
I'm quitting in January. Photop 81-1:15 Ja '72
Forum. Photop 81-2:28 F '72
How they abuse their bodies to please their men. Photop 81-4:
    36 Ap '72
Her fears and her future. Mod Screen 66-5:20 My '72
It happened in Las Vegas. Photop 81-6:16 Je '72
On location. Photop 82-2:34 Ag '72
Fayard, J. Recovery on a diet of liquid pizza. Life 73:87 N
    24 '72
Interview with Roger Smith. Mod Screen 66-12:57 D '72
Filmog. Film Dope 1:42 D '72
Crippled for life? Photop 82-6:30 D '72
Interview. Photop 83-1:31 Ja '73
Interview with her mother. Photop 83-2:52 F '73
Whitney, D. Nothin' stops the champ. TV Guide 21-12:26 Mr
    24 '73
At last, I'm a mother. Photop 83-4:48 Ap '73
Her grief. Photop 83-5:46 My '73
John Wayne made me more of a woman. Photop 83-6:60 Je '73
Why she goes to AA. Photop 84-4:41 O '73
Her husband's jealousy. Photop 85-3:42 Mr '74
Klemesrud, J. Come to the nightclub old chum. N.Y. Times
    sec 2:15 Ap 7 '74
Ann-Margret. Photop 85-4:54 Ap '74
Sabol, B. Vegas Vargas. Interview 4-5:14 My '74
A British birthday party. Photop 86-2:66 Ag '74

ANSARA, MICHAEL
    Here come the heroes. TV Guide 4-37:28 S 15 '56

ANTONY, SCOTT
    Next stop stardom. Films Illus 1-12:10 Je '72
    d'Arcy, S. Second race. Films Illus 3-32:312 Ap '74

AOKI, TSURU
    Field, C. K. In moving pictures. Sunset 37:25 Jl '16
    Gaddis, P. Sketch. Motion Pic Classic 3:18 D '16

APPLEBY, DOROTHY
    Careers for four, please. Silver S 2-1:43 N '31

APPLEGATE, EDDIE
    Maynard, J. 17, going on 30. TV Guide 12-42:12 O 17 '64

APPLEWHITE, ERIC
    Obit. Screen World p231 '74

ARBUCKLE, ROSCOE "FATTY"
  Sketch.  Motion Pic 9:94 Jl '15
  Moore, R. F.  Interview.  Motion Pic Classic 3:45 N '16
  How he got in moving pictures.  Motion Pic 14:92 S '17
  The cost of a laugh.  Motion Pic 15:69 Mr '18
  Remont, F.  Interview.  Motion Pic Classic 6:39 Jl '18
  Arbuckle will star once more.  Am Project 5-2:17 Ap '27
  Calhoun, D.  Interview.  Motion Pic Classic 25:45 Jl '27
  Winters, D.  Sketch.  Motion Pic Classic 33:26 Jl '31
  Grant, J.  Does he deserve a break?  Motion Pic 42:40 S '31
  Jackson, G.  His fight to return to the screen.  Movie Classic
    3:29 S '32
  Jolly comic or brutal killer?  Classic Film Collect 15:27 Sum '66
  Peeples, S. A.  The sad clown.  Classic Film Collect 17:6 Win/
    Spg '67
  Mrs. Al St. John reminisces about the Arbuckle affair.  Classic
    Film Collect 22:29 Fall/Win '68
  Peeples, S. A.  Films on 8 & 16.  Films In R 24-2:102 F '73
  Carley, C. E.  Fatty.  Classic Film Collect 43:24 Sum '74
  Mundy, R.  Some Hollywood scandals of the twenties.  After Dark
    7-7:32 N '74

ARCHER, POLLY
  Sketch.  Photop 26:50 O '24

ARDEN, EVE
  Service, F.  Is love a handicap?  Silver S 14-12:28 O '44
  Turner, J.  Eve knows her apples.  Silver S 16-3:50 Ja '46
  Bawden, J. E. A.  Eve Arden; filmog.  Films In R 24-1:58 Ja
    '73

ARDEN, JANE
  Beatty, J.  The highest salaried extra in the movies.  Am Mag
    110:30 Jl '30
  Hollywood's most beautiful extra girl.  Silver S 1-1:42 N '30

ARENA, MAURIZIO
  These faces will win top places during 1959.  Films & Filming
    5-7:18 Ap '59

ARKIN, ALAN
  On the scene.  Playboy 13-10:163 O '66
  Biography.  Cur Bio 28:3 O '67
    Same.  Cur Bio Yrbk 1967:11 '68
  Inspector Clouseau and The heart is a lonely hunter.  Time 92:82
    Ag 9 '68
  Amory, C.  Trade Winds.  Sat R 52:8 S 6 '69
  Arkin, A.  Catch-22 family album.  Show 1-3:39 Mr '70
  Some are more Yossarian than others.  Time 95:66 Je 15 '70
  Greenfield, J.  Go ahead; interview me.  N. Y. Times Bio Ed Je
    21 '70

What directors are saying.  Action 5-4:30 Jl/Ag '70
Cohen, L.  Making of Little murders.  Sat R 53:19 Ag 8 '70
Farrell, B.  Yossarian in Connecticut.  Life 69:51 O 2 '70
Salute of the week.  Cue 40-9:1 F 27 '71
Opposite direction; bio note.  Films Illus 1-5:30 N '71
Carragher, B.  I'm not against women's lib, but I'd prefer peo-
   ple's liberation.  Show 2-6:40 S '72
Filmog.  Film Dope 1:46 D '72
Who is the last of the red hot lovers?  Films Illus 2-21:26 Mr
   '73
Bio note; filmog.  Films & Filming 20-9:69 Je '74

ARLEDGE, JOHN
   Sketch.  Photop 41:59 D '31

ARLEN, BETTY
   Uselton, R. A.  The Wampus baby stars.  Films In R 21-2:73
   F '70

ARLEN, JUDITH
   Uselton, R. A.  The Wampus baby stars.  Films In R 21-2:73
   F '70

ARLEN, RICHARD
   York, C.  Sketch.  Photop 32:76 S '27
   Spencer, M.  Sketch.  Motion Pic Classic 26:55 O '27
   Hyland, R.  Sketch.  Photop 34:59 Jl '28
   Ramsey, W.  Interview.  Motion Pic 38:50 Ag '29
   Fender, R.  Interview.  Motion Pic Classic 33:65 Mr '31
   Churchill, E.  Does being a good sport pay?  Silver S 1-9:35
   Jl '31
   Prior, N.  His married life.  Movie Classic 4:52 Ap '33
   Pine, D.  Interview.  Motion Pic 53:39 My '37
   Vallee, W. L.  Man of action.  Silver S 14-7:30 My '44

ARLEN, ROXANNE
   The wiggle goes straight.  TV Guide 10-35:27 S 1 '62

ARLETTY
   Performing Sartre for the screen.  Films & Filming 2-1:7 O '55
   Hartwell, C.  Letter.  Films In R 22-3:184 Mr '71

ARLISS, GEORGE
   A chat with his Satanic majesty.  Theatre 8:262 '08
   Dodge, W. P.  Interview.  Theatre 10:119 D '09
   His memories of King Edward.  Green Bk Album 4:89 Jl '10
   Parsons, C. L.  Interview.  N. Y. Dram 67:5 F 14 '12
   White, M. Jr.  At home.  Munsey 47:273 My '12
   Service, F.  Interview.  Classic 15:22 O '22
   Wilson, B. F.  Autocrat of the stage.  Theatre 42:22 O '25
   The cough and the drama.  Van Fair 29:52 F '28
   Should an actor submerge his emotions?  Threatre 49:22 F '29
   Belfrage, C.  Interview.  Motion Pic Classic 30:44 O '29

Cruikshank, H.   Interview.   Motion Pic 40:66 S '30
Sketch.   Fortune 2:40 O '30
Mr. Arliss talks on Hollywood.   Lit Dig 110:18 Jl 11 '31
Littlejohn, J.   Interview.   Motion Pic 42:42 S '31
Collins, F. L.   Sketch.   Good House 94:44 Je '32
Hall, G.   Sketch.   Movie Classic 2:26 Je '32
Mendmore, W. S.   Arliss talks.   Windsor 76:367 Ag '32
Powell, S. M.   George Arliss.   Cinema Dig 1-13:14 O 31 '32
Moffitt, C. F.   Censorship for interviews Hollywood's latest wild
    ideas.   Cinema Dig 2-5:9 Ja 9 '33
Mosley, L. O.   Knighthood for him seems certain.   Movie Clas-
    sic 3:51 F '33
Melcher, E.   George Arliss.   Cinema Dig 3-7:11 My 1 '33
Haddon, A.   Could he portray Shakespeare?   Theatre World 22:
    61 Ag '34
Sellmer, R.   The Arliss menage.   Stage 12:37 Je '35
Corneau, E.   I remember George Arliss.   Classic Film Collect
    30:47 Spg '71
Contratti, L.   A look at George Arliss.   Classic Film Collect
    41:27 Win '73

ARMENDARIZ, PEDRO
    Obit.   Film R p34 '63/64

ARMETTA, HENRY
    Keats, P.   Picture savers.   Silver S 5-5:32 Mr '35

ARMIDA
    York, C.   Sketch.   Photop 37:57 F '30
    Schwarzkopf, J.   Sketch.   Motion Pic 54:15 S '37

ARMSTRONG, LOUIS
    Swing stars.   Lions R 2-4:no p# Ap '43
    Marill, A. H.   Louis Armstrong; filmog.   Films In R 21-10:653
        D '70
    (Only citations concerning his film career researched.)

ARMSTRONG, MICHAEL
    Bio note.   Films Illus 4-40:130 D '74

ARMSTRONG, ROBERT
    Cruikshank, H.   Sketch.   Motion Pic Classic 28:43 Ja '29
    York, C.   Sketch.   Photop 37:41 D '29
    Calhoun, D.   Sketch.   Motion Pic Classic 30:20 Ja '30
    Martin, B.   Personalities prominent in the press.   Cinema Dig
        1-6:5 Jl 25 '32
    Calhoun, D.   Home of.   Motion Pic 48:52 Ja '35
    Obit.   Classic Film Collect 39:extra 1 Sum '73
        Film R p18 '73/74
        Screen World p231 '74

ARNALL, JULIA
    Rising stars.   Film R p34 '56/57

ARNAZ, DESI SR.
  His marriage to Lucille Ball.   Photop 18:93 F '41
  Arnaz, L. B.   The man I married.   Silver S 18-1:36 N '47
  TV Team.   Newsweek 39:67 F 18 '52
  Unaverage situation.   Time 59:73 F 18 '52
  Sher, J. & Sher, M.   Cuban and the red head.   Am Mag 154:26
    S '52
  Biography.   Cur Bio S '52
  Harris, E.   Why I love Lucy.   McCalls 80:24 Ja '53
  Desilu formula for top TV.   Newsweek 41:56 Ja 19 '53
  Gould, J.   Why millions love Lucy.   N. Y. Times Mag p16 Mr 1
    '53
  Lucy's boys.   Life 34:89 Ap 6 '53
  TV Guide goes backstage.   TV Guide 1-5:12 My 1 '53
  Shipp, C.   Our babies will be happy.   Womans Home C 80:40
    My '53
  Morris, J. K.   We love little Desi.   Parents 28:38 Je '53
  Roll out the red carpet.   TV Guide 1-16:4 Jl 17 '53
  Johnson, G.   What's the secret of I love Lucy?   Coronet 34:36
    Jl '53
  From rumba band to businessman.   TV Guide 2-18:15 Ap 30 '54
  Arnaz, D.   Who's quitting?   TV Guide 2-31:3 Jl 31 '54
  Stump, A.   America has been good to me.   Am Mag 159:22 F
    '55
  Minoff, P.   Young man of property.   Cue 24-19:10 My 14 '55
  Still in the driver's seat.   TV Guide 3-50:13 D 10 '55
  Bergquist, L.   Desi and Lucy.   Look 20:74 D 25 '56
  You can't stand still.   TV Guide 5-44:8 N 2 '57
  New tycoon.   Time 71:69 Ap 7 '58
  Ager, C.   From gags to riches.   N. Y. Times Mag p32 Ap 20 '58
  Martin, P.   I call on Lucy and Desi.   Sat Eve Post 230:32 My
    31 '58
  $30 million Desilu gamble.   Life 45:24 O 6 '58
  Clown in a new mood.   Newsweek 52:77 O 20 '58
  Scott, J. A.   How to be a success in show business.   Cosmop
    145:67 N '58
  Christian, F.   Lucille Ball's serious life with Desi Arnaz.   Cos-
    mop 148:68 Ja '60
  Slater, L.   Way it happened.   McCalls 87:106 S '60
  Whitney, D.   I sez I'm gonna get outa here, Lucy.   TV Guide
    17-5:42 F 1 '69
  Bell, J.   Interview with Desi Jr.   Good House 172:14 Mr '71
  Bowers, R. L.   Lucille Ball; Arnaz filmog.   Films In R 22-6:
    321 Je/Jl '71
  Interview.   Photop 80-6:21 D '71
  Ball, L.   Patty Duke used my son and victimized us.   Photop
    80-6:19 D '71
  Interview.   Photop 80-6:21 D '71
  Desi's (Jr.) intimate confession to his dad about Liza.   Photop
    82-1:52 Jl '72

ARNAZ, DESI JR.
  Morris, J. K.   We love little Desi.   Parents 28:38 Je '53

One year old.  Look 18:76 Ja 26 '54
Raddatz, L.  Just like the kids next door.  TV Guide 17-9:24
   Mr 1 '69
Our mother the boss.  Look 33:M Je 24 '69
Desi Arnaz talks turkey.  Seventeen 30:98 Ja '71
Patty Duke pregnant by man she won't name.  Photop 79-2:77 F
   '71
Interview.  Good House 172:14 Mr '71
Let me and my baby live here with you.  Photop 79-5:32 My '71
Don't disgrace me.  Photop 79-5:92 My '71
I'm pregnant again.  Photop 80-2:89 Ag '71
Is he troubled?  Photop 80-3:36 S '71
Patty Duke tells how Lucille Ball defeated her.  Photop 80-3:37
   S '71
Patty Duke crushed as Desi begs new girl to live with him.
   Photop 80-4:82 O '71
Ball, L.  Patty Duke used my son and victimized us.  Photop
   80-6:19 D '71
Interview with Desi Sr.  Photop 80-6:21 D '71
Why Patty stops me from seeing my baby.  Photop 81-2:76 F '72
Desi and Liza.  Mod Screen 66-3:38 Mr '72
Duke, P.  Desi was the biggest mistake of my life.  Photop 81-
   3:70 Mr '72
Ball, L.  My son has finally found the right girl.  Photop 81-3:
   69 Mr '72
I want to marry Liza.  Photop 81-4:54 Ap '72
Go back to your husband.  Photop 81-5:38 My '72
Desi gives Liza a wedding ring.  Photop 81-6:45 Je '72
Intimate confession to his dad.  Photop 82-1:52 Jl '72
Will Liza and Desi take Patty Duke's son?  Mod Screen 66-9:52
   S '72
Desi and Liza's wedding day.  Photop 82-3:60 S '72
In Tokyo with Desi and Liza.  Photop 82-4:62 O '72
Don't marry Desi!  Mod Screen 66-11:44 N '72
Why Liza lives with Lucille Ball.  Photop 83-1:24 Ja '73
Whitney, D.  We wrote the baby into the script.  TV Guide 21-
   13:4 Mr 31 '73
Liza's first interview with Lucille Ball.  Mod Screen 67-4:26 Ap
   '73
Desi answers lies about life with Liza.  Photop 84-1:48 Jl '73
Meet Desi's new girl.  Photop 84-3:49 S '73
Liza and Desi's new love arrangement.  Photop 84-5:40 N '73

ARNAZ, LUCIE
   Raddatz, L.  Just like the kids next door.  TV Guide 17-9:24 Mr
      1 '69
   Our mother the boss.  Look 33:M Je 24 '69
   Altman, C.  Doing it her way.  People 1-12:60 My 20 '74

ARNE, PETER
   Person of promise.  Films & Filming 3-1:17 O '56

ARNESS, JAMES
    De Roos, R.   The Greta Garbo of Dodge City.   TV Guide 14-50:
        19 D 10 '66
    The dangers of galloping inflation.   TV Guide 16-14:14 Ap 6 '68
    Clipper, P. M.   The brothers Aurness.   TV Guide 18-29:16 Jl
        18 '70
    The marshall breaks the law.   Photop 78-1:56 Jl '70
    Whitney, D.   It looked like O' Matt was through.   TV Guide 18-
        34:20 Ag 22 '70
    Busy day at the office.   TV Guide 19-5:20 Ja 30 '71
    James Arness meets the mother of his maybe bride.   Photop 79-
        4:68 Ap '71
    Scott, V.   Gunsmoke's mysterious James Arness.   Ladies Home
        J 88:90 My '71
    The Aurness album.   TV Guide 21-29:11 Jl 21 '73
    What makes Jim Arness TV's favorite lover?   Photop 84-4:47 O
        '73

ARNGRIM, STEFAN
    Buy melon crates!   TV Guide 18-2:14 Ja 10 '70

ARNO, SIG
    Exhibition of his paintings.   Newsweek 25:106 Je 18 '45

ARNOLD, EDWARD
    Churchill, E.   Everything is rosy--now.   Silver S 5-9:51 Jl '35
    Conlin, S.   Story of.   Movie Classic 10:50 Ag '36
    Zeitlin, I.   Sketch.   Motion Pic 53:43 My '37
    Arnold, E.   Arnold's diary.   Screen Book 19-2:60 S '37
    Biographical note; filmog.   Movies & People 2:3 '40
    Hopper, H.   Sketch.   Photop 19:36 S '41
    Hollywood chairman.   Lions R 1-3:no p# N '41
    Benedict, P.   Energetic Eddie.   Silver S 12-9:42 Jl '42
    Let Eddie do it.   Lions R 2-1:no p# S/O '42
    Arnold, E.   My old theatrical trunk.   Lions R 2-2:no p# N '42
    (He) writes a letter to his son.   Lions R 2-4:no p# Ap '43
    Lovable villain.   Lions R 3-5:no p# D '44
    Jobs wanted.   Lions R 3-5:no p# D '44
    (He) writes to his daughter.   Lions R 4-1:no p# F '45

ARNST, BOBBE
    Service, F.   Interview.   Motion Pic 44:60 S '32

ARQUETTE, CLIFF (Charlie Weaver)
    Dennis Day's handiest man.   TV Guide 2-13:23 Mr 26 '54
    This bumpkin's smart.   Newsweek 52:74 Jl 28 '58
    Almost like a letter from mama.   TV Guide 7-52:10 D 26 '59
    Master of the paunch line.   TV Guide 8-3:17 Ja 16 '60
    Obit.   N. Y. Daily News p4 S 24 '74
        N. Y. Times p44 S 24 '74
        Same.   N. Y. Times Bio Ed p1196 S '74

ARTAUD, ANTONIN
  Esslin, M.  Theater of cruelty.  N. Y.  Times Mag p22 Mr 6 '66
  Chiaromonte, N.  Antonin Artaud.  Encounter 28:44 Ag '67
  Hardison, F.  Brothers under the skin.  Educ Theatre J 19:455
    D '67
  De Gramont, S.  Vocation for madness.  Am Heritage 12:49 Spg
    '70
  Gadoffre, G. F. A.  Antonin and the avant-garde theatre.  John
    Rylands Lib Bul 53:329 Spg '71
  Kestner, J. A. II.  Stevenson & Artaud:  The master of Ballan-
    trae.  Film Heritage 7-4:19 Sum '72
  Bio note.  Screen 14-1/2:228 Spg/Sum '73

ARTHUR, BEATRICE
  Type casting.  Newsweek 80:63 O 9 '72
  Flatley, G.  Gene, for heaven's sake, help me!  TV Guide 20-
    47:28 N 18 '72
  Stone, J.  She gave Archie his first comeuppance.
    N. Y.  Times sec 2:17 N 19 '72
  Same.  N. Y.  Times Bio Ed p1921 N '72

ARTHUR, GEORGE K.
  Donnell, D.  Sketch.  Motion Pic Classic 22:36 D '25
  Thorp, D.  The Mutt & Jeff of the movies.  Motion Pic Classic
    26:41 S '27
  Tozzi, R.  George K. Arthur; filmog.  Films In R 13-3:151 Mr
    '62

ARTHUR, JEAN
  Calhoun, D.  Interview.  Motion Pic 35:71 Jl '28
  Goldbeck, E.  Sketch.  Motion Pic 41:76 My '31
  Maddox, B.  Story of.  Motion Pic 50:49 D '35
  Morley, D.  A thousand teachers.  Silver S 6-4:24 F '36
  Lee, S.  Interview.  Motion Pic 52:38 Ag '36
  Towne, T.  Story of.  Movie Classic 11:84 Ja '37
  Hartley, K.  She didn't take it with her.  Screen Book 21-3:30
    O '38
  Franchey, J.  Comeback girl.  Screen Book 22-6:64 Ja '40
  Home life.  Life 8:59 Mr 11 '40
  Bio note; filmog.  Movies & People 2:3 '40
  Story of.  Photop 18:44 Ja '41
  Hamman, M.  Sketch.  Good House 112:16 Ap '41
  Uselton, R. A.  The Wampus baby stars.  Films In R 21-2:73
    F '70
  Very personal garden of...  House & Gard 138:70 Jl '70
  Springer, J.; Bressan, A. & Moran, M.  Great star as great
    lady.  Interview 22:22 Je '72
  Flatley, G.  From Mr. Deeds goes to town to Miss Arthur goes
    to Vassar.  N. Y.  Times sec 2:11 My 14 '72
  Same.  N. Y.  Times Bio Ed My 14 '72
  Filmog.  Film Dope 1:48 D '72
  Stars in an animal epic.  Classic Film Collect 39:13 Sum '73

ARTHUR, JOHNNY
   Maltin, L.  Our gang; Our Gang filmog.   Film Fan Mo 66:3 D
      '66
   Marlowe, L.  Johnny Arthur.  Classic Film Collect 31:15 Sum
      '71

ARTHUR, MAUREEN
   She out-talked 299 rivals.   TV Guide 4-51:12 D 22 '56
   Ooh, I just love War and peace.   TV Guide 9-7:25 F 18 '61

ARTHUR, PHIL
   Frances faces life.   TV Guide 2-33:23 Ag 14 '54

ARTHUR, ROBERT
   Parsons, L. O.   Cosmop's citation for the best supporting role
      of the month.   Cosmop 125:12 Jl '48

ASHER, JANE
   Filmog.   Film Dope 1:51 D '72

ASHLEY, ELIZABETH
   The Hollywood swingers.   Show 3-11:89 N '63
   Elizabeth Ashley.   Vogue 143:158 F 1 '64
   Two in the center.   Time 83:64 Mr 6 '64
   Star at odds with her career.   Life 57:87 D 4 '64
   Considine, S.   The rise and fall of a Broadway prom queen.
      After Dark 6-10:65 F '74
   Barthel, J.   A 'cat' in search of total approval.   N.Y. Times
      sec 2:1 S 22 '74
   Same.   N.Y. Times Bio Ed p1197 S '74
   Davis, C.   Ashley keeps Maggie the cat alive.   People 2-15:64
      O 7 '74
   Note; filmog.   Films Illus 4-39:91 N '74

ASHTON, SYLVIA (As Actress)
   Handy, T. B.   Interview.   Motion Pic 24:28 Ag '22
   Hall, G.   Gives up cinema to open a tea-room.   Motion Pic 27:
      46 F '24

ASKEW, LUKE
   Filmog.   Films & Filming 21-3:58 D '74

ASKWITH, ROBIN
   Tomorrow people.   Films Illus 3-35:441 Jl '74

ASNER, EDWARD
   So who's afraid of a big bad paunch?   TV Guide 19-21:31 My 22
      '71
   My child.   Photop 81-2:32 F '72
   Strout, E.   Interview.   Mod Screen 66-9:72 S '72
   Cohn, E.   Mary Tyler Moore's irascible boss is a pussycat.
      N.Y. Times sec 2:19 S 23 '73
   Same.   N.Y. Times Bio Ed p1425 S '73

Robison, R. J.   Edward Asner; filmog.   Films In R 24-10:631
  D '73

ASSAN, RATNA
  Butterfly girl.   Playboy 21-2:151 F '74

ASTAIRE, FRED
  Sketch.   Theatre World 21:10 Ja '34
  Dowling, M.   Sketch.   Movie Classic 6:71 Mr '34
  Asher, J.   Dancing genius.   Movie Classic 7:40 Ja '35
  Hartley, K.   Embarrassed by fame.   Movie Classic 8:30 Mr '35
  Harrison, H.   Interview.   Movie Classic 8:28 Jl '35
  Rhea, M.   Wants to act and not dance.   Motion Pic 50:24 Ag '35
  Maxwell, V.   The seven neckties that conquered Hollywood.   Silver S 5-11:22 S '35
  Sketch.   Theatre World 24:107 S '35
  French, W. F.   Sketch.   Motion Pic 50:34 N '35
  Sullivan, E.   The great Astaire.   Silver S 6-1:20 N '35
  Appreciation.   Delin 127:68 D '35
  Lewis, F.   His private life.   Photop 48:26 D '35
  Craig, C.   Interview.   Movie Classic 9:30 D '35
  Rhea, M.   His personality.   Movie Classic 10:36 Mr '36
  Broderick, H.   Story of.   Movie Classic 10:44 My '36
  Langford, H.   An open letter to.   Motion Pic 52:54 S '36
  Reid, J.   His dancing a masterpiece of rhythm and originality.
    Movie Classic 11:34 N '36
  Horton, H.   He dances in his sleep.   Screen Book 19-2:28 S '37
  Fred Astaire and Ginger Rogers.   Visages 31:entire issue Ja '39
  Ager, C.   To produce the life of Vernon and Irene Castle on the
    screen.   Stage 16:20 F '39
  Appreciation as Vernon Castle.   Stage 16:41 Ap 1 '39
  Jacobs, M.   Will Powell and Astaire click?   Screen Book 22-5:
    87 D '39
  Bio note; filmog.   Movies & People 2:4 '40
  Vallee, W. L.   Keeping in step with Astaire.   Silver S 11-4:42
    F '41
  Astaire "had it" in Europe.   Lions R 4-1:no p# F '45
  Sketch.   Theatre Arts 29:473 Ag '45
  Astaire's farewell to films.   Cue 15-41:11 O 12 '46
  Astaireway to rhythm opens to New Yorkers.   Cue 16-10:11 Mr
    8 '47
  Astaire dances his way back.   Cue 17-25:12 Je 19 '48
  Niemeyer, J.   Take it from his stand-in!   Silver S 18-9:24 Jl
    '48
  Astaire and Rogers reunited in new film.   Cue 18-9:12 F 26 '49
  Torme, M.   Of singing and singers.   Metronome 66:22 My '50
  Two musicals coming with Fred Astaire.   Cue 19-29:16 Jl 22 '50
  Zunser, J.   50 years a hoofer.   Cue 26-8:12 F 23 '57
  An Astaire "special."   Cue 27-41:11 O 11 '58
  Astaire spins-off Ava Records to two Texans; he'll retain 10%
    interest.   Variety 235:49 Je 24 '64
  Gotta sing! gotta dance!   Film 40:9 Sum '64
  Terry, W.   Dancing on TV.   Sat R 52:42 Mr 1 '69

Raddatz, L.   Astaire.   TV Guide 18-15:18 Ap 11 '70
Astaire, F.   Letter to Films In Review.   Films In R 21-7:445
   Ag/S '70
The love teams.   Screen Greats 1-2:10 Sum '71
Collins, F. L.   The real romance in the life of Fred Astaire.
   Liberty 1-4:32 Spg '72
Filmog.   Film Dope 1:53 D '72
Astaire and Rogers; filmog.   Screen Greats 1-7:entire issue '72
Shipley, G.   Some notes on some of film's dancers.   Filmograph
   3-1:15 '72
Gardner, P.   Groups here to tip their hats to Astaire.   N. Y.
   Times Bio Ed p211 F '73
Harris, D.   Fred Astaire, singer.   N. Y. Times sec 2:28 Ap 29
   '73
Kisselgoff, A.   Astaire comes back to town in Philharmonic gala.
   N. Y. Times p49 My 1 '73
Maltin, L.   Astaire.   Film Fan Mo 143:3 My '73
Saltus, C.   Interview.   Interview 33:10 Je '73
Spiegel, E.   Fred and Ginger meet Van Nest Polglase.   Velvet
   Light 10:17 Fall '73
Lederer, G.   Fred Astaire remembers.   After Dark 6-6:55 O
   '73
Buckley, M.   Account of Astaire evening at '73 N. Y. film festi-
   val.   Films In R 25-4:256 Ap '74

ASTHER, NILS
   Biery, R.   Interview.   Photop 34:42 O '28
   Alpert, K.   Interview.   Photop 35:32 F '29
   Belfrage, C.   Interview.   Motion Pic 37:33 Mr '29
   Walker, H. L.   Interview.   Motion Pic 38:48 Ag '29
   Hall, G.   Interview.   Photop 38:44 Ja '30
   French, J.   Interview.   Photop 38:53 Ag '30
   Hall, G.   Returns to the screen.   Motion Pic Classic 32:33 Ag
      '31
   Hall, G.   Sketch.   Motion Pic 43:50 Jl '32
   Maddox, B.   Can't stay in love.   Silver S 3-12:22 O '33
   Hamilton, S.   Sketch.   Photop 20:53 D '41

ASTIN, JOHN
   A tale of two zanies.   TV Guide 10-48:16 D 1 '62
   Durslag, M.   From a fifth-floor walkup to a haunted house.   TV
      Guide 13-44:15 O 3 '65
   Duke, P.   Desi was the biggest mistake of my life.   Photop 81-
      3:70 Mr '72
   What it's like living with Patty Duke.   Photop 82-4:22 O '72
   Their wedding.   Photop 82-5:59 N '72
   Parents to be.   Photop 83-4:61 Ap '73
   John and Patty Duke Astin's second son.   Photop 84-3:38 S '73

ASTIN, PATTY DUKE
   (See: DUKE, PATTY)

ASTOR, GERTRUDE
  St. Johns, I.  Sketch.  Photop 32:72 Jl '27

ASTOR, MARY
  Morena, M.  Sketch.  Met Mag 57:36 Je '23
  Roberts, W. A.  Sketch.  Motion Pic 30:54 O '25
  Todd, J.  Sketch.  Motion Pic 31:1 F '26
  Calhoun, D.  Interview.  Motion Pic 39:40 Ap '30
  Sketch.  Photop 37:44 My '30
  Manners, D.  Interview.  Motion Pic 40:44 Ja '31
  Walker, H. L.  Sketch.  Motion Pic Classic 33:65 My '31
  Astor, M.  Six weeks of hell made me an actress.  Silver S 1-
    9:24 Jl '31
  Manners, D.  Sketch.  Motion Pic 43:44 F '32
  Her marital problems.  Time 28:42 Ag 17 '36
  Calhoun, D.  Her tragic story.  Motion Pic 52:38 N '36
  Hall, G.  Interview.  Motion Pic 53:22 Jl '37
  Franchey, J. R.  Correction please.  Silver S 12-2:36 D '41
  Hamilton, S.  Sketch.  Photop 22:45 Mr '43
  She's no fake.  Lions R 3-1:no p# S '43
  Autobiographical.  Cosmop 115:56 N '43
  Contrary Mary!  Lions R 3-2:no p# Ja '44
  Astor, M.  Give me the good old days.  Lions R 4-1:no p# F '45
  Yours for fun.  Lions R 4-1:no p# F '45
  Astor, M.  What it was like to kiss Clark Gable.  Read Dig 94:
    49 Je '69
  Uselton, R. A.  The Wampus baby stars.  Films In R 21-2:73
    F '70
  Gets her Oscar--30 years later.  Classic Film Collect 35:7X
    Sum '72
  Filmog.  Film Dope 2:6 Mr '73

ATKINS, EILEEN
  Chase, C.  Vivat! Vivat Eileen Atkins, actress.  N. Y. Times
    Bio Ed Ja 30 '72
  Connolly, R.  Extraordinary Atkins.  Plays & Players 20-2:32
    N '72

ATKINS, ROBERT
  Obit.  N. Y. Times p40 F 11 '72

ATTENBOROUGH, RICHARD
  Cowie, P.  The face of '63--Great Britain.  Films & Filming
    9-5:19 F '63
  Star of the year; filmog; list of awards.  Film R p18 '65/66
  An actor's actor; interview.  Cinema (BH) 3-2:9 Mr '66
  Attenborough, R.  Why I became a director.  Action 5-1:15 Ja/
    F '69
  Gow, G.  Elements of truth; interview.  Films & Filming 15-9:
    4 Je '69
  What directors are saying.  Action 4-5:32 S/O '69

Biography.  British Book Yr 1970:138 '70
Opposite director; bio note.  Films Illus 1-5:30 N '71
Young Winston; filmog.  Films Illus 2-13:12 Jl '72
Rose, T.  Interview.  Movie Maker 6-9:616 S '72
Filmog.  Film Dope 2:8 Mr '73
What directors are saying.  Action 8-3:37 My/Je '73
Castell, D.  His 10-year obsession.  Films Illus 37:24 S '74

ATWILL, LIONEL
Beach, B.  Interview.  Motion Pic Classic 8:18 Jl '19
Harper, C.  Interview.  National Mag 58:451 Jl '30
Service, F.  Sketch.  Motion Pic 45:52 Jl '33
Obit.  Cur Bio '46
Bryant, D. & Rehrauer, G.  Lionel Atwill; filmog. of sound
   films.  Film Fan Mo 139:21 Ja '73
Borst, R.  His life and times.  Gore Creatures #23 '74

AUBREY, SKYE
Hobson, D.  Television's child.  TV Guide 19-29:31 Jl 17 '71

AUCLAIR, MICHAEL
Bio note.  Unifrance 10:7 Je '51

AUDRAN, STEPHANE
Elley, D.  Bio note; filmog.  Focus On F 12:10 Win '72
Filmog.  Film Dope 2:9 Mr '73

AUDRET, PASCALE
Bio note.  Unifrance 45:6 D '57

AUER, MISCHA
Williams, W.  Wild boy of Siberia.  Silver S 7-5:28 Mr '37
Zeitlin, I.  Sketch.  Motion Pic 54:48 S '37
Obit.  Film R p21 '66/68

AUGUST, EDWIN
Sketch.  Motion Pic 9:108 Mr '15
Zeidman, B.  An August scenario.  Motion Pic 10:108 D '15
Obit.  Screen World 16:219 '65

AUMONT, JEAN-PIERRE
Jean-Pierre Aumont.  Visages 23:entire issue Mr '38
Stars of tomorrow.  Lions R 1-11/12:no p# Jl/Ag '42
New friends for Pierre.  Lions R 2-4:no p# Ap '43
Hall, G.  Before I go.  Silver S 13-7:46 My '43
Manners, M. J.  Second love for Maria.  Silver S 13-9:34 Jl '43
One of the fifty million.  Lions R 3-2:no p# Ja '44
Dudley, F.  Ideal family man.  Silver S 16-3:48 Ja '46
Autobiographical.  Photop 29:17 Jl '46
Palmer, C.  The happy Aumonts.  Silver S 16-10:35 Ag '46
Hall, G.  This is the way I am.  Silver S 17-5:37 Mr '47

AUSTIN, GENE
  Walsh, J.  Gene Austin.  Hobbies 61:34 F '57; 62:30 Mr '57
  It's show business.  Newsweek 49:78 My 6 '57
  Smith, H. A.  Crooner comes back.  Sat Eve Post 230:25 Ag 31
    '57
  Pitts, M. R.  Pop singers on the screen; filmog.  Film Fan Mo
    112:15 O '70
  Obit.  New York Times p38 Ja 25 '72
    Newsweek 79:79 F 7 '72
    Time 99:80 F 7 '72

AUSTIN, PAMELA
  The Pearl White of the hard sell.  TV Guide 14-34:13 Ag 20 '66
  Calamity Pam.  Time 89:64 Ja 13 '67

AUTRY, GENE
  Williams, W.  Singing cowboy.  Screen Book 19-1:66 Ag '37
  James, E.  Paradox on horseback.  Screen Book 22-2:78 S '39
  Vallee, W. L.  He took Will Rogers' advice.  Silver S 10-1:40
    N '39
  Biographical note; filmog.  Movies & People 2:4 '40
  People.  Cue 10-40:34 O 4 '41
  Vallee, W. L.  Gene Autry's advice about dude ranches.  Silver
    S 12-8:26 Je '42
  Churchill, R. & B.  Streamlining the horse opera.  Silver S 20-
    6:44 Ap '50
  Minoff, P.  Back in the saddle.  Cue 19-31:9 Ag 5 '50
  Autry, G.  Keep trying.  Music 28:4 N/D '50
  LaBadie, D. W.  The last roundup.  Show 2-9:74 S '62
  Meanwhile, back at the ranch...  Screen Greats 1-2:73 Sum '71
  Biographical note.  Cinema Trails 2:20 n. d.

AVALON, PHIL
  Barra, M.  Playgirl's man for November.  Playgirl 2-6:64 N
    '74

AVEDON, DOE
  Lady of few words.  TV Guide 4-18:20 My 5 '56

AVERY, PATRICIA
  Uselton, R. A.  The Wampus baby stars.  Films In R 21-2:73
    F '70

AVERY, PHYLLIS
  Back in skirts.  TV Guide 3-4:13 Ja 22 '55
  Don't call us...we'll call you.  TV Guide 6-20:20 My 17 '58

AVON, VIOLET
  Uselton, R. A.  The Wampus baby stars.  Films In R 21-2:73
    F '70

AXELL, JANE
  Aspiring young actresses.  Show 2-2:64 S '71

AYARS, ANN
    Cinderella in Hollywood.    Lions R 1-5:no p# Ja '42
    Self-taught.    Lions R 1-7:no p# Mr '42
    Hamilton, S.    Sketch.    Photop 21:47 Jl '42
    Stars of tomorrow.    Lions R 1-11/12:no p# Jl/Ag '42
    Myrna Loy's protege.    Lions R 2-1:no p# S/O '42
    Pen portrait.    Lions R 2-4:no p# Ap '43

AYE, MARYON
    Uselton, R. A.    The Wampus baby stars.    Films in R 21-2:73
        F '70

AYRES, AGNES
    A Fifth ave. beauty.    Photop 14-6:56 N '18
    Hall, G.    Sketch.    Motion Pic Classic 7:34 D '18
    Sketch.    Photop 17:44 Ap '20
    Cheatham, M. S.    Interview.    Motion Pic Classic 10:58 Ag '20
    Goldbeck, M.    Interview.    Motion Pic 21:56 My '21
    Shelley, H.    Interview.    Motion Pic Classic 13:34 N '21
    Bishop, R.    Interview.    Motion Pic 24:72 N '22
    Reachi, M.    How it feels to be a star's husband.    Motion Pic
        30:33 Ja '26
    Bahm, C. B.    Quoting Agnes...    Cinema Dig 4-2:10 My 22 '33

AYRES, LEW
    Gray, C.    Sketch.    Motion Pic Classic 31:45 Je '30
    Standish, J.    Sketch.    Motion Pic 41:50 Mr '31
    Ayres, L. as told to S. R. Mook.    My life.    Silver S 1-5:51
        Mr '31
    Standish, J.    His marriage.    Movie Classic 1:40 D '31
    Sharon, M.    The love of Lew and Lola.    Silver S 2-3:20 Ja '32
    Hall, G.    Interview.    Movie Classic 3:37 D '32
    Townsend, L.    Sketch.    Movie Classic 5:46 S '33
    English, R.    Sketch.    Motion Pic 47:42 Jl '34
    Palmborg, R. P.    His marriage.    Movie Classic 7:32 Ja '35
    Morgan, L.    Stand back!    Silver S 9-4:51 F '39
    Bio note; filmog.    Movies & People 2:4 '40
    Manners, M. J.    Doctor Kildare after office hours.    Silver S
        11-9:26 Jl '41
    Meet the doctor.    Lions R 1-5:no p# Ja '42
    He kissed Garbo.    Lions R 1-9:no p# My '42
    Where are they now?    Newsweek 71:20 Ap 15 '68
    Whatever happened to your favorite Dr. Kildare?    Photop 85-3:
        24 Mr '74

AZNAVOUR, CHARLES
    Flash on...    Unifrance 50:8 Jl/S '59
    Acting on my emotions.    Films & Filming 7-1:17 O '60
    Faces of anybody.    New Yorker 39:33 Ap 6 '63
    Tu parles Charles.    Time 81:62 Ap 12 '63
    Sad star.    Newsweek 61:32 Ap 15 '63
    Graham, P.    The face of '63--France.    Films & Filming 9-8:13
        My '63

Bell, L.  He even makes married love sound exciting.   Life 56:
   18 My 22 '64
Of love and deeper sorrows.   Time 86:102 O 22 '65
Tiny Troubador.   Newsweek 66:102 O 25 '65
Bio.   Cur Bio 29:5 F '68
   Same.   Cur Bio Yrbk 1968:40 '69
Salute of the week.   Cue 39-6:1 F 7 '70
Popkin, M.  His music is an exact equivalent of romance.   N. Y.
   Times sec 2:33 O 22 '72
Filmog.   Film Dope 2:20 Mr '73


BABS, ALICE
   Dance, H.   God has those angels.   Sat R 51:60 Ap 13 '68

BABY CHARLES (SPOFFORD)
   Baby Charles.   Classic Film Collect 33:27 Win '71

BABY LeROY
   Hamilton, S.   Sketch.   Photop 43:60 My '33
   Grant, J.   Sketch.   Motion Pic 45:40 Je '33
   Goldbeck, E.   How they get him to act his parts.   Motion Pic
   47:46 My '34
   Rivalry with Ricky Arlen.   Photop 45:40 My '34
   Johnston, A.   Story of.   Womans Home C 61:10 Ag '34

BABY PEGGY
   Goldbeck, W.   Interview.   Classic 15:40 O '22
   Sketch.   Photop 23:42 F '23
   Whitehill, D.   Sketch.   Motion Pic 25:42 Mr '23

BABY SANDY
   Where is Baby Sandy?   Movie Dig 1-2:39 Mr '72

BACALL, LAUREN
   Journey to Bacall.   Cue 14-7:10 F 17 '45
   Dudley, F.   What now, Lauren?   Silver S 15-7:22 My '45
   London, E.   And so they are one.   Silver S 15-11:32 S '45
   Asher, J.   And how are things with the Bogarts?   Silver S 17-9:
   52 Jl '45
   Colby, A.   Story of.   Photop 31:62 O '47
   Graham, S.   Story of.   Photop 36:38 Ag '49
   Hall, G.   Baby exposes Bogey.   Silver S 24-6:36 Ap '54
   Bacall's a "Designing woman. "   Cue 26-12:11 Mr 23 '57
   Burke, T.   And don't call her Bogey's baby.   N. Y. Times Bio
   Ed Mr 22 '70
   Biography.   Cur Bio 31:5 Mr '70
      Same.   Cur Bio Yrbk 1970:21 '71
   Farrell, B.   Applause for Bacall.   Life 68:54A Ap 3 '70
   Salute of the week.   Cue 39-14:1 Ap 4 '70
   Botts, L.   Betty Bacall takes a musical trip.   Look 34:M Ap 21
   '70

The love story of Bogie and his Betty.   Screen Greats 1-2:54
  Sum '71
English, P.   Age cannot wither a new woman.   New Woman 1-8:
  44 F '72
Ast, P.   No chicken for Bacall.   Interview 27:12 N '72
Baker, R.   Interview.   Films Illus 2-21:28 Mr '73
Filmog.   Film Dope 2:21 Mr '73

BACKUS, JIM
  Rieder, H.   Memories of Mr. Magoo.   Cinema J 8-2:17 Spg '69
  Backus, J. & H.   Guess what?   Coronet 12-2:36 F '74

BACLANOVA, OLGA
  Spensley, D.   Sketch.   Motion Pic 36:34 S '28
  Obit.   N. Y. Times Bio Ed p1204 S '74

BADDELEY, HERMIONE
  Sketch.   Theatre World 41:29 Jl '45

BADGLEY, HELEN
  Those Thanhouser kids.   Photop 7-3:134 F '15

BAER, BUDDY
  Shane, D.   The biggest man in Hollywood.   Silver S 24-6:39 Ap
  '54

BAER, JOHN
  The adventures of John Baer.   TV Guide 1-18:A-10 Jl 31 '53

BAER, MAX SR.
  Baskette, K.   Sketch.   Photop 44:34 N '33
  Service, F.   Interview.   Movie Classic 5:51 F '34
  Reynolds, Q.   Sketch.   Colliers 93:11 Ja 27 '37
  Obit.   Screen World 11:215 '60
  (Only references to his film career were researched.)

BAER, MAX JR.
  A lot of hostility.   TV Guide 13-21:13 My 22 '65

BAGGOT, KING
  Gates, H. H.   Sketch.   N. Y. Drama 69:43 Ja 15 '13
  Sketch.   Blue Book 19:469 Jl '14
  Stanhope, S. A.   Work of.   Motion Pic Supp 1:54 O '15
  Sleuthing as a fine art.   Photop 15-4:59 Mr '19
  Naylor, H. S.   Interview.   Motion Pic Classic 13:26 O '21
  Filmog (as actor, director, writer).   Film Dope 2:26 Mr '73

BAILEY, PEARL
  Sketch.   Vogue 108:140 Ag 1 '46
  Pearl in the raw.   Newsweek 70:110 D 4 '67
  Prideaux, T.   Big new deal for Dolly--hello Pearl.   Life 63:128
  D 8 '67
  Lewis, E.   A string of Pearls.   Cue 37-1:13 Ja 6 '68

Salute of the week.  Cue 38-11:1 Mr 15 '69
To be or not to be nude.  Current 109:18 Ag '69
Bio.  Cur Bio 30:5 O '69
   Same.  Cur Bio Yrbk 1969:23 '70
Davidson, B.  Pearl Bailey says "hello" to TV.  TV Guide 19-13:
   40 Mr 27 '71
Cook, J.  She needled her way through 22 cities.  N. Y. Times
   Bio Ed D 16 '71

BAILEY, RAYMOND
   The banker's friend.  TV Guide 13-38:34 S 18 '65
   He finally dropped anchor at a bank.  TV Guide 18-28:16 Jl 11
   '70

BAIN, BARBARA
   Who's afraid of Liz Taylor?  TV Guide 11-22:26 Je 1 '63
   Gordon, S.  Computer-age Mata Hari.  Look 31:73 N 28 '67
   Conversation with the Landaus.  TV Guide 16-18:30 My 4 '68
   Ephron, N.  Marriage: impossible?  Good House 167:60 N '68
   I felt I had never been away.  TV Guide 19-40:18 O 2 '71

BAIN, CONRAD
   He has become a household face.  TV Guide 22-2:21 Ja 12 '74

BAIN, SHERRY
   Raddatz, L.  Farewell to the check-out counter.  TV Guide 20-
   26:31 Je 24 '72

BAINTER, FAY
   Interview.  N. Y. Drama 76:5 O 28 '16
   Sketch.  Theatre 26:96 Ag '17
   The serious playgoer and lost illusions.  Drama 11:264 My '21
   Sketch.  Stage 9:2 Je '32
   Sketch.  Photop 53:68 Mr '39
   Biographical note; filmog.  Movies & People 2:4 '40
   The challenge of the movies.  Lions R 1-5:no p# Ja '42
   Fay Bainter serves.  Lions R 2-1:no p# S/O '42
   Bainter, F.  Looking ahead.  Lions R 2-3:no p# D '42
   "Ma" Bainter.  Lions R 3-1:no p# S '43
   Captain of the cover(all) girls.  Lions R 3-2:no p# Ja '44
   Obit.  N. Y. Times p47 Ap 17 '68
      Newsweek 71:62 Ap 29 '68
      Time 91:90 Ap 26 '68

BAIRD, LEAH
   Sketch.  Motion Pic 8:116 Ja '15
   Sketch.  Green Book 13:243 F '15
   Baird, L.  Two exciting experiences.  Movie Pic 2-6:9 D '15
   Reid, J.  Interview.  Motion Pic 18:60 D '19
   Obit.  Screen World 23:235 '72

BAKER, ART
   Obit.  Screen World 18:232 '67

38                                    Motion Picture Performers

BAKER, BOB
   Bio note.   Cinema Trails 2:21 n. d.

BAKER, CARROLL
   LaBadie, D. W.   Free agent.   Show 1-3:60 D '61
   Leppard, S.   This is Carroll Baker.   Sound Stage 1-2:5 F '65
   Matteo, P. F. Jr.   From Baby Doll to Harlow; filmog.   Screen
      Legends 1-1:39 My '65
   Filmog.   Film Dope 2:28 Mr '73

BAKER, DIANE
   McClelland, D.   Where all that old-time glamour went.   Film
      Fan Mo 75:11 S '67
   Raddatz, L.   Dear Diane: where did I fail?   TV Guide 18-44:20
      O 31 '70
   McClelland, D.   Diane Baker; filmog.   Films In R 23-2:117 F
      '72

BAKER, EDDIE
   Obit.   Screen World 20:231 '69

BAKER, ELSIE
   Obit.   Screen World 23:235 '72

BAKER, GEORGE
   The stars of tomorrow.   Film R p43 '55/56
   Rising stars.   Film R p31 '57/58

BAKER, JOE DON
   Note; filmog.   Films Illus 4-39:91 N '74

BAKER, KENNY
   Arthur, P.   One of the best.   Silver S 8-7:59 My '38
   Hendrick, K.   Five points of a star.   CS Mon Mag p8 O 9 '48

BAKER, PHIL
   Tells about his public.   Stage 12:60 Ja '35
   $64 question.   Time 43:86 Mr 6 '44
   Vincent, P.   The $64 question man.   Silver S 14-8:38 Je '44
   Beatty, J.   Brains and dough.   America 139:33 My '45
   Bio.   Cur Bio N '46
      Same.   Cur Bio Yrbk 1946

BAKER, STANLEY
   Nolan, J. E.   Films on TV.   Films In R 21-1:40 Ja '70
   Tarratt, M. & Gough-Yates, K.   Playing the game; interview;
      filmog.   Films & Filming 16-11:34 Ag '70
   Filmog.   Film Dope 2:29 Mr '73

BAKER, TOM
   Tom Baker.   Look 35-21:60 O 19 '71
   d'Arcy, S.   Baker on the deadline.   Films Illus 3-31:258 Ja '74

BAKEWELL, WILLIAM
Manners, D.   Sketch.   Motion Pic Classic 28:55 Ja '29
York, C.   Sketch.   Photop 37:40 D '29
Biery, R.   Interview.   Motion Pic Classic 31:41 Mr '30
Hall, G.   Sketch.   Motion Pic Classic 33:73 Mr '31
Churchill, E.   That darned fool.   Silver S 1-7:20 My '31
Cheatham, M.   Bill Bakewell says.   Silver S 3-6:23 Ap '33

BAL, JEANNE
The most surprising dropout of the school year.   TV Guide 12-
27:13 Jl 4 '64

BALFOUR, BETTY
My work for British films.   Graphic 118:315 N 19 '27
Slide, A.   Britain's queen of happiness.   Silent Pic 2:10 Spg '69

BALFOUR, KATHERINE
Theater Arts introduces.   Theater Arts 33:21 Je '49

BALL, LUCILLE
Martin, S.   Sketch.   Movie Classic 11:45 O '36
Hamilton, S.   Sketch.   Photop 52:68 Ja '38
Smithson, E. J.   Something on the Ball.   Screen Book 21-2:39
S '38
Hamilton, S.   Sketch.   Photop 54:29 Ag '40
Manners, M. J.   Her "good fellow" days are over.   Silver S 11-
1:40 N '40
Her marriage.   Photop 18:93 F '41
Wilson, E.   The odds were 100 to 1.   Silver S 12-8:36 Je '42
Ball, L.   Just between you and me.   Lions R 2-4:no p# Ap '43
Hayseed in her hair.   Lions R 3-1:no p# S '43
Haas, D. B.   The serious side of Lucille Ball.   Silver S 13-12:
26 O '43
Lucille Ball's golden day.   Lions R 3-3:no p# Ap '44
Hall, G.   A star is reborn.   Silver S 14-7:32 My '44
Rand, M.   Interview.   Photop 27:22 N '45
Ball, L.   What I've learned about living.   Silver S 16-5:35 Mr
'46
Pritchett, F.   Sketch.   Photop 29:43 S '45
Arnaz, L. B.   The man I married.   Silver S 18-1:36 N '47
Holland, J.   Here's a girl who knows the answers.   Silver S 19-
3:24 Ja '49
Ball, L.   Complexes are silly!   Silver S 19-11:30 S '49
Ball, L.   My favorite funnyman.   Silver S 20-6:36 Ap '50
Ball, L.   Ten ways to lose a man.   Silver S 21-5:22 Mr '51
Lucy's $50,000,000 baby.   TV Guide 1-1:5 Ap 3 '53
TV Guide goes backstage.   TV Guide 1-5:12 My 1 '53
That funny looking Lucy.   TV Guide 1-28:18 O 9 '53
Marsh, P.   Lucy looks into her future.   Silver S 23-12:36 O '53
Still in the driver's seat.   TV Guide 3-50:13 D 10 '55
Minoff, P.   The lowdown from Lucy.   Cue 26-15:14 Ap 13 '57
Fletcher, F.   Broadway bow for Lucy.   Cue 29-50:11 D 10 '60
Defining Lucy: the realist who really cares.   Broadcasting

73:117 Jl 31 '67
$54,000,000 bonanza.    Vogue 151:216 My '68
Thomas, B.    Lady millionaire, Hollywood style.    Good House
    166:50 Je '68
Our mother the boss.    Look 33:M Je 24 '69
Bacon, J.    All I could see was Elizabeth and that rock.    TV
    Guide 18-36:16 S 5 '70
Is this why Lucille Ball stopped laughing?    Photop 78-3:48 S '70
Bell, J. N.    My mother, Lucille Ball.    Good House 172:14 Mr
    '71
The first ten years were the easiest.    Photop 79-4:74 Ap '71
Let me and my baby live here with you.    Photop 79-5:32 My '71
Don't disgrace me.    Photop 79-5:92 My '71
Bowers, R. L.    Lucille Ball; filmog.    Films In R 22-6:321 Je/
    Jl '71
I'm pregnant again.    Photop 80-2:89 Ag '71
Letters.    Films In R 22-7:448 Ag/S '71
Bergquist, L.    The star that never sets.    Look 35-18:54 S 7 '71
Patty Duke tells how Lucille Ball defeated her.    Photop 80-3:37
    S '71
Patty Duke used my son and victimized us.    Photop 80-6:19 D
    '71
Interview with Desi Sr.    Photop 80-6:21 D '71
Carter, J.    Lucy stopped me from killing myself.    Mod Screen
    66-2:56 F '72
Ball, L.    My son has finally found the right girl.    Photop 81-3:
    69 Mr '72
Ski accident.    Mod Screen 66-4:41 Ap '72
How she suffered for success.    Mod Screen 66-7:51 Jl '72
Birmingham, F. A.    Everybody loves Lucy.    Sat Eve Post 244:
    60 Win '72
Why Liza lives with Lucille Ball.    Photop 83-1:24 Ja '73
Higham, C.    Is Lucy having a ball as Mame?    N. Y. Times sec
    2:15 F 18 '73
    Same.    N. Y. Times Bio Ed p217 F '73
Whitney, D.    We wrote the baby into the script.    TV Guide 21-
    13:4 Mr 31 '73
Liza's first interview about Lucille Ball.    Mod Screen 67-4:26
    Ap '73
Lucy today.    Photop 84-3:46 S '73
Stoop, N. M.    Here's Lucy...as Mame.    After Dark 6-6:33 O
    '73
Pearce, C.    They still love Lucy.    Show 3-8:31 N '73
Paskin, B.    The other Mame.    Films Illus 3-29:186 N '73
Watters, J.    Lucy is 'Mame'--high-kicking, 63 and full of brass.
    People 1-3:34 Mr 18 '74
Interview.    Dialogue 3-6:entire issue My/Je '74
Gale Gordon talks about Lucille Ball.    Photop 85-6:48 Je '74
O'Flaherty, T.    TV will never be quite the same again.    TV
    Guide 22-27:15 Jl 6 '74
Mrs. Ross Martin talks about Lucille Ball.    Photop 86-5:39 N
    '74

BALL, SUZAN
  (Incorrectly spelled Susan in First Volume)
  Ball, S.  My cooking had nothing to do with it.   Silver S 23-1:46
    N '52
  Connolly, M.  She'll never walk alone.   Silver S 24-6:40 Ap '54

BALLARD, KAYE
  Just don't call her Jerry Lewis.   TV Guide 2-46:20 N 13 '54
  Watt, D.  Tables for two.   New Yorker 33:48 D 21 '57
  Eimeri, S.  Can women be funny?   Mlle 56:150 N '62
  Efron, E.  She offers no threat to the housewives.   TV Guide
    14-38:26 S 17 '66
  Hano, A.  She lives from one trauma to another.   TV Guide 16-
    29:16 Jl 20 '68
  Bio.  Cur Bio 30:6 S '69
    Same.  Cur Bio Yrbk 1969:25 '70
  The Christmas that taught me the meaning of love.   Mod Screen
    66-1:46 Ja '72
  Orton, C.  An open letter to Gertrude Berg.   After Dark 6-6:30
    O '73

BALLEW, SMITH
  Where is Smith Ballew?   Movie Dig 1-6:138 N '72

BALLIN, MABEL
  Fletcher, A. W.  Interview.   Motion Pic 21:38 Je '21
  Fletcher, A. W.  Interview.   Motion Pic Classic 13:20 O '21
  Evans, D.  Sketch.   Photop Ap '22
  Oettinger, M. H.  Interview.   Motion Pic 24:30 N '22
  Sketch.   Motion Pic 32:55 N '26

BALSAM, MARTIN
  Milne, T.  Bio note; filmog.   Focus On F 6:7 Spg '71
  Filmog.   Film Dope 2:32 Mr '73
  Stoop, N. M.  All media actor.   After Dark 6-8:42 D '73

BAMATTRE, MARTHA
  Obit.   Screen World 22:235 '71

BANCROFT, ANNE
  Gittel with guitar.   Cue 27-35:12 Ag 30 '58
  Hammel, F.  The second miracle.   Cue 28-42:18 O 17 '59
  Funke, L. & Booth, J. E.  On acting; interview.   Show 1-1:88
    O '61
  Rising stars.   Film R p41 '63/64
  Salute of the week.   Cue 39-7:1 F 14 '70
  Young Winston.   Films Illus 2-13:12 Jl '72
  Filmog.   Film Dope 2:32 Mr '73
  Interview.   Viva 1-3:89 D '73
  Burke, T.  Annie.   TV Guide 22-47:16 N 23 '74

BANCROFT, GEORGE
  Wells, H. K.  Sketch.   Motion Pic Classic 22:35 Ja '26

Walker, H. L.  Interview.  Motion Pic 34:33 N '27
Walker, H. L.  Interview.  Motion Pic 36:67 D '28
Goldbeck, E.  Interview.  Motion Pic 39:50 Mr '30
Lang, H.  Sketch.  Photop 38:35 O '30
Hall, G.  What women ask his advice about.  Motion Pic 40:49
    D '30
Alpert, D.  Women don't understand themselves.  Silver S 1-6:
    16 Ap '31
Keen, J. H.  Cinema indigestion.  Cinema Dig 1-3:8 Je 13 '32
Johnston, J.  What's happened to Geo. Bancroft?  Screen Book
    19-1:20 Ag '37
Filmog.  Film Dope 2:33 Mr '73

BANKHEAD, TALLULAH
    Cruikshank, H.  Sketch.  Motion Pic 41:33 Je '31
    Cohen, J. S. Jr.  Sketch.  Photop 40:46 Ag '31
    Wilson, E.  The toughest break in pictures.  Silver S 2-4:22 F
        '32
    Spensley, D.  Sketch.  Movie Classic 2:54 Mr '32
    Biery, R.  Sketch.  Photop 41:46 Ap '32
    Grayson, C.  The star that has Hollywood guessing.  Motion Pic
        43:58 Ap '32
    Carvel, M.  Hollywood's opinion of...  Movie Classic 2:26 My
        '32
    Hall, G.  Interview.  Motion Pic 44:47 S '32
    Hefferman, H.  Tallulah.  Cinema Dig 1-11:11 O 3 '32
    Bell, N. B.  Tallulah.  Cinema Dig 1-13:15 O 31 '32
    Cheasley, C. W.  Her numberscope.  Movie Classic 3:51 O '32
    Keen, J. H.  Tallulah... yes?  Cinema Dig 2-3:10 D 12 '32
    Patrick, C.  Tallulah... no?  Cinema Dig 2-3:10 D 12 '32
    Moffitt, C. F.  Censorship for interviews Hollywood's latest wild
        idea...  Cinema Dig 2-5:9 Ja 9 '33
    Melcher, E.  Tallulah.  Cinema Dig 2-10:9 F 20 '33
    Mosley, L. O.  Interview.  Motion Pic 45:35 F '33
    Green, E. M.  Sketch.  Theatre World 26:231 N '36
    Her country house.  Vogue 102:56 Jl 1 '43
    Tallulah talks about life and Lifeboat.  Cue 13-3:6 Ja 15 '44
    Fletcher, A. W.  Story of.  Photop 24:51 Ap '44
    Tallulah comes to Stamford.  Cue 13-25:14 Je 17 '44
    Wilson, E.  Tallulah's Royal scandal.  Silver S 15-4:24 F '45
    The Pollyanna kid.  Cue 14-10:12 Mr 10 '45
    Linen, J. A.  Getting an interview with Miss Bankhead.  Time
        52:14 D 6 '48
    Tattling on Tallulah.  Cue 21-39:12 S 27 '52
    Yoo hoo, Talloo!  TV Guide 2-33:8 Ag 14 '54
    Tallulah tees off.  Cue 23-37:15 S 11 '54
    Where are they now?  Newsweek 71:14 Mr 18 '68
    Tallulah.  Newsweek 72:80 D 23 '68
    Obit.  Brit Book Yr 1969:566 '69
        Cur Bio Yrbk 1969:463 '70
        Film R. p21 '69/70
        N. Y. Times pl D 13 '68
    Loos, A.  Unforgettable Tallulah.  Read Dig 95:130 Jl '69

Ace, G. Tallulah. Sat R 55:8 My 20 '72
Holt's new photo-biography shows another Tallulah.   Pub W 202:
   35 Ag 14 '72
Gill, B. Profiles.   New Yorker 48:45 O 7; 50 O 14 '72
Gill, B. Tallulah.   Harp Baz 106:102 N '72
Filmog.   Films & Filming 19-2:62 N '72
Filmog.   Film Dope 2:34 Mr '73
Pin-up of the past.   Films & Filming 19-10:68 Jl '73
Eugenia Rawls remembers...   Interview 4-4:10 Ap '74

BANKS, MONTY
Spensley, D. Sketch.   Photop 32:67 Ag '27
Shelton, G. Sketch.   Motion Pic Classic 34:66 D '27
Obit.   Time 55:76 Ja 16 '50

BANKY, VILMA
Sheldon, J. Interview.   Motion Pic 30:24 N '25
Curran, D. Interview.   Motion Pic Classic 22:30 D '25
York, C. Sketch.   Photop 29:1 Ap '26
Denbo, D. Sketch.   Motion Pic Classic 24:58 Ja '27
Kenworthy, M. Interview.   Photop 31:84 Ap '27
Biery, R. Interview.   Photop 33:48 Mr '28
Why she is not to play with Ronald Colman.   Motion Pic 35:31
   Ap '28
Donnell, D. Interview.   Motion Pic Classic 29:18 Ag '29
Lewis, G. American filmog.   Films In R 24-2:123 F '73
Miller, N. Partial filmog.   Films In R 25-5:315 My '74

BANNEN, IAN
Ian Bannen talks about Sophia Loren.   Photop 85-6:41 Je '74

BANNER, JOHN
Hobson, D. Achtung!...please.   TV Guide 15-18:16 My 6 '67
Obit.   Screen World p231 '74

BANNISTER, HARRY C.
Calhoun, D. Sketch.   Motion Pic 41:48 Je '31
Grant, J. Sketch.   Motion Pic Classic 33:54 Jl '31
Sykes, L. His divorce.   Movie Classic 2:28 Je '32
Real reasons for his divorce.   Motion Pic 43:40 Je '32
Burden, J. Sketch.   Movie Classic 3:28 O '32
Grant, J. Will he remarry Ann Harding?   Motion Pic 45:32 Ap
   '33

BARA, LORI
Maxwell, V. Experiences in the jungle during the filming of
   Samarang.   Photop 44:50 S '33

BARA, THEDA
Bell, A. The vampire woman.   Theatre 22:246 N '15
Sketch.   Green Book 15:263 F '16
Sketch.   Motion Pic Classic 2:26 Ap '16
Her defense.   Motion Pic 12:99 Ag '16

Courtlandt, R.   Sketch.   Motion Pic Classic 3:25 O '16
Courtlandt, R.   Sketch.   Motion Pic 13:59 Ap '17
Ghostly Belva barks at Bara.   Photop 11-6:74 My '17
Home of.   Motion Pic Classic 5:27 D '17
McKelvie, M. G.   Interview.   Motion Pic Classic 7:24 S '18
Smith, F. J.   Interview.   Motion Pic Classic 7:16 F '19
Metcalfe, J. S.   From the movies to the legitimate stage.   Life
   75:610 Ap 1 '20
Smith, A.   Confessions of.   Photop 18:56 Je '20
Woollcott, A.   Stage debut.   Cent 100:413 Jl '20
Bara, P. L.   The real Theda Bara.   Motion Pic Classic 11:19
   D '20
Bara, P.   Bio sketch.   Motion Pic Classic 11:19 D '20
Hall, G. & Fletcher, A. W.   Interview.   Motion Pic 24:20 N '22
Henning, O.   What is a vamp?   Motion Pic 35:71 Je '28
Towne, C. H.   O, vanished vampire!   Cue 4-44:4 Ag 29 '36
Bio note.   Harp Baz 82:191 S '48
Whitehall, R.   The face of the vampire.   Cinema (BH) 3-3:11
   Jl '66
Brock, A.   The unfilled dream of a star.   Classic Film Collect
   28:6 Fall '70

BARBEAU, ADRIENNE
   From Broadway to TV--in one unlikely hop.   TV Guide 21-6:14
      F 10 '73

BARCROFT, ROY
   Obit.   Those Enduring Idols 1-3:35 F/Mr '70

BARD, BEN
   Manners, D.   Sketch.   Motion Pic Classic 24:56 N '26

BARDOT, BRIGITTE
   Bio note.   Unifrance 23:10 F '53
   They didn't plan to be movie stars.   Unifrance 56:no p# Spg '62
   Feinstein, H.   My gorgeous darling sweetheart angels.   Film Q
      15-3:66 Spg '62
   Graham, P.   The face of '63--France.   Films & Filming 9-8:13
      My '63
   Maurois, A.   The sex kitten grows up.   Playboy 11:84 Jl '64
   Silke, J. R.   The tragic mask of Bardolatry.   Cinema (BH) 2-2:
      27 '64
   Discontented countess.   Life 64:85 My 3 '68
   Rollin, B. B.   Brigitte Bardot, Coco Chanel and me.   Look 33:
      13 Ap 1 '69
   Fetching new symbol of France.   Time 97:32 Mr 22 '71
   Society of the spectacle; interview.   Cineaste 4-4:18 Spg '71
   Brigitte Bardot.   Show 2-9:42 N '71
   De Vilallonga, J. L.   Sensational Brigitte Bardot.   Vogue 160:
      168 N 1 '72
   Filmog.   Film Dope 2:34 Mr '73
   Williamson, B.   Bardot.   Oui 2-4:31 Ap '73

BARDOT, MIJANOU
A flash on.   Unifrance 48:7 O '58
Any more at home like Brigitte?  Yes.   Life 45:101 N 24 '58

BARI, LYNN
Hamilton, S.   Sketch.   Photop 54:29 My '40
Franchey, J. R.   Bari the baddie.   Silver S 13-7:39 My '43
A mistake I wouldn't make again.   Photop 22:47 My '43
Wilson, E.   Meet the missus!   Silver S 14-7:38 My '44
What she and Mr. Luft argue about.   Photop 27:60 Jl '45
Holland, J.   How to get over a love affair.   Silver S 15-10:32
   Ag '45
Garvin, R.   Filmog.   Films In R 21-8:516 O '70
Madden, J. C.   Letter; additional filmog.   Films In R 21-9:584
   N '70
Letters; additional filmog.   Films In R 22-2:113 F '71

BARKER, JESS
Holland, J.   Life with the Barkers.   Silver S 16-12:40 O '46
Barker, J.   My life with Susan.   Silver S 20-5:30 Mr '50

BARKER, LEX
Tarzan X.   Cue 18-13:19 Mr 26 '49
The tenth and newest of movie Tarzans.   Life 26:159 My 16 '49
Churchill, R. & B.   So you want to be like Tarzan.   Silver S
   20-8:44 Je '50
Rising stars.   Film R p27 '50
Dahl, A.   Here's why our marriage will last.   Silver S 21-10:22
   Ag '51
Hall, G.   For as long as we both shall live.   Silver S 22-9:24
   Jl '52
Reid, L.   Lana tries marriage again.   Silver S 24-2:35 D '53
Glanz, B.   Partial filmog.   Films In R 18-1:60 Ja '67
Marill, A. H.   Partial filmog.   Films In R 18-4:253 Ap '67
In memory.   Show 3-6:74 S '73
Obit.   Classic Film Collect 40:58 Fall '73
   Film R p18 '73/74
   Screen World p231 '74

BARNES, BARRY K.
Obit.   Film R p45 '65/66

BARNES, BINNIE
Lee, S.   Sketch.   Motion Pic 48:59 D '34
Hall, H.   Sketch.   Movie Classic 7:54 D '34
Sketch.   Stage 12:33 Je '35
Reed, D.   Interview.   Movie Classic 8:38 Jl '35
Hall, H.   Binnie's a bit all right.   Silver S 6-1:25 N '35
Donnell, D.   Interview.   Motion Pic 51:24 My '36
Lee, S.   Interview.   Movie Classic 10:50 My '36
Bombshell Barnes.   Lions R 3-1:no p# S '43
Double trouble.   Lions R 3-4(sup):no p# Jl '44
Maltin, L.   Interview; filmog.   Film Fan Mo 151:3 Ja '74

BARNES, CARMEN
  Churchill, E.  Hollywood's newest genius.  Silver S 1-7:59 My
    '31
  Autobiographical.  Motion Pic Classic 33:80 Je '31
  Hall, J.  Sketch.  Motion Pic 41:58 Je '31
  Pryor, N.  Sketch.  Motion Pic Classic 32:72 Ag '31

BARNES, JOANNA
  The Hollywood swingers.  Show 3-11:88 N '63
  Amory, C.  Trade winds.  Sat R 54:8 F 20 '71

BARNES, THOMAS ROY
  Goldbeck, W.  Sketch.  Motion Pic Classic 14:46 My '22

BARNETT, CHESTER
  Wade, P.  Interview.  Motion Pic Classic 3:56 O '16
  Lamb, G.  Interview.  Motion Pic 17:53 My '19

BARNETT, VINCE
  Baskette, K.  The man all Hollywood fears.  Photop 44:28 N '33
  Sketch.  Time 26:42 Jl 29 '35
  Spencer, E. L.  Five-alarm rib.  Sat Eve Post 217:6 D 9 '44

BARON, LITA
  Walker, H. L.  Her wedding.  Photop 33:24 N '48
  Honeymoon at Ojai Valley inn.  Photop 34:66 D '48
  Noel, T.  Watch out for Rory.  Silver S 24-9:24 Jl '54

BARON, SANDY
  The hoods were his heroes.  TV Guide 15-19:30 My 13 '67

BAROUX, LUCIEN
  Obit.  N. Y. Times p47 My 23 '68

BARRAT, ROBERT
  Obit.  N. Y. Times p33 Ja 9 '70
    Screen World 22:235 '71

BARRAULT, JEAN LOUIS
  Klein, L. & A.  Interview.  Theatre Arts 31:24 O '47
  Note.  Vogue 113:103 Mr 15 '49
  Bentley, E.  Traveler's report.  Theatre Arts 33:43 My '49
  Note.  Harp Baz 83:74 Jl '49
  Bentley, E.  Child of silence.  Theatre Arts 33:28 O '49
  Bentley, E.  Actor as thinker.  Theatre Arts 34:31 Ap '50
  Artists and statesmen.  Life 29:77 Ag 7 '50
  Hobson, H.  Barrault-Renaud in Anouilh play.  CS Mon Mag p9
    N 11 '50
  Hill, R. K.  Man at work.  Theatre Arts 35:40 O '51
  Hewes, H.  French family Barrault.  Sat R 35:28 N 8 '52
  Barrault on Broadway.  Cue 21-45:13 N 8 '52
  Barrault on Broadway.  Life 33:69 N 17 '52
  Feinstein, M.  Avant-garde theatre that won an audience.  Theatre

Arts 36:21 N '52
Hayes, R.  Renaud-Barrault company.  Commonweal 57:223 D
    5 '52
Marshall, M.  Barrault's Hamlet.  Nation 175:562 D 13 '52
Brown, J. M.  Barrault's Hamlet.  Sat R 35:24 D 27 '52
Hewes, H.  Se moquer ou ne pas se moquer.  Sat R 36:25 Ja
    24 '53
Nathan, G. J.  Latest Hamlet.  Theatre Arts 37:24 F '53
Bio.  Cur Bio Mr '53
Hope-Wallace, P.  Barrault offstage.  N. Y.  Times Mag p20 Ja
    20 '57
Hewes, H.  Total theatre.  Sat R 40:22 Ja 26 '57
Great audience.  New Yorker 33:27 F 23 '57
Clurman, H.  Theatre.  Nation 184:174 F 23 '57
Bentley, E.  One-man dialogue.  New Rep 136:20 Mr 18 '57
Mr. Harper.  Master of mime.  Harper 214:85 Ap '57
Bowers, F.  Renaud-Barrault company.  Theatre Arts 41:20 Ap
    '57
Why the French need Shakespeare.  Horizon 4:102 S '61
Genet.  Letter from Paris.  New Yorker 40:102 F 22 '64
Oliver, E.  Off Broadway.  New Yorker 40:112 Mr 14 '64
Life force.  Newsweek 63:96 Mr 16 '64
Smith, P. J.  Interview.  Opera N 30:8 S 25 '65
Gutman, J.  With honor and insolence.  Opera N 30:17 Ap 9 '66
Dance of life.  Time 90:50 D 22 '67
Saal, H.  Return of Carmen.  Newsweek 70:68 D 25 '67
Pilikian, H. I.  Dialogue with.  Drama 89:50 Sum '68
Last bow for Barrault?  Time 92:86 S 13 '68
Letter from Paris.  New Yorker 44:173 S 21 '68
French side of it.  Yachting 125:66 F '69
In the words of.  Cue 38-40:12 O 4 '69
Gruen, J.  I've taken risks for 30 years.  N. Y.  Times Bio Ed
    My 17 '70
Salute of the week.  Cue 39-20:1 My 23 '70
Carlson, J.  Rabelais!  Show 1-6:54 O '70
Ansorge, P.  Interview.  Plays & Players 18-7:18 Ap '71
Filmog.  Film Dope 2:42 Mr '73

BARRAULT, MARIE-CHRISTINE
    Cowie, P.  Marie-Christine Barrault.  Focus On F 1:14 Ja/F
        '70

BARRETT, CLAUDIA
    Claudia and the tree stump.  TV Guide 8-36:28 S 3 '60

BARRETT, JUDITH
    Blackstock, L.  Sketch.  Motion Pic 53:25 F '37

BARRIE, BARBARA
    Winsome Barbara Barrie.  TV Guide 12-48:10 N 28 '64

BARRIE, ELAINE
    Garvey, L.  Why she married John Barrymore.  Movie Classic

11:32 F '37
Exploits of.   Time 35:55 F 12 '40
Zeitlin, I.   Interview.   Photop 54:26 Je '40

BARRIE, MONA
Sketch.   Photop 46:72 Jl '34
Clever changes of hairdress.   Movie Classic 8:64 Ag '35

BARRIE, NIGEL
Interview.   N. Y.   Drama 72:18 Ag 12 '14
Landy, G. & Smith, A.   Both Englishmen.   Photop 16-6:78 N '19
Roberts, S.   Interview.   Motion Pic 19:54 Ap/My '20

BARRIE, WENDY
Sketch.   Time 25:61 Ap 22 '35
Surmelian, L.   Hong Kong's contribution.   Silver S 6-2:25 D '35
Zeitlin, I.   Interview.   Motion Pic 53:45 Ap '37
Walker, H. L.   Wendy learned about men from men.   Silver S
   10-4:46 F '40
Hamilton, S.   Sketch.   Photop 54:31 S '40
Sketch.   Photop 34:95 F '49

BARRIS, MARTI
Something for the boys of all ages.   TV Guide 8-31:29 Jl 30 '60

BARRISCALE, BESSIE
How she became a photoplayer.   Motion Pic 9:96 Je '15
Willis, R.   Natural.   Movie Pic 2-3:18 S '15
Sketch.   Motion Pic 10:106 Ja '16
Use your mind.   Film Players Herald 2-7:31 F '16
Does immorality exist in the moving-picture studios?   Motion Pic
   12:79 S '16
Willis, R.   Sketch.   Motion Pic Classic 5:25 S '17
Peltret, E.   Sketch.   Motion Pic 16:32 Ja '19
Cheatham, M. S.   Interview.   Motion Pic 19:44 Mr '20
Bio note.   Silent Pic 14:20 Spg '72

BARRY, DON "RED"
King of the redheads.   Those Enduring Idols 1-6:63 S '70
Don "Red" Barry appeals to fan.   Classic Film Collect 29:58
   Win '70
Danard, D.   Filmog.   Films In R 23-4:250 Ap '72

BARRY, GENE
Hall, G.   Every actor needs a wife.   Silver S 24-9:44 Jl '54
Hobson, D.   All for one and one for all?   Well, hardly!   TV
   Guide 17-13:20 Mr 29 '69
Loving one woman is the toughest game in town.   Photop 77-6:
   50 Je '70
Whitney, D.   The real Gene Barry.   TV Guide 19-11:28 Mr 13
   '71
Have I got a partner for you.   Show 2-5:6 Jl '71

BARRY, PATRICIA
Miss Barry likes gumption.  TV Guide 7-13:25 Mr 28 '59
She made them yell zowie!  TV Guide 10-47:27 N 24 '62

BARRY, WESLEY
Yost, R. M. Jr.  Wes Barry-American.  Photop 16-3:41 Ag '19
Keene, M. S.  Interview.  Motion Pic Classic 9:24 F '20
Sketch.  Photop 17:96 My '20
Interview.  Motion Pic 24:36 O '22

BARRYMORE, DIANA
Sketch.  Life 7:56 Jl 31 '39
Sketch.  Vogue 95:84 Mr 15 '40
Sketch.  Vogue 98:78 D 1 '41
Story of.  Vogue 98:78 D 1 '41
Vallee, W. L.  Daughter Diana.  Silver S 12-6:42 Ap '42

BARRYMORE, ETHEL
Her great stage speeches.  Theatre 9:26 Ja '09
Sketch.  Green Bk Album 1:1020 My '09
Sketch of career.  Womans Home C 37:21 Ja '10
Sketch of career.  Munsey 43:134 Ap '10
Eaton, W. P.  Sketch.  America 72:631 S '11
Wolf, R.  Bio sketch.  Green Book 9:641 Ap '13
Bio sketch.  Harp Baz 48:14 N '13
Guiterman, A.  ...and her family.  Womans Home C 41:24 Mr
   '14
Dale, A.  Interview.  Cosmop 56:697 Ap '14
White, M. Jr.  Sketch.  Munsey 54:537 Ap '15
Dale, A.  Bio sketch.  Green Book 14:1065 D '15
Wagstaffe, W.  Interview.  Theatre 23:80 F '16
Frohman, D. & Marcosson, I. F.  As a star.  Cosmop 61:368
   Ag '16
Gaddis, P.  Sketch.  Motion Pic Classic 4:43 Je '17
Interview.  Theatre 34:32 Jl '21
Porter, K.  Interview.  World Today 52:589 N '28
Collins, F. L.  Her successor.  Womans Home C 56:9 Ap '29
Wilson, E.  Lionel, Ethel and John.  Silver S 2-12:14 O '32
Moffitt, C. F.  Censorship for interviews Hollywood's latest wild
   idea.  Cinema Dig 2-5:9 Ja 9 '33
Barrymore, J.  Lionel, Ethel and I.  Am Mag 115:12 F '33 &
   following issues.
Fortieth anniversary on the stage.  Time 37:84 F 17 '40
Story of.  Vogue 101:50 Ap 1 '43
Miss Barrymore is back.  Cue 12-18:12 My 1 '43
St. Johns, A. R.  Story of.  Cosmop 115:8 S '43
A clan named Barrymore.  Lions R 3-2:no p# Ja '44
"Dame" Ethel the incomparable.  Cue 18-34:18 Ag 20 '49
Williams, E.  Tribute (in verse).  Theatre World 45:10 S '49
Obit.  Screen World 11:215 '60
Filmog.  Film Dope 2:43 Mr '73
(See Also: BARRYMORE FAMILY)

BARRYMORE, JOHN
Heredity on the stage.  Greek Bk Album 1:626 Mr '09
Barry, O.  Sketch.  Green Bk Album 4:1102 N '10
Sketch.  N. Y.  Drama 70:9 S 3 '13
Playing a juvenile lead.  Theatre 19:304 Je '14
Ten Eyck, J.  Interview.  Green Book 13:25 Ja '15
Ten Broeck, H.  From comedy to tragedy.  Theatre 24:23 Jl '16
Sermolino, M.  Interview with his barber.  Theatre 30:22 S '19
Bio.  Dramatic Mirror 82:1163 Je 5 '20
Seymour, W.  Some Richards I have seen.  Theatre 31:502 Je
    '20
Lewishon, L.  A note on acting.  Nation 111:569 N 17 '20
His views on moving pictures.  Motion Pic Classic 21:59 Ag '25
Confessions of an actor.  Ladies Home J 42:3 O '25 and following
    issues.
Ryan, D.  Barrymore on the movies.  Motion Pic Classic 23:20
    Ap '26
St. Johns, A. R.  Interview.  Photop 31:58 D '26
Miller, H.  Compared to Emil Jannings.  Motion Pic Classic
    26:33 S '27
Perry, R.  Sketch.  Motion Pic Classic 26:25 F '28
Belfrage, C.  Filming Tempest.  Motion Pic Classic 27:25 Ap
    '28
Smith, R.  An amazing personality.  Theatre 17:23 Ap '28
Fairbanks, D. Jr.  Appreciation.  Vanity Fair 35:67 S '30
Sketch.  Fortune 2:40 O '30
Chapman, J. B.  The legendary Barrymore.  Motion Pic Classic
    32:30 N '30
Hall, L.  Sketch.  Photop 39:38 Ja '31
Fender, R.  Sketch.  Motion Pic Classic 33:30 Mr '31
Lang, H.  Interview.  Movie Classic 1:24 F '32
Wilson, E.  Lionel, Ethel and John.  Silver S 2-12:14 O '32
Moffitt, C. F.  Censorship for interviews Hollywood's latest
    wild idea.  Cinema Dig 2-5:9 Ja 9 '33
Barrymore, J.  Lionel, Ethel and I.  Am Mag 115:12 F '33 &
    following issues.
Jones, C.  John Barrymore.  Cinema Dig 3-5:11 Ap 17 '33
Jones, C.  Barrymores and doubtful taste?  Cinema Dig 3-8:8 My
    8 '33
Ten years ago.  Photop 44:110 Ag '33
Lynn, H.  How he makes love.  Photop 44:103 Ag '33
Temperamental romance.  Lit Dig 112:26 N 21 '36
Schallert, E.  His separation from Elaine Barrie.  Motion Pic
    53:34 Ap '37
Clowning in My dear children.  Time 34:32 N 6 '39
Clowning in My dear children.  Life 7:50 D 4 '39
Bio note; filmog.  Movies & People 2:4 '40
McEvoy, J. P.  Story of.  Stage 1:27 Ja '41
Obit.  Ill Lon N 200:662 Je 6 '42
A clan named Barrymore.  Lions R 3-2:no p# Ja '44
Lyon, R. L.  Incredibly perfect.  8mm Collect 9:9 S '64
Maltin, L.  John Barrymore; filmog.  Film Fan Mo 61/62:3
    Jl/Ag '66

Peeples, S. A.   Films on 8 and 16.   Films In R 21-5:300 My
  '70
Bodeen, D.   John Barrymore and Dolores Costello; filmog.
  Focus on F 12:17 Win '72
Filmog.   Film Dope 2:44 Mr '73
Kanin, G.   The day (he) threw the little girl across the set.
  People 2-9:43 Ag 26 '74
(See Also: BARRYMORE FAMILY)

BARRYMORE, JOHN DREW
Zunser, J.   The newest Barrymore.   Cue 18-53:15 D 31 '49
Barrymore, J. Jr.   My kind of girl.   Silver S 22-1:42 N '51
Barrymore Jr. views heritage at show here.   8mm Collect 9:9
  S '64

BARRYMORE, LIONEL
Smith, F. J.   Interview.   Motion Pic Classic 12:16 Ap '21
Fletcher, A. W.   Interview.   Motion Pic 27:22 Mr '24
de Revere, F. W.   Sketch.   Motion Pic 29:42 Ap '25
Belfrage, C.   Interview.   Motion Pic Classic 28:58 N '28
Hall, L.   Sketch.   Photop 41:53 F '32
Kirkley, D.   The Barrymore tortoise passes the Barrymore
  hare.   Cinema Dig 1-2:5 My 30 '32
Wilson, E.   Lionel, Ethel and John.   Silver S 2-12:14 O '32
Moffitt, C. F.   Censorship for interviews Hollywood's latest wild
  idea.   Cinema Dig 2-5:9 Ja 9 '33
Barrymore, J.   Lionel, Ethel and I.   Am Mag 115:12 F '33 and
  following issues.
Grant, J.   Work of in Sweepings.   Motion Pic 45:40 Ap '33
Jones, C.   Barrymores and doubtful taste?   Cinema Dig 3-8:8
  My 8 '33
Keen, E.   When Lionel acts.   Silver S 3-8:25 Je '33
Reid, J.   Story of.   Motion Pic 54:26 S '37
Reid, J.   Star of valor.   Screen Book 22-2:62 S '39
Sketch.   Photop 54:41 F '40
Bio note; filmog.   Movies & People 2:4 '40
Barrymore, L.   Looking backward and forward.   Lions R 1-5:no
  p# Ja '42
Barrymore, L.   Hollywood's ghost landmarks stir Barrymore
  memories.   Lions R 1-11/12:no p# Jl/Ag '42
Barrymore looks at Van Heflin.   Lions R 2-3:no p# D '42
Busy Barrymore.   Lions R 2-3:no p# D '42
Fiftieth milestone.   Lions R 2-5:no p# Jl '43
A clan named Barrymore.   Lions R 3-2:no p# Ja '44
Painters may "ham" but actors dare not.   Lions R 3-3(sup):no
  p# Ap '44
Barrymore, L.   The march of the movies.   Lions R 3-4:no p#
  Jl '44
Barrymore, L.   Idols, too, have idols.   Lions R 4-1:no p# F
  '45
My Easter prayer.   Photop 26:43 Ap '45
Parsons, L. O.   Cosmop's citation for one of the best perform-
  ances of the month.   Cosmop 122:98 Ja '47

Letters.    Films In R 13-5:312 My '62
Filmog.    Film Dope 2:45 Mr '73
(See also: BARRYMORE FAMILY)

BARRYMORE FAMILY
Ten Broeck, H.    The Barrymores and Augustus Thomas.    Theatre
    27:210 Ap '18
Wilson, B. F.    Sketch.    Motion Pic Classic 21:32 Mr '25
Harris, J.    First-night tradition of the Drews and Barrymores.
    Theatre 53:14 Ap '31
Schallert, E.    The "royal family" of Hollywood.    Motion Pic 44:
    34 S '32
Babcock, M.    Their headline career.    Movie Classic 3:42 F '33
Hall, G.    The Barrymore traditions.    Movie Classic 11:38 O '36

BARTHELMESS, RICHARD
Brewster, E.    Sketch.    Motion Pic 15:86 Je '18
Taylor, M. K.    Sketch.    Motion Pic Classic 7:39 F '19
Smith, F. J.    Sketch.    Motion Pic Classic 9:19 Ja '20
Naylor, H. S.    Interview.    Motion Pic 19:56 F '20
Hall, G.    Interview.    Motion Pic 21:22 Ap '21
A star in the making.    Motion Pic Classic 14:44 Je '22
Fletcher, A. W.    Interview.    Motion Pic 24:21 O '22
Service, F.    Work of.    Classic 15:18 D '22
Kenyon, D.    Interview.    Classic 18:14 Ja '24
Wilson, B.    Interview.    Classic 19:38 Ag '24
de Revere, F. W.    Sketch.    Motion Pic 29:41 F '25
My leading women.    Motion Pic 30:56 Ja '26
Lamm, L. M.    Sketch.    Motion Pic 34:36 N '27
Wilson, B.    Sketch.    Motion Pic Classic 29:51 My '29
Gray, C.    Sketch.    Motion Pic 39:42 F '30
Hall, G.    Interview.    Motion Pic 39:44 Jl '30
Steele, J. H.    The greatest star in Hollywood.    Silver S 1-3:32
    Ja '31
Cruikshank, H.    Sketch.    Motion Pic 41:66 Mr '31
Conrad, S.    He's got his own number.    Silver S 1-11:38 S '31
Steele, J. H.    Sketch.    Motion Pic 42:51 Ja '32
Fairbanks, D. Jr.    Appreciation.    Vanity Fair 38:60 Mr '32
Carlisle, J.    Barthelmess pictures.    Silver S 3-8:21 Je '33
Hall, G.    Interview.    Motion Pic 47:33 My '34
Castle, M.    The famous quintet of movie stars.    Photop 52:18
    Jl '38
Kearns, M.    About Richard Barthelmess.    8mm Collect 6:12 N
    '63
Obit.    8mm Collect 6:12 N '63
    Film R p44 '64/65
Note; filmog.    Film Dope 3:96 Ag '73

BARTHOLOMEW, FREDDIE
Samuels, L.    Born to act.    Silver S 5-6:51 Ap '35
Dew, G.    Sketch.    Motion Pic 47:39 My '35
Hartley, K.    Sketch.    Motion Pic 49:26 Jl '35
Hall, G.    Interview.    Child Life 14:306 Jl '35

Zeitlin, I.   Sketch.   Movie Classic 9:32 S '35
Zeitlin, I.   Interview.   Movie Classic 10:38 Mr '36
Rhea, M.   Guardianship controversy.   Movie Classic 10:22 Jl
   '36
Foye, T.   Pals.   Silver S 7-5:40 Mr '37
A letter from...   Child Life 16:161 Ap '37
Zeitlin, I.   Interview.   Motion Pic 54:31 Ag '37
Rich, G.   Auntie said no.   Screen Book 19-1:94 Ag '37
Willson, D.   Story of.   Child Life 17:327 Jl '38
Bio note; filmog.   Movies & People 2:5 '40
Bartholomew, F.   I knew Mickey Rooney when...   Lions R 2-1:
   no p# S/O '42
Rooney, M.   I knew Freddie Bartholomew when...   Lions R 2-1:
   no p# S/O '42
Minoff, P.   New future for Freddie.   Cue 20-11:14 Mr 17 '51
The kids.   Screen Greats 1-2:50 Sum '71
Lardner, R. W. Jr.   Will Hollywood spoil Freddie Bartholomew?
   Liberty 1-4:82 Spg '72

BARTON, BUZZ
Calhoun, D.   Sketch.   Motion Pic 35:41 Ap '28

BARTON, DAVID
Martin, R.   You read it here first.   TV Guide 16-46:28 N 16
   '68

BARZELL, WOLFE
Obit.   Screen World 21:233 '70

BASEHART, RICHARD
Parsons, L. O.   Cosmop's citation for the best starring per-
   formance of the month.   Cosmop 126:12 Ja '49
Sketch.   Photop 36:81 O '49
Asher, J.   I hated Hollywood!   Silver S 22-11:34 S '52

BASILE, NADINE
Bio note.   Unifrance 23:10 F '53

BASKETT, JAMES
Parsons, L. O.   Cosmop's citation for the best starring performance of the month.   Cosmop 121:65 D '46

BASQUETTE, LINA
Uselton, R. A.   The Wampus baby stars.   Films In R 21-2:73
   F '70

BASSERMAN, ALBERT
Hamilton, S.   Sketch.   Photop 54:33 N '40

BASSETT, RUSSELL
Obit.   Dramatic Mirror 78:747 My 25 '18

BATES, ALAN
  Rising stars.  Film R p58 '64/65
  Platt, D.  Among the best.  Harp Baz 102:118 Mr '69
  Bio.  Cur Bio 30:3 Mr '69
    Same.  Cur Bio Yrbk 1969:33 '70
  A pride of Hamlets.  Plays & Players 18-5:16 F '71
  Gow, G.  Reflections; interview; filmog.  Films & Filming 17-9:
    22 Je '71
  Buckley, P.  An actor who prefers to be anonymous.  Show 2-3:
    41 My '72
  Chase, C.  Who says nice girls finish last?  N. Y. Times sec
    2:1 O 29 '72
    Same.  N. Y. Times Bio Ed p1740 O '72
  Colors of Bates.  Time 100:111 N 6 '72
  Warhol, A.  Interview.  Interview 29:12 Ja '73
  Note; filmog.  Film Dope 3:100 Ag '73
  McAsh, I.  Bates is Butley.  Films Illus 3-29:196 N '73

BATES, BARBARA
  Sketch.  Am Mag 144:113 D '47
  Crivello, K.  Barbara Bates; filmog.  Film Fan Mo 105:15 Mr
    '70
  Obit.  Film R p15 '70/71
    Screen World 21:233 '70

BATSON, SUSAN
  Stasio, M.  The stars of tomorrow on stage today.  Cue 38-9:9
    Mr 1 '69

BATTEN, TOMMY
  Gosh!  Lions R 3-3:no p# Ap '44

BATTISTA, MIRIAM
  Patterson, A.  Sketch.  Photop 22:27 Jl '22
  Hall, G.  Interview.  Motion Pic 24:40 D '22
  Sketch.  National 52:230 O '23

BAUR, ELIZABETH
  See, G.  I'm there to show the boys are normal.  TV Guide
    17-11:25 Mr 15 '69
  Adler, D.  New girl on the force.  TV Guide 20-6:24 F 5 '72

BAVIER, FRANCES
  Home is where the part is.  TV Guide 12-2:12 Ja 11 '64

BAXTER, ANNE
  Wilson, E.  Living alone and liking it.  Silver S 13-9:44 Jl '43
  Mulvey, K.  Sketch.  Womans Home C 70:75 O '43
  Wilson, E.  Get acquainted with Anne.  Silver S 14-4:28 F
    '44
  Pointers on Anne.  Photop 27:42 Jl '45

Should a woman tell her age?  Photop 28:52 Ap '46
Baxter, A.  Men are too mousey!  Silver S 16-6:52 Ap '46
Parsons, L. O.  Cosmop's citation for the best supporting role
  of the month.  Cosmop 124:13 Je '48
Autobiographical.  Photop 33:48 Jl '48
Parsons, L. O.  Cosmop's citation for the best feminine stellar
  performance of the month.  Cosmop 125:13 S '48
Maddox, B.  How to handle actors.  Silver S 19-6:29 Ap '49
Mulvey, K.  Her reputation as a hostess.  Photop 36:54 Ag '49
Baxter, A.  Your slip always shows.  Silver S 21-3:26 Ja '51
MacDonald, E.  Letter to a star.  Silver S 21-10:30 Ag '51
Baxter, A.  Pleasing my husband comes first with me.  Silver S
  22-10:32 Ag '52
Reid, L.  How to lose a husband.  Silver S 23-8:40 Ja '53
Sheridan, M.  Is Anne on a merry-go-round?  Silver S 24-5:26
  Mr '54
A single parent's problems.  Photop 79-4:14 Ap '71
Klemesrud, J.  From All about Eve to all about Anne.  N. Y.
  Times Bio Ed Ag 22 '71
Same.  N. Y. Times sec 2:1 Ag 22 '71
Salute of the week.  Cue 40-37:1 S 11 '71
Bio.  Cur Bio 33:5 My '72
The best Christmas of my life.  Photop 83-1:27 Ja '73
Note; filmog.  Film Dope 3-102:13 Ag '73

BAXTER, KEITH
  In the words of Keith Baxter.  Cue 39-51:21 D 19 '70
  Zadan, C.  Funny old Maureen.  After Dark 3-12:18 Ag '71
  Colaciello, R.  Keith Baxter.  Interview 21:40 My '72

BAXTER, MEREDITH
  Bridget and Bernie.  Mod Screen 67-1:39 Ja '72
  Durslag, M.  The girl who loves Bernie.  TV Guide 20-40:30 S
    30 '72
  Klemesrud, J.  Birney and his 'Irish' rose.  N. Y. Times sec
    2:21 O 29 '72
  Same.  N. Y. Times Bio Ed p1748 O '72
  How Bernie stole Bridget from David Cassidy.  Photop 83-2:30
    F '73
  Lovers on fire!  Mod Screen 67-4:44 Ap '73
  Watters, J.  A real-life rerun.  People 1-18:30 Jl 1 '74

BAXTER, WARNER
  Peltret, E.  Sketch.  Motion Pic Classic 14:52 Ap '22
  Cheatham, M.  Interview.  Classic 16:24 Jl '23
  Tilton, J.  Interview.  Motion Pic 31:53 My '26
  Hall, G.  Sketch.  Motion Pic 37:50 My '29
  Hall, J.  Interview.  Motion Pic 39:44 My '30
  Rice, L.  His character read from his handwriting.  Motion Pic
    44:60 D '32
  Hall, G.  Interview.  Movie Classic 5:19 Ja '34

Babcock, M. Baxter in the garage business. Silver S 4-4:23
  F '34
Lane, J. Sketch. Motion Pic 47:68 Ap '34
Lee, S. His kidnaping. Movie Classic 6:29 Ap '34
Brundidge, H. T. His wife and boarding house keepers respon-
  sible for his success. Movie Classic 7:34 F '35
Tully, J. Story of. Movie Classic 9:26 Ja '36
Langford, H. Interview. Motion Pic 51:42 Mr '36
Orme, M. Appreciation. Ill Lon N 188:948 My 30 '36
Zeitlin, I. Interview. Motion Pic 52:37 D '36
Zeitlin, I. Interview. Motion Pic 52:37 D '36
Home of. Photop 52:45 F '38
Castle, M. The famous quintet of movie stars. Photop 52:18
  Jl '38
Bio note; filmog. Movies & People 2:5 '40
Obit. Screen World 3:177 '53
Corneau, E. N. I remember Warner Baxter. Classic Film
  Collect 26:27 Win '70
Williams, N. All the Cisco Kids; Cisco Kid filmog. Filmograph
  1-2:33 '70

BAYLY, FRANK G.
  Bayly, J. Frank G. Bayly. Silent Pic 13:30 Win/Spg '72

BAYNE, BEVERLY
  Sixteen a perfect age for 'Juliet' on screen. Classic Film Col-
    lect 22:18 Fall/Win ·68
  Fulbright, T. Presenting Miss Beverly Bayne. Classic Film
    Collect 29:6 Win '70; 30:8 Spg; 31:9 Sum; 32:6 Fall '71; 34:32
    Spg; 35:33 Sum '72

BEAIRD, BETTY
  Raddatz, L. She's a nutty mom. TV Guide 17-42:40 O 18 '69

BEAL, JOHN
  Reed, E. Roster of new faces. Theatre Arts 18:64 Ja '34
  Asher, J. Beal. Silver S 5-6:24 Ap '35
  Where show folks show their hobbies. Am Mag 147:114 Ap '49

BEAL, ROYAL
  Obit. N. Y. Times p27 Je 21 '69
    Screen World 21:233 '70

BEAL, SCOTT
  Obit. Screen World p231 '74

BEAN, ORSON
  It's Bean: lots of fun. TV Guide 2-32:10 Ag 7 '54
  The blue angel. TV Guide 2-33:21 Ag 14 '54
  Bio. Cur Bio Yrbk 1967:24 '68

BEARD, MATTHEW JR. ("Stymie")
  Maltin, L. Our gang; Our Gang filmog. Film Fan Mo 66:3

D '66

Balling, F. D.  The day the comedy turned to tragedy.  Movie
Dig 1-2:80 Mr '72

BEATLES, The
Interview.  Playboy 12:51 F '65
Sugg, A. R.  The Beatles and film art.  Film Heritage 1-4:3
Sum '66
Messengers.  Time 90:60 S 22 '67
Same abridged with title Four little Beatles and how they grew.
Read Dig 91:229 D '67
Beatles inc.  Newsweek 71:68 My 27 '68
Davies, H.  Excerpts from The Beatles; biography.  Life 65:86
S 13; 60 S 20 '68
Zimmerman, P. D.  Inside Beatles.  Newsweek 72:106 S 30 '68
Lydon, S.  Would you want your sister to marry a Beatle?
Ramp Mag 7:65 N 30 '68
Aronowitz, A. G.  Wisdom of their years.  Life 66:12 Ja 31 '69
Willis, E.  Records:  rock, etc.  New Yorker 44:55 F 1 '69
Fager, C. E.  Apple corps four.  Chr Cent 86:386 Mr 19 '69
Gabree, J.  Beatles' ninety-minute bore, and the Rolling Stones'
Beggars' banquet.  Hi Fi 19:84 Mr '69
Goldman, A.  Beatles decide to let it be--apart.  Life 68:38 Ap
24 '70
Worm in the apple.  Newsweek 73:84 My 12 '69
Beatles besieged.  Time 93:78 My 30 '69
Luce, P. A.  Great rock conspiracy.  Nat R 21:959 S 23 '69
Cheerful coherence.  Time 94:57 O 3 '69
Beatles in the web.  Newsweek 74:130 O 20 '69
Sander, E.  Beatles:  Abbey Road.  Sat R 52:69 O 25 '69
Newsmakers.  Newsweek 74:62 N 3 '69
Norman, P.  The circus has left town.  Show 1-1:50 Ja '70
Hello, goodbye, hello.  Time 95:57 Ap 20 '70
Saal, H.  Beatles minus one.  Newsweek 75:95 Ap 20 '70
Spector of the Beatles.  Time 95:64 My 18 '70
Morgenstern, J.  Swan songs.  Newsweek 75:93 Je 8 '70
Goldstein, R.  New culture.  Vogue 156:99 Ag 1 '70
Beatle roundup.  Newsweek 76:85 S 7 '70
Beatledammerung.  Time 97:55 Ja 25 '71
Scoppa, B.  Beatles to remember, Beatles to forget.  Sr Schol
98:29 Mr 29 '71
Playboy interview:  Allen Klein.  Playboy 18-11:89 N '71
Scoppa, B.  Beatles apart.  Sr Schol 100:28 Ja 31 '72
A decade after.  People 1-10:58 My 6 '74
(See also:  HARRISON, GEORGE; LENNON, JOHN; McCARTNEY,
PAUL; STARR, RINGO)

BEATTY, WARREN
Beatty, W.  The first ten seconds--they shape the way ahead.
Films & Filming 7:6 Ap '61
Rising stars.  Film R p33 '62/63
Bean, R.  Will there be film stars in 1974?  Films & Filming
10-10:9 Jl '64

Interview.  Cinema (BH) 3-5:7 D '66
Reed, R.  Will the real Warren Beatty please stand up.  Esquire
   68:93 Ag '67
Thompson, T.  Under the gaze of the charmer.  Life 64:86 Ap
   26 '68
Davidson, M.  Public image vs. private man.  Good House 171:
   85 Ag '70
Ehrlich, H.  Warren and Julie: together at last.  Look 35:70
   Je 1 '71
Atlas, J. & Guerin, A.  Robert Altman, Julie Christie and War-
   ren Beatty make the western real.  Show 2-6:18 Ag '71
Chase, C.  ... Stars in the great McGovern money hunt.  Life
   72:69 Je 23 '72
Hay, R. C.  Beatty on the bandwagon.  Interview 22:14 Je '72
Reeves, R.  Stars shown bright on George McGovern.  Sat R
   55:5 Jl 8 '72
Flamini, R.  His political life.  Harp Baz 106:20 N '72
Wilmington, M.  The sweet smell of success; filmog.  Velvet
   Light 7:29 Win '72/73
Wilmington, M. & Peary, G.  Interview.  Velvet Light 7:32 Win
   '72/73
Note; filmog.  Film Dope 3:104 Ag '73
Klemesrud, J.  Back where he belongs?  N. Y. Times sec 2:15
   Mr 17 '74
   Same.  N. Y. Times Bio Ed p310 Mr '74
Note; filmog.  Films Illus 4-39:91 N '74

BEAUMONT, HARRY
   Interview.  Motion Pic 9:102 Mr '15
   How he became a photoplayer.  Motion Pic 9:95 Je '15
   Sketch.  Motion Pic 10:113 D '15
   A pioneer harks back.  Lions R 3-5:no p# D '44

BEBAN, GEORGE
   Meriden, O.  Silent and spoken drama.  Theatre 22:62 Ag '15
   Ames, H.  Sketch.  Motion Pic Classic 2:56 My '16
   Brewster, E.  Work of.  Motion Pic Classic 6:36 Mr '18
   Interview.  Dramatic Mirror p1067 D 4 '20

BECK, THOMAS
   Hamilton, S.  Sketch.  Photop 52:69 Ja '38

BECKETT, SCOTTY
   Maltin, L.  Our gang; Our Gang filmog.  Film Fan Mo 66:3 D
   '66
   Obit.  N. Y. Times p47 My 16 '68
   Brunas, J.  Scotty Beckett.  Film Fan Mo 105:3 Mr '70

BEDELIA, BONNIE
   Actresses who are real people.  Life 68:44 My 29 '70

BEDFORD, BRIAN
   In the words of.  Cue 39-10:13 Mr 7 '70

Gruen, J.  Funny--but suicide runs in the family.  N. Y. Times
   sec 2:1 Mr 28 '71
   Same.  N. Y. Times Bio Ed Mr 28 '71

BEDOYA, ALPHONSO
   Norman, M.  Alphonso Bedoya in America; filmog.  Cinema
   (BH) 5-4:17 Win '69

BEE, MOLLY
   Rinzler, C.  When she coughs, dozens of people clutch their
   checks.  TV Guide 13-24:13 Je 12 '65

BEECHER, JANET
   Sketch.  Green Bk Album 3:627 Mr '10
   Sketch.  N. Y. Drama 70:9 Ag 13 '13
   Interview.  Theatre 20:14 Jl '14
   Dowling, M.  Sketch.  Movie Classic 6:16 Mr '34

BEECHER, MARGARET
   Hall, G.  Interview.  Motion Pic Classic 12:57 Ap '21

BEECHER, SYLVIA
   Biery, R.  Sketch.  Photop 34:101 Je '28

BEER, JACQUELINE
   Silent partner.  TV Guide 9-50:12 D 16 '61

BEERY, CAROL ANN
   Beery, W.  My daughter will be a star.  Screen Book 22-5:62
   D '39
   Presenting Carol Ann.  Lions R 3-3:no p# Ap '44

BEERY, NOAH SR.
   Cheatham, M.  Interview.  Motion Pic 22:59 Ja '22
   St. Johns, I.  Sketch.  Photop 31:82 D '26

BEERY, NOAH JR.
   Rhea, M.  Sketch.  Photop 53:67 S '39

BEERY, WALLACE
   Beery, W.  The art of make-up defined by explanations and ex-
   amples.  Film Players Herald 2-7:23 F '16
   Cheatham, M.  Interview.  Motion Pic 25:76 Je '23
   Carr, H.  Sketch.  Classic 22:35 N '24
   Roberts, W. A.  Sketch.  Motion Pic 29:36 Mr '25
   de Revere, F. V.  Sketch.  Motion Pic 29:65 My '25
   Benthall, D.  Interview.  Motion Pic 33:55 Ap '27
   My face is my fortune.  Theatre 47:32 Mr '28
   Walker, H. L.  Interview.  Motion Pic Classic 28:55 N '28
   Goldbeck, E.  Sketch.  Motion Pic Classic 32:41 S '30
   Dressler, M.  Appreciation.  Motion Pic 41:32 Ap '31
   Service, F.  Sketch.  Motion Pic 43:52 Ap '32
   Collins, F. L.  Sketch.  Good House 94:45 Je '32

Moffitt, C. F. Censorship for interviews Hollywood's latest wild
   idea. Cinema Dig 2-5:9 Ja 9 '33
Logan, C. A. "The champ" learned his lesson. Silver S 2-4:21
   F '32
Pryor, N. Interview. Movie Classic 2:25 Ap '32
Grant, L. It's my fatal beauty. Silent S 3-6:64 Ap '33
Hall, G. His friendship with Marie Dressler. Movie Classic 5:
   28 D '33
Hall, G. Interview. Movie Classic 6:33 Ag '34
Brownfield, L. Interview. Motion Pic 50:30 O '35
Ergenbright, E. L. Interview. Movie Classic 10:45 Ap '36
Beery, W. My daughter will be a star. Screen Book 22-5:62 D
   '39
Sketch. Photop 54:41 F '40
Bio note; filmog. Movies & People 2:5 '40
Beery, W. Things I learned from the army. Lions R 1-5:no
   p# Ja '42
The things he does for MGM. Lions R 1-11/12:no p# Jl/Ag '42
Beery, W. His first forty years. Lions R 3-1:no p# S '43
Salute to Wally. Lions R 3-1:no p# S '43
He never won an argument. Lions R 3-3:no p# Ap '44
Presenting Carol Ann. Lions R 3-3:no p# Ap '44
Hollywood's hardy perenial. Lions R 3-4(sup):no p# Jl '44
Obit. Ill Lon N 214:582 Ap 30 '49
   Screen World 1:233 '49
Made for each other. Screen Greats 1-2:68 Sum '71
Anderson, E. Wallace Beery. Films In R 24-6:330 Je/Jl '73
Braff, R. E. Filmog. Films In R 24-6:330; 24-7:415 Je/Jl
   Ag/S '73


BEGLEY, ED
Taylor, T. Stage right, stage left. Cue 26-23:12 Je 8 '57
Zunser, J. An actor's actor. Cue 32-31:10 Ag 3 '63
Obit. Brit Bk Yr 1971:557 '71
   Classic Film Collect (reprint Washington Evening Post) 27:60
   Spg/Sum '70
   Cur Bio 31:45 Je '70
   Same. Cur Bio Yrbk 1970:460 '71
   Film R p13 '71/72
   N.Y. Times p41 Ap 29; p35 Ap 30 '70
   Same. N.Y. Times Bio Ed Ap 30 '70
   Newsweek 75:110 My 11 '70
   Screen World 22:235 '71
   Time 95:89 My 11 '70


BEKASSY, STEPHEN
Bio note; filmog. Films & Filming 19-6:59 Mr '73


BELAFONTE, HARRY
Voices and modern jazz. Metronome 66:29 Je '50
Taylor, T. Busy balladeer. Cue 26-10:13 Mr 9 '57
Taylor, T. After dark. Cue 27-49:13 D 6 '58
Zunser, J. Young man in a hurry. Cue 28-17:19 Ap 25 '59

Personality of the month. Films & Filming 6-3:3 D '59
Belafonte power. Newsweek 71:101 F 19 '68
Kotlowitz, R.  Making of The angel Levine.   Harper 239:98 Jl
    '69
Belafonte plays angel on and off the screen.   Ebony 24:76 O '69
Harry and Lena off the cuff.   Ebony 25:128 Mr '70
Higgins, R.  Harry and Lena.  TV Guide 18-12:14 My 21 '70
Salute of the week.  Cue 39-34:1 Ag 22 '70
Goodman, G.  Durango: Poitier meets Belafonte.   Look 35-17:
    56 Ag 24 '71
Flatley, G.  About Belafonte. N. Y.  Times Bio Ed p1274 Jl '72
Interview.  Photop 82-3:14 S '72
Morley, S.  Control and conscience; interview.   Films & Filming
    18-12:26 S '72

BELFORD, CHRISTINE
    Sketch.  Movie Dig 1-6:28 N '72
    Off came the white gloves.  TV Guide 21-17:34 Ap 28 '73

BELGADO, MARIA
    Obit.  Screen World 21:233 '70

BELITA (Jepson-Turner)
    Sketch.  Newsweek 23:82 Ap 17 '44
    Watkins, W.  Ballerina on blades.  Silver S 14-9:46 Jl '44
    Ballet dancing under water.  Life 10:14 Ag 27 '45

BELL, REX
    Henning, O.  Sketch.  Motion Pic Classic 27:63 Jl '28
    Bow, C.  He is the ideal husband.  Photop 43:28 F '33
    Obit.  Screen World 14:221 '63
    Corneau, E. N.  I remember Rex Bell.  Classic Film Collect
        25:36 Fall '69

BELL, TOM
    Rising stars.  Film R p40 '63/64

BELLAMY, MADGE
    Beach, B.  Interview.  Motion Pic Classic 11:46 Ja '21
    Jordan, J.  Sketch.  Photop 19:54 Mr '21
    Gassawy, G.  Interview.  Motion Pic Classic 14:36 Mr '22
    Gebhart, M.  Interview.  Motion Pic 23:54 Ap '22
    Smith, A.  Her new personality.  Photop 30:31 O '26
    Milne, P.  Sketch.  Motion Pic Classic 25:34 Ap '27
    Wilson, H. D.  Sketch.  Motion Pic Classic 33:29 Jl '31
    Schwartz, W.  Madge Bellamy; filmog.  Films In R 24-4:256 Ap
        '70
    Teichert, R. E.  Letter.  Films In R 21-5:314 My '70
    Pack, A. C.  Partial filmog.  Films In R 21-6:392 Je/Jl '70
    Madge Bellamy needs autobiographical help.  Classic Film Col-
        lect 26:4 Win '70

BELLAMY, RALPH
  New faces for the electric lights.   Silver S 2-4:38 F '32
  Hamilton, S.   Sketch.   Photop 41:46 F '32
  Bellamy, R.   Mr. Bellamy's little boy.   Silver S 2-9:43 Jl '32
  Tully, J.   His success.   Movie Classic 8:32 Mr '35
  Reed, D.   And he enjoys it.   Silver S 8-9:34 Jl '38
  Brown, C.   Good guy.   Screen Book 22-5:83 D '39
  Bio note; filmog.   Movies & People 2:5 '40
  Vallee, W. L.   Casanova.   Silver S 15-6:50 Ap '45
  Here comes the heroes.   TV Guide 4-37:28 S 15 '56
  It's the sponsor who pays.   TV Guide 4-37:24 S 15 '56
  Zunser, J.   Bellamy portrays the 32nd president.   Cue 27-4:10
    Ja 25 '58
  Maltin, L.   Interview.   Film Fan Mo 111:3 S '70

BELMONDO, JEAN-PAUL
  Personality of the month.   Films & Filming 7-1:5 O '60
  Two actors; interview.   Films & Filming 7-1:13 O '60
  Graham, P.   The face of '63--France.   Films & Filming 9-8:13
    My '63
  Towne, R.   Bogart and Belmondo.   Cinema (BH) 3-1:4 D '65
  What makes Belmondo jump?   Films Illus 1-11:19 My '72
  Seven-year love scandal ends.   Mod Screen 66-9:42 S '72
  Climbing up the curtains.   Films Illus 2-20:8 F '73
  Note; filmog.   Film Dope 3:109 Ag '73

BELOKHVOSTIKOVA, NATALYA
  Note.   Int F. G.   10:335 '73

BENADERET, BEA
  Busy Bea.   TV Guide 2-31:22 Jl 31 '54
  Raddatz, L.   Gertrude Gearshift is now a star.   TV Guide 12-6:
    16 F 8 '64
  Obit.   N. Y. Times p47 O 14 '68
    Newsweek 72:72 O 28 '68
    Screen World 20:232 '69
    Time 92:98 O 25 '68

BENCHLEY, ROBERT
  Return of the actors.   Yale R 23:504 Mr '34
  Strunsky, R.   Benchley cases.   Sat R 14:14 My 9 '36
  Chips off the old Benchley.   Read Dig 29:74 Jl '36
  Excerpt from Of all things.   Scholastic 29:19 D 10 '36
    (Same abridged.   Read Dig 32:29 F '38)
  Winterich, J. T.   Benchley boom.   Sat R 15:19 D 26 '36
  Bio note.   Sat R 17:22 Ja 8 '38
  Bryan, J.   Funny man.   Sat Eve Post 212:10 S 23; 32 O 7 '39
  Bio.   Cur Bio 2:63 '41
    Same.   Cur Bio Yrbk '41
  O'Hara, J.   Thisa and thata.   Newsweek 18:54 Jl 21 '41
  Benchley's back.   Lions R 3-2:no p# Ja '44
  Buffoonery by Benchley.   Lions R 3-3:no p# Ap '44
  Obit.   Cur Bio '46

New Yorker 21:138 D 1 '45
Pub W 148:2448 D 1 '45
Time 46:72 D 3 '45
Wilson Lib Bul 20:328 Ja '46
Robert Benchley: 1889-1945.  Newsweek 26:90 D 3 '45
Benet, W. R.  Phoenix nest.  Sat R 28:31 D 15 '45
Benchley anecdotes.  New Yorker 21:18 Ja 5 '46
Polyp with a past.  Scholastic 48:13 F 25 '46
Sullivan, F.  Knight of wonderful nonsense.  Scholastic 48:14 F
    25 '46
One and only Benchley.  Read Dig 48:27 F '46
Excerpt from Benchley or else.  Read Dig 51:55 O '47
Benchley, N.  Birds, beasts and Benchley.  Good House 127:187
    N '48
Excerpt from Chips off the old Benchley.  Life 27:23 O 10 '49
Excerpt from Benchley or else.  Read Dig 60:126 Ja '52
Benchley, N.  Bon-voyage Benchley.  Holiday 15:83 Je '54
Stewart, D. O.  Mr. Humor.  Nation 179:343 O 16 '54
Excerpt from Benchley beside himself.  Read Dig 66:113 F '55
Benchley, N.  Businessman Benchley.  Holiday 17:73 Mr '55
O'Hara, J.  Appointment with O'Hara.  Colliers 137:6 Ja 6 '56
Benchley, N.  Excerpt from bio.  Read Dig 68:49 F '56
Excerpt from My ten years in a quandary.  Read Dig 81:101 S
    '62
Connelly, M.  Most unforgettable character I've met.  Read Dig
    86:72 My '65
The films of Robert Benchley; filmog.  Film Fan Mo 59:3 My '66
Zimmerman, P. D.  Funny gentleman.  Newsweek 75:94 Mr 30
    '70
Note; filmog.  Film Dope 3:110 Ag '73
(See Readers' Guide for additional references to his creative
    writing.)

BENDER, RUSSELL
    Obit.  Screen World 21:233 '70

BENDIX, WILLIAM
    Hamilton, S.  Sketch.  Photop 22:45 Mr '43
    Movie man.  Cue 12-16:14 Ap 17 '43
    Franchey, J. R.  Magnificent mug!  Silver S 13-9:30 Jl '43
    Should a girl propose?  Photop 24:43 F '44
    Bendix, T.  Sketch.  Photop 25:48 Ag '44
    Sketch.  Time 44:95 S 11 '44
    My biggest lie.  Photop 26:56 Mr '45
    The role I liked best.  Sat Eve Post 218:90 F 2 '46
    Bendix, W.  Gimme the simple life.  Silver S 17-2:50 D '46
    Reid, L.  Bill finally gets his wish.  Silver S 18-11:36 S '48
    His friendship with Babe Ruth.  Photop 34:82 Ja '49
    Note; filmog.  Film Dope 3:111 Ag '73

BENEDICT, DIRK
    Sketch.  Films Illus 3-29:197 N '73

BENHAM, HARRY
    How he became a photoplayer.    Motion Pic 9:114  F '15
    Wilkinson, C.   Harry Benham.    Films In R 13-6:378  Je/ Jl '62

BENHAM, LELAND
    Those Thanhouser kids.    Photop 7-3:134  F '15

BENJAMIN, RICHARD
    Higgins, R.   The great, crazy love affair of him and her.    TV
        Guide 15-40:21  O 7  '67
    Lear, M. W.   Dick Benjamin and Paula Prentiss.    Redbook 134:
        55  Ja '70
    Amory, C.   Trade winds.    Sat R 134:54  Ja '70
    Miller, E.   Interview.    Seventeen 29:46  Jl '70
    Zimmerman, P. D.   Harrowing voyage.    Newsweek 76:72  Ag 10
        '70
    Burke, T.   Alexander Portnoy--this is your life.    N. Y. Times
        Bio Ed D 5  '71
    MacDonough, S.   The coming of age of Paula Prentiss and
        Richard Benjamin.    Show 2-4:18  Je '71
    Biskin, S.   The sexiest schnook in the movies.    Movie Dig 1-4:
        55  Jl '72
    Fields, S.   Those impossible years.    N. Y. Daily News p57  O
        29  '73
    Kushner, T. D.   Do you know Richard Benjamin?    Interview 4-
        2:18  F '74
    Photoplay forum.    Photop 86-1:34  Jl '74

BENNER, YALE D.
    How he became a photoplayer.    Motion Pic 11:87  Ap '16

BENNETT, BARBARA
    Maxwell, V.   Interview.    Photop 44:47  Jl '33
    Obit.   Screen World 10:221  '59

BENNETT, BELLE
    St. Johns, A. R.   Billy Bennett's mother.    Photop 29:58  Ja '26
    Work of.   Motion Pic 31:23  F '26
    Redway, S.   Interview.    Motion Pic Classic 22:18  F '26
    Hall, G.   Sketch.    Motion Pic 36:48  D '28
    Sketch.   Movie Classic 3:24  Ja '33

BENNETT, BRUCE
    Miller, D.   Remember Bruce Bennett.    Applause 1-9:13  Ja 19
        '72

BENNETT, CONSTANCE
    Redway, S.   Interview.    Motion Pic Classic 21:36  Ag '25
    Belfrage, C.   Sketch.    Motion Pic 38:82  S '29
    Gray, C.   Interview.    Motion Pic Classic 30:39  Ja '30
    Sketch.   Photop 37:74  Ja '30
    Spensley, D.   Sketch.    Motion Pic 40:44  S '30
    Sketch.   Photop 39:1  Mr '31

Sharon, M.   What is love doing to her?  Silver S 1-9:59 Jl '31
Manners, D.   Sketch.  Motion Pic 41:8 Je '31
Jamison, J.   Women do not like her.  Motion Pic 42:27 S '31
Benton, C.   Will she marry the Marquis de la Falaise?  Movie
    Classic 1:37 O '31
Fairbanks, D. Jr.   Appreciation.  Vanity Fair 37:52 Ja '32
Pryor, N.   Her marriage.  Movie Classic 1:30 F '32
Brawley, B.   Sketch.  Motion Pic 43:60 F '32
Babcock, M.   Her career during 1919-1932.  Movie Classic 2:20
    Mr '32
Cheasley, C. W.   Her marriage.  Motion Pic 43:42 Ap '32
Mook, S. R.   Parties.  Silver S 2-6:18 Ap '32
Churchill, E.   Sketch.  Motion Pic 43:34 Je '32
Manners, D.   Her motherhood revealed.  Movie Classic 2:38 Jl
    '32
Balfour, J.   Those extraordinary Bennetts.  Silver S 2-12:18 O
    '32
Maynard, C.   Discovers she has a friend.  Movie Classic 3:52
    F '33
Keen, J.   Bennett, et al.  Cinema Dig 4-2:11 My 22 '33
Pryor, N.   How does she rate with women?  Movie Classic 4:47
    Je '33
Ergenbright, E. L.   Interview.  Movie Classic 4:18 Jl '33
Chapman, J. B.   Different sides of her character.  Motion Pic
    46:32 S '33
Hall, G.   Interview.  Motion Pic 47:42 Mr '34
Mook, S. R.   Women and men equal.  Silver S 4-6:22 Ap '34
Brock, C.   Her moods.  Movie Classic 6:49 Ap '34
Standish, J.   Divorce rumors denied.  Movie Classic 7:39 D '34
Packer, E.   What, no Cinderella?  Silver S 5-6:28 Ap '35
Lane, V.   Style secrets.  Movie Classic 10:48 Ap '36
Crowley, G.   Why Hollywood fears her.  Motion Pic 51:43 Jl '36
Bio sketch.   Delin 130:10 Ja '37
Bergere, R.   Is she becoming human?  Screen Book 19-4:39 N
    '37
Home of.   Photop 52:44 F '38
Young, G.   I work for her.  Screen Book 21-6:27 Ja '39
Bio note; filmog.   Movies & People 2:6 '40
Steen, A.   Versatile is right.  Silver S 15-11:23 S '45
Letters.   Films In R 16-9:585 N '65
Pin-ups of the past.   Films & Filming 17-3:72 D '70
Note; filmog.   Film Dope 3:116 Ag '73

BENNETT, ENID
Remont, F.   Interview.  Motion Pic Classic 6:27 Ag '18
Cheatham, M.   Interview.  Motion Pic Classic 10:32 Jl '20
Hall, G.   Interview.  Motion Pic 20:44 D '20
Goldbeck, W.   Interview.  Motion Pic Classic 13:48 F '22
Curly, K.   Interview.  Motion Pic 23:28 Jl '22
Sketch.   Photop 22:48 S '22
Her darkest hour.   Classic 16:66 Mr '23
Home of.   Photop 24:54 O '23
Obit.   N. Y. Times p33 My 17 '69
    Screen World 21:233 '70

BENNETT, HYWEL
Sketch. Films Illus 1-16:26 O '72

BENNETT, JILL
People of promise. Films & Filming 1-5:23 F '55
Gow, G.   Making it in a man's world.   Plays & Players 19-12:
   20 S '72

BENNETT, JOAN
Manners, D.   Interview.   Motion Pic 38:82 Ag '29
Cruikshank, H.   Sketch.   Motion Pic Classic 31:51 Mr '30
Sketch.   Photop 38:1 S '30
Manners, D.   Interview.   Motion Pic 42:26 Ja '31
Taviner, R.   Interview.   Motion Pic 41:64 My '31
Parsons, H.   Her own worst enemy.   Silver S 1-7:35 My '31
Mook, S. R.   Joan says "yes. "   Silver S 2-8:24 Je '32
Pryor, N.   Sketch.   Motion Pic 43:60 Jl '32
Balfour, J.   Those extraordinary Bennetts.   Silver S 2-12:18 O
   '32
Sylvia.   How her posture has improved.   Photop 44:54 Jl '33
Pope, J.   Her idea.   Silver S 3-11:68 S '33
Hall, G.   Her home life.   Motion Pic 48:44 D '34
Ergenbright, E. L.   Interview.   Movie Classic 7:37 F '35
Hill, G.   Interview.   Movie Classic 8:24 Je '35
Osborn, K.   Her hints on beauty.   Motion Pic 50:50 S '35
Wilson, B. F.   Her success.   Movie Classic 9:1 D '35
Wilson, E.   She has everything.   Silver S 6-4:51 F '36
Hill, G.   Story of.   Motion Pic 51:46 Mr '36
Lane, V. T.   Interview.   Motion Pic 52:34 D '36
Bio sketch.   Delin 130:10 Ja '37
Hall, G.   Her, 10 commandments for a mother.   Movie Classic
   11:26 Ja '37
Messer, G.   Interview.   Photop 51:16 Jl '37
Wilson, E.   Projection.   Silver S 8-12:30 O '38
Her rebellion against the advertising of her part in The house-
   keeper's daughter.   Newsweek 14:33 D 11 '39
Wilson, E.   Experiences she'd love to relive.   Silver S 10-2:24
   D '39
Bio note; filmog.   Movies & People 2:6 '40
Wilson, E.   Don't kid the public.   Silver S 11-10:22 Ag '41
Things I wish men would do.   Photop 20:44 Ja '42
Manners, M. J.   Hints for husband-hunters.   Silver S 14-5:38
   Mr '45
Marsh, P.   I detest the girls I play.   Silver S 16-10:42 Ag '46
Maddox, B.   Bachelor girl, beware.   Silver S 19-11:40 S '49
Look of a garden five floors up.   House & Gard 132:110 Ag '67
Bennett, J.   Hopes for spring.   Girl Talk 2-3:9 Ap '71
Pin-up of the past.   Films & Filming 18-10:71 Jl '72
Note; filmog.   Film Dope 3-117:26 Ag '73

BENNETT, JULIE
This lady talks with animals.   TV Guide 10-29:27 Jl 21 '62

BENNETT, MICKEY
Sketch.  Photop 25:82 F '24

BENNETT, RICHARD
Sketch.  Theatre 9:64 F '09
Parsons, C. L.  Interview.  N. Y.  Drama 65:11 Ap 19 '11
White, M.  Jr.  The man behind "Damaged goods. "  Munsey 50:
   93 O '13
Shannon, B.  A cheerful anarchist.  Photop 11-5:49 Ap '17
Beckley, Z.  Home of.  Theatre 29:222 Ap '19
Smith, F. J.  Interview.  Motion Pic Classic 13:20 Ja '22
Wilson, B. F.  The Bennett family.  Classic 19:36 Jl '24
Beckley, Z.  Interview.  Theatre 44:12 O '26
Interview.  Motion Pic 42:39 O '31
Obit.  Cur Bio 5 '44

BENNISON, LOUIS
Mantle, B.  Sketch.  Green Book 17:799 My '17
Smith, R. E.  Sketch.  Motion Pic 17:35 Ap '19

BENNY, JACK
Goldbeck, E.  Interview.  Motion Pic Classic 30:60 O '29
Morgan, L.  Head man of the air waves.  Silver S 7-9:22 Jl '37
Harlan, B.  Story of.  Motion Pic 54:38 Ag '37
Benny, M. L.  Romance in reverse.  Silver S 9-12:38 O '39
Mason, A.  A friendship built on gags and insults.  Silver S 10-
   9:24 Jl '40
Bio note; filmog.  Movies & People 2:6 '40
Haas, D.  A Benny for your thoughts.  Silver S 12-10:26 Ag '42
Mulvey, K.  Sketch.  Womans Home C 70:22 Ja '43
Jack Benny steals a march.  Cue 14-4:8 Ja 27 '45
Kaufman, S.  Behind the mike with Jack Benny.  Silver S 15-8:32
   Je '45
High spots in his life.  Life 21:93 S 30 '46
Zolotow, M.  The fiddler from Waukegan.  Cosmop 123:48 O '47
Getting material for a personality sketch.  Cosmop 123:14 O '47
The story behind his switch from NBC to CBS.  Newsweek 32:56
   D 6 '48
List of his shows on CBS.  Life 26:63 Ja 3 '49
Holiday in Hawaii.  TV Guide 1-26:10 S 25 '53
Gehman, R.  It 's Jack and Natty.  TV Guide 12-51:15 D 19 '64
Stern, I.  Euterpe by any other name?  N. Y.  Times Bio Ed O
   11 '70
Five happy moments.  Esquire 74:138 D '70
Toast to two funny old pals.  Life 72:78 My 26 '72
Note; filmog.  Film Dope 3-119:28 Ag '73

BENTON, BARBI
Barbi 's back.  Playboy 20-12:143 D '73
Interview.  Interview 4-8:26 S '74

BENTON, SUSANNE
Bent on stardom; photos.  Playboy 17-5:137 My '70

BERADINO, JOHN
What am I doing here?  TV Guide 12-20:8 My 16 '64

BERARD, ROXANE
No ooh-la-la's for her.   TV Guide 9-41:29 O 14 '61

BERENSON, MARISA
Marisa Berenson takes the lotus position.   Vogue 156:104 Jl '70
Hughes, F.  Interview.  Interview 2-4:16 Jl '71
Meet Marisa.  Playboy 18-10:103 O '71
Colaciello, R. & O'Brien, G.  Interview.  Interview 20:6 Mr '72
Many moods of Marisa.  Vogue 159:88 Ap 15 '72
Klemesrud, J.  Make room for the Berenson sisters.  N. Y.
   Times Bio Ed p551 Ap '73

BERESFORD, VERA
Mother-not-ashamed-of-her-daughter.  Photop 15-2:61 Ja '19

BERGEN, CANDICE
Little women.  Esquire 71:136 My '69
Paley, M.  Miss Bergen protests--but not too much.  Life 69:40
   Jl 24 '70
Miller, E.  She's a great girl.  Seventeen 29:240 Ag '70
Princess who belched.  Time 96:83 N 2 '70
Knight, A. & Alpert, H.  Sex stars of 1970.  Playboy 17-12:220
   D '70
Robbins, F.  Interview.  Photop 79-2:8 F '71
Ebert, R.  Candy's sweet on acting now.  N. Y. Times Bio Ed
   Ap 11 '71
Her California house.  Vogue 157:74 Je '71
Greenfield, J.  What can you say about a sleeping beauty; inter-
   view.  Redbook 137:58 Jl '71
Lee Marvin and Paul Newman.  Vogue 158:146 O 1 '71
Was Mike Nichols the Svengali who changed her life?  Mod
   Screen 65-12:26 D '71
I thought they might hiss.  Life 72:90 Ap 21 '72
Graves, R.  Meryman is our man but Candy is dandy.  Life 72:
   3 Ap 21 '72
Righter, C.  Star of the month; horoscope.  Mod Screen 66-5:50
   My '72
Gregory, J.  The girl who grew up in Charlie McCarthy's room.
   Movie Dig 1-4:20 Jl '72
Bernie Cornfield honors his mother.  Esquire 78:152 N '72
Eyles, A.  Note; filmog.  Focus On F 7:8 n. d.

BERGEN, EDGAR
Charlie McCarthy and his feud with W. C. Fields.  Life 3:57 Jl
   26 '37
Spensley, D.  Story of.  Motion Pic 54:56 N '37
Babcock, G.  The man who plays with a doll.  Screen Book 19-
   4:24 N '37
Story of Bergen and Charlie McCarthy.  Time 33:28 Mr 20 '39
Spensley, D.  Story of.  Photop 53:44 Jl '39

Bio note; filmog.  Movies & People 2:6 '40
Smith, H. A.  The story of Bergen and McCarthy.  Cosmop 117:
   8 Ag '44
Charlie at the Waldorf.  Cue 13-46:11 N 11 '44
On U. S. tour with Charlie McCarthy.  Time 46:72 N 26 '45
Kaufman, S.  Benny confides about Charlie and his guests.  Sil-
   ver S 16-4:49 F '46
Minoff, P.  Mr. Bergen climbs aboard the quiz bandwagon.  Cue
   25-2:39 Ja 14 '56
Lewis, F.  The private life of Charlie McCarthy.  Liberty 1-7:
   61 Win '72

BERGEN, POLLY
   Rugged individualist.  TV Guide 4-39:8 S 29 '56
   Taylor, T.  The girl on the piano.  Cue 26-18:17 My 4 '57
   Beauty and the beast.  Newsweek 72:104 O 7 '68
   Portrait, E.  The world of beauty welcomes Hollywood's beautiful
      women.  Cue 38-46:11 N 15 '69
   Photoplay forum.  Photop 80-5:10 N '71
   Schanche, D. A.  I assure you, beauty is its own tyranny.  To-
      days Health 50:36 Ag '72
   Stanke, D.  A portrait of Polly Bergen; filmog.  Filmograph 3-2:
      32 '72

BERGER, HELMUT
   Jabara, P.  Rich, young and decidedly decadent.  After Dark 5-
      12:18 Ap '73
   Berger as Ludwig.  Films Illus 3-26:76 Ag '73

BERGGREN, THOMMY
   Note; filmog.  Film Dope 3-122:30 Ag '73
   Thommy Berggren; filmog.  Film 60:14 n. d.

BERGMAN, INGRID
   Hamman, M.  Sketch.  Good House 110:57 Ja '40
   Hamilton, S.  Sketch.  Photop 54:14 Ja '40
   Sketch.  Life 10:46 F 24 '41
   Nice girl?  Lions R 1-1:no p# S '41
   Sketch.  Harp Baz 76:88 Ag '42
   Manners, M. J.  Nice and naughty.  Silver S 13-4:32 F '43
   Manners, M. J.  The mystery of.  Silver S 14-2:30 D '43
   Incognito as usual.  Lions R 3-3(sup):no p# Ap '44
   My most unforgettable moment overseas.  Photop 25:52 Je '44
   De Rig, M.  Advice from Ingrid.  Silver S 15-2:22 D '44
   Oil painting by Alexander Brook.  Life 18:37 Ja 15 '45
   Walker, H. L.  Easy does it.  Silver S 15-12:24 O '45
   Second place in Companion poll of favorite stars.  Womans Home
      C 73:7 Je '46
   Steele, J. H.  Incidents in her life.  Photop 29:42 Jl '46
   Parsons, L. O.  Cosmop's citation for the best feminine star-
      ring performance of the month.  Cosmop 121:68 Ag '46
   Work of in Joan of Larraine.  Newsweek 28:94 D 2 '46
   Prize winner in 1946.  Photop 30:37 F '47

Wilson, E. Dream of her life come true. Silver S 18-4:28 F
'48
Oakey, V. How she influenced the life of a boy who was a
stranger to her. Ladies Home J 65:46 Je '48
Bergman is screen's Maid of Orleans. Cue 17-27:10 Jl 3 '48
Ferrer, J. Is the Bergman legend true? Silver S 18-11:24 S
'48
Bright star meets top director. Cue 17-41:17 O 9 '48
Work of in Joan of Arc. Life 25:35 N 15 '48
Winner of Photoplay gold medal for 1948. Photop 34:33 Mr '49
Reid, J. Ingrid's fulfillment as a woman. Silver S 24-1:24 N
'53
Gow, G. The quest for realism; discussion. Films & Filming
4-3:13 D '57
Star of the year; filmog. Film R p15 '59/60
One thing at a time. Time 90:53 S 8 '67
Prideaux, T. Shining return for Ingrid. Life 63:63 O 13 '67
Fallaci, D. Interview. Look 32:26 Mr 5 '68
Newsmakers. Newsweek 73:55 F 24 '69
Davidson, M. The new happiness in her life. Good House 168:
82 My '69
Lurie, D. (She) speaks out. Ladies Home J 87:141 O '70
Serene at 55. N. Y. Times Bio Ed Mr 20 '71
Still going great. Screen Greats 1-2:78 Sum '71
Koch, H. The making of Casablanca. New York 6-18:74 Ap 30
'73
Note; filmog. Film Dope 3-124:32 Ag '73
Bourget, J-L. Romantic dramas of the forties. Film Comment
10-1:48 Ja/F '74
Wood, R. Bergman on Rossellini; interview. Film Comment
10-4:12 Jl/Ag '74

BERGNER, ELIZABETH
Sketch. Threatre World 19:270 Je '33
Troy, W. Work of in Catherine the Great. Nation 138:285 Mr
7 '34
Norden, H. B. Appreciation. Vanity Fair 42:46 Mr '34
Sketch. Vanity Fair 42:52 My '34
Hayden, K. Puppet or genius? Photop 46:26 Je '34
Aydelotte, W. Sketch. Motion Pic 47:52 Je '34
Appreciation. Time 25:60 Ja 28 '35
Phillips, H. A. Work of. Stage 12:8 F '35
Motherwell, H. Work of in Escape me never. Stage 12:22 Mr
'35
Green, E. M. Sketch. Stage 12:15 Mr '35
Sketch. Theatre World 23:180 Ap '35
Phillips, H. A. Story of. Motion Pic 49:19 Ap '35
Grimstead, H. Personal sketch. Windsor 82:741 N '35
Baker, G. The great Bergner! Silver S 5-8:53 Je '38
Brent, R. Appreciation. Stage 14:48 Ja '37
Work of in Stolen life. Stage 16:32 My 15 '39
What they are doing now. Show 2-7:108 Jl '62
Chierichetti, D. San Francisco salutes Elizabeth Bergner. Film

Fan Mo 90:6 D '68
Bookley, G. D.  Letter; filmog.  Films In R 25-5:318 My '74

BERLE, MILTON
Vallee, W. L.  Merrymaker Milton.  Silver S 12-11:44 S '42
Berle is berling.  Newsweek 21:88 Mr 15 '43
Kilgallen, D.  Sketch.  Photop 23:21 Je '43
Bright star shines in the nightclubs.  Cue 15-9:11 Mr 2 '46
Gag machine.  Time 49:94 Mr 31 '47
Carson, S.  Morgan and Berle.  New Rep 116:40 Mr 31 '47
The Berle radio show.  Time 49:94 Mr 31 '47
Week's work.  New Rep 117:36 Ag 25 '47
Gourmet.  Colliers 122:30 O 23 '48
Sylvester, R.  Strange career of Milton Berle.  Sat Eve Post
   221:38 Mr 19 '49
Milton's marathon.  Life 26:112 Ap 25 '49
Child wonder.  Time 53:70 My 16 '49
Television's top.  Newsweek 33:56 My 16 '49
Bio.  Cur Bio 10:4 Je '49
Mr. Television.  Time 54:58 O 3 '49
Hamburger, P.  Television.  New Yorker 25:91 O 29 '49
Milton tries Hollywood again.  Cue 18-45:19 N 5 '49
Millstein, G.  Bringing things to a Berle.  N. Y. Times Mag p17
   Ap 8 '51
Edwards, J.  Behind the scenes with Berle.  Coronet 29:83 Ap
   '51
Lords of laughter.  Coronet 30:78 O '51
Berle and his ace.  Newsweek 40:60 S 29 '52
Shayon, R. L.  Old star with new tricks.  Sat R 35:41 O 4 '52
Minoff, P.  Change in Berle format doesn't ring the bell.  Cue
   21-42:7 O 18 '52
Ace, G.  Berle's still Berling.  Look 17:52 Ap 7 '53
Mr. television.  TV Guide 1-11:10 Je 12 '53
The great comeback.  TV Guide 1-12:13 Je 19; 1-13:20 Je 26 '53
It's bigger than both of us!  TV Guide 1-23:8 S 4 '53
Mama remembers Milton's forty years in show business.  Look
   17:115 N 3 '53
Minoff, P.  Behind the scenes with Uncle Miltie.  Cue 23-6:12
   F 6 '54
Out in front.  TV Guide 2-41:8 O 9 '54
How Gleason got Berle's job.  TV Guide 3-5:3 Ja 29 '55
Berle directs Berle.  TV Guide 3-6:17 F 5 '55
What Berle didn't tell.  TV Guide 3-43:5 O 22 '55
The rise and fall of...  TV Guide 4-31:5 Ag 4 '56
Lardner, J.  Air.  New Yorker 33:199 N 23 '57
Bester, A.  Good old days of Mr. Television.  Holiday 23:97 F
   '58
Return of an old ham.  Time 71:46 Mr 3 '58
Mr. TV off the shelf.  Newsweek 51:92 My 12 '58
Neither new nor old.  Time 72:55 O 20 '58
What new Milton Berle?  TV Guide 7-2:17 Ja 10 '59
Milton Berle offbeat.  Newsweek 53:118 Ap 27 '59
Now he co-stars with a bowling ball.  TV Guide 8-46:25 N 12 '60

Nichols, M.  Berle goes bowling along.  Coronet 49:14 N '60
Frank, G.  Milton Berle.  McCalls 91:94 Mr '64
Whitney, D.  How to make millions without really working.  TV
  Guide 12-23:4 Je 6 '64
Uncle Miltie's back.  Newsweek 68:60 S 12 '66
Nathan, P.  Berle, Benson, Bleeck.  Pub W 196:46 O 13 '69
Ace, G.  I've known Milton Berle, man and woman, for about 30
  years.  TV Guide 21-47:6 N 24 '73
Wilson, E.  Everything for a laugh.  Liberty 1-7:58 Win '72

BERLIN, JEANNIE
  Gruen, J.  More than Elaine May's daughter.  N. Y.  Times sec
    2:13 Ja 7 '73
  Same.  N. Y.  Times Bio Ed p14 Ja '73
  Clein, H.  Betting on Berlin.  After Dark 5-9:30 Ja '73
  Manners, D.  I nominate for stardom.  Mod Screen 67-4:16 Ap
    '73

BERLINGER, WARREN
  Rising stars.  Film R p20 '60/61

BERMAN, SHELLEY
  Minoff, P.  Man with a telephone.  Cue 27-22:15 My 31 '58
  Confession comedy.  Time 73:56 Ja 12 '59
  Berman, inside and out.  Newsweek 55:103 F 15 '60
  Alone on the telephone.  Time 77:66 Ja 20 '61
  Jamison, P. A.  Interview.  Seventeen 20:94 Ja '61
  Miller, E.  Berman off the record.  Seventeen 21:76 Jl '62
  Shayon, R. L.  Pussy cats and propriety.  Sat R 45:17 Ag 11
    '62
  Seeing Shelley plain.  Newsweek 60:56 Ag 13 '62

BERNARD, BUTCH
  (See NOLAN, TOMMY)

BERNARD, DOROTHY
  Burgess, B.  The girl on the cover.  Photop 10-3:92 Ag '16
  Seitz, C. W.  Sketch.  Motion Pic 14:69 S '17

BERNARD, JACQUES
  Bio note.  Unifrance 10:9 Je '51

BERNARD, SUE
  Growing up glamorous.  Playboy 13-12:174 D '66
  Hobson, D.  I spent a lot of time at the water cooler.  TV Guide
    18-33:10 Ap 15 '70

BERNARDI, HERSCHEL
  A matter of maturity.  TV Guide 9-27:17 Jl 8 '61
  Davidson, B.  Hesh the Greek.  TV Guide 18-41:24 O 10 '70
  Enjoying a long run.  TV Guide 19-2:10 Ja 9 '71
  I'm still not used to not being dead.  Mod Screen 66-2:37 F '72

BERRY, KEN
  Hobson, D.  I'm the original dull guy.  TV Guide 14-19:19 My
    7 '66
  Durslag, M.  Ken Berry keeps a small town in the big time.
    TV Guide 17-11:37 Mr 15 '69
  Swisher, V. H.  Ken Berry.  Dance 43:22 Jl '69
  I thought I had cancer and I prepared to die.  Photop 78-2:70
    Ag '70

BERTI, MARINA
  Sexy signore.  Life 31:63 S 3 '51
  Which is glamor?  Colliers 131:34 Ja 3 '52
  Mullins, J.  Filmog.  Films In R 23-1:61 Ja '72

BERTRAM, VEDAH
  Doyle, B. H.  Vedah Bertram.  Films In R 12-9:574 N '61

BESSELL, TED
  He said good-by and walked into a closet.  TV Guide 15-39:22
    S 30 '67

BEST, EDNA
  Kahn, J. M.  Sketch.  Photop 39:74 My '31
  Sketch.  Photop 41:38 D '31
  Work of in There's always Juliet.  Theatre Guild 9:29 Ap '32
  Standish, J.  Marital troubles.  Movie Classic 6:42 Jl '34
  Obit.  N. Y. Times p46 S 19 '74
    Same.  N. Y. Times Bio Ed p1207 S '74

BESWICK, MARTINE
  Note; filmog.  Film Dope 3-136:40 Ag '73

BETHUNE, ZINA
  Efron, E.  The nurses.  TV Guide 10-50:22 D 15 '62
  Gill, A.  Zina is a lonely child.  TV Guide 12-9:11 F 29 '64
  Efron, E.  What happens to a ballerina with a sore foot?  TV
    Guide 14-4:33 N 19 '66

BETZ, CARL
  More than a stick of furniture.  TV Guide 11-26:15 Je 29 '63
  Fessier, M. Jr.  A mere matter of life or death.  TV Guide
    16-15:25 Ap 13 '68

BEVANS, PHILIPPA
  Obit.  N. Y. Times p35 My 11 '68
  Screen World 20:232 '69

BEY, TURHAN
  Holland, J.  Is he another Valentino.  Silver S 14-4:44 F '44
  A romance I can't forget.  Photop 24:54 Mr '44
  From kisses to Hepburn.  Lions R 3-4:no p# Jl '44
  Why I'm still single.  Photop 25:56 N '44

BIANCHI, DANIELA
  Hamilton, J.   Secret agent James Bond's second girl friend.
  Look 27:71 D 31 '63
  Rising stars.   Film R p55 '64/65

BIANCHI, REGINA
  Lane, J. F.   The face of '63--Italy.   Films & Filming 9-7:11
  Ap '63

BICE, ROBERT
  Lucky Bice.   Lions R 3-4:no p# Jl '44

BICKFORD, CHARLES
  Spensley, D.   Sketch.   Motion Pic 38:66 N '29
  Goldbeck, E.   Interview.   Motion Pic 39:64 Jl '30
  Ramsey, W.   Interview.   Motion Pic Classic 32:38 S '30
  Hall, G.   Sketch.   Motion Pic 41:65 F '31
  Carvel, M.   Sketch.   Movie Classic 2:29 Ap '32
  Hall, G.   Sketch.   Movie Classic 2:52 Jl '32
  My faith.   Photop 24:49 My '44
  Dudley, F.   Swoon man of the senior league.   Silver S 16-9:48
  Jl '46
  Obit.   Brit Book Yr 1968:587 '68
  New York Times p47 N 10 '67
  Newsweek 70:98 N 20 '67
  Time 90:102 N 17 '67

BIDDLE, CRAIG JR.
  How he became an actor.   Photop 24:31 Je '23

BIKEL, THEODORE
  Minoff, P.   Conversation with Bikel.   Cue 27-49:10 D 6 '58

BILLINGS, FLORENCE
  Hall, G.   Interview.   Motion Pic 19:73 Je '20
  Irwin, D.   Some letters to.   Motion Pic Classic 11:57 Ja '21

BILLINGSLEY, BARBARA
  An expert on the male.   TV Guide 9-8:11 F 25 '61

BILLINGTON, FRANCELIA
  Squier, E. L.   Interview.   Motion Pic Classic 10:24 Ap/My '20

BING, HERMAN
  Hamilton, S.   Story of.   Photop 52:21 My '38

BINNEY, CONSTANCE
  Boone, A.   A race for stardom.   Photop 15-4:50 Mr '19
  Michaels, E. S.   Interview.   Motion Pic 19:73 Mr '20
  As her own hat-maker.   Photop 17:70 Ap '20
  Boone, A.   Sketch.   Photop 18:28 S '20
  Bruce, B.   Interview.   Motion Pic 20:33 N '20
  Smith, F. J.   Interview.   Motion Pic Classic 11:16 Ja '21

Curly, K.  Interview.  Motion Pic 23:44 My '22
Adams, B.  (She) came to our Christmas party.  Classic Film
   Collect 39:11 Sum '73
Adams, B.  Constance Binney receives 'rosemary.'  Classic
   Film Collect 43:1 Sum '74

BINNEY, FAIRE
   Service, F.  Interview.  Motion Pic Classic 7:36 F '19
   Boone, A.  A race for stardom.  Photop 15-4:50 Mr '19
   Boone, A.  Sketch.  Photop 18:28 S '20

BIRD, CHARLOT
   Sketch.  Motion Pic Classic 22:54 D '25

BIRD, JOHN
   Bird of prey.  Time 90:68 N 17 '67

BIRD, LAURIE
   On the road with the new Hollywood.  Show 2-1:16 Mr '71

BIRELL, TALA
   Sketch.  Motion Pic 43:26 My '32
   Sketch.  Photop 41:74 My '32
   Service, F.  Sketch.  Motion Pic 48:47 Jl '32

BIRKIN, JANE
   Baby Jane.  Newsweek 75:61 Ja 5 '70
   Je t'aime, Jane (Pictorial).  Playboy 17-11:113 N '70

BIRNEY, DAVID
   Bridget and Bernie.  Mod Screen 67-1:39 Ja '72
   Durslag, M.  The girl who loves Bernie.  TV Guide 20-40:30 S
      30 '72
   Klemesrud, J.  Birney and his 'Irish' rose.  N.Y. Times sec
      2:21 O 29 '72
   Same.  N.Y. Times Bio Ed p1748 O '72
   How Bernie stole Bridget from David Cassidy.  Photop 83-2:30
      F '73
   Lovers on fire!  Mod Screen 67-4:44 Ap '73
   I want a wife...  Photop 83-4:59 Ap '73
   Schoenstein, R.  Return with us now to Abie's Irish rose.  TV
      Guide 21-26:18 Je 30 '73
   Watters, J.  A real-life rerun.  People 1-18:30 Jl 1 '74

BIRNS, TOM
   From grip-electrician to movie actor and back.  Am Cinematog
      52-12:1242 D '71

BISHOP, JOEY
   Joey at the summit.  Time 75:74 F 22 '60
   A dead-pan comic's lively wit.  TV Guide 8-51:24 D 17 '60
   Millstein, G.  Portrait of a well, well, well comic.  N.Y.
      Times Mag p12 Ja 1 '61

My small war against prejudice.  Ebony 16:63 Ap '61
Fletcher, F.  Chat with Joey.  Cue 30-32:10 Ag 12 '61
Steuer, A.  Call me the candy store.  Esquire 56:110 S '61
De Roos, R.  The comedian who does not confuse common with
    coarse.  TV Guide 9-48:9 D 2 '61
Sick, Sick, Sick.  TV Guide 10-11:16 Mr 17 '62
Gehman, R.  The man who'd rather do it himself.  TV Guide
    11-52:23 D 28 '63
Here's Johnny.  Newsweek 69:114 My 8 '67
Lewis, R. W.  The show is over at 1 a.m.  TV Guide 16-8:26
    F 24 '68
Williams, L.  (He) tries harder.  Look 32:57 My 28 '68
Kid from Philly.  Newsweek 72:41 S 2 '68
Comedy is a form of religion.  TV Guide 16-43:14 O 26 '68
Battle of the talk shows.  Newsweek 74:42 S 1 '69
Good-by Joey, hello Dick.  Newsweek 74:84 D 8 '69


BISHOP, JULIE
    (Also known as Jacqueline Wells)
    Her ideas of love.  Photop 23:41 N '43
    Walker, H. L.  Private life of...  Silver S 14-8:26 Je '44
    Uselton, R. A.  The Wampus baby stars.  Films In R 21-2:73
        F '70
    Briggs, C. G.  Filmog.  Films In R 21-8:516 O '70
    Spangenberg, J. A.  Letter; additional filmog.  Films In R 22-2:
        113 F '71


BISHOP, WILLIAM
    Stars of tomorrow.  Lions R 1-11/12:no p# Jl/Ag '42
    Obit.  Screen World 11:215 '60


BISSET, JACQUELINE
    Ehrlich, H.  Sinatra's English import.  Look 32:71 Mr 19 '68
    It's a drag to be pretty.  Life 68:80 F 13 '70
    Hallowell, J.  Beauty can't be disguised in a blonde wig.  Show
        1-13:28 S 17 '70
    Mothner, I.  Now faces.  Look 34-22:77 N 3 '70
    Klemesrud, J.  A good roommate is hard to find.  N. Y. Times
        Bio Ed D 20 '70
    Knight, A. & Alpert, H.  Sex stars of 1970.  Playboy 17-12:220
        D '70
    Hollywood's hot new sex queens.  Mod Screen 66-1:34 Ja '72
    Married in all but name.  Mod Screen 66-11:26 N '72
    MacDonough, S.  Actress and woman.  Show 3-1:26 Mr '73
    Note; filmog.  Film Dope 3-141:45 Ag '73
    I hide in a corner until it's time to go crazy.  Films Illus 3-29:
        177 N '73
    Considine, S.  Bisset.  Interview p7 F '74
    Filmog.  Films & Filming 20-11:68 Ag '74


BIXBY, BILL
    The abstract world of...  TV Guide 12-5:14 F 1 '64
    Hobson, D.  So who wants marriage?  TV Guide 18-27:24 Jl 4 '70

What generation gap?   TV Guide 19-25:12 Je 19 '71
I'll go through with the wedding.   Silver S 41-10:75 O '71
Wed.   Photop 80-4:79 O '71
Strout, D.   Interview.   Mod Screen 66-6:62 Je '72
Windeler, R.   Courtship and marriage of Eddie's father.   Good
   House 175:24 Jl '72
Hano, A.   ...beats boredom to death.   TV Guide 21-48:17 D 1
   '73
Presto!   Change-o!   Playboy 20-12:176 D '73

BJORNSTRAND, GUNNAR
Burke, P. E.   The man who would make his mistakes again.
   Films & Filming 5-1:8 O '58
Cowie, P.   Note; filmog.   Focus On F 5:12 Win '70
Note; filmog.   Film Dope 3-143:46 Ag '73

BLACK, KAREN
Burke, T.   From Easy rider to Easy pieces, she's easy to
   love.   N. Y. Times Bio Ed N 22 '70
Women first.   Vogue 157:113 Mr 1 '71
Mulligan, T.   There's stardom in her future.   Show 2-3:20 My
   '71
Monkey shines.   Newsweek 80:79 Jl 24 '72
Sketch.   Movie Dig 1-6:25 N '72
Jack Nicholson comments on (her).   Dialogue 1:23 '72
Milam, M. S.   Interview.   Playgirl 1-2:48 Jl '73
Note; filmog.   Film Dope 3-144:48 Ag '73
Eyles, A.   Karen Black.   Focus On F 7:6 n. d.

BLACKFORD, MARY
Calhoun, D.   Sketch.   Movie Classic 7:36 F '35

BLACKMAN, HONOR
Musel, M.   Violence can be fun.   TV Guide 12-19:12 My 9 '64
Rising stars.   Film R p53 '65/66
The avengers.   Castle of F 7:56 n. d.

BLACKMER, SIDNEY
Patterson, A.   Sketch.   Theatre 35:106 F '22
Goldbeck, E.   Interview.   Motion Pic 40:44 O '30
Long, long ago.   Theatre Arts 34:38 S '50
Morehouse, W.   First forty years are the toughest.   Theatre
   Arts 43:76 S '59
Obit.   Classic Film Collect 41:53 Win '73
   Films & Filming 20-3:81 D '73
   N. Y. Times Bio Ed p1603 O '73
   Screen World p231 '74

BLACKTON, CHARLES
Montanye, L.   Sketch.   Motion Pic 18:57 N '19

BLACKTON, JACK
Como, W.   Beneath the sheets of morning.   After Dark 5-5:32
   S '72

BLACKTON, PAULA
  Olmsted, S. Art of. Motion Pic Classic 4:52 Mr '17
  Gregory, N. D. Appreciation. Motion Pic 13:99 Jl '17

BLACKTON, VIOLET
  Montanye, L. Sketch. Motion Pic 18:57 N '19

BLACKWELL, CARLYLE
  Sketch. Blue Book 19:12 My '14
  Willis, R. Carlyle Blackwell. Movie Pic 2-4:6 O '15
  Warren, M. Sketch. Motion Pic 11:114 Mr '16
  How to get into motion pictures. Motion Pic 11:115 Jl '16
  Montanye, L. Interview. Motion Pic Classic 6:24 Je '18
  Leon, S. Carlyle Blackwell. Films In R 22-9:583 N '71

BLACKWELL, IRENE
  Alleson, D. You win! Photop 15-1:59 D '18

BLAGOI, GEORGE
  Obit. Screen World 23:235 '72

BLAINE, VIVIAN
  Vallee, W. L. Weight off her mind. Silver S 17-3:55 Ja '47
  Fulton, M. J. Sketch. Photop 33:88 S '48
  Oderman, S. Vivian Blaine; filmog. Film Fan Mo 130:7 Ap '72

BLAIR, JANET
  Sketch. Life 12:55 Ap 6 '42
  Manners, M. J. Red Riding Hood and the Hollywood wolves.
    Silver S 12-12:38 O '42
  Mulvey, K. Sketch. Womans Home C 70:26 Ap '43
  The type of man she likes. Photop 22:51 Ap '43
  Manners, M. J. Love insurance for war brides. Silver S 14-1:
    34 N '43
  Watkins, W. Worth a gamble. Silver S 16-3:25 Ja '46
  What changed my life. Photop 28:60 My '46
  Churchill, R. & B. Ten new ways to get a man. Silver S 18-4:
    24 F '48
  Minoff, P. New bride for Caesar. Cue 25-37:12 S 15 '56
  When a woman needs a lift. TV Guide 7-28:17 Jl 11 '59
  ...advises fashions. TV Guide 7-29:17 Jl 18 '59
  Oderman, S. Janet Blair; filmog. Film Fan Mo 107:3 My '70
  Photoplay forum. Photop 81-3:14 Mr '72
  Davidson, B. Janet Blair regrets. TV Guide 20-20:16 My 13
    '72

BLAIR, JUNE
  She goes for the hero but not his horse. TV Guide 8-49:24 D
    3 '60

BLAIR, LINDA
  The Exorcist's possessed child. Photop 85-5:52 My '74

BLAIR, PAT
   New ammunition for The Rifleman.   TV Guide 10-45:26 N 10 '62
   She slaves all day over a hot stove.   TV Guide 13-34:12 Ag 21
   '65

BLAIR, RUTH
   Sketch.   Green Book 15:897 My '16

BLAKE, AMANDA
   Raddatz, L.   An open letter to my wife.   TV Guide 12-23:15 Je
   6 '54
   Her hair is her own.   TV Guide 5-12:20 Mr 23 '57
   She who never gets kissed.   TV Guide 6-11:8 Mr 15 '58
   Gordon, S.   Private life of Gunsmoke's Kitty.   Look 22:60 N 25
   '58
   Mona Lisa of the long branch.   TV Guide 8-50:25 D 10 '60

BLAKE, BOBBY
   Bobby Blake at 8.   Lions R 1-8:no p# Ap '42

BLAKE, ETTA
   Aspiring young actresses.   Show 2-2:64 S '71

BLAKE, JEAN
   She wants to forget her past.   TV Guide 8-47:21 N 19 '60

BLAKE, PAMELA
   Stars of tomorrow.   Lions R 1-11/12:no p# Jl/Ag '42
   B for Blake.   Lions R 2-2:no p# N '42

BLAKE, ROBERT
   On the scene.   Playboy 17-10:179 O '70

BLAKE, WHITNEY
   People took a chance.   TV Guide 6-24:20 Je 14 '58
   Like being a spectator at a tennis match.   TV Guide 11-11:27
   Mr 16 '63

BLAKELEY, JIMMY
   Whitehead, H.   Sketch.   Motion Pic 52:21 N '36

BLAKELY, COLIN
   Old times.   Plays & Players 18-10:22 Jl '71

BLAKELY, SUSIE
   Hickey, N.   This fake smile is worth $100,000 a year.   TV
   Guide 22-35:20 Ag 24 '74

BLANC, MEL
   One-man menagerie.   TV Guide 3-33:15 Ag 13 '55
   Barber, R.   Cheer, cheer for Bugs Bunny tech.   TV Guide 20-
   24:16 Je 10 '72

BLANCHAR, PIERRE
  Pierre Blanchar.    Visages 16:entire issue S '37
  Obit.    Film R p46 '64/65
    Screen World 15:219 '64

BLANCHARD, MARI
  O'Leary, D.    Is Mari the girl for Greg?    Silver S 24-7:35 My
    '54
  Bradley, A.    Mari Blanchard, filmog.    Films In R 21-7:446 Ag/S
    '70
  Crivello, K.    Mari Blanchard was a "bad" girl.    Classic Film
    Collect 28:ex p2 Fall '70
  Obit.    Screen World 22:235 '71

BLANCHE, FRANCIS
  Eyles, A.    Francis Blanche; filmog.    Focus On F 4:10 S/O '70

BLAND, R. HENDERSON
  Sketch.    Photop 40:76 Ag '31

BLANE, SALLY
  Manners, D.    Sketch.    Motion Pic 37:59 Jl '29
  Sketch.    Photop 37:52 Mr '30
  Uselton, R. A.    The Wampus baby stars.    Films In R 21-2:73
    F '70

BLESSED, BRIAN
  Twice Blessed.    Films Illus 2-19:10 Ja '73

BLETCHER, BILLY
  Ware, H. & Barrier, M.    Billy Bletcher; filmog.    Films In R
    21-5:318 My '70

BLINN, HOLBROOK
  Sketch.    Theatre 9:144 My '09
  Parsons, C. L.    Interview.    N. Y. Drama 65:11 Mr 1 '11
  Experiment in the production of one-act plays.    Theatre 17:186
    Je '13
  Wallace, D. H.    Interview.    N. Y. Drama 70:3 S 17 '13
  Seitz, C. W.    Interview.    Motion Pic Classic 6:52 Ap '18
  How I create my bad men.    Theatre 44:22 O '26

BLOCKER, DAN
  A whale of a hero.    TV Guide 8-10:7 Mr 5 '60
  Seay, S.    TV's gentle giants.    Look 26:66 Ja 30 '62
  Whitney, D.    There's no place to hide.    TV Guide 12-39:22 S 26
    '64
  Lewis, R. W.    Bonanza.    Sat Eve Post 238:84 D 4 '65
  Obit.    N. Y. Daily News My 15 '72
    N. Y. Times p34 My 15 '72
    Same.    N. Y. Times Bio Ed My 15 '72
    Newsweek 79:78 My 29 '72
    Time 99:85 My 29 '72

Stowers, C.  They remember (him).  TV Guide 19-33:24 Ag 14
   '71
Too soon, the final curtain for a gentle giant.  Mod Screen 66-8:
   50 Ag '72
He was a big man in every way.  Photop 82-2:26 Ag '72

BLONDELL, JOAN
Halprin, M.  Breezy Joan Blondell.  Silver S 2-1:26 N '31
Horton, H.  Sketch.  Motion Pic 42:66 Ja '32
Chapman, J. B.  Sketch.  Movie Classic 2:19 Ap '32
Keats, P.  Booked solid.  Silver S 3-9:19 Jl '33
Manners, D.  Does not want sex appeal.  Movie Classic 5:26 S
   '33
Wilson, E.  The maddest set in Hollywood.  Silver S 4-7:26 My
   '34
Williams, W.  Her climb to fame and fortune.  Movie Classic
   11:42 O '36
Cheatham, M.  Two blonde menaces.  Silver S 7-1:27 N '36
Hartley, K.  Interview.  Motion Pic 52:36 D '36
McHenry, M.  Her love story.  Movie Classic 11:20 Ja '37
Williams, W.  Her popularity.  Motion Pic 53:30 Jl '37
Wilson, E.  Projections.  Silver S 7-10:28 Ag '37
Henderson, J.  Danger--blonde at work!  Screen Book 20-4:22
   My '38
Hover, H.  Blondell--where to?  Screen Book 21-8:25 Mr '39
Wilson, E.  Don't get those Powells wrong.  Silver S 10-10:26
   Ag '40
Bio note; filmog.  Movies & People 2:6 '40
Wilson, E.  Joanie gets a bustle at last.  Silver S 12-3:24 Ja
   '42
The letter from Liza.  Silver S 13-4:90 F '43
My secret dream.  Photop 23:55 O '43
Bare facts of a camp tour.  Lions R 3-2:no p# Ja '44
Uselton, R. A.  The Wampus baby stars.  Films In R 21-2:73
   F '70
Barthel, J.  Quartet of queens.  Life 70:60 F 19 '71
Johnson, D.  The original Miss Show Biz.  After Dark 4-8:38
   D '71
Bowers, R. L.  Joan Blondell; filmog.  Films In R 23-4:193 Ap
   '72
Koch, M.  The great golddigger is still digging Hollywood.  In-
   terview 24:24 Ag '72
Higham, C.  Joanie's still bright, brash and Blondell.  N. Y.
   Times Bio Ed p1444 Ag '72
Cosgrove, J.  Letter.  Films In R 23-7:443 Ag/S '72
Starring Joan Blondell and--TV Guide 20-39:14 S 23 '72
Chances are I've done everything.  Photop 84-1:64 Jl '73
Note; filmog.  Film Dope 4:149 Mr '74


BLOOM, CLAIRE
Baker, P.  A star without the limelight.  Films & Filming 2-6:
   5 Mr '56
The year of the Steigers; interview.  Cinema (BH) 3-2:19 Mr '66

Barthel, J.  Interview.  Redbook 133:98 Jl '69
Bloom, C.  Cue salutes Charles Chaplin.  Cue 39-13:34 Mr 28
   '70
Klemesrud, J.  The man Claire wanted to kill.  N. Y.  Times
   Bio Ed F 7 '71
In the words of Claire Bloom.  Cue 40-10:10 Mr 6 '71
Prideaux, T.  As Nora and Hedda.  Life 70:10 Mr 12 '71
Roman, R. C.  In Bloom.  After Dark 4-1:20 My '71
Buck, J.  Interview.  Plays & Players 20-6:18 Mr '73
Note; filmog.  Film Dope 4:150 Mr '74

BLOOM, VERNA
   Actresses.  Newsweek 76:74 D 7 '70
   Note; filmog.  Film Dope 4:151 Mr '74

BLORE, ERIC
   McFee, F.  Blore's a funny bloke!  Screen Book 19-5:38 D '37
   Hamilton, S.  Story of.  Photop 52:21 My '38
   Obit.  Film R p10 '59/60
      Screen World 11:215 '60

BLUE, BEN
   Two shades of Blue.  Lions R 3-3:no p# Ap '44

BLUE, MONTE
   Private Blue!  Photop 15-4:35 Mr '19
   Delvigne, D.  Interview.  Motion Pic 18:57 O '19
   Hall, G.  Interview.  Motion Pic Classic 11:37 Ja '21
   Bruce, B.  Interview.  Motion Pic 21:69 F '21
   Hall, G.  Interview.  Motion Pic 24:75 Ag '22
   Autobiography.  Motion Pic 28:32 S '24
   Tully, J.  Sketch.  Photop 27:42 F '25
   Currie, H.  Sketch.  Motion Pic 29:35 Jl '25
   Interview.  Theatre 44:40 D '26
   Knighton, P.  Sketch.  Motion Pic Classic 26:55 D '27
   Calhoun, D.  Making White shadows of the South Seas.  Motion
      Pic 36:31 Ag '28
   Biery, R.  Interview.  Motion Pic Classic 29:37 My '29
   Gray, J.  Monte Blue; filmog.  Films In R 14-5:313 My '63
   Scott, K. W.  Monte Blue.  Films In R 14-8:508 O '63
   Pitts, M. B.  The career of...; filmog.  Classic Film Collect
      30:22 Spg '71
   Additional filmog.  Classic Film Collect 31:43 Sum '71
   Monte Blue; filmog.  Cinema Trails 2:14 n. d.

BLYDEN, LARRY
   Fletcher, F.  The busy Blydens.  Cue 28-12:18 Mr 21 '59
   He would like to sell more tickets.  TV Guide 10-38:13 S 22 '62

BLYTH, ANN
   Should teenagers marry?  Photop 30:66 D '46
   Vallee, W. L.  Blyth spirit.  Silver S 17-6:61 Ap '47
   Sketch.  Photop 31:98 S '47

Her costumes for Mr. Peabody and the mermaid.  Life 24:91 F
   9 '48
O'Leary, D.  That brand new Blyth.  Silver S 18-5:40 Mr '48
Maddox, B.  What's ahead for Ann?  Silver S 18-11:34 S '48
Mulvey, K.  Her Valentine's day party.  Photop 34:52 F '49
Blyth, A.  Having fun with Bing and Barry.  Silver S 19-7:42
   My '49
Saunders, A. W.  What's in a cast?  Life With Music 2:10 My
   '49
O'Leary, D.  I'm not ready for marriage.  Silver S 21-1:48 N
   '50
Gerard, M.  The home life for Ann.  Silver S 23-1:38 N '52
Hewitt, M.  Ann finally said yes.  Silver S 23-8:24 Je '53
Holland, J.  Ann's plans for motherhood.  Silver S 24-7:23 My
   '54
Borie, M.  We visit with (her) today.  Movie Dig 1-2:87 Mr '72
Interview.  Photop 83-2:26 F '73

BLYTHE, BETTY
   The family name is Blythe.  Photop 14-4:99 S '18
Hall, G.  Sketch.  Motion Pic 16:74 D '18
Montanye, L.  Interview.  Motion Pic 18:60 O '19
Star or starve.  Photop 17-1:63 D '19
Cheatham, M. S.  Interview.  Motion Pic Classic 9:20 F '20
Naylor, H. S.  Sketch.  Motion Pic 21:22 F '21
Smith, F. J.  Interview.  Motion Pic Classic 12:16 Ag '21
Interview.  Motion Pic 22:23 Ag '21
Service, F.  Interview.  Motion Pic Classic 14:16 Ap '22
Carr, H.  Sketch.  Motion Pic 29:1 F '25
Obit.  Film R p15 '72/73
   N. Y. Times p71 Ap 9 '72
Same.  Classic Film Collect 35:8x Sum '72
Same.  N. Y. Times Bio Ed Ap 9 '72

BOARDMAN, BILLIE (Billie Boy)
Mount, C.  Sketch.  Motion Pic Classic 4:31 Mr '17

BOARDMAN, ELEANOR
Cheatham, M.  Interview.  Classic 18:34 F '24
Interview by radio.  Motion Pic 29:44 Jl '25
Lane, T.  Sketch.  Motion Pic Classic 21:64 Ag '25
Thorp, D.  Sketch.  Motion Pic 31:1 Jl '26
Wingate, R.  Separated from King Vidor.  Movie Classic 3:28
   S '32
Uselton, R. A.  The Wampus baby stars.  Films In R 21-2:73
   F '70
Bodeen, D.  Eleanor Boardman; filmog.  Films In R 24-10:593
   D '73

BOARDMAN, VIRGINIA TRUE
Walsh, R. E.  Sketch.  Motion Pic Classic 3:23 F '17
Obit.  Classic Film Collect 33:46 Win '71

BOGARDE, DIRK
  My favorite role.    Film R p32 '51/52
  Personality of the month.    Films & Filming 1-11:3 Ag '55
  My favorite role.    Film R p27 '55/56
  The screen answers back.    Films & Filming 8-8:12 My '62
  Star of the year; filmog.    Film R p18 '62/63
  Cowie, P.    The face of '63--Great Britain.    Films & Filming
      9-5:19 F '63
  Bio.    Cur Bio Yrbk 1967:34 '68
  Guerin, A.    His love affair with the camera.    Show 1-5:57 My
      '70
  Alpert, H.    Directors at work; Visconti in Venice.    Sat R 53:16
      Ag 8 '70
  Visconti, L.    Reply to Alpert.    Sat R 53:20 D 19 '70
  Gow, G.    Interview; filmog.    Films & Filming 17-8:42 My '71
  When Dirk Bogarde turns disc jockey...    Films Illus 3-29:171
      N '73
  Note; filmog.    Film Dope 4:156 Mr '74
  Castell, D.    Bogarde.    Films Illus 34:387 Je '74

BOGART, HUMPHREY
  Mack, G.    Story of.    Motion Pic 52:34 Ja '37
  Albert, D.    Bad boy Bogart.    Screen Book 21-9:27 Ap '39
  Holland, J.    Everything happens to Humphrey.    Silver S 10-2:42
      D '39
  Bogart, H.    Why Hollywood hates me.    Screen Book 22-6:66 Ja
      '40
  Bio note; filmog.    Movies & People 2:6 '40
  Wilson, E.    Easy does it Bogie.    Silver S 12-2:26 D '41
  Sheridan, A. as told to D. B. Haas.    Brother Bogie.    Silver S
      13-3:22 Ja '43
  Bogart, H. as told to D. B. Haas.    Sister Annie.    Silver S 13-
      5:26 Mr '43
  Mulvey, K.    Sketch.    Womans Home C 70:20 My '43
  Bogart, H. as told to J. Holland.    How to keep your marriage
      alive.    Silver S 14-1:30 N '43
  A romance I can't forget.    Photop 24:55 Mr '44
  Hall, G.    "Listen, Kreep. "    Silver S 15-8:22 Je '45
  London, E.    And so they are one.    Silver S 15-11:32 S '45
  Asher, J.    And how are things with the Bogarts?    Silver S 17-9:
      52 Jl '47
  Bogart, H.    Imagine me a father!    Silver S 19-7:24 My '49
  Awarded Photoplay's citation for 1948.    Photop 35:59 My '49
  Bogie sides the law in The enforcer.    Cue 19-48:16 D 2 '50
  Bogart, H. as told to J. Hyams.    Movie making beats the devil.
      Cue 22-48:14 N 28 '53
  Hall, G.    Baby exposes Bogey.    Silver S 24-6:36 Ap '54
  Barnes, P.    Gunman No. 1.    Films & Filming 1-12:12 S '55
  Towne, R.    Bogart and Belmondo; where it was and where it's
      at.    Cinema (BH) 3-1:4 D '65
  Tynan, K.    Here's looking at you kid.    Playboy 13-6:110 Je '66
  Crowther, B.    The career and the cult.    Playboy 13-6:110 Je
      '66

A Bogart quiz. Playboy 13-6:112 Je '66
Bibliog. and filmog. Playboy 13-6:166 Je '66
Dawson, W. J. Bogart-mania. Films In R 17-6:391 Je/Jl '66
Condon, B. Bubbling Bogart. Scanlans 1-5:67 Jl '70
Marlowe, D. The man, Bogie. Classic Film Collect 30:31 Spg
    '71
Davis, P. Bogart, Hawks and The big sleep revisited--frequent-
    ly. Film J 1-2:3 Sum '71
The love story of Bogie and his Betty. Screen Greats 1:54 Sum
    '71
Bogart; filmog. Screen Greats 1-2: entire issue '71
Truffaut, F. Truffaut on Bogart. Sat R Arts 1-3:31 Mr '73
Koch, H. The making of... Casablanca. New York 6-18:74 Ap
    30 '73
Note; filmog. Film Dope 4:157 Mr '74
Bressi, J. F. Huston and Bogart. Mise-en-Scene 1:66 n. d.

BOLAND, MARY
Sketch. Green Book 3:342 F '10
Interview. Cosmop 55:411 Ag '13
Work in My lady's dress. Strand (NY) 49:119 F '15
Sketch. Cosmop 58:462 Mr '15
Sketch. Theatre 45:30 Mr '27
Obit. Film R p21 '66/68

BOLES, JOHN
Carlisle, H. Sketch. Motion Pic 35:72 Jl '28
Hall, G. Interview. Motion Pic 38:44 D '29
Manners, D. Interview. Motion Pic Classic 30:27 D '29
Ramsey, W. Interview. Motion Pic Classic 31:26 Jl '30
Cruikshank, H. Sketch. Motion Pic 39:74 Jl '30
Hall, G. Interview. Motion Pic 41:48 Mr '31
Conrad, S. What women should know about men. Silver S 1-8:
    25 Je '31
Costello, T. Interview. Movie Classic 3:52 N '32
Cheatham, M. John Boles 'em over. Silver S 3-4:20 F '33
Lathem, M. Interview. Movie Classic 6:51 Jl '34
Borden, L. Interview. Movie Classic 7:55 D '34
Chrisman, J. E. An open letter to (him). Motion Pic 50:38 S
    '35
Reply to Chrisman. Motion Pic 50:56 O '35
Blackford, M. Interview. Movie Classic 9:25 N '35
Haddon, J. L. Interview. Motion Pic 51:39 F '36
Silver, G. R. Grateful. Silver S 6-5:54 Mr '36
Harrison, P. Interview. Motion Pic 53:35 Ap '37
Bio note; filmog. Movies & People 2:7 '40
Meet the colonel. Lions R 3-2:no p# Ja '44
Obit. Classic Film Collect 23:46 Spg '69
    Film R p13 '71/72
    N. Y. Times p39 F 28 '69
    Newsweek 73:93 Mr 10 '69
    Screen World 21:234 '70
    Time 93:80 Mr 7 '69

BOLGER, RAY
  Pringle, H. F. Luck of the Bolgers. Colliers 98:11 Ag 1 '36
  Bio. Cur Bio 3:93 '42
  Beiswanger, G. All-out theatre man. Theatre Arts 27:85 F '43
  Entertaining overseas. Theatre Arts 28:194 Ap '44
  Strictly for round actors. Theatre Arts 28:235 Ap '44
  Three to make ready. Life 20:67 Mr 25 '46
  Anecdote. Am Mag 143:68 F '47
  Sketch. Vogue 112:118 O 15 '48
  Work of in Where's Charley? Life 25:85 N 8 '48
  Story of. Life 25:62 D 27 '48
  Bolger butts in. Life 26:38 Mr 21 '49
  Here's Bolger. Newsweek 34:72 Jl 18 '49
  Zolotow, M. Muscles with a sense of humor. Sat Eve Post
    222:32 Jl 30 '49
  Lords of laughter. Coronet 30:84 O '51
  Seldes, G. Comic spirit. Sat R 36:32 Ja 10 '53
  Here's Bolger. Newsweek 42:75 O 19 '53
  Minoff, P. New Bolger series could use alterations. Cue 22-45:
    9 N 7 '53
  How people talk about me. Colliers 132:68 D 11 '53
  Mr. Stiltlegs. Look 17:83 D 15 '53
  Bolger's Thursday. Dance 28:34 Ap '54
  Still dancing at 50. TV Guide 2-28:9 Jl 9 '54
  Minoff, P. Notes on TV. Cue 23-40:34 O 2 '54
  Eight ways to ask for a raise. McCalls 83:21 N '55
  Bolger's tour of Greenwich Village. TV Guide 4-42:12 O 20 '56
  Minoff, P. The medium finally does right by Mr. Bolger. Cue
    25-44:15 N 3 '56
  Rubberlegs. Time 68:44 D 3 '56
  Minoff, P. I'm no dancer. Cue 26-12:10 Mr 23 '57
  Mr. rubberlegs. Newsweek 55:80 My 16 '60
  Bolger breezes by. Life 52:84 My 25 '62
  Oz revisited. TV Guide 18-11:38 Mr 14 '70
  Interview. Interview 4-10:37 O '74
  Bolger, R. Playing the Palace. Nostalgia Illus 1-2:6 D '74

BOLKAN, FLORINDA
  Robbins, F. Interview. Photop 77-5:76 My '70
  Beauty of Bolkan. Harp Baz 104:82 Ap '71
  Note; filmog. Film Dope 4:161 Mr '74

BOLLING, TIFFANY
  Tiffany's a gem. Playboy 19-4:153 Ap '72

BOLOGNA, JOSEPH
  Adler, D. Joe and Renee. New York 4-50:35 D 13 '71
  Johnson, D. Taylor-made for each other. After Dark 4-11:44
    Mr '72
  MacDonough, S. Made for each other. Show 2-1:20 Mr '72

BONADUCE, DANNY
  Adler, D. What is a freckled-faced Partridge? TV Guide 21-14:
    21 Ap 7 '73

BONANOVA, FORTUNIO
  Obit.  Screen World 21:234 '70

BOND, GARY
  Buck, J.  Interview.  Plays & Players 20-4:14 Ja '73
  Leech, M. T.  ...of the amazing technicolor rock musical.  Af-
    ter Dark 6-5:34 S '73

BOND, LILLIAN
  Uselton, R. A.  The Wampus baby stars.  Films In R 21-2:73
    F '70

BOND, TOMMY
  Maltin, L.  Our gang; Our gang filmog.  Film Fan Mo 66:3 D
    '66

BOND, WARD
  The winning Bond.  Lions R 3-2:no p# Ja '44

BONDARCHUK, SERGEI
  Director of the year; filmog.  International Film G 6:9 '69
  Gillett, J.  Thinking big.  Sight & Sound 39-3:135 Sum '70
  Lind, J.  filmog (as actor and director).  Focus On F 4:24 S/O
    '70
  The coming of the Russians.  Action 6-2:4 Mr/Ap '71
  The Russians are here.  Making Films 5-3:10 Je '71
  Note; filmog.  Film Dope 4:165 Mr '74

BONDI, BEULAH
  Hamilton, S.  Sketch.  Photop 54:28 My '40
  Springer, J.  Letter.  Films In R 14-6:374 Je/Jl '63

BONERZ, PETER
  Lochte, D.  Friendship by appointment.  TV Guide 22-19:24 My
    11 '74

BONNE, SHIRLEY
  She's practically type-cast.  TV Guide 9-1:24 Ja 7 '61

BONNER, MARJORIE
  Manners, D.  Sketch.  Motion Pic Classic 25:43 Ag '27

BONNER, PRISCILLA
  Interview.  Motion Pic Classic 11:18 Ja '21
  Interview.  Motion Pic 22:68 O '21
  Manners, D.  Sketch.  Motion Pic Classic 25:43 Ag '27

BOONE, PAT
  Zunser, J.  Throwback to the Merriwell boys?  Cue 26-20:17
    My 18 '57
  Rising stars.  Film R p30 '58/59
  Cross and the switchblade.  Chr. Today 14:52 O 10 '69
  Newsmakers.  Newsweek 77:67 Ap 19 '71

People.  Time 97:30 Ap 19 '71
Lynch, D. M.  Interview.  Chr.  Cent 88:1167 O 6 '71
Why I was kicked out of my church.  Photop 80-4:85 O '71
How I tell my child the story of Christmas.  Photop 81-1:51 Ja
   '72
Burke, T.  Gospel according to Boone.  Esquire 77:146 Ap '72
Photoplay forum.  Photop 81-5:7 My '72
Strout, D.  Interview.  Mod Screen 66-7:63 Jl '72
Filmog.  Films & Filming 19-7:66 Ap '73
His family.  Photop 86-3:45 S '74
(Pat Boone had a column in Photoplay Magazine in 1974)

BOONE, RICHARD
   Minoff, P.  Doctor in the house.  Cue 24-17:14 Ap 30 '55
   Schickel, R.  Angry gun.  Show 1-2:50 N '61
   From dauber to dobbin.  Show 2-7:73 Jl '62
   Issue in priorities.  Current 113:40 D '69
   Adler, D.  Had gun, traveled, is back in TV.  TV Guide 19-39:
      16 S 25 '71
   Gardella, K.  Back as Heck Ramsey.  N. Y. Sun News sec 3:19
      O 8 '72
   Berkvist, R.  Meaner than ever.  N. Y. Times sec 2:23 D 10 '72
   Same.  N. Y. Times Bio Ed p2117 D '72
   The Boone method.  TV Guide 21-20:13 My 19 '73
   Davidson, B.  Interview.  TV Guide 22-8:25 F 23 '74
   Note; filmog.  Film Dope 4:166 Mr '74

BOOTH, ADRIAN
   (See GRAY, LORNA)

BOOTH, ANITA
   Montanye, L.  Sketch.  Motion Pic Classic 11:1 S '20

BOOTH, EDWINA
   Alpert, K.  Experiences making Trader Horn.  Photop 37:46 Mr
      '30
   Goldbeck, E.  Experiences making Trader Horn.  Motion Pic
      39:66 Ap '30
   Calhoun, D.  Her sob story.  Motion Pic Classic 32:29 S '30
   Calhoun, D.  Sketch.  Motion Pic 40:8 Ja '31
   Derr, E.  Jungle malady prevents her return to films.  Movie
      Classic 3:33 F '33
   Calhoun, D.  Her illness.  Movie Classic 6:32 Ag '34
   Riggan, B.  Damn the crocodiles...  Am Heritage 19:38 Je '68
   Cabana, R. Jr.  Concerning Trader Horn.  Views & Rs 3-1:35
      Sum '71
   Tuska, J.  Trader Horn.  Views & Rs 3-1:51 Sum '71

BOOTH, SHIRLEY
   Bio sketch.  Cur Bio 3:96 '42
   Keating, J.  The Tree's brightest blossom.  Cue 20-21:14 My
      26 '51
   Water, R.  Time for Shirley.  Cue 21-42:15 O 18 '52

Culman, D.  Star of 3-C!  Silver S 23-10:38 Ag '53
Tough day of a star.  Cue 23-12:15 Mr 20 '54
Gow, G.  The quest for realism; discussion.  Films & Filming
  4-3:13 D '57
Salute of the week.  Cue 39-45:1 N 7 '70
Valentry, D.  My fight with loneliness.  Harvest Yrs 12:48 Mr
  '72
Hano, A.  Back from the Gobi Desert.  TV Guide 21-19:17 My
  12 '73

BOOTH, SUZETTE
Breaking into the movies in California.  Motion Pic 12:69 Ja '17
  and following issues.

BORDEN, OLIVE
Leslie, A.  Sketch.  Motion Pic 31:56 Je '26
York, C.  Sketch.  Photop 31:1 Ja '27
Clark, F.  Sketch.  Photop 31:50 My '27
Reid, J.  Sketch.  Motion Pic 33:24 Jl '27
Wells, H. K.  Sketch.  Motion Pic Classic 27:25 Jl '28
Ramsey, W.  Sketch.  Motion Pic Classic 30:62 N '29
Uselton, R. A.  The Wampus baby stars.  Films In R 21-2:73
  F '70

BORDONI, IRENE
Her love affair.  Cosmop 54:414 F '13
Home of.  Theatre 43:42 Ap '26
Biery, R.  Interview.  Motion Pic Classic 30:25 S '29
York, C.  Sketch.  Photop 37:40 D '29
Obit.  Newsweek 41:70 Mr 30 '53
  Time 61:82 Mr 30 '53

BOREL, LOUIS
Obit.  Screen World p231 '74

BORELLI, CARLA
Carla.  TV Guide 17-48:19 N 29 '69

BORG, VEDA ANN
Letters.  Films In R 16-6:393 Je/Jl '65
Obit.  Classic Film Collect 41:53 Win '73
  Screen World p231 '74

BORGNINE, ERNEST
Bell, A.  Borgnine's a softie.  N. Y. Times Bio Ed p931 Je '73

BORIO, JOSEPHINE
Thornton, J.  Sketch.  Motion Pic 35:67 Ap '28

BORISENKO, DON
Person of promise.  Films & Filming 8-9:27 Je '62

BORZAGE, RAYMOND
    Heffernan, H.  Personalities prominent in the press.  Cinema
        Dig 1-3:7 Je 13 '32

BOSE, LUCIA
    Note; filmog.  Film Dope 4:171 Mr '74

BOSLEY, TOM
    Discusses his child.  Photop 86-5:25 N '74

BOSWORTH, HOBART
    Work in The sea wolf.  Nation 47:277 My '18
    Cheatham, M.  Interview.  Motion Pic Classic 9:18 D '19
    Beach, B.  Interview.  Motion Pic 23:42 F '22
    Parker, R.  Sketch.  National 53:469 Je '25
    Belfrage, C.  Hollywood's first movie actor.  Motion Pic 35:34
        Ap '28
    Martin, B.  Hobart Bosworth.  Cinema Dig 1-10:9 S 19 '32
    Obit.  Newsweek 23:12 Ja 10 '44
        Time 43:82 Ja 10 '44

BOTHWELL, JOHN F.
    Obit.  Screen World 19:228 '68

BOTTOMS, JOSEPH
    Tomorrow people.  Films Illus 3-35:442 Jl '74
    Stoop, N. M.  Joseph Bottoms and The Dove.  After Dark 7-6:
        34 O '74
    The Bottomses are reaching for the top.  People 2-20:45 N 11
        '74

BOTTOMS, SAM
    The Bottomses are reaching for the top.  People 2-20:45 N 11
        '74

BOTTOMS, TIMOTHY
    I've got to get married young.  Mod Screen 66-2:42 F '72
    Miller, E.  Interview.  Seventeen 31:66 Mr '72
    Faces going far.  Films Illus 1-10:21 Ap '72
    Interview.  Photop 81-6:46 Je '72
    Up from the top.  Playboy 21-6:176 Je '74
    The Bottomses are reaching for the top.  People 2-20:45 N 11
        '74

BOUCHER, VICTOR
    Victor Boucher.  Visages 32:entire issue.  F '39

BOUCHET, BARBARA
    Ease of Europa.  Esquire 61:114 Ap '64
    Rising stars.  Film R p53 '65/66

BOUCHIER, CHILI
    Silent films remembered.  Films & Filming 17-5:39 F '71

BOUDREAUX, JOSEPH CARL
  Story of the star of Louisiana story.   Life 26:137 My 2 '49

BOULDEN, EDWARD
  How he became a photoplayer.   Motion Pic 9:117 Ap '15

BOUQUET, MICHEL
  Note; filmog.   Film Dope 4:176 Mr '74

BOURVIL
  Cayatte, A.   My friend Bourvil.   Unifrance 48:170 '58
  Trying to find my style.   Films & Filming 7-1:14 O '60
  Obit.   Film R p13 '71/72
    N. Y. Times p50 S 24 '70
    Same.   N. Y. Times Bio Ed S 24 '70
    Screen World 22:235 '71

BOUTON, BETTY
  Peltret, E.   Interview.   Motion Pic Classic 11:38 O '20

BOW, CLARA
  Sketch.   Motion Pic Classic 13:63 Ja '22
  Perry, M.   Interview.   Classic 15:66 S '22
  Carr, H.   Sketch.   Motion Pic Classic 21:1 Je '25
  Chaffin, G.   Sketch.   Photop 28:78 Je '25
  Tildesley, A. L.   Interview.   Motion Pic Classic 23:1 Je '26
  Howe, M.   Sketch.   Motion Pic Classic 24:59 F '27
  Manners, D.   Interview.   Motion Pic 34:24 Ag '27
  Evoking emotions is no child's play.   Theatre 46:42 N '27
  Cummings, A.   How to tell her from Sue Carol.   Motion Pic
    Classic 27:28 Ag '28
  Biery, R.   Interview.   Motion Pic 36:44 N '28
  Belfrage, C.   Sketch.   Classic 28:22 D '28
  Whitaker, A.   Home of.   Photop 36:64 S '29
  Biery, R.   Sketch.   Motion Pic 39:8 Mr '30
  Belfrage, C.   Her sex appeal.   Motion Pic Classic 32:36 S '30
  Goldbeck, E.   Interview.   Motion Pic 40:48 S '30
  Sketch.   Fortune 2:37 O '30
  Manners, D.   Her new beau.   Motion Pic Classic 32:48 N '30
  Benham, L.   Why can't the "It" girl keep her man?   Silver S
    1-1:31 N '30
  Hall, G.   Sketch.   Motion Pic 40:28 Ja '31
  Taviner, R.   Sketch.   Motion Pic 41:8 Ap '31
  Donnell, D.   Sketch.   Motion Pic Classic 33:1 Ap '31
  The girl who needs a friend.   Silver S 1-6:51 Ap '31
  Walker, H. L.   Sketch.   Motion Pic Classic 33:65 My '31
  Her headline career.   Motion Pic Classic 32:34 Ag '31
  Hall, L.   Sketch.   Photop 40:55 Ag '31
  Gallant, T.   Can she ever come back?   Movie Classic 1:20 S '31
  Rivers, A.   She will come back.   Movie Classic 1:22 S '31
  Clara Bow--past, present and future.   Silver S 1-11:22 S '31
  Dibble, S.   Sketch.   Movie Classic 1:28 F '32
  Lee, S.   Interview.   Movie Classic 2:20 Ap '32

Sykes, L.  Signs big contract.  Movie Classic 2:32 Jl '32
Belfrage, C.  Her return to the screen.  Motion Pic 44:40 Ag
    '32
Melcher, E.  Clara Bow.  Cinema Dig 1-10:9 S 19 '32
Crosley, H.  Her return to the screen.  Photop 42:27 N '32
Manners, D.  Her future life-story.  Motion Pic 44:1 N '32
Moffitt, C. F.  Censorship for interviews Hollywood's latest wild
    idea.  Cinema Dig 2-5:9 Ja 9 '33
Keats, P.  Clara Bow's return bout.  Silver S 3-3:22 Ja '33
Schallert, E.  Interview.  Movie Classic 4:42 Ap '33
Her European diary.  Photop 43:28 My '33
Wilson, E.  Bow goes Hoopla!  Silver S 4-2:20 D '33
Sylvia's beauty helps.  Photop 45:34 F '34
Shaffer, R.  Her prospective motherhood.  Movie Classic 6:39
    Ag '34
Estes, O. Jr.  High voltage in the middle twenties!  8mm Col-
    lect 11:21 Spg '65
Obit.  8mm Collect 13:10 Fall/Win '65
    Film R p21 '66/68
Robinson, D.  Show people.  Sight & Sound 37:199 Aut '68
Uselton, R. A.  The Wampus baby stars.  Films In R 21-2:73
    F '70
Lee, R.  The magic that was Hollywood.  Classic Film Collect
    27:36 Spg/Sum '70
Note; filmog.  Film Dope 4:179 Mr '74

BOWDEN, DORIS
    Hamilton, S. & Morse, W. Jr.  Sketch.  Photop 54:20 Mr '40
    MacDonald, J.  She didn't wait for lady luck.  Silver S 10-6:38
        Ap '40
    Hamilton, S.  Sketch.  Photop 23:35 Je '43
    Perkins, R.  Actress wife.  Silver S 13-10:42 Ag '43

BOWERS, JOHN
    Kingsley, R.  Interview.  Motion Pic 18:48 Ag '19
    He hasn't been home since.  Photop 16-3:61 Ag '19
    Peltret, E.  Sketch.  Motion Pic Classic 9:20 Ja '20
    Roberts, S.  Interview.  Motion Pic 20:80 Ja '21
    Goldbeck, W.  Interview.  Motion Pic Classic 12:32 Ag '21

BOWERS, KENNY
    He wants to be a dumb guy.  Lions R 3-3:no p# Ap '44

BOWKER, JUDI
    Headliners.  Photop 84-1:14 Jl '73

BOWMAN, LEE
    Hamilton, S.  Sketch.  Photop 54:18 F '40
    Lindsay, M.  Sketch.  Photop 18:30 Ja '41
    Two who help make Married bachelor a joy.  Lions R 1-2:no p#
        O '41
    (His) lucky rain.  Lions R 1-4:no p# D '41
    Six-love!  Lions R 1-6:no p# F '42

Bowman's progress.  Lions R 1-8:no p# Ap '42
Stars of tomorrow.  Lions R 1-11/12:no p# Jl/Ag '42
Just the type.  Lions R 2-3(sup):no p# Ja '43
His marriage.  Photop 27:60 Je '45
Ames, A.  It took time, but...  Silver S 15-8:42 Je '45
Fisher, G.  Not very public.  Silver S 16-12:48 O '46

BOYD, BETTY
    Uselton, R. A.  The Wampus baby stars.  Films In R 21-2:73
    F '70

BOYD, STEPHEN
    Rising star.  Film R p31 '57/58
    Giving up gratefully.  Films Illus 3-28:136 O '73

BOYD, WILLIAM
    Tildsley, A. L.  Interview.  Motion Pic Classic 23:18 Ap '26
    Spensley, D.  Sketch.  Photop 30:91 N '26
    Hanlon, J.  Sketch.  Motion Pic Classic 26:33 Ja '28
    Donnell, D.  Sketch.  Motion Pic Classic 29:45 Ap '29
    Hall, G.  Sketch.  Motion Pic Classic 31:63 Jl '30
    Alpert, K.  Sketch.  Photop 42:31 O '32
    Tully, J.  His story.  Photop 45:54 Mr '34
    Hopalong Cassidy enterprises and sidelines.  Time 54:68 Ag 29
    '49
    St. Johns, A. R.  Bill Boyd's alter ego... Hopalong Cassidy.
    Cue 19-22:12 Je 3 '50
    LaBadie, D. W.  The last roundup.  Show 2-9:74 S '62
    Obit.  Classic Film Collect 36:extra 2 Fall '72
        Film R p11 '73/74
        N. Y. Times Bio Ed p1601 S '72

BOYER, CHARLES
    Goldbeck, E.  A new lover from Paris.  Motion Pic 48:50 Ja
    '35
    Sketch.  Time 25:48 Mr 25 '35
    Sketch.  Stage 12:36 My '35
    His fine acting in Break of hearts.  Lit Dig 119:25 Je 1 '35
    Crowley, G.  Hollywood's new heartthrob.  Motion Pic 49:33 Jl
    '35
    Samuels, L.  The Boyer charm.  Silver S 5-10:23 Ag '35
    Reed, D.  His charm.  Movie Classic 9:30 Ja '36
    Zeitlin, I.  His story.  Motion Pic 51:39 Je '36
    Reed, D.  An irrestible actor.  Silver S 7-3:52 Ja '37
    Surmelian, L.  His popularity.  Motion Pic 53:32 F '37
    Charles Boyer.  Visages 10:entire issue Mr '37
    Appreciation in Conquest.  Stage 15:21 Je '38
    Wilson, E.  Projection of...  Silver S 8-9:56 Jl '38
    Magee, T.  Behind the scenes with...  Screen Book 21-1:34 Ag
    '38
    Bio note; filmog.  Movies & People 2:7 '40
    Hopper, H.  His married life.  Photop 22:26 My '43
    A romance I can't forget.  Photop 24:55 Mr '44

Hisses instead of kisses.   Lions R 3-3(sup):no p# Ap '44
Talmey, A.   His work in establishing the French research
    foundation in Hollywood.   Vogue 105:130 Mr 15 '45
Pritchett, F.   Boyer breaks down.   Silver S 16-3:34 Ja '46
Boyer, C.   Advanced training for film workers:  France.   Holly-
    wood Q 1-3:287 Ap '46
Parsons, L. O.   Cosmop's citation for the best performance of
    the month.   Cosmop 123:46 N '47
Screen's wonder Boyer.   Cue 17-49:20 D 4 '48
Rattigan, R.   A good lover never cools.   Silver S 24-4:38 F '54
Failure makes good.   TV Guide 4-38:25 S 22 '56
Boyer-Colbert are back again.   Cue 27-43:11 O 25 '58
Hair-raising stories from the stars.   Photop 78-1:62 Jl '70
Monsees, R. A.   Charles Boyer; filmog.   Films In R 22-5:258
    My '71
Passalacqua, J. C.   Letter; response to Monsees.   Films In R
    22-6:377 Je/Jl '71
Letters.   Films In R 22-7:447 Ag/S '71
The continental lover.   Screen Greats 1-2:71 Sum '71
Letter.   Films In R 24-3:190 Mr '73
Note; filmog.   Film Dope 4:181 Mr '74

BOYLE, PETER
    Klemesrud, J.   His happiness is a thing called Joe.   N. Y.
        Times Bio Ed Ag 2 '70
    Durham, M.   Reluctant hero of the hardhats.   Life 69:69 O 16
        '70
    Johnson, A.   A man of many roles.   Show 2-10:18 D '71
    Miller, G.   Interview.   Interview 29:31 Ja '73

BOZYK, MAX
    Obit.   N. Y. Times p43 Ap 8 '70
    Same.   N. Y. Times Bio Ed Ap 8 '70
    Screen World 22:235 '71

BRACKEN, EDDIE
    Sketch.   Photop 24:38 D '43
    In the movies with Bracken.   Cue 13-39:16 S 23 '44
    Walker, H. L.   No more elegance for Eddie.   Silver S 15-2:40
        D '44
    His new radio program.   Newsweek 25:94 F 19 '45
    Watkins, W.   Pluperfect family man.   Silver S 17-4:58 F '47
    Interview; filmog.   Film Fan Mo 64:3 O '66
    Maltin, L.   Our gang; Our Gang filmog.   Film Fan Mo 66:3 D
        '66
    Nordheimer, J.   Bracken battles losses in a 'most tragic role.'
        N. Y. Times Bio Ed D 27 '71

BRADDOCK, MICKEY
    Here comes the heroes.   TV Guide 4-37:28 S 15 '56

BRADFORD, LANE
    Obit.   Screen World p231 '74

BRADFORD, RICHARD
  Filmog.   Films & Filming 20-10:64 Jl '74

BRADFORD, VIRGINIA
  West, M.   Sketch.   Photop 32:66 S '27
  Wheaton, J.   Sketch.   Motion Pic 35:74 F '28
  Standish, B.   Sketch.   Motion Pic Classic 27:58 Mr '28
  Belfrage, C.   Sketch.   Motion Pic 36:58 D '28
  Biery, R.   Interview.   Motion Pic 37:44 Mr '29

BRADLEY, GRACE
  Bradley, G.   I'm a bad girl.   Screen Book 19-2:78 S '37

BRADNA, OLYMPE
  Williams, W.   Who will win the golden apple of success?   Silver
    S 8-1:24 N '37
  Holland, J.   Bewitching.   Silver S 8-10:51 Ag '38

BRADY, ALICE
  Interview.   Cosmop 57:702 O '14
  Reynolds, W.   Interview.   Green Book 12:802 N '14
  Randolph, A.   Sketch.   National 41:464 D '14
  The business of dressing.   Green Book 14:484 S '15
  LaRoche, E. M.   Sketch.   Motion Pic Classic 5:46 O '17
  Montanye, L.   Interview.   Motion Pic Classic 6:47 My '18
  Shunwood, C. B.   Interview.   Motion Pic Classic 7:24 Ja '19
  Fletcher, A. W.   Interview.   Motion Pic 20:32 Ag '20
  Her town house.   Theatre 35:118 F '22
  Hall, G.   Interview.   Motion Pic 24:24 O '22
  Smith, F. J.   Interview.   Photop 22:20 O '22
  Movies and mummers.   Drama 14:46 N '23
  Irwin, L.   Up from the Theatre Guild!   Silver S 4-3:20 Ja '34
  Brady, A.   Let Hollywood teach you.   Screen Book 19-5:47 D
    '37
  Service, F.   Interview.   Movie Classic 5:45 S '38
  Walker, H. L.   A peek into her lovely home.   Silver S 9-7:52 My
    '39

BRADY, FRED
  Poet with a pickaxe.   Lions R 2-5:no p# Jl '43

BRADY, PAT
  Obit.   Classic Film Collect 35:8X Sum '72
    Film R p16 '72/73
    N. Y. Times F 29 '72
    Same.   N. Y. Times Bio Ed F 29 '72
  Jones, K.   Passing parade.   Film Collect Reg 4-3:11 My/Je '72

BRADY, SCOTT
  Baer, M. M.   The romantic Mr. Brady.   Silver S 23-4:24 F '53
  My child.   Photop 85-5:6 My '74

BRAMLEY, FLORA
    Uselton, R. A.   The Wampus baby stars.   Films In R 21-2:73
        F '70

BRAND, JOLENE
    A match for Zorro.   TV Guide 6-40:25 O 4 '58

BRAND, NEVILLE
    Heavies?  Who is?   TV Guide 8-18:23 Ap 30 '60

BRANDO, MARLON
    Bio sketch.   Vogue 108:173 Ag 15 '46
    Actor Marlon Brando.   Cue 18-17:22 Ap 23 '49
    Hall, G.   It isn't that I don't like glamour girls.   Silver S 20-9:
        46 Jl '50
    Rising star.   Film R p39 '51/52
    Sheridan, M.   The enigma of Marlon.   Silver S 22-7:24 My '52
    Zunser, J.   Streetcar to Shakespeare.   Cue 21-51:16 D 20 '52
    Richardson, J. W.   This time I've had it.   Silver S 23-9:36 Jl
        '53
    Really Mr. Christian.   Show 3-3:108 Mr '63
    Fenin, G.   The face of '63--U.S.   Films & Filming 9-6:55 Mr
        '63
    Sarris, A.   Oddities and one shots.   Film Cult 28:45 Spg '63
    Steele, R.   Meet Marlon Brando.   Film Heritage 2-1:2 Fall '66
    Jeremiah.   The stars' stars; astrology.   Show 1-1:22 Ja '70
    Lane, J. F.   Is (he) really necessary?   Show 1-1:46 Ja '70
    Greenfeld, J.   Rapping and zapping in Morocco.   Life 68:59 Mr
        13 '70
    For ten years he made my life a living hell.   Photop 77-5:42 My
        '70
    Knight, A.   Star time?   Sat R 53:56 N 21 '70
    Why his common-law wife won't marry him.   Photop 79-1:37 Ja
        '71
    Shooting The godfather.   Newsweek 77:89 Je 28 '71
    Bio note.   Films Illus 1-5:30 N '71
    Alexander, S.   Grandfather of all cool actors becomes The god-
        father.   Life 72:40 Mr 10 '72
    Zimmerman, P. D.   Triumph for Brando.   Newsweek 79:56 Mr
        13 '72
    Making of Godfather.   Time 99:57 Mr 13 '72
    People are talking about.   Vogue 159:132 My '72
    The love torment even divorce couldn't end.   Mod Screen 66-6:51
        Je '72
    Brando fights for his son.   Photop 81-6:66 Je '72
    McGillivray, D.   Note; filmog.   Focus On F 11:6 Aut '72
    Conversation with Brando.   Oui 1-1:71 Oct '72
    You asked for it.   Photop 82-6:34 D '72
    Self-portrait of an angel and monster.   Time 101-4:51 Ja 22 '73
    Craig, H. A. L.   Brando at top of his form again.   New York 6-
        6:60 F 5 '73
    Hirsch, F.   The ultimate Brando cad.   After Dark 5-10:42 F '73
    Brando's last tango.   Films Illus 2-21:8 Mr '73

Guerin, A.  Topol on Brando.  Show 3-2:23 Ap '73
Kashfi, A.  How (he) loves and hurts a woman.  Photop 83-5:22
  My '73
How the Indians feel about him.  Photop 84-1:66 Jl '73
The night Brando punched out Galella.  Show 3-7:17 O '73
Note; filmog.  Film Dope 4:190 Mr '74
Thomas, B.  Comeback of the rebel.  Playgirl 1-12:85 My '74
Sarris, A.  A tribute to Brando.  Film Comment 10-3:33 My/Je
  '74
Brando's Oscar speech.  Cineaste 5-4:62 n. d.
Hano, A.  When Brando walks in, everybody turned to stone.
  TV Guide 22-46:4 N 16 '74
Gow, G.  The Brando boom.  Films & Filming 21-2:10 N '74

BRANDON, MICHAEL
  Note; filmog.  Films & Filming 20-2:67 N '73

BRANDS, X.
  This man is called X.  TV Guide 7-21:28 My 23 '59

BRANNUM, TOM
  Leonard Sillman's New faces of 1971.  Cue 40-8:8 F 20 '71

BRASSELLE, KEEFE
  Rising star.  Film R p31 '50
  Rising star.  Film R p106 '52/53
  Waters, H. F.  Worm's eye view.  Newsweek 72:59 S 23 '68

BRASSEUR, PIERRE
  Bio note.  Unifrance 45:9 D '57
  Note; filmog.  Film Dope 4:191 Mr '74

BRAVERMAN, BART
  Johnson, D.  The brothers Braverman.  After Dark 5-11 Mr '73

BRAY, ROBERT
  Raddatz, L.  The man with dog appeal.  TV Guide 13-33:15 Ag
  14 '65

BRAZZI, ROSSANO
  Zunser, J.  No love? No movies!  Cue 26-50:13 D 14 '57

BREAKSTONE, GEORGE P.
  Obit.  Screen World p232 '74

BREAMER, SYLVIA
  Lamb, G.  Interview.  Motion Pic Classic 7:28 N '14
  Brewster, E.  Sketch.  Motion Pic 15:64 Jl '18
  Reid, J.  Motion Pic 21:44 F '21
  McGaffey, K.  Interview.  Motion Pic Classic 13:32 D '21
  Fifteen years ago.  Photop 45:108 D '33

BRECK, KATHLEEN
    Rising stars.  Film R p56 '64/65

BRECK, PETER
    Hano, A.  How to survive on ketchup soup.  TV Guide 14-38:30
        S 17 '66
    My child.  Photop 85-6:14 Je '74

BREEN, BOBBY
    Hall, G.  Interview.  Child Life 16:122 Mr '37
    Bio note; filmog.  Movies & People 2:8 '40
    Doherty, E.  The private life of Bobby Breen.  Liberty 1-8:71
        Spg '73

BREJCHOVA, JANA
    Note; filmog.  Film 60:14 n. d.

BREMER, LUCILLE
    Meet Lucille Bremer.  Lions R 4-1:no p# F '45

BRENDEL, EL
    Belfrage, C.  Interview.  Motion Pic Classic 31:52 My '30
    Obit.  Film R p46 '64/65
        Screen World 16:219 '65

BRENNAN, EILEEN
    Arrival.  New Yorker 35:26 Ja 16 '60
    I'm with the sexiest guys in Hollywood.  Photop 83-6:50 Je '73

BRENNAN, WALTER
    DeKolty, J.  He can do anything.  Silver S 7-10:51 Ag '37
    Joseph, R.  Story of.  Motion Pic 54:50 Ag '37
    Rhea, M.  Sketch.  Photop 53:31 Jl '39
    Hamilton, S.  Sketch.  Photop 18:47 My '41
    Bio.  Cur Bio 2:99 '41
    Battling Brennan.  Lions R 2-3:no p# D '42
    Brennan, the great lover.  Lions R 2-4:no p# Ap '43
    Goodby to makeup.  TV Guide 6-7:28 F 15 '58
    Pigeon, go away!  TV Guide 13-11:12 Mr 13 '65
    Grandma Curry comes to town.  TV Guide 19-36:13 S 4 '71
    (He) speaks from Hollywood.  Harvest Yrs 12:46 My '72
    Obit.  N. Y. Daily News p56 S 23 '74
        N. Y. Times Bio Ed p1213 S '74

BRENT, EVE
    She's out of the jungle.  TV Guide 10-11:27 Mr 17 '62

BRENT, EVELYN
    From extra to stardom.  Motion Pic Classic 5:39 S '17
    Thornton, J.  Sketch.  Motion Pic 35:70 F '28
    Hall, G.  Confessions of.  Motion Pic Classic 29:28 Jl '29
    Hall, G.  Interview.  Motion Pic 39:45 Mr '30
    Hall, G.  What women ask her advice about.  Motion Pic 40:48

D '30
Hall, G.   Sketch.   Motion Pic Classic 32:54 Ag '31
Uselton, R. A.   The Wampus baby stars.   Films In R 21-2:73
  F '70

BRENT, GEORGE
Maddox, B.   Brent from Dublin.   Silver S 2-7:23 My '32
Sketch.   Motion Pic 43:26 My '32
Grayson, C.   Sketch.   Motion Pic 43:47 Je '32
Pryor, N.   Sketch.   Movie Classic 2:18 Je '32
Hall, G.   Interview.   Movie Classic 3:26 S '32
The Chatterton-Brent romance.   Movie Classic 3:15 O '32
Cheasley, C. W.   His numberscope.   Movie Classic 3:51 N '32
Manners, D.   Sketch.   Motion Pic 45:49 F '33
Grant, J.   His marriage.   Movie Classic 4:26 Mr '33
Dillon, F.   Separated from Chatterton.   Movie Classic 6:32 Je
  '34
Dillon, F.   Interview.   Movie Classic 7:33 O '34
Jones, C.   Where you going?   Silver S 5-2:21 D '34
Grant, J.   Interview.   Movie Classic 8:16 Mr '35
Sketch.   Photop 49:86 F '36
Lang, H.   Why he shuns romance.   Movie Classic 10:37 Ag '36
Craig, C.   Story of.   Motion Pic 54:35 S '37
Dew, G.   I love danger.   Screen Book 21-8:24 Mr '39
Waterbury, R.   Sketch.   Photop 53:13 My '39
Walker, H. L.   If I had my life to live over.   Silver S 10-6:52
  Ap '40
Sketch.   Time 36:70 Jl 15 '40
Bio note; filmog.   Movies & People 2:8 '40
Wilson, E.   If Ann Sheridan becomes Mrs. George Brent...   Sil-
  ver S 11-7:22 My '41
Reid, J.   Why Ann changed her mind.   Silver S 12-7:22 My '42
Here comes the heroes.   TV Guide 4-37:28 S 15 '56
Watkins, F.   George Brent; filmog.   Film Fan Mo 136:3 O '72

BRESSART, FELIX
Two who make Married bachelor a joy.   Lions R 1-2:no p# O '41
Man of many mustachios.   Lions R 2-5:no p# Jl '43

BREWER, BETTY
Letter from.   Photop 18:10 Ja '41

BREWSTER, DIANE
The understanding type.   TV Guide 5-50:28 D 14 '57

BRIALY, JEAN-CLAUDE
Person of promise.   Films & Filming 4-10:10 Jl '58
Flash on Jean-Claude Brialy.   Unifrance 51:7 O/D '59
White, J. & Connel, E.   Interview.   Interview 2-2:28 n. d.

BRIAN, DAVID
Parsons, L. O.   Cosmop's citation for the best supporting performance of the month.   Cosmop 126:13 My '49

Birthday party.  Photop 36:13 N '49
Brian, A. B.  The man I married.  Silver S 20-2:30 D '49
Brian, D.  How private is an actor's life?  Silver S 21-11:24 S
    '41

BRIAN, MARY
    Sketch.  Motion Pic 29:36 Jl '25
    Manner, D.  Interview.  Motion Pic 37:58 Mr '29
    Sketch.  Photop 37:14 My '30
    Goldbeck, E.  Interview.  Motion Pic 40:55 Ag '30
    Busby, M.  The most popular girl in Hollywood.  Silver S 1-6:12
        Ap '31
    Fender, R.  Interview.  Motion Pic 41:76 Jl '31
    Albert, D.  OK'd by (her).  Silver S 3-11:28 S '33
    Latham, M.  Interview.  Motion Pic 46:60 Ja '34
    Maddox, B.  Her admirers.  Motion Pic 48:42 N '34
    Uselton, R. A.  The Wampus baby stars.  Films In R 21-2:73
        F '70

BRIANT, SHANE
    Straight on till stardom.  Films Illus 2-14:23 Ag '72

BRICE, FANNY
    Interview.  N. Y. Drama 71:20 Ap 22 '14
    Seldes, G.  Demoniac in the American theatre.  Dial 75:303 S
        '23
    Wilson, B.  Interview.  Classic 19:34 Je '24
    Feel of the audience.  Sat Eve Post 198:10 N 21 '25
    Home of.  Theatre 48:59 S '28
    Sherwood, A. M. Jr.  Appreciation.  Outlook 151:69 Ja 9 '29
    Clothes are a big thing in my life.  Theatre 49:31 Je '29
    They stand out from the crowd.  Lit Dig 117:9 F 10 '34
    Kutner, N.  Story of.  Good House 116:38 Mr '34
    In support of the moon-struck.  Lit Dig 117:20 Je 2 '34
    Autobiographical.  Cosmop 100:20 F '36 and following issues
    Pinchot, A.  Not in the picture.  Delin 128:19 My '36
    Returns to the Follies.  Newsweek 8:27 S 26 '36
    Sugrue, T.  Little jumbo.  Am Mag 123:48 Ja '37
    Her married life not happy.  Life 3:46 N 29 '37
    As Baby Snooks.  Time 37:42 Mr 10 '41
    Kutner, N.  If you were daughter to Baby Snooks.  Good House
        116:38 Mr '43
    Her new radio character, Irma Potts.  Time 44:56 O 2 '44
    Grandmother Snooks.  Newsweek 27:60 Mr 11 '46
    Bio.  Cur Bio Je '46
        Same.  Cur Bio Yrbk '46
    Zolotow, M.  Story of.  Cosmop 121:24 S '46 and following is-
        sue.
    She couldn't make them cry.  Coronet 25:24 Mr '49
    Obit.  Hobbies 56:23 Ag '51
        Newsweek 37:71 Je 11 '51
        Time 57:106 Je 11 '51
    Katkov, N.  Fabulous Fannie.  Ladies Home J 69:50 N; 44 D '52;

48 Ja; 60 F '53
Same Abridged.   Read Dig 62:149 Mr '53
Memories of Brice.   Newsweek 41:100 F 16 '53
Debus, A. G.   Records of Fannie.   Hobbies 61:34 Mr '56
Rose, B.   Girl named Fannie.   McCalls 90:52 S '63
Collins, F. L.   The private life of Baby Snooks.   Liberty 1-7:65
    Win '72
Kupferberg, A.   Fannie Brice.   Film Fan Mo 147:21 S '73

BRICE, ROSETTA
How she became a photoplayer.   Motion Pic 9:95 Je '15

BRICKELL, BETH
Crail, T.   You don't have to be Ma Kettle.   TV Guide 15-47:17
    N 25 '67

BRIDGES, BEAU
Eyles, A.   Note; filmog.   Focus On F 1:15 Mr/Ap '70
Harmetz, A.   Beau Bridges.   N. Y. Times Bio Ed My 3 '70
Barthel, J.   Of fathers, sons and love.   Life 68:61 My 15 '70
Beau Bridges starts a new family.   Ebony 25:96 O '70

BRIDGES, JEFF
Second generation.   Films Illus 1-10:12 Ap '72
Klemesrud, J.   Bridges going up, going up.   N. Y. Times sec
    2:19 O 22 '72
Just enjoying the trip (to the top).   Films Illus 2-24:17 Je '73

BRIDGES, LLOYD
Barthel, J.   Of fathers, sons and love.   Life 68:61 My 15 '70
Stone, J.   Out of the depths.   TV Guide 19-18:23 My 1 '71
A fish out of water.   TV Guide 20-22:14 My 27 '72
O'Hallaren, B.   And then Lloyd Bridges got sick.   TV Guide
    22-9:14 Mr 2 '74

BRIGGS, SUZANNE
Kroll, J.   Girls! girls! girls!   Newsweek 79:105 My 22 '72

BRILL, FRAN
Hall, J.   Take it from a widow.   TV Guide 22-42:19 O 19 '74

BRION, FRANÇOISE
Person of promise.   Films & Filming 7-1:16 O '60

BRISCOE, LOTTIE
Rodgers, J. J.   Interview.   Green Book 12:1043 D '14
Leading men I have known.   Green Book 13:513 Mr '15
Placing the blame for unsatisfactory films.   Motion Pic 9:77 My
    '15
Sketch.   Motion Pic 9:118 My '15
My leading men.   Photop 8-2:135 Jl '15
How is the film playing talent really developed?   Film Players
    Herald 2-7:22 F '16
Obit.   Screen World 2-233 '51

BRISSON, CARL
    Park Ave. Sinatra. Newsweek 23:84 My 1 '44
    Engaging grandfather. Time 43:48 My 29 '44
    Grandpa still sends 'em. Am Mag 143:138 My '47
    Obit. Screen World 10:221 '59

BRITT, MAY
    Newsmakers. Newsweek 70:52 D 4 '67

BRITTON, BARBARA
    Vallee, W. L. Boquets for Barbara. Silver S 13-2:48 D '42

BRITTON, PAMELA
    Obit. N. Y. Times Bio Ed p801 Je '74

BRITTON, TONY
    Rising star. Film R p34 '57/58

BROCKWELL, GLADYS
    In reply to yours. Photop 12-1:72 Je '17
    Blackstone, L. Sketch. Motion Pic 13:109 Jl '17
    Evans, C. D. Interview. Motion Pic Classic 5:22 O '17
    McKelvie, M. G. Interview. Motion Pic 17:45 Je '19
    Handy, T. B. Interview. Classic 15:36 S '22

BRODERICK, HELEN
    Hamilton, S. Story of. Photop 52:20 My '38

BROLIN, JAMES
    Hano, A. The actor who looks like a star--but sounds like a tax
        accountant. TV Guide 17-39:22 S 27 '69
    Brolin and son. Photop 77-5:34 My '70
    My husband, his girlfriend and me. Photop 78-2:63 Ag '70
    For 4 months my son-in-law was just a voice on the phone.
        Photop 80-5:56 N '71
    The Brolins expecting again. Photop 80-6:80 D '71
    Halberstam, M. J. An M. D. reviews Dr. Welby. N. Y. Times
        Mag p12 Ja 16 '72
    How I tell my child the story of Christmas. Photop 81-1:51 Ja
        '72
    Durslag, M. Second stethoscope--for how long? TV Guide 20-
        11:32 Mr 11 '72
    Leech, M. T. Off we go! After Dark 4-11:36 Mr '72
    Baby's a movie star! Mod Screen 66-5:29 My '72
    Now we'll adopt a baby. Photop 81-5:44 My '72
    Brolin's son steals the show. Photop 81-6:40 Je '72
    Our second baby. Mod Screen 66-6:22 Je '72
    I had to learn to love my second child. Photop 82-6:32 D '72
    ...gives a boy courage to live. Photop 83-4:42 Ap '73
    How a woman's faith saved him. Mod Screen 67-4:38 Ap '73

BROMBERG, J. EDWARD
    Appreciation of his acting. Stage 11:13 N '33

BROMFIELD, JOHN
  Churchill, R. & B.   My honeymoon never ended.   Silver S 22-9:
    20 Jl '52
  An out-of-town boy makes good.   TV Guide 6-1:20 Ja 4 '58

BROMILEY, DOROTHY
  Person of promise.   Films & Filming 2-4:33 Ja '56

BRONCHO BILLY
  (See ANDERSON, GILBERT MAXWELL)

BRONSON, BETTY
  Sketch.   Photop 26:58 O '24
  Carr, H.   Sketch.   Classic 20:51 N '24
  Wyckoff, C.   Sketch.   Motion Pic Classic 22:52 D '25
  St. John-Brenon, A.   Sub-deb of the film set.   Photop 29:110
    Ja '26
  Clark, F.   Sketch.   Photop 31:81 Mr '27
  Fletcher, A. W.   Sketch.   Motion Pic 35:34 Jl '28
  Obit.   Classic Film Collector 33:46 Win '71
    Film R p14 '72/73
    N. Y.   Times p42 O 22 '71
    N. Y.   Times Bio Ed O 22 '71
    Screen World 23:236 '72
  Everson, W. K.   Betty Bronson.   Film Fan Mo 125:19 N '71
  Lewis, G.   Betty Bronson; filmog.   Films In R 23-5:319 My '72
  Bodeen, D.   Betty Bronson; filmog.   Films In R 25-10:577 D '74

BRONSON, CHARLES
  A conversation with Charles Bronson.   Cinema (BH) 3-1:8 D '65
  Whitmore, J.   Here comes Charlie.   Newsweek 79:83 My 29 '72
  Is he the #1 sex symbol?   Films Illus 2-18:26 D '72
  Robbins, F.   Interview.   Photop 82-6:22 D '72
  Bio note.   Playboy 20-1:28 Ja '73
  Interview.   Photop 86-1:54 Jl '74
  Vespa, M.   Bronson finally becomes a star at home.   People
    2-8:17 Ag 19 '74
  Davidson, B.   America discovers a 'sacred monster. '   N. Y.
    Times Mag p18 S 22 '74
  Same.   N. Y.   Times Bio Ed p1214 S '74

BROOK, CLIVE
  Bruce, N.   Sketch.   Motion Pic Classic 21:32 Ag '25
  Bailey, H.   Interview.   Motion Pic Classic 26:33 D '27
  Waterbury, R.   Sketch.   Photop 33:29 Mr '28
  Belfrage, C.   Interview.   Motion Pic 37:55 F '29
  Walker, H. L.   How women annoy us.   Motion Pic 40:70 D '30
  Walker, H. L.   Sketch.   Motion Pic Classic 31:52 Je '31
  Hall, G.   Interview.   Motion Pic 42:58 Ag '31
  Moffitt, C. F.   Censorship for interviews Hollywood's latest wild
    idea.   Cinema Dig 2-5:9 Ja 9 '33
  Hall, G.   Interview.   Motion Pic 5:23 O '33
  Samuels, L.   Clive Brook returns.   Silver S 5-7:51 My '35

Sketch. Lit Dig 119:26 Je 15 '35
Roberts, F.  Home of.  Theatre World 28:232 N '37
Castle, M.  The famous quintet of movie stars.  Photop 52:18
    Jl '38
Grimstead, H.  Bio sketch.  Windsor 89:629 Ap '39

BROOK, RAY
    Vallance, T. & Darvell, M.  The actor; filmog.  Film 65:5 Spg
    '72

BROOKE, HILARY
    Kapel, K.  Hilary Brooke; filmog.  Films In R 23-2:124 F '72

BROOKS, GERALDINE
    Sketch.  Photop 30:94 Ap '47
    Firth, R.  Sketch.  Life 23:157 O 13 '47
    Holland, J.  She's apt to fool you.  Silver S 18-11:44 S '48
    Fulton, M. J.  Sketch.  Photop 34:18 D '48
    The American picks a future star.  Am Mag 148:105 Jl '49
    Maddox, B.  Bachelor girl, beware!  Silver S 19-11:40 S '49
    They peeled off the makeup to find an actress.  TV Guide 13-8:
    18 F 20 '65
    Vespa, M.  Budd Schulberg and Gerri Brooks escape Hollywood.
    People 2-11:28 S 9 '74

BROOKS, IRIS
    Macdonough, S.  They started in skin flicks.  Show 2-10:46 D
    '71

BROOKS, JAN
    Best-looking cop on the beat.  TV Guide 7-44:28 O 31 '59

BROOKS, JEAN
    McClelland, D.  Jean Brooks at RKO; RKO filmog.  Film Fan
    Mo 155:19 My '74

BROOKS, LOUISE
    Waterbury, R.  Sketch.  Photop 29:58 Ap '26
    Johnston, C.  Sketch.  Motion Pic Classic 26:53 S '27
    Reynolds, R.  National press revives interest in (her).  8mm
    Collect 12:2 Sum '65
    Brooks, L.  Charlie Chaplin remembered.  Film Cult 40:5 Spg
    '66
    Sarris, A.  Editore eyrie.  Cahiers (Eng) 2:67 '66
    Brooks, L.  The other faces of W. C. Fields.  Sight & Sound
    40-2:92 Spg '71
    Brooks, L.  On location with Billy Wellman.  Film Cult 53/54/
    55:145 Spg '72
    Brooks, L.  On location with Billy Wellman.  Focus On F 12:51
    Win '72
    Brooks, L.  Actors and the Pabst spirit.  Focus On F 8:45 n. d.

BROOKS, PAULINE
  Obit.  Screen World 19:229 '68

BROOKS, PHYLLIS
  Smithson, E. J.  A model young girl.  Screen Book 20-6:41 Jl
    '38
  Williams, W.  Phyllis keeps them guessing.  Silver S 9-8:34 Je
    '39
  Manners, M. J.  My South Sea island flight with Gary Cooper.
    Silver S 14-7:22 My '44

BROOKS, STEPHEN
  Raddatz, L.  Dossier on...  TV Guide 14-30:31 Jl 23 '66

BROOKS, VIRGINIA
  Dust off 4 pedestals in the hall of fame.  Silver S 2-3:36 Ja '32

BROPHY, SALLIE
  This is what became of Sallie.  TV Guide 13-35:20 Ag 28 '65

BROWN, CHELSEA
  Living breathing picture gallery.  Ebony 24:54 Ap '69
  Hudson, P.  From go-go dancer to hotline social worker.  Sr
    Schol 97:20 O 12 '70
  Rediscovering Chelsea.  TV Guide 18-47:21 N 21 '70

BROWN, GEORG STANFORD
  Love makes our interracial marriage work.  Mod Screen 67-3:48
    Mr '73
  Goode, B.  Don't call him "cop."  Sepia 23-3:54 Mr '74
  Greenberg, P.  And he didn't like cops.  TV Guide 22-18:21 My
    4 '74

BROWN, JAMES (Jim L.)
  Second fiddle to a dog.  TV Guide 5-42:28 O 19 '57

BROWN, JIM
  Brown power.  Newsweek 71:75 Ja 15 '68
  Playboy interviews.  Playboy 15-2:51 F '68
  Steinem, G.  The black John Wayne.  New York 1-32:35 N 11 '68
  Sanders, C. L.  Film star Jim Brown.  Ebony 24:192 D '68
  Woodley, R.  He likes to keep you psyched.  Life 66:69 My 23
    '69
  Sheppard, R. Z.  Ultimate locker room.  Time 97:92 Ap 5 '71
  Brown, J.  Approach it as business (on Black movies).  N. Y.
    Times sec 2:19 D 17 '72
  I'll date any woman I want.  Photop 83-5:67 My '73
  Anderson, D.  The movie star and O. J.  N. Y. Times sec 5:4
    N 4 '73
  Same.  N. Y. Times Bio Ed p1761 N '73
  Kushner, T. D.  Big Jim Brown.  Interview p28 D '73
  Dancoff, J.  Playgirl's man for September; centerfold.  Playgirl
    2-4:68 S '74

BROWN, JOE E.
  Ramsey, W.   Sketch.   Motion Pic 37:82 Jl '29
  Walker, H. L.   Sketch.   Motion Pic Classic 31:65 Jl '30
  Goldbeck, E.   Sketch.   Motion Pic 41:76 Ap '31
  Grayson, C.   Mascot of the University of California.   Movie
    Classic 4:48 Ag '33
  Mulgrave, J.   Batting out laughs.   Silver S 3-10:20 Ag '33
  Lee, S.   His ambition--to make people laugh.   Motion Pic 48:42
    Ja '35
  Barton, R.   Interview.   Movie Classic 7:35 F '35
  Appreciation.   Stage 12:18 S '35
  Appreciation.   Lit Dig 121:20 My 9 '36
  Mack, G.   Bartender Brown.   Screen Book 19-4:40 N '37
  Bio note; filmog.   Movies & People 2:8 '40
  Hopper, H.   His married life.   Photop 22:26 My '43
  My faith.   Photop 24:49 My '44
  Walker, H. L.   His heart's as big as his mouth.   Silver S 15-5:
    38 Mr '45
  Miller, A.   His souvenirs of baseball.   Colliers 123:43 Ap 9 '49
  Joe E.   Baseball.   TV Guide 1-23:A-8 S 4 '54
  Obit.   Classic Film Collect 40:58 Fall '73
    Films & Filming 20-2:80 N '73
    N. Y. Times Bio Ed p1097 Jl '73
    Screen World p232 '74

BROWN, JOHN MACK
  Dawson, C.   Sketch.   Motion Pic Classic 27:42 Ag '28
  Albert, K.   Sketch.   Photop 34:59 N '28
  Gray, C.   Sketch.   Motion Pic 38:42 O '29
  Walker, H. L.   Sketch.   Motion Pic Classic 31:58 Ag '30
  Manners, D.   Interview.   Motion Pic Classic 33:63 Mr '31
  What they are doing now.   Show 2-8:106 Ag '62
  Big jocks.   Esquire 73:128 Ap '70
  Cocchi, J.   John Mack Brown; filmog.   Film Fan Mo 108-122.
    Je '70 thru Ag '71
  Hoaglin, J. L.   Down memory lane.   Hollywood Stu 6-8:31 D
    '71
  Obit.   N. Y. Post p72 N 15 '74

BROWN, JOHN MOULDER
  Partial filmog.   Films & Filming 20-2:67 N '73

BROWN, PAMELA
  Up, up and away.   Newsweek 76:30 O 5 '70
  Flight of a lovely folly.   Life 69:39 O 23 '70

BROWN, PETER
  Mother was the dragon lady.   TV Guide 36-9:18 S 3 '60
  Going down to the sea without ships.   Oui 3-11:43 N '74

BROWN, ROBERT
  Goodwin, F.   The first real hunk of man since Errol Flynn.
    TV Guide 16-40:16 O 5 '68

Interview. Mod Screen 66-3:56 Mr '72
At home with the Robert Browns. Photop 81-6:63 Je '72

BROWN, RUSS
  Gray, B. Russ Brown. Films In R 15-10:647 D '64
  Obit. Screen World 16:220 '65

BROWN, TOM
  Horton, H. Tom Brown's hobby. Silver S 3-1:22 N '32
  Lee, H. Tom Brown's school days. Silver S 5-1:24 N '34
  Fraser, P. Tom Brown's runaway marriage. Screen Book 19-
    3:22 O '37
  Raddatz, L. The Dodge City gang. TV Guide 20-12:14 Mr 18
    '72

BROWN, VANESSA
  Keating, J. Visit with Vanessa. Cue 22-33:14 Ag 15 '53
  Leather luxury. TV Guide 1-24:22 S 11 '53
  Brown, V. George Seaton. Action Jl/Ag '70
  Brown, V. Interview with Billy Wilder. Action 5-6:16 N/D '70

BROWNE, CORAL
  Johns, E. Discusses why she chose Maugham's Lady Frederick.
    Theatre World 43:29 Ja '47
  Buck, J. Interview. Plays & Players 19-10:31 Jl '72

BROWNE, IRENE
  Obit. Screen World 17:234 '66

BROWNE, KATHIE
  A petticoat for the Ponderosa. TV Guide 12-3:24 Ja 18 '64

BROWNE, LUCILE
  Malcomson, R. M. The sound serial. Views & Rs 3-1:13 Sum
    '71

BRUCE, CAROL
  Breeziest young starlet in Louisiana purchase. Life 9:48 Jl 1
    '40
  New York has made her its summer darling. Life 9:84 S 9 '40
  I have to say no 20 times a day. Am Mag 132:20 Jl '41

BRUCE, NIGEL
  Hamilton, S. Sketch. Photop 54:30 Jl '40
  The films of Nigel Bruce; filmog. Film Fan Mo 65:3 N '66

BRUCE, VIRGINIA
  Service, F. To marry John Gilbert. Movie Classic 2:42 Ag
    '32
  Coleman, W. He's at it again. Silver S 2-10:17 Ag '32
  Lathem, M. Interview. Movie Classic 7:46 O '34
  Babcock, M. The girl from Fargo. Silver S 5-6:56 Ap '35
  Dixe, M. Her cure for heartache. Movie Classic 8:14 Jl '35

Donnell, D. Interview. Motion Pic 50:35 O '35
Lane, V. Her bag of fashion tricks. Movie Classic 9:44 N '35
Her requirements for romance. Movie Classic 10:44 Je '36
Spensley, D. Her love code. Motion Pic 53:37 Je '37
Gibbs, W. K. I will marry again. Screen Book 19-4:43 N '37
Dillon, F. (She) speaks out. Screen Book 21-1:26 Ag '38
Wilson, E. Projection of. Silver S 9-1:18 N '38
Walters, H. Hollywood's hidden glamor girl. Screen Book 21-11:32 Je '39
Hall, G. Marriage is not enough. Silver S 10-13:36 O '40
Bio note; filmog. Movies & People 2:8 '40
Pinup of the past. Films & Filming 19-1:61 O '72

BRUNETTE, FRITZI
A Brunette by name and nature. Photop 11-6:119 My '17

BRYAN, DORA
Rising stars. Film R p109 '53/54

BRYAN, JANE
Williams, W. Which will win the golden apple of success? Silver S 8-1:24 N '37
Hamilton, S. Sketch. Photop 52:68 Ja '38
Joseph, L. R. You can't make me a star. Screen Book 20-2:44 Mr '38
Williams, B. Starlet on Broadway. Silver S 9-5:34 Mr '39
Roberts, K. Story of. Colliers 103:20 Ap 8 '39
Story of. Life 7:86 N 26 '39
Hall, G. Her own worst enemy. Silver S 10-4:24 F '40
Bio note; filmog. Movies & People 2:8 '40

BRYAN, WINI
Colaciello, R. Interview. Interview 2-6:12 O '71

BRYLSKA, BARBARA
Bio note; filmog. Focus On F 3:18 My/Ag '70

BRYNNER, YUL
Rising stars. Film R p34 '57/58
Marill, A. H. Yul Brynner; filmog. Films In R 21-8:457 O '70
Holmes, N. The music would go waroomph. TV Guide 20-38:28 S 16 '72
Super human superstar. Films & Filming 20-1:8 O '73
d'Arcy, S. The gentle giant. Films Illus 3-32:307 Ap '74
Bio note; filmog. Focus On F 17:6 Spg '74
Crawley, T. & Flatley, G. Interview. Game 1-2 D '74

BRYSON, BETTY
Uselton, R. A. The Wampus baby stars. Films In R 21-2:73 F '70

BRYSON, WINIFRED
Cheatham, M. Interview. Classic 16:24 Jl '23

BUA, GENE
Efron, E.   Their names are Bull and Bua.   TV Guide 19-9:14
    F 27 '71

BUCHANAN, EDGAR
Heffer, B. J.   Partial filmog.   Films In R 20-1:61 Ja '69
Maltin, E.   Interview; filmog.   Film Fan Mo 120:20 Je '71

BUCHANAN, JACK
Corathiel, E.   Interview.   Theatre World 21:166 Ap '34
Pinups of the past.   Films & Filming 19-7:69 Ap '73

BUCHHOLZ, HORST
Fenin, G.   The face of '63-United States.   Films & Filming 9-
    6:55 Mr '63
Slingo, C.   Partial filmog.   Films In R 23-1:61 Ja '72
Busch, S.   Letter; additional filmog.   Films In R 23-3:189 Mr
    '72
The Buchholz formula.   Films Illus 2-19:4 Ja '73

BUCKLEY, FLOYD
Obit.   Time 68:88 N 26 '56
Manski, A. B.   Floyd Buckley.   Films In R 8-7:361 Ag/S '57

BUJOLD, GENEVIEVE
Ruddy, J.   Saint Joan.   TV Guide 15-48:28 D 2 '67
Williams, L.   Canada's Joan of Arc.   Look 31:M16 D 12 '67
Miller, E.   Interview.   Seventeen 28:140 N '69
Kitten purring Beethoven.   Time 95:90 Mr 30 '70
Actresses who are real people.   Life 68:45 My 29 '70
Robbins, F.   Director Cacoyannis and his Trojan women.   Show
    2-8:32 O '71
McLarty, J.   Interview.   Motion p36 Ja/F '74
McLarty, J.   Genevieve Bujold.   Motion p12 My/Je '74

BUKA, DONALD
Pritchett, F.   Buka's bound to suit ya!   Sil S 19-1:34 N '48

BULIFANT, JOYCE
Delicate--like an oak tree.   TV Guide 11-33:19 Ag 17 '63

BULL, PETER
Bull, P.   How bawdy can a movie become?   Films & Filming
    15-8:66 My '69

BULL, TONI
Efron, E.   Bull and Bua of Love of life.   TV Guide 19-9:14 F 27
    '71

BUNDY, BROOKE
She got tired of pretending to be a lemon.   TV Guide 12-51:20
    D 19 '64

BUNKER, RALPH
   Obit.  Screen World 18:232 '67

BUNNY, JOHN
   Work of.  Sat R 117:466 Ap 11 '14
   Interview.  Blue Book 19:4 My '14
   The serious side of being funny.  Blue Book 19:912 S '14
   Lanier, H. W.  Work of.  World's Work 29:566 Mr '15
   How he became a photoplayer.  Motion Pic 9:91 My '15
   Duncan, H.  John Bunny.  Silent Pic 1:no p# Win '68/69
   Gill, S.  Filmog.  Silent Pic 15:8 Sum '72

BUONO, VICTOR
   A breed apart.  TV Guide 11-26:19 Je 29 '63

BURGE, JAMES
   Leonard Sillman's New faces of 1971.  Cue 40-8:9 F 20 '71

BURGHOFF, GARY
   Stump, A.  Burghoff is for the birds.  TV Guide 22-32:24 Ag 10
      '74
   Tucker, R.  About men.  Playgirl 2-5:28 O '74

BURKE, BILLIE
   Her experiences.  Green Bk Album 3:543 Mr '10
   Patterson, A.  Her life when off the stage.  Green Bk Album 5:
      961 My '11
   Patterson, A.  Home life of.  Theatre 17:28 Ja '13
   White, M. Jr.  Work of.  Munsey 49:152 Ap '13
   Stearns, H. E.  Interview.  N. Y. Drama 69:3 My 14 '13
   Dale, A.  Interview.  Cosmop 56:842 My '14
   How the red-haired woman should dress.  Green Book 12:21 Jl
      '14
   Wolf, R.  Marriage and home life.  Green Book 12:843 N '14
   Sketch.  Motion Pic 10:114 D '15
   White, M. Jr.  Work of.  Munsey 58:515 Ag '16
   Courtlandt, R.  Sketch.  Motion Pic Classic 2:59 Ag '16
   Personal reminiscences.  Theatre 24:122 S '16
   Courtlandt, R.  Home of.  Motion Pic 13:91 Ap '17
   Sherwood, C. B.  Sketch.  Motion Pic Classic 8:22 My '19
   Gaddis, P.  Interview.  Motion Pic Classic 6:57 Ag '18
   The nursery in her home at Hastings-on-Hudson.  House & Gard
      35:35 Ap '19
   Hall, G.  Interview.  Motion Pic 18:52 S '19
   Your daughter on the stage--why not?  Theatre 51:30 F '30
   Calhoun, D.  Interview.  Motion Pic 49:51 Mr '35
   Obit.  Brit Book Yr 1971:557 '71
      Classic Film Collect 27:60 Spg/Sum '70
      Film R p13 '71/72
      N. Y. Times p1 My 16 '70
      Same.  N. Y. Times Bio Ed My 16 '70
      Newsweek 75:55 My 25 '70
      Screen World 22:235 '71

    Time 95:79 My 25 '70
Brock, A.   The Ziegfield girl.   Classic Film Collect 32:34 Fall
    '71
Davis, H. R.   Billie Burke; filmog.   Films In R 21-10:648 D
    '70
Sutherland, S.   Broadway's most famous love affair.   Liberty 1-
    14:47 Fall '74

BURKE, KATHLEEN
    Derr, E.   The panther woman in The island of lost souls.   Movie
       Classic 3:24 D '32
    Sharpe, D.   We'll keep this one.   Silver S 3-8:24 Je '33

BURKE, MARGARET (Fatty)
    The Split reel.   Film Players Herald 2-7:28 F '16

BURKE, PAUL
    A dog's best friend.   TV Guide 5-1:17 Ja 5 '57
    Star with a wall around him.   TV Guide 10-20:6 My 19 '62
    Prelutsky, B.   Flying into the wild blue yonder.   TV Guide 14-
       6:24 F 5 '66

BURNETT, CAROL
    Love song to Mr. Dulles.   Life 43:99 Ag 19 '57
    Singer and song writer.   Life 46:114 Je 15 '59
    Miss frenetic and Miss flabbergasted.   TV Guide 8-42:9 O 15 '60
    Garvin, A.   Who's news.   Good House 151:34 N '60
    America's greatest face maker.   Look 25:102 My 23 '61
    Nichols, M.   I.O.U. to success.   Coronet 49:14 My '61
    Millstein, G.   Happiest when slobby.   TV Guide 9-39:13 S 30 '61
    Boeth, R.   On stage.   Horizon 4:80 S '61
    Martin, P.   Backstage with...   Sat Eve Post 235:36 Mr 10 '62
    Kelly, V.   A wacky TV caper.   Look 26:80 Je 19 '62
    Carol the clown.   Time 79:56 Je 22 '62
    Eimeri, S.   Can women be funny?   Mlle 56:150 N '62
    Havemann, E.   Only girl who acts with her front and back too.
       Life 54:85 F 22 '63
    Efron, E.   The girl in the rubber mask.   TV Guide 11-8:7 F 23
       '63
    Stuart, N. G.   Life, love and laughter.   Ladies Home J 80:72
       Ap; 80:34 My '63
    Hochstein, R.   One battle I had to win.   Good House 156:86 My
       '63
    Adventures of (her) in her movie bow.   Look 27:90 S 24 '63
    Ebert, A.   What did you want most at 17?   Seventeen 22:130 S
       '63
    The wildest flower of the old west.   TV Guide 11-45:6 N 9 '63
    Markel, H.   My friend Julie Andrews.   Good House 157:34 N '63
    Redbook dialogue.   Redbook 122:60 D '63
    Gift of love.   McCalls 94:73 D '66
    Barthel, J.   The makeup of (her).   TV Guide 15-52:18 D 30 '67
    Ephron, N.   Cockeyed optimist.   Good House 167:68 O '68
    See, C.   Speaking of life styles.   TV Guide 18-15:30 Ap 11 '70

Hair-raising stories from the stars.    Photop 78-2:50 Ag '70
How I learned to love my husband's eight children.    Photop 78-2:
   75 Ag '70
Christy, G.    Interview.    Good House 171:68 D '70
As others see her.    TV Guide 19-8:14 F 20 '71
Carol Burnett show.    Life 70:10 Ap 2 '71
Downs, J.    Here's to you, Mrs. Hamilton.    Life 70:92 My 14
   '71
When Carol kisses me.    Photop 79-5:60 My '71
The Burnett body.    Photop 79-6:62 Je '71
Why I loved (her) and why I lost her.    Photop 80-2:62 Ag '71
Davidson, B.    As if someone had turned up the bright yellow
   lights.    TV Guide 19-49:14 D 4 '71
Carol Burnett has never looked better.    Ladies Home J 88:100
   D '71
Macdonough, S.    I want to be Susan Hayward.    Show 2-10:38 D
   '71
Stewart-Gordon, J.    Human cyclone.    Read Dig 100:119 Ja '72
Andrews, J.    My friend, Carol Burnett.    Good House 174:57 Ja
   '72
Brodkey, H.    Why is this woman funny.    Esquire 77:122 Je '72
Whitney, D.    Carol and Joe and Fred and Marge.    TV Guide 20-
   27:10 Jl 1 '72
Johnson, D.    It's about time.    Show 2-10:36 Ja '73
Berkvist, R.    Is (she) forever?    N. Y. Times sec 2:17 Je 3 '73
   Same.    N. Y. Times Bio Ed p937 Je '73
Watters, J.    Carol and Rock make summer theater dynamite.
   People 2-3:39 Jl 15 '74
Please tell us...    Photop 86-6:42 D '74


BURNETTE, SMILEY
   Williams, N.    Three comedians of the horse opera; partial
      filmog.    Filmograph 1-4:19 '70


BURNHAM, BEATRICE
   Goldbeck, W.    Interview.    Motion Pic Classic 11:24 N '20


BURNS, BOB ("Bazooka")
   Local bazookist makes good.    Newsweek 6:29 D 14 '35
   McHenry, M.    Story of.    Movie Classic 11:34 F '37
   Surmelian, L.    Interview.    Motion Pic 53:51 Je '37
   Stuart, G.    No glamour--just happiness.    Screen Book 19-3:64
      O '37
   Wilson, E.    Projection.    Silver S 8-11:17 S '38
   Bio sketch.    Time 32:26 O 31 '38
   Cobb, I. S.    Appreciation.    Photop 52:23 D '38
   Peterson, E. T.    Interview.    Bet Homes & Gard 17:13 F '39
   Armstrong, D.    (he) gave me $5,000.    Screen Book 21-10:58
      My '39
   Bio note; filmog.    Movies & People 2:8 '40
   Burns treks thru Arkansas.    Newsweek 18:63 S 29 '41
   Obit.    Newsweek 47:67 F 13 '56
      Screen World 8:221 '57
      Time 67:88 F 13 '56

BURNS, CATHERINE (Cathy)
   Howard, J.   Flowering of a late bloomer.   Life 67:83 N 21 '67
   Clein, H.   The real people.   Show 1-8:14 Jl 9 '70

BURNS, DAVID
   Obit.   N. Y. Times p75 Mr 14 '71
      Same.   N. Y. Times Bio Ed Mr 13 '71
      Newsweek 77:76 Mr 22 '71
   Channing, C.   David Burns 1902-71.   N. Y. Times sec 2:14 Mr
      28 '71

BURNS, GEORGE
   Albert, D.   Interview.   Photop 51:44 Ap '37
   Best, K.   Story of.   Stage 16:35 My 1 '39
   Sketch.   Time 42:58 D 13 '43
   Holiday in Hawaii.   TV Guide 1-26:10 S 25 '53
   Toast to two funny old pals.   Life 72:78 My 26 '72
   (See also: BURNS AND ALLEN)

BURNS, MICHAEL
   A boy who's doing a man's job.   TV Guide 12-45:15 N 7 '64

BURNS, PIERETTE
   Bio note.   Unifrance 23:10 F '53

BURNS AND ALLEN
   Hall, G.   Private life of.   Movie Classic 6:56 My '34
   Best, K.   Career of.   Stage 16:28 My 15 '39
   Hit New York.   Cue 13-50:11 D 9 '44
   Set a zany pace.   Cue 20-1:13 Ja 6 '51
   Collins, F. L.   The man in (her) life.   Liberty 1-7:74 Win '72
   (See also: ALLEN, GRACIE; BURNS, GEORGE)

BURR, EUGENE
   Br-r-r-r-r-r!   The villain!   Photop 15-3:40 F '19
   See the players well bestowed.   Theatre Arts 38:68 D '54

BURR, RAYMOND
   The court will recess.   TV Guide 7-28:28 Jl 11 '59
   Letters, filmog.   Films In R 19-6:389 Je/ Jl '68
   My Naitauba.   Travel & Camera 33:46 Ja '70
   Ironside was a teenage outlaw.   Photop 77-6:62 Je '70
   Adams, C.   Ironside is also a chief in Fiji.   TV Guide 18-45:39
      N 7 '70
   Burr faces paralysis.   Photop 79-2:60 F '71
   Who's the man behind the beard?   TV Guide 20-4:12 Ja 22 '72
   How I find peace of mind.   Mod Screen 66-9:62 S '72
   A psychologist tackles the rumors about (him).   Photop 82-4:58
      O '72
   Whitney, D.   And now the man who became Pope John.   TV
      Guide 21-16:15 Ap 21 '73
   Am I dying?   Photop 84-5:46 N '73
   Raymond Burr.   Photop 85-5:64 My '74

BURSTON, JANET
    Maltin, L.  Our gang; Our Gang filmog.  Films Fan Mo 66:3 D
        '66

BURSTYN, ELLEN
    Klemesrud, J.  What's her next picture show about?  N. Y.
        Times Bio Ed Ja 23 '72
    Guerin, A.  The lady in The king of Marvin Gardens.  Show 2-9:
        30 D '72
    Photoplay forum.  Photop 85-5:34 My '74

BURTON, RICHARD
    Marsh, P.  The astonishing Mr. Burton.  Silver S 23-9:40 Jl
        '53
    Rising star.  Film R p113 '53/54
    Brinson, P.  Prince of Wales.  Films & Filming 1-8:13 My '55
    Interview.  Playboy 10:51 S '63
    Lawrenson, H.  The nightmare of the iguana.  Show 4-1:46 Ja
        '64
    Peter Glenville talks about the Burtons.  Vogue 150:282 S 1 '67
    Pepper, C. G.  Voyage of the Burtons.  McCalls 95:56 Ja '68
    Sheed, W.  Burton and Taylor must go.  Esquire 70:173 O '68
    Thompson, T.  While Burton romances Rex, Liz weighs her
        power and her future.  Life 66:65 Ja 17 '69
    Birstein, A.  What it is like to be walking investments.  Vogue
        153:100 F 15 '69
    Who cares about Wales?  I care.  Look 33:74 Je 24 '69
    Love is losing 40 pounds and giving it to your husband.  Photop
        77-5:36 My '70
    Roddy, J.  How do I love thee?  Look 34:28 Je 16 '70
    Why do they call my son girlie?  Photop 78-1:68 Jl '70
    Attacked for nude beach party.  Photop 78-2:56 Ag '70
    Bacon, J.  All I could see was Elizabeth and that rock.  TV
        Guide 18-36:16 S 5 '70
    Burton, L.  Last game Richard Burton lost.  Vogue 157:102 Ja
        1 '71
    What it's like to be in bed with Burton.  Photop 79-1:45 Ja '71
    Burton, R.  Traveling with Elizabeth.  Vogue 157:68 Ap 15 '71
    Bain, J.  Our marriage; interview.  Ladies Home J 88:89 Ap
        '71
    Liz walks out on him.  Photop 80-2:64 Ag '71
    Knapp, D.  On location in Mexico.  Show 2-7:18 S '71
    Dauntless travelers.  Vogue 158:130 O 15 '71
    Will Richard want a younger woman now.  Mod Screen 65-11:27
        N '71
    Liz saves Burton's life.  Photop 80-6:66 D '71
    Thompson, T.  Happy 40th, dear Liz.  Life 72:57 F 25 '72
    Scandalize guests at decadent French party.  Mod Screen 66-3:34
        Mr '72
    Bain, R.  Ten years since scandal time.  Harp Baz 105:126 Ap
        '72
    Why we want to adopt another baby.  Photop 82-1:49 Jl '72
    Public passion.  Mod Screen 66-9:33 S '72

Burton & Taylor; filmog. Films Illus 1-16:19 O '72
Musel, R. Not bad for 40 years old, eh? TV Guide 21-5:16 F
    3 '73
The right and wrong way to love. Photop 83-5:54 My '73
Edwards, J. P. His story. Liberty 1-10:53 Fall '73
Liz tells all. Photop 84-4:56 O '73
After the divorce. Photop 84-5:26 N '73
We find Burton's two girlfriends. Photop 85-1:32 Ja '74
Why I took Richard back. Photop 85-3:34 Mr '74
Stone, J. The klansman. Playgirl 2-2:85 Jl '74
New scandal. Photop 86-1:17 Jl '74
No more men... no more marriages. Photop 86-3:60 S '74
Burton tumbles for a new Liz. People 2-19:4 N 4 '74
Burton, R. The shock of his presence was like a blow under the
    heart. TV Guide 22-47:6 N 23 '74
Burton, R. To play Churchill is to hate him. N. Y. Times sec
    2:1 N 24 '74
Burton berated for attack on Churchill; letters. N. Y. Times sec
    2:1 D 8 '74

BUSCH, MAE
Petersen, E. Sketch. Motion Pic Classic 3:26 S '16
Wells, W. Interview. Motion Pic Classic 12:44 Ap '21
Howe, H. Motion Pic 22:40 N '21
Carr, H. Sketch. Motion Pic 28:44 N '24
Roberts, W. A. Sketch. Motion Pic 30:70 Ag '25
Summers, M. A tribute to Mae Busch; filmog. Filmograph 1-1:
    23 '70

BUSH, PAULINE
Bush, P. Pretenses of Pauline. Movie Pictorial 2-2:18 Ag; 2-4:
    13 O; 2-6:7 D '15; 2-7:16 F '16
McKelvie, M. G. Sketch. Motion Pic 12:82 O '16
Thayer, J. Farewell to a lovely lady. Classic Film Collect 31:
    20 Sum '71

BUSHMAN, FRANCIS X.
Interview. Motion Pic 9:89 F '15
How he became a photoplayer. Motion Pic 9:91 My '15
Bushman, F. X. A thrilling parallel. Photop 7-6:121 My '15
Bushman, F. X. How I keep my strength. Photop 8-1:59 Je '15
Briscoe, J. Sketch. Motion Pic 11:79 Jl '16
Romeo and Juliet in moving pictures. Motion Pic 12:111 S '16
How to get into moving pictures. Motion Pic 12:72 D '16
Eubanks, L. E. Personality of. Motion Pic Classic 3:22 D '16
Reid, E. Home of. Motion Pic Classic 4:33 Mr '17
Brady, S. E. Interview. Classic 16:22 Je '23
What they are doing now. Show 2-8:106 Ag '62
Obit. Classic Film Collector (Reprints Des Moines Register;
    Chicago Daily News; Minneapolis Tribune; Variety) 16:43 Fall
    '66
    Film R p21 '66/68
Hyams, J. Ex-star pines for lost son. Classic Film Collect
    34:35 Spg '72

BUTLER, DAVE
Yost, R. M. Jr.   Fat boy--tight pants.   Photop 16-4:43 S '19

BUTLER, LOIS
Fulton, M. J.   Sketch.   Photop 33:4 N '48

BUTLER, ROYAL
Obit.   Screen World p232 '74

BUTTERWORTH, CHARLES
Savage, R.   His zigzag trail to Broadway.   Theatre 44:24 D '26
Autobiographical.   Theatre 48:20 N '28
Sketch.   Photop 45:90 Ja '34
Craig, C.   Story of.   Motion Pic 53:51 Ap '37
Obit.   Cur Bio '46

BUTTONS, RED
Minoff, P.   Red Buttons arrives.   Cue 21-45:14 N 8 '52
Minoff, P.   Bouncing with Buttons.   Cue 23-32:12 Ag 7 '54
Minoff, P.   Mr. Buttons conducts another experiment.   Cue 24-6:
   35 F 12 '55
Minoff, P.   Big break for Buttons.   Cue 26-5:10 F 2 '57
Eyles, A.   Bio note; filmog.   Focus On F 3:6 My/Ag '70

BUZZI, RUTH
Girls from Laugh In.   Newsweek 73:62 Ja 27 '69
Whitney, D.   Life was not kind to Gladys Ormphby.   TV Guide
   17-31:14 Ag 2 '69
Zolotow, M.   She put the African violets in the bathroom.
   TV Guide 20-23:38 Je 3 '72
Raddatz, L.   Six who bowed out.   TV Guide 20-38:23 S 16 '72
Johnson, D.   Television's laughing lady.   Show 3-1:22 Mr '73

BYINGTON, SPRING
Hamilton, S.   Sketch.   Photop 54:30 S '40
Obit.   Classic Film Collect 32:62 Fall '71
   Cur Bio 32:43 O '71
   Same.   Cur Bio Yrbk 1971:461 '72
   Film R p 15 '72/73
   N. Y. Times p46 S 9 '71
   Same.   N. Y. Times Bio Ed S 9 '71
   Newsweek 78:71 S 20 '71
   Screen World 23:236 '72
   Time 98:58 S 20 '71

BYRD, RALPH
Obit.   Screen World 4:176 '53
Malcomson, R. M.   The sound serial.   Views & Rs 3-1:13 Sum
   '71

BYRNES, EDD
My child.   Photop 83-2:46 F '73

BYRON, WALTER
  Sketch.  Photop 34:42 Jl '28
  Belfrage, C.  Interview.  Motion Pic 36:42 Ag '28


CAAN, BRIAN
  Hano, A.  I'm too old for violence.  TV Guide 20-47:12 N 18
    '72

CAAN, JAMES
  Movie personality for March.  After Dark 4-11:12 Mr '72
  Godsons.  Time 99:70 Ap 3 '72
  Carragher, B.  The godfather's oldest son.  Show 2-2:18 Ap '72
  Feiden, R.  His godfather's son.  Interview 21:10 My '72
  Fiore, M. & Scott, V.  Story behind The godfather by the men
    who lived it.  Ladies Home J 89:62 Je '72
  Miller, E.  Interview.  Seventeen 31:274 Ag '72
  What every woman who wants him should know.  Photop 82-2:51
    Ag '72
  McGillivray, D.  Note; filmog.  Focus On F 11:6 Aut '72
  Lardine, B.  I want to have fun all the time.  N. Y. News Mag
    p36 O 8 '72
  Harmetz, A.  What's a son of the godfather doing in a rodeo?
    N. Y. Times sec 2:13 Ja 14 '73
  Same.  N. Y. Times Bio Ed p37 Ja '73
  Brand him two stars.  Films Illus 2-24:25 Je '73
  The boy who played recklessly.  Photop 84-3:42 S '73
  Fremont, V.  Interview.  Interview p20 Ja '74
  Interview.  Viva 1-8:61 My '74
  Next superstar?  People 2-27:76 D 30 '74

CABOT, BRUCE
  Horton, H.  His romance with Adrienne Ames.  Photop 45:52 D
    '33
  Schallert, E.  Interview.  Motion Pic 47:60 F '34
  Samuels, L.  A natural.  Silver S 6-6:28 Ap '36
  Wilson, E.  Cabot on reservation.  Silver S 11-12:24 O '41
  Obit.  Classic Film Collector 35:8X Sum '72 (Reprint N. Y. Times)
    Film R p11 '73/74
  N. Y. Post p25 My 4 '72
  N. Y. Times p48 My 4 '72
  Same.  N. Y. Times Bio Ed My 4 '72
  Newsweek 79:58 My 15 '72
  Time 99:88 My 15 '72

CAESAR, SID
  New Laurels for Caesar.  Cue 19-16:16 Ap 22 '50
  Mr. Caesar, Mr. Liebman.  Newsweek 37:56 Mr 19 '51
  Bio.  Cur Bio Ap '51
  Lords of laughter.  Coronet 30:74 O '51
  Backstage with Imogene & me.  Coronet 31:109 D '51
  Coca, I.  I married somebody else's husband.  Colliers 129:22
    F 23 '52

Zolotow, M.  TV gives him nightmares.  Sat Eve Post 225:26
  My 16 '53
Lonely Saturday nights?  Newsweek 43:83 F 15 '54
Last time together.  Life 36:63 Je 21 '54
Caesar vs. Coca.  Newsweek 44:66 O 11 '54
Sid and Imogene go it alone.  Life 37:57 O 18 '54
Minoff, P.  Notes on TV.  Cue 23-43:39 O 23 '54
The man who wanted to be an ant.  TV Guide 3-8:5 F 19 '55
Zolotow, M.  I'm home at last.  Cosmop 138:30 My '55
So I'm a baby sitter?  Coronet 38:45 Je '55
New Caesar.  Look 20:114 Mr 20 '56
Bester, A.  Two worlds of Caesar.  Holiday 20:71 S '56
Gehman, R.  What psychoanalysis did for me.  Look 20:48 O 2 '56
Goldberg, H.  It's wonderful being a third wife.  Cosmop 141:26
  D '56
Caesar's fretful hour.  Newsweek 49:63 Ap 8 '57
Hollow victory.  TV Guide 5-21:17 My 25 '57
Where Caesar stands.  Newsweek 49:100 My 27 '57
Decline of the comedians.  Time 69:72 My 27 '57
Sid Caesar, tv-dp?  Cath World 185:146 My '57
Minoff, P.  It wouldn't be the same with Caesar.  Cue 26-22:14
  Je 1 '57
Shanley, J. P.  Television.  America 97:290 Je 1 '57
Back together again.  Newsweek 50:87 Ag 5 '57
Roth, J.  Hurdles of satire.  New Rep 137:22 S 9 '57
Pow! Bang! Blam!  TV Guide 6-4:17 Ja 25 '58
Barrett, M. E. & M.  TV: the things which are Mr. Caesar's.
  Good House 146:17 Ja '58
Rebirth of a time.  Cue 27-5:11 F 1 '58
Lardner, J.  Air.  New Yorker 34:67 Mr 29 '58
Return of a talented trio.  Coronet 43:18 Ap '58
Langman, A. W.  Television.  McCalls 86:6 My '59
Davidson, B.  Hail Caesar!  Colliers 126:24 N 11 '59
O mighty Caesar.  Newsweek 58:74 O 30 '61
The comedy business.  TV Guide 9-45:4 N 11 '61
Cuniff, R.  Cool jazz to comedy.  Show 2-7:71 Jl '62
Little me's man.  N. Y. Times Mag p75 N 4 '62
Conquest of the seven Caesars.  Newsweek 60:51 N 26 '62
Hail Caesar.  Time 80:53 N 30 '62
Make way for clowns.  Life 53:113 N 30 '62
Gehman, R. & B.  Seven Caesars.  Theatre Arts 46:17 N '62
People are talking about.  Vogue 140:122 D '62
Barber, R.  Hail Caesar!  Sat Eve Post 236:28 F 16 '63
Gehman, R.  It was my medium.  TV Guide 11-7:18 F 16; 11-8:
  20 F 23 '63
Cohane, T.  How to pitch a ball game in five hours.  Look 27:99
  F 26 '63
Great Caesar's ghost.  Esquire 77:138 My '72
Ace, G.  Aftermath.  Esquire 78:193 O '72
Torre, M.  Hail Caesar!  Show 3-4:20 Je '73
Zolotow, M.  First we'll eat, then we'll talk.  TV Guide 22-26:
  23 Je 29 '74

CAGNEY, JAMES
Grayson, C.   Sketch.   Movie Classic 1:60 O '31
Keen, J. H.   Cagney.   Cinema Dig 1-2:6 My 30 '32
Townsend, L.   Why he left the movies.   Motion Pic 44:40 S '32
Fidler, J.   Interview.   Movie Classic 3:22 F '33
Ergenbright, E. L.   Interview.   Movie Classic 5:48 O '33
Hall, G.   Interview.   Movie Classic 5:26 Ja '34
Appreciation in Jimmy the Gent.   Lit Dig 117:43 Ap 7 '34
Wilson, E.   The maddest set in Hollywood.   Silver S 4-7:26 My
   '34
Orme, M.   Criticism.   Ill Lon N 185:146 Jl 28 '34
Appreciation in Here comes the navy.   Lit Dig 118:26 Ag 4 '34
Hartley, K.   Cagney.   Movie Classic 7:47 O '34
French, W. F.   Interview.   Motion Pic 48:51 N '34
James, K.   Chosen for leading role in A midsummer night's
   dream.   Motion Pic 47:32 My '35
Hartley, K.   The unholy three.   Motion Pic 50:49 O '35
Zeitlin, I.   Interview.   Movie Classic 9:35 D '35
Makes good in Great guy.   Newsweek 8:37 D 26 '36
Craig, C.   His return to the screen.   Motion Pic 52:24 Ja '37
Ferguson, O.   Appreciation.   New Rep 92:271 O 13 '37
Lorton, T.   Can he come back?   Screen Book 20-5:32 Je '38
Crouse, R.   Story of.   Stage 16:10 D '38
Rankin, R.   Spots what it takes.   Silver S 9-4:30 F '39
Reid, J.   The Cagney legend.   Screen Book 22-1:62 Ag '39
McFee, F.   Cagney and Cagney, Inc.   Screen Book 22-6:59 Ja
   '40
Holland, J.   Try anything once!   Silver S 10-3:38 Ja '40
Bio note; filmog.   Movies & People 2:9 '40
Hopper, H.   Sketch.   Photop 19:37 S '41
Mook, D.   Privacy preferred.   Silver S 12-9:36 Jl '42
His performance in Blood on the sun.   Newsweek 26:101 Jl 9 '45
Cheatham, M.   The ideal realist.   Silver S 18-1:40 N '47
Maddox, B.   The same old Jimmy.   Silver S 20-1:45 N '49
That Cagney look.   Cue 19-40:18 O 7 '50
Zunser, J.   Look ma, it's Jimmy.   Cue 26-30:11 Jl 27 '57
Roman, R. C.   Yankee doodle Cagney.   Dance 41:58 Jl '67
Where are they now?   Newsweek 71:16 Ap 22 '68
When hoods were heroes.   Screen Greats 1-2:34 Sum '71
Bogdanovich, P.   Hollywood.   Esquire 78:34 Jl '72
McGilligan, P.   The actor as auteur; filmog.   Velvet Light 7:3
   Win '72/73
Screen veteran.   Cue 42-12:64 Mr 24 '73
McGilligan, P.   Just a dancer gone wrong.   Take One 4-5:22
   My/Je '73
Harmetz, A.   The man who got away.   N. Y. Times Bio Ed p319
   Mr '74
Harmetz, A.   The man who got away.   N. Y. Times sec 2:1 Mr
   3 '74
Cagney comes back to take a bow.   People 1-2:56 Mr 11 '74
Sayre, N.   To the star, it's long ago and far away.   N. Y. Times
   p44 Mr 14 '74
Lawrence, K. G.   Homage to Cagney.   Films In R 25-5:286

My '74
A tribute to Hollywood's tough guy.  Photop 86-1:63 Jl '74

CAGNEY, JEANNE
    McFee, F.  Cagney and Cagney, Inc.  Screen Book 22-6:59 Ja
    '40

CAGNEY, WILLIAM
    Rankin, R.  Sketch.  Photop 44:75 O '33

CAINE, MICHAEL
    On the scene.  Playboy 13-4:160 Ap '66
    Interview.  Playboy 14:47 Jl '67
    Wolf, W.  The able Mr. Caine.  Cue 36-49:16 D 9 '67
    Bio.  Cur Bio 29:5 My '68
        Same.  Cur Bio Yrbk 1968:72 '69
    Sweeney, L.  Male of the species.  TV Guide 16-52:15 D 28 '68
    Austen, D.  Playing dirty; interview.  Films & Filming 15-7:4
    Ap '69
    Austen, D.  Making it or breaking it.  Films & Filming 15-8:15
    My '69
    Interview.  Mod Screen 66-11:30 N '72
    Flythe, S.  Interview.  Holiday 52:32 N '72
    I got him to marry me by living with him.  Mod Screen 67-4:55
    Ap '73
    Eyles, A.  Note; filmog.  Focus On F 14:10 Spg '73
    d'Arcy, S.  Raising Caine.  Films Illus 3-33:346 My '74

CALDWELL, ORVILLE
    Obit.  Screen World 19:229 '68

CALDWELL, ZOE
    Gussow, M.  Zoe in her prime.  Newsweek 71:81 F 5 '68
    Weales, G.  Without that spark.  Reporter 38:43 Mr 7 '68
    People are talking about.  Vogue 151:177 Ap 1 '68
    Keast, L. S.  A great taste of life.  After Dark 12-3:42 Jl '70
    Tierney, M.  Jumping at Lady Hamilton.  Plays & Players 18-
    1:20 O '70
    Bio.  Cur Bio 31:8 D '70
        Same.  Cur Bio Yrbk 1970:64 '71

CALHERN, LOUIS
    Maughan, R.  Meanie Calhern.  Silver S 18-3:43 Ja '48
    Maugham, R.  Is age so important?  Silver S 21-6:31 Ap '51

CALHOUN, ALICE
    Malvern, P.  Interview.  Motion Pic Classic 10:62 Je '20
    Boone, A.  Sketch.  Photop 19:27 My '21
    Bruce, B.  Interview.  Motion Pic 21:37 Jl '21
    Ashworth, C. W.  Interview.  Motion Pic 13:16 O '21
    Curly, K.  Interview.  Motion Pic 23:48 Jl '22
    Obit.  Screen World 18:232 '67

CALHOUN, RORY
    Honeymoon at Ojai Valley.   Photop 34:66 D '48
    Noel, T.   Watch out for Rory.   Silver S 24-9:24 Jl '54

CALLEIA, JOSEPH
    Note; filmog.   Movies & People 2:9 '40
    Whorf, R.   As I see them.   Lions R 3-2:no p# Ja '44

CALTHROP, DONALD
    Truscott, H.   Donald Calthrop.   Silent Pic 18:13 Fall '73

CALVERT, CATHERINE
    Ames, H.   Interview.   Motion Pic 15:53 Ap '18
    Allison, D.   Team work.   Photop 15-4:66 Mr '19
    Fletcher, A. W.   Interview.   Motion Pic Classic 12:18 Je '21
    Obit.   N. Y. Times p40 Ja 19 '71
        Screen World 23:236 '72

CALVERT, PHYLLIS
    Howard, M.   Lady of distinction.   Silver S 19-5:40 Mr '49

CALVET, CORRINE
    Calvet, C.   Memories of me.   Silver S 20-2:36 D '49
    Calvet, C.   Does marriage ruin sex appeal?   Silver S 20-6:22
        Ap '50
    Rising star.   Film R p30 '50
    Churchill, R. & B.   Outsmart the other woman.   Silver S 21-11:
        22 S '51
    Churchill, R. & B.   My honeymoon never ended.   Silver S 22-9:
        20 Jl '52
    Walker, H. L.   I'm so-o-o sorry for American husbands.   Silver
        S 23-4:33 F '53

CAMBRIDGE, GODFREY
    Dunbar, E.   (He) turns white.   Look 33:57 D 30 '69
    Bio.   Cur Bio Yrbk 1969:67 '70
    What the FBI has on me.   Esquire 76:140 D '71

CAMERON, JOANNA
    Manners, D.   I nominate for stardom.   Mod Screen 66-5:16 My
        '72

CAMERON, ROD
    Cameron, R.   How to remain a Hollywood bachelor.   Silver S
        20-10:22 Ag '50

CAMPANELLA, JOSEPH
    Davidson, B.   Say, Mac, you're my favorite actor and I know
        your name, but I can't think of it.   TV Guide 20-24:22 Je 10
        '72

CAMPBELL, COLIN
    Obit.   Screen World 18:232 '67

CAMPBELL, ERIC
  Grossman, A.  Eric Campbell.  Films In R 14-1:62 Ja '63

CAMPBELL, GLEN
  Man from Delight.  Newsweek 71:65 Ap 15 '68
  Living proof of what a diet of hawg jowls can do.  TV Guide 16-
    24:16 Je 15 '68
  Country hipster.  Life 65:82 S 6 '68
  Miller, E.  Sweet singing man.  Seventeen 28:148 Mr '69
  Diehl, D.  Selling the concept of the all-American boy.  TV
    Guide 17-24:16 Je 14 '69
  Eyles, A.  Note; filmog.  Focus On F 1:9 Ja/F '70
  Smothers, T.  Never gonna be a country boy again.  Look 34:70
    F 24 '70
  Dowty, L.  Interview.  Good House 170:42 F '70
  My good times and bad.  Ladies Home J 87:62 F '70
  Condon, M. J.  They remember Glen.  TV Guide 18-18:26 My 2
    '70
  I was in love with Glen Campbell but I let my sister marry him.
    Photop 78-1:59 Jl '70
  Robbins, F.  On location with (him).  Photop 80-3:71 S '71
  It's only six miles from Hillman.  TV Guide 19-44:13 O 30 '71
  Stoop, N. M.  Duet with Glen Campbell.  After Dark 6-6:19 O
    '73

CAMPBELL, LOUISE
  Smithson, E. J.  A Campbell is coming.  Screen Book 21-3:44
    O '38
  Bio note; filmog.  Films & Filming 19-5:58 F '73

CAMPBELL, WEBSTER
  Sketch.  Motion Pic 10:117 N '15
  His most difficult scene.  Motion Pic 15:47 Ap '18
  Bruce, B.  Interview.  Motion Pic 20:68 O '20

CAMPBELL, WILLIAM
  Rising star.  Film R p36 '56/57

CAMPEAU, FRANK
  Boone, A.  The devil's violet.  Photop 16-3:81 Ag '19

CANARY, DAVID
  Whitney, D.  New boy on Bonanza.  TV Guide 16-9:21 Mr 2 '68

CANNON, DYAN
  Honey, are you in pictures.  TV Guide 8-46:29 N 12 '60
  Battelle, P.  Mrs. Cary Grant talks about marrying and divorcing
    him.  Ladies Home J 85:106 Ap '68
  Mrs. Cary Grant suffers sad collapse.  Photop 77-5:71 My '70
  I just gave birth to Cary Grant's baby.  Photop 77-6:28 Je '70
  Gordon, S.  Dyan Cannon booms.  Look 34:73 Jl 14 '70
  Her fears for Jennifer--real or imaginery?  Mod Screen 65-11:
    32 N '71

Skin touch. Time 99:46 Ja 17 '72
Johnson, D. Preminger made her cry but Such good friends
   should make her crow. Show 12:33 F '72
Faces going far. Films Illus 1-10:21 Ap '72
Enoff, J. The primal scream of Dyan Cannon. Viva 1-4:42 Ja
   '74
Klemesrud, J. Come to the nightclub old chum. N. Y. Times
   sec 2:15 Ap 7 '74
Natale, R. Interview. Interview 4-4:7 Ap '74
Johnson, D. Dyan Cannon--broadside. After Dark 7-6:56 O '74

CANNON, J. D.
   Bercovici, L. New York actor goes Hollywood. TV Guide 22-21:
      20 My 25 '74

CANOVA, JUDY
   Wilson, E. Hill-billy queen. Silver S 10-9:36 Jl '40
   Perkins, R. Glamour girl. Silver S 13-1:44 N '42

CANTINFLAS
   Sketch. Time 36:34 Ag 26 '40
   Zunser, J. Mexico's millionaire mirthquake. Cue 27-34:11 Ag
      23 '58

CANTOR, EDDIE
   Benchley, R. C. Appreciation. Life 79:18 My 4 '22
   Benchley, R. C. Songs sung by. Life 82:18 Jl 26 '23
   Freeman, D. Sketch. Theatre 49:28 My '29
   Fender, R. Sketch. Motion Pic Classic 31:48 Ag '30
   Crawford, R. Sketch. Photop 38:83 O '30
   Brundidge, H. T. Interview. Motion Pic 48:28 Ja '34
   Fender, R. Divorce rumors to gain publicity. Movie Classic
      5:46 Ja '34
   Jamison, J. It's that man again. Silver S 4-6:23 Ap '34
   Orme, M. Appreciation. Ill Lon N 186:198 F 9 '35
   Radio star. Newsweek 5:26 F 9 '35
   Wedding anniversary to his wife. Am Mag 123:43 Ja '37
   Value of his eyes. Delin 130:46 Mr '37
   What is behind the popular song? Etude 58:804 D '40
   Bio Note; filmog. Movies & People 2:9 '40
   Salute! Cue 10-39:3 S 27 '41
   The trouble with women. Cosmop 114:56 Ja '43
   Beatty, J. Story of. Am Mag 111:36 Jl '43
   His debut as movie producer. Newsweek 23:104 My 22 '44
   Team work. Am Mag 139:64 F '45
   Obit. Film R p45 '65/66
   Bio. NCAB 52:106 '70
   Mikelides, N. Eddie Cantor; filmog. Films In R 22-9:582 N '71

CAPRI, ANNA
   A flap-eyed femme fatale. TV Guide 12-16:26 Ap 18 '64

CAPRICE, JUNE
  Wallace, R.  Sketch.  Motion Pic 12:116 Ja '17
  Gaddis, P.  Sketch.  Motion Pic 13:27 Je '17
  Rosemon, E.  Playing extra with.  Motion Pic Classic 5:37 D
    '17
  Montanye, L.  Interview.  Motion Pic 21:38 My '21

CAPUCINE
  Zunser, J.  From la belle France.  Cue 29-30:11 Jl 23 '60
  Rising star.  Film R p33 '61/62

CARDINALE, CLAUDIA
  Lane, J. F.  The face of '63-Italy.  Films & Filming 9-7:11 Ap
    '63
  Bean, R.  Will there be film stars in 1974?  Films & Filming
    10-10:9 Jl '64
  Canham, C.  In search of an actress.  Film Fan Mo 87:7 S '68
  Claudia Cardinale.  Show 2-9:43 N '71

CARETTE, JULIEN
  Obit.  Screen World 18:233 '67

CAREW, ORA
  Kingston, R.  Sketch.  Motion Pic 17:81 F '19
  Cheatham, M.  Interview.  Motion Pic Classic 13:50 O '21

CAREWE, RITA
  Uselton, R. A.  The Wampus baby stars.  Films In R 21-2:73
    F '70

CAREY, HARRY SR.
  Cheyenne Harry from New York.  Photop 15-2:27 Ja '19
  Cheatham, M.  Interview.  Motion Pic Classic 11:18 F '21
  Cheatham, M.  Interview.  Motion Pic Classic 13:36 N '21
  Adair, C. H.  His trading-post.  Motion Pic Classic 24:62 N '26
  People.  Cue 10-29:16 Jl 19 '41
  Phillips, A.  Screen immortal.  8mm Collect 13:14 Fall/Win '65
  Cabana, R. Jr.  Concerning Trader Horn.  Views & Rs 3-1:35
    Sum '71
  Tuska, J.  Trader Horn.  Views & Rs 3-1:51 '71

CAREY, MACDONALD
  Young, A.  Sketch.  Photop 22:6 Ja '43
  Proctor, K.  Carey calls it quits.  Silver S 13-5:44 Mr '43
  Parsons, L. O.  Cosmop's citation for the best supporting role
    of the month.  Cosmop 122:66 Ap '47
  Hall, G.  Suddenly it's stardom.  Silver S 19-2:42 D '48
  Gibson, W.  Women just aren't fair.  Silver S 20-6:49 Ap '50
  Carey, M.  You can love your in-laws.  Silver S 22-2:42 D '51
  Photoplay forum.  Photop 81-2:28 F '72
  My child.  Photop 82-6:36 D '72

CAREY, PHIL
   Here comes the heroes.  TV Guide 4-37:28 S 15 '56

CARLIN, GEORGE
   Pop of the news.  Newsweek 69:41 Ja 9 '67
   He may not look like Jackie Gleason.  TV Guide 15-32:10 Ag 12
     '67
   Gottfried, M.  Freewheeling funnyman.  Vogue 159:80 My '72

CARLIN, LYNN
   Klemesrud, J.  Lynn went along as mom.  N. Y. Times Bio Ed
     Ap 18 '71
   Interview with Milos Forman.  Dialogue 3:5 '72

CARLISLE, KITTY
   Reed, E.  Roster of new faces.  Theatre Arts 18:59 Ja '34
   Roberts, K.  Six o'clock stars.  Colliers 94:13 O 13 '34
   Samuels, L.  (She) throws her mask away.  Silver S 5-4:47 F
     '34
   Dew, G.  Interview.  Motion Pic 49:44 Mr '35
   Cooley, D.  Interview.  Movie Classic 8:51 Mr '35
   Knight, A.  Story of.  Motion Pic 53:37 My '37
   About the author.  Theatre Arts 33:58 O '49
   Fuller, J. G.  Autographing of Act one at Woolworth's.  Sat R
     43:6 O 22 '60
   Why I love my man, Moss.  Cosmop 149:74 N '60
   Daniels, R. D.  Interview.  Opera N 31:26 Ja 7 '67

CARLISLE, LUCILLE
   Carlisle, H.  Interview.  Motion Pic 23:59 Ap '22

CARLISLE, MARY
   Sketch.  Theatre Arts 18:56 Ja '34
   Sylvia's beauty helps.  Photop 46:56 O '34
   Uselton, R. A.  The Wampus baby stars.  Films In R 21-2:73
     F '70

CARLSON, RAY
   Efron, E.  Under five.  TV Guide 18-46:32 N 14 '70

CARLSON, RICHARD
   Sketch.  Photop 53:69 Mr '39
   Reid, J.  Unpredictable Dick.  Silver S 11-3:42 Ja '41
   The unpredictable Mr. Carlson.  Lions R 1-11/12:no p# Jl/Ag
     '42
   Stars of tomorrow.  Lions R 1-11/12:no p# Jl/Ag '42
   Ham, he loves it.  Lions R 2-2:no p# N '42
   College professor and the movie queens.  Lions R 2-4: no p# Ap
     '43
   Mr. Carlson--ball of fire.  Lions R 3-1:no p# S '43
   Between pictures--huh!  Lions R 3-1:no p# S '43
   Sketch.  Womans Home C 73:14 Je '46

CARLSON, VERONICA
  Bio note.  Black Oracle 2:20 n. d.

CARMEN, JEAN
  Uselton, R. A.  The Wampus baby stars.  Films In R 21-2:73
    F '20

CARMEN, JEANNE
  Jeanne's having a ball.  TV Guide 6-2:28 Ja 11 '58

CARMEN, JEWEL
  A queen of blondes.  Photop 12-2:108 Jl '17
  Peltret, E.  Interview.  Motion Pic 15:68 N '18
  Ashworth, C. W.  Interview.  Motion Pic Classic 13:16 D '21

CARMICHAEL, HOAGY
  Hamilton, S.  Story of.  Photop 30:90 My '47
  Minoff, P.  His revue needs an awful lot of work.  Cue 22-25:18
    Je 20 '53
  Freeman, B.  Interview.  Sat R 52:43 Je 26 '69
  Efron, E.  Play it again, Hoagy.  TV Guide 18-51:6 D 19 '70

CARMICHAEL, IAN
  John, M.  Why we all love Wimsey.  Cue 43-34:10 S 9 '74

CARMINATI, TULLIO
  Dowling, M.  Sketch.  Movie Classic 6:16 Mr '34
  Sketch.  Motion Pic 48:45 D '34
  Calhoun, D.  Interview.  Movie Classic 8:42 Ap '35
  French, W. F.  Bio sketch.  Photop 47:46 Ap '35
  Carroll, J.  His love for Eleonora Duse.  Movie Classic 9:33 D
    '35
  Obit.  N. Y. Times p30 F 27 '71

CARNE, DAGNE
  Hickey, N.  From hatha yoga to women's liberation.  TV Guide
    18-28:27 Jl 11 '70

CARNE, JUDY
  Durslag, M.  Brash, confident, scared!  TV Guide 14-42:21 O
    15 '66
  Gordon, S.  Sock it to 'em Judy.  Look 32:72 O 1 '68
  Lewis, R. W.  Frankly, it has become a big, bloody bore.  TV
    Guide 17-4:12 Ja 25 '69
  Girls from Laugh In.  Newsweek 73:62 Ja 27 '69
  A good marriage almost destroyed us.  Photop 82-2:33 Ag '72
  Raddatz, L.  Six who bowed out.  TV Guide 20-38:23 S 16 '72

CARNELL, SUZI
  He'll never get over the shock.  TV Guide 11-13:26 Mr 30 '63

CARNEY, ALAN
  Obit.  Classic Film Collect 40:59 Fall '73
    Screen World p232 '74

CARNEY, ART
  Harvey, E.   Comedians' comedian.   Colliers 129:20 Ap 5 '52
  Second banana.   TV Guide 1-6:15 My 8 '53
  Art Carney weighs in.   Newsweek 43:52 Mr 8 '54
  Millstein, G.   TV's number one second comedian.   N. Y. Times
     Mag p19 Ap 18 '54
  Long, J.   Don't kid your kid brother.   Am Mag 158:24 D '54
  The man in the manhole.   TV Guide 3-12:4 Mr 19 '55
  Gleason's pal.   Look 19:30 Je 14 '55
  No guts, I guess.   Newsweek 52:58 D 8 '58
  Major clown.   Time 74:83 O 12 '59
  Langman, A. W.   Television.   McCalls 87:60 '59
  A new perspective of.   TV Guide 7-48:5 N 28 '59
  Ewald, B.   Up from the sewer.   Newsweek 54:59 N 30 '59
  Two great comics.   Vogue 135:150 F 1 '60
  Carney steps out and up.   Life 48:53 My 9 '60
  Kuhn, R.   Actor without ego.   Sat Eve Post 234:22 Ja 21 '61
  Fathers the boys watch for.   Seventeen 20:102 F '61
  Talk with a star.   Newsweek 59:48 Ja 1 '62
  Rollin, B.   A second honeymoon for The honeymooners.   Look
     30:76 N 15 '66
  Crail, T.   Carney goes on a second honeymoon.   TV Guide 15-2:
     20 Ja 14 '67
  Hickey, N.   Carney the clown.   TV Guide 16-38:12 S 21 '68
  How I faced my drinking problem.   Photop 78-4:60 O '70
  Wilkins, B.   Art Carney wins in a film--and over alcoholism.
     People 2-17:43 O 21 '74

CAROL, MARTINE
  A few moments with...   Unifrance 19:11 Jl/Ag '52
  Zunser, J.   Goodbye to cheesecake?   Cue 26-33:10 Ag 17 '57
  Obit.   Film R p21 '66/68

CAROL, SUE
  Smith, F. J.   Interview.   Motion Pic Classic 12:16 Je '21
  Jordan, J.   Sketch.   Photop 22:22 Ag '22
  Biery, R.   Interview.   Photop 33:63 Mr '28
  Dickey, J.   Sketch.   Motion Pic 35:55 Mr '28
  Cummings, A.   How to tell her from Clara Bow.   Motion Pic
     Classic 27:28 Ag '28
  Hall, G.   Interview.   Motion Pic Classic 30:18 O '29
  Biery, R.   Her secret marriage.   Motion Pic 39:8 F '30
  Donnell, D.   Her women fans.   Motion Pic 40:55 N '30
  Sketch.   Photop 38:86 N '30
  Fender, R.   Sketch.   Photop 39:54 Ja '31
  Dudley, F.   Pattern for a perfect marriage.   Silver S 15-4:32
     F '45
  Uselton, R. A.   The Wampus baby stars.   Films In R 21-2:73
     F '70

CARON, LESLIE
  Hendricks, H.   The latest thing from gay Paree.   Silver S 22-6:
     38 Ap '52

Rising star.   Film R p107 '52/53
Reid, L.   Lonely Leslie.   Silver S 24-7:36 My '54
Zunser, J.   Farewell to the dance.   Cue 27-19:11 My 10 '58
Photoplay forum.   Photop 85-4:4 Ap '74

CARPENTER, NANCEE
Aspiring young actresses.   Show 2-2:64 S '71

CARPENTER, PAUL
Obit.   Screen World 16:220 '65

CARR, BETTY ANN
Adler, D.   The ballad of Betty Bigfinger.   TV Guide 20-13:34
Mr 25 '72

CARR, JANE
Think of a dumpy lady.   Films Illus 1-12:8 Je '72

CARR, MARY
Montanye, L.   Interview.   Motion Pic 21:38 Mr '21
Sketch.   Photop 19:72 Mr '21
Carlisle, H.   Interview.   Motion Pic 28:62 S '24
Obit.   Classic Film Collect 40:58 Fall '73
Screen World p232 '74

CARRADINE, DAVID
de Roos, R.   Rides the new wave--in a saddle.   TV Guide 14-
51:24 D 17 '66
Stump, A.   Wild man of Laurel Canyon.   TV Guide 20-46:18 N
11 '72
Burke, T.   King of 'Kung Fu. '   N. Y. Times Bio Ed p560 Ap '73
Same.   N. Y. Times sec 2:17 Ap 29 '73
A little off the top--the hard way.   TV Guide 21-25:30 Je 23 '73
Leider, R. A.   Raising Caine.   Show 3-6:25 S '73
Davidson, B.   Does not the pebble, entering the water, begin
fresh journeys?   TV Guide 24-4:21 Ja 26 '74
Lardine, B.   I say 'no' to everything and everybody.   Sunday
N. Y. News Mag p14 F 10 '74
The Carradines:  the first family of film.   People 1-2:61 Mr 11
'74
Rebel with a cause.   Photop 86-5:65 N '74

CARRADINE, JOHN
Sculptor of character.   Lions R 2-5:no p# Jl '43
To be or not to be?   Lions R 3-4(sup):no p# Jl '44
Pitts, M. R.   Partial filmog.   Films In R 19-5:316 My '68
Carradine, J.   The company remembers Stagecoach.   Action 6-
5:29 S/O '71
Carradine makes a comeback.   Cinefantastique 1-2:39 Win '71
Parish, J. R.  & Pitts, M. R.   John Carradine; filmog.   Focus
On F 15:31 Sum '73
Mank, G.   John Carradine; filmog.   Film Fan Mo 143:3 O '73
The Carradines:  the first family of film.   People 1-2:61 Mr 11
'74

CARRADINE, KEITH
    The Carradines: the first family of film.    People 1-2:61 Mr 11
    '74
    Corliss, R.   Interview.    Film Comment 10-3:14 My/Je '74

CARRADINE, ROBERT
    The Carradines: the first family of film.    People 1-2:61 Mr 11
    '74

CARREL, DANY
    Do you know Dany Carrel?    Unifrance 39:no p# Mr/Ap '56
    Bio note.    Unifrance 45:8 D '57

CARRILLO, LEO
    Mantle, B.  Sketch.    Green Book 18:984 D '17
    Interview.    Dramatic Mirror Je 19 '20
    Chrisman, J. E.  Sketch.    Movie Classic 2:41 My '32
    Ludlam, H. F.    Carrillo the "Gringo. "  Silver S 4-12:48 O '34
    Ganley, H.  Leo Carrillo.    Motion Pic 50:49 N '35
    Obit.    Film R p17 '62/63

CARROLL, DIAHANN
    The entertainer of the year.    Cue 30-52:9 D 30 '61
    Wolff, A.    A new kind of glamour on TV.    Look 32:66 O 29 '68
    Wonderful world of color.    Time 92:70 D 13 '68
    Hochstein, R.    (her) juggling act.    Good House 168:38 My '69
    (She) presents the Julia dolls.    Ebony 24:148 O '69
    See, C.    I'm a black woman with a white image.    TV Guide 18-
    11:26 Mr 14 '70
    Shayon, R. L.    Changes.    Sat R 53:46 Ap 18 '70
    Evers, M.    Tales of two Julias; interview.    Ladies Home J 87:
    60 My '70
    Julia models a look for the beach.    Ebony 26:106 Ja '71
    I love her.    Photop 79-1:54 Ja '71
    O, marry me.    Photop 79-4:71 Ap '71
    Secretly married?    Mod Screen 65-11:37 N '71
    Pierce, P.    To begin with, I am an individual.    McCalls 99:92
    F '72
    Now they're engaged.    Photop 82-1:23 Jl '72
    Prime time to get married.    Life 73:97 N 17 '72
    Wedding plans.    Mod Screen 67-2:52 F '73
    Surprise wedding.    Photop 83-6:38 Je '73
    Black women reveal how they suffer for their white men.    Photop
    84-6:54 D '73
    Diahann Carroll on love and responsibility.    Viva 2-1:112 O '74

CARROLL, GEORGIA
    Her marriage.    Photop 27:61 Je '45
    Gorgeous Georgia.    Am Mag 139:126 Je '45

CARROLL, JOHN
    Hamilton, S. & Morse, W. Jr.  Sketch.    Photop 54:21 Mr '40
    Franchey, J. R.    Incredible John Carroll.    Silver S 12-1:38

N '41
Hollywood--port of call.    Lions R 1-8:no p# Ap '42
John Carroll's crag.    Lions R 1-11/12:no p# Jl/Ag '42
Corporal John Carroll.    Lions R 2-4:no p# Ap '43
Franchey, J. R.    Eight men in her life.    Silver S 13-8:34 Je '43

CARROLL, LEO G.
    Obit.    Classic Film Collect 37:59 Win '72
    Film R p12 '73/74
    N. Y. Times Bio Ed p1755 O '72

CARROLL, MADELEINE
    Spensley, D.    Story of.    Motion Pic 52:34 O '36
    Sketch.    Life 3:94 S 13 '37
    Wilson, E.    Projections of...    Silver S 8-1:28 N '37
    Lee, S.    An actress must live dangerously.    Screen Book 19-4:32
        N '37
    Wilson, E.    (She) is not to be misunderstood.    Silver S 9-9:28
        Jl '39
    Wallace, G.    What--no oomph?    Screen Book 22-3:56 O '39
    Bryan, K.    Story of.    Photop 54:34 S '40
    Walker, H. L.    Sketch.    Photop 54:40 O '40
    Vallee, W. L.    Getting confidential with (her).    Silver S 11-1:35
        N '40
    Bio note; filmog.    Movies & People 2:9 '40
    Why I joined the United seamen's service.    Cosmop 114:46 Ap '43
    Reid, L.    Fabulous femme.    Silver S 18-5:44 Mr '48
    Film star voted Woman of the year.    Cue 17-22:14 My 29 '48
    Pin-up of the past.    Films & Filming 18-1:80 O '71
    Rode, D.    Madeleine Carroll; filmog.    Film Fan Mo 159:3 S '74

CARROLL, NANCY
    Thornton, J.    Sketch.    Motion Pic 35:34 Mr '28
    Lubou, D.    Interview.    Motion Pic 37:42 Jl '29
    Manners, D.    Interview.    Motion Pic Classic 30:31 Ja '30
    Harris, R.    Portrait of a rising star.    Silver S 1-6:27 Ap '31
    Goldbeck, E.    Interview.    Motion Pic 41:84 Je '31
    Carroll, N.    The story of my life.    Silver S 1-8:16 Je '31; 1-9:
        48 Jl '31
    What they are doing now.    Show 2-9:108 S '62
    Obit.    Classic Film Collect 16:22 Fall '66 (reprint L. A. Times)
    Martin, A.    Commemorates career of talkie star in book.    Clas-
        sic Film Collect 23:41 Spg '69
    Pin-up of the past.    Films & Filming 17-8:144 My '71

CARROLL, PAT
    Aw, gee, I'm not that funny.    TV Guide 3-29:12 Jl 16 '55
    That certain feeling.    TV Guide 5-5:24 F 2 '57
    Miss Carroll has an underwhelming ego.    TV Guide 11-23:13 Je
        8 '63

CARSON, JACK
    Carson, Mrs. J.    Care and feeding of a comedian.    Silver S

14-11:46 S '44
Holland, J. I'll never do it again. Silver S 16-8:53 Je '46
Gift for his son. Am Mag 147:114 Ja '49
Obit. Film R p34 '63/64

CARSON, JEANNIE
Minoff, P. Notes on T. V. Cue 25-38:45 S 22 '56

CARSON, L. M. KIT
Carson, L. M. K. More notes from the underground. Cinema
(BH) 5-1:20 Spg '69
Carson, L. M. K. A voice-over. Film Lib Q 2-3:20 Sum '69
Carson, L. M. K. The loser here. Show 1-1:39 Ja '70
Zadan, C. An American dreamer. After Dark 3-11:18 Mr '71
Colaciello, R. Interview. Interview 2-3:22 n. d.
Carson, L. M. K. The mask falls... and there's life. AFI Re-
port 3:12 N '72

CARTER, HELENA
Story of. Life 25:33 N 8 '48
Briggs, C. Filmog. Films In R 24-7:446 Ag/S '73

CARTER, JACK
Lucy stopped me from killing myself. Mod Screen 66-2:56 F '72

CARTER, JANIS
Parsons, L. O. Cosmop's citation for the best supporting per-
formance of the month. Cosmop 127:13 N '49
Tobin, M. Janis Carter; filmog. Films In R 20-10:648 D '69
Briggs, C. Filmog. Films In R 24-7:446 Ag/S '73

CARTER, NAN
May, L. Interview. Motion Pic Classic 2:28 Je '16

CARTWRIGHT, ANGELA
Femme fatale. TV Guide 7-45:8 N 7 '59
I'm just happy, I guess. TV Guide 17-43:48 O 25 '69

CARVER, KATHRYN
Carlisle, H. Interview. Motion Pic 35:34 F '28
Tennant, M. Estranged from husband. Movie Classic 3:27 Ja
'33

CARVER, LYNNE
Reynolds, Q. Sketch. Colliers 102:20 D 24 '38

CASE, ALLEN
Musical-comedy singer goes west. TV Guide 8-25:23 Je 18 '60

CASE, KATHLEEN
Rising star. Film R p38 '56/57

CASH, JOHNNY
Aronowitz, A. G. Music behind the bars. Life 65:12 Ag 16 '68
Empathy in the dungeon. Time 92:52 Ag 30 '68
Wren, C. S. Restless ballad of... Look 33:68 Ap 29 '69
Cashing in. Time 93:94 Je 6 '69
Goldstein, R. Something rude showing. Vogue 154:46 Ag 15 '69
Dearmore, T. First angry man of country singers. N. Y. Times
    Mag p32 S 21 '69
Frook, J. Hard times king of song. Life 67:44 N 21 '69
Cantwell, M. Boy named Johnny. Mlle 70:162 N '69
Saal, H. On the spot. Newsweek 75:84 F 2 '70
Hudson, P. It's a boy, but not named Sue. Sr Schol 96:22 Ap
    6 '70
We find (his) first wife. Photop 77-5:58 My '70
My baby was nearly killed the day before he was born. Photop
    77-6:46 Je '70
Fox, W. P. He ain't like nobody. TV Guide 18-24:26 Je 13 '70
Sakol, J. Grit and grace of... McCalls 97:28 Jl '70
(His) love letter to God. Photop 78-2:68 Ag '70
Graham, B. The Johnny Cash I know. Photop 78-3:73 S '70
Miller, F. Back from drugs. Read Dig 97:85 S '70
Shockley, D. G. & Freeman, R. L. Cash on prison reform.
    Chr Cent 87:1157 S 30 '70
Miller, E. Interview. Seventeen 29:122 O '70
Braun, S. Good ole boy. Playboy 17-11:138 N '70
Pitts, M. R. Popular singers on the screen; filmog. Film Fan
    Mo 114:26 D '70
Hickey, N. His mother-in-law is a legend. TV Guide 19-3:41
    Ja 16 '71
My wife's in love with a very young man. Photop 79-2:41 F '71
The house that Cash built. TV Guide 19-13:14 Mr 27 '71
Gallagher, D. I'm growing, changing, becoming. Redbook 137:
    61 Ag '71
Wren, C. S. Winners get scars too. McCalls 98:99 Ag '71
The night (he) watched his brother die. Photop 80-3:76 S '71
Minister of God. Photop 82-4:42 O '72
Vecsey, G. Cash's Gospel Road is renaissance for him. N. Y.
    Times Bio Ed p1919 D '73

CASH, ROSEMARY
Is it better to be Shaft than Uncle Tom? Conversation with Rose-
    mary Clark, Donald Boyle, Heywood Hale Broun. N. Y. Times
    sec 2:11 Ag 26 '73

CASSAVETES, JOHN
Zunser, J. His'n and her'n. Cue 27-23:11 Je 7 '58
Taylor, J. R. Cassavetes in London. Sight & Sound 29-4:177
    Aut '60
Young, C. & Bachman, G. New wave or gesture. Film Q 14-3:
    6 Spg '61
Young, C. West Coast report. Sight & Sound 30-3:137 Sum '61
Mekas, J. Cassavetes, the improvisation. Film Cult 24:8 Spg
    '62

Incoming tide, interview.  Cinema (BH) 1-1:34 '62
Fenin, G.  The face of '63--United States.  Films & Filming 9-
  6:55 Mr '63
Sarris, A.  Oddities and one shots.  Film Cult 28:45 Spg '63
Faces interview.  Cinema (BH) 4-1:33 Spg '68
Austen, D.  Interview.  Films & Filming 14-12:4 S '68
AuWerter, R.  A talk with Cassavetes.  Action 5-1:12 Ja/F '69
Faces of the husbands.  New Yorker 45:32 Mr 15 '69
Guerin, A.  A film to keep the man-child alive.  Life 66:53 My
  9 '69
Bio.  Cur Bio Yrbk 1969:74 '70
Haskell, M.  Three husbands hold court.  Show 1-2:67 F '70
On the scene.  Playboy 17-4:183 Ap '70
New Hollywood is old Hollywood.  Time 96:72 D 7 '70
Gillett, J.  Bio note; filmog.  Focus On F 6:11 Spg '71
Interview.  Playboy 18-7:55 Jl '71
Gittelson, N.  Merry nepotism, 1971.  Harp Baz 105:74 D '71
Harmetz, A.  I'm sorry I couldn't interview Gena...  N. Y.
  Times sec 2:11 F 13 '72
Galluzzo, T.  Movie Making; interview.  Mod Phot 36:32 Je '72
Cassavetes, J.  What's wrong with Hollywood.  Film Cult 19:4
  n. d.
Robert Aldrich comments on Cassavetes.  Dialogue 2:7 '72
Interview with Cassavetes and Peter Falk; Cassavetes filmog as
  director; Biblio.  Dialogue 4:entire issue '72
Interview: on movies, madness and myth.  Viva 2-3:61 D '74
Nolan, J. E.  Films on TV.  Films In R 25-10:616 D '74

CASSEL, JEAN-PIERRE
  Discreet charm, in the French style.  Films Illus 2-22:18 Ap
  '73

CASSIDY, DAVID
  I wanted her to be mean to me.  Photop 79-1:52 Ja '71
  Win a stepson--lose a husband.  Photop 79-3:53 Mr '71
  Raddatz, L.  Dear David--I am 9 years old.  TV Guide 19-21:24
    My 22 '71
  Why too much love turns him off.  Photop 79-5:69 My '71
  David Cassidy's real mother talks.  Photop 79-6:70 Je '71
  David a go-go.  TV Guide 19-33:14 Ag 14 '71
  David!  Newsweek 78:82 Ag 30 '71
  (He) saved my life.  Photop 80-2:95 Ag '71
  David and the whale.  TV Guide 19-42:37 O 16 '71
  Faynard, J.  David.  Life 71:1 O 29 '71
  Surgeons keep him from dying.  Photop 80-4:63 O '71
  David Cassidy and Susan Dey.  Mod Screen 65-12:33 D '71
  First interview with his hush-hush girlfriend.  Photop 80-6:68
    D '71
  The night (he) cried out for his father.  Photop 81-2:45 F '72
  I find (him) very sexy.  Mod Screen 66-2:32 F '72
  Graves, R.  D-day sound was a high-c shriek.  Life 72:3 Mr 24
    '72
  Interview.  Photop 81-3:26 Mr '72

Elvis! David!  New Yorker 48:28 Je 24 '72
Whitney, D.  It's practically a branch of the U.S. mint.  TV
    Guide 20-29:24 Jl 15 '72
I watched drugs kill my best friend.  Mod Screen 66-9:41 S '72
How Bernie stole Bridget from (him).  Photop 83-2:30 F '73
Amid scenes of chaos, David departs.  People 1-16:30 Je 17 '74

CASSIDY, JACK
Win a stepson--lose a husband.  Photop 79-3:53 Mr '71
(His) side of the story.  Silver S 41-10:49 O '71
Shirley Jones walks out on marriage.  Mod Screen 66-4:45 Ap
    '72
Shirley Jones walks out on her husband forever.  Photop 81-4:67
    Ap '72
Shirley Jones is a woman in love--and the man is still Jack Cas-
    sidy.  Photop 82-3:80 S '72
I never stopped loving Jack.  Mod Screen 66-12:30 D '72
Automobile accident.  Photop 83-2:51 F '73

CASSIDY, TED
Rising to the occasion.  TV Guide 13-36:26 S 4 '65

CASSINELLI, DOLORES
Montanye, L.  Interview.  Motion Pic Classic 10:36 Je '20

CASSON, LEWIS
Guthrie, T.  After 20 years, re-enter Dame Sybil.  N.Y. Times
    Mag p62 Ja 27 '57
Sir Lewis and Dame Sybil.  Vogue 129:60 F 15 '57
Team.  New Yorker 33:26 Mr 2 '57
Obit.  N.Y. Times p33 My 17 '69
    Time 93:95 My 23 '69

CASTELLANO, RICHARD
Flatley, G.  The bigger-than-life, classic-tough-guy-with-gentle-
    heart.  TV Guide 20-28:40 Jl 8 '72

CASTLE, DON
Obit.  Screen World 18:232 '67

CASTLE, IRENE
Artists of the tango.  Cosmop 55:408 Ag '13
Patterson, A.  Success of.  Green Book 11:191 F '14
Patterson, A.  Sketch.  Theatre 19:126 Mr '14
Rankin, L.M.  Sketch.  National 40:280 My '14
What is a thé dansant?  Delin 84:10 My '14
Mr. and Mrs. Vernon Castle's new dances for this winter.
    Ladies Home J 31:38 O; 22 N; 24 D '14
Foote, E.  Sketch.  Theatre 21:112 Mr '15
Her gowns.  Green Book 13:1089 Je '15
Duryea, B.  Interview.  Green Book 14:1025 D '15
Ames, H.  Sketch.  Motion Pic Classic 3:30 F '17
Monde, N.  Adventures of a girl reporter in trailing Mrs.

Castle.   Motion Pic 14:117 O '17
Bartlett, R.   Our Irene was the village queen.   Photop 12-6:42
    N '17
Allison, D.   Irene Castle will carry on.   Photop 14-5:79 O '18
Sherwood, C. B.   Interview.   Motion Pic Classic 7:20 O '18
My memories of Vernon Castle.   Everybodys 39:22 N '18 & fol-
    lowing issues.
Naylor, H. S.   Sketch.   Motion Pic 17:32 Je '19
Her summer gowns.   Ladies Home J 39:33 Jl '19
Interview.   Delin 96:166 Ap '20
Hall, G.   Interview.   Motion Pic 20:54 O '20
Patterson, A.   Interview.   Photop 20:42 Je '21
I bobbed my hair.   Ladies Home J 38:1240 '21
Fletcher, A. W.   Interview.   Motion Pic 22:22 N '21
Putting your best foot forward.   Met Mag 56:36 O '22
Dress to suit your personality.   Met Mag 56:42 N '22
My life out of doors.   Met Mag 56:38 D '22
Every woman's duty to look her best.   Met Mag 56:44 Ja '23
At the Embassy Club, London.   Graphic 107:875 Je 16 '23
Terhune, A. P.   Gone to the dogs.   Good House 95:34 N '32
They stand out from the crowd.   Lit Dig 116:9 Jl 29 '33
Allen, F. L.   When America learned to dance.   Scrib 102:11 S
    '37
    Same abridged.   Read Dig 31:104 O '37
Returns to stage.   Newsweek 14:30 Ag 14 '39
Sketch.   Life 7:18 Ag 21 '39
Adler, B. S.   Then and now.   N. Y. Times Mag p42 D 10 '50
Duncan, D.   Irene Castle in 1956.   Dance 30:87 O '56
Duncan, D.   Irene Castle comeback.   Dance 32:74 Mr '58
Flesh of the stars.   Newsweek 52:97 D 8 '58
Castles in the air; excerpt.   Dance 33:67 Ja '59
Stainton, W. H.   Irene Castle; filmog.   Films In R 13-6:347 Je/
    Jl '62
Smith, F. L.   Irene Castle.   Films In R 13-7:441 Ag/S '62
Obit.   Classic Film Collect 23:46 Spg '69 (Reprint Washington
    Post)
Brock, A.   The story of.   Classic Film Collect 24:18 Sum '69

CASTLE, JO ANN
    Photoplay forum.   Photop 80-4:8 O '71
    How I told my children about my divorce.   Photop 82-4:56 O '72

CASTLE, PEGGY
    Apple of the marshal's eye.   TV Guide 8-23:9 Je 4 '60
    Crivello, K.   Peggy Castle; filmog.   Films In R 25-1:64 Ja '74
    Obit.   Classic Film Collect 41:53 Win '73
        Screen World p232 '74

CASTLETON, BARBARA
    Blame (her)--and Cleopatra!   Photop 15-4:40 Mr '19

CAULFIELD, JOAN
    Sketch.   Life 14:41 Ap 12 '43

Littlefield, C.   A blonde with brains.   Silver S 17-1:58 N '46
Franchey, J.   Interviewer's delight.   Silver S 18-10:34 Ag '48
Caulfield, J.   Don't ever sell glamour short.   Silver S 20-5:40
   Mr '50
Minoff, P.   Cover girl makes good.   Cue 23-39:13 S 25 '54

CAVALIERI, LINA
   Shorey, J.   The romance of Cavalieri and Muratore.   Photop
      15-4:32 Mr '19
   Obit.   Etude 62:193 Ap '44

CAVANAUGH, HOBART
   Obit.   Screen World 2:233 '51

CAVANI, LILIANA
   Note; filmog.   Films Illus 4-39:84 N '74

CAZALE, JOHN
   Godsons.   Time 99:71 Ap 3 '72

CERUSICO, ENZO
   Goodwin, F.   The operation was a failure...but the patient sur-
      vived.   TV Guide 17-22:12 My 31 '69

CESANA, RENZO
   Latin lover.   Time 58:104 N 5 '51
   Lonesome guy.   Newsweek 38:58 N 5 '51
   Woo-pitcher gets network.   Life 32:63 F 11 '52
   Obit.   Screen World 22:236 '71

CHADWICK, HELENE
   Rosemon, E.   Interview.   Motion Pic Classic 7:41 Ja '19
   Lee, D.   Interview.   Motion Pic p44 Ag '20
   Sketch.   Photop 18:29 Ag '20
   Fletcher, A. W.   Interview.   Motion Pic Classic 11:22 Ja '21
   Naylor, H. S.   Interview.   Motion Pic 21:24 Jl '21
   Shelley, H.   Interview.   Motion Pic 14:62 Mr '22
   Handy, T. B.   Interview.   Motion Pic 24:20 Ag '22

CHAGRIN, JULIAN
   Morley, S.   Three is one.   Plays & Players 16-8:32 My '69

CHAKIRIS, GEORGE
   Zunser, J.   Chat with Chakiris.   Cue 31-33:10 Ag 18 '62
   Catching up with...   Mod Screen 66-2:29 F '72

CHALMERS, THOMAS
   Obit.   Screen World 18:233 '67

CHAMBERLAIN, RICHARD
   Rising star.   Film R p43 '63/64
   Kildare as Hamlet.   Time 96:70 N 16 '70
   A pride of Hamlets.   Plays & Players 18-5:17 F '71

Alas, Poor Ilyich.   Vogue 157:70 Mr 15 '71
Kalem, T. E.   New Barrymore.   Time 97:74 Ap 26 '71
Andrews, E.   The change in (him).   Films Illus 1-7:6 Ja '72
Buck, J.   Interview.   Plays & Players 19-11:23 Ag '72
Buck, J.   (He) is not dull!   Interview 25:15 S '72
Chamberlain as Byron; the first pop star.   Films Illus 2-17:12
    N '72
Gow, G.   Interview; filmog.   Films & Filming 19-2:13 N '72
Stoop, N. M.   Lady Caroline Lamb and Richard Chamberlain.
    After Dark 5-12:22 Ap '73
Stoneman, E.   The renaissance of Richard Chamberlain.   Show
    3-3:38 My '73
Whatever happened to your favorite Dr. Kildare?   Photop 85-3:
    24 Mr '74

CHAMBERS, MARILYN
    Cohen, S.   Interview.   Interview 3-9:9 S '73
    Showcase.   Show 3-6:36 S '73
    Goldstein, A.   Conversation with Marilyn Chambers.   Oui 3-2:69
        F '74

CHAMBLISS, WOODY
    Raddatz, L.   The Dodge City gang.   TV Guide 20-12:14 Mr 18
        '72

CHAMPION, GOWER
    Television revue team.   Life 26:25 Mr 7 '49
    Rising star.   Film R p113 '53/54
    Lewis, E.   The dancing Champions.   Cue 24-10:12 Mr 12 '55
    It's the sponsor who pays.   TV Guide 4-37:24 S 15 '56
    Whitney, D.   Jazzing up Oscar.   TV Guide 17-15:25 Ap 12 '69
    Salute of the week.   Cue 39-36:1 S 5 '70
    Stasio, M.   ...and still Champion.   Cue 43-37:9 S 30 '74
    Stock, E.   Mack and Mabel; getting the show off the road.   New
        York 7-40:49 O 7 '74
    Bio note.   Films Illus 4-38:46 O '74

CHAMPION, MARGE
    Television revue team.   Life 26:25 Mr 7 '49
    Rising star.   Film R p113 '53/54
    Lewis, E.   The dancing Champions.   Cue 24-10:12 Mr 12 '55
    It's the sponsor who pays.   TV Guide 4-37:24 S 15 '56
    Dancing for the Lord.   Newsweek 80:98 O 9 '72

CHANDLER, HELEN
    Hall, G.   Sketch.   Motion Pic 42:66 N '31
    Vine, N. N.   Cute.   Silver S 2-3:62 Ja '32
    Obit.   Film R p21 '66/68
        Screen World 17:234 '66

CHANDLER, JEFF
    My favorite role.   Film R p25 '55/56
    Obit.   Film R p28 '61/62

CHANDLER, JOHN DAVIS
    Note; partial filmog.   Films & Filming 19-9:66 Je '73

CHANDLER, LANE
    Carlisle, H.   Interview.   Motion Pic Classic 27:55 Je '28

CHANEY, LON SR.
    Cheatham, M. S.   Interview.   Motion Pic 10:38 Mr '20
    Winship, M.   Interview.   Photop 20:25 Jl '21
    His makeup.   Photop 21:43 Mr '22
    His darkest hour.   Classic 15:47 S '22
    Handy, T. B.   Interview.   Motion Pic 24:42 Ja '23
    Goldbeck, W.   The star sinister.   Classic 18:62 N '23
    Currie, H.   Interview.   Motion Pic 30:44 S '25
    Howe, M.   The man who made homeliness pay.   Motion Pic
        Classic 23:34 Mr '26
    St. Johns, I.   Sketch.   Photop 31:58 F '27
    Master craftsman of makeup.   Motion Pic 34:32 Ag '27
    Why I prefer the grotesque characters.   Theatre 46:36 O '27
    Tully, J.   Work of.   Vanity Fair 29:55 F '28
    Steele, J. H.   Sketch.   Motion Pic Classic 27:23 My '28
    Nyvelt, E. B.   The mystery man of the movies.   World Today
        53:265 F '29
    Cruikshank, H.   Sketch.   Motion Pic Classic 29:43 Mr '29
    York, C.   Sketch.   Photop 30:49 Je '30
    Ramsey, W.   Interview.   Motion Pic Classic 31:24 Je '30
    Hall, G.   Interview.   Motion Pic 39:59 Jl '30
    Obit.   Lit Dig 106:37 S 13 '30
    Chrisman, J. E.   The friend of the crook.   Motion Pic Classic
        32:41 O '30
    In memoriam.   Silver S 1-1:51 N '30
    Donnell, D.   A martyr to the movies.   Motion Pic 40:34 D '30
    Webster, M.   Interview.   Movie Classic 2:33 Ap '32
    Pryor, N.   Interview.   Movie Classic 3:54 Ja '33
    In memoriam.   Motion Pic 45:53 Je '33
    Phillips, A.   Man of a thousand faces.   8mm Collect 10:8 Win
        '64
    Filmog.   8mm Collect 10:10 Win '64
    Davy, D.   I heard Lon Chaney.   Film Fan Mo 61/62:22 Jl/Ag
        '66
    Braff, R. E.   A Lon Chaney index; filmog.   Films In R 21-4:217
        Ap '70
    Letters.   Films In R 21-5:312 My '70
    Bodeen, D.   Man of a thousand faces; filmog.   Focus On R 3:21
        My/Ag '70
    Mr. Monster.   Famous Monsters 69:6 S '70
    Case, D. E.   Letter.   Films In R 21-8:517 O '70
    Poston, D. H.   Letter.   Films In R 22-2:112 F '71
    Ames, A.   Letter.   Films In R 22-3:182 Mr '71
    Star, S. A.   (His) favorite joke.   Gore Creatures 20:21 S '71
    Shay, D.   Letter.   Focus On F 12:16 Win '72
    Peed, B.   In defense of...   Classic Film Collect 38:6 Spg '73

CHANEY, LON JR.
Valler, W. L.   Sentimental monster.   Silver S 13-9:42 Jl '43
Son of Chaney.   Castle of Frankenstein 4:8 '64
Bojarski, R.   The Lon Chaney Jr. story.   Castle of Frankenstein
7:38 n. d.
Filmog.   Castle of Frankenstein 7:44 n. d.
Interview.   Castle of Frankenstein 10:26 F '66
Interview.   Photon #20 n. d.
Obit.   Classic Film Collect 40:58 Fall '73 (Reprint N. Y. Daily
News)
Film 2-7:15 O '73
Films & Filming 20-2:80 N '73
N. Y. Daily News p4 Jl 14 '73
N. Y. Times Bio Ed p1109 Jl '73
Screen World p232 '74
Parish, J. R. & Pitts, M. R.   Lon Chaney Jr.; filmog.   Films
In R 24-9:529 N '73
Lazear, W.   Letter.   Films In R 25-6:383 Je/Jl '74

CHANEY, NORMAN "Chubby"
Maltin, L.   Our gang; Our gang filmog.   Film Fan Mo 66:3 D
'66

CHANNING, CAROL
Water, R.   A vamp there is.   Cue 24-43:13 O 29 '55
The wide-eyed Miss Channing.   TV Guide 6-1:17 Ja 4 '58
Back to burlesque for the third time.   TV Guide 14-50:12 D 10
'66
Salute of the week.   Cue 38-11:1 Mr 15 '69
Mann, R.   Channing's prime time.   N. Y. Times Bio Ed S 6 '70
Pacheco, P.   Gentlemen prefer Carol.   After Dark 6-6:24 O '73
Pacheco, P.   Getting heady over Halston.   After Dark 7-3:68
Jl '74
Hay, R. C.   She's her own best friend.   Interview 4-11:41 N '74

CHAPIN, BENJAMIN
Conlon, L.   Impersonation of Abraham Lincoln.   Motion Pic 15:
46 Mr '18

CHAPIN, LAUREN
Readin' ritin' and rehearsal.   TV Guide 4-38:20 S 22 '56

CHAPLIN, CHARLES
Eubank, V.   Interview.   Motion Pic 9:75 Mr '15
Sketch.   Motion Pic 9:93 Jl '15
McGuirk, C. J.   Motion Pic 9:121 Jl '15 (and following issues)
How I made my success.   Theatre 22:120 S '15
Gaddis, I.   Sketch.   Motion Pic 11:47 Ap '16
Fiske, M. M.   Art of.   Harper 62:494 My 6 '16
Grau, R.   Salary of.   Harper 62:496 My 6 '16
Raymond, C. S.   Sketch.   Green Book 16:204 Ag '16
Todd, S. W.   Personal side of.   Motion Pic Classic 3:41 S '16
Moore, R. F.   Falling, on and off the screen.   Motion Pic

13:39 Mr '17
Briscoe, J.   Sketch.   Motion Pic 13:43 Ap '17
Cram, M.   Taking Charlie seriously.   Theatre 26:10 Jl '17
Hilbert, J. E.   A day with Chaplin on location.   Motion Pic 14:
    59 N '17
Carr, M. C.   Sketch.   Motion Pic Classic 8:18 Ap '19
Visit to London.   Graphic 104:296 S 10 '21
Sketch.   Sat R 132:400 O 1 '21
Swaffer, H.   Visit to London.   Graphic 104:434 O 15 '21
Impressions of travels in Europe.   Photop 21:64 D '21 (and fol-
    lowing issues)
Sheridan, C.   The strange little man with the great big heart.
    Met Mag 55:27 F '22
Sketch.   Canadian Bookman 4:130 Ap '22
Leight, E.   How Charlie does it.   World Work (Lon) 39:441 Ap
    '22
Carr, H.   Interview.   Motion Pic 23:22 My '22
Carr, H.   Compared with Harold Lloyd.   Motion Pic 24:55 N '22
Birthplace in London.   Mus Courier 86:8 Je 7 '23
Higgins, B.   Appreciation.   Spectator 131:318 S 8 '23
Carr, H.   His production of A woman in Paris.   Motion Pic 25:
    28 D '23
Becomes a motion picture reformer.   Cur Opin 75:708 D '23
Wilson, B. F.   Interview.   Theatre 39:20 Ja '24
Hall, G. & Fletcher, A. W.   Interview.   Motion Pic 27:24 F '24
Grein, J. T.   As film producer.   Ill Lon N 164:462 Mr 15 '24
Tully, J.   The loneliest man in Hollywood.   Classic 19:40 Mr '24
Carr, H.   Interview.   Motion Pic 30:31 N '25
Underhill, H.   That Chaplin complex.   Motion Pic Classic 23:56
    Ap '26
Hall, M.   The changeable Chaplin.   Motion Pic Classic 23:16 Ag
    '26
Ennis, B.   How fame came to him with borrowed clothes.   Mo-
    tion Pic Classic 23:36 Jl '26
Green, I. E.   Who made Chaplin?   Motion Pic 32:49 S '26
St. Johns, A. R.   Matrimonial troubles.   Photop 31:30 Ja '27
Manners, D.   The riddle of the Chaplin marriage.   Motion Pic
    33:39 Mr '27
Gilmore, F.   The change in Chaplin.   Motion Pic Classic 26:21
    Ja '28
Smith, R.   Has he lost his humor?   Theatre 48:22 S '28
Donnell, D.   His mother.   Motion Pic 36:31 D '28
Hall, G.   Interview.   Motion Pic 37:28 My '29
Whitaker, A.   Home of.   Photop 36:40 Je '29
To play Napoleon?   Graphic 127:508 Mr 29 '30
Fairbanks, D. Jr.   Appreciation.   Vanity Fair 34:47 Ag '30
Bravermann, B. G.   Charlie.   Theatre Guild 7-12:23 S '30
Kendall, S.   Why Chaplin won't talk.   Silver S 1-1:16 N '30
Frink, C.   Sketch.   Motion Pic Classic 32:30 Ja '31
Ockham, D.   Tribute to genius.   Sat R 151:299 F 28 '31
Two Chaplins.   Graphic 131:346 Mr 7 '31
Mr. Chaplin throws a party.   Graphic 131:322 Mr 7 '31
Betts, E.   Chaplin's pantomime.   Weekend R 3:354 Mr 7 '31

Dumb shows and noise.  R of Rs (Lon) 81:42 Mr '31
Chaplin abroad.   Liv Age 340:410 Je '31
Vantine, W. C. K.   Sketch.   Motion Pic 41:34 Je '31
Spensley, D.   Hollywood wants him to return.   Motion Pic 42:49
     S '31
Manners, D.   What love has cost him.   Movie Classic 1:24 N '31
Shallert, E.   Sketch.   Movie Classic 2:42 Je '32
Janeway, D.   His sons enter the movies.   Movie Classic 3:30 S
     '32
Derr, E.   His latest romance.   Movie Classic 3:29 O '32
Babcock, M.   His headline history.   Movie Classic 3:42 N '32
Moffitt, C. F.   Censorship for interviews Hollywood's latest wild
     idea...   Cinema Dig 2-5:9 Ja 9 '33
Schallert, E.   Sketch.   Motion Pic 44:34 Ja '33
Taviner, R.   In search of happiness.   Photop 43:34 My '33
Romance with Paulette Goddard.   Movie Classic 4:20 Ag '33
Autobiographical.   Womans Home C 59:7 S '33 (and following is-
     sues)
Lee, S.   Immortals of the screen.   Motion Pic 46:32 O '33
Schallert, E.   Expenditures for his sons.   Motion Pic 46:41 Ja
     '34
Nicholai, B.   Story of his marriage to Goddard.   Movie Classic
     6:40 Je '34
Tully, J.   Can he come back?   Motion Pic 49:30 Jl '35
Hogarth, D.   His quest for love.   Movie Classic 9:30 O '35
Eastman, M.   Appreciation.   Stage 13:26 N '35
Simpson, G.   Groucho tells how he "discovered" the genius of
     Chaplin.   Motion Pic 51:39 My '36
Wilson, C.   Sketch.   Photop 50:25 S '36
Waley, H. D.   Is this Charlie?   Sight & Sound 7-25:10 Spg '38
Sketch.   Photop 53:46 Ap '39
Hyde, F.   Chaplin.   Cue 7-25:9 Ap 15 '39
Kalich, J.   Exploding the Chaplin myth.   Screen Book 22-6:70 Ja
     '40
His marriage to Oona O'Neill.   Life 14:31 Je 28 '43
His marriage to Oona O'Neill.   Newsweek 21:46 Je 28 '43
His marriage to Oona O'Neill.   Time 41:70 Je 28 '43
Kilgallen, D.   Sketch.   Photop 23:21 Je '43
Reproduction of early screen plays.   New Statesman 26:232 O 9
     '43
The case of Carol Ann.   Newsweek 25:40 Ja 15 '45
Huff, T.   Index to his films.   Sight & Sound (sup) #3 Mr '45
Scheuer, P. K.   From rags to riches.   Colliers 119:15 Ap 12 '47
His role in Monsieur Verdoux.   Newsweek 29:98 Ap 28 '47
Brown, J. M.   Charlie-into-Charles.   Sat R 30:24 My 3 '47
His new film Monsieur Verdoux.   Time 49:98 My 5 '47
Lewis, R.   Story of.   Theatre Arts 31:32 Je '47
Payne, R.   The man whose comic genius and pathos have given
     pleasure to millions.   World R 2:34 Ap '49
Agee, J.   Early work of.   Life 27:76 S 5 '49
Stonier, G. W.   After Limelight?   New Statesman 45:581 My 16
     '53
Gibbons, T.   Chaplin as Chaplin.   Film 3:16 F '55

Dyer, P. J.   The true face of man.   Films & Filming 4-12:13
   S '58
Beaumont, C.   Chaplin.   Playboy 7:81 Mr '60
Sarris, A.   Pantheon directors; filmog.   Film Cult 28:2 Spg '63
Brownlow, K.   Watching Chaplin direct A countess from Hong
   Kong.   Film Cult 40:2 Spg '66
Brooks, L.   Chaplin remembered.   Film Cult 40:5 Spg '66
Ginsberg, A. & Orlovsky, P.   A letter to Chaplin.   Film Cult
   40:7 Spg '66
Brownlow, K.   The Countess set.   Film 46:4 Sum '66
Hoover, M. L.   Chaplin on Chaplinism.   Tulane Drama R 11:
   188 Fall '66
The complete screenplay of The gold rush compiled by Timothy
   J. Lyons.   Cinema (BH) 4-2:17 Sum '68
Rosen, P. G.   The Chaplin world-view.   Cinema J 9-1:2 Fall
   '69
Chaplin's Monsieur Verdoux press conference.   Film Comment
   5-4:34 Win '69
Hickey, T.   Political and moral offences accusations.   Film
   Comment 5-4:44 Win '69
Quixote with a bowler.   Time 95:54 Ja 5 '70
Bloom, C.   Cue salutes.   Cue 39-13:34 Mr 28 '70
Mills, I.   Chaplin's Mutual films.   Velvet Light 3:2 Win '71/72
What directors are saying.   Action 7-1:36 Ja/F '72
Phillips, G. D.   Chaplin revisits us.   America 126:261 Mr 11
   '72
Wolf, W.   Welcome back; interview.   Cue 41-12:2 Mr 18 '72
People are talking about.   Vogue 159:126 Ap 1 '72
Schickel, R.   Hail Chaplin, the early Chaplin.   N. Y. Times
   Mag p12 Ap 2 '72
Kanfer, S.   Re-enter... smiling and waving.   Time 99:65 Ap 10
   '72
Reborn.   New Yorker 48:37 Ap 15 '72
Like old times.   Time 99:72 Ap 17 '72
Oberbeck, S. K.   Charlie comes home.   Newsweek 79:94 Ap 17
   '72
Bergen, C.   Love feast for Charlie; interview.   Life 72:86 Ap
   21 '72
Meryman, R.   Interview.   Life 72:89 Ap 21 '72
Graves, R.   Meryman is our man, but Candy is dandy.   Life
   72:3 Ap 21 '72
Modern times.   Nation 214:518 Ap 24 '72
Handel medallion presented by Mayor Lindsay.   New Yorker 48:
   33 Ap 29 '72
DeLucovich, J. P.   Chaplin comes home.   Harp Baz 105:132 Ap
   '72
Knight, A.   One man's movie.   Sat R 55:14 My 6 '72
The tramp for television.   Films & Filming 18-8:14 My '72
Dunne, G. H.   I remember Chaplin.   Commonweal 96:303 Je 2
   '72
Wolf, W.   Elder statesman of the arts.   Show 2-4:33 Je '72
Lyons, T. J.   Roland Totheroh interviewed on Chaplin films.
   Film Cult 53/54/55:230 Spg '72

Sieger, E.   Chaplin.   Focus 7:33 Spg '72
Frederickson, P.   Goodbye Charlie.   Sat Eve Post 244:56 Sum
    '72
Lee, R.   The five Chaplins.   Classic Film Collect 37:36 Win '72
Morgan, E. P.   Letter.   Filmograph 3-1:47 '72
Canby, V.   Bravo Chaplin! Bravo Tati!   N. Y. Times sec 2:1 Jl
    8 '73
Canby, V.   Once a king always a king.   N. Y. Times sec 2:1 Ja
    20 '74
Evans, C.   The sounds of silence.   Mise-en-Scene 1:23 n. d.
Eyman, S.   The once and future king.   Classic Film Collect 44:
    10 Fall '74
Tuch, R.   Chaplin and the American avant garde.   F. Lib Q 7-
    2:17 '74

CHAPLIN, SYDNEY (1885-1965)
    Sketch.   Photop 18:63 Jl '20
    Carr, H.   Interview.   Classic 19:21 Ap '24
    Ryan, D.   Interview.   Motion Pic Classic 22:38 Ja '26
    Obit.   Film R p45 '65/66
        Film R p21 '66/68

CHAPLIN, SYDNEY (1926-)
    Water, R.   The sage of Sydney.   Cue 26-2:12 Ja 12 '57

CHAPLIN, VICTORIA
    Newsmakers.   Newsweek 76:65 D 14 '70
    People.   Time 96:45 D 14 '70

CHAPMAN, EDYTHE
    Peltret, E.   Interview.   Motion Pic Classic 11:34 N '20

CHAPMAN, LEIGH
    Portrait of a worried woman.   TV Guide 14-27:20 Jl 2 '66

CHAPMAN, MARGUERITE
    Hendricks, H.   A kid sister grows up.   Silver S 13-12:34 O '43
    Wilson, E.   A change in Maggie.   Silver S 17-7:37 My '47

CHARISSE, CYD
    Tildesley, A. L.   Cyd's secrets of romance.   Silver S 24-5:36
        Mr '54

CHARLESON, MARY
    Sketch.   Motion Pic Supp 1:62 O '15
    McKelvie, M. G.   Interview.   Motion Pic 14:77 O '17
    Haskins, H.   Sketch.   Motion Pic 17:47 F '19

CHARRIER, JACQUES
    Spotlight on...   Unifrance 49:12 Ja '59

CHASE, BARRIE
    She became a star in 60 minutes.   TV Guide 6-50:12 D 13 '58

CHASE, CHARLIE
   Gill, S. The funnymen. 8mm Collect 11:12 Spg '65; 12:6 Sum
      '65

CHASE, ILKA
   The philosophy of being a woman. Vogue 98:78 N 15 '41
   Are you attractive to women? Vogue 100:52 N 15 '42
   Open letter from. Vogue 102:82 S 15 '43
   She can bake a cherry pie. Cue 12-51:10 D 18 '43
   Me and my clothes. Vogue 107:142 Mr 15 '46
   Sketch. Ladies Home J 63:4 My '46

CHATBURN, JEAN
   New face. Cinema Arts 1-1:38 Je '37

CHATTERTON, RUTH
   Tinee, M. Interview. Green Book 9:1062 Je '13
   Collins, C. W. Success of. Green Book 12:413 S '14
   Interview. Cosmop 58:328 F '15
   Sketch. Strand (NY) 49:271 Mr '15
   How she plans her gowns. Green Book 14:261 Ag '15
   Albert, K. Sketch. Photop 35:64 My '29
   Hall, G. Sketch. Motion Pic 37:50 Jl '29
   Conti, M. Shopping with. Motion Pic 38:68 N '29
   Sketch. Photop 37:1 F '30
   Walker, H. L. Interview. Motion Pic 40:33 Ag '30
   Ramsey, W. Interview. Motion Pic Classic 32:38 O '30
   Sketch. Fortune 2:40 O '30
   Hall, L. Sketch. Photop 39:38 Ja '31
   Lane, J. That amazing girl. Silver S 1-5:27 Mr '31
   Biery, R. Interview. Photop 39:64 Ap '31
   Rush, D. The unknown Chatterton. Silver S 1-11:35 S '31
   Rivers, A. Sketch. Movie Classic 1:37 Ja '32
   Burden, J. Sketch. Movie Classic 2:34 My '32
   Pryor, N. Sketch. Motion Pic 44:56 Ag '32
   Bannon, J. Divorced from Ralph Forbes. Movie Classic 3:31
      S '32
   The Chatterton-Brent romance. Movie Classic 3:15 O '32
   Moffitt, C. F. Censorship for interviews Hollywood's latest wild
      idea. Cinema Dig 2-5:9 Ja 9 '33
   Hall, G. Her second marriage. Motion Pic 44:50 Ja '33
   Grant, J. Her divorce and marriage. Movie Classic 4:26 Mr
      '33
   Lee, S. She tells what's wrong with movies. Motion Pic 45:
      50 Je '33
   Five years ago today. Photop 45:108 D '33
   Lee, S. Interview. Movie Classic 5:21 D '33
   How Sylvia changed her nose and figure. Photop 45:36 Ja '34
   Dillon, F. Separated from George Brent. Movie Classic 6:32
      Ja '34
   Returns to films. Lit Dig 121:20 Ja 11 '36
   Sketch. Newsweek 11:23 F 7 '38

CHATTERTON, THOMAS
    Sketch.  Motion Pic 9:110 Ap '15
    How to get in moving pictures.  Motion Pic 12:123 Ag '16
    Courtlandt, R.  Home of.  Motion Pic Classic 4:15 Ag '17

CHATTON, SYDNEY
    Obit.  Screen World 18:233 '67

CHEKHOV, MICHAEL
    Chekhov--from Moscow.  Lions R 3-2:no p# Ja '44

CHERKASOV, NIKOLAI
    Buck, T.  Cherkasov's Don Quixote.  Sight & Sound 27-6:320
        Aut '58
    Obit.  Screen World 18:233 '67

CHERRILL, VIRGINIA
    Matthews, J.  Sketch.  Movie Classic 2:31 My '32
    Harrison, H.  The Grant that took Virginia.  Silver S 4-7:47 My
        '34

CHEVALIER, MAURICE
    Macaulay, T.  Sketch.  Theatre 48:46 S '28
    Moen, L.  Sketch.  Motion Pic 36:76 D '28
    Reeve, W.  Interview.  Motion Pic 37:50 Je '29
    Hall, G.  Sketch.  Motion Pic Classic 30:23 N '29
    Cruikshank, H.  Interview.  Motion Pic 39:44 Je '30
    Busby, M.  Compared with Lawrence Tibbett.  Photop 38:34 Je
        '30
    Sketch.  Fortune 2:41 O '30
    Williams, V.  Sketch.  Graphic 130:440 D 6 '30
    Goldbeck, E.  Sketch.  Motion Pic Classic 32:33 D '30
    Grayson, C.  Sketch.  Motion Pic 41:48 F '31
    Harris, R.  The man with two souls.  Silver S 1-8:59 Je '31
    Fairbanks, D. Jr.  Appreciation.  Vanity Fair 37:55 N '31
    Service, F.  Interview.  Motion Pic 43:26 F '32
    Winters, D.  Sketch.  Movie Classic 2:29 Mr '32
    Collins, F. L.  Sketch.  Good House 94:44 Je '32
    Hall, G.  Sketch.  Motion Pic 43:44 Je '32
    The bubble of fame.  Windsor 76:244 Jl '32
    Rice, L.  Sketch.  Motion Pic 44:33 O '32
    Calhoun, D.  His divorce.  Movie Classic 3:42 O '32
    Moffitt, C. F.  Censorship for interviews Hollywood's latest wild
        idea.  Cinema Dig 2-5:9 Ja 9 '33
    Maxwell, V.  His divorce.  Photop 43:69 F '33
    Ewin, D.  Maurice Chevalier's code.  Silver S 3-5:26 Mr '33
    Hall, G.  Interview.  Movie Classic 4:51 Ap '33
    Ergenbright, E. L.  Answers questions about himself.  Motion
        Pic 45:58 Je '33
    Lyon, H.  How he makes love.  Photop 44:30 Ag '33
    Manners, D.  Romance rumors.  Motion Pic 46:49 S '33
    Sketch.  Theatre World 24:34 Jl '35
    Maurice Chevalier.  Visages 5:entire issue O '36

His one-man show in Manhattan.   Time 49:66 Mr 24 '47
The mature Chevalier.   Newsweek 30:87 N 3 '47
Maughan, R.   Man about town at home.   Silver S 18-4:44 F '48
Notes from his memory book.   Vogue 114:128 O 1 '49
Minoff, P.   Notes on TV.   Cue 24-50:25 D 17 '55
Corneau, E. N.   I remember Chevalier.   Classic Film Collect
     28:16 Fall '70
Phillips, M.   Chevalier here to lure readers, not listeners.
     N. Y. Times Bio Ed O 6 '70
Obit.   Classic Film Collect 34:X-3 Spg '72
     Cur Bio 33:45 F '72
     Film R p12 '72/73
     N. Y. Times p1 Ja 2 '72
     N. Y. Times Bio Ed Ja 2 '72
     Newsweek 79:68 Ja 10 '72
     Time 99:74 Ja 10 '72
Cooper, A.   Magnificent Maurice.   Newsweek 79:68 Ja 10 '72
Sketch.   Time 99:74 Ja 10 '72
Mamoulian, Maurice Chevalier 1888-1972.   N. Y. Times Bio Ed
     Ja 16 '72
People.   Time 99:31 Ja 24 '72
Adieu Maurice.   Continental Film R p10 F '72
Farewell to a legend.   Show 2-1:41 Mr '72
There is joy.   Photop 81-4:68 Ap '72
Monsees, R. A.   Maurice Chevalier 1888-1972; filmog.   Films
     In R 23-5:267 My '72


CHIEF THUNDER CLOUD
     (See WILLIAMS, SCOTT T.)


CHILDERS, NAOMI
     Sketch.   Green Book 13:1070 Je '15
     Handy, T. B.   Interview.   Motion Pic Classic 9:26 F '20
     Delvigne, D.   Interview.   Motion Pic 20:68 N '20
     Bruce, B.   Interview.   Motion Pic 22:52 O '21


CHOUREAU, ETCHIKA
     Do you know (her)?   Unifrance 33:28 D '54/Ja '55
     Nichols, M.   Foreign accent in starlets.   Coronet 40:52 Ag '56


CHRISTIAN, LINDA
     Sketch.   Life 19:53 S 3 '45
     Schroeder, C.   Sketch.   Photop 32:48 My '48
     MacDonald, E.   Truly a love story.   Silver S 19-7:30 My '49
     Pritchett, F.   Love story of the stars.   Silver S 20-5:26 Mr
          '50
     Power, Mrs. T.   So it is with Ty and me.   Silver S 21-1:22 N
          '50
     Balling, F. D.   Happy parents at last.   Silver S 22-7:42 My '52
     MacDonald, E.   Exploding those Ty-Linda rumors.   Silver S 23-
          10:40 Ag '53
     Wilson, E.   Once more for Linda.   Silver S 24-2:24 D '53

CHRISTIANS, MADY
    Sketch.    Stage 11:13 D '33
    Sketch.    Vanity Fair 42:51 Ap '34
    Hamilton, S.    Sketch.    Photop 46:70 S '34
    Keats, P.    The girl all Hollywood is talking about.    Silver S 5-2:
        18 D '34
    Gresham, W. L.    Interview.    Theatre Arts 29:219 Ap '45
    Bio Sketch.    Cur Bio 6 '45

CHRISTIE, JULIE
    Rising stars.    Film R p53 '65/66
    (She) talks about working with directors.    Action 1-2:12 N/D '66
    Ehrlich, H.    Warren & Julie, together at last.    Look 35:70 Je 1
        '71
    Atlas, J. & Guerin, A.    Robert Altman, Julie Christie and War-
        ren Beatty make the western real.    Show 2-6:18 Ag '71
    Eyles, A.    Bio note; filmog.    Focus On F 16:9 Aut '73
    Filmog.    Films and Filming 20-10:64 Jl '74

CHRISTINA, MARIA
    Palmer, C.    The happy Aumonts.    Silver S 16-10:35 Ag '46

CHRISTINE, VIRGINIA
    Hoaglin, J. L.    The face is familiar.    Hollywood Stu 6-8:10 D
        '71

CHRISTOPHER, JORDAN
    Lerman, L.    Four most likely to succeed.    Mlle 65:158 S '67

CHRISTY, ANN
    Uselton, R. A.    The Wampus baby stars.    Films In R 21-2:73
        F '70

CHRYSLER, BARBARA
    Pounding home a point.    TV Guide 20-8:10 F 19 '72

CHURCHILL, MARGUERITE
    Hall, G.    Sketch.    Motion Pic 39:40 F '30
    York, C.    Sketch.    Photop 37:68 My '30
    Reid, M.    Leading lady--aged 19.    Silver S 1-2:36 D '30

CHURCHILL, SARAH
    Sarah's on her own.    Cue 18-36:15 S 3 '49
    Minoff, P.    Charm ain't enough.    Cue 20-44:22 N 3 '51
    Sarah and Shakespeare.    TV Guide 2-16:17 Ap 16 '54

CHURSINA, LYUDMILA
    Note.    Int F G 10:335 '73

CIANELLI, EDUARDO
    Sketch.    Photop 51:4 S '37
    Williams, W.    But not so wicked.    Silver S 7-12:28 D '37
    Poles, P.    Cianelli's films; filmog.    Films In R 20-10:640 D '69

Obit.   Classic Film Collect 25:extra 2 Fall '69
  Film R p15 '70/71
  N. Y. Times p47 O 10 '69
  Screen World 21:234 '70
Letters.   Films In R 21-2:124 F '70

CILENTO, DIANE
  The stars of tomorrow.   Film R p47 '55/56
  Separated, but more than friends.   Mod Screen 66-3:36 Mr '72

CIOFFI, CHARLES
  Taylor, F.   How to make it in pictures... if you don't mind being
    the villain.   Hollywood Stu 6-8:36 D '71

CITTI, FRANCO
  Lane, J. F.   The face of '63--Italy.   Films & Filming 9-7:11
    Ap '63

CLAIR, ETHLYNE
  Uselton, R. A.   The Wampus baby stars.   Films In R 21-2:73
    F '70

CLAIRE, BERNICE
  Manners, D.   Sketch.   Motion Pic Classic 30:51 F '30
  Sketch.   Photop 37:53 Mr '30
  Hollywood cavalcade.   Classic Film Collect 33:27 Win '71

CLAIRE, INA
  Smith, F. J.   Interview.   N. Y. Drama Ag 6 '13
  Autobiographical.   Green Book 10:559 O '13
  Dodge, W. P.   Sketch.   Theatre 24:70 Ag '16
  Mantle, B.   Sketch.   Green Book 18:985 D '17
  Interview.   Music Courier 77:6 Ag 8 '18
  Patterson, A.   Sketch.   Theatre 31:168 Mr '20
  Sloan, J. V.   Appreciation.   Drama 17:107 Ja '27
  Waterbury, R.   Marries John Gilbert.   Photop 36:30 Jl '29
  Hall, G.   Sketch.   Motion Pic 38:58 Ag '29
  Calhoun, D.   Her wedding to John Gilbert.   Motion Pic 38:50 S
    '29
  Spensley, D.   Interview.   Motion Pic 39:58 Mr '30
  Manners, D.   Sketch.   Motion Pic Classic 33:24 My '31
  Calhoun, D.   Her divorce from John Gilbert.   Movie Classic
    1:36 O '31
  Calhoun, D.   Why her marriage with John Gilbert failed.   Motion
    Pic 42:28 N '31
  Walker, H. L.   What Hollywood has done to her.   Motion Pic
    Classic 43:34 Ap '32
  Moffitt, C. F.   Censorship for interviews Hollywood's latest wild
    idea.   Cinema Dig 2-5:9 Ja 9 '33
  Sketch.   Stage 10:25 F '33
  Work of.   Players 11:11 Mr/Ap '35
  Nathan, G. J.   Work of.   Vogue 87:115 Ap 1 '36
  Sketch.   Stage 15:24 Mr '38

Her victorian house in San Francisco.   Vogue 105:118 O 15 '45
Her return to Broadway.   Newsweek 28:94 D 2 '46
Lewis, E.   Confidential chat with Ina Claire.   Cue 23-5:10 Ja 30
   '54

CLARE, MARY
   Obit.   Film R p13 '71/72
   Screen World 22:236 '71

CLARIDGE, SHAARON
   Raddatz, L.   She speaks to the police in their own language.   TV
   Guide 17-52:20 D 27 '69

CLARK, CANDY
   Bio note; filmog.   Focus On F 17:9 Spg '74

CLARK, DANE
   Hamilton, S.   Sketch.   Photop 25:55 Ag '44
   Vallee, W. L.   Unmelancholy Dane.   Silver S 16-11:35 S '46
   Here come the heroes.   TV Guide 4-37:28 S 15 '56

CLARK, FRED
   Obit.   Film R p18 '69/70

CLARK, JOHNNY
   Obit.   Screen World 19:229 '68

CLARK, MARGUERITE
   Career.   Pearson (NY) 22:231 Ag '09
   Playing a child's part.   Green Book 9:879 My '13
   Ten Eyck, J.   Interview.   Green Book 11:390 Mr '14
   Disadvantages of being girlish.   Theatre 19:188 Ap '14
   Interview.   Cosmop 59:72 Je '15
   Autobiographical.   Motion Pic 9:113 Jl '15
   Dale, A.   Sketch.   Green Book 16:161 Jl '16
   How to get into motion pictures.   Motion Pic 12:125 Ag '16
   Sketch.   Motion Pic 13:103 F '17
   Lowell, H.   Interview.   Motion Pic Classic 5:45 O '17
   Brooke, M.   Sketch.   Motion Pic 14:85 N '17
   Autobiographical.   Motion Pic 15:60 Jl '18
   Phelps, T. A.   Interview.   Theatre 30:112 Ag '19
   de Piquet, A.   Sketch.   Motion Pic 18:64 Ag '19
   Sketch.   Photop 17:28 Ja '20
   Smith, F. J.   Interview.   Motion Pic Classic 12:44 Jl '21

CLARK, PETULA
   My favorite role.   Film R p18 '52/53
   Levy, A.   Is (she) another Julie Andrews?   Good House 168:88
   Mr '69
   Miller, E.   Hollywood scene.   Seventeen 28:130 Ag '69
   Hamilton, J.   Petula Clark, Mrs. Chips.   Look 33:50 O 7 '69
   Cross, C. S.   Petula Clark; filmog.   Films In R 20-10:647 D
   '69

And the Pet goes on.  Time 95:59 F 23 '70
Bio.  Cur Bio 31:10 F '70
    Same.  Cur Bio Yrbk 1970:83 '71
Shawcross, G.  Letter.  Films In R 23-2:121 F '72

CLARK, SUSAN
    Actresses who are real people.  Life 68:45 My 29 '70
    Johnson, D.  Gets a chance to be herself.  Show 2-10:29 D '71
    Sketch.  Movie Dig 1-6:29 N '72
    Manners, D.  I nominate for stardom.  Mod Screen 66-12:15 D
        '72
    Headliners.  Photop 85-3:40 Mr '74

CLARKE, BETTY ROSS
    Remont, F.  Interview.  Motion Pic Classic 12:32 Mr '21

CLARKE, GARY
    How I let the one I love get away.  Photop 82-2:72 Jl '72

CLARKE, GORDON
    Obit.  N. Y. Times p46 Ja 12 '72
        Same.  N. Y. Times Bio Ed Ja 12 '72

CLARKE, MAE
    Sketch.  Photop 40:69 Jl '31
    Pryor, N.  Sketch.  Motion Pic 42:70 N '31
    Shirley, L.  Her story.  Movie Classic 2:41 Ag '32
    Sylvia's beauty helps.  Photop 45:52 Ap '34
    Blontman, J. W.  Grapefruit for girls.  Silver S 4-9:22 Jl '34
    Stevens, J.  Story of.  Movie Classic 11:41 F '37
    Lewis, G.  Mae Clarke; filmog.  Films In R 23-2:127 F '72

CLARY, CHARLES
    Owen, K.  A gentleman of France.  Photop 12-4:136 S '17
    Kingsley, R.  Interview.  Motion Pic 17:64 Je '19

CLARY, ROBERT
    The other Frenchman.  Metronome.  66:18 Je '50
    New faces.  Theatre Arts 36:21 Ag '52
    French letter.  Time 60:58 N 24 '52
    Hobson, D.  The strange history of A-5714.  TV Guide 14-47:23
        N 19 '66

CLAUSEN, CONNIE
    So you want to be a TV star?  TV Guide 1-5:8 My 1 '53
    I love you honey but the season's over.  Read Dig 76:86 Ap '60

CLAYTON, ETHEL
    Sketch.  New England Mag 45:618 F '12
    Courtlandt, R.  Interview.  Motion Pic 12:55 Ag '16
    The cover lady.  Photop 11-5:72 Ap '17
    McGaffey, K.  Sketch.  Motion Pic 15:41 N '18
    Peltret, E.  Interview.  Motion Pic Classic 8:50 Mr '19

Sketch.   Photop 17:63 Ap '20
Delvigne, D.   Interview.   Motion Pic 19:52 Ap/My '20
Interview.   Dramatic Mirror 1169 D 18 '20
Fletcher, A. W.   Interview.   Motion Pic 21:44 Ap '21
Cheatham, M.   Interview.   Motion Pic Classic 13:36 O '21
Home of.   Classic 16:40 Mr '23

CLAYTON, JAN
... of Carousel.   Cue 14-19:10 My 12 '45
Dog opera heroine.   TV Guide 2-50:12 D 11 '54
Lindsay, C.   McCalls visits.   McCalls 84:22 F '57

CLAYTON, MARGUERITE
Sketch.   Motion Pic 8:118 Ja '15
How she became a photoplayer.   Motion Pic Supp 1:49 S '15
How to get into moving pictures.   Motion Pic Classic 3:40 O '16
Lee, C.   Her war-time gowns.   Motion Pic Classic 5:250 '17
McKelvie, M. G.   Sketch.   Motion Pic Classic 6:27 My '18

CLEMENT, AURORE
Tomorrow people.   Films Illus 3-35:440 Jl '74

CLEMENT, DONALD
Obit.   N. Y. Times p33 Jl 30 '70

CLEMENTI, PIERRE
Millinaire, C.   Interview.   Interview 4-6:24 Je '74

CLIFFORD, KATHLEEN
Interview.   N. Y. Drama 71:33 Mr 4 '14
Owen, K.   Col. Kathleen, some boy.   Photop 12-3:19 Ag '17
Dunning, O.   Interview.   Motion Pic 36:50 Ag '28

CLIFFORD, RUTH
The knothole astronomer.   Photop 13-5:87 Ap '18
Delvigne, D.   Sketch.   Motion Pic 17:58 My '19

CLIFFORD, THOMAS
Sketch.   Photop 37:42 F '30

CLIFT, MONTGOMERY
Cosmop's citation for the best male starring performance of the
   month.   Cosmop 125:12 Ag '48
Sketch.   Life 25:24 D 6 '48
Downing, H.   Story of.   Photop 34:52 D '48
Hall, G.   The amazing Mr. Clift.   Silver S 19-3:22 Ja '49
Kilgallen, D.   Sketch.   Photop 34:29 Ja '49
Graham, S.   Sketch.   Photop 35:64 My '49
Blake, A.   Life with Monty in Berlin.   Silver S 20-3:26 Ja '50
Gibson, M.   The mood-man repents.   Silver S 24-4:33 F '54
Zunser, J.   Monty's dilemma.   Cue 26-38:10 S 21 '57
Fenin, G.   The face of '63-U.S.   Films & Filming 9-6:55 Mr
   '63

The Hallucinogenic hotel room (pictorial).   Playboy 13-11:110 O
    '66
Obit.   Film R p21 '66/68
Filmog.   Films & Filming 19-2:62 N '72
Brode, D.   The actor who never won a fight, but refused to give
    up the war; filmog.   Show 2-9:26 D '72

CLIVE, COLIN
    Mank, G.   Colin Clive, partial filmog.   Films In R 24-9:573 N
        '73
    The monster maker remembered.   Gore Creatures #23 '74

CLOSE, IVY
    Wade, P.   Sketch.   Motion Pic Classic 3:39 N '16

CLUNES, ALEC
    Obit.   N. Y. Times p31 Mr 14 '70
    Trewin, J. C.   Alec Clunes.   Plays & Players 17-9:49 Je '70

CLYDE, ANDY
    Sketch.   Photop 39:68 Ja '31
    Obit.   Classic Film Collect 18:40 Sum '67 (Reprint N. Y. Times)
        N. Y. Times My 18 '67

CLYDE, JUNE
    Belfrage, C.   Sketch.   Motion Pic Classic 31:51 Jl '30
    Denton, F.   Her amazing story.   Photop 42:84 Ag '32
    Uselton, R. A.   The Wampus baby stars.   Films In R 21-2:73
        F '70

COBB, EDMUND
    Williams, N.   A tribute to; filmog.   Filmograph 2-2:30 '71
    McKay, A. C. with B. McDowell, N. Williams, M. Summers.
        Filmog 1913-1966.   Filmograph 3-1:7 '72
    Partial filmog.   Filmograph 4-2:48 '74

COBB, JOE FRANK
    Maltin, L.   Our gang; inc Our Gang filmog.   Film Fan Mo 66:3
        D '66

COBB, LEE J.
    Peck, S.   ... creates the grand illusion.   Cue 18-10:17 Mr 5 '49
    Sketch.   Photop 34:72 Ap '49
    Enter the Virginians electronically.   TV Guide 10-49:23 D 8 '62
    As flies to wanton boys.   Time 92:92 N 15 '68

COBURN, CHARLES
    Franchey, J. R.   Actor's actor.   Silver S 12-3:42 Ja '42
    Franchey, J. R.   Free as a lark.   Silver S 15-11:50 S '45
    Mr. Coburn's Green years.   Cue 15-13:13 Mr 30 '46

COBURN, GLADYS
    She wearied of the juleps.   Photop 11-6:73 My '17

COBURN, JAMES
  On the scene.   Playboy 13-7:119 Jl '66
  Redbook dialogue.   Redbook 129:64 O '67
  Interview.   Cinema (BH) 3-1:11 n. d.
  We live in a house of travel treasures.   House & Gard 138:42 Jl
    '70
  Robbins, F.   Interview.   Photop 82-4:32 O '72
  Cool killer.   Films Illus 37:27 S '74

COCA, IMOGENE
  Coca's a sketch.   Cue 18-17:17 Ap 23 '49
  Havemann, E.   Girl with the rubber face.   Life 30:53 F 5 '51
  Bio.   Cur Bio Ap '51
  Lords of laughter.   Coronet 30:76 O '51
  Caesar, S.   Backstage with Imogene and me.   Coronet 31:109 D
    '51
  Gentauer, E.   Coca goes to the gallery.   Theatre Arts 35:28 D
    '51
  I married somebody else's husband.   Colliers 129:22 F 23 '52
  Harris, E.   Imogene Coca.   McCalls 80:40 N '52
  Seldes, G.   Comical gentlewomen.   Sat R 36:37 My 2 '53
  Shy-type star.   TV Guide 1-29:15 O 16 '53
  Gould, J.   TV's top comediennes.   N. Y. Times Mag p16 D 27
    '53
  Whitcomb, J.   Dear valentine.   Cosmop 136:90 F '54
  Lonely Saturday nights?   Newsweek 43:83 F 15 '54
  Last time together for a great pair.   Life 36:63 Je 21 '54
  Caesar vs. Coca.   Newsweek 44:66 O 11 '54
  Sid and Imogene go it alone.   Life 37:57 O 18 '54
  What makes Coca tired?   TV Guide 2-51:5 D 18 '54
  St. John, A.   Me and my shadows.   Womans Home C 81:4 D '54
  McCarthy, J.   Imogene Coca.   Cosmop 137:26 D '54
  Girl meets wolf.   McCalls 82:6 F '55
  How to be an actress.   Coronet 37:49 Ap '55
  Minoff, P.   A video artist returns in a wobbly vehicle.   Cue 25-
    10:39 Mr 10 '56
  Coca question.   Newsweek 47:73 Mr 12 '56
  Back together again.   Newsweek 50:87 Ag 5 '57
  Roth, P.   Hurdles of satire.   New Rep 137:22 S 9 '57
  Pow. Bang. Blam.   TV Guide 6-4:17 Ja 25 '58
  Barrett, M. E. & M.   The things which are Caesar's.   Good
    House 146:17 Ja '58
  Rebirth of a team.   Cue 27-5:11 F 1 '58
  Return of a talented trio.   Coronet 43:18 Ap '58

COCHRAN, STEVE
  Cochran, S.   I knew Ruth Roman when.   Silver S 21-8:40 Je '51
  Cochran, T.   Telling on pappy.   Silver S 22-2:36 D '51
  Shane, D.   He plays hard to get but...   Silver S 23-1:44 N '52

COCO, JAMES
  Bosworth, P.   Fat and forty--and red hot.   N. Y. Times Bio Ed
    Ja 4 '70

The editors bless.   Show 1-2:14 F '70
Summer, A.   The quixotic adventures of James Coco.   After
   Dark 6-1:20 My '73

CODMAN, JOHN
   East, J. M.   The Codmans.   Silent Pic 13:24 Win/Spg '72

CODY, LEW
   Peltret, E.   Interview.   Motion Pic Classic 9:18 F '20
   Hall, G.   Interview.   Motion Pic 21:24 Je '21
   Hammond, M.   Interview.   Motion Pic Classic 13:58 N '21
   Brady, S. E.   Interview.   Classic 15:24 F '23
   Getting married and unmarried.   Classic 18:62 D '23
   Carlisle, H.   Interview.   Motion Pic 27:46 Mr '24
   Hall, G.   Sketch.   Motion Pic 28:66 O '24
   Walker, H. L.   Interview.   Motion Pic 31:45 Je '26
   Spensley, D.   Sketch.   Photop 31:82 Ja '27
   The tribulations of a motion picture star.   Theatre 47:32 F '28
   Hall, G.   Sketch.   Motion Pic Classic 29:26 My '29
   Hall, G.   Sketch.   Motion Pic Classic 32:57 N '30

COGHLAN, JUNIOR
   Calhoun, D.   Sketch.   Motion Pic 37:82 Ap '29

COHAN, GEORGE M.
   Cohan, G. M.   My beginnings.   Theatre 7:52 F '07
   What he thinks of himself.   Green Bk Album 1:341 F '09
   Dodge, W. P.   Sketch.   Theatre 13:60 F '11
   Cohan, G. M.   Sketch.   Green Book 7:1220 Je '12
   Wolf, R.   Work of.   Green Book 9:40 Ja '13
   Dale, A.   Interview.   Cosmop 54:547 Mr '13
   Macfarlane, P. C.   Original character-sketch.   Everybodys 30:
      107 Ja '14
   Is (he) to be regarded as a joke or a genius?   Cur Opin 56:192
      Mr '14
   What the American flag has done for me.   Theatre 19:286 Je '14
   Porter, V. H.   Bio sketch.   Green Book 12:964 D '14
   Cohan, G. M. & Porter, V. H.   Life story of.   Green Book 13:
      38 Ja '15 and following issues.
   Rhodes, H.   Appreciation.   Met Mag 41:43 Mr '15
   Eaton, W. P.   As a writer of burlesque.   Am Mag 79:42 My '15
   How can I put it over without a flag?   Photop 11-4:42 Mr '17
   The art of adapting plays.   Theatre 26:284 N '17
   Flavor of the cities.   Am Mag 84:36 N '17
   Ten Broeck, H.   How he picks winners.   Theatre 28:40 Jl '18
   Johnson, J.   Cohan and the movies.   Photop 15-3:27 F '19
   Mullet, M. B.   His definition of one who is "on the level."   Am
      Mag 88:19 Ag '19
   Any other form.   Theatre 32:254 N '20
   Home of.   Theatre 34:406 D '21
   Cohan, Mrs. H. C.   His childhood.   Theatre 35:312 My '22
   Sketch.   National 52:282 N '23
   Sketch.   National 52:451 Ap '24

Sketch.  Theatre 39:22 Ap '24
Why my plays succeed.  Theatre 39:58 My '24
Why American plays succeed in London.  Theatre 47:17 Mr '28
His career.  Theatre 52:31 '30
Pryor, N.  Enters the movies.  Movie Classic 3:21 S '32
Hall, H. R.  (He) speaks out of turn.  Cinema Dig 1-11:4 O 3 '32
Kennedy, J. B.  Broadway knight.  Colliers 90:14 O 8 '32
Affrontery and ignorance.  Cinema Dig 1-13:15 O 31 '32
Work of.  Stage 10:37 F '33
Stage trouper.  Newsweek 2:22 S 30 '33
Sketch.  Time 22:26 O 9 '33
Song and dance man.  Theatre Arts 17:744 O '33
As a song writer.  Time 23:29 F 5 '34
Motherwell.  Appreciation.  Stage 11:17 My '34
Able and enviable.  Lit Dig 118:10 N 10 '34
Returns to home town.  Newsweek 4:28 N 10 '34
Writes a play about Cohan.  Lit Dig 121:18 Ja 25 '36
Garland, R.  Story of.  Cosmop 104:8 Je '38
His 60th birthday.  Newsweek 12:30 Jl 18 '38
Recollection.  Stage 15:47 Ag '38
To whom it may concern.  Good House 107:19 N '38
Ready Cohan.  Time 33:34 My 8 '39
Phillips, H. A.  I like small-town audiences.  Rotarian 55:10 S '39
Play on life of Cohan.  Time 35:45 Ja 1 '40
Cohan's return.  Life 8:72 My 27 '40
Musical biography.  Theatre Arts 24:516 Jl '40
Owen, R.  Yankee doodle dandy.  N. Y. Times Mag p14 Mr 1 '42
Yankee doodle Cagney.  Newsweek 19:56 Je 8 '42
Cagney as Cohan.  Life 12:64 Je 15 '42
Obit.  Cur Bio '43
    Newsweek 20:93 N 16 '42
    Time 40:82 N 16 '42
Wyatt, E. V.  Keep it clean.  Cath World 156:335 D '72
Morehouse, W.  George M. Cohan.  Theatre Arts 28:53 Ja '44
Cerf, B.  Sweet notes for music week.  Sat R 27:14 Ja 22 '44
Morehouse, W.  Prince of the American theatre.  Theatre Arts 28:255 Ap '44
Rose, K. D.  Patriotic music.  Hobbies 49:113 Ag '44
Morehouse, W.  Prince of the American theatre.  N. Y. Hist 27:520 O '46
Vincent, H.  Heart of Broadway.  Coronet 32:124 My '52
Debus, A. G.  Current collectors recordings.  Hobbies 59:27 D '54
Hammerstein, O. 2nd.  Tribute to.  N. Y. Times Mag p14 My 5 '57
    Reply by C. Parmer p2 Je 20 '57
Latham, L.  The films of.  Classic Film Collect 35:32 Sum '72

COHAN, HELEN
    Uselton, R. A.  The Wampus baby stars.  Films In R 21-2:73 F '70

COLBERT, CLAUDETTE

Cruikshank, H.   Sketch.   Motion Pic Classic 31:44 My '30
Harris, R.   Young woman of Manhattan.   Silver S 1-1:14 N '30
Orme, M.   Criticism.   Ill Lon N 178:108 Ja 17 '31
Conrad, S.   What men should know about women.   Silver S 1-8: 24 Je '31
Sketch.   Photop 40:1 Jl '31
Wilson, E.   The trans-continental wife.   Silver S 2-1:39 N '31
Wilson, E.   The girl on the cover.   Silver S 2-4:61 F '32
Service, F.   Her separation marriage.   Motion Pic 44:47 Ag '32
Henderson, J.   Claudette Colbert.   Cinema Dig 1-10:9 S '19 '32
Donnell, D.   As Empress Poppaea.   Movie Classic 3:31 N '32
Melcher, E.   Colbert and I cover the waterfront.   Cinema Dig 2-9:10 F 13 '33
Fidler, J. M.   Talking to myself.   Silver S 3-5:25 Mr '33
Patrick, C.   Claudette's Eve dive.   Cinema Dig 4-3:15 My 29 '33
Walker, H. L.   Interview.   Movie Classic 4:17 Jl '33
Wilson, E.   (She) explains how to wear clothes elegantly.   Silver S 3-12:14 O '33
Goldbeck, E.   Interview.   Motion Pic Classic 32:52 F '34
Played Cleopatra in spite of illness.   Movie Classic 6:6 Jl '34
Goldbeck, E.   Interview.   Movie Classic 6:51 Ag '34
Brundidge, H. T.   Sketch.   Motion Pic 49:28 F '35
Grant, J.   Threatened after wearing million dollars in gems.   Movie Classic 7:6 F '35
Appreciation.   Lit Dig 119:36 Ap 13 '35
Weybright, V.   Sketch.   Motion Pic 49:27 Ap '35
Calhoun, D.   Interview.   Movie Classic 8:30 My '35
Gaines, W. P.   No. 1 lady of the screen.   Motion Pic 49:32 Je '35
Sullivan, E.   Claudette is not going to stop there.   Silver S 5-8:20 Je '35
Lane, V.   Interview.   Movie Classic 8:28 Ag '35
Ullman, W. A.   Jr.   Interview.   Motion Pic 50:24 S '35
Appreciation.   Lit Dig 120:26 O 5 '35
Hartley, K.   Interview.   Movie Classic 9:28 O '35
Zeitlin, I.   Interview.   Motion Pic 51:42 F '36
Chapman, J.   An actress in real life.   Movie Classic 9:46 F '36
Rankin, R.   The busiest girl in Hollywood.   Silver S 6-5:24 Mr '36
Mack, G.   Her story.   Motion Pic 51:33 Je '36
Wilson, E.   Projections of...   Silver S 6-10:16 Ag '36
Albert, K.   Sketch.   Motion Pic 52:7 D '36
Claudette Colbert.   Visages 11:entire issue Ap '37
Craig, C.   Interview.   Motion Pic 53:28 Jl '37
Bunch, H.   Don't be a copycat.   Screen Book 19-1:28 Ag '37
Wilcox, G.   You can have everything.   Screen Book 19-5:32 D '37
Liza.   Nothing to worry about.   Silver S 8-5:34 Mr '38

Deane, C.   Colbert's teen rules for success.   Screen Book 20-3:22 Ap '38

Wilson, E.   Claudette goes to her picture.   Silver S 9-5:30 Mr '39

Reid, J.   She censors the censors.   Screen Book 21-10:20 My '39

Wilson, E.   Claudette's like that.   Silver S 10-11:22 S '40

Smalley, J.   Interview.   Photop 54:73 O '40

Trotter, M.   Astrological forecast.   Photop 18:31 F '41

Hamman, M.   Sketch.   Good House 112:16 Ap '41

Mulvey, K.   Sketch.   Womans Home C 68:37 Je '41

Wilson, E.   Want to cry or laugh?   Silver S 12-12:28 O '42

Wilson, C.   Her advice to Cheryl.   Silver S 13-10:34 Ag '43

Letter from Liza.   Silver S 14-10:41 Ag '44

Parsons, L. O.   Cosmop's citation for the best performance of the month.   Cosmop 119:61 D '45

Colbert, C.   Answers problems.   Photop '45 thru '49.

Fourth place in Companion poll of favorite stars.   Womans Home C 73:7 Je '46

Letter from Liza.   Silver S 17-6:52 Ap '47

Palmer, C.   She speaks up.   Silver S 17-8:35 Je '47

Parsons, L. O.   Cosmop's citation for the best female performance of the month.   Cosmop 126:15 Mr '49

O'Leary, D.   You need a sense of humor.   Silver S 21-9:40 Jl '51

Boyer-Colbert are back again.   Cue 27-43:11 O 25 '58

Maltin, L.   Claudette Colbert; filmog.   Film Fan Mo 106:3 Ap '70

Pacheco, J. B. Jr.   Claudette Colbert; filmog.   Films In R 21-5:268 My '70

Letters.   Films In R 21-7:448 Ag 15 '70

Pin-up of the past.   Films & Filming 17-7:70 Ap '71

Here's to the ladies.   Screen Greats 1-2:26 Sum '71

Corneau, C.   The Colbert story.   Classic Film Collect 37:30 Win '72

Mank, G.   Claudette Colbert returns.   Film Fan Mo 152:19 F '74

COLBY, ANITA
Miss Colby's remarks.   Time 45:8 F 5 '45
Her 32nd birthday celebrated in Hollywood by a South Seas party. Life 21:135 S 23 '46

COLE, DENNIS
Interview.   Mod Screen 66-1:20 Ja '72
Stoop, N. M.   Women have always been my Achilles' heel.   After Dark 5-2:52 Je '72

COLE, MICHAEL
de Roos, R.   He has a hard time even saying good morning. TV Guide 17-28:20 Jl 12 '69
Michael Cole to wed his 7-year love.   Photop 80-3:84 S '71
A kiss for Mr. Cole.   Photop 80-6:35 D '71

A lifetime of love.   Mod Screen 65-12:45 D '71
Now we are three.   Mod Screen 67-1:31 Ja '72
Each time I look at my wife I see my unborn child.   Photop 81-
    2:39 F '72
We don't want to stop having babies.   Photop 82-3:48 S '72
Hopes and fears for his expected baby.   Mod Screen 66-9:35 S
    '72
New baby.   Photop 83-4:63 Ap '73

COLE, NAT KING
    Fiddlers three.   Newsweek 28:97 Ag 12 '46
    King Cole trio.   Opportunity 25:28 Ja '47
    Remember the public.   Time 58:63 Jl 30 '51
    Hubler, R. G.   $12,000 a week preacher's boy.   Sat Eve Post
        227:30 Jl 17 '54
    Melancholy monarch.   Look 19:119 Ap 19 '55
    Unscheduled appearance.   Time 67:31 Ap 23 '56
    Who the hoodlums are.   Newsweek 47:31 Ap 23 '56
    Swift justice.   Time 67:23 Ap 30 '56
    Asbell, B.   King Cole cuts a biscuit.   Playboy 3:35 N '56
    King's own show.   Newsweek 50:90 Jl 15 '57
    Pioneer.   Time 70:66 Jl 15 '57
    A step in the right direction.   TV Guide 5-36:15 S 7 '57
    Host of the month.   Time 70:56 S 23 '57
    Nat King Cole twins.   Ebony 18:106 Ag '63
    King.   Time 85:60 F 26 '65
    Thompson, T.   A friend remembers him.   Life 58:36 F 26 '65
    Soft answers.   Newsweek 65:81 Mr 1 '65
    Robinson, L.   Life and death of Nat King Cole.   Ebony 20:123
        Ap '65
    Obit.   Screen World 17:235 '66

COLE, TINA
    Felton, D.   She moved in with her husband's people.   TV Guide
        16-7:14 F 17 '68
    Tina Cole splits with husband.   Photop 77-5:52 My '70

COLEMAN, FRANK B.
    Obit.   N. Y. Times p50 D 11 '70

COLEMAN, NANCY
    Hall, G.   Diary of a damsel in distress.   Silver S 13-4:34 F
        '43
    A mistake I wouldn't make again.   Photop 22:47 My '43
    Service, F.   Can an average girl succeed in the movies?   Silver
        S 14-1:24 N '43
    Sketch.   Photop 24:49 D '43
    Asher, J.   Revelations of a red-head.   Silver S 14-9:32 Jl '44

COLEMAN, VINCENT
    Service, F.   Interview.   Motion Pic Classic 11:18 O '20
    Ashworth, W.   Interview.   Motion Pic Classic 13:46 O '21

COLEMAN, WARREN
    Obit.  N. Y. Times p39 Ja 16 '68

COLLIER, CONSTANCE
    Stage career.  Pearson (NY) 23:100 Ja '10
    Character study.  Strand (NY) 42:491 N '11
    Dale, A.  Interview.  Cosmop 57:120 Je '14
    Zeschin, R.  Ladies of the libretto.  Opera N 36:29 Mr 18 '72

COLLIER, LOIS
    Kerlee, C.  Success story.  Screen Book 20-3:76 Ap '38

COLLIER, WILLIAM (Buster) Jr.
    Sherwood, C. B.  Interview.  Motion Pic Classic 11:58 O '20
    Curran, D.  Sketch.  Motion Pic Classic 22:38 O '25
    Tildesley, R. M.  Interview.  Motion Pic 35:71 My '28
    Tildesley, R.  Sketch.  Motion Pic 36:42 S '28
    Obit.  Cur Bio Mr '44

COLLINGE, PATRICIA
    Interview.  Cosmop 58:680 My '15
    Dickinson, J.  Interview.  Green Book 13:929 My '15
    Why I don't write a play.  Stage 14:46 N '36
    Bio note.  Scholastic 33:5 O 1 '38
    Another part of the Hubbards.  New Yorker 23:29 Mr 15 '47
    Obit.  N. Y. Times Bio Ed p493 Ap '74
    (Patricia Collinge's creative writing appeared frequently in New
       Yorker, Vogue, Saturday Review, others)

COLLINS, CHARLES
    Sketch.  Movie Classic 10:15 My '36

COLLINS, CORA SUE
    Sketch.  Photop 45:37 D '33
    Sketch.  Photop 45:90 F '34

COLLINS, DOROTHY
    Listen for opportunity's knock.  TV Guide 1-3:17 Ap 17 '53
    Her blouses went to the laundry.  TV Guide 7-1:24 Ja 3 '59
    Haas, A. D.  Musical house for a musical family.  Pop Mech
       112:126 S '59
    Once and future follies.  Time 97:70 My 3 '71

COLLINS, GARY
    Who?  TV Guide 13-45:14 N 6 '65
    My child.  Photop 80-5:6 N '71
    Raddatz, L.  It wasn't ESP.  TV Guide 20-21:34 My 20 '72
    The Collins family.  Photop 82-2:32 Jl '72

COLLINS, JOAN
    A star is born.  Film R p101 '52/53
    Cole, C.  Two faces of...  Films & Filming 2-3:20 D '55
    Filmog.  Films Illus 1-1:31 Jl '71

COLLINS, RUSSELL
    Obit.   Screen World 17:235 '66
    Tributary to professional.   Theatre Arts 22:528 Jl '38

COLLYER, JUNE
    Hall, G.  Sketch.  Motion Pic 35:47 Ap '28
    Manners, D.  Sketch.  Motion Pic Classic 28:40 D '28
    Goldbeck, E.  Sketch.  Motion Pic 38:82 Ja '30
    Dorman, J.  Her marriage to Stuart Erwin.  Movie Classic 1:38
       O '31
    Ellis, T.  Her romance.  Photop 40:32 O '31
    Minoff, P.  The double life of the Erwins.  Cue 20-18:14 My 5
       '51
    Obit.  N. Y. Times p47 Mr 19 '68
       Screen World 20:233 '69
    Uselton, R. A.  The Wampus baby stars.  Films In R 21-2:73
       F '70

COLMAN, RONALD
    Brenton, A.  Sketch.  Photop 27:66 D '24
    Autobiographical.  Motion Pic 29:32 Mr '25
    The next Romeo.  Motion Pic Classic 21:37 Jl '25
    Darrow, I.  Sketch.  Motion Pic Classic 22:32 D '25
    Leslie, J.  Interview.  Motion Pic 33:60 Ap '27
    Carlisle, H.  Why he is not to play with Vilma Banky.  Motion
       Pic 35:31 Ap '28
    Spensley, D.  Interview.  Motion Pic 37:50 F '29
    Hall, G.  Interview.  Motion Pic Classic 31:52 Ap '30
    Fender, R.  Sketch.  Motion Pic Classic 31:52 Ag '30
    Shaffer, R.  His married life.  Motion Pic 41:50 F '31
    Service, F.  Interview.  Movie Classic 1:50 O '31
    Whitchel, J. A.  Yo ho! for a six months' vacation.  Silver S
       2-3:21 Ja '32
    Pryor, N.  Sketch.  Motion Pic 43:48 F '32
    Maxwell, V.  His trip abroad.  Motion Pic 43:52 Je '32
    Bahn, C. B.  Ronald Colman.  Cinema Dig 1-13:15 O 31 '32
    Fairbanks, D. Jr.  Appreciation.  Vanity Fair 39:39 O '32
    Shaffer, R.  Interview.  Motion Pic 44:40 D '32
    Hall, G.  Interview.  Motion Pic 45:49 Mr '33
    Schellert, E.  Divorce rumors.  Movie Classic 6:50 Je '34
    Fender, R.  Interview.  Movie Classic 8:56 Mr '35
    Mack, G.  His private life.  Motion Pic 50:38 N '35
    Hartley, K.  Interview.  Movie Classic 10:44 Jl '36
    Lang, H.  Story of.  Motion Pic 51:32 Jl '36
    Steele, J. H.  Sketch.  Movie Classic 11:16 F '37
    Hosic, R.  Exploding the Colman myths.  Screen Book 21-5:40
       D '38
    Mulvey, K.  Sketch.  Womans Home C 67:7 Mr '40
    Bio note; filmog.  Movies & People 2:10 '40
    The Colman tradition.  Lions R 2-3:no p# D '44
    Parsons, L. O.  Cosmop's citation for the best performance of
       the month.  Cosmop 124:12 Mr '48
    It's the sponsor who pays.  TV Guide 4-37:24 S 15 '56

Richards, J.   Ronald Colman and the cinema of empire; filmog.
    Focus On F 4:42 S/O '70
Schatz, G. A.   Tribute to a gentleman; filmog.   Classic F Col-
    lect 29:18 Win '70
Perfect gentleman.   Screen Greats 1-2:66 Sum '71
Fox, J.   Colman.   Films & Filming 18-6:26 Mr '72
Fox, J.   Study of a career.   Films & Filming 18-7:35 Ap '72
Pin-up of the past.   Films & Filming 19-18:64 S '73

COLONNA, JERRY
    Sketch.   Newsweek 27:64 F 25 '46

COLUMBO, RUSS
    Yawitz, P.   Sketch.   Movie Classic 2:56 My '32
    Obit.   Movie Classic 7:37 N '34
    Palmborg, R. P.   His friendship with Lansing Brown.   Motion
        Pic 43:47 D '34
    Liquori, J.   Russ Columbo.   Films In R 13-6:381 Je/Jl '62
    Pitts, M. R.   Popular singers on the screen; filmog.   Film Fan
        Mo 112:150 O '70; 114:26 D '70

COLVIG, PINTO (VANCE)
    Want to hear a noise?   Am Mag 138:128 Ag '44
    Obit.   N. Y. Times p39 O 6 '67
        Time 90:104 O 13 '67

COMBS, FREDERICK
    Zadan, C.   Frederick Combs' 35th part.   After Dark 3-10:48 F
        '71

COMINGORE, DOROTHY
    (Also known as Kay Winters; Linda Winters)
    Crichton, K.   Forward fawn.   Colliers 107:13 Ja 18 '41
    Success story.   Cue 10-24:3 Je 14 '41
    Dorothy Comingore finds the committee cute.   Film Comment
        50/51:65 Fall/Win '70
    Obit.   Classic Film Collect 34:X-3 Spg '72
        N. Y. Times p22 D 31 '71
        Same.   N. Y. Times Bio Ed D 31 '71
        Screen World 23:236 '72
    Crivello, K.   The second Mrs. Kane; filmog.   Focus On F 9:31
        Spg '72

COMO, PERRY
    Talmey, A.   Sketch.   Vogue 102:102 O 1 '43
    At the Versailles--ecco homo Como.   Cue 13-8:8 F 19 '44
    Supper club with Como.   Cue 14-1:9 Ja 6 '45
    Next.   Newsweek 26:69 Jl 30 '45
    Hubba, hubba, hubba.   Time 47:49 Mr 18 '46
    O Como mio.   Newsweek 28:93 S 16 '46
    Bio.   Cur Bio Ap '47
    Henderson, H. & Shaw, S.   King of the jukes.   Colliers 119:59
        Je 21 '47

Kass, R.  Film and TV.  Cath World 175:467 S '52
Perry Como cuts a disc.  Colliers 130:34 N 8 '52
Casual Perry Como.  TV Guide 1-14:14 Jl 3 '53
Crazy for Como.  TV Guide 2-12:8 Mr 19 '54
Peace of mind at any price.  TV Guide 3-20:13 My 14 '55
Battle of the giants.  Newsweek 46:111 S 26 '55
Kass, R.  Perry Como.  Cath World 182:140 N '55
World of nice guys.  Time 66:46 D 19 '55
Drury, M.  Nice guys finish first.  Colliers 137:26 Ja 6 '56
Millstein, G.  How to relax.  N. Y. Times Mag p19 Ja 29 '56
Jackie, Perry and a TV row.  Life 40:47 F 13 '56
Kass, R.  Films and TV.  Cath World 182:465 Mr '56
Whatta setup for a barber shop.  TV Guide O 20 '56
Twenty-year-old's ideal.  Life 41:143 D 24 '56
What 20 years have wrought.  TV Guide 5-12:24 Mr 23 '57
Bester, A.  Relaxed man.  Holiday 21:113 Mr '57
McCarthy, J.  Is he really Mr. Nice Guy?  Look 21:126 Ap 16
    '57
Placid Perry.  TV Guide 6-12:4 Mr 22 '58
Durable star.  Newsweek 51:69 Mr 24 '58
They killed the fatted calf.  TV Guide 6-42:8 O 18 '58
Big cheese.  Time 73:65 Mr 16 '59
Eells, G.  How much is his $25,000,000 worth?  Look 23:47 My
    12 '59
It's better than cutting hair.  TV Guide 7-46:8 N 14 '59
Martin, P.  I call on...  Sat Eve Post 233:19 N 12; 33 N 19; 34
    N 26 '60
What do they expect me to do?  TV Guide 9-2:4 Ja 14 '61
Market, H.  He speaks out on privacy.  Good House 152:32 Je
    '61
Adams, C.  Como the comic.  TV Guide 11-2:6 Ja 16 '63

COMPSON, BETTY
    Peltret, E.  Interview.  Motion Pic Classic 9:16 D '19
    Smith, F. J.  Interview.  Motion Pic Classic 10:16 Je '20
    Interview.  Dramatic Mirror 909 N 13 '20
    Naylor, H. S.  Sketch.  Motion Pic 21:44 Mr '21
    Montanye, L.  Interview.  Motion Pic Classic 12:22 Je '21
    Goldbeck, W.  Interview.  Motion Pic 23:24 Mr '22
    Hall, G.  Interview.  Motion Pic 25:48 My '23
    Home of.  Classic 20:36 N '24
    Pryor, N.  Returns to the screen.  Motion Pic Classic 27:23
        Jl '28
    Hall, G.  Her confessions.  Motion Pic Classic 28:16 D '28
    Howe, H.  Sketch.  Photop 35:51 Ap '29
    Donnell, D.  Interview.  Motion Pic 38:64 Ja '30
    Sketch.  Motion Pic 39:8 Jl '30
    The Comptons and the Compsons.  Photop 38:66 N '30
    Compson, B. as told to E. R. Moak.  Ex-wives make the best
        wives.  Silver S 1-5:36 Mr '31
    Walker, H. L.  Interview.  Motion Pic Classic 33:73 Je '31
    Keen, J. H.  Betty Compson.  Cinema Dig 1-8:6 Ag 22 '32
    Sketch.  Photop 54:40 F '40

Joyful, silent memories.   Classic Film Collect 30:extra 1 Spg
   '71
Mazurki, J.   Glendale star from silent film era feted.   Classic
   Film Collect 33:13 Win '71
Mazurki, J.   Best bad girl of the silent era still sparkles, lives
   with her memories.   Classic Film Collect 34:X-4 Spg '72
Leonard, W. T.   The story of Betty Compson.   Classic Film
   Collect 36:9 Fall; 37:42 Win '72
Obit.   Classic Film Collect 43:X6 Sum '74
   N. Y. Times Bio Ed p494 Ap '74

COMPTON, JOHN
He eats bees and sometimes ants.   TV Guide 7-22:17 My 30 '59

COMPTON, JOYCE
The Comptons and the Compsons.   Photop 38:66 N '30
Uselton, R. A.   The Wampus baby stars.   Films In R 21-2:73
   F '70

COMPTON, JULIETTE
Hall, G.   Sketch.   Motion Pic Classic 30:24 Ja '30
The Comptons and the Compsons.   Photop 38:66 N '30

CONDON, JACKIE
Maltin, L.   Our gang; Our gang filmog.   Film Fan Mo 66:3 D
   '66

CONKLIN, CHESTER
Sketch.   Motion Pic 9:115 Je '15
McAubrey, M.   Interview.   Motion Pic Classic 9:92 Ja '20
Kibbe, V.   Interview.   Motion Pic Classic 22:54 F '26
His work in motion pictures.   Graphic 116:502 Je 18 '27
Spensley, D.   Sketch.   Motion Pic Classic 29:63 Mr '29
Lamberto, N.   A lonely boy who never came back to Iowa.
   Classic Film Collect 24:15 Sum '69
Obit.   Classic Film Collect 32:62 Fall '71
   Film R p11 '72/73
   N. Y. Times p46 O 12 '71
   Same.   N. Y. Times Bio Ed O 12 '71
   Screen World 23:236 '72
   Time 98:82 O 25 '71

CONKLIN, PEGGY
Quigg, M.   This little Peggy went to town.   Screen Book 21-5:69
   D '38

CONNELLY, BOBBY
Obit.   N. Y. Clipper 70:30 Jl 12 '22

CONNELLY, CHRIS
Hobson, D.   What is (his) secret hatred.   TV Guide 16-32:24 Ag
   10 '68

CONNELLY, EDWARD
    Cheatham, M.  Interview.   Motion Pic Classic 14:63 Ap '22

CONNELLY, PEGGY
    We're both a little wacky.   TV Guide 8-42:24 O 15 '60

CONNERY, SEAN
    Interview.  Playboy 12-11:75 N '65
    (He) strikes again (pictures).   Playboy 13-7:75 Jl '66
    Sweeney, L.  Male of the species.   TV Guide 16-52:15 D 28 '68
    Campbell, R.  Bio note; filmog.  Focus On F 3:11 My/Ag '70
    Evans, P.  The ghost of Connery's past.  Show 2-11:42 Ja '72
    Separated, but more than friends.  Mod Screen 66-3:36 Mr '72
    Gow, G.  Interview; filmog.  Films & Filming 20-6:22 Mr '74

CONNOLLY, WALTER
    Sketch.  Photop 46:72 O '34
    Brundidge, H. T.  Interview.  Movie Classic 7:56 Ja '35
    Vandour, C.  He supplies the background.  Silver S 8-6:33 Ap
        '38

CONNORS, JOAN
    Just call him Barry--and keep him at a distance.  TV Guide 11-
        32:7 Ag 10 '63

CONNORS, MIKE
    (Also known as Touch Connors)
    Hudson, P.  Mannix:  where the action is; interview.  Sr Schol
        97:40 O 26 '70
    Mannix's perfect marriage.  Photop 79-5:88 My '71
    Why he's Hollywood's most persistent lover.  Photop 80-4:48 O
        '71
    Schroeder, C.  Interview.  Good House 174:40 Ap '72
    I watched my father being beaten to death.  Photop 81-4:51 Ap
        '72
    Davidson, B.  The sweet smell of (his) success.  TV Guide 20-
        26:20 Je 24 '72
    Mike and Mary Lou Connors.  Mod Screen 66-9:18 S '72
    Miron, C.  The private eye who is an average Joe.  Show 2-8:
        38 N '72
    The best Christmas of my life.  Photop 83-1:27 Ja '73

CONRAD, ROBERT
    Denton, C.  The slings and arrows of out-raged critics.  TV
        Guide 10-33:6 Ag 18 '62
    Lewis, E.  The kid with the golden sandbox.  TV Guide 13-49:
        14 D 4 '65
    Photoplay forum.  Photop 80-5:10 N '71
    Adler, D.  If things go bad, he can always take his shirt off.
        TV Guide 20-42:38 O 14 '72

CONRAD, WILLIAM
    Adler, D.  Fat is beautiful.  TV Guide 19-45:32 N 6 '71

Nolan, J. E.   Films on TV; partial TV filmog.   Films In R
    23-10:639 D '72
Adler, D.   How old Bill Conrad? Old Bill Conrad fine--and fat.
    TV Guide 21-9:18 Mr 3 '73
Note; filmog.   Films & Filming 19-18:56 S '73

CONRIED, HANS
    Hans across the TV screen.   TV Guide 4-21:12 My 26 '56
    Maltin, L.   Hans Conried; filmog.   Film Fan Mo 107:14 My '70

CONSIDINE, TIM
    The boys from Triple R.   TV Guide 5-22:28 Je 1 '57

CONSTANT, YVONNE
    Right out of Glass Face Inc.   TV Guide 12-19:23 My 9 '64

CONSTANTINE, EDDIE
    The star who didn't come home.   Show 2-5:10 My '62
    Interview.   Cinema (BH) 4-4:16 n.d.

CONSTANTINE, MICHAEL
    Funny, you don't look Greek.   TV Guide 18-39:22 S 26 '70

CONTE, JOHN
    Seen: a voice!   Lions R 3-5:no p# D '44
    The man with 3,000,001 wives.   TV Guide 5-17:28 Ap 27 '57

CONTE, RICHARD
    Vallee, W. L.   No aspirant was he.   Silver S 17-2:47 D '46
    Kamp, S.   Story of.   Photop 30:104 My '47

CONTI, ALBERT
    Obit.   Screen World 19:229 '68

CONTI, AUDREY
    She changed lines.   TV Guide 4-11:12 Mr 17 '56

CONVERSE, FRANK
    Efron, E.   This man plays a cop.   TV Guide 17-18:18 My 3 '69
    Stoneman, E. D.   Hot footing it back to television.   After Dark
        6-8:76 D '73

CONWAY, CURT
    Obit.   N.Y. Times Bio Ed p494 Ap '74

CONWAY, GARY
    He refuses to sound like he looks.   TV Guide 12-32:15 Ag 8 '64
    See, C.   How's life among the giants these days?   TV Guide
        17-4:30 Ja 25 '69
    Holt, T.   Handsome man, handsome life; centerfold.   Playgirl
        1-3:72 Ag '73

CONWAY, PAT
   All work and no Jack.   TV Guide 11-27:15 Jl 6 '63

CONWAY, SHIRL
   Sketch.   Theatre World 44:33 Ap '48
   Keating, J.   Shirl on a whirl.   Cue 24-7:14 F 19 '55
   Efron, E.   The wonderful woman in white.   TV Guide 11-28:7 Jl
      13 '63

CONWAY, TIM
   Talk about type casting.   TV Guide 11-42:12 O 19 '63
   Hano, A.   The tinsmith's son from Chagrin Falls.   TV Guide
      15-24:15 Je 17 '67

CONWAY, TOM
   Obit.   Film R p21 '66/68
   Thiede, K. S.   The Falcon saga.   Views & Rs 3-4:52 '72

COOGAN, BOBBY
   Sketch.   Photop 39:71 Ap '31
   Lang, H.   Sketch.   Photop 40:28 Je '31

COOGAN, JACKIE
   Shelly, H.   His work in The kid.   Motion Pic Classic 12:24 My
      '21
   Smith, F. J.   Interview.   Motion Pic 22:28 S '21
   Howe, H.   Interview.   Motion Pic Classic 14:18 Ap '22
   Handy, T. B.   Interview.   Motion Pic 23:32 Je '22
   Home of.   Photop 23:40 Ja '23
   Carr, H.   What of his future?   Motion Pic 25:21 My '23
   Sangster, M.   How he is being trained.   Photop 23:36 My '23
   Service, F.   Frank Lloyd's opinion of him.   Classic 16:42 Je
      '23
   In Circus days.   Ladies Home J 40:42 N '23
   Sketch.   National 52:450 Ap '24
   His suit for money earned when a child actor.   Life 4:50 Ap 25
      '38
   Roberts, W. A.   Making a man of him.   Everybody's 55:36 Jl
      '26
   Sketch.   Photop 31:74 D '26
   The youngest rancher.   Photop 32:115 Ag '27
   Belfrage, C.   Interview.   Motion Pic 35:42 F '28
   Hughes, M.   To return to pictures.   Photop 38:35 Ag '30
   Pryor, N.   Returns to the movies.   Motion Pic Classic 32:41
      N '30
   Reid, M.   The kid even genius can't spoil.   Silver S 1-1:30 N
      '30
   Grant, J.   Better than Jackie.   Silver S 1-11:19 S '31
   Jackson, G.   Interview.   Motion Pic 49:42 F '35
   Return of The kid.   Cue 15-13:12 Mr 30 '46
   His baby.   Life 26:5 Ja 3 '49
   To make his Broadway debut in Fatty.   Classic Film Collect 16:
      22 Fall '66

The kids.   Screen Greats 1-2:50 Sum '71
Harmetz, A.   Remember?   N. Y. Times Bio Ed Ap 2 '72
Adler, D.   Making a TV time capsule.   TV Guide 30-36:6 S 2
   '72

COOK, ELISHA JR.
   Reed, E.   Work of.   Theatre Arts 18:57 Ja '34

COOK, JOE
   Adams, F. P.   You ought to see Joe Cook.   Colliers 71:22 Ja
      13 '23
   Mullett, M. B.   Joe Cook does more stunts than anyone else on
      the stage.   Am Mag 97:34 Ja '24
   Leamy, H.   Interview.   Colliers 83:14 Ja 26 '29
   What makes 'em laugh.   Am Mag 111:38 F '31
   Full of ideas.   Am Mag 113:54 My '32
   Powers, J.   Joe Cook completes the circuit.   Scholastic 40:24
      F 16 '42
   Obit.   Screen World 11:216 '60

COOK, MARIANNE
   Person of promise.   Films & Filming 3-8:8 My '57

COOLIDGE, PHILIP
   Obit.   Screen World 19:230 '68

COOPER, GARY
   Sketch.   Photop 31:75 Ap '27
   Cross, J.   Sketch.   Motion Pic 33:70 Je '27
   Manners, D.   Interview.   Motion Pic Classic 25:54 Je '27
   Goldbeck, E.   Sketch.   Motion Pic Classic 28:43 F '29
   Walker, H. L.   Interview.   Motion Pic 37:48 Ap '29
   Goldbeck, E.   Sketch.   Motion Pic 39:55 Je '30
   Standish, J.   Interview.   Motion Pic Classic 33:52 Mr '31
   Jamison, J.   Sketch.   Motion Pic Classic 33:48 Jl '31
   Wilson, E.   (He) discovers Manhattan island.   Silver S 2-3:18 Ja
      '32
   Goldbeck, E.   Interview.   Movie Classic 1:22 Ja '32
   Menner, E.   Sketch.   Movie Classic 2:22 Jl '32
   Wingate, R.   His pet chimpanzee.   Movie Classic 2:31 Ag '32
   Moffitt, C. F.   Censorship for interviews Hollywood's latest wild
      idea...   Cinema Dig 2-5:9 Ja 9 '33
   Melcher, E.   Gary Cooper.   Cinema Dig 2-6:8 Ja 16 '33
   Goldbeck, E.   Brings African jungle to Beverly Hills.   Motion
      Pic 44:40 Ja '33
   Parsons, H.   Small town habits.   Silver S 3-7:20 My '33
   Service, F.   Interview.   Movie Classic 4:34 Je '33
   Fidler, J.   Interview.   Movie Classic 4:26 Jl '33
   Pryor, N.   How he rates with men.   Movie Classic 4:30 Jl '33
   Lynn, H.   A farewell to arms.   Photop 44:31 Ag '33
   Ergenbright, E. L.   Interview.   Movie Classic 5:49 O '33
   Biery, R.   Women puzzle him.   Motion Pic 46:40 N '33
   Kellum, F.   Sketch.   Photop 45:56 D '33

Sinclaire, V.  His engagement to Sandra Shaw.  Motion Pic 47: 32 F '34

Grant, J. & Busby, M.  His marriage.  Movie Classic 6:8 Mr '34

MacDonald, B.  Is Hollywood killing its leading men?  Silver S 4-9:30 Jl '34

Ulman, W. A. Jr.  On location with...  Silver S 5-3:50 Ja '35

Daniels, J. A.  Fighting man of all nations.  Motion Pic 49:7 F '35

Brundidge, H. T.  Sketch.  Motion Pic 49:28 F '35

Daniels, J. A.  Sketch.  Photop 47:25 F '35

Daniels, J. A.  Work of.  Movie Classic 7:7 F '35

Brundidge, H. T.  How he got into the movies.  Motion Pic 49: 34 Jl '35

Tully, J.  Sketch.  Motion Pic 50:49 Ag '35

Harrison, H.  Interview.  Movie Classic 9:25 O '35

Ulman, W. A. Jr.  Interview.  Movie Classic 10:42 Ap '36

Swanson, P.  Sketch.  Movie Classic 10:33 Je '36

Lang, H.  His story.  Motion Pic 51:32 Je '36

Lane, V. T.  Producers battle over him.  Movie Classic 11:28 Ja '37

Hartley, K.  His popularity.  Motion Pic 53:44 Mr '37

Gary Cooper.  Visages 12:entire issue.  My '37

Appreciation.  Stage 14:46 Jl '37

DeKolty, J.  Old pals' ranch.  Silver S 8-3:50 Ja '38

Reid, J.  Gary Gary quite contrary.  Silver S 10-7:22 My '40

Bio note; filmog.  Movies and People 2:10 '40

Hall, G.  I try to keep in touch with the guy I was.  Silver S 11-9:22 Jl '41

People.  Cue 10-36:16 S 6 '41

I like women.  Cosmop 113:33 Jl '42

Hall, G.  Pulling no punches.  Silver S 13-2:22 D '42

Trotter, M.  His horoscope.  Photop 22:31 F '43

Hopper, H.  His married life.  Photop 22:26 My '43

Brooks, P.  My South Sea Island flight with (him).  Silver S 14-7:22 My '44

My most unforgettable moment overseas.  Photop 25:52 Je '44

Garrulous Gary.  Cue 13-36:10 S 2 '44

Hall, G.  Actor-hyphen-producer.  Silver S 15-11:38 S '45

Mann, M.  Who says he won't talk?  Silver S 19-1:24 N '48

Mann, M.  (He) speaks his mind!  Silver S 20-7:36 My '50

Cowboy Cooper rides the range again.  Cue 19-51:14 D 23 '50

Sheridan, M.  The strange second life of Cooper.  Silver S 23- 12:24 O '53

Boase, A.  The passing of the personalities.  Film J (Aus) 18:22 O '61

Obit.  Film R p17 '61/ 62

Captain America.  Screen Greats 1-2:17 Sum '71

Schwartz, W.  Filmog of shorts.  Films In R 24-1:63 Ja '73

Guy, R.  Gary Cooper was a great actor...; filmog.  Cinema (BH) 2-3:15 n. d.

Gary Cooper; filmog.  Screen Greats 1-6:entire issue n. d.

COOPER, GLADYS
  In The letter.  Graphic 115:421 Mr 12 '27
  Grein, J. T.  Miss Cooper and the critics.  Ill Lon N 170:374
    Mr 8 '30
  Johns, E.  Her return to the English stage.  Theatre World 44:
    20 Ap '48
  Lewis, E.  About New York.  Cue 25-3:22 Ja 21 '56
  Tierney, M.  Nothing like a Dame; interview.  Plays & Players
    18-6:24 Mr '71
  Obit.  Broadcasting 81:79 N 29 '71
    Classic Film Collect 34:X-2 Spg '72
    Film R p14 '72/73
    N. Y. Times p50 N 18 '71
    Same.  N. Y. Times Bio Ed N 18 '71
    Newsweek 78:65 N 29 '71
    Screen World 23:236 '72
    Time 98:85 N 29 '71
  Von Furstenberg, B.  Gladys Cooper 1889-1971.  N. Y. Times
    Bio Ed N 28 '71
  Anderson, E.  Dame of the British empire; filmog.  Films In
    R 25-6:321 Je/Jl '74

COOPER, JACKIE
  Lang, H.  Sketch.  Photop 40:28 Je '31
  Churchill, E.  Cooper tells all.  Silver S 1-9:26 Jl '31
  His salary.  Outlook 150:68 S 16 '31
  Calhoun, D.  Sketch.  Motion Pic 42:32 D '31
  Manners, D.  Hollywood's opinions of.  Movie Classic 2:52 Ap
    '32
  Chandler, L.  Sketch.  Photop 42:56 Jl '32
  Service, F.  Outgrowing his roles.  Motion Pic 46:51 Ja '34
  Samuels, L.  Jackie.  Silver S 5-2:25 D '34
  Hall, G.  His diary while working in O'Shaughnessey's boy.
    Child Life 14:500 D '35
  Smalley, R. E.  Home of.  Movie Classic 11:46 N '36
  Carson, C.  His hobbies.  Leisure 5:26 Ag '38
  Williams, W.  Jitterbug.  Screen Book 22-6:82 Ja '40
  Holland, J.  Will Jackie and Bonita wed?  Silver S 12-2:38 D
    '41
  O'Leary, D.  His advice to Butch Jenkins.  Silver S 17-10:46
    Ag '47
  Water, R.  Broadway speedster.  Cue 23-32:13 Ag 7 '54
  Minoff, P.  Cooper for councilman.  Cue 24-35:12 S 3 '55
  Readin' ritin' and rehearsal.  TV Guide 4-38:20 S 22 '56
  Maltin, L.  Our gang; inc Our gang filmog.  Film Fan Mo 66:3
    D '66
  The kids.  Screen Greats 1-2:50 Sum '71
  Maltin, L.  Interview.  Film Fan Mo 156:19 Je '74

COOPER, MELVILLE
  Blackstock, L.  Sketch.  Motion Pic 54:15 N '37
  Obit.  Classic Film Collect 39:extra 1 Sum '73
    Film R p17 '73/74

N. Y. Times Bio Ed p566 Ap '73
Screen World p232 '74

COOPER, MIRIAM
Fletcher, A. W.  Interview.  Motion Pic 19:32 Mr '20
Sketch.  Photop 18:57 S '20
Cheatham, M.  Interview.  Motion Pic 22:36 Ag '21
Howe, H.  Interview.  Motion Pic 23:52 Je '22
Spotter.  Am Mag 123:102 F '37
O'Dell, P.  Forgotten star; filmog.  Silent Pic 4:5 Aut '69
Miriam Cooper; partial filmog.  Silent Pic 6:20 Spg '70
Miriam Cooper Walsh.  Classic Film Collect 26:ex 4 Win '70
Blackford, F.  Former film star lives quietly in Charlottesville.
    Classic Film Collect 42:35 Spg '74
Rubin, J.  Interview.  Classic Film Collect 44:6 Fall '74
Gitt, R; Herndon, B; Slide A.  Interview.  Silent Pic 19:41 '74

COPAGE, JOHN
Whitney, D.  Superchild meets his public.  TV Guide 17-26:10 Je
    28 '69

CORBETT, GLENN
And he hasn't crumpled a fender yet.  TV Guide 11-27:11 Jl 6
    '63

CORBIN, VIRGINIA LEE
Ames, H.  How she got in the movies.  Motion Pic 15:41 Je '18
Metcalfe, L.  Extry! Great Hollywood disaster.  Photop 15-5:55
    Ap '19
Goldbeck, E.  Sketch.  Motion Pic 39:70 My '30

CORBY, ELLEN
Stanks, D.  Ellen Corby; filmog.  Film Fan Mo 151:22 Ja '74

CORCORAN, NOREEN
It all started with mother's arthritis.  TV Guide 9-5:25 F 4 '61

CORD, ALEX
Lewis, S.  In the era of the anti-hero.  After Dark 11-9:16 Ja
    '70

CORDAY, PAULA
(Also known as Paula Croset; Rita Corday)
Benson, E.  Letter.  Films In R 17-7:459 Ag/S '66

CORDAY, RITA
(See CORDAY, PAULA)

COREY, WENDELL
Parsons, L. O.  Cosmop's citation for the best male supporting
    performance of the month.  Cosmop 126:13 Ja '49
Holliday, K.  A man of contradictions.  Silver S 19-11:35 S '49
Asher, J.  Why go on hating?  Silver S 21-2:37 D '50

Obit.   Film R p17 '69/70
  N. Y.  Times p33 N 9 '68
  Newsweek 72:137 N 18 '68
  Time 92:58 N 22 '68

CORLAN, ANTHONY
  Filmog.   Films & Filming 19-3:62 D '72

CORNWALL, ANNE
  Handy, T. B.   Interview.   Motion Pic Classic 11:22 O '20
  Uselton, R. A.   The Wampus baby stars.   Films In R 21-2:73
    F '70

CORRI, ADRIENNE
  Fighting talk.   Films Illus 3-28:153 O '73

CORRIGAN, LLOYD
  Obit.   N. Y. Times p21 N 8 '69
  Screen World 21:234 '70

CORSAUT, ANITA
  Making a career out of being a nice girl.   TV Guide 10-14:27
    Ap 7 '62
  Raddatz, L.   Anita Corsaut.   TV Guide 15-20:17 My 20 '67

CORTESE, VALENTINA
  Elley, D.   Valentina Cortese; filmog.   Focus On F 14:11 Spg '73
  Klemesrud, J.   It's my fault--I never followed the rules.   N. Y.
    Times sec 2:17 F 17 '74
    Same.   N. Y. Times Bio Ed p178 F '74

CORTEZ, RICARDO
  Fender, R.   Interview.   Motion Pic Classic 33:63 Jl '31
  Lieber, E.   His comeback.   Photop 41:45 D '31
  Grant, J.   Sketch.   Movie Classic 2:56 Ap '32
  Keats, P.   The busy Mr. Cortez.   Silver S 4-7:21 My '34
  Brundidge, H. T.   How he got into the movies.   Motion Pic 49:
    34 Jl '35

CORTLAND, NICHOLAS
  Stoop, N. M.   Suddenly now, I'm Rin Tin Tin.   After Dark 4-11:
    18 Mr '72

COSBY, BILL
  Riiight.   Newsweek 61:89 Je 17 '63
  Raceless Cosby.   Ebony 19:131 My '64
  Spy.   Newsweek 64:51 D 14 '64
  Mee, C. L.   That's the truth and other Cosby stories.   N. Y.
    Times Mag p96 Mr 14 '65
  Hemming, R.   Interview.   Sr Schol 86:17 Mr 18 '65
  Karnow, S.   Variety is the life of spies.   Sat Eve Post 238:86
    S 25 '65
  I spy.   Ebony 20:65 S '65

de Roos, R.   The spy who came in for the gold.   TV Guide 13-43:14 O 23 '65
Color him funny.   Newsweek 67:76 Ja '66
Life with Cosby.   Ebony 21:34 S '66
Simonds, C. H.   Primarily a guy.   Nat R 18:1007 O 4 '66
Long, J.   Interview.   Seventeen 26:94 Ja '67
Flagler, J. M.   Spy off duty.   Look 31:M16 My 30 '67
Stang, J.   Private world of...   Good House 164:26 Je '67
Cosby comes back to 11th and Green.   TV Guide 15-33:4 Ap 19 '67
Silver throat's crusade.   Newsweek 70:78 S 4 '67
Hallowell, J.   Interview.   Life 64:37 Mr 15 '68
Birstein, A.   Cosby special.   Vogue 151:134 Ap 1 '68
Color-blind comic.   Newsweek 71:92 My 20 '68
The regular way.   Playboy 15:115 D '68
Bio.   Cur Bio Yrbk 1967:82 '68
Morgan, T. B.   I am two people.   Life 66:74 Ap 11 '69
Interview.   Playboy 16-5:73 My '69
Robinson, L.   Pleasures and problems of being Cosby.   Ebony 24:144 Jl '69
Fat Albert and friends.   TV Guide 17-31:12 Ag 2 '69
Lewis, R. W.   Cosby takes over.   TV Guide 17-40:12 O 4 '69
Cosby on chicken football.   Look 33:94 N 4 '69
How to win at basketball: cheat.   Look 34:65 Ja 27 '70
Davison, M.   The man, his work, his world.   Good House 170:86 Mr '70
Pretty good going for the son of a wino.   Photop 78-1:61 Jl '70
Robinson, L.   Man and boy.   Ebony 26:42 Ap '71
Davidson, M.   Follow-up: command performance.   Good House 172:50 Je '71
Davidson, M.   Celebrating with the Cosbys.   Good House 175:64 D '72
Ryan, C.   The man in studio 41.   TV Guide 21-5:28 F 3 '73
Davidson, M.   It isn't playing at the Bijou.   TV Guide 21-33:28 Ag 18 '73

COSTELLO, DOLORES
Wells, H. K.   Sketch.   Motion Pic Classic 22:34 N '25
Interview.   Motion Pic 31:26 My '26
Johnston, C.   Sketch.   Motion Pic Classic 26:53 O '27
Marries John Barrymore.   Photop 35:29 F '29
Returns to pictures.   Time 27:48 Mr 23 '36
Harrison, P.   Her return to the screen.   Motion Pic 51:36 Ap '36
Uselton, R. A.   The Wampus baby stars.   Films In R 21-2:73 F '70
Bodeen, D.   John Barrymore and Dolores Costello; filmog.   Focus On F 12:17 Win '72

COSTELLO, HELLENE
Spensley, D.   Her sob-story.   Motion Pic Classic 31:29 My '30
Shaffer, R.   Sketch.   Movie Classic 1:28 F '32
Dowling, M.   Her divorce.   Movie Classic 2:24 Ag '32

Uselton, R. A.   The Wampus baby stars.   Films In R 21-2:73
  F '70

COSTELLO, LOU
  Reid, J.   Still up to their old tricks.   Silver S 12-2:34 D '41
  I'm Costello.   Lions R 1-8:no p# Ap '42
  Eddy, D.   Story of Abbott and Costello.   Am Mag 135:42 Ja '43
  Wilson, E.   Meet the box-office champs.   Silver S 13-6:34 Ap
    '43
  Wilson, E.   At Costello's bedside.   Silver S 13-12:28 O '43
  I'm a m-a-a-d boy!   Lions R 3-5:no p# D '44
  Frank, S.   Sketch.   Colliers 120:24 N 8 '47
  Obit.   Film R p10 '59/60
    Screen World 11:216 '60
  Comedians.   Screen Greats 1-2:62 Sum '71
  Peary, D.   Top comics of the forties.   Velvet Light 5:30 Sum
    '72

COSTELLO, MAURICE
  How egotism shows in moving pictures.   Blue Book 19:690 Ag '14
  Cummings, A.   Sketch.   Motion Pic Classic 26:18 Ja '28
  Obit.   Screen World 2:233 '51
  Leon, S.   Letter.   Films In R 22-4:248 Ap '71

COSTELLO, WARD
  The evolution of the have-not kid.   TV Guide 12-25:26 Je 20 '64

COSTELLO, WILLIAM
  Obit.   Classic Film Collect 33:46 Win '71
    N. Y. Times p47 O 12 '71

COTLER, SHIRLEY
  Young hopefuls do bit parts now.   TV Guide 1-7:20 My 15 '53

COTTEN, JOSEPH
  Hamilton, S.   Sketch.   Photop 20:54 F '42
  Wilson, E.   Not just another guy named Joe.   Silver S 12-7:24
    My '42
  Since you went away for America.   Cue 13-30:8 Jl 22 '44
  Bio.   Cur Bio 4 '43
  Trotter, M.   Prediction for 1944.   Photop 24:27 Ja '44
  Pickin' Cotten.   Lions R 3-3(sup):no p# Ap '44
  Hall, G.   Cotten talks.   Silver S 14-10:32 Ag '44
  Dudley, F.   Relax and enjoy life.   Silver S 17-3:37 Ja '47
  Caskin, B.   Cool and charming Cotten.   Silver S 17-9:66 Jl '47
  Here come the heroes.   TV Guide 4-37:28 S 15 '56
  It's the sponsor who pays.   TV Guide 4-37:24 S 15 '56
  Special report--Orson Welles.   Action 4-3:23 My/Je '69

COTTON, LUCY
  Service, F.   Interview.   Motion Pic Classic 11:24 S '20

COUGHLAN, FRANK JR.
  Whatever happened to Frank Coughlan Jr. ?    Those Enduring
    Idols 1-3:35 F/Mr '70

COULOURIS, GEORGE
  Gilling, T.   Interview with Coulouris and Bernard Herrman.
    Sight & Sound 41-2:71 Spg '72

COURT, HAZEL
  Gee whiz!   TV Guide 6-9:26 Mr 1 '58

COURTENAY, TOM
  Cowie, P.   The face of '63--Great Britain.    Films & Filming
    9-5:19 F '63
  Rising star.   Film R p38 '63/64
  Guerin, A.   One day in the life of Ivan Denisovich--and Courtenay
    loves it.   Show 2-6:26 Ag '71
  Loney, G. M.   Interview.   Interview 1-9:10 n. d.

COURTLAND, JEROME
  Courtland, J.   I believe in young Hollywood marriages.   Silver S
    20-12:40 O '50
  They make ladies' hearts go pitty pat.   TV Guide 5-28:8 Jl 13
    '57

COURTNEIDGE, CICELY
  Tierney, M.   Interview.   Plays & Players 19-5:28 F '72

COURTOT, MARGUERITE
  How she became a photoplayer.   Motion Pic 8:75 Ja '15
  Sketch.   Motion Pic 9:116 Je '15
  Courtlandt, R.   Interview.   Motion Pic 10:98 D '15
  Wynden-Vail, G.   Home life of.   Motion Pic Classic 2:41 Jl '16
  How she got in moving pictures.   Motion Pic 14:60 Ja '18
  Montanye, L.   Interview.   Motion Pic 19:73 F '20
  Cummings, J.   Interview.   Motion Pic Classic 14:44 My '22

COWAN, JEROME
  Sketch.   Photop 31:85 S '47
  Obit.   Classic Film Collect 34:X-3 Spg '72
      Film R p15 '72/73
    N. Y. Times p4 Ja 27 '72
    Same.   N. Y. Times Bio Ed Ja 26 '72
  Jewell, J.   Letter; partial filmog.   Films In R 23-7:447 Ag/S
    '72

COWL, JANE
  Romantic realist.   Cosmop 54:703 Ap '13
  Why a reputation for being a beauty is a handicap.   Am Mag 84:
    50 Ag '17
  How I kept myself from being a failure.   Ladies Home J 36:35
    Je '19
  Watch sharply--the next time you get to the theatre.   Am Mag

88:36 S '19
Lewisahn, L.  Juliet.  Nation 116:200 F 14 '23
Bernhardt memorial.  Drama 14:11 O '23
Jane Cowl's story.  Delin 104:10 Ap '24
Cole, C. C.  What Jane Cowl does for beauty.  Delin 106:22
    Mr '25
My beauty secret.  Ladies Home J 42:22 N '25
Kennedy, J. B.  Jane Cowl's only job.  Colliers 78:9 Jl 3 '26
Collapse of the drama.  Pict R 30:27 S '29
Roberts, K.  Good gracious!  Colliers 84:28 O 9 '29
Actress appeals to her audience.  No Am 229:7 Ja '30
Rebirth of glamour.  Cent 120:113 Ja '30
Young, S.  Miss Cowl.  New Rep 71:100 Je 8 '32
Jane Cowl: playwright.  Lions R 1-2:no p# O '41
Obit.  Newsweek 36:47 Jl 3 '50
    Screen World 2:233 '51
    Time 56:74 Jl 3 '50
Brock, A.  Backstage with the stars.  Classic Film Collect 36:
    30 Fall '72


COX, RONNY
    Whitney, D.  If he plays his cards right.  TV Guide 22-30:20 Jl
       27 '74


COX, WALLY
    Discless disc-jockey show.  New Yorker 27:29 O 13 '51
    Mr. Peepers emerges.  Life 33:78 Jl 7 '52
    Mr. Peepers.  Time 60:42 Jl 28 '52
    Who's who?  Newsweek 40:66 N 10 '52
    Barry, I.  Mr. Cox and his alter ego.  Cue 21-49:19 D 6 '52
    Poling, J.  Wally Cox is Mr. Peepers.  Colliers 131:66 Ja 3
      '53
    Gilroy, H.  Peep at Mr. Peepers.  N. Y. Times Mag p14 Ja 11
      '53
    Mr. Peepers grows bold.  Look 17:46 My 5 '53
    Back to school with Mr. Peepers.  TV Guide 1-23:5 S 4 '53
    Long, J.  Love life of Mr. Peepers.  Am Mag 156:26 O '53
    Gehman, R.  The man behind Mr. Peepers.  Cosmop 135:122 O
      '33
    Marshall, F.  Mr. Peepers does his homework.  Pop Mech 101:
      110 F '54
    Real Mr. Peepers.  Newsweek 43:84 Ap 12 '54
    Morrow, E.  Other Mr. Peepers.  Sat Eve Post 227:26 Ap 16
      '55
    Taylor, T.  Wally Cox and Mr. Peepers.  Coronet 37:91 Ap '55
    The rise and fall of Mr. Peepers.  TV Guide 3-31:20 Jl 30 '55
    New power for Peepers.  Life 41:155 O 8 '56
    Minoff, P.  You can't keep a good little man down.  Cue 25-43:
      14 O 27 '56
    Back to the kitchen.  TV Guide 5-7:12 F 16 '57
    Cox, W.  Whatever happened to me?  TV Guide 9-6:25 F 11 '61
    My life as a small boy.  Good House 153:99 N '61
    Frankel, H.  On the fringe.  Sat R 49:31 Mr 19 '66

Goodwin, F.   Taking another look at Mr. Peepers.   TV Guide
15-46:30 N 18 '67
Obit.   N. Y. Times p40 F 16 '73
Same.   N. Y. Times Bio Ed p232 F '73
In memory of.   Show 3-3:66 My '73

COXEN, EDWARD
Sketch.   Motion Pic 8:116 Ja '15
Courtlandt, R.   Sketch.   Motion Pic 10:115 Ag '15

COY, JOHNNY
Osborne, B.   Johnny Coy; filmog.   Films In R 25-6:381 Je/Jl
'74

CRABBE, LARRY "BUSTER"
Janeway, D.   Sketch.   Movie Classic 3:29 Ja '33
Nominated for stardom.   Motion Pic 45:42 F '33
Sketch.   Photop 44:82 Jl '33
Miller, M.   Swimming champion.   Photop 44:38 Jl '33
Dowling, M.   His success.   Motion Pic 47:66 Jl '34
Minoff, P.   Calisthenics by Crabbe!   Cue 20-17:19 Ap 28 '51
Malcomson, R. M.   The sound serial.   Views & Rs 3-1:13 Sum
'71
Cutter, R. A.   Flash Gordon lives, but up in Rye?   After Dark
4-10:32 F '72
Rubin, J.   Interview.   Classic Film Collect 43:9 Sum '74
Shay, D.   Interview.   Kaleidoscope 1-1:18 n. d.

CRAIG, CAROLYN
She wants to be her age.   TV Guide 6-11:24 Mr 15 '58

CRAIG, CATHERINE
Preston, C. C.   The movies and I.   Films In R 8-7:334 Ag/S
'57

CRAIG, JAMES
Franchey, J. R.   Recipe for renown.   Silver S 12-12:48 O '42
Hi, o...Maude!   Lions R 2-2:no p# N '42
Strictly business.   Lions R 2-3(sup):no p# Ja '43
Butter and egg man.   Lions R 2-4:no p# Ap '43
Haas, D. B.   Just one of the "Joes. "   Silver S 13-8:30 Je '43
Real life actor.   Lions R 2-5:no p# Jl '43
James Craig.   Lions R 3-2:no p# Ja '44
Credit to laughter.   Lions R 3-2:no p# Ja '44
So he didn't get the gal.   Lions R 3-5:no p# D '44
Craig, J.   Texan from Texas.   Lions R 3-5:no p# D '44

CRAIG, MAY
Obit.   N. Y. Times p46 F 10 '72
Time 99:68 F 21 '72

CRAIG, MICHAEL
People of promise.   Films & Filming 1-10:11 Jl '55

CRAIG, NELL
Sketch.   Green Book 16:985 D '16
Naylor, H. S.   Sketch.   Motion Pic 13:66 Ap '17
Obit.   Screen World 17:235 '66

CRAIG, NOEL
Stoop, N. M.   Two stars on the horizon.   After Dark 5-3:36 Jl
'72

CRAIG, YVONNE
Making a graceful entry into TV.   TV Guide 6-26:24 Je 28 '58
Swinging Yvonne.   Look 24:146 O 25 '60
The dynamic duo becomes a terrific trio.   TV Guide 15-44:14 N
4 '67

CRAIN, JEANNE
My biggest lie.   Photop 26:56 My '44
Bowers, L.   Lucky in love.   Silver S 17-1:35 N '46
Colby, A.   Story of.   Photop 30:48 D '46
Bowers, L.   Jeanne's new look.   Silver S 18-4:53 F '48
O'Leary, D.   Can a girl stay natural in Hollywood?   Silver S 18-
10:28 Ag '48
Story of.   Life 27:39 O 17 '49
Morris, J.   Jeanne really means it.   Silver S 21-2:42 D '50
Crain, J.   I object!   Silver S 22-3:24 Ja '52
Churchill, R. & B.   Hollywood's greatest sin.   Silver S 23-4:22
F '53
Churchill, R. & B.   You wouldn't know Jeanne now.   Silver S
24-9:42 Jl '54
Jeanne Crain answers your questions on marriage and children.
Movie Dig 1-2:73 Mr '72; 1-4:130 Jl '72

CRAMER, SUSANNE
The exceptional Miss Cramer.   TV Guide 14-28:19 Jl 9 '66

CRANE, BOB
Dern, M.   Man in pursuit of himself.   TV Guide 13-9:16 F 27
'65
Efron, E.   Think John Wayne.   TV Guide 16-31:25 Ag 3 '68

CRANE, DAGNE
Hickey, N.   From hatha yoga to women's liberation.   TV Guide
18-28:26 Jl 11 '70

CRANE, JAMES L.
Sketch.   N. Y. Drama 74:12 O 30 '15

CRANE, NORMA
Obit.   Films & Filming 20-3:81 D '73
N. Y. Times p65 S 30 '73
Screen World p233 '74

CRANE, RICHARD
    Why I'm still single.  Photop 25:57 N '44
    Raker, A.  Filmog.  Films In R 20-6:386 Je/Jl '69

CRANE, WARD
    Bruce, B.  Interview.  Motion Pic 20:64 D '20

CRANSHAW, PAT
    Zolotow, M.  The ballad of toothless Cranshaw.  TV Guide 22-
        44:12 N 2 '74

CRAVEN, FRANK
    Interview.  N.Y. Drama 76:5 S 30 '16
    Sketch.  Theatre 26:146 S '17
    Woolcott, A.  Sketch.  Everybodys 44:54 F '21
    Bio sketch.  Theatre Arts 11:534 Jl '27
    Sketch.  Theatre Guild 9:7 Ap '32
    Obit.  Cur Bio 6 '45

CRAWFORD, BRODERICK
    Vallee, W. L.  Actor by conquest.  Silver S 11-10:40 Ag '41
    Wilson, E.  They always knew he had it.  Silver S 20-7:26 My
        '50
    Whitney, D.  Crawford reminisces.  TV Guide 19-10:34 Mr 6 '71

CRAWFORD, HOWARD MARION
    Obit.  Film R p15 '70/71

CRAWFORD, JOAN
    Denbo, D.  Interview.  Motion Pic 33:48 Ap '27
    Interview.  Motion Pic 34:56 N '27
    Belfrage, C.  Sketch.  Motion Pic Classic 27:37 Jl '28
    Biery, R.  Sketch.  Motion Pic Classic 28:40 Ja '29
    St. Johns, I.  Sketch.  Photop 31:71 My '29
    Goldbeck, E.  Sketch.  Motion Pic Classic 29:55 Jl '29
    Whitaker, A.  Home of.  Photop 36:64 Ag '29
    Manners, D.  Interview.  Motion Pic Classic 30:16 S '29
    Manners, D.  Sketch.  Motion Pic Classic 30:51 O '29
    Sketch.  Photop 37:10 Mr '30
    Biery, R.  Sketch.  Motion Pic 39:66 My '30
    Fairbanks, D. Jr.  Appreciation.  Vanity Fair 34:55 Jl '30
    Sketch.  Fortune 2:39 O '30
    Busby, M.  Interview.  Photop 38:57 O '30
    Hall, G.  Interview.  Motion Pic 41:49 Mr '31
    Harris, R.  The real Joan Crawford.  Silver S 1-7:21 My '31
    Manners, D.  Interview.  Motion Pic 41:66 My '31
    Service, F.  Sketch.  Motion Pic 41:48 Jl '31
    Walker, H. L.  Compared with Shearer and Garbo.  Movie Clas-
        sic 1:23 S '31
    Jamison, J.  Faked divorce rumors.  Movie Classic 1:36 N '31
    Maddox, B.  Give (her) credit.  Silver S 2-3:25 Ja '32
    Sherman, J.  Sketch.  Movie Classic 1:50 Ja '32
    Chensley, C. W.  Sketch.  Motion Pic 43:42 Mr '32

Albert, K.  Sketch.  Photop 41:40 Mr '32
Rice, L.  Her handwriting.  Movie Classic 2:51 Je '32
Gallant, T.  Faciology of Crawford.  Movie Classic 2:24 Jl '32
Horton, H.  When Joan comes into her own.  Silver S 2-9:22 Jl
  '32
Wilson, E.  First shots of Rain.  Silver S 2-10:18 Ag '32
Melcher, E.  Pitfalls of publicity.  Cinema Dig 1-9:7 S 5 '32
Manners, D.  Will her career wreck her marriage.  Motion Pic
  44:1 S '32
Wilson, E.  The premiere of Rain.  Silver S 3-1:44 N '32
Manners, D.  Her first trip to Europe.  Motion Pic 44:47 D '32
North, J.  Recovers her sense of humor.  Photop 43:72 D '32
Moffitt, C. F.  Censorship for interviews Hollywood's latest wild
  idea.  Cinema Dig 2-5:9 Ja 9 '33
Crawford receives her medal.  Silver S 3-3:46 Ja '33
Service, F.  The star who never rests.  Movie Classic 3:38 Ja
  '33
Wilson, E.  Crawford rebels.  Silver S 3-4:18 F '33
Taviner, R.  Divorce rumors.  Photop 43:31 Ap '33
Fidler, J.  Interview.  Movie Classic 4:22 Ap '33
Grantham, K.  When Crawford was a school girl.  Silver S 3-7:
  24 My '33
Cates, F.  Interview.  Movie Classic 4:20 My '33
Her separation from D. Fairbanks Jr.  Motion Pic 45:26 My '33
Bahn, C. B.  Joan Crawford...  Cinema Dig 4-5:10 Je 12 '33
Pryor, N.  How does she rate with women.  Movie Classic 4:47
  Je '33
Fidler, J.  Doug is courting her again.  Motion Pic 45:56 Je
  '33
Manners, D.  Her rivalries.  Movie Classic 4:23 Jl '33
French, W. F.  Interview.  Photop 44:30 Jl '33
Parker, M.  Her best friend.  Photop 44:50 Ag '33
Lynn, H.  How she makes love.  Photop 44:31 Ag '33
Manners, D.  Does not want sex appeal.  Movie Classic 5:26 S
  '33
Fidler, J. M.  The Gardenia girl.  Silver S 3-11:16 S '33
Crawford wins the Silver Screen Gold Medal.  Silver S 3-11:50
  S '33
Keats, P.  Our Dancing lady.  Silver S 3-12:24 O '33
Biery, R.  Easy to hurt.  Silver S 4-1:12 N '33
Hall, G.  Interview.  Motion Pic 46:42 D '33
Walker, H. L.  Crawford--the most remarkable girl in Holly-
  wood.  Silver S 4-3:24 Ja '34
Walker, H. L.  A weekend with Crawford.  Silver S 4-11:18 S
  '34
Maddox, B.  Joan on the phone.  Silver S 5-1:26 N '34
Ergenbright, E. L.  Her success secret.  Motion Pic 48:40 Ja
  '35
Ergenbright, E. L.  Interview.  Motion Pic 49:56 F '35
Mook, S. R.  Interview.  Motion Pic 49:19 Mr '35
Ramsey, W.  These things have counted.  Silver S 5-6:20 Ap '35
Hartley, K.  Interview.  Motion Pic 49:28 My '35
Lee, S.  Answers her critics.  Movie Classic 8:26 Je '35

Babcock, M.   Through Crawford's clothes closet.   Silver S 5-8: 24 Je '35

Samuels, L.   Beautiful Joan.   Silver S 5-9:24 Jl '35

Brundidge, H. T.   How she got into movies.   Motion Pic 49:35 Jl '35

Brundidge, H. T.   Interview.   Motion Pic 50:27 Ag '35

Mook, S. R.   Interview.   Movie Classic 9:34 O '35

Sullivan, E.   Garbo is right.   Silver S 6-3:12 Ja '36

Lee, S.   Why she married Franchot Tone.   Motion Pic 51:35 F '36

Lieber, E.   Story.   Movie Classic 9:32 F '36

Asher, J.   Cocktails with Joan.   Silver S 6-8:53 Je '36

Lee, S.   The new Joan.   Motion Pic 51:30 Jl '36

Wilson, E.   Projections of Crawford.   Silver S 6-12:26 O '36

Hall, G.   Interview.   Movie Classic 11:30 N '36

Experience with.   Photop 50:16 D '36

Albert, K.   Interview.   Motion Pic 52:22 Ja '37

Sketch.   Life 2:46 Mr 1 '37

Spensley, D.   The most copied girl in the world.   Motion Pic 53:30 My '37

Lee, S.   Crawford's amazing plans.   Screen Book 19-3:52 O '37

Joan Crawford.   Visages 17:entire issue O '37

Wilson, E.   She's dancing again.   Silver S 9-3:10 Ja '39

Reid, J.   I like Hollywood.   Screen Book 21-7:31 F '39

Waterbury, R.   Interview.   Photop 53:12 Ag '39

Danger! High explosives!   Screen Book 22-2:58 S '39

Franchey, J. R.   Joan's own way to snag a man.   Silver S 10-10:22 Ag '40

Bio note; filmog.   Movies & People 2:10 '40

Franchey, J. R.   Bachelor mother.   Silver S 12-10:38 Ag '42

Sketch.   Harp Baz 76:88 Ag '42

Crawford's jobs.   Lions R 2-3(sup):no p# Ja '43

Manners, M. J.   Crawford's wartime philosophy.   Silver S 13-5: 24 Mr '43

A mistake I wouldn't make again.   Photop 22:46 My '43

An idea is born.   Lions R 2-5:no p# Jl '43

My secret dream.   Photop 23:55 O '43

Letter from Liza.   Silver S 14-12:55 O '44

My favorite possession.   Photop 26:57 My '45

Story of.   Newsweek 26:102 O 15 '45

Dudley, F.   Untold tales about Crawford.   Silver S 16-2:22 D '45

O'Leary, D.   None can compare.   Silver S 16-8:40 Je '46

Parsons, L. O.   Cosmop's citation for the best performance of the month.   Cosmop 121:72 N '46

Bio.   Cur Bio 7 '46

Marsh, P.   Newspapermen's delight.   Silver S 18-1:24 N '47

Graham, S.   Sketch.   Photop 33:40 N '48

O'Leary, D.   There are no bad girls.   Silver S 19-5:22 Mr '49

Crawford, J.   Tricks that don't fool women.   Silver S 20-2:24 D '49

Maxwell, E.   Sketch.   Photop 36:35 D '49

Lane, F.   Behind closed doors with informative Joan.   Silver S 20-8:40 Je '50

O'Leary, D.  One Joan to another.  Silver S 21-7:26 My '51
MacDonald, E.  A letter to a star.  Silver S 22-1:30 N '51
Baer, M. M.  How I live, love and stay happy.  Silver S 23-9:
   26 Jl '53
Hull, W.  No better friend.  Silver S 24-6:46 Ap '54
Gow, G.  The quest for realism; discussion.  Films & Filming
   4-3:13 D '57
Hill, T. G.  Letter; TV appearances.  Films In R 17-7:457 Ag/
   S '66
Uselton, R. A.  The Wampus baby stars.  Films In R 21-2:73
   F '70
Art of looking beautiful; excerpt from My way of life.  McCalls
   98:55 Jl '71
Still going great.  Screen Greats 1-2:78 Sum '71
Moore, T.  (She) refuses to play Miss Mushy Mouth.  Life 71:
   81 O 15 '71
Kula, S.  The dancing lady remembers.  AFI Report p4 O '71
Montgomery, T.  The Crawford style.  Hollywood Stu 6-8:17 D
   '71
Cooking with a star.  Mod Screen 66-1:60 Ja '72
Albert, K.  Waitress to glamour girl.  Liberty 1-4:58 Spg '72
Bosworth, P.  I'm still an actress!  N. Y. Times sec 2:21 S 24
   '72
   Same.  N. Y. Times Bio Ed p1624 S '72
Interview.  Mod Screen 66-9:36 S '72
Basinger, J.  Letter reply to P. Bosworth.  N. Y. Times sec
   2:19 O 15 '72
A tribute to Joan Crawford.  Film Fan Mo 138:29 D '72
Tuska, J.  Rain.  Views & Rs 3-4:4 '72
Basinger, J.  The films of Joan Crawford.  AFI Report 4-1:10
   F '73
The tales their houses tell.  Mod Screen 67-2:36 F '73
Phillips, M.  Many eras, many fans (at Town Hall).  N. Y.
   Times p36 Ap 10 '73
Crawford, J.  I deplore going back (comment on obscenity rul-
   ing).  N. Y. Times sec 2:11 Ag 5 '73
Bowers, R.  Legendary ladies of the movies.  Films In R 24-6:
   321 Je/Jl '73
Kobal, J.  Working with...; interview with Vincent Sherman.
   Film 2-9:12 D '73
Bourget, J-L.  Romantic dramas of the forties.  Film Comment
   10-1:48 Ja/F '74

CRAWFORD, JOHNNY
   An old pro at 12.  TV Guide 7-19:24 My 9 '59

CRAWFORD, MICHAEL
   Miller, E.  Michael of the movies; interview.  Seventeen 28:104
      D '69
   The actor as acrobat.  Plays & Players 18-11:14 Ag '71

CREGAR, LAIRD
   Haas, D. B.  Setbacks to fame.  Silver S 12-8:52 Je '42

Hendricks, H.   Maniac at ease!   Silver S 14-3:30 Ja '44
My Christmas wish.   Photop 26:47 Ja '45
Obit.   Cur Bio 6 '45
Mank, G.   Laird Cregar; filmog.   Film Fan Mo 150:3 D '73

CRENNA, RICHARD
Filmog.   Films & Filming 20-6:52 Mr '74

CRESPI, TODD
Schaefer, S.   Todd Crespi.   Photop 85-5:66 My '74

CRESPO, JOSE
Spensley, D.   His difficulties in entering the U.S.   Motion Pic
   40:33 N '30
Movie double-talk.   Inter Am 5:26 F '46

CREWS, LAURA HOPE
Career.   Pearson (NY) 24:95 Jl '10
Patterson, A.   Interview.   Theatre 39:12 Ap '24
Miller, L.   Fifty years of acting.   Motion Pic 46:54 O '33

CRISP, DONALD
Willis, R.   Three rough-necks from The escape.   Photop 7-3:
   136 F '15
Henry, W. M.   Crisp is right.   Photop 11-2:133 Ja '17
Kingsley, R.   Sketch.   Motion Pic 18:49 S '19
Hamilton, S.   Sketch.   Photop 54:28 My '40
Crisp's third war.   Lions R 3-1:no p# S '43
Talks about the movie greats he knew as child stars.   Classic
   Film Collect 42:35 Spg '74
Obit.   Classic Film Collect 43:X6 Sum '74
   N.Y. Times p20 My 27 '74
   Same.   N.Y. Times Bio Ed p660 My '74

CROCKER, HARRY
Lindsay, M.   Sketch.   Photop 18:30 Ja '41
R-day for the 21-year-olds.   C.S. Mon Mag p5 Je 14 '41
Assignment in Hollywood (various issues) Good House to Je '48

CROMWELL, RICHARD
Jarvis, P.   Sketch.   Photop 39:56 F '31
Sketch.   Motion Pic 41:78 Mr '31
Duncan, C.   Mr. Cinderella.   Silver S 1-6:37 Ap '31
Sketch.   Photop 42:40 S '32
Sketch.   Photop 45:78 D '33
Manners, D.   Interview.   Motion Pic 47:55 F '34
Obit.   Screen World 12:219 '61

CRONYN, HUME
Whorf, R.   As I see them.   Lions R 3-2:no p# Ja '44
Mr. & Mrs. --24 hours a day.   Lions R 3-4(sup):no p# Jl '44
Whorf, R.   Cronyn's a character.   Lions R 4-1:no p# F '45
It's the sponsor who pays.   TV Guide 4-37:24 S 15 '56

Eyles, A.  Cronyn; filmog.  Focus On F 1:16 Mr/Ap '70
Chase, C.  Tandy and Cronyn are wed to the theatre, too.  N. Y.
    Times sec 2:1 Mr 24 '74
    Same.  N. Y. Times Bio Ed p443 Mr '74

CROSBY, BING
    Sketch.  Motion Pic 43:51 F '32
    Manners, D.  Interview.  Motion Pic 47:51 Mr '34
    Sketch.  Photop 45:87 Mr '34
    Sketch.  Photop 45:71 My '34
    Hall, G.  Interview.  Motion Pic 47:42 Je '34
    Donnell, D.  Interview.  Movie Classic 6:30 Je '34
    Keats, P.  She loves me not.  Silver S 4-10:26 Ag '34
    Standish, J.  Father of twin boys.  Movie Classic 7:40 O '34
    French, W. F.  Interview.  Motion Pic 49:57 F '35
    Tally, J.  Sketch.  Motion Pic 49:32 Mr '35
    Walker, H. L.  Two life stories that became one.  Silver S 5-8:
        26 Je '35
    Sherwin, T.  As a father.  Motion Pic 50:30 Ag '35
    Lee, D.  As a husband.  Movie Classic 8:26 Ag '35
    Ulman, W. A. Jr.  Story of.  Motion Pic 50:50 O '35
    Mercer, M.  Home of.  Movie Classic 9:41 N '35
    Williams, F.  Interview.  Motion Pic 51:36 F '36
    Kent, J.  Interview.  Movie Classic 10:6 Ap '36
    Lang, H.  His popularity explained.  Motion Pic 52:32 S '36
    Reid, J.  Story of.  Movie Classic 11:44 N '36
    Sketch.  Photop 52:38 My '38
    Maddox, B.  Bing and all that money.  Silver S 8-10:52 Ag '38
    Story of.  Life 5:54 S 5 '38
    Simpson, G.  Meet "lonely hearts" Crosby.  Screen Book 22-2:
        60 S '39
    Walker, H. L.  If I had my life to live over.  Silver S 10-6:
        52 Ap '40
    Bio note; filmog.  Movies & People 2:10 '40
    Reid, J.  Actors aren't sissies!  Silver S 11-7:26 My '41
    Mook, D.  Bing comes out of his shell.  Silver S 12-11:36 S '42
    Hopper, H.  His married life.  Photop 22:27 My '43
    Manners, M. J.  Dottie tells on Bob and Bing.  Silver S 14-6:30
        Ap '44
    Der Bingle and Dinah are back.  Cue 13-43:11 O 21 '44
    Bangs, B.  Concerning Bing.  Silver S 15-1:24 N '44
    Pritchett, F.  Overseas with Bing.  Silver S 15-4:22 F '45
    In France.  Harp Baz 79:92 F '45
    Revises Kraft music hall radio show.  Newsweek 25:93 F 19 '45
    His world-wide popularity.  Time 45:88 Mr 26 '45
    Crosby, B.  Yes, I guess I've changed.  Silver S 16-3:38 Ja '46
    Awarded Photoplay Gold Medal for 1945.  Photop 28:29 F '46
    Story of.  Vogue 107:154 Mr 15 '46
    First place in Companion poll of favorite stars.  Womans Home
        C 73:8 Je '46
    Crosby, E.  Brother Bing.  Silver S 17-11:22 S '46
    Parsons, L. O.  Cosmop's citation for the best actor of the
        month.  Cosmop 121:66 S '46

Prize winner for 1946.    Photop 30:38 F '47
My favorite tree.    Am For 54:74 F '48
Maxwell, E.    Story of.    Photop 33:44 Ag '48
Holland, J.    Bing's new leading lady.    Silver S 19-1:42 N '48
Rogers, B.    Crosby research foundation.    Cue 18-12:18 Mr 19
    '49
Winner of Photop gold medal for 1948.    Photop 34:32 Mr '49
Blyth, A.    Having fun with Bing and Barry.    Silver S 19-7:42
    My '49
Crosby, B.    My favorite role, and why.    Film R p15 '50
Minoff, P.    The world is their oyster.    Cue 21-49:16 D 6 '52
O'Leary, D.    The true meaning of Christmas.    Silver S 23-2:22
    D '52
Sheridan, M.    Bing's romantic future.    Silver S 23-8:26 Je '53
Bing goes dramatic.    Cue 23-48:13 N 27 '54
Plimpton, G.    A block on the road to yaksville.    Show 2-4:95
    Ap '62
Raddatz, L.    How Crosby has mellowed.    TV Guide 12-50:6 D
    12 '64
Davis, D.    Fishing with Bing.    Travel & Camera 32:84 Ag '69
Crosby, B.    Remembering Leo McCarey.    Action 4-5:12 S/O '69
Stone, J.    I'll be dreaming of a white Christmas again.    N. Y.
    Times D 13 '70
    Same.    N. Y. Times Bio Ed D 13 '70
Song and dance men.    Screen Greats 1-2:42 Sum '71
Whitney, D.    Life with Bing.    TV Guide 20-51:24 D 16 '72
Collins, F. L.    America's richest actor.    Liberty 1-8:57 Spg
    '73
Kent, R.    The Crosby experience.    Interview 3-9:17 S '73
It's Bing's special, but Kathy is the Crosby to watch these days.
    People 2-25:34 D 16 '74

CROSBY, GARY
    Davidson, M.    A man's victory over alcoholism.    Good House
        165:93 S '67
    How I faced my drinking problem.    Photop 78-4:60 O '70
    Whitney, D.    Life with Bing.    TV Guide 20-51:24 D 16 '72
    Raddatz, L.    Three heroes have disappeared.    TV Guide 22-22:14
        Je 1 '74

CROSBY, PHIL
    The Hollywood swingers.    Show 3-11:91 N '63

CROSET, PAULA
    (See CORDAY, PAULA)

CROSSE, RUPERT
    Obit.    Screen World p233 '74

CROWLEY, KATHLEEN
    Miss Egg Harbor of 1949.    TV Guide 6-28:25 Jl 12 '58
    Crowley works hard for stardom.    TV Guide 9-32:17 Ag 12 '61

CROWLEY, PAT
    Perkens, R.  It simply isn't true.  Silver S 24-7:30 My '54

CRUZ, BRANDON
    What generation gap?  TV Guide 19-25:12 Je 19 '71

CUADRA, MARIA
    Cobos, J.  The face of '63--Spain.  Films & Filming 10-1:39 O
        '63

CUGAT, XAVIER
    Rhumba king.  Newsweek 18:74 O 13 '41
    Eet ees deesgosting!  Time 40:56 D 28 '42
    Bio.  Cur Bio '42
    Vallee, W. L.  His royal rumba majesty.  Silver S 13-12:38 O
        '43
    Kilgallen, D.  Rhumba one man.  Colliers 112:18 N 20 '43
    Rhumba me round again, Willie.  Cue 13-1:10 Ja 1 '44
    Good will ambassador.  Lions R 3-3(sup):no p# Ap '44
    Wood, W.  Music in the South American way.  Etude 62:317 Je/
        Jl '44
    Cugat versus May.  Cue 13-28:10 Jl 8 '44
    Faces his fortune.  Lions R 3-4:no p# Jl '44
    Personality.  Time 48:43 Jl 29 '46
    Power of a woman.  Newsweek 37:53 Je 18 '51
    Kassel, A. M.  A painter as well as a musician.  Show 2-8:42
        N '72

CULVER, CAL
    (Also known as Casey Donovan, which see)
    Como, W.  Yeah, but can he do dialogue?  After Dark 5-3:27
        Jl '72
    McClelland, D.  Meet Cal Culver.  Filmograph 3-2:40 '72
    The naked athlete; photos.  Viva 1-9:76 Je '74

CULVER, HOWARD
    Raddatz, L.  The Dodge City gang.  TV Guide 20-12:14 Mr 18
        '72

CUMMING, RUTH
    Obit.  Screen World 19:230 '68

CUMMINGS, CONSTANCE
    Jones, C. P.  Constance Cummings.  Cinema Dig 2-2:11 N 28
        '32
    Moak, B.  Up and Cummings.  Silver S 3-2:20 D '32
    Costello, T.  Sketch.  Motion Pic 44:47 Ja '33
    Sketch.  Photop 43:92 Ja '33
    Sylvia.  How I gave her a new figure.  Photop 43:54 Mr '33
    Sketch.  Newsweek 9:25 Ap 10 '37
    Johns, E.  Interview.  Theatre World 42:19 O '46
    Uselton, R. A.  The Wampus baby stars.  Films In R 21-2:73
        F '70

Constance Cummings talks to M. Tierney.   Plays & Players 19-
4:32 Ja '72

CUMMINGS, ROBERT
Rhea, M.   Sketch.   Photop 53:31 Jl '39
Wilson, E.   Gable was never like this.   Silver S 11-1:42 N '40
Cummings, R.   Is a husband ever a boss?   Silver S 16-6:35 Ap
'46
Parsons, L.   Cosmop's citation for one of the best performances
of the month.   Cosmop 124:13 Mr '48
Cummings, R. K.   This is my son.   Silver S 18-12:47 O '48
Cummings, R.   This business of being a husband.   Silver S 21-
12:22 O '51
Minoff, P.   A fine comic is wasted in silly video series.   Cue
21-50:9 D 13 '52
Minoff, P.   New ventures for Bob Cummings.   Cue 24-2:47 Ja
15 '55
Minoff, P.   Comeback for Cummings.   Cue 25-15:16 Ap 14 '56
Gehman, R.   Bob Cumming's foundation of youth.   TV Guide 9-
32:12 Ag 12 '61

CUMMINGS, SUSAN
This could be expensive.   TV Guide 5-12:16 Mr 23 '57
Competition from a locomotive.   TV Guide 8-7:25 F 13 '60

CUMMINGS, VICKI
Obit.   N. Y. Times p55 D 2 '69
Time 94:87 D 12 '69

CUMMINS, PEGGY
Dudley, F.   Bernhardt from Britain.   Silver S 16-8:60 Je '46
Dudley, F.   It was only a dented fender.   Silver S 17-8:50 Je
'47
Vallee, W. L.   Peggy gets around.   Silver S 19-12:40 O '49

CUNARD, GRACE
How she became a photoplayer.   Motion Pic 9:117 Mr '15
Willis, R.   Interview.   Motion Pic 9:98 Jl '15
Sketch.   Motion Pic Classic 1:48 Ja '16
Leon, S.   Letter.   Films In R 23-2:124 F '72
Everett, E. K.   The great Cunard-Ford mystery.   Classic Film
Collect 39:22 Sum '73

CUNNINGHAM, CECIL
McClelland, D.   Cecil Cunningham.   Film Fan Mo 132:9 Je '72

CUNNINGHAM, ZAMAH
Obit.   Screen World 19:230 '68

CURLEY, PAULINE
Remont, F.   Interview.   Motion Pic Classic 8:34 Mr '19
Cheatham, M. S.   Interview.   Motion Pic 18:52 O '19

CURRAN, PAMELA
    See if you can capture some of the quicksilver on paper.    TV
        Guide 10-18:10 My 5 '62

CURRIE, FINLAY
    Obit.    N. Y. Times p35 My 11 '68

CURRY, STEVE
    O'Brien, G.    Interview.    Interview 2-6:24 O '71

CURTIS, ALAN
    Smithson, E. J.    A model young man.    Screen Book 20-3:36 Ap
        '38
    Taxicab to Hollywood.    Lions R 2-5:no p# Jl '43

CURTIS, CHRISTOPHER
    Walker, H. L.    Story of.    Photop 26:42 My '45

CURTIS, DICK
    Dick Curtis; filmog.    Cinema Trails 2:8 n.d.
    Smith, H. A.    Just like a movie.    Sat Eve Post 222:32 Ja 28
        '50

CURTIS, JACKIE
    Wicked women on the moon.    Interview 1-4:20 n.d.
    The love life of Jackie Curtis.    Interview 2-3:15; 2-4:26 Jl '71
    Abagnalo, G.    Interview.    Interview 4-7:24 Ag '74

CURTIS, TONY
    Leigh, J.    What I like about Tony Curtis.    Silver S 21-6:26 Ap
        '51
    Leigh, J.    And so we were married.    Silver S 21-12:26 O '51
    Rowland, R. C.    So happily ever after.    Silver S 22-5:36 Mr
        '52
    Curtis, T.    At last I'm carrying the ball.    Silver S 22-12:28 O
        '52
    Rising star.    Film R p108 '52/53
    Maddox, B.    Untold tales about Janet and Tony.    Silver S 23-5:
        40 Mr '53
    Leigh, J.    The real facts about Tony and me.    Silver S 24-2:29
        D '53
    Curtis, T.    Any girl can be charming.    Silver S 24-8:42 Je '54
    Zunser, J.    Boy into man.    Cue 27-31:10 Ag 2 '58
    Lewis, R. W.    It's a brand new ball game.    Sat Eve Post 241:
        39 Mr 23 '68
    Weinraub, B.    The cool and the chutzpah.    N. Y. Times Bio Ed
        Ag 23 '70
    Kasindorf, M.    Xanadu for sale.    Newsweek 79:66 Ja 24 '72
    Musel, R.    The oddest couple.    TV Guide 20-15:12 Ap 8 '72
    Cassa, A.    Tony Curtis; filmog.    Films In R 24-1:63 Ja '73
    Partial filmog.    Films & Filming 19-7:66 Ap '73
    Garland, W.    Tony Curtis; filmog.    Films In R 25-5:312 My '74

CUSHING, PETER
   Bio note.  Black Oracle 2:20 n. d.
   Interview.  Black Oracle 5:6 Spg '71
   Cushing, P.  Letter.  Cinefantastique 1-4:4 Fall '71
   Castell, D.  Professor Van Helsing is alive and well...; filmog.
      Films Illus 1-6:6 D '71
   Knight, C. & Nicholson, P.  A chat with Peter Cushing.  Cine-
      fantastique 2-2:5 Sum '72
   Knight, C.  London scene.  Cinefantastique 2-4:43 Sum '73
   Cushing on Frankenstein and others.  Films Illus 3-28:150 O '73

CUTTS, PATRICIA
   Scatty.  TV Guide 6-31:29 Ag 2 '58

CYBULSKI, ZBIGNIEW
   The Polish cinema.  Film 31:25 Spg '62
   Obit.  Screen Ed 39:54 My/Je '67
   Minchinton, J.  Zbigniew Cybulski.  Film 48:26 Spg '67
   Pin-up of the past.  Films & Filming 18-9:72 Je '72

DADE, FRANCES
   Uselton, R. A.  The Wampus baby stars.  Films In R 21-2:73
      F '70

DAGMAR
   Breathing, just breathing.  Time 58:60 Jl 9 '51
   Week with Dagmar.  Life 31:132 Jl 16 '51
   Steinberg, J.  Day and night with Dagmar.  Am Mer 73:79 S '51
   Dieting ain't fun but it's sure rewarding.  TV Guide 1-6:21 My 8
      '53
   Leonard Sillman's New faces of 1971.  Cue 40-8:9 F 20 '71
   Now you see 'em, now you don't.  Look 35-18:70 S 7 '71

DAGOVER, LIL
   Dibble, S.  Makes tour of U. S.  Movie Classic 1:39 D '31
   Goldbeck, E.  Sketch.  Motion Pic 43:66 Mr '32

DAHL, ARLENE
   Sketch.  Life 27:43 S 19 '49
   Dahl, A.  Men's worst date faults.  Silver S 20-7:22 My '50
   Dahl, A.  Here's why our marriage will last.  Silver S 21-10:
      22 Ag '51
   Hall, G.  For as long as we both shall live.  Silver S 22-9:24
      Jl '52
   Sheridan, M.  Hollywood's most criticized romance.  Silver S
      23-10:29 Ag '53
   Mathews, L.  Arlene's hidden desire.  Silver S 24-5:19 Mr '54
   Portrait, E.  The world of beauty welcomes Hollywood's beauti-
      ful women.  Cue 38-46:11 N 15 '69

DAILEY, DAN
   Hamilton, S.  Sketch.  Photop 18:37 Mr '41
   Dan-of-all-trades.  Lions R 1-8:no p# Ap '42
   He's in the army now.  Lions R 1-9:no p# My '42
   Lane, L.  Mrs. Dailey's problem husband.  Silver S 19-5:42 Mr
     '49
   Parsons, L. O.  Cosmop's citation for the best male performance
     of the month.  Cosmop 126:14 Mr '49
   Dailey, D.  What's a talent anyway?  Silver S 21-4:44 F '51
   Lane, L.  What does Dan Dailey want?  Silver S 22-6:24 Ap '52
   Pine, D.  Is Dailey having fun, or what?  Silver S 24-2:26 D '53
   Dailey's loved by two women.  Photop 77-5:69 My '70
   I was in a mental hospital.  Photop 84-6:45 D '73
   Albert, J. E.  Dan Dailey; filmog.  Film Fan Mo 153:3 Mr '74

DAILEY, IRENE
   Perils of Irene.  Time 76:57 Jl 18 '60
   Zeicer, A.  Irene Dailey: she's still here.  After Dark 4-5:33
     S '71

DAILY, BILL
   Raddatz, L.  I'll never make it as an actor.  TV Guide 17-14:11
     Ap 5 '69

DAILY, BOB
   My child.  Photop 85-1:51 Ja '74

DALBERT, SUZANNE
   Puso, L.  Obit; filmog.  Classic Film Collect 31:20 Sum '71
   Brandley, A.  Letter; filmog.  Films In R 22-6:379 Je/Jl '71

d'ALCY, JEHANNE
   Eisner, L.  The passing of the first film star.  Film 11:4 Ja/F
     '57

DALE, CHARLES
   What this country needs.  Theatre 53:14 Ja '31
   And why not more repertory?  Theatre 53:14 F '31
   First birthday party.  Theatre 53:14 Mr '31
   Obit.  N. Y. Times p50 N 17 '71
     Newsweek 78:65 N 29 '71
     Screen World 23:236 '72
     Time 98:85 N 29 '71

DALE, JIM
   Up hill and down Dale.  Films Illus 2-21:14 Mr '73
   Filmog.  Films & Filming 20-6:52 Mr '74
   Hess, J. L.  Scapino star, a new Danny Kaye.  N. Y. Times
     Bio Ed p665 My '74
   Barthel, J.  What makes Jim Dale run and jump and skid and
     dance?  N. Y. Times sec 2:3 Je 30 '74
     Same.  N. Y. Times Bio Ed p817 Je '74
   Jim Dale's ten-thousand moments.  After Dark 7-8:52 D
     '74

DALE, MARGARET
    Obit.   N. Y. Times p44 Mr 24 '72

DALEY, CASS
    Sketch.   Life 10:12 Mr 17 '41
    Stanke, D.   Cass Daley; filmog.   Film Fan Mo 130:23 Ap '72

DALL, JOHN
    Service, F.   It takes much more than patience.   Silver S 15-10:
        50 Ag '45
    Obit.   Classic Film Collect 30:extra 3 Spg '71
        N. Y. Times p35 Ja 18 '71
        Same.   N. Y. Times Bio Ed Ja 18 '71
        Screen World 23:236 '71

DALLESANDRO, JOE
    Pearsall, A.   How some of the magic went out of Stanley Sweet-
        heart's Garden.   Show 1-3:69 Mr '70
    Raynes, T.   Interview.   Cinema (Lon) 6/7:42 Ag '70
    Zadan, C.   Factory brothers.   After Dark 13-8:22 D '70
    People are talking about.   Vogue 157:128 Ap 15 '71
    Interview.   Viva 1-9:47 Je '74
    Photos.   Oui 3-7:41 Jl '74

DALLESANDRO, ROBERT
    Zadan, C.   Factory brothers.   After Dark 13-8:22 D '70

DALLIMORE, MAURICE
    Obit.   Screen World p233 '74

DALTON, ABBY
    Pin-up and patients.   TV Guide 8-1:28 Ja 2 '60
    Eells, G.   A television original.   Look 24:123 My 24 '60
    Outdoor Abby is in with Hennesy.   TV Guide 8-48:8 N 26 '60
    Never a bridesmaid.   TV Guide 11-4:7 Ja 26 '63
    Fessier, M. Jr.   Old Abby, 8 years later.   TV Guide 16-24:12
        Je 15 '68

DALTON, ARLENE
    Once upon a time.   TV Guide 2-1:17 Ja 1 '54

DALTON, AUDREY
    Her brief interlude has lasted 10 years.   TV Guide 10-17:11 Ap
        28 '62

DALTON, DOROTHY
    Sheridan-Bickers, H.   Sketch.   Motion Pic 14:87 S '17
    Naylor, H. S.   Sketch.   Motion Pic 14:119 N '17
    Hall, G.   Interview.   Motion Pic 16:57 O '18
    Dorothy Dalton's Hollywood home.   Photop 15-4:56 Mr '19
    Interview.   Motion Pic Classic 8:43 Ag '19
    Interview.   Dramatic Mirror N 6 '20
    Fletcher, A. W.   Motion Pic 20:52 N '20

Willoughby, L.  Interview.  Motion Pic Classic 12:46 Ag '21
Dalton, J. H.  My daughter.  Filmplay J F '22
Carr, H.  Interview.  Motion Pic Classic 14:20 My '22
Bishop, R.  Motion Pic 24:56 S '22
Obit.  Classic Film Collect 35:8X Sum '72
   N. Y. Times p34 Ap 15 '72
   Same.  N. Y. Times Bio Ed Ap 15 '72
Bio note.  Silent Pic 14:20 Spg '72

DALTON, TIMOTHY
  Miller, E.  How handsome the hero; interview.  Seventeen 29:
    110 D '70
  Heathcliff!  Life 70:52 Mr 5 '71
  Ansorge, P.  In and out of disguise.  Plays & Players 19-12:31
    S '72

DALY, JAMES
  See, C.  Nothing personal.  TV Guide 18-8:26 F 21 '70
  My little black granddaughter.  Photop 79-5:66 My '71

DALYA, JACQUELINE
  Hall, G.  The luckiest girl in town.  Silver S 16-3:22 Ja '46

DAMITA, LILI
  Sketch.  Photop 34:43 Jl '28
  Moen, L.  Interview.  Motion Pic 36:72 Ag '28
  Walker, H. L.  Interview.  Motion Pic 37:48 Mr '29
  Biery, R.  Interview.  Motion Pic 38:44 Ag '29
  Cruikshank, H.  Interview.  Motion Pic 39:45 Je '30
  Hall, G.  Sketch.  Motion Pic 41:58 Ap '31
  Horton, H.  Her love affairs.  Movie Classic 1:36 D '31
  Hamilton, S.  Interview.  Movie Classic 2:15 Mr '32
  Hall, L.  Her married life.  Photop 51:32 F '37

DAMONE, VIC
  Da Moan.  Time 50:60 Jl 21 '47
  After hours.  Harper 195:381 O '47
  Da moment for Da Moan.  Newsweek 31:52 Ja 5 '48
  Vic Damone cuts a record.  Coronet 29:118 D '50
  My life in Hollywood.  Silver S 21-7:24 My '51
  Interview.  TV Guide 5-35:28 Ag 31 '57
  Jennings, D.  What a mess I've made of things.  Sat Eve Post
    230:19 F 22 '58
  Efron, E.  Seeking the right note.  TV Guide 15-22:11 Je 3 '67

DANA, BILL
  Jo, jo, jo--it's Hosay Himanez.  TV Guide 8-35:24 Ag 27 '60
  The rest is jistory.  TV Guide 12-7:9 F 15 '64
  We demand equal time.  TV Guide 12-46:26 N 14 '64
  Higgins, B.  He rang the bell with bellhops.  TV Guide 13-1:15
    Ja 2 '65
  Pop goes the network.  Newsweek 69:90 My 15 '67

DANA, VIOLA
  White, J. Jr.  Interview.  Munsey 49:289 My '13
  Ten Eyck, J.  Interview.  Green Book 10:841 N '13
  How a child became a tragedienne.  Theatre 20:82 Ag '14
  Sketch.  Motion Pic 10:109 Ag '15
  Courtlandt, R.  Interview.  Motion Pic 12:51 S '16
  A double twinkler.  Photop 11-3:74 F '17
  Sketch.  Motion Pic 14:79 O '17
  McKelvie, M. G.  Interview.  Motion Pic Classic 6:41 Jl '18
  Service, F.  Sketch.  Motion Pic Classic 7:52 Ja '19
  Evans, N.  Interview.  Motion Pic 18:64 S '19
  Galeson, E.  Interview.  Motion Pic Classic 9:43 O '19
  Her make-up as Madame Butterfly.  Photop 17:37 F '20
  Shelley, H.  Sketch.  Motion Pic Classic 11:44 N '20
  Brooks, R.  Interview.  Motion Pic Classic 12:56 Je '21
  Howe, H.  Motion Pic 23:36 F '22
  Goldbeck, W.  Interview.  Motion Pic Classic 14:60 Ap '22
  Sketch.  Photop 23:47 My '23
  Carr, H.  Her career.  Motion Pic 28:20 D '24
  de Revere, F. V.  Face analysis.  Motion Pic 29:70 Je '25
  Spensley, D.  Sketch.  Photop 30:38 Je '26

DANE, KARL
  Sketch.  Motion Pic Classic 22:56 F '26
  Thorp, D.  The Mutt & Jeff of the movies.  Motion Pic Classic
    26:41 S '27

DANE, PATRICIA
  Hamilton, S.  Sketch.  Photop 20:53 D '41
  Great Dane.  Lions R 1-5:no p# Ja '42
  Glamour for defense.  Lions R 1-9:no p# My '42
  Menace.  Am Mag 134:84 Jl '42
  Stars of tomorrow.  Lions R 1-11/12:no p# Jl/Ag '42
  Pat Dane's impulses.  Lions R 2-3(sup):no p# Ja '43

DANIEL, VIORA
  Cheatham, M.  Interview.  Motion Pic Classic 11:51 O '20

DANIELL, HENRY
  Hamilton, S.  Sketch.  Photop 52:69 Ja '38
  Murder without crime.  Cue 12-34:11 Ag 21 '43
  Obit.  Film R p46 '64/65

DANIELS, BEBE
  Remont, F.  Interview.  Motion Pic Classic 8:42 My '19
  Blame the League of Nations.  Photop 16-2:79 Jl '19
  Cheatham, M.  Interview.  Motion Pic 18:32 N '19
  Handy, T. B.  Interview.  Motion Pic 20:36 S '20
  Her imprisonment for speeding.  Photop 20:52 Jl '21
  Tulley, J.  Interview.  Motion Pic 21:13 S '21
  Naylor, H. S.  Interview.  Motion Pic 22:28 N '21
  Gordon, R.  Interview.  Motion Pic 23:22 Ap '22
  Her darkest hour.  Classic 16:66 Mr '23

Lamb, G.  Sketch.  Classic 18:32 N '23
Home of.  Classic 20:40 S '24
Adams, E.  Her horoscope.  Photop 26:34 N '24
Roberts, W. A.  Sketch.  Motion Pic 28:57 Ja '25
de Revere, F. V.  Face analysis of.  Motion Pic 29:41 F '25
York, C.  Sketch.  Photop 29:1 F '26
Carr, H.  Interview.  Motion Pic 31:31 F '26
Donnell, D.  Sketch.  Motion Pic 31:1 My '26
Belfrage, C.  Interview.  Motion Pic 35:34 My '28
My twenty-four hours a day.  Theatre 48:22 Jl '28
Johnston, C.  Sketch.  Motion Pic Classic 28:51 D '28
Hall, G.  Confessions.  Motion Pic Classic 28:16 Ja '29
Lessons in love.  Motion Pic Classic 30:30 N '29
Hall, G.  A new-born Bebe.  Motion Pic 38:58 D '29
Hall, G.  Interview.  Motion Pic 40:59 Ag '30
Calhoun, D.  Her marriage.  Motion Pic 40:8 S '30
Calhoun, D.  Interview.  Motion Pic 41:48 My '31
Donnell, D.  Interview.  Motion Pic Classic 32:24 Ag '31
Lee, S.  Sketch.  Motion Pic 44:56 Ja '33
What they are doing now.  Show 2-8:106 Ag '62
Letters.  Films In R 15-8:514 O '64
Pin-up of the past.  Films & Filming 16-9:128 Je '70
Lyon, B. & Slide, A.  Bebe Daniels; conversation.  Silent Pic
    10:no p# Spg '71
Various.  Bebe.  Silent Pic 11/12:no p# Sum/Aut '71
Obit.  Classic Film Collect 30:extra 2 Spg '71
    Film R p13 '71/72
    N.Y. Times p40 Mr 16 '71
    Same.  N.Y. Times Bio Ed Mr 16 '71
    Newsweek 77:58 Mr 29 '71
    Screen World 23:236 '72
    Time 97:84 Mr 29 '71

DANIELS, MICKEY
    Maltin, L.  Our gang; Our gang filmog.  Film Fan Mo 66:3 D
    '66

DANIELS, WILLIAM
    That fellow in the star-spangled underwear.  TV Guide 15-6:30
    F 11 '67
    Archibald, L.  William Daniels.  Show 2-10:42 Ja '73

DANNER, BLYTHE
    Boxer, T.  On the rise.  Show 1-3:48 Mr '70
    Durslag, M.  How do you follow Katharine Hepburn?  TV Guide
    21-43:21 O 27 '73

DANTINE, HELMUT
    Watkins, W.  Vengeful protege.  Silver S 13-10:52 Ag '43
    Mulvey, K.  Sketch.  Womans Home C 70:74 O '43
    Why I'm still single.  Photop 25:56 N '44
    Pritchett, F.  Dynamic combination.  Silver S 16-1:42 N '45
    The song I remember.  Photop 29:58 Je '46
    The eagle has two heads.  Films Illus 34:408 Je '74

D'ARBANVILLE, PATTI
    Colaciello, R.   Interview.   Interview 31:8  Ap '73

DARBY, KIM
    Miller, E.   New name, a new life.   Seventeen 28:117 Je '69
    Eyles, A.   Kim Darby; filmog.   Focus On F 1:9 Ja/F '70
    Diehl, D.   Darby has rich girl's shoulders.   Show 1-2:53  F '70
    Actresses who are real people.   Life 68:40 My 29 '70

DARCEL, DENISE
    Rising star.   Film R p107  '52/53

DARCY, GEORGINE
    When is a pigtail a braid?   TV Guide 9-2:25 Ja 14 '61

D'ARCY, ROY
    Perrin, H.   Sketch.   Motion Pic Classic 22:59 N '25
    Home of.   Motion Pic Classic 23:57 Ag '26
    Smith, A.   Interview.   Photop 31:90 Ja '27
    Sketch.   Theatre 45:40 Ja '27
    Palmberg, R. P.   Interview.   Motion Pic 31:58 Ap '27
    Obit.   N.Y. Times p55 N 19 '69
        Screen World 21:234 '70

DARIN, BOBBY
    Rising star.   Film R p31  '62/63
    Raddatz, L.   Bobby Darin--15 years later.   TV Guide 20-35:28
        Ag 26 '72
    Obit.   N.Y. Times Bio Ed p1935 D '73
        Screen World p233 '74

DARK, CHRISTOPHER
    Obit.   Screen World 23:236 '72

DARK, MICHAEL
    Donnell, D.   Interview.   Classic 20:36 D '24

DARLING, CANDY
    Colaciello, R.   Interview.   Interview 20:37 Mr '72
    Berger, T.   Films.   Esquire 77:30 Ap '72

DARLING, JEAN
    Our Gang's Darling.   Am Mag 140:150 D '45
    Maltin, L.   Our gang; Our gang filmog.   Film Fan Mo 66:3 D
        '66

DARLING, JOAN
    To all the Friedas of the world.   TV Guide 21-11:14 Mr 17 '73

DARMOND, GRACE
    What are the qualifications of the film players?   Film Players
        Herald 2-7:22 F '16
    Heinemann, E. M.   Sketch.   Motion Pic 14:106 D '17

DARNELL, LINDA
  Condon, F.  Sketch.  Colliers 104:14 N 11 '39
  Rhea, M.  Sketch.  Photop 53:31 N '39
  Hall, G.  All flew into the cuckoo's nest.  Silver S 10-1:38 N
    '39
  Sketch.  Life 7:58 D 18 '39
  Eddy, D.  Sketch.  Am Mag 130:24 Jl '40
  Manners, M. J.  The problem of sharing a husband.  Silver S
    10-11:26 S '40
  Leighton, J.  Interview.  Photop 18:35 Ja '41
  Manners, M. J.  A new Linda steps out!  Silver S 12-2:24 D
    '41
  Cheatham, M.  Awakened beauty.  Silver S 15-1:24 N '44
  Darnell, L.  Watch out, kids.  Silver S 16-7:42 My '46
  Marley, L. D.  The man I married.  Silver S 18-11:22 S '48
  Holland, J.  What makes a great lover?  Silver S 19-8:26 Je
    '49
  Holland, J.  Are we really the weaker sex?  Silver S 21-2:26
    D '50
  Obit.  Film R p45 '65/66
  Here's to the ladies.  Screen Greats 1-2:30 Sum '71
  Corneau, E.  Hollywood's tragic beauty.  Classic Film Collect
    42:21 Win '73
  McElwee, J.  The delightful duo: Darnell and Power.  Classic
    Film Collect 41:32 Win '73

DARREN, JAMES
  Rumors of his romance with Dean Martin's wife.  Photop 86-1:57
    Jl '74
  James Darren.  Photop 86-2:58 Ag '74

DARRIEUX, DANIELLE
  Danielle Darrieux.  Visages 13:entire issue Je '37
  Sketch.  Life 3:59 O 25 '37
  Babcock, M.  Meet Darrieux.  Screen Book 20-2:22 Mr '38
  Sketch.  Life 5:39 Jl 4 '38
  Bio note; filmog.  Movies & People 2:11 '40
  Collaborating with the Nazis.  Newsweek 28:9 Ja 17 '44
  Collaborating with the Nazis.  Time 43:37 Ja 17 '44
  Bio note.  Unifrance 10:10 Je '51
  Billard, G.  Seeks new horizons.  Films & Filming 2-1:10 O '55
  Whitehall, R.  Filmog.  Films & Filming 8-3:45 D '61
  Blanch, L.  Love is not child's play.  Show 2-6:91 Je '62
  Curtiss, T. Q.  Danielle prepares for Coco.  N.Y. Times Bio
    Ed Jl 16 '70
  Simon, J.  Forever Danielle.  New Yorker 3-34:59 Ag 24 '70
  Tierney, M.  The music: view points.  Plays & Players 19-3:
    20 D '71

DARROW, HENRY
  See, C.  Zap!  TV Guide 16-44:21 N 2 '68

DARVAS, LILI
   Drutman, I.   A movie star is born at 70.   N. Y.   Times Bio Ed
      p395 Mr '73
   Obit.   N. Y.  Times Bio Ed p935 Jl '74

DARVI, BELLA
   Egyptian Belle.   Films & Filming 1-2:25 N '54
   Obit.   Film R p12 '72/73
      N. Y.  Times p32 S 18 '71
      Same.   N. Y.  Times Bio Ed S 18 '71
      Newsweek 78:77 S 27 '71
      Screen World 23:236 '72

DARWELL, JANE
   Hamilton, S.   Sketch.   Photop 54:25 Ap '40
   Obit.   Cur Bio 28:43 O '67
      Same.   Cur Bio Yrbk 1967:474 '68
      N. Y.  Times p39 Ag 15 '67
      Newsweek 70:73 Ag 28 '67
      Time 90:65 Ag 25 '67

DA SILVA, HOWARD
   Hammel, F.   Director in love.   Cue 30-38:12 S 23 '61

DAVENPORT, DORIS
   Hamilton, S.   Sketch.   Photop 54:28 Ag '40

DAVENPORT, DOROTHY
   Sketch.   Motion Pic 10:113 D '15
   Courtlandt, R.   Interview.   Motion Pic Classic 2:30 Jl '16
   How to hold a husband.   Photop 20:20 N '21
   Handy, T. B.   Interview.   Motion Pic 23:245 F '22

DAVENPORT, HARRY
   Hamilton, S.   Sketch.   Photop 54:30 S '40
   How to live and love it.   Lions R 4-1:no p# F '45
   Obit.   Screen World 1:233 '49
   Purvis, H.   Partial filmog.   Films In R 17-8:529 O '66

DAVIDSON, JOHN
   Higgins, R.   Soloist who's eager to harmonize.   TV Guide 14-31:
      12 Jl 30 '66
   Buckley, P.   The square that never was.   After Dark 11-4:30
      Ag '69
   My child.   Photop 81-4:10 Ap '72
   Lewis, R. W.   The boy with nothing extra.   TV Guide 22-23:24
      Je 8 '74

DAVIDSON, MAX
   Obit.   Screen World 2:233 '51

DAVIES, DIANE
   Miss soft sell.   Show 1-2:26 F '70

DAVIES, MARION
    Sheridan, V.   Sketch.   Motion Pic 15:51 Ag '18
    For future reference.   Photop 15-3:29 F '19
    Bruce, B.   Interview.   Motion Pic 19:68 Je '20
    Fletcher, A.   Interview.   Motion Pic 20:52 S '20
    Shulsinger, R.   The different Marion Davies.   Dramatic Mirror
        1257 D 25 '20
    How I keep in condition.   Photop 21:47 Ja '22
    Service, F.   Interview.   Classic 15:22 S '22
    Roberts, W. A.   Sketch.   Motion Pic 30:70 Ag '25
    Sketch.   Motion Pic Classic 22:26 F '26
    Tilton, J.   Sketch.   Motion Pic 31:36 Je '26
    Sketch.   Theatre 45:40 Ja '27
    Hall, G.   Sketch.   Motion Pic Classic 25:53 Mr '27
    Fairfield, L.   Hostess to Col. Lindbergh in Hollywood.   Motion
        Pic 34:39 Ja '28
    Defends Hollywood.   Motion Pic 42:58 S '31
    Moffit, J. C.   Choice of Davies brings squawk.   Cinema Dig 1-
        6:7 Jl 25 '32
    Fairbanks, D. Jr.   Appreciation.   Vanity Fair 39:46 N '32
    Colman, W.   Hostell to the famous.   Silver S 9-3:26 Jl '33
    Busby, M.   Social queen of Hollywood.   Motion Pic 46:50 Ag '33
    Manners, D.   Does not want sex appeal.   Movie Classic 5:26 S
        '33
    Home of.   Photop 45:42 Ja '34
    Sketch.   Motion Pic 48:27 Ja '35
    Percy, E.   Appreciation.   Movie Classic 9:31 S '35
    Obit.   Film R p17 '62/63
    Milne, T.   Show people.   Sight & Sound 37:200 Aut '68
    Kendall, P.   Marion Davies; filmog.   Silent Pic 7:2 Sum '70
    Pin-up of the past.   Films & Filming 17-5:70 F '71
    Anderson, E.   Marion Davies; filmog.   Films In R 23-6:321 Je/
        Jl '72

DAVIS, ANN B.
    Interview.   Photop 86-3:8 S '74

DAVIS, BETTE
    Sketch.   Photop 41:61 Ap '32
    Fidler, J. M.   The best Bette in pictures.   Silver S 2-7:26 My
        '32
    Goldbeck, E.   Her love life.   Movie Classic 2:13 Ag '32
    Peabody, A.   Davis and numerology.   Silver S 2-12:43 O '32
    Heller, G.   Davis gives a party.   Silver S 3-8:20 Je '33
    White, K.   Sketch.   Movie Classic 6:52 Jl '34
    Crichton, K.   Her story.   Colliers 94:18 N 17 '34
    Sylvia's beauty hints.   Photop 46:48 N '34
    Dowling, M.   Interview.   Motion Pic 48:30 N '34
    Jones, C.   Not that kind of a girl.   Silver S 5-1:23 N '34
    Williams, W.   Just hard work.   Silver S 5-3:23 Ja '35
    Chrisman, J. E.   An open letter to.   Motion Pic 49:33 Je '35
    Davis, B.   Reply.   Motion Pic 49:38 Jl '35
    Hartley, K.   Interview.   Movie Classic 8:25 Ag '35

Fender, R.   Interview.   Motion Pic 50:37 S '35
Calhoun, D.   Interview.   Motion Pic 50:49 Ja '36
Dowling, M.   Interview.   Movie Classic 9:47 F '36
Wood, V.   Bette from Boston.   Silver S 6-7:53 My '36
Lee, S.   Best actress.   Motion Pic 51:36 Je '36
Baird, F.   Interview.   Photop 50:54 Ag '36
Surmelian, L.   Interview.   Movie Classic 10:38 S '56
Wilson, E.   Projections of Davis.   Silver S 6-11:22 S '36
Kellum, F.   Sketch.   Motion Pic 52:24 O '36
Gardner, L.   Impressions of Davis.   Movie Classic 11:58 N '36
Lang, H.   Interview.   Motion Pic 53:33 Ap '37
Beauty not necessary to success in the movies.   Cosmop 103:48
    N '37
Lee, S.   Davis discusses dangerous loves.   Screen Book 19-6:
    26 Ja '38
Holland, J.   She likes to be bad.   Silver S 8-4:26 F '38
Work of.   Time 31:33 Mr 28 '38
Work of in Jezebel.   Stage 15:12 Ap '38
Appreciation.   Stage 15:20 Je '38
Rankin, R.   Story of.   Photop 52:10 Ag '38
Her party.   Life 5:62 S 5 '38
Lee, S.   Ten don'ts for the career girl.   Screen Book 21-4:20
    N '38
Rankin, R.   What happened to her marriage?   Photop 52:24 D
    '38
Busch, N. F.   Story of.   Life 6:52 Ja 23 '39
Wins Academy award second time.   Stage 16:29 Je '39
Bette Davis.   Visages 35:entire issue Je '39
Maddox, B.   Who'll win the 1939 Oscars?   Silver S 9-10:38 Ag
    '39
Rankin, R.   Bette Davis--star maker.   Screen Book 22-2:80 S
    '39
Hall, G.   I'd never marry an actor.   Silver S 10-9:22 Jl '40
Code for American girls in war time.   Photop 54:17 S '40
Bio note; filmog.   Movies & People 2:11 '40
Don't be a draft bride.   Photop 18:26 Ja '41
Heyn, E. V.   Story of.   Photop 18:17 F '41
Birthday party in her honor.   Life 10:126 Ap 28 '41
William, B.   At home with the Farnsworths.   Silver S 11-9:34
    Jl '41
Autobiographical.   Ladies Home J 58:16 Jl '41
Sketch.   Womans Home C 68:58 O '41
Elected president of Academy.   Newsweek 18:56 N 17 '41
Bio.   Cur Bio 2:206 '41
The husband of a career woman.   Ladies Home J 59:18 Ap '42
Haas, D. B.   Dangerous age for women.   Silver S 12-11:24 S
    '42
Answers problems.   Photop 22:36 D '42 and following issues.
Death of her husband.   Photop 23:69 N '43
Oil painting by Alexander Brook.   Life 17:73 N 20 '44
Her marriage to Wm. Sherry.   Photop 28:27 F '46
Third place in Companion poll of favorite stars.   Womans Home
    C 73:7 Je '46

Asher, J.  Bette lets her hair down.  Silver S 17-4:30 F '47
Great roles.  Theatre Arts 31:56 Mr '47
My luckiest day.  Cosmop 122:106 Je '47
Davis, B.  Let's take Hollywood out of the kitchen.  Silver S
    18-6:24 Ap '48
As a comedienne in June bride.  Newsweek 32:91 N 8 '48
Charles, G.  Tribulation of Davis.  Cue 21-48:12 N 29 '52
Raper, M.  Mannerisms in the grand manner.  Films & Filming
    1-12:7 S '55
Stine, W.  Letter.  Films In R 15-9:577 N '64
When I was sixteen.  Good House 167:99 O '68
She was something else.  TV Guide 18-4:23 Ja 24 '70
Carey, G.  The lady and the director; Davis and Wm. Wyler.
    Film Comment 6-3:18 Fall '70
Taylor, A.  Bette Davis.  N. Y. Times Bio Ed D 8 '70
Guerin, A.  On screen and off.  Show 2-2:28 Ap '71
Guerin, A.  Davis on the new films.  Show 2-3:28 My '71
Still going great.  Screen Greats 1-2:78 Sum '71
Madame Sin tells all.  Films Illus 1-5:5 N '71
Hinxman, M.  Bette.  Sight & Sound 41-1:17 Win '71/72
Cooking with a star.  Mod Screen 66-4:76 Ap '72
Mansfield, D.  Big screen originals; letter.  Films & Filming
    18-11:6 Ag '72
Graham, R.  Fasten your seatbelts; interview.  After Dark 5-5:
    40 D '72
Hay, R. C.  Interview.  Interview 28:14 D '72
Lambert, G.  The making of Gone with the wind.  Atlantic 231-
    2:46 F '73
Davis at Town Hall.  Film Fan Mo 140:18 F '73
Marshack, L.  She couldn't wait to get back into her act.  TV
    Guide 21-12:12 Mr 24 '73
Interview.  Photop 83-6:66 Je '73
Bowers, R.  Legendary ladies of the movies.  Films In R 24-6:
    321 Je/Jl '73
Appleton, J. S.  Here comes (there goes) Bette now.  N. Y.
    Times sec 2:15 Ag 26 '73
Kobal, J.  Working with Bette Davis; interview with Vincent
    Sherman.  Film 2-9:12 D '73
Dyer, R.  The nervy vitality of the great Bette--on film and on
    the road.  N. Y. Times sec 2:11 Jl 21 '74
Gardner, P.  A star views directors.  Action 9-5:10 S/O '74
Hogan, W. H.  Larger than life.  Nostalgia Illus 1-2:63 D '74

DAVIS, CLIFTON
    Talent on approval.  Time 99:97 Je 26 '72
    Melba Moore-Clifton Davis show.  Life 73:17 Jl 14 '72

DAVIS, GAIL
    Girl of the golden west.  TV Guide 2-9:8 F 26 '54
    Ride 'em, cowgirl.  TV Guide 3-24:13 Je 11 '55
    It's the woman who pays.  TV Guide 5-28:12 Jl 13 '57
    She who was shorn.  TV Guide 8-43:11 O 22 '60

DAVIS, JACKIE
  Maltin, L.   Our gang; Our gang filmog.   Film Fan Mo 66:3 D
    '66

DAVIS, JIM
  Stars of tomorrow.   Lions R 1-11/12:no p# Jl/Ag '42

DAVIS, JOAN
  Smithson, E. J.   Hollywood's clown princess.   Screen Book 21-
    1:37 Ag '38
  Hunt, M.   That screwball, Davis.   Screen Book 21-11:10 Je '39
  Sketch.   Time 40:76 N 16 '42
  Vallee, W. L.   Queen of comedy.   Silver S 14-9:24 Jl '44
  Obit.   Film R p28 '61/62

DAVIS, MILDRED
  Gray, F.   Interview.   Motion Pic Classic 10:62 Jl '20
  Willis, R.   Interview.   Motion Pic 20:78 Ag '20
  Cheatham, M.   Interview.   Motion Pic 22:36 S '21
  Jordon, J.   Interview.   Photop 21:45 Ja '22
  Montanye, L.   Interview.   Motion Pic Classic 14:32 My '22
  Goldbeck, W.   Interview.   Motion Pic 24:42 O '22
  Tildesley, A. L.   Interview.   Motion Pic 31:26 F '26
  Dillon, F.   Champion Housekeeper.   Motion Pic 44:57 S '32
  Spensley, D.   Her home life.   Movie Classic 7:54 Ja '35
  Obit.   N. Y. Times p47 Ag 20 '69
    Screen World 21:234 '70

DAVIS, NANCY
  Gordon, S.   California's leading lady.   Look 31:37 O 31 '67
  Harris, E.   What is (she) really, really like?   Look 31:40 O
    31 '67
  Didion, J.   Pretty Nancy.   Sat Eve Post 241:20 Je 1 '68
  Klemesrud, J.   She may be shy, but she still takes a stand.
    N. Y. Times Bio Ed F 3 '71
  Ronnie and Nancy: stepping down but not out.   People 2-12:64
    S 16 '74

DAVIS, OSSIE
  Hammel, F.   Two for the theatre.   Cue 28-47:20 N 21 '59
  Curtis, R.   Cinema comes to Harlem.   Action 4-6:12 N/D '69
  Bio.   Cur Bio 30:18 O '69
    Same.   Cur Bio Yrbk 1969:114 '70

DAVIS, OWEN JR.
  Pennington, M.   His success in the movies.   Movie Classic 10:
    46 S '36
  Schwarzkopf, J.   Sketch.   Motion Pic 53:21 Ap '37
  Obit.   Newsweek 33:58 My 30 '49

DAVIS, PHYLLIS ELIZABETH
  They don't throw stones at her window any more.   TV Guide 19-
    19:44 My 8 '71

DAVIS, ROGER
   He kidnapped the woman he loved.   Photop 82-5:48 N '72
   I don't expect my wife to sit at home and wait for me.   Mod
     Screen 67-2:35 F '73

DAVIS, SAMMY JR.
   Taylor, T.   Young Mr. Versatility.   Cue 25-6:13 F 11 '56
   The golden boy.   Show 4-8:23 S '64
   Lewis, E.   New York's golden boy.   Cue 34-1:11 Ja 2 '65
   Interview.   Playboy 13:99 D '66
   Because money don't make you free.   N. Y. Times Bio Ed Ap 18
     '71
   Davis, S.   Peace of mind.   Look 35-15:27 Jl 27 '71
   Bacon, J.   How Frank Sinatra taught me friendship.   Todays
     Health 49:30 N '71
   Drink after drink I was dying.   Photop 81-1:62 Ja '72
   Be brave in your handicap.   Photop 81-6:32 Je '72
   Why I went to the troops.   Ebony 27:141 Je '72
   Young voters for the president rally.   Life 73:2 S 1 '72
   Conaway, J.   (He) has bought the bus.   N. Y. Times Mag p32 O
     15 '72
     Same.   N. Y. Times Bio Ed p1767 O '72
   How I told my children about my divorce.   Photop 82-4:56 O '72
   Whitney, D.   A man has to grow up sometime.   TV Guide 21-45:
     22 N 10 '73
   Now we want a baby.   Photop 85-6:38 Je '74

DAVISON, DAVEY
   Her name is Davey.   TV Guide 12-12:27 Mr 21 '64

DAVISON, DICK
   He's balmy, but he's bright.   TV Guide 15-51:26 D 23 '67

DAVISON, GRACE
   Montanye, L.   Interview.   Motion Pic 20:35 Ag '20

DAW, EVELYN
   Obit.   Screen World 22:236 '71

DAWKINS, IRMA L.
   Thayer, J. E.   A diamond in the sky.   Classic Film Collect 39:
     51 Sum '73

DAWN, HAZEL
   Sketch.   Strand (NY) 48:274 S '14
   Interview.   Cosmop 57:698 O '14
   First aids to loveliness.   Green Book 13:673 Ap '15
   Naughty parts in plays.   Theatre 29:278 My '19
   Brenon, A.   Sketch.   Motion Pic Classic 8:31 Je '19
   Returns in new comedy.   Cue 16-37:10 S 13 '47
   Dawn of a bright era.   Theatre Arts 43:29 S '59
   What they are doing now.   Show 2-3:96 Mr '62
   Brock, A.   Younger than spring time.   Classic Film Collect 34:
     30 Spg '72

DAWN, ISABEL
  Obit.  Screen World 18:233 '67

DAWSON, DORIS
  Manners, D.  Sketch.  Motion Pic Classic 27:42 Jl '28
  Uselton, R. A.  The Wampus baby stars.  Films In R 21-2:73
    F '70

DAWSON, KURT
  Stoop, N. M.  Two for the show.  After Dark 5-9:27 Ja '73

DAY, ALICE
  Standish, B.  Sketch.  Motion Pic Classic 26:58 D '27
  Johnston, C.  Sketch.  Motion Pic Classic 28:51 F '29
  Uselton, R. A.  The Wampus baby stars.  Films In R 21-2:73
    F '70

DAY, DORIS
  Vallee, W. L.  Day break for Day.  Silver S 18-5:45 Mr '48
  Mulvey, K.  Her recipe for a picnic in the park.  Photop 33:60
    N '48
  Success of the year.  Metronome 65:17 F '49
  Parsons, L. O.  Cosmop's citation for the best performance of
    month.  Cosmop 126:12 Ap '49
  Kinney, V.  Interview.  Music 28:42 N/D '50
  Keats, P.  Busiest blonde in town.  Silver S 21-5:38 Mr '51
  My favorite role.  Film R p29 '51/52
  O'Leary, D.  Her own hit parade.  Silver S 22-6:22 Ap '52
  Carlson, T.  Sweetheart of the U. S. S. Juneau.  Silver S 23-7:42
    My '53
  My favorite role.  Film R p21 '53/54
  Noel, T.  There'll be no changes made.  Silver S 24-8:31 Je '54
  Taylor, T.  A new Day for Doris.  Cue 25-19:12 My 12 '56
  Rollin, B.  Miss Apple Pie hits TV.  Look 32:54 N 26 '68
  I won't settle for being his mistress.  Photop 77-5:60 My '70
  Hair-raising stories from the stars.  Photop 78-2:50 Ag '70
  She's in love!  Photop 78-4:66 O '70
  This is the man she will marry.  Photop 79-1:56 Ja '71
  Davidson, B.  The change in (her).  TV Guide 19-8:30 F 20 '71
  My son acts like my father.  Photop 79-2:54 F '71
  Where they never raise the rent.  TV Guide 19-15:16 Ap 10 '71
  Tragedy strikes again.  Photop 79-4:36 Ap '71
  Our children want to get married.  Photop 79-6:69 Je '71
  Enraged Dean Martin takes daughter from (her) son.  Photop 80-
    4:72 O '71
  Why she started drinking again.  Photop 80-5:38 N '71
  The Christmas that taught me the meaning of love.  Mod Screen
    66-1:45 Ja '72
  The most fateful decision I ever made.  Mod Screen 66-3:45 Mr
    '72
  Amory, C.  The dog catcher of Beverly Hills.  TV Guide 20-24:
    34 Je 10 '72
  At son's bedside.  Photop 82-2:36 Jl '72

How she suffered for success.  Mod Screen 66-7:51 Jl '72
Melcher, T.  Why I'm suing mom.  Mod Screen 66-8:38 Ag '72
Doris Day to wed?  Photop 82-4:24 O '72
Favorite animal stories.  Mod Screen 66-11:34 N '72
The tales their houses tell.  Mod Screen 67-4:30 Ap '73
What's happened to Doris Day?  Photop 85-4:43 Ap '74
Armstrong, L.  Doris Day has her day in court.  People 2-15:
   36 O 7 '74

DAY, EDITH
   There's nothing to it, says Edith.  Photop 16-1:43 Je '19
   Obit.  N.Y. Times p40 My 3 '71

DAY, LARAINE
   Hamilton, S.  Sketch.  Photop 54:15 Ja '40
   Hilton, J.  Story of.  Photop 54:21 Jl '40
   Smith, F. J.  Dawn of a new Day.  Silver S 10-9:26 Jl '40
   Trotter, M.  Astrological forecast.  Photop 18:74 F '41
   A new Day.  Lions R 1-3:no p# N '41
   Her little theatre.  Lions R 1-4:no p# D '41
   Dudley, F.  Interview.  Photop 20:34 Ja '42
   Sketch.  Cosmop 112:29 F '42
   Hall, G.  Her unsolvable problem.  Silver S 12-6:38 Ap '42
   She doesn't want a city.  Lions R 1-9:no p# My '42
   Stars of tomorrow.  Lions R 1-11/12:no p# Jl/Ag '42
   The rise of Laraine Day.  Lions R 2-3:no p# D '42
   The type of man she likes.  Photop 22:50 Ap '43
   Perkins, R.  Confidential report on Day.  Silver S 13-7:30 My
      '43
   Wilson, E.  Men I have kissed.  Silver S 14-6:24 Ap '44
   Pritchett, F.  Naughty but nice.  Silver S 15-11:42 S '45
   Dudley, F.  Strange case of Lippy and Laraine.  Silver S 17-8:
      30 Je '47
   Minoff, P.  Highlights and sidelights on the video circuit.  Cue
      22-20:7 My 16 '53
   America we love; excerpt.  Ladies Home J 88:64 Jl '71
   My child.  Photop 85-3:10 Mr '74

DAY, LYNDA
   (See: GEORGE, LYNDA DAY)

DAY, MARCELINE
   Standish, B.  Sketch.  Motion Pic Classic 26:58 D '27
   Wheaton, J.  Sketch.  Motion Pic 35:74 F '28
   Tildesley, R. M.  Wanted: a husband.  Motion Pic 36:67 Ja '29
   Uselton, R. A.  The Wampus baby stars.  Films In R 21-2:73
      F '70

DAY, MARJORIE
   Courtlandt, R.  Sketch.  Motion Pic 11:37 Jl '16
   Peltret, E.  Interview.  Motion Pic Classic 8:48 Ap '19
   Sheridan, M.  Interview.  Motion Pic 17:47 Ap '19
   Sketch.  Photop 17:97 F '20

Cheatham, M. S.  Interview.  Motion Pic Classic 10:20 Mr '20
Peltret, E.  Interview.  Motion Pic 20:64 S '20
Leslie, G.  Interview.  Motion Pic Classic 12:16 Jl '21
deRevere, F. V.  Face analysis.  Motion Pic 29:64 My '25

DAY, SHANNON
    Squier, E.  Interview.  Motion Pic Classic  11:36 N '20
    Shelley, H.  Interview.  Motion Pic Classic 14:32 Ap '22

DAY, VERA
    Person of promise.  Films & Filming 1-11:13 Ag '55

DAYAN, ASSAF
    Devlin, P.  Young and stung with love and war.  Vogue 154:130
        S 15 '69

DEACON, RICHARD
    The stare, the long take, and yyu-uch.  TV Guide 10-35:20 S 1
        '62

DEAD END KIDS
    Readin' ritin' and rehearsal.  TV Guide 4-38:20 S 22 '56

DEAN, JAMES
    Kazan kid.  Films & Filming 1-9:25 Je '55
    Rebel with a cause.  Films & Filming 2-2:20 N '55
    The stars of tomorrow.  Film R p44 '55/56
    Taylor, T.  His name was Dean.  Cue 25-39:11 S 29 '56
    Ringgold, G.  His life and his legend; filmog; list of TV and
        radio performances.  Screen Legends 1-1:3 My '65
    Ringgold, G.  A Jas. Dean album; filmog.  Nostalgia Illus 1-1:28
        N '74

DEAN, JIMMY
    Good country boy.  Time 70:64 Jl 1 '57
    Joy of the corn.  Newsweek 50:46 Jl 1 '57
    Happy as a clam.  TV Guide 5-36:17 S 7 '57
    Quick rise of an early riser.  Life 43:78 O 7 '57
    Efron, E.  A drawl, a pocket of country songs...  TV Guide 12-
        1:15 Ja 4 '64
    Gehman, R.  Lemme do it mah way.  TV Guide 13-27:24 S 13
        '65

DEAN, JULIA
    Briscoe, J.  Sketch.  Green Bk Album 4:371 Ag '10
    Wallace, D. H.  Interview.  N. Y. Drama 70:3 O 1 '13
    Mantle, B.  Stage career.  Munsey 51:125 F '14
    What women like best in plays today.  Green Book 11:961 Je '14
    Her gowns.  Green Book 14:66 Jl '15
    Obit.  Screen World 4:176 '53

DEAN, PRISCILLA
    In name only.  Photop 14-6:70 N '18

Remont, F.   Interview.   Motion Pic Classic 7:30 F '19
Squier, E.   Interview.   Motion Pic 18:72 O '19
Peltret, E.   Interview.   Motion Pic 19:62 Mr '20
Keene, M.   Interview.   Motion Pic Classic 10:24 Je '20
Howe, H.   Interview.   Motion Pic 22:36 D '21
Handy, T. B.   Interview.   Classic 15:36 O '22
Sketch.   Motion Pic 29:46 Jl '25
Summers, M.   Have you seen Priscilla Dean in Universal pic-
   tures? with note by Priscilla Dean; filmog.   Filmograph 1-2:
   3 '70
Phillips, A.   Priscilla Dean and censors.   Filmograph 1-4:49
   '70
Brock, A.   Unforgettable Priscilla Dean.   Classic Film Collect
   30:6 Spg '71

DEAN, RAYE
   May, L.   Interview.   Motion Pic Classic 12:44 Mr '21

DEAN, ROY
   Swisher, V. H.   Poet of the camera.   After Dark 11-9:47 Ja '70

de AQUINAGA, PEDRO
   Zuker, J.   Pedro de Aquinaga.   Interview 21:20 My '72

De AUBRY, DIANE
   Obit.   Screen World 21:234 '70

DEAVER, NANCY
   May, L.   Interview.   Motion Pic Classic 11:60 D '20

de BORDA, DOROTHY
   Maltin, L.   Our gang; our gang filmog.   Film Fan Mo 66:3 D
   '66

De CAMP, ROSEMARY
   Everybody's mother.   TV Guide 4-35:28 S 1 '56

DeCARLO, YVONNE
   Vallee, W. L.   Go west, young gal.   Silver S 15-12:50 O '45
   DeCarlo, Y.   Mistakes I've made in love.   Silver S 19-6:42 Ap
   '49
   Shane, D.   Is distance a danger to love?   Silver S 22-1:22 N
   '51
   Crivello, K.   Whatever happened to the most beautiful girls in
   the world?   Film Fan Mo 109/110:38 Jl/Ag '70
   Flatley, G.   Three show-biz girls and how they grew.   N. Y.
   Times Bio Ed Ap 4 '71
   Once and future follies.   Time 97:70 My 3 '71

De CONDE, SYN
   Pinto, A.   Letter; filmog.   Films In R 25-8:512 O '74

De CORDOBA, PEDRO
  Obit.  Screen World 2:233 '51

de CORDOVA, ARTURO
  Franchey, J. R.  Great lover under wraps.  Silver S 14-9:26 Jl
    '44
  New sensation from Mexico.  Cue 13-37:16 S 9 '44
  Obit.  Classic Film Collect 42:35 Spg '74
    N. Y. Times p85 N 4 '73
    Same.  N. Y. Times Bio Ed p1769 N '73
    Screen World p233 '74

DEE, FRANCES
  York, C.  Sketch.  Photop 39:81 D '30
  Sketch.  Motion Pic Classic 33:51 Ap '31
  Manners, D.  Sketch.  Motion Pic 41:84 Ap '31
  Costello, T.  Her success.  Movie Classic 1:26 D '31
  Cohen, H.  Praising players of minor importance.  Cinema Dig
    3-6:12 Ap 24 '33
  March, J.  Dee.  Silver S 3-10:49 Ag '33
  Wilson, I.  All aboard for wedded bliss.  Silver S 4-3:21 Ja '34
  Beauty hints.  Motion Pic 49:50 Jl '35
  Mack, G.  Interview.  Movie Classic 8:37 Ag '35
  Lane, V. T.  Her return to the screen.  Motion Pic 53:38 Ap
    '37
  Uselton, R. A.  The Wampus baby stars.  Films In R 21-2:73
    F '70

DEE, RUBY
  Hammel, F.  Two for the theatre.  Cue 28-47:20 N 21 '59
  Bosworth, P.  Every black woman is Lena.  N. Y. Times Bio
    Ed Jl 12 '70
  Salute of the week.  Cue 39-39:1 S 26 '70
  Weales, G.  Stage.  Commonweal 93:47 O 9 '70
  Bio.  Cur Bio 31:3 N '70
    Same.  Cur Bio Yrbk 1970:107 '71

DEE, SANDRA
  Rising star.  Film R p21 '60/61
  Catching up with.  Mod Screen 66-12:32 D '72

DEEL, SANDRA
  Songs, dances and funny sayings.  TV Guide 4-8:12 F 25 '56

DeFORE, DON
  Perkins, R.  Big dumb ox, eh?  Silver S 16-2:48 D '45

deGARDE, ADELE
  Sketch.  Motion Pic Classic 2:13 My '16
  Lincks, A. S.  Sketch.  Motion Pic 15:64 My '18

DEGERMARK, PIA
  Hamilton J.  Sweden's school girl star.  Look 32:52 Ap 16 '68
  The new candid girl.  Harp Baz 101:84 Jl '68

De GORE, JANET
  Saved by the bell.   TV Guide 9-9:29 Mr 4 '61

DeHART, FLORINE FINDLAY
  Sketch.   Classic 16:49 Jl '23

De HAVEN, CARTER
  Tinee, M.   Interview.   Green Book 11:739 My '14
  Cheatham, M. S.   Interview.   Motion Pic Classic 9:36 N '19
  Cheatham, M.   Interview.   Motion Pic 23:76 Ap '22
  Slide, A.   Interview.   Silent Pic 15:26 Sum '72

De HAVEN, GLORIA
  Actress by heritage.   Lions R 3-3(sup):no p# Ap '44
  Born in a trunk.   Lions R 3-3:no p# Ap '44
  Sketch.   Photop 24:56 My '44
  Tin Type.   Lions R 4-1:no p# F '45
  Her mother's daughter.   Lions R 4-1:no p# F '45
  Mitchell, M.   Morning Gloria.   After Dark 12-3:19 Jl '70
  Catching up with...   Mod Screen 66-3:31 Mr '72

de HAVILLAND, OLIVIA
  Dixe, M.   Interview.   Movie Classic 9:15 O '35
  Lee, S.   Her success.   Motion Pic 52:38 S '36
  Reed, D.   Ready for love.   Silver S 7-4:25 F '37
  Caine, D.   Beauty secrets.   Motion Pic 53:16 F '37
  Lane, V. T.   Interview.   Movie Classic 11:35 F '37
  Williams, W.   How it's done.   Silver S 7-9:24 Jl '37
  Sketch.   Photop 51:6 Ag '37
  Reid, J.   Interview.   Motion Pic 54:42 Ag '37
  Wood, V.   One of the fearless five.   Screen Book 19-4:36 N '37
  Dillon, F.   I won't marry an Irishman.   Screen Book 21-5:28 D '38
  Service, F.   Strange pact!   Silver S 10-2:38 D '39
  Bio note; filmog.   Movies & People 2:12 '40
  Hall, G.   Olivia decides on a fling for herself.   Silver S 11-3:22 Ja '41
  Wilson, E.   It's too bad about Olivia...   Silver S 12-1:22 N '41
  Wilson, E.   Olivia decides to reform.   Silver S 12-11:28 S '42
  Walker, H. L.   Sketch.   Photop 21:42 N '42
  Skolsky, S.   Her story.   Photop 23:50 S '43
  Hall, G.   I am tired of my past.   Silver S 14-5:42 Mr '44
  My Easter prayer.   Photop 26:42 Ap '45
  Wilson, E.   What the doctor didn't order.   Silver S 16-1:32 N '45
  Parsons, L. O.   Cosmop's citation for best performance of month.   Cosmop 121:67 Jl '46
  Holland, J.   Olivia catches up.   Silver S 16-11:58 S '46
  Lane, L.   No longer but a dream.   Silver S 17-5:47 Mr '47
  Fink, H.   Her feud with Joan Fontaine.   Photop 31:36 Je '47
  Story of.   Photop 31:70 O '47
  Marsh, P.   Marriage.   Silver S 18-4:22 F '48
  Her home life.   Photop 34:46 Ap '49
  Mann, M.   No wonder she's happy.   Silver S 19-9:30 Jl '49

Graham, S.   Story of.   Photop 36:39 Ag '49
Romeo and Olivia.   Cue 20-9:10 Mr 3 '51
The love teams.   Screen Greats 1-2:10 Sum '71
Olivia de Havilland; filmog.   Films Illus 1-4:32 O '71
Chierichetti, D.   Olivia in London.   Film Fan Mo 124:3 O '71
Raddatz, L.   (She) returns to Hollywood.   TV Guide 20-5:12 Ja
   29 '72
The lady's in love with love.   Photop 81-5:74 My '72
Lambert, G.   The making of Gone with the wind.   Atlantic 231-
   2:48 F; 231-3:56 Mr '73
de Havilland seminar; filmog.   Dialogue 4-3:24 D '74

DEHNER, JOHN
   56 and never been kissed.   TV Guide 19-48:12 N 27 '71

DEKKER, ALBERT
   Hamilton, S.   Sketch.   Photop 54:28 My '40
   Obit.   N.Y. Times p47 My 7 '68
      Newsweek 71:73 My 20 '68
      Time 91:86 Mr 17 '68

de LACY, PHILIPPE
   Carr, H.   Sketch.   Classic 18:26 S '23
   Jansen, L.   Sketch.   Photop 26:81 S '24
   Calhoun, D.   Interview.   Motion Pic 35:67 Je '28

de la MOTTE, MARGUERITE
   Marguerite's dancing fingers.   Photop 16-2:58 Jl '19
   Sketch.   Motion Pic 18:34 Ag '19
   Drew, L.   Interview.   Motion Pic Classic 11:52 F '21
   Gassaway, G.   Interview.   Motion Pic Classic 14:48 Je '22
   Handy, T. B.   Interview.   Motion Pic 23:22 Jl '22
   Carr, H.   Sketch.   Classic 20:38 S '24
   Obit.   Screen World 2:233 '51

DELANEY, CHARLES
   Lawler, P.   Sketch.   Motion Pic Classic 26:58 Ja '28
   Obit.   Screen World 12:219 '61

de la TOUR, FRANCES
   Berkvist, R.   The funny girl in Brook's dream.   N.Y. Times
      Bio Ed F 28 '71
   Tomorrow belongs to us.   Plays & Players 20-10:24 Jl '73

DELGADO, ROGER
   Obit.   Screen World p233 '74

DELL, CLAUDIA
   Manners, D.   Sketch.   Motion Pic 40:48 Ag '30
   York, C.   Sketch.   Photop 38:68 N '30
   Hall, G.   Sketch.   Motion Pic 42:26 N '31
   Keats, P.   The rebel blonde.   Silver S 2-4:62 F '32

DELL, DOROTHY
  Sketch.   Time 23:32 Ap 2 '34
  Sketch.   Photop 45:38 My '34
  Grant, J.   Her death.   Movie Classic 6:6 Ag '34

DELL, GABRIEL
  How tough are the Dead End Kids?   Screen Book 21-6:28 Ja '39
  Berg, B.   This little Dead End Kid made good.   N.Y. Times
    Bio Ed Je 26 '72

DELON, ALAIN
  Lyons, D.   Interview.   Interview 1-10:3 n.d.
  A flash on (him).   Unifrance 48:8 O '58
  Graham, P.   The face of '63--France.   Films & Filming 9-8:13
    My '63
  Bean, R.   Will there be film stars in 1974?   Films & Filming
    10-10:9 Jl '64
  Rising stars.   Film R p55 '64/65
  Nolan, J. E.   Films on TV; filmog.   Films In R 21-4:229 Ap
    '70
  Bean, R.   Creating with a passion; interview; filmog.   Films &
    Filming 16-9:7 Je '70
  Klemesrud, J.   The French think he's good when he's bad.
    N.Y. Times Bio Ed Ag 16 '70
  Eyles, A.   Alain Delon; filmog.   Focus On R 4:6 S/O '70
  Delon's stepping stones.   Films Illus 2-14:12 Ag '72
  DeChamil, H.   The Markovic affair.   Oui 3-11:41 N '74

DE LON, JACK
  Obit.   N.Y. Times p35 Jl 2 '70

DEL RIO, DOLORES
  Renthall, D.   Interview.   Motion Pic Classic 25:48 Mr '27
  St. Johns, I.   Sketch.   Photop 32:66 Je '27
  Caverley, A.   Interview.   Motion Pic 34:22 S '27
  Autobiographical.   Theatre 47:18 F '28
  Goldbeck, E.   Interview.   Motion Pic Classic 27:23 Ag '28
  Waterbury, R.   Going Hollywood.   Photop 35:30 F '29
  Donnell, D.   Death of Jaime Del Rio.   Motion Pic 37:31 Mr '29
  Hall, G.   Interview.   Motion Pic 39:59 Je '30
  Grayson, C.   Sketch.   Motion Pic 41:50 Ap '31
  Manners, D.   Sketch.   Motion Pic Classic 33:50 Ap '31
  Hall, G.   Interview.   Movie Classic 1:24 S '31
  Home of.   Motion Pic 42:50 O '31
  Hall, G.   Interview.   Motion Pic 43:44 Jl '32
  Parsons, H.   Magic!   Silver S 4-8:18 Je '34
  Calhoun, D.   Home of.   Motion Pic 48:48 N '34
  Chrisman, J. E.   Interview.   Movie Classic 9:31 O '35
  Russell, A.   Dolores Del Rio's fan mail.   Silver S 6-1:29 N '35
  As a hostess.   Photop 49:74 F '36
  Harrison, P.   Interview.   Motion Pic 51:26 F '36
  Seymore, H.   Interview.   Photop 50:30 S '36
  Wilson, C.   Sketch.   Photop 50:25 S '36

Cummings, M.  Interview.  Photop 52:32 Mr '38
Cheatham, M.  Holiday's end.  Silver S 10-6:26 Ap '40
Berliner, M.  Del Rio festival.  Classic Film Collect 19:21 Fall/
  Win '67
Gomez-Sicre, J.  Dolores Del Rio; excerpts.  Americas 19:8
  N '67
Uselton, R. A.  The Wampus baby stars.  Films In R 21-2:73
  F '70
Braun, E.  Queen of Mexico.  Films & Filming 18-10:34 Jl '72
Dickson, D.  Letter.  Films & Filming 18-11:4 Ag '72

DELROY, IRENE
  Manners, D.  Interview.  Motion Pic 40:82 D '30

De LUISE, DOM
  Happy to be miserable.  TV Guide 15-2:28 Ja 14 '67
  Crail, T.  He bought his wife a bugle for Christmas.  TV Guide
    16-30:12 Jl 27 '68
  Lochte, D.  I grew up with garbage.  TV Guide 22-5:17 F 2 '74

De MARNEY, TERENCE
  Obit.  Film R p13 '71/72

de MARRAIS, JOAN
  Television's own promising starlets.  TV Guide 3-37:10 S 10 '55

DeMAVE, JACK
  Raddatz, L.  Lassie is better than some of the actresses I've
    played opposite.  TV Guide 17-34:22 Ag 23 '69

DeMILLE, KATHERINE
  Walker, H. L.  New girls to satisfy Hollywood's insatiable de-
    mand.  Silver S 4-8:30 Je '34

DEMONGEOT, MYLENE
  Bio note.  Unifrance 45:6 D '57

DEMPSTER, CAROL
  Smith, F. J.  Interview.  Motion Pic Classic 11:16 O '20
  Hall, G.  Interview.  Motion Pic 23:40 Jl '22
  Roberts, W. A.  Sketch.  Motion Pic 29:45 Jl '25
  Carr, H.  Sketch.  Motion Pic Classic 22:38 D '25
  Herzog, D.  Sketch.  Photop 29:36 Mr '26
  Hall, G.  Interview.  Motion Pic Classic 24:53 O '26
  Peterson, E. B.  Sketch.  Motion Pic 32:27 Ja '27
  Peterson, E.  Sketch.  Motion Pic 31:33 Ap '27
  Schonert, V. L.  Carol Dempster; filmog.  Film Fan Mo 125:22
    N '71
  Dorr, J.  The movies, Mr. Griffith and Carol Dempster.  Cine-
    ma (BH) 7-1:23 Fall '71

DENBERG, SUSAN
  Photos.  Playboy 13-8:86 Ag '66

DENEUVE, CATHERINE
  They didn't plan to be movie stars.   Unifrance 56:no p# Spg '62
  France's Deneuve wave; photos.   Playboy 12-10:88 O '65
  Belle de jour.   Time 91:106 Ap 26 '68
  Ehrlich, H.   Catherine Deneuve.   Look 32:62 Ap 30 '68
  Making it in America.   Newsweek 72:42 Ag 26 '68
  Off the set and on the town.   Newsweek 72:44 Ag 26 '68
  Liber, N.   Interview.   Life 66:32 Ja 24 '69
  Sheehan, E. F.   Interview.   Holiday 46:48 Ag '69
  Bio.   Brit Bk Yr 1969:148 '69
  Knight, A. & Alpert, H.   Sex stars of 1970.   Playboy 17-12:220
    D '70
  Hidden lovers.   Photop 80-2:82 Ag '71
  Mastroianni and Deneuve.   Show 2-10:35 D '71
  How she got Mastroianni away from his wife.   Mod Screen 66-8:
    48 Ag '72
  Chelminski, R.   Interview.   People 2-10:29 S 2 '74

De NIRO, ROBERT
  Flatley, G.   Look, Bobby's slipping into Brando's shoes.   N. Y.
    Times sec 2:13 N 4 '73
  Same.   N. Y. Times Bio Ed p1774 N '73

DENNING, DOREEN
  Person of promise.   Films & Filming 3-5:16 F '57

DENNING, RICHARD
  Sketch.   Photop 54:28 Ag '40

DENNIS, BEVERLY
  In the cast.   TV Guide 1-6:13 My 8 '53

DENNIS, SANDY
  Warga, W.   Girl with a good grip on chaos.   Life 64:65 F 9 '68
  Bio.   Cur Bio 30:3 Ja '69
    Same.   Cur Bio Yrbk 1969:121 '70

DENNY, REGINALD
  Sketch.   Photop 24:28 Je '23
  de Revere, F. V.   Face analysis.   Motion Pic 28:44 O '24
  Penn, V.   Interview.   Motion Pic 30:34 N '25
  Eddy, D.   Sketch.   Motion Pic Classic 24:48 S '26
  Reid, J.   Interview.   Motion Pic 33:45 O '26
  Fairfield, L.   As an aviator.   Motion Pic 35:41 My '28
  Manners, D.   Sketch.   Motion Pic Classic 28:55 O '28
  The new revolution in pictures.   Theatre 48:24 N '28
  Morse, W. Jr.   Sketch.   Motion Pic 38:74 O '29
  Gray, C.   Interview.   Motion Pic Classic 31:33 Ag '30
  Severin, R.   Maker of model airplanes.   Leisure 5:26 Jl '38
  Obit.   Brit Bk Yr 1968:588 '68
    Classic Film Collect 18:40 Sum '67

DENT, VERNON
    Lee, R.  Vernon Dent.  Films In R 15-1:59 Ja '64

DENVER, BOB
    Like what are beatniks big daddy.  TV Guide 8-8:8 F 20 '60
    He's the Robinson Crusoe of the beatnik set.  TV Guide 13-4:15
        Ja 23 '65

de PUTTI, LYA
    Fraenkel, H.  Famous Hungarian screen beauty.  Motion Pic
        Classic 23:18 My '26
    Waterbury, R.  Interview.  Photop 31:63 F '27
    Service, F.  Interview.  Motion Pic Classic 25:38 Mr '27
    Cruikshank, H.  Interview.  Motion Pic 34:54 Ja '28
    The movie as a means of world unity.  Theatre 47:26 Ap '28
    Interview regarding Hollywood.  Liv Age 336:382 Jl '29
    Miller, N.  Letter.  Films In R 16-2:125 F '65

DEREK, JOHN
    Stevens, B.  Handsomest guy in Hollywood.  Silver S 19-8:35 Je
        '49
    Pritchett, F.  Speaking of love and kisses.  Silver S 20-6:40 Ap
        '50
    Derek, Mrs. J.  Our third year of marriage.  Silver S 21-5:37
        Mr '51
    Rowland, R.  The last of Mr. Pretty Boy.  Silver S 24-8:24 Je
        '54
    Enchore; photos of Ursula Andress by Derek.  Playboy 20-11:103
        N '73
    Hanson, C. L.  Derek directs his second feature with pictorial
        bravura.  Cinema (BH) 3-3:17 n. d.

de REMER, RUBY
    Interview.  Theatre 29:189 Mr '19
    Bio sketch.  Motion Pic Classic 8:20 Ag '19
    Malverne, P.  Interview.  Motion Pic Classic 11:26 F '21
    How I keep in condition.  Photop 20:45 S '21
    Gassaway, G.  Interview.  Motion Pic 23:72 Ap '22
    Amoret, J.  Interview.  Classic 15:22 N '22

DERN, BRUCE
    Young, C.  Filmog.  Films In R 21-2:124 F '70
    Delson, J.  Interview.  Take One 3-10:8 Mr/Ap '72
    Anderson, K. & Meech, S.  Silent running; interview.  Cinefan-
        tastique 2-2:8 Sum '72
    Wohlfert, L.  'Gatsby' is a green light for Dern.  People 1-9:22
        Ap 29 '74

de ROCHE, CHARLES
    Obit.  Screen World 4:176 '53

DESHON, FLORENCE
    Morris, M.  Greenwich Village as it ain't.  Photop 15-1:30 D '18

DESMOND, FLORENCE
  Ruddy, J. M.  Clever mimic.  Motion Pic 47:64 Mr '34
  Hunter, L.  Sketch.  Motion Pic 48:14 Ja '35
  Roberts, F.  Home of.  Theatre World 26:130 S '36
  Johns, E.  Work of.  Theatre World 37:18 My '42

DESMOND, JOHNNY
  Inside McCalls.  McCalls 82:6 Ja '55
  Taylor, T.  Up and down with Desmond.  Cue 24-37:14 S 17 '55
  Her blouses went to the laundry.  TV Guide 7-1:24 Ja 3 '59

DESMOND, WILLIAM
  O'Hara, K.  Desmond of Dublin.  Photop 12-3:82 Ag '17
  Despard, L.  Interview.  Motion Pic 15:93 F '18
  Fleming, S.  Sketch.  Motion Pic Classic 6:53 Jl '18
  Roberts, S.  Interview.  Motion Pic Classic 7:18 Ja '19
  Obit.  Screen World 1:233 '49
  Bio note.  Silent Pic 14:20 Spg '72
  Bio note.  Cinema Trails 2:20 n. d.

DESMONDE, JERRY
  Obit.  Film R p21 '66/68

DESNY, IVAN
  Rising star.  Film R p28 '50

DESTE, LULI
  Whitehead, H.  Sketch.  Motion Pic 53:9 Je '37

DEUEL, GEOFF
  The Duel brothers.  Films Illus 1-9:18 Mr '72

DEUTSCH, ERNST
  Obit.  N. Y. Times p93 Mr 23 '69
    Screen World 21:234 '70

DEVERY, JAMES
  That man is back.  TV Guide 8-16:12 Ap 16 '60

DEVI, KAMALA
  The prettiest Indian he ever came across.  TV Guide 12-36:10
    S 5 '64

DEVINE, ANDY
  Gebhart, M.  (His) story.  Silver S 2-12:21 O '32
  Ducas, D.  Home of.  Photop 53:32 Je '39
  Kaufman, S.  Meet the weighty mayor of Van Nuys.  Silver S 16-
    1:50 N '45
  The company remembers Stagecoach.  Action 6-5:29 S/O '71

DEVORE, DOROTHY
  Cheatham, M.  Interview.  Motion Pic 21:54 Mr '21
  Shelley, H.  Interview.  Motion Pic Classic 11:34 D '21

Donnell, D.   Interview.   Motion Pic 30:51 Ja '26
Uselton, R. A.   The Wampus baby stars.   Films In R 21-2:73
    F '70
Slide, A.   Interview.   Silent Pic 15:16 Sum '72

DEWHURST, COLLEEN
    Clurman, H.   Theatre.   Nation 183:314 O 13 '56
    Maiden voyage for two.   Theatre Arts 41:69 Ap '57
    Pryce-Jones, A.   Cleo in the park.   Theatre Arts 47:16 Jl '63
    Mothner, I.   New York is a stage.   Look 28:121 F 11 '64
    Chase, C.   She has Broadway 'Moon'-struck.   N. Y. Times sec
        2:1 F 17 '74
        Same.   N. Y. Times Bio Ed p185 F '74

de WILDE, BRANDON
    Obit.   Classic Film Collector 36:extra 2 Fall '72
        Film R p11 '73/74
        N. Y. Times Bio Ed p1299 Jl '72

deWIT, JACQUELINE
    Go-getter.   Lions R 3-4:no p# Jl '44

De WOLFE, BILLY
    Sketch.   Photop 32:10 Mr '48
    Sketch.   Vogue 98:76 O 1 '48
    Obit.   N. Y. Post p13 Mr 6 '74
        N. Y. Times Bio Ed p335 Mr '74

DEXTER, ANTHONY
    Valentino.   Cue 19-44:15 N 4 '50
    O'Leary, D.   His life is unbelievable.   Silver S 21-6:42 Ap '51

DEXTER, ELLIOTT
    Stars he has loved.   Theatre 26:408 D '17
    Women I have loved.   Photop 13-6:18 My '18
    McGaffey, K.   Sketch.   Motion Pic 17:35 F '19
    Yorke, M.   Interview.   Motion Pic Classic 9:104 Ja '20
    St. Johns, A. R.   Sketch.   Photop 17:89 My '20
    Montanye, L.   Interview.   Motion Pic Classic 13:34 O '21
    Goldbeck, W.   Interview.   Motion Pic 24:24 D '22

DEY, SUSAN
    Vachon, B.   Becoming Susan Dey.   Look 35-15:64 Jl 27 '71
    Why our daughter fears the men she dates.   Photop 80-4:64 O
        '71
    David Cassidy and Susan Dey.   Mod Screen 65-12:33 D '71
    How a little girl lost became a woman overnight.   Photop 81-3:
        51 Mr '72
    Photop forum.   Photop 81-4:28 Ap '72
    Cooking with a star.   Mod Screen 66-5:62 My '72
    From loneliness to... marriage?   Photop 81-5:50 My '72
    Adler, D.   Now, really!   TV Guide 21-2:15 Ja 13 '73

DHIEGH, KHIGH
Meyers, R.   (He) digs i ching.   TV Guide 19-8:45 F 20 '71

DICKENS, CHARLES STAFFORD
Obit.   N. Y. Times p27 O 14 '67

DICKINSON, ANGIE
Rising star.   Film R p33 '61/62
Hollywood swingers.   Show 3-11:93 N '63
Burt Bacharach:  Hollywood's sexy music man.   Photop 78-4:46
   O '70
Davidson, M.   Private world of a golden couple.   Good House
   174:82 Mr '72
He's the family star now.   People 1-15:49 Je 10 '74

DICKSON, DOROTHY
Wilson, B. F.   Interview.   Motion Pic Classic 11:48 N '20
Roberts, F.   Home of.   Theatre World 27:82 F '37

DICKSON, GLORIA
Lane, J.   Sketch.   Motion Pic 54:58 N '37
Caine, D.   Sketch.   Motion Pic 54:6 D '37
Hamilton, S.   Sketch.   Photop 52:68 Ja '38
Manzi, I. A.   Filmog.   Films In R 16-1:56 Ja '65
Crivello, K.   Gloria Dickson; filmog.   Classic Film Collect 32:
   17 Fall '71

DIERKES, JOHN
Shuman, L.   John Dierkes; filmog.   Films In R 22-10:648 D '71

DIETRICH, MARLENE
Jordan, A.   Two first-rate girls who refuse to be seconds.   Sil-
   ver S 1-2:14 D '30
Manners, D.   Sketch.   Motion Pic 40:50 Ja '31
Hall, L.   The Garbo-Dietrich rivalry.   Photop 39:50 F '31
Tolishus, O.   Sketch.   Photop 39:28 Ap '31
Friedkin, E. Z.   The true story.   Silver S 1-9:18 Jl '31
Manners, D.   Will she stay in America?   Motion Pic 42:56 S
   '31
Sued by director's wife.   Movie Classic 1:37 N '31
Benton, C.   Sketch.   Movie Classic 1:37 D '31
Hall, G.   Interview.   Movie Classic 1:20 Ja '32
Rice, L.   Sketch.   Movie Classic 2:51 My '32
Manners, D.   Interview.   Movie Classic 2:19 My '32
Dillon, F.   Sketch.   Movie Classic 2:20 Jl '32
Cheasley, C. W.   Her numberscope.   Motion Pic 43:32 Jl '32
Calhoun, D.   Will she be deported?   Motion Pic 43:28 Jl '32
Barden, J.   Gets kidnap threat.   Movie Classic 2:28 Ag '32
Keats, P.   She is amazing in Blonde Venus.   Silver S 1-10:14
   Ag '32
Dillon, F.   Annoyances that may drive her out America.   Movie
   Classic 3:22 S '32
Potter, M.   Marlene Dietrich.   Cinema Dig 1-13:14 O 31 '32

Moffitt, C. F.   Censorship for interviews Hollywood's latest wild
   idea...   Cinema Dig 2-5:9 Ja 9 '33
Melcher, E.   Marlene Dietrich.   Cinema Dig 2-10:10 F 20 '33
Manners, D.   Her future films to be made in Germany.   Movie
   Classic 4:28 Mr '33
Hall, H.   Dietrich would buy it for a song.   Cinema Dig 3-3:4
   Ap 3 '33
Keen, E.   Her trousers started something.   Silver S 3-6:52 Ap
   '33
Shaffer, R.   Why she wears men's clothes.   Motion Pic 45:54
   Ap '33
Wilson, E.   Goodbye Dietrich.   Silver S 3-8:18 Je '33
Lee, S.   Sketch.   Motion Pic 45:26 Je '33
Sketch.   Lit Dig 116:22 Ag 5 '33
Schallert, E.   Is she indifferent to her public?   Motion Pic 46:
   31 S '33
Lee, S.   Interview.   Motion Pic 46:49 Ja '34
Perry, E.   Interview.   Movie Classic 5:24 Ja '34
Wilson, E.   The loveliest star.   Silver S 4-4:20 F '34
Vegtel, M.   Compared with Garbo.   Vanity Fair 42:28 Je '34
Hall, G.   Why she leads a solitary life.   Motion Pic 47:34 Je
   '34
Keats, P.   Beautiful Dietrich.   Silver S 5-1:28 N '34
French, W. F.   What price glamour?   Motion Pic 48:5 N '34
Cruikshank.   Interview.   Motion Pic 49:24 Je '35
Hartley, K.   Fashions follow her lead.   Movie Classic 8:38 Ag
   '35
Zeitlin, I.   The real Dietrich.   Motion Pic 51:37 My '36
Liza.   Unlucky lady.   Silver S 6-8:25 Je '36
Marlene Dietrich.   Visages 2:entire issue Je '36
Reid, J.   Work of.   Movie Classic 10:44 Ag '36
Boehael, W.   Story of.   Motion Pic 53:35 Je '37
Wilson, E.   Projections of.   Silver S 7-11:34 S '37
Fisher, J.   Symbol of today's glamour.   Photop 51:5 N '37
Decline in popularity.   Life 4:18 Ja 3 '38
Sullivan, E.   Glamour lets down its hair.   Silver S 10-5:42 Mr
   '40
Hall, G.   Marlene tells tales out of school.   Silver S 11-2:22 D
   '40
Bio note; filmog.   Movies & People 2:12 '40
Hamman, M.   Sketch.   Good House 112:16 Ap '41
Story of.   Vogue 100:34 Jl 1 '42
Manners, M. J.   Dietrich's ten most exciting moments.   Silver
   S 13-2:36 D '42
Her makeup for Kismet.   Life 15:119 N 29 '43
Savo savvies Dietrich.   Cue 13-5:10 Ja 29 '44
Lerman, L.   Somewhere in Italy.   Vogue 104:154 Ag 15 '44
Here's a Dietrich you may not know.   Lions R 3-5:no p# D '44
Entertaining in Germany.   Time 45:70 Ja 29 '45
As USO entertainer in Germany.   Life 18:49 Mr 5 '45
Hall, G.   Marlene minces no words.   Silver S 17-7:30 My '47
Wilson, E.   Glamourous Grandma.   Silver S 18-12:24 O '48
Atterbury, C.   Marlene's birth certificate.   Films In R 15-6:375

Je/ Jl '64
Old gal in town.   Time 90:84 O 20 '67
Kroll, J.   The Kraut.   Newsweek 70:113 O 23 '67
Bio.   Cur Bio 29:10 F '68
   Same.   Cur Bio Yrbk 1968:112 '69
Silver, C.   A love letter to Marlene.   Classic Film Collect 20:9
   Spg '68
Lady doth protest.   Newsweek 72:58 S 16 '68
Crinkley, R.   Quintessential sultry female.   Nat R 21:134 F 11
   '69
Bowers, R. L.   Dietrich '54-70; updated filmog.   Films In R
   22-1:17 Ja '71
Der Krauts.   Screen Greats 1-2:58 Sum '71
Corneau, E.   Glamorous Grandma.   Classic Film Collect 31:26
   Sum '71
Flinn, T.   Joe, where are you?   Velvet Light 6:9 Fall '72
Calendo, J.   Dietrich and the devil.   Interview 26:27 O '72
Rheuban, J.   The scientist and the vamp.   Sight & Sound 42-1:35
   Win '72/73
Taylor, A.   Dietrich at 68 (or 71) still a terror, still an angel.
   N. Y. Times Bio Ed p2145 D '72
Marlene rides again.   Time 101:57 Ja 15 '73
Gow, G.   Alchemy: Dietrich and Sternberg.   Films & Filming
   20-9:57 Je '74

DILLER, PHYLLIS
   Erwin, R.   Diller begins her own comic script.   Ed & Pub 101:
      37 Ja 6 '68
   Bio.   Cur Bio Yrbk 1967:98 '68
   McDonald, E.   The plant lady?   House Beaut 122:202 Ap '70
   Stoginski, J.   Filmog.   Filmograph 2-1:44 '71
   Tells about a facelift--hers.   Life 72:73 F 11 '72
   How my facelift changed my life.   Photop 81-6:48 Je '72
   How I find peace of mind.   Mod Screen 66-9:62 S '72
   Diller, P.   Bring back the violins.   Viva 1-11:112 Ag '74

DIX, RICHARD
   Bryers, L.   Interview.   Motion Pic 22:50 Ja '22
   Shelley, H.   Interview.   Motion Pic Classic 13:37 F '22
   His darkest hour.   Classic 15:58 Ja '23
   Gassaway, G.   Interview.   Motion Pic 25:30 F '23
   Donnell, D.   Interview.   Classic 18:64 F '24
   Adams, E.   His horoscope.   Photop 26:35 N '24
   de Revere, F. V.   Face analysis of.   Motion Pic 28:48 N '24
   Autobiographical.   Motion Pic 30:28 O '25
   Diary while making The vanishing American.   Motion Pic 30:50
      D '25
   Wins popularity contest.   Motion Pic Classic 23:16 Jl '26
   Hall, H. R.   Interview.   Motion Pic Classic 24:54 Ja '27
   Smith, F. J.   Sketch.   Photop 31:30 F '27
   Redway, S.   Interview.   Motion Pic 31:26 Mr '27
   Johnston, C.   Sketch.   Motion Pic Classic 25:53 Ag '27
   Manners, D.   Interview.   Motion Pic 34:24 D '27

Why I welcome talking pictures.   Theatre 49:28 My '29
Calhoun, D.   Interview.   Motion Pic 39:64 Mr '30
Martin, E.   Interview.   Photop 38:55 Je '30
Walker, H. L.   Sketch.   Motion Pic 39:40 Jl '30
Larnard, P.   Sketch.   Motion Pic Classic 32:53 Ja '31
Lane, J.   Sketch.   Movie Classic 1:40 Ja '32
His marriage.   Photop 41:27 Ja '32
Cruikshank.   How marriage changed him.   Motion Pic 43:50 Je
    '32
Lieber, E.   Sketch.   Motion Pic 50:39 D '35
Calhoun, D.   His marriage with Virginia Webster.   Movie Classic
    10:51 Mr '36
Zeitlin, I.   Interview.   Motion Pic 53:51 Mr '37
Bio note; filmog.   Movies & People 2:12 '40
Obit.   Screen World 1:233 '49

DIXON, IVAN
    The sergeant's hard climb from the ranks.   TV Guide 15-37:35
        S 16 '67

DOAT, ANNE
    They didn't plan to be movie stars.   Unifrance 56:no p# Spg '62

DOBSON, TAMARA
    Klemesrud, J.   Not superfly but super woman.   N.Y. Times sec
        2:11 Ag 19 '73
    Cutrone, R. & Fremont, V.   Interview.   Interview 3-8(35):14 Ag
        '73

DODD, CLAIRE
    Sketch.   Time 25:38 Ap 15 '35
    Garvin, R.   Filmography.   Films In R 21-8:516 O '70
    Obit.   Classic Film Collect 42:34 Spg '74
        N.Y. Times Bio Ed p1776 N '73
        Screen World p233 '74

DODD, NEAL
    Parson.   Am Mag 129:80 Je '40
    Chaplain to the movies.   Time 42:76 Ag 2 '43
    Kellick, H. W.   Hollywood's marrying parson.   Sat Eve Post
        222:128 Ap 15 '50
    Obit.   Screen World 18:234 '67

DODSON, JACK
    Mother's boy grows up.   TV Guide 19-25:37 Je 19 '71

DOERMER, CHRISTIAN
    The image shapers.   Films & Filming 9-3:76 D '62
    Bean, R.   The face of '63--Germany.   Films & Filming 9-9:41
        Je '63

DOLENZ, MICKY
    (See:  MONKEES, THE)

DOMERGUE, FAITH
Rising star.   Film R p40 '51/52

DONAHUE, ELINOR
She's still the girl next door.   TV Guide 8-2:17 Ja 9 '60

DONAHUE, PAT
Just then something else happened.   TV Guide 9-27:25 Jl 8 '61

DONAHUE, TROY
Rising star.   Film R p22 '60/61
Denton, C.   The slings and arrows of outraged critics.   TV
   Guide 10-33:6 Ag 18 '62

DONALD, PETER
Unmasked.   TV Guide 4-15:13 Ap 14 '56

DONALDSON, ARTHUR
Bryce, J.   The original Prince of Pilsen.   Photop 7-3:78 F '15
Hoffman, H.   Wizard of makeup.   Motion Pic 11:44 My '16

DONALDSON, TED
Hamilton, S.   Sketch.   Photop 25:54 Ag '44

DONAT, ROBERT
Sketch.   Theatre World 22:206 N '34
Ruddy, J. M.   Interview.   Motion Pic 48:39 Ja '35
Sketch.   Photop 48:80 D '35
Biery, R.   Interview.   Movie Classic 9:51 Ja '36
Lieber, R.   Interview.   Motion Pic 51:36 My '36
Sketch.   Theatre World 32:176 N '39
Bio note; filmog.   Movies & People 2:12 '40
Mr. Chips goes to town.   Lions R 3-1:no p# S '43
Parsons, L. O.   Cosmop's citation for the best starring per-
   formance of the month.   Cosmop 120:45 F '46
Obit.   Film R p10 '59/60
Maltin, L.   Robert Donat; filmog.   Film Fan Mo 76:3 O '67
Richards, J.   A star without armour; filmog.   Focus On R 8:17
   n. d.

DONLEVY, BRIAN
Sketch.   Motion Pic 52:62 Ja '37
Holland, J.   There's drama in his life.   Screen Book 19-5:86 D
   '37
Rhea, M.   Sketch.   Photop 53:30 N '39
Sketch.   Time 36:48 Ag 26 '40
Bio note; filmog.   Movies & People 2:12 '40
Reid, J.   Shake hands with an ex-villain.   Silver S 11-9:44 Jl
   '41
Tough guy Donlevy.   Lions R 2-3:no p# D '42
Franchey, J. R.   Soft-hearted brute.   Silver S 14-6:31 Ap '44
Brian Donlevy, American.   Lions R 3-4:no p# Jl '44
My favorite possession.   Photop 26:57 My '45

Pritchett, F. Women battle him. Silver S 16-6:58 Ap '46
Maltin, L. The films of...; filmog. Film Fan Mo 70:3 Ap '67
Mank, G. Brian Donlevy; filmog. Films In R 22-1:55 Ja '71
Pitts, M. R. Letter. Films In R 22-3:182 Mr '71
Obit. Classic Film Collect 35:8X Sum '72
   Film R p16 '72/73
   Mod Screen 66-7:16 Jl '72
   N. Y. Times p38 Ap 7 '72
   Same. N. Y. Times Bio Ed Ap 6 '72
   Newsweek 79:93 Ap 17 '72
   Time 99:62 Ap 17 '72

DONLIN, MIKE
Pinto, A. Mike Donlin; filmog. Films In R 25-5:316 My '74

DONNELL, JEFF
Stanke, D. Jeff Donnell; filmog. Film Fan Mo 137:19 N '72

DONNELLY, RUTH
Cohen, H. Praising players of minor importance. Cinema Dig
   3-6:12 Ap 24 '33

DONOVAN, CASEY
(Also known as Cal Culver, which see)
Buckley, P. A dirty movie is a dirty movie is a dirty movie
   is... Films & Filming 18-11:29 Ag '72

DORAINE, LUCY
Hall, G. Sketch. Motion Pic Classic 28:22 S '28

DORALDINA
Handy, T. B. I'm a wild woman! Photop 16-5:59 My '19

DORAN, MARY
York, C. Sketch. Photop 38:51 S '30
Ladies of lenses! Silver S 2-7:43 My '32

DORIAN, ANGELA
Screen gem. Playboy 14-9:126 S '67

DORLEAC, FRANCOISE
Obit. Newsweek 70:98 Jl 10 '67
Delbos, C. Letter; filmog. Films In R 19-4:249 Ap '68

DORN, PHILIP
Hamilton, S. Sketch. Photop 18:59 Ja '41
Amateur photographer expert actor. Lions R 1-11/12:no p# Jl/
   Ag '42
Stars of tomorrow. Lions R 1-11/12:no p# Jl/Ag '42
Incident in Holland. Lions R 2-3(sup):no p# Ja '43
Hollander in Hollywood. Lions R 4-1:no p# F '45
Ragan, D. The secret courage of a star whose luck ran out.
   Movie Dig 1-6:126 N '72

DORO, MARIE
Her unusual facial expressions.  Theatre 8:70 Mr '08
History.  Pearson (NY) 22:376 S '09
Warwick, A.  Sketch.  Green Book 11:733 My '14
Dale, A.  Sketch.  Green Book 15:1121 Je '16
Pollock, A.  Sketch.  Motion Pic 13:38 Ap '17
Naylor, H. S.  Sketch.  Motion Pic Classic 8:20 Mr '19
Her New York home.  Theatre 35:252 Ap '22

DORS, DIANA
Hill, D.  A window on Dors.  Films & Filming 1-7:10 Ap '55
A young star speaks.  Film R p21 '55/56
Zunser, J.  Lend-lease from Britain.  Cue 25-32:14 Ag 11 '56
Braun, E.  On her own terms.  Films & Filming 19-5:23 F '73
Coveney, M.  Interview.  Plays & Players 21-10:14 Jl '74

D'ORSAY, FIFI
Belfrage, C.  Sketch.  Motion Pic Classic 30:58 F '30
Cartwright, D.  Sketch.  Movie Classic 1:43 O '31
Benton, C.  Sketch.  Movie Classic 2:33 Mr '32
Rosado, L.  Sketch.  Movie Classic 3:32 F '33
What they are doing now.  Show 2-8:106 Ag '62
Handsaker, G.  Fifi still wows 'em.  Classic Film Collect:X1
    Fall '70
Stanke, D.  Fifi D'Orsay; filmog.  Film Fan Mo 128:21 F '72

DOSCHER, DORIS
Obit.  Screen World 22:236 '71

DOTRICE, KAREN
Filmog.  Films & Filming 19-6:59 Mr '73

DOTRICE, MICHELE
Filmog.  Films & Filming 19-6:59 Mr '73

DOTRICE, ROY
Oliver, E.  Theatre.  New Yorker 43:46 D 30 '67
Clurman, H.  Theatre.  Nation 206:92 Ja 15 '68
Morley, S.  Three is one.  Plays & Players 16-8:32 My '69
Filmog.  Films & Filming 19-6:59 Mr '73

DOUGLAS, DONNA
The evolution of Dot Smith.  TV Guide 9-46:11 N 18 '61
Haute couture hillbilly style.  TV Guide 11-10:6 Mr 9 '63
They're still single.  TV Guide 13-9:22 F 27 '65

DOUGLAS, KIRK
Douglas, K.  I don't like career women.  Silver S 18-10:44 Ag
    '48
Keats, P.  Hottest star in pictures.  Silver S 20-1:26 N '49
Sable, M.  Must genius come from a garret?  Silver S 21-7:40
    My '51
Douglas, K.  I've very decided news about women.  Silver S

22-5:24 Mr '52
O'Leary, D.   You've got to be tough.   Silver S 23-1:32 N '52
Morris, G.   Watch out, Pier.   Silver S 24-1:26 N '53
Miller, E.   More than a chip off the old block (primarily about
    Michael Douglas).   Seventeen 28:330 Ag '69
Ebert, R.   Kirk Douglas at large.   Esquire 73:89 F '70
Castell, D.   Kirk Douglas.   Films Illus 1-11:10 My '72
Gow, G.   Impact; interview; filmog.   Films & Filming 18-12:10
    S '72
Kelly, K.   Interview.   Interview p6 Ja '74
Eyles, A.   Kirk Douglas; filmog.   Focus On F 7:5 n. d.

DOUGLAS, LAWRENCE
    New faces.   Films Illus 1-7:11 Ja '72

DOUGLAS, MELVYN
    New faces for the electric lights.   Silver S 2-4:38 F '32
    Keats, P.   Why Garbo is great; interview.   Silver S 2-8:16 Je
        '32
    Schwarzkopf, J.   Sketch.   Motion Pic 51:21 Je '36
    Hall, G.   Eluding stardom.   Silver S 7-6:20 Ap '37
    Joseph, L. R.   There are always three women.   Screen Book
        20-6:38 Jl '38
    Bio note; filmog.   Movies & People 2:13 '40
    Hall, G.   I cover the set.   Silver S 11-8:22 Je '41
    Caught napping.   Lions R 1-3:no p# N '41
    He dances, too.   Lions R 1-6:no p# F '42
    And so, an actor.   Lions R 2-3(sup):no p# Ja '43
    Minoff, P.   One misplaced actor.   Cue 22-23:9 Je 6 '53
    Zunser, J.   A daarlin' man.   Cue 28-8:10 F 21 '59
    It was much more hazardous, but more fun.   TV Guide 19-43:26
        O 23 '71

DOUGLAS, MICHAEL
    Miller, E.   More than a chip off the old block.   Seventeen 28:
        330 Ag '69
    Considine, S.   I never sang for my father.   After Dark 4-3:18
        Jl '71
    Second generation.   Films Illus 1-10:11 Ap '72
    Note; filmog.   Films & Filming 18-11:60 Ag '72
    Kiester, E. Jr.   My father and I are very different people.   TV
        Guide 22-7:25 F 16 '74
    Photoplay forum.   Photop 85-6:8 Je '74
    Is out-of-wedlock no longer in?   People 2-10:50 S 2 '74

DOUGLAS, PAUL
    Sketch.   Time 53:86 Ja 17 '49
    Bowers, L.   This Douglas guy.   Silver S 19-7:35 My '49
    New movie tailored to fit Paul Douglas.   Cue 18-42:14 O 15 '49
    Reid, L.   The taming of the 'big brute. "   Silver S 20-12:46 O
        '50
    Rising star.   Film R p30 '50
    Service, F.   Completely nuts about the guy.   Silver S 21-11:38

S '51
Water, R.  Conversation with Douglas.  Cue 26-16:11 Ap 20 '57
Obit.  Film R p10 '60/61
    Screen World 11:216 '60
Pickard, R.  Paul Douglas; filmog.  Films In R 24-8:507 O '73

DOUGLAS, ROBERT
    Meyer, J.  Robert Douglas; filmog.  Film Fan Mo 132:18 Je '72

DOUGLASS, KENT
    Grayson, C.  Some call him a genius.  Silver S 2-1:20 N '31

DOVE, BILLIE
    Sketch.  National 51:33 Je '22
    Gassaway, G.  Interview.  Classic 15:36 N '22
    St. Johns, I.  Sketch.  Photop 31:38 Ap '27
    Johnston, C.  Sketch.  Motion Pic Classic 26:53 D '27
    Donnell, D.  Sketch.  Motion Pic 35:33 Je '28
    Conti, M.  Shopping with Billie Dove.  Motion Pic 37:69 F '29
    Goldbeck, E.  Interview.  Motion Pic 38:48 N '29
    Hall, G.  Interview.  Motion Pic 39:45 My '30
    Walker, H. L.  Interview.  Motion Pic Classic 33:63 Ap '31
    Manners, D.  Her tragedy.  Motion Pic D '31
    Goldbeck, E.  The new Billie Dove.  Movie Classic 1:50 D '31
    Ten years ago.  Photop 44:116 O '33
    What they are doing now.  Show 2-8:106 Ag '62
    Phillips, A.  Letter; partial filmog.  Films In R 19-2:123 F '68
    Case, D. E.  Partial filmog.  Films In R 21-8:517 O '70
    Hoaglin, J. L.  Down memory lane.  Hollywood Stu 6-8:31 D '71

DOW, PEGGY
    Hall, G.  Thank goodness for men.  Silver S 20-8:47 Je '50
    Rising star.  Film R p27 '50
    Dow, P.  My lessons in love so far.  Silver S 21-8:24 Je '51

DOW, TONY
    Beaver's big brother.  TV Guide 7-22:20 My 30 '59
    His mother detests child actors.  TV Guide 10-4:27 Ja 27 '62

DOWLING, CONSTANCE
    New golden-haired Goldwyn find.  Cue 13-9:6 F 26 '44
    Hall, G.  Cinderella Dowling.  Silver S 14-8:32 Je '44
    Obit.  N. Y. Times p52 O 29 '69
        Screen World 21:236 '70

DOWNES, EDWARD RAY
    Obit.  N. Y. Times p39 Mr 15 '68

DOWNS, JOHNNY
    Williams, W.  Don't be a child star.  Screen Book 21-6:14 Ja
        '39
    Maltin, L.  Our gang; Our gang filmog.  Film Fan Mo 66:3 D
        '66

Farlekas, C.  The reign of the King of the Hollywood B movies.
    Classic Film Collect 41:51 Win '73

DRAKE, BETSY
    Parsons, L.  Cosmop's citation for the best supporting perform-
        ance of the month.  Cosmop 125:12 D '48
    Norman, D. C.  Sketch.  Ladies Home J 96:65 S '49
    Land, I. S.  First novelists.  Lib J 96:3165 O 1 '71
    Bannan, A.  Authors & editors.  Pub W 200:15 S 27 '71

DRAKE, DONA
    Story of.  Life 12:60 Ja 19 '42
    Franchey, J. R.  The nonesuch.  Silver S 13-116:42 S '43

DRAKE, DOROTHY
    Uselton, R. A.  The Wampus baby stars.  Films In R 21-2:73
        F '70

DRAKE, FRANCES
    Walker, H. L.  New girls to satisfy Hollywood's insatiable de-
        mand.  Silver S 4-8:30 Je '34

DRAKE, TOM
    Young man with a hunch.  Lions R 3-3(sup):no p# Ap '44
    Study in contrasts.  Lions R 3-5:no p# D '44
    (His) debut.  Lions R 4-1:no p# F '45

DRAPER, T. WALN-MORGAN
    Muenchener, J.  Super the great.  Photop 8-5:67 O '15

DRESSER, LOUISE
    Sketch.  Theatre 16:24 Jl '12
    Sketch.  Green Book 8:600 O '12
    Interview.  Cosmop 57:123 Je '14
    Patterson, A.  Interview.  Green Book 15:161 Ja '16
    Sketch.  Motion Pic 32:43 Ag '26
    Donnell, D.  Sketch.  Motion Pic Classic 23:25 S '28
    Interview.  Motion Pic 38:40 N '29
    Fifty years of acting.  Motion Pic 46:55 O '33
    McGregor, D.  Will the real Louise Dresser please stand up.
        Interview 1-3:16 n. d.
    Obit.  8mm Collector 12:7 Sum '65
    Dresser, L.  My gal Sal.  Classic Film Collect 18:36 Sum '67

DRESSLER, MARIE
    Goldbeck, E.  Sketch.  Motion Pic Classic 31:58 Je '30
    Ruth, J. W.  New success in pictures.  Theatre 52:39 O '30
    Sketch.  Cosmop 89:19 N '30
    Kutten, J.  Sketch.  Motion Pic 40:31 Ja '31
    Walker, H.  Sketch.  Motion Pic Classic 33:68 Mr '31
    Beery, W.  Appreciation.  Motion Pic 41:32 Ap '31

Walker, H.  Sketch.  Motion Pic 41:55 My '31
Busby, M.  It's not your age but what you can do that counts.
  Silver S 1-8:35 Je '31
Sketch.  Motion Pic Classic 33:28 Jl '31
Dibble, S.  As a cook.  Motion Pic 42:78 N '31
Spensley, D.  Sketch.  Motion Pic 43:26 Ap '32
Jones, C. P.  Marie Dressler.  Cinema Digest 2-3:10 D 12 '32
Moffitt, C. F.  Censorship for interviews Hollywood's latest wild
  idea.  Cinema Dig 2-5:9 Ja 9 '33
Moak, E. R.  Box office champion.  Silver S 3-6:16 Ap '33
St. Johns, A. R.  Hollywood's six greatest women.  Silver S 3-
  12:20 O '33
Lee, S.  Immortals of the screen.  Motion Pic 46:32 O '33
Miller, L.  Fifty years of acting.  Motion Pic 46:54 O '33
Hall, G.  Her friendship with Wallace Beery.  Movie Classic 5:
  28 D '33
Service, F.  Her sixty-second birthday.  Motion Pic 47:52 F '34
Death of.  Lit Dig 118:8 Ag 4 '34
Ergenbright, E. L.  Her last illness.  Movie Classic 7:40 S '34
Sherman, J.  Her most faithful friend.  Movie Classic 7:44 O
  '34
Driscoll, M.  Tribute paid at burial rites.  Silver S 4-12:4 O
  '34
Ergenbright, E. L.  Her courage and determination to succeed.
  Motion Pic 48:41 Ja '35
Wheeler, J.  An anecdote.  Movie Classic 7:16 Ja '35
St. Johns, A. R.  Recollections of.  Photop 25:30 Ag '44
Made for each other.  Screen Greats 1-2:68 Sum '71
Carley, C. E.  Marie Dressler; filmog; list of stage appear-
  ances.  Classic F Collect 35:20 Sum '72

DREW, ELLEN
  Vallee, W. L.  The girl from the five and ten.  Silver S 9-12:
    42 O '39
  Bio note; filmog.  Movies & People 2:13 '40
  Asher, J.  What I learned from the other woman.  Silver S 17-
    8:46 Je '47

DREW, S. RANKIN
  Schaefer, F.  S. Rankin of the clan Drew.  Photop 11-5:115 Ap
    '17

DREXEL, NANCY
  Manners, D.  Interview.  Motion Pic 36:72 N '28

DREYFUSS, RICHARD
  Bio note; filmog.  Focus On F 17:8 Spg '74
  McLarty, J.  A view of us.  Motion p58 Jl/Ag '74
  A Dreyfuss fund of acting talent.  People 2-7:50 Ag 12 '74
  Hinxman, M.  Dynamic Dreyfuss.  Films Illus 37:14 S '74
  Klemesrud, J.  He has already written his Oscar speech.  N. Y.
    Times sec 2:17 O 27 '74

DRISCOLL, BOBBY
    Letter from Liza.   Silver S 17-5:67 Mr '47
    Epstein, F.   The lonely death of a star.   Movie Dig 1-4:99 Jl
        '72

DRISCOLL, PAT
    Hot it up a bit.   TV Guide 5-45:14 N 9 '57

DRIVAS, ROBERT
    Zachary, R.   I don't want to be the boy next door.   After Dark
        p16 Ag '69
    Tayor, C.   The good habits of Robert Drivas.   After Dark 7-2:
        62 Je '74

DRU, JOANNE
    Haymes, J. D.   The man I married.   Silver S 18-2:28 D '47
    Walker, H. L.   New magic for Joanne.   Silver S 22-11:32 S '52

DRURY, JAMES
    Enter the Virginians electronically.   TV Guide 10-49:23 D 8 '62

DUBOIS, MARIE
    They didn't plan to be movie stars.   Unifrance 56:no p# Spg '62

DuBREY, CLAIRE
    Sketch.   Motion Pic 18:54 S '19
    A want-ad vampire.   Photop 16-3:66 Ag '19
    Slide, A.   Interview.   Silent Pic 14:7 Spg '72

DUDLEY, DORIS
    Gives Halloween party.   Life 9:92 N 4 '40

DUEL, PETER
    Gardella, K.   Pete's not convinced he's lucky.   N. Y. Sun News
        p520 Ap 25 '71
    Stone, J.   He's alias Smith or alias Jones.   TV Guide 19-20:28
        My 15 '71
    Obit.   N. Y. Times p17 Ja 1 '72
        Time 99:63 Ja 10 '72
    The Duel brothers.   Films Illus 1-9:18 Mr '72
    Why Peter Duel took his life.   Photop 81-4:82 Ap '72

DUFF, HOWARD
    Kilgallen, D.   Sketch.   Photop 34:28 Ja '49
    Duff, H. G.   My son Howard.   Silver S 19-5:41 Mr '49
    Shane, D.   Who's boss--Ida or Howard?   Silver S 23-10:36 Ag
        '53
    Minoff, P.   Non-private lives.   Cue 26-3:12 Ja 19 '57

DUFF-McCORMICK, CARA
    The super-duper original time machine.   After Dark 6-3:28 Jl
        '73

DUKE, PATTY
  Rising star.  Film R p41 '63/64
  Rollins, B.  Dames in the Valley of the dolls.   Look 31:56 S 5
    '67
  Nine minds in trouble.   Photop 78-3:56 S '70
  Fast Patty.   Photop 78-3:18 S '70
  A look at two lost virgins.   Photop 78-4:55 O '70
  Pregnant by man she won't name.   Photop 79-2:77 F '71
  Let me and my baby live here with you.   Photop 79-5:32 My '71
  Don't disgrace me.   Photop 79-5:92 My '71
  Her baby.   Photop 79-6:64 Je '71
  Her husband talks.   Photop 79-6:67 Je '71
  I'm pregnant again.   Photop 80-2:89 Ag '71
  Tells how Lucille Ball defeated her.   Photop 80-3:37 S '71
  Crushed as Desi begs new girl to live with him.   Photop 80-4:
    82 O '71
  Interview.   Silver S 41-10:34 O '71
  Interview with Desi Sr.   Photop 80-6:21 D '71
  Her search to find a father for her son.   Photop 81-1:67 Ja '72
  A new leaf, a new life.   Mod Screen 66-1:40 Ja '72
  Desi was the biggest mistake of my life.   Photop 81-3:70 Mr '72
  Bring my baby to me.   Photop 81-5:58 My '72
  Will Liza and Desi take Patty's son?   Mod Screen 66-9:52 S '72
  What it's like living with Patty.   Photop 82-4:22 O '72
  Their wedding.   Photop 82-5:59 N '72
  Her wild wedding night.   Mod Screen 66-11:46 N '72
  Parents to be.   Photop 83-4:61 Ap '73
  Her miracle story.   Photop 83-6:36 Je '73
  John and Patty's second son.   Photop 84-3:38 S '73

DULLEA, KEIR
  Salute of the week.   Cue 39-28:1 Jl 11 '70
  Bio.   Brit Book Yr p580 '70
  Bio.   Cur Bio 31:12 Je '70
    Cur Bio Yrbk 1970:119 '71
  A view of us.   Motion p58 Ja/F '74
  Veljkovic, M. & Z.   The London lives of Kier Dullea.   After
    Dark 7-2:50 Je '74

DUMBRILLE, DOUGLASS
  Obit.   Classic Film Collect 43:X6 Sum '74
    N. Y. Times Bio Ed p503 Ap '74

DUMONT, MARGARET
  Obit.   Film R p45 '65/66

DUNA, STEFFI
  Lane, V. T.   Sketch.   Motion Pic 52:43 Ag '36

DUNAWAY, FAYE
  Day or night Faye's a girl with go.   Life 64:74 Ja 12 '68
  Maas, P.   New fashion star is born.   Ladies Home J 85:75 F
    '68

Star, symbol, style.   Newsweek 71:42 Mr 4 '68
Beauty register.   Vogue 151:220 My '68
Hamilton, J.   Faye and the Italian.   Look 33:44 Ja 21 '69
Knight, A. & Alpert, H.   Sex stars of 1970.   Playboy 17-12:220
    D '70
Judge, D.   The classic capricorn.   Show 2-4:30 Je '71
Classic modern setting for a fascinating woman.   House & Gard
    140:60 Jl '71
Milne, T.   Bio note; filmog.   Focus On F 6:7 Spg '71
Bio.   Cur Bio 33:8 F '72
How I let the one I love get away.   Photop 82-1:72 Jl '72
Darrach, B.   A gauzy grenade called Dunaway.   People 2-5:35
    Jl 29 '74
Gussow, M.   Only Faye Dunaway knows what she's hiding.   N. Y.
    Times sec 2:1 O 20 '74
Beauty closeup.   Photop 86-5:28 N '74
Marriage to Peter Wolf.   Photop 86-6:46 D '74
A panther of an actress springs back to the top.   People 2-27:
    21 D 30 '74

DUNBAR, DIXIE
    Green, C.   Sketch.   Photop 49:38 Ap '36

DUNCAN, BUD
    Ames, H.   Sketch.   Motion Pic Classic 2:41 Mr '16
    Henry, W. M.   Ham and Bud.   Photop 10-3:95 Ag '16

DUNCAN, MARY
    Hampton, E.   Sketch.   Photop 34:62 Je '28
    Hall, G.   Sketch.   Motion Pic 36:53 S '28
    Conti, M.   Shopping with.   Motion Pic 37:68 My '29
    Gray, C.   Sketch.   Motion Pic 39:42 Ap '30
    Hall, G.   Interview.   Motion Pic 40:42 N '30

DUNCAN, PAMELA
    Into each life some rain must fall.   TV Guide 7-31:28 Ag 1 '59

DUNCAN, PETER
    First floor, going up.   Films Illus 37:27 S '74

DUNCAN, SANDY
    Futures, great.   Vogue 156:90 Jl '70
    Johnson, D.   Stage door Sandy.   After Dark 12-5:45 S '70
    Bio note.   Films Illus 1-2:29 Ag '71
    Hano, A.   Funny face.   TV Guide 19-38:34 S 18 '71
    Miller, E.   Interview.   Seventeen 30:72 S '71
    Show stealer against the odds.   Life 71:8 N 26 '71
    Davidson, M.   Exciting new TV star goes into orbit.   Good
        House 173:102 N '71
    Double tragedy.   Photop 80-6:62 D '71
    Stardom isn't as wonderful as I thought it would be.   Mod
        Screen 65-12:31 D '71
    Fights to live.   Photop 81-2:43 F '72

Her amazing operation.   Mod Screen 66-2:57  F  '72
Frook, J.   Interview.   Life 72:66  F 18  '72
A nightmare of suffering taught me how to live.   Photop 81-3:31
   Mr  '72
Righter, C.   Star of the month; horoscope.   Mod Screen 66-3:50
   Mr  '72
To wed her doctor.   Photop 81-4:48  Ap  '72
Her new life after she became blind in one eye.   Mod Screen
   66-4:33  Ap  '72
Whitney, D.   When I got up and walked out of there... success or
   failure... didn't seem to matter.   TV Guide 20-19:30 My 6  '72
Be brave in your handicap.   Photop 81-6:32  Je  '72
A day with Sandy in her home town.   TV Guide 20-31:14  Jl 29
   '72
Her secret wedding.   Photop 82-3:31  S  '72
No more secrets.   Photop 82-4:28  O  '72
I have to marry Tom.   Mod Screen 66-12:58  D  '72
I'm never going to be alone again.   Mod Screen 67-3:28  Mr  '73
Runaway marriage.   Photop 83-4:40  Ap  '73
Sugar and spice.   Show 3-6:28  S  '73

DUNCAN, WILLIAM
   Remont, F.   Sketch.   Motion Pic 16:40  Ja  '19
   His own boss on the lot.   Photop 16-6:86  N  '19
   The business of making thrills.   Photop 21-28  F  '22

DUNN, EMMA
   Solis-Cohen, J. Jr.   Interview.   N. Y. Drama 67:11  Je 5  '12
   Sketch.   Green Book 15:103  Ja  '16
   Ten Broeck, H.   A famous "old woman" of our stage.   Theatre
      25:28  Ja  '17
   Cheatham, M. S.   Interview.   Motion Pic 19:65  Ap/My  '20

DUNN, JAMES
   Costello, T.   Sketch.   Movie Classic 1:59  N  '31
   Mook, S. R.   O. K. Jimmie.   Silver S 2-1:38  N  '31
   Gallant, T.   His face reveals all his secrets.   Movie Classic
      2:25  My  '32
   Donnell, D.   Sketch.   Movie Classic 2:31  Jl  '32
   Pryor, N.   Sketch.   Motion Pic 44:60  N  '32
   Goldbeck, E.   Interview.   Motion Pic 46:57  N  '33
   Hartley, K.   The Shirley Temple influence in his life.   Movie
      Classic 7:32  F  '35
   Comeback for Jimmy Dunn.   Cue 14-10:13  Mr 10  '45
   Creelman, E.   This time it's serious.   Silver S 15-9:32  Jl  '45
   What they are doing now.   Show 2-7:108  Jl  '62
   Obit.   N. Y. Times p21  S 4  '67
      Newsweek 70:89  S 18  '67

DUNN, JOSEPHINE
   Manners, D.   Sketch.   Motion Pic 36:71  D  '28
   Uselton, R. A.   The Wampus baby stars.   Films In R 21-2:73
      F  '70

DUNN, MICHAEL
 Obit.  Classic Film Collect 41:53 Win '73
 N. Y. Times Bio Ed p1288 Ag '73
 Screen World p233 '74

DUNNE, IRENE
 Walker, H. L.  Sketch.  Motion Pic Classic 32:51 F '31
 Moak, B.  Happiness guaranteed.  Silver S 2-6:23 Ap '32
 Burden, J.  Parted but happily married.  Motion Pic 43:26 Jl
  '32
 Cruikshank.  Irene gets the plum.  Silver S 3-12:60 O '33
 French, W. F.  Her love story.  Motion Pic 48:59 Ja '35
 McDonough, J.  Sketch.  Movie Classic 9:37 S '35
 Interview.  Motion Pic 50:39 S '35
 Ludlam, H. F.  Dunne "nucleus."  Silver S 5-9:20 Jl '35
 French, W. F.  Interview.  Movie Classic 10:36 My '36
 Surmelian, R.  Interview.  Motion Pic 51:38 Jl '36
 Wilson, E.  Projections of Dunne.  Silver S 7-1:30 N '36
 Lee, S.  Interview.  Motion Pic 53:39 Mr '37
 Heebner, J. D.  An anecdote.  Photop 51:10 S '37
 Zeitlin, I.  Motion Pic 54:32 N '37
 Rankin, R.  Found, one happy actress.  Screen Book 19-6:33 Ja
  '38
 Wilson, E.  Dunne's advice to wives-to-be.  Silver S 10-7:36
  My '40
 Bio notes; filmog.  Movies & People 2:13 '40
 Wilson, E.  Men she'll remember.  Silver S 11-6:22 Ap '41
 Letter from Liza.  Silver S 13-9:61 Jl '43
 My secret dream.  Photop 23:54 O '43
 A gal named Dunne.  Lions R 3-2:no p# Ja '44
 Memos for the boss.  Lions R 3-4:no p# Jl '44
 Service, F.  My screen selves and I.  Silver S 14-10:22 Ag '44
 Holland, J.  The lady speaks her mind.  Silver S 16-7:35 My
  '46
 My luckiest day.  Cosmop 121:90 O '46
 Palmer, G.  If I were 21.  Ladies Home J 64:86 Ja '47
 Parsons, L. O.  Cosmop's citation for best performance of
  month.  Cosmop 124:12 Ap '48
 Receives Laetare medal from Notre Dame university.  Time 53:
  40 Ap 4 '49
 Receives Laetare medal from Notre Dame university.  Newsweek
  34:51 Jl 11 '49
 Saunders, A. W.  Irene remembers mama.  Life With Music 2:
  10 N '49
 Dunne, I.  Do you have a problem?  Silver S S '47 through My
  '52
 Madden, J. C.  Irene Dunne; filmog.  Films In R 20-10:605 D
  '69
 Hall, J. B.  Letter.  Films In R 21-1:59 Ja '70
 Chierichetti, D.  Irene Dunne today.  Film Fan Mo 116:3 F '71

DUPEA, TATZUMBIA
 Obit.  Classic Film Collect 27:60 Spg/Sum '70

DUPREZ, JUNE
 Vallee, W. L.   Her father said No.   Silver S 11-2:36 D '40

DURANTE, JIMMY
 Sketch.   Photop 41:58 D '31
 Grant, J.   Interview.   Movie Classic 1:50 Ja '32
 Costello, T.   Interview.   Motion Pic 43:62 Je '32
 Keats, P.   Kings in Hollywood.   Silver S 3-4:22 F '33
 Fidler, J.   Interview.   Movie Classic 4:52 My '33
 The trouble with women.   Cosmop 115:62 O '43
 Dream man.   Cue 12-51:9 D 18 '43
 Parker, D.   Returns to the movies.   Colliers 113:24 Ja 1 '44
 Me and me girls.   Lions R 3-3(sup):no p# Ap '44
 An instrumentality.   Lions R 4-1:no p# F '45
 Little interview with Durante.   Cue 14-15:10 Ap 14 '45
 Hamilton, S.   Tribute to.   Photop 29:124 N '46
 How he wrecks a baby grand piano.   Life 25:14 S 20 '48
 Keating, J.   Durante the durable.   Cue 18-49:17 D 3 '49
 Taylor, T.   After dark.   Cue 28-4:8 Ja 24 '59
 Reynolds, Q.   The indestructible enigma.   Show 2-2:61 F '62
 Mangel, C.   Pinocchio lives.   Look 33:93 Mr 4 '69
 Whitney, D.   Da Schnozz.   TV Guide 17-52:22 D 27 '69

DURBIN, DEANNA
 Farwell, H. C.   Story of.   Movie Classic 11:8 Ja '37
 Reese, B.   Story of.   Motion Pic 53:38 My '37
 Lynn, J.   Sweet and lovely.   Screen Book 19-2:56 S '37
 A letter from.   Child Life 16:405 S '37
 McGinnis, E. W.   Sketch.   St. Nich 64:39 S '37
 Her fifteenth birthday party.   Life 3:74 D 20 '37
 Gillespie-Hayck, A.   The girl with the glorious gift.   Silver S
  8-2:30 D '37
 Churchill, D. W.   Appreciation.   Stage 15:58 F '38
 Visits New York.   Life 4:32 Mr 14 '38
 Talmey, A.   Sketch.   Vogue 91:93 My 1 '38
 Sharon, M.   Deanna's price for fame.   Screen Book 20-4:29 My
  '38
 Sketch.   Life 5:32 O 3 '38
 Arvey, V.   Story of.   Etude 57:434 Jl '39
 MacKaye, M.   Sketch.   Ladies Home J 57:19 S '40
 Hamilton, S.   Sketch.   Photop 54:47 D '40
 Bio note; filmog.   Movies & People 2:13 '40
 Baldwin, F.   Sketch.   Photop 18:27 Ap '41
 Heyn, E. V.   Letters from and to Mussolini.   Photop 19:26 S
  '41
 Wilson, E.   Deanna faces 21.   Silver S 13-1:38 N '42
 Trotter, M.   Her horoscope.   Photop 22:32 F '43
 MacDonald, J.   End of a love story.   Silver S 14-3:28 Ja '44
 Her role in Christmas holiday.   Newsweek 24:88 Jl 10 '44
 Holland, J.   What divorce has done to Deanna.   Silver S 15-1:22
  N '44
 Palmer, C.   Ten years of good fortune.   Silver S 17-5:35 Mr
  '47

Maddox, B.  Deanna's dos and don'ts.  Silver S 17-12:38 O '47
Parsons, L. O.  Cosmop's citation for the best performance of
    the month.  Cosmop 123:55 O '47
Benedict, P.  Why Deanna and Shirley won't return.  Silver S
    23-10:42 Ag '53
Slide, A.  I gave my heart to Deanna.  Classic F Collect 23:46
    Spg '69
The kids.  Screen Greats 1-2:48 Sum '71
We hear from Deanna Durbin.  Mod Screen 66-1:30 Ja '72
Lewis, F.  The private life of Deanna.  Liberty 1-8:55 Spg '73


DURFEE, MINTA
    Queen of silver screen lauded on 80th birthday.  Classic F Col-
        lect 25:22 Fall '69


DURIEUX, TILLA
    Obit.  N. Y. Times p32 F 22 '71


DURKIN, JUNIOR
    His opinion of Mitzi Green.  Photop 39:36 Ja '31


DURYEA, DAN
    Hall, G.  Villain unmasked.  Silver S 15-12:32 O '45
    Hendricks, H.  Daniel and the lionesses.  Silver S 18-3:46 Ja
        '48
    Obit.  Film R p15 '69/70
        N. Y. Times p31 Je 8 '68
        Newsweek 71:88 Je 17 '68
        Time 91:88 Je 14 '68
    Johnson, D.  Dan Duryea; filmog.  Films In R 22-6:348 Je/Jl
        '71


DURYEA, GEORGE
    Henning, O.  Sketch.  Motion Pic 35:55 Ap '28
    Collier, H.  Sketch.  Photop 34:57 O '28


DUVAL, PAULETTE
    Sketch.  Motion Pic Classic 22:41 Ja '26


DUVALL, ROBERT
    Eyles, A.  Robert Duvall; filmog.  Focus On F 1:9 Ja/F '70
    Godsons.  Time 99:71 Ap 3 '72
    Chase, C.  About Duvall.  N. Y. Times Bio Ed Ap 23 '72
    Man of many faces.  Newsweek 80:99 S 18 '72
    On the scene.  Playboy 20-1:208 Ja '73
    Stoop, N. S.  Interview.  After Dark 6-5:18 S '73


DUVALL, SHELLEY
    Bosworth, P.  New girl on the screen.  Show 2-2:37 Ap '71
    Corliss, R.  Interview.  Film Comment 10-3:14 My/Je '74


DVORAK, ANN
    Jones, C.  Dreams come through.  Silver S 2-8:22 Je '32

Lee, S.  Her marriage.  Motion Pic 43:56 Je '32
Sketch.  Motion Pic 43:26 Je '32
Keen, J. H.  Showin' 'em...  Cinema Dig 1-6:6 Jl 25 '32
Slave drivers...  Cinema Dig 1-6:27 Jl 25 '32
Costello, F.  Sketch.  Movie Classic 2:13 Jl '32
Donnell, D.  Sketch.  Movie Classic 3:30 O '32
Ergenbright, E.  Leaves Hollywood.  Movie Classic 4:17 Mr '33
Lane, J.  Sketch.  Motion Pic 46:50 S '33
McVeigh, G.  Chevalier's welcoming arms.  Silver S 4-2:47 D '33
Hall, G.  Interview.  Motion Pic 49:45 F '35
Beauty advice.  Motion Pic 49:50 My '35
Goldbeck, E.  Motion Pic 50:33 Ag '35
Dvorak, A.  You can't pull your punches in Hollywood.  Silver S 17-6:44 Ap '47
Parsons, L. O.  Cosmop's citation for the best supporting role of the month.  Cosmop 123:47 N '47
Canham, K.  Ann Dvorak; filmog.  Films In R 25-7:443 Ag/S '74

DWAN, DOROTHY
Sketch.  Motion Pic 32:43 D '26
Manners, D.  Sketch.  Motion Pic 35:42 My '28


EAGELS, JEANNE
Patterson, A.  Interview.  Theatre 38:19 S '23
Mullett, B.  Interview.  Am Mag 96:34 N '23
Wilson, B.  Interview.  Motion Pic Classic 20:33 Ja '25
Sketch.  Theatre 43:12 Ja '26
Alias Sadie Thompson.  Colliers 80:14 O 1 '27
Cummings, A.  Interview.  Motion Pic Classic 26:21 D '27
The actor more important than the play.  Theatre 47:20 Ja '28
Cruikshank, H.  Sketch.  Motion Pic 38:8 Ja '30
Goldbeck, E.  The real Jeanne Eagels.  Motion Pic 40:48 O '30
In memoriam.  Motion Pic 45:52 Je '33

EAMES, VIRGINIA
Obit.  Screen World 23:236 '72

EARLE, EDWARD
Donnell, D.  Interview.  Motion Pic 9:104 Je '15
Wade, P.  Interview.  Motion Pic 13:72 Mr '17
Howe, H.  Sketch.  Motion Pic 15:72 Ag '18
Earle, E.  If you have no farm, borrow one.  Photop 14-5:26 O '18
Montanye, L.  Interview.  Motion Pic Classic 12:60 Mr '21

EASTMAN, JOAN
Obit.  N. Y. Times p35 Ag 25 '69

EASTON, ROBERT
   Clein, H.  The real people:  featuring Hollywood's new breed of
      character actors.  Show 1-8:14 Jl 9 '70

EASTWOOD, CLINT
   How to keep fit.  TV Guide 7-33:20 Ag 15 '59
   Miller, E.  Interview.  Seventeen 28:116 O '69
   Jeremiah.  The stars' stars; astrology.  Show 1-2:23 F '70
   Guerin, A.  Eastwood as Mr. Warmth.  Show 1-2:82 F '70
   Knight, A. & Alpert, H.  Sex stars of 1970.  Playboy 17-12:220
      D '70
   Fayard, J.  Who can stand 32,580 seconds of Eastwood?  Life
      71:45 Jl 23 '71
   Bio.  Cur Bio 32:13 O '71
      Same.  Cur Bio Yrbk 1971:113 '72
   That self-sufficient thing.  Time 93:66 D 6 '71
   Play Misty for Clint; filmog.  Films Illus 1-8:29 F '72
   Pushover for pullovers; photos.  Playboy 19-3:123 Mr '72
   Bodeen, D.  A fistful of fame; filmog.  Focus On F 9:12 Spg '72
   My wife lets me go my own way.  Mod Screen 66-7:58 Jl '72
   Photoplay forum.  Photop 82-1:10 Jl '72
   Eastwood, C.  Play Misty for me.  Action 8-2:6 Mr/Ap '73
   Note; filmog.  Films & Filming 20-2:67 N '73
   Interview.  Playboy 21-2:57 F '74

EATON, JAY
   Obit.  Screen World 22:236 '71

EATON, MARY
   Mother of three "Follies" girls.  Colliers 76:8 Jl 25 '25
   Cruikshank, H.  Interview.  Motion Pic 38:50 O '29

EBSEN, BUDDY
   Cast as a Beverly hillbilly.  TV Guide 10-45:15 N 10 '62
   New breed of racing catamaran.  Pop Sci 194:86 F '69
   Raddatz, L.  After striking oil, what do you do for an encore?
      TV Guide 20-6:14 F 5 '72
   Whitney, D.  Too rich to work?  TV Guide 21-34:21 Ag 25 '73

EBURNE, MAUDE
   Sketch.  Strand (NY) 47:681 Je '14
   Work of.  Theatre 20:171 O '14
   McClelland, D.  Maude Eburne; filmog.  Film Fan Mo 149:22 N
      '73

EDDY, HELEN JEROME
   McGaffey, K.  Helpful Helen.  Photop 14-1:65 Je '18
   Peltret, E.  Interview.  Motion Pic 18:58 S '19
   Peltret, E.  Interview.  Motion Pic Classic 10:55 Mr '20
   Beach, B.  Interview.  Motion Pic 21:28 My '21
   Jordon, J.  Sketch.  Photop 22:22 Ag '22
   Gassaway, G.  Interview.  Motion Pic 24:63 Ja '23

EDDY, NELSON
  Sketch.  Mus Courier 107:17 Jl 29 '33
  Acting experience in films for operatic artists.  Mus Courier
    107:15 Ag 5 '33
  Baxter, H. C.  A voice, a phonograph and brains.  Silver S 5-
    7:56 My '35
  Sketch.  Stage 12:35 My '35
  Spensley, D.  Interview.  Movie Classic 9:28 S '35
  Brundidge, H. T.  Hollywood's new sensation.  Motion Pic 50:30
    S '35
  Liza.  With Jeanette and Nelson on location.  Silver S 6-2:18 D
    '35
  Ergenbright, E. L.  Interview.  Motion Pic 51:39 Mr '36
  Ergenbright, E. L.  Interview.  Movie Classic 10:32 Mr '36
  Ludlam, H. F.  The romantic Nelson Eddy.  Silver S 6-9:26
    Jl '36
  Hartley, K.  His popularity.  Movie Classic 10:28 Jl '36
  His rescue mission.  Movie Classic 11:40 O '36
  Service, F.  Interview.  Motion Pic 53:32 Mr '37
  Wilson, E.  Projections.  Silver S 8-4:32 F '38
  Quigg, M.  Royal rhythmatician.  Screen Book 20-1:41 F '38
  Henderson, J.  A hidden chapter from (his) life.  Screen Book
    21-3:22 O '38
  Reid, J.  Are his fans hurting him?  Screen Book 21-6:22 Ja
    '39
  The joy of singing.  Etude 57:427 Jl '39
  Bio note; filmog.  Movies & People 2:13 '40
  You haven't seen Nelson Eddy yet.  Lions R 1-3:no p# N '41
  The business of being a movie star.  Lions R 1-8:no p# Ap '42
  My most unforgettable moment overseas.  Photop 25:52 Je '44
  Luck is where you find it.  Lions R 3-5:no p# D '44
  Nelson Eddy, baritone.  Mus Amer 69:16 My '49
  Obit.  Film R p21 '66/68
  Looking Hollywood way.  Good Old Days 6-1:26 Jl '69
  The love teams.  Screen Greats 1-2:10 Sum '71
  Banta, H.  Nelson Eddy: 1901-1965; filmog.  Films In R 25-2:
    83 F '74

EDELMAN, HERB
  See, C.  My-son-the-bum finds happiness.  TV Guide 16-46:34
    N 16 '68

EDEN, BARBARA
  Miss self-improvement of 1966.  TV Guide 14-6:15 F 5 '66
  Watch Jeannie's smoke.  TV Guide 14-39:7 S 24 '66
  Whitney, D.  When the genie comes out of the bottle.  TV Guide
    16-27:17 Jl 6 '68
  The day the doctors told me your baby is dead.  Photop 81-2:85
    F '72
  Balling, F. D.  My child.  Photop 85-2:38 F '74

EDEN, CHANA
  Old soldiers don't always fade away.  TV Guide 10-5:27 F 3 '62

EDMONDS, ANN
   Sketch.   Photop 20:50 Mr '42

EDWARDS, CLIFF (Ukulele Ike)
   Walker, H. L.   Sketch.   Motion Pic Classic 30:44 S '29
   Hamilton, S.   Sketch.   Photop 54:70 Je '40
   Jiminy Cricket!   It's Cliff Edwards!   TV Guide 4-26:12 Je 30 '56
   Obit.   Classic F Collect 32:62 Fall '71
      Film R p11 '72/73
      N. Y. Times p36 Jl 22 '71
      Same.   N. Y. Times Bio Ed Jl 22 '71
      Newsweek 78:59 Ag 2 '71
      Screen World 23:236 '72

EDWARDS, EDNA PARK
   Obit.   Screen World 19:232 '68

EDWARDS, JAMES
   Obit.   N. Y. Times p41 Ja 8 '70
      Same.   N. Y. Times Bio Ed Ja 8 '70
      Newsweek 75:95 Ja 19 '70
      Screen World 22:236 '71
      Time 95:49 Ja 19 '70

EDWARDS, JODY
   Obit.   N. Y. Times p45 O 30 '67

EDWARDS, MARK
   New faces.   Films Illus 1-7:10 Ja '72

EDWARDS, MEREDITH
   Rising star.   Film R p28 '50

EFRON, MARSHALL
   Who took the lemons out of mom's pie?   Bsns W p23 F 6 '71
   Barrett, M.   TV's tiny terror.   Vogue 158:91 S 15 '71

EGAN, PETER
   Tierney, M.   Interview.   Plays & Players 19-10:22 Jl '72
   d'Arcy, S.   All about Egan.   Films Illus 3-31:271 Ja '74

EGE, JULIE
   The gift from Norway.   Show 2-9:24 N '71

EGGAR, SAMANTHA
   Cowie, P.   The face of '63--Great Britain.   Films & Filming
      9-5:19 F '63
   Rising stars.   Film R p54 '64/65
   Hanson, C. L.   Samantha and the look.   Cinema (BH) 3-2:15 Mr
      '66
   Campbell, R.   Bio note; filmog.   Focus On F 3:11 My/Ag '70

EGGERTH, MARTA
    Stars of tomorrow.  Lions R 1-11/12:no p# Jl/Ag '42
    Singing siren.  Lions R 2-2:no p# N '42
    Bio.  Cur Bio '43

EILERS, SALLY
    Ramsey, W.  Sketch.  Motion Pic 39:42 Jl '30
    Uselton, R. A.  The Wampus baby stars.  Films In R 21-2:73
      F '70

EINSTEIN, HARRY
    Obit.  Screen World 10:222 '59

EISLEY, ANTHONY
    Raddatz, L.  I didn't know how to do anything else.  TV Guide
      19-45:22 N 6 '71

EK, ANDERS
    Cowie, P.  Anders Ek; filmog.  Focus On F 5:13 Win '70

EKBERG, ANITA
    Minoff, P.  Anita's double exposure.  Cue 24-36:12 S 10 '55

EKLAND, BRITT
    Ehrlich, H.  But can she act?  Look 35:41 Mr 9 '71
    Living with Peter Sellers is impossible.  Photop 84-3:60 S '73

EKMAN, HASSE
    Gohrn-Ohm, M.  Hasse Ekman.  Am Scandinavian R 36:47 Mr
      '48
    Note.  International Film G 2:41 '65

ELAM, JACK
    Rising star.  Film R p39 '51/52

ELDER, RUTH
    Biery, R.  Interview.  Motion Pic 37:44 Jl '29

ELDRIDGE, FLORENCE
    Goldbeck, E.  Sketch.  Motion Pic Classic 30:51 S '29
    Cohen, H.  Praising players of minor importance.  Cinema D
      3-6:12 Ap 24 '33
    Hunt, J. L.  Interview.  Photop 46:49 O '34
    MacDonald, J.  Marriage and the Marches.  Silver S 10-9:38 Jl
      '40
    Lewis, E.  Mr. and Mrs. Fredric March.  Cue 19-4:13 Ja 28
      '50

ELG, TAINA
    Rising star.  Film R p29 '58/59
    Kingslex-Smith, T.  Letter.  Films In R 25-10:637 D '74

ELHARDT, KAYE
   It's tough to be serious.   TV Guide 7-9:20 F 28 '59

ELINE, MARIE
   The Thanhouser kid.   Photop 4-4:36 S '13

ELLIMAN, YVONNE
   Brown, L.   Everyone knows how to love her.   After Dark 5-4:
      22 Ag '72

ELLIOT, BIFF
   Tough guy from TV.   TV Guide 1-30:10 O 23 '53

ELLIOTT, (WILD) BILL
   From the 100 finest westerns: Overland.   Views & Reviews 1-4:
      18 n. d.
   Obit.   Film R p21 '66/68
   Letters.   Films In R 20-7:452 Ag/S '69

ELLIOTT, DENHOLM
   Rising star.   Film R p107 '53/54

ELLIOTT, MARY
   Canfield, A.   Her marriage.   Photop 27:64 Je '45

ELLIS, EDWARD
   Obit.   Screen World 4:176 '53

ELLIS, MARY
   Patterson, A.   Work of.   Theatre 43:22 Ap '26
   Sketch.   Theatre 45:30 Ja '27
   Sketch.   Theatre World 19:114 Mr '33
   Grein, J. T.   Appreciation.   Ill Lon N 182:852 Je 10 '33
   Corathiel, E.   Interview.   Theatre World 20:113 S '33
   Calhoun, D.   Story of.   Motion Pic 49:49 Je '35
   Sketch.   Theatre World 29:89 F '38

ELLIS, MONIE
   And the winner is...   TV Guide 19-42:17 O 16 '71

ELLIS, PATRICIA
   Sylvia's beauty helps.   Photop 45:72 Mr '34
   Goldbeck, E.   Sketch.   Movie Classic 6:52 My '34
   Uselton, R. A.   The Wampus baby stars.   Films In R 21-2:73
      F '70
   Hughson, D. E.   Patricia Ellis; filmog.   Films In R 21-6:388
      Je/Jl '70
   Obit.   Classic Film Collect 27:60 Spg/Sum '70
      N. Y. Times p27 Mr 28 '70
      N. Y. Times Bio Ed Mr 28 '70
      Screen World 22:236 '71

ELLIS, PAUL
    Carr, H.  Interview.  Motion Pic 29:25 Ap '25

ELLIS, ROBERT
    Obit.  Screen World p233 '74

ELLISON, JAMES
    Schwarzkopf, J.  Sketch.  Motion Pic 54:9 Ag '37
    Smithson, E. J.  Fugitive from horse opera.  Screen Book 21-4:
        36 N '38
    Hamilton, S.  Sketch.  Photop 54:29 Ag '40

ELMORE, STEVE
    Confessions of a soap-opera veteran.  TV Guide 22-40:14 O 5
        '74

ELTINGE, JULIAN
    Sketch.  Green Bk Album 2:1096 D '09
    Advent of the male prima donna.  Cur Lit 51:550 N '11
    How I portray a woman on the stage.  Theatre 18:56 Ag '13
    Wolf, R.  Bio sketch.  Green Book 10:793 N '13
    Sketch.  Strand (NY) 48:693 D '14
    Troubles of a man who wears skirts.  Green Book 13:813 My '15
    McGaffey, K.  Clothes do not make the woman.  Photop 13-2:84
        Ja '18
    His Italian castle in California.  Photop 14-6:22 N '18
    Home of.  House & Gard 35:46 F '19
    Residence at Los Angeles.  Architecture 39:57 Mr '19
    Grey, E.  Residence of.  Arch Rec 49:98 F '31
    Sturges, M.  Interview.  Met Mag 57:37 S '23
    Obit.  Cur Bio '41
        Time 37:63 Mr 17 '41

ELVEY, MAURICE
    Obit.  N. Y. Times p37 Ag 29 '67

ELVIDGE, JUNE
    Sketch.  Green Book 13:1131 Je '15
    A June bride in mid-November.  Photop 15-3:71 F '19
    Smith, F. J.  Interview.  Motion Pic Classic 8:31 Jl '19
    Bruce, B.  Interview.  Motion Pic 20:64 O '20

ELY, RON
    Lewis, R. W.  It shouldn't happen to an ape man.  TV Guide
        14-48:22 N 26 '66
    The dangers of galloping inflation.  TV Guide 16-14:14 Ap 6 '68

EMERSON, FAYE
    Plea for help to find her sister.  Photop 24:66 My '44
    United with sister.  Photop 25:34 Ag '44
    Asher, J.  Fabulous Fayezie.  Silver S 14-10:46 Ag '44
    Her debut in The play's the thing.  Life 24:85 My 24 '48

EMERY, GILBERT
    Letters.  Films In R 17-3:195 Mr '66
    Shellhase, G.  Gilbert Emery; filmog.  Films In R 18-10:661 D
        '67

EMHARDT, ROBERT
    A breed apart.  TV Guide 11-26:19 Je 29 '63

ENGEL, GEORGIA
    She even gets laughs on her straight lines.  TV Guide 21-49:25
        D '73
    Summer flair.  Photop 85-6:33 Je '74

ENGSTROM, JEAN
    No time for stardom.  TV Guide 6-36:28 S 6 '58

ERARD, CATHERINE
    Bio note.  Unifrance 23:10 F '53

ERICKSON, LEIF
    Hamilton, S.  Sketch.  Photop 21:51 O '42
    Just a baby sitter at heart.  Photop 79-1:39 Ja '71

ERICSON, JOHN
    They make ladies' hearts go pitty pat.  TV Guide 5-28:8 Jl 13
        '57
    Holt, T.  John Ericson; centerfold.  Playgirl 1-8:64 Ja '74

ERNEST, GEORGE
    Hamilton, S.  Sketch.  Photop 52:31 S '38

ERROL, LEON
    Patterson, A.  Work of.  Theatre 28:74 Ag '18
    Bird, C.  Interview.  Theatre 34:8 Jl '21
    Walker, H. L.  Interview.  Motion Pic Classic 32:70 Ja '31
    Obit.  Screen World 3:177 '53
    Maltin, L.  Leon Errol; filmog.  Film Fan Mo 109/110:3 Jl/Ag
        '70

ERSKINE, MARILYN
    Portrait of an actress at work.  TV Guide 5-35:20 Ag 31 '57
    Rx for an actress.  TV Guide 5-40:16 O 5 '57
    One little word.  TV Guide 9-9:18 Mr 4 '61

ERWIN, STUART
    York, C.  Sketch.  Photop 37:69 My '30
    Fender, R.  Sketch.  Motion Pic Classic 32:75 Ja '31
    Samuels, L.  "Stu"--not such a boob!  Silver S 5-1:47 N '34
    Bio note; filmog.  Movies & People 2:13 '40
    Minoff, P.  The double life of the Erwins.  Cue 20-18:14 My 5
        '51
    Obit.  N. Y. Times p31 D 22 '67
        Newsweek 71:41 Ja 1 '68

ESMOND, CARL
  Miller, N.  Letter.  Films In R 16-2:125 F '65

ESMOND, JILL
  Service, F.  Sketch.  Motion Pic 44:50 S '32

ESSEX, DAVID
  Not your picture book Jesus.  Films Illus 2-22:44 Ap '73
  Essex repeats a success.  Films Illus 4-38:56 O '74

ESSLER, FRED
  Obit.  Screen World p233 '74

ESTELITA (RODRIGUEZ)
  Obit.  Screen World 18:239 '67

ETTING, RUTH
  Shine on, harvest girl.  Newsweek 29:54 F 3 '47
  Harvest moon.  Time 49:54 My 19 '47
  Gimp is back, still rough on Ruth.  Life 38:67 Je 20 '55
  Moshier, W. F.  Ruth Etting today; interview.  Film Fan Mo
    159:19 S '74
  Maltin, L.  Ruth Etting's short subjects; filmog.  Film Fan Mo
    159:25 S '74

EVANKO, ED
  Stoop, N. M.  Where were you when we auditioned in New York?
    After Dark 4-11:50 Mr '72

EVANS, DALE
  Marsh, P.  Kissless heroine.  Silver S 17-8:61 Je '47

EVANS, DOUGLAS
  Obit.  Screen World 20:234 '69

EVANS, EDITH
  Sketch.  Theatre 40:26 Ja '25
  Sketch.  Theatre Guild 9:38 Ja '32
  The stage as I see it.  Theatre World 18:87 Ag '32
  Sketch.  Theatre World 10:38 Ja '33
  Hast, N.  Sketch.  Theatre World 24:257 D '35
  Sketch.  Theatre World 26:183 O '36
  Sketch.  Play Pict 70 F '37
  Sketch.  Theatre World 42:32 Ap '46
  Enter Dame Smith.  Cue 19-37:17 S 16 '50
  Goodwin, I.  Grand Dame.  Newsweek 71:88 Ap 1 '68
  Tierney, M.  Nothing like a Dame; interview.  Plays & Players
    18-7:20 Ap '71

EVANS, HARVEY
  Zadan, C.  Everybody has to go through stages like that.  After
    Dark 4-6:18 O '71

EVANS, JOAN
  Schoolgirl star.    Cue 17-43:18 O 23 '48
  Stars in her first picture.    Newsweek 34:89 S 29 '49
  Hall, G.    Mother knows best.    Silver S 20-3:33 Ja '50
  MacDonald, E.    Misunderstood Miss.    Silver S 21-3:38 Ja '51
  O'Leary, D.    One Joan to another.    Silver S 21-7:26 My '51
  Maddox, B.    Are you mature about love?    Silver S 21-12:38 O
    '51
  Rising star.    Film R p41 '51/52
  MacDonald, E.    Letter to a star.    Silver S 22-8:42 Je '52

EVANS, LINDA
  Raddatz, L.    The Linda Evans story.    TV Guide 14-52:12 D 24
    '66

EVANS, MADGE
  Pauvre enfant?  Merci-non!    Photop 14-4:76 S '18
  Wheelwright, F.    Veteran trooper.    Silver S 1-12:35 O '31
  Sketch.    Photop 40:80 N '31
  Grayson, C.    Heading for stardom.    Motion Pic 42:26 D '31
  Pryor, N.    Sketch.    Motion Pic 44:26 S '32
  Maddox, B.    She actually obeys her fan mail.    Silver S 3-8:16
    Je '33
  Fifteen years ago.    Photop 44:84 N '33
  Lee, S.    Marriage plans.    Movie Classic 6:26 Mr '34
  English, R.    Sketch.    Motion Pic 47:59 My '34
  Her dressing table secrets.    Motion Pic 48:61 Ja '35
  Sketch.    Lit Dig 120:24 Jl 13 '35
  Brundidge, H. T.    How she got into the movies.    Motion Pic
    49:35 Jl '35
  Evans, W.    The girl who has many friends.    Silver S 7-3:31 Ja
    '37
  Wilson, E.    Projections.    Silver S 7-7:36 My '37
  Bio note; filmog.    Movies & People 2:14 '40
  Maltin, L.    Interview; filmog.    Film Fan Mo 138:3 D '72
  Postscript: partial filmog.    Film Fan Mo 139:30 Ja '73

EVANS, MAURICE
  Sketch.    Theatre World 24:258 D '35
  Making up to play Falstaff.    Life 6:64 F 13 '39
  Harriman, M. C.    Story of.    Cosmop 108:11 Mr '40
  Green, E. M.    His G. I. version of Hamlet.    Theatre World 42:
    28 F '46
  Jackson, B.    His production of Hamlet.    Theatre Arts 30:734 D
    '46
  His U. S. movie debut.    Cue 20-22:15 Je 2 '51
  What can television do for Shakespeare?    TV Guide 2-48:8 N 27
    '54
  Minoff, P.    He has another go at the Bard.    Cue 23-50:47 D 11
    '54
  Guestward ho.    Time 90:82 D 8 '67
  Winogura, D.    Dialogues on apes, apes and more apes.    Cine-
    fantastique 2-2:29 Sum '72

EVANS, MICHAEL
  Whitney, D.  The boy next door to the Bunkers.   TV Guide 21-
    22:28 Je 2 '73

EVANS, MURIEL
  Aids to beauty.   Motion Pic 46:46 Ja '34

EVANS, RENEE
  Obit.   Screen World 23:236 '72

EVANS, REX
  Obit.   Screen World 21:236 '70

EVANS, ROBERT
  Taylor, T.  Lightning struck twice.   Cue 26-32:12 Ag 10 '57
  Three to get ready.   Time 91:104 Ap 12 '68
  Mills, J.  Why should he have it?   Life 66:62 Mr 7 '69
  Ali MacGraw: a return to basics.   Time 97:43 Ja 11 '71
  Ali forced to choose?   My husband or my son.   Mod Screen 65-
    11:55 N '71
  Why she turned to McQueen.   Photop 82-5:64 N '72
  Power; symposium.   Playboy 19-12:189 D '72
  I'm taking Ali, you can't stop me.   Mod Screen 66-12:48 D '72

EVELYN, JUDITH
  Success story.   Cue 11-2:1 Ja 10 '42
  Sketch.   Harp Baz 76:78 F '42
  Sketch.   Life 16:42 F 21 '44

EVEREST, BARBARA
  Obit.   N.Y. Times p92 F 11 '68

EVERETT, CHAD
  Hegedorn, R.  Letter; filmog.   Films In R 20-10:643 D '69
  Chad as a child.   Photop 78-1:81 Jl '70
  Hobson, D.  Tab, Rock and now Chad.   TV Guide 18-38:22 S 19
    '70
  How he saved his baby from fire.   Photop 79-1:48 Ja '71
  Saves his wife.   Photop 79-2:64 F '71
  Why I let a woman support me.   Photop 79-5:78 My '71
  When my wife is pregnant I can't love her enough.   Photop 80-4:
    41 O '71
  He's on his way to a harem.   Photop 80-5:89 N '71
  Announce arrival of second daughter.   Mod Screen 65-11:29 N '71
  How I tell my child the story of Christmas.   Photop 81-1:51 Ja
    '72
  Passion and quarrels.   Photop 81-5:54 My '72
  Kasindorf, J.  I have three horses and three dogs...and a wife.
    TV Guide 20-34:14 Ag 19 '72
  The six months that changed my life.   Photop 82-2:75 Ag '72
  He builds his dream house.   Mod Screen 66-9:24 S '72
  Elvis or Chad?   Photop 82-4:50 O '72
  The best Christmas of my life.   Photop 83-1:27 Ja '73

A place for lovers.  Photop 83-1:35 Ja '73
The innocent have been hurt enough.   Photop 84-6:38 D '73
Chad and Shelby's second wedding.   Photop 85-1:18 Ja '74
Talks about his daughter.   Photop 85-6:20 Je '74

EVERS, JASON
    Davidson, M.   Professor without diploma.   TV Guide 12-3:15 Ja
        18 '64

EWELL, TOM
    Lewis, E.   His eighteen year itch.   Cue 21-50:16 D 13 '52
    Peck, I.   At last, he's shaken the seven year itch.   N. Y.
        Times Bio Ed Ag 29 '71

EYETON, BESSIE
    Sketch.   Motion Pic 10:103 Ja '16

EYTHE, WILLIAM
    Sketch.   Photop 24:66 Mr '44
    Sketch.   Photop 25:53 N '44
    Benedict, P.   Intense is the word.   Silver S 15-7:40 My '45
    My first kiss.   Photop 29:58 S '46

EYTON, CHARLES
    Home of.   Classic 16:34 My '23


FABARES, SHELLEY
    The many sides of Shelley.   TV Guide 8-25:25 Je 18 '60
    Miller, E.   Teens are looking at Shelley.   Seventeen 21:52 N
        '62
    Stump, A.   She's on the kinipopo.   TV Guide 21-15:18 Ap 14 '73

FABIAN (FORTE)
    Rising star.   Film R p33 '61/62
    The new Fabian; centerfold.   Playgirl 1-4:64 S '73

FABIAN, FRANCOISE
    Cowie, P.   Francoise Fabian; filmog.   Focus On F 1:14 Ja/F
        '70
    Ross, W. S.   And now--my day at Maud's.   N. Y. Times Bio
        Ed Je 6 '71

FABRAY, NANETTE
    Fabray is gay.   Cue 17-46:13 N 13 '48
    Test pattern makes good.   TV Guide 2-45:20 N 6 '54
    Minoff, P.   Caesar's new girl.   Cue 24-5:12 F 5 '55
    Why does she cry?  To make you laugh.   TV Guide 3-11:8 Mr
        12 '55
    Caesar's wife.   TV Guide 3-45:13 N 5 '55
    After the stage weight fell.   TV Guide 4-5:16 F 4 '56
    Nanette said no!   TV Guide 4-16:20 Ap 21 '56

Just an old cut up.   TV Guide 4-47:8 N 24 '56
Who wants to be a housewife.   TV Guide 9-7:14 F 18 '61
Maltin, L.   Our gang; Our gang filmog.   Film Fan Mo 66:3 D
    '66

FABRIZI, ALDO
    Work of in Open city.   Theatre Arts 30:194 Ap '46

FAHEY, MYRNA
    Leopard skins on leotards.   TV Guide 6-19:20 My 20 '58

FAIR, ELINOR
    Delvigne, D.   Interview.   Motion Pic 17:55 Je '19
    Montanye, L.   Interview.   Motion Pic 21:60 F '21
    Chapman, M. B.   Sketch.   Motion Pic Classic 23:56 Je '26
    Uselton, R. A.   The Wampus baby stars.   Films In R 21-2:73
        F '70

FAIR, JOYCE
    Sketch.   Strand (NY) 48:110 Ag '14
    Sketch.   Cosmop 57:558 S '14

FAIRBANKS, DOUGLAS SR.
    Sketch.   Green Bk Album 4:1216 D '10
    Interview.   Theatre 14:178 N '11
    His style in farce.   Green Book 9:93 Ja '13
    Wallace, D. H.   Interview.   NY Drama 70:3 Ag 13 '13
    Ten Eyck, J.   Interview.   Green Book 12:624 O '14
    The split reel.   Film Players Herald 2-7:28 F '16
    Fairbanks as a father.   Green Book 16:136 Jl '16
    Ames, H.   Sketch.   Motion Pic Classic 2:18 Jl '16
    Seitz, C. W.   Interview.   Motion Pic 12:65 D '16
    Hornblow, A. Jr.   Interview.   Motion Pic Classic 4:48 Mr '17
    Personal reminiscences.   Theatre 25:220 Ap '17
    Combining play with work.   Am Mag 83:33 Jl '17
    Smith, F. J.   Interview.   Motion Pic Classic 5:46 S '17
    Laugh and live.   Hearst 32:387 N '17
    How he got in motion pictures.   Motion Pic 14:116 N '17
    Lachmund, M. G.   Interview.   Motion Pic Classic 5:54 D '17
    Douglas Fairbanks' own page.   Photop N '17 through Ap '18
    Naylor, H. S.   Interview.   Motion Pic 17:30 F '19
    Bates, B.   The Pickford-Fairbanks wooing.   Photop 18:70 Je '20
    Interview.   Motion Pic 20:30 N '20
    Sketch.   Photop 20:30 N '21
    Cheatham, M.   His darkest hour.   Motion Pic Classic 14:49 Ag
        '22
    Kind of crazy.   Motion Pic 24:42 N '22
    Chapple, J. M.   Interview.   National 51:365 Ja '23
    His Robin Hood awarded gold medal of honor.   Photop 25:61 D
        '23
    Adams, E.   His horoscope.   Photop 26:35 N '24
    de Revere, F. V.   Sketch.   Motion Pic 28:43 Ja '25
    Henning, C.   Daredevil Doug.   Motion Pic 30:40 O '25

Fletcher, A. W.   A Hollywood idyl.   Motion Pic 32:20 Ag '26
St. Johns, A. R.   The married life of Doug and Mary.   Photop
   31:34 F '27
Manners, D.   Interview.   Motion Pic Classic 28:21 N '28
Woods, K.   Mary and Doug.   World Today 53:69 D '28
MacCulloch, C.   Interview.   Theatre 48:24 D '28
Whitaker, A.   Pickfair, a real home.   Photop 35:34 My '29
Biery, R.   His sob-story.   Motion Pic Classic 31:29 Mr '30
Fairbanks, D. Jr.   Appreciation.   Vanity Fair 34:75 My '30
Manners, D.   Sketch.   Motion Pic 41:55 F '31
Matthews, P.   Home of.   Motion Pic Classic 33:36 Mr '31
Service, F.   Sketch.   Motion Pic 41:48 Jl '31
Webster, M.   Interview.   Motion Pic 42:73 Ja '32
Home of.   Photop 41:32 Ap '32
Hall, G.   The haunted house of Pickfair.   Motion Pic 43:29 Ap
   '32
Grant, J.   The romance Hollywood couldn't destroy.   Motion Pic
   43:28 My '32
Literary digest find.   Cinema Dig 1-6:27 Jl 25 '32
Quirk, M. A.   Opinions of his son.   Photop 43:52 F '33
Babcock, M.   His headline career.   Movie Classic 4:48 Mr '33
Schallert, E.   The breaking up of Pickfair.   Movie Classic 5:22
   S '33
Hayden, K.   Interview.   Photop 44:30 N '33
Calhoun, D.   Has he deserted Hollywood?   Motion Pic 47:40 F
   '34
Lee, S.   His side of the story.   Motion Pic 47:32 Mr '34
Hall, G.   His son's opinion of him.   Movie Classic 6:21 Mr '34
Donnell, D.   Returns to America.   Movie Classic 7:41 O '34
Are he and Mary reconciled?   Movie Classic 7:38 N '34
Homespun superman.   Films & Filming 1-3:13 D '54
Silke, J. R.   His production of Robin Hood.   Cinema (BH) 1-3:
   20 '63
McWilliams, W. A.   Douglas Fairbanks.   8mm Collect 13:8
   Fall/Win '65
Estes, O. Jr.   Filmog.   8mm Collect 13:9 Fall/Win '65
Finney, E. A.   Doug; filmog.   Classic F Collect 18:4 Sum '67
Bodeen, D.   Douglas Fairbanks; filmog.   Focus On F 5:17 Win
   '70
When silence was golden.   Screen Greats 1-2:77 Sum '71
Schickel, R.   Superstar of the silents.   Am Heritage 23:4 D '71
The inside of the bowl.   Liberty 1-4:76 Spg '72
Gow, G.   Doug; filmog.   Films & Filming 19-8:34 My '73
Robinson, D.   The hero.   Sight & Sound 42-2:98 Spg '73

FAIRBANKS, DOUGLAS JR.
Biery, R.   Sketch.   Motion Pic Classic 28:37 F '29
Gold, E.   Sketch.   Motion Pic Classic 29:55 Jl '29
Hall, G.   Interview.   Motion Pic 40:58 S '30
Lang, H.   Sketch.   Photop 38:64 N '30
Fairbanks, D. jr. as told to D. Alpert.   Four rules of married
   love.   Silver S 1-5:37 Mr '31
Sketch.   Motion Pic 43:47 My '32

Jones, C. Interview. Photop 42:71 O '32

Moffitt, C. F. Censorship for interviews Hollywood's latest wild idea. Cinema Dig 2-5:9 Ja 9 '33

Opinions of his father. Photop 43:52 F '33

Divorce rumors. Photop 43:31 Ap '33

His separation from Joan Crawford. Motion Pic 45:26 My '33

Cates, F. Separation from Crawford. Movie Classic 4:20 My '33

Fidler, J. Courting Joan again. Motion Pic 45:56 Je '33

Hayden, K. Interview. Photop 45:54 F '34

Hall, G. Interview. Movie Classic 6:21 Mr '34

Larkin, M. Interview. Movie Classic 6:38 My '34

Grayson, C. What marriage has done to him. Motion Pic 42:56 Ag '34

Donnell, D. Remains in London indefinitely. Movie Classic 7:41 O '34

Calhoun, D. His romance with Gertrude Lawrence. Movie Classic 7:53 D '34

Biery, R. Becomes a film producer. Motion Pic 51:46 Je '36

St. Johns, A. R. Story of. Photop 50:14 Jl '36

Craig, C. Interview. Motion Pic 53:46 Je '37

Magee, T. Like father-like son. Screen Book 20-4:37 My '38

Bio note; filmog. Movies & People 2:14 '40

Vallee, W. L. Ambassador with a grin. Silver S 11-9:36 Jl '41

Vallee, W. L. In there pitching again. Silver S 16-7:52 My '46

Carson, R. Sketch. Photop 31:105 Jl '47

Wilson, E. Don't let his films fool you. Silver S 18-3:28 Ja '48

Made honorary Knight of the Order of the British empire. Ill Lon N 214:476 Ap 9 '49

Same. Newsweek 34:38 Jl 25 '49

Douglas Fairbanks and his family. Vogue 114:186 S 1 '49

Minoff, P. A couple of smoothies roll out the barrels. Cue 22-6:7 F 7 '53

Bary, S. The antiquarian Mr. Fairbanks. TV Guide 1-26:A2 S 25 '53

Chierichetti, D. Interview. Film Fan Mo 108:18 Je '70

Raddatz, L. It's lovely to be back. TV Guide 20-42:29 O 14 '72

FAIRBANKS, MARION AND MADELINE

Darnell, J. Marion and Madeline. Photop 4-5:64 O '13

Those Thanhouser kids. Photop 7-3:134 F '15

FAIRE, VIRGINIA BROWN

Allen, B. Interview. Motion Pic Classic 10:46 Je '20

Cheatham, M. Interview. Motion Pic 21:28 Jl '21

Uselton, R. A. The Wampus baby stars. Films In R 21-2:73 F '70

FALANA, LOLA

Dancers go dramatic. Ebony 24:38 S '69

Lola; photos.   Playboy 17-6:89 Je '70
Knight, A. & Alpert, H.   Sex stars of 1970.   Playboy 17-12:220
    D '70
Durslag, M.   Triple threat-with interest.   TV Guide 21-25:19
    Je 23 '73

FALK, PETER
    Clein, H.   Husbands.   Entertainment World 1-4:7 O 24 '69
    Haskell, M.   Three husbands hold court.   Show 1-2:67 F '70
    Milne, T.   Bio note; filmog.   Focus On F 6:11 Spg '71
    Chase, C.   Peter picked a pip.   N. Y. Times Bio Ed N 28 '71
    Mutt for all seasons.   Time 98:64 D 13 '71
    Hudson, P.   Interview.   Sr Schol 100:30 F 28 '72
    Guerin, A.   He really is an actor.   Show 12:29 F '72
    Hobson, D.   America discovers Columbo.   TV Guide 20-13:28
        Mr 25 '72
    Bio.   Cur Bio 33:13 Jl '72
    Real Columbo.   Newsweek 8:93 N 13 '72
    Interview with John Cassavetes and Peter Falk.   Dialogue 4:en-
        tire issue '72
    Condon, M.   In Ossining, he is a legend.   TV Guide 21-18:27
        My 5 '73
    Why you're in love with Columbo.   Photop 84-3:36 S '73
    Interview: on movies, madness and myth.   Viva 2-3:61 D '74

FALKENBERG, JINX
    Davis, L. & Cleveland, J.   Story of.   Colliers 106:11 O 12 '40
    Jensen, O.   Story of.   Life 10:34 Ja 27 '41
    Franchey, J. K.   Jinx the minx.   Silver S 12-9:34 Jl '42
    Story of her family.   Newsweek 20:60 Ag 17 '42
    Mulvey, K.   Sketch.   Womans Home C 70:22 N '43
    Deere, D.   Story of.   Photop 24:46 Mr '44
    The Falkenburg-O'Brien troupe...   Life 18:22 Ja 1 '45
    She weds in a flurry.   Life 18:28 Je 25 '45
    Franchey, J. R.   She bids farewell to Hollywood.   Silver S 16-9:
        58 Jl '46
    Radio and television schedules.   Newsweek 30:52 Ag 25 '47
    Maughan, R.   Television...   Silver S 18-5:28 Mr '48
    Tex and Jinx back in print.   Newsweek 34:56 Ag 15 '49
    Beatty, J.   Tex's lucky Jinx.   Am Mag 148:79 S '49
    Falkenberg, J.   Telescope (column).   Silver S various '49
    Family affair.   New Yorker 26:25 Ap 15 '50
    Minoff, P.   Jinx does a solo.   Cue 21-36:15 S 6 '52
    Ten things that make my heart beat faster.   Good House 141:140
        Ag '55
    Her scrapbook.   McCalls 82:8 Ag '55

FANT, KENNE
    Note.   International Film G 2:41 '65

FARENTINO, JAMES
    Klemesrud, J.   Stanley Kowalski loves Gittel Mosca.   N. Y.
        Times sec 2:1 Je 10 '73
        Same.   N. Y. Times Bio Ed p959 Je '73

FARINA (Allen Clayton Hoskins)
  Howe, H.   Sketch.   Photop 24:35 S '23
  Albert, K.   Interview.   Photop 35:39 Mr '29
  Hall, L.   Sketch.   Photop 40:35 Je '31
  Maltin, L.   Our gang; inc. Our Gang filmog.   Film Fan Mo 66:
    3 D '66

FARKAS, KARL
  Obit.   N. Y. Times p38 My 17 '71

FARMER, FRANCES
  Lang, H.   Sketch.   Movie Classic 11:36 N '36
  Hall, G.   Her story.   Motion Pic 53:34 Mr '37
  Darnton, C.   An inside job?   Silver S 7-6:34 Ap '37
  Williams, W.   How it's done.   Silver S 7-9:24 Jl '37
  Surmelian, L.   Interview.   Motion Pic 54:36 O '37
  Farmer, F.   Learn acting on the stage.   Screen Book 19-5:46
    D '37
  Sketch.   Life 4:24 Ja 17 '38
  Hamilton, S.   Sketch.   Photop 54:30 S '40
  Mentally ill.   Newsweek 21:29 Ja 25 '43
  Lane, C.   Letter.   Films In R 18-4:254 Ap '67
  Obit.   Classic Film Collect 28:ex p3 Fall '70
    Film R p13 '71/72
    N. Y. Times p57 Ag 2 '70
    Same.   N. Y. Times Bio Ed Ag 2 '70
    Newsweek 76:59 Ag 17 '70
    Screen World 22:236 '71
    Time 96:52 Ag 17 '70
  Stangen, B.   Frances Farmer; filmog.   Films In R 21-10:656 D
    '70

FARNUM, DUSTIN
  Interview.   Theatre 6:272 O '06
  Gridschmid, P.   Sketch.   Motion Pic Classic 2:16 Ap '16
  How to get in moving pictures.   Motion Pic Classic 2:46 Ag '16
  McKelvie, M.   Interview.   Motion Pic 12:67 N '16
  Eubanks, L. E.   Personality of.   Motion Pic Classic 3:22 D '16
  Wright, W.   Interview.   Motion Pic 17:47 Mr '19
  Cheatham, M.   Sketch.   Motion Pic Classic 9:56 D '19
  Cheatham, M.   Interview.   Motion Pic 19:33 F '20
  Peltret, E.   Interview.   Motion Pic Classic 14:68 Ap '22
  Corneau, E. N.   The Farnum brothers.   Classic Film Collect
    23:24 Spg '69

FARNUM, FRANKLIN
  Delvigne, D.   Sketch.   Motion Pic 17:59 Ap '19
  Obit.   Screen World 13:221 '62

FARNUM, WILLIAM
  Gaddis, P.   Interview.   Motion Pic 10:100 D '15
  How to get in moving pictures.   Motion Pic 12:104 S '16
  Hall, G.   Interview.   Motion Pic 17:52 F '19

Roseman, E.  Interview.  Motion Pic 20:32 S '20
Montanye, L.  Interview.  Motion Pic 14:66 Je '22
Carr, H.  Interview.  Motion Pic 28:114 D '24
Schader, F. H.  Story of his illness and recovery.  Photop 33:
    30 Ja '28
Comfort, J. J.  William Farnum.  Classic Film Collect 16:39
    Fall '60
Corneau, E. N.  The Farnum brothers.  Classic Film Collect
    23:24 Spg '69

FARR, FELICIA
    Eyles, A.  Bio note; filmog.  Focus On F 9:7 Spg '72
    Parsons, L. O.  Felicia Farr arrives in Hollywood.  Fuller
    Brush Mag: entire issue.  n. d.

FARRELL, CHARLES
    Chapman, M. B.  Sketch.  Motion Pic Classic 23:57 Jl '26
    Manners, D.  Sketch.  Motion Pic Classic 24:54 N '26
    Manners, D.  Interview.  Motion Pic 34:18 N '27
    Newcomb, M.  Sketch.  Motion Pic 27:58 My '28
    Biery, R.  Compared to Charles Rogers.  Motion Pic 36:55 D
    '28
    Shopping with (him).  Motion Pic 37:68 Jl '29
    Gray, C.  Sketch.  Motion Pic 38:42 D '29
    Manners, D.  Sketch.  Motion Pic Classic 30:29 F '30
    Manners, D.  Interview.  Motion Pic 42:39 S '31
    Simpson, G.  Turkey and stuffing.  Silver S 2-1:35 N '31
    Home of.  Movie Classic 3:50 N '32
    Moffitt, C. F.  Censorship for interviews.  Cinema Dig 2-5:9
    Ja 9 '33
    Lee, S.  Screen divorce from Gaynor.  Movie Classic 3:64 F
    '33
    Williams, W.  Returns to the screen.  Motion Pic 46:60 O '33
    Brundidge, H. T.  Sketch.  Motion Pic 49:28 F '35
    Mains, M.  Not so hard-hearted.  Silver S 8-12:59 O '38
    Campbell, S.  The man who came back.  Screen Book 21-4:28
    N '38
    What they are doing now.  Show 2-8:106 Ag '62
    Yesterday's sweethearts today.  Photop 85-6:56 Je '74

FARRELL, GLENDA
    Nominated for stardom.  Motion Pic 45:42 F '33
    Costello, T.  Interview.  Motion Pic 45:50 Mr '33
    Cohen, H.  Praising players of minor importance.  Cinema Dig
    3-6:12 Ap 24 '33
    Birchard, M.  Interview.  Movie Classic 5:55 O '33
    Sylvia's beauty helps.  Photop 45:54 My '34
    Manners, D.  Interview.  Movie Classic 6:27 Ag '34
    Farrell, T.  Her son's opinion of her.  Photop 47:43 My '35
    Cheatham, M.  Two blonde menaces.  Silver S 7-1:27 N '36
    Home of.  Movie Classic 11:44 F. '37
    Spensley, D.  Interview.  Motion Pic 53:45 Mr '37
    Janisch, A.  I won't marry again.  Screen Book 19-4:42 N '37

Walker, H. L.   Glenda's castle.   Silver S 9-3:22 Ja '39
The girl on the cover.   Cue 11-17:1 Ap 25 '42
Interview.   Photon #20 n. d.
Obit.   Classic Film Collect 31:62 Sum '71
    Film R p13 '71/72
    N. Y. Times p74 My 2 '71
    Same.   N. Y. Times Bio Ed My 2 '71
    Newsweek 77:70 My 17 '71
    Screen World 23:236 '72
    Time 97:70 My 17 '71
Kanin, G.   Glenda Farrell--1904-1971.   N. Y. Times Bio Ed My
    16 '71
Dalton, E.   Meet Torchy Blane; Torchy Blane filmog.   Film Fan
    Mo 133/134:37 Jl/Ag '72
Zinman, D.   Torchy Blane and Glenda Farrell; Torchy Blane
    filmog.   Filmograph 3-3:38 '73

FARRELL, SHARON
    Zadan, C.   You've come a long way from Sioux City; interview.
        After Dark 11-11:54 Mr '70
    Opinions on liberation.   Photop 78-3:78 S '70
    When you can't have another child.   Photop 79-2:6 F '71

FARROW, MIA
    Hamilton, J.   Working Sinatras.   Look 31:86 O 31 '67
    Newsmakers.   Newsweek 70:52 D 4 '67
    Tabori, L.   Interview.   Ladies Home J 85:59 Ag '68
    Cocks, J.   Moonchild and the fifth Beatle.   Time 93:50 F 7 '69
    Mia Farrow.   Vogue 153:156 My '69
    Devlin, P.   Her thin-skinned courage.   Vogue 153:80 My '69
    Chapman, D.   Mia is a trip.   Look 33:47 Ag 26 '69
    Bio.   Cur Bio 31:11 Ap '70
        Same.   Cur Bio Yrbk 1970:132 '71
    Motherhood.   Photop 77-5:26 My '70
    Denied home because of illegitimate children.   Photop 77-6:56 Je
        '70
    Nine minds in trouble.   Photop 78-3:56 S '70
    Was it worth it?   Photop 78-4:41 O '70
    Knight, A. & Alpert, H.   Sex stars of 1970.   Playboy 17-12:220
        D '70
    Kanin, G.   Mia comes to rest.   McCalls 98:64 Ap '71
    Raddatz, L.   Mia.   TV Guide 19-42:30 O 16 '71
    Why she left Andre Previn.   Silver S 41-10:43 O '71
    What secrets has Mia been hiding?   Photop 80-5:93 N '71
    Sirmans, J.   'Rosemary'? She's Andre's baby now.   N. Y.
        Times Bio Ed O 17 '71
    How she suffered for success.   Mod Screen 66-7:52 Jl '72
    Games to save a marriage.   Mod Screen 66-10:50 O '72
    Mia's back and Gatsby's got her.   People 1-1:32 Mr 4 '74
    Elizabeth Taylor gave me courage.   Photop 86-1:42 Jl '74
    Hauptfuhrer, F.   On the symphony circuit, now it's Andre and
        Mia.   People 2-13:26 S 23 '74

FARROW, TISA
   Checking out First Avenue.  Holiday 45:38 My '69
   Klemesrud, J.  Being Mia's sister was Tisa's burden.  N. Y.
      Times Bio Ed Ja 8 '70
   Actresses who are real people.  Life 68:46 My 29 '70
   Miller, E.  Juliet to a rebelious Romeo; interview.  Seventeen
      29:136 Je '70
   Chapman, D.  Will Mia's sister make it?  Look 34:48 S 22 '70
   Second generation.  Films Illus 1-10:12 Ap '72

FAULKNER, GRAHAM
   Headliners.  Photop 84-1:14 Jl '73

FAWCETT, GEORGE
   Patterson, A.  Interview.  Theatre 18:46 Ag '13
   Valentine, S.  Sketch.  Photop 18:64 Jl '20
   Oettinger, M.  Interview.  Motion Pic 24:54 D '22
   A plea for the old school of acting.  Theatre 47:32 Ap '28
   Why acting has declined.  Lit Dig 22:3 My 26 '28
   Calhoun, D.  Interview.  Motion Pic 36:40 D '28
   How sound films will affect legitimate drama.  Theatre 49:32 Mr
      '29

FAY, FRANK
   Harvey's friend.  New Yorker 20:23 N 18 '44
   Zolotow, M.  Frank Fay.  Life 18:55 Ja 8 '45
   Bio.  Cur Bio Ag '45
   Field, J.  L'affaire Frank Fay.  New Rep 113:900 D 31 '45
   Frank Fay and friends.  Newsweek 27:78 Ja 28 '46
   Letts, W.  Fays at the Abbey theatre.  Fortnightly 163:420 Je
      '48
   Obit.  Screen World 13:222 '62

FAYE, ALICE
   Goldbeck, E.  Sketch.  Motion Pic 47:39 Jl '34
   Sketch.  Photop 46:74 N '34
   Sketch.  Time 27:28 Ja 6 '36
   Harrison, P.  Interview.  Motion Pic 50:33 Ja '36
   Cheatham, M.  Interview.  Motion Pic 53:51 F '37
   Wilson, E.  Projections.  Silver S 7-9:30 Jl '37
   Spensley, D.  Story of.  Motion Pic 54:28 S '37
   Why Alice Faye almost missed stardom.  Screen Book 19-3:48
      O '37
   Bradford, S.  She never took a lesson.  Screen Book 20-4:36
      My '38
   Wilson, E.  Righting wrong impressions.  Silver S 9-10:22 Ag
      '39
   Bio note; filmog.  Movies & People 2:14 '40
   Hall, G.  Should women feel sorry for Alice Faye?  Silver S
      11-5:22 Mr '41
   Sketch.  Photop 24:48 D '43
   Bubbly, bouncy and blonde.  Screen Greats 1-2:52 Sum '71
   Vlasek, K.  Alice Faye; filmog.  Film Musical Q 1-1:entire

issue Win '71
McClelland, D.  Good news from Alice Faye.  After Dark 6-8:36
   D '73
Watters, J.  On stage.  People 1-7:29 Ap 15 '74
This time it's not just a movie plot.  Cue 43-49:1 D 23 '74

**FAYE, JULIA**
McGaffey, K.  Introducing the vampette.  Photop 15-4:47 Mr '19
Peltret, E.  Sketch.  Motion Pic Classic 12:34 Ag '21

**FAZENDA, LOUISE**
How to get in moving pictures.  Motion Pic 12:71 D '16
Evans, D.  Sketch.  Motion Pic 14:91 D '17
Carr, H.  Work of.  Motion Pic 16:61 Ja '19
Autobiographical.  Motion Pic Classic 8:34 My '19
Goldbeck, W.  Sketch.  Motion Pic Classic 11:48 F '21
Goldbeck, W.  Interview.  Motion Pic 22:52 N '21
Carr, H.  Sketch.  Motion Pic Classic 21:1 Ap '25
St. Johns, A. R.  The most versatile girl in Hollywood.  Photop
   28:84 Je '25
How she planned her home.  Motion Pic 31:40 Mr '26
Walker, H. L.  Sketch.  Motion Pic 36:71 S '28
Cruikshank, H.  Interview.  Motion Pic 38:32 O '29
Conti, M.  Christmas shopping with her.  Motion Pic 38:68 Ja
   '30
Cruikshank, H.  Sketch.  Motion Pic Classic 33:70 Mr '31

**FEALY, MAUDE**
Interview.  Blue Book 19:460 Jl '14
Roat, A. L.  Reminiscences of.  Motion Pic 9:115 F '15
Sketch.  N. Y. Drama 77:9 Ja 6 '17
Obit.  Classic Film Collect 33:53 Win '71
   Screen World 23:236 '72
Altamirano, A.  Maude Fealy; partial filmog.  Films In R 23-5:
   319 My '72

**FEARS, PEGGY**
Sketch.  Stage 9:39 Je '32
Sabine, L.  That elusive something; interview.  Ind Woman 13:71
   Mr '34
d'Arcy, R. J.  Interview on clothes.  Motion Pic 48:54 D '34

**FEDDON, MARGARET**
Obit.  Screen World 20:234 '69

**FELDARY, ERIC**
Obit.  Screen World 20:234 '69

**FELDMAN, MARTY**
Musel, R.  He'd like to redesign the human body.  TV Guide
   20-25:38 Je 17 '72

FELDON, BARBARA
    Sic 'em tigers.   Newsweek 65:92 My 3 '65
    Hobson, D.   Wholesome agent 99.   TV Guide 14-35:17 Ag 27 '66
    Whitney, D.   Spoofy they call her.   TV Guide 16-16:26 Ap 20
        '68

FELIX, MARIA
    Sketch.   Vogue 105:143 O 1 '45
    Minoff, P.   Mexico's torrid tamale.   Cue 25-23:13 Je 9 '56

FELL, NORMAN
    The workaday cop.   TV Guide 10-17:7 Ap 28 '62

FELLOWES, ROCKCLIFFE
    Obit.   Screen World 2:233 '51

FELLOWS, EDITH
    Schwarzkopf, J.   Sketch.   Motion Pic 51:21 Jl '36
    Hall, G.   Interview.   Child Life 15:507 N '36
    Hamilton, S.   Sketch.   Photop 52:31 S '38

FELTON, VERNA
    $500 a word star.   TV Guide 3-23:12 Je 4 '55
    TV's happiest outlaws.   Look 19:178 D 13 '55
    The female of the species.   TV Guide 5-38:17 S 21 '57
    Obit.   Screen World 18:234 '67

FENHOLT, JEFF
    Sparn, E.   Interview.   Sr Schol 99:10 D 13 '71
    Summer, A.   Once during the gethsemane soliloquey...   After
        Dark 5-7:18 N '72

FENTON, LESLIE
    Alpert, K.   Interview.   Photop 39:45 F '31
    Howe, H.   Sketch.   Photop 36:41 N '29
    Jones, C.   Dreams come through.   Silver S 2-8:22 Je '32

FERGUSON, ELSIE
    Sketch.   Theatre 9:69 F '09
    Rapid promotion of.   Pearson (NY) 22:502 O '09; 22:663 N '09
    How she became a star.   Green Bk Album 3:385 F '10
    Advice to stage aspirants.   Greek Bk 9:599 Ap '13
    Interview.   Cosmop 58:458 Mr '15
    Dress philosophy.   Green Bk 13:833 My '15
    Sketch.   N.Y. Drama 61:25 Ag 7 '15
    Success of.   Green Bk 294:9 Ag '15
    Interview.   Motion Pic Classic 5:48 F '18
    Naylor, H. S.   Sketch.   Motion Pic 15:34 S '18
    Sears, G.   America's own actress.   Theatre 29:208 My '19
    Helping wounded soldiers thru the Red Cross.   Motion Pic 17:28
        Je '19
    Smith, F. J.   Interview.   Motion Pic Classic 8:18 Je '19
    Hall, G.   Interview.   Motion Pic 19:30 F '20

Interview.  Dram Mir 82:606 Mr 27 '20
Clothes and good taste.  Photop 17:57 Mr '20
Patterson, A.  Sketch.  Theatre 32:20 Jl/Ag '20
Haskins, H.  Sketch of her trip around world.  Motion Pic Classic 12:43 Mr '21
Naylor, H. S.  Interview.  Motion Pic 21:22 My '21
Hall, G. & Fletcher, A. W.  Interview.  Motion Pic 22:22 O '21
de Revere, F. V.  Face analysis of.  Theatre 43:12 Mr '26
Bodeen, D.  Letter.  Films In R 16-1:53 Ja '65

FERGUSON, HELEN
Cheatham, M. S.  Interview.  Motion Pic 20:45 O '20
Autobiographical.  Motion Pic Classic 14:24 Ap '22
Handy, T. B.  Interview.  Motion Pic 23:30 My '22
Uselton, R. A.  The Wampus baby stars.  Films In R 21-2:73 F '70

FERNANDEL
Fernandel.  Visages 25:entire issue Jl '38
Personality of the month.  Films & Filming 1-8:3 My '55
Hume, R.  French face man.  Films & Filming 2-5:31 F '56
I'm an actor, not a comedian.  Films & Filming 7-1:15 O '60
Obit.  Classic Film Collect 30:extra 3 Spg '71
  Cur Bio 32:45 Ap '71
  Cur Bio Yrbk 1971:463 '72
  Film R p13 '71/72
  N. Y. Times p60 F 26 '71
  Same.  N. Y. Times Bio Ed F 28 '71
  Newsweek 77:63 Mr 8 '71
  Screen World 23:236 '72
  Time 97:62 Mr 8 '71
Domke, G.  Fernandel; filmog.  Films In R 24-4:248 Ap '73
Romer, J. C.  Letter.  Films In R 24-7:444 Ag/S '73
Domke, G.  Additions & Corrections to filmog.  Films In R 24-8:512 O '73

FERNANDEZ, BIJOU
Downing, R.  Bijou Fernandez; letter.  Films In R 13-1:60 Ja '62

FERRADAY, LISA
I luf TV.  TV Guide 4-31:25 Ag 4 '56

FERRARE, CHRISTINA
Sketch.  Movie Dig 1-6:30 N '72

FERRER, JOSE
Ferrer, J.  Is the Bergman legend true?  Silver S 18-11:24 S '48
His portrayal of the tramp in The silver whistle.  Newsweek 32:86 D '48
Sketch.  Photop 36:120 O '49

Ferrer as Cyrano.   Cue 19-38:17 S 23 '50
Holliday, K.   No one in the world like him.   Silver S 21-3:42
    Ja '51
Keating, J.   Man of parts.   Cue 21-17:11 Ap 26 '52
One-man repertory.   Cue 22-45:16 N 7 '53
Carlson, T.   Come closer darling.   Silver S 24-4:31 F '54
London, J.   The two faces of Ferrer.   Films & Filming 4-9:12
    Je '58
The screen answers back.   Films & Filming 8-8:12 My '62

FERRER, MEL
Holliday, K.   Fabulous Ferrer.   Silver S 20-9:41 Jl '50
Hall, G.   Ever meet a quinto phreniac?   Silver S 23-5:24 Mr
    '53

FERRIS, AUDREY
Uselton, R. A.   The Wampus baby stars.   Films In R 21-2:73
    F '70

FERRIS, BARBARA
People are talking about.   Vogue 151:109 Ja 1 '68

FETCHIT, STEPIN
Goldbeck, E.   Interview.   Motion Pic 37:76 Jl '29
Thompson, H. G.   Appreciation.   Stage 13:70 Ja '36
Where are they now?   Newsweek 70:22 N 20 '67
Black power casualties.   Nat R 21:701 Jl 15 '69
McBride, J.   Stepin Fetchit talks back.   Film Q 24-4:20 Sum '71
Whatever happened to Lincoln Perry?   Ebony 27:202 N '71
Charlie Chan in Egypt.   Views & Rs 3-3:48 Win '72
Bogle, D.   The first black movie stars.   Sat R Arts 1-2:25 F
    '73

FEUILLADE, LOUIS
Schofer, P.   See Fantomas.   Velvet Light 9:1 Sum '73

FEUILLERE, EDWIGE
Edwige Feuillere.   Visages 22:entire issue Ap '38
Caloosa, U.   Paris model, 1946.   Colliers 117:16 F 16 '46

FICKETT, MARY
Flame and sympathy.   TV Guide 3-25:12 Je 18 '55

FIELD, BETTY
Hamilton, S.   Sketch.   Photop 54:15 Ja '40
Vallee, W. L.   Betty made it the hard way.   Silver S 10-4:40
    F '40
Michaels, J.   Exposing the allergy girl.   Silver S 15-2:46 D '44
Parsons, L. O.   Cosmop's citation for best supporting actress.
    Cosmop 127:13 Ag '49
Obit.   Classic Film Collect 41:53 Win '73
    N. Y. Daily News p4 S 15 '73
    N. Y. Times Bio Ed p1466 S '73

Screen World p233 '74
Kalter, D.  Betty Field 1918-1973.  N. Y.  Times sec 2:4 O 14
'73
Same.  N. Y.  Times Bio Ed p1641 O '73

FIELD, MARY
McClelland, D.  Mary Field; filmog.  Films In R 22-7:454 Ag/S
'71
Witmer, T.  Partial filmog.  Films In R 22-9:581 N '71
McClelland, D.  A toast to Mary Field; filmog.  Film Fan Mo
148:25 O '73

FIELD, SALLY
Raddatz, L.  Gidget.  TV Guide 14-22:16 My 28 '66
de Roos, R.  Her feet are on the ground.  TV Guide 15-39:16
S 30 '67
Rollin, B.  The flying nun.  Look 31:M18 N 14 '67
Whitney, D.  I didn't want to play a nun.  TV Guide 16-11:21
Mr 16 '68
Grounded!  TV Guide 21-41:43 O 13 '73

FIELD, SHIRLEY ANN
Rising star.  Film R p35 '61/62
Cowie, P.  The face of '63--Great Britain.  Films & Filming
9-5:19 F '63

FIELD, VIRGINIA
Hamilton, S.  Sketch.  Photop 54:30 Jl '40
Fulton, M. J.  Sketch.  Photop 35:97 My '49
Raker, A. & McClelland, D.  Virginia Field; filmog.  Film Fan
Mo 142:24 Ap '73

FIELDING, ROMAINE
Baker, K. W.  Romaine Fielding; interview.  Photop 7-4:33 Mr
'15
Everett, E. K.  The search for Romaine Fielding.  Classic
Film Collect 44:32 Fall '74

FIELDS, BENNY
Debus, A. G.  Current collectors' records.  Hobbies 59:24 Mr
'54

FIELDS, GRACIE
Grein, J. T.  Appreciation.  Ill Lon N 175:1044 D 14 '29
Grimstead, H.  Personal sketch.  Windsor 82:597 O '35
People.  Cue 10-17:20 Ap 26 '41
Beavan, J.  Sketch.  World R 5:19 Jl 9 '41
Sketch.  Vogue 100:60 Jl 15 '42
Sketch.  Harp Baz 76:71 D '42
Your own Gracie.  Cue 12-32:10 Ag 7 '43
Vallee, W. L.  At long last.  Silver S 14-2:42 D '43
My biggest lie.  Photop 26:57 Mr '45
Minoff, P.  Gracie goes "legit."  Cue 25-20:17 My 19 '56

It's the sponsor who pays.  TV Guide 4-37:24 S 15 '56
Pinup of the past.  Films & Filming 19-5:64 F '73

FIELDS, LEW
  That reminds me...  Photop 12-5:54 O '17
  Obit.  Cur Bio '41
    Newsweek 18:54 Jl 28 '41
    Time 38:53 Jl 28 '41
  Fabulous Fields family.  Life 14:41 F 22 '43

FIELDS, TOTI
  Higgins, R.  Everyone's favorite size 44.  TV Guide 17-1:32
    Ja 4 '69

FIELDS, W. C.
  Redway, S.  Interview.  Motion Pic Classic 22:32 S '25
  Roberts, W. A.  Sketch.  Motion Pic 30:54 D '25
  Hanemann, H.  Interview.  Motion Pic 32:39 Ag '26
  Thorp, D.  Sketch.  Motion Pic Classic 24:38 S '26
  Autobiographical.  Theatre 48:44 O '28
  Tully, J.  Sketch.  Photop 45:60 Ja '34
  Sketch.  Vanity Fair 42:32 Je '34
  Ferguson, O.  Appreciation.  New Rep 79:320 Ag 1 '34
  Grant, J.  Proud of his big nose.  Movie Classic 7:56 F '35
  Tully, J.  Sketch.  Motion Pic 49:33 Mr '35
  Cheatham, M.  Juggler of laughs.  Silver S 5-6:30 Ap '35
  Ferguson, O.  A minor Falstaff.  New Rep 84:48 Ag 21 '35
  Sullivan, E.  That lovable liar.  Silver S 5-11:16 S '35
  Autobiographical.  Motion Pic 50:49 S '35
  Sketch.  Photop 49:46 Je '36
  His feud with Charlie McCarthy.  Life 3:26 Jl '37
  Reid, J.  Story of.  Motion Pic 54:37 O '37
  Darnton, C.  Mr. Fields wins by a nose.  Screen Book 19-4:34
    N '37
  Gillespie-Hayek, A.  Oh what a dummy.  Silver S 7-12:18 D '37
  Bio note; filmog.  Movies & People 2:14 '40
  Obit.  Ill Lon N 210:19 Ja 4 '47
  Ford, C.  One and only W. C. Fields.  Harpers 235:65 O '67
  Ford, C.  The one and only.  Read Dig 91:158 N '67
  McVay, D.  Elysian Fields.  Film 50:22 Win '67
  Kindler, J.  Elysian Fields.  Playboy 16:116 Mr '69
  Gilliatt, P.  Current cinema.  New Yorker 45:86 Je 21 '69
  Lee, R.  The brabbling boozer returns.  Classic Film Collect
    24:46 Sum '69
  Van Dyke, W.  Cue salutes.  Cue 39-13:54 Mr 28 '70
  Marlowe, D.  Fieldsiana.  Classic Film Collect 28:48 Fall '70
  Filmog. of screen plays.  Film Com 6-4:101 Win '70/71
  Cooper, A.  His last Chickadee.  Newsweek 77:92 Je 21 '71
  Brooks, L.  The other faces of W. C. Fields.  Sight & Sound
    40-2:92 Spg '71
  Comedians.  Screen Greats 1-2:64 Sum '71
  Flinn, T.  Out of the past.  Velvet Light 3:6 Win '71/72
  Fowler, W.  Sleigh bells gave me nausea.  Life 73:42 D 15 '72

Thomas, J. C.  Uncle Willie, where are you now that we need
   you?  Moviegoer 2-1:22 n. d.
Evans, C.  The sounds of silence.  Mise-en-Scene 1:23 n. d.
W. C. Fields and Mae West.  Nostalgia Illus 1-1:40 N '74

FIERMONTE, ENZO
   They stand out from the crowd.  Lit Dig 118:10 Jl 14 '34
   What they are doing now.  Show 2-3:97 Mr '62

FINCH, JON
   Buckley, P.  Fresh faces from the British cinema.   After Dark
      4-3:38 Jl '71
   New faces.  Films Illus 1-7:9 Ja '72
   On the scene.  Playboy 19-4:176 Ap '72
   Sketch.  Movie Dig 1-6:33 N '72
   Crossing London for a brand of beer; filmog.  Films Illus 2-19:
      32 Ja '73
   Milinaire, C.  Interview.  Interview 31:15 Ap '73
   Note; filmog.  Films & Filming 19-11:58 Ag '73

FINCH, PETER
   Bio sketch.  Theatre World 45:31 My '49
   Finch, P.  How I learned to laugh at myself.  Films & Filming
      4-12:7 S '58
   Cowie, P.  The face of '63--Great Britain.  Films & Filming
      9-5:19 F '63
   Desert island films.  Films & Filming 9-11:11 Ag '63
   Gow, G.  The mind's eye; interview; filmog.  Films & Filming
      16-11:5 Ag '70
   Filmog.  Films Illus 1-1:26 Jl '71
   Kramer, F.  Peter Finch finally makes it to Shangri-La.  Movie
      Dig 1-4:8 Jl '72
   McAsh, I.  I am fascinated by human frailty.  Films Illus 2-19:
      34 Ja '73
   The year of Peter Finch.  Films Illus 2-23:20 My '73

FINLAY, FRANK
   Gow, G.  Interview.  Plays & Players 21-2:31 N '73

FINLAY, GRACE
   Evanchuck, P.  Grace Finlay.  Motion p15 My/Je '74

FINLEY, NED
   Henry, M.  Interview.  Motion Pic 15:89 Je '18

FINNEY, ALBERT
   Rising star.  Film R p31 '61/62
   Cowie, P.  The face of '63--Great Britain.  Films & Filming
      9-5:19 F '63
   Bean, R.  Will there be film stars in 1974?  Films & Filming
      10-10:9 Jl '64
   Robinson, D.  Case histories of the next renascence.  Sight &
      Sound 38:40 Win '68

Musical Scrooge: bah!  Look 34:28 D '70
Opposite direction; bio note.  Films Illus 1-5:31 N '71
Head, M.  He digs this Sam Spade.  N. Y. Times sec 2:11 Ap
    30 '72

FIORE, BILL
    Higgins, R.  Recognize yourself?  TV Guide 18-32:24 Ag 8 '70

FIRTH, PETER
    Gruen, J.  Equus makes a star of Firth.  N. Y. Times sec 2:1
        O 27 '74

FISCHER, MARGARITA
    Willis, R.  Margarita Fischer.  Movie Pictorial 2-1:8 Jl '15
    Sketch.  Motion Pic Classic 4:41 My '17
    Courtlandt, R.  Interview.  Motion Pic Classic 5:48 S '17
    Kingsley, R.  Interview.  Motion Pic 17:30 My '19
    Kingsley, G.  Interview.  Motion Pic Classic 27:42 Mr '28

FISHER, CAROLINE
    Reynolds, Q.  Hollywood sweepstakes.  Colliers 102:20 D 24 '38

FISHER, EDDIE
    Private first class Fisher, crooner.  Life 33:89 O 13 '52
    Eddie's back.  Newsweek 41:92 Ap 20 '53
    Minoff, P.  Still can't believe it.  Cue 22-25:12 Je 20 '53
    Now it's Eddie.  Colliers 131:64 Je 27 '53
    Bonanza, country style.  Time 62:38 Jl 27 '53
    Eddie Fisher.  Cosmop 135:124 Ag '53
    Beatty, J.  Wail and get wealthy.  Am Mag 156:26 N '53
    Roddy, J.  Every day's the greatest.  Look 18:56 Mr 23 '54
    Debbie and Eddie announce it.  Life 37:45 Jl 27 '54
    He throws a fan party.  Womans Home C 81:16 Jl '54
    Millionaire.  TV Guide 2-36:15 S 4 '54
    Teen-age tizzy.  Life 37:185 S 13 '54
    Debbie and Eddie.  Look 19:22 F 22 '55
    Eddie Fisher, boy corporation.  TV Guide 3-23:7 Je 4 '55
    Debbie's ring on at last.  Life 39:59 O 10 '55
    No time is their time.  Look 20:105 Mr 6 '56
    Wheatland, C. M. & Sharpe, E.  Young Hollywood at home.
        Ladies Home J 73:88 N '56
    Say it isn't so, boys.  TV Guide 5-47:17 N 23 '57
    Just friends.  Time 72:44 S 22 '58
    Tale of Debbie, Eddie and the widow Todd.  Life 45:39 S 22 '58
    That's show biz.  Newsweek 52:77 S 22 '58
    Gehman, R.  Debbie's story.  McCalls 86:48 Mr '59
    Fast divorce OK by Debbie.  Life 46:41 Ap 13 '59
    Life of the senses.  Time 73:65 Ap 13 '59
    Eddie's comeback.  Time 74:72 N 30 '59
    Boeth, R.  Aftermath of a scandal.  McCalls 87:36 Ja '60
    Martin, P.  I call on Debbie Reynolds.  Sat Eve Post 232:28 Mr
        26 '60
    Oh!  my sincerity.  Time 77:42 My 26 '61

Liz, Liz, Liz.   Newsweek 57:70 My 29 '61
Slater, L.   Interview.   McCalls 89:74 Ja '62
Eddie Fisher at the Winter Garden.   Theatre Arts 46:13 N '62
Richardson, J.   Mr Fisher is open.   Esquire 60:158 D '63
Funny thing happened on the way to decorum.   Time 83:56 Ja 3
   '64
(Additional citings to material relating to the Debbie Reynolds-
   Eddie Fisher-Elizabeth Taylor-Richard Burton involvements
   may be found under Reynolds and Taylor in the first volume
   of this bibliography, published 1971.)

FISHER, GAIL
   Radditz, L.   My mother is a very strong lady.   TV Guide 16-42:
      23 O 19 '68
   The girl from Mannix.   Ebony 24:140 O '69
   Berkvist, R.   Too bad Liz Taylor's already beaten me to Cleo-
      patra.   N. Y. Times Bio Ed Ap 9 '72
   The perfect secretary.   Photop 81-5:60 My '72
   Her favorite dish.   Mod Screen 67-3:20 Mr '73

FISHER, GEORGE
   Remont, F.   Interview.   Motion Pic 15:40 Jl '18

FITZGERALD, BARRY
   Sketch.   Time 43:90 My 1 '44
   Crosby, B.   Appreciation.   Cosmop 117:14 Jl '44
   Bruce, J.   Barry the bachelor.   Silver S 15-8:24 Je '45
   Parsons, L. O.   Cosmop's citation for best supporting role of
      the month.   Cosmop 119:61 D '45
   Parsons, L. O.   Cosmop's citation for best supporting perform-
      ance of month.   Cosmop 122:65 Je '47
   Parsons, L. O.   Cosmop's citation as best film star of month.
      Cosmop 124:13 F '48
   Sketch.   Photop 33:116 Je '48
   Blyth, A.   Having fun with Bing and Barry.   Silver S 19-7:42
      My '49
   Obit.   Film R p17 '61/62

FITZGERALD, CISSY
   Spensley, D.   Interview.   Photop 31:67 Ap '27
   Obit.   Cur Bio '41

FITZGERALD, GERALDINE
   Rhea, M.   Sketch.   Photop 53:30 Jl '39
   Bio note; filmog.   Movies & People 2:15 '40
   Hall, G.   Ida Lupino, Bette Davis and Olivia de Havilland talk
      about (her).   Silver S 11-6:26 Ap '41
   Wilson, E.   A mind of her own.   Silver S 16-11:42 S '46
   Fulton, M. J.   Sketch.   Photop 33:89 O '48
   Burke, T.   Geraldine's long journey.   N. Y. Times Bio Ed Je
      13 '71
   Gardella, K.   What's on TV?   N. Y. Daily News p107 Mr 14 '74
   Rode, D.   Geraldine Fitzgerald, Filmog.   Film Fan Mo 156:3

Je '74
Hoffman, L.   Interview.   Interview 4-8:33 S '74

FITZMAURICE, MICHAEL T.
   Obit.   Screen World 19:232 '68

FLAGG, FANNIE
   Grandma Fannie turned out to be a cow.   TV Guide 21-22:19 Je
   2 '73

FLAHERTY, PAT J. Sr.
   Obit.   Screen World 22:236 '71

FLANAGAN, BUD
   Obit.   N. Y. Times p47 O 21 '68

FLANDERS, ED
   Gent, G.   'Ages' to cheers in O'Neill play.   N. Y. Times Bio
   Ed p42 Ja '74

FLEETWOOD, SUSAN
   Gow, G.   Shakespeare lib.   Plays & Players 20-9:18 Je '73

FLEMING, ERIC
   Obit.   Screen World 18:234 '67

FLEMING, RHONDA
   Holland, J.   Bing's new leading lady.   Silver S 19-1:42 N '48
   Tildesley, A. L.   If I should marry.   Silver S 21-4:42 F '51

FLETCHER, BRAMWELL
   Stars of tomorrow.   Lions R 1-11/12:no p# Jl/Ag '42

FLETCHER, LOUISE
   Out of the crowd.   TV Guide 7-14:20 Ap 4 '59

FLICK, GINGER
   And the winner is...   TV Guide 19-42:17 O 16 '71

FLINT, HELEN
   Obit.   Screen World 19:232 '68

FLIPPIN, JAY C.
   Obit.   Classic Film Collect 30:extra 4 Spg '71
      Film R p13 '71/72
      N. Y. Times p34 F 5 '71
      Same.   N. Y. Times Bio Ed F 5 '71
      Newsweek 77:74 F 15 '71
      Screen World 23:236 '72
   Glaub, A. M.   Jay C. Flippen.   Films In R 22-7:456 Ag/S '71

FLOOD, ANN
   Condemned to wholesomeness.   TV Guide 11-9:20 Mr 2 '63

FLORELLE
  Nolan, J. E.   Florelle.   Films In R 15-4:247 Ap '64

FLOWERS, BESS
  Rosterman, R.   Letter.   Films In R 13-1:54 Ja '62
  Harris, W. G.   Bess Flowers.   Film Fan Mo 127:21 Ja '72

FLUGRATH, EDNA
  Interview.   Nash 55:451 Je '15
  Spensley, D.   Sketch.   Photop 30:38 Je 26 '26

FLUGRATH, LEONIE
  Interview.   Motion Pic Classic 3:45 S '16

FLYNN, ERROL
  Hart, M. G.   The gentleman from New Guinea.   Silver S 6-3:16
    Ja '36
  King, S.   Story of.   Movie Classic 9:35 Ja '36
  Sherwin, T.   Story of.   Motion Pic 51:34 Mr '36
  Ulman, W. Jr.   His life story.   Movie Classic 10:28 My '36 &
    following issues
  Reid, J.   Sketch.   Motion Pic 52:39 Ag '36
  Decker, M.   Story of.   Motion Pic 52:51 Ja '37
  Darnton, C.   His greatest enemy.   Screen Book 19-4:48 N '37
  Wilson, E.   Projection.   Silver S 8-5:24 Mr '38
  A legend lives on.   Cue 6-29:10 My 14 '38
  Sketch.   Life 4:64 My 23 '38
  Maddox, B.   Is he just plain lucky?   Silver S 9-11:44 S '39
  McFee, F.   Errant knight.   Screen Book 22-3:87 O '39
  Hall, G.   He gives himself a grilling!   Silver S 10-6:36 Ap '40
  Bio Note; filmog.   Movies & People 2:15 '40
  Trotter, M.   Astrological forecast.   Photop 18:31 F '41
  MacDonald, J.   Desperate journey.   Silver S 12-10:46 Ag '42
  Watkins, W.   Flynn without flim flam.   Silver S 13-1:26 N '42
  Trotter, M.   His horoscope.   Photop 22:31 F '43
  Mulvey, K.   Sketch.   Womans Home C 68:49 Ja '44
  Franchey, J.   Victim of rumors.   Silver S 17-12:27 O '47
  Hamilton, S.   His life on Navy Island.   Photop 34:58 D '48
  Wymore, P.   My life with (him).   Silver S 21-9:24 Jl '51
  Kaufman, H.   Is there a new Errol?   Silver S 24-7:38 My '54
  Letters.   Films In R 11-3:182 Mr '60
  Obit.   Screen World 11:219 '60
  Cutts, J.   Requiem for a swashbuckler.   Cinema (BH) 3-5:17
    Sum '67
  Wilkinson, H.   Looking Hollywood way.   Good Old Days 6-6:25
    D '69
  Behlmer, R.   Collaboration may be the answer.   Films In R
    21-3:129 Mr '70
  Cutts, J.   Requiem for a swashbuckler.   Films & Filming 17-1:
    14 O '70
  The love teams.   Screen Greats 1-2:10 Sum '71
  Kobal, J.   Working with Flynn; interview with Vincent Sherman.
    Film 2-9:12 D '73
  Errol Flynn; filmog.   Screen Greats 10:entire issue. n. d.

FLYNN, JOE
   An actor can get too many laughs.   TV Guide 11-32:27 Ag 10
      '63
   The second banana who knows his place.   TV Guide 13-5:26 Ja
      30 '65

FLYNN, SEAN
   Bad trip.   Newsweek 75:101 Ap 20 '70
   Missing in Cambodia.   Time 95:43 Ap 20 '70
   Young, P. D.   Two of the missing.   Harper 245:84 D '72
   Filmog.   Films & Filming 20-8:61 My '74

FO, FARIA
   Italian incendiary.   Time 93:72 Mr 21 '69

FOCH, NINA
   Minoff, P.   Elementary for Nina.   Cue 20-17:11 Ap 28 '51

FONDA, HENRY
   Chrisman, J. E.   Sketch.   Movie Classic 8:40 Ag '35
   Zeitlin, I.   His story.   Motion Pic 50:42 O '35
   Samuels, L.   They ought to shoot actors who mug.   Silver S 6-
      5:26 Mr '36
   Stevens, G.   Interview.   Photop 49:36 My '36
   McHenry, M.   His love tangle.   Movie Classic 10:36 Je '36
   Liza.   The eligible heart-breakers.   Silver S 6-9:51 Jl '36
   Zeitlin, I.   His love story.   Motion Pic 52:33 Ja '37
   Morrison, D.   His love story.   Movie Classic 11:48 Ja '37
   Jacobs, M.   Snobs beware!   Screen Book 21-11:54 Je '39
   Morse, W. Jr.   Story of.   Photop 54:26 N '40 & following is-
      sue.
   Bio note; filmog.   Movies & People 2:15 '40
   Frenchey, J. R.   Close-up of a hermit.   Silver S 11-8:34 Je '41
   Hopper, H.   Sketch.   Photop 19:37 S '41
   Marsh, P.   Henry, homelife and Hank.   Silver S 17-12:46 O '47
   My current reading.   Sat R 31:29 Jl 31 '48
   Hall, G.   How happy can you get?   Silver S 18-11:28 S '48
   Keating, J.   Mariner on a marathon.   Cue 19-36:14 S 9 '50
   Medallion theater.   TV Guide 1-23:14 S 4 '53
   Failure makes good.   TV Guide 4-38:25 S 22 '56
   Reflections on forty years of make believe; interview.   Cinema
      (BH) 3-4:11 D '66
   In the words of Henry Fonda.   Cue 38-51:12 D 20 '69
   Raddatz, L.   He never made it as a journalist.   TV Guide 18-2:
      30 Ja 10 '70
   Cronin, M.   Quiet evening with the family; Interview.   Time 95:
      61 F 16 '70
   Flying Fondas and how they grew.   Time 95:58 F 16 '70
   Logan, J.   Fonda memories.   Show 1-4:6 Ap '70
   Innocent revisited.   Time 95:54 Je 29 '70
   Still going great.   Screen Greats 1-2:78 Sum '71
   Cooking with a star.   Mod Screen 67-1:20 Ja '72
   Ostroff, R.   Interview.   Take One 3-10:14 Mr/Ap '72

An evening with Henry Fonda.   AFI Report p10 #1 '72
Nogueira, R.   Fonda on Ford.   Sight & Sound 42-2:85 Spg '73
Fonda seminar; filmog; stage appearances; TV appearances; bib-
   liography.   Dialogue 3-2:entire issue N '73
Gussow, M.   Still excited by the theater.   N. Y. Times Bio Ed
   p343 Mr '74
Hogan, W.   The Fonda kind of magic; filmog.   Nostalgia Illus
   1-1:64 N '74

FONDA, JANE
   Zunser, J.   Hank's little girl.   Cue 33-9:12 F 29 '64
   Bennett, J.   Hollywood's apples fall close to the tree.   Sound
      Stage 1-3:4 My '65
   The French Fonda (pictures).   Playboy 13-8:66 Ag '66
   Thompson, T.   Up and away with Jane.   Life 64:66 Mr 29 '68
   Ehrlich, H.   Shining in two roles.   Look 33:70 My 13 '69
   Lear, M. W.   Whatever happened to Mr. Fonda's baby Jane?
      Redbook 133:66 Ag '69
   Burke, T.   Conversation with Jane.   Holiday 46:44 S '69
   Cronin, M.   Interview.   Time 95:61 F 16 '70
   Flying Fondas and how they grew.   Time 95:58 F 16 '70
   Bosworth, P.   Astonish me!   McCalls 97:14 Ap '70
   The night (her) husband flew off with another woman.   Photop
      77-5:38 My '70
   Eyles, A.   Bio note; filmog.   Focus On F 3:5 My/Ag '70
   Two young successes: Liza Minelli and Jane Fonda.   Vogue 155:
      106 Je '70
   Lerman, L.   Interview.   Mlle 71:329 Ag '70
   Amory, C.   Trade winds.   Sat R 52:14 O 10 '70
   Cause celeb.   Newsweek 76:65 N 16 '70
   Knight, A. & Alpert, H.   Sex stars of 1970.   Playboy 17-12:220
      D '70
   Fallaci, O.   I'm coming into focus; interview.   McCalls 98:123
      F '71
   Left face.   New Rep 164:9 Mr 13 '71
   Jane Fonda takes on the world.   Show 2-1:44 Mr '71
   Frook, J.   Nonstop activist.   Life 70:51 Ap 23 '71
   Nothing plain about Jane.   Photop 79-5:74 My '71
   Ace, G.   You Jane, me fellow.   Sat R 54:5 Je 5 '71
   Roman, M.   Whatever happened to Baby Jane?   Sr Schol 99:36
      N 29 '71
   The new Jane Fonda.   Mod Screen 65-12:39 D '71
   Typhoon Jane.   Time 99:71 Ja 3 '72
   Hollywood's hot new sex queens.   Mod Screen 66-1:34 Ja '72
   Alan Pakula, Jane Fonda, Klute.   Films Illus 1-8:4 F '72
   Second generation.   Films Illus 1-10:12 Ap '72
   Hollywood's happiest hooker.   Mod Screen 66-7:57 Jl '72
   Filmog.   Films & Filming 18-10:64 Jl '72
   Buckley, W. F. Jr.   Secretary Fonda.   Nat R 24:918 Ag 18 '72
   Miller, E.   Interview.   Seventeen 31:134 S '72
   Show the Pentagon couldn't stop.   Ramparts 11:29 S '72
   Peary, G.   Fonda on tour.   Take One 4-4:24 Mr/Ap '73
   Tuska, J.   A note on Jane Fonda.   Views & Rs 4-4:3 Sum '73

Athas, D.   How Jane continues her search since the roles don't fit; poem.   After Dark 6-4:54 Ag '73
Choate, G.   People you should forget.   Viva 1-1:110 O '73
Kasindorf, M.   Fonda; a person of many parts.   N. Y. Times Mag p16 F 3 '74
    Same.   N. Y. Times Bio Ed p197 F '74
Interview.   Playboy 21-4:67 Ap '74
Hochman, S.   Interview.   Changes 90:15 N '74

FONDA, PETER
    Rising stars.   Film R p51 '64/65
    Reed, R.   Holden Caulfield at 27.   Esquire 69:70 F '68
    Ewing, I. & Reif, T.   Interview.   Take One 2-3:6 Ja/F '69
    Space odyssey 1969.   Time 94:73 Jl 25 '69
    Not so easy riders.   Vogue 154:129 Ag 1 '69
    Fonda, P.   Thoughts and attitudes about Easy rider.   Film 56: 24 Aut '69
    Cronin, M.   Quiet evening with the family; interview.   Time 95:61 F 16 '70
    Flying Fondas and how they grew.   Time 95:58 F 16 '70
    Interview.   Playboy 17-9:85 S '70
    Knight, A. & Alpert, H.   Sex stars of 1970.   Playboy 17-12:220 D '70
    Man and the sea.   Vogue 158:43 Ag 1 '71
    Castell, D.   Fonda the third.   Films Illus 1-6:36 D '71
    Interview.   Mod Screen 66-10:37 O '72
    Shevey, S.   Interview.   Playgirl 1-10:57 Mr '74
    Lorber, R.   Interview.   Interview 1-1:22 n. d.

FONG, BENSON
    Raddatz, L.   No. 1 son is now Master Po.   TV Guide 21-25:27 Je 23 '73

FONTAINE, JOAN
    Schwarzkopf, J.   Sketch.   Motion Pic 53:13 Jl '37
    Craig, C.   Interview.   Motion Pic 54:43 Ag '37
    Lynn, J.   Sunshine and showers.   Screen Book 19-4:76 N '37
    Ruddy, J. M.   Fontaine the youthful.   Screen Book 19-4:94 N '37
    Hamilton, S.   Sketch.   Photop 52:68 Ja '38
    Her wedding.   Life 7:78 S 11 '39
    Service, F.   Strange past.   Silver S 10-2:38 D '39
    Sketch.   Time 35:96 Ap 15 '40
    Waterbury, R.   Story of.   Photop 21:34 Je '42 and following issue.
    Wilkinson, L. A.   Story of.   Cosmop 113:8 N '42
    A mistake I wouldn't make again.   Photop 22:46 My '43
    Mabon, M. F.   Story of.   Harp Baz 78:92 Ap '44
    Notes about.   Photop 26:62 F '45
    Palmer, C.   Alone and happy!   Silver S 15-5:24 Mr '45
    Maughan, R.   Putting men under a microscope.   Silver S 15-9: 38 Jl '45
    Holland, J.   I can't be hurt anymore.   Silver S 16-4:38 F '46

Should a woman tell her age.   Photop 28:53 Ap '46
Hall, G.   Longer than forever.   Silver S 16-11:30 S '46
Parsons, L. O.   Cosmop's citation for the best performance of
   the month.   Cosmop 123:54 Ag '47
Gwynn, E.   Gives a dinner party.   Photop 31:56 S '47
Her home.   Photop 32:62 Ja '48
Hall, G.   Are you a "now" person.   Silver S 18-5:24 Mr '48
Holliday, K.   The delicate Joan Fontaine?   Silver S 19-7:36 My
   '49
Graham, S.   Story of.   Photop 36:38 Ag '49
Maxwell, E.   Sketch.   Photop 36:34 D '49
Hall, G.   Parisian escapades of Joan.   Silver S 22-4:22 F '52
Gibson, M.   A cautious gambler on Broadway.   Cue 23-35:14 Ag
   28 '54
Her Paris outfits.   TV Guide 4-42:24 O 20 '56
Here's to the ladies.   Screen Greats 1-2:32 Sum '71
Bourget, J-L.   The coming of age of Joan Fontaine.   Film Com
   10-1:47 Ja/ F '74

FORAN, DICK
   Sketch.   Photop 46:79 Ag '34
   Sketch.   Photop 51:82 F '37
   Hamilton, S.   Sketch.   Photop 54:46 D '40

FORBES, RALPH
   Millet, J.   Interview.   Photop 31:81 D '26
   Dickey, J.   Sketch.   Motion Pic Classic 26:40 F '28
   Goldbeck, E.   Interview.   Motion Pic Classic 31:30 Mr '30
   Cruikshank, H.   Sketch.   Motion Pic Classic 32:41 Ja '31
   Hall, G.   Interview.   Motion Pic 41:50 My '31
   Busby, M.   A gentleman of contrasts.   Silver S 1-7:38 My '31
   Burden, J.   Sketch.   Movie Classic 2:34 My '32
   Grant, J.   His divorce.   Movie Classic 4:26 Mr '33
   Standish, J.   His marriage.   Movie Classic 7:40 N '34
   Obit.   Screen World 3:177 '53

FORBES, SCOTT
   The wild frontiersman.   TV Guide 5-10:12 Mr 9 '57

FORD, FRANCIS
   How he became a photoplayer.   Motion Pic 9:112 F '15
   Willis, R.   Interview.   Motion Pic 9:101 Je '15
   Obit.   N. Y. Times p19 S 7 '53
   Everett, E. K.   The great Cunard-Ford mystery.   Classic Film
      Collect 39:22 Sum '73

FORD, GLENN
   Smith, F. J.   Miracle boy.   Silver S 11-7:44 My '41
   Haas, D. B.   Change for the better.   Silver S 16-2:42 D '45
   Should teenagers marry?   Photop 30:67 D '46
   A letter from Glenn to his son.   Silver S 17-6:35 Ap '47
   Holland, J.   He drives his wife crazy.   Silver S 21-5:42 Mr '51
   Ford, G.   Why not listen to your parents?   Silver S 22-4:24 F

'52
MacDonald, E.  Glenn shares a secret.  Silver S 22-9:48 Jl '52
Bruce, J.  The truth about the Fords.  Silver S 23-4:36 F '53
Holland, J.  If you were Glenn's guest.  Silver S 24-7:42 My '54
Star gardener.  Am Home 73:24 Ap '70
His son gets married.  Photop 79-3:48 Mr '71
His house is full of memories.  Photop 80-4:60 O '71
Could you make this man marry again?  Silver S 41-10:46 O '71
A man who is afraid of love is a fool.  Mod Screen 66-2:35 F
   '72
His sensuous secrets.  Photop 81-2:72 F '72
Cooking with a star.  Mod Screen 66-3:54 Mr '72
Diehl, D.  The western today.  TV Guide 20-14:20 Ap 1 '72
He brings Hope Lange home to meet the family.  Mod Screen
   66-4:55 Ap '72
Photoplay forum.  Photop 81-4:28 Ap '72
His fight against blindness.  Photop 81-5:76 My '72
How I let the one I love get away.  Photop 82-1:72 Jl '72
His real romance.  Photop 82-3:42 S '72
Dad's better off being a bachelor.  Mod Screen 66-10:29 O '72
The best Christmas of my life.  Photop 83-1:27 Ja '73

FORD, HARRISON
Sketch.  Motion Pic Classic 7:27 D '18
Cheatham, M. S.  Interview.  Motion Pic 19:68 Mr '20
Bruce, B.  Interview.  Motion Pic 21:48 My '21
Montanye, L.  Interview.  Motion Pic Classic 13:43 F '22
Gassaway, G.  Interview.  Motion Pic 24:56 N '22
Redway, S.  Interview.  Motion Pic Classic 22:60 O '25
West, M.  Sketch.  Photop 29:54 My '26

FORD, JAMES
Belfrage, C.  Interview.  Motion Pic 36:71 Ja '29

FORD, RUTH
Colaciello, R.  Interview.  Interview 2-5:4 n. d.
Rader, D.  I'd never settle for anything dull.  After Dark 6-11:
   40 Mr '74

FORD, VICTORIA
Sketch.  Motion Pic 9:94 Jl '15
Wallace, R.  Sketch.  Motion Pic Classic 3:22 N '16
Sketch.  Photop 39:36 F '31

FORD, VIRGINIA ANN
Debut.  Show 1-7:56 Je 25 '70

FORD, WALLACE
Hall, G.  Sketch.  Motion Pic 43:88 Mr '32
Sketch.  Photop 41:60 Ap '32
Pedelty, D.  Success chains the wanderer.  Silver S 2-8:23 Je
   '32
Whorf, R.  As I see them.  Lions R 3-2:no p# Ja '44
Obit.  Film R p21 '66/68

FOREST, FRANK
  Housel, S.  Sketch.  Movie Classic 11:24 O '36
  Opera under canvas.  Time 74:51 Ag 10 '59

FORMAN, FAN
  Courtlandt, R.  Sketch.  Motion Pic 11:69 Jl '16

FORMAN, TOM
  Sketch.  Motion Pic 10:113 D '15
  McGaffey, K.  Return to motion pictures.  Motion Pic 17:36 Je
    '19
  Boone, A.  Rich men, poor men and actors.  Photop 16-5:36 O
    '19
  Shelley, H.  Rise of.  Motion Pic Classic 11:32 N '20
  Boone, A.  Interview.  Photop 19:55 Ja '21
  Underhill, H.  Interview.  Motion Pic 21:72 F '21

FORQUET, PHILIPPE
  Rising stars.  Film R p59 '64/65

FORREST, ALLAN
  Delvigne, D.  Interview.  Motion Pic 19:46 Mr '20

FORREST, ANN
  Remont, F.  Interview.  Motion Pic Classic 11:34 S '20
  Cheatham, M.  Interview.  Motion Pic 20:62 N '20
  Naylor, H. S.  Interview.  Motion Pic 22:44 O '21
  My homecoming.  Motion Pic Classic 14:60 Je '22
  Fredericks, J.  Interview.  Motion Pic 24:40 N '22

FORREST, FREDERIC
  Stoop, N. M.  Twenty-eight is a magic number.  After Dark
    5-6:24 O '72
  Burke, T.  How long must a pizza waiter wait?  Very long.
    N. Y. Times sec 2:13 Mr 25 '73
    Same.  N. Y. Times Bio Ed p407 Mr '73

FORREST, MABEL
  LeBerthon, T.  Interview.  Motion Pic 25:25 Ja '24

FORREST, SALLY
  Parsons, L. O.  Cosmop's citation for the best performance by
    a newcomer.  Cosmop 127:13 S '49
  Rowland, R. C.  It takes more than talent.  Silver S 22-2:38 D
    '51

FORREST, STEVE
  They make ladies' hearts go pitty pat.  TV Guide 5-28:8 Jl 13
    '57
  Favorite animal story.  Mod Screen 66-11:34 N '72

FORSTER, ROBERT
  Klemesrud, J.  How to succeed in flops.  N. Y. Times Bio Ed

Je 4 '72
Secret man.  Photop 83-1:54 Ja '73

FORSYTH, ROSEMARY
  Girl with a goal.  Show 2-8:76 Ag '62
  I paid $20,000 to share his bed.  Photop 77-6:38 Je '70
  Whitney, D.  David likes the tailored look.  TV Guide 19-35:28
    Ag 28 '71
  Cooking with a star.  Mod Screen 65-11:51 N '71
  A love that was too good to last?  Mod Screen 65-12:36 D '71
  Forsyth, R.  After our 3-year love affair... how I learned to live
    again.  Photop 81-1:42 Ja '72

FORSYTHE, JOHN
  Whitney, D.  Just slightly rhomboid.  TV Guide 18-25:24 Je 20
    '70

FORTE, FABIAN
  (See:  FABIAN)

FORTH, JANE
  Robin, S.  A woman's face.  After Dark 11-12:56 Ap '70
  Just plain Jane.  Life 69:54 Jl 4 '70

FOSS, DARRELL
  Delvigne, D.  Interview.  Motion Pic 19:66 Mr '20

FOSTER, BUDDY
  Hano, A.  He is too tired to come out and play.  TV Guide 18-
    30:15 Jl 25 '70

FOSTER, GLORIA
  Robinson, L.  Star couple.  Ebony 25:142 Mr '70

FOSTER, HELEN
  Uselton, R. A.  The Wampus baby stars.  Films In R 21-2:73
    F '70

FOSTER, JODIE
  Galanoy, T.  Raising kid stars for fun and profit.  TV Guide 22-
    46:27 N 16 '74

FOSTER, JULIA
  Tierney, M.  Interview.  Plays & Players 17-10:22 Jl '70

FOSTER, NORMAN
  Service, F.  His separation marriage.  Motion Pic 44:47 Ag '32
  Ludlam, H.  As a grid star, makes good.  Silver S 6-1:32 N
    '35

FOSTER, PRESTON
  Nominated for stardom.  Motion Pic 44:42 Ja '33
  Proctor, K.  Interview.  Motion Pic 53:38 Jl '37

Bio note; filmog.   Movies & People 2:15 '40
Haas, D. B.   Perennial Preston.   Silver S 13-10:44 Ag '43
Obit.   Classic Film Collect 28:ex p3 Fall '70
    Film R p13 '71/72
    N. Y. Times p39 Jl 15 '70
    Same.   N. Y. Times Bio Ed Jl 15 '70
    Newsweek 76:79 Jl 27 '70
    Screen World 22:236 '71

FOSTER, SUSANNA
    My teenage mistake.   Photop 25:59 Jl '44
    Watkins, W.   Stardom hasn't changed her.   Silver S 14-12:30 O
      '44

FOULGER, BYRON
    Obit.   Film R p15 '70/71

FOX, EDWARD
    Sketch.   Films Illus 2-17:6 N '72

FOX, FRANKLYN
    Obit.   N. Y. Times p86 N 5 '67

FOX, HARRY
    Obit.   Screen World 11:219 '60

FOX, LUCY
    Montanye, L.   Interview.   Motion Pic Classic 12:54 My '21

FOX, SIDNEY
    Goldbeck, E.   Interview.   Motion Pic 42:70 Ag '31
    Sketch.   Photop 41:60 Ap '32
    How Sylvia brightened her life.   Photop 44:52 Ag '33
    Uselton, R. A.   The Wampus baby stars.   Films In R 21-2:73
      F '70
    Schuster, M.   Sidney Fox; filmog.   Film Fan Mo 121/122:9 Jl/
      Ag '71

FOX, VIRGINIA
    Goldbeck, W.   Interview.   Motion Pic Classic 12:42 Mr '21
    Cheatham, M.   Interview.   Motion Pic Classic 13:37 Ja '22

FOXE, CYRINDA
    Calendo, J.   Interview.   Interview 28:10 D '72

FOXE, EARLE
    How he got in moving pictures.   Motion Pic 14:38 Ag '17
    Seitz, C. W.   Sketch.   Motion Pic 14:103 S '17
    Cruikshank, H.   Interview.   Motion Pic Classic 28:63 O '28

FOXX, REDD
    Robinson, L.   Prince of clowns.   Ebony 22:91 Ap '67
    Feather, L.   Interview.   Penthouse 2-7:60 Mr '71

Gardner, P.   The quick Redd Foxx jumps into a new kettle of
   fish.   N. Y. Times Bio Ed F 6 '72
All in the black family.   Time 99:74 Ap 17 '72
Adler, D.   Look what they found in a junkyard.   TV Guide 20-20:
   28 My 13 '72
Robinson, L.   Sanford and son.   Ebony 27:52 Jl '72
Davidson, B.   The world's funniest dishwasher is still cleaning
   up.   TV Guide 21-11:26 Mr 17 '73
The waiting game is no game at all.   People 1-14:14 Je 3 '74

FRANCEN, VICTOR
   Victor Francen.   Visages 34:entire issue My '39

FRANCHI, SERGIO
   He's only a part-time panther.   TV Guide 12-36:26 S 5 '64
   Flagg, T.   Opera singer, pop singer, movie actor and painter.
      After Dark 11-8:16 D '69

FRANCIOSA, TONY
   Hyams, J.   Tough new star.   Cue 26-26:12 Je 29 '57
   Loving one woman is the toughest game in town.   Photop 77-6:50
      Je '70

FRANCIS, ALEC B.
   Henderson, F.   His foot on the soft pedal.   Photop 16-4:59 S '19
   Peltret, E.   Interview.   Motion Pic Classic 10:32 Je '20
   Cheatham, M.   Interview.   Motion Pic Classic 14:20 Jl '22
   Sheldon, J.   Interview.   Motion Pic 31:54 F '26
   Denbo, D.   Sketch.   Motion Pic Classic 24:62 D '26
   Benton, H.   Reminiscences.   Photop 43:71 Mr '33

FRANCIS, ANNE
   Rising star.   Film R p105 '52/53
   Francis, A.   How modern should a young wife be?   Silver S 23-
      2:33 D '52
   The stars of tomorrow.   Film R p43 '55/56
   Parillo, B.   Letter; filmog.   Films In R 24-2:125 F '73
   Michaels, G.   Partial filmog.   Films In R 25-4:256 Ap '74

FRANCIS, ARLENE
   For the girls at home.   Newsweek 43:92 Mr 15 '54
   Minoff, P.   At home with Arlene.   Cue 23-16:14 Ap 17 '54
   TV's busiest woman.   Look 18:52 My 4 '54
   This is our line.   Theatre Arts 38:92 My '54
   What's her line?   TV Guide 2-28:4 Jl 9 '54
   The queen of television.   Newsweek 44:50 Jl 19 '54
   Terzian, S.   Reply, with rejoinder.   Newsweek 44:3 Ag 9 '54
   Tunley, R.   You don't have to be beautiful.   Am Mag 158:114
      O '54
   Our cover picture.   Ind Woman 34:81 Mr '55
   Whitcomb, J.   Arlene Francis.   Cosmop 138:76 Ap '55
   Conniff, J. C. G.   The lady is a wit.   Coronet 39:53 F '56
   Bester, A.   At home with Arlene.   Holiday 20:79 O '56

No place for home.  Newsweek 49:98 Je 10 '57
Minoff, P.  Non-stop Arlene.  Cue 26-32:11 Ag 10 '57
Perils of Arlene.  Time 70:81 S 9 '57
Scott, J. A.  How to be a success in show business.  Cosmop
  145:70 N '58
Francis, A.  Just be yourself.  TV Guide 8-36:5 S 3 '60
Redbook dialogue.  Redbook 118:50 Mr '62
Gehman, R.  The amazing Armenian.  TV Guide 10-25:19 Je 23;
  10-26:25 Je 30 '62
Private agonies of being in the public eye.  McCalls 89:61 Ag
  '62
Efron, E.  She dazzles you with footwork.  TV Guide 14-25:22
  Je 18 '66
Memorable minutes on What's my line?  McCalls 96:88 Mr '69

FRANCIS, CONNIE
  Career vs. college.  TV Guide 7-27:28 Jl 4 '59

FRANCIS, KAY
  Goldbeck, E.  Sketch.  Motion Pic 38:66 Ag '29
  Walker, H. L.  Sketch.  Motion Pic 40:42 S '30
  Walker, H. L.  How men annoy us.  Motion Pic 40:71 D '30
  Sketch.  Photop 39:12 D '30
  Rush, D.  The aristocrat of the screen.  Silver S 2-4:41 F '32
  Service, F.  Interview.  Motion Pic 44:50 N '32
  Roberts, K.  Sketch.  Photop 43:34 D '32
  Moffitt, C. F.  Censorship for interviews Hollywood's latest wild
    idea...  Cinema Dig 2-5:9 Ja 9 '33
  Lynn, H.  How she makes love.  Photop 44:103 Ag '33
  Hall, G.  Interview.  Motion Pic 46:31 Ag '33
  Keats, P.  (She) 'as 'eard the East a'callin'.  Silver S 4-3:49
    Ja '34
  Fidler, J.  Spiking the rumors.  Silver S 4-10:29 Ag '34
  Rankin, R.  O-Kay Francis!  Silver S 6-3:17 Ja '36
  Grant, J.  Interview.  Movie Classic 10:32 S '36
  Cheatham, M.  Interview.  Motion Pic 53:59 Mr '37
  Lane, J.  Plenty has happened to (her).  Screen Book 19-1:56
    Ag '37
  Magee, T.  (She) signs a lifetime contract.  Screen Book 20-6:
    24 Jl '38
  Bio note; filmog.  Movies & People 2:16 '40
  Mook, D.  She wanted to be forgotten.  Silver S 11-6:46 Ap '41
  O-Kay for sound.  Lions R 1-2:no p# O '41
  Obit.  Classic Film Collect 22:51 Fall/Win '68
    Film R p19 '69/70
    N. Y. Times p41 Ag 27 '68
    Newsweek 72:103 S 9 '68
    Time 92:68 S 6 '68
  Kay Francis: 1903-1968.  Film Fan Mo 88:22 O '68
  Parish, J. R.  But did (she) have a 5th husband?  Classic Film
    Collect 22:51 Fall/Win '68
  Pin-ups of the past.  Films & Filming 17-1:78 O '70

FRANCISCO, BETTY
  Goldbeck, W.  Interview.  Motion Pic Classic 13:44 D '21
  Obit.  Screen World 2:234 '51
  Uselton, R. A.  The Wampus baby stars.  Films In R 21-2:73 F '70

FRANCISCUS, JAMES
  Raddatz, L.  Bringing Mr. Novak up to date.  TV Guide 19-43:34
    O 23 '71
  Barber, R.  Man for all seasons.  TV Guide 22-12:20 Mr 23 '74

FRANCKS, DON
  The man in the orange harris tweed.  TV Guide 14-50:30 D 10 '66

FRANKEN, STEPHEN
  Well-heeled heel.  TV Guide 10-31:27 Ag 4 '62

FRANKLIN, JUDY
  And the winner is...  TV Guide 19-42:17 O 16 '71

FRANKLIN, PAMELA
  Miller, E.  On my own at last!  Seventeen 28:96 Ja '69
  Clein, H.  An innocent who took to the skies.  After Dark 5-4:52 Ag
    '72

FRANQUELLI, FELY
  Meet the cover(all) girls.  Lions R 3-2:no p# Ja '44

FRASCA, MARY
  (Also known as La Sorrentina)
  Obit.  Screen World p234 '74

FRASER, ELISABETH
  Sgt. Hogan is a blonde.  TV Guide 4-20:13 My 19 '56

FRASER, JOHN
  Person of promise.  Films & Filming 2-6:12 Mr '56
  How to get into films by the people who got in themselves.  Films &
    Filming 9-10:11 Jl '63

FRASER, ROBERT
  Rising star.  Film R p42 '63/64

FRAZEE, JANE
  Franchey, J. R.  The melodious Miss from Duluth.  Silver S 13-6:
    48 Ap '43 .
  McClelland, D.  Queen of B musicals; filmog.  Film Fan Mo 113:3
    N '70

FRAZER, ROBERT
  Sketch.  Photop 26:55 S '24
  Tully, J.  Sketch.  Motion Pic Classic 21:36 Ap '25

FRAZIER, JAMEL
   Whatever happened to Buckwheat?   Ebony 27:170 My '72

FRAZIER, SHEILA
   The super cops.   Photop 84-6:41 D '73

FRECHETTE, MARK
   Sullivan, A.  Interview.  Interview 1-1:8 n. d.

FREDERICK, LYNNE
   New faces.  Films Illus 1-7:11 Ja '72
   Note; filmog.  Films Illus 4-39:84 N '74

FREDERICK, PAULINE
   From the chorus to legitimate dramatic star.   Theatre 17:172 Je
      '13
   Interview.  Cosmop 58:95 D '14
   Sketch.  Nat Mag 41:705 Ja '15
   Why I forsook the stage.  Theatre 22:241 N '15
   May, L.  Interview.  Motion Pic Classic 2:27 Je '16
   How to get in moving pictures.  Motion Pic Classic 3:39 O '16
   Lee, C.  Interview.  Motion Pic Classic 3:22 Ja '17
   Seitz, C. W.  Sketch.  Motion Pic Classic 5:37 S '17
   Gregory, N. D.  Sketch.  Motion Pic Classic 5:26 N '17
   Autobiographical.  Motion Pic 16:63 D '18
   Home of.  Photop 29:52 S '21
   Bryers, L.  Interview.  Motion Pic 23:46 F '22
   Gassaway, G.  Interview.  Motion Pic Classic 14:18 My '22
   Sketch.  Theatre 37:12 Ap '23
   Wilson, B.  Interview.  Motion Pic Classic 29:40 Mr '29
   Sketch.  Theatre Guild 9:10 Ap '32
   Elwood, M.  Pauline on and off the stage.  Sat R 21:19 F 10 '40

FREDERICKS, CHARLES
   Obit.  Screen World 22:236 '71

FREDERICKS, DEAN
   The cartoon that came to life.  TV Guide 7-1:20 Ja 3 '59

FREEMAN, HOWARD
   Obit.  N. Y. Times p44 D 13 '67

FREEMAN, JOAN
   She plays the slentem.  TV Guide 9-39:29 S 30 '61

FREEMAN, KATHLEEN
   Clein, H.  The real people.  Show 1-8:14 Jl 9 '70

FREEMAN, MONA
   Freeman, M.  Alan's no mystery man.  Silver S 21-4:26 F '51
   Reid, L.  Mixed up Mona.  Silver S 24-2:32 D '53

FRENCH, VALERIE
   Rising star.  Film R p36 '56/57
   Miss French, your freckles are showing.   TV Guide 6-39:28 S
      27 '58

FRESNAY, PIERRE
   Pierre Fresnay.  Visages 36:entire issue Jl '39
   Bio note.  Unifrance 10:12 Je '51

FREY, LEONARD
   Zadan, C.  Just one of the boys.  After Dark 11-10:22 F '70
   Frey, L.  A view of us.  Motion p29 S/O '73

FREY, NATHANIEL
   Obit.  N. Y. Times p44 N 9 '70
      Same.  N. Y. Times Bio Ed N 9 '70

FRIC, MARTIN
   Dewey, L.  Czechoslovakia; silence into sound.  Film 60:5 n. d.

FRID, JONATHAN
   Turned-on vampire.  Newsweek 75:102 Ap 20 '70

FRIGANZA, TRIXIE
   Obit.  Screen World 7:223 '56
      Time 65:92 Mr 14 '55

FRISCO, JOE
   Hayes, P. L.  M-m-m-meet J-J-J-Joe F-F-F-Frisco.  Colliers
      128:20 D 1 '51
   Obit.  Screen World 10:222 '59

FRITSCH, WILLY
   Obit.  Films & Filming 20-2:80 N '73
   Passalacqua, J.  Willy Fritsch; filmog.  Films In R 25-3:187
      Mr '74

FRYE, DAVID
   Bonquartz, R.  Deformita perfetta of Richard Nixon, Lyndon
      Johnson and other heroes.  Esquire 75:70 F '71

FRYE, DWIGHT
   Mank, G. W.  Dwight Frye; filmog.  Films In R 24-10:638 D
      '73
   Coughlin, J. T.  Dwight Frye; filmog.  Film Fan Mo 154:3 Ap
      '74

FUCCELLO, TOM
   Calendo, J.  Interview.  Interview 28:37 D '72

FULLER, DALE
   Shallert, E.  Interview.  Motion Pic 24:52 N '22

FULLER, MARY
  Gates, H. H. Interview. N. Y. Drama 69:29 F 26 '13
  Katterjohn, M. M. Interview. Green Book 10:321 Ag '13
  My ambition. Blue Book 19:919 S '14
  Advice to movie-struck girls. Green Book 12:785 N '14
  Popularity of. Green Book 13:30 Ja '15
  Interview. Cosmop 56:413 F '15
  Anecdote. Motion Pic 9:98 F '15
  Morals behind the screen and curtain. Motion Pic 9:85 F '15
  Autobiographical. Green Book 13:650 Ap '15
  Interview. Cosmop 58:678 My '15
  Sketch. Motion Pic 9:118 My '15
  Meriden, O. Interview. Theatre 22:185 O '15
  Keynote of smart dressing. Green Book 14:737 O '15
  Van Loan, H. H. Interview. Motion Pic 11:77 Ap '16
  Hornblow, A. How she got into motion pictures. Motion Pic
    Classic 2:23 My '16
  How to get into motion pictures. Motion Pic 12:62 N '16
  Van Loan, H. H. Sketch. Motion Pic 13:112 Ap '17
  Smith, F. J. Interview. Photop 26:58 Ag '24

FULLER, NANCY BELLE
  McCaughna, D. A terribly personal business. Motion p16 Jl/
    Ag '74

FULLER, ROBERT
  He's hot in Japan. TV Guide 9-36:6 S 9 '61
  Raddatz, L. The gentle brawler. TV Guide 11-49:19 D 7 '63
  Whitney, D. Anybody want to buy a pair of boots? TV Guide
    21-33:24 Ag 18 '73

FULLERTON, FIONA
  Meet Alice. Films Illus 2-14:6 Ag '72
  Miller, E. Interview. Seventeen 31:52 O '72

FULTON, EILEEN
  Efron, E. Love those poison-pen letters. TV Guide 13-34:22
    Ag 21 '65

FUNICELLO, ANNETTE
  Fair weather ahead. TV Guide 6-21:28 My 24 '58
  So long, Mickey. TV Guide 7-8:17 F 21 '59
  She's the idol of little boys--and big ones too. TV Guide 11-41:
    12 O 12 '63
  Interview. Look 35:71 S 7 '71
  My child. Photop 86-1:6 Jl '74

FURNESS, BETTY
  Cohen, H. Praising players of minor importance. Cin Dig 3-6:
    12 Ap 24 '33
  Her requirements for romance. Movie Classic 10:44 S '36
  Morehead, A. America's top saleswoman. Cosmop 134:135 F
    '53

Dalmas, H.   No. 1 saleswoman.   Coronet 34:36 O '53
Harris, E.   I had to start over.   Womans Home C 81:38 Je '54
Ramsey, B. J.   Quick-change artist.   Good House 150:36 Je '60
Abrams, M.   Letter; filmog.   Films In R 18-9:581 N '67
Newsmakers.   Newsweek 78:44 Jl 26 '71
People.   Time 98:34 Jl 26 '71
(Citations to Betty Furness' career in Consumer Affairs not
   documented. )

## FYODOROVA, VIKTORIA
Note.   Int F. G.   10:334 '73


## GAAL, FRANCISKA
Holland, J.   Miss Gaal tells all.   Screen Book 21-2:45 S '38

## GABIN, JEAN
Jean Gabin.   Visages 21:entire issue My '38
Sketch.   Harp Baz 75:61 Je '41
Manners, M.   Glamour girls adore him!   Silver S 11-11:22 '41
Sketch.   Newsweek 19:54 My 4 '42
Duvillars, P.   (He) is instinctual man.   Films In R 2-3:28 Mr
   '51
25 years experience, 50 years of age, 50 films.   Unifrance 32:
   17 O/N '54
Delanney, J.   Gabin, the modest man.   Unifrance 49:3 Ja '59
Graham, P.   The face of '63--France.   Films & Filming 9-8:13
   My '63

## GABLE, CLARK
Sketch.   Photop 40:68 Jl '31
Busby, M.   Nothing's been easy for (him).   Silver S 1-9:21 Jl
   '31
Goldbeck, E.   Interview.   Motion Pic 42:51 Ag '31
Calhoun, D.   His marriage.   Movie Classic 1:42 S '31
Calhoun, D.   His fight for fame.   Movie Classic 1:20 D '31
Gallant, T.   His popularity.   Movie Classic 1:26 Ja '32
Cheasley, C. W.   Predictions of success.   Motion Pic 42:42 Ja
   '32
Chrisman, J. E.   Interview.   Motion Pic 43:28 F '32
Henry, D.   Oh Clark, do you remember?   Silver S 2-4:24 F '32
Manners, D.   Hollywood's opinions of him.   Movie Classic 2:16
   Mr '32
Vonnell, C.   Sketch.   Photop 41:30 Ap '32
Rice, L.   His handwriting.   Movie Classic 2:51 Ap '32
Keats, P.   The new Clark Gable in Strange Interlude.   Silver S
   2-7:16 My '32
Collins, F. L.   Sketch.   Good House 94:44 Je '32
Calhoun, D.   Trials of his ex-wife.   Movie Classic 2:24 Je '32
Hall, G.   He denies divorce rumors.   Movie Classic 2:14 Ag
   '32
Moffitt, C. F.   Censorship for interviews Hollywood's latest wild

idea.  Cinema Dig 2-5:9 Ja 9 '33
Hall, G.  His New Year's resolutions.  Movie Classic 3:13 Ja
   '33
Answers questions of fans.  Motion Pic 45:56 Ap '33
Pryor, N.  Interview.  Movie Classic 4:34 My '33
Parsons, H.  Small town habits.  Silver S 3-7:20 My '33
Letters from his former wife.  Motion Pic 44:27 Jl '33
Pryor, N.  How he rates with men.  Movie Classic 4:30 Jl '33
Lynn, H.  How he makes love.  Photop 44:32 Ag '33
Fidler, J. M.  Just to make it tough for the girls.  Silver S 3-
   10:50 Ag '33
Chapman, J. B.  Is the future threatening him?  Motion Pic 46:
   42 O '33
Biery, R.  Loses interest in his career.  Movie Classic 5:34
   Ja '34
Hall, G.  Interview.  Motion Pic 46:42 Ja '34
Hall, G.  Interview.  Motion Pic 47:51 Ap '34
St. Johns, A. R.  In person.  Silver S 4-7:18 My '34
Lee, S.  Appreciation.  Motion Pic 47:31 Jl '34
MacDonald, B.  Is Hollywood killing its leading men?  Silver S
   4-9:30 Jl '34
Mead, E.  Interview.  Movie Classic 6:29 Ag '34
Winner, V.  Silver Screen gold medal for 1934.  Silver S 5-2:
   20 D '34
Lee, S.  Interview.  Movie Classic 7:28 F '34
Calhoun, D.  Interview.  Motion Pic 50:24 O '35
Memories of his boyhood.  St Nich 63:21 N '35
Mook, S. R.  Has he changed?  Movie Classic 9:24 Ja '36
Samuels, L.  Gable returns.  Silver S 6-3:48 Ja '36
Packer, E.  Interview.  Motion Pic 51:32 F '36
Biery, R.  His separation from his wife.  Movie Classic 10:35
   Mr '36
Hall, G.  His opinion of Jean Harlow.  Movie Classic 10:34 My
   '36
Kellum, F.  His plans for the future.  Motion Pic 51:31 My '36
St. Johns, A. R.  Pursuit of the Hollywood he-man.  Photop 49:
   14 Je '36
Clark Gable.  Visages 3:entire issue Jl '36
Lang, H.  His sense of humor.  Motion Pic 52:32 Ag '36
Lee, S.  His re-creation.  Movie Classic 10:36 S '36
Surmelian, L.  Why Gable remains Hollywood's king.  Screen
   Book 20-5:22 Je '38
Wilson, E.  Swell guy.  Silver S 9-4:20 F '39
Marriage to Lombard.  Time 33:52 Ap 10 '39
Home of.  Photop 53:57 Je '39
Reid, J.  Gable debunks stardom.  Screen Book 21-11:48 Je '39
Myrick, S.  Training in southern accent for Gone with the wind.
   Colliers 104:20 D 16 '39
Rhett Butler among the most memorable roles I have played.
   Womans Home C 67:17 Ja '40
Wilson, E.  How to bring out the Gable in any man.  Silver S
   10-4:22 F '40
Bio note; filmog.  Movies & People 2:16 '40

Roughing it is the best fun.   Cosmop 110:21 Mr '41
Gable meets Lana Turner in Honky Tonk.   Lions R 1-2:no p#
    O '41
Gable, C.   Excitement.   Lions R 1-2:no p# O '41
Wilson, E.   What about those Lombard rumors?   Silver S 12-5:
    26 Mr '42
Personal history.   Lions R 2-1:no p# S/O '42
Trotter, M.   Prediction for 1944.   Photop 24:26 Ja '44
Parsons, L. O.   Cosmop's citation for the best performance of
    month.   Cosmop 120:55 Ja '46
The great Gable is back.   Cue 15-6:12 F 9 '46
Third place in Companion poll of favorite stars.   Womans Home
    C 73:8 Je '46
Peters, S.   Story of.   Photop 29:38 Ag '46
Colby, A.   His preferences in feminine beauty.   Photop 30:62
    Mr '47
Dudley, F.   She made Gable change his mind.   Silver S 17-9:62
    Jl '47
Dudley, F.   Clark's still The King.   Silver S 17-10:22 Ag '47
Mann, M.   Gable speaks out.   Silver S 18-12:22 O '48
Stanwyck, B.   The new Gable.   Silver S 19-8:24 Je '49
Parsons, L. O.   Cosmop's citation for best performance of
    month.   Cosmop 127:13 Ag '49
Kielty, B.   Sketch.   Ladies Home J 66:14 O '49
Mann, M.   Catching up with Gable.   Silver S 20-3:30 Ja '50
Balling, F. D.   The King takes a queen.   Silver S 20-6:26 Ap
    '50
Gable shoots two overseas.   Cue 22-13:17 Mr 28 '53
Lee, E.   Why the king still reigns.   Silver S 23-8:35 Je '53
Benedict, P.   Gable's Parisian escapade.   Silver S 24-5:29 Mr
    '54
Zunser, J.   The man, actor, institution.   Cue 27-10:10 Mr 15
    '58
Boase, A.   The passing of the personalities.   Film J (Aus) 18:
    22 O '61
Obit.   Film R p17 '61/62
Astor, M.   What it was like to kiss Gable.   Read Dig 94:49 Je
    '69
Clark Gable; filmog.   Screen Greats 1-2:entire issue Sum '71
The terror that threatens his son.   Mod Screen 66-1:50 Ja '72
Pin-up of the past.   Films & Filming 18-12:62 S '72
Tuska, R.   Notes on the establishment of a star.   Views & Rs
    4-1:46 Fall; 4-2:28 Win '72
Kurlfinke, D.   Women in the life of dear Mr. Gable.   After
    Dark 7-2:30 Je '74

GABOR, EVA
    Taylor, T.   I'm bored with Gabors.   Cue 22-24:10 Je 13 '53
    Bio.   Cur Bio 29:19 Jl '68
        Same.   Cur Bio Yrbk 1968:136 '69
    Opinions on liberation: my man and me.   Photop 78-3:78 S '70
    Filmog.   Films & Filming 20-7:63 Ap '74

GABOR, ZSA ZSA
  Rowland, R. C.   It's easy to entice.   Silver S 22-6:42 Ap '52
  Hall, G.   Never turn off the heat.   Silver S 23-7:32 My '53
  Taylor, T.   I'm bored with the Gabors.   Cue 22-24:10 Je 13
    '53
  Portrait, E.   The world of beauty welcomes Hollywood's beauti-
    ful women.   Cue 38-46:11 N 15 '69
  Salute of the week.   Cue 39-27:1 Jl 4 '70
  Photoplay forum.   Photop 81-5:7 My '72
  Guerin, A.   George and Zsa Zsa.   Show 2-5:38 Jl '72
  Guerin, A.   A forty carat smash on Broadway.   Show 1-11:32
    Ag 20 '70
  Calendo, J.   The Zsa Zsa story.   Interview 24:18 Ag '72
  Goodbye my love.   Photop 82-2:40 Ag '72
  Filmog.   Films & Filming 20-7:63 Ap '74

GAGE, BEN
  Fink, H.   His honeymoon in Mexico.   Photop 28:42 Mr '46

GAGE, PATRICIA
  McLarty, J.   Patricia Gage.   Motion p14 Mr/Je '74
  Keil, M.   On acting.   Motion p35 S/O '74

GAINES, RICHARD
  Success story.   Cue 11-5:1 Ja 31 '42

GALE, JEAN
  Uselton, R. A.   The Wampus baby stars.   Films In R 21-2:73
    F '70

GALAJEV, PETER
  Interview.   Film J 1-3/4:17 Fall/Win '72

GALLAGHER, CAROLE
  Stars of tomorrow.   Lions R 1-11/12:no p# Jl/Ag '42

GALLAGHER, HELEN
  Lewis, E.   Is she Broadway's next star?   Cue 22-5:12 Ja 31
    '53
  Poling, J.   Broadway's busiest babe.   Colliers 131:17 F 14 '53
  Little girl they had to star.   Life 34:102 Mr 9 '53
  Dancing dolls on Broadway.   Coronet 33:52 Mr '53
  Burke, T.   The Gallagher who gives Nanette its sheen.   N. Y.
    Times Bio Ed F 21 '71
  Considine, S.   Get a load of Gallagher!   After Dark 3-11:26
    Mr '71

GALLAGHER, RAYMOND
  West, V.   Interview.   Motion Pic 9:99 Mr '15

GALLERY, THOMAS S.
  Stuart, C.   Interview.   Motion Pic 22:69 N '21

GALLIAN, KETTI
  Dillon, F.   Sketch.   Movie Classic 7:62 N '34
  Hartley, K.   Sketch.   Movie Classic 8:31 Ap '35

GALLOWAY, DON
  See, C.   And then what happened?   TV Guide 18-3:25 Ja 17 '70

GAM, RITA
  Service, F.   Please don't get me wrong.   Silver S 23-7:31 My
      '53
  Rising star.   Film R p107 '53/54
  Hall, G.   Things happen to Rita.   Silver S 24-8:44 Je '54
  Schuster, M.   Interview; filmog.   Filmograph 4-1:2 '73

GAMMELTOFT, HELEN
  Montanye, L.   Interview.   Motion Pic Classic 10:41 Ap/My '20

GARAT, HENRI
  Maxwell, V.   Chosen as leading man for Janet Gaynor.   Photop
      43:35 Ap '33
  Moffitt, J.   Henri Garat.   Cinema Dig 4-4:10 Je 5 '33
  Sketch.   Photop 44:71 Jl '33
  Obit.   Screen World 11:219 '60

GARBO, GRETA
  Tildesley, A. L.   Sketch.   Motion Pic Classic 23:52 My '26
  Palmborg, R. P.   Sketch.   Motion Pic 31:54 My '26
  Markham, D.   Interview.   Motion Pic 32:23 D '26
  Smith, A.   Her romance with John Gilbert.   Photop 31:32 F '27
  York, C.   Sketch.   Photop 31:29 Ap '27
  Sketch.   Motion Pic Classic 25:36 Ag '27
  Autobiographical.   Theatre 46:86 D '27
  Palmborg, R. P.   Interview.   Motion Pic 35:58 F '28
  Tully, J.   Estimate.   Vanity Fair 30:66 Je '28
  Palmborg, R. P.   Sketch.   Motion Pic Classic 28:21 F '29
  Biery, R.   Sketch.   Motion Pic Classic 30:18 Ja '30
  York, C.   Sketch.   Photop 30:49 Je '30
  Albert, K.   What she thinks of Hollywood.   Photop 38:64 Ag '30
  Sketch.   Fortune 2:38 O '30
  Parsons, H.   24 hours with Garbo.   Silver S 1-3:12 Ja '31
  Chapman, J. B.   Sketch.   Motion Pic Classic 33:32 Mr '31
  Bisch, L. E.   Why Garbo is the world's love ideal.   Silver S
      1-7:16 My '31
  Grant, J.   Sketch.   Motion Pic Classic 33:34 Je '31
  Churchill, E.   Is Garbo doomed?   Silver S 1-8:23 Je '31
  Wilson, H. D.   Story of.   Motion Pic 42:26 Ag '31
  Palmborg, R. P.   A love affair.   Photop 40:32 S '31
  Service, F.   Insomnia has robbed her of happiness.   Movie
      Classic 1:41 S '31
  Walker, H. L.   Compared with Crawford and Shearer.   Movie
      Classic 1:23 S '31
  Gallant, T.   Study of her features.   Movie Classic 1:23 O '31
  Babcock, M.   Will television mean the end of Garbo?   Motion

Pic 42:32 O '31

Keen, E.   Garbo "played the game. "   Silver S 1-12:18 O '31

Grant, J.   Sketch.   Motion Pic 42:28 Ja '32

Brokaw, C. B.   The great Garbo.   Vanity Fair 37:63 F '32

Rondon, F.   Interview.   Movie Classic 1:18 F '32

Manners, D.   Romance rumors.   Motion Pic 43:44 Mr '32

Hall, G.   Sketch.   Movie Classic 2:28 Mr '32

Keen, E.   Garbo's daring new character.   Silver S 2-5:46 Mr
   '32

Vonnell, C.   Sketch.   Photop 41:31 Ap '32

Appreciation of acting in Grand Hotel.   Lit Dig 113:15 My 7 '32

Cheasley, C. W.   Her numberscope says she will not marry.
   Motion Pic 43:42 My '32

Calhoun, D.   Sketch.   Motion Pic 43:28 Je '32

Keats, P.   Why Garbo is great; interview with Melvyn Douglas.
   Silver S 2-8:16 Je '32

Calhoun, D.   Sketch.   Movie Classic 2:26 Jl '32

Calhoun, D.   Will she be deported?   Motion Pic 43:28 Jl '32

Garbo at sea.   Cinema Dig 1-8:30 Ag 22 '32

Babcock, M.   Her headline career.   Movie Classic 2:29 Ag '32

Biery, R.   The Garbo jinx on her leading men.   Photop 42:34 S
   '32

Garbo's gone, scribes relax.   Cinema Dig 2-5:14 Ja 9 '33

Garbo--the fans are waiting.   Silver S 3-5:28 Mr '33

Martin, H.   Garbo.   Cinema Dig 3-4:11 Ap 10 '33

Garbo greater?   Cinema Dig 3-8:3 My 8 '33

Nordstrom, S.   Her plans for the future.   Motion Pic 45:28 My
   '33

Taine, W.   The beautiful homecoming.   Silver S 3-7:43 My '33

Stone, D.   Interview.   Movie Classic 4:34 Jl '33

Chapman, J. B.   Her rival, Mae West.   Motion Pic 44:28 Jl '33

Wren, H.   The photo that made Garbo.   Photop 44:26 Ag '33

Receives $12,500 a week.   Photop 44:27 Ag '33

Schallert, E.   The new Garbo.   Movie Classic 5:19 S '33

Biery, R. & Packer, E.   Garbo has changed.   Silver S 3-11:26
   S '33

Lee, S.   Immortals of the screen.   Motion Pic 46:32 O '33

Appreciation.   Delin 123:30 O '33

Chapman, J. B.   Why she came back.   Motion Pic 46:28 O '33

Is her glamour real?   Movie Classic 5:5 N '33

St. Johns, A. R.   The great Garbo.   Silver S 4-1:16 N '33

Hill, J.   How she lives.   Movie Classic 5:17 F '34

Fidler, J. M.   Woman of mystery.   Motion Pic 47:49 Mr '34

Nicolai, B.   Marriage rumors.   Movie Classic 6:22 Mr '34

Baskette, K.   Compared with Katharine Hepburn.   Photop 45:28
   Mr '34

Colnik, G.   Why women look up to Garbo.   Movie Classic 6:31
   My '34

Calhoun, D.   Is her popularity declining?   Movie Classic 6:52
   Je '34

Hall, G.   Why she leads a solitary life.   Motion Pic 47:34 Je
   '34

Vegtel, M.   Compared with Marlene Dietrich.   Vanity Fair 42:28

Je '34

Troy, W. Work of in The painted veil. Nation 139:721 D 19 '34

Lee, S. Why she is a genius. Motion Pic 48:27 D '34

Wilson, E. Garbo vs. Lombard. Silver S 5-2:16 D '34

Hull, H. The Garbo fear. Motion Pic 49:31 Ap '35

Calhoun, D. Why her friends dare not talk. Motion Pic 49:28 Jl '35

Adrian. Her costumes in Anna Karenina. Movie Classic 8:34 Jl '35

Packer, E. Garbo smiles again. Silver S 5-10:47 Ag '35

Sherwin, T. A glimpse of the true Garbo. Motion Pic 50:26 S '35

Sedgwick, R. W. The great Garbo mystery. Stage 13:32 O '35

Bjelke, G. Interview. Movie Classic 9:35 O '35

Hartley, K. How she has helped other players. Motion Pic 50:24 D '35

Greta Garbo. Visages 1:entire issue My '36

Asher, J. Giving Garbo away. Silver S 6-7:28 My '36

Zeitlin, I. Still queen. Motion Pic 52:37 Ag '36

Wilson, C. Sketch. Photop 50:25 S '36

Schallert, E. Will she retire? Motion Pic 52:38 D '36

Gillespie-Hayek, A. The Sphinx has melted. Silver S 7-2:22 D '36

Surmelian, L. A close-up of the incomparable Garbo. Movie Classic 11:31 F '37

Fairweather, D. Appreciation. Theatre World 27:186 Ap '37

Palmborg, R. P. Is she becoming Americanized? Motion Pic 54:34 S '37

Her early life. Life 3:81 N 8 '37

Sullivan, E. When Greta isn't Garbo. Silver S 9-12:22 O '39

Underhill, D. Garbo goes on forever. Screen Book 22-6:57 Ja '40

Sullivan, E. Glamour lets down its hair. Silver S 10-5:42 Mr '40

Bio note; filmog. Movies & People 2:16 '40

The gay Garbo. Lions Roar 1-3:no p# N '41

How Cukor directs Garbo. Lions R 1-3:no p# N '41

The Garbo myth. Lions R 1-3:no p# N '41

She works with Garbo. Lions R 1-3:no p# N '41

St. Johns, A. R. Story of. Photop 25:30 Ag '44

On the French Riviera. Newsweek 30:46 S 8 '47

Rippy, F. W. She embodies all qualities necessary to portray tragedy. Arizona Q 5:35 Spg '49

Her return to motion pictures. Harp Baz 83:157 O '49

Legendary star. World R 10:43 D '49

Gronowicz, A. Garbo and my book. Contemporary R 198:679 D '60

Zierold, N. Garbo and her court; excerpt from Garbo. McCalls 96:52 Ag '62

Greta Garbo. Screen Ed 21:60 S/O '63

Kroll, J. Garbo. Newsweek 72:76 Jl 22 '68

Zierold, N. Garbo; excerpts. McCalls 96:53 Ag '69

Nordberg, C. E. Her secret; filmog. Film Comment 6-2:27 Sum '70
Bainbridge, J. Garbo is 65. Look 34:48 S 8 '70
Canham, K. Her early talkies. Film 61:33 Spg '71
Great Garbo. Screen Greats 1-2:44 Sum '71
A recent footnote. Life 71:86 N 12 '71
Culff, R. Her Hollywood silents. Sil Pic 16:4 Aut '72
Garbo still looks great at 67. Harp Baz 106:84 N '72
Bodeen, D. Memories of Garbo; filmog. Focus On F 15:19 Sum '73
St. Johns, A. R. The mystery of Hollywood. Liberty 1-10:35 Fall '73
Haskell, M. Garbo revisited. Viva 1-4:36 Ja '74
Garbo; filmog. Screen Greats 1-8:entire issue. n. d.

GARCIA, HENRY
Obit. Screen World 22:236 '71

GARDENIA, VINCENT
Walker, G. The flowering of Vincent Gardenia. N. Y. Times sec 2:5 D 8 '74

GARDINER, REGINALD
Should a girl propose? Photop 24:42 F '44

GARDNER, AVA
You ought to be in pictures. Lions R 3-3(sup):no p# Ap '44
Beautiful but--wise. Lions R 3-5:no p# D '44
Palmer, C. The farmer's number one daughter. Silver S 17-11:44 S '47
Fulton, M. J. Sketch. Photop 31:81 O '47
Letter from Liza. Silver S 18-7:42 My '48
Bowers, L. Venus modern style. Silver S 18-9:28 Jl '48
Graham, S. Sketch. Photop 33:40 N '48
Howe, H. Story of. Photop 34:54 D '48
Sketch. Photop 36:66 Je '49
O'Leary, D. Making friends in Hollywood. Silver S 21-5:26 Mr '51
Morris, J. Ava faces a problem. Silver S 21-6:24 Ap '51
Rogers, V. What about Ava's career? Silver S 22-5:28 Mr '52
Rowland, R. C. I can take it on the chin. Silver S 22-11:36 S '52
Wilson, E. My pal Ava. Silver S 23-8:22 Je '53
Balling, F. D. Just because of Ava. Silver S 23-10:24 Ag '53
Reid, L. Don't let Ava fool you. Silver S 24-5:24 Mr '54
Star without shoes. Cue 23-33:12 Ag 14 '54
Lawrenson, H. The nightmare of the iguana. Show 4-1:46 Ja '64
Caldwell, R. Twilight of a goddess. Ladies Home J 89:108 Jl '72
Untamed. Photop 83-4:66 Ap '73

GARDNER, CRAIG
  Raddatz, L.   Three heroes have disappeared.   TV Guide 22-22:
    14 Je 1 '74

GARFIELD, JOHN
  Green, E. M.   Sketch.   Theatre World 30:184 O '38
  Mook, S. R.   Another East side genius.   Silver S 9-2:51 D '38
  Towers, J.   Slums to stardom.   Screen Book 21-5:37 D '38
  Cooper, M.   Once was enough.   Silver S 10-7:38 My '40
  Bio note; filmog.   Movies & People 2:16 '40
  The battle of Garfield.   Lions R 1-9:no p# My '42
  Benedict, P.   His greatest adventure.   Silver S 12-10:42 Ag '42
  Walker, H. L.   Overseas report from Garfield.   Silver S 14-10:
    26 Ag '44
  My Easter prayer.   Photop 26:42 Ap '45
  The role I liked best.   Sat Eve Post 218:94 Ja 12 '46
  Palmer, C.   Quiet guy.   Silver S 16-12:37 O '46
  Work of.   Cosmop 123:168 O '47
  Churchill, R. & B.   Women--they're dynamite.   Silver S 19-2:
    22 D '48
  Obit.   Screen World 4:176 '53
  When hoods were heroes.   Screen Greats 1-2:34 Sum '71
  Ford, A.   His defiant look spoke for an age; filmog.   Show 2-8:
    39 O '71
  Pinup of the past.   Films & Filming 18-7:72 Ap '72
  Waterbury, R.   Closeup of Garfield.   Liberty 1-4:50 Spg '72
  Gelman, H.   Hollywood was the dead end; filmog.   Velvet Light
    7:16 Win '72/73

GARGAN, WILLIAM
  North, J.   Sketch.   Photop 42:60 S '32
  Sketch.   Motion Pic 44:42 N '32
  Townsend, L.   Sketch.   Motion Pic 44:59 D '32
  Mook, D.   Reformation of a loudmouth.   Silver S 11-7:46 My '41
  Gumshoe Gargan.   Lions R 2-4:no p# Ap '43
  William Gargan.   Cue 12-27:11 Jl 3 '43
  Bio.   Cur Bio 30:6 Ja '69
    Same.   Cur Bio Yrbk 1969:156 '70
  Gargan, W.   Why me? excerpts.   Good House 168:92 Mr '69
  Tuska, J.   Rain.   Views & Rs 3-4:4 '72

GARLAND, BEVERLY
  McClelland, D.   TV: where all that old-time glamour went.
    Film Fan Mo 75:11 S '67
  Hano, A.   If she can be Fred MacMurray's wife, why can't I?
    TV Guide 18-2:20 Ja 10 '70
  I'm a new mother and a new grandmother.   Photop 79-5:38 My
    '71

GARLAND, JUDY
  Becomes member of Sigma Chi of Ohio State University.   Life
    4:66 Mr 28 '38
  Manners, M. J.   The ugly duckling who became a swan.   Silver

S 10-8:36 Je '40
Willson, D. Story of. Photop 54:32 S '40
Bio note; filmog. Movies & People 2:16 '40
Her engagement announced. Photop 19:6 S '41
Judy's life of song. Lions R 1-5:no p# Ja '42
Mickey and me. Cosmop 112:28 Mr '42
Hall, G. Mistakes I'll never make again. Silver S 13-1:28 N
  '42
She's a trouper. Lions R 2-2:no p# N '42
She who dances. Lions R 2-2:no p# N '42
Sammis, F. R. Her separation from David Rose. Photop 22:4
  Ap '43
Garland, J. Don't get me wrong. Lions R 2-4:no p# Ap '43
Rooney, M. Deat Jootes. Lions R 3-1:no p# S '43
Garland, J. He's terrific. Lions R 3-1:no p# S '43
St. Johns, A. R. Story of. Photop 25:30 Ag '44
Graham, B. J. If you knew Judy. Lions R 4-1:no p# F '45
St. Johns, A. R. Her engagement to Vincente Minnelli. Photop
  26:28 Ap '45 & following issues.
St. Johns, E. Her daughter Liza. Photop 29:60 N '46
Holland, J. (She) has her say. Silver S 19-2:24 D '48
Sheridan, M. What's ahead for Judy? Silver S 22-11:22 S '52
Sheridan, M. The unhappy life of Judy Garland. Silver S 23-7:
  26 My '53
Hyams, J. A star is reborn. Cue 23-10:12 Mr 6 '54
Brinson, P. The great comeback. Films & Filming 1-3:4 D
  '54
Minoff, P. Notes on TV. Cue 25-16:18 Ap 21 '56
Readin' ritin' and rehearsal. TV Guide 4-38:20 S 22 '56
Johnson, A. Conversation with Roger Edens. Sight & Sound
  27-4:179 Spg '58
McVay, D. Filmography. Films & Filming 8-1:39 O '61
Letters. Films In R 13-5:311 My '62
Gotta sing! gotta dance! Film 40:9 Sum '64
Seance at the Palace. Time 90:40 Ag 18 '67
Plot against Judy. Ladies Home J 84:64 Ag '67
Korall, B. Garland phenomenon. Sat R 50:66 S 30 '67
Davidson, M. My mom and I; interview with Liza Minnelli.
  Good House 167:72 Jl '68
Goldman, W. Judy floats. Esquire 71:78 Ja '69
Obit. Brit Bk Yr 1970:581 '70
  Classic Film Collect 24:14 Sum '69
  Cur Bio 30:46 S '69
  Same. Cur Bio Yrbk 1969:467 '70
  Film 55:19 Sum '69
  Film R p15 '70/71
  N. Y. Times p47 Je 5 '69
  Screen World 21:236 '70
End of the rainbow. Time 94:64 Jl 4 '69
Notes and comment. New Yorker 45:19 Jl 5 '69
Schulberg, B. Farewell to Judy. Life 67:26 Jl 11 '69
Deans, M. Her last tragic months. Look 33:84 O 7 '69
Bolger, R. Cue salutes. Cue 39-13:48 Mr 28 '70

Nine minds in trouble.   Photop 78-3:56 S '70
The kids.   Screen Greats 1-2:48 Sum '71
The love teams.   Screen Greats 1-2:10 Sum '71
Harper & Row lands bio. of Garland.   Pub W 201:52 Je 26 '72
Lorna Luft interview.   McCalls 100:14 N '72
Judy and Mickey; filmog.   Screen Greats 8:entire issue.   n. d.
Special tribute issue published by Skywald Pub Corp.   Entire
   issue:n. d.

GARNER, JAMES
   Zunser, J.   Maverick goes straight.   Cue 31-9:10 Mr 3 '62
   Wells, D.   His new act.   Motor T 21:74 Je '69
   About 7. 5 on the Richter scale.   TV Guide 19-47:14 N 20 '71
   Stump, A.   Crusader rabbit rides again.   TV Guide 19-50:33 D
      11 '71
   Gardner, P.   Why interview me?   N. Y. Times Bio Ed D 19 '71

GARNER, PEGGY ANN
   Sketch.   Photop 24:57 My '44
   Story of.   Newsweek 25:103 F 19 '45
   Fulton, M. J.   Sketch.   Photop 34:95 Mr '49
   The kids.   Screen Greats 1-2:50 Sum '71
   Filmog.   Films & Filming 19-18:56 S '73

GARON, PAULINE
   Service, F.   Interview.   Classic 16:32 My '23
   Uselton, R. A.   The Wampus baby stars.   Films In R 21-2:73
      F '70

GARRETT, BETTY
   Deere, D.   Story of.   Photop 30:54 My '47
   Betty Garrett; filmog.   Film Fan Mo 84 Je '68
   Filmog.   Films & Filming 20-6:52 Mr '74
   Whitney, D.   One day she met a kid from Kansas.   TV Guide
      22-17:21 Ap 27 '74

GARRICK, JOHN
   Sketch.   Photop 37:53 Mr '30

GARRISON, MICHAEL
   Obit.   Screen World 18:235 '67

GARSON, GREER
   Sketch.   Theatre World 24:53 Ag '35
   Sketch.   Theatre World 25:13 Ja '36
   Rhea, M.   Sketch.   Photop 53:66 S '39
   Proctor, K.   "Chips" Garson.   Screen Book 22-5:64 D '39
   Bio note; filmog.   Movies & People 2:17 '40
   Green, E. M.   Sketch.   Theatre World 35:57 S '41
   Sketch.   Theatre World 37:18 Mr '42
   Garson meets the people.   Lions R 1-9:no p# My '42
   Hilton, J.   Story of.   Cosmop 113:8 O '42
   Hall, G.   Salute to the spotlight.   Silver S 12-12:24 O '42

Legs Garson.   Lions R 2-3:no p# D '42
Sketch.   Vogue 101:54 Mr 1 '43
Garson discovers Marie Curie.   Lions R 3-2:no p# Ja '44
Manners, M. J.   Heart to heart talk with Garson.   Silver S 14-
    8:22 Je '44
Dark beauty.   Lions R 3-5:no p# D '44
My Christmas wish.   Photop 26:46 Ja '45
My Easter prayer.   Photop 26:42 Ap '45
Awarded Photoplay gold medal award for 1945.   Photop 28:28 F
    '46
First place in Companion poll of favorite stars.   Womans Home
    C 73:7 Je '46
The thrill of winning a gold medal.   Photop 29:127 Je '46
Christmas story.   Photop 30:22 Ja '47
Her divorce from Richard Ney.   Life 23:50 O 6 '47
Her acrobatic role in Julia misbehaves.   Life 24:20 Je 7 '48
Parsons, L. O.   Interview.   Photop 34:44 D '48
Cosmop's citation for performance of the month.   Cosmop 127:12
    N '49
Her marriage to Mr. Fogelson.   Photop 36:11 O '49
Minoff, P.   Broadway gets another Mame.   Cue 27-3:12 Ja 12
    '58
The love teams.   Screen Greats 1-2:10 Sum '71
The lady has class.   Photop 82-4:47 O '72

GARVER, KATHY
    Hobson, D.   How do you upstage two kids and a beard?   TV
        Guide 16-46:16 N 16 '68

GARWOOD, WILLIAM
    Willis, R.   A man with a mission and a message.   Photop 6-4:
        86 S '14
    Sketch.   Motion Pic 9:119 My '15
    Interview.   Motion Pic 9:102 Jl '15
    Sketch.   Motion Pic 13:47 Mr '17
    Gregory, N. D.   Sketch.   Motion Pic 14:77 S '17

GASSMAN, VITTORIO
    Gassman, V.   Let me tell you about my Shelley.   Silver S 24-4:
        36 F '54
    Lane, J. F.   The face of '63--Italy.   Films & Filming 9-7:11
        Ap '63
    On the scene.   Playboy 12-1:183 Ja '65

GATTEY, BENNYE
    Why she took her sister's bike.   TV Guide 7-30:25 Jl 25 '59

GAUNTIER, GENE
    Obit.   Classic Film Collect 17:41 Win/Spg '67
        Screen World 18:235 '67

GAVIN, JOHN
    Rising star.   Film R p34 '62/63

Pacheco, P.  The surprising John Gavin.  After Dark 6-7:30 N
    '73

GAXTON, WILLIAM
    Broadway Bill.  Lions R 3-1:no p# S '43
    Your bit part may be a star role.  Read Dig 55:81 N '49
    Shepherd.  New Yorker 37:17 Jl 1 '61

GAYE, HOWARD
    Dunham, H.  Letter.  Films In R 22-9:577 N '71

GAYE, LISA
    The girl with 94 cats.  TV Guide 6-37:24 S 13 '58
    Meow!  TV Guide 7-37:21 S 12 '59

GAYLOR, ANNA
    Rising star.  Film R p30 '58/59

GAYNOR, JANET
    Waterbury, R.  Sketch.  Photop 31:62 Ja '27
    Manners, D.  Interview.  Motion Pic 34:34 Ag '27
    Calhoun, D.  Sketch.  Motion Pic Classic 26:37 S '27
    Biery, R. L.  Sketch.  Photop 32:35 O '27
    Wheaton, J.  Sketch.  Motion Pic 35:74 F '28
    Spensley, D.  Interview.  Photop 35:50 Ja '29
    Calhoun, D.  Sketch.  Motion Pic 39:8 Ap '30
    Sketch.  Fortune 2:38 O '30
    Wilson, K.  The story behind the signing of the Gaynor-Fox pact
        of peace.  Silver S 1-1:28 N '30
    Pryor, N.  Sketch.  Motion Pic 41:58 F '31
    Sketch.  Photop 39:38 Ap '31
    Babcock, M.  Sketch.  Motion Pic 41:51 Je '31
    Gebhart, M.  Anecdotes of Janet Gaynor.  Silver S 2-1:21 N '31
    Manners, D.  Sketch.  Motion Pic 42:54 D '31
    Chensley, C. W.  Numbers tell the truth about her.  Motion Pic
        43:42 Je '32
    She is making a great picture.  Silver S 3-1:48 N '32
    Rice, L.  Sketch.  Motion Pic 44:33 N '32
    Ergenbright, E.  Interview.  Movie Classic 3:44 D '32
    Jones, C. P.  Janet Gaynor.  Cinema Dig 2-6:9 Ja 16 '33
    Her divorce.  Motion Pic 43:27 Mr '33
    Tennant, M.  Her divorce.  Movie Classic 4:30 Mr '33
    Moffitt, J.  Sheehan and Gaynor?  Cinema Dig 4-4:10 Je 5 '33
    Fidler, J. M.  Janet's "hideaway."  Silver S 3-9:22 Jl '33
    Lynn, H.  How she makes love.  Photop 44:32 Ag '33
    Five years ago.  Photop 44:110 Ag '33
    Manners, D.  Does she want sex appeal?  Movie Classic 5:26
        S '33
    Slater, A.  Unfounded rumors.  Movie Classic 7:43 S '34
    Dowling, M.  Interview.  Movie Classic 7:27 O '34
    Brundidge, H. T.  Interview.  Motion Pic 48:34 N '34
    Maddox, B.  Janet is Janet.  Silver S 5-2:48 D '34
    Lewis, L.  Secret of her popularity.  Movie Classic 9:26 S '35

Smalley, J.  Story of.  Movie Classic 10:32 My '36
Lane, J.  Her popularity.  Motion Pic 52:30 S '36
Lang, H.  Her amazing coup.  Screen Book 19-1:30 Ag '37
Story of.  Motion Pic 54:38 S '37
Hartley, K.  She minds her own business.  Screen Book 21-4:29
    N '38
Liza.  Interview.  Silver S 10-1:16 N '39
Bio note; filmog.  Movies & People 2:17 '40
Sketch.  Vogue 105:82 Ja 1 '45
Osborne, R.  Letter.  Films In R 11-3:183 Mr '60
Uselton, R. A.  The Wampus baby stars.  Films In R 21-2:73
    F '70
Hamilton, J.  Where oh where are the beautiful girls?  Look 34-
    22:67 N 3 '70
Gordon, A.  Gaynor at Fox.  Film Fan Mo 135:25 S '72
Roud, R.  People we like.  Film Comment 10-1:37 Ja/F '74
Yesterday's sweethearts today.  Photop 85-6:56 Je '74

GAYNOR, MITZI
Gaynor, M.  I knew what I wanted.  Silver S 22-2:30 D '51
MacDonald, E.  Letter to a star.  Silver S 22-5:40 Mr '52
A star is born.  Film R p101 '52/53
Bruce, J.  I learned about love the hard way.  Silver S 23-9:42
    Jl '53
Mitzi makes it on the rebound.  Cue 25-13:15 Mr 31 '56

GAZZARA, BEN
Lewis, E.  New look actor.  Cue 24-11:13 Mr 19 '55
Lewis, R. W.  See how he runs.  TV Guide 14-8:19 F 19 '66
Bio.  Cur Bio 28:19 N '67
    Same.  Cur Bio Yrbk 1967:134 '68
Clein, H.  Husbands.  Entertainment World 1-4:7 O 24 '69
Haskell, M.  Three husbands hold court.  Show 1-2:67 F '70
Milne, T.  Bio note; filmog.  Focus On F 6:11 Spg '71
Crichton, M.  My neck was out.  TV Guide 20-48:14 N 25 '72

GEDDES, BARBARA BEL
Sketch.  Photop 32:84 Ja '48

GEER, WILL
Eyles, A.  Bio note; filmog.  Focus On F 12:8 Win '72
Stone, J.  To the Devil and back.  N.Y. Times sec 2:23 D 17
    '72
    Same.  N.Y. Times Bio Ed p2167 D '72
Grandpa Walton meets Shakespeare.  People 1-11:55 My 13 '74
The world's oldest hippie.  TV Guide 22-43:21 O 26 '74

GEESON, JUDY
Wolf, W.  The London look in films.  Cue 37-11:10 Mr 16 '68

GELLEN, AUDREY
Wood sprite who can write.  TV Guide 7-29:24 Jl 18 '59

GEMMA, GIULIANO
  Filmog.  Films & Filming 20-11:68 Ag '74

GENEVIEVE
  Genevieve.  TV Guide 9-16:17 Ap 22 '61
  Poling, J.  American men are easier to love than understand.
    Redbook 117:34 S '61

GEORGE, ANTHONY
  A woman came along.  TV Guide 8-51:17 D 17 '60
  All for one and one for all.  TV Guide 10-28:15 Jl 14 '62

GEORGE, CHRISTOPHER
  Efron, E.  Go to the heart of danger.  TV Guide 15-20:10 My
    20 '67
  Hano, A.  A most unhappy warrior.  TV Guide 18-46:27 N 14 '70
  Pregnant wife, panicked husband.  Photop 81-5:18 My '72
  New baby girl.  Photop 82-5:50 N '72
  Hardeman, M.  Playgirl's man for June; centerfold.  Playgirl
    2-1:76 Je '74

GEORGE, CHIEF DAN
  Zimmerman, P. D.  The chief.  Newsweek 77:80 Ja 25 '71
  Nobel non-savage.  Time 97:76 F 15 '71
  Klemesrud, J.  Dustin calls him Grandpa.  N. Y. Times Bio Ed
    F 21 '71
  Chief Dan George stars in a hunt.  Life 71:85 N 12 '71
  McLarty, J.  More than an actor.  Motion p6 Jl/Ag '73

GEORGE, FLORENCE
  Don't tell a soul.  TV Guide 1-3:A-2 Ap 17 '53

GEORGE, GLADYS
  Astor, T.  Interview.  Motion Pic Classic 13:48 N '21
  Camp, D.  Interview.  Motion Pic 52:43 Ja '37
  Smithson, E. J.  Story of.  Movie Classic 11:6 Ja '37
  Proctor, K.  Interview.  Motion Pic 54:38 D '37
  Bio note; filmog.  Movies & People 2:17 '40
  Brunas, J.  Gladys George; filmog.  Film Fan Mo 129:9 Mr '72

GEORGE, LYNDA DAY
  Wasserman, J. L.  This woman will not self-destruct.  TV
    Guide 20-4:32 Ja 22 '72
  Pregnant wife, panicked husband.  Photop 81-5:18 My '72
  New baby girl.  Photop 82-5:50 N '72

GEORGE, MAUDE
  Sewell, J.  Interview.  Motion Pic Classic 14:44 Ap '22

GEORGE, SUSAN
  She won't holler uncle.  TV Guide 5-45:21 N 9 '57
  Flatley, G.  The girl who made Straw dogs bark.  N. Y. Times
    Bio Ed Mr 5 '72
  Sketch.  Mov Dig 1-6:26 N '72

GERAGHITY, CARMELITA
  Uselton, R. A.   The Wampus baby stars.   Films In R 21-2:73
    F '70

GERARD, TEDDY
  Montanye, L.   Interview.   Motion Pic Classic 13:66 N '21

GEREWAL, SIMI
  Louie, E.   The courtesan Kamala.   Viva 1-2:117 N '73

GERRARD, DOUGLAS
  Obit.   Screen World 2:234 '51

GERRITSEN, LISA
  Lisa.   TV Guide 19-18:15 My 1 '71

GERVIS, JOHN JR.
  Lewis, R. W.   Hello stardom!   TV Guide 15-12:21 Mr 25 '67

GETWELL, ANETHA
  Fredericks, J.   Interview.   Motion Pic 19:47 Mr '20

GHENT, DEREK
  Squier, E. L.   Sketch.   Motion Pic Classic 12:61 Je '21

GHOSTLEY, ALICE
  Lewis, E.   New funny-face on Broadway.   Cue 21-26:14 Je 28
    '52
  Clein, H.   The real people.   Show 1-8:14 Jl 9 '70

GIBSON, HELEN
  Ames, H.   Sketch.   Motion Pic 13:114 Je '17
  Gibson, H. as told to Mike Kornick.   In very early days.   Films
    In R 19-1:28 Ja '68
  Slide, A.   The Kalem serial queens.   Silent Pic 1:no p# Win
    '68/69

GIBSON, HENRY
  Raddatz, L.   Six who bowed out.   TV Guide 20-38:23 S 16 '72

GIBSON, HOOT
  St. Johns, I.   Interview.   Photop 29:40 Mr '26
  Fairfield, L.   Interview.   Motion Pic Classic 27:58 Ap '28
  Belfrage, C.   Interview.   Motion Pic Classic 31:63 Mr '30
  LaBadie, D. W.   The last roundup.   Show 2-9:76 S '62
  Reynolds, R.   Hollywood's silent western stars lived active, ad-
    venturous lives.   8mm Collect 5:3 Ag 15 '63
  Reynolds, R.   The Hoot Gibson story.   8mm Collect 10:24 Win
    '64
  Phillips, A.   Hoot.   8mm Collect 10:24 Win '64
  Lucky terror.   Views & Rs 2-3:42 Win '71
  Spurs: from 100 finest westerns.   Views & Rs 4-2:53 Win '72

294                                    Motion Picture Performers

GIBSON, MARGARET
    Sketch.  Motion Pic 9:106 Mr '15

GIBSON, WYNNE
    Sketch.  Photop 40:68 Jl '31
    Manners, D.  Interview.  Motion Pic 42:66 S '31
    Look out Garbo! Here we come.  Silver S 2-5:52 Mr '32

GIELGUD, JOHN
    Interview.  Theatre World 18:166 O '32
    Corathiel, E.  Interview.  Theatre World 20:85 Ag '33
    Sedgwick, R. W.  Sketch.  Stage 12:17 O '34
    Hast, N.  Sketch.  Theatre World 23:9 Ja '35
    Sketch.  Theatre World 24:73 Ag '35
    Roberts, F.  Gielgud at home.  Theatre World 24:284 D '35
    Looking at the New York theatre.  Theatre World 27:61 F '37
    His return to London.  Theatre World 27:183 Ap '37
    Interview.  Theatre World 28:65 Ag '37
    Hast, N.  Pictorial record of his career.  Play Pict 75:18 S '39
    Johns, E.  Interview.  Theatre World 37:7 D '42
    Bio sketch.  Vogue 105:151 O 1 '45
    Johns, E.  His return to London.  Theatre World 42:3 Ag '46
    Sketch.  Vogue 109:183 Mr 15 '47
    Gibbs, P.  Who is Britain's first actor?  World R p58 Jl '47
    Unveiling statue of Shakespeare.  Ill Lon N 213:146 Ag 7 '48
    Return to London.  Theatre World 45:29 Ja '49
    MacNeice, L.  Comments on his production of The lady's not for
        burning.  World R 4:19 Je '49
    Film and Sir John Gielgud.  Film 7:19 Ja/F '56
    Hobson, H.  Interview.  Show 2-1:58 Ja '62
    Gielgud, J.  A note on Hamlet.  Show 4-2:74 F '64
    Gielgud, J.  Herne's oak has fallen.  Plays & Players 16-10:34
        Jl '69
    In the words of Sir John Gielgud.  Cue 39-45:8 N 7 '70
    Palmer, T.  Don't ask Sir John about Hamlet.  N.Y. Times Bio
        Ed N 15 '70
    Tierney, M.  Knights at work.  Plays & Players 18-12:19 S '71
    Gruen, J.  Interview.  Vogue 158:86 N 15 '71
    I had nothing to do for a couple of months.  TV Guide 20-7:20
        F 12 '72
    Buckley, P.  In the distinguished company of John Gielgud.
        Plays & Players 20-2:27 N '72
    Guerin, A.  Theatre's greatest star.  Show 2-11:39 F '73
    Bryden, R.  Plays a suicidal William Shakespeare.  N.Y. Times
        sec 2:3 Ag 25 '74

GIFFORD, FRANCES
    Sketch.  Time 37:52 My 12 '41
    Meet the cover(all) girls.  Lions R 3-2:no p# Ja '44
    So long, sarong!  Lions R 3-5:no p# D '44
    Reid, L.  Bad beginning.  Silver S 15-12:44 O '45
    Service, F.  The other side of me.  Silver S 17-7:42 My '47

GIFTOS, ELAINE
    Raddatz, L. When myopia is an asset. TV Guide 19-12:33 Mr
      20 '71

GILBERT, BILLY
    Maltin, L. Our gang; inc Our gang filmog. Film Fan Mo 66:3
      D '66
    Maltin, L. Billy Gilbert; partial filmog. Film Fan Mo 88:15 O
      '68
    Obit. Classic Film Collect 32:62 Fall '71
      Film R p11 '72/73
      N. Y. Times p44 S 24 '71
      Same. N. Y. Times Bio Ed S 24 '71
      Newsweek 78:90 O 4 '71
      Screen World 23:236 '72
      Time 98:76 O 4 '71

GILBERT, HELEN
    Hall, G. All flew into the cuckoo's nest. Silver S 10-1:38 N
      '39
    Hamilton, S. Sketch. Photop 54:18 F '40
    Quilting bee. Wilson Lib Bul 14:653 My '40

GILBERT, JODY
    Hunter, G. W. Letter; filmog. Films In R 21-4:253 Ap '70

GILBERT, JOHN
    Cheatham, M. Interview. Motion Pic Classic 13:49 D '21
    Autobiographical. Motion Pic 29:37 My '25
    Donnell, D. Sketch. Motion Pic Classic 22:33 N '25
    The screen's man of the moment. Motion Pic Classic 22:52 Ja
      '26
    Herzog, D. The man who wouldn't be second-rate. Motion Pic
      31:32 Mr '26
    Home of. Photop 30:68 Je '26
    Home of. Motion Pic 31:50 Jl '26
    Home of. Theatre 44:48 Jl '26
    Miller, H. Appreciation. Motion Pic Classic 24:20 D '26
    Smith, A. The romance of Gilbert and Garbo. Photop 31:32 F
      '27
    Interview. Theatre 45:40 Mr '27
    Hall, G. & Fletcher, A. W. Interview. Motion Pic 33:34 Ap
      '27
    Manners, D. Interview. Motion Pic 34:19 N '27
    Appreciation. Vanity Fair 30:85 My '28
    Smith, R. Symbol of a vanishing type in motion pictures.
      Theatre 49:22 Ap '29
    Calhoun, D. Marries Ina Claire. Motion Pic 38:50 S '29
    Babcock, M. His first marriage. Motion Pic 40:58 D '30
    Spensley, D. Sketch. Motion Pic 41:48 Ap '31
    Manners, D. Sketch. Motion Pic Classic 33:24 My '31
    Churchill, E. In this lies tragedy. Silver S 1-12:21 O '31
    Calhoun, D. His separation from Ina Claire. Mov Classic 1:36

O '31
Hall, L.  Separation from Claire.  Photop 40:31 O '31
Calhoun, D.  Why his marriage failed.  Motion Pic 42:28 N '31
Babcock, M.  His headline career 1922-1931.  Movie Classic
    1:24 D '31
Service, F.  To marry Virginia Bruce.  Movie Classic 2:42 Ag
    '32
Coleman, W.  He's attic again!  Silver S 2-10:17 Ag '32
Moffitt, C. F.  Censorship for interviews Hollywood's latest wild
    idea...  Cinema Dig 2-5:9 Ja 9 '33
Schallert, E.  Interview.  Motion Pic 44:28 Ja '33
Manners, D.  Interview.  Movie Classic 5:25 N '33
Hall, G.  Sketch.  Movie Classic 7:50 S '34
Wilson, C.  Sketch.  Photop 50:25 S '36
The magic that was Hollywood.  Classic Film Collect 25:41 Fall
    '69

GILBERT, RUTH
    It's bigger than both of us.  TV Guide 1-23:8 S 4 '53
    Great American two weeks.  Look 18:120 Je 15 '54

GILCHRIST, CONNIE
    Meet the cover(all) girls.  Lions R 3-2:no p# Ja '44
    Greenwich Village in Hollywood.  Lions R 3-3:no p# Ap '44
    Stanke, D.  Connie Gilchrist; filmog.  Films In R 25-3:151 Mr
        '74

GILLIAM, DAVID
    Stoop, N. M.  The drop that hits the pool of water.  After Dark
        7-8:73 D '74

GILLIN, LINDA
    Pearsall, A.  How some of the magic went out of Stanley Sweet-
        heart's garden.  Show 1-3:69 Mr '70

GILLINGWATER, CLAUDE
    Talks on vaudeville.  N.Y. Drama 74:25 D 25 '15
    Goldbeck, W.  Interview.  Motion Pic 23:44 F '22
    Gassaway, G.  Interview.  Motion Pic Classic 14:22 Ag '22
    Obit.  Newsweek 14:6 N 13 '39

GILLMORE, MARGALO
    Sketch.  Theatre 43:32 Je '26
    The ups and downs of a career.  Met 56:39 Ja '39

GILMAN, TONI
    In the cast.  TV Guide 1-9:21 My 29 '53

GILMORE, VIRGINIA
    Enters the movies.  Life 7:32 N 27 '39
    Hamilton, S.  Sketch.  Photop 18:36 Mr '41
    Franchey, J. R.  Indifference did the trick.  Silver S 11-7:34
        My '41

Turton, T. P.  Virginia Gilmore; filmog.  Films In R 22-1:49
    Ja '71

GING, JACK
    Davidson, M.  The I don't care actor who cares too much.  TV
        Guide 11-25:11 Je 22 '63

GINGOLD, HERMIONE
    Sketch.  Theatre World 37:20 F '42
    Sketch.  Theatre World 42:29 Jl '46
    Bio. sketch.  Vogue 109:186 Mr 15 '47
    Johns, E.  La belle dame sans merci.  Theatre World 45:25 Ja
        '49
    Keating, J.  Hermione is here to stay.  Cue 23-26:14 Je 26 '54
    Minoff, P.  The Gingold gal is "live" again.  Cue 28-10:18 Mr
        7 '59
    Gingold, H.  A tribute to Maurice Chevalier.  Show 2-1:44 Mr
        '72

GIRACI, MAE
    Lee, R.  The magic that was Hollywood.  Classic Film Collect
        22:14 Fall/Win '68

GIRARDOT, ANNIE
    Bio note.  Unifrance 45:8 D '57
    Eyles, A.  Annie Girardot; filmog.  Focus On F 4:9 S/O '70
    Curtiss, T. Q.  New first lady of French cinema.  N. Y. Times
        Bio Ed F 15 '72

GISH, DOROTHY
    Keefe, W. E.  Sketch.  Motion Pic 9:109 Je '15
    Rex, W.  Dorothy and Mae tell secrets.  Film Players Herald
        2-7:11 F '16
    Wright, E.  Interview.  Motion Pic 13:78 Je '17
    Gish, L.  My sister and I.  Theatre 46:14 N '17
    Remont, F.  Sketch.  Motion Pic Classic 6:45 My '18
    Robbins, E. M.  Interview.  Motion Pic Classic 7:54 Ja '19
    Cheatham, M. S.  Interview.  Motion Pic 18:30 Ag '19
    Beach, B.  Interview.  Motion Pic Classic 9:20 N '19
    Hall, G.  Sketch.  Motion Pic 21:39 Jl '21
    Carr, H.  Her return to the screen.  Motion Pic 25:21 Ag '23
    Why we are glad to get home.  Motion Pic 28:25 O '24
    de Revere, F. V.  Face analysis of.  Motion Pic 28:49 N '24
    Roberts, W. A.  Sketch.  Motion Pic 29:44 Je '25
    Borden, E.  Sketch.  Photop 28:90 Ag '25
    Redway, S.  Interview.  Motion Pic Classic 22:62 S '25
    Gish, L.  My sister and I.  Theatre 40:14 N '27
    Wilson, B.  Sketch.  Motion Pic 37:55 Ap '29
    The Gish girls gallop again.  Cue 11-46:16 N 14 '42
    Dottie comes back.  Cue 12-49:10 D 4 '43
    Fragile is not the word for this Gish sister.  Cue 19-8:16 F 25
        '50
    Lee, R.  Little Miss mischief.  Classic Film Collect 21:25

Sum '68
Obit.   Brit Bk Yr 1969:570 '69
    Classic Film Collect 21:49 Sum '68
    Cur Bio 29:41 S '68
    Cur Bio Yrbk 1968:455 '69
    Film R p20 '69/70
    N. Y. Times p47 Je 6 '68
    Newsweek 71:88 Je 17 '68
    Time 91:88 Je 14 '68

GISH, LILLIAN
Sketch.   Motion Pic 8:117 Ja '15
How to get in moving pictures.   Motion Pic 12:128 Ag '16
Zeidman, B.   Sketch.   Motion Pic 12:134 O '16
McKelvie, M. G.   Interview.   Motion Pic 15:81 Ag '18
Robbins, E. M.   Interview.   Motion Pic Classic 7:54 Ja '19
Biographical.   Dram Mir 82:642 Ap 3 '20
Hall, G.   Interview.   Motion Pic 19:30 Ap/My '20
Hall, G.   Interview.   Motion Pic Classic 12:26 Je '21
Smith, F. J.   Interview.   Motion Pic Classic 13:16 N '21
Hall, G. and Fletcher, A. W.   Interview.   Motion Pic 23:47 My
    '22
Interview.   Photop 21:39 My '22
Her darkest hour.   Classic 15:43 D '22
Service, F.   Interview.   Classic 15:18 F '23
Fletcher, A. W.   Interview.   Motion Pic 25:21 D '23
Why we are glad to get home.   Motion Pic 28:24 O '24
de Revere, F. V.   Face analysis of.   Motion Pic 28:48 N '24
Roberts, W. A.   Sketch.   Motion Pic 28:56 Ja '25
Carr, H.   Sketch.   Motion Pic 30:27 D '25
The evolution of a star.   Motion Pic 31:51 F '26
Hall, G.   Sketch.   Motion Pic Classic 25:53 Jl '27
My sister and I.   Theatre 46:14 N '27
Gish, D.   My sister Lillian.   Theatre 46:32 D '27
Goldbeck, E.   Sketch.   Motion Pic 39:50 My '30
Gish revives town.   Cinema Dig 1-7:28 Ag 8 '32
Recollections.   Stage 14:100 Ja '37
Simple arithmetic.   Cue 6-5:10 N 27 '37
The Gish girls gallop again.   Cue 11-46:16 N 14 '42
Parsons, L. O.   Cosmop's citation for the best supporting per-
    formance of the month.   Cosmop 120:45 F '46
Vidor, K.   Lillian Gish in opera.   Films & Filming 1-4:4 Ja '55
Desert island films.   Films & Filming 9-11:11 Ag '63
Stern, S.   Lillian Gish.   Film Culture 36:49 Spg/Sum '65
Still a trouper.   8mm Collect 13:10 Fall/Win '65
Thomas, B.   Not ready for museum, says Lillian at 69.   Classic
    Film Collect 15:38 Sum '66
Lee, R.   First lady of the screen.   Classic Film Collect 16:27
    Fall '66
Thompson, H.   Lillian Gish, the author, talks on D. W. Griffith.
    Classic Film Collect 24:15 Sum '69
Radcliffe, D.   Gish recalls birth of the films.   Classic Film
    Collect 25:extra 2 Fall '69

Bodeen, D.  Lillian Gish.  Silent Pic 4:2 Aut '69
Lillian Gish--director.  Silent Pic 6:12 Spg '70
Pin-up of the past.  Films & Filming 17-12:72 S '71
Kauffmann, S.  D. W. Griffith's Way down east.  Horizon 14:50
    Spg '72
Women directors.  Film Comment 8-4:40 N '72
Rubin, J.  Interview.  Classic Film Collect 39:10 Sum '73
Rubin, J.  The Lillian Gish lecture.  Classic Film Collect 40:44
    Fall '73
Bowers, R.  Gish's bicentennial proposal.  Films In R 25-8:467
    O '74

GLASS, GASTON
    Shaw, O.  Interview.  Motion Pic Classic 11:50 O '20

GLASS, KATHY
    Whitney, D.  They wanted a girl with "Mia vibes. "  TV Guide
        20-52:20 D 23 '72

GLAUM, LOUISE
    How she became a photoplayer.  Motion Pic 9:92 My '15
    Lee, C.  Work of.  Motion Pic Classic 4:44 Mr '17
    Howe, H.  Sketch.  Motion Pic Classic 5:52 D '17
    Milton, M.  Interview.  Motion Pic Classic 6:29 Ag '18
    Taylor, M. K.  Interview.  Motion Pic Classic 8:48 Je '19
    Bruce, B.  Interview.  Motion Pic 20:62 S '20
    Drew, R.  Interview.  Motion Pic 23:72 Mr '22
    Obit.  Classic Film Collect 30:extra 4 Spg '71
        Screen World 22:237 '71
    Bio note.  Silent Pic 14:20 Spg '72

GLEASON, JACKIE
    Fashionable fat fellow.  Cue 13-25:12 Je 17 '44
    Robinson, M.  Gleeful Goliath.  Colliers 128:18 Ag 25 '51
    Gleason gets girls and awa-a-ay he goes!  Life 33:87 S 29 '52
    Keep it corny.  Newsweek 40:66 O 6 '52
    Minoff, P.  A dan, dan dandy comic.  Cue 21-43:13 O 25 '52
    Make me laugh!  TV Guide 1-4:5 Ap 24 '53
    Boal, S.  Many sides of Gleason.  Coronet 34:61 My '53
    Gleason plays Hamlet.  TV Guide 1-14:8 Jl 3 '53
    On with the girls.  Life 35:113 O 19 '53
    McCarthy, J.  Ten men in one.  Cosmop 135:24 N '53
    Minoff, P.  Gleason's "Portrettes. "  Cue 22-52:14 D 26 '53
    For fat circulation.  Newsweek 43:72 Mr 1 '54
    TV's good time Charlie.  TV Guide 2-13:5 Mr 26; 2-14:15 Ap 2;
        2-15:13 Ap 9 '54
    Rosten, L.  Mr. Saturday nite.  Look 18:23 Je 1 '54
    Rosten, L.  Fat, sad and funny.  Look 18:88 Je 15 '54
    Businessman's heyday.  Newsweek 45:60 Ja 3 '55
    Jack for Jackie.  Time 65:52 Ja 3 '55
    Gleason drives himself harder.  Life 38:32 Ja 24 '55
    How Gleason got Berle's job.  TV Guide 3-5:3 Ja 29 '55
    Drury, M.  E pluribus Gleason.  Colliers 135:34 Mr 18; 36 Ap

1 '55
Traveling music.   Newsweek 46:66 Ag 8 '55
Tops in tunesmiths.   Coronet 38:73 Ag '55
Battle of the giants.   Newsweek 46:111 S 26 '55
One of these days, Alice.   TV Guide 3-40:13 O 1 '55
What Berle didn't tell.   TV Guide 3-43:5 O 22 '55
Jackie, Perry and a TV row.   Life 40:47 F 13 '56
Bishop, J.   Life story of Gleason.   Look 20:34 F 7; 77 F 21;
     86 Mr 6 '56
O'Hara, J.   Appointment with O'Hara.   Colliers 137:6 Mr 16 '56
How to tell a story.   Good House 142:68 Mr '56
Inside the comedians.   Newsweek 47:58 Je 25 '56
Too much for Gleason.   Newsweek 48:68 S 24 '56
De Blois, F.   And away we go.   TV Guide 4-39:5 S 29 '56
Minoff, P.   It's no joke.   Cue 26-2:10 Ja 12 '57
Elias, A. J.   Composer, conductor, comedian.   Etude 75:22 Ja
     '57
Shanley, J. P.   Television.   America 97:290 Je 1 '57
And away he goes.   TV Guide 5-24:7 Je 15 '57
Martin, P.   I call on Gleason; interview.   Sat Eve Post 230:36
     Jl 6 '57
Pensioner.   Newsweek 51:60 Ja 6 '58
Big comebacks.   Newsweek 51:66 Je 16 '58
Jackie's unfamiliar face.   Life 45:105 O 13 '58
Neither new nor old.   Time 72:55 O 20 '58
Lardner, J.   Air.   New Yorker 34:200 D 13 '58
Prideaux, T.   Gentlefolk and the bum.   Life 47:122 N 2 '59
His round house.   Pop Mech 113:88 Ap '60
Away you go.   Newsweek 56:90 S 12 '60
Gleason, J.   Dear old dad.   Good House 151:74 N '60
This is a panel show?   Newsweek 57:72 Ja 30 '61
Jackie ties off again.   TV Guide 9-7:8 F 18 '61
Jackie acts himself.   Life 50:107 Ap 14 '61
Magnificent muttonhead.   Time 77:52 My 5 '61
Gleason sinks his teeth in Paris.   Life 51:106 Jl 14 '61
Big hustler.   Time 78:34 D 29 '61
Mine host.   Newsweek 60:62 Ag 20 '62
And away we go again.   Life 53:111 O 5 '62
Brossard, C.   A new partner.   Look 26:84 O 9 '62
Gehman, R.   The great one.   TV Guide 10-41:16 O 13; 10-42:10
     O 20; 10-43:22 O 27 '62
McCarthy, J.   Indomitable Gleason.   Holiday 32:131 D '62
Interview.   Playboy 9:63 D '62
Reddy, J.   TV's vast waistband.   Read Dig 82:132 F '63
June Taylor dancers open with tap.   Dance 37:42 Je '63
Rising star.   Film R p41 '63/64
Bester, A.   The hollow clown.   Show 4-1:70 Ja '64
Efron, E.   Gleason on sin, music, Plato, pity and other sub-
     jects.   TV Guide 13-6:15 F 6 '65
Morgan, T. B.   How sweet it is--or is it?   TV Guide 13-39:20
     S 25 '65
Kobrin, J.   Why Gleason got the headlines.   TV Guide 14-19:12
     My 7 '66

Second honeymoon.   Time 88:108 O 14 '66
Rollin, B.   Gleason and Carney.   Look 30:76 N 15 '66
Davidson, B.   Anything I can't lick appeals to me.   Sat Eve
   Post 240:30 F 11 '67
King of Miami.   Newsweek 69:104 F 13 '67
Crail, T.   His majesty Jackie the first.   TV Guide 15-11:16 Mr
   18 '67
Crail, T.   Waiting for Jackie.   TV Guide 16-10:24 Mr 9 '68
King, L.   Gleason on Gleason.   TV Guide 17-25:16 Je 21 '69
Miller, M.   Gleason wants you in Miami tomorrow morning.   TV
   Guide 17-47:6 N 22 '69
Crail, T.   How he lost 61 pounds.   TV Guide 18-12:20 Mr 21
   '70
Musel, R.   Why pay to keep me off the air?   TV Guide 18-50:
   36 D 12 '70
Metz, R.   And awaaayy Gleason goes again.   N. Y. Times sec
   2:15 Ag 5 '73
   Same.   N. Y. Times Bio Ed p1298 Ag '73
Robbins, F.   Interview.   Gallery 2-7:27 Jl '74

GLEASON, JAMES
   Sketch.   Theatre 42:18 Ag '25
   He spelled success with a "z. "   Lions R 3-2:no p# Ja '44
   Obit.   Film R p10 '59/60
      Screen World 11:219 '60

GLENN, ROY
   Obit.   Screen World 23:237 '72

GLYNNE, DEREK
   St. Johns, I.   Sketch.   Photop 25:53 My '24

GOBEL, GEORGE
   Hot from the saloons.   Newsweek 44:65 O 18 '54
   Low pressure comic with a high rating.   N. Y. Times Mag p17
      N 7 '54
   Pretty mixed up.   Time 64:52 N 22 '54
   Gobel bowls 'em over.   TV Guide 2-49:5 D 4 '54
   Wainright, S.   Believe thee George.   Life 37:69 D 27 '54
   Gobel: 1954's contribution to comedy.   Newsweek 44:44 D 27 '54
   People are talking about.   Vogue 124:124 D '54
   Life and times of Gobel.   TV Guide 3-18:10 Ap 30 '55
   You can be a handyman.   Home & Gard 33:82 Ap '55
   Child guidance and all like that.   Colliers 135:90 My 13 '55
   Harris, E.   George Gobel.   Look 19:78 My 31 '55
   Confessions of a southpaw.   Am Mag 160:26 Jl '55
   Will second year jinx get Gobel?   TV Guide 3-43:17 O 22 '55
   Kanter, H.   One quarter inch from the truth.   Coronet 39:66 N
      '55
   Seldes, G.   Envying the dead.   Sat R 39:24 Ap 7 '56
   Cerf, B.   Trade winds.   Sat R 39:5 Ap 21 '56
   A new cup of tea.   TV Guide 4-42:8 O 20 '56
   Why George did it.   TV Guide 4-47:24 N 24 '56

Shanley, J. P. Television. America 97:290 Je 1 '57
Say it isn't so, boys. TV Guide 5-47:17 N 23 '57
How to take command at the perfume counter. Vogue 130:132 D
    '57
All about lonesome George. TV Guide 7-5:17 Ja 31 '59
As George goes and sues. Newsweek 53:92 Je 8 '59

GODDARD, MARK
    Something on the ball. TV Guide 10-30:26 Jl 28 '62

GODDARD, PAULETTE
    Derr, E. Sketch. Movie Classic 3:29 O '32
    Romance with Chaplin. Movie Classic 4:20 Ag '33
    Dillon, F. Interview. Movie Classic 6:46 Ag '34
    Lee, S. Chaplin's mystery girl. Movie Classic 10:37 Mr '36
    Garvey, L. Can she overcome the Chaplin jinx? Motion Pic
        11:33 N '36
    Wilson, E. It's in the stars. Silver Screen 10-3:26 Ja '40
    Bio note; filmog. Movies & People 2:18 '40
    Wilson, R. The new mystery of Mr. and Mrs. Chaplin. Photop
        18:56 Ja '41
    Franchey, J. R. Canny campaigner. Silver S 13-2:40 D '42
    Franchey, J. R. The constant imp. Silver S 13-10:24 Ag '43
    Hendricks, H. Madame Cheesecake in the Far East. Silver S
        14-11:26 S '44
    Goddard plays rags to riches in new film. Cue 15-3:13 Ja 19
        '46
    Service, F. They don't come any smarter. Silver S 16-4:25
        F '46
    Sketch. Photop 30:103 Ap '47
    My luckiest day. Cosmop 123:84 O '47
    Home of. Photop 33:56 Ag '48
    Maxwell, E. Sketch. Photop 36:35 D '49
    Pinups of the past. Films & Filming 16-12:110 S '70
    Barthel, J. Quartet of queens. Life 70:62 F 19 '71
    Here's to the ladies. Screen Greats 1-2:28 Sum '71
    Amory, C. Interview. Sat R 55:8 Mr 11 '72
    People are talking about. Vogue 159:60 Mr 15 '72
    Sheppard, E. Interview. Harp Baz 105:12 Jl '72
    Lambert, G. The making of Gone with the wind. Atlantic 231-
        2:49 F '73
    Bowman, C. H. Jr. Letter. Films In R 24-4:252 Ap '73
    Gorney, J. Paulette Goddard; filmog. Films In R 25-7:401 Ag/
        S '74

GODFREY, ARTHUR
    Frank, S. Tycoons of the turntable. Colliers 119:18 Mr 22 '45
    Sneers after breakfast. Newsweek 26:76 S 3 '45
    Early bird. Time 48:87 S 2 '46
    Beatty, J. Chitchat and song. Am Mag 143:38 Je '47
    Man with a briery voice. Newsweek 30:48 D 8 '47
    Havemann, A. G. Godfrey. Life 24:89 Je 7 '48
        Same abridged. Read Dig 53:63 S '48

Bio.   Cur Bio Jl '48
Bobby-sox silencer.   Newsweek 34:58 N 21 '49
Hughes, C.   What's (his) secret?   Coronet 27:158 D '49
Oceans of empathy.   Time 55:72 F 27 '50
Godfrey replies.   Newsweek 35:48 Ap 3 '50
Who, me?   Life 55:44 Ap 3 '50
Hamburger, P.   Television.   New Yorkers 26:70 Je 10 '50
Shriver, W. H.   Jr.   Radio and television.   Cath W 171:386 Ag
   '50
CBS's barefoot boy.   Newsweek 38:55 Ag 6 '51
Winchester, J. A.   Pilot Godfrey sells aviation to America.
   Coronet 31:22 Ja '52
My favorite stories.   Coronet 31:32 Ap '52
Godfrey is TV proof.   Newsweek 39:62 My 19 '52
Gallery, D. V.   My pal.   Sat Eve Post 225:25 Jl 19 '52
Taves, L.   Why women love (him).   McCalls 80:46 O '52
She sings for Godfrey's supper.   McCalls 80:24 Ap '53
Davidson, B.   Godfrey and his fan mail.   Colliers 131:11 My 2
   '53
Godfrey surgery.   TV Guide 1-6:4 My 8 '53
Operation Godfrey.   Time 61:67 My 25 '53
Operation no one.   Newsweek 41:88 My 25 '53
Slocum, W. J.   Godfrey you never see.   Coronet 34:70 Je '53
Godfrey's return.   TV Guide 1-15:5 Jl 10 '53
Whitcomb, J.   Backstage with Godfrey's friends.   Cosmop 135:48
   Ag '53
Godfrey is back.   Newsweek 42:52 Ag 10 '53
Wilson, J.   Godfrey himself.   Look 17:29 S 22; 45 O 6; 51 O
   20 '53
Godfrey's first movie.   TV Guide 1-30:7 O 23 '53
It's the humility.   Newsweek 42:51 N 2 '53
Cogley, J.   Humility.   Commonweal 59:110 N 6 '53
Godfrey vs. La Rosa.   TV Guide 1-33:A-2 N 13 '53
Godfrey and his happy-hunting friends.   Newsweek 42:90 N 30 '53
Kass, R.   Films and TV.   Cath W 178:226 D '53
Like a divorce.   Time 63:70 Ja 18 '54
Good deal of buzzing.   Newsweek 43:56 Ja 25 '54
Wild blue yonder.   Time 63:47 Ja 25 '54
Godfrey not expected to fight CAA action.   Aviation W 60:13 F 1
   '54
Cloud and sunshine.   Time 63:59 F 1 '54
CAA weighs Godfrey version of takeoff.   Aviation W 60:14 F 8
   '54
O'Brian, J.   Facts about Godfrey.   Am Mer 78:3 Mr '54
In the soup.   Time 63:88 My 24 '54
What's Godfrey's hold on women?   TV Guide 2-23:5 Je 4 '54
Virtue reigns.   Time 64:37 Jl 26 '54
Stahl, B.   Godfrey snaps back at "untruths."   TV Guide 2-32:13
   Ag 7 '54
Munro, C.   Must our teachers be underprivileged?   Look 18:42
   S 21 '54
Meegan, J.   When Godfrey met Helen Hayes.   Coronet 37:25 D
   '54

Stahl, B. Godfrey talks.   TV Guide 3-2:5 Ja 8; 3-3:13 Ja 15 '55
One man's meat.   Newsweek 45:90 Ap 25 '55
Ex-friends.   Time 65:49 Ap 25 '55
Is this the end of Godfrey?   TV Guide 3-19:3 My 7 '55
Unrequited love.   Newsweek 45:56 My 30 '55
Here's to Hawaii.   Coronet 38:43 My '55
Godfrey again.   Newsweek 45:94 Je 20 '55
Crosby, J.  It doesn't seem like old times.   Colliers 136:27 S 3
     '55
Godfrey's feud with the press.   TV Guide 3-37:5 S 10; 3-38:13 S
     17 '55
Godfrey faces inquiry.   Aviation W 63:139 S 19 '55
Storm center.   Newsweek 46:58 S 26 '55
Godfrey pays penalty.   Aviation W 63:18 O 10 '55
I'll quit in '65.   Newsweek 46:103 O 17 '55
Martin, P.   This is my story.   Sat Eve Post 228:19 N 5; 20 N
     12; 28 N 19; 32 N 26; 36 D 3; 28 D 10; 25 D 17; 20 D 24 '55
Discussion.   Colliers 136:24 N 11 '55
All about authors.   Newsweek 46:74 D 5 '55
Blow, counterblow.   Newsweek 46:84 D 19 '55
What's Godfrey like off the air.   TV Guide 4-1:4 Ja 7 '56
Godfrey and ex-friends; letters.   Sat Eve Post 228:4 Ja 14 '56
The grind that Godfrey couldn't take.   TV Guide 4-19:10 My 12
     '56
Real meaning of air power; address.   Vital Speeches 22:645 Ag
     15 '56
Sullivan, E.   My story.   Colliers 138:71 S 28 '56
The stuff that stars are made of.   TV Guide 5-1:8 Ja 5 '57
White hunter.   Time 69:40 Ap 1 '57
Mr. Godfrey of Miami Beach.   Cosmop 142:48 Ap '57
Helicopter safari in Africa.   Life 42:80 Je 10 '57
Interview.   Look 21:50 Je 11 '57
And now a byline.   Newsweek 50:52 Jl 29 '57
Godfrey deplores a TV trend.   TV Guide 6-10:5 Mr 8 '58
New Arthur Godfrey.   Newsweek 51:79 Mr 10 '58
Still friends.   Newsweek 52:80 Ag 18 '58
Down on the farm.   TV Guide 6-36:13 S 6 '58
Greenwood, J. R.   Aviation's man.   Flying 63:40 O '58
Lardner, J.   Air.   New Yorker 34:200 D 13 '58
Candid photos of an old pro at work.   TV Guide 6-52:8 D 27 '58
TV's supersalesman discusses commercials.   TV Guide 7-11:20
     Mr 14 '59
Lardner, J.   Godfrey's lament.   Newsweek 53:87 Mr 16 '59
Subbing for the readhead.   Newsweek 53:64 My 4 '59
Grace and courage.   Time 73:74 My 11 '59
Facing a cruel fact.   Newsweek 53:77 My 11 '59
Godfrey phenomenon.   Newsweek 53:65 My 25 '59
David, L.   Interview.   Am Mer 88:97 My '59
To live without fear.   TV Guide 7-37:8 S 12 '59
I'm thankful I'm alive.   McCalls 87:45 N '59
Wolters, L.   His fight against cancer.   Todays Health 37:23 N
     '59
Rooney, A. A.   The Godfrey you don't know.   Look 23:80 D

22 '59
Kamm, H.  Interview.  Look 24:107 My 10 '60
Godfrey's back.  TV Guide 8-41:18 O 8 '60
Godfrey on camera.  Newsweek 56:49 D 16 '60
Robin, A.  Living legends.  Todays Health 40:78 Mr '62
Godfrey, J. & K.  All the little Godfreys.  Good House 154:70
    Ap '62
Gill, A.  I feel like I could lick the world.  TV Guide 11-51:15
    D 21 '63
Francis, D.  Interview.  Pop Sci 189:134 O '66
Challenge of the seventies.  Esquire 72:8 N '69
Godfrey hangs out a new pollution line.  Bsns W p38 F 21 '70
Confessions of a polluter.  Read Dig 97:60 S '70
Man and his environment.  PTA Mag 65:2 S '70
Address July 13, 1971.  Conservationist 26:8 O '71
Schoenstein, R.  Stay young regimen of Godfrey.  Todays Health
    50:28 Ja '72
Godfrey receives Horticulture award.  Horticulture 50:24 My '72

GODFREY, PETER
    Morris, G.  From Gate to Gate.  Theatre Arts 29:58 Ja '45
    Obit.  Screen World 22:237 '71

GODOWSKY, DAGMAR
    Interview.  Motion Pic Classic 11:32 Ja '21
    Concerning my husband.  Motion Pic 23:62 Jl '22

GOETZ, THEO
    Papa's not kaput.  TV Guide 5-43:17 O 26 '57

GOLITZIN, NATALIE
    Glyn, E.  Her romantic story.  Photop 34:39 O '28

GOLONKA, ARLENE
    Hano, A.  What's an Arlene Golonka?  TV Guide 17-21:18 My
        24 '69

GOLOVINA, SVETLANA
    Note.  Int Film G 10:335 '73

GOMBELL, MINNA
    Obit.  Classic Film Collect 39:extra 1 Sum '73
        Screen World p234 '74

GOMEZ, THOMAS
    Heavies?  Who us?  TV Guide 8-18:23 Ap 30 '60
    Obit.  Classic Film Collect 31:62 Sum '71
        N.Y. Times p50 Je 20 '71
        Same.  N.Y. Times Bio Ed Je 20 '71
        Screen World 23:237 '72

GOODE, JACK
    Obit.  N.Y. Times p38 Je 25 '71
        Screen World 23:237 '72

GOODMAN, DODY
    Taylor, T.  Is Dody for real?  Cue 26-38:12 S 21 '57
    Blond called Dody.  Newsweek 50:94 O 28 '57
    Dody defies description.  TV Guide 6-4:12 Ja 25 '58
    Girl that Jack built.  Time 71:61 Mr 24 '58

GOODRICH, EDNA
    How to get into motion pictures.  Motion Pic Classic 3:39 D '16
    Hall, G.  Interview.  Motion Pic 16:35 D '18

GOODWIN, BILL
    Announcing Bill Goodwin.  Lions R 3-4:no p# Jl '44

GORCEY, BERNARD
    Cummings, A.  Interview.  Motion Pic Classic 27:21 Mr '28

GORCEY, LEO
    How tough are the Dead End Kids?  Screen Book 21-6:28 Ja '39
    Obit.  Classic Film Collect 24:14 Sum '69
        N. Y. Times p47 Je 4 '69
        Newsweek 73:71 Je 16 '69
        Screen World 21:236 '70
        Time 93:90 Je 13 '69

GORDON, GALE
    Danger!  Principal at work!  TV Guide 3-13:5 Mr 26 '55
    Master of the slow burn.  TV Guide 10-31:22 Ag 4 '62
    The night he helped a woman escape from jail.  Photop 77-6:58
       Je '70
    Gordon talks about Lucille Ball.  Photop 85-6:48 Je '74

GORDON, GAVIN
    Goldbeck, E.  Sketch.  Motion Pic 40:77 N '30
    Hillson, A.  The strange case of 99.  Silver S 1-8:39 Je '31
    Sketch.  Theatre World 19:219 My '33

GORDON, HUNTLEY
    Hall, G.  Interview.  Motion Pic 23:57 F '22
    Tully, J.  Interview.  Motion Pic Classic 20:24 F '25
    St. Johns, I.  Sketch.  Photop 28:76 Je '25
    Wells, H. K.  Sketch.  Motion Pic Classic 23:38 Ag '26

GORDON, KITTY
    Obit.  N. Y. Times Bio Ed p689 My '74

GORDON, ROBERT
    Lamb, G.  Interview.  Motion Pic 18:47 S '19
    Sketch.  Dram Mir 82:1075 My 22 '20
    Herbert, H.  Interview.  Motion Pic 20:56 O '20
    Obit.  Screen World 23:237 '72

## GORDON, RUTH
Young, S.  Compared with Helen Hayes.   New Rep 69:163 D 23
    '31
An open letter to.   Theatre Guild 9:14 Mr '32
Laughton, C.  Work of.   Stage 14:44 D '36
She works with Garbo.   Lions R 1-3:no p# N '41
Sketch.   Harp Baz 78:50 Ja '44
Lydon, S.  Faa-bu-lous long run of Gordon and Kanin.   N. Y.
    Times Mag p64 O 5 '69
...20, 21, 73 and courting.   Vogue 154:173 N 1 '69
Myself among others; excerpts.   Vogue 157:138 Mr 1; 102 Mr
    15; 126 Ap 1 '71
Kent, L.  A boy of 20 and a woman of 80.   N. Y. Times Bio
    Ed Ap 4 '71
Amory, C.  Trade winds.   Sat R 54:8 My 22 '71
Authors and editors; interview.   Pub W 199:63 My 31 '71
O'Brien, G.  Interview.   Interview 20:32 Mr '72
Bio.   Cur Bio 33:15 Ap '72
Mr. and Mrs.  Films Illus 1-11:19 My '72

## GORDONE, CHARLES
Quiet talk with myself.   Esquire 73:78 Ja '70
Keneas, A.  From the Muthah lode.   Newsweek 75:95 My 25 '70
Garland, P.  Prize winners.   Ebony 25:29 Jl '70

## GORMAN, CLIFF
Man from The boys in the band.   Life 68:49 My 8 '70
Cliff Gorman as Lenny.   Vogue 158:75 Ag 1 '71
Gussow, M.  Gorman reflects on role as Lenny.   N. Y. Times
    sec 2:20 My 28 '71
Flatley, G.  Gorman is a cool Lenny.   N. Y. Times Bio Ed Je
    6 '71
Zelcer, A.  Coitus interrupted.   After Dark 4-8:18 D '71

## GORMAN, TOM
Obit.   N. Y. Times p42 O 4 '71

## GORNEY, KAREN
Lang, B.  The trouble with Tara.   TV Guide 19-41:24 O 9 '71

## GORSHIN, FRANK
Zadan, C.  Out of town with "Jimmy. "   After Dark 11-7:17 N
    '69

## GORTNER, MARJOE
Schickel, R.  Con man on the sawdust trail.   Life 73:18 Jl 28
    '72
Zimmerman, P. D.  Thank you, Jesus.   Newsweek 80:62 Jl 30
    '72
Hollow holiness.   Time 100:45 Ag 14 '72

Preacher-turned-actor.   Pub W 202:67 Ag 21 '72
Forbes, C. A.   Rapped in celluloid.   Chr. Today 16:28 Ag 25
    '72
Lichtenstein, G.   Does somebody up there like...?   N. Y. Times
    Bio Ed p1478 Ag '72
Stoop, N. M.   Twenty-eight is a magic number.   After Dark 5-
    6:24 O '72
Speak of the devil.   Newsweek 80:94 N 27 '72
On the scene.   Playboy 19-11:191 N '72
Glantz, S. T.   Marjoe (about the film).   Film. Newsletter 6-1:
    20 N '72
Speak of the devil.   Newsweek 80:94 N 27 '72
Feighan, F.   Interview.   Penthouse 4-6:86 F '73
Gortner, M.   Who was guru Maharaj Ji?   Oui 3-5:91 My '74

GOSFIELD, MAURICE
    Russia's secret weapon.   TV Guide 5-5:12 F 2 '57

GOSSETT, LOU
    Stone, J.   Did we always eat watermelon?   N. Y. Times Bio Ed
        Ag 30 '70
    Ronan, M.   Interview.   Sr Schol 100:15 Ja 31 '72

GOUDAL, JETTA
    Carr, H.   Sketch.   Classic 20:20 O '24
    Autobiographical.   Motion Pic 30:47 Ag '25
    Donnell, D.   Interview.   Motion Pic Classic 22:36 F '26
    Clark, F.   Interview.   Photop 32:34 Ag '27
    Reid, M.   Her quarrel with Lupe Velez.   Motion Pic Classic 28:
        58 D '28
    Donnell, D.   Sketch.   Motion Pic Classic 28:22 F '29
    Cruikshank, H.   Sketch.   Motion Pic Classic 27:40 Jl '29
    Walker, H. L.   Her return to the screen.   Movie Classic 1:64
        N '31
    Bodeen, D.   Jetta Goudal; filmog.   Films In R 25-8:449 O '74
    Davis, H. R.   Letter.   Films In R 25-10:639 D '74

GOUGH, JOHN
    Obit.   Screen World 20:235 '69

GOULD, ELLIOT
    Paley, M.   Steamrollered to stardom.   Life 67:R D 12 '69
    Greenfeld, J.   Funnyboy makes good.   Show 1-2:44 F '70
    On the scene.   Playboy 17-2:168 F '70
    Kasindorf, M.   Mallomar kid.   Newsweek 75:88 Mr 9 '70
    Salute of the week.   Cue 39-26:1 Je 27 '70
    The Urban Don Quixote.   Time 96:35 S 7 '70
    Mayer, M.   Gould as the entrepreneur.   Fortune 82:109 O '70
    Live together? No.  Love together? Yes.   Photop 78-4:48 O '70
    Solid Gould (pictorial).   Playboy 17-10:99 O '70
    Mothner, I.   Now faces.   Look 34:77 N 3 '70
    Interview.   Playboy 17-11:77 N '70
    Knight, A. & Alpert, H.   Sex stars of 1970.   Playboy 17-12:220

D '70
Bio.   Cur Bio 32:7 F '71
The sex problem that kept the army from taking me.   Photop
   79-3:64 Mr '71
Crackup.   Photop 79-6:84 Je '71
Bio.   Brit Bk Yr 1971:141 '71
Bio.   Cur Bio Yrbk 1971:167 '72
Flatley, G.   Gould is back.   N.Y. Times Bio Ed p425 Mr '73
Mills, B.   A new M*A*S*H-terpiece for Elliot and Don?   N.Y.
   Times sec 2:13 S 16 '73
The short hello.   Films Illus 3-27:115 S '73
McAsh, I.   As good as Gould.   Films Illus 3-31:273 Ja '74
City boy meets country girl.   Photop 86-3:52 S '74
Wilkins, B.   Career?   Up again.   Love life?   Blah.   People
   2-13:20 S 16 '74

GOULD, SANDRA
   Raddatz, L.   A caricature she sadly admits.   TV Guide 18-28:
      12 Je 11 '70

GOULET, ROBERT
   Well, it's an asset.   TV Guide 10-36:26 S 8 '62
   Good knight.   Newsweek 60:73 N 19 '62
   Arbus, D.   Hear your heroes.   Seventeen 22:64 Ja '63
   Hamblin, D. J.   Gangway for Goulet.   Life 54:86 Ap 26 '63
   Millstein, G.   Go-go-go of Goulet.   Sat Eve Post 236:24 Ap 27
      '63
   Hockstein, R.   Goulet goes to Hollywood.   Good House 157:30
      S '63
   Lewis, R. W.   Before the blue light went out.   TV Guide 14-34:
      24 Ag 20 '66
   My child.   Photop 80-4:16 O '71

GRABLE, BETTY
   Vallee, W. L.   Grable makes good again.   Silver S 10-10:40 Ag
      '40
   Wilson, E.   The boys all go for Betty.   Silver S 11-9:24 Jl '41
   Manners, M. J.   Are women natural born feudists?   Silver S
      13-1:24 N '42
   Wilson, E.   Betty's tour of the army camps.   Silver S 13-2:24
      D '42
   Letter from Liza.   Silver S 13-7:89 My '43
   Her legs a Hollywood landmark.   Life 14:82 Je 7 '43
   Autobiographical.   Cosmop 115:40 O '43
   Her new baby.   Life 16:32 My 8 '44
   Her new baby.   Photop 24:27 My '44
   Items from her life.   Photop 26:42 D '44
   What she and Mr. James argue about.   Photop 27:61 Jl '45
   Sharpe, H.   Betty and the simple life.   Silver S 16-7:30 My '46
   The song I remember.   Photop 29:58 Je '46
   Marsh, P.   Betty Grable as a mother.   Silver S 18-2:22 D '47
   Lane, F.   I'm sorry about those rumors.   Silver S 20-7:30 My
      '50

Churchill, R. & B.  Off-screen Betty.  Silver S 21-9:22 Jl '51
My favorite role.  Film R p31 '51/52
Why I got tired of it all.  Silver S 22-10:36 Ag '52
The pin-up girls.  Screen Greats 1-2:20 Sum '71
The queen of hearts.  Photop 82-3:66 S '72
Kendall, R.  Grable's gorgeous gams.  Hollywood Stu 7-7:20 N
    '72
Shipley, G.  Some notes on some of film's dancers.  Filmograph
    3-1:15 '72
Obit.  N. Y. Times Bio Ed p1146 Jl '73
Basinger, J.  Betty Grable 1916-1973.  N. Y. Times sec 2:9 Jl
    15 '73
    Same.  N. Y. Times Bio Ed p1147 Jl '73
Basinger, J.  Remembering Betty Grable.  Film Fan Mo 145/
    146:3 Jl/Ag '73
Baker, R.  Grable remembered.  Films Illus 3-26:76 Ag '73
Girney, J.  Betty Grable--1916-1973; filmog.  Films In R 24-7:
    385 Ag/S '73
In memory.  Show 3-6:74 S '73
Richardson, J. D.  Betty Grable 1916-1973.  After Dark 6-5:50
    S '73
Polunsky, B.  Flicker footlights.  Classic Film Collect 40:42
    Fall '73
Notables throng Grable rites.  Classic Film Collect 40:58 Fall
    '73
The men in her life remember her.  Photop 84-4:51 O '73
Obit.  Screen World p234 '74
Letters.  Films In R 25-1:57 Ja '74

GRACE, DICK
    Lubon, D.  Sketch.  Motion Pic Classic 28:58 Ja '29
    Daredeviling in air and water for the movies.  Lit Dig 103:24 D
        21 '29
    Calhoun, D.  Interview.  Motion Pic Classic 31:51 Ap '30

GRACE, ROBYN
    Robyn's biography is for the birds.  TV Guide 12-5:32 F 1 '64

GRAD, GENEVIEVE
    They didn't plan to be movie stars.  Unifrance 56:no p# Spg '62

GRADY, DON
    Grady's on the move.  TV Guide 13-41:13 O 9 '65

GRAFF, WILTON
    Obit.  Screen World 21:236 '70

GRAFTON, GLORIA
    Meet the cover(all) girls.  Lions R 3-2:no p# Ja '44

GRAHAME, GLORIA
    Local girl makes good.  Lions R 4-1:no p# F '45
    Marsh, P.  Girl with the sinful stare.  Silver S 23-7:35 My '53

Walker, H. L.   Try and figure her out.   Silver S 24-1:33 N '53
Rogers, V.   Grahame can take a beating.   Silver S 24-6:31 Ap
  '54

GRANDIN, ETHEL
  Katterjohn, M. M.   Interview.   Green Book 12:255 Ag '14

GRANELLI, MIREILLE
  A flash on Granelli.   Unifrance 48:9 O '58

GRANGER, FARLEY
  Letter to Roddy McDowall.   Photop 27:59 O '45
  Kilgallen, D.   Sketch.   Photop 34:29 Ja '49
  Mann, M.   What women mean to him.   Silver S 19-12:36 O '49
  Wilson, E.   Girls can wait.   Silver S 20-8:26 Je '50
  Tildesley, A. L.   So in the mood for love.   Silver S 23-8:38 Je
    '53
  Gow, G.   Out into the world; filmog.   Films & Filming 20-1:15
    O '73

GRANGER, STEWART
  Holland, J.   The man Jean Simmons married.   Silver S 21-6:36
    Ap '51
  My favorite role.   Film R p22 '52/53
  See, C.   One of the originals returns.   TV Guide 18-51:10 D 19
    '70

GRANT, BARRA
  Adler, D.   Girl with definite edges.   TV Guide 21-37:35 S 15 '73

GRANT, CARY
  Norris, L.   Sketch.   Movie Classic 2:52 Ag '32
  Melcher, E.   Cary Grant.   Cinema Dig 1-13:14 O 31 '32
  Maddox, B.   They keep "Bachelor's Hall."   Silver S 3-5:20 Mr
    '33
  Goldbeck, E.   Interview.   Motion Pic 45:60 My '33
  Harrison, H.   The Grant that took Virginia.   Silver S 4-7:47 My
    '34
  Sketch.   Vanity Fair 43:52 N '34
  Jackson, G.   Sketch.   Movie Classic 7:37 Ja '35
  Grant, J.   Sketch.   Movie Classic 8:83 Ap '35
  Crowley, G.   Interview. Motion Pic 50:38 Ja '36
  Harmel, E.   Sketch.   Movie Classic 11:40 D '36
  Mack, G.   Story of.   Motion Pic 52:35 D '36
  Rankin, R.   A hair-raising story.   Silver S 7-8:51 Je '37
  Sketch.   Photop 51:4 Je '37
  Sullivan, E.   Ascending.   Silver S 8-6:26 Ap '38
  Henderson, J.   Valiant is the word for Cary.   Screen Book 21-1:
    33 Ag '38
  Churchill, E.   True story of his stand-in.   Silver S 8-11:30 S
    '38
  Best, K.   Work of.   Stage 16:34 Ap 15 '39
  Mulvey, K.   Sketch.   Womans Home C 66:7 O '39

Reid, J.  Cary plays the game his own way.   Silver S 10-12:24
     O '40
Bio note; filmog.   Movies & People 2:18 '40
Trotter, M.  Astrological forecast.   Photop 18:31 F '41
Wood, V.  The foibles of the fabulous Cary.   Silver S 12-2:22
     D '41
His marriage to Barbara Hutton.   Newsweek 20:31 Jl 20 '42
One of the best liked men in Hollywood.   Photop 23:8 N '43
Maddox, B.  Reaching the unreachable.   Silver S 17-4:44 F '47
Dudley, F.  Story of.   Photop 30:19 My '47
Parsons, L. O.  Cosmop's citation for best performance of
     month.   Cosmop 123:54 Ag '47
Sheridan, A.  The guy.   Silver S 19-11:20 S '49
Balling, F. D.  Why every bachelor should be married.   Silver
     S 20-9:22 Jl '50
Perennial lover boy.   Cue 26-34:12 Ag 24 '57
Star of the year; filmog.   Film R p15 '60/61
Cary Grant.   Look 27:87 D 17 '63
Battelle, P.  Mrs. Cary Grant talks about marrying and divorcing
     him.   Ladies Home J 85:107 Ap '68
Levy, R.  To catch a star.   Dun's R 92:90 S '68
How a star fits a director's chair.   Bsns W p92 D 21 '68
I just gave birth to Cary Grant's baby.   Photop 77-6:28 Je '70
My baby is Cary Grant's.   Photop 78-1:66 Jl '70
Nine minds in trouble.   Photop 78-3:56 S '70
This is Cary Grant's baby.   Photop 78-4:51 O '70
Lilly, D.  Day at the office with Cary Grant.   Ladies Home J
     87:142 N '70
Mangel, C.  The new women in the life of Cary Grant.   Look
     35-4:59 F 23 '71
Perfect gentlemen.   Screen Greats 1-2:66 Sum '71
Dyan Cannon's fears for little Jennifer.   Mod Screen 65-11:32 N
     '71
Bogdanovich, P.  Hollywood.   Esquire 77:82 Ap '72
Flatley, G.  Cary, from Mae to September.   N. Y. Times sec
     2:1 Jl 22 '73
     Same.   N. Y. Times Bio Ed p1148 Jl '73
Sharpe, H.  Dimple in his chin.   Liberty 1-10:50 Fall '73
Allan, I.  Cary Grant.   Film Album 3:entire issue.  n. d.

GRANT, KATHY
     Rising star.   Film R p22 '60/61
     What Bing Crosby is doing for golf, his wife is doing for golf
          fashions.   N. Y. Times Bio Ed D 26 '71
     It's Bing's special, but Kathy is the Crosby to watch these days.
          People 2-25:34 D 16 '74

GRANT, LEE
     Considine, S.  Hollywood starlet.   After Dark 11-8:24 D '69
     Burke, T.  The lady who ran off with the landlord.   N. Y. Times
          Bio Ed Jl 5 '70
     Blevins, W.  A study in courage.   Show 2-5:23 Jl '71
     People are talking about.   Vogue 160:85 Jl '72

Oberon, G.  No regrets.  Interview 24:20 Ag '72
Townsend, R.  Being an actress is such hell.  Movie Dig 1-6:
    35 N '72
Grant, L.  Selling out to Hollywood, or home is where the work
    is.  N. Y. Times sec 2:1 Ag 12 '73
Interview.  Viva 1-10:47 Jl '74

GRANT, VALENTINE
    Boone, J. A.  Sketch.  Motion Pic Classic 1:43 Ja '16
    Nelson, E. M.  Interview.  Motion Pic Classic 4:46 Jl '17
    Naylor, H. S.  Interview.  Motion Pic 15:31 Ap '18

GRANVILLE, BONITA
    Schwarzkopf, J.  Sketch.  Motion Pic 51:21 Jl '36
    Hamilton, S.  Sketch.  Photop 52:31 S '38
    Hamilton, S.  Sketch.  Photop 54:30 Jl '40
    Bonita grows up.  Lions R 1-1:no p# S '41
    Holland, J.  Will Jackie and Bonita wed?  Silver S 12-2:38 D '41
    Vallee, W. L.  She made it the easy way.  Silver S 13-8:42 Je
        '43
    Trotter, M.  Prediction for 1944.  Photop 24:26 Ja '44
    The Brat grows up.  Lions R 3-3:no p# Ap '44
    Vallee, W. L.  Bonita and her crushes.  Silver S 14-10:38 Ag
        '44
    Vermilye, J.  Bonita Granville; filmog.  Film Fan Mo 150:19 D
        '73

GRANVILLE, LOUISE
    Obit.  Screen World 20:235 '69

GRAPEWIN, CHARLES
    Bailey, P. H.  Woodworking is his hobby.  Leisure 4:32 D '37

GRASSBY, BERTRAM
    Trepel, B.  Interview.  Motion Pic 20:76 Ja '21

GRAVES, PETER
    Clepper, P. M.  The brothers Aurness.  TV Guide 18-29:16 Jl
        18 '70
    The Aurness album.  TV Guide 21-29:11 Jl 21 '73

GRAVES, RALPH
    Remont, F.  Interview.  Motion Pic Classic 9:18 N '19
    Naylor, H. S.  Interview.  Motion Pic 19:32 Je '20
    Service, F.  Interview.  Motion Pic Classic 13:26 N '21
    Naylor, H. S.  Interview.  Motion Pic 23:27 Ap '22

GRAVES, TERESA
    Lewis, R. W.  Then time out for Bible study.  TV Guide 22-48:
        20 N 30 '74

GRAVET, FERNAND (Also GRAVEY)
    Caine, D.  Interview.  Motion Pic 53:59 Ap '37

Cruikshank,  H.  Story of.  Motion Pic 53:51 My '37
Crichton,  K.  Fernand the great.  Colliers 101:15 Mr 19 '38
Fernand Gravey.  Visages 28:entire issue O '38
Bio note; filmog.  Movies & People 2:18 '40
Obit.  Film R p13 '71/72
    N. Y.  Times p50 N 4 '70
    N. Y.  Times Bio Ed N 4 '70
    Screen World 22:237 '71
    Time 96:85 N 16 '70


GRAVINA, CARLA
    These faces will win top places during 1959.  Films & Filming
    5-7:18 Ap '59


GRAY, ALEXANDER
    York, C.  Sketch.  Photop 36:68 N '29
    Spensley, D.  Sketch.  Motion Pic Classic 30:59 Ja '30


GRAY, COLEEN
    Sketch.  Photop 32:76 D '47
    Farmer's daughter.  Am Mag 145:111 Mr '48
    Marsh, P.  Hitting the jackpot double.  Silver S 19-2:34 D '48
    Gray, C.  I had a lulu of an inferiority complex.  Silver S 20-
    10:40 Ag '50
    Gray, C.  What men should mean to you.  Silver S 21-10:38 Ag
    '51


GRAY, DOLORES
    Johns, E.  Her ideas of the fallacy of achieving stardom in a
    night.  Theatre World 43:27 O '47
    Dolores scores a bullseye.  Cue 20-32:12 Ag 11 '51


GRAY, GILDA
    The blues.  Cur Opinion 67:165 S '19
    My new idea.  Met 56:38 S '22
    Smith, A.  Sketch.  Photop 28:38 O '25
    York, C.  Sketch.  Photop 29:84 Mr '26
    Thorpe, D.  How she does her stuff.  Motion Pic 32:40 S '26
    Redway, S.  Sketch.  Motion Pic 31:26 Ap '27
    Clyce, C.  Sketch.  Motion Pic Classic 25:54 Jl '27
    Carlisle, H.  In the Devil dance.  Motion Pic 34:45 Ja '28
    Cruikshank, H.  Sketch.  Motion Pic Classic 27:37 Je '28
    Home of.  Theatre 48:60 O '28
    Obit.  Screen World 11:219 '60


GRAY, GORDON
    Sketch.  Motion Pic Classic 3:68 Ja '17
    Sketch.  Motion Pic Classic 5:59 S '17


GRAY, JANINE
    This is Janine Gray.  TV Guide 13-26:19 Je 26 '65

GRAY, LAWRENCE
Edmonton, S.   Sketch.   Motion Pic Classic 22:64 S '25
Obit.   Screen World 22:237 '71

GRAY, LORNA
(Also known as Adrian Booth)
Brian, A. B.   The man I married.   Silver S 20-2:30 D '49
Malcomson, R. M.   The sound serial.   Views & Rs 3-1:13 Sum
'71

GRAY, NADIA
Rising star.   Film R p41 '51/52

GRAY, SALLY
Pinups of the past.   Films & Filming 19-2:68 N '72

GRAYSON, KATHRYN
Stars of tomorrow.   Lions R 1-11/12:no p# Jl/Ag '42
Hall, G.   The rumors no longer are true.   Silver S 13-9:48 Jl
'43
DeRig, M.   I've always known what I wanted.   Silver S 17-4:40
F '47
Hall, G.   Wedding bells for Kathryn.   Silver S 17-11:40 S '47
Ament, A.   Curiosity comes in handy.   Life With Music 2:14
Mr '49
Holland, J.   The kind of wife I am.   Silver S 20-10:30 Ag '50
Balling, F. D.   Lonely?  Not me.   Silver S 23-1:42 N '52
Maddox, B.   Must a woman be mysterious?  Silver S 23-8:37 Je
'53

GREAZA, WALTER N.
Obit.   N. Y. Times Bio Ed p967 Je '73
Same.   N. Y. Times p57 Je 3 '73
Screen World p234 '74

GRECO, JULIETTE
Wild one.   Time 68:40 Jl 16 '56
Accent on the French.   Newsweek 49:64 Ap 15 '57
Ghostly wild one.   Life 42:67 Ap 29 '57
Titi and Lorelei.   Time 69:42 My 6 '57
Rising star.   Film R p29 '58/59
Double role of Juliette.   Life 48:81 My 23 '60
Paris in Japan.   Newsweek 58:58 D 18 '61
Darryl vs. Desdemona.   Show 3-2:98 F '63
Genet.   Letter from Paris.   New Yorker 42:151 O 8 '66

GREELEY, EVELYN
Interview.   Green Book 13:706 Ap '15
Montanye, L.   Interview.   Motion Pic Classic 6:24 Je '18
Work of.   Motion Pic Classic 8:53 Ag '19

GREEN, DOROTHY
She dyed for her art.   TV Guide 5-48:28 N 30 '57
Obit.   Screen World 15:220 '64

GREEN, KENNETH
    Obit.  Screen World 21:237 '70

GREEN, MITZI
    Manners, D.  Sketch.  Motion Pic 40:74 S '30
    Her opinion of Junior Durkin.  Photop 39:36 Ja '31
    Albert, D.  The private life of Mitzi.  Silver S 1-7:39 My '31
    Story of.  Life 3:20 D 27 '37
    She's a big girl now.  Cue 18-8:21 F 19 '49
    Minoff, P.  New ventures for Mitzi.  Cue 24-2:47 Ja 15 '55
    Obit.  Classic Film Collect 24:14 Sum '69
        Film R p15 '70/71
        N. Y. Times p81 My 25 '69
        Newsweek 73:123 Je 9 '69
        Screen World 21:237 '70
        Time 93:98 Je 6 '69

GREENE, KEMPTON
    Courtlandt, R.  Interview.  Motion Pic 10:114 S '15
    How he became a photoplayer.  Motion Pic Classic 1:40 F '16

GREENE, LORNE
    Bio.  Cur Bio Yrbk 1967:149 '68
    She gives me hell and I'm happy.  Photop 77-6:40 Je '70
    Klemesrud, J.  The man who struck it rich with Bonanza.  N. Y.
        Times sec 2:23 O 8 '72

GREENE, RICHARD
    Lee, S.  Hollywood's new heart breaker.  Screen Book 21-1:24
        Ag '38
    Waterbury, R.  His love story.  Photop 52:11 N '38
    Rhea, M.  Sketch.  Photop 53:66 S '39
    Sullivan, E.  Not in keeping with the rule.  Silver S 10-7:26 My
        '40
    Bio note; filmog.  Movies & People 2:18 '40

GREENE, WILLIAM
    Hartung, P. T.  Bugs & and the movies.  Commonweal 57:38 O
        17 '52
    Obit.  N. Y. Times p39 Mr 13 '70

GREENSTREET, SYDNEY
    Hamilton, S.  Sketch.  Photop 23:34 Je '43
    Made for each other.  Screen Greats 1-2:68 Sum '71
    Pickard, R.  Sydney Greenstreet; filmog.  Films In R 23-7:385
        Ag/S '72
    Pepper, L.  Hollywood's heaviest heavy; filmog.  Velvet Light
        7:21 Win '72/73

GREENWOOD, CHARLOTTE
    Metcalfe, J. S.  High-kicking ability.  Life 74:899 N 27 '19
    Coates, R. M.  Making an art of awkwardness.  Theatre 46:37
        S '27

Why not homely movie stars?   Motion Pic 34:54 D '27
Walker, H. L.   Interview.   Motion Pic Classic 30:59 D '29
Sketch.   Theatre World 21:218 My '34

GREENWOOD, WINIFRED
Interview.   Motion Pic Classic 1:55 D '15
Doyle, B. H.   Letter; partial filmog.   Films In R 13-1:63 Ja
   '62

GREER, JANE
Wilson, E.   Let's be frank and cozy.   Silver S 19-5:36 Mr '49
Greer, J.   It's good to have Bob back again.   Silver S 19-9:42
   Jl '49
Greer, J.   No equal rights for me.   Silver S 20-12:45 O '50
Greer, J.   The seven deadly sins of romance.   Silver S 22-6:30
   Ap '52
McClelland, D.   Jane Greer; filmog.   Film Fan Mo 77:3 N '67

GREER, MICHAEL
Pearsall, A.   How some of the magic went out of Stanley Sweetheart's garden.   Show 1-3:69 Mr '70

GREGG, VIRGINIA
Raker, A.   Filmog.   Films In R 18-10:659 D '67

GREGOR, NORA
Pinto, A.   Letter.   Films In R 14-1:56 Ja '63

GREGORY, ENA
Uselton, R. A.   The Wampus baby stars.   Films In R 21-2:73
   F '70

GREGSON, JOHN
Gregson, J.   Sixty years of cinema.   Films & Filming 2-11:12
   Ag '56

GRENFELL, JOYCE
Topolski, F.   Sketch.   Vogue 111:92 Ap 15 '48

GREY, GLORIA
Uselton, R. A.   The Wampus baby stars.   Films In R 21-2:73 F
   '70

GREY, JOEL
New star on Broadway.   Newsweek 68:106 D 19 '66
Apparition of success.   Time 89:57 Ja 27 '67
Interview.   New Yorker 43:34 Mr 4 '67
Stasio, M.   Wilkommen, Joel Grey.   Cue 36-18:15 My 6 '67
People are talking about.   Vogue 151:116 Je '68
Prideaux, T.   Birth of Yankee Doodle Dandy.   Life 65:58 Ag 23
   '68
Easy going cosmos of a star.   House & Gard 134:80 D '68
Mandelstam, J.   Interview.   Sr Schol 94:18 Ja 17 '69

318                                           Motion Picture Performers

Goldman, A.   After 25 years, an actor.   TV Guide 18-35:21 Ag
    29 '70
Goldsmith, B.   Joel Grey.   Harp Baz 105:94 F '72
Vallance, T.   Bio note; filmog.   Focus On F 10:7 Sum '72
Sketch.   Films & Filming 20-1:58 O '73

GREY, LITA
    York, C.   Her unromantic wedding.   Photop 27:35 F '25
    Manners, D.   The riddle of the Chaplin marriage.   Motion Pic
        33:39 Mr '27
    Sketch.   Photop 37:38 Mr '30
    Schallert, E.   Controversy with Chaplin.   Motion Pic 46:41 Ja
        '34

GREY, NAN
    Hamilton, S.   Sketch.   Photop 54:70 Je '40

GREY, OLGA
    How she learned to act.   Motion Pic 12:69 D '16
    A vamp with a goulash name.   Photop 11-3:73 F '17

GREY, VIRGINIA
    Mook, D.   The girl nobody knows.   Silver S 11-12:34 O '41
    Hollywood born.   Lions R 1-9:no p# My '42

GRIBBON, EDDIE T.
    Obit.   Screen World 17:237 '66

GRIEM, HELMUT
    Bio note; filmog.   Films & Filming 19-7:66 Ap '73
    Portnoy, E.   Helmut Griem and Children of rage.   After Dark
        7-8:46 D '74

GRIER, ROSEY
    Ellis, W. D.   This is our house, y'see.   Read Dig 95:65 D '69
    Durslag, M.   How to satisfy your mind without expanding your
        body.   TV Guide 18-23:10 My 30 '70
    Klemesrud, J.   Rosey now does needle point.   N. Y. Times Bio
        Ed p1651 O '73

GRIFFIES, ETHEL
    The toast of the town.   Cue 18-31:13 Jl 30 '49
    Bio.   Cur Bio 29:19 Ja '68
        Same.   Cur Bio Yrbk 1968:169 '69

GRIFFIN, MERV
    (Film Career citations only)
    McClelland, D.   Mervyn of the movies; filmog.   Filmograph 1-4:
        11 '70

GRIFFIN, STEPHANIE
    Going up.   TV Guide 4-19:12 My 12 '56
    New girl makes the old Hollywood try.   Look 18:117 N 16 '54
    Restyling of Stephanie.   Life 41:59 Jl 2 '56

GRIFFITH, ANDY
   Lewis, E.  Ridge-runner with talent.  Cue 24-44:16 N 5 '55
   Zunser, J.  Big deal for Andy.  Cue 26-14:10 Ap 6 '57
   Rising star.  Film R p21 '59/60
   Davidson, B.  His $3,500,000 misunderstanding.  TV Guide 19-
      2:34 Ja 9 '71
   I thought I was a born loser.  Photop 79-2:70 F '71
   McAllister, J.  Running scared.  TV Guide 19-42:45 O 16 '71

GRIFFITH, CORINNE
   Smith, F. J.  Interview.  Motion Pic Classic 8:20 Ap '19
   Bruce, B.  Interview.  Motion Pic 19:64 Mr '20
   Boone, A.  Sketch.  Photop 18:67 Jl '20
   Fletcher, A. W.  Interview.  Motion Pic Classic 12:18 Mr '21
   How I keep in condition.  Photop 20:33 N '21
   Smith, F. J.  Interview.  Motion Pic 22:36 Ja '22
   de Revere, F. V.  What I read in her face.  Motion Pic 28:44
      O '24
   Autobiographical.  Motion Pic 28:27 D '24
   Driver, M. W.  Sketch.  Motion Pic 30:35 Ag '25
   Home of.  Photop 29:82 Ja '26
   Tildesley, A. L.  Sketch.  Motion Pic Classic 23:30 Je '26
   Fletcher, A. W.  Interview.  Motion Pic 33:56 Jl '27
   Carpen, F.  Sketch.  Motion Pic Classic 27:37 Ag '28
   Hall, G.  Confessions.  Motion Pic Classic 29:18 My '29
   Whitaker, A.  Home of.  Photop 36:70 Jl '29
   Conti, M.  Shopping with her.  Motion Pic 38:68 D '29
   Hall, G.  Interview.  Motion Pic 39:45 Ap '30
   Palmborg, R. P.  How she handles her money.  Motion Pic 39:
      74 My '30
   Sketch.   Photop 41:70 My '32
   Derr, E.  Makes comeback abroad.  Movie Classic 2:31 Je '32
   Letters.  Films In R 10-10:630 D '59
   What they are doing now.  Show 2-3:96 Mr '62
   The Orchid lady claims she is not the girl she was.  Classic
      Film Collect 15:27 Sum '66

GRIFFITH, LINDA
   Obit.  Screen World 1:234 '49

GRIFFITH, RAYMOND
   Howe, H.  Sketch.  Photop 27:39 My '25
   Robinson, S.  Sketch.  Motion Pic 31:35 My '26
   His part in All quiet on the western front.  Photop 38:33 Jl '30

GRILLO, JOHN
   Ford, J.  Two for the road.  Plays & Players 18-9:22 Je '71

GRIMES, GARY
   Miller, E.  Interview.  Seventeen 31:78 F '72
   Linkletter, A.  The movie performance I will always remember.
      Movie Dig 1-4:108 Jl '72

GRIMES, TAMMY
  Are you a kook?   TV Guide 9-35:5 S 2 '61

GRIZZARD, GEORGE
  Chase, C.  Grizzard is ready for his 'Seven year itch. '  N. Y.
    Times Bio Ed Ap 9 '72

GRODIN, CHARLES
  Guerin, A.  Grodin and The heartbreak kid, and the funny things
    that happen on the way to success.   Show 3-1:43 Mr '73
  On the scene.   Playboy 21-3:174 Mr '74
  Stoop, N. M.   Custom-made armor.   After Dark 7-8:40 D '74

GROOM, SAM
  Evanchuck, A. M.  A view of us.   Motion p7 N/D '74

GROVE, BETTY ANN
  Television's own promising starlets.   TV Guide 3-37:10 S 10 '55

GROVER, MARY
  Raddatz, L.  The blonde with the electronic oven.   TV Guide
    18-16:47 Ap 18 '70

GROVES, REGINA
  Without advice of counsel.   TV Guide 11-18:8 My 4 '63

GRUNDGENS, GUSTAV (Gustaf)
  Hull, D. S.  Gustaf Grundgens.   Films In R 14-10:634 D '63
  Donaldson, G.  Grundgens' films; filmog.   Films In R 16-1:63
    Ja '65
  Luft, H. G.  Letter.   Films In R 16-3:185 Mr '65

GUARD, KIT
  Obit.   Screen World 13:222 '62

GUBITOSI, MICKEY
  Maltin, L.  Our gang; inc. Our Gang filmog.   Film Fan Mo.
    66:3 D '66

GUGLIELMI, ALBERTO
  (See: VALENTINO, ALBERTO)

GUILBEAULT, LUCE
  McLarty, J.  Time's on my side.   Motion p12 Ja/F '74
  McLarty, J.  Luce Guilbeault.   Motion p20 My/Je '74

GUILBERT, ANN MORGAN
  So this is who Ann Morgan Guilbert is.   TV Guide 13-49:12 D 4
    '65

GUILD, NANCY
  Sketch.   Life 19:140 S 17 '45
  Should teenagers marry?   Photop 30:66 D '46

Dudley, F.  As wholesome as buttermilk.  Silver S 17-11:46 S
'47
Her honeymoon.  Photop 32:38 D '47

## GUINAN, TEXAS
Sketch.  N. Y. Drama 58:22 O 11 '13
Craig, J.  The state of excitement.  Photop 14-3:76 Ag '18
St. Johns, A. R.  Guinan of the guns.  Photop 16-3:59 Ag '19
Vreeland, F.  Her padlocks of 1927.  Motion Pic Classic 26:30
O '27
Shaw, C. G.  Sketch.  Vanity Fair 29:68 N '27
Belfrage, C.  Her reception in Hollywood.  Motion Pic Classic
28:22 N '28
Bolitho, W.  Two stars.  Delin 118:15 Ja '31
Fender, R.  Interview.  Movie Classic 5:56 D '33
Remen, N.  Estimate.  Photop 45:40 Ja '34

## GUINNESS, ALEC
Work of.  Theatre World 30:228 N '38
Bio sketch.  Vogue 110:52 Jl 1 '47
Keating, J.  Life of the party.  Cue 19-6:16 F 11 '50
A man of parts.  Cue 19-16:18 Ap 22 '50
My favorite role.  Film R p19 '52/53
Hill, D.  Man of many faces.  Films & Filming 1-5:12 F '55
Guinness goes to Paris.  Cue 24-11:12 Mr 19 '55
Star of the year; filmog; stage appearances.  Film R p17 '58/59
The screen answers back.  Films & Filming 8-8:12 My '62
Cowie, P.  The face of '63--Great Britain.  Films & Filming
9-5:19 F '63
People are talking about.  Vogue 151:65 Ja 15 '68
Tierney, M.  Knights at work.  Plays & Players 18-12:19 S '71
Gruen, J.  I cannot possibly make Hitler sympathetic.  N. Y.
Times sec 2:9 S 10 '72
Same.  N. Y. Times Bio Ed p1645 S '72
Phillips, G.  Talent has many faces; filmog.  Focus On F 11:17
Aut '72

## GULAGER, CLU
Billy the kidder.  TV Guide 8-48:24 N 26 '60
Denton, C.  The slings and arrows of outraged critics.  TV
Guide 10-33:6 Ag 18 '62

## GULLIVER, DOROTHY
Sketch.  Motion Pic 36:76 O '28
Uselton, R. A.  The Wampus baby stars.  Films In R 21-2:73
F '70

## GUMPILIL, DAVID
Rupard, R.  Interview.  Interview 2-5:18 Ag '71
Downs, J.  Just in from the outback.  Life 71:72 S 17 '71

## GUNN, MOSES
Rolling thunder.  Time 95:62 Ap 6 '70

GURIE, SIGRID
    Story of.   Life 4:28 Ap 18 '37
    Craig, C.   Interview.   Motion Pic 54:37 N '37
    Reid, J.   Sketch.   Photop 51:48 N '37
    Hall, G.   The Gurie brand of glamour.   Silver S 10-2:22 D
        '39
    Bio note; filmog.   Movies & People 2:18 '40
    Obit.   N. Y. Times p35 Ag 15 '69
        Screen World 21:237 '70
    Crivello, K.   The mystery of Sigrid Gurie; filmog.   Classic Film
        Collect 30:29 Spg '71

GUTHRIE, ARLO
    Woody's boy.   Newsweek 67:112 My 23 '66
    Interview.   New Yorker 43:18 Ja 6 '68
    Woody's boy.   Time 91:50 Ja 12 '68
    Arlo.   Take One 2-1:9 S/O '68
    Hedgepeth, W.   Successful anarchist.   Look 33:60 F 4 '69
    Miller, E.   Hollywood scene.   Seventeen 28:42 F '69
    Stickney, J.   Family of folk song becomes a movie.   Life 66:43
        Mr 28 '69
    Braudy, S.   As (he) sees it.   N. Y. Times Mag p56 Ap 27
        '69
    Alice's restaurant children.   Newsweek 74:101 S 29 '69
    Joyful happening.   Time 94:66 O 17 '69
    Braun, S.   Alice and Ray and yesterday's flowers.   Playboy 16:
        120 O '69

GWENN, EDMUND
    Corathiel, E.   Interview.   Theatre World 22:39 Jl '34
    Story of.   Photop 32:10 D '47
    Parsons, L. O.   Cosmop's citation for best performance of
        month.   Cosmop 125:13 N '48
    Obit.   Film R p10 '60/61
        Screen World 11:220 '60

GWILLIM, DAVID
    Keeping it in the family.   Films Illus 4-39:94 N '74

GWYNNE, ANNE
    Hamilton, S.   Sketch.   Photop 19:62 O '41
    Manners, M. J.   Homemade glamour girl makes good.   Silver
        S 12-9:40 Jl '42

GWYNNE, FRED
    An offbeat pair on the beat.   TV Guide 9-42:13 O 21 '61
    He can do more with a pencil than write a parking ticket.   TV
        Guide 10-26:3 Je 30 '62
    The bluecoat blues.   TV Guide 11-3:6 Ja 19 '63
    Lewis, R. W.   Putting a new face on his career.   TV Guide 13-
        28:15 Jl 10 '65

HAAS, HUGO
    Obit.   Film R p21 '69/70
        Screen World 20:235 '69

HABER, JOYCE
    Hair-raising stories from the stars.    Photop 78-1:62 Jl '70
    Hollywood looks at Henry (Kissinger).   Harp Baz 106:128 N '72

HACKATHORNE, GEORGE
    Goldbeck, W.    Interview.   Motion Pic Classic 13:31 Ja '22
    Gassaway, G.    Interview.   Motion Pic 23:58 My '22

HACKETT, BUDDY
    Keating, J.   Level-headed lunatic goes legit.   Cue 24-2:14 Ja
        15 '55
    Taylor, T.   Hilarious Hackett.   Cue 25-7:11 F 18 '56
    Minoff, P.   Visit with "Stanley."   Cue 25-43:12 O 27 '56
    Born to be funny.   TV Guide 4-46:9 N 17 '56
    Wolf, W.   Harnessing comic energy for new movie laughter.
        Cue 38-18:7 My 3 '69

HACKETT, JOAN
    McClelland, D.   TV: where all that old-time glamour went.
        Film Fan Mo 75:11 S '67
    Flatley, G.   Making a racket over Hackett.   N.Y. Times Bio Ed
        Mr 12 '72
    MacDonough, S.   I'm not an intellect, I'm a psychic.   Show 2-7:
        31 O '72

HACKETT, RAYMOND
    Babcock, M.   Sketch.   Photop 36:37 Jl '29
    Biery, R.   Interview.   Motion Pic 38:66 O '29
    Gray, C.   Interview.   Motion Pic Classic 31:36 Ap '30

HACKMAN, GENE
    Farber, S.   A cops and crooks movie that doesn't cop out.   N.Y.
        Times Bio Ed N 21 '71
    Flamini, R.   Interview.   Time 99:69 Ap 24 '72
    Kupfer, M.   Interview.   Newsweek 79:108 My 1 '72
    Strout, D.   Interview.   Mod Screen 66-5:65 My '72
    Bio.   Cur Bio 33:16 Jl '72
    Cort, G.   The aftermath of the Oscars.   Show 2-5:24 Jl '72
    Filmog.   Films & Filming 20-5:58 F '74
    Talks about The conversation.   Films Illus 3-35:437 Jl '74
    Eyles, A. & Billings, P.   Bio sketch; filmog.   Focus On F 8:4
        n. d.
    Hamill, P.   Hackman.   Film Comment 10-5:40 S/O '74

HADDON, DAYLE
    Manners, D.   I nominate for stardom.   Mod Screen 67-1:18 Ja
        '72
    Disney's latest hit; pictorial.   Playboy 20-4:147 Ap '73

HADLEY, NANCY
    More than a stick of furniture.  TV Guide 5-33:24 Ag 17 '57

HAGEN, UTA
    Bio.  Cur Bio 5 '44
    Stars born in Chicago.  Life 26:36 Ja 31 '49
    Firm sense of role.  Time 81:82 My 10 '63
    Loney, G.  Don't call me madam; interview.  Opera N 335:6 Ja
        23 '71

HAGMAN, LARRY
    Did mother really know best?  TV Guide 14-53:12 D 31 '66
    Whitney, D.  Who's in charge here?  TV Guide 19-44:21 O 30
        '71
    To each his home.  TV Guide 22-3:12 Ja 19 '74

HAINES, WILLIAM
    Redway, S.  Sketch.  Motion Pic 31:58 My '26
    Paton, C.  Sketch.  Motion Pic Classic 24:59 Ja '27
    Weller, S. M.  Interview.  Motion Pic Classic 26:42 D '27
    Manners, D.  Sketch.  Motion Pic 38:50 N '29
    Fender, R.  Sketch.  Motion Pic 40:66 Ag '30
    Grayson, C.  Sketch.  Motion Pic Classic 33:48 Ap '31
    Lang, H.  Sketch.  Photop 39:58 My '31
    Fairbanks, D. Jr.  Appreciation.  Vanity Fair 38:40 Ap '32
    Summers, M.  Film career of Haines; filmog.  Filmograph 3-3:
        3; 3-4:21 '73
    Obit.  Classic Film Collect 42:34 Spg '74
        Screen World p234 '74

HAIRSTON, JESTER
    Ramsey, W.  Afro-American ambassador.  Music J 28:33 O '70

HALE, ALAN SR.
    Alan of all trades.  Photop 12-4:97 S '17
    Hall, G.  Sketch.  Motion Pic Classic 27:25 Je '28
    Manners, D.  Interview.  Motion Pic 49:72 F '35
    Conlon, S.  His 1,000 ideas.  Screen Book 19-2:94 S '37
    Hale, A.  How to smash a saloon.  Screen Book 21-11:74 Je '39
    Hamilton, S.  Sketch.  Photop 54:41 F '40
    Reid, J.  Picture saver No. 1.  Silver S 11-2:38 D '40
    Obit.  Screen World 2:234 '51

HALE, BARBARA
    Palmer, C.  When dreams come true.  Silver S 16-11:60 S '46
    O'Leary, D.  The "girl next door" grows up.  Silver S 20-7:44
        My '50

HALE, CHANIN
    Oderman, S.  A modern unsung heroine.  Film Fan Mo 87:15 S
        '68
    Whitney, D.  Just one surprise after another.  TV Guide 17-50:
        22 D 13 '69

HALE, CREIGHTON
   Gordon, K.  Sketch.  Motion Pic 12:64 Ja '17
   How he got into motion pictures.  Motion Pic 14:92 S '17
   Roberts, S.  Interview.  Motion Pic 8:43 Je '19
   Leon, S.  Letter; partial filmog.  Films In R 20-6:388 Je/Jl '69

HALE, GEORGIA
   Edmonton, S.  Sketch.  Motion Pic Classic 21:60 Jl '25
   York, C.  Sketch.  Photop 29:76 D '25
   Thorp, D.  Sketch.  Motion Pic Classic 24:58 S '26

HALE, GEORGIA
   McAsh, I.  Hale storm.  Films Illus 3-33:356 My '74

HALE, LOUISE CLOSSER
   Interview.  N. Y. Drama 65:11 Mr 15 '11
   Sketch.  Womans Home C 52:100 Ja '25

HALE, SONNIE
   Obit.  N. Y. Times p37 Je 10 '59

HALEY, JACK
   Taviner, R.  Story of.  Motion Pic 54:58 O '37
   Oz revisited.  TV Guide 18-11:38 Mr 14 '70
   Maltin, L.  Jack Haley today.  Film Fan Mo 123:3 S '71

HALL, CHARLIE
   Maltin, L.  Our gang; Our gang filmog.  Film Fan Mo 66:3 D
      '66

HALL, CONRAD
   Shedlin, M.  Interview.  Film Q 24:2 Spg '71

HALL, DICKIE
   Prodigy.  Lions R 1-3:no p# N '41
   Sketch.  Photop 20:56 Ja '42
   Mulvey, K.  Sketch.  Womans Home C 69:22 Ja '42

HALL, DONALD
   Interview.  Motion Pic 8:108 Ja '15

HALL, DORA
   Finnigan, J.  Hubby spent $400,000, so now she is featured in a
      TV show.  TV Guide 19-34:9 Ag 21 '71

HALL, DOROTHY
   Sketch.  Photop 21:52 F '22
   Sketch.  Photop 23:52 Mr '23
   Look out Garbo.  Silver S 2-5:52 Mr '32

HALL, ELLA
   Sketch.  Motion Pic 9:111 Ap '15
   Owen, K.  Bob and Ella.  Photop 8-6:87 N '15

HALL, GERALDINE
  Obit.  Screen World 22:237 '71

HALL, GRAYSON
  Efron, E.  Out of the shadows.  TV Guide 19-4:17 Ja 23 '71

HALL, HUNTZ
  How tough are the Dead End Kids?  Screen Book 21-6:28 Ja '39

HALL, JAMES
  Carlisle, H.  Sketch.  Motion Pic 32:33 D '26
  Hall, G.  Sketch.  Motion Pic 36:71 Ag '28
  Spensley, D.  Interview.  Motion Pic Classic 28:40 S '28
  Obit.  Cur Bio p361 '40
    N. Y.  Times p15 Je 8 '40

HALL, JON
  Service, F.  Story of.  Motion Pic 54:95 N '37
  Hamilton, S.  Sketch.  Photop 52:69 Ja '38
  Corton, E.  Is Jon Hall on the spot?  Screen Book 20-5:35 Je
    '38
  Sullivan, E.  Hall's most amazing love story.  Silver S 10-11:34
    S '40
  Hamilton, S.  Sketch.  Photop 54:30 S '40
  Kilgallen, D.  Sketch.  Photop 23:21 Je '43
  Manners, M. J.  The truth about Frances Langford and Hall.
    Silver S 14-3:24 Ja '44

HALL, PORTER
  Unsung heroes.  Film Fan Mo #84 Je '68

HALL, RUTH
  New faces for the electric lights.  Silver S 2-4:38 F '32
  Uselton, R. A.  The Wampus baby stars.  Films In R 21-2:73
    F '70

HALL, WILLIAM
  Marlowe, D.  William Hall.  Classic Film Collect 34:X-1 Spg
    '72

HALLIDAY, JOHN
  Bio note; filmog.  Movies & People 2:18 '40

HALLOR, EDITH
  Fletcher, A. W.  Interview.  Motion Pic 19:52 F '20

HALLS, ETHEL MAY
  Obit.  Screen World 19:233 '68

HALOP, BILLY
  How tough are the Dead End Kids?  Screen Book 21-6:28 Ja '39
  Mizzell, R. T.  Filmog.  Films In R 19-2:127 F '68

HALPRIN, DARIA
    Miller, E.   Interview.   Seventeen 30:52 O '71
    Sullivan, A.   Interview.   Interview 1-1:8 n. d.

HALSEY, BRETT
    Denton, C.   The slings and arrows of outraged critics.   TV
        Guide 10-33:6 Ag 18 '62

HAMER, RUSTY
    Daddy's boy.   TV Guide 2-37:20 S 11 '54
    Readin' Ritin' and Rehearsal.   TV Guide 4-38:20 S 22 '56

HAMILTON, GEORGE
    Zunser, J.   Young man on the go.   Cue 29-10:9 Mr 5 '60
    Fenin, G.   The face of '63--United States.   Films & Filming
        9-6:55 Mr '63

HAMILTON, JOHN
    Obit.   N. Y. Times p37 Jl 13 '67

HAMILTON, JOHN F.
    Obit.   Screen World 19:233 '68

HAMILTON, KIM
    No longer trying to reach the moon.   TV Guide 11-36:27 S 7 '63

HAMILTON, LLOYD V.
    Ames, H.   Sketch.   Motion Pic Classic 2:41 Mr '16
    Henry, W. M.   Ham & Bud.   Photop 10-3:95 Ag '16
    Capron, F.   Sketch.   Motion Pic Classic 24:62 F '27
    Gray, C.   His comeback.   Motion Pic Classic 30:39 N '29
    Gill, S.   The funnymen.   8mm Collect 14:8 Spg '66

HAMILTON, MAHLON
    The career of hero Hamilton.   Photop 11-6:132 My '17
    Peltret, E.   Interview.   Motion Pic 17:64 Mr '19
    Winship, M.   Interview.   Photop 19:55 Mr '21
    Beach, B.   Interview.   Motion Pic 21:46 Ap '21

HAMILTON, MARGARET
    Young, S.   Her work in impersonations.   New Rep 71:181 Je 29
        '32
    Oz revisited.   TV Guide 18-11:38 Mr 11 '70
    Roman, R. C.   Ding Dong, the witch isn't dead.   After Dark
        11-11:48 Mr '70
    Stein, J.   A wonderful witch of Oz; filmog.   Focus On F 3:40
        My/Ag '70
    Margaret Hamilton.   Focus On F 4:16 S/O '70

HAMILTON, NEIL
    Cone, S.   Sketch.   Motion Pic 30:36 O '25
    Hagen, L.   Sketch.   Motion Pic Classic 22:60 N '25
    Ramsey, W.   Sketch.   Motion Pic Classic 29:58 My '29

Calhoun, D.  Sketch.  Motion Pic 39:35 My '30
Sommers, M.  More darned fun.  Silver S 1-9:25 Jl '31
Donnell, D.  The Hamiltons adopt a daughter.  Motion Pic Classic 32:29 Ag '31
Lee, S.  Interview.  Motion Pic 32:29 Ag '31

HAMMERSTEIN, ELAINE
Boone, A.  Sketch.  Photop 16-6:51 N '19

HAMMOND, FREEMAN
Obit.  N. Y. Times p53 Mr 13 '68

HAMMOND, HARRIET
Goldbeck, W.  Interview.  Motion Pic Classic 11:22 F '21
Shelley, H.  Interview.  Motion Pic Classic 13:18 O '21
Bishop, R.  Interview.  Motion Pic 23:40 Mr '22

HAMPDEN, WALTER
Briscoe, J.  Sketch.  Green Bk Album 4:373 Ag '10
Bio sketch.  N. Y. Drama 70:9 Jl 2 '13
Stratton, C.  A new Hamlet.  Drama 9:82 F '19
Brown, F. C.  Shakespeare, Hampden and Bragdon.  Drama 11: 184 Mr '21
The changing drama.  Drama 11:184 Mr '21
Hampden and the American stage.  Outlook 128:100 My 18 '21
Bird, C.  Work of.  Theatre 34:104 Ag '21
Sketch.  Theatre 39:22 Ap '24
Wanted: a leader in our theatre.  Theatre 39:9 Jl '24
Bolce, H.  Interview.  Theatre 47:10 Ap '28
A comedy with Walter Hampdon.  Cue 14-8:8 F 24 '45

HAMPER, GENEVIEVE
Obit.  N. Y. Times p30 F 20 '71

HAMPSHIRE, SUSAN
Rising stars.  Film R p53 '65/66
Zinner, J.  Partial filmog.  Films In R 20-10:645 D '69
Klemesrud, J.  Road to adulation.  N. Y. Times Bio Ed Mr 30 '70
Jobin, J.  A most villainous villainess whom everybody loves.  TV Guide 18-24:38 Je 13 '70
Hampshire sage.  Time 95:53 Je 22 '70
Ehrlich, H.  Susan Hampshire.  Look 35:28 F 23 '71
Perint, G.  At home in Paris.  Harp Baz 104:70 My '71
Miller, E.  Interview.  Seventeen 31:64 Ap '72

HAMPTON, HOPE
Hall, G.  Interview.  Motion Pic 20:62 D '20
Hernon, J.  Interview.  Motion Pic Classic 11:50 F '21
Hall, G.  Interview.  Motion Pic Classic 12:54 Jl '21
Evans, D.  Sketch.  Photop 20:42 N '21
Home of.  Theatre 47:50 Ap '28
Dennis, S.  Story of.  Motion Pic 54:43 D '37

HANCOCK, SHEILA
  Franey, R.   Choosing the masses.   Plays & Players 20-12:19 S
    '73

HANCOCK, TONY
  Hancock, T.   Punch & Judy man.   Films & Filming 8-11:9 Ag
    '62
  Obit.   N. Y. Times p41 Je 25 '68

HANDWORTH, OCTAVIA
  How she became a photoplayer.   Motion Pic Supp 1:50 S '15

HANEY, CAROL
  Peck, S.   Up and coming actress.   N. Y. Times Mag p38 My 23
    '54
  Harvey, E.   Something new in steam heat.   Colliers 133:30 Je
    25 '54
  Fireworks on 44th St.   Cue 23-27:12 Jl 3 '54
  Sockeroo's sockeroo.   New Yorker 30:18 Jl 10 '54
  Entertainment highlights.   Dance 28:26 Jl '54
  People are talking about.   Vogue 124:52 Jl '54
  Knight, A.   Pajama Game and Carol Haney.   Dance 31:36 Ag '57
  Haney views Haney.   McCalls 84:6 S '57
  Alpert, H.   Old friends in new jobs.   Dance 32:52 D '58
  Fletcher, F.   The busy Blydens.   Cue 28-12:18 Mr 21 '59
  Hazard, E.   Product is the star.   Dance 36:42 D '62

HANLEY, BRIDGET
  Durslag, M.   She plays Candy with a difference.   TV Guide 17-
    19:21 My 10 '69

HANLEY, JENNY
  The private sex life of Sherlock Holmes.   Show 1-2:79 F '70

HANLEY, JIMMY
  Obit.   Film R p15 '70/71

HANLON, BERT
  Obit.   N. Y. Times p42 Ja 21 '72

HANNA, DOLLY
  Donnell, D.   Sketch.   Motion Pic Classic 28:37 Ja '29

HANSEN, JOHN
  Did playing Christine Jorgensen ruin my career?   Mod Screen
    66-8:56 Ag '72

HANSEN, JUANITA
  Without benefit of custard.   Photop 14-4:98 S '18
  Peltret, E.   Interview.   Motion Pic 17:30 Ja '19
  Interview.   Dram Mir p589 O 2 '20
  Service, F.   Interview.   Motion Pic Classic 11:58 D '20
  Smith, L. F.   Letter.   Films In R 13-3:191 Mr '62

Fulbright, T.   The poppyseed girl.   Classic Film Collect 23:10
    Spg; 24:6 Sum '69

HANSON, LARS
    Sketch.   Motion Pic Classic 22:40 Ja '26
    Palmborg, R. P.   Interview.   Motion Pic 33:56 Je '27
    Sketch.   Photop 32:35 Jl '27
    Palmborg, R. P.   Sketch.   Motion Pic 35:47 Mr '28

HANTZ, BOB
    The super cops.   Photop 84-6:41 D '73

HARA, SETSUKO
    Harvey, S.   People we like.   Film Comment 10-6:34 N/D '74

HARDIE, RUSSELL
    Obit.   N. Y. Times Bio Ed p1159 Jl '73
        Screen World p234 '74

HARDING, ANN
    Biery, R.   Interview.   Motion Pic Classic 29:25 Jl '29
    Busby, M.   Interview.   Photop 36:41 O '29
    Sketch.   Photop 38:6 Je '30
    Belfrage, C.   Sketch.   Motion Pic 39:82 Jl '30
    Shirley, L.   Home of.   Photop 38:66 O '30
    Autobiographical.   Theatre 52:37 O '30
    Her feud with her father.   Motion Pic 40:10 D '30
    Calhoun, D.   Sketch.   Motion Pic 41:48 Je '31
    Grant, J.   Sketch.   Motion Pic Classic 33:34 Jl '31
    Sharon, M.   (She) isn't contented.   Silver S 1-11:59 S '31
    Her double.   Movie Classic 1:42 N '31
    Sykes, L.   Her divorce.   Movie Classic 2:28 Je '32
    Her divorce.   Motion Pic 43:40 Je '32
    Henderson, J.   Tear up contract?   Cinema Dig 1-6:7 Jl 25 '32
    Winters, D.   Wants to leave pictures.   Movie Classic 3:34 S '32
    Moffitt, C. F.   Censorship for interviews Hollywood's latest wild
        idea.   Cinema Dig 2-5:9 Ja 9 '33
    Jones, C. B.   Ann Harding.   Cinema Dig 2-6:8 Ja 16 '33
    Patrick, C.   Her future?   Cinema Dig 2-7:13 Ja 23 '33
    Grant, J.   Remarriage rumors.   Motion Pic 45:32 Ap '33
    Melcher, E.   Ann Harding.   Cinema Dig 3-7:11 My 1 '33
    How Sylvia improved her posture.   Photop 44:54 N '33
    Harrison, H.   Interview.   Movie Classic 9:24 O '35
    Borton, E.   Interview.   Motion Pic 50:51 Ja '36
    St. Johns, A. R.   The Harding-Bannister fight over the daughter.
        Photop 50:14 Ag '36
    Ryan, D.   Interview.   Movie Classic 2:64 My '37
    Ann Harding's return.   Lions R 2-2:no p# N '42
    Mulvey, K.   Sketch.   Womans Home C 70:12 Je '43
    Ringgold, G.   Ann Harding; filmog.   Films In R 23-3:129 Mr '72
    Anderson, E.   Letter.   Films In R 23-10:646 D '72

HARDWICKE, CEDRIC
  Work of.   Stage 14:66 My '37
  Whorf, R.   As I see them.   Lions R 3-2:no p# Ja '44
  Obit.   Film R p45 '65/66

HARDY, OLIVER
  Bio note; filmog.   Movies & People 2:19 '40
  Laurel, S.   My stooge.   Lions R 2-4:no p# Ap '43
  (See also:  LAUREL & HARDY)

HARDY, SAM B.
  Smith, A.   Interview.   Photop 32:53 Jl '27
  Hall, G.   Sketch.   Movie Pic Classic 30:43 S '29

HARE, WILL
  Phillips, M.   Actor takes a long road to success.   N. Y. Times
    Bio Ed Mr 2 '72

HARKER, GORDON
  Obit.   Film R p21 '66/68
  Scannell, A. T.   Gordon Harker.   Films In R 22-5:319 My '71
  Shawcross, G.   Filmog.   Films In R 22-7:453 Ag/S '71

HARKINS, JIM
  Obit.   N. Y. Times p48 O 27 '70

HARLAN, KENNETH
  Delvigne, D.   Interview.   Motion Pic 18:56 D '19
  Malverne, P.   Sketch.   Motion Pic Classic 11:38 D '20
  Adams, E.   His horoscope.   Photop 26:109 N '24
  Donnell, D.   Marie & Ken.   Motion Pic Classic 28:26 O '28
  Obit.   Classic Film Collect 17:47 Win/Spg '67

HARLAN, MACEY
  The second mate of villainy.   Photop 11-6:128 My '17

HARLOW, JEAN
  Pryor, N.   Sketch.   Motion Pic 40:77 O '30
  Benham, L.   Hell's smartest angel.   Silver S 1-3:18 Ja '31
  Haydon, H.   Sketch.   Motion Pic Classic 32:33 F '31
  Manners, D.   Sketch.   Motion Pic Classic 33:61 Jl '31
  Leiber, R.   Sketch.   Photop 40:71 N '31
  Grayson, C.   Sketch.   Movie Classic 2:50 Mr '32
  Whitchel, J. A.   The girl who changed the stars.   Silver S 2-7:
    22 My '32
  Janeway, D.   Sketch.   Movie Classic 2:29 Jl '32
  Personality changed by red wig.   Photop 42:69 Ag '32
  Jean is wed.   Silver S 2-11:17 S '32
  Donnell, D.   Her marriage.   Motion Pic 44:64 S '32
  Costello, T.   Sketch.   Movie Classic 3:40 S '32
  Rice, L.   Sketch.   Movie Classic 3:51 S '32
  Jones, C. P.   Jean Harlow and Rain.   Cinema Dig 2-1:11 N 14
    '32

Calhoun, D.  Tragic death of her husband.  Movie Classic 3:16 N '32

Manners, D.  Interview.  Movie Classic 3:15 D '32

Wilson, E.  Jean seeks forgetfulness.  Silver S 3-2:43 D '32

Babcock, M.  Her headline career.  Motion Pic 44:30 D '32

Jamison, J.  She takes up life again.  Silver S 3-6:28 Ap '33

Fidler, J.  Interview.  Motion Pic 45:27 Ap '33

Pryor, N.  How does she rate with women?  Movie Classic 4:44 Je '33

Ergenbright, E. L.  Answers questions.  Motion Pic 45:54 Jl '33

Manners, D.  Her rivalries.  Movie Classic 4:23 Jl '33

Hampton, J.  Sketch.  Photop 44:72 Ag '33

Keats, P.  It's easier in fast company.  Silver S 3-11:21 S '33

Manners, D.  Her psychic powers.  Motion Pic 46:41 S '33

How Sylvia insured her success.  Photop 44:70 S '33

Wilson, E.  You're going to talk about Bombshell.  Silver S 4-1: 18 N '33

Manners, D.  Her marriage explained.  Motion Pic 46:51 D '33

Hall, G.  Turns author.  Movie Classic 6:42 Ap '34

Walker, H. L.  I'm that way.  Silver S 4-6:24 Ap '34

Manners, D.  Her salary.  Motion Pic 47:42 My '34

Calhoun, D.  Home of.  Motion Pic 47:48 Je '34

Fidler, J. M.  Whispering tongues.  Silver S 4-8:51 Je '34

Lee, S.  Her marriage collapsed.  Movie Classic 6:44 Jl '34

Donnell, D.  Fate that shadows her marriages.  Movie Classic 7:41 S '34

Grant, J.  Her mother's story.  Movie Classic 7:49 O '34

French, W. F.  What price glamour?  Motion Pic 48:29 N '34

Lee, S.  Interview.  Motion Pic 48:49 Ja '35

Grant, J.  Interview.  Motion Pic 49:30 F '35

Foster, B.  Interview.  Motion Pic 49:24 My '35

Grant, J.  1934 her dark year.  Movie Classic 8:52 Ap '35

Packer, E.  Interview.  Motion Pic 50:33 S '35

Ambition pinch-hitting for love.  Silver S 6-4:28 F '36

Cheatham, M.  Interview.  Motion Pic 51:38 Mr '36

Harrison, H.  Interview.  Movie Classic 10:39 Ap '36

Hall, G.  Her opinion of Gable.  Movie Classic 10:34 My '36

Jean Harlow.  Visages 4:entire issue Ag '36

The evolution of Harlow.  Movie Classic 10:32 Ag '36

Wilson, C.  Sketch.  Photop 50:24 S '36

Altman, M.  Her hair.  Movie Classic 11:28 O '36

Schallert, E.  Interview.  Motion Pic 52:32 N '36

Beall, H. H.  Interview.  Movie Classic 11:34 Ja '37

Reid, J.  Interview.  Motion Pic 53:30 Mr '37

Craig, C.  Teamed with Robert Taylor.  Motion Pic 53:56 My '37

Service, F.  Appreciation.  Motion Pic 54:24 S '37

Draper, L.  This was Jean Harlow; filmog.  Sound Stage 1-2:5 F '65

Hair-raising stories from the stars.  Photop 78-1:62 Jl '70

Tragedy was their co-star.  Screen Greats 1-2:38 Sum '71

Fry, R.  Hughes, Harlow and Hell's angels.  Nostalgia Illus 1-1: 59 N '74

HARLOWE, JUNE
  Maltin, L.   Our gang; Our gang filmog.    Film Fan Mo 66:3 D
    '66

HARPER, JOHN
  Raddatz, L.   The Dodge City gang.    TV Guide 20-12:14 Mr 18
    '72

HARPER, RON
  The workaday cop.   TV Guide 10-17:7 Ap 28 '62
  Whitney, D.   A 3-time loser tries again.    TV Guide 15-47:20 N
    25 '67

HARPER, VALERIE
  Raddatz, L.   She used to be a snowflake in South Orange, New
    Jersey.   TV Guide 19-6:17 F 6 '71
  Berkvist, R.   Henny Penny goes to Harper.    N. Y. Times Bio
    Ed Ap 11 '71
  Righter, C.   Star of the month; horoscope.    Mod Screen 66-9:49
    S '72
  Stevens, J.   The second banana of the Mary Tyler Moore show.
    Show 3-2:27 Ap '73
  Rhoda gets her own show (plus husband).   People 2-11:35 S 9 '74
  Hano, A.   Say goodbye to Minnesota fats.    TV Guide 22-41:26
    O 12 '74
  Davidson, B.   Rhoda alone, married.    N. Y. Times Mag p34 O
    20 '74
  Rhoda's a winner on her own and so much for TV taboos.   Peo-
    ple 2-27:54 D 30 '74

HARRIGAN, WILLIAM
  Obit.   Screen World 18:236 '67

HARRINGTON, PAT JR.
  Gambling on Guido.   Time 73:52 Je 1 '59
  He has hit a new green.   TV Guide 7-42:28 O 17 '59

HARRIS, BARBARA
  Lewis, E.   Broadway's new golden girl.   Cue 35-53:13 D 31 '66
  Bio.   Cur Bio 29:14 Ap '68
    Same.   Cur Bio Yrbk 1968:173 '69
  Gussow, M.   Barbara Harris on role playing.    N. Y. Times Bio
    Ed My 24 '72

HARRIS, JONATHAN
  One case where evil triumphs.   TV Guide 14-25:12 Je 18 '66

HARRIS, JULIE
  Young actress makes hit.   Cue 17-50:26 D 11 '48
  Keating, J.   Name in lights.   Cue 21-3:12 Ja 19 '52
  Bernhardt to Marlowe to Hayes to Harris.   Theatre Arts 37:15
    Mr '53
  Zunser, J.   You can't say that.   Cue 24-30:12 Jl 30 '55

Gow, G.   The quest for realism; discussion.   Films & Filming
   4-3:13 D '57
Vallance, T.   Julie Harris.   Film 35:21 Spg '63
Salute of the week.   Cue 38-3:1 Ja 18 '69
In the words of Julie Harris.   Cue 38-50:10 D 13 '69
Keith, D. L.   Me?   Play a girl who has an abortion?   After
   Dark 4-7:22 N '71
Flatley, G.   What's a great actress doing in a pickle factory?
   TV Guide 21-31:15 Ag 4 '73

HARRIS, KAY
   Hamilton, S.   Sketch.   Photop 19:63 O '41

HARRIS, MILDRED
   Stage experience?  None.   Photop 14-5:43 O '18
   Sheridan, M.   Sketch.   Motion Pic 15:52 N '18
   Cheatham, M. S.   Interview.   Motion Pic p30 Je '20

HARRIS, PHIL
   Hamilton, S.   His marriage with Alice Faye.   Photop 19:26 Ag
      '41

HARRIS, RICHARD
   Rising star.   Film R p38 '63/64
   Interview.   Cinema (BH) 2-5:19 Mr/Ap '65
   Borgzinner, J.   Limerick lad in Arthur's court.   Life 63:70 S
      22 '67
   Ginger man sings.   Newsweek 71:88 Je 17 '68
   Just for laughs.   Look 33:87 Ap 29 '69
   Miller, E.   Irishman with impact; interview.   Seventeen 29:152
      Mr '70
   Campbell, R.   Bio note; filmog.   Focus On F 3:11 My/Ag '70
   Hair-raising stories from the stars.   Photop 78-2:50 Ag '70
   Opposite direction; bio note.   Films Illus 1-5:31 N '71
   Clark, C.   Really Irish.   Applause 1-9:22 Ja 19 '72
   Song and film man.   After Dark 4-9:14 Ja '72
   Flatley, G.   Is Philharmonic hall ready for him?   N. Y. Times
      Bio Ed Mr 26 '72
   Shevey, S.   Interview.   Playgirl 1-6:52 N '73
   Bio note.   Films Illus 4-38:44 O '74

HARRIS, ROSEMARY
   Bio.   Cur Bio 28:18 S '67
   Same.   Cur Bio Yrbk 1967:162 '68
   Ehrlich, H.   Actors' favorite actress.   Look 32:M15 O 15 '68

HARRISON, GEORGE
   Beatle roundup.   Newsweek 76:85 S 7 '70
   Bender, W.   Letting George do it.   Time 96:57 N 30 '70
   Willis, E.   George and John.   New Yorker 47:95 F 27 '71
   Rarest rock show of all.   Life 71:20 Ag 13 '71
   Concert.   New Yorker 47:29 Ag 14 '71
   Costa, J. C.   Colossal event.   Sr Schol 99:32 S 27 '71

Notes and comment.  New Yorker 47:25 F 5 '72
The Playboy jazz and pop hall of fame.  Playboy 19-2:159 F '72
The quiet Beatle revs up for a crash comeback.  People 2-20:26
    N 11 '74
(See also: BEATLES, The)

HARRISON, KATHLEEN
    The screen answers back.  Films & Filming 8-8:12 My '62

HARRISON, LINDA
    Lewis, R. W.  In Bracken's world live beautiful people.  TV
        Guide 18-7:29 F 14 '70

HARRISON, NOEL
    Prelutsky, B.  Something must have gone wrong.  TV Guide 15-
        10:14 Mr 11 '67
    How I faced my drinking problem.  Photop 78-4:60 O '70

HARRISON, REX
    Parsons, L. O.  Cosmop's citation for best performance of
        month.  Cosmop 121:68 Ag '46
    Lane, L.  Regal, romantic and regular.  Silver S 16-11:37 S '46
    Harrison, L. P.  What about the Rex Harrisons?  Silver S 18-
        10:22 Ag '48
    Maxwell, E.  His opinion of Hollywood.  Photop 34:50 Mr '49
    Keating, J.  The Harrisons observed.  Cue 21-8:10 F 23 '52
    Rex Harrison; filmog.  Sound Stage 1-1:11 D '64
    Wolf, W.  A dapper Dr. Dolittle.  Cue 36-50:12 D 16 '67
    King Rex.  Newsweek 71:84 Ja 29 '68
    Bradshaw, J.  Oozing charm from every pore.  Esquire 78:102
        Jl '72
    Musel, R.  Harrison is not your ordinary star.  TV Guide 21-
        15:14 Ap 14 '73
    Coveney, M.  Interview.  Plays & Players 21-6:14 Mr '74

HARRON, JOHN
    Goldbeck, W.  Interview.  Motion Pic Classic 12:59 Je '21

HARRON, ROBERT
    Willis, R.  Three rough-necks from The escape.  Photop 7-3:136
        F '15
    The split reel.  Film Players Herald 2-7:28 F '16
    Handy, T. B.  Sketch.  Motion Pic 18:60 S '19
    Smith, F. J.  Interview.  Motion Pic Classic 10:16 Jl '20
    Obit.  N. Y. Clipper 68:34 S 8 '20
    North, J.  Career of.  Photop 18:52 O '20
    Hall, G.  Sketch.  Motion Pic 20:66 D '20
    Siglin, C.  Letter.  Films In R 15-4:250 Ap '64
    Mae Marsh, Robert Harron and D. W. Griffith; filmog.  Silent
        Pic 4:10 Aut '69

HART, DIANE
    Doffing the cloth cap.  Time 95:31 Je 15 '70

HART, DOROTHY
    Movie sculptress molds a snow maid.    Life 21:110 D 23
        '46
    Sweet Hart.    TV Guide 3-37:12 S 10 '55
    Minoff, P.    TV's queen of the charades.    Cue 26-33:12 Ag 17
        '57
    Newsmakers.    Newsweek 76:50 S 28 '70
    Wolf, A. M.    Why I became a nun.    Ladies Home J 88:94 My
        '71

HART, NEAL
    Obit.    N. Y. Times p23 Ap 4 '49
    Everett, E. K.    The educated cowboy.    Classic Film Collect 40:
        36 Fall '73

HART, RICHARD
    Obit.    Screen World 3:177 '53

HART, TEDDY
    Obit.    N. Y. Times p30 F 20 '71

HART, WILLIAM S.
    How he became a photoplayer.    Motion Pic 9:80 My '15
    Gordon, G.    Sketch.    Motion Pic Classic 2:48 Mr '16
    Sketch.    Motion Pic 12:117 N '16
    Briscoe, J.    Sketch.    Motion Pic 12:93 Ja '17
    McKelvie, M. G.    Sketch.    Motion Pic 13:103 Ap '17
    Living your character.    Motion Pic 13:71 My '17
    Naylor, H. S.    Interview.    Motion Pic Classic 5:32 N '17
    How he got in moving pictures.    Motion Pic 14:77 D '17
    Fuir, C. W.    His horse, Fritz.    Motion Pic 14:95 Ja '18
    Moore, W.    Interview.    Motion Pic 14:41 Ja '18
    Duffy, G. C.    Sketch.    Motion Pic Classic 7:43 O '18
    Service, F.    Sketch.    Motion Pic Classic 7:31 Ja '19
    Naylor, H. S.    Sketch.    Motion Pic 17:32 Mr '19
    Hart, W. S.    Cowpunchers of the Antipodes.    Photop 15-5:32 Ap
        '19
    Impressions of his leading ladies.    Motion Pic 18:38 Ag '19
    Cheatham, M. S.    Interview.    Motion Pic Classic 10:46 Ag '20
    Patterson, A.    His love story.    Photop 19:36 Ja '21
    Cheatham, M.    Interview.    Motion Pic 21:58 Ap '21
    Fletcher, A. W.    Interview.    Motion Pic 23:22 F '22
    Cheatham, M.    His darkest hour.    Motion Pic Classic 14:51 Jl
        '22
    Carr, H.    Interview.    Motion Pic 24:24 S '22
    Carlisle, H.    Interview.    Motion Pic 25:21 N '23
    Carlisle, H.    A day with him on his ranch.    Motion Pic 28:20
        O '24
    Sketch.    National 54:313 Mr '26
    Calhoun, D.    Interview.    Motion Pic Classic 26:23 O '27
    Hall, G.    Sketch.    Motion Pic Classic 30:21 O '29
    LaBadie, D. W.    The last roundup.    Show 2-9:75 S '62

Reynolds, R.   Hollywood's silent western stars lived active, ad-
venturous lives.   8mm Collect 5:3 Ag 15 '63
Estes, O. Jr.   His film career.   8mm Collect 11:14 Spg '65
Griggs, J.   A visit to his ranch.   8mm Collect 11:16 Spg '65
Tasoff, R.   The Hart ranch.   Film Fan Mo 61/62:19 Jl/Ag '66
Wilkinson, H.   Even "two gun" Bill made it with the song writ-
ers.   Classic Film Collect 16:39 Fall '66
White, J.   William S. Hart revisited.   Classic Film Collect 18:
22 Sum '67
Bio note.   Silent Pic 14:20 Spg '72
The stage career of W. S. Hart.   Silent Pic 16:17 Aut '72
Cawelti, J. G.   The romantic western of the 1920s.   Velvet
Light 12:7 Spg '74
Mitchell, C. R. & Scheide, F.   The reformation of the good
badman.   Velvet Light 12:11 Spg '74
From the 100 finest westerns: Tumbleweeds.   Views & Rs 1-4:
18 n. d.

HARTE, BETTY
Obit.   Screen World 17:237 '66

HARTLEY, MARIETTE
Hollywood swingers.   Show 3-11:88 N '63
Hartley is a young... take your choice.   TV Guide 12-37:26 S 12 '64
Robison, R.   Mariette Hartley; filmog & TV roles.   Films In R
25-6:376 Je/Jl '74

HARTMAN, DAVID
Hano, A.   He's never had an experience he didn't like.   TV
Guide 17-23:18 Je 7 '69
Durslag, M.   Summer on the rubber-chicken circuit.   TV Guide
19-38:18 S 18 '71
The Christmas that taught me the meaning of love.   Mod Screen
66-1:48 Ja '72
Kiester, E. Jr.   On the go with David Hartman.   TV Guide 22-
51:16 D 21 '74

HARTMAN, ELIZABETH
Miller, E.   Daydreamer talks; interview.   Seventeen 27:130 N
'68

HARTMAN, GRETCHEN
Her work.   Theatre 9:6 Ja '09
Recollections by.   Green Bk Album 2:528 S '09

HARTMAN, PAUL
Minoff, P.   Mr. Hartman beats a new challenge.   Cue 23-1:12
Ja 2 '54
Raddatz, L.   He's not going anyplace.   TV Guide 16-12:29 Mr
23 '68
Obit.   Films & Filming 20-3:81 D '73
N. Y. Times Bio Ed p1655 O '73
Screen World p235 '74

HARTY, PATRICIA
Do not fold, mutilate or staple.   TV Guide 14-44:12 O 29 '66

HARVEY, LAURENCE
Thorpe, E.   Shooting stars.   Films & Filming 1-10:8 Jl '55
Fenin, G.   The face of '63--United States.   Films & Filming
9-6:55 Mr '63
Lawrenson, H.   1/5 of Harvey.   Esquire 70:93 Ag '68
Opposite direction; bio note.   Films Illus 1-5:31 N '71
I got him to marry me by living with him.   Mod Screen 67-4:55
Ap '73
Julianelli, J.   An afternoon with Laurence.   Interview 3-9:10 O
'73
Obit.   Classic Film Collect 42:34 Spg '74
N. Y. Times Bio Ed p1793 N '73
Screen World p235 '74

HARVEY, LILIAN*
Her arrival in Germany.   Graphic 134:437 D 12 '31
Germany sends another blonde Venus.   Motion Pic 45:64 Ap '33
Mosley, L. O.   Marriage rumors.   Movie Classic 4:26 My '33
Fidler, J.   Answers questions.   Movie Classic 4:26 Ag '33
Wilson, E.   In harmony with Hollywood.   Silver S 3-10:30 Ag '33
Biery, R.   Marriage plans.   Movie Classic 5:56 O '33
Lee, S.   Interview.   Movie Classic 6:51 My '34
Smalley, J.   Marriage postponed.   Movie Classic 7:42 S '34
Trepanier, S.   Partial filmog.   Films In R 16-1:57 Ja '65
Donaldson, G.   Letter.   Films In R 16-3:187 Mr '65
Obit.   Brit Bk Yr 1969:571 '69
Film R p19 '69/70
N. Y. Times p65 Jl 28 '68
Pinto, A.   Lilian Harvey; filmog.   Films In R 21-8:478 O '70
*Incorrectly spelled Lillian in 1st volume.

HARVEY, VERNA
Faces going far.   Films Illus 1-10:21 Ap '72

HASSO, SIGNE
Stars of tomorrow.   Lions R 1-11/12:no p# Jl/Ag '42
Zing girl.   Lions R 2-4:no p# Ap '43
Lady lucky.   Lions R 3-4(sup):no p# Jl '44
Service, F.   What an actress really should be like.   Silver S
14-11:38 S '44
Manzi, I.   Letter; partial filmog.   Films In R 19-2:124 F '68

HASSOM, JAMIEL
Calhoun, D.   Interview.   Motion Pic 36:40 N '28

HATCHER, MARY
Hine, A.   The life of a movie starlet.   Holiday 3:138 Mr '48

HATFIELD, HURD
Newcomer.   Lions R 3-4:no p# Jl '44

Reid, L.  A sinister start.  Silver S 15-9:30 Jl '45
Zoerink, R.  Dorian Gray gone country squire.  After Dark 7-
8:78 D '74

## HATTON, RAYMOND
Remont, F.  Sketch.  Motion Pic Classic 7:41 D '18
Cheatham, M. S.  Interview.  Motion Pic 19:58 Jl '20
Tulley, J.  Interview.  Motion Pic Classic 12:34 Jl '21
Shelley, H.  Interview.  Motion Pic Classic 13:22 F '22
Tully, J.  Sketch.  Motion Pic Classic 20:32 F '25
Chaffin, G.  The part Mrs. Hatton played in her husband's
career.  Motion Pic Classic 23:55 Je '26
Williams, N.  A tribute to Raymond Hatton; filmog.  Filmograph
1-3:3 '70
Harris, G. Jr.  Raymond Hatton and westerns.  Filmograph 2-
1:48 '71
Obit.  Classic Film Collect 33:45 Win '71
Film R p11 '72/'73
N.Y. Times p36 O 23 '71
Same.  N.Y. Times Bio Ed O 23 '71
Screen World 23:237 '72
Brennen, T.  Farewell to Ray Hatton.  Classic Film Collect 33:
45 Win '71

## HAVER, JUNE
Wilson, E.  Lucky year for June.  Silver S 16-1:44 N '45
A date with Peter Lawford.  Photop 29:62 N '46
Haver, J.  I'll marry if...  Silver S 17-4:61 F '47
Sammis, F. R.  Her separation from Jimmy Zito.  Photop 31:33
S '47
Loper, D.  Sketch.  Photop 32:93 Ja '48
Holland, J.  I've learned my lesson.  Silver S 18-12:32 O '48
Graham, S.  Sketch.  Photop 33:41 N '48
Parsons, L. O.  Cosmop's citation for best performance of
month.  Cosmop 126:12 Je '49
Haver, J.  Education is where you find it.  Silver S 20-5:36 Mr
'50
Haver, J.  I'm so different now.  Silver S 21-12:31 O '51
MacMurray, J. H.  Magic of a good marriage.  Good House
173:94 O '71

## HAVER, PHYLLIS
Goldbeck, W.  Interview.  Motion Pic Classic 12:32 My '21
Lake, J. M.  Interview.  Motion Pic Classic 14:46 Ap '22
Handy, T. B.  Interview.  Motion Pic 25:36 Ap '23
Calhoun, D.  Sketch.  Motion Pic 34:42 S '27
Waterbury, R.  Sketch.  Photop 32:32 O '27
Walker, H. L.  Sketch.  Motion Pic 35:44 F '28
Johnston, C.  Sketch.  Motion Pic Classic 28:51 O '28
Belfrage, C.  Sketch.  Motion Pic 37:50 Ap '29
Bodeen, D.  Phyllis Haver; filmog.  Focus On F 19:39 Aut '74

HAVOC, JUNE
Vallee, W. L.   Devastating June.   Silver S 12-7:38 My '42
The type of man she likes.   Photop 22:51 Ap '43
Sketch.   Life 21:115 O 28 '46
Keating, J.   New lady of affairs.   Cue 20-23:14 Je 9 '51
Minoff, P.   A comely counselor begins to hit her stride.   Cue
  24-13:35 Ap 2 '55
Minoff, P.   Love letter to an actress.   Cue 26-25:14 Je 22 '57
Taylor, T.   About New York.   Cue 26-46:15 N 16 '57
Sullivan, R.   Your obedient servant, Lady Dynamo.   After Dark
  11-10:19 F '70

HAWKINS, JACK
Sketch.   Theatre World 30:130 S '38
Sketch.   Theatre World 42:8 S '46
My favorite role.   Film R p21 '52/53
Rising star.   Film R p107 '53/54
Personality of the month.   Films & Filming 1-6:3 Mr '55
Hall, D. J.   Gentleman Jack.   Films & Filming 16-12:75 S '70
McAsh, I.   Fighting back to stardom.   Films Illus 1-16:10 O
  '72
Obit.   Classic Film Collect 40:58 Fall '73
  Films & Filming 19-18:79 S '73
  N. Y. Daily News p91 Jl 19 '73
  N. Y. Times Bio Ed p1159 Jl '73
  Screen World p235 '74

HAWLEY, ORMI
Interview.   Cosmop 56:555 Mr '14

HAWLEY, WANDA
Harris, C. L.   Sketch.   Motion Pic Classic 7:32 O '18
The open season for salamanders.   Photop 15-5:41 Ap '19
Squier, E. L.   Interview.   Motion Pic 18:60 N '19
Handy, T. B.   Interview.   Motion Pic 20:52 Ag '20
Powers, E.   Interview.   Motion Pic Classic 13:22 S '21

HAWN, GOLDIE
Girls from Laugh In.   Newsweek 73:62 Ja 27 '69
People are talking about.   Vogue 153:192 My '69
Burke, T.   Goldie rush.   McCalls 97:81 O '69
Rollin, B.   Goofy little Goldie.   Look 33:75 D 2 '69
How golden to be Goldie.   Life 68:76 Je 26 '70
Barber, R.   You can take Goldie out of the chorus, but...   TV
  Guide 19-7:29 F 13 '71
Wilkie, J.   Goldie Hawn.   Good House 172:55 My '71
Righter, C.   Star of the month; horoscope.   Mod Screen 65-11:
  46 N '71
Bio.   Cur Bio 32:15 D '71
  Same.   Cur Bio Yrbk 1971:183 '72
Raddatz, L.   Six who bowed out.   TV Guide 20-38:23 S 16 '72
Fury, K. D.   All that glitters is really Goldie.   Redbook 140:10
  Ja '73

Burke, T.  All that glitter is Goldie's.  N. Y. Times sec 2:13
  Ja 28 '73
  Same.  N. Y. Times Bio Ed p75 Ja '73

HAY, MARY
  Denton, F.  Sketch.  Photop 18:68 S '20
  Haskins, H.  Sketch.  Motion Pic Classic 11:44 O '20
  de Revere, F. V.  Face analysis of.  Motion Pic 29:40 F '25
  Underhill, H.  Interview.  Photop 27:38 My '25
  Obit.  Screen World 9:223 '58

HAYAKAWA, SESSUE
  Field, C. K.  In moving pictures.  Sunset 37:22 Jl '16
  Gaddis, P.  Sketch.  Motion Pic Classic 3:18 D '16
  Easterfield, H. C.  Interview.  Motion Pic 15:33 Ap '18
  Carr, H. C.  Sketch.  Motion Pic Classic 7:22 Ja '19
  Fletcher, A. W.  Interview.  Motion Pic 20:52 O '20
  McGaffey, K.  Interview.  Motion Pic Classic 13:58 S '21
  Bryers, L.  Interview.  Motion Pic 23:54 Mr '21
  Carr, H.  Interview.  Motion Pic Classic 14:31 Jl '22
  Redway, S.  Interview.  Motion Pic Classic 23:54 My '26
  Reeve, W. E.  Why he left the American screen.  Motion Pic
    36:33 Ja '29
  Willis, B.  Returns to the screen.  Motion Pic 42:44 O '31
  Returns to American screen.  Newsweek 34:90 N 14 '49
  Brock, A.  American style.  Classic Film Collect 27:12 Spg/
    Sum '70
  Obit.  Classic Film Collect 42:34 Spg '74
    N. Y. Times Bio Ed p1793 N '73
    Screen World p235 '74

HAYDEN, LINDA
  Bio note.  Black Oracle 3:10 Mr '70
  Stuart, A.  Assurance; interview; filmog.  Films & Filming 19-
    9:28 Je '73

HAYDEN, NORA
  Occupation: red herring.  TV Guide 7-42:24 O 17 '59

HAYDEN, STERLING
  Smith, F. J.  100,000 miles to Hollywood.  Silver S 11-4:52 F
    '41
  Hamilton, S.  Sketch.  Photop 18:46 My '41
  Sketch.  Harp Baz 76:60 Je '41
  Pritchett, F.  A very serious young man.  Silver S 17-9:69 Jl
    '47
  Gow, G.  Interview; filmog.  Films & Filming 20-3:17 D '73

HAYDN, RICHARD
  Clein, H.  The real people.  Show 1-8:14 Jl 9 '70
  McClelland, D.  Richard Haydn; filmog.  Film Fan Mo 160:3 O
    '74

HAYDON,  JULIE
  Sketch.   Stage 12:34 Je '35
  Asher, J.   Her story.   Motion Pic 50:37 O '35
  Asher, J.   Enchanting hopeful.   Silver S 6-12:29 O '36
  Actress.   Scrib.   104:4 Ag '38
  Manning, M.   Interview.   Am Home 37:26 D '46

HAYES,  BILL
  TV's gift to Broadway.   TV Guide 1-24:9 S 11 '53

HAYES,  GEORGE  "GABBY"
  Corneau, E.   The gol durndest sidekick in westerns.   Classic
      Film Collect 24:23 Sum '69
  Obit.   Classic Film Collect 23:46 Spg '69
      Film R p20 '69/70
      N. Y. Times p39 F 10 '69
      Newsweek 73:101 F 24 '69
      Screen World 21:237 '70
      Time 93:67 F 21 '69
  Williams, N.   Three comedians of the horse opera; partial
      filmog.   Filmograph 1-4:19 '70
  Meanwhile, back at the ranch.   Screen Greats 1-2:73 Sum '71
  Tuska, J.   Gabby Hayes in the Hoppy series.   Filmograph 2-3:
      49 '71

HAYES,  HAZEL
  Uselton, R. A.   The Wampus baby stars.   Films In R 21-2:73
      F '70

HAYES,  HELEN
  Woollcott, A.   The child actor grows up.   Everybodys 42:57 F
      '20
  Patterson, A.   Sketch.   Theatre 33:26 Ja '21
  Skinner, R. D.   Success in What every woman knows.   Indep
      116:580 My 15 '26
  Beckley, Z.   How she learned the gentle art of playing Barrie
      heroines.   Theatre 44:32 N '26
  Babcock, M.   Interview.   Movie Classic 1:40 S '31
  Goldbeck, E.   Sketch.   Motion Pic 42:26 O '31
  Tribute to.   Ill Lon N 179:1016 D 19 '31
  Young, S.   Compared with Ruth Gordon.   New Rep 69:163 D 23
      '31
  Packer, E.   Are you Helen Hayes conscious?   Silver S 2-2:25
      D '31
  Sketch.   Photop 41:45 Ja '32
  Janeway, D.   Sued by husband's former wife.   Movie Classic
      2:32 Ag '32
  Wilson, E.   Helen Hayes.   Silver S 2-11:17 S '32
  Service, F.   Her marriage ledger.   Motion Pic 44:31 O '32
  Melcher, E.   Helen Hayes.   Cinema Dig 2-7:12 Ja 23 '33
  Jones, C. P.   Helen Hayes.   Cinema Dig 2-9:10 F 13 '33
  Donnell, D.   Acclaimed best actress.   Movie Classic 3:30 F '33
  Chandler, J.   Interview.   Motion Pic 47:59 Ap '34

Motherwell, H.   Work of in Mary of Scotland.   Stage 11:14 My
    '34
Maxwell, V.   How she makes her marriage happy.   Silver S 4-
    11:47 S '34
Smalley, J.   Interview.   Motion Pic 49:34 Ap '35
Lee, S.   One of Hollywood's greatest funsters.   Movie Classic
    8:42 My '35
Her creed for happiness.   Ladies Home J 53:8 Ap '36
Story of.   Life 1:32 N 23 '36
Her makeup for Victoria Regina.   Life 4:62 Ap 11 '38
Home life of.   Vogue 94:44 Jl 15 '39
Home life of.   Life 7:82 N 13 '39
Role in the Hayes.   Cue 12-9:12 F 27 '43
Anecdote.   Am Mag 141:108 F '46
Cushman, W.   Mother and daughter have similar tastes in dress
    fashions.   Ladies Home J 64:60 Jl '47
Story of.   Theatre World 44:33 S '48
Interview.   Life 25:77 N 8 '48
Keating, J.   Lady in retirement.   Cue 21-14:12 Ap 5 '52
Lewis, E.   About New York.   Cue 23-51:18 D 18 '54
Miss Hayes' half-century.   Cue 24-49:14 D 10 '55
Downing, R.   Her golden jubilee; filmog.   Films In R 7-2:62 F
    '56
Funke, L. & Booth, J. E.   On acting; interview.   Show 1-1:88
    O '61
Salute of the week.   Cue 38-42:1 O 18 '69
Calta, L.   Helen Hayes raises sights to 70-year stage career.
    N. Y. Times Bio Ed Mr 3 '70
In the words of Helen Hayes.   Cue 39-15:20 Ap 11 '70
Mothner, I.   Let's not get sentimental about Helen Hayes.   Look
    34:M+ O 6 '70
Newsmakers.   Newsweek 77:42 Je 21 '71
People.   Time 97:34 Je 21 '71
How we taught our son to love.   Photop 79-6:42 Je '71
Grand slam.   TV Guide 19-41:16 O 9 '71
How I find peace of mind.   Mod Screen 66-9:62 S '72
Skolsky, S.   Showing up.   Show 2-11:13 F '73
Miss Hayes meets Alice Cooper.   TV Guide 22-9:6 Mr 2 '74
Castell, D.   The first lady.   Films Illus 4-38:64 O '74

HAYES, PAUL
    Obit.   N. Y. Times p39 Jl 30 '69

HAYES, PETER LIND
    New comic in Manhattan.   Time 47:74 Je 24 '46
    Newest comedy star.   Life 21:60 Ag 12 '46
    Sounding out Hayes.   Newsweek 28:65 S 23 '46
    M-M-M-Meet J-J-J-Joe F-F-F-Frisco.   Colliers 128:20 D 1 '51
    Moore, G.   Final curtain.   Coronet 33:149 Ap '53
    Hayes, P. L.   Stop thief.   TV Guide 1-3:8 Ap 17 '53
    Washington's strangest statue.   Coronet 36:33 Jl '54
    Godfrey's substitute.   TV Guide 3-49:13 D 3 '55
    Hayes has hats by the hundreds.   TV Guide 7-9:12 F 28 '59

--- and HEALY, MARY
 Five thousand fingers of the Hayeses. Theatre Arts 37:16 D 1
  '51
 Jon Whitcomb's page. Cosmop 134:12 Mr '53
 Ten things that make our hearts beat faster. Good House 141:
  244 N '55
 Double life of Peter Lind Hayes. Look 29:46 S 4 '56
 Crafty commuters. TV Guide 4-36:8 S 8 '56
 Weekend yachtsman. McCalls 84:14 Ag '57
 Peter and Mary make their bid. Cue 27-9:12 Mr 1 '58
 Martin, P. I call on... Sat Eve Post 231:26 D 27 '58
 Hayes, P. L. The family that plays together stays together.
  TV Guide 8-42:6 O 15 '60
 Shane, G. Aboard the 36' cruiser Queen Mary. Motor Boat
  115:60 '65

HAYMES, DICK
 Vallee, W. L. Rival of Crosby and Sinatra. Silver S 14-8:24
  Je '44
 Betz, B. Sketch. Womans Home C 72:118 Mr '45
 Warner, S. All about the Haymes-James Inc. Silver S 16-1:
  38 N '45
 O'Leary, D. Hi ho, Haymes. Silver S 16-10:58 Ag '46
 Haymes, J. D. The man I married. Silver S 18-2:28 D '47
 The Dick Haymes story. Song Hits 13:6 Jl '49
 In person. Metron 66:20 D '50
 Sherwood, P. Rita sticks her neck out again. Silver S 24-1:31
  N '53

HAYNES, LLOYD
 Hobson, D. Superteacher calls his class to order. TV Guide
  17-44:31 N 1 '69
 Why Lloyd Haynes must get not one but two divorces. Photop
  78-1:79 Jl '70
 Raddatz, L. His message: look up. TV Guide 21-37:21 S 15
  '73

HAYS, KATHRYN
 McClelland, D. TV: where all that old-time glamour went.
  Film Fan Mo 75:11 S '67

HAYS, WILL
 Filmog. Films & Filming 20-7:63 Ap '74

HAYWARD, LOUIS
 Mack, G. Interview. Motion Pic 53:43 Je '37
 Rhea, M. Sketch. Photop 53:30 Jl '39
 Harvey, G. Unmasking the man in the iron mask. Silver S
  9-11:48 S '39
 Bio note; filmog. Movies & People 2:19 '40
 Parsons, L. O. Cosmops citation for best supporting role of
  the month. Cosmop 120:61 Ap '46

HAYWARD, SUSAN
    The girl on the cover.    Cue 11-11:1 Mr 14 '42
    Franchey, J. R.    Mistreated miss.    Silver S 12-8:24 Je '42
    My first date.    Cosmop 113:41 N '42
    Franchey, J. R.    Eight men in her life.    Silver S 13-8:34 Je '43
    Holland, J.    Life with the Barkers.    Silver S 16-12:40 O '46
    Wilson, E.    Not so sweet Susan.    Silver S 18-2:46 D '47
    Barker, J.    My life with Susan.    Silver S 20-5:30 Mr '50
    Bruce, J.    Do women expect too much?    Silver S 21-9:30 Jl '51
    Churchill, R. & B.    Why wait for romance?    Silver S 22-8:22 Je
        '52
    Lee, T.    You never can tell about Susan.    Silver S 23-5:28 Mr
        '53
    Churchill, R. & B.    Redhead who doesn't care.    Silver S 23-12:
        29 O '53
    Actress around the world.    Cue 24-15:13 Ap 16 '55
    Davidson, B.    Just like Paramount in 1945.    TV Guide 20-9:18
        F 26 '72
    A woman is a woman and a man is a man.    Photop 81-2:53 F
        '72
    Verity, F.    Actress and writer; letter.    Filmograph 3-2:47 '72
    Keith, D. L.    Flame-haired blizzard from Brooklyn.    After Dark
        5-9:40 Ja '73

HAYWORTH, RITA
    Hamilton, S.    Sketch.    Photop 54:28 Ag '40
    Franchey, J. R.    Sultry siren.    Silver S 11-4:36 F '41
    Teltscher, H. O.    Analysis of her handwriting.    Photop 19:62
        Je '41
    Sketch.    Life 11:33 Ag 11 '41
    Rumors of marital trouble.    Photop 19:32 N '41
    How I keep my husband from getting jealous.    Silver S 12-6:26
        Ap '42
    Mulvey, K.    Sketch.    Womans Home C 70:60 F '43
    Manners, M. J.    Rita announces her marriage plans.    Silver S
        13-8:24 Je '43
    Hendricks, H.    Why Rita really married Orson Welles.    Silver
        S 14-2:24 D '43
    Notes about.    Photop 27:50 S '45
    Watkins, W.    Catching up with Rita.    Silver S 16-1:22 N '45
    Parsons, L. O.    Cosmop's citation for best performance of
        month.    Cosmop 120:60 Ap '46
    In London at world premiere of Down to earth.    Time 50:33 Ag
        4 '47
    Graham, S.    Sketch.    Photop 33:40 N '48
    Parsons, L. O.    Cosmop's citation for best performance of
        month.    Cosmop 125:12 N '48
    Flight with Aly Khan.    Life 26:51 F 7 '49
    The Cansinos and Prince Aly.    Newsweek 33:47 My 30 '49
    Peterson, E.    And so they were married.    Silver S 19-11:24 S
        '49
    Hall, G.    A tip to teenagers from Rita.    Silver S 21-7:22 My
        '51

Holland, J.   Dancing with joy.   Silver S 22-12:22 O '52
Wilson, E.   The regal Rita.   Silver S 23-7:19 My '53
Sherwood, P.   Rita sticks her neck out again.   Silver S 24-1:31
   N '53
Hallowell, J.   Don't put the blame on me, boys.   N. Y. Times
   Bio Ed O 25 '70
Hamilton, J.   Where, oh where are the beautiful girls?   Look
   34-22:62 N 3 '70
The pin-up girls.   Screen Greats 1-2:20 Sum '71
I have no regrets.   Photop 81-6:23 Je '72
Kobal, J.   The time, the place and the girl; filmog.   Focus On
   F 10:15 Sum '72
Additional filmog.   Focus On F 11:15 Aut '72
Stanke, D.   Rita Hayworth; filmog.   Films In R 23-9:527 N '72
Note about vocal dubbing.   Focus On F 12:15 Win '72
Hayworth, R.   This was my favorite role.   Movie Dig 2-1:55 Ja
   '73
The strange case of Rita Hayworth.   Mod Screen 67-3:13 Mr '73
Letters.   Films In R 24-4:251; 255 Ap '73
Varble, S.   An untitled adulation of Rita Hayworth.   Special Hay-
   worth edition.   Interview 1-11:3 n. d.

HAZELL, HY
   Obit.   Film R p15 '70/71

HAZLETT, ZOE
   From turnips to television.   TV Guide 6-17:12 Ap 26 '58

HEAD, MURRAY
   Buckley, P.   Fresh faces from the British cinema.   After Dark
      4-3:38 Jl '71
   Andrews, E.   Head of hair.   Films Illus 1-3:14 S '71
   Stoop, N. M.   Side A of Murray Head.   After Dark 6-2:44A Je
      '73
   Head lines.   Films Illus 3-27:115 S '73
   McGillivray, D.   Bio note; filmog.   Films & Filming 20-12:57
      S '74

HEALY, MARY
   (See HAYES, PETER LIND and HEALY, MARY)

HEALY, TED
   Fender, R.   Interview.   Movie Classic 6:51 Mr '34

HEATHERTON, JOEY
   Rising stars.   Film R p53 '65/66
   Manners, D.   I nominate for stardom.   Mod Screen 66-7:18 Jl
      '72
   Saal, H.   Just a little girl.   Newsweek 80:85 S 25 '72

HECHT, TED
   Obit.   N. Y. Times p41 Je 26 '69
      Screen World 21:237 '70

HECKART, EILEEN
  Johnson, D.   Everybody's favorite "mum" in the movies plays
    her again in Butterflies are free.   Show 2-4:20 Je '72
  Klemesrud, J.   After the Oscar, she went on unemployment.
    N.Y. Times sec 2:13 My 6 '73

HEDLEY, NANCY
  Her secret weapons--lessons.   TV Guide 7-7:24 F 14 '59

HEDREN, TIPPI
  Rising stars.   Film R p59 '64/65

HEEREN, ASTRID
  Hamilton, J.   Ascent of Astrid.   Look 33:86 Ap 1 '69

HEFLIN, VAN
  Sailor on Broadway.   Lions R 1-2:no p# O '41
  There's a sailor in the cast.   Lions R 1-5:no p# Ja '42
  The picture he didn't make.   Lions R 1-9:no p# My '42
  Haas, D. B.   Young man from the sea.   Silver S 12-9:52 Jl '42
  Stars of tomorrow.   Lions R 1-11/12:no p# Jl/Ag '42
  Barrymore looks at Van Heflin.   Lions R 2-3:no p# D '42
  That man Van.   Lions R 2-4:no p# Ap '43
  Holliday, K.   Just call him rugged.   Silver S 17-7:54 My '47
  Heflin, F. N.   The man I married.   Silver S 18-7:22 My '48
  Heflin, V.   Don't be afraid to take a chance.   Silver S 22-3:26
    Ja '52
  Taylor, T.   A view of Van Heflin.   Cue 24-38:14 S 24 '55
  Obit.   Classic Film Collect 32:62 Fall '71
    Cur Bio 32:44 S '71
    Cur Bio Yrbk 1971:464 '72
    Film R p13 '72/73
    N.Y. Times p28 Jl 24 '71
    Same.   N.Y. Times Bio Ed Jl 24 '71
    Newsweek 78:59 Ag 2 '71
    Screen World 23:237 '72
    Time 98:60 Ag 2 '71
  Marrill, A. H.   Van Heflin; filmog.   Films In R 24-1:1 Ja '73
  Davis, F.   Van Heflin.   Films In R 24-4:250 Ap '73

HEILBRON, VIVIEN
  New faces.   Films Illus 1-7:11 Ja '72

HELL, ERIK
  Cowie, P.   Eric Hell; filmog.   Focus On R 5:13 Win '70

HELM, ANNE
  From My sister Eileen to Elvis Presley.   TV Guide 10-19:7 My
    12 '62

HELTON, PERCY
  Weisenreder, E. B.   Percy Helton.   Films In R 19-9:592 N '68
  Obit.   N.Y. Times p44 S 14 '71
    Screen World 23:237 '72

HEMING, VIOLET
    West, M. F.   Sketch.   Green Book 9:52 Ja '13
    Sketch.   N. Y. Drama 70:5 S 17 '13
    Sketch.   Strand (NY) 50:70 Ag '15
    Cades, H. R.   Interview.   Womans Home C 50:76 Ap '23

HEMMINGS, DAVID
    Ehrlich, H.   Light brigade charges again.    Look 32:58 F 6 '68
    Redbook dialogue.   Redbook 131:70 Jl '68
    Macdonough, S.   Young man of all mediums.    Show 2-2:24 S '71
    The 14.   Films Illus 1-16:16 O '72
    Hemmings and ambition.   Films Illus 2-19:6 Ja '73
    Gow, G.   Interview; filmog.   Films & Filming 19-8:13 My '73
    Cowie, P.   David Hemmings; filmog.   Focus On F 7:4 n. d.

HEMSLEY, ESTELLE
    Obit.   N. Y. Times p47 N 8 '68
    Screen World 20:235 '69

HENABERY, JOSEPH H.
    Cohn, A. A.   Sketch.   Photop 17:88 Ja '20

HENDERSON, DEL
    Obit.   N. Y. Times p39 D 5 '56
    Screen World 8:222 '57

HENDERSON, FLORENCE
    Today's woman.   TV Guide 8-3:29 Ja 16 '60
    Landau, G. M.   My kids are real stars.   Parents 42:42 Ag '67
    Hano, A.   Suzie sweet she ain't.   TV Guide 18-6:40 F 7 '70
    Tips on winter beauty.   Parents 45:23 D '70
    Bio.   Cur Bio 32:15 Ap '71
        Same.   Cur Bio Yrbk 1971:187 '72
    The Christmas that taught me the meaning of love.   Mod Screen
        66-1:46 Ja '72
    Battelle, P.   Mother of TV's Brady bunch.   Good House 175:36
        S '72

HENDERSON, MARCIA
    This is a sports writer?   TV Guide 3-10:13 Mr 5 '55

HENDRIX, WANDA
    Parsons, L. O.   Cosmop's citation for the best supporting role
        of month.   Cosmop 123:12 D '47
    Sketch.   Photop 32:31 F '48
    Gwynn, E.   Her wardrobe on sailing for Italy.   Photop 33:68
        N '48
    Graham, S.   Sketch.   Photop 33:41 N '48
    O'Leary, D.   So you want to be an actress?   Silver S 19-3:33
        Ja '49
    Her coming marriage to Audie Murphy.   Photop 34:24 Ja '49
    Hendrix, W.   A man called Power.   Silver S 19-9:24 Jl '49
    Hendrix, W.   Are older men dangerous dates?   Silver S 20-12:38

O '50
My favorite role.   Film R p20 '52/53
Cohen, J.   Filmog.   Films In R 19-2:126 F '68

HENDRY, IAN
Rising star.   Film R p44 '63/64
Filmog.   Films & Filming 19-5:58 F '73
Hendry on Theatre of blood.   Films Illus 2-22:32 Ap '73

HENIE, SONJA
Sketch.   Life 2:57 Ja 11 '37
Lane, V. T.   Story of.   Motion Pic 52:44 Ja '37
Sketch.   Leisure 4:36 Ja '37
Sketch.   Photop 51:80 My '37
Sullivan, E.   Champions vs. the screen.   Silver S 7-8:22 Je '37
Castle, M.   Interview.   Motion Pic 54:29 Ag '37
Surmelian, L.   Darling of the ice.   Silver S 8-3:22 Ja '38
Surmelian, L.   My daughter Sonja.   Screen Book 20-2:26 Mr '38
She's the tops.   Cue 7-12:9 Ja 14 '39
How she keeps her feet in trim.   Life 6:66 Ja 23 '39
Brown, C.   Take a skating lesson from Sonja.   Screen Book 21-
   6:29 Ja '39
Cheatham, M.   Still laughing at love.   Silver S 10-3:36 Ja '40
Bio note; filmog.   Movies & People 2:19 '40
Reasons why an ice queen keeps her crown.   Cue 10-3:12 Ja 18
   '41
The girl on the cover.   Cue 11-3:1 Ja 17 '42
Reid, J.   Busy as a B-25.   Silver S 12-10:54 Ag '42
Sonja's coming back.   Cue 13-3:9 Ja 15 '44
New Henie ice revue.   Cue 14-2:7 Ja 13 '45
Vallee, W. L.   Other side of Sonja.   Silver S 15-7:42 My '45
Ice queen eternal is woman of the week.   Cue 16-3:9 Ja 18 '47
Fink, H.   Her party.   Photop 30:52 Ja '47
The lady cometh.   Cue 19-2:17 Ja 14 '50
What they are doing now.   Show 2-3:97 Mr '62
Obit.   Brit Bk Yr 1970:582 '70
   Cur Bio 31:44 N '70
   Cur Bio Yrbk 1970:464 '71
   Film R p15 '70/71
   Screen World 21:237 '70
Bubbly, bouncy and blonde.   Screen Greats 1-2:52 Sum '71

HENLEY, HOBART
Ames, H.   Sketch.   Motion Pic 11:72 My '16
Van Loan, H. H.   Sketch.   Motion Pic Classic 4:35 Ap '17
Shaw, O.   Interview.   Motion Pic Classic 10:28 Mr '20
Fredericks, J.   Interview.   Motion Pic 20:68 S '20
Obit.   N. Y. Times p23 My 23 '64
   Screen World 16:220 '64

HENNECKE, CLARENCE R.
Obit.   Screen World 21:237 '70

HENNING, PAT
   Obit.  N. Y. Times Bio Ed p617 Ap '73
      Screen World p235 '74

HENNING-JENSEN, ASTRID
   Bio note.  Int F G 6:61 '69

HENREID, PAUL
   Sketch.  Theatre Arts 26:188 Mr '42
   Sharpe, H.  Story of.  Photop 22:36 Ja '43
   Wilson, E.  The man with the smoldering eyes.  Silver S 13-3:
      24 Ja '43
   Bio.  Cur Bio '43
   Hall, G.  Women who have been kind to me.  Silver S 14-4:32
      F '44
   A romance I can't forget.  Photop 24:55 Mr '44
   O'Leary, D.  End of fantasy.  Silver S 17-1:37 N '46
   Nolan, J. E.  Films on TV.  Films In R 20-5:305 My '69
   The director-actor: a conversation.  Action 5-1:21 Ja/F '70

HENRY, CHARLOTTE
   Sketch.  Photop 45:37 D '33
   Calhoun, D.  Her fame in title role of Alice in Wonderland.
      Movie Classic 5:5 Ja '34

HENRY, EMMALINE
   Just call her the rock.  TV Guide 11-20:15 My 18 '63

HENRY, WILLIAM
   Hamilton, S. & Morse, W. Jr.  Sketch.  Photop 54:20 Mr '40
   Haynes, H.  Interview.  Photop 18:48 Ap '41

HENRY, WILLIAM E.
   When the money runs out.  Todays Ed 59:54 Mr '70
   Actors' search for self.  Trans-Action 7:57 S '70

HENSON, NICKY
   Nicky and Una, together again for the first time; filmog.  Films
      Illus 2-22:24 Ap '73

HENVILLE, SANDRA LEE (Sandy)
   Story of.  Life 7:38 Ag 14 '39
   Hamman, M.  Story of.  Good House 109:42 N '39

HEPBURN, AUDREY
   Keating, J.  Girl hard to find.  Cue 20-46:15 N 17 '51
   Rising star.  Film R p108 '52/53
   Hollywood's new Hepburn.  Cue 22-29:14 Jl 18 '53
   No mermaid more magical.  Cue 23-13:12 Mr 27 '54
   Wilson, E.  Is Hollywood shifting its accent on sex?  Silver S
      24-9:40 Jl '54
   Viotti, S.  Britain's Hepburn.  Films & Filming 1-2:7 N '54
   My favorite role.  Film R p26 '55/56

Feinstein, H.   My gorgeous darling sweetheart angel.   Film Q
    15-3:65 Spg '62
Gotta sing.   Gotta dance.   Film 40:9 Sum '64
Audrey Hepburn; filmog.   Sound Stage 1-1:19 D '64
Dowty, L.   Hepburn makes the scene.   Good House 165:84 Ag
    '67
Audrey and Andrea.   Vogue 153:109 Mr 15 '69
Barry, J.   New life, a new love; Hepburn at 40.   McCalls 96:57
    Jl '69
Pepper, C. B.   Interview.   Vogue 157:94 Ap 1 '71
Ringgold, G.   Audrey Hepburn; filmog.   Films In R 22-10:585 D
    '71

HEPBURN, KATHARINE
Who is Katharine Hepburn?   Stage 9-8:30 My '32
Sketch.   Motion Pic 44:42 D '32
Larnard, P.   Sketch.   Movie Classic 3:47 D '32
Fidler, J.   Answers 20 startling questions.   Movie Classic 4:22
    Mr '33
Melcher, E.   Screen sensation of the year.   Cinema Dig 3-5:9
    Ap 17 '33
Cohen, H.   Hepburn.   Cinema Dig 3-7:12 My 1 '33
Lee, S.   Her "mystery. "   Motion Pic 45:34 My '33
Lynn, H.   How she makes love.   Photop 44:32 Ag '33
Appreciation.   Lit Dig 116:16 S 2 '33
Biery, R.   She's not a one picture girl.   Silver S 3-12:18 O '33
Pope, N.   Changes in her since her first picture.   Motion Pic
    46:30 N '33
Orme, M.   Appreciation.   Ill Lon N 183:818 N 18 '33
Mannes, M.   Compared with Miriam Hopkins.   Vogue 83:24 Ja 1
    '34
Biery, R.   Interview.   Motion Pic 47:30 F '34
Baskette, K.   Compared with Garbo.   Photop 45:28 Mr '34
Champion, C.   Hepburn, West and sex appeal.   Motion Pic 47:
    28 Mr '34
Benedict, D.   Her radio broadcasting.   Movie Classic 6:32 Ap
    '34
Norden, H. B.   Appreciation.   Vanity Fair 42:50 Ap '34
Calhoun, D.   Sketch.   Movie Classic 6:33 Jl '34
Slater, A.   Her divorce.   Movie Classic 6:40 Jl '34
Rogers, B.   Has she married Leland Hayward?   Photop 47:26
    Mr '35
Putnam, N. W.   Sketch.   Motion Pic 49:21 Mr '35
Fairweather, D.   Criticism.   Theatre World 23:182 Ap '35
Asher, J.   On location.   Motion Pic 47:42 My '35
Martin, E.   How men have changed her.   Motion Pic 49:24 Jl
    '35
Blake, N.   Hepburn the person.   Movie Classic 8:24 Jl '35
French, W. F.   Interview.   Motion Pic 51:47 F '36
Craig, C.   As her designer sees her.   Movie Classic 9:40 F '36
Lane, V.   A never before revealed story.   Movie Classic 10:32
    Je '36
Reid, J.   Queening it as Mary of Scotland.   Motion Pic 51:33

Jl '36
Camp, D. Her hobbies. Motion Pic 53:40 F '37
Asher, J. Explaining the real Hepburn. Motion Pic 53:26 Jl
    '37
Katharine Hepburn. Visages 15:entire issue Ag '37
Hall, G. Story of. Motion Pic 54:26 D '37
Sketch. Life 5:12 Jl 25 '38
Hartford Philly. Cue 7-22:9 Mr 25 '39
Nathan, G. J. Appreciation. Newsweek 13:28 Ap 10 '39
Story of. Harp Baz 73:52 Ag '39
Hall, G. Has Hepburn changed? Silver S 11-1:22 N '40
The girls on the cover. Cue 11-5:1 Ja 31 '42
Call her Kate. Lions R 1-6:no p# F '42
Franchey, J. K. Don't be nice to Katie. Silver S 12-6:34 Ap
    '42
Sketch. Harp Baz 76:89 Ag '42
Hepburn's challenge. Lions R 2-3:no p# D '42
Unpredictable Hepburn. Lions R 3-4:no p# Jl '44
Franchey, J. R. Hepburn gets confidential. Silver S 14-12:22
    O '44
Watkins, W. The Hepburn candor. Silver S 15-8:46 Je '45
Lewis, E. Katie meets the Bard. Cue 19-3:16 Ja 21 '50
Katie set to explode here. Cue 21-40:16 O 4 '52
Zunser, J. Stratford: Ryan, Hepburn, et al. Cue 29-31:8 Jl
    30 '60
Fenin, G. The face of '63--United States. Films & Filming
    9-6:55 Mr '63
Hamilton, J. Last visit with two undimmed stars. Look 31:26
    Jl 11 '67
Israel, L. Last of the honest-to-God ladies. Esquire 68:14 N
    '67
Arkadin. Film clips. Sight & Sound 37-1:48 Win '67/68
Newsmakers. Newsweek 71:36 Ja 1 '68
Frook, J. Aunt Kat. Life 64:61 Ja 5 '68
Miller, E. Kath and her Aunt Kate. Seventeen 27:134 F '68
Feibleman, P. S. Unsinkable Kate. Look 32:63 Ag 6 '68
Graham, S. Spencer Tracy and Katharine Hepburn. Ladies
    Home J 85:94 D '68
Tynan, K. Great Kate. Vogue 153:87 Ap 15 '69
The career of Hepburn at Museum of Modern Art. Classic Film
    Collect 24:25 Sum '69
Cronin, B. The very expensive Coco. Time 94:86 N 7 '69
Kate and Co Co. Newsweek 74:75 N 10 '69
Salute of the week. Cue 38-46:1 N 15 '69
Bio. Cur Bio 30:21 N '69
    Same. Cur Bio Yrbk 1969:209 '70
Kanin, G. Private Kate. McCalls 97:57 F '70
Brooks, D. Cue salutes. Cue 39-13:32 Mr 28 '70
Bowers, R. L. Hepburn since '57; filmog. Films In R 21-7:
    423 Ag/S '70
The love teams. Screen Greats 1-2:10 Sum '71
Forbes, B. Kate; filmog. Films Illus 1-3:17 S '71
Robbins, F. Director Cacoyannis and his Trojan women. Show

2-8:29 O '71

Kanin, G.   He-she chemistry of Hepburn and Tracy; excerpt
    from Tracy and Hepburn.   Vogue 158:142 N 1 '71

One of the pre-eminent women of our time.   New Woman 1-7:
    82 D '71

Cutts, J.   Long shot.   Films & Filming 18-3:26 D '71

Kanin, G.   Katie and the hard hats; excerpt from Tracy and
    Hepburn.   Read Dig 100:213 F '72

Reingold, C. B.   A very special love.   Movie Dig 1-2:16 Mr '72

Hepburn and Tracy.   Mod Screen 66-3:48 Mr '72

St. Johns, A.   The private life of Katharine Hepburn.   Liberty
    1-4:52 Spg '72

Canby, V.   Tracy and Hepburn, the potato and the dessert.
    N. Y. Times sec 2:1 S 17 '72

Gilliatt, P.   Current cinema.   New Yorker 48:64 S 23 '72

Lambert, G.   The making of Gone with the wind.   Atlantic 231-
    2:46 F '73

Israel, L.   That's no lady, that's Katharine Hepburn.   MS 1-8:
    25 F '73

McAsh, I.   Maintaining a delicate balance.   Films Illus 2-23:16
    My '73

Higham, C.   Private and proud and Hepburn.   N. Y. Times sec
    2:3 D 9 '73

Same.   N. Y. Times Bio Ed p1956 D '73

Musel, R.   The day they stole her trousers.   TV Guide 21-50:31
    D 15 '73

Kate and Duke team up to make Hollywood history.   People 2-21:
    8 N 18 '74

Tracy and Hepburn; filmog.   Screen Greats 1-5:entire issue n. d.

Classy rider.   TV Guide 22-52:2 D 28 '74

HERBERT, HOLMES
    Calhoun, D.   Sketch.   Motion Pic Classic 21:50 Je '25

HERBERT, HUGH
    Dowling, M.   Sketch.   Movie Classic 6:16 Mr '34
    Hall, G.   Interview.   Motion Pic 52:57 N '36
    Harrison, H.   Woo-woo.   Silver S 8-10:58 Ag '38
    A day with Herbert.   Lions R 3-5:no p# D '44
    Obit.   Screen World 4:176 '53

HERNANDEZ, JUANO
    Obit.   N. Y. Times p27 Jl 20 '70
        N. Y. Times Bio Ed Jl 20 '70
        Screen World 22:237 '71

HERSHEY, BARBARA
    (See also: SEAGULL, BARBARA)
    Raddatz, L.   Bring on the chocolate mousse.   TV Guide 15-18:20
        My 6 '67
    Miller, E.   Essence of Barbara; interview.   Seventeen 29:132 F
        '70
    Coffin, H. A.   The unconventional star of Last summer and The

baby maker is a triumph of intuition over intellect.   Show 1-
7:33 Je 25 '70
Mothner, I.   Now faces.   Look 34:73 N 3 '70
Actresses.   Newsweek 76:74 D 7 '70
Wilson, J.   Up in a tree house with Barbara.   Cosmop 172-4:
158 Ap '72

HERSHOLT, JEAN
Sketch.   Photop 28:76 S '25
Sketch.   Motion Pic 30:58 Ja '26
York, C.   Sketch.   Photop 31:71 D '26
Milne, P.   Work of.   Motion Pic Classic 24:26 F '27
Hall, G.   Sketch.   Motion Pic Classic 27:55 Ag '28
Hall, G.   Sketch.   Motion Pic Classic 29:42 Ap '29
Palmborg, R. P.   How he handles his money.   Motion Pic 39:68
F '30
Hall, G.   Sketch.   Motion Pic Classic 32:73 Ja '31
Chrisman, J. E.   Motion Pic Classic 33:56 Ap '31
Samuels, L.   Made by the "quints."   Silver S 6-9:28 Jl '36
Hersholt, J.   We can't forget.   Screen Book 22-4:78 N '39
Haas, D.   Keeping him healthy.   Silver S 11-7:36 My '41
Dr. Christian and Mr. Hersholt.   Cue 15-26:11 Je 29 '46
Finney, E.   The Jean Hersholt story; interview with Allan Her-
sholt.   Classic Film Collect 25:18 Fall '69

HERVEY, IRENE
Home of.   Photop 54:56 S '40
McClelland, D.   Irene Hervey; filmog.   Film Fan Mo 126:7 D
'71

HERVEY, RICHARD
How to be an actor.   TV Guide 7-41:20 O 10 '59

HESTON, CHARLTON
Swift, J.   He has all Hollywood talking about him.   Silver S 22-
1:36 N '51
I married an actress.   Silver S 24-8:46 Je '54
The questions no one asks about Willy (Wyler).   Films & Filming
4-11:9 Ag '58
Heston, C.   Ben-Hur diaries.   Cinema (BH) 2-2:10 '64
"War" article on Heston and Major Dundee.   Cinema (BH) 2-3:
6 O/N '64
Heston, C.   Greatest story diaries.   Cinema (BH) 2-4:4 D '64/
Ja '65
What I want, and don't want, from my director.   Action 2-1:19
Ja/ F '67
1968: a new year in better shape.   Vogue 151:67 Ja 1 '68
Austin, D.   It's all a matter of size.   Films & Filming 14-7:4
Ap '68
Quotemanship.   Action 3-3:20 Jl/Ag '68
Delson, J.   Heston on Welles; interview.   Take One 3-6:7 Jl/Ag
'71
One-day in the life of Heston; filmog.   Films Illus 1-2:4 Ag '71

Bio note.  Films Illus 1-5:31 N '71
Gow, G.  Actor's country; interview; filmog.  Films & Filming
  18-8:18 My '72
Winogura, D.  Dialogues on apes, apes and more apes; inter-
  view.  Cinefantastique 2-2:28 Sum '72
Interview; biblio.  Dialogue 1:1 '72
American Film Institute University advisory committee seminar.
  Dialogue 2-1:entire issue '72
A bleak view of the future.  Films Illus 3-26:56 Ag '73
Interview.  Film Heritage 10-1:1 Fall '74
Answers questions from readers.  Photop 86-5:48 N '74

HEYBURN, WELDON
  Obit.  Screen World 3:177 '53

HEYL, JOHN
  Carragher, B.  There really was a super suicide society.  N. Y.
    Times sec 2:1 O 8 '72
  Lyons, D.  Interview.  Interview 29:28 Ja '73

HIATT, RUTH
  Uselton, R. A.  The Wampus baby stars.  Films In R 21-2:73
    F '70

HICKEY, DONNA LEE
  (See:  WYNN, MAY)

HICKMAN, DARRYL
  Shades of Mickey Rooney.  Lions R 1-11/12:no p# Jl/Ag '42
  Hollywood's youngest character actor.  Lions R 3-2:no p# Ja '44
  His TV success.  TV Guide 9-32:24 Ag 12 '61
  McClelland, D.  Darryl Hickman; filmog.  Film Fan Mo 153:18
    Mr '74

HICKMAN, HOWARD
  Bickers, H. S.  Sketch.  Motion Pic 13:59 My '17
  Willis, R.  Sketch.  Motion Pic Classic 5:25 S '17
  Peltret, E.  Sketch.  Motion Pic 16:32 Ja '19

HICKOX, HARRY
  The sound-and-fury boys.  TV Guide 13-26:6 Je 26 '65

HICKSON, JOAN
  Tierney, M.  Interview.  Plays & Players 19-4:32 Ja '72

HIERS, WALTER
  Bishop, R.  Interview.  Motion Pic 25:44 Ap '23

HIGGINS, DONNA
  Once upon a time there was a little girl.  TV Guide 12-27:27 Jl
    4 '67

HIGGINS, JOE
    Commercial successes.    Newsweek 76:100 O 19 '70

HILBURN, BETTY
    Smith, F. J.  Interview.    Motion Pic Classic 12:16 Mr '21

HILL, ARTHUR
    Berkvist, R.  One S. O. B. was enough.  N. Y. Times Bio Ed
      O 24 '71
    Barber, R.  The plainsman in lotus land.  TV Guide 20-7:41 F
      12 '72
    Ehrlich, H.  Nice men cometh.  McCalls 99:22 My '72
    Robbins, F.  Interview.  Photop 83-4:12 Ap '73

HILL, DORIS
    Manners, D.  Interview.  Motion Pic 38:86 N '29
    Uselton, R. A.  The Wampus baby stars.  Films In R 21-2:73
      F '70

HILL, JOSEPHINE
    Goldbeck, W.  Interview.  Motion Pic Classic 11:20 S '20
    Lake, M.  Sketch.  Motion Pic Classic 13:38 D '21

HILL, MARIANNA
    A Schwarzkopf by another name.  TV Guide 8-41:21 O 8 '60

HILLER, WENDY
    Interview.  Theatre World 23:179 Ap '35
    Patch, H.  O'Neill's Josie Hogan.  Cue 26-17:8 Ap 27 '57
    Verdugo, E.  The movie performance I will always remember.
      Movie Dig 1-6:141 N '72

HILLIARD, HARRIET
    (See: NELSON, HARRIET)

HILLYER, SHARYN
    The world's most low-pressure actress.  TV Guide 13-19:27 My
      8 '65

HINDS, SAMUEL S.
    Riches to movies.  Lions R 1-9:no p# My '42
    Purvis, H.  Partial filmog.  Films In R 17-8:529 O '66

HINES, CONNIE
    Connie really knows Mr. Ed.  TV Guide 10-40:25 O 6 '62

HINES, HARRY
    Obit.  Screen World 19:233 '68

HINES, JOHNNY
    Courtlandt, R.  Sketch.  Motion Pic 11:37 Jl '16
    May, L.  Interview.  Motion Pic 17:81 Mr '19
    Pike, C.  Everybody calls him "Johnny."  Photop 15-5:43 Ap '19

Crooker, H.   Discoverer of screen stars.   Motion Pic 32:30 Ag
'26
Johnston, C.   Sketch.   Motion Pic Classic 27:51 Jl '28
Baubie, J. A. & Clayton, F.   (He) laughs his way to fame.
(Reprint from Pittsburgh Press F 11 '31) Classic Film Col-
lect 16:21 Fall '66
Obit.   Classic Film Collect 29:15 Win '70 (Reprint from Holly-
wood Reporter)

HINGLE, PAT
Minoff, P.   Hingle "arrives."   Cue 26-52:11 D 28 '57

HINZ, MICHAEL
Bean, R.   The face of '63--Germany.   Films & Filming 9-9:41
Je '63

HITCHCOCK, PATRICIA
Cue says watch.   Cue 11-8:1 F 21 '42
Pattie the boo.   Am Mag 134:75 Jl '42
Pat in Violet.   Cue 13-43:10 O 21 '44

HITCHCOCK, RAYMOND
Interview.   Dram Mir 77:4 Jl 21 '17
The art of the curtain speech.   Theatre 26:1920 '17
Hitchcock to return to pictures?   Photop 14-5:34 O '18

HOBART, ROSE
Goldbeck, E.   Interview.   Motion Pic Classic 32:65 N '30
Manners, D.   Hobart leaves Hollywood.   Motion Pic 43:47 Ap '32

HODGES, JOY
Meyer, D.   Little Miss Publicity.   Screen Book 22-3:60 O '39

HODIAK, JOHN
Franchey, J. R.   Meet Hodiak the rocket.   Silver S 14-11:30 S
'44
Willing pawn of fate.   Lions R 3-5:no p# D '44
Dear Johnnie.   Lions R 3-5:no p# D '44
Creelman, E.   He wants a wife.   Silver S 16-1:24 N '45
Tildesley, A. L.   Don't they think we're human?   Silver S 18-4:
46 F '48
Stanke, D.   John Hodiak; filmog.   Film Fan Mo 123:7 S '71

HOFFMAN, DUSTIN
Zeitlin, D.   Homely non-hero.   Life 63:111 N 24 '67
I plummeted to stardom.   Newsweek 71:86 Ja 22 '68
On the scene.   Playboy 15-8:131 Ag '68
Chapman, D.   Graduate turns bum.   Look 32:66 S 17 '68
Gossow, M.   Dustin.   McCalls 95:66 S '68
Lear, M. W.   The man behind the smile.   Redbook 131:66 S '68
Wilkes, P.   The burden of making Dustin shine.   New York 1-34:
42 N 25 '68
Gilman, R.   High level acting.   New Rep 160:32 Ja 25 '69

Cooks, J.   Moonchild and the fifth Beatle.   Time 93:50 F 7 '69
Salute of the week.   Cue 38-24:1 Je 14 '69
Dusty and the Duke.   Life 67:36 Jl 11 '69
Bio.   Cur Bio 30:12 D '69
    Same.   Cur Bio Yrbk 1969:215 '70
Bio.   Brit Bk Yr 1969:152 '69
Kempton, S.   Little big man clings to life.   Esquire 74:78 Jl '70
Merryman, R.   Old age of Dustin; interview.   Life 69:75 N 20
    '70
Knight, A. & Alpert, H.   Sex stars of 1970.   Playboy 17-12:220
    D '70
Wilson, E.   Friends call him Dusty.   Moviegoer 2-1:28 '70
The miracle of makeup.   Making Films 5-2:22 Ap '71
Miller, E.   Interview.   Seventeen 30:138 My '71
Milne, T.   Bio note; filmog.   Focus On F 6:7 Spg '71
Boxer, T.   A very public actor.   Show 2-6:40 Ag '71
Our baby nearly choked to death.   Mod Screen 66-7:54 Jl '72
The bonds that hold Dustin and his wife together.   Mod Screen
    67-4:35 Ap '73
Filmog.   Films & Filming 19-18:56 S '73

HOLBROOK, HAL
    Barber, R.   Long distance actor.   TV Guide 19-9:21 F 27 '71
    Irony of a success de Emmy.   Life 70:11 Je 18 '71
    Berkvist, R.   Looking for trouble?   Look for Holbrook.   N. Y.
        Times sec 2:19 Mr 25 '73
        Same.   N. Y. Times Bio Ed p434 Mr '73
    Fleming, A. T.   Interview.   Playgirl 1-4:52 S '73
    Holbrook shifts from Twain to Lincoln.   People 2-9:40 Ag 26 '74
    Lightman, H. A.   The filming of Sandberg's Lincoln.   Am Cine-
        matographer 55-9:1042 S '74

HOLDEN, FAY
    Maternal instinct in wartime.   Lions R 2-3:no p# D '42
    Obit.   Classic Film Collect 40:58 Fall '73
        Films & Filming 19-18:79 S '73
        N. Y. Times Bio Ed p975 Je '73
        Screen World p235 '74
    In memory.   Show 3-6:74 S '73

HOLDEN, JOYCE
    Riding the comeback trail.   TV Guide 4-49:12 D 8 '56

HOLDEN, WILLIAM
    Proctor, K.   Lady luck's protege.   Screen Book 21-12:86 Jl '39
    Reid, J.   Gilding Golden Boy.   Silver S 9-12:26 O '39
    Cheatham, M.   Casually captured.   Silver S 12-1:24 N '41
    Parsons, L. O.   Cosmop's citation for best supporting perform-
        ance of month.   Cosmop 123:55 Ag '47
    Holland, J.   Is the press fair to actors?   Silver S 21-9:46 Jl
        '51
    Hyams, J.   Hollywood's busiest leading man.   Cue 23-17:12 Ap
        24 '54

Harmetz, A. Don't get personal with (him). N. Y. Times Bio
  Ed Jl 4 '71
Marill, A. H. William Holden; filmog. Films In R 24-8:449 O
  '73

HOLDING, THOMAS
  Shelley, H. Sketch. Motion Pic Classic 13:26 D '21

HOLDRIDGE, CHERYL
  The general's daughter grows up. TV Guide 10-49:26 D 8 '62

HOLLAND, JOHN
  Hall, G. Sketch. Motion Pic Classic 32:52 D '30

HOLLAND, KRISTINA
  Raddatz, L. Five words a week. TV Guide 19-50:26 D 11 '71

HOLLIDAY, JUDY
  Sketch. Life 21:7 Jl 22 '46
  Vallee, W. L. The exception to the rule. Silver S 20-9:44 Jl
    '50
  Rising star. Film R p30 '50
  Tennant, S. Judy Holliday. Film 3:19 F '55
  Lewis, E. Revuers reunited. Cue 25-47:15 N 24 '56

HOLLIDAY, MARJORIE
  Obit. Screen World 21:237 '70

HOLLINGSWORTH, ALFRED F.
  Case, D. E. Filmog. Films In R 21-8:517 O '70

HOLLISTER, ALICE
  Sketch. Motion Pic 9:94 F '15
  Shelley, H. Interview. Motion Pic Classic 12:62 Jl '21

HOLLOWAY, CAROL
  Peltret, E. Interview. Motion Pic 17:69 Je '19

HOLLOWAY, STANLEY
  A remarkable solution to the servant problem. TV Guide 10-44:
    15 N 3 '62

HOLLOWAY, STERLING
  Sketch. Photop 44:96 O '33
  Holloway house. TV Guide 12-57:24 D 19 '64

HOLLY, ELLEN
  Drake, R. Black, but not black enough. TV Guide 20-12:38 Mr
    18 '72

HOLM, CELESTE
  Celeste at the Plaza. Cue 14-2:8 Ja 13 '45
  Fulton, M. J. Sketch. Photop 34:63 Ja '49

Bruce, J.   Are marital vacations necessary?   Silver S 20-3:46
   Ja '50
Gibson, M.   Here's how to get that first date.   Silver S 21-1:37
   N '50
Efron, E.   Look who's in Nancy.   TV Guide 18-50:53 D 12 '70
Loney, G.   Holm is where the heart is.   After Dark 6-1:60 My
   '73
Headliners.   Photop 84-1:8 Jl '73
Pickard, R.   Celeste Holm; filmog.   Films In R 24-10:633 D '73
Davis, F.   Celeste Holm.   Films In R 25-7:445 Ag/S '74

## HOLM, ELEANOR
Dirkson, E.   Interview.   Colliers 30:9 Jl 16 '32
Olympic dismissal.   Time 28:21 Ag 3 '36
Eleanor's show.   Time 34:31 Ag 21 '39
Billy Rose and wife.   Life 8:112 My 13 '40
Roses with thorns.   Newsweek 40:23 Ag 18 '52
War of the Roses.   Time 60:58 Ag 18 '52
Billy comes marching down the hill.   Life 33:40 S 22 '52
Faded Roses.   Newsweek 40:36 S 22 '52
Costly battle of sexes.   Newsweek 43:25 Ja 18 '54
Uselton, R. A.   The Wampus baby stars.   Films In R 21-2:73
   F '70
Johnson, W.   Ex-decorator.   Sports Illus 37:30 Jl 17 '72

## HOLM, IAN
Alexander, C.   Which way now?   Films Illus 1-5:16 N '71

## HOLMAN, LIBBY
Kennedy, J. B.   Stop the show.   Colliers 84:34 N 16 '29
Blues in the night.   Newsweek 20:70 N 23 '42
Bad news.   Time 56:17 Ag 28 '50
Old favorite in Manhattan.   Time 64:76 O 18 '54
Cartwright, M.   American troubadour.   Negro Hist Bul 18:180
   My '55
Re-racinated.   Newsweek 64:85 S 14 '64
Obit.   N. Y. Times p39 Je 22 '71
   Newsweek 78:65 Jl 5 '71
   Time 98:49 Jl 5 '71

## HOLMES, GERDA
Her art's votary.   Movie Pictorial 2-4:12 O '15
Brodie, A. D.   Sketch.   Motion Pic Classic 1:37 F '16
Holmes, G.   Plans back of the production of harmonious screen
   effects.   Film Players Herald 2-7:23 F '16
Milady Gerda of the Danes.   Photop 11-4:133 Mr '17

## HOLMES, HELEN
Sketch.   Green Bk Album 3:877 Ap '10
Sketch.   Motion Pic 9:111 Ap '15
How she became a photoplayer.   Motion Pic Sup 1:49 S '15
Work of.   Green Bk 15:741 Ap '16
Gaddis, P.   Sketch.   Motion Pic 13:102 Mr '17

Gregory, N. D.  Sketch.  Motion Pic 13:59 Jl '17
Courtlandt, R.  Sketch.  Motion Pic Classic 4:54 Ag '17
How she got in moving pictures.  Motion Pic 14:115 N '17
Obit.  Screen World 2:234 '51
Slide, A.  The Kalem serial queens.  Silent Pic 2:15 Spg '69
Everett, K.  The railroad girl.  Classic Film Collect 41:37 Win '73

HOLMES, HERBERT
Brady, S. E.  Interview.  Classic 15:59 O '22

HOLMES, PHILLIPS
Gray, C. W.  Sketch.  Motion Pic 38:42 N '29
Manners, D.  Sketch.  Motion Pic Classic 32:58 F '31
Benham, L.  Holmes sweet Holmes.  Silver S 1-5:15 Mr '31
Goldbeck, E.  Sketch.  Motion Pic Classic 32:41 Ag '31
Costello, T.  Sketch.  Motion Pic 43:51 Ap '32
Melcher, E.  Personalities prominent in the press.  Cinema Dig 1-2:4 My 30 '32
Mook, S. R.  Phil has had his fill of melancholy.  Silver S 2-11:24 S '32
Moffitt, C. F.  Censorship for interviews Hollywood's latest wild idea.  Cinema Dig 2-5:9 Ja 9 '33
Obit.  Newsweek 20:8 Ag 24 '42

HOLMES, RALPH
The art of character acting and its relation to other acting.  Film Players Herald 2-7:24 F '16

HOLMES, STUART
Owen, K.  An admirable villain.  Photop 11-1:34 D '16
Courtlandt, R.  Work of.  Motion Pic Classic 4:24 Jl '17
Lee, R.  Villainy of a velvet touch.  Classic Film Collect 28:47 Fall '70
Obit.  Screen World 23:238 '72

HOLMES, TAYLOR
Interview.  Bk News 32:289 F '13
Sketch.  Strand (NY) 48:405 O '14
Brewster, E.  Sketch.  Motion Pic 15:72 My '18
Allison, D.  Early to breakfast.  Photop 14-5:66 O '18
Obit.  Screen World 11:220 '60

HOLOUBEK, GUSTAW
The Polish cinema.  Film 31:25 Spg '62

HOLT, GEORGE
Willis, R.  Interview.  Motion Pic Sup 1:53 N '15

HOLT, JACK
Headin' south.  Photop 14-3:56 Ag '18
Taylor, M. K.  Interview.  Motion Pic Classic 7:29 Ja '19
Cheatham, M.  Interview.  Motion Pic 22:44 N '21

Autobiographical.  Motion Pic 28:38 Ja '25
Tully, J.  Sketch.  Motion Pic Classic 21:31 Jl '25
Manners, D.  Interview.  Motion Pic Classic 25:58 Mr '27
Carlisle, H.  Sketch.  Motion Pic Classic 27:26 Jl '28
Carson, A.  Twenty years a star.  Movie Classic 11:56 N '36
Obit.  Screen World 3:177 '53

HOLT, JACKIE
Pop was a movie producer.  TV Guide 6-49:24 D 6 '58

HOLT, TIM
Henderson, J.  He's no carbon copy.  Screen Book 21-5:16 D
    '38
Sketch.  Photop 32:31 My '48
Obit.  Classic Film Collect 38:57 Spg '73
    Film R p15 '73/74
    N.Y. Times p42 F 16 '73
    Same.  N.Y. Times Bio Ed p251 F '73
    Screen World p235 '74
    Washington Post pB6 F 17 '73
In memory.  Show 3-3:66 My '73

HOLTER, CHRIS
Whitney, D.  The problem to sell milk.  The answer: Chris
    Holter.  TV Guide 21-38:17 S 22 '73

HOLZER, BABY JANE
Way-out Baby Jane is really in.  Life 58:121 Mr 19 '65
Malanga, G.  Let's be serious: a profile of Baby Jane Holzer.
    Film Culture 45:35 Sum '67
Where are they now?  Newsweek 73:22 My 19 '69
Jane Holzer the lion-hearted.  Vogue 154:210 N 1 '69

HOMEIER, SKIP
Skippy off-stage.  Cue 14-2:8 Ja 13 '45
Failure makes good.  TV Guide 4-38:25 S 22 '56

HOMOLKA, OSCAR
Sketch.  Theatre World 23:229 My '35
McAsh, I.  Oscar Homolka.  Films Illus 3-35:447 Jl '74

HONG, JAMES
Raddatz, L.  No. 1 son is now Master Po.  TV Guide 21-25:27
    Je 23 '73

HOOD, DARLA
Maltin, L.  Our gang; Our gang filmog.  Film Fan Mo 66:3 D
    '66

HOOKS, ROBERT
Efron, E.  He hasn't forgotten the rats.  TV Guide 16-6:22 F
    10 '68
Stasio, M.  Man alive.  Cue 37-14:12 Ap 6 '68

Bio.   Cur Bio 31:20 Mr '70
   Same.   Cur Bio Yrbk 1970:189 '71
   In the words of Robert Hooks.   Cue 39-20:10 My 16 '70

HOOSER, WILLIAM S.
   May, L.   Sketch.   Motion Pic Classic 3:21 Ja '17

HOPE, BOB
   Rhea, M.   Sketch.   Photop 53:30 Ap '39
   Harvey, G.   Fate, Hope and hilarity.   Silver S 9-9:24 Jl '39
   Bio note; filmog.   Movies & People 2:19 '40
   Salute.   Cue 10-28:3 Jl 12 '41
   Reid, J.   Do women have a sense of humor?   Silver S 11-10:26
     Ag '41
   French, W. F.   The Bob Hope you don't know.   Silver S 12-5:
     24 Mr '42
   Mulvey, K.   Sketch.   Womans Home C 69:28 Ap '42
   Program for a day.   Harp Baz 76:16 Jl '42
   The trouble with women.   Cosmop 114:58 My '43
   Sketch.   Vogue 102:82 O 1 '43
   Benedict, P.   Hope's phenomenal war activities.   Silver S 13-12:
     24 O '43
   Manners, M. J.   Dottie tells on Bob and Bing.   Silver S 14-6:30
     Ap '44
   The great American Hopeful.   Cue 14-5:8 F 3 '45
   Watkins, W.   Inside Hope's dressing room.   Silver S 16-10:30
     Ag '46
   Parsons, L. O.   Cosmop's citation for best male role of month.
     Cosmop 122:67 Ap '47
   Radio acceptance poll names Hope worst comedian on the air.
     Time 50:78 N 17 '47
   Discusses the art of Christmas shopping.   Cosmop 123:11 D '47
   Hope, B.   The woman I married.   Silver S 19-1:38 N '48
   Awarded Photoplay's gold medal.   Photop 35:56 My '49
   Ball, L.   My favorite funnyman.   Silver S 20-6:36 Ap '50
   Minoff, P.   A matter of Hope.   Cue 19-23:12 Je 10 '50
   My favorite role.   Film R p22 '50
   Anthony, V.   That's the way he is.   Silver S 22-1:40 N '51
   Minoff, P.   The world is their oyster.   Cue 21-49:16 D 6 '52
   Hull, W.   Could be you.   Silver S 24-5:46 Mr '54
   Hope on golf.   Playboy 1:15 S '54
   Failure makes good.   TV Guide 4-38:25 S 22 '56
   Plimpton, G.   A block on the road to yaksville.   Show 2-4:95
     Ap '62
   Whitney, D.   American institution.   TV Guide 13-3:15 Ja 16 '65
   Comedian as hero.   Time 90:58 D 22 '67
   Rollin, B.   Bob Hope hits the road he never left.   Look 32:44
     Ja 23 '68
   Wright, A.   Golf is a game of Hope.   Sports Illus 28:44 F 12
     '68
   Robinson, D.   Eight famous Americans tell of the day I was
     proudest of my wife; interview.   Good House 167:75 Ag '68
   Sharpless, D. R.   In support of Hope.   Parks & Rec 4:12 D '69

364  Motion Picture Performers

I get a lot more than I give.  Read Dig 96:177 Ja '70

McVay, D.  In a dirty glass: a tribute to Bob Hope; filmog. Focus On F 1:15 Ja/F '70

Harger, A.  On the road to riches.  Show 1-7:14 Je 25 '70

Van Gelder, L.  Comedian and patriot.  N. Y. Times Bio Ed Jl 4 '70

Lukas, J. A.  This is Bob (politician-patriot-publicist) Hope. N. Y. Times Bio Ed O 4 '70

Barthel, J.  The road gets rougher.  Life 70:48 Ja 29 '71

Bowers, R. L.  Bob Hope; filmog.  Films In R 22-3:121 Mr '71

Raddatz, L.  I'm very happy to be here for my annual insult. TV Guide 19-15:25 Ap 10 '71

Letters.  Films In R 22-6:378 Je/Jl '71

The gentleman from Ohio.  Sat Eve Post 243:68 Sum '71

Still going great.  Screen Greats 1-2:78 Sum '71

Importance of having fun.  Read Dig 100:49 Ja '72

Interview.  Nations Bsns 60:43 F '72

Heffelfinger, L.  Merry Christmas--or else; letter.  Playboy 19-4:61 Ap '72

Muhan, T.  Thanks for the memory.  Sat R 55:82 O 21 '72

Gage, J.  Interview.  Ladies Home J 89:68 D '72

Interview.  Playboy 20-12:97 D '73

Hickey, N.  The comedian turns serious.  TV Guide 22-3:21 Ja 19 '74

Hickey, N.  Thanks for the memories.  TV Guide 24-4:32 Ja 26 '74


HOPKINS, ANTHONY

Note; filmog.  Films & Filming 19-11:58 Ag '73

Headliners.  Photop 84-5:12 N '73


HOPKINS, BO

Filmog.  Films & Filming 21-3:58 D '74


HOPKINS, MIRIAM

Pryor, N.  Sketch.  Movie Classic 1:59 O '31

Service, F.  Sketch.  Motion Pic 43:58 F '32

Walker, H. L.  Her marriage tangle.  Movie Classic 2:33 Jl '32

Keats, P.  Happy Hopkins.  Silver S 3-2:25 D '32

Service, F.  Interview.  Movie Classic 4:34 Ap '33

Quirk, M. A.  Sketch.  Photop 44:62 Jl '33

Chapman, J. B.  Her movie moral code.  Movie Classic 5:21 O '33

Mannes, M.  Compared with K. Hepburn.  Vogue 83:24 Ja 1 '34

Samuels, L.  Design for starring.  Silver S 4-5:27 Mr '34

Keats, P.  She loves me not.  Silver S 4-10:26 Ag '34

Smalley, J.  Her unusual love affair.  Movie Classic 8:28 Mr '35

Davis, D.  Interview.  Motion Pic 49:36 Ap '35

Home of.  Vogue 85:48 Je 15 '35

Harris, R.  The new gorgeous screen.  Silver S 5-8:32 Je '35

Reeve, M. W.   Interview.   Movie Classic 9:30 S '35
Chrisman, J. E.   An open letter to.   Motion Pic 50:15 N '35
Hogarth, D.   Begins a new life.   Movie Classic 9:27 D '35
Reply to Chrisman letter.   Motion Pic 50:15 Ja '36
Liza.   La Hopkins.   Silver S 6-5:27 Mr '36
Douglas, E.   The so-illusive lady.   Silver S 6-6:29 Ap '36
Haddon, J. L.   Sketch.   Movie Classic 10:36 Ag '36
Schallert, E.   Interview.   Motion Pic 53:65 F '37
Walker, H. L.   In keeping with Miriam.   Silver S 9-9:42 Jl '39
William, B.   Now I understand (her).   Silver S 10-10:42 Ag '40
Bio note; filmog.   Movies & People 2:19 '40
Pin-up of the past.   Films & Filming 17-6:70 Mr '71
Obit.   Classic Film Collect 37:59 Win '72
    Film R p12 '73/74
    N. Y. Times Bio Ed p1795 O '72
Kobal, J.   Working with Hopkins; interview with Vincent Sher-
    man.   Film 2-9:12 D '73

HOPKINS, MURIEL
    Keats, P.   On location.   Silver S 3-10:18 Ag '33

HOPKINS, SHIRLEY KNIGHT
    (Formerly known as Shirley Knight)
    Burke, T.   Whatever Shirley thinks, Shirley says.   N. Y. Times
        Bio Ed p223 F '74

HOPPER, DENNIS
    Space odyssey.   Time 94:73 Jl 25 '69
    Not so easy riders: Hopper and Fonda.   Vogue 154:129 Ag 1 '69
    Macklin, A.   The initiation of Hopper.   Film Heritage 5-1:1 Fall
        '69
    What directors are saying.   Action 4-5:32 S/O '69
    Dennis Hopper, riding high.   Playboy 16-12:250 D '69
    Darrack, B.   Easy rider runs wild in the Andes.   Life 68:48
        Je 19 '70
    Nolan, T.   You can bring Hopper to Hollywood but you can't take
        Dodge City out of Kansas.   Show 1-9:20 Jl 23 '70
    Miller, E.   Hopper makes The last movie in Peru.   Seventeen
        29:92 Jl '70
    Burke, T.   Dennis Hopper saves the movies.   Esquire 74:139
        S '70
    Flatley, G.   Dennis Hopper.   N. Y. Times Bio Ed O 18 '70
    Movies: and everybody's doing it.   Look 34-22:42 N 3 '70
    Knight, A. & Alpert, H.   Sex stars of 1970.   Playboy 17-12:
        220 D '70
    Hopkins, H.   Dennis Hopper's America.   Art In America 59:87
        My '71
    Goodwin, M.   Home is the Hopper.   Interview 2-4:25 Jl '71
    Bio note.   Films Illus 1-5:31 N '71
    O'Brien, G. & Netter, M.   Interview.   Interview 19:24 F '72
    Sarne, M.   The American dreamer.   Films & Filming 19-4:24
        Ja '73
    Bell, A.   Easy rider on a bum trip.   Viva 1-6:73 Mr '74

HOPPER, WILLIAM
  Life with mother.   TV Guide 10-35:10 S 1 '62
  Obit.   Classic Film Collect 27:60 Spg/Sum '70
    N. Y. Times p31 Mr 7 '70
    Same.   N. Y. Times Bio Ed Mr 7 '70
    Newsweek 75:114 Mr 16 '70
    Screen World 22:237 '71
    Time 95:74 Mr 16 '70

HORN, CAMILLA
  Pryor, N.   Sketch.   Motion Pic 35:67 Mr '28
  Reeve, W.   Interview.   Motion Pic Classic 29:21 Mr '29

HORNE, LENA
  Honey, sweet and hot.   Lions R 2-4:no p# Ap '43
  Hamilton, S.   Sketch.   Photop 23:65 S '43
  Call her tomorrow.   Lions R 3-2:no p# Ja '44
  Box-office honey.   Lions R 3-3(sup): no p# Ap '44
  Talent in triplicate.   Lions R 3-3:no p# Ap '44
  Horne, L.   I just want to be myself.   Show 3-9:62 S '63
  Higgins, R.   Harry and Lena.   TV Guide 18-12:14 My 21 '70
  Klemesrud, J.   Lena Horne.   N. Y. Times Bio Ed Ap 23 '71
  Gruen, J.   Interview.   Vogue 159:92 Je '72
  Hay, R. C.   Interview.   Interview 29:20 Ja '73

HORTON, CLARA MARIE
  Condon, M.   The littlest leading lady.   Photop 6-6:89 N '14
  Handy, T. B.   Sweet sixteen-plus.   Photop 16-4:67 S '19
  Lester, A.   Interview.   Motion Pic Classic 11:60 F '21

HORTON, EDWARD EVERETT
  Spensley, D.   Sketch.   Motion Pic Classic 29:23 My '29
  Moving pictures cannot supplant the stage.   Theatre 50:22 Ag '29
  Interview.   Motion Pic Classic 30:45 F '30
  Keats, P.   The picture savers.   Silver S 5-5:32 Mr '35
  Reid, L.   Sketch.   Movie Classic 11:34 D '36
  Reid, J.   Story of.   Motion Pic 53:44 My '37
  Cardwell, R.   Eddie Horton's strange "pals."   Screen Book 19-
    3:88 O '37
  Hamilton, S.   Story of.   Photop 52:21 My '38
  Vallee, W. L.   He's fuss budget No. 1.   Silver S 16-2:44 D '45
  Stein, J.   Fusspot and fortune's fool; filmog.   Focus On F 1:30
    Ja/F '70
  Obit.   Classic Film Collect 29:15 Win '70
    Cur Bio 31:44 N '70
    Same.   Cur Bio Yrbk 1970:464 '71
    Film R p13 '71/72
    N. Y. Times p44 O 1 '70
    Same.   N. Y. Times Bio Ed O 1 '70
    Newsweek 76:84 O 12 '70
    Screen World 22:237 '71
    Time 96:62 O 12 '70

HORTON, ROBERT
  Conversation piece.   TV Guide 6-44:24 N 1 '58
  The dangers of galloping inflation.   TV Guide 16-14:14 Ap 6 '68

HOSKINS, BOB
  Ford, J.  Two for the road.   Plays & Players 18-9:22 Je '71

HOSKINS, ALLEN CLAYTON
  (See:  FARINA)

HOSSEIN, ROBERT
  Bio note.   Unifrance 45:8 D '57
  Graham, P.  The face of '63--France.   Films & Filming 9-8:13
    My '63

HOSTETLER, BARRY
  Williams, L.  Barry Hostetler; centerfold.   Playgirl 1-9:64 F
    '74

HOUDINI, HARRY
  Magician who mistrusts spirits.   Lit Dig 73:54 Je 3 '22
  When magic didn't work.   Colliers 75:20 Ap 18 '25
  Wilson, E.  Houdini.   New Rep 43:125 Je 24 '25
  Warning against spiritualism.   Lit Dig 86:32 Jl 18 '25
  Obit.   Outlook 144:330 N 10 '26
  Man who laughed at locksmiths.   Lit Dig 91:45 N 20 '26
  Houdini.   Sci Am 136:12 Ja '27
  Kennedy, J. B.  The wonder-worker.   Mentor 14:62 Ja '27
  Buranelli, P.  Interview.   Bookman 64:611 Ja '27
  Kellock, H.  His life and some of his secrets.   Am Mag 105:7
    Mr; 56 Ap; 24 My; 52 Je; 106:40 Jl '28
  The escape king.   Lit Dig 97:34 Je 16 '28
  Byron, M.  Self-made magician.   Outlook 149:554 Ag 1 '28
  Wilson, E.  Great magician.   New Rep 56:248 O 17 '28
  Great silence.   Time 28:48 N 9 '36
  Wickware, F. S.  Hairbreadth Houdini.   Read Dig 42:61 Mr '43
  Great Houdini.   Life 34:119 Je 22 '53
  Gresham, W. L.  No prison can hold me.   Coronet 38:149 Jl
    '55
  Helfer, H.  Magician tricked.   Coronet 40:145 Jl '56
  Escapist.   Time 74:45 Ag 10 '59
  Grossman, A.  Houdini on the screen; filmog.   Films In R 12-9:
    572 N '61
  White, J. R.  Houdini: his movies.   Classic Film Collect 29:46
    Win '70
  Ronnie, A.  Excerpt from Locklear.   Am Heritage 23:106 Ap
    '72

HOUGHTON, KATHARINE
  Frook, J.  Hepburn comes on big bringing a niece who calls her
    Aunt Kat.   Life 64:60 Ja 5 '68
  Miller, E.  Kath and her Aunt Kate.   Seventeen 27:134 F '68

HOUSE, BILLY
    Obit.   Screen World 13:222 '62

HOUSEMAN, JOHN
    Lost fortnight.   Harper 231:55 Ag '65
    Chase, C.   Suddenly they're all sending for Houseman.   N.Y.
        Times sec 2:1 Ap 21 '74
        Same.   N.Y. Times Bio Ed p529 Ap '74
    Houseman's new career.   Films Illus 3-32:312 Ja '74
    Houston, P.   Minister of energy.   Sight & Sound 44-1:25 Win
        '74/75

HOUSMAN, ARTHUR
    Sketch.   Motion Pic 9:115 Je '15

HOVEY, ANN
    Uselton, R. A.   The Wampus baby stars.   Films In R 21-2:73
        F '70

HOVIS, GENE
    Host to the swinging set.   Ebony 23:107 Mr '68

HOVIS, LARRY
    Hobson, D.   Invisible actor.   TV Guide 18-32:12 Ag 8 '70

HOWARD, ALAN
    Morley, S.   Two actors.   Plays & Players 16-12:51 S '69
    A pride of Hamlets.   Plays & Players 18-5:18 F '71

HOWARD, CLINT
    You get 5 cards for a pack of bubble gum.   TV Guide 13-11:24
        Mr 13 '65

HOWARD, ESTHER
    Obit.   Screen World 17:237 '66

HOWARD, JOHN
    Sketch.   Movie Classic 10:7 Je '36
    Spensley, D.   Story of.   Motion Pic 53:50 Jl '37
    Dudley, F.   Interview.   Photop 19:58 Jl '41
    Sketch.   Photop 22:67 Mr '43

HOWARD, KEN
    Salute of the week.   Cue 39-31:1 Ag 1 '70
    Miller, E.   Interview.   Seventeen 31:74 N '72
    Archibald, L.   Ken Howard.   Show 2-10:44 Ja '73
    He's the kind who proposed on his knees.   Photop 84-4:33 O '73

HOWARD, LESLIE
    Strange experience.   Theatre 46:24 S '27
    I try out a one-man theatre.   Vanity Fair 29:80 Ja '28
    Henderson, R.   Sketch.   Theatre 47:21 My '28
    The high functions of the theatre.   Theatre 51:38 Je '30

Service, F. Interview. Motion Pic 42:49 O '31
Sketch. Theatre Guild 9:38 Ja '32
Sketch. Theater Guild 9:8 Mr '32
Melcher, E. Personalities prominent in the press. Cinema Dig 1-3:6 Je 13 '32
Hall, G. Why he is the man of the moment. Movie Classic 4:44 Mr '33
Grant, J. Sketch. Motion Pic 45:50 Jl '33
Lynn, H. How he makes love. Photop 44:30 Ag '33
Manners, D. Interview. Motion Pic 46:40 O '33
Reed, D. Tea-timing with the horsey Mr. Howard. Silver S 5-5:26 Mr '35
Crichton, K. Story of. Colliers 95:24 My 4 '35
Reilly, P. Sketch. Motion Pic 49:26 My '35
Anthony, W. Interview. Movie Classic 10:43 Mr '36
Lang, H. Sketch. Motion Pic 51:33 My '36
Camp, D. Story of. Motion Pic 54:22 S '37
Mann, M. Howard's bitter triumph. Screen Book 22-3:58 O '39
Bio note; filmog. Movies & People 2:20 '40
Williams, J. D. Discussion on film of the future. World R p11 Ap '41
Appreciation. Spectator 170:516 Je 4 '43
Sketch. New Statesman 25:281 Je 12 '43
Frisbie, C. In memoriam. Photop 23:93 S '43
Perfect gentlemen. Screen Greats 1-2:66 Sum '71
Lambert, G. The making of Gone with the wind. Atlantic 231-3:56 Mr '73
Pinup of the past. Films & Filming 19-9:69 Je '73

HOWARD, MARY
Hamilton, S. Sketch. Photop 54:28 My '40

HOWARD, NORAH
Obit. N. Y. Times p87 My 5 '68

HOWARD, RONNY
Not so elementary, my dear Watson. TV Guide 2-51:20 D 18 '54
A small boy with a modest outlook. TV Guide 11-28:11 Jl 13 '63
You get five cards for a pack of bubble gum. TV Guide 13-11:24 Mr 13 '65
Bio note; filmog. Focus On F 17:8 Spg '74
Raddatz, L. Dear Mickey Rooney, wherever you are. TV Guide 22-24:24 Je 15 '74
My real days are happy too. Photop 86-2:40 Ag '74

HOWARD, TREVOR
My favorite role. Film R p37 '51/52
Howard, T. The stage, the screen and the actor. Int F Ann 1:90 '57
Double trouble: "Really Mr. Christian." Show 3-3:108 Mr '63

HOWELL, ALICE
  She's a rough gal!   Photop 12-3:133 Ag '17

HOWELL, ARLENE
  Ah'm from the south you-all.   TV Guide 7-24:20 Je 13 '59

HOWELL, JEAN
  Just her type.   TV Guide 7-43:24 O 24 '59

HOWES, BOBBY
  Obit.  N.Y. Times p44 Ap 28 '72

HOWES, SALLY ANN
  Efron, E.  She looks like a Goddess...  TV Guide 13-36:12 S 4
    '65

HOXIE, AL
  Kinkade, H.  Interview.  8mm Collect 14:24 Spg '66
  Al Hoxie out to pasture; a word from Hoxie himself.   Filmograph
    1-1:11 '70
  Shipley, G.  Jack Hoxie & Al Hoxie.  Filmograph 1-4:48 '70
  Rainey, B.  Al Hoxie and his cow-dung westerns; filmog.   Filmo-
    graph 4-1:22 '73

HOXIE, JACK
  Lahue, K. C.  The Jack Hoxie story.   8mm Collect 12:15 Sum
    '65
  Coriell, V.  Hoxie almost Tarzan No. 3.   8mm Collect 12:15
    Sum '65
  Shipley, G.  Jack Hoxie and Al Hoxie.  Filmograph 1-4:48 '70
  Brennen, T.  Hoxie, artist or idiot?  Classic Film Collect 31:6
    Sum '71
  Brennen, T.  Hoxie progress report.  Classic Film Collect 32:30
    Fall '71
  Leonard, W. T.  The hazards of Hoxie.  Classic Film Collect
    32:30 Fall '71
  Everson, W. K.  Stands pat on Hoxie "hand."  Classic Film
    Collect 32:31 Fall '71

HUBBARD, ELIZABETH
  Efron, E.  Look what's happened to Slugger.  TV Guide 17-14:38
    Ap 5 '69

HUBBARD, JOHN
  Hamilton, S.  Sketch.  Photop 54:31 Jl '40

HUBER, GUSTI
  A gal named Gusti.  Cue 21-11:14 Mr 15 '52

HUDSON BROTHERS (Bill, Mark, Brett)
  Edelman, R.  Hi!  We're the Hudson Brothers.  TV Guide 22-
    31:10 Ag 3 '74

HUDSON, JOHN
    They make ladies' hearts go pitty pat.    TV Guide 5-28:8  Jl 13
        '57

HUDSON, ROCHELLE
    Spensley, D.   Sketch.   Motion Pic 43:58 Mr '32
    Ladies for lenses.   Silver S 2-7:43 My '32
    Spensley, D.   Interview.   Motion Pic 48:39 N '34
    Meyers, A. E.   Sketch.   Motion Pic 50:35 N '35
    Dixe, M.   Sketch.   Movie Classic 9:14 N '35
    Hartley, K.   Her love hoax.   Movie Classic 10:42 Je '36
    Harte, C.   Sketch.   Motion Pic 52:54 O '36
    Williams, W.   She's 21.   Silver S 7-10:34 Ag '37
    Bio note; filmog.   Movies & People 2:20 '40
    Uselton, R. A.   The Wampus baby stars.   Films In R 21-2:73
        F '70
    Crivello, K.   Passing parade.   Film Collect Reg 4-3:25 My/ Je
        '72
    Obit.   Classic Film Collect 34:X-3 Spg '72
        N. Y. Times p40 Ja 19 '72
        Same.   N. Y. Times Bio Ed Ja 19 '72
        Newsweek 79:55 Ja 31 '72
    Puzo, L.   Letter; filmog.   Films In R 23-7:447 Ag/S '72

HUDSON, ROCK
    Hudson, R.   Before I marry.   Silver S 22-12:46 O '52
    Maddox, B.   Five ways to win Rock Hudson.   Silver S 24-1:29
        N '53
    Maddox, B.   Rock Hudson's frankest confession.   Silver S 24-8:
        29 Je '54
    Zunser, J.   What makes Rock No. 1 dreamboat?   Cue 25-11:13
        Mr 17 '56
    I did not marry Jim Nabors.   Photop 80-5:63 N '71
    Barber, R.   Roy Fitzgerald takes some time to reminisce.   TV
        Guide 20-18:24 Ap 29 '72
    Rock Hudson's last words of love to Marilyn Maxwell.   Photop
        82-1:19 Jl '72
    Rock Hudson in head-on crash.   Photop 82-3:46 S '72
    Righter, C.   Star of the month; horoscope.   Mod Screen 66-11:
        65 N '72
    I want to be your daddy.   Photop 82-6:72 D '72
    Hano, A.   Lunch ended up a smashing success.   TV Guide 21-7:
        30 F 17 '73
    Feiden, R. & Colaciello, R.   Interview.   Interview 2-2:12 n. d.
    Shevey, S.   Interview.   Playgirl 1-9:53 F '74
    Superstar?  Just call me a survivor.   Photop 85-3:42 Mr '74
    Watters, J.   Carol and Rock make summer theater dynamite.
        People 2-3:39 Jl 15 '74

HUFF, LOUISE
    How she became a photoplayer.   Motion Pic 9:115 Ap '15
    Sketch.   Motion Pic 9:117 My '15
    McGaffey, K.   She discovered Columbus.   Photop 12-6:21 N '17

Baremore, R. W.   Sketch.   Motion Pic 15:74 Ap '18
Smith, F. J.   Interview.   Motion Pic 16:56 D '18
Service, F.   Interview.   Motion Pic Classic 9:16 N '19
Smith, F. J.   Interview.   Motion Pic Classic 10:18 Ag '20
Obit.   Classic Film Collect 41:53 Win '73
     N. Y. Times Bio Ed p1386 Ag '73
     Screen World p235 '74

HUGHES, CAROL
     Schwarzkopf, J.   Sketch.   Motion Pic 51:25 Je '36

HUGHES, KATHLEEN
     Wilson, E.   She'd like to pose for a calendar, too.   Silver S
     24-6:24 Ap '54

HUGHES, LLOYD
     Forrester, M.   Interview.   Motion Pic Classic 10:92 Ap/My '20
     McGregor, J.   Confessions of a free-lance.   Motion Pic 28:88
     Ja '25
     Mabury, M.   Sketch.   Motion Pic 30:62 D '25
     Hall, G.   Sketch.   Motion Pic 39:74 Mr '30

HUGHES, MARY BETH
     Hamilton, S.   Sketch.   Photop 54:32 N '40
     Manners, M. J.   A blonde with a red-head's personality.   Silver
     S 11-2:44 D '40
     Turton, T. P.   Mary Beth Hughes; filmog.   Films In R 22-8:
     485 O '71

HUGUENY, SHARON
     Too old for summer camp.   TV Guide 9-23:27 Je 10 '61

HULETTE, GLADYS
     May, L.   Interview.   Motion Pic Classic 13:18 Ja '22

HULL, DIANNE
     Pearsall, A.   How some of the magic went out of Stanley Sweet-
     heart's Garden.   Show 1-3:69 Mr '70

HULL, HENRY
     Sketch.   Theatre 25:18 Ja '17
     Plea for clean drama and audience aid.   Theatre 49:35 F '29
     Rand, E.   Enters the movies.   Movie Classic 7:36 D '34
     Hull, H.   A word about audiences.   Cue 5-46:6 S 11 '37
     Brock, A.   Backstage with the stars.   Classic Film Collect 36:
     30 Fall '72

HULL, JOSEPHINE
     Keating, J.   A star at long last.   Cue 19-46:19 N 18 '50

HULL, WARREN
     Sketch.   Motion Pic 52:25 N '36

HUME, BENITA
Hall, G.  Interview.  Motion Pic 45:50 My '33
Obit.  N. Y. Times p86 N 5 '67
   Newsweek 70:67 N 13 '67

HUMES, FRED
Bio note.  Cinema Trails 2:21 n. d.

HUMPERDINCK, ENGELBERT
Musel, R.  ... by any other name.  TV Guide 17-49:43 D 6 '69

HUMPHRIES, BARRY
Morley, S.  Three is one.  Plays & Players 16-8:32 My '69
Aunt Edna lives.  Films Illus 3-29:196 N '73

HUNNICUTT, GAYLE
A show trio.  Show 2-1:34 Mr '72
Gayle force.  Films Illus 3-27:96 S '73
Filmog.  Films & Filming 21-3:58 D '74

HUNT, MARSHA
Babcock, G.  She snapped her fingers and won a contract.
   Screen Book 19-3:24 O '37
Her model career.  Lions R 1-6:no p# F '42
Perfectionist.  Lions R 1-8:no p# Ap '42
Sergeant Marsha.  Lions R 1-11/ 12:no p# Jl/Ag '42
Stars of tomorrow.  Lions R 1-11/ 12:no p# Jl/Ag '42
Benedict, P.  Marsha put over a fast one.  Silver S 13-2:44 D
   '42
Hollywood war widow.  Lions R 2-4:no p# Ap '43
Tips from Marsha.  Lions R 2-5:no p# Jl '43
Women of Bataan.  Lions R 3-2:no p# Ja '44
Something on the side.  Lions R 3-2:no p# Ja '44
Broyles, M. H.  My sister, Marsha.  Lions R 4-1:no p# F '45
Elliot, F.  Sweetie-sweet farewell.  Silver S 17-5:61 Mr '47
Patrick, S.  Marsha Hunt; filmog.  Films In R 23-4:249 Ap '72

HUNT, MARTITA
Gallic fantasy in the theatre.  Cue 18-3:13 Ja 15 '49
Obit.  Brit Bk Yr 1970:583 '70
   Film R p15 '70/71
   N. Y. Times p33 Je 14 '69
   Screen World 21:237 '70
   Time 93:72 Je 20 '69

HUNTER, GLENN
Hall, G.  Interview.  Motion Pic Classic 14:31 Mr '22
Lamb, G.  Interview.  Motion Pic 24:38 S '22
Brady, S. E.  Interview.  Classic 16:20 My '23
Croy, H.  Interview.  Classic 18:36 D '23
Burr, E. T.  Sketch.  Motion Pic 25:42 D '23
Beckley, Z.  From park bench to stardom.  Theatre 44:12 Jl '26
Beckley, Z.  Interview.  Womans Home C 57:123 Jl '30

HUNTER, IAN
   Sketch.  Theatre World 22:11 Jl '34
   Hartley, K.  Interview.  Motion Pic 53:46 Ap '37
   Hamilton, S.  Sketch.  Photop 54:70 Je '40
   Bio note; filmog.  Movies & People 2:20 '40
   Hall, G.  Meet the two-way man.  Silver S 12-11:48 S '42

HUNTER, JEFFREY
   Rising star.  Film R p30 '57/58
   Obit.  Film R p15 '70/71
      Screen World 21:237 '70
   Filmog.  Films & Filming 18-10:64 Jl '72
   Meyer, J.  Notes on Hunter and his films; filmog.  Filmograph
      4-2:2 '74

HUNTER, KIM
   Rising star.  Film R p106 '53/54
   Winogura, D.  Dialogues on apes, apes and more apes.  Cine-
      fantastique 2-2:31 Sum '72

HUNTER, ROSS
   Davidson, B.  Ross Hunter: the last dream merchant.  Show
      2-8:74 Ag '62
   Morgan, D.  Hunter kicks the youth kick.  Todays Filmmaker
      1-1:22 Ag '71
   Shangri-la in Burbank.  Time 100:73 Jl 17 '72
   Castell, D.  The chance to dream again; filmog. as producer.
      Films Illus 2-22:26 Ap '73
   Leider, R. A.  Hunter vs. the critics.  Show 3-6:32 S '73

HUNTER, TAB
   Zachary, R.  What's a Tab Hunter?  After Dark 11-11:16 Mr
      '70
   Polk, B.  Interview.  Interview 4-11:25 N '74

HUNTINGTON, JOAN
   She also cooks like a French chef.  TV Guide 11-6:26 F 9 '63

HUNTLEY, HUGH
   May, L.  Interview.  Motion Pic Classic 12:65 Jl '21

HURD, HUGH
   Hoover, C.  Interview.  Film Comment 1-4:24 n. d.

HURLOCK, MADELINE
   Sketch.  Photop 28:88 Je '25
   Uselton, R. A.  The Wampus baby stars.  Films In R 21-2:73
      F '70

HURST, DAVID
   People of promise.  Films & Filming 1-8:7 My '55
   Portrait of a prize winner.  Theatre Arts 43:7 Jl '59
   Weston, M.  On stage.  Horizon 3:100 Ja '61

HUSSEY, OLIVIA
  People are talking about.  Vogue 150:88 Ag 1 '67
  Miller, E.  Love is the sweetest thing.  Seventeen 27:83 Ja '68
  Dean Martin's swinging son secretly married?  Photop 79-3:47
    Mr '71
  Manners, D.  I nominate for stardom.  Mod Screen 66-9:16 S
    '72

HUSSEY, RUTH
  Surmelian, L.  Screen 'debs. '  Silver S 9-4:24 F '39
  Maddox, B.  Can a girl really be moral in Hollywood?  Silver
    S 11-3:40 Ja '41
  Demure allure.  Lions R 1-2:no p# O '41
  Ruth answers a fan letter.  Lions R 1-4:no p# D '41
  Walker, H. L.  Popularity is something you earn.  Photop 21:49
    Jl '42
  Stars of tomorrow.  Lions R 1-11/12:no p# Jl/Ag '42
  A new Hussey.  Lions R 1-11/12:no p# Jl/Ag '42
  Autobiographical.  Cosmop 113:39 S '42
  Sketch.  Photop 24:49 D '43

HUSTON, ANGELICA
  Miller, E.  Extraordinary debut.  Seventeen 27:138 O '68
  Ehrlich, H.  Angelica.  Look 32:66 N 12 '68
  Devlin, P.  Young and stung with love and war.  Vogue 154:130
    S 15 '69
  Berenson, B.  Miss Angelica Huston; interview.  Interview 25:39
    S '72
  Kent, R.  Jack Nicholson and Angelica Huston.  Interview 4-4:12
    Ap '74

HUSTON, KAREN
  Raddatz, L.  Actress-equestrienne with a problem.  TV Guide
    20-30:16 Jl 22 '72

HUSTON, WALTER
  Belfrage, C.  His portrayal of Abraham Lincoln.  Motion Pic
    39:40 My '30
  Belfrage, C.  His portrayal of Abraham Lincoln.  Motion Pic
    Classic 31:51 Je '30
  Pryor, N.  Sketch.  Motion Pic 40:33 Ja '31
  Biery, R.  His friendship with Lupe Velez.  Photop 42:46 N '32
  Service, F.  Interview.  Movie Classic 3:17 Ja '33
  Samuels, L.  A giant on Broadway.  Silver S 4-8:26 Je '34
  Motherwell, H.  Appreciation of his acting.  Stage 11:16 My '34
  Service, F.  Interview.  Motion Pic 52:40 D '36
  His views of the failure of his Othello.  Stage 14:54 Mr '37
  Bio note; filmog.  Movies & People 2:21 '40
  Success the hard way.  Lions R 3-4:no p# Jl '44
  Bio sketch.  Harp Baz 80:183 Mr '46
  Obit.  Screen World 2:234 '51
  Letters.  Films In R 11-3:183 Mr '60

HUTCHEONS, BOBBY "WHEEZER"
    Maltin, L.   Our gang; Our gang filmog.   Film Fan Mo 66:3 D
        '66

HUTCHINS, WILL
    More than meets the eye.   TV Guide 6-9:17 Mr 1 '58
    Hano, A.   Hutchins' hidden hostilities.   TV Guide 14-52:15 D 24
        '66

HUTCHINSON, CHARLES
    Lehue, K. C.   Stunt king.   Classic Film Collect 17:13 Win/Spg
        '67

HUTTON, BETTY
    Proctor, K.   Can Betty keep up her terrific pace.   Silver S 13-
        3:36 Ja '43
    Holland, J.   Romantic comic.   Silver S 14-2:34 D '43
    Trotter, M.   Prediction for 1944.   Photop 24:26 Ja '44
    The trouble with men.   Cosmop 117:63 N '44
    Wilson, E.   Record-breaking Betty.   Silver S 15-3:38 Ja '45
    Receives Gizmo statuette from Marine corps magazine Leather-
        neck.   Newsweek 25:76 Mr 5 '45
    Sketch.   Life 19:70 Ag 27 '45
    Palmer, C.   Paramount's pride and joy.   Silver S 15-11:30 S '45
    Wilson, E.   A shower for Betty.   Silver S 16-3:53 Ja '46
    Watkins, W.   Let's pay a call on Betty.   Silver S 17-2:44 D '46
    Bowers, L.   You'd never know Betty these days.   Silver S 17-9:
        60 Jl '47
    Parsons, L. O.   Cosmop's citation for best comedy role of
        month.   Cosmop 123:58 Jl '47
    Fraker, B.   Story of her baby.   Photop 31:34 O '47
    Hutton, M.   My little sister, Betty.   Silver S 19-4:30 F '49
    Letter from Liza.   Silver S 19-4:44 F '49
    Hall, G.   Betty has two problems.   Silver S 21-2:38 D '50
    Marsh, P.   I hated him at first.   Silver S 23-5:44 Mr '53
    Barthel, J.   Quartet of queens.   Life 70:64 F 19 '71
    Bubbly, bouncy and blonde.   Screen Greats 1-2:52 Sum '71
    Gregory, J.   I want to be a star again.   Movie Dig 2-1:40 Ja '73
    Wilson, E.   Betty the blonde bombshell.   Liberty 1-8:74 Spg '73
    The cook.   N. Y. Post p11 Ap 13 '74

HUTTON, LAUREN
    Halsy's girl.   Show 1-1:45 Ja '70
    Interview.   Vogue 157:116 Ap 15 '71
    Darling, C.   Interview.   Interview p14 O '73

HUTTON, ROBERT
    Service, F.   He makes you blink.   Silver S 17-2:55 D '46

HYAMS, LEILA
    Howe, M.   Sketch.   Motion Pic Classic 25:63 Ag '27
    Manners, D.   Sketch.   Motion Pic 39:76 Je '30
    Cranford, R.   Sketch.   Photop 38:52 Ag '30

Varden, H.  Interview.  Movie Classic 1:60 S '31
Leiber, R.  Sketch.  Photop 40:70 N '31
Moak, B.  Artists' model makes good.  Silver S 2-2:21 D '31
Leila Hyams' beach house.  Silver S 2-6:20 Ap '32
Henderson, J.  Personalities prominent in the press.  Cinema
    Dig 1-6:5 Jl 25 '32

HYER, MARTHA
What it takes to be a starlet.  Am Mag 145:136 F '48
Stanke, D.  Martha Hyer; filmog.  Films In R 22-4:196 Ap '71
Letters.  Films In R 22-6:376 Je/Jl '71
Meyer, J.  A conversation with Martha Hyer.  Filmograph 2-4:
    9 '72

HYLAND, DIANA
This year's cool blonde.  TV Guide 11-43:16 O 26 '63
Prelutsky, B.  Dear Abby, I fell in love with the minister's
    wife.  TV Guide 16-21:46 My 25 '68

HYLAND, PEGGY
Conlon, L.  Sketch.  Motion Pic 12:127 S '16
The art of makeup.  Motion Pic Classic 3:15 F '17
Montanye, L.  Interview.  Motion Pic Classic 4:46 My '17


IHNAT, STEVE
Obit.  N. Y. Times p36 My 20 '72
Robison, R. J.  Steve Ihnat; filmog.  Films In R 23-9:572 N '72

INESCORT, FRIEDA
Douglas, C.  Interview.  Met 58:34 O '23

INGELS, MARTY
A tale of two zanies.  TV Guide 10-48:16 D 1 '62
Hobson, D.  Rapping about the wrap.  TV Guide 19-35:13 Ag 28
    '71

INGRAM, JACK
Obit.  Screen World 21:237 '70

INGRAM, REX
River boy.  Lions R 2-4:no p# Ap '43
Maltin, L.  Rex Ingram.  Film Fan Mo 89:3 N '68
Obit.  Classic Film Collect (reprint N. Y. Times) 25:extra 2 Fall
    '69
    Film R p15 '70/71
    N. Y. Times p29 S 20 '69
    Newsweek 74:98 S 29 '69
    Screen World 21:238 '70
    Time 94:57 S 26 '69

IRELAND, JILL
 My husband David.   TV Guide 14-23:25 Je 4 '66

IRWIN, MAY
 Dolliver, A.   First appearance.   Green Bk Alb 1:196 Ja '09
 Patterson, A.   Home of.   Green Bk Alb 5:520 Mr '11
 Views on woman.   Green Bk 8:1057 D '12
 Interview.   Theatre 17:175 Je '13
 Autobiographical.   Green Book 10:441 S '13
 Randolph, A.   Sketch.   National 38:1101 S '13
 Patterson, A.   Twenty years a star.   Theatre 22:236 N '15

ISBERT, JOSE
 Cobos, J.   The face of '63--Spain.   Films & Filming 10-1:39 O
  '63

ITURBI, JOSE
 Leonard, F.   Interview.   Etude 48:239 Ap; 321 My '30
 Sanborn, P.   Little giant of the piano.   Outlook 156:355 O 29 '30
 When Iturbi enchants children.   Lit Dig 108:17 F 14 '31
 Bio sketch.   Musician 36:4 Jl '31
 Leonard, F.   Outline and atmosphere in piano music.   Etude
  50:89 F '32
 Thomajan, P. K.   A temperament-silhouette.   Musician 39:5 Jl
  '34
 Mexico dates music from Iturbi.   Newsweek 6:30 Jl 6 '35
 Leonard, F.   Honesty in piano study.   Etude 53:716 D '35
 Iturbi troubles.   Time 28:28 S 7 '36
 Turbulent Iturbi.   Time 30:38 Ag 23 '37
 Iturbi's week.   Time 39:60 F 2 '42
 Comfort, A.   Keyboard mechanics.   Etude 60:730 N '42
 Bio.   Cur Bio '43
 Iturbi, by a knockout.   Lions R 3-2:no p# Ja '44
 Jesters in tail coats.   Lions R 3-3(sup): no p# Ap '44
 Maestro for millions.   Lions R 4-1:no p# F '45
 Royce, J.   How strong is your foundation?   Etude 63:144 Mr '45
 Piano playboy.   Time 47:57 Je 17 '46
 Martin, P.   Prodigious senor.   Sat Eve Post 220:30 O 25 '47
 What happened to Jose?   Time 57:101 My 21 '51
 Carnegie Hall recital.   Mus Am 76:21 N 15 '56
 Contracts and cheesecake.   Newsweek 48:64 D 17 '56

IVAN, ROSILAND
 Filmog.   Films & Filming 18-11:60 Ag '72

IVES, BURL
 That wayfaring stranger.   Cue 13-18:12 Ap 29 '44
 Best of the ballad boys.   Cue 13-30:9 Jl 22 '44
 Lewis, E.   Mr. and Mrs. Burl Ives.   Cue 18-48:12 N 26 '49
 It's the sponsor who pays.   TV Guide 4-37:24 S 15 '56
 Rising star.   Film R p20 '59/60
 McGinniss, J.   Big Daddy smells a rat.   TV Guide 18-16:33 Ap
  18 '70

IWASHITA, SHIMA
  Svensson, A.   Shima Iwashita; filmog.   Focus On F 1:6 Mr/Ap
    '70


JABARA, PAUL
  Auder, M.   Interview.   Interview 2-5:32 Ag '72

JACKSON, ANNE
  Hammel, F.   The Wallachs at home.   Cue 32-21:10 My 25 '63
  Robinson, D.   Eight famous Americans tell of the day I was
    proudest of my wife; interview.   Good House 167:77 Ag '68
  Eyles, A.   Anne Jackson; filmog.   Focus On F 4:12 S/O '70
  I like having a husband but I don't want to be a wife; interview.
    House B 113:35 O '71

JACKSON, FREDA
  Sketch.   Theatre World 37:29 Ag '42
  Sketch.   Theatre World 39:26 Ag '43

JACKSON, GLENDA
  Oakes, P.   Ken & Glenda & Peter & Nina.   Show 1-3:57 Mr '70
  Futures, great.   Vogue 156:92 Jl '70
  Ehrlich, H.   They hardly ever make passes at Glenda Jackson.
    Look 34:36 D 29 '70
  Knight, A. & Alpert, H.   Sex stars of 1970.   Playboy 17-12:220
    D '70
  Sheppard, E.   She lives two lives.   Moviegoer 2-1:10 n. d.
  Flatley, G.   Must Glenda always be so neurotic?   N. Y. Times
    Bio Ed F 7 '71
  Reign of Glenda Jackson.   Vogue 157:159 Ap 1 '71
  Talented Mrs. Hodges.   Time 97:53 Ap 26 '71
  Williams, J.   Oscar, Oscar; filmog.   Films Illus 1-1:17 Jl '71
  Irving, C.   Reluctant Oscars.   McCalls 98:12 Jl '71
  Buckley, P.   Everybody knows about Glenda Jackson.   Show 2-9:
    36 N '71
  Miller, E.   Interview.   Seventeen 30:38 D '71
  Bio.   Cur Bio 32:19 D '71
    Same.   Cur Bio Yrbk 1971:208 '72
  We go to London to visit Glenda Jackson.   Mod Screen 66-2:39
    F '72
  Stockwood, J.   Glenda Jackson.   Harp Baz 105:96 F '72
  Williams, J.   Why I'll give up acting.   Films Illus 2-14:17 Ag
    '72
  Leech, M. T.   More than a touch of class.   After Dark 6-5:32
    S '73

JACKSON, GORDON
  Musel, R.   The man from downstairs.   TV Guide 22-52:24 D
    28 '74

JACKSON, KATE
    Raddatz, L.   Attention Mrs. America.   TV Guide 21-8:11 F 24
        '73
    I'll never give up my career for marriage.   Photop 85-5:61 My
        '74

JACKSON, MARY ANN
    Maltin, L.   Our Gang; Our gang filmog.   Film Fan Mo 66:3 D
        '66

JACKSON, SAMMY
    de Roos, R.   Sammy Jackson of No time for sergeants.   TV
        Guide 12-49:22 D 5 '64
    That drip, he said...   TV Guide 13-30:11 Jl 24 '65

JACKSON, SHERRY
    Harbert, R.   Assignment in Hollywood.   Good House 137:17 D '53
    A vintage year for Sherry.   TV Guide 3-3:12 Ja 15 '55
    Readin' ritin' and rehearsal.   TV Guide 4-38:20 S 22 '56

JACKSON, THOMAS
    Obit.   Screen World 19:233 '68

JACOBI, DEREK
    Tierney, M.   Of saints and sinners; interview.   Plays & Players
        17-11:22 Ag '70

JACOBS, BILLIE
    A man of many mothers.   Photop 12-3:99 Ag '17

JACOBSSON, ULLA
    A fresh new face from Sweden.   TV Guide 9-42:20 O 21 '61

JADE, CLAUDE
    Gross, L.   Claude Jade.   Look 34:M Ap 7 '70

JAECKEL, RICHARD
    Sketch.   Photop 24:56 My '44
    Weisenreder, E. B.   Richard Jaeckel.   Films In R 24-10:636 D
        '73

JAFFE, CHAPELLE
    McCaughna, D.   A terribly personal business.   Motion p16 Jl/Ag
        '74

JAGGER, CHRIS
    Hay, R. C.   Interview.   Interview 4-7:15 Ag '74

JAGGER, DEAN
    Hamilton, S.   Sketch.   Photop 54:32 N '40
    His lust for life.   Lions R 2-2:no p# N '42

JAGGER, MICK
  Saal, H. Rolling again. Newsweek 74:137 N 17 '69
  Sander, E. The Stones keep rolling. Sat R 52:67 N 29 '69
  Coren, A. Head Stone. Playboy 16:162 N '69
  People are talking about. Vogue 155:168 F 1 '70
  Newman, D. & Benton, R. Transitional sex figures. Mlle 71:
    102 Jl '70
  Knight, A. & Alpert, H. Sex stars of 1970. Playboy 17-12:220
    D '70
  Jagger and the future of rock. Newsweek 77:44 Ja 4 '71
  Schickel, R. Apocalypse at Altamont. Life 70:12 Ja 29 '71
  Gimme shelter obituary for Woodstock nation. Show 2-1:49 Mr
    '71
  Pagan event. Newsweek 77:36 My 24 '71
  Thompson, T. Stones blast through the land. Life 73:30 Jl 14
    '72
  Heckman, D. As Cynthia Sagittarius says... N.Y. Times Mag
    p10 Jl 16 '72
  Hughes, R. Stones and the triumph of Marsyas. Time 100:44
    Jl 17 '72
  Southern, T. Reply with rejoinder. N.Y. Times p60 Ag 6 '72
  Goldschlager, S. Michael P. Jagger and company. Newsweek
    80:55 Ag 7 '72
  Mick Jagger talks to Lee Radziwill. Interview 25:7 S '72
  Calendo, J. Dietrich and the devil. Interview 27:23 N '72
  Elman, R. Bitch. Oui 1-3:43 D '72
  Marks, J. Interview. Gallery 1-10:53 Ag '73

JAMES, FRANCESCA
  Drake, R. Meet one of All my children. TV Guide 20-48:19 N
    25 '72

JAMES, GARDNER
  Sketch. Photop 26:50 O '24
  Sketch. Motion Pic 32:58 O '26
  Thorp, D. Sketch. Motion Pic Classic 26:26 F '28

JAMES, GLADDEN
  Fletcher, A. W. Interview. Motion Pic 18:52 Ja '20

JAMES, HARRY
  Gabriel of the big top. Lions R 3-1:no p# S '43
  Young man with a horn. Lions R 3-3(sup):no p# Ap '44
  Gabriel over Hollywood. Lions R 3-4:no p# Jl '44
  Vallee, W. L. Trumpet man at ease. Silver S 14-11:24 S '44
  Warner, S. All about the Haymes-James Inc. Silver S 16-1:38
    N '45

JAMES, SHEILA
  Hardly a femme fatale. TV Guide 10-18:16 My 5 '62
  James, S. It's the first minute that hurts. TV Guide 15-21:25
    My 27 '67

JAMESON, HOUSE
    In the cast.   TV Guide 1-13:12 Je 26 '53
    Obit.   N. Y. Times p32 Ag 24 '71

JAMESON, JOYCE
    When Alice fell through the looking glass.   TV Guide 12-33:19
        Ag 15 '64
    Hobson, D.   Confessions of a dumb blonde.   TV Guide 15-27:10
        Jl 8 '67

JAMISON, MIKKI
    What's an agent?   TV Guide 11-30:27 Jl 27 '63

JANIS, ELSIE
    Randolph, M.   Two enthusiasts.   Photop 7-4:88 Mr '15
    Story of my life.   Am Mag 84:33 N '17
    Home again.   Good House 69:27 S '19
    Is imitation the sincerest flattery?   Sat Eve Post 198:14 S 26 '25
    Flirting with the famous.   Colliers 77:7 Je 19 '26
    Should an actress marry?   Pict R 29:2 O '27
    Who said Hollywood was wild?   Pict R 29:4 My '28
    NBC's first woman announcer.   Newsweek 5:24 Ja 12 '35
    Janis turns back on Mammon.   Newsweek 8:26 Jl 18 '36
    Orders from G. H. Q.   Time 28:37 Jl 20 '36
    Obit.   Newsweek 47:74 Mr 12 '56
        Screen World 8:223 '57
        Time 67:110 Mr 12 '56
    Debus, A. G.   Current collectors' recordings.   Hobbies 61:31
        Jl '56

JANNINGS, EMIL
    Autobiographical.   Motion Pic Classic 22:20 D '25
    Smith, F. J.   Interview.   Photop 31:64 D '26
    Hall, G.   Sketch.   Motion Pic 33:24 F '27
    Wells, H. K.   The real Jannings.   Motion Pic Classic 25:16 Mr
        '27
    Glassgold, C. A.   The Americanization of Jannings.   Arts 12:
        114 Ag '27
    Miller, H.   Compared to John Barrymore.   Motion Pic Classic
        26:33 S '27
    Intimate facts about himself and his work.   Theatre 46:42 O '27
    Tulley, J.   Estimate of.   Vanity Fair 29:77 N '27
    Calhoun, D.   Interview.   Motion Pic 34:20 Ja '28
    Reniers, P.   Appreciation.   Indep 121:330 O 6 '28
    Smith, R.   Jannings, the moan-maker.   Theatre 49:24 Ja '29
    Walker, H. L.   Sketch.   Motion Pic Classic 29:26 Mr '29
    Bahn, C.   Jannings-Laughton "duel?"   Cinema Dig 3-5:9 Ap 17
        '33
    Five years ago.   Photop 44:116 O '33
    Obit.   Screen World 2:234 '51
    Truscott, H.   Emil Jannings; a personal view.   Silent Pic 8:5
        Aut '70

JANOWSKA, ALINA
   Janowska, A.   Truth behind a mask.   Films & Filming 8-2:10
     N '61

JANSSEN, DAVID
   Bio.   Cur Bio Yrbk 1967:196 '68
   I paid $20,000 to share his bed.   Photop 77-6:38 Je '70
   Cooking with a star.   Mod Screen 65-11:51 N '71
   Meredith, J.   How a weekend with David changed my life.   Pho-
     top 80-6:70 D '71
   A love that was too good to last?   Mod Screen 65-12:36 D '71
   Forsyth, R.   After our 3-year love affair...   Photop 81-1:42 Ja
     '72
   Hobson, D.   Eyeball to eyeball with Janssen.   TV Guide 20-5:16
     Ja 29 '72
   My son, the actor.   TV Guide 20-5:18 Ja 29 '72

JARRETT, RENNE
   Wasserman, J. L.   A good girl nowadays is hard to find.   TV
     Guide 18-45:28 N 7 '70
   The most fateful decision I ever made.   Mod Screen 66-3:47 Mr
     '72

JARVIS, SCOTT
   At Ohio State... the biggest thing on campus.   After Dark 4-11:52
     Mr '72

JASON, SYBIL
   March, M.   Sketch.   Motion Pic 50:42 N '35
   Marianne.   Sketch.   Photop 51:67 N '37
   Rhea, M.   Sketch.   Photop 53:30 Jl '39

JAYNES, BETTY
   Sketch.   Time 28:65 D 14 '36
   Mimi.   Am Mag 123:100 Ap '37

JAYSTON, MICHAEL
   Andrews, E.   Star Tsar.   Films Illus 1-6:32 D '71
   Nicholas and director Franklin Schaffner.   Show 2-11:35 Ja '72
   Feiden, R.   Interview.   Interview 20:31 Mr '72

JEAN, GLORIA
   Story of.   Life 7:54 S 18 '39
   Hall, G.   She'll take Deanna's place.   Silver S 9-11:26 S '39
   Rhea, M.   Sketch.   Photop 53:30 N '39
   Catching up with Gloria Jean.   Mod Screen 66-7:41 Jl '72
   Lewis, G.   Gloria Jean; filmog.   Films In R 24-9:513 N '73

JEANMARIE, RENEE
   Reid, L.   Ballerina from Paris.   Silver S 22-11:30 S '52
   Lewis, E.   French firecracker in Pink tights.   Cue 23-7:14 F
     23 '54
   Old-fashioned insouciance.   Time 96:62 Jl 13 '70

JEANS, ISABEL
  Beaton, C.  In Beaton's view.    Plays & Players 19-7:28 Ap '72
  Obit.  Screen World p236 '74

JEFFRIES, LIONEL
  Opposite direction; bio note.    Films Illus 1-5:31 N '71
  Star to director.  Film 60:2 n. d.
  Interview.  Film R p41 '73/74

JENKINS, ALLEN
  Cohen, H.   Praising players of minor importance.    Cinema Dig
    3-6:12 Ap 24 '33
  Obit.  N. Y. Daily News p53 Jl 22 '74
    N. Y. Times Bio Ed p973 Jl '74

JENKINS, BUTCH
  Boy called Butch.    Lions R 2-4:no p# Ap '43
  O'Leary, D.   Jackie Cooper's advice to Butch Jenkins.    Silver
    S 17-10:46 Ag '47
  The kids.   Screen Greats 1-2:50 Sum '71

JENNINGS, CLAUDIA
  Playmate of the year; photos.    Playboy 17-6:140 Je '70
  Turner, P.   Claudia observed.    Playboy 21-12:129 D '74

JENS, SALOME
  Williams, N.   Interview; filmog & Playlist.    Filmograph 2-3:10
    '71
  Schmidt, R. W.   (Her) first film; letter.    Filmograph 2-4:42 '72
  Addendum to filmog.    Filmograph 3-1:45 '72

JENSEN, KAREN
  The starlet, 1967.    TV Guide 15-15:9 Ap 15 '67
  Lewis, R. W.   In Bracken's world live beautiful people.    TV
    Guide 18-7:29 F 14 '70
  Coffin, H.   Va-va-voom on TV.    Show 1-10:32 Ag 6 '70
  Opinions on liberation; my man and me.    Photop 78-3:78 S '70
  The most fateful decision I ever made.    Mod Screen 66-3:47 Mr
    '72

JEPSON-TURNER, BELITA
  (See: BELITA)

JESSEL, PATRICIA
  Three stars brighter than ever.    Vogue 125:89 Ap 15 '55
  Television's own promising starlets.    TV Guide 3-37:10 S 10 '55
  Obit.  Film R p18 '69/70
    N. Y. Times p47 Je 11 '68
    Newsweek 71:110 Je 24 '68
    Time 91:76 Je 21 '68

JESSUP, SALLY
  La Cossitt, H.   I want both:  my love and my career.    Womans
    Home C 80:50 S '53

JEWELL, ISABEL
  Biery, R.  Her story.  Movie Classic 5:30 D '33
  Samuels, L.  Isabel on her own.  Silver S 4-12:27 O '34
  Hall, G.  Interview.  Motion Pic 49:38 Ap '35
  Interview.  Movie Classic 10:54 My '36
  Williams, W.  Only a "bit" girl.  Silver S 6-11:53 S '36
  Lee, S.  Interview.  Motion Pic 52:41 D '36
  Hall, J. B.  Isabel Jewell.  Films In R 21-10:652 D '70
  Budelli, P. U.  Letter; partial filmog.  Films In R 23-2:123 F
    '72
  Obit.  Classic Film Collect (reprint L. A. Herald Examiner) 35:
    8X Sum '72
    Film R p15 '72/73
    N. Y. Times p38 Ap 7 '72
    Same.  N. Y. Times Bio Ed Ap 7 '72

JILLSON, JOYCE
  Wasserman, J. L.  The girl at the end of the hot line.  TV
    Guide 16-20:23 My 18 '68
  Bonfante, J.  Cash on the line.  Life 65:32B N 22 '68

JIMINEZ, SOLEDAD
  Obit.  Screen World 18:237 '67

JOHAR, I. S.
  Rising star.  Film R p22 '59/60

JOHNS, GLYNIS
  Cinderella from South Africa.  Lions R 3-1:no p# S '43
  Rogers, V.  Do you have upside-down eyes?  Silver S 23-9:33
    Jl '53
  Parsons, L. O.  Cosmop's citation for best performance of
    month.  Cosmop 126:13 My '49
  Shawcross, G.  Filmog.  Films In R 22-7:453 Ag/S '71
  Berkvist, R.  Miss Johns hits a high note.  N. Y. Times sec 2:1
    Mr 11 '73
    Same.  N. Y. Times Bio Ed p443 Mr '73
  Richardson, J. D.  A little Johns music.  After Dark 6-10:36 F
    '74

[OLSEN AND] JOHNSON
  Reid, J.  Still up to their old tricks.  Silver S 12-2:34 D '41

JOHNSON, ARTE
  On the scene.  Playboy 16-10:191 O '69
  TV's tallest short man.  TV Guide 17-46:18 N 15 '69
  Hudson, P.  Want a walnetto?  Sr Schol 95:18 Ja 12 '70
  Raddatz, L.  Six who bowed out.  TV Guide 20-38:23 S 16 '72

JOHNSON, BEN
  Johnson, G.  Bashful Ben of the bang-bangs.  Colliers 124:28 O
    22 '49
  Ronan, M.  Two screen cowboys talk about the reel west and the

real west.   Sr Schol 99:11 D 6 '71
Kleiner, D.   The kind deed that changed his life forever.   Movie
    Dig 2-1:56 Ja '73

JOHNSON, CELIA
    Sketch.   Theatre World 21:270 Je '34
    Winner of N. Y. film critic's award.   Harp Baz 81:77 Jl '47
    Interview.   Theatre World 44:25 F '48

JOHNSON, DON
    Pearsall, A.   How some of the magic went out of Stanley Sweet-
        heart's Garden.   Show 1-3:69 Mr '70

JOHNSON, EDITH
    Remont, F.   Interview.   Motion Pic Classic 9:36 F '20
    Winship, M.   Interview.   Photop 19:45 Mr '21

JOHNSON, EMORY
    Obit.   Screen World 12:222 '61

JOHNSON, GEORGIANN
    Pitch girl from Iowa.   TV Guide 2-20:15 My 14 '54

JOHNSON, HAROLD
    Obit.   Film R p17 '62/63

JOHNSON, JAY
    Zadan, C.   Factory brothers.   After Dark 13-8:22 D '70

JOHNSON, JED
    Zadan, C.   Factory brothers.   After Dark 13-8:22 D '70

JOHNSON, KANDI
    Rotsler, W.   Kandi is dandi; interview.   Adam F World 4-7:10
        Ag '73

JOHNSON, KAY
    Burton, S.   Sketch.   Photop 37:37 D '29
    Pryor, N.   Interview.   Motion Pic Classic 31:30 Jl '30

JOHNSON, MELODIE
    The easy way.   TV Guide 15-1:16 Ja 7 '67

JOHNSON, OLIVIA
    Kingsley, G.   The baby or the bow?   Photop 8-3:33 Ag '15

JOHNSON, PAULINE
    Hall, W.   Film hunt for Pauline, star of the '20s.   Classic Film
        Collect 19:21 Fall/Win '67

JOHNSON, RAFER
    New role for Rafer.   Ebony 21:181 D '65
    How they all played Roman games.   Photop 77-6:64 Je '70

JOHNSON, RITA
  Schwarzkopf, J.  Sketch.  Motion Pic 54:19 N '37
  Hamilton, S.  Sketch.  Photop 54:30 Jl '40
  McClelland, D.  The perfect "other woman"; filmog.  Film Fan
    Mo 118:19 Ap '71

JOHNSON, VAN
  Stars of tomorrow.  Lions R 1-11/12:no p# Jl/Ag '42
  New leading man-power.  Lions R 2-3:no p# D '42
  Hamilton, S.  Sketch.  Photop 22:45 Mr '43
  You know Van.  Lions R 2-5:no p# Jl '43
  Inside information.  Lions R 2-5:no p# Jl '43
  Moving Van.  Lions R 3-2:no p# Ja '44
  Dr. Gillespie makes a diagnosis.  Lions R 3-3(sup):no p# Ap '44
  The kid next door.  Lions R 3-3(sup):no p# Ap '44
  Stranger than fiction.  Lions R 3-5:no p# D '44
  My Christmas wish.  Photop 26:46 Ja '45
  Vim, vigor and Van.  Lions R 4-1:no p# F '45
  Betz, B.  Sketch.  Womans Home C 72:121 Ap '45
  Pritchett, F.  Van gets clubby.  Silver S 15-10:22 Ag '45
  Hall, G.  The luckiest girl in town.  Silver S 16-3:22 Ja '46
  My luckiest day.  Cosmop 122:98 Ja '47
  Pritchett, F.  Let Van give answers.  Silver S 19-12:30 O '49
  Baer, M. M.  Van comes back better than ever.  Silver S 22-1:
    26 N '51
  Bruce, J.  Look at him now.  Silver S 24-7:32 My '54
  Zunser, J.  Juvenile comes of age.  Cue 23-30:12 Jl 24 '54
  Post revives movie footage to promote fortified oat flakes.  Ad-
    vertising Age p194 Ag 14 '70
  The all-American boy.  Screen Greats 1-2:70 Sum '71
  The Dr. Kildares.  Photop 85-3:24 Mr '74

JOHNSTON, JOHNNIE
  Young man from Missouri.  Cue 13-44:15 O 28 '44
  Hall, G.  Wedding bells for Kathryn.  Silver S 17-11:40 S '47

JOHNSTON, JULANNE
  Uselton, R. A.  The Wampus baby stars.  Films In R 21-2:73
    F '70

JOHNSTONE, JUSTINE
  Evans, D.  Sketch.  Photop 19:60 D '20
  Lamb, G.  Interview.  Motion Pic 20:52 Ja '21
  Wrong roads to beauty.  Ladies Home J 43:33 Je '26
  Sketch.  Harp Baz 74:52 Jl '40

JOLSON, AL
  Training an audience to laugh.  Theatre 18:134 O '13
  Sketch.  Strand (NY) 49:278 Mr '15
  Making people laugh.  Green Book 14:333 Ag '15
  The art of minstrelsy.  Theatre 27:290 My '18
  Sketch.  Harp Baz 58:178 O '23
  Benchley, R.  Continued applause.  Life 85:18 Ja 29 '25

Sketch. National 53:269 Ja '25

Nathan, G. J. Appreciation. Am Mer 4:375 Mr '25

Gilmore, F. Interview. Motion Pic Classic 26:25 N '27

Clifton, B. Appreciation. Motion Pic 34:35 D '27

Sketch. National 56:314 Mr '28

Cruikshank, H. Interview. Motion Pic 36:33 N '28

Johnston, C. Sketch. Motion Pic Classic 28:51 Ja '29

Feels lost when not in intimate contact with his audience.
Theatre 50:43 Jl '29

Belfrage, C. Interview. Motion Pic 38:28 Ag '29

Belfrage, C. Sketch. Motion Pic 39:66 F '30

Lee, S. Gives up two million dollars. Motion Pic 44:31 Ag '32

Moffitt, C. F. Censorship for interviews Hollywood's latest wild
idea. Cinema Dig 2-5:9 Ja 9 '33

Lorentz, P. In Hallelujah I'm a bum. Vanity Fair 40:43 Ap '33

French, W. F. His comeback. Photop 44:37 N '33

Grant, J. Leaving the movies. Movie Classic 6:46 Ap '34

French, W. F. His love story. Motion Pic 49:36 Mr '35

Staunton, D. Test for lovers, Hollywood style. Silver S 5-7:27
My '35

Cheatham, M. Interview. Movie Classic 8:31 Je '35

French, W. F. His happy marriage. Motion Pic 51:40 My '36

Lang, H. Interview. Movie Classic 10:28 Je '36

O'Hara, J. Appreciation. Newsweek 16:50 S 23 '40

Parsons, L. O. An untold story. Photop 30:38 D '46

Jolson resurgent. Cue 16-18:12 My 3 '47

Obit. Screen World 2:234 '51

Kobal, J. Al Jolson and Wonder-bar. Film 59:21 Sum '70

Who are you Bill Eckstine and why are you saying those silling
things about Al Jolson? Liberty 1-7:13 Win '72

The re-creation of Al Jolson. Making Films 7-5:22 O '73

JONES, ALLAN

Camp, D. His success. Motion Pic 53:39 Ap '37

Morgan, L. Born with it. Silver S 8-1:54 N '37

Lee, S. The true life story. Screen Book 19-5:44 D '37; 19-6:
46 Ja '38

Home of. Photop 54:56 S '40

Leiber, L. No work and all pay. Silver S 10-11:40 S '40

Russell, J. You're a lucky fellow Mr. Jones. Silver S 14-4:26
F '44

Gilmour, P. Allan Jones; filmog. Films In R 21-5:320 My '70

Jordan, H. Letter. Films In R 22-1:52 Ja '71

JONES, ANISSA

See, C. A family is a family is a family. TV Guide 17-22:18
My 31 '69

Fitzgerald, R. For Buffy & Jody, two very special rooms.
House B 112:37 D '70

JONES, "BUCK" CHARLES

Burden, J. Hero to 2 million kids. Motion Pic 45:64 F '33

French, W. F. His love story. Motion Pic 49:59 F '35

LaBadie, D. W.   The last roundup.   Show 2-9:76 S '62
Reynolds, R.   Hollywood's silent western stars lived active, ad-
    venturous lives.   8mm Collect 5:3 Ag 15 '63
Bio note.   8mm Collect 8:5 My '64
Gordon, A.   The Buck Jones story.   Classic Film Collect 15:4
    Sum '66
Corneau, E. N.   I remember Buck Jones.   Classic Film Collect
    27:28 Spg/Sum '70
Men without law.   Views & Rs 3-1:27 Sum '71

JONES, CAROLYN
    Whitney, D.   Addams' Eve.   TV Guide 12-44:23 O 31 '64
    Bio.   Cur Bio Yrbk 1967:208 '68

JONES, CHRISTOPHER
    Knight, A. & Alpert, H.   Sex stars of 1970.   Playboy 17-12:220
        D '70
    Filmog.   Films & Filming 18-10:64 Jl '72

JONES, DAVID
    Mismatch of the century.   Ebony 23:58 My '68
    Now you see 'em, now you don't.   Look 35-18:70 S 7 '71
    (See Also: MONKEES, The)

JONES, DEAN
    My child.   Photop 81-1:18 Ja '72
    Favorite animal stories.   Mod Screen 66-11:34 N '72

JONES, EDGAR
    How he became a photoplayer.   Motion Pic 9:115 Ap '15
    Rollins, F.   Interview.   Motion Pic 9:105 My '15

JONES, EMRYS
    Obit.   Film R p11 '73/74

JONES, JAMES EARL
    Dynamo.   Newsweek 62:68 D 2 '63
    Actor still climbing.   Ebony 20:98 Ap '65
    Jones by a knockout.   Newsweek 72:66 O 21 '68
    Hellman, P.   The great black hope.   New York 1-29:41 O 21 '68
    People are talking about.   Vogue 152:166 N 1 '68
    Bio.   Cur Bio 30:18 S '69
        Same.   Cur Bio Yrbk 1969:225 '70
    Gussow, M.   Jones sighs for Bossman and Lena.   N. Y. Times
        Bio Ed Je 22 '70
    Resnik, M.   Now a short message from James Earl Jones.   New
        York 3-41:58 O 12 '70
    Kalem, T. E.   Wounded animal.   Time 97:75 Ap 26 '71
    Fraser, C. G.   Stage unites two Jones generations.   N. Y. Times
        Bio Ed p228 F '74
    Novak, R.   A classical actor enjoys a pop movie hit.   People
        1-17:40 Je 24 '74
    Barber, R.   Great bear of a polar man.   TV Guide 22-41:13 O
        12 '74

JONES, JENNIFER
    Story of.   Am Mag 135:28 My '43
    Hall, G.   Who is Jennifer Jones?   Silver S 13-10:30 Ag '43
    Her ideas about love.   Photop 23:41 N '43
    My faith.   Photop 24:48 My '44
    On location for Duel in the sun.   Life 18:99 Ap 23 '45
    Wilson, E.   Quite a change for Jennifer.   Silver S 15-9:24 Jl '45
    Costumes for Duel in the sun.   Womans Home C 73:138 N '46
    Parsons, L. O.   Cosmop's citation for best performance of
       month.   Cosmop 122:67 Ja '47
    Maxwell, E.   Sketch.   Photop 36:35 D '49
    Lewis, E.   Portrait of Jennifer.   Cue 23-49:16 D 4 '54
    Married.   Time 97:77 Je 14 '71
    Newsmakers.   Newsweek 77:56 Je 14 '71
    Here's to the ladies.   Screen Greats 1-2:32 Sum '71

JONES, L. Q.
    Filmog.   Films & Filming 19-7:66 Ap '73

JONES, PAUL
    Buckley, P.   Conduct unbecoming becomes Paul Jones.   After
       Dark 12-5:29 S '70

JONES, SAMANTHA
    Knapp, D.   A documentary screenplay.   Show 1-9:34 Jl 23 '70
    Raddatz, L.   Just call her Sam.   TV Guide 18-45:47 N 7 '70

JONES, SHIRLEY
    Taylor, T.   That Jones girl.   Cue 24-34:13 Ag 27 '55
    Rising star.   Film R p30 '57/58
    Raddatz, L.   You might not believe it but...   TV Guide 18-42:26
       O 17 '70
    I wanted her to be mean to me.   Photop 79-1:52 Ja '71
    Win a stepson--lose a husband.   Photop 79-3:53 Mr '71
    Davidson, B.   Her struggle for family success.   Good House
       173:31 Ag '71
    The man Shirley will always grieve for.   Photop 80-3:47 S '71
    Shirley's side of the story.   Silver S 41-10:49 O '71
    Interview.   Photop 80-5:8 N '71
    I find David Cassidy very sexy.   Mod Screen 66-2:32 F '72
    How the years have changed her.   Photop 81-3:61 Mr '72
    She walks out on husband forever.   Photop 81-4:67 Ap '72
    She walks out on marriage.   Mod Screen 66-4:45 Ap '72
    Righter, C.   Star of the month; horoscope.   Mod Screen 66-4:50
       Ap '72
    Alone, but still smiling.   Mod Screen 66-5:25 My '72
    Her new men.   Photop 82-2:46 Jl '72
    How I find peace of mind.   Mod Screen 66-9:56 S '72
    She is a woman in love and the man is still Jack Cassidy.   Pho-
       top 82-3:80 S '72
    Favorite animal stories.   Mod Screen 66-11:34 N '72
    I never stopped loving Jack.   Mod Screen 66-12:30 D '72
    Automobile accident.   Photop 83-2:51 F '73

Lochte, D. Life is not a situation comedy. TV Guide 22-10:15
Mr 9 '74

JONES, T. C. (Thomas Craig)
Water, R. Boy meets girls. Cue 25-27:14 Je 7 '56
Clurman, H. Theatre. Nation 185:230 O 5 '57
Mask and gown. Theatre Arts 41:17 N '57
Impersonator. Time 74:70 Jl 20 '59
Obit. Screen World 23:238 '72

JONES, TOM
Carthew, A. My name is Tom Jones. N. Y. Times Mag p67 N
14 '65
Welsh rare bit. Newsweek 73:94 Ja 20 '69
Musel, R. Singing Welshman. TV Guide 17-21:34 My 24 '69
On the scene. Playboy 16-6:184 Je '69
Ladies' man. Time 94:54 Jl 11 '69
Baer, B. Tom Jones. Look 33:96 N 4 '69
Diehl, D. He's the apostle of life after 30. TV Guide 18-4:16
Ja 24 '70
His wife stops him from jumping to his death. Photop 78-1:71
Jl '70
Bonfante, J. Ladies' men of music. Life 69:46 S 18 '70
Why Tom has a bra collection. Photop 78-3:71 S '70
The night Tom's wife found him with another woman. Photop 79-
3:71 Mr '71
Doctors warn him to stop singing. Mod Screen 66-7:39 Jl '72
I don't trust women. Photop 85-1:44 Ja '74
Kidnap threat. Photop 86-2:68 Ag '74

JORDAN, BOBBY
Hamilton, S. Sketch. Photop 52:31 S '38
How tough are the Dead End Kids? Screen Book 21-6:28 Ja '39
Obit. Screen World 17:238 '66

JORDAN, DOROTHY
Goldbeck, E. Sketch. Motion Pic Classic 30:52 Ja '30
York, C. Sketch. Photop 37:56 F '30
Walker, H. L. Sketch. Motion Pic Classic 33:71 Ap '31
Dodd, M. Sketch. Motion Pic 42:75 D '31
Sharon, M. The Dorothy boosters. Silver S 2-11:21 S '32

JORDAN, JOANNE
Nine to five? Not for her. TV Guide 3-53:12 D 31 '55

JORDAN, MIRIAM
Nominated for stardom. Motion Pic 45:42 Mr '33
Marion, J. Interview. Photop 44:44 S '33

JORDAN, TED
Raddatz, L. The Dodge City gang. TV Guide 20-12:14 Mr 18
'72

## JORY, VICTOR
Spensley, D.   Sketch.   Motion Pic 46:58 Ag '33
O'Dell, C. N.   Victor Jory.   Silver S 3-11:47 S '33
The story of Victor Jory.   Cue 14-9:9 Mr 3 '45
Autobiographical sketch.   Theatre Arts 30:177 Mr '46
Nolan, J. E.   Films on TV.   Films In R 19-6:370 Je/Jl '68
Victor Jory.   Photop 82-1:65 Je '72
Robert Young: best friend tells all about him.   Photop 82-2:64
   Jl '72

## JOURDAN, LOUIS
Sketch.   Vogue 107:172 Ag 15 '46
Bio note.   Vogue 111:143 Mr 15 '48
Bruce, J.   Import from Paris.   Silver S 18-6:44 Ap '48
Parsons, L. O.   Cosmop's citation as best male star of month.
   Cosmop 124:13 My '48
Graham, S.   Sketch.   Photop 35:65 My '49
Randall, T. L.   Formula for Happiness.   Silver S 21-7:36 My '51
Bio note.   Unifrance 23:10 F '53
Bio.   Cur Bio Yrbk 1967:211 '68

## JOUVET, LOUIS
Allard, S.   Jouvet as a designer.   Theatre Arts 12:437 Je '28
Les quatre.   Theatre Arts 13:177 Mr '29
Larkin, O. W.   Two French directors and their two theatres.
   Theatre Arts 15:42 Ja '31
Elizabethan theatre.   Theatre Arts 20:222 Mr '36
Success.   Theatre Arts 20:354 My '36
Profession of the producer.   Theatre Arts 20:942; 21:56 D '36,
   Ja '37
Moliere.   Theatre Arts 21:686 S '37
Bio.   Cur Bio O '49
Jouvet.   New Yorker 27:18 Mr 31 '51
Obit.   Newsweek 38:57 Ag 27 '51
   Screen World 3:177 '53
   Time 58:87 Ag 27 '51
Genet.   Letter from Paris.   New Yorker 27:65 S 1 '51
Venezky, A.   Reflections of an actor.   Theatre Arts 35:18 D '51
Knapp, B. L.   Madwoman and a master.   Theatre Arts 41:67
   Mr '57

## JOY, GLORIA
McKelvie, M. G.   Sketch.   Motion Pic 17:49 F '19

## JOY, LEATRICE
Cheatham, M. S.   Interview.   Motion Pic Classic 10:15 Ap/My
   '20
Van Dyck, E.   Interview.   Motion Pic Classic 13:62 S '21
Goldbeck, W.   Interview.   Motion Pic 24:52 Ag '22
Handy, T. B.   Interview.   Motion Pic Classic 14:16 Ag '22
Her darkest hour.   Classic 15:52 F '23
Autobiographical.   Motion Pic 28:26 Ag '24
Driver, M. W.   Leatrice and her baby.   Motion Pic 29:52 Jl '25

York, C.  Sketch.   Photop 29:86 My '26
Calhoun, D.  Interview.   Motion Pic 38:64 N '29
Patterson, G. G.  At film revivals with... in attendance.   Film-
  ograph 3-4:9 '73

JOYCE, ALICE
Chamberlin, M.  Bio sketch.   Theatre 17:17 My '13
Sketch.   Motion Pic 8:118 Ja '15
Her work in moving pictures.   Nash & Pall Mall 54:579 F '15
Courtlandt, R.  Interview.   Motion Pic Classic 2:35 Ag '16
Sketch.   Green Book 16:878 N '16
How she got into moving pictures.   Motion Pic 14:77 Ap '17
Sketch.   Motion Pic 14:83 O '17
Smith, F. J.  Interview.   Motion Pic Classic 7:18 D '18
Seadler, S.  Interview.   Motion Pic 17:65 Jl '19
Patterson, A.  Sketch.   Photop 17:47 F '20
Bruce, B.  Interview.   Motion Pic 19:42 Ap/My '20
Hall, G.  Interview.   Motion Pic 19:52 Jl '20
Roberts, W. A.  The real Alice Joyce.   Motion Pic 29:61 My
  '25
Redway, S.  Interview.   Motion Pic Classic 23:32 Mr '26
York, C.  Sketch.   Photop 30:74 O '26
Hall, G.  Sketch.   Motion Pic 33:24 Mr '27
Cruikshank, H.  Sketch.   Motion Pic Classic 30:41 F '30

JOYCE, BRENDA
Hover, H.  Co-ed to co-star.   Screen Book 22-4:83 N '39
Hall, G.  All flew into the cuckoo's nest.   Silver S 10-1:38 N
  '39
Cheatham, M.  Love comes first.   Silver S 11-3:36 Ja '41
Manners, M. J.  Brenda and the glamour girl baby cycle.   Sil-
  ver S 13-11:30 S '43

JOYCE, NATALIE
Uselton, R. A.  The Wampus baby stars.   Films In R 21-2:73
  F '70

JOYCE, PEGGY HOPKINS
Redway, S.  Interview.   Motion Pic Classic 23:22 My '26
Manners, D.  The secret of her fascination.   Motion Pic 45:64
  My '33
Lee, S.  Romance rumors.   Movie Classic 4:17 Je '33

JUDD, EDWARD
Bio note; filmog.   Films & Filming 21-3:58 D '74

JUDGE, ARLINE
Janeway, D.  Interview.   Movie Classic 2:52 Je '32
New faces for the electric lights.   Silver S 2-4:38 F '32
Sketch.   Photop 42:71 N '32
Sketch.   Movie Classic 3:40 D '32
Stanley, G.  Why she continues her movie career.   Motion Pic
  49:37 Jl '35

Obit.   Classic Film Collect 42:34 Spg '74
N. Y. Times Bio Ed p227 F '74
Passalacqua, J.  Arline Judge; filmog.   Films In R 25-7:447
Ag/S '74

JURGENS, CURT
Conrad, D.  Success was not enough for Sunset Blvd.   Films &
Filming 4-9:9 Je '58

KABBIBLE, ISH
College of musical knowledge.   TV Guide 2-33:20 Ag 14 '54

KAHN, MADELINE
Considine, S.  The kaleidoscopic Madeline Kahn.   After Dark
6-3:32 Jl '73
Scott, A.  Boom boom girl.  Interview p12 D '73
Berkvist, R.  Woses are wed, Madeline's a wow.   N. Y. Times
sec 2:13 Mr 24 '74
Same.  N. Y. Times Bio Ed p377 Mr '74

KALLMAN, DICK
Fessier, M. Jr.  Move over, Laurence Olivier.   TV Guide 14-
9:22 F 26 '66

KAMINSKA, IDA
Bio.  Cur Bio 30:24 N '69
Same.  Cur Bio Yrbk 1969:228 '70
Rothstein, R.  Kaminska plays new role as a teacher in Queens.
N. Y. Times Bio Ed N 14 '71

KANE, CAROL
Furey, L.  Something about her eyes.   After Dark 6-5:52 S '73

KANE, GAIL
Geffen, Y. D.  Sketch.  Theatre 20:291 D '14
Her gowns.  Green Book 13:225 F '15
Sketch.  Cosmop 58:331 F '15
May, L.  Interview.  Motion Pic 12:101 Ag '16
Lowell, A.  Interview.  Motion Pic 17:47 Jl '19

KANE, HELEN
Manners, D.  Interview.  Motion Pic Classic 30:25 O '29
Huston, H.  Sketch.  Photop 36:39 O '29
Esterow, M.  Then and now.  N. Y. Times Mag p49 Mr 18 '56
What they are doing now.  Show 3-10:130 O '63
Obit.  Screen World 18:237 '67

KANE, JOHN
The actor as acrobat.  Plays & Players 18-11:14 Ag '71

KAPOOR, SHASHI
    Sketch.  Films Illus 1-16:8 O '72

KARDELL, LILI
    I wish people would forget I was Swedish.  TV Guide 9-26:25 Jl
        1 '61

KARINA, ANNA
    Person of promise.  Films & Filming 7-12:23 S '61
    They didn't plan to be movie stars.  Unifrance 56:no p# Spg '62
    Graham, P.  The face of '63--France.  Films & Filming 9-8:
        13 My '63
    I didn't always understand him (Jean-Luc Godard).  Film 2-2:16
        My '73
    Warhol, A.  Anna Karina.  Interview p6 Mr '74

KARLOFF, BORIS
    Sketch.  Motion Pic 43:66 Ap '32
    Calhoun, D.  Trials of his ex-wife.  Movie Classic 2:24 Je '32
    Walker, H. L.  The mystery man in real life.  Motion Pic 46:
        55 D '33
    Kent, J.  Interview.  Movie Classic 10:26 Jl '36
    Bio note; filmog.  Movies & People 2:21 '40
    Cue says go!  Cue 10-1:15 Ja 4 '41
    Benedict, P.  Lament of a monster.  Silver S 11-6:40 Ap '41
    Her horror party on Friday the 13th.  Life 12:122 Mr 30 '42
    Vallee, W. L.  Meet a most charming monster.  Silver S 16-6:
        50 Ap '46
    Big, bad bogey man goes benevolent.  Cue 17-9:14 F 28 '48
    Beale, K.  Master of horror.  Castle of Frankenstein 1:42 Ja
        '62
    Letters.  Films In R 15-8:511 O '64
    Rosenburg, S.  Horrible truth about Frankenstein.  Life 64:74C
        Mr 15 '68
    Peeples, S. A.  Films on 8 & 16.  Films In R 19-7:450 Ag/S
        '68
    Obit.  Brit Bk Yr 1970:589 '70
        Cur Bio 30:44 Mr '69
        Cur Bio Yrbk 1969:468 '70
        Film R p14 '69/70
        N. Y. Times p1 F 4 '69
        Screen World 21:238 '70
        Time 93:81 F 14 '69
    Gentle monster.  Newsweek 73:100 F 17 '69
    Rayns, T.  Boris Karloff.  Cinema (Lon) 2:31 Mr '69
    Santora, P.  The mellow monster (reprint from N. Y. Daily
        News).  Classic Film Collect 23:46 Spg '69
    Gordon, A.  Boris Karloff; filmog.  Cinema (BH) 5-1:2 Spg '69
    Karloff.  Famous Monsters 56:entire issue Jl '69
    Harwood, J.  Mad monster of the movies; filmog.  Classic Film
        Collect 24:26 Sum; 25:41 Fall '69
    Gerard, L.  The man behind the myth.  Film Comment 6-1:46
        Spg '70

Marlow, D.  Karloff.  Classic Film Collect 29:36 Win '70

Pitts, M. R.  Boris Karloff; partial filmog.  Films In R 21-9: 578 N '70

Letter.  Films In R 22-2:117 F '71

Roman, R. C.  How William Henry Pratt became the cinema's second greatest horror presence.  After Dark 3-10:44 F '71

Two guys from Transylvania.  Screen Greats 1-2:72 Sum '71

Karloff, B.  Houses I have haunted.  Liberty 1-4:80 Spg '72

Bates, D.  Targets: Karloff's legacy.  Castle of Frankenstein 15:25 n. d.

In memoriam.  Castle of Frankenstein 14:10 n. d.

Karloff, B.  My life as a monster.  Castle of Frankenstein 14: 14 n. d.

Dello Stritto, F.  An investigation of a cinema phenomenon.  Photon 21:15 n. d.

KARLOV, SONIA

Graham, C.  Sketch.  Photop 33:76 F '28

Cummings, A.  Sketch.  Motion Pic Classic 27:37 Ap '28

KARNS, ROSCOE

Parsons, H.  Roscoe Karns.  Silver S 3-12:26 O '33

Obit.  N. Y. Times p81 F 8 '70

Same.  N. Y. Times Bio Ed F 8 '70

Screen World 22:237 '71

KARR, DARWIN

How to get into moving pictures.  Motion Pic 12:104 O '16

KARRAS, ALEX

Maule, T.  Big man who wasn't there.  Sports Illus 19:76 S 30 '63

Back in bounds.  Newsweek 63:54 Mr 30 '64

Plimpton, G.  Detroit Lions' remarkable screwball.  Harper 232:76 Ja '66

Plimpton, G.  Meet Mr. Twinkletoes and his friends.  Sports Illus 33:22 O 12 '70

Cutting the mad duck.  Newsweek 78:101 S 27 '71

Lion at large.  Time 98:49 D 27 '71

Durslag, M.  Is TV ready for Alex Karras?  TV Guide 20-10:39 Mr 4 '72

Morris, J.  Trying to prove he's not a 500-pound jerk.  Life 73:89 D 8 '72

Goodman, M.  Over the tube.  People 2-18:45 O 28 '74

KASHFI, ANNA

For ten years he made my life a living hell.  Photop 77-5:42 My '70

Brando fights for his son.  Photop 81-6:66 Je '72

The love torment even divorce couldn't end.  Mod Screen 66-6:51 Je '72

KAUFMANN, CHRISTINE
  Rising star.  Film R p32 '62/63

KAYE, DANNY
  Sketch.  Vogue 97:77 Mr 1 '41
  Sketch.  Cosmop 112:28 F '42
  Work of.  Theatre World 37:28 S '42
  Sketch.  Life 16:115 Mr 6 '44
  Sketch.  Newsweek 23:90 Mr 13 '44
  Perkins, R.  Broadway sensation.  Silver S 14-6:44 Ap '44
  A comedian puts new irons in the fire.  Cue 15-10:11 Mr 9 '46
  Parsons, L. O.  Cosmop's citation for best performance of
    month.  Cosmop 120:70 Mr '46
  Agee, J.  As a screen comedian.  Nation 162:636 My 25 '46
  Miller, L.  Story of.  Photop 34:62 D '48
  Recipe for laughter.  Film R p13 '48
  London appearance.  Spectator 182:574 Ap 29 '49
  Edwards, A.  Kaye-leidoscopic.  Silver S 19-6:40 Ap '49
  His English tour.  Theatre World 45:3 Je '49
  Beavan, J.  Sketch.  World R 5:20 Jl '49
  Winsten, S.  A visit with Bernard Shaw.  World R 5:21 Jl '49
  Danny Kaye does double duty in new film.  Cue 18-52:12 D 24
    '49
  Kaye does a double take.  Cue 20-15:15 Ap 14 '51
  Hyams, J.  Kaye plays the Palace.  Cue 21-1:16 Ja 3 '53
  Minoff, P.  Mr. Kaye's on the move again.  Cue 23-15:12 Ap
    10 '54
  Baker, P.  Kaye's dreams are hard to capture on film.  Films
    & Filming 2-3:3 D '55
  Miller, D.  Films on TV.  Films In R 9-6:341 Je/Jl '58
  Dworkin, M. S.  The clownings of Danny Kaye.  Screen Ed 15:43
    Jl/Ag '62
  Spicy side of Danny Kaye.  Look 34:36 Mr 10 '70
  Burke, T.  Just a guy who can't say Noah.  N. Y. Times Bio Ed
    N 8 '70
  Salute of the week.  Cue 39-46:1 N 14 '70
  Kaye, S. F.  All work and no play.  Vogue 156:168 D '70
  People are talking about.  Vogue 156:166 D '70
  Stasio, M.  The many happy faces of Danny Kaye.  Cue 40-2:8
    Ja 9 '71
  Benchley, P.  A clown for all seasons returns to Broadway.
    Travel & Leisure 1-1:20 F/Mr '71
  Saal, H.  Danny Kaye of the Met.  Newsweek 81:36 Ja 15 '73
  Buckley, M.  Danny Kaye; filmog.  Films In R 24-5:263 My '73
  Berkow, G.  Letter.  Films In R 25-5:314 My '74

KEACH, STACY
  Salute of the week.  Cue 38-44:1 N 1 '69
  I'm a good case study as a lesson in patience.  Life 67:68 N 7
    '69
  Kroll, J.  Grand young man.  Newsweek 74:135 N 24 '69
  Clein, H.  The real people: featuring Hollywood's new breed of
    character actors.  Show 1-8:14 Jl 9 '70

Keach, S.   A screen actor in search of his character.   New
    York 3-34:60 Ag 24 '70
On the scene.   Playboy 18-2:169 F '71
Miller, E.   Interview.   Seventeen 30:62 My '71
Bio.   Cur Bio 32:16 N '71
    Same.   Cur Bio Yrbk 1971:213 '72
Charlton, L.   For Keach, acting is magic--with perseverance.
    N. Y. Times Bio Ed Je 30 '72
Kalem, T. E.   Willy Loman at Elsinore.   Time 100:72 Jl 10
    '72
Hewes, H.   Princely rain.   Sat R 55:64 Jl 22 '72
Kauffmann, S.   Requiem for Keach?   New Rep 167:18 Ag 19 '72
Feiden, R.   Stacy Keach acting up.   Interview 24:30 Ag '72
Westerbeck, C. L.   Travail of Stacy Keach.   Commonweal 97:14
    O 6 '72
Atlas, J.   Renaissance man of drama.   Show 2-7:18 O '72
Whitman, M.   Crusader with a sense of conscience.   Films Illus
    2-18:12 D '72
Jack, E.   The long reach of Stacy Keach.   Movie Dig 2-1:37 Ja
    '73
Fisher, R.   Acting for films; interview.   Filmmakers Newsletter
    6-8:28 Je '73
Shevey, S.   Interview.   Playgirl 1-7:52 D '73
Gow, G.   Charisma for the '70s.   Films & Filming 20-8:54 My
    '74

KEAN, JANE
    Double trouble.   Cue 12-40:9 O 2 '43
    Crazy Keans.   Look 20:53 F 21 '56

KEANE, DORIS
    Sketch.   Pearson (NY) 22:501 '09
    Sketch.   Green Bk Alb 3:1111 My '10
    Stearns, H. E.   Interview.   N. Y. Drama 69:3 Mr 5 '13
    Dale, A.   Star of romance.   Cosmop 55:121 Je '13
    Ten Eyck, J.   Interview.   Green Bk 10:627 O '13
    How shall we speak Shakespeare?   Lit Dig 62:29 Jl 12 '19
    Hall, G.   Interview.   Motion Pic 20:54 Ag '20
    Sumner, K.   More than 2,000 nights in one play.   Am Mag 92:
        34 N '21
    Young, S.   Miss Doris Keane.   New Rep 29:340 F 15 '22
    Indoor kennel of Doris Keane.   Int Studio 94:56 O '29
    Young, S.   Appreciation.   New Rep 113:798 D 10 '45
    Obit.   Cur Bio 7 '46

KEANE, RAYMOND
    Obit.   Screen World p236 '74

KEARNEY, CAROLYN
    A square with curves.   TV Guide 11-23:23 Je 8 '63

KEATING, FRED
    Sketch.   Photop 47:90 Ap '35

KEATING, LARRY
    In the cast.   TV Guide 1-32:20 N 6 '53

KEATON, BUSTER
    Van Dyke, S.   Oh Buster.   You wouldn't kid us, would you?
        Silver S 2-6:22 Ap '32
    Minoff, P.   Even the veteran comics are putting it on film.
        Cue 22-1:7 Ja 3 '53
    Adieu Buster.   Cahiers (Eng.) 2:5 '66
    Kanfer, S.   Great stone face.   Time 96:94 N 2 '70
    Evans, C.   The sounds of silence.   Mise-en-Scene 1:23 n. d.

KEATON, DIANE
    Gage, J.   Woody was as scared of me as I was of him.   N. Y.
        Times Bio Ed My 28 '72
    Carragher, B.   The girl from the Godfather and Play it again
        Sam wants to do Chekhov.   Show 2-5:44 Jl '72
    Sketch.   Movie Dig 1-6:26 N '72
    Rosin, M.   Straight talk and forthright fashion.   Harp Baz 106:
        66 D '72

KEDROV, MIKHAIL NIKOLAEVICH
    Obit.  N. Y. Times p44 Mr 24 '72

KEEFE, ZENA
    Reid, J.   Interview.   Motion Pic 18:30 Ja '20
    Sherwood, C. B.   Interview.   Motion Pic Classic 10:48 Mr '20
    Fulbright, T.   The baby of old Vitagraph.   Classic Film Collect
        35:16 Sum '72

KEEL, HOWARD
    MacArthur, M.   That happy combination sort of guy.   Silver S
        21-10:36 Ag '51
    Oppenheimer, P. J.   Just don't force him.   Silver S 23-5:36
        Mr '53
    Patch, H.   Singing swashbuckler.   Cue 24-49:17 D 10 '55
    Druxman, M. B.   Howard Keel; filmog.   Films In R 21-9:549
        N '70

KEELER, RUBY
    Lee, S.   Enters the movies.   Movie Classic 3:29 N '32
    Wilson, E.   The Stepping star.   Silver S 3-6:20 Ap '33
    Walker, B.   Sketch.   Movie Classic 4:17 Ap '33
    Nominated for stardom.   Motion Pic 45:42 Ap '33
    Manners, D.   Not quitting the screen.   Motion Pic 46:41 N '33
    French, W. F.   How love story.   Motion Pic 49:36 Mr '35
    Staunton, D.   Test for lovers, Hollywood style.   Silver S 5-7:27
        My '35
    Cheatham, M.   Interview.   Movie Classic 8:31 Je '35
    Hogarth, D.   Dancing thru.   Silver S 6-7:34 My '36
    French, W. F.   Her happy marriage.   Motion Pic 51:40 My '36
    Lang, H.   Interview.   Movie Classic 10:28 Je '36
    Bio note; filmog.   Movies & People 2:21 '40

Calta, L.   Ruby Keeler says Yes Yes to role in No No Nanette.
    N. Y. Times Bio Ed Je 25 '70
Gorton, D.   Busby and Ruby.   Newsweek 76:63 Ag 3 '70
Roman, R. C.   Back to Broadway after 40 years.   Dance 44:62
    D '70
Flatley, G.   Yes, yes, Ruby.   N. Y. Times Bio Ed Ja 10 '71
Botto, L.   Ruby Keeler is alive and tapping.   Look 35-3:70 F 9
    '71
O'Malley, W. S.   Ruby came back.   Film Fan Mo 121/122:3 Jl/
    Ag '71
Bowers, R. L.   Ruby Keeler; filmog.   Films In R 22-7:405 Ag/
    S '71
The love teams.   Screen Greats 1-2:10 Sum '71
Sus, A.   Letter.   Films In R 22-10:645 D '71
Bio.   Cur Bio 31:21 D '71
    Same.   Cur Bio Yrbk 1971:215 '72
Dunn, D.   Backstage with No No Nanette.   New York 5-13:49
    Mr 27; 5-14:40 Ap 3 '72
Keeler, R.   Horray for Busby Berkeley.   Films In R 24-8:471
    O '73

KEENAN, FRANK
    My beginnings.   Theatre 8:78 Mr '08
    Interview.   N. Y. Drama 64:6 N 30 '10
    Patterson, A.   Interview.   Theatre 20:286 D '14
    What Keenan did at high noon.   Photop 11-6:77 My '17
    Interview.   Motion Pic Classic 8:56 Ag '19
    Cope, H.   Not The grand old man.   Photop 16-6:46 N '19
    Goldbeck, W.   Interview.   Motion Pic 25:52 Mr '23

KEENE, TOM
    Hall, G.   Sketch.   Movie Classic 4:24 Jl '33
    Edwards, J.   Tom Keene; filmog.   Films In R 14-8:502 O '63

KEENER, HAZEL
    Uselton, R. A.   The Wampus baby stars.   Films In R 21-2:73
        F '70

KEITH, BRIAN
    Tough company.   Films & Filming 1-11:20 Ag '55
    Eyles, A.   Brian Keith; filmog.   Focus On F 1:15 Mr/Ap '70
    Brian Keith and babies who went on his honeymoon.   Photop 77-
        5:64 My '70

KEITH, IAN
    Cruikshank, H.   Sketch.   Motion Pic 38:74 D '29
    Merrick, C.   His marital troubles.   Movie Classic 1:40 O '31

KEITH, JANE
    Rodgers, J. J.   Interview.   Green Book 15:41 Ja '16
    How she became a photoplayer.   Motion Pic 11:117 F '16

KELETY, JULIA
    Obit.   N. Y. Times p36 Ja 4 '72

KELLAWAY, CECIL
    Obit.   Classic Film Collect 39:Extra 1 Sum '73
        Film R p16 '73/74
        N. Y. Times Bio Ed p445 Mr '73
        Screen World p236 '74

KELLER, HIRAM
    Colaciello, R. & Smith, M.  Interview.  Interview 30:9 Mr '73
    Lawrence, D.  Interview.  Interview 4-10:31 O '74

KELLERMAN, SALLY
    The biggest feet since Garbo.   TV Guide 13-16:23 Ap 17 '65
    McClelland, D.   TV: where all that old-time glamour went.
        Film Fan Mo 75:11 S '67
    Actresses.   Newsweek 76:73 D 7 '70
    Knight, A. & Alpert, H.   Sex stars of 1970.   Playboy 17-12:220
        D '70
    Walters, J.   New found fame of Hot Lips.   Life 70:58 F 5 '71
    The barge is sailing along.   Time 97:40 Mr 8 '71
    Zadan, C.   Flashing her navel.   After Dark 3-12:32 Ap '71
    Not bad for a waitress from L. A.   Photop 80-2:92 Ag '71
    Lucky to be successful while she can still walk.   Movie Dig 1-2:
        49 Mr '72
    Castell, D.   Break-in.   Films Illus 2-23:22 My '73

KELLIN, MIKE
    The man with the lived-in face.   TV Guide 14-17:26 Ap 23 '66

KELLOGG, BRUCE
    Beery's new buddy.   Lions R 3-4(sup):no p# Jl '44

KELLY, BRIAN
    Crail, T.   Dear Mr. Kelly.   TV Guide 14-28:15 Jl 9 '66

KELLY, CLAIRE
    I am not a Hollywood dingaling.   TV Guide 5-49:21 D 7 '57

KELLY, DOROTHY
    Brodie, A. D.   Sketch.   Motion Pic Classic 2:43 Ap '16
    Duryea, B.   Sketch.   Green Book 16:170 Jl '16
    Lachmund, M. G.   Sketch.   Motion Pic 13:118 Je '17

KELLY, GENE
    Stars of tomorrow.   Lions R 1-11/12:no p# Jl/Ag '42
    Meet Pal Joey.   Lions R 2-2:no p# N '42
    Kelly, G.   A letter to my daughter Kerry.   Silver S 13-5:30
        Mr '43
    Tintype.   Lions R 2-4:no p# Ap '43
    Mrs. Kelly's boy.   Lions R 2-5:no p# Jl '43
    The man on the flying trapeze.   Lions R 3-2:no p# Ja '44

Kelly ain't kickin'.  Lions R 3-2:no p# Ja '44
O'Leary, D.  Always on his toes.  Silver S 17-6:40 Ap '47
Hyams, J.  All the world loves to dance.  Cue 22-18:12 My 2
     '53
Bruce, J.  He changes their lives.  Silver S 24-8:40 Je '54
Personality of the month.  Films & Filming 2-4:3 Ja '56
Sarris, A.  Oddities and one shots.  Film Culture 28:45 Spg '63
Gotta sing.  Gotta dance.  Film 40:9 Sum '64
Interview.  Cinema (BH) 3-4:24 D '66
Swisher, V.  Gene and Jack and the beanstalk.  Dance 41:52 F
     '67
Kelly, G.  Directing Dolly.  Action 4-2:8 Mr/Ap '69
What directors are saying.  Action 5-3:30 My/Je '70
Shipley, G.  Some notes on some of film's dancers.  Filmograph
     3-1:15 '72
Paskin, B.  Living the life of Kelly.  Films Illus 3-30:212 D '73
Gene Kelly goes legit again after 33 years.  People 2-2:54 Jl 8
     '74
22 years later it's Uncle Gene and his umbrella.  People 2-16:
     38 O 14 '74
Castell, D.  Song and dance man.  Films Illus 4-39:98 N '74

KELLY, GRACE
Holland, J.  Witches with halos.  Silver S 24-4:29 F '54
Little land of the big wheel.  Playboy 4:24 My '57
Interview.  Playboy 13:69 Ja '66
Arthur, W. B.  Princess Grace turns forty; interview.  Look
     33:96 D 16 '69
Mann, R.  How a royal beauty stays beautiful.  Ladies Home J
     87:101 My '70
Princess Grace has a lot to say about mothers.  Life 71:63 Jl
     30 '71
Why mothers should breast-feed their babies.  Ladies Home J
     88:56 Ag '71
The princess who'd rather be a movie star.  Silver S 41-10:26
     O '71
We go to Monaco to visit Princess Grace.  Mod Screen 65-12:34
     D '71
Pepper, C. B.  Interview.  Vogue 158:108 D '71
Nemy, E.  Kelly women together at a Philadelphia party.  N. Y.
     Times p82 Ap 8 '73

KELLY, JACK
Kelly get your gun.  TV Guide 6-20:8 My 17 '58
Funniest brother act since the Marxes.  TV Guide 7-3:17 Ja 17
     '59
Shooting for laughs.  TV Guide 7-36:17 S 5 '59
The last of the mavericks.  TV Guide 10-22:15 Je 2 '62
Professional amateur.  Sat Eve Post 244:80 Win '72

KELLY, KITTY
Obit.  Screen World 20:235 '69

KELLY, NANCY
   Rhea, M.  Sketch.  Photop 53:31 Ap '39

KELLY, PATSY
   Sketch.  Photop 49:80 Mr '36
   Gwin, J.  It comes out here.  Silver S 6-5:58 Mr '36
   Hall, G.  Interview.  Motion Pic 52:32 Ja '37
   Maltin, L.  Interview; filmog.  Film Fan Mo 117:3 Mr '71

KELLY, PAUL
   Fairfield, L.  Sketch.  Movie Classic 2:34 Jl '32
   Hall, H.  Sketch.  Motion Pic 47:72 Je '34
   Donnell, D.  Sketch.  Movie Classic 10:24 S '36
   Crowley, G.  Interview.  Motion Pic 52:53 O '36

KELLY, PAULA
   Paula adds zip to Sweet Charity.  Ebony 24:86 Je '69
   Paula Kelly.  Playboy 19-7:139 Jl '72
   Swisher, V. H.  The dazzling imperfections of Paula Kelly.  After Dark 5-10:52 F '73

KELLY, TOMMY
   McGinnis, E. W.  To play Tom Sawyer.  St Nich 64:39 S '37
   Reay, N. W.  Meet Tom Sawyer.  Screen Book 19-5:36 D '37
   Willson, D.  Story of.  Child Life 17:367 Ag '38

KELTON, PERT
   Masters, G.  Pert in name and nature.  Silver S 3-11:49 S '33
   Manners, D.  Interview.  Motion Pic 46:41 D '33
   Obit.  N. Y. Times p43 O 31 '68
    Screen World 20:236 '69

KEMP, VALLI
   McAsh, I.  Straight up from down under.  Films Illus 1-10:32 Ap '72
   Knight, C. & Nicholson, P.  On the set of Phibes II.  Cinefantastique 2-2:38 Sum '72

KEMPINSKI, TOM
   Tomorrow belongs to us.  Plays & Players 20-10:24 Jl '73

KENDALL, KAY
   Hard way up.  Films & Filming 2-6:10 Mr '56
   Zunser, J.  Kay, the beautiful clown.  Cue 26-44:13 N 2 '57
   Obit.  Film R p10 '60/61
    Screen World 11:220 '60

KENDALL, SUZY
   Wolf, W.  The London look in films.  Cue 37-11:10 Mr 16 '68

KENNEDY, ADAM
   Adam led six lives.  TV Guide 6-6:25 F 8 '58

KENNEDY, ARTHUR
    Hamilton, S.   Sketch.   Photop 19:62 O '41
    Hendricks, H.   Salty guy from Worcester.   Silver S 20-10:36 Ag
       '50
    Marill, A. H.   Arthur Kennedy; filmog.   Films In R 25-3:129
       Mr '74

KENNEDY, DOUGLAS
    Obit.   Screen World p236 '74

KENNEDY, EDGAR
    Maltin, L.   Our Gang; Our Gang filmog.   Film Fan Mo 66:3 D
       '66

KENNEDY, GEORGE
    Canham, C.   A day in the life of Gaily Gaily.   Cineaste 2-3:13
       Win '68/69
    Eyles, A.   George Kennedy; filmog.   Focus On F 1:16 Mr/Ap
       '70
    Clein, H.   The real people; featuring Hollywood's new breed of
       character actors.   Show 1-8:14 Jl 9 '70
    Raddatz, L.   They needed big guys to beat up.   TV Guide 19-49:
       57 D 4 '71
    Richter, C.   Star of the month; horoscope.   Mod Screen 66-2:46
       F '72

KENNEDY, MADGE
    Sketch.   Cosmop 58:200 Ja '15
    Sketch.   Green Bk 14:879 N '15
    The art of being innocently devilish.   Green Bk 16:137 Jl '16
    Her best lines.   Everybodys 34:496 Jl '16
    Interview.   Dram Mir 77:10 Jl 7 '17
    Naylor, H. S.   Interview.   Motion Pic 15:74 Mr '18
    Lamb, G.   Interview.   Motion Pic Classic 7:28 O '18
    The art of Madge Kennedy.   Photop 16-6:66 N '19
    Fletcher, A. W.   Interview.   Motion Pic 19:30 Je '20
    Hall, G.   Interview.   Motion Pic Classic 11:20 D '20
    Bruce, B.   Interview.   Motion Pic 22:52 Ja '22
    Hall, G.   Interview.   Motion Pic Classic 14:34 Jl '22
    Oetinger, M.   Interview.   Motion Pic 25:40 F '23
    Kenyon, D.   The klan of Kenyon and Kennedy.   Motion Pic 28:24
       S '24
    Brock, A.   Day dreams come true.   Classic Film Collect 26:52
       Win '70

KENNEDY, MARY
    Courtlandt, R.   Sketch.   Motion Pic 11:36 Jl '16

KENT, BARBARA
    Uselton, R. A.   The Wampus baby stars.   Films In R 21-2:73
       F '70

KENT, CRAWFORD
Montanye, L. Interview. Motion Pic 16:71 O '18
Montanye, L. Interview. Motion Pic Classic 13:70 S '21
Obit. Screen World 5:208 '54

KENT, LARRY
Standish, B. Sketch. Motion Pic Classic 27:40 Je '28

KENYON, DORIS
Montanye, L. Sketch. Motion Pic Classic 4:47 Je '17
The birth of a smile. Photop 14-2:81 Jl '18
Montanye, L. M. Interview. Motion Pic 16:43 D '18
Fletcher, A. W. Interview. Motion Pic Classic 13:50 S '21
Fletcher, A. W. Interview. Motion Pic 24:62 Ag '22
Cades, H. R. Interview. Womans Home C 50:76 Ap '23
Service, F. Interview. Classic 19:24 Mr '24
The klan of Kenyon and Kennedy. Motion Pic 28:24 S '24
de Revere, F. V. Face analysis of. Motion Pic 29:43 Ap '25
Selection of color. Motion Pic Classic 21:59 Jl '25
Roberts, W. A. Sketch. Motion Pic 30:58 S '25
Sketch. Motion Pic 32:49 Ag '26
York, C. Sketch. Photop p78 Ag '26
Green, E. Sketch. Motion Pic 31:45 Ap '27
Thorp, D. Interview. Motion Pic 36:58 N '28

KERNESS, DONNA
Cowan, B. Interview. Take One 1-8:22 n. d.

KERR, DEBORAH
Parsons, L. O. Cosmop's citation for best performance of month. Cosmop 122:66 My '47
Dudley, F. She made Gable change his mind. Silver S 17-9:62 Jl '47
Bartley, D. K. The man I married. Silver S 18-6:28 Ap '48
Mulvey, K. Story of. Photop 35:74 My '49
Parsons, L. O. Cosmop's citation for best performance of month. Cosmop 127:13 Jl '49
Hendricks, H. If you knew Deborah. Silver S 23-1:30 N '52
Kerr, D. Dream wife wakes up. Silver S 23-4:38 F '53
Taylor, T. Debut for Deborah. Cue 22-38:15 S 19 '53
Wilson, E. The rebellious Miss Kerr. Silver S 24-5:32 Mr '54
Kerr, D. The young giant. Int F Ann 1:9 '57
Lawrenson, H. The nightmare of the iguana. Show 4-1:46 Ja '64
Braun, E. A code of behavior. Films & Filming 16-7:24 Ap '70
Braun, E. From here to esteem. Films & Filming 16-8:22 My '70
Braun, E. With deep sincerity. Films & Filming 16-9:108 Je '70
Clein, H. The real people; featuring Hollywood's new breed of character actors. Show 1-8:14 Jl 9 '70
Enjoy falling in love. Vogue 159:114 Mr 1 '72
Travels with Deborah. Films & Filming 19-10:8 Jl '73

KERRIGAN, J. WARREN
    Baker, H. G.   Sketch.   Motion Pic 9:99 My '15
    West, V.   Interview.   Motion Pic Supp 1:51 S '15
    Letters received by.   Green Bk 14:512 S '15
    Kerrigan, J. W.   Why do we remember and admire certain
        players?   Film Players Herald 2-7:22 F '16
    How to get into motion pictures.   Motion Pic 12:99 S '16
    Peterson, E.   Home life of.   Motion Pic Classic 3:21 D '16
    Robinson, C. R.   Sketch.   Motion Pic Classic 5:62 O '17
    Remont, F.   Interview.   Motion Pic 15:70 My '18
    Chapman, J. B.   Interview.   Motion Pic 18:64 O '19
    Sketch.   Photop 24:53 Jl '23
    Carlisle, H.   Interview.   Motion Pic 25:24 O '23
    Kingsley, G.   Sketch.   Motion Pic 36:72 S '28

KERRY, NORMAN
    Naylor, H. S.   Interview.   Motion Pic 18:32 Ag '19
    Handy, T. B.   Interview.   Motion Pic Classic 10:22 Mr '20
    Cheatham, M. S.   Interview.   Motion Pic 20:67 Ag '20
    Walker, H. L.   Sketch.   Motion Pic 31:67 Jl '26
    Waterbury, R.   Sketch.   Photop 32:97 Ag '27
    Ramsey, W.   Sketch.   Motion Pic Classic 29:55 Mr '29

KERSH, KATHY
    Some monkeys have all the luck.   TV Guide 12-24:26 Je 13 '64

KERT, LARRY
    Salute of the week.   Cue 40-19:1 My 8 '71
    Stoop, N. M.   Tony and Larry and Bobby and Larry.   After
        Dark 4-2:40 Je '71

KEY, KATHLEEN
    Obit.   Screen World 6:224 '55
    Uselton, R. A.   The Wampus baby stars.   Films In R 21-2:73
        F '70

KEYES, EVELYN
    Franchey, J. R.   Three-career Keyes.   Silver S 14-4:40 F '44
    Green, P. D.   Glamour is a dreary business.   Silver S 16-2:52
        D '45
    Parsons, L. O.   Cosmop's citation for best performance of
        month.   Cosmop 127:13 N '49
    Churchill, R. & B.   Evelyn's seven keys to allure.   Silver S
        21-1:30 N '50
    Hall, G.   Let's confide about romance.   Silver S 23-12:38 O '53
    Catching up with Evelyn Keyes.   Mod Screen 66-4:29 Ap '72

KIBBEE, GUY
    Cohen, H.   Praising players of minor importance.   Cinema Dig
        3-6:12 Ap 24 '33

KID, MARY
    Pinto, A.   Mary Kid; filmog.   Films In R 23-1:63 Ja '72

KIDDER, MARGOT
    Whitney, D.  Less an actress than a happening.  TV Guide 20-
      11:16 Mr 11 '72

KIER, UDO
    Udo meets Monique.  Interview 4-5:20 My '74

KILBRIDE, PERCY
    Roman, R. C.  Percy Kilbride; filmog.  Films In R 23-5:315
      My '72

KILBURN, TERRY
    Poetic justice.  Theatre Arts 38:15 Ja '54
    Limbacher, J. L.  Terry Kilburn; filmog.  Film Fan Mo 124:21
      O '71

KILEY, RICHARD
    Richard Kiley and The little prince.  Films Illus 3-35:454 Jl '74

KIMBROUGH, JOHN
    Hall, G.  Jarrin' John jolts Hollywood.  Silver S 12-2:42 D '41

KING, ALAN
    King of the crab-grass set.  TV Guide 8-53:15 D 31 '60
    Fun of living in the suburbs.  McCalls 89:46 S '62
    Wilner, N.  Kniberg in the crabgrass.  Esquire 58:126 S '62
    Fit for what?  McCalls 90:46 F '63
    To the finest little old sanitation men in the whole world.  Mc-
      Calls 91:44 D '63
    How I feel about banks is unbalanced.  McCalls 91:42 Ja '64
    King, A.  A show soliloquy.  Show 4-5:85 My '64
    Kitman, M.  Large, loud mouth of Alan King.  Sat Eve Post
      237:68 N 28 '64
    Offend institutions.  Newsweek 66:118 N 15 '65
    Chopped liver a la King.  Time 87:43 My 13 '66
    Efron, E.  King of the fast burn.  TV Guide 15-8:6 F 25 '67
    Bio.  Cur Bio Yrbk 1970:224 '71
    Nemy, E.  How did Alan King's son become an addict?  Both
      try to explain.  N. Y. Times Bio Ed p1345 Jl '72
    Chase, C.  Setting 'em up at Grant's Tomb.  TV Guide 20-30:18
      Ag 12 '72
    Robbins, F.  Interview.  Gallery 2-11:91 D '74

KING, ANDREA
    Cohen, J.  Filmog.  Films In R 19-2:126 F '68

KING, ANITA
    Field, C. K.  Work of.  Sunset 37:30 S '16
    Courtlandt, R.  Sketch.  Motion Pic 12:117 O '16

KING, CHARLES
    Hall, G.  Sketch.  Motion Pic Classic 29:37 Jl '29

KING, DENNIS
  Merton, P.   Sketch.   Photop 37:98 D '29
  Goldbeck, E.   Interview.   Motion Pic 38:50 Ja '30
  Obit.   Classic Film Collect (reprint Baltimore Sun) 31:62 Sum
    '71
    N. Y.   Times p61 My 23 '71
    Screen World 23:238 '72
    Time 97:74 My 31 '71

KING, JOHN
  Blackstock, L.   Sketch.   Motion Pic 54:13 Ag '37

KING, JOHN
  Last miles.   Theater Arts 41:12 My '57

KING, MOLLIE
  Sketch.   N. Y.   Drama 70:9 Jl 23 '13
  Roberts, S.   Interview.   Motion Pic Classic 8:50 My '19
  May, L.   Interview.   Motion Pic 21:72 Mr '21

KING, PEGGY
  Hardly King size.   TV Guide 3-1:12 Ja 1 '55
  That wonderful feeling.   TV Guide 3-47:17 N 19 '55

KING, PERRY
  Stoop, N. M.   Two stars on the horizon.   After Dark 5-3:36 Jl
    '72
  Colacello, B.   Interview.   Interview 4-12:16 D '74

KING, YOLANDA DENISE
  Jablow, M.   Interview.   Seventeen 31:92 Ja '72

KING, ZALMAN
  Shayne, B.   Leading man named Zalman?   N. Y. Times Bio Ed F
    28 '71
  Hobson, D.   A shaggy lawyer story.   TV Guide 19-16:43 Ap 17
    '71

KINGSTON, NATALIE
  Kibbe, V.   Interview.   Motion Pic Classic 22:50 N '25
  Uselton, R. A.   The Wampus baby stars.   Films In R 21-2:73
    F '70

KIRBY, DURWARD
  In the cast.   TV Guide 1-26:14 S 25 '53
  Onward and upward.   TV Guide 8-11:29 Mr 12 '60
  TV's triple threat.   Look 26:48d Je 5 '62

KIRBY, GEORGE
  Where else?   Newsweek 60:44 D 24 '62
  Mammouth of mimicry.   Ebony 20:57 Je '65
  Crail, T.   George is ready.   TV Guide 18-29:13 Jl 18 '70

KIRK, ALYN
Malcomson, R. M.  The sound serial.  Views & Rs 3-1:13 Sum
'71

KIRK, PHILLIS
O'Leary, D.  Bachelor girl with brains.  Silver S 23-4:44 F '53
Perkins, R.  Fearless Phyllis.  Silver S 23-12:43 O '53

KIRKBY, OLLIE
Mount, C.  Sketch.  Motion Pic 13:28 F '17

KIRKE, DONALD
Bio note.  Cinema Trails 2:21 n. d.

KIRKLAND, ALEXANDER
Evans, W.  An artist to his finger tips.  Silver S 2-8:26 Je '32
Lane, J.  Sketch.  Motion Pic 44:61 Ja '33
Miss Gypsy Rose Lee, author, weds Broadway actor.  Life 13:
41 S 14 '42
Last of the twenties.  Theatre Arts 33:22 S '49
Matterhorn at twilight.  Theatre Arts 33:26 N '49
Woman from Yalta.  Theatre Arts 33:28 D '49

KIRKLAND, MURIEL
Martin, B.  Personalities prominent in the press.  Cinema Dig
1-6:6 Jl 25 '32
Obit.  N. Y. Times p38 S 27 '71
Same.  N. Y. Times Bio Ed S 27 '71
Screen World 23:238 '72

KIRKMAN, KATHLEEN
Delvigne, D.  Interview.  Motion Pic 18:54 Ja '20
Peltret, E.  Interview.  Motion Pic Classic 11:36 S '20

KIRKWOOD, JAMES
Keith, D. L.  Good times getting better.  After Dark 4-10:18 F
'72

KISHIDA, KYOKO
A conversation with two Japanese film stars.  Film Comment
3-1:61 Win '65

KITT, EARTHA
Lewis, E.  Miss Kitt goes earthy.  Cue 23-48:14 N 27 '54
Santa's baby is back on Broadway.  Playboy 2:36 Ja '55
Down to Eartha.  Time 91:14 Ja 26 '68
Word from Miss Kitt.  Newsweek 71:23 Ja 29 '68
C'est si bon.  Newsweek 78:61 N 22 '71
Black women reveal how they suffer for their white men.  Photop
84-6:54 D '73

KLEIN-ROGGE, RUDOLF
Estes, O. Jr.  The German Chaney.  Classic Film Collect 32:
22 Fall '71

KLUGMAN, JACK
  The odd couple drops in.  TV Guide 18-31:12 Ag 1 '70
  Odd squad.  Time 96:74 O 26 '70
  Interview.  Photop 81-2:48 F '72
  Whitney, D.  Off-camera too, they are an odd couple.  TV Guide
    20-36:14 S 2 '72
  Durslag, M.  Lights, camera, place your bets.  TV Guide 22-
    15:27 Ap 13 '74

KNAPP, EVELYN
  Manners, D.  Sketch.  Motion Pic 41:78 Ap '31
  Andrews, C.  An old man's darling.  Silver S 1-8:50 Je '31
  Thomas, G. M.  A broken back and a stiff upper lip.  Silver S
    2-3:50 Ja '32
  Burden, J.  Sketch.  Movie Classic 2:28 Jl '32
  Uselton, R. A.  The Wampus baby stars.  Films In R 21-2:73
    F '70

KNEF, HILDEGARDE
  (Also known as Hildegard Neff)
  Lewis, E.  From Berlin to Broadway.  Cue 23-53:14 Ja 1 '55
  Cooper, A.  Bitter goddess.  Newsweek 78:73 Jl 5 '71
  Darrach, B.  Quality of her truth.  Time 98:72 Jl 5 '71
  Authors and editors.  Pub W 200:39 Jl 12 '71
  Orshefsky, M.  Hildegard rides again.  Life 71:36 Jl 23 '71
  Cox, R.  Berlin, your face has freckles.  Holiday 51:38 Ja '72
  Nolan, J. E.  Films on TV.  Films In R 24-4:221 Ap '73

KNIGHT, FUZZY
  Cohen, H.  Praising players of minor importance.  Cinema Dig
    3-6:12 Ap 24 '33

KNIGHT, JUNE
  Walker, B.  Sketch.  Motion Pic 45:60 Je '33
  Hall, H.  Her story.  Motion Pic 47:68 My '34
  Her rules for health and beauty.  Motion Pic 48:52 N '34
  French, W. F.  Sketch.  Movie Classic 7:66 N '34

KNIGHT, SANDRA
  How can she hide in public?  TV Guide 9-31:29 Ag 5 '61

KNIGHT, SHIRLEY
  (See: HOPKINS, SHIRLEY KNIGHT)

KNIGHT, TED
  Tadewurz Wladzui Konopka: (also known as) Ted Baxter and Ted
    Knight.  TV Guide 19-32:14 Ag 7 '71

KNOTTS, DON
  Minoff, P.  A new Allen's Alley.  Cue 26-25:11 Je 22 '57
  Poston to Knotts to Nye.  TV Guide 6-40:17 O 4 '58
  If they can help Don Knotts...  TV Guide 12-3:18 Ja 18 '64
  Raddatz, L.  Look who's a star.  TV Guide 18-43:26 O 24 '70

KNOWLDEN, MARILYN
  Sketch.   Photop 48:78 Jl '35

KNOWLES, PATRICK
  Whitehead, H.  Sketch.   Motion Pic 54:16 D '37
  Parsons, L. O.   Cosmop's citation for best supporting perform-
    ance of month.   Cosmop 120:55 Ja '46

KNOX, ELYSE
  Pin-up technique of Ray Jones.   Life 16:18 Mr 27 '44

KNUTSON, GUNILLA
  Hickey, N.  Not just another little shaver.   TV Guide 20-7:24 F
    12 '72

KOBE, GAIL
  All this and courage.   TV Guide 6-12:20 Mr 22 '58
  McClelland, D.   TV: where all that old-time glamour went.
    Film Fan Mo 75:11 S '67

KOHLER, FRED
  Ramsey, W.  Sketch.   Motion Pic Classic 29:57 Ap '29

KOHNER, SUSAN
  The screen answers back.   Films & Filming 8-8:12 My '62

KOLLMAR, RICHARD TOMPKINS
  Wiley, J. M.  At home with Dorothy and Dick.   Am Home 38:42
    N '47
  Bio.   Cur Bio F '52
  Dorothy and Dick's New York.   See various issues of Cosmopoli-
    tan to April 1953.
  Obit.   Cur Bio 32:46 F '71
    N. Y. Times p30 Ja 9 '71
    Newsweek 77:49 Ja 18 '71
    Time 97:47 Ja 18 '71

KOMACK, JIMMIE
  Hobson, D.  The renaissance man of the orthicon tube.   TV
    Guide 19-22:18 My 29 '71

KOOPMAN, WILLI
  Whitney, D.  The trouble with Willi.   TV Guide 17-13:26 Mr 29
    '69

KORENE, VERA
  Vera Korene.   Visages 29:entire issue N '38

KORMAN, HARVEY
  So there he was muttering Shakespeare in a freight yard.   TV
    Guide 13-31:24 My 22 '65
  Strengthening the weak and frightened child.   Photop 80-3:7 S '71
  Johnson, D.  King-size comic with a serious side.   After Dark
    7-2:46 Je '74

KORNMAN, MARY
  Maltin, L.  Our Gang; Our gang filmog.  Film Fan Mo 66:3 D
    '66
  Obit.  Classic Film Collect 40:58 Fall '73
    Screen World p236 '74

KORTNER, FRITZ
  Obit.  Film R p13 '71/72
    N. Y. Times p31 Jl 24 '70
    Same.  N. Y. Times Bio Ed Jl 24 '70
    Screen World 22:238 '71

KORWIN, CHARLES
  Bruce, J.  Romeo with a punch.  Silver S 16-5:48 Mr '46
  Korwin, C.  On the Berlin Express.  Silver S 18-4:62 F '48

KOSLECK, MARTIN
  Larkin, F.  Sketch.  Classic Film Collect 37:35 Win '72

KOSLOFF, THEODORE
  Obit.  Screen World 8:223 '57

KOVACS, ERNIE
  Kovacs, E.  Notes on TV.  Cue 21-30:6 Jl 26 '52
  Kovacs makes a new star... the TV camera.  TV Guide 2-42:A-2
    O 16 '54
  Minoff, P.  That krazy Kovacs.  Cue 25-28:12 Jl 14 '56
  Schickel, R.  The real Ernie Kovacs is standing up.  Show 1-3:
    81 D '61
  Rising star.  Film R p20 '60/61
  Talking about people.  Film 32:6 Sum '62
  Obit.  Film R p17 '62/63
  Gelanoy, T.  Ode to a bottomless bathtub.  Playboy 19-8:88 Ag
    '72

KOZELKOVA, YELENA
  Shenkman, A.  Two actresses.  CTVD 9-3:22 Spg '73

KRAFFTOWNA, BARBARA
  Donaldson, G.  Filmog.  Films In R 17-3:197 Mr '66

KRAUSS, WERNER
  Obit.  Screen World 11:220 '60

KRESKI, CONNIE
  Playmate review.  Playboy 16-1:187 Ja '69

KREUGER, KURT
  York, C.  Sketch.  Photop 28:20 D '45

KRIEGER, LEE
  Obit.  Screen World 19:235 '68

KRISTEN, MARTA
  Norwegian cinderella.   TV Guide 13-47:32 N 20 '65

KRISTENSEN, JANNI PIA
  Soft logic.   Oui 3-11:63 N '74

KRISTOFFERSON, KRIS
  McGregor, C.  I'm nobody's best friend.   N. Y. Times Bio Ed
    Jl 26 '70
  Hemphill, P.   Kristofferson is the new Nashville sound.   N. Y.
    Times Bio Ed D 6 '70
  Miller, E.   Interview.   Seventeen 30:130 Ap '71
  Axthelm, P.   Pilgrim's progress.   Newsweek 77:105 My 24 '71
  New minstrels.   Harp Baz 104:57 Je '71
  Hedgepeth, W.   Superstars, poets, pickers, prophets.   Look 35:
    30 Jl 13 '71
  Bloom, H.   Oxford ashtrays and Bobby McGee.   Circus 6-2:32
    N '71
  On the scene.   Playboy 20-7:169 Jl '73

KRUGER, OTTO
  Sketch.   Theatre 25:18 Ja '17
  Sketch.   Photop 44:60 N '33
  Service, F.   Interview.   Movie Classic 6:34 Mr '34
  Hall, G.   Sketch.   Motion Pic 47:48 Jl '34
  Hartley, K.   Interview.   Motion Pic 48:51 D '34
  Partial filmog.   Films & Filming 19-4:58 Ja 73
  Obit.   N. Y. Daily News p13 S 7 '74
    N. Y. Times Bio Ed p1278 S '74

KULKY, HENRY
  No wonder he can act.   TV Guide 8-19:29 My 7 '60
  Obit.   Screen World 17:238 '66

KULLE, JARL
  Filmmaking in Sweden.   Interview 1-7:25 n. d.

KULP, NANCY
  Hathaway of the hillbillies.   TV Guide 11-33:27 Ag 17 '63
  They're still single.   TV Guide 13-9:22 F 27 '65

KUPCHENKO, IRINA
  Note.   Int Film G 10:336 '70

KURSTON, ROBERT
  Hoaglin, J. L.   He's headed for Hollywood.   Hollywood Stu 7-7:
    22 N '72

KURTY, LEE
  Hano, A.   Lee Kurty is a klutz.   TV Guide 14-8:14 F 19 '66

KURTZ, MARCIA JEAN
  Stasio, M.   The stars of tomorrow on stage today.   Cue 38-9:9
    Mr 1 '69

KUWA, GEORGE
    Connor, E.   The 6 Charlie Chans; Chan filmog.   Films In R 6-
        1:23 Ja '55

KWAN, NANCY
    Rising star.   Film R p32 '61/62

KYO, MICHIKO
    Richie, D.   The face of '63--Japan.   Films & Filming 9-10:15
        Jl '63

KYSER, KAY
    Franchey, J. R.   The merry music maker.   Silver S 11-2:34 D
        '40
    Professor of mirth.   Lions R 3-2:no p# Ja '44
    Manners, M. J.   No time for romance.   Silver S 14-10:44 Ag
        '44
    College of musical knowledge.   TV Guide 2-33:20 Ag 14 '54


LAAGE, BARBARA
    Bio note.   Unifrance 23:10 F '53

LA BADIE, FLORENCE
    Sketch.   Blue Book 19:27 My '14
    Interview.   Blue Book 19:909 S '14
    Kellette, J. W.   Sketch.   Motion Pic 8:111 Ja '15
    How to get into motion pictures.   Motion Pic Classic 2:22 Jl '16
    Obit.   Dram Mir 77:18 O 20 '17

LADD, ALAN
    Sketch.   Life 12:48 Je 22 '42
    Sketch.   Harp Baz 76:22 Jl '42
    Mook, D.   A Ladd on top of the ladder.   Silver S 12-12:42 O '42
    Trotter, M.   Prediction for 1944.   Photop 24:27 Ja '44
    Dudley, F.   Pattern for a perfect marriage.   Silver S 15-4:32
        F '45
    My Easter prayer.   Photop 26:43 Ap '45
    My favorite possession.   Photop 26:56 My '45
    Open letter to movie magazines.   Silver S 15-10:28 Ag '45
    What changed my life.   Photop 28:60 My '46
    Littlefield, C.   Alan's new philosophy.   Silver S 17-3:44 Ja '47
    Parsons, L. O.   Cosmop's citation for best performance of
        month.   Cosmop 126:13 F '49
    Awarded Photoplay's gold medal.   Photop 35:57 My '49
    Maddox, B.   Things keep happening to Alan.   Silver S 19-7:26
        My '49
    Ladd, A.   Those I'll never forget.   Silver S 20-4:24 F '50
    My favorite role.   Film R p16 '50
    Freeman, M.   Alan's no mystery man.   Silver S 21-4:26 F '51
    Maddox, B.   Women I admire most.   Silver S 22-9:22 Jl '52
    Oppenheimer, P. J.   Is it a life of Riley?   Silver S 23-9:29

Jl '53
Todd, W.   Alan Ladd.   Films In R 9-9:543 N '58
Letters.   Films In R 15-5:315 My '64
Letters.   Films In R 15-6:381 Je/ Jl '64
Obit.   Film R p42 '64/ 65
    Screen World 16:223 '65
The love teams.   Screen Greats 1-2:10 Sum '71
Pin-up of the past.   Films & Filming 18-3:70 D '71
Fox, J.   The good bad Ladd.   Films & Filming 18-9:28 Je '72
Fox, J.   Spirit of the West.   Films & Filming 18-10:38 Jl '72

LADD, DAVID
Filmog.   Films & Filming 18-11:60 Ag '72

LADD, DIANE
Out of the chorus.   TV Guide 7-32:24 Ag 8 '59

LAFAYETTE, ANDREE
Carr, H.   The girl who plays Trilby.   Classic 16:34 Ag '23

LA FOLLETTE, FOLA
Pierre Curie.   New Rep 40:sup7 O 1 '24
Obit.   N.Y. Times p47 F 18 '70

LAFORET, MARIE
Bio note.   Unifrance 50:12 Jl/ S '59
L'exploration de Laforet.   Esquire 55:106 Ap '61
Like Europe, Marie is strummin' along.   Life 54:50 F 1 '63

LAHR, BERT
Underhill, D.   Hamlet of burleycue.   Screen Book 22-1:82 Ag '39
He knew them when.   Lions R 1-9:no p# My '42
Lahr the lion-hunter.   Lions R 3-3:no p# Ap '44
Lahr upstages himself in a new comedy.   Show 3-1:48 Ja '63
A comedians' comedian.   Cue 33-6:10 F 8 '64
Notes and comment.   New Yorker 43:37 D 16 '67
Obit.   Brit Bk Yr 1968:593 '68
    Cur Bio 29:46 F '68
    Same.   Cur Bio Yrbk 1968:457 '69
    N.Y. Times p1 D 5 '67
    Newsweek 70:70 D 18 '67
    Time 90:104 D 15 '67
Wolff, G.   Laugh, clown, laugh.   Newsweek 74:123 N 24 '69
Where the laughs came from.   Time 94:104 D 12 '69

LAINE, FRANKIE
Masin, H. L.   Real gone guy.   Scholastic 53:23 Ja 5 '49
He has learned how to put on a show.   Time 53:77 F 7 '49
Feels good that way.   Time 53:77 F 14 '49
Jennings, D.   That lucky old Laine.   Colliers 126:28 Ag 12 '50
Favor for a friend.   Time 64:49 Ag 16 '54
Jennings, D.   Case of the screaming troubador.   Sat Eve Post
    227:18 D 11 '54

Godfrey's pinch hitter.  TV Guide 3-34:13 Ag 20 '55
Laine and Littler inc.  Life 40:163 My 14 '56
Pitts, M. R.  Popular singers on the screen; filmog.  Film Fan
    Mo 114:26 D '70
Filmog.  Films & Filming 19-5:58 F '73

LAKE, ALICE
Remont, F.  Interview.  Motion Pic Classic 9:22 D '19
North, G.  Sketch.  Photop 17:46 My '20
Robinson, R. D.  Interview.  Motion Pic 19:42 Je '20
Interview.  Dram Mir p227 Ag 7 '20
Peltret, E.  Interview.  Motion Pic Classic 12:32 Ap '21
Howe, H.  Interview.  Motion Pic 23:36 F '22
Sketch.  Motion Pic Classic 21:68 Ap '25

LAKE, ARTHUR
Belfrage, C.  Sketch.  Motion Pic 39:82 Mr '30
York, C.  Sketch.  Photop 37:68 My '30
French, J.  Interview.  Photop 38:51 O '30
Anecdote.  Am Mag 142:92 Ag '46
My luckiest day.  Cosmop 123:175 D '47

LAKE, JANET
Her beauty makes men stare.  TV Guide 9-15:8 Ap 15 '61

LAKE, VERONICA
Hamilton, S.  Sketch.  Photop 18:36 Mr '41
Vallee, W. L.  Lady villain.  Silver S 11-8:44 Je '41
Sketch.  Am Mag 132:69 S '41
Her hair.  Life 11:58 N 24 '41
Reid, J.  Veronica lets her hair down.  Silver S 12-9:22 Jl '42
Sketch.  Harp Baz 76:89 Ag '42
All this and Veronica too.  Cue 11-43:14 O 24 '42
Franchey, J. R.  Little Miss One Eye.  Silver S 13-4:22 F '43
Sketch.  Life 14:39 Mr 8 '43
Like women and make them like you.  Cosmop 114:50 Je '43
Bangs, B.  Problem child with good intentions.  Silver S 15-5:
    32 Mr '45
Letter from Liza.  Silver S 15-7:28 My '45
Watkins, W.  The home life of a glamour queen.  Silver S 16-11:
    40 S '46
Howard, M.  The amazing de Toths.  Silver S 17-9:43 Jl '47
Wilson, E.  What love can do.  Silver S 18-6:36 Ap '48
Arkadin.  Film clips.  Sight & Sound 38-2:105 Spg '69
Klemesrud, J.  For Veronica Lake, the past is something to
    write about.  N. Y. Times p38 Mr 10 '71
    Same.  N. Y. Times Bio Ed Mr 10 '71
The love teams.  Screen Greats 1-2:10 Sum '71
Obit.  Classic Film Collect (reprint N. Y. Times) 40:59 Fall '73
    Films & Filming 20-2:80 N '73
    N. Y. Times Bio Ed p1183 Jl '73
    Screen World p236 '74
    Washington Post pC8 Jl 8 '73
Braun, E.  Hollywood comet.  Films & Filming 20-8:30 My '74

LA MARR, BARBARA
  Goldbeck, W.  Sketch.  Motion Pic 23:43 Jl '22
  Goldbeck, W.  Sketch.  Motion Pic 24:64 N '22
  Ferguson, H.  Interview.  Classic 19:34 My '24
  Wilson, B.  Interview.  Met Mag 59:44 Ag '24
  Home of.  Classic 20:40 D '24
  de Revere, F. V.  Face analysis of.  Motion Pic 28:42 Ja '25
  The business of being a vampire.  Motion Pic 29:43 Mr '25
  Roberts, W. A.  Sketch.  Motion Pic 30:71 Ag '25
  Hamilton, F.  Sketch.  Motion Pic 31:63 F '26
  Ennis, B.  Sketch.  Motion Pic 37:40 F '29
  Calhoun, D.  What if she had lived?  Motion Pic 40:28 D '30
  In memoriam.  Motion Pic 45:52 Je '33
  Lee, R.  She walks in beauty like the night.  Classic Film Col-
    lect 35:35 Sum '72

LAMARR, HEDY
  Story of.  Life 5:27 Jl 25 '38
  McFee, F.  Garbo's headache.  Screen Book 21-5:26 D '38
  Joseph, R.  Hedy's here.  Silver S 9-2:34 D '38
  Wilson, E.  Lamarr and the angry blondes.  Silver S 9-6:16 Ap
    '39
  Karel, P.  They took this woman.  Screen Book 21-10:25 My
    '39
  Fletcher, A. W.  Story of.  Photop 53:28 Je '39
  Hall, G.  Marriage and Lamarr.  Silver S 9-9:18 Jl '39
  Sketch.  Life 7:38 Ag 28 '39
  McFee, F.  Lamarr and Bob Taylor--lovers.  Screen Book 22-1:
    58 Ag '39
  Bio note; filmog.  Movies & People 2:21 '40
  Trotter, M.  Astrological forecast.  Photop 18:76 F '41
  Hall, G.  I live for today.  Silver S 11-4:22 F '41
  Lamarr profile.  Lions R 1-4:no p# D '41
  The girl on the cover.  Cue 11-18:1 My 2 '42
  Lamarr, H.  Escape from glamor.  Lions R 1-9:no p# My '42
  I, Hedy Lamarr, confess...  Lions R 1-11/12:no p# Jl/Ag '42
  Hall, G.  Has Hedy changed?  Silver S 12-10:24 Ag '42
  Getting acquainted with Tondelayo.  Lions R 2-2:no p# N '42
  Her men friends.  Photop 22:60 Ja '43
  The trouble with men.  Cosmop 114:57 Ja '43
  Hendricks, H.  Loneliest woman in Hollywood.  Silver S 13-4:26
    F '43
  Her wedding.  Photop 23:98 Ag '43
  Hedy Lamarr--American.  Lions R 3-2:no p# Ja '44
  Autobiographical.  Photop 26:54 Mr '44
  Wilson, E.  Informal chat with Hedy.  Silver S 14-9:22 Jl '44
  De Rig, M.  Do you interest men?  Silver S 15-4:38 F '45
  Her baby.  Life 19:42 O 1 '45
  Maddox, B.  The drastic change in Hedy.  Silver S 19-1:22 N
    '48
  Birmingham, S.  Would you believe I was once a famous star?
    It's the truth.  N. Y. Times Bio Ed Ag 23 '70
  Der Krauts.  Screen Greats 1-2:58 Sum '71

Young, C.  Hedy Lamarr.  Films In R 23-1:62 Ja '72
Luft, H.  Letter.  Films In R 23-4:255 Ap '72
Edison, B.  Interview.  Films In R 25-6:350 Je/Jl '74

## LAMAS, FERNANDO
Balling, F. D.  You can dream of Lamas.  Silver S 22-8:30 Je '52
Shane, D.  A not-so-lousey Latin lover.  Silver S 23-7:24 My '53
Sheridan, M.  Hollywood's most criticized romance.  Silver S 23-10:29 Ag '53
Bruce, J.  The trouble with men is women.  Silver S 24-1:36 N '53

## LAMBERT, TOBY JOSEPH
(Also known as SKINNY in the Our Gang Comedies)
Obit.  Classic Film Collect 36:extra 2 Fall '72

## LAMONT, LILLIAN
Hunt, J. L.  Her marriage.  Photop 50:30 N '36

## LAMOUR, DOROTHY
Morgan, L.  Beauty meets success.  Silver S 7-11:27 S '37
Gardner, M.  Her story.  Motion Pic 54:46 N '37
Van Wyck, C.  Interview.  Photop 52:10 D '38
Cheatham, M.  What really makes a woman dangerous?  Silver S 10-1:24 N '39
Manners, M. J.  Lamour and the stage door Johnnies of Hollywood.  Silver S 10-12:22 O '40
Walker, H. L.  Sketch.  Photop 54:41 O '40
Bio note; filmog.  Movies & People 2:21 '40
French, W. F.  Patti learned a lot from Dottie.  Silver S 11-8:38 Je '41
Her portrait a favorite pin-up with the army.  Life 11:34 Jl 7 '41
Dudley, F.  Interview.  Photop 19:59 Jl '41
Reid, J.  Lamour and allure.  Silver S 12-4:24 F '42
The trouble with men.  Cosmop 114:59 My '43
Harris, E.  Story of.  Cosmop 116:60 F '44
Manners, M. J.  Dottie tells on Bob and Bing.  Silver S 14-6:30 Ap '44
Hall, G.  Crossroads for Dottie.  Silver S 14-11:32 S '44
Wilson, E.  Dottie gets her wish.  Silver S 15-7:30 My '45
Should a woman tell her age?  Photop 28:52 Ap '46
Liza.  Perfect role for Dottie.  Silver S 16-9:37 Jl '46
Palmer, C.  With a heart full of love.  Silver S 17-10:38 Ag '47
Maddox, B.  The typical girl next door.  Silver S 18-12:36 O '48
Baer, M. M.  A riping time for Dottie.  Silver S 21-1:40 N '50
Hall, G.  Lamour's miracle.  Silver S 22-5:26 Mr '52
Minoff, P.  The world is their oyster.  Cue 21-49:16 D 6 '52
Hamilton, J.  Where, oh where are the beautiful girls?  Look 34-22:64 N 3 '70
Here's to the ladies.  Screen Greats 1-2:30 Sum '71

Catching up with Dorothy Lamour.   Mod Screen 63-12:18 D '71
Lamour, D.  This was my favorite role.   Movie Dig 1-2:70 Mr
'72
Mrs. Wm. Howard always carries a sarong.   Photop 82-1:60 Jl
'72
Chierichetti, D.  Dorothy Lamour today; filmog.   Film Fan Mo
133/134:3 Jl/Ag '72
Thompson, K.  Queen of the sarong.   Films Illus 3-32:318 Ap
'74

LAMPERT, ZOHRA
Person of promise.   Films & Filming 7-7:23 Ap '61

LANCASTER, BURT
Parsons, L. O.   Cosmop's citation for best supporting role of
month.   Cosmop 121:73 O '46
Bio sketch.   Vogue 111:143 Mr 15 '48
Graham, S.  Sketch.   Photop 35:64 My '49
My favorite role.   Film R p28 '51/52
Asher, J.  Diary of a beachcomber.   Silver S 23-5:34 Mr '53
Zunser, J.  Sweet smell of success.   Cue 26-23:11 Je 8 '57
Burt force.   Time 97:97 Ap 26 '71
Cutts, J.  Long shot.   Films & Filming 18-3:26 D '71
Williams, J.  Between takes; filmog.   Films Illus 1-16:12 O '72
Gow, G.  Interview; filmog.   Films & Filming 19-4:14 Ja '73
Lancaster on...   Films Illus 3-27:92 S '73

LANCHESTER, ELSA
Grein, J. T.  Criticism of her work.   Ill Lon N 170:388 Mr 5
'27
Lanchester's spice.   Lions R 3-1:no p# S '43

LANCTOT, MICHELINE
Keil, M.  On acting.   Motion p35 S/O '74

LANDAU, MARTIN
Conversation with the Landaus.   TV Guide 16-18:30 My 4 '68
Ephron, N.  Marriage: impossible?  Good House 167:60 N '68
Filmog.   Films & Filming 19-11:58 Ag '73

LANDEAU, GEORGIA
Young hopefuls do bit parts now.   TV Guide 1-7:20 My 15 '53

LANDERS, HARRY
Bette Davis made a phone call.   TV Guide 11-39:12 S 28 '63

LANDI, ELISSA
Grayson, C.  Sketch.   Motion Pic 42:66 Ag '31
Evans, W.  Elusive Elissa.   Silver S 2-2:35 D '31
Hamilton, S.  Sketch.   Movie Classic 1:17 F '32
Her story about her grandmother.   Movie Classic 2:42 Ap '32
Hall, G.  Interview.   Motion Pic 44:26 D '32
Grant, J.  Interview.   Movie Classic 5:48 N '33

Lee, S. Sues for divorce. Movie Classic 6:41 Ag '34
Secrets of the dressing table. Motion Pic 49:62 F '35
Hutchinson, H. Interview. Movie Classic 8:18 Ag '35
Piper, B. M. Filmog. Films In R 24-6:382 Je/Jl '73
Bookey, G. D. Elissa Landi; filmog. Films In R 25-5:313 My
    '74

LANDI, MARLA
    Gray, M. Unknown star. Films & Filming 3-12:11 S '57

LANDIN, HOPE
    Obit. Screen World p236 '74

LANDIS, CAROLE
    Reid, J. No advice to the lovelorn. Silver S 11-5:36 Mr '41
    Sketch. Life 10:59 Je 30 '41
    Teltscher, H. O. Analysis of handwriting. Photop 19:63 Je '41
    Hall, G. Interview. Photop 20:36 D '41
    Vallee, W. L. If I were Victor Mature. Silver S 12-9:26 Jl
        '42
    Proctor, K. I don't want to be an angel. Silver S 13-2:30 D
        '42
    Fletcher, A. W. Interview. Photop 23:22 Je '43
    My secret dream. Photop 23:55 O '43
    Her ideas about love. Photop 23:40 N '43
    Hall, G. Meet the new Landis. Silver S 14-1:26 N '43
    Marsh, P. Now it's for keeps. Silver S 16-9:52 Jl '46
    Landis, C. Do you think I was wrong? Silver S 17-11:53 S '47
    29 years ago in Life. Life 72:20 F 4 '72
    Crivello, K. Carole Landis; filmog. Film Fan Mo 149:3 N '73

LANDIS, CULLEN
    Hunt, J. Play ball. Photop 16-6:88 N '19
    Schermerhorn, J. One thing or another. Classic Film Collect
        (reprint Detroit News Mag.) 18:37 Sum '67
    Goldsworthy, J. The Cullen Landis story; filmog. Classic Film
        Collect 27:6 Spg/Sum '70

LANDIS, JESSIE ROYCE
    Lewis, E. The London stage. Cue 25-6:14 F 11 '56
    Obit. N.Y. Times p36 F 3 '72
        Same. N.Y. Times Bio Ed F 3 '72
    Newsweek 79:86 F 14 '72

LANDIS, JOHN
    Winogura, D. Interview. Cinefantastique 3-1:24 Fall '73

LANDON, MICHAEL
    Javelin thrower on horseback. TV Guide 10-1:15 Ja 6 '62
    Lewis, R. W. He plays cowboys and indians for $13.00 a week.
        TV Guide 15-29:17 Jl 22 '67

Happiness is a slice of salami.   TV Guide 17-48:25 N 29 '69
Photoplay forum.   Photop 80-4:8 O '71
Our baby must live.   Photop 80-4:86 O '71
The new girl in his life.   Mod Screen 66-5:60 My '72
Wilkins, B.   Little Joe in 'Little house' is a big man now.
   People 2-16:32 O 14 '74
Davidson, B.   General contractor.   TV Guide 22-49:36 D 7 '74

LANDOWSKA, YONA
   The beautiful unknown; interview.   Photop 7-4:118 Mr '15

LANE, ABBE
   A singer of dimension.   TV Guide 5-17:8 Ap 27 '57
   Lardner, R.   Those madcap Cugats.   Coronet 44:118 Ag '58
   The Abbe Lane story.   TV Guide 13-11:20 Mr 13 '65

LANE, ADELE
   How she became a photoplayer.   Motion Pic 8:77 Ja '15

LANE, ALLAN ("Rocky")
   Would they become famous stars or forgotten faces.   Silver S
   2-2:36 D '31
   Quigg, M.   Allan's Lane to fame.   Screen Book 21-1:36 Ag '38
   Obit.   Classic Film Collector 42:35 Spg '74
      Screen World p236 '74

LANE, JOCELYN
   Heiress apparent.   Playboy 13-9:118 S '66

LANE, LOLA
   Hall, G.   Sketch.   Motion Pic Classic 30:27 Ja '30
   Her romance.   Photop 40:42 N '31
   Standish, J.   Her marriage.   Movie Classic 1:40 D '31
   Sharon, M.   The love of Lew and Lola.   Silver S 2-3:20 Ja '32
   Bio note; filmog.   Movies & People 2:21 '40
   (See also: LANE SISTERS)

LANE, LUPINO
   Calhoun, D.   Interview.   Motion Pic 34:30 Ag '27
   Barcia, R.   His horoscope.   Theatre World 37:28 Je '42
   Sketch.   Theatre World 37:18 S '42
   Sketch.   Theatre World 39:30 O '43
   Obit.   Screen World 11:220 '60

LANE, PRISCILLA
   Sketch.   Life 5:62 S 12 '38
   Talmey, A.   Sketch.   Vogue 92:74 O 1 '38
   Holland, J.   The Lanes fight it out.   Screen Book 21-12:26 Jl
   '39
   Lane, J.   Priscilla's romance test.   Silver S 9-10:14 Ag '39

Ducas, D.  Home of.  Photop 53:40 D '39
Bio note; filmog.  Movies & People 2:22 '40
Mulvey, K.  Sketch.  Womans Home C 68:21 F '41
In Million dollar baby.  Life 10:60 Je 16 '41
Manners, M. J.  Wedding bells that didn't ring.  Silver S 12-7:
   26 My '42
Palmborg, R. P.  Sketch.  Photop 21:34 S '42
(See also: LANE SISTERS)

LANE, ROSEMARY
   Wood, V.  "R" is for Rosemary.  Screen Book 20-4:40 My '38
   Sketch.  Life 5:62 S 12 '38
   Holland, J.  The Lanes fight it out.  Screen Book 21-12:26 Jl
      '39
   Ducas, D.  Home of.  Photop 53:40 D '39
   Bio note; filmog.  Movies & People 2:22 '40
   Mulvey, K.  Sketch.  Womans Home C 68:21 F '41
   Teltscher, H. O.  Analysis of her handwriting.  Photop 19:62
      Je '41
   Walker, H. L.  Pointer on popularity.  Photop 21:48 Jl '42
   Wilson, E.  The strange case of Rosemary Lane.  Silver S 13-
      5:42 Mr '43
   Obit.  N. Y. Times p40 N 27 '74
   (See also: LANE SISTERS)

LANE, SARA
   Raddatz, L.  Her skirts cover her knees.  TV Guide 15-25:24
      Je 24 '67

LANE SISTERS
   (LOLA, PRISCILLA, ROSEMARY)
   Maddox, B.  Three Lanes to fame.  Silver S 8-7:26 My '38
   Vallee, W. L.  Why the Lane Sisters broke up.  Silver S 11-5:
      26 Mr '41
   Lane, C. B.  Five daughters and a prayer.  Liberty 1-4:70 Spg
      '72

LANG, ALOIS
   Obit.  N. Y. Times p28 D 24 '71

LANG, BARBARA
   Crivello, K.  The mystery of Barbara Lang; filmog.  Classic
      Film Collect 30:41 Spg '71

LANG, JUNE
   Schwarzkopf, J.  Sketch.  Motion Pic 51:63 My '36
   Sketch.  Movie Classic 10:15 My '36
   Gillespie-Hayck, A.  Venus under contract.  Silver S 7-3:25 Ja
      '37
   Zeitlin, I.  Interview.  Motion Pic 53:37 Jl '37

LANGDON, HARRY
   Curran, D.  Sketch.  Motion Pic Classic 21:62 Jl '25

Matzen, M.  Sketch.  Motion Pic 32:36 D '26
Herzog, D.  Sketch.  Motion Pic 34:18 O '27
The serious side of comedy making.  Theatre 46:22 D '27
Hall, L.  Sketch.  Photop 36:59 Je '29
Lee, S.  Sketch.  Motion Pic 44:56 Ja '33
Obit.  Cur Bio 6 '45
Hall, L.  Hey! hey! Harry's coming back.  Photop 36-1:59 Je
   '59
Taylor, J. R.  A Harry Langdon revelation (reprint from Lon-
   don Times) Classic Film Collect 19:21 Fall/Win '67
Schonert, V. L.  Harry Langdon; filmog.  Films In R 18-7:470
   O '67
Letters.  Films In R 18-9:583 N '67
Gilliatt, P.  Current cinema.  New Yorker 47:130 Ap 24 '71
Leary, R.  Capra and Langdon.  Film Comment 8-4:15 N/D '72
Truscott, H.  Harry Langdon.  Silent Pic 13:2 Win/Spg '72
Watz, E.  The unsung genius.  Classic Film Collect 43:33 Sum
   '74

LANGDON, SUE ANN
Sean Connery strikes again (pictorial).  Playboy 13-7:75 Jl '66
How's your orange juice, Arnie?  TV Guide 19-46:24 N 13 '71
The Christmas that taught me the meaning of love.  Mod Screen
   66-1:48 Ja '72
Favorite animal stories.  Mod Screen 66-11:34 N '72
Cooking with a star.  Mod Screen 66-12:43 D '72

LANGE, HOPE
Rising star.  Film R p22 '59/60
Raddatz, L.  Mrs. Muir, Mrs. Van Dyke and Hope Lange.  TV
   Guide 20-17:38 Ap 22 '72
Glenn Ford brings Hope Lange home to meet the family.  Mod
   Screen 66-4:55 Ap '72
The best Christmas of my life.  Photop 83-1:27 Ja '73
To each his home.  TV Guide 22-3:12 Ja 19 '74

LANGELLA, FRANK
Gussow, M.  Film success spurs Langella's career.  N. Y.
   Times Bio Ed Ag 19 '70
Robin, S.  The essential Frank Langella.  After Dark 12-4:46
   Ag '70
On the scene.  Playboy 18-11:198 N '71

LANGFORD, FRANCES
Sullivan, E.  Hollywood's most amazing love story.  Silver S
   10-11:34 S '40
Manners, M. J.  The truth about Langford and Jon Hall.  Silver
   S 14-3:24 Ja '44
Entertains service men.  Life 16:122 Je 5 '44
On overseas tour with Bob Hope.  Life 17:41 Ag 7 '44
Schwartz, W.  Filmog.  Films In R 17-8:599 O '66

LANPHIER, JAMES F.
  Obit.  Screen World 21:238 '70

LANSBURY, ANGELA
  Angela in wonderland.  Lions R 3-3(sup):no p# Ap '44
  Bio sketch.  Vogue 106:109 N 15 '45
  Haas, D. B.  Good little bad girl.  Silver S 16-3:44 Ja '46
  Sketch.  Am Mag 142:123 Ag '46
  Vallee, W. L.  Angela wants the moon.  Silver S 17-9:58 Jl '47
  Shaw, P.  I married an angel.  Silver S 20-6:30 Ap '50
  Bio.  Cur Bio 28:21 S '67
    Same.  Cur Bio Yrbk 1967:237 '68
  Salute of the week.  Cue 38-7:1 F 15 '69
  Clein, H.  The real people featuring Hollywood's new breed of
    character actors.  Show 1-8:14 Jl 9 '70
  Irving, C.  Prime of Miss Angela Lansbury.  McCalls 99:12 O
    '71
  Castell, D.  She came, she saw, she conquered.  Filmog.
    Films Illus 1-5:18 N '71
  Gow, G.  I was a young woman of parts; interview; filmog.
    Films & Filming 18-3:18 D '71
  A true story of faith and courage.  Mod Screen 66-5:48 My '72
  Gilling, T.  Safety zone.  Sight & Sound 41-3:140 Sum '72
  Gow, G.  Interview.  Plays & Players 20-10:16 Jl '73
  Leech, M. T.  Sing out, Angela.  After Dark 6-6:21 O '73
  Lansbury on Mame and other dames.  Films Illus 3-29:184 N '73
  Porter, J.  Angela Lansbury takes a turn at riveting Rose.  Cue
    43-35:2 S 16 '74
  Watters, J.  A thorny Rose by Angela Lansbury.  People 2-12:
    48 S 16 '74

LANSING, JOI
  Obit.  Classic Film Collect (reprint L.A. Times) 36:extra 2
    Fall '72
    N.Y. Times Bio Ed p1503 Ag '72
  Akuda, T.  Remember Joi Lansing; filmog.  Classic Film Col-
    lect 43:38 Sum '73

LANSING, ROBERT
  The workaday cop.  TV Guide 10-17:7 Ap 28 '62
  Photop forum.  Photop 81-6:42 Je '72

LANZA, MARIO
  Hollywood musical presents much publicized young tenor.  Mus
    Amer 69:24 O '49
  Lanza, M.  I learned to sing by accident.  Etude 67:9 D '49
  The great Caruso.  Cue 20-16:12 Ap 21 '51
  Lanza, M.  The 12 loves of my life.  Silver S 21-8:36 Je '51
  Lanza, M.  What really makes a woman irresistible?  Silver S
    22-8:20 Je '52
  Obit.  Screen World 11:220 '60

LA PLANTE, BEATRICE
Squier, E. L.  Interview.  Motion Pic Classic 11:32 S '20

LA PLANTE, LAURA
Kibbe, V.  Sketch.  Motion Pic Classic 23:34 Ap '26
St. Johns, I.  Interview.  Photop 31:37 My '27
Bartol, M.  Interview.  Motion Pic 34:66 N '27
Tully, J.  Her rise to stardom.  Vanity Fair 29:71 Ja '28
Belfrage, C.  To play in Show Boat.  Motion Pic Classic 28:40
    O '28
Conti, M.  Shopping with.  Motion Pic 38:68 Ag '29
Palmborg, R. P.  How she handles her money.  Motion Pic 39:
    74 Ap '30
Summers, M.  Laura La Plante:  reminescences on her real
    life.  Filmograph 2-3:22 '71
Uselton, R. A.  The Wampus baby stars.  Films In R 21-2:73
    F '70
Summers, M.  Her reel life; filmog.  Filmograph 2-4:20 '72
Letters.  Filmograph 2-4:44 '72
Summers, M.  ... exhibits sculpting work.  Filmograph 3-1:46
    '72

LARKEN, SHEILA
When you're 26, bright and involved.  TV Guide 19-3:20 Ja 16
    '71

LARKIN, GEORGE
Welsh, R. E.  Work of.  Motion Pic Classic 3:47 Ja '17
Lincks, P.  Interview.  Motion Pic 15:123 Je '18

LARKIN, JOHN
They wrote him out of town.  TV Guide 9-50:26 D 16 '61
Obit.  Screen World 17:238 '66

LA ROCQUE, ROD
Six feet, nineteen.  Photop 14-6:41 N '18
Notice of.  Motion Pic Classic 8:48 Ag '19
Fletcher, A. W.  Interview.  Motion Pic 19:54 Jl '20
Hall, G.  Interview.  Motion Pic Classic 12:24 Mr '21
Sketch.  Photop 25:76 My '24
Carlisle, H.  Interview.  Motion Pic 27:25 My '24
de Revere, F. V.  Face analysis of.  Motion Pic 29:64 My '25
Roberts, W. A.  Sketch.  Motion Pic 29:44 Je '25
Calhoun, D.  Interview.  Motion Pic 31:61 Mr '27
Home of.  Photop 31:68 Ap '27
Biery, R.  Interview.  Photop 33:48 Mr '28
Cummings, A.  Sketch.  Motion Pic Classic 27:26 My '28
Obit.  Classic Film Collect 25:extra 2 (reprint N.Y. Times)
    Fall '69
    Film R p15 '70/71
    N.Y. Times p47 O 17 '69
    Newsweek 74:86 O 27 '69
    Screen World 21:238 '70

Time 94:99 O 24 '69
Joynson, E. A.   Rod La Rocque; filmog.   Films In R 25-3:189
    Mr '74

LA ROY, RITA
    Horton, H.   Interview.   Motion Pic Classic 32:30 F '31

LARSEN, KEITH
    Young whip snapper.   TV Guide 4-38:8 S 22 '56
    A professional failure takes the plunge.   TV Guide 8-53:25 D 31
        '60

LARSON, SUSAN
    Foster, C.   Story of.   Photop 23:52 S '43

LA RUE, DANNY
    Coveney, M.   Interview.   Plays & Players 21-4:24 Ja '74

LA RUE, JACK
    Cohen, H.   Praising players of minor importance.   Cinema Dig
        3-6:12 Ap 24 '33
    Donnell, D.   Work of.   Movie Classic 4:31 My '33
    Calhoun, D.   Interview.   Motion Pic 45:49 Jl '33
    Orr, J.   He makes his own breaks.   Silver S 3-9:43 Jl '33
    Hall, H.   Attempt on his life.   Movie Classic 7:42 N '34

LASSER, LOUISE
    Alpern, D. M.   Lasser went 'Bananas. '   N. Y. Times Bio Ed
        Jl 11 '71

LATELL, LYLE
    Obit.   Screen World 19:235 '68

LATIMER, CHERIE
    Clein, H.   Dream girl from Alex in wonderland.   Show 1-12:29
        S 3 '70

LATIMORE, FRANK
    Should teenagers marry?   Photop 30:67 D '46

LAUGHLIN, TOM
    Kroll, J.   Out of the sun.   Newsweek 78:76 Ag 30 '71
    Ostroff, R.   The following is NOT an interview with Billy Jack.
        Take One 3-11:24 My/Je '72
    Siminoski, T.   The Billy Jack phenomenon.   Velvet Light 13:36
        Fall '74

LAUGHTON, CHARLES
    Sketch.   Theatre Guild 9:26 Mr '32
    Sketch.   Photop 42:71 N '32
    Grayson, C.   Sketch.   Motion Pic 44:33 D '32
    Bahn, C.   Jannings-Laughton duel?   Cinema Dig 3-5:9 Ap 17 '33
    Reynolds, Q.   Interview.   Colliers 95:9 F 2 '35

Putnam, N. W.  His secret.  Movie Classic 8:38 Ap '35
Fender, R.  Interview.  Motion Pic 49:19 My '35
His makeup as Rembrandt.  Photop 51:6 F '37
Vallee, W. L.  Villainy as you like it.  Silver S 10-5:24 Mr '40
He looks at preview of They knew what they wanted.  Life 9:47
    S 30 '40
Bio note; filmog.  Movies & People 2:22 '40
Admirable admiral.  Lions R 2-3:no p# D '42
Laughing at Laughton.  Lions R 3-1:no p# S '43
Speaking of spooks.  Lions R 3-4(sup):no p# Jl '44
His art collection.  Vogue 105:136 F 1 '45
Bartlett, N.  Charles Laughton.  Film 35:22 Spg '63
Sarris, A.  Oddities and one shots.  Film Cult 28:45 Spg '63
Obit.  Film R p31 '63/64
Plagemann, B.  My most unforgettable character.  Read Dig
    91:127 D '67

LAUREL, STAN
Walker, H. L.  Interview.  Motion Pic Classic 31:70 Je '30
Peet, C.  Sketch.  Outlook 155:632 Ag 20 '30
Glaze, A.  Divorce rumors.  Movie Classic 3:28 F '33
Moak, E. R.  Bio sketch.  Photop 44:40 Je '33
Bio note; filmog.  Movies & People 2:22 '40
Hardy, O.  My stooge.  Lions R 2-4:no p# Ap '43
Meet a gentleman.  8mm Collect 7:9 F '64
Bacon, J.  Stan Laurel at 70: I'm all washed up.  8mm Collect
    11:10 Spg '65
Stan Laurel, forgotten man of Hollywood.  8mm Collect 11:11
    Spg '65
Stan Laurel suffers fatal heart attack.  8mm Collect 11:11 Spg
    '65
Thomson, B.  Was the salute to Stan Laurel really a salute?
    8mm Collect 14:30 Spg '66
Mazurki, J.  Stan's daughter recalls comic.  Classic Film Col-
    lect 32:53 Fall '71
(See also:  LAUREL AND HARDY)

LAUREL AND HARDY
(Stan Laurel and Oliver Hardy)
Hurley, J.  Laurel & Hardy editorialized...  Cinema Dig 1-6:8
    Jl 25 '32
Robinson, D.  The lighter people.  Sight & Sound 24-1:39 Jl/S
    '54
Barnes, P.  Cuckoo.  Films & Filming 6-11:15 Ag '60
Reynolds, R.  Creative craftsmen taken for granted.  8mm Col-
    lect 3:3 D 31 '62
Maher, R.  The twiddle, the look, the cry; how they happened.
    8mm Collect 7:10 F '64
The screen's funniest comics.  8mm Collect 7:8 F '64
Of Mr. Laurel and Mr. Hardy.  8mm Collect 7:8 F '64
Laurel & Hardy's "hardy" screen life; filmog.  8mm Collect 7:9
    F '64
Polacek, M.  My hobby, Laurel & Hardy.  8mm Collect 7:9 F

'64
Laurel & Hardy; au revoir.  8mm Collect 11:11 Spg '65
Laurel & Hardy cult.  Time 90:74 Jl 14 '67
Pope, D. & Norvell, O.  Laurel & Hardy.  Film 49:32 Aut '67
Warwick, R.  A life of comedy.  Classic Film Collect 20:10
   Spg '68
Gifford, D.  Laurel & Hardy.  Classic Film Collect 21:36 Sum
   '68
Gifford, D.  The latter days of Laurel & Hardy.  Classic Film
   Collect 22:46 Fall/Win '68
Hoffman, A.  The twilight years.  Classic Film Collect 24:49
   Sum '69; 25:54 Fall '69
Marlowe, D.  Highlights.  Classic Film Collect 27:38 Spg/Sum
   '70
Atherton, R.  The legend grows.  Classic Film Collect 26:35
   Win '70
Hoffman, A.  The twilight years.  Classic Film Collect 26:52
   Win '70; 30:26 Spg '71
Comedians.  Screen Greats 1-2:64 Sum '71
Marshall, J.  Comic couple now a cult.  Classic Film Collect
   32:53 Fall '71
Cooper, R.  Two minds without a single thought.  Sat Eve Post
   243:94 Fall '71
A fan club for famous comedy duo.  Classic Film Collect 35:7X
   Sum '72
Everson, W. K.  The crazy world of Laurel and Hardy.  Take
   One 1-9:16 n. d.
Evans, C.  The sounds of silence.  Mise-en-Scene 1:23 n. d.
(See Also:  HARDY, OLIVER; LAUREL, STAN)

LAURELL, KAY
   Evans, D.  A sweet gal.  Photop 16-5:44 O '19

LAURET, LARYSSA
   Efron, E.  Portrait of a husband-stealer.  TV Guide 16-36:12 S
      7 '68

LAURIE, PIPER
   Balling, F. D.  Courageous carrot top.  Silver S 21-7:30 My '51
   Laurie, P.  No eloping for me.  Silver S 23-2:44 D '52
   Rising star.  Film R p108 '52/53

LAUTER, HARRY
   Mezerow, J.  Filmog.  Films In R 20-10:646 D '69

LAVI, DALIAH
   Rising stars.  Film R p53 '65/66

LAW, JOHN PHILLIP
   Confessions of an international lover.  Mod Screen 65-12:22 D
      '71
   Castell, D.  Walking tall; filmog.  Films Illus 1-7:12 Ja '72
   Gow, G.  Vibrations; interview; filmog.  Films & Filming

18-7:19 Ap '72
Eyles, A.   Bio sketch; filmog.   Focus On R 8:11 n. d.

LAW, WALTER
Bernd, A. B.   Sketch.   Motion Pic 12:88 N '16

LAWFORD, PETER
O'Leary, D.   Tickets please.   Silver S 16-9:44 Jl '46
If I had one wish.   Photop 29:60 O '46
Kilgallen, D.   Sketch.   Photop 34:29 Ja '49
Pritchett, F.   Peter is changing.   Silver S 19-7:40 My '49
Hurst, T.   Is eligible bachelor no. 1 about to wed?   Silver S
    20-9:42 Jl '50
Rowland, R.   You simply can't figure him out.   Silver S 22-4:
    42 F '52
Hull, W.   Neighborly Pete.   Silver S 24-4:43 F '54

LAWLOR, MARY
Manners, D.   Sketch.   Motion Pic Classic 31:70 Ag '30

LAWRENCE, BARBARA
Vallee, W. L.   A foxy babe in the Hollywoods.   Silver S 19-2:
    43 D '48

LAWRENCE, CAROL
Just for kicks.   TV Guide 7-37:13 S 12 '59
Carol Lawrence.   TV Guide 11-40:27 O 5 '63
My child.   Photop 80-4:16 O '71

LAWRENCE, FLORENCE
Interview.   N. Y. Drama 68:13 Jl 31 '12
Sketch.   Green Bk 11:841 My '14
Interview.   Blue Book 19:922 S '14
Why she returned to the screen.   Motion Pic 11:129 Mr '16
Bahn, C. B.   Personalities prominent in the press.   Cinema
    Dig 1-3:7 Je 13 '32

LAWRENCE, GERTRUDE
What I believe.   Forum 100:238 N '38
Eustis, M.   Footlight parade.   Theatre Arts 23:714 O '39
Reynolds, Q.   Kids grew up.   Colliers 105:11 F 10 '40
Bio.   Cur Bio 1940
Gertie the great.   Time 37:53 F 3 '41
Vernon, G.   Leading American actress.   Commonweal 33:423 F
    14 '41
Salute.   Cue 10-21:8 My 24 '41
Strauss, T.   Gertrude Lawrence.   Theatre Arts 26:284 My '42
Gertie takes the air.   Cue 12-39:8 S 25 '43
Gertie's air.   Newsweek 22:97 O 11 '43
Pilot's bracelet.   Am Mag 137:60 F '44
Kilgallen, D.   Lawrence in America.   Colliers 113:71 Mr 11 '44
I swam ashore.   Life 17:106 N 27 '44
Star danced; autobio.   Ladies Home J 62:20 Jl '45

Gibbs, W.  O. K. Zanuck, take it away.  New Yorker 21:61 Ag
4 '45

Eliza crossing the land.  Theatre Arts 31:22 My '47

Noel and Gertie.  Life 23:101 D 8 '47

Lewis, E.  Mr. and Mrs. Richard Aldrich.  Cue 19-23:16 Je
10 '50

Church, L. R.  Real cool home I have.  Am Home 44:22 Ag '50

Poling, J.  Gertie and the King of Siam.  Colliers 127:24 Ap 7
'51

Garden and I.  House & Gard 100:72 Jl '51

Last dance.  Time 60:65 S 15 '52

Star falls.  Newsweek 40:93 S 15 '52

Brown, J. M.  Blithe spirit.  Sat R 35:24 S 27 '52

Bio.  Cur Bio S '52

Hart, M.  How a lady kept a playwright in the dark.  Theatre
Arts 36:80 N '52

Memorial exhibition.  Theatre Arts 37:16 Ap '53

Aldrich, R. S.  Gertrude Lawrence as Mrs. A.  Ladies Home J
72:16 Jl; 30 Ag; 40 S; 66 O; 68 N '54

Aldrich, R. S.  Gertrude Lawrence as Mrs. A; condensation.
Read Dig 66:169 Ap '55

Zill, J. A.  Julie plays Gertie.  Look 31:63 S 19 '67

Frankel, H.  Filming of Star.  Sat Eve Post 241:28 Je 29 '68


LAWRENCE, MARC
Actor Lawrence speaking out: where have all the faces gone?
Entertainment World 1-12:48 D '69


LAWRENCE, MURIEL
Waters, K.  Muriel Lawrence.  Films In R 15-1:61 Ja '64
Jordan, D.  Letter.  Films In R 15-2:126 F '64


LAWRENCE, PAUL
Kitchen, K. K.  He didn't want to do it.  Photop 10-6:139 N '16


LAWRENCE, VICKI
Raddatz, L.  What can a girl do if she looks like Carol Burnett?
TV Guide 16-18:16 My 4 '68
Hano, A.  What am I doing in this show?  TV Guide 22-11:29
Mr 16 '74


LAWRENCE, WILLIAM
Obit.  N. Y. Clipper 69:34 Mr 23 '21


LAWSON, LEIGH
Howes, J.  Progress for Percy.  Films Illus 3-32:313 Ap '74


LAWSON, LINDA
Her accent comes from a book.  TV Guide 8-8:29 F 20 '60


LAWTON, FRANK
Sketch.  Theatre World 23:83 F '35
Calhoun, D.  His romance.  Movie Classic 8:42 Mr '35

Obit.   N. Y. Times p47 Je 13 '69
   Screen World 21:238 '70

LAYE, EVELYN
   Kennedy, J. B.   A star by right.   Colliers 85:17 Ap 5 '30
   Manners, D.   Sketch.   Motion Pic Classic 32:48 Ja '31
   Some American experiences.   Windsor 74:39 Je '31
   Baskette, K.   Her dual personalities.   Photop 47:36 Mr '35
   Calhoun, D.   Her romance.   Movie Classic 8:42 Mr '35
   Samuels, L.   London is different.   Silver S 5-5:27 Mr '35
   Johns, E.   Interview with her dresser.   Theatre World 28:40 Jl
      '37
   Sketch.   Theatre World 28:12 Jl '37

LAYTON, DOROTHY
   Uselton, R. A.   The Wampus baby stars.   Film In R 21-2:73 F
      '70

LAZENBY, GEORGE
   Which man would you pick as the new James Bond?   Life 65:120
      O 11 '68
   Newsmakers.   Newsweek 72:62 O 21 '68

LEA, JENIFER
   Wall St. was never like this.   TV Guide 6-29:28 Jl 19 '58

LEACHMAN, CLORIS
   Lassie's new lady.   TV Guide 5-52:8 D 28 '57
   Confessions of a happy caterpillar.   TV Guide 11-26:13 Je 29 '63
   Raddatz, L.   There are two types of actresses.   TV Guide 20-3:
      19 Ja 15 '72
   O'Brien, G.   Interview.   Interview 19:16 F '72
   Cuskelly, R.   I've been good, but I could be great.   Show 2-2:
      28 Ap '72
   Kupfer, M.   Woman scorned; interview.   Newsweek 79:108 My 1
      '72
   Super-mom.   Mod Screen 66-5:56 My '72
   My child.   Photop 82-5:29 N '72
   Milam, M. S.   Playgirl plays it back.   Playgirl 1-1:48 Je '73
   Rick Rosenberg and Robert Christensen comment on Cloris
      Leachman.   Dialogue 2-10:5 Ag '73
   d'Arcy, S.   Interview.   Films Illus 3-30:216 D '73
   Goodman, M.   Actress in demand, mother of 5, practicing
      looney.   People 2-24:63 D 9 '74

LEAHY, MARGARET
   Uselton, R. A.   The Wampus baby stars.   Films In R 21-2:73
      F '70

LEANDER, ZARAH
   Pin-up of the past.   Films & Filming 20-2:68 N '73

LEARN, BESSIE
Show she became a photoplayer.   Motion Pic 9:115 Mr '15
Sketch.   Motion Pic Supp 1:53 S '15

LEARNED, MICHAEL
Pearce, C.   Very much a lady.   Show 3-7:48 O '73
Efron, E.   On Walton's mountain or off...   TV Guide 21-47:20
   N 24 '73
Sketch.   Photop 86-2:50 Ag '74

LEASE, REX
Pryor, N.   His marital troubles.   Movie Classic 1:36 S '31
Obit.   Screen World 18:237 '67

LEAUD, JEAN-PIERRE
Alive and well in Paris.   Sat R 52:18 F 8 '69
Ross, W. S.   Jean-Pierre.   N.Y. Times Bio Ed Je 28 '70
Turim, M.   Child of the French cinema.   Velvet Light 7:41 Win
   '72/73
Dawson, J.   Getting beyond the looking glass.   Sight & Sound
   43-1:46 Win '73/74
Aumont, J-P.   Son of Truffaut.   Oui 2-12:48 D '73
Fox, T. K.   Jean-Pierre explains himself.   Coq 1-2:21 F '74

LeBEAU, MADELEINE
Three little girls in tune.   Lions R 4-1:no p# F '45

LEBEDEFF, IVAN
Donnell, D.   Sketch.   Motion Pic 35:28 F '28
Palmborg, R. P.   Sketch.   Motion Pic 37:67 Jl '29
Hall, G.   Sketch.   Motion Pic Classic 29:45 Ag '29
Hall, G.   Interview.   Motion Pic 39:44 Mr '30
Hall, G.   His love life.   Motion Pic 42:42 O '31

LEDERER, FRANCIS
Lederer, J. P.   Sketch.   Windsor 74:727 N '31
In Autumn crocus.   Lit Dig 114:14 D 24 '32
Talmey, A.   Sketch.   Stage 10:22 Ja '33
Shannon, B.   Sketch.   Motion Pic 46:40 Ag '33
Anderson, E.   Interview.   Movie Classic 5:21 N '33
Jackson, G.   Sketch.   Movie Classic 5:25 F '34
Grant, J.   Sketch.   Movie Classic 7:6 O '34
Hill, G.   The pursuit of Lederer.   Silver S 5-3:22 Ja '35
Bailey, J.   Only one of his kind in Hollywood.   Motion Pic 49:44
   F '35
Smalley, J.   A man of action.   Motion Pic 49:42 Ap '35
Grant, J.   His romance.   Movie Classic 8:27 My '35
Reed, D.   Sketch.   Movie Classic 9:29 N '35
Lawton, J.   Sketch.   Movie Classic 10:31 Ag '36
Surmelian, L.   Interview.   Motion Pic 52:36 Ag '36
Asher, J.   They found it better to bend than to break.   Silver S
   9-8:24 Je '39
Bio note; filmog.   Movies & People 2:22 '40

Romance by Lederer.   Cue 13-14:8 Ap 1 '44
Wilson, E.   A matinee idol from the farm.   Silver S 14-8:30 Je '44
What they are doing now.   Show 3-1:108 Ja '63

LEE, ANNA
  Holland, J.   Conquered coquette.   Silver S 11-12:26 O '41
  Hendricks, H.   Am I so terribly shocking?   Silver S 13-6:26 Ap '43
  Hendricks, H.   Anna Lee's vital message.   Silver S 14-7:26 My '44
  My most unforgettable moment overseas.   Photop 25:53 Je '44

LEE, BELINDA
  Person of promise.   Films & Filming 2-1:11 O '55
  Obit.   Film R p17 '61/62
    Screen World 13:222 '62

LEE, BILLY
  Hamilton, S.   Sketch.   Photop 52:30 S '38

LEE, BRENDA
  She'd druther ketch frogs.   TV Guide 4-51:20 D 22 '56

LEE, BRUCE
  Ochs, P.   Requiem for a dragon departed.   Take One 4-3:20 Ja/F '73
  Obit.   Films & Filming 20-2:80 N '73
    N. Y. Times Bio Ed p1184 Jl '73
    Screen World p236 '74
  Fighting fit.   Films Illus 3-26:77 Ag '73
  Bruce Lee.   Films Illus 3-27:114 S '73
  When I kick, I really kick.   Films Illus 3-30:222 D '73
  Bio note.   Films & Filming 20-9:69 Je '74
  Golden, C.   Interview.   Interview 4-11:31 N '74
  Flanigan, B. P.   Kung Fu Krazy.   Cineaste 6-3:9 '74
  The best of Bruce Lee.   Special publication of Rainbow Publications '74
  Dennis, F. & Atyeo, D.   King of Kung-Fu.   Special publication by arrangement with Bunch Books '74 (Book in magazine format)

LEE, CAROLYN
  Vallee, W. L.   Shirley's successor.   Silver S 11-6:38 Ap '41

LEE, CHRISTOPHER
  The many faces of Lee.   Castle of Frankenstein 2:4 n. d.
  Horror film acting.   Castle of Frankenstein 7:59 n. d.
  Interview.   Castle of Frankenstein 10:12 F '66
  Interview.   Castle of Frankenstein 12:28 n. d.
  Bio note.   Black Oracle 3:10 Mr '70
  Clarke, F. S.   Rasputin on film.   Cinefantastique 1-1:6 Fall '70
  Many bloodsuckers; filmog.   Films Illus 1-2:8 Ag '71

Interview; filmog. Famous Film Stars 1:entire issue '71
Castell, D. Will the real Dracula stand up. Films Illus 1-6:
34 D '71
"Vampire" filmog. Films & Filming 19-7:66 Ap '73
Knight, C. London scene. Cinefantastique 2-4:43 Sum '73
Parish, J. R. & Pitts, M. R. Christopher Lee; with introduc-
tion by Peter Cushing; afterword by Terence Fisher. Cine-
fantastique 3-1:5 Fall '73
Christopher Lee and Anthony N. Keys discuss their newly formed
Charlemagne Productions. Cinefantastique 2-3:24 Win '73
I'm refusing to be labelled. Films Illus 3-30:223 D '73
Keeping it in the family. Films Illus 3-37:28 S '74

LEE, DAVEY
Hastings, T. Sketch. Photop 35:29 Ja '29

LEE, DIXIE
Manners, D. Her love story. Motion Pic 47:51 Mr '34
Walker, H. L. Two life stories that became one. Silver S 5-8:
26 Je '35
Taviner, R. Story of. Photop 48:65 Jl '35
Stanley, G. Why she continues her movie career. Motion Pic
49:36 Jl '35
Bing Crosby as a husband. Movie Classic 8:26 Ag '35
Mrs. Bing Crosby's hobbies. Hobbies 47:63 O '42
Obit. Screen World 4:177 '53

LEE, DORIS
Miss what's-my-name? Photop 14-3:66 Ag '18

LEE, DOROTHY
Ramsey, W. Interview. Motion Pic Classic 31:71 Jl '30
York, C. Sketch. Motion Pic 38:69 N '30
Albert, K. Sketch. Photop 39:138 Mr '31
Bryon, J. She packs a wallop. Silver S 1-6:17 Ap '31

LEE, EUGENE "PORKY"
Maltin, L. Our gang; inc. Our gang filmog. Film Fan Mo 66:
3 D '66

LEE, FRANCES
Uselton, R. A. The Wampus baby stars. Films In R 21-2:73
F '70

LEE, GWEN
Albert, K. Sketch. Motion Pic 34:23 D '27
Ames, E. Sketch. Motion Pic Classic 26:63 F '28
Uselton, R. A. The Wampus baby stars. Films In R 21-2:73
F '70

LEE, GYPSY ROSE
Makes screen debut. Newsweek 10:22 Ag 7 '37
Mack, G. Story of. Motion Pic 54:37 S '37

Gypsy Rose and muse.   Cue 12-29:8  Jl 17 '43
Wilson, E.  Gypsy's back in Hollywood.   Silver S 14-10:28 Ag
   '44
Gypsy Rose finds a new world to conquer.   Cue 17-45:20 N 6
   '48
TV Guest star.   Cue 19-41:15 O 14 '50
Obit.   Classic Film Collect (reprint L. A. Advertiser) 27:60 Spg/
   Sum '70
   Cur Bio Yrbk 1970:466 '71
   Film R p13 '71/72
   N. Y. Times Bio Ed Ap 28 '70
   Newsweek 75:44 My 11 '70
   Screen World 22:238 '71

LEE, JANE
   Rosemon, E.   Sketch.   Motion Pic Classic 7:57 D '18

LEE, JENNIE
   Mother of many.   Photop 11-5:141 Ap '17

LEE, JOANNA
   Joanna Lee is a good talker.   TV Guide 13-10:34 Mr 6 '65

LEE, LILA
   Vail, M. V.   Sketch.   Motion Pic Classic 7:37 S '18
   Doing a pirate picture.   Motion Pic 16:53 D '18
   Cheatham, M. S.   Interview.   Motion Pic Classic 11:64 O '20
   Goldbeck, W.   Interview.   Motion Pic 21:56 Ap '21
   Shelley, H.   Interview.   Motion Pic Classic 12:48 Ag '21
   Naylor, H. S.   Interview.   Motion Pic 23:60 F '22
   Cheatham, M.   Her darkest hour.   Motion Pic Classic 14:51 Jl
      '22
   Fletcher, A. W.   Interview.   Motion Pic 25:26 Mr '23
   Service, F.   Sketch.   Classic 18:40 N '23
   Walker, H. L.   Interview.   Motion Pic 37:58 F '29
   Hall, G.   Interview.   Motion Pic Classic 32:48 S '30
   Manners, D.   To return to the screen.   Motion Pic Classic 33:
      20 Ag '31
   Fidler, J. M.   The new life of Lila Lee.   Silver S 2-2:45 D '31
   Chrisman, J. E.   Sketch.   Movie Classic 1:27 F '32
   Standish, J.   Her love affairs.   Movie Classic 4:33 Mr '33
   Uselton, R. A.   The Wampus baby stars.   Films In R 21-2:73
      F '70
   Lewis, G.   Letter.   Films In R 23-4:253 Ap '72
   Obit.   Classic Film Collect 41:53 Win '73
      N. Y. Times Bio Ed p1803 N '73
      Screen World p237 '74

LEE, LOIS
   Goldbeck, W.   Sketch.   Motion Pic 23:43 Jl '22

LEE, LUANA
   Rising star.   Film R p38 '56/57

LEE, MICHELE
  The improbable Miss Lee.   TV Guide 16-21:21 My 25 '68
  Klemesrud, J.   Stanley Kowalski loves Gittel Mosca.   N.Y.
    Times sec 2:1 Je 10 '73
    Same.   N.Y. Times Bio Ed p959 Je '73
  Summer, A.   It's not where you start, it's where you finish.
    After Dark 6-4:30 Ag '73

LEE, PEGGY
  Sweet Peggy Lee.   Newsweek 30:56 Jl 28 '47
  Busy singer.   Life 24:101 Mr 29 '48
  Story of a songbird.   Cue 17-32:14 Ag 7 '48
  Long, J.   Wild about Peggy.   Am Mag 146:28 O '48
  Tanner, P.   Meet the Barbours.   Mel Mak 25:8 S 3 '49
  Masin, H. L.   Do-re-Lee.   Scholastic 56:26 O 19 '49
  Singer with instinct.   Time 59:64 Je 16 '52
  Jon Whitcomb visits Peggy Lee.   Cosmop 138:56 F '55
  Lady and the tramp.   Look 19:18 My 31 '55
  Slater, L.   McCalls visits.   McCalls 85:12 F '58
  As hot as a torch.   Newsweek 55:115 Mr 21 '60
  Wheeler, T. C.   Timeless charm of Peggy.   Sat Eve Post 237:
    24 O 10 '64
  Red hot.   Newsweek 65:92 Mr 15 '65
  Parsimonious Peggy.   Time 90:46 N 3 '67
  Lees, G.   Consummate artistry of Peggy Lee.   Hi Fi 18:96 Jl
    '68
  Boe, E.   An artist tunes up for the Waldorf.   Cue 38-14:14 Ap
    5 '69
  Hemming, R.   Interview.   Sr Schol 97:19 O 5 '70
  Miss Peggy Lee.   New Yorker 48:31 Mr 18 '72
  McCormack, E.   The last of the red hot mamas comes to the
    Waldorf.   Interview 21:36 My '72
  Considine, S.   Miss Peggy Lee.   After Dark 7-2:38 Je '74
  Peggy's loss is her admirers' gain.   People 1-14:48 Je 3 '74

LEE, PINKY
  Youhoo, it's me.   Newsweek 44:71 Jl 5 '54
  Up from burlesque.   TV Guide 2-30:10 Jl 24 '54
  Nobody loves him--but the kids.   TV Guide 3-42:13 O 15 '55
  Marsano, W.   Baby sitter of the '50s.   TV Guide 19-2:25 Ja 9
    '71
  Botto, L.   Interview.   Look 35:73 S 7 '71

LEE, RAYMOND
  Lee, R.   The Franklin Kid pix; letter.   Films In R 24-3:189
    Mr '73
  (Raymond Lee contributes frequently to Classic Film Collector)

LEE, RUTA
  Dream came true.   TV Guide 6-3:20 Ja 18 '56

LEEDS, ANDREA
  Hamilton, S.   Sketch.   Photop 52:68 Ja '38
  Lee, S.   The girl said no.   Screen Book 20-2:35 Mr '38

LE GUERE, GEORGE
  Sketch.   N. Y.  Drama 69:7 Je 18 '13
  He's a deadly sinner, girls.   Photop 11-6:46 My '17
  Hall, G.  Interview.   Motion Pic 18:77 N '19

LEHR, LEW
  Crichton, K.   Looney Lew.   Colliers 102:11 Jl 9 '38
  Underhill, D.   Stalking the Lew in its Lehr.   Screen Book 21-5:
    24 D '38
  Obit.   Newsweek 35:56 Mr 20 '50
    Time 55:93 Mr 13 '50

LEHRMAN, HENRY
  Obit.   N. Y. Times p17 N 9 '46

LEIBER, FRITZ
  Schem, L. C.   Two latter-day Hamlets.   Dial 66:228 Mr 8 '19
  Firkins, O. W.   New star in Shakespeare.   Review 4:60 Ja 19
    '21
  Krutch, J. W.   Shakespeare without pain.   Nation 130:446 Ap
    16 '30
  Obit.   Screen World 1:234 '49
    Time 55:99 O 24 '49

LEIBMAN, RON
  Stasio, M.   The stars of tomorrow on stage today.   Cue 38-9:9
    Mr 1 '69
  Bosworth, P.   Ron Lunt and Linda Fontanne?   N. Y. Times Bio
    Ed My 31 '70
  On the scene.   Playboy 19-10:173 O '72
  The super cops.   Photop 84-6:41 D '73

LEIGH, JANET
  Pidgeon, W.   Naive is the word.   Silver S 18-7:36 My '48
  Norman, D. C.   Sketch.   Ladies Home J 96:65 S '49
  Holliday, K.   Is the Cinderella girl changing.   Silver S 20-2:42
    D '49
  Leigh, J.   And so we were married.   Silver S 21-12:26 O '51
  Rowland, R. C.   So happily ever after.   Silver S 22-5:36 Mr
    '52
  Morris, J.   When I look back.   Silver S 23-1:34 N '52
  Maddox, B.   Untold tales about Janet and Tony.   Silver S 23-5:
    40 Mr '53
  Leigh, J.   Every wife must be an actress.   Silver S 23-9:34 Jl
    '53
  Leigh, J.   The real facts about Tony and me.   Silver S 24-2:
    29 D '53
  Holland, J.   Her marriage secrets.   Silver S 24-9:35 Jl '54
  Nogueira, R.   Psycho, Rosie and a touch of Orson; interview.
    Sight & Sound 39-2:66 Spg '70
  Photop forum.   Photop 81-1:12 Ja '72

LEIGH, VIRGINIA
    The stars of tomorrow.  Film R p47 '55/56
    Bio note; filmog.  Films & Filming 20-12:57 S '74

LEIGH, VIVIEN
    To play Scarlet O'Hara.  Time 33:26 Ja 23 '39
    Rhea, M.  Sketch.  Photop 53:30 Ap '39
    Hover, A.  Why she got the Scarlett O'Hara role.  Screen Book
      21-9:20 Ap '39
    Holland, J.  Vivien breezes in.  Silver S 9-7:26 My '39
    Wilson, E.  That gay Southern gal from London.  Silver S 9-11:
      46 S '39
    Sketch.  Vogue 95:76 My 1 '40
    Mulvey, K.  Sketch.  Womans Home C 68:28 Ap '41
    Stranger in Hollywood.  Lions R 3-5:no p# D '44
    Hall, G.  Those amazing Oliviers.  Silver S 16-12:30 O '46
    Johns, E.  Miss Leigh's approach to A streetcar named Desire.
      Theatre World 45:9 D '49
    Canfield, A.  A lady in love.  Silver S 21-3:36 Ja '51
    Venezky, A.  Enter the Oliviers.  Cue 20-49:10 D 8 '51
    Reid, L.  The story behind Vivien's tragic collapse.  Silver S
      23-9:38 Jl '53
    Raper, M.  They called her a Dresden Shepherdess.  Films &
      Filming 1-11:5 Ag '55
    Obit.  Brit Bk Yr 1968:594 '68
      Cur Bio 28:44 O '67
      Cur Bio Yrbk 1967:479 '68
      Life 63:32 Jl 21 '67
      N. Y. Times p1 Jl 9 '67
      Newsweek 70:82 Jl 17 '67
      Time 90:88 Jl 14 '67
    Lambert, G.  The making of Gone with the wind.  Atlantic 231-
      3:56 Mr '73
    South, R.  Letter.  Films In R 25-2:125 F '74
    Bowers, R.  Letter.  Films In R 25-5:315 My '74
    Evans, C.  Letter.  Films In R 25-10:637 D '74

LEIGHTON, MARGARET
    My favorite role.  Film R p38 '51/52
    Morley, S.  Ladies only; interview.  Plays & Players 17-5:24 F
      '69

LELAND, DAVID
    He's had the fattest roles on TV.  TV Guide 8-9:28 F 27 '60

LE MAT, PAUL
    Bio note; filmog.  Focus On F 17:9 Spg '74

LEMMON, JACK
    The stars of tomorrow.  Film R p42 '55/56
    Zunser, J.  Just call me lucky Lemmon.  Cue 25-9:13 Mr 3 '56
    Interview.  Playboy 11:57 My '64
    Redbook dialogue.  Redbook 130:50 D '67

Baltake, J.   Jack Lemmon; filmog.   Films In R 21-1:1 Ja '70
Salute of the week.   Cue 39-24:1 Je 13 '70
Berkvist, R.   He sings, he dances, he plays piano.   N. Y. Times
  Bio Ed Ja 16 '72
Thomas, B.   I never had a bad experience in my life.   Action
  7-1:6 Ja/ F '72
Eyles, A.   Bio note; filmog.   Focus On F 9:6 Spg '72
Archibald, L.   Twenty years after.   Show 3-3:46 My '73
Greenberg, S.   Interview.   Film Comment 9-3:27 My/ Je '73
Castell, D.   Still trying to speak to George.   Films Illus 3-26:
  70 Ag '73
Darrach, B.   The sweet taste of success again.   People 1-16:36
  Je 17 '74

LENARD, MARK
  Raddatz, L.   When is a villain not a villain?   TV Guide 18-11:
    35 Mr 14 '70

LENIHAN, DEIRDRE
  Whitney, D.   Who's afraid of the old pros?   TV Guide 21-44:25
    N 3 '73

LENNON, JOHN
  Cott, J.   John Lennon talks.   Vogue 153:170 Mr 1 '69
  Rollin, B.   Top pop merger: Lennon/Ono inc.   Look 33:36 Mr
    18 '69
  Sander, E.   John and Yoko give peace a chance.   Sat R 52:46
    Je 28 '69
  Childs, C.   Interview.   Penthouse 1-2:28 O '69
  Opening of the show of erotic lithographs.   New Yorker 46:29 F
    21 '70
  Beatle roundup.   Newsweek 76:85 S 7 '70
  McCarry, D.   John Rennon's excrusive gloupie.   Esquire 74:205
    D '70
  People.   Time 97:34 Ja 18 '71
  Saal, H.   Confessions of a Beatle.   Newsweek 77:50 Ja 18 '71
  Beatledammerung.   Time 97:55 Ja 25 '71
  Simonds, C. H.   Settlin' down.   Nat R 23:145 F 9 '71
  Willis, E.   George and John.   New Yorker 47:96 F 27 '71
  Buckley, W. F. Jr.   John Lennon's almanac.   Nat R 23:39 Ap
    6 '71
  Kopkind, A.   I wanna hold your hand; Lennon after the fall.
    Ramp Mag 9:18 Ap '71
  Blackburn, R. & Ali, T.   Interview.   Ramp Mag 10:43 Jl '71
  Goldman, J.   Two women who broke up the Beatles.   McCalls
    98:72 Jl '71
  Everywhere's somewhere.   New Yorker 47:28 Ja 8 '72
  Jahn, M.   Waiting for Lennon: the myth and the silence.   Cue
    41-15:2 Ap 8 '72
  O'Hara, J. D.   Talking through their heads.   New Rep 166:30
    My 20 '72
  Warhol, A.   Morrissy, P. & O'Brien, G.   John & Yoko, some-
    times in New York and sometimes in the big apple.   Interview

22:6 Je '72
Gitlin, T.   Lennon speaking.   Commonweal 96:500 S 22 '72
Hertzberg, H.   Reporter at large.   New Yorker 48:138 D 9 '72
Lennon, J. & Ono, Y.   Our films.   Filmmaker's Newsletter 6-
   8:25 Je '73
Interview.   Interview 4-11:11 N '74
(See also:  BEATLES, The)

LENYA, LOTTE
   Kaye, D.   Interview.   Sat R 55:70 Mr 25 '72
   Filmog.   Films & Filming 20-6:52 Mr '74

LEONARD, JACK E.
   Minoff, P.   The man in the spinning panama.   Cue 20-26:14 Je
      30 '51
   Jack E. Leonard, M. I.*   TV Guide 6-51:10 D 20 '58

LEONARD, SHELDON
   Minoff, P.   TV's triple threat.   Cue 23-25:13 Je 19 '54
   Leonard, S.   It's time we junked model T techniques.   Action 2-
      1:14 Ja/F '67
   Leonard, S.   Miss MacLaine goes East.   TV Guide 19-39:20 S
      25 '71

le ROUX, MADELEINE
   Johnson, D.   Madeleine le Roux, entre nouse.   After Dark 3-10:
      18 F '71

LE ROY, HAL
   Maltin, L.   Hal Le Roy; filmog.   Film Fan Mo 131:21 My '72

LESLIE, BETHEL
   The face ought to be familiar.   TV Guide 9-22:29 Je 3 '61
   The great escape.   TV Guide 12-10:12 Mr 7 '64

LESLIE, GLADYS
   Howe, H.   A truly ingenuous ingenue.   Photop 14-2:27 Jl '18
   Naylor, H. S.   Interview.   Motion Pic 17:36 Ag '19
   Smith, F. J.   Sketch.   Motion Pic Classic 12:16 My '21
   Underhill, H.   Interview.   Motion Pic 21:46 Je '21

LESLIE, JOAN
   Success story.   Cue 10-29:3 Jl 19 '41
   Franchey, J. R.   My sisters and I.   Silver S 11-11:36 S '41
   The girl on the cover.   Cue 11-14:1 Ap 4 '42
   Crucial moments.   Photop 23:58 S '43
   Wilson, E.   Now that she's 18.   Silver S 14-1:44 N '43
   Lane, L.   Now 21.   Silver S 16-5:40 Mr '46
   Bowers, L.   Somebody special.   Silver S 16-11:55 S '46
   Wells, H.   We visit Joan Leslie today.   Movie Dig 1-4:62 Jl '72

LESLIE, NAN
   Hardly the dull type.   TV Guide 5-39:24 S 28 '57
   Whitney, D.   The cowboy's lament.   TV Guide 6-36:9 S 6 '58

LESTER, MARK
    Bio note; filmog.   Films Illus 3-36:474 Ag '74

LETCHWORTH, EILEEN
    A soap star's face-lift is part of the script.   People 2-11:60 S
        9 '74

LEUWERIK, RUTH
    Gordon, A.   Letter; partial filmog.   Films In R 22-1:50 Ja '71
    Buchet, J. M.   Letter; filmog.   Films In R 22-4:247 Ap '71

LEVANT, OSCAR
    Zolotow, M.   The little world of Levant.   Playboy 6:37 Jl '59
    Levant, O.   'S wonderful, 's marvelous, 's Gershwin.   TV
        Guide 20-3:24 Ja 15 '72
    Obit.   Classic Film Collect (reprint Variety) 36:extra 2 Fall '72
        New York Times Bio Ed p1505 Ag '72
        Newsweek 80:55 Ag 28 '72
        Time 100:38 Ag 28 '72
    Green, A.   Oscar Levant 1906-72.   N. Y. Times Bio Ed p1506
        Ag '72
    Kolodin, I.   Trouble with Oscar.   Sat R 55:13 S 9 '72

LEVENE, SAM
    Hollywood-Broadway commuter.   Lions R 1-2:no p# O '41
    Gussow, M.   Stars share espirit of Sunshine boys.   N. Y. Times
        Bio Ed p2096 D '72

LE VEQUE, EDDIE
    Erwin, B.   Native El Pasoan only original Keystone Kop still in
        pictures (reprint El Paso Times) Classic Film Collect 19:21
        Fall/Win '67
    Le Veque, E.   The last Keystone Kop.   Classic Film Collect
        28:25 Fall '70

LEWIS, AL
    A volcano called Schnauzer.   TV Guide 11-10:10 Mr 9 '63

LEWIS, CATHY
    Pair of Lewises.   Newsweek 31:54 Mr 15 '48
    Obit.   N. Y. Times p47 N 23 '68
        Screen World 20:236 '69

LEWIS, DIANA
    Stars of tomorrow.   Lions R 1-11/12:no p# Jl/Ag '42
    Meet the cover(all) girls.   Lions R 3-2:no p# Ja '44

LEWIS, FIONA
    Filmog.   Films Illus 1-1:32 Jl '71

LEWIS, GEORGE
    Manners, D.   Interview.   Motion Pic Classic 29:65 Je '29
    Manners, D.   Sketch.   Motion Pic 38:48 D '29
    College for gagsters.   Am Mag 143:128 Je '47

LEWIS, JERRY
   Parsons, L. O.   Cosmop's citation for best newcomer of the
      month.   Cosmop 127:12 O '49
   MacDonald, E.   Letter to a star.   Silver S 22-7:36 My '52
   Martin, D.   It wasn't my idea.   Silver S 24-9:38 Jl '54
   Minoff, P.   Time for Martin & Lewis to take inventory.   Cue
      24-20:59 My 21 '55
   Hume, R.   Are their critics wrong?   Films & Filming 2-6:10
      Mr '56
   Taylor, T.   New soloist in town.   Cue 26-6:12 F 9 '57
   Nine-channel spectacular.   TV Guide 6-7:4 F 15 '58
   Fenin, G.   The face of '63--United States.   Films & Filming
      9-6:55 Mr '63
   Sarris, A.   Oddities and one shots.   Film Culture 28:45 Spg
      '63
   Hanson, C. L.   Point of view.   Cinema (BH) 3-4:50 D '66
   Madsen, A.   Interview.   Cahiers (in Eng.) 4:27 '66
   Manes, S.   Lewis as auteur.   Focus 3/4:21 '68
   What directors are saying.   Action 4-5:32 S/O '69
   Lewis, J.   Five happy moments.   Esquire 74:137 D '70
   What directors are saying.   Action 6-1:30 Ja/F '71
   Newsmakers.   Newsweek 77:63 My 10 '71
   Camper, F.   Essays in visual style.   Cinema (Lon) 8:32 '71
   What directors are saying.   Action 7-1:36 Ja/F '72
   Comedy is the mirror we hold up to life; interview.   Focus 7:4
      Spg '72
   Higham, C.   Jerry isn't just clowning around now.   N.Y. Times
      Bio Ed p1353 Jl '72
   Stern, M. A.   Emulsion compulsion.   Focus 8:45 Aut '72
   Michener, C.   That's my boy.   Newsweek 80:74 D 25 '72

LEWIS, JOE E.
   O'Hara, J.   Good man in a room.   Newsweek 17:58 Je 30 '41
   Reynolds, Q.   Comeback in comedy.   Colliers 110:22 Jl 4 '42
   Lewis goes to a fight.   Cue 12-39:10 S 25 '43
   Lewisite.   Newsweek 22:89 O 18 '43
   Songs of the bedeviled.   Cue 13-19:12 My 6 '44
   Dude (photos).   Colliers 123:48 Ja 15 '49
   Watt, D.   Tables for two.   New Yorker 28:123 O 11 '52
   Taylor, T.   Same old Joe E. back at the brand new Copa.   Cue
      24-38:15 S 24 '55
   Churchill, A.   Six men of the world.   Sat R 38:18 D 17 '55
   Cohn, A.   Joker is wild; condensation.   Coronet 40:83 My '56
   Obit.   N.Y. Times p32 Je 5 '71
      Newsweek 77:93 Je 14 '71
      Time 97:77 Je 14 '71

LEWIS, MITCHELL
   Remont, F.   Sketch.   Motion Pic Classic 8:21 Mr '19
   St. John, A. R.   Trapping a vagabond.   Photop 16-1:81 Je '19

LEWIS, RALPH
   Mack, M.   Interview.   Motion Pic 23:68 Mr '22
   Stern, S.   Ralph Lewis.   Film Cult 36:42 Spg/Sum '65

LEWIS, ROBERT Q.
  Unsettled comedian.  Newsweek 35:49  F 13 '50
  Always a champion.  Coronet 34:137 My '53
  Robert Q. Lewis.  Look 17:86 Je 30 '53
  Breeder of champions.  Coronet 34:95 Je '53
  Baseball's clown prince.  Coronet 34:63 Jl '53
  Sergeant's choice.  Coronet 34:158 S '53
  How to take care of a record collection.  House & Gard 104:206
    D '53
  Robert Q. on his own.  TV Guide 2-4:17 Ja 22 '54
  Whitcomb, J.  Favorite records of all time.  Cosmop 136:42 Ap
    '54
  Sailor's secret.  Coronet 36:71 My '54
  Taves, I.  He finally replaced himself.  Coronet 136:124 Je '54
  Where I first met you.  Coronet 37:167 Mr '55
  Lewis, R. Q.  Notes on TV.  Cue 24-29:35 Jl 23 '55

LEWIS, RONALD
  Person of promise.  Films & Filming 2-2:25 N '55
  Como, W.  Las Vegas scene.  Dance 40:14 Ag '66

LEWIS, SHELDON
  Pack, A. C.  Filmog.  Films In R 18-9:585 N '67

LIBERACE (Wladziu Valentino)
  His father thought he'd better be an undertaker.  TV Guide 1-18:
    A-8 Jl 31 '53
  Popular piano.  Time 62:51 O 5 '53
  Kidding on the keys.    Life 35:88 D 7 '53
  Piano with a flair.  Newsweek 43:96 F 22 '54
  Don't laugh at the piano player.  TV Guide 2-9:5 F 26 '54
  Jenkins, D.  How Liberace faced his greatest challenge.  TV
    Guide 3-10:4 Mr 5 '55
  Taubman, H.  Square looks at hot shot.  N. Y. Times Mag p20
    Mr 14 '54
  Monroe, K.  Liberace and his piano.  Coronet 36:118 My '54
  Liberace.  New Yorker 30:23 Je 5 '57
  Goose pimples for all.  Time 63:50 Je 7 '54
  Great Liberace.  Look 18:62 Je 29 '54
  Virtuoso or ham?  TV Guide 2-35:10 Ag 28 '54
  Donovan, R.  Nobody loves me but the people.  Colliers 134:28
    S 3; 72 S 17 '54
  The Liberace legend.  TV Guide 2-38:5 S 18 '54
  Discussion.  Colliers 134:16 O 15 '54
  Why women idolize Liberace.  Look 18:101 O 19 '54
  Witt, E.  Mature women are the best.  Coronet 37:79 D '54
  Hubler, R. G.  Liberace.  Cosmop 137:104 D '54
  Cooke, J. F.  Musical showmanship.  Etude 73:58 My '55
  Lion of the lot.  TV Guide 3-46:5 N 12 '55
  Mud on the stars.  Newsweek 48:58 O 8 '56
  Liberace and the nonbelievers.  Time 68:58 O 15 '56
  He's still crying all the way to the bank.  TV Guide 6-18:18 My
    3 '58

Candelabra and the quill.   Newsweek 53:33 Je 22 '59
Liberace show.   Time 73:48 Je 22 '59
Jealousy.   Time 73:34 Je 29 '59
Whatever happened to Buster Keys?   Time 86:89 O 1 '65
Musel, R.   Liberace at the halfway mark.   TV Guide 17-32:11
    Ag 9 '69

LIGHT, PAMELA
    Fighting it on her own lines.   TV Guide 5-47:20 N 23 '57

LIGHTNER, WINNIE
    Belfrage, C.   Interview.   Motion Pic Classic 30:65 F '30
    Weltman, M.   Broadway favorite.   Classic Film Collect 19:9
        Fall/Win '67
    Obit.   N. Y. Times p30 Mr 6 '71
        Screen World 23:238 '72

LIGON, TOM
    Stoop, N. M.   Opposites attract; complex Tom Ligon.   After
        Dark 4-5:16 S '71

LILLIE, BEATRICE
    Wilson, B.   Interview.   Classic 19:34 Je '24
    Carlisle, H.   Sketch.   Motion Pic 32:38 D '26
    Appearing in a new theatre.   Graphic 129:427 S 13 '30
    Horton, H.   Interview.   Motion Pic Classic 32:54 N '30
    Sketch.   Theatre Guild 9:38 Ap '32
    Grein, J. T.   Work of.   Ill Lon N 183:932 D 9 '33
    Appreciation.   Lit Dig 120:18 N 2 '35
    Adventures with audiences.   Stage 14:41 F '37
    Appreciation.   Theatre World 29:280 Je '38
    Johns, E.   Appreciation.   Theatre World 40:25 Ag '44
    At last we have Lillie.   Cue 13-46:13 N 11 '44
    Radio appearance in New York.   Newsweek 24:100 N 20 '44
    Kilgallen, D.   The real Bea Lillie.   Cosmop 118:8 Mr '45
    Sketch.   Theatre World 42:3 Je '46
    Poling, J.   Lillie's in the U. S. A.   Colliers 121:24 My 15 '48
    Starring in Inside U. S. A.   Life 24:135 My 17 '48
    Hogan, F.   Night I sang Carmen at the Met.   Opera N 33:12 Mr
        15 '69
    Sillman, L.   Cue salutes.   Cue 39-13:52 Mr 28 '70
    Clarke, G.   Blithe spirit.   Time 99:E9 Ap 3 '72

LILO
    Keating, J.   Mlle from Montmartre.   Cue 22-24:13 Je 13 '53
    Taylor, T.   After dark.   Cue 25-14:17 Ap 7 '56

LINCOLN, ABBEY
    For love of Ivy.   Ebony 23:52 O '68

LINCOLN, CARYL
    Uselton, R. A.   The Wampus baby stars.   Films In R 21-2:73
        F '70

LINCOLN, EDWARD X.
  Boone, J. A.  Sketch.  Motion Pic 13:114 F '17
  La Roche, E. M.  Bio sketch.  Motion Pic Classic 6:27 Je '18

LINCOLN, ELMO
  A Yankee maciste.  Photop 16-2:91 Jl '19
  The first movie Tarzan.  Life 26:159 My 16 '49
  Obit.  Screen World 4:177 '53
  Coriell, V.  Elmo, the mighty.  Classic Film Collect 20:12
    Spg; 21:28 Sum; 22:25 Fall/Win '68
  Couto, D.  The original Tarzan; filmog.  Classic Film Collect
    44:33 Fall '74

LINDELAND, LIV
  There's a lot to Liv.  Playboy 18-1:136 Ja '71
  Playmate of the year.  Playboy 19-6:156 Je '72

LINDEN, ERIC
  Will they become famous stars or forgotten faces?  Silver S 2-
    2:36 D '31
  Churchill, E.  Sketch.  Silver S 2-4:40 F '32
  Hamilton, S.  Sketch.  Photop 41:47 F '32
  North, J.  Sketch.  Photop 43:40 Ja '33
  Grayson, C.  Life continues.  Silver S 3-5:50 Mr '33

LINDEN, HAL
  Linden, H.  Now, what are those reasons for not going to the
    theatre lately?  Cue 40-25:9 Je 19 '71

LINDEN, MARTA
  Mother Eve in Hollywood.  Lions R 2-3:no p# D '42

LINDER, MAX
  Chandler, C. F.  Return to moving pictures.  Motion Pic 13:
    129 F '17 and following issues.
  Kimball, R. I.  Sketch.  Motion Pic Classic 4:23 Ap '17
  La Roche, E. M.  Sketch.  Motion Pic 13:80 Ap '17
  Goldbeck, W.  Interview.  Motion Pic 22:32 Ag '21
  Dodd, A.  The golden era's forgotten comic.  8mm Collect 7:6
    F '64
  Spears, J.  More on Linder.  Films In R 16-6:391 Je/Jl '65

LINDFORS, VIVECA
  Sketch.  Time 48:104 D 9 '46
  Lindfors, V.  Beginning again.  Viva 1-10:112 Jl '74

LINDSAY, JOHN V. (as actor)
  Hall, W.  Once a politician always an actor.  N. Y. Times Bio
    Ed p1130 Ag '74

LINDSAY, LEX
  Obit.  N. Y. Times p50 Ap 28 '71

LINDSAY, MARGARET
    Maddox, B.  Interview.  Motion Pic 47:59 Jl '34
    Vallee, W. L.  The Iowa girl from England.  Silver S 10-8:26
        Je '40
    Bio note; filmog.  Movies & People 2:23 '40

LINDSEY, GEORGE
    Next to frozen chickens, he's Jasper's biggest asset.  TV Guide
        15-43:12 O 28 '67

LINDT, CINDY
    Opportunity U. S. A.  TV Guide 5-14:8 Ap 6 '57

LINVILLE, JOANNE
    Chorus-line graduate, cum laude.  TV Guide 12-15:25 Ap 11 '64

LIPTON, PEGGY
    Is that a face!  TV Guide 16-44:12 N 2 '68
    I want to make love to a Negro.  Photop 77-6:34 Je '70
    Hair-raising stories from the stars.  Photop 78-1:62 Jl '70
    Robbins, F.  Interview.  Photop 78-3:28 S '70
    Meryman, R.  Can two TV beauties survive TV? interview.
        Life 70:54 Ja 22 '71
    I'm not just a nice Jewish girl anymore.  Photop 79-1:58 Ja '71
    Berkvist, R.  Bored?  Creatively, I'm bored, but...  N. Y.
        Times Bio Ed Mr 19 '72
    Sinatra's got a new young love.  Mod Screen 66-7:42 Jl '72

LIPTON, ROBERT
    Lewis, S.  A sole survivor surveys a failure.  After Dark 12-
        1:16 My '70

LISI, VIRNA
    Virna Lisi.  Show 4-7:73 Jl/Ag '64
    Brown, A.  Filmog.  Films In R 16-6:393 Je/Jl '65
    Rising stars.  Film R p53 '65/66
    Beauty in a classic way.  Vogue 158:66 Ag '71

LITEL, JOHN
    Sketch.  Stage 12:34 Je '35
    Hamilton, S.  Sketch.  Photop 54:30 S '40
    Obit.  Classic Film Collect 34:X-3 Spg '72
        N. Y. Times p32 F 5 '72
        Same.  N. Y. Times Bio Ed F 5 '72

LITTLE, ANNA
    How she became a photoplayer.  Motion Pic 8:77 Ja '15
    Sketch.  Motion Pic 9:108 Mr '15
    Sketch.  Motion Pic 11:112 Mr '16
    McGaffey, K.  Sketch.  Motion Pic 16:62 O '18
    Shirk, A. H.  Interview.  Motion Pic Classic 7:36 Ja '19

LITTLE, ANITA
    Bartlett, R.   Little Miss Lochinvar.   Photop 11-6:117 My '17

LITTLE, CLEAVON
    Garland, P.   Prize winners.   Ebony 25:29 Jl '70
    Kaiser, R. B.   This doctor might become a patient.   TV Guide
        21-17:11 Ap 28 '73

LITTLEFIELD, LUCIEN
    Hall, G.   Interview.   Motion Pic 37:67 Je '29

LIVINGSTON, MARGARET
    Tully, J.   Sketch.   Motion Pic Classic 12:60 Je '21
    Spensley, D.   Sketch.   Photop 29:57 F '26
    Cruikshank, H.   Sketch.   Motion Pic 35:58 Mr '28
    Hall, G.   Interview.   Motion Pic 37:58 Je '29
    Dyer, A.   Her romance.   Movie Classic 1:35 N '35

LIVINGSTON, ROBERT
    Haber, J.   Robert Livingston.   Films In R 8-10:542 D '57

LIVINGSTON, STANLEY
    ...and no cracks, please.   TV Guide 10-21:15 My 26 '62

LLOYD, DORIS
    York, C.   Sketch.   Photop 39:80 D '30

LLOYD, HAROLD
    Granger, F.   Sketch.   Motion Pic 17:48 Je '19
    Blame the League of Nations.   Photop 16-2:79 Jl '19
    Laurel, M.   Interview.   Motion Pic Classic 9:34 O '19
    Fredericks, J.   Interview.   Motion Pic 19:38 Ap/My '20
    Furman, B.   Interview.   Motion Pic 22:34 Ag '21
    Peltret, E.   Interview.   Motion Pic Classic 13:33 Ja '22
    Home of.   Photop 22:68 Jl '22
    Hall, G. & Fletcher, A. W.   Interview.   Motion Pic 23:20 Jl
        '22
    Sketch.   Classic 15:46 O '22
    Carr, H.   Compared with Chaplin.   Motion Pic 24:55 N '22
    His darkest hour.   Classic 15:52 F '23
    Perlman, P.   His boyhood.   Motion Pic 25:38 Jl '23
    Home of.   Classic 18:40 O '23
    de Revere, F. V.   Analysis of his face.   Motion Pic 29:40 F
        '25
    Calhoun, D. D.   Interview.   Motion Pic 29:59 My '25
    Autobiographical.   Motion Pic 30:40 D '25
    Criticism.   Graphic 115:380 Mr 5 '27
    Sketch.   Theatre 45:39 My '27
    Howe, M.   Interview.   Motion Pic 33:24 My '27
    Donnell, D.   Story of.   Motion Pic 34:18 S '27
    Johnston, C.   Sketch.   Motion Pic Classic 26:53 N '27
    Stevens, J.   The making of Speedy.   Motion Pic 35:67 F '28
    Sketch.   National 56:542 Ag '28

Home of.  Motion Pic Classic 29:56 Mr '29
Home of.  Photop 37:34 My '30
Hall, G.  Interview.  Motion Pic 40:58 O '30
Calhoun, D.  First story about his son.  Motion Pic Classic 33:
    30 My '31
Hall, G.  His home life.  Photop 42:58 S '32
Hall, G.  Interview.  Motion Pic 46:40 S '33
Brundidge, H. T.  Interview.  Motion Pic 48:45 N '34
Spensley, D.  His home life.  Movie Classic 7:54 Ja '35
Ganley, H.  Story of.  Motion Pic 51:40 F '36
Goldbeck, E.  As an artist.  Movie Classic 9:34 F '36
Camp, D.  As a scientist.  Motion Pic 54:27 D '37
The perennial Mr. Harold Lloyd.  Cue 6-38:9 Jl 16 '38
Home of.  Life 5:28 Ag 1 '38
Home of.  Photop 52:28 Ag '38
Pine, D.  Exploding the Lloyd legend.  Screen Book 21-2:44 S
    '38
Bio note; filmog.  Movies & People 2:23 '40
Destruction of irreplacable negatives of his silent comedies.
    Newsweek 22:8 Ag 16 '43
He revives the glass character.  Cue 14-5:9 F 3 '45
Wilson, E.  A great comic returns.  Silver S 16-6:37 Ap '46
A funny guy with glasses comes back.  Cue 18-26:18 Je 25 '49
Bio.  Cur Bio 10:37 S '49
Harold's back again.  Cue 19-46:14 N 18 '50
Lipton, N. C.  An ardent photographer, stereo fan.  Pop Phot
    69:50 Ag '51
Zunser, J.  Comedy is no laughing matter.  Cue 31-22:10 Je 2
    '62
Just an ordinary millionaire.  Sound Stage 1-3:25 My '65
Cowie, D.  Lloyd and his world of slapstick; filmog.  Int F
    G 2:43 '65
Reynolds, R.  Lloyd visits Rochester for film festival.  8mm
    Collect 14:2 Spg '66
McCaffrey, D.  The mutual approval of Keaton and Lloyd.
    Cinema J 6 '66/67
Jim Beauchamp reports on symposium with Harold Lloyd.  Clas-
    sic Film Collect 17:33 Win/Spg '67
Green, L. J.  Comic, 75, turns nostalgic.  Classic Film Col-
    lect 21:58 Sum '68
Lloyd, H.  The serious business of being funny.  Film Comment
    5-3:46 Fall '69
Obit.  Classic Film Collect 30:extra 3 (reprint N. Y. Times) Spg
    '71
    Cur Bio 32:46 Ap '71
    Same.  Cur Bio Yrbk 1971:466 '72
    Film R p13 '71/72
    N. Y. Times p1 Mr 9 '71
    Same.  N. Y. Times Bio Ed Mr 9 '71
    Screen World 23:238 '72
    Time 97:60 Mr 22 '71
Zimmermann, P. D.  Comic Merriwell.  Newsweek 77:110 Mr
    22 '71

Funeral. Classic Film Collect:extra 3 Spg '71
A tribute to Harold Lloyd. Film Fan Mo 118:3 Ap '71
Slide, A. Interview. Silent Pic 11/12:no p# Sum/Aut '71
Flinn, T. Out of the past. Velvet Light 3:6 Win '71/72
Kaminsky, S. A reassessment of his film comedy. Silent Pic
16:21 Aut '72
Gleason, B. Automaniac. Film 2-15:17 Je '74
Evans, C. The sounds of silence. Mise-en-Scene 1:23 n.d.

LLOYD, NORMAN
Nolan, J. E. Films on TV. Films In R 25-5:298 My '74

LOCHER, FELIX
Obit. Screen World 21:238 '70

LOCKE, KATHERINE
Pringle, H. F. Girl meets fame. Colliers 99:16 Je 19 '37

LOCKHART, CALVIN
Klemesrud, J. Champagne, yes, Coca-Cola, no. N.Y. Times
Bio Ed Ap 19 '70
Knight, A. & Alpert, H. Sex stars of 1970. Playboy 17-12:220
D '70

LOCKHART, JUNE
Firth, R. Sketch. Photop 30:99 F '47
Takes Broadway by storm. Newsweek 30:84 N 14 '47
New star on Broadway. Cue 16-47:19 N 22 '47
Hats off to Fall. TV Guide 1-28:22 O 9 '53

LOCKWOOD, GARY
The Hollywood swingers. Show 3-11:90 N '63

LOCKWOOD, HAROLD
How he became a photoplayer. Motion Pic 9:111 F '15
Sketch. Motion Pic 9:119 My '15
Willis, R. Interview. Motion Pic 10:111 S '15
Zeidman, B. Sketch. Motion Pic 13:98 Mr '17
Courtlandt, R. Sketch. Motion Pic Classic 4:34 My '17
How he got into motion pictures. Motion Pic 14:92 S '17
Pike, C. It never can happen again. Photop 13-3:61 F '18
Funny happenings in the movie world. Motion Pic 15:59 Je '18
& following issues.
Obit. Dram Mir 79:660 N 2 '18
Photop 15-2:51 Ja '19
Tribute. Motion Pic 16:71 Ja '19
Bodeen, D. Lockwood and Allison; filmog. Films In R 22-5:275
My '71

LOCKWOOD, KING
Obit. Screen World 23:238 '72

LOCKWOOD, MARGARET
    Receives National film award.   Ill Lond N 210:494 My 10 '47
    Sketch.   Life 25:84 N 1 '48

LODEN, BARBARA
    Best of all worlds.   Newsweek 63:78 F 10 '64
    People are talking about.   Vogue 143:96 Mr 15 '64
    Women worth watching.   McCalls 95:30 Ja '68
    Melton, R.   Loden on Wanda.   Film J 1-2:11 Sum '71
    Butterfield, M.   After a long silence Loden speaks on film.
        Show 2-5:39 Jl '71
    Involved.   Harp Baz 105:40 Jl '72
    Women directors; filmog.   Film Comment 8-4:42 N '72

LODER, JOHN
    Bradley, E.   Sketch.   Photop 35:53 Mr '29
    Interview.   Motion Pic Classic 29:55 My '29
    Parsons, L. O.   His separation from Hedy Lamarr.   Photop 31:
        36 S '47

LODER, LOTTI
    Gray, C.   Sketch.   Motion Pic Classic 32:70 S '30

LODGE, JOHN
    (Film Career citations only)
    Hall, G.   Sketch.   Movie Classic 4:24 Jl '33
    Cunniff, R.   From law to leading man and back again.   Show 2-
        7:73 Jl '62

LOFF, JEANETTE
    Prior, N.   Sketch.   Motion Pic 35:58 My '28
    Manners, D.   Interview.   Motion Pic 39:50 F '30
    Cranford, R.   Sketch.   Photop 38:36 Je '30
    Hall, G.   Sketch.   Motion Pic Classic 31:41 Ag '30

LOGAN, BOB
    A new F. P. for 77 Sunset Strip.   TV Guide 9-40:17 O 7 '61

LOGAN, ELLA
    Sketch.   Motion Pic 53:19 Mr '37
    Obit.   Classic Film Collect 24:14 (reprint Washington Evening
        Star) Sum '69
        N. Y. Times p43 My 2 '69
        Newsweek 73:69 My 12 '69
        Screen World 21:238 '70
        Time 93:100 My 9 '69

LOGAN, JACQUELINE
    Peltret, E.   Interview.   Motion Pic Classic 12:34 Je '21
    Powers, E.   Interview.   Motion Pic Classic 13:32 O '21
    Wadleigh, W.   Sketch.   Motion Pic Classic 24:20 F '27
    Calhoun, D.   Her love for animals.   Motion Pic 35:49 Je '28
    Biery, R.   Interview.   Motion Pic 37:44 Je '29

Uselton, R. A.  The Wampus baby stars.  Films In R 21-2:73
  F '70
Lewis, G.  Letter.  Films In R 23-4:254 Ap '72

## LOGAN, JANICE
Hamilton, S.  Sketch.  Photop 54:71 Je '40
Vallee, W. L.  From riches to rags.  Silver S 10-8:44 Je '40

## LOGGIA, ROBERT
Last miles.  Theatre Arts 41:12 My '57
Davy Crockett, move over.  TV Guide 6-46:22 N 15 '58
Raddatz, L.  Fine feline fellow.  TV Guide 15-13:12 Ap 1 '67

## LOLLOBRIGIDA, GINA
Wilson, E.  Marilyn, beware.  Silver S 23-12:22 O '53
Water, R.  Visit with Gina.  Cue 23-43:14 O 23 '54
La Lollo.  Films & Filming 1-2:13 N '54
Lollo in Paris.  Cue 24-46:13 N 19 '55
Lane, J. F.  The face of '63--Italy.  Films & Filming 9-7:11
  Ap '63
Gina says.  Interview 33:17 Je '73
Lollobrigida, G.  Last word.  Viva 1-4:127 Ja '74

## LOMBARD, CAROLE
Belfrage, C.  Interview.  Motion Pic 37:58 My '29
O'Malley, A.  Sketch.  Motion Pic Classic 29:45 Je '29
Cruikshank, H.  Sketch.  Motion Pic 40:74 N '30
Goldbeck, E.  Interview.  Motion Pic Classic 33:73 Ap '31
Biery, R.  Sketch.  Photop 40:49 Je '31
Biery, R.  Her love story.  Photop 40:55 S '31
Hall, G.  Why she married William Powell.  Motion Pic 42:58
  D '31
Goldbeck, E.  Bill Powell talks about his wife.  Movie Classic
  3:15 N '32
How Sylvia changed her figure.  Photop 43:50 Ap '33
Service, F.  Interview.  Movie Classic 4:51 My '33
Hall, G.  Interview.  Photop 44:50 O '33
Wilson, E.  That funny divorce.  Silver S 4-6:20 Ap '34
Keene, D.  Carole gets her own way.  Silver S 4-7:20 My '34
Lee, S.  Interview.  Motion Pic 47:5 My '34
Calhoun, D.  Home of.  Motion Pic 47:40 My '34
Wilson, E.  Garbo vs. Lombard.  Silver S 5-2:16 D '34
Lee, S.  Interview.  Movie Classic 7:37 D '34
Wilson, E.  Tripping to New York.  Silver S 5-6:18 Ap '35
Best dressed star.  Movie Classic 8:28 My '35
Harrison, H.  Sincerely, Carole Lombard.  Silver S 5-9:31 Jl
  '35
French, W. F.  Interview.  Motion Pic 50:28 Ag '35
Lane, V.  Her clothes match her moods.  Movie Classic 9:44 S
  '35
Lee, S.  Self-made woman.  Movie Classic 9:32 D '35
Wilson, E.  Everything has been done before; interview.  Silver
  S 6-3:18 Ja '36

Thompson, M.   One of Hollywood's practical jokers.   Cosmop
    120:58 Mr '46
Dowling, M.   Interview.   Motion Pic 51:36 Jl '36
Wilson, E.   Projections.   Silver S 7-3:22 Ja '37
Lang, H.   Her home life.   Motion Pic 53:36 F '37
Williams, W.   Hazing.   Silver S 7-11:53 S '37
Story of.   Life 5:9 O 17 '38
McFee, F.   Why is she hiding out from Hollywood?   Screen
    Book 21-3:28 O '38
Schrott, E.   Hollywood's goofy gal goes glamorous.   Screen
    Book 21-7:28 F '39
Her marriage.   Time 33:52 Ap 10 '39
Underhill, D.   Homemaker Lombard.   Screen Book 22-4:52 N
    '39
She looks at preview of They knew what they wanted.   Life 9:47
    S 30 '40
Mulvey, K.   Sketch.   Womans Home C 67:15 D '40
Bio note; filmog.   Movies & People 2:23 '40
Wilson, E.   It looked good for a laugh at the time.   Silver S
    11-3:26 Ja '41
Lane, J.   Story of.   Photop 18:48 F '41
Wilson, E.   What about those Lombard rumors?   Silver S 12-5:
    26 Mr '42
Manners, M. J.   Killed in action.   Silver S 12-6:22 Ap '42
Letters.   Films In R 12-3:182 Mr '61
Pinup of the past.   Films & Filming 19-8:70 My '73
St. Johns, A. R.   A gallant lady.   Liberty 1-10:43 Fall '73

LOMNICKI, TADEUSZ
    Bio note; filmog.   Focus On F 3:18 My/Ag '70

LON, ALICE
    Alice tells why she still wears a size 7.   TV Guide 5-31:28 Ag
        3 '57

LONDON, BABE
    Chatterton, R. W.   From prat falls to portraits.   Classic Film
        Collect 18:21 Sum '67
    Slide, A.   Interview.   Silent Pic 15:4 Sum '72

LONDON, JULIE
    Taylor, T.   Julie comes to Manhattan.   Cue 25-2:13 Ja 14 '56
    Taylor, T.   Out of the dragnet.   Cue 26-3:11 Ja 19 '57
    Choen, J.   Filmog.   Films In R 20-3:188 Mr '69
    Reichenthal, C.   Letter.   Films In R 20-5:323 My '69
    Hano, A.   She's on hand to provide the basic femininity.   TV
        Guide 20-25:18 Je 17 '72

LONG, RICHARD
    Should teenagers marry?   Photop 30:66 D '46
    Sketch.   Photop 31:18 Jl '47

LONG, SALLY
   Uselton, R. A.   The Wampus baby stars.   Films In R 21-2:73
     F '70

LONG, WALTER
   Walter the wicked.   Photop 12-2:67 Jl '17
   Cheatham, M.   Interview.   Classic 16:36 Jl '23
   Obit.   Screen World 4:177 '53
   Estes, O. Jr.   Versatile villain.   Classic Film Collect 15:14
     Sum '66

LONGET, CLAUDINE
   The surrender of Leslie Raddatz.   TV Guide 16-5:12 F 3 '68
   Christy, G.   Holiday with music.   Good House 169:40 D '69

LOO, RICHARD
   Raddatz, L.   No. 1 son is now Master Po.   TV Guide 21-25:27
     Je 23 '73

LOOMIS, MARGARET
   Cheatham, M.   Interview.   Motion Pic Classic 11:34 F '21

LOR, DENISE
   In the cast.   TV Guide 1-12:12 Je 19 '53

LORD, JACK
   I made my wife agree she'd never have my baby.   Photop 77-2:
     54 Ag '70
   How I faced my drinking problem.   Photop 78-4:60 O '70
   They were two brutes.   Photop 79-5:81 My '71
   Whitney, D.   Jack Lord, superstar.   TV Guide 19-36:24 S 4 '71
   The 16 hours that changed his life.   Photop 80-4:76 O '71
   Working together, keeping apart.   Photop 80-6:53 D '71
   My life is filled with miracles.   Photop 85-3:42 Mr '74

LORD, MARJORIE
   Danny Thomas's TV wife.   Look 24:46b Mr 1 '60
   Meet Danny's Missus.   TV Guide 9-11:20 Mr 18 '61

LORD, PAULINE
   Obit.   New Rep 123:23 N 6 '50
     Newsweek 36:65 O 23 '50
     Screen World 2:234 '51
     Time 56:99 O 23 '50

LORD, PHILLIPS HAYNES
   Sketch.   National 59:245 Mr '31

LORDE, ATHENA
   Obit.   Screen World p237 '74

LOREN, SOPHIA
   Zunser, J.   Sophia makes the grade.   Cue 26-9:11 Mr 2 '57

Zunser, J.   Conversation with Sophia.   Cue 30-31:10 Ag 5 '61
Moravia, A.   This is your life, Sophia Loren.   Show 2-9:55 S
     '62
Ponti, C.   At home with Sophia.   Show 2-9:56 S '62
Sweigart, W. R.   Letter concerning English translations of titles
     of her Italian films.   Films In R 14-2:125 F '63
Lane, J. F.   The face of '63--Italy.   Films & Filming 9-7:11
     Ap '63
Sweigart, W. R.   Letter.   Films In R 14-8:504 O '63
Silke, J. R.   Earth mother.   Cinema (BH) 2-1:20 F/Mr '64
Cheever, J.   Sophia.   Sat Eve Post 240:33 O 21 '67
Her greatest role:  wife and mother.   Vogue 153:202 Ap 1 '69
Barry, J.   Her baby.   McCalls 96:124 Ap '69
Blum, S.   Sophia and Carlo talk about their new baby.   Redbook
     133:81 My '69
Levy, A.   A woman was born to have children.   Good House
     169:86 N '69
Sophia's miscarriage since son's birth.   Photop 77-6:69 Je '70
Burke, T.   Now I am a complete woman.   N. Y. Times Bio Ed
     O 4 '70
Questions at Radio City News conference.   New Yorker 46:20 O
     3 '70
Sophia Loren.   Vogue 156:124 D '70
Arras, J. & Hickey, N.   What Miss Loren is wearing this sea-
     son.   TV Guide 19-2:26 Ja 9 '71
Hershey, L.   Sophia.   Serenely female; interview.   Ladies Home
     J 88:48 Ja '71
The mystery men who want to destroy them.   Photop 79-5:85 My
     '71
My life depends on having another baby.   Photop 81-1:70 Ja '72
We go to Rome to visit Sophia and son.   Mod Screen 66-3:65 Mr
     '72
Sophia's packing plan.   Vogue 159:52 Ap 15 '72
In the kitchen with love; excerpts.   Ladies Home J 89:83 Mr;
     140 Ap '72
The last of the love goddesses.   Show 2-3:26 My '72
Sophia's expecting again.   Mod Screen 66-11:51 N '72
Evans, P.   Glamour queen locked in the asylum of fame.   Mov
     Dig 2-1:19 Ja '73
Child threatened.   Photop 83-1:52 Ja '73
Sophia sings.   Films Illus 2-19:13 Ja '73
Ian Bannen talks about Loren.   Photop 85-6:41 Je '74
Efron, E.   An appreciation.   TV Guide 22:45:10 N 9 '74

LORNE, MARION
     Roberts, F.   Interview.   Theatre World 25:36 Ja '36
     Returns to stage.   Theatre World 29:135 Mr '38
     In the cast.   TV Guide 1-36:20 D 4 '53
     Professional flibbertigibbet.   TV Guide 6-5:29 F 1 '58
     Miss frenetic and Miss flabbergasted.   TV Guide 8-42:9 O 15 '60
     Obit.   N. Y. Times p47 My 10 '68

LORRAINE, LOUISE
  Gassaway, G.   Interview.   Motion Pic Classic 14:36 Jl '22
  Lahue, K. C.   Louise Lorraine.   8mm Collect 13:5 Fall/Win
    '65
  Uselton, R. A.   The Wampus baby stars.   Films In R 21-2:73
    F '70

LORRE, PETER
  Service, F.   Interview.   Motion Pic 49:60 F '35
  Williams, W.   The world's greatest actor.   Silver S 5-10:22 Ag
    '35
  Surmelian, L.   Story of.   Motion Pic 51:51 Je '36
  Lang, H.   He's an "inside" actor.   Screen Book 19-5:49 D '37
  Bio note; filmog.   Movies & People 2:23 '40
  Whorf, R.   As I see them.   Lions R 3-2:no p# Ja '44
  Benedict, P.   Mild mannered maniac.   Silver S 14-12:26 O '44
  Obit.   Film R p41 '64/65
  Made for each other.   Screen Greats 1-2:68 Sum '71
  Everson, W. K.   The Peter Lorre story.   Castle of Franken-
    stein 5:14 n. d.
  Bojarski, R.   Lorre 1904-1964 Castle of Frankenstein 5:18 n. d.
  The Lorre story; filmog.   Famous Monsters (special issue) n. d.

LOSEE, FRANK
  Let Frank do it.   Photop 11-6:115 My '17

LOUDON, DOROTHY
  Zolotow, M.   She was the screaming end.   TV Guide 11-22:8
    Je 1 '63
  Millstein, G.   Lowdown on Loudon.   Sat Eve Post 236:70 Ap 6
    '63

LOUIS, WILLARD
  Tilton, J.   Interview.   Motion Pic 31:51 Ap '27

LOUISE, ANITA
  Hartley, K.   How she became a star.   Motion Pic 51:26 Jl '36
  March, M.   Sketch.   Movie Classic 10:36 Jl '36
  Harrison, H.   Beautiful veteran.   Silver S 6-10:29 Ag '36
  Campbell, S.   Was this the dangerous age?   Screen Book 21-1:
    41 Ag '38
  Uselton, R. A.   The Wampus baby stars.   Films In R 21-2:73
    F '70
  Obit.   Classic Film Collect (reprint Washington Post) 27:60 Spg/
    Sum '70
    Film R p13 '71/72
    N. Y. Times p33 Ap 27 '70
    Same.   N. Y. Times Bio Ed Ap 27 '70
    Newsweek 75:110 My 11 '70
    Screen World 22:238 '71
    Time 95:89 My 11 '70

LOUISE, TINA
    Durslag, M.   Speaks of men, marriage and the Mets.   TV Guide
        12-49:12 D 5 '64

LOVE, BESSIE
    Zeidman, B.   Interview.   Motion Pic 12:85 O '16
    From extra to stardom.   Motion Pic Classic 5:41 S '17
    Todd, S.   The rise of Bessie Love.   Motion Pic 14:330 '47
    How she got into motion pictures.   Motion Pic 14:61 Ja '18
    Montanye, L.   Interview.   Motion Pic 15:79 Ap '18
    Rosemon, E.   A day with Bessie Love.   Motion Pic Classic
        6:54 My '18
    Peltret, E.   Interview.   Motion Pic 11:16 S '20
    Curley, K.   Interview.   Motion Pic 23:70 My '22
    Gassaway, G.   Interview.   Motion Pic Classic 14:38 Ag '22
    Carr, H.   Her return to the screen.   Motion Pic 25:21 Ag '23
    de Revere, F. V.   Analysis of her face.   Motion Pic 29:55 Mr
        '25
    Be true to your type.   Motion Pic Classic 21:62 My '25
    Hall, G.   Confessions.   Motion Pic Classic 29:20 Je '29
    On working behind the camera.   Films & Filming 8-10:16 Jl '62
    Uselton, R. A.   The Wampus baby stars.   Films In R 21-2:73
        F '70
    Hollander, Z.   Bessie Love, 74 years young and still acting in
        films (reprint South Middlesex News) Classic Film Collect
        36:extra 3 Fall '72

LOVE, MONTAGU
    Bartlett, R.   Montague encounters a Capulet.   Photop 12-2:95 Jl
        '17
    Hall, G.   Sketch.   Motion Pic Classic 7:30 D '18
    Malvern, P.   Interview.   Motion Pic Classic 11:48 S '20
    Clarke, F. S.   Rasputin on film.   Cinefantastique 1-1:6 Fall '70

LOVEJOY, FRANK
    Rising star.   Film R p108 '52/53

LOVELACE, LINDA
    Blumenthal, R.   Porno chic.   N. Y. Times Mag p28 Ja 21 '73
    Hill, R.   My Linda Lovelace problem (and yours).   Oui 2-2:71
        F '73

LOVELY, LOUISE
    Owen, K.   The lady of the names.   Photop 12-2:46 Jl '17
    Sheridan, P.   Sketch.   Motion Pic Classic 6:19 Mr '18
    Kingsley, R.   Interview.   Motion Pic Classic 9:36 O '19

LOWE, EDMUND
    Hall, G.   Interview.   Motion Pic 19:68 Ap/My '20
    Hall, G.   Interview.   Motion Pic Classic 10:51 Ag '20
    Interview.   Motion Pic Classic 26:58 N '27
    Wells, H. K.   Struggling along on $50,000 a year.   Motion Pic
        Classic 26:55 F '28

Manners, D.   Interview.   Motion Pic 37:67 F '29
Belfrage, C.   Sketch.   Motion Pic Classic 29:28 Ap '29
Gray, C.   Sketch.   Motion Pic 39:42 My '30
Traviner, R.   Why he married an actress.   Photop 43:52 Mr '33
Advice for the well-dressed young man.   Photop 47:54 Mr '35
Bio note; filmog.   Movies & People 2:23 '40
Obit.   Classic Film Collect 31:62 (reprint N. Y. Times) Sum '71
   Film R p13 '71/72
   N. Y. Times p40 Ap 23 '71
   Same.   N. Y. Times Bio Ed Ap 23 '71
   Newsweek 77:82 My 3 '71
   Screen World 23:238 '72

LOWELL, JOAN
   Calhoun, D.   Her story.   Motion Pic 38:40 S '29
   Filming Adventure girl.   Photop 46:52 N '34

LOWELL, LOUISE
   The first camera-maid.   Photop 17:80 F '20
   Peterson, E. B.   Sketch.   Motion Pic 20:75 Ja '21

LOWERY, ROBERT
   Obit.   Classic Film Collect 34:X-3 Spg '72
      N. Y. Times p30 D 27 '71
      Same.   N. Y. Times Bio Ed D 27 '71
      Screen World 23:238 '72
   Puzo, L.   Robert Lowery; filmog.   Films In R 23-2:117 F '72

LOWRY, JUDITH
   81 is a vintage year.   Life 71:83 O 8 '71
   Rosenbaum, H.   Profile: Judith Lowry.   TV N. Y. 1-2:19 N '72

LOY, MYRNA
   Donnell, D.   Sketch.   Motion Pic Classic 25:55 Ag '27
   Moak, E. R.   Loy a victim of sudden success.   Silver S 3-5:18
     Mr '33
   Hall, G.   Interview.   Movie Classic 4:51 Je '33
   Fidler, J. M.   Romance rumors.   Motion Pic 46:41 Ag '33
   Keats, P.   I'm in love.   Silver S 4-5:16 Mr '34
   Keats, P.   Myrna's "School for wives."   Silver S 5-3:18 Ja '35
   Samuels, L.   Loyal to Loy.   Silver S 5-11:19 S '35
   Ulman, W. A. Jr.   Her success in pictures with William Pow-
     ell.   Movie Classic 10:40 Mr '36
   Hamilton, S.   Sketch.   Motion Pic 51:33 Ap '36
   Harrison, H.   Interview.   Movie Classic 10:38 Ap '36
   Williams, W.   She's swell.   Silver S 6-9:29 Jl '36
   Mack, G.   Crises in her life.   Movie Classic 10:36 Jl '36
   Zeitlin, I.   Interview.   Motion Pic 52:36 N '36
   Reid, J.   Sketch.   Motion Pic 53:30 Ap '37
   Sketch.   Life 3:46 O 11 '37
   Cheatham, M.   The perfect wife has a past.   Screen Book 20-1:
     24 F '38
   Wilson, E.   Projection.   Silver S 8-6:54 Ap '38

Myrna Loy and William Powell.   Visages 26:entire issue Ag '38

Hartley, K.   Just call her Queenie.   Screen Book 21-2:28 S '38

Proctor, K.   You're next, Mrs. Hornblow...   Screen Book 21-11:
    34 Je '39

Sullivan.   Virtue is still its own reward.   Silver S 10-10:34 Ag
    '40

Bio note; filmog.   Movies & People 2:24 '40

Trotter, M.   Astrological forecast.   Photop 18:31 F '41

Baldwin, F.   Sketch.   Photop 18:27 Ap '41

They call her Min.   Lions R 1-3:no p# N '41

Myrna Loy's protégé.   Lions R 2-1:no p# S/O '42

The things I do for Nora.   Lions R 4-1:no p# F '45

My luckiest day.   Cosmop 121:155 D '46

Parsons, L. O.   Cosmop's citation for best performance of
    month.   Cosmop 122:67 Ja '47

Grant, C.   Tribute to.   Photop 33:50 Ag '48

It's the sponsor who pays.   TV Guide 4-37:24 S 15 '56

Letters.   Films In R 14-3:184 Mr '63

Letters.   Films In R 14-4:247 Ap '36

Lauritzen, E.   Letter.   Films In R 14-5:318 My '63

Braun, E.   Myrna Loy on comedy.   Films & Filming 14-6:9 Mr
    '68

Hemming, R.   We're not second-class citizens or sad sacks.
    Sr Schol 93:13 O 25 '68

Barthel, J.   Quartet of queens.   Life 70:66 F 19 '71

Grand slam.   TV Guide 19-41:16 O 9 '71

It was much more hazardous, but more fun.   TV Guide 19-43:26
    O 23 '71

The love teams.   Screen Greats 1-2:10 Sum '71

Carr, L.   A lovely lady talks about her past.   Movie Dig 1-4:120
    Jl '72

Chierichetti, D.   Myrna Loy today.   Film Fan Mo 141:3 Mr '73

Bowers, R.   Legendary ladies of the movies.   Films In R 24-6:
    321 Je/Jl '73


LU, LISA
    Hao-chi-la.   TV Guide 7-12:28 Mr 21 '59
    Zunser, J.   Hollywood goes East.   Cue 29-11:9 Mr 12 '60


LUCAS, GAIL
    Efron, E.   The nurses.   TV Guide 10-50:22 D 15 '62


LUCAS, NICK
    Pitts, M. R.   Pop singers on the screen; filmog.   Film Fan Mo
        112:15 O '70


LUCAS, WILFRED
    How he became a photoplayer.   Motion Pic 9:118 Mr '15


LUCCI, SUSAN
    Drake, R.   What a handicap.   TV Guide 19-23:27 Je 5 '71

LUCKINBILL, LAURENCE
  Carragher, B.  The man with Such good friends.  Show 12:37 F
    '72
  Barber, R.  Mark Spitz he ain't.  TV Guide 21-13:26 Mr 31 '73

LUDEN, JACK
  Thorp, D.  Sketch.  Motion Pic Classic 26:63 Ja '38

LUFT, LORNA
  Newsmakers.  Newsweek 78:61 D 13 '71
  Wilson, J. S.  Another kid in the family of singers.  N. Y.
    Times Bio Ed p1820 O '72
  Headliners.  Photop 83-5:14 My '73
  Colacello, B.  Lorna Luft.  Interview p12 Mr '74

LUGOSI, BELA
  Hall, G.  Interview.  Motion Pic Classic 32:33 Ja '31
  Is he the second Chaney?  Silver S 1-3:51 Ja '31
  Sinclair, J.  Master of horrors.  Silver S 2-3:44 Ja '32
  Coulter, H.  Cold chills and cold cash.  Cinema Progress 3-2:
    16 My/Je '38
  Hall, G.  Memos of a madman.  Silver S 11-9:52 Jl '41
  Letters.  Films In R 15-9:579 N '64
  Brown, B.  Lugosi's tragic drug addiction.  Castle of Franken-
    stein 10:8 F '66
  Everson, W. K.  The last days of Bela Lugosi.  Castle of
    Frankenstein 8:18 n. d.
  Horror film acting.  Castle of Frankenstein 7:59 n. d.
  Borland, C.  What makes Lugosi tick.  Famous Monsters 39:38
    Je '66
  Dracula.  Famous Monsters 49:4 n. d.
  Clarke, F. S.  Rasputin on film.  Cinefantastique 1-1:6 Fall '70
  Marlowe, D.  Lugosi.  Classic Film Collect 26:46 Win '70
  Two guys from Transylvania.  Screen Greats 1-2:72 Sum '71
  del Olmo, F.  Afraid of Dracula?  His son never was.  Classic
    Film Collect 32:53 Fall '71
  Fernett, G.  Bela Lugosi.  Classic Film Collect 36:28 Fall '72
  Dillard, R. H.  Three lines: poetry.  Film J 1-3/4:35 Fall/
    Win '72
  Lennig, A.  The raven.  Film J 2-2:53 Ja/Mr '73
  Dello Stritto, F.  An investigation of a cinema phenomenon.
    Photon 21:15 n. d.

LUKAS, PAUL
  Sammis, E. R.  Sketch.  Motion Pic Classic 27:58 Je '27
  Hall, G.  Sketch.  Motion Pic Classic 32:56 N '30
  Hall, G.  Sketch.  Movie Classic 1:59 D '31
  Churchill, E.  The luck of Lukas.  Silver S 2-2:40 D '31
  Lane, J.  Interview.  Movie Classic 2:15 Jl '32
  Hamilton, S.  Sketch.  Photop 54:31 S '40
  Strauss, T.  Work of.  Theatre Arts 26:96 F '42
  Bio.  Cur Bio 3:534 '42
  Watkins, F.; Tillmany, J.; Maltin, L.  Paul Lukas; filmog.

Film Fan Mo 112:3 O '70
Obit.   Classic Film Collect 32:62 Fall '71
Cur Bio 32:43 O '71
Same.   Cur Bio Yrbk 1971:466 '72
Film R p14 '72/73
N. Y. Times p38 Ag 17 '71
Same.   N. Y. Times Bio Ed Ag 17 '71
Newsweek 78:55 Ag 30 '71
Screen World 23:238 '72
Time 98:51 Ag 30 '71
Shawcross, G.   Paul Lukas; filmog.   Films In R 23-2:125 F '72

LUKE, KEYE
Chinese Aubrey Beardsley.   Lions R 2-3:no p# D '42
Actor, artist and scholar.   Lions R 2-5:no p# Jl '43
Student turns teacher.   Lions R 3-3(sup):no p# Ap '44
Albert, J. E.   Keye Luke; filmog.   Film Fan Mo 143:25 My '73
Raddatz, L.   No. 1 son is now Master Po.   TV Guide 21-25:27
Je 27 '73

LULLI, FOLCO
Obit.   Film R p13 '71/72

LUND, DEANNA
Crail, T.   It never hurts to arrive by fire engine.   TV Guide
17-7:12 F 15 '69
Only we were there.   Photop 78-1:53 Jl '70
We almost lost our baby on the day she was born.   Photop 80-6:
59 D '71

LUND, JOHN
Dudley, F.   Mr. Gold Mine.   Silver S 17-4:37 F '47
Parsons, L. O.   Cosmop's citation for the best performance of
month.   Cosmop 125:12 D '48
O'Leary, D.   John looks anew at the ladies.   Silver S 19-2:38 D
'48

LUND, LUCILLE
Uselton, R. A.   The Wampus baby stars.   Films In R 21-2:73
F '70

LUNDIGAN, WILLIAM
Schwarzkopf, J.   Sketch.   Motion Pic 54:13 O '37
Hamilton, S.   Sketch.   Photop 54:28 My '40
Lindsay, M.   Sketch.   Photop 18:31 Ja '41
He trained on the air.   Lions R 1-9:no p# My '42
Stars of tomorrow.   Lions R 1-11/12:no p# Jl/Ag '42
Call him Bill.   Lions R 2-1:no p# S/O '42
Lundigan, W.   I never knew.   Lions R 2-3(sup):no p# Ja '43
Athlete in wheelchair.   Lions R 2-5:no p# Jl '43
Booker, J. H.   Private Lundigan, USMC.   Lions R 3-1:no p#
S '43
Balling, F. D.   The boys from Syracuse.   Silver S 20-2:40 D '49
Failure makes good.   TV Guide 4-38:25 S 22 '56

LUPINO, IDA
Sketch. Photop 44:60 N '33
Goldbeck, E. Sketch. Movie Classic 6:52 My '34
Hall, G. Interview. Motion Pic 52:37 O '36
Castle, M. Story of. Motion Pic 54:45 N '37
Hamilton, S. & Morse, W. Jr. Sketch. Photop 54:21 Mr '40
Sketch. Newsweek 16:36 Jl 29 '40
Service, F. She's as crazy as a fox. Silver S 11-1:24 N '40
Mulvey, K. Sketch. Womans Home C 68:27 Mr '41
Vallee, W. L. Hostess extraordinary. Silver S 12-5:38 Mr '42
Hopper, H. Sketch. Photop 21:28 Ag '42
St. Johns, A. R. Story of. Cosmop 114:46 Ja '43 & following
    issues.
Trotter, M. Her horoscope. Photop 22:30 F '43
Embarrassing moment. Photop 23:59 S '43
Should a girl propose? Photop 24:43 F '44
My faith. Photop 24:48 My '44
Bangs, B. Ida with a lilt. Silver S 15-4:42 F '45
Hall, G. Ida reads her tea leaves. Silver S 16-1:30 N '45
Lupino, I. The trouble with men is women. Silver S 17-6:36
    Ap '47
Lupino, I. Who says men are people? Silver S 18-8:22 Je '48
Nelson, K. Keep it simple. Silver S 18-12:44 O '48
Waterbury, R. Home of. Photop 34:56 F '49
Lupino, I. I cannot be good. Silver S 19-8:42 Je '49
Keats, P. Ida takes over in no-woman's land. Silver S 20-8:36
    Je '50
Shane, D. Who's boss--Ida or Howard? Silver S 23-10:36 Ag
    '53
Director only? Films & Filming 1-4:26 Ja '55
The director and the public; a symposium. Film Culture 1-2:15
    Mr/Ap '55
Minoff, P. Non-private lives? Cue 26-3:12 Ja 19 '57
A new twist. TV Guide 5-28:28 Jl 13 '57
Sarris, A. Oddities and one shots. Film Culture 28:45 Spg '63
Lupino, I. Me, mother directress. Action 2-3:14 My/Je '67
Nolan, J. E. Ida Lupino; director; directing filmog. Film Fan
    Mo 89:8 N '68
What directors are saying. Action 4-5:32 S/O '69
Gardner, P. Lupino in comeback after 15 years. N. Y. Times
    Bio Ed p1821 O '72
Lupino, I. This was my favorite role. Movie Dig 1-6:20 N '72
Catching up with Ida Lupino. Mod Screen 66-11:68 N '72
Women directors; directing filmog. Film Comment 8-4:42 N '72
The best Christmas of my life. Photop 83-1:27 Ja '73
Parker, F. Discovering Ida Lupino. Action 8-4:19 Jl/Ag '73

LUPTON, JOHN
Here come the heroes. TV Guide 4-37:28 S 15 '56
Stalking the trail of success. TV Guide 5-40:6 O 5 '57

LUPUS, PETER
Workout with Lupus. TV Guide 16-15:19 Ap 13 '68

Mission: accomplished. Photop 77-1:76 Jl '70
Woods, B. Television hero takes a healthy view of life. N. Y.
Daily News p60 Mr 22 '74
Playgirl's man for April; centerfold. Playgirl 1-11:68 Ap '74

LUTHER, ANNA
Bruner, F. V. Sketch. Motion Pic 17:74 Je '19
Sketch. Photop 18:28 Ag '20
Obit. Screen World 12:222 '61

LYNCH, ALFRED
Rising star. Film R p38 '63/64

LYNCH, HELEN
Uselton, R. A. The Wampus baby stars. Films In R 21-2:73
F '70

LYNDE, PAUL
Wilkie, J. That what's-his-name is a very funny fellow. TV
Guide 17-29:15 Jl 19 '69
Johnson, D. Now let's hear it for Paul Lynde. After Dark 5-
7:52 N '72
Raddatz, L. If he ever calms down he'll be in trouble. TV
Guide 21-6:24 F 10 '73
Strout, D. Interview. Mod Screen 67-2:32 F '73
At home with Paul. Photop 83-5:62 My '73
To each his home. TV Guide 22-3:11 Ja 19 '74

LYNLEY, CAROL
Zunser, J. Star? Don't be silly! Cue 28-29:18 Jl 18 '59
Rising star. Film R p21 '60/61
Leiter, S. Sweet and not so sweet. Show 4-3:64 Mr '64
Carol grows up; photos. Playboy 12-3:108 Mr '65
Strout, D. Interview. Mod Screen 67-1:27 Ja '72

LYNN, DIANA
Hamilton, S. Sketch. Photop 25:54 Ag '44
Sketch. Photop 25:52 N '44
My biggest lie. Photop 26:56 Mr '45
Notes about. Photop 27:52 Ag '45
Franchey, J. R. Fugitive from glamour. Silver S 15-12:38 O
'45
The role I liked best. Sat Eve Post 218:100 Ja 26 '46
Pritchett, F. Sketch. Photop 29:43 S '46
Should teenagers marry? Photop 30:67 D '46
Letter from Liza. Silver S 18-5:42 Mr '48
Vallee, W. L. Warning to a young man in love. Silver S 18-6:
22 Ap '48
Norman, D. Sketch. Ladies Home J 96:65 S '49
Howard, M. What every girl desires. Silver S 20-3:42 Ja '50
Vallee, W. L. How careerish can you get? Silver S 21-7:44
My '51
Obit. Classic Film Collect 34:X-3 Spg '72

Lynn, Jeffrey                                                    463

    Cur Bio 33:46 F '72
    N. Y. Times p60 D 19 '71
    N. Y. Times Bio Ed D 19 '71
    Newsweek 78:63 D 27 '71
    Screen World 23:238 '72
  Brock, A.  Backstage with the stars.   Classic Film Collect 36:
    30 Fall '72

LYNN, JEFFREY
  Joseph, R.  He delivers the goods.   Silver S 9-1:52 N '38
  Smithson, E. J.  A line on Lynn.   Screen Book 21-7:22 F '39
  Rhea, M.  Sketch.   Photop 53:30 Ap '39
  Asher, J.  Eligible bachelor.   Silver S 10-12:38 O '40
  Bio note; filmog.  Movies & People 2:24 '40
  Dudley, F.  Interview.   Photop 29:25 Ja '42
  Blair, E.  High spots for Jeffrey.   Silver S 12-7:36 My '42

LYON, BEN
  de Revere, F. V.  Face analysis of.   Motion Pic 28:44 D '24
  Vampires I have known.   Photop 27:28 F '25
  Day, D.  Interview.   Motion Pic 29:27 Mr '25
  Redway, S.  Interview.   Motion Pic Classic 2:56 Ja '26
  Hall, H. R.  Sketch.   Motion Pic Classic 24:54 F '27
  Dressen, M.  His ideas on marriage.   Motion Pic 36:33 S '28
  Calhoun, D.  Interview.   Motion Pic Classic 31:51 My '30
  Fender, D.  His honeymoon.   Motion Pic Classic 32:30 S '30
  Calhoun, D.  Interview.   Motion Pic 41:48 My '31
  Cooper, J.  Lyon's up in the air.   Silver S 2-3:41 Ja '32
  His broadcasts for servicemen.   Time 40:40 D 28 '42
  What they are doing now.   Show 2-8:106 Ag '62
  Lyon, B. and Slide, A.  Bebe Daniels; conversation.   Silent Pic
    10:no p# Spg '71
  Ben Lyon filmog.   Silent Pic 10:no p# Spg '71

LYON, SUE
  Niebuhr, R.  Lolita.   Show 2-8:69 Ag '62
  Rising star.   Film R p44 '63/64
  Lawrenson, H.  The nightmare of iguana.   Show 4-1:46 Ja '64

LYONS, EDDIE
  Willis, R.  They call him Smiling Eddie.   Photop 7-3:130 F '15

LYONS, ROBERT F.
  Debut.   Show 1-10:56 Ag 6 '70

LYS, LYA
  Flake, K.  Flight to freedom.   Screen Book 21-12:52 Jl '39
  William, B.  Whirling around with Lya.   Silver S 10-1:46 N '39

LYTELL, BERT
  Peltret, E.  The essential ingredient.   Photop 14-5:41 O '18
  Kingston, R.  Sketch.   Motion Pic 15:45 N '18
  Peltret, E.  Interview.   Motion Pic Classic 9:22 N '19

Peltret, E.   Interview.   Motion Pic 20:64 Ag '20
Interview.   Dram Mir 369 Ag 28 '20
Service, F.   Interview.   Motion Pic Classic 11:25 O '20
A lesson in love.   Photop 19:43 F '21
Peltret, E.   Sketch.   Motion Pic Classic 13:61 Ja '22
Naylor, H. S.   Interview.   Motion Pic 23:79 Jl '22
de Revere, F. V.   Analyses of his face.   Motion Pic 28:45 D
   '24
Leon, S.   Letter.   Films In R 24-4:252 Ap '73


MacARTHUR, JAMES
   Fenin, G.   The face of '63--United States.   Films & Filming 9-
      6:55 Mr '63
   Marriage on the rocks.   Photop 78-4:45 O '70
   Helen Hayes discusses:   how we taught our son to love.   Photop
      79-6:42 Je '71
   How a divorced dad and his new wife make the most of his kids.
      Mod Screen 65-11:60 N '71
   Working together, keeping apart.   Photop 80-6:53 D '71
   Second generation.   Films Illus 1-10:12 Ap '72
   Cooking with a star.   Mod Screen 66-7:34 Jl '72
   Davidson, B.   Hawaii's happy almond.   TV Guide 21-38:21 S 22
      '73

MacCAULAY, JOSEPH
   Obit.   N. Y. Times p45 O 12 '67

MACCHIA, JOHN
   Obit.   Screen World 19:235 '68

MacDERMOTT, MARC
   Sketch.   Motion Pic 9:106 Mr '15
   Sketch.   Motion Pic 13:73 My '17
   Frederick, J. S.   Movie '49er.   Photop 12-5:104 O '17
   Naylor, H. S.   Interview.   Motion Pic 17:40 Jl '19
   Hall, G.   Interview.   Motion Pic 20:74 Ja '21

MacDONALD, DONALD
   Taylor, M. K.   Interview.   Motion Pic Classic 8:22 Mr '19

MacDONNALD J. FARRELL
   Obit.   Screen World 4:177 '53

MacDONALD, J. FARRELL
   Hall, G.   Sketch.   Motion Pic Classic 31:45 Mr '30
   York, C.   Sketch.   Photop 37:69 My '30
   Sketch.   Photop 38:10 Jl '30
   Goldbeck, E.   Interview.   Motion Pic Classic 32:41 D '30
   Reid, M.   Looks, lyrics and legs.   Silver S 1-3:33 Ja '31
   Her appearance in London.   Graphic 133:470 O 3 '31
   Grant, J.   Unfounded rumors of her death.   Movie Classic 1:43

S '31
Grant, J.  Interview.  Motion Pic 42:43 N '31
Willis, B.  Interview.  Motion Pic 43:26 Mr '32
Rice, L.  Analysis of her handwriting.  Movie Classic 2:51 Jl
    '32
Pryor, N.  Interview.  Motion Pic 45:26 F '33
Jeanette MacDonald.  Cinema Dig 3-6:11 Ap 24 '33
Cruikshank.  Interview.  Motion Pic 46:49 D '33
Sharon, M.  Hollywood has always spelt good luck for me.  Sil-
    ver S 4-12:21 O '34
Her beauty treatments.  Motion Pic 49:50 Je '35
Dixe, M.  Her romance.  Movie Classic 8:14 Ag '35
Liza.  With Jeanette and Nelson on location.  Silver S 6-2:18 D
    '35
As a hostess.  Photop 49:74 Mr '36
Kent, J.  Story of her success.  Movie Classic 10:34 Mr '36
Hartley, K.  No longer conservative.  Motion Pic 51:47 Je '36
Seymore, H.  Interview.  Photop 50:31 S '36
Hall, G.  Her advice to girls in love.  Motion Pic 53:36 Ap '37
Wolf, A. L.  Don't cry over spilt milk.  Silver S 7-7:26 My '37
Hill, M.  Jeanette dances.  Screen Book 19-2:58 S '37
Wilson, E.  Projections.  Silver S 7-12:22 D '37
Van Wyck, C.  The secret of her beauty.  Photop 53:10 My '39
Smithson, E. J.  She made it the hard way.  Screen Book 21-10:
    46 My '39
Wilson, E.  On tour with a prima donna.  Silver S 10-8:22 Je
    '40
Walker, H. L.  Sketch.  Photop 54:40 O '40
Bio note; filmog.  Movies & People 2:24 '40
Hall, G.  Most in love couple in Hollywood.  Silver S 11-12:22
    O '41
Dual personality.  Lions R 1-2:no p# O '41
Sketch.  Womans Home C 68:15 D '41
Study in contrasts.  Lions R 1-8:no p# Ap '42
Wilson, E.  Jeanette falls in line.  Silver S 12-10:28 Ag '42
Trills on the high Cs.  Lions R 2-1:no p# S/O '42
Questions about her.  Photop 23:80 O '43
Should a girl propose?  Photop 24:42 F '44
The drama behind the music.  Lions R 3-5:no p# D '44
Marsh, P.  Jeanette reconsiders.  Silver S 17-10:44 Ag '47
Letters.  Films In R 16-4:259 Ap '65
Looking Hollywood way.  Good Old Days 6-1:26 Jl '69
The love teams.  Screen Greats 1-2:10 Sum '71

MacDONALD, KATHERINE
Harris, C. L.  Interview.  Motion Pic Classic 7:22 N '18
Our incandescent icicle.  Photop 16-3:38 Ag '19
Cheatham, M. S.  Interview.  Motion Pic 18:30 O '19
Squier, E. L.  Interview.  Motion Pic Classic 10:22 Jl '20
Peltret, E.  Interview.  Motion Pic 21:28 Mr '21
Dickson, M.  Her marital troubles.  Movie Classic 1:41 O '31

MacDONALD, RAY
Hamilton, S.  Sketch.   Photop 19:63 O '41
Two babes from Broadway.   Lions R 1-5:no p# Ja '42
MacDonald, R.  Hoofing to Hollywood.   Lions R 1-6:no p# F '42
Stars of tomorrow.   Lions R 1-11/12:no p# Jl/Ag '42
Obit.   Screen World 11:223 '60

MACDONALD, RYAN
Allards, J.  Presenting Ryan Macdonald.   Playgirl 1-1:84 Je '73

MacDONALD, WALLACE
Goldbeck, W.  Interview.   Motion Pic Classic 13:46 S '21

MACE, FRED
Sketch.   Motion Pic 10:109 N '15
Obit.   Dram Mir 77:10 Mr 3 '17
N. Y. Drama 64:23 Mr 3 '17

MacFADDEN, GERTRUDE "MICKEY"
Obit.   Screen World 19:235 '68

MacFARLAND, GEORGE "SPANKY"
Crichton, K.  Sketch.   Colliers 98:22 N 21 '36
Maltin, L.  Our gang; Our gang filmog.   Film Fan Mo 66:3 D
   '66

MacGOWRAN, JACK
Salute of the week.   Cue 39-51:1 D 19 '70
Obit.   Film R p15 '73/74
N. Y. Times Bio Ed p118 Ja '73
Screen World p237 '74

MacGRATH, LEUREEN
Big week for Leureen.   Cue 20-6:34 F 10 '51

MacGRAW, ALI
New princess.   Newsweek 73:108 My 5 '69
Girl who has everything, just about.   Time 93:102 My 9 '69
One film turns life upside down.   Life 66:46 Je 20 '69
People are talking about.   Vogue 154:82 Ag 15 '69
The making of a star.   McCalls 96:78 S '69
Wilkes, P.  Ali MacGraw.   Look 34:26 Ag 11 '70
Five young beauties and how they got that way.   Mlle 72:135 N
   '70
Salute of the week.   Cue 40-1:1 Ja 2 '71
A return to basics.   Time 97:40 Ja 11 '71
Ronan, M.  Is there a new now?; interview.   Sr Schol 98:3 F
   15 '71
Carro, G.  Life story.   Ladies Home J 88:87 F '71
Miller, E.  Interview.   Seventeen 30:130 F '71
Robbins, F.  Interview.   Photop 79-3:6 Mr '71
Why I'm afraid for my baby.   Photop 79-4:43 Ap '71
The day she believed she was scarred for life.   Photop 79-6:92
   Je '71

Martin, P.  Interview.  Sat Eve Post 243:50 Sum '71
We're rich and we love it.  Photop 80-3:74 S '71
Forced to choose?  My husband or my son.  Mod Screen 65-11:
    55 N '71
What's wrong with Ali?  Mod Screen 66-4:58 Ap '72
Ali and baby.  Photop 81-5:31 My '72
Movie star.  Mlle 75:290 Ag '72
Kopoecky, G.  Private world of Ali MacGraw.  Ladies Home J
    89:84 O '72
Games to save a marriage.  Mod Screen 66-10:50 O '72
Why she turned to Steve McQueen.  Photop 82-5:64 N '72
Bell, J. N.  Interview.  Good House 175:96 N '72
I'm taking Ali, you can't stop me.  Mod Screen 66-12:48 D '72
Robbins, A.  Interview.  Photop 83-1:6 Ja '73
Harmetz, A.  I was the golden girl.  N. Y.  Times sec 2:13 Mr
    11 '73
Same.  N. Y.  Times Bio Ed p456 Mr '73
Lovers on fire.  Mod Screen 67-4:42 Ap '73
We catch Ali and Steve...  Photop 83-6:34 Je '73
We go to Steve and Ali's wedding.  Photop 84-4:48 O '73

MacIVOR, MARY
    Remont, F.  Sketch.  Motion Pic Classic 9:24 Ja '20

MACK, CHARLES
    Tildesley, A. L.  Sketch.  Motion Pic Classic 23:54 Jl '26
    Kennedy, J. B.  Two black crows.  Colliers 81:13 Ja 21 '28
    Lewis, L.  Sketch.  New Rep 54:124 Mr 14 '28
    Walker, H. L.  Sketch.  Motion Pic Classic 29:53 Je '29
    Goldbeck, E.  Sketch.  Motion Pic Classic 31:52 Jl '30

MACK, HELEN
    Allen, S. S.  A sprouting career.  Silver S 3-9:60 Jl '33
    Sketch.  Photop 44:82 S '33
    McKenzie, G.  Her career.  Movie Classic 10:42 Mr '36

MACK, HUGHIE
    Obit.  Screen World 4:177 '53

MACK, WILBUR
    Obit.  Screen World 16:223 '65

MACKAILL, DOROTHY
    Carr, H.  Interview.  Classic 20:24 D '24
    de Revere, F. V.  Analysis of her face.  Motion Pic 29:65 My
        '25
    York, C.  Sketch.  Photop 30:106 Jl '26
    Darby, J.  Interview.  Motion Pic 37:58 Ap '29
    Biery, R.  Interview.  Motion Pic 37:44 My '29
    Biery, R.  Interview.  Motion Pic Classic 30:30 D '29
    Sketch.  Photop 39:6 F '31
    Manners, D.  Interview.  Motion Pic Classic 32:65 F '31
    Hall, G.  Interview.  Motion Pic Classic 33:58 Je '31

Walker, H. L.   Her love life.   Motion Pic Classic 32:38 Ag '31
Kingsley, B.   Crazy to get married.   Silver S 1-12:59 O '31
Her marriage.   Photop 41:27 Ja '32
Harlan, M.   Sketch.   Motion Pic 43:52 F '32
Wood, B.   Silent screen star has moonday brightened up.   Clas-
    sic Film Collect 25:extra 3 Fall '69
Uselton, R. A.   The Wampus baby stars.   Films In R 21-2:73
    F '70
Minton, E.   Considering some surviving films of two 'lost' stars.
    Filmograph 1-2:26 '70

MacKAYE, NORMAN
    Obit.   Screen World 20:236 '69

MacKENNA, KENNETH
    Belfrage, C.   Sketch.   Motion Pic Classic 31:70 Ap '30
    Obit.   Screen World 14:225 '63

MacLACHLAN, JANET
    Stone, J.   Janet is beginning to see the light.   N. Y. Times sec
        2:17 Ag 12 '73
    Same.   N. Y. Times Bio Ed p1323 Ag '73
    Black women reveal how they suffer for their white men.   Photop
        84-6:54 D '73

MacLAINE, SHIRLEY
    Rising star.   Film R p38 '56/57
    Zunser, J.   The 3 faces of Shirley.   Cue 27-17:11 Ap 26 '58
    Rising star.   Film R p20 '59/60
    Hamilton, J.   Shirley as Sweet Charity.   Look 32:56 Jl 9 '68
    Hochstein, R.   Crusades and capers of Shirley.   Good House 168:
        52 Je '69
    Free to love or free-love?   Photop 78-4:73 O '70
    Miss Vanilla.   N. Y. Times Bk R p38 N 15 '70
    Notables.   Time 96:60 D 28 '70
    Keneas, A.   Adventures of Shuri.   Newsweek 77:83C Ja 11 '71
    Morris, B.   Shirley MacLaine.   N. Y. Times Bio Ed Ja 15 '71
    Kronenberger, J.   Interview.   Look 35:35 Ja 26 '71
    Amory, C.   Interview.   Sat R 54:8 F 6 '71
    Alpert, H.   Diversification of Shirley MacLaine.   Sat R 54:43 F
        27 '71
    MacDonough, S.   A lady in her prime.   Show 2-3:36 My '71
    Klemesrud, J.   Let's tax diapers.   N. Y. Times Bio Ed Ag 8 '71
    Leonard, S.   Miss MacLaine goes East.   TV Guide 19-39:20 S
        25 '71
    She wants to free love...   Mod Screen 65-11:57 N '71
    People I love are not conventional.   McCalls 99:12 Mr '72
    How she suffered for success.   Mod Screen 66-7:52 Jl '72
    Women, the convention and brown paper bags.   N. Y. Times Mag
        p14 Jl 30 '72
    Peer, E.   Shirley's road show.   Newsweek 80:36 S 25 '72
    Cincinelli, R.   Tribute to Shirley MacLaine at San Francisco
        Film Festival.   Films In R 25-2:126 F '74

Klemesrud, J.   Come to the nightclub old chum.   N. Y. Times
  sec 2:15 Ap 7 '74
Shirley's a chorus girl at heart.   People 2-5:48 Jl 29 '74
Kaiser, R. B.   Militant lover; interview.   Playgirl 2-4:57 S '74
Bell, A.   Interview.   Viva 2-1:77 O '74

MacLANE, BARTON
  Obit.   Film R p22 '69/70
    N. Y. Times p29 Ja 2 '69
    Newsweek 73:61 Ja 13 '69
    Screen World 21:239 '70
  Dalton, E.   Meet Torchy Blane; Blane filmog.   Film Fan Mo
    133/134:37 Jl/Ag '72

MacLAREN, MARY
  How she got into motion pictures.   Green Book 17:404 Mr '17
  From extra to stardom.   Motion Pic Classic 5:39 S '17
  Kingsley, R.   Sketch.   Motion Pic 17:38 Mr '19
  Anderson, L. C.   An everyday Diana.   Photop 17-1:56 D '19
  Peltret, E.   Interview.   Motion Pic Classic 10L38 Ap/My '20
  Valentine, S.   Interview.   Photop 19:36 D '20
  Mohr, M.   Flickers queen hasn't slowed down (reprint from Hol-
    lywood Citizen-News).   Classic Film Collect 26:ex 4 Win '70
  Topor, T.   Silent film star remembers when.   N. Y. Post p64
    Ap 2 '74

MacLEAN, DOUGLAS
  North, G.   Interview.   Photop 18:76 Ag '20
  Naylor, H. S.   Interview.   Motion Pic 20:36 N '20
  Montanye, L.   Interview.   Motion Pic 21:51 Jl '21
  Curran, D.   Sketch.   Motion Pic Classic 22:42 S '25
  Howe, H.   Sketch.   Photop 29:75 Ja '26
  Trouping with Maude Adams.   Photop 30:81 S '26
  Denbo, D.   Sketch.   Motion Pic Classic 24:57 N '26
  Hunter, L.   Sketch.   Motion Pic 48:14 Ja '35
  Obit.   N. Y. Times p37 Jl 11 '67
    Screen World 19:236 '68

MacLEOD, GAVIN
  Lochte, D.   Lovable at last.   TV Guide 20-52:14 D 23 '72
  All he wants for Christmas is more Kewpie dolls.   TV Guide
    22-51:8 D 21 '74

MacMAHON, ALINE
  Fidler, J. M.   Take a letter Miss MacMahon.   Silver S 2-10:21
    Ag '32
  Sketch.   Photop 42:70 N '32
  Sketch.   Motion Pic 44:42 N '32
  Harrison, H.   Sketch.   Motion Pic 46:57 O '33
  Recipe for realism.   Lions R 3-4:no p# Jl '44

MacMURRAY, FRED
  Sheldon, D. P.   Sketch.   Movie Classic 8:39 Je '35

Zeitlin, I.   Interview.   Motion Pic 51:40 Ap '36
Facts about him.   Movie Classic 10:24 Ag '36
Hale, R.   His honeymoon diary.   Movie Classic 11:22 O '36
Vandour, C.   Interview.   Motion Pic 52:36 O '36
Wood, V.   He's just the boy next door.   Silver S 7-1:35 N '36
I'm heckled over hobbies.   Leisure 4:16 My '37
Home of.   Photop 51:42 D '37
Magee, T.   Why am I an actor?   Screen Book 20-5:28 Je '38
Reid, J.   Surprising things about Fred.   Silver S 10-2:36 D '39
Bio note; filmog.   Movies & People 2:24 '40
Mulvey, K.   Sketch.   Womans Home C 68:31 Jl '41
Asher, J.   If he lived next door.   Silver S 11-11:26 S '41
Musical MacMurray.   Lions R 2-5:no p# Jl '43
Bruce, J.   Just a guy named Fred.   Silver S 15-6:30 Ap '45
Maddox, B.   No faking for Fred.   Silver S 17-10:36 Ag '47
Parsons, L. O.   Cosmop's citation for best performance of
   month.   Cosmop 125:12 O '48
Bio.   Cur Bio Yrbk 1967:273 '68
Schroeder, C.   Magic of a good marriage.   Good House 173:94
   O '71
Cooking with a star.   Mod Screen 67-1:20 Ja '72
Corneau, E.   The most likable guy.   Classic Film Collect 35:38
   Sum '72


MACNEE, PATRICK
   Musel, M.   Violence can be fun.   TV Guide 12-19:12 My 9 '64
   On the scene.   Playboy 14-3:143 Mr '67
   Bauer, I.   Best dressed man in the world.   Look 35:51 O 5 '71
   The avengers.   Castle of Frankenstein 12:24 n. d.


MacRAE, ELIZABETH
   Gomer's learning about women from her.   TV Guide 16-10:20
      Mr 9 '68


MacRAE, GORDON
   Balling, F. D.   The boys from Syracuse.   Silver S 20-2:40 D
      '49
   He grabbed the brass ring.   Cue 25-3:19 Ja 21 '56


MacRAE, MEREDITH
   Lewis, R. W.   Petticoat Junction is not her only station.   TV
      Guide 18-3:14 Ja 17 '70


MacRAE, SHEILA
   Keeping it in the can.   TV Guide 4-28:4 Jl 15 '56
   Efron, E.   Finally out of the cave.   TV Guide 15-38:28 S 23 '67


MACRAE, DUNCAN
   Obit.   Brit Bk Yr 1968:594 '68
      Screen World 19:236 '68


MACREADY, GEORGE
   Heavies?   Who us?   TV Guide 8-18:23 Ap 30 '60

Obit.  Classic Film Collect 40:58 Fall '73
Films & Filming 20-2:80 N '73
N.Y. Times Bio Ed p1193 Jl '73
Screen World p237 '74

MACY, BILL
Stump, A.  Steady work for a former floater.  TV Guide 21-24:
26 Je 16 '73

MADDEN, DAVE
Knapp, D.  The peacemaker of The Partridge family.  Show 2-2:
29 S '71
Television's blond baby sitter.  TV Guide 19-51:28 D 18 '71

MADHUBALA
Patel, B.  Stardom in India.  Films In R 2-1:32 Ja '51
Cort, D.  Biggest star in the world.  Theatre Arts 36:24 Ag '52

MADISON, CLEO
How she became a photoplayer.  Motion Pic 9:118 Ap '15
Sketch.  Motion Pic 9:115 Je '15
How to get into motion pictures.  Motion Pic Classic 2:45 Ag '16
Van Loan, H. H.  Sketch.  Motion Pic 12:35 D '16

MADISON, ELLEN
Ellen takes the stand.  TV Guide 13-9:28 F 27 '65

MADISON, GUY
Parsons, L. O.  Cosmop's citation for best supporting perform-
ance.  Cosmop 121:66 Jl '46
Mulvey, K.  Story of.  Photop 34:60 Ap '49
Russell, G.  Why I waited 4 years to marry Guy.  Silver S 20-
4:22 F '50
Reid, L.  He learned to relax.  Silver S 24-8:33 Je '54

MAGNANI, ANNA
Bio sketch.  Harp Baz 83:124 F '49
Queen of Italian films.  Life 26:58 Ap 11 '49
Magnani in Hollywood.  Cue 24-44:15 N 5 '55
Lane, J. F.  The face of '63--Italy.  Films & Filming 9-7:11
Ap '63
Crist, J.  Evviva, Magnani.  New York 2-44:58 N 3 '69
Obit.  Classic Film Collect 41:53 Win '73
Films & Filming 20-2:80 N '73
N.Y. Daily News p4 S 27 '73
N.Y. Times Bio Ed p1502 S '73
Screen World p237 '74
Thousands attend tribute to Anna Magnani in Rome.  N.Y. Daily
News S 29 '73

MAHARIS, GEORGE
Wolf, W.  New Yorker on the rise.  Cue 34-19:10 My 8 '65
Photoplay forum.  Photop 82-2:10 Ag '72

McClelland, D.   George Maharis; filmog.   Films In R 24-3:188
  Mr '73
Holt, T.   Bold and beautiful; centerfold.   Playgirl 1-2:68 Jl '73

MAHONEY, JOCK
  Sanford, H.   Stunt men.   Films In R 6-10:537 D '55

MAIN, MARJORIE
  The voice.   Lions R 1-2:no p# O '41
  Glamour ain't everything.   Lions R 1-5:no p# Ja '42
  She collects characters.   Lions R 1-11/12:no p# Jl/Ag '42
  Glamour isn't everything.   Lions R 1-11/12:no p# Jl/Ag '42
  Marjorie Main plus Mary Roberts Rinehart.   Lions R 2-4:no p#
    Ap '43
  The other Main.   Lions R 2-4:no p# Ap '43
  If you call on Marjorie.   Lions R 4-1:mo p# F '44
  She's good to the old lady.   Lions R 3-3:no p# Ap '44

MAISON, EDNA
  How she became a photoplayer.   Motion Pic 8:78 Ja '15
  Ames, H.   Sketch.   Motion Pic Supp 1:59 N '15

MAJORS, LEE
  The Big Valley's Lee Majors.   TV Guide 14-8:30 F 19 '66
  Raddatz, L.   Owen Marshall's back-up quarterback.   TV Guide
    20-43:10 O 21 '72
  Davidson, B.   Bionic man to the rescue.   TV Guide 22-20:24
    My 18 '74

MALA, RAY
  Obit.   Screen World 4:177 '53

MALDEN, KARL
  Fenin, G.   The face of '63--U. S.   Films & Filming 9-6:55 Mr
    '63
  What the hell, I'm a frank guy; interview.   Cinema (BH) 2-1:26
    F/Mr '64
  Eyles, A.   Bio note; filmog.   Focus On F 3:15 My/Ag '70
  Lochte, D.   He was always the guy who got the cab for Marlon
    Brando.   TV Guide 21-21:14 My 26 '73

MALLESON, MILES
  Obit.   Brit Bk Yr 1970:585 '70
    Film R p21 '69/70

MALLORY, PATRICIA (BOOTS)
  Goldbeck, E.   Interview.   Movie Classic 3:22 Ja '33
  Manners, D.   Romance doesn't mean love.   Movie Classic 4:43
    Ag '33
  Uselton, R. A.   The Wampus baby stars.   Films In R 21-2:73
    F '70

**MALONE, DOROTHY**
Baer, M. M.  The romantic Mr. Brady.  Silver S 23-4:24 F '53
It took so long to say I love you.  Photop 81-1:44 Ja '72
How I told my children about my divorce.  Photop 82-4:56 O '72

**MALONE, MARY**
Peltret, E.  Interview.  Motion Pic Classic 11:60 S '20
Goldbeck, W.  Interview.  Motion Pic Classic 12:44 Je '21

**MALONE, NANCY**
Miss Malone and Miss Madrigal.  TV Guide 7-3:25 Ja 17 '59

**MAMEDOV, GASAN**
Aliev, A.  Gasan Mamedov.  Soviet Film 5(192):40 '73

**MANFREDI, NINO**
Lane, J. F.  The face of '63--Italy.  Films & Filming 9-7:11
Ap '63

**MANGANO, SILVANA**
Squalid roles lead to movie success.  Life 27:108 N 7 '49
Morris, G.  A puzzle called Silvana.  Silver S 24-4:40 F '54
Pepper, C. B.  Secret star.  Vogue 160:154 N 1 '72

**MANN, FRANKIE**
Fletcher, A. W.  Interview.  Motion Pic 19:60 F '20

**MANN, HANK**
Obit.  N.Y. Times p34 N 27 '71
Screen World 23:238 '72

**MANN, MARGARET**
Schader, F. H.  Sketch.  Photop 33:66 Ap '28
Watson, E.  Her success in Four sons.  Motion Pic 35:55 My
'28
Reilly, R. S.  Her career in the movies.  Am Mag 106:61 D
'28
Reilly, R. S.  How her dreams came true.  Am Mag 106:61 D
'28
York, C.  Sketch.  Photop 35:50 Ap '29
Maltin, L.  Our gang; inc. Our gang filmog.  Film Fan Mo 66:3
D '66

**MANNERS, DAVID**
Belfrage, C.  Sketch.  Motion Pic 40:74 O '30
York, C.  Sketch.  Photop 39:81 D '30
Simpson, G.  Sketch.  Silver S 25:26 Mr '32
Brock, D.  After the movies.  Classic Film Collect 41:42 Win
'73

**MANNING, IRENE**
Hamilton, S.  Sketch.  Photop 21:50 O '42
Franchey, J. R.  I walked out 3 times.  Silver S 13-3:38 Ja '43

MANNING, JACK
  American classic.   TV Guide 1-23:A-6 S 4 '53
  Deschin, J.   He gets to the core of a story fast.   Pop Phot 67:
    24 D '70

MANNING, MILDRED
  Lamb, M.   Interview.   Motion Pic 14:72 Ag '17
  Frederick, J. S.   An ingenue who won't ingenue.   Photop 12-4:
    35 S '17
  Conlon, L.   Sketch.   Motion Pic Classic 5:50 N '17
  Her pets.   Motion Pic 15:83 Ap '18

MANON, MARCIA
  Mistley, M.   Interview.   Motion Pic 16:51 D '18
  Smith, F. J.   Interview.   Motion Pic Classic 8:18 My '19
  Cheatham, M.   Interview.   Motion Pic Classic 12:34 My '21
  Handy, T. B.   Interview.   Motion Pic Classic 14:24 Jl '22

MANSFIELD, JAYNE
  Water, R.   Hollywood bound.   Cue 24-39:12 O 1 '55
  McClure, M.   Defense of Jayne Mansfield.   Film Culture 32:24
    Spg '64
  Obit.   N. Y. Times p19 Jl 4 '67
    Newsweek 70:98 Jl 10 '67
    Time 90:79 Jl 7 '67
  Jayne was a lovely little girl.   Photop 83-5:28 My '73

MANSFIELD, MARTHA
  Sherwood, C. B.   Interview.   Motion Pic Classic 8:23 Je '19
  May, L.   Interview.   Motion Pic 20:56 Ja '21

MANTOOTH, RANDOLPH
  Swisher, V. H.   Hollywood's professional training ground.   After
    Dark 13-7:36 N '70
  Weldon, D.   Hardly your orthodox, all-American boy.   TV Guide
    21-42:20 O 20 '73

MAPLE, AUDREY
  Obit.   N. Y. Times p40 Ap 19 '71

MARA, ADELE
  Fulton, M. J.   Sketch.   Photop 36:105 Ag '49

MARAIS, JEAN
  With Jean Marais from stage to screen.   Unifrance 23:14 F '53
  With Jean Marais.   Unifrance 39:no p# Mr/Ap '56

MARCEAU, MARCEL
  (as relates to films only)
  Conversation with Marceau.   Oui 2-9:67 S '73
  Harmetz, A.   Look ma, he's talking.   N. Y. Times Bio Ed p1817
    N '73

MARCELLUS, IRENE
Keane, M.  Interview.  Motion Pic Classic 11:20 F '21

MARCH, DELLA
Obit.  Classic Film Collect 40:59 Fall '73

MARCH, FREDRIC
Walker, H. L.  Sketch.  Motion Pic 37:76 My '29
Hall, G.  Sketch.  Motion Pic 38:30 D '29
Lee, S.  Sketch.  Motion Pic 46:60 D '30
Harris, R.  The March lamb.  Silver S 1-3:27 Ja '31
Jarvis, P.  Sketch.  Photop 39:142 F '31
Goldbeck, E.  Interview.  Motion Pic Classic 33:71 Mr '31
Mook, S. R.  The career of Fredric March.  Silver S 2-4:26 F
    '32
Dunham, E.  As Mr. Hyde in Dr. Jekyll and Mr. Hyde.  Movie
    Classic 2:31 Mr '32
Lane, J.  Interview.  Movie Classic 2:14 Jl '32
Manners, D.  Interview.  Motion Pic 44:58 Ja '33
Donnell, D.  Wins title of best actor.  Movie Classic 3:30 F '33
Cheatham, M.  Judge March.  Silver S 3-9:45 Jl '33
Service, F.  Sketch.  Motion Pic 46:49 Ag '33
Gwin, J.  Shakespeare? No!  Silver S 4-9:23 Jl '34
MacDonald, B.  Is Hollywood killing its leading men?  Silver S
    4-9:30 Jl '34
Hunt, J.  His adopted children.  Photop 46:49 O '34
Manners, D.  Defends Hollywood's morals.  Motion Pic 48:31 N
    '34
Calhoun, D.  Home of.  Motion Pic 49:52 F '35
Brownfield, L.  Interview.  Movie Classic 8:24 Ap '35
Gay, V.  Hollywood hero No. 1.  Movie Classic 8:33 Ag '35
Tully, J.  Story of.  Motion Pic 50:27 D '35
Hartley, K.  Story of.  Motion Pic 51:36 Mr '36
Lang, H.  Interview.  Movie Classic 10:46 My '36
Osborn, K.  Story of.  Motion Pic 52:35 O '36
Cheatham, M.  Just "lucky."  Silver S 7-4:51 F '37
Vandour, C.  Story of.  Motion Pic 54:31 D '37
Home of.  Photop 52:44 F '38
Story of.  Stage 16:20 My 15 '39
MacDonald, J.  Marriage and the Marchs.  Silver S 10-9:38 Jl
    '40
Bio note; filmog.  Movies & People 2:24 '40
The American March Twain.  Cue 13-18:14 Ap 29 '44
Parsons, L. O.  Cosmop's citation for best performance of
    month.  Cosmop 122:67 Ja '47
Lewis, E.  Mr. and Mrs. Fredric March.  Cue 19-4:12 Ja 28
    '50
Uselton, R. A.  Fredric March.  Films In R 10-4:249 Ap '59
Zunser, J.  Conversation with March.  Cue 30-28:11 Jl 15 '61
Pinup of the past.  Films & Filming 18-2:72 N '71

MARCH, HAL
Minoff, P.  Comedy on the March.  Cue 24-10:13 Mr 12 '55

Forward, March.  TV Guide 4-9:13 Mr 3 '56
Obit.  N. Y. Times Bio Ed Ja 20 '70
    Screen World 22:238 '71

MARCH, KENDALL
    Leonard Sillman's New faces of 1971.  Cue 40-8:9 F 20 '71

MARCH, LORI
    Cohn, E.  Calm eye in the secret storm.  TV Guide 19-11:37
    Mr 13 '71

MARCHAL, ARLETTE
    Sketch.  Motion Pic Classic 22:55 D '25
    St. Johns, I.  Interview.  Photop 31:43 F '27
    York, C.  Sketch.  Photop 31:76 Mr '27

MARCHAND, CORINNE
    They didn't plan to be movie stars.  Unifrance 56:no p# Spg '62

MARCUSE, THEODORE
    Obit.  Screen World 19:236 '68

MARGO
    Williams, W.  Margo.  Silver S 5-5:30 Mr '35
    Jackson, G.  Story of.  Movie Classic 10:39 Mr '36
    Calhoun, D.  Interview.  Motion Pic 51:41 Ap '36
    Sketch.  Movie Classic 11:21 N '36
    Sketch.  Photop 50:75 N '36
    Sketch.  Movie Classic 11:63 D '36
    Reid, J.  Interview.  Motion Pic 52:26 Ja '37

MARGOLIN, STUART
    An actor hears from some young fans.  TV Guide 20-7:27 F 12
    '72

MARICLE, LEONA
    Whitehead, H.  Sketch.  Motion Pic 53:21 Mr '37

MARIE, ROSE
    Whatever became of Baby Rose Marie?  TV Guide 11-2:15 Ja 12
    '63
    Durslag, M.  She goes along.  TV Guide 18-16:22 Ap 18 '70

MARINOFF, FANIA
    Obit.  N. Y. Times p51 N 17 '71

MARION, EDNA
    Uselton, R. A.  The Wampus baby stars.  Films In R 21-2:73
    F '70

MARION, SID
    Obit.  Screen World 17:239 '66

MARIS, MONA
   Goldbeck, E.   Sketch.   Motion Pic Classic 31:70 Mr '30
   Red-head and dark duds.   Lions R 1-10:no p# Je '42
   Letters; filmog.   Films In R 18-1:60 Ag/S '60

MARITZA, SARI
   Burden, J.   Sketch.   Movie Classic 2:31 Ap '32
   Service, F.   Sketch.   Motion Pic 43:50 My '32
   Sketch.   Photop 41:74 My '32
   Goldbeck, E.   Interview.   Motion Pic 45:50 F '33

MARJOE
   (See GORTNER, MARJOE)

MARKEY, ENID
   Hall, G.   Interview.   Motion Pic 18:75 Ag '19
   Lee, L.   Sketch.   National 52:224 O '23
   Bio note.   Silent Pic 14:21 Spg '72

MARKHAM, MONTE
   de Roos, R.   I sound like a fathead.   TV Guide 15-52:12 D 30
      '67

MARKS, ALFRED
   Tierney, M.   Interview.   Plays & Players 20-11:32 Ag '73

MARKS, JOE E.
   In memory.   Show 3-6:74 S '73

MARLBOROUGH, LEAH
   East, J. M.   The Codmans.   Silent Pic 13:24 Win/Spg '72

MARLOWE, HUGH
   Opportunity knocks once...twice...thrice.   Lions R 3-5:no p#
      D '44

MARLOWE, JUNE
   Copeland, D. M.   Letter; filmog.   Films In R 20-10:644 D '69
   Uselton, R. A.   The Wampus baby stars.   Films In R 21-2:73
      F '70

MARLY, FLORENCE
   Marly, F.   How to make life more interesting--for men.   Silver
      S 22-7:30 My '52

MARMONT, PERCY
   Service, F.   Interview.   Motion Pic Classic 8:30 My '19
   Landy, G. & Smoth, A.   Both Englishmen.   Photop 16-6:78 N
      '19
   Fletcher, A. W.   Interview.   Motion Pic 19:46 Je '20
   Oettinger, M. H.   Interview.   Motion Pic 24:64 S '22
   Gordon, L.   Interview.   Motion Pic 27:34 Ap '24
   Slide, A.   Percy Marmont's Hollywood; interview.   Silent Pic
      8:15 Aut '70

MARQUAND, CHRISTIAN
  Bio note.   Unifrance 45:8 D '57

MARR, SALLY
  The lifestyle of a starlet.   TV Guide 18-47:30 N 21 '70

MARSH, HOWARD
  Obit.   N. Y. Times p25 Ag 9 '69

MARSH, JEAN
  Jordan, H. B.   Lady Marjorie would swoon.   TV Guide 22-7:16
    F 16 '74
  Over the tube.   People 1-7:58 Ap 15 '74
  Hall, W.   Thanks to Rose, Jean's got it maid.   N. Y. Times sec
    2:17 Ap 21 '74
  Same.   N. Y. Times Bio Ed p558 Ap '74

MARSH, JOAN
  Will they become famous stars or forgotten faces?   Silver S 2-2:
    36 D '31
  Grant, J.   How she reduced.   Movie Classic 6:34 My '34
  Uselton, R. A.   The Wampus baby stars.   Films In R 21-2:73
    F '70

MARSH, MAE
  Sketch.   Green Bk 13:527 Mr '15
  Sketch.   Motion Pic 9:107 Mr '15
  Sketch.   Motion Pic 10:118 Ag '15
  Rex, W.   Dorothy and Mae tell secrets.   Film Players Herald
    2-7:11 F '16
  Zeidman, B.   Sketch.   Motion Pic Classic 3:42 O '16
  Naylor, H. S.   Interview.   Motion Pic Classic 6:29 Je '18
  Where is Mae Marsh?   Photop 16-2:65 Jl '19
  Smith, F. J.   Interview.   Motion Pic Classic 10:16 Mr '20
  Cheatham, M.   Interview.   Motion Pic 21:54 F '21
  Fletcher, A. W.   Interview.   Motion Pic 25:26 My '23
  Carlisle, H.   Interview.   Motion Pic 27:25 Mr '24
  Babcock, M.   Sketch.   Motion Pic Classic 33:30 Jl '31
  Sketch.   Photop 41:45 Mr '32
  Stern, S.   Mae Marsh.   Film Culture 36:46 Spg/Sum '65
  Obit.   Classic Film Collect 20:43 (reprint N. Y. Times & L. A.
    Times) Spg '68
    N. Y. Times p47 F 14 '68
    Newsweek 71:93 F 26 '68
    Time 91:73 F 23 '68
  The girl with a thousand expressions.   (reprint from the Picture
    Show) Classic Film Collect 20:43 Spg '68
  Mae Marsh, Robert Harron and D. W. Griffith; filmog.   Silent
    Pic 4:10 Aut '69
  Cushman, R. B.   Interview.   Silent Pic 17:7 Spg '73

MARSH, MARGUERITE
  Montayne, L.   Interview.   Motion Pic 18:75 S '19

MARSH, MARIAN
Sketch.  Photop 39:31 Ap '31
Service, F.  Her success.  Motion Pic 42:58 N '31
Jones, C.  Afraid of love.  Silver S 2-4:20 F '32
Maddox, B.  Marsh twinkles.  Silver S 2-5:21 Mr '32
Kent, J.  Her return to the screen.  Movie Classic 9:50 F '36
Uselton, R. A.  The Wampus baby stars.  Films In R 21-2:73
  F '70

MARSHAL, ALAN
Sketch.  Motion Pic 53:23 F '37
Hamilton, S.  Sketch.  Photop 54:28 My '40
A horse on Alan Marshal.  Lions R 3-4:no p# Jl '44

MARSHALL, BRENDA
Hall, G.  All flew into the cuckoo's nest.  Silver S 10-1:38 N
  '39
Frenchey, J. R.  A love that strangely didn't last.  Silver S 11-
  1:44 N '40
Hamilton, S.  Sketch.  Photop 54:32 N '40
Cheatham, M.  Casually captured.  Silver S 12-1:24 N '41
Mulvey, K.  Sketch.  Womans Home C 69:20 S '42

MARSHALL, CONNIE
Filmog.  Films & Filming 19-18:56 S '73

MARSHALL, E. G.
Crichton, M.  My neck was out.  TV Guide 20-48:14 N 25 '72

MARSHALL, EVERETT
Sketch.  Mus Cour 96:12 My 31 '28
Belfrage, C.  Sketch.  Motion Pic Classic 32:52 S '30
They stand out from the crowd.  Lit Dig 118:12 Ag 4 '34

MARSHALL, HERBERT
Biery, R.  His love story.  Photop 42:50 S '32
Manners, D.  Sketch.  Movie Classic 3:44 S '32
Keats, P.  Marshall law declared.  Silver S 2-11:20 S '32
Tennant, M.  Sketch.  Movie Classic 3:26 D '32
Goldbeck, E.  Interview.  Movie Classic 5:48 Ja '34
Hogarth, D.  Secret of his irresistible attraction for women.
  Movie Classic 7:36 Ja '35
Hall, G.  Sketch.  Motion Pic 53:46 My '37
Bio note; filmog.  Movies & People 2:25 '40
Herbert Marshall, gentleman.  Lions R 1-4:no p# D '41
An actor in his stride.  Lions R 3-1:no p# S '43
Strolling minstrel.  Lions R 3-3:no p# Ap '44
The man who killed the fly; farewell to Herbert Marshall.  Fa-
  mous Monsters 39:8 Je '66
Obit; filmog.  Cahiers (in Eng.) 7:64 Ja '67

MARSHALL, JOAN
Just an old sea dog.  TV Guide 6-33:24 Ag 16 '58

MARSHALL, SARAH
   Spotlight.  Life 51:115 O 27 '61
   Miss Marshall has taken over in spades.   TV Guide 10-28:12 Jl
      14 '62

MARSHALL, TULLY
   Career of.  Theatre 11:89 Mr '10
   Gordon, G.  Work of.  Motion Pic Classic 3:32 F '17
   Home of.  Classic 15:38 F '23
   Greene, H. W.  Home of.  Arch & B 55:35 Ap '23
   Obit.  Time 41:44 Mr 22 '43

MARSHALOV, BORIS
   Obit.  N. Y. Times p47 O 17 '67

MARTEN, HELEN
   Sketch.  Motion Pic Classic 2:43 My '16

MARTIN, ANDRA
   Tale of a blighted troth.  Life 45:24 S 1 '58
   A press agent's dream.  TV Guide 7-4:20 Ja 24 '59

MARTIN, ANDREA
   McCaughna, D.  A terribly personal business.  Motion p16 Jl/
      Ag '74

MARTIN, CYE
   Obit.  N. Y. Times p40 Mr 30 '72

MARTIN, DEAN
   MacDonald, E.  Letter to a star.  Silver S 22-7:36 My '52
   Martin, D.  It wasn't my idea.  Silver S 24-9:38 Jl '54
   Minoff, P.  Time for Martin & Lewis to take inventory.  Cue
      24-20:59 My 21 '55
   Hume, R.  Are their critics wrong?  Films & Filming 2-6:10
      Mr '56
   Thomas, B.  Is there a real Dean Martin?  Good House 165:96
      N '67
   Fallaci, O.  Dean Martin talks...  Look 31:78 D 26 '67
   TV Christmas with the Martins and the Sinatras.  Look 31:76 D
      26 '67
   All that glamour and a hug for the boss, too.  TV Guide 18-16:
      15 Ap 18 '70
   Why Dean's the lover who can't stay up late.  Photop 77-5:45
      My '70
   Off booze on blondes.  Photop 78-1:49 Jl '70
   How they live together but love others.  Photop 79-2:63 F '71
   We're having a wonderful divorce.  Photop 79-4:50 Ap '71
   Billy Graham converting Dean Martin?  Photop 80-2:97 Ag '71
   Martin fearful for Sinatra's health.  Photop 80-3:65 S '71
   Enraged, he takes daughter from Doris Day's son.  Photop 80-4:
      72 O '71
   I'm going to drink, play golf and make love.  Silver S 41-10:40

O '71
How Cathy Hawn is luring Dean into marriage.  Photop 80-5:79
N '71
The baby that binds Dean to Kathy.  Mod Screen 65-12:29 D '71
Dean to adopt Cathy Hawn's child?  Photop 80-6:83 D '71
Why Jeanne Martin held up Dean's wedding.  Mod Screen 67-1:36
Ja '72
Hawn, C.  I'm Mrs. Dean Martin.  Photop 81-1:49 Ja '72
Martin, J.  Why I let Dean love another woman.  Photop 81-2:68
F '72
Dean and Cathy's honeymoon cottage.  Photop 81-3:24 Mr '72
Dean and Cathy's elopement.  Mod Screen 66-4:34 Ap '72
Passion and quarrels.  Photop 81-5:54 My '72
Righter, C.  Star of the month; horoscope.  Mod Screen 66-6:31
Je '72
Dean and Jeanne battle it out.  Photop 83-1:17 Ja '73
Dean and Cathy, why they had to marry.  Photop 84-1:34 Jl '73
Interviews with Dean's ex-loves.  Photop 84-1:36 Jl '73
Jeanne in hospital again.  Photop 84-6:43 D '73
Visits doctor.  Photop 85-2:63 F '74
Concerning Dino's arrest.  Photop 85-4:38 Ap '74
Rumors of wife's romance with James Darren.  Photop 86-1:57
Jl '74

MARTIN, DINO
Guerin, T.  Dino jr; interview.  Interview 27:29 N '72
Concerning his arrest.  Photop 85-4:38 Ap '74
Escapes jail.  Photop 86-3:38 S '74

MARTIN, EDIE
Obit.  Film R p45 '64/65

MARTIN, LORI
Girl on horseback.  Newsweek 56:108 S 26 '60
She wants to grow up.  TV Guide 9-14:18 Ap 8 '61

MARTIN, MARION
Crivello, K.  Adrian and Martin...best of the tough dames.
Film Collect Registry 4-3:5 My/Je '72
Here is Marion Martin.  Movie Dig 1-6:139 N '72

MARTIN, MARY
Sketch.  Life 5:29 D 19 '38
Story of.  Life 7:58 D 4 '39
Hamilton, S.  Sketch.  Photop 54:14 Ja '40
McIllwaine, R.  Mother knew best.  Silver S 10-5:44 Mr '40
Manners, M. J.  Making the honeymoon last.  Silver S 11-5:44
Mr '41
Walker, H. L.  Sketch.  Photop 21:42 N '42
Star loves New York and vice versa.  Cue 13-34:8 Ag 19 '44
London award for performance in One touch of Venus.  Theatre
World 40:26 O '44
Her ingenuity with hats and clothes.  Life 17:70 N 27 '44

Story of.   Photop 27:61 Je '45

Her impressions of theatre-going in London.   Theatre World 43:
35 F '45

Two girls four notes make record history.   TV Guide 1-33:11 N
13 '53

Halliday, H.   Flying is fun.   Cue 23-42:15 O 16 '54

Minoff, P.   Notes on TV.   Cue 24-11:47 Mr 19 '55

Minoff, P.   Miss Martin returns.   Cue 28-45:19 N 7 '59

Pages from my needlepoint book; excerpt.   McCalls 96:84 Ap '69

Martin's life off Broadway--in Brazil.   N. Y. Times Bio Ed Ap
4 '71

Where are they now?   Newsweek 80:12 S 4 '72

Herman, H.   Fame is a song.   Liberty 1-8:48 Spg '73


MARTIN, MILLICENT

Musel, R.   She looked in the mirror and cried help.   TV Guide
19-31:13 Jl 31 '71


MARTIN, STROTHER

A breed apart.   TV Guide 11-26:19 Je 29 '63

Eyles, A.   Strother Martin; filmog.   Focus On F 1:9 Ja/F '70

Diehl, D.   What we have here is a failure to communicate.
Show 1-8:21 Jl 9 '70

Filmog.   Films & Filming 20-8:61 My '74


MARTIN, TONY

Bio note; filmog.   Movies & People 2:25 '40

York, C.   His friendship with Lana Turner.   Photop 18:30 Mr
'41

Hodgkins, B.   Tony's life.   Metron 66:17 Mr '49

Comeback?   What comeback?   TV Guide 3-14:5 Ap 2 '55

Singing a different tune.   TV Guide 4-4:20 Ja 28 '56

Pitts, M.   Actor Tony Martin; filmog.   Classic Film Collect
34:10 Spg '72


MARTIN, VIVIAN

Interview.   Cosmop 55:413 Ag '13

Ames, H.   Facial expression.   Motion Pic Classic 5:34 F '18

Remont, F.   Sketch.   Motion Pic 16:51 O '18

Carter, C. F.   Sketch.   Motion Pic 17:63 Mr '19

Lane, M.   Interview.   Motion Pic Classic 9:22 O '19

Alexander, S.   Ingenue from the eyes down.   Photop 17-1:108 D
'19

Interview.   Dram Mir 694 O 16 '20

Mantanye, L.   Interview.   Motion Pic 20:40 Ja '21


MARTINDEL, EDWARD

Howe, M.   Sketch.   Motion Pic Classic 23:30 Ap '26


MARTINELLI, ELSA

Rising star.   Film R p28 '58/59

MARTINI, NINO
  Trogus, M.   High-lights on Martini.   Screen Book 19-4:41 N
    '37

MARVIN, LEE
  Re-creating a footnote to history.   TV Guide 8-13:10 Mr 26 '60
  Wolf, W.   Dynamic Lee Marvin.   Cue 36-19:17 My 13 '67
  Redbook dialogue.   Redbook 130:74 N '67
  Interview.   Playboy 16-1:59 Ja '69
  Fool's gold.   Time 94:100 O 24 '69
  Eyles, A.   Lee Marvin; filmog.   Focus On F 5:5 Win '70
  Ebert, R.   Saturday at Lee--ing Marvin's.   Esquire 74:148 N
    '70
  Bergen, C.   Lee Marvin and Paul Newman.   Vogue 158:146 O 1
    '71
  Stone, J.   The Klansman.   Playgirl 2-2:85 Jl '74
  Paskin, B.   Life begins at 50.   Films Illus 3-35:438 Jl '74

MARX, CHICO
  Obit.   Film R p17 '62/63
  (See also:  MARX BROTHERS)

MARX, GROUCHO
  Simpson, G.   Tells how he "discovered" the genius in Chaplin.
    Motion Pic 51:39 My '36
  Note.   Vogue 111:147 Ap 1 '48
  Hyams, J.   The givin' is easy.   Cue 23-14:17 Ap 3 '54
  Gibbons, T.   Groucho Marx.   Film 4:22 Mr '55
  Any number can play.   TV Guide 4-37:30 S 15 '56
  Groucho writes.   Take One 1-11:14 My/Je '68
  Ebert, R.   Groucho remembers mama.   N. Y. Times Bio Ed Mr
    1 '70
  Portrait of an artist as an old man.   Take One 3-1:10 S/O '70
  Ace, G.   Report on Groucho.   Sat R 55:4 Ap 1 '72
  Shenker, I.   Groucho, at 81, discusses favorite topic:  women.
    N. Y. Times Bio Ed My 4 '72
  Lax, E.   Secret word is Groucho.   Life 72:82 My 12 '72
  Fleming, E.   Interview.   Vogue 160:88 Jl '72
  Ebert, R.   Living legend rated R.   Esquire 78:140 Jl '72
  Foreman, B.   Groucho sent me.   TV Guide 20-41:52 O 7 '72
  Anobile, R. J.   Interview.   Penthouse 5-4:106 D '73
  Interview.   Playboy 21-3:59 Mr '74
  (See also:  MARX BROTHERS)

MARX, HARPO
  Woollcott, A.   Sketch.   Colliers 84:29 Jl 20 '29
  Wilson, E.   Roses, love and guns hots.   Silver S 2-9:24 Jl '32
  Woollcott, A.   His strange career.   Cosmop 96:56 Ja '34
  Levant, O.   Story of.   Vogue 94:62 O 1 '39
  Hayes, F.   Story of.   Colliers 109:14 Ja 31 '42
  Work of in Love happy.   Life 26:84 F 7 '49
  Kerouac, J.   To Harpo Marx; poem.   Playboy 6:44 Jl '59
  Obit.   Film R p45 '65/66
  (See also:  MARX BROTHERS)

MARX BROTHERS
(Chico, Groucho, Harpo, Zeppo)
Kennedy, J. B.   Slapstick stuff.   Colliers 78:28 Jl 10 '26
In moving pictures.   Motion Pic Classic 26:48 F '28
Golden, S. B.   Confessions of.   Theatre 49:48 Ja '29
Hamilton, S.   Sketch.   Photop 42:27 Jl '32
Birrell, F.   The humor of in Horse feathers.   New Statesman
   4:374 O 1 '32
The humor of in Horse feathers.   R of Rs (Lon) 82:77 O '32
Moffitt, C. F.   Censorship for interviews Hollywood's latest
   wild idea.   Cinema Dig 2-5:9 Ja 9 '33
Sammis, E. R.   Story of.   Photop 49:26 F '36
Johnston, A.   Story of.   Womans Home C 63:12 S '36
Lang, H.   A day with the Marxes.   Motion Pic 53:38 Je '37
Glendenning, A.   Originality of performance in Room service.
   19th Cent 125:92 Ja '39
Bio note; filmog.   Movies & People 2:25 '40
Agee, J.   In A night in Casablanca.   Nation 162:636 My 25 '46
Mosdell, D.   Character sketch.   Can Forum 26:138 S '46
Rowland, R.   American classic.   Hollywood Q 2-3:264 Ap '47
Perelman, S. J.   The winsome foursome.   Show 1-2:35 N '61
Kroll, J.   Sam's boys.   Newsweek 72:116 N 25 '68
Comedians.   Screen Greats 1-2:64 Sum '71
Brown, G.   The Marx Brothers.   Cinema (Lon) 8:29 '71
Donnelly, W.   A theory of the comedy of The Marx Bros.   Vel-
   vet Light 3:8 Win '71/72
Adamson, J.   Nothing but amok.   Views & Rs 4-1:4 Fall; 4-2:
   10 Win '72
Beranger, C.   The woman who taught her children to be fools.
   Liberty 1-7:54 Win '72


MASIELL, JOE
Stoop, N. M.   Back to reality.   After Dark 4-8:54 D '71


MASINA, GIULIETTA
Wolf, W.   Italy's movie greats.   Cue 34-45:14 N 6 '65
Kast, P.   Giulietta and Federico.   Cahiers (Eng) 5:24 '66


MASKELL, VIRGINIA
Rising star.   Film R p22 '59/60
Coulson, A. A.   Letter; filmog.   Films In R 19-10:659 D '68
McClelland, D.   What might have been...; filmog.   Filmograph
   3-4:14 '73


MASON, DON
How he became a photoplayer.   Motion Pic 9:112 F '15


MASON, JAMES
His direction of Bathsheba.   Theatre World 43:28 Ap '47
Howard, M.   The extraordinary Mr. Mason.   Silver S 19-4:40
   F '49
Graham, S.   Sketch.   Photop 35:65 My '49
Shane, D.   The truth about the James Masons.   Silver S 22-11:26

S '52

Mason, J.    Stage vs. screen.    Films & Filming 1-2:5 N; 1-3:7
  D '54
Mason, J.    Max Ophuls.    Sight & Sound 27-1:49 Sum '57
Mason, J.    Andrew Stone, the man who wants men of steel.
  Films & Filming 4-11:6 Ag '58
Mason, J.    The film spectacular.    Film R p67 '65/66
Nogueira, R.    Mason talks about his career in the cinema; filmog.
  Focus On F 1:19 Mr/Ap '70
Canby, V.    Mason--is he better than ever?    N. Y. Times sec
  2:1 Jl 29 '73
Graham, T.    Second Tehran International film festival.    Ameri-
  can Cinematog. 55-2:176 F '74
Efron, E.    Dickens performed a function now being performed
  by TV.    TV Guide 22-46:17 N 16 '74

MASON, MARLYN
  The Hollywood swingers.    Show 3-11:88 N '63
  Will someone please send this girl flowers.    TV Guide 13-20:20
    My 15 '65
  Diehl, D.    Well, you have to laugh a lot.    TV Guide 20-18:18
    Ap 29 '72

MASON, MARSHA
  Bio note; filmog.    Films Illus 4-40:131 D '74

MASON, SHIRLEY
  Ames, H.    Sketch.    Motion Pic 12:124 N '16
  Shapely Shirley of the sins.    Photop 11-4:89 Mr '17
  Olden, J.    Sketch.    Motion Pic Classic 4:23 Je '17
  Beatty, J.    Sketch.    Motion Pic 14:115 S '17
  Lamb, G.    Interview.    Motion Pic Classic 7:30 S '18
  Boone, A.    Surely, Shirley, surely.    Photop 14-6:42 N '18
  Handy, T. B.    Interview.    Motion Pic Classic 10:22 Ap/My '20
  Ramsey, N.    Sketch.    Photop 18:28 Jl '20
  Peltret, E.    Interview.    Motion Pic 20:44 Ja '21
  Shelley, H.    Interview.    Motion Pic Classic 13:48 O '21
  Lamb, G.    Interview.    Motion Pic 23:57 Ap '22
  Spensley, D.    Sketch.    Photop 30:38 Je '26

MASSARI, LEA
  Lane, J. F.    The face of '63--Italy.    Films & Filming 9-7:11
    Ap '63
  Bean, R.    Will there be film stars in 1974?    Films & Filming
    10-10:9 Jl '64

MASSEY, ILONA
  Franchey, J. R.    Beauty and brains do go together.    Silver S
    10-5:22 Mr '40
  And Genghis Khan.    Cue 12-35:10 Ag 28 '43
  O'Leary, D.    Adventures of Ilona.    Silver S 16-7:58 My '46
  Dillon, F.    Melodic menace.    Screen Book 22-3:84 O '39
  Wilkinson, G. R.    Ilona Massey; filmog.    Films In R 22-1:21

Ja '71
Brock, A.  The magic of Ilona Massey.   Classic Film Collect
40:X2 Fall '73
Obit.  N. Y. Times Bio Ed p1138 Ag '74

MASSEY, RAYMOND
Corathiel, E.  Interview.   Theatre World 19:31 Ja '33
Sketch.   Theatre World 23:229 My '35
Sketch.   Theatre World 29:231 My '38
Sketch.   Canadian Mag 90:37 D '38
Hamilton, S. & Morse, W. Jr.  Sketch.   Photop 54:20 Mr '40

MASSIE, PAUL
Massie, P.  What Asquith did for me.   Films & Filming 4-5:11
F '58

MASTERS, MARIE
Drake, R.  Ooh, what she said.   TV Guide 20-34:32 Ag 19 '72

MASTERS, RUTH
Obit.  N. Y. Times p47 S 23 '69

MASTROIANNI, MARCELLO
These faces will win top places during 1959.   Films & Filming
5-7:18 Ap '59
Zunser, J.  Movie idol with a mind.   Cue 32-16:12 Ap 20 '63
Lane, J. F.  The face of '63--Italy.   Films & Filming 9-7:11
Ap '63
Interview.   Playboy 12-7:49 Jl '65
Fellini, F.  Mastroianni at home; is he?   Vogue 152:134 N 15
'68
Hamilton, J.  Faye and the Italian.   Look 33:44 Ja 21 '69
Marcello makes a big scandalo.   N. Y. Times Bio Ed Je 21 '70
Hidden lovers.   Photop 80-2:82 Ag '71
Fallaci, O.  X ray of a man.   McCalls 98:88 S '71
Mastroianni and Deneuve.   Show 2-10:35 D '71
How I let the one I love get away.   Photop 82-1:72 Jl '72
How Catherine Deneuve got Mastroianni away from his wife.
Mod Screen 66-8:48 Ag '72

MATHER, JACK
Obit.  Screen World 18:238 '67

MATHERS, JERRY
Tom Sawyer (Junior grade).   TV Guide 6-5:17 F 1 '58
TV's eager beaver.   Look 22:67 My 27 '58
Busy as a beaver.   TV Guide 6-26:8 Je 28 '58

MATHESON, DON
Only we were there.   Photop 78-1:53 Jl '70
We almost lost our baby.   Photop 80-6:59 D '71

MATHEWS, CAROLE
She loves to pack.   TV Guide 7-8:29 F 21 '59

MATTHAU, WALTER
Jennings, C. R.   Matthau in full flower.   Esquire 70:193 D '68
Lear, M. W.   Interview.   Redbook 132:69 Ja '69
We've given our house a country look.   House & Gard 138:38 Jl '70
A new leaf.   Show 1-13:26 S 17 '70
Kanfer, S.   Triumph of a one-man trio.   Time 97:86 My 24 '71
Salute of the week.   Cue 40-23:1 Je 5 '71
Meehan, T.   What the OTB bettor can learn from Matthau.
   N. Y. Times Mag p6 Jl 4 '71
   Same.   N. Y. Times Bio Ed Jl 4 '71
Eyles, A.   Bio note; filmog.   Focus On F 9:6 Spg '72
Man of many faces; filmog.   Film 65:20 Spg '72
Sonnett, S.   How did Matthau get mixed up in murder?   N. Y.
   Times sec 2:11 Ap 21 '74
   Same.   N. Y. Times p561 Ap '74
Darrach, B.   (His) love for the long shot.   People 1-18:41 Jl 1
   '74

MATTHEWS, A. E.
   Obit.   Film R p17 '61/62

MATTHEWS, ANNE
Cole, R.   Searching for Sardi's in Bucks County.   After Dark
   7-2:43 Je '74

MATTHEWS, JESSIE
Sketch.   Time 25:32 Ja 21 '35
Sketch.   Time 27:43 Ja 13 '36
Biery, R.   Sketch.   Movie Classic 9:49 F '36
Sketch.   Newsweek 7:27 My 23 '36
Grimstead, H.   Interview.   Windsor 86:45 Je '37
Albert, J. E.   Jessie Matthews; filmog.   Film Fan Mo 139:3
   Ja '73

MATTINGLY, HEDLEY
The day Noel Coward bowed to me.   TV Guide 15-41:13 O 14 '67

MATTIOLI, RAF
These faces will win top places during 1959.   Films & Filming
   5-7:18 Ap '59

MATURE, VICTOR
Hamilton, S.   Sketch.   Photop 54:71 Je '40
Love, E.   I might have married her, but...   Silver S 11-5:42
   Mr '41
Vallee, W. L.   If I were Victor Mature.   Silver S 12-9:26 Jl
   '42
Franchey, J. R.   Specialist in confusion.   Silver S 13-1:36 N
   '42

Trotter, M.  Horoscope.  Photop 22:31 F '43
Manners, M. J.  Rita announces her marriage plans.  Silver S
    13-8:24 Je '43
Manners, M. J.  The lowdown on the Mature-Anne Shirley ro-
    mance.  Silver S 14-4:24 F '44
Palmer, C.  Advice from a ladies' man.  Silver S 16-5:37 Mr
    '46
Parsons, L. O.  Cosmop's citation for best supporting perform-
    ance of month.  Cosmop 121:73 N '46
Holland, J.  What makes a woman exciting?  Silver S 17-5:55
    Mr '47
Maughan, R.  Marriage and Mr. Mature.  Silver S 18-9:44 Jl
    '48
Balling, F. D.  Me, I'm the cautious type.  Silver S 19-6:26
    Ap '49
Graham, S.  Sketch.  Photop 35:65 My '49
Maxwell, E.  Sketch.  Photop 36:35 D '49
Manners, M. J.  The softest job in the world.  Silver S 20-10:
    42 Ag '50
Karns, K.  Vic finally learns about life.  Silver S 23-7:36 My
    '53
Churchill, R. & B.  I love my work.  Silver S 24-2:30 D '53
Harmetz, A.  That beautiful hunk of man, at 55.  N. Y. Times
    Bio Ed D 12 '71
Marks, J.  Victor Mature.  Interview 21:19 My '72

MAUCH, BILLY and BOBBY
    Sketch.  Newsweek 9:20 My 8 '37
    Lane, V. T.  Story of.  Motion Pic 53:56 Je '37
    Sketch.  Photop 51:8 D '37
    A letter from the Mauch twins.  Child Life 17:42 Ja '38

MAUNDER, WAYNE
    Raddatz, L.  He survived Custer's last stand.  TV Guide 18-21:
        18 My 23 '70
    Raddatz, L.  Three heroes have disappeared.  TV Guide 22-22:
        14 Je 1 '74

MAURICE, MARY
    Sketch.  Motion Pic 9:116 Je '15
    Bio sketch.  Delin 87:9 Ag '15
    Brodie, A. D.  Sketch.  Motion Pic Sup 1:41 O '15
    Sketch.  Motion Pic 13:32 Je '17
    Obit.  Dram Mir 78:747 My 25 '18
        Motion Pic Classic 6:72 Jl '18

MAXWELL, MARILYN
    Stars of tomorrow.  Lions R 1-11/12:no p# Jl/Ag '42
    Marilyn, the eye-filler.  Lions R 2-5:no p# Jl '43
    Introducing Marilyn.  Lions R 3-1:no p# S '43
    The calamity kid.  Lions R 3-2:no p# Ja '44
    The girl who belongs.  Lions R 3-3(sup):no p# Ap '44
    What price glamour?  Lions R 3-5:no p# D '44

You never know who's listening. Lions R 4-1:no p# F '45
Marsh, P. She plays her cards well. Silver S 17-9:65 Jl '47
Sketch. Photop 32:17 Mr '48
Churchill, R. & B. You can be popular if... Silver S 20-2:22
  D '49
Obit. Classic Film Collect (reprint L. A. Times) 35:8X Sum '72
  Mod Screen 66-6:84 Je '72
N. Y. Times p44 Mr 21 '72
Same. N. Y. Times Bio Ed Mr 21 '72
Newsweek 79:73 Ap 3 '72
Time 99:63 Ap 3 '72
Crivello, K. Profile. Film Collect Registry 4-3:28 My/Je '72
Rock Hudson's last words to her. Photop 82-1:19 Jl '72
Crivello, L. Letter; filmog. Films In R 23-7:446 Ag/S '72
Stanke, D. Marilyn Maxwell; filmog. Film Fan Mo 135:3 S '72
Letter. Films In R 24-2:128 F '73

MAY, ANN
Montanye, L. Interview. Motion Pic Classic 11:36 D '20

MAY, DORIS
Delvigne, D. Sketch. Motion Pic 18:48 N '19
Hernon, J. Interview. Motion Pic 23:66 Mr '22
Gassaway, G. Interview. Motion Pic Classic 14:62 My '22
Interview. Motion Pic Classic 21:34 Je '25

MAY, EDNA
Baker, G. Sketch. Motion Pic 11:144 Mr '16
Frohman, D. & Marcosson, I. F. Career of. Cosmop 61:76
  N '16
Nathan, G. J. Reminiscences of. McClure 52:24 Jl '20

MAY, ELAINE
Their line is laughter. TV Guide 7-20:22 My 16 '59
Salute of the week. Cue 38-38:1 S 20 '69
What directors are saying. Action 5-2:16 Mr/Ap '70
Baer, B. If Mike can, Elaine may. Look 34:M F 10 '70
Matthau, W. A new leaf. Show 1-13:26 S 17 '70
Castell, D. First of May. Films Illus 1-6:33 D '71
Behind the lens. Time 99:92 Mr 20 '72
Women directors; directing filmog. Film Comment 8-4:42 N '72

MAYFIELD, JULIEN
Legitimacy of black revolution. Nation 206:541 Ap 22 '68
New mainstream. Nation 206:638 My 13 '68
Up tight. Ebony 24:46 N '68

MAYNARD, BILL
Tierney, M. Interview. Plays & Players 19-10:22 Jl '72

MAYNARD, KEN
Wooldridge, D. Interview. Motion Pic Classic 27:55 My '28
Cruikshank, H. Sketch. Motion Pic Classic 29:60 Je '29

Belfrage, C.  Interview.  Motion Pic Classic 31:33 Jl '30
Hall, G.  Sketch.  Movie Classic 4:24 Jl '33
LaBadie, D. W.  The last roundup.  Show 2-9:74 S '62
Reynolds, R.  Hollywood's silent western stars lived active, ad-
   venturous lives.  8mm Collect 5:3 Ag 15 '63
McKay, A. C.  Maynard guest on Mike Douglas show.  Classic
   Film Collect 20:62 Spg '68
Warga, W.  Maynard's empty saddle in old corral.  Classic Film
   Collect 23:40 Spg '69
Tuska, J.  In retrospect.  Views & Rs 1-1:6 Sum '69; 1-2:23
   Fall '69; 1-3:22 Win '70
Thiede, K.  Filmog.  Views & Rs 1-3:43 Win '70
The trail drive.  Views & Rs 2-2:31 Fall '70
Williams, N.  Letter.  Filmograph 1-2:42 '70
Ken Maynard book finished.  Classic Film Collect 35:1X Sum '72
The red raiders.  Views & Rs 3-3:27 Win '72
Appreciation.  Views & Rs 4-3:1 Spg '73
Obit.  Classic Film Collect 39:extra 1 Sum '73
   Film R p17 '73/74
   Films & Filming 19-9:79 Je '73
   N. Y. Times p71 Mr 25 '73
   Same.  N. Y. Times Bio Ed p459 Mr '73
   Screen World p237 '74
Fernett, G.  His death stirs many memories among his fans.
   Classic Film Collect 39:6 Sum '73

MAYNARD, KERMIT
Williams, N.  Maynard as western star and stunt man; filmog.
   Filmograph 2-1:24 '71
Maynard, K.  Rocky and me.  Filmograph 2-1:37 '71
Letters.  Filmograph 2-2:48 '71
Letters.  Filmograph 2-3:44 '71
Obit.  Classic Film Collect 30:extra 4 Spg '71
   Film R p13 '71/72

MAYNIEL, JULIETTE
Spotlight on Juliette Mayniel.  Unifrance 49:13 Ja '59

MAYNOR, ASA
A long way from Tobacco Road.  TV Guide 9-10:22 Mr 11 '61

MAYO, EDNA
How she became a photoplayer.  Motion Pic Sup 1:49 S '15
Young, Z. Z.  Interview.  Green Book 15:680 Ap '16
How to get in moving pictures.  Motion Pic Classic 2:47 Ag '16
Gaddis, P.  Sketch.  Motion Pic 12:123 O '16
How she got in moving pictures.  Motion Pic 14:108 O '17
Maskell, R. R.  What happened to Edna Mayo?  Classic Film
   Collect 29:3 Win '70
Maskell, R. R.  What happened to Edna Mayo?  Classic Film
   Collect 34:29 Spg '72

MAYO, FRANK
  Sketch.  Photop 17:40 My '20
  Cheatham, M. S.  Interview.  Motion Pic 20:72 S '20
  Squier, E. L.  Interview.  Motion Pic Classic 11:44 Ja '21
  Lake, M.  Interview.  Motion Pic Classic 13:60 D '21
  Mayo, D. G.  His wife's views concerning him.  Motion Pic 23:
    62 Jl '22
  Is woman's love greater than man's?  Motion Pic 25:58 Ag '23

MAYO, VIRGINIA
  Vallee, W. L.  Goldilock 1945.  Silver S 15-10:24 Ag '45
  Letter from Liza.  Silver S 16-4:40 F '46
  My first kiss.  Photop 29:58 S '46
  Parsons, L. O.  Cosmop's citation for best performance of
    month.  Cosmop 122:99 Ja '47
  Wilson, E.  Stardom wasn't easy.  Silver S 17-11:48 S '47
  Gentry, C.  Things are different now for Virginia.  Silver S 19-
    3:38 Ja '49
  Hall, G.  She wishes on a star.  Silver S 20-12:30 O '50
  Vallee, W. L.  Anatomy award winner speaks.  Silver S 22-7:40
    My '52
  Tildesley, A. L.  The mystery of Mayo.  Silver S 23-1:25 N '52
  Rowland, R. C.  Maybe I'm too much woman.  Silver S 23-10:
    31 Ag '53

McALISTER, MARY
  Evans, D.  Bobo's Billie.  Photop 13-1:52 D '17
  Naylor, H. S.  Interview.  Motion Pic 15:62 Ag '18
  Uselton, R. A.  The Wampus baby stars.  Films In R 21-2:73
    F '70

McANENY, PATRICIA
  And the winner is...  TV Guide 19-42:17 O 16 '71

McAVOY, MAY
  Hall, G.  Interview.  Motion Pic 21:58 Je '21
  Goldbeck, W.  Interview.  Motion Pic Classic 12:44 Ag '21
  Jordan, J.  Interview.  Photop 20:34 N '21
  Naylor, H. S.  Interview.  Motion Pic 22:40 Ja '22
  Service, F.  Interview.  Motion Pic Classic 14:20 Je '22
  Her darkest hour.  Classic 15:58 Ja '23
  MacGregor, D.  Sketch.  Motion Pic 25:38 Je '23
  Fairfield, L.  Interview.  Motion Pic 30:27 N '25
  Denbo, D.  Sketch.  Motion Pic Classic 24:34 D '26
  Mahlon, M.  Sketch.  Photop 31:49 Ap '27
  Wells, H. K.  Struggling along on $50,000 a year.  Motion Pic
    Classic 26:55 F '28
  Calhoun, D.  Her reputation.  Motion Pic Classic 28:37 D '28
  Fulbright, T.  Selected for first 1973 "rosemary."  Classic
    Film Collect 37:4 Win '72

McBRIDE, JIM
  Ditlea, S.  After the holocaust:  McBride's Glen and Randa.  Show
    2-3:44 My '71

McCALLA, IRISH
    Sheena is also a Mexican acrobat.    TV Guide 4-24:4 Je 16 '56

McCALLISTER, LON
    Maddox, B.    Too busy for love.    Silver S 17-2:48 D '46
    A fellow needs a girl.    Photop 33:46 S '48
    Carlyle, J.    Lon McCallister; filmog.    Films In R 23-7:405 Ag/
        S '72

McCALLUM, DAVID
    Gauguin, L.    Judas is a man from UNCLE.    Sound Stage 1-3:38
        My '65
    Partial filmog.    Films Illus 1-2:38 Ag '71
    The man from MONSTER.    Castle of Frankenstein 8:8 n. d.

McCAMBRIDGE, MERCEDES
    Here come the heroes.    TV Guide 4-37:28 S 15 '56
    How I faced my drinking problem.    Photop 78-4:60 O '70
    Ross, M. T.    Choose life instead of death.    Movie Dig 1-2:42
        Mr '72
    Higham, C.    Will the real devil speak up? Yes!    N. Y. Times
        Bio Ed p87 Ja '74
    The exorcist's possessed child.    Photop 85-5:52 My '74

McCANN, CHUCK
    Our second windjammer winner.    Applause 1-9:44 Ja 19 '72

McCARTNEY, PAUL
    Of rumor, myth and a Beatle.    Time 94:41 O 31 '69
    Bacon, D.    Interview.    Life 67:105 N 7 '69
    Neary, J.    Magical McCartney mystery.    Life 67:103 N 7 '69
    Newsmakers.    Sr Schol 95:15 N 10 '69
    Saal, H.    Beatles minus one.    Newsweek 75:95 Ap 20 '70
    Hello, goodbye, hello.    Time 95:57 Ap 20 '70
    Sander, E.    McCartney on his own.    Sat R 53:53 My 30 '70
    Beatle roundup.    Newsweek 76:85 S 7 '70
    Meeryman, R.    Interview on the Beatle breakup.    Life 70:52 Ap
        16 '71
    Goldman, J.    Two women who broke up the Beatles.    McCalls
        98:72 Jl '71
    Schwartz, F.    He love me, yeah, yeah, yeah.    Penthouse 4-3:56
        N '72
    Alterman, L.    Paul's grooves will grab you.    N. Y. Times sec
        2:32 D 2 '73
    Interview.    Viva 1-4:69 Ja '74
    (See also: BEATLES, The)

McCARTY, MARY
    Theatre Arts introduces.    Theatre Arts 32:18 Ag '48
    No more braces.    New Yorker 24:24 O 2 '48
    Twenty years' trouping pays off.    Cue 17-42:14 O 16 '48
    Youth on Broadway.    Newsweek 32:84 D 6 '48
    She sings about rich wild West.    Life 26:81 Ja 24 '49

Harbert, R.   Home-town girl makes good.   Good House 138:16
  Mr '54

McCAY, PEGGY
  The real McCay.   TV Guide 2-34:12 Ag 21 '54

McCLURE, DOUG
  Denton, C.   The slings and arrows of outraged critics.   TV
    Guide 10-33:6 Ag 18 '62
  Enter The Virginian electronically.   TV Guide 10-49:23 D 8 '62
  Prehistoric range rider.   Films Illus 37:29 S '74

McCOMAS, CARROLL
  Sketch.   Cosmop 59:203 Jl '15
  Sketch.   Green Book 16:876 N '16
  Sketch.   Photop 25:48 Ja '24

McCONNELL, GLADYS
  Donnell, D.   Interview.   Motion Pic 37:68 Mr '29
  Uselton, R. A.   The Wampus baby stars.   Films In R 21-2:73
    F '70

McCORD, KENT
  Prelutsky, B.   The making of a cop.   TV Guide 17-27:21 Jl 5 '69
  Photoplay forum.   Photop 81-1:12 Ja '72

McCORMACK, PATTY
  Normal little girl with differences.   TV Guide 5-28:20 Jl 13 '57

McCORMICK, MYRON
  Reed, E.   Some actors.   Theatre Arts 20:444 Je '36
  Obit.   Screen World 14:225 '63

McCOWEN, ALEC
  Tynan, K.   Man who plays the man who plays Pope Hadrian VII.
    Vogue 153:124 Ja 1 '69
  Paranoid as pope.   Time 93:68 Ja 17 '69
  Dreams of glory.   Newsweek 73:80 Ja 20 '69
  Flink, S.   Prophetic pope on Broadway.   Look 33:M1 Ja 21 '69
  Interview.   New Yorker 44:22 Ja 25 '69
  Hewes, H.   Eminence of Alec McCowen.   Sat R 52:44 Ja 25 '69
  Gilman, R.   High-level acting.   New Rep 160:32 Ja 25 '69
  Salute of the week.   Cue 38-4:1 Ja 25 '69
  Bio.   Cur Bio 30:29 O '69
    Same.   Cur Bio Yrbk 1969:272 '70
  Gow, G.   Interview.   Plays & Players 20-7:28 Ap '73
  Eyles, A.   Alec McCowen; filmog.   Focus On F 14:17 Spg '73

McCOY, GERTRUDE
  Interview.   Cosmop 56:702 Ap '14
  Sketch.   Blue Book 19:8 My '14
  Obit.   Screen World 19:236 '68

McCOY, TIM
  Paton, C.  Sketch.  Motion Pic Classic 26:38 O '27
  Standish, B.  Camping out.  Motion Pic 35:66 F '28
  Johnston, C.  Sketch.  Motion Pic Classic 27:51 My '28
  Dawson, C.  Interview.  Motion Pic 35:72 Je '28
  Kinkade, H. Jr.  Tim McCoy, a rough sketch; filmog.  Filmo-
    graph 1-1:14 '70
  Tuska, J.  In retrospect.  Views & Rs 2-1:10 Sum '70; 2-2:12
    Fall '70; 2-3:23 Win '71; 2-4:13 Spg '71
  Thiede, K.  Filmog.  Views & Rs 2-4:42 Spg '71

McCRACKEN, JOAN
  Note.  Harp Baz 83:110 Je '49

McCREA, JODY
  Rising stars.  Film R p52 '64/65

McCREA, JOEL
  Manners, D.  Sketch.  Motion Pic 41:51 Jl '31
  Sketch.  Photop 40:69 Jl '31
  Reid, M.  He's the prince of juveniles.  Silver S 2-1:50 N '31
  Hall, G.  Interview.  Motion Pic 43:44 Jl '32
  Willis, B.  Sketch.  Movie Classic 3:21 N '32
  Manners, D.  Interview.  Motion Pic 46:41 O '33
  Wilson, I.  All aboard for wedded bliss.  Silver S 4-3:21 Ja '34
  Borden, L.  Interview.  Movie Classic 7:53 F '35
  Home of.  Photop 48:46 Jl '35
  Mack, G.  His love story.  Movie Classic 8:37 Ag '35
  Dowling, M.  His success.  Motion Pic 52:42 O '36
  Service, F.  Interview.  Motion Pic 53:24 Jl '37
  Maddox, B.  Thinking of the other fellow.  Silver S 10-1:36 N '39
  Bio note; filmog.  Movies & People 2:25 '40
  Leighton, J.  Interview.  Photop 18:34 Ja '41
  Mulvey, K.  Sketch.  Womans Home Comp 68:8 Ag '41
  My most unforgettable moment overseas.  Photop 25:53 Je '44
  Maddox, B.  Independent in a nice way.  Silver S 17-5:50 Mr '47
  Hall, G.  Solving the man of mystery.  Silver S 18-8:28 Je '48
  Pinup of the past.  Films & Filming 18-11:66 Ag '72
  The Dr. Kildares.  Photop 85-3:24 Mr '74

McDANIEL, HATTIE
  Hamilton, S.  Sketch.  Photop 54:71 Je '40
  Obit.  Screen World 4:177 '53
  Bogh, D.  The first black movie stars.  Sat R Arts 1-2:25 F '73

McDEVITT, RUTH
  Pistol in petticoats.  TV Guide 14-52:24 D 24 '66

McDONALD, FRANCIS
  Obit.  Screen World 20:237 '69

McDONALD, GRACE
  Dancer who couldn't walk.  Am Mag 136:108 Jl '43
  Holland, J.  The girl and the costume.  Silver S 13-10:48 Ag '43

McDONALD, MARIE
  Crivello, K.    The body.    Films In R 16-10:655 D '65
  Crivello, K.    Whatever happened to the most beautiful girls in
    the world?    Film Fan Mo 109/110:38 Jl/Ag '70
  Crivello, K.    Marie McDonald; filmog.    Film Fan Mo 143:7 My
    '73

McDOWALL, RODDY
  Cue says watch.    Cue 11-4:1 Ja 24 '42
  Perkins, R.    Master McDowall--master actor.    Silver S 13-8:46
    Je '43
  This, his magic land.    Lions R 3-1:no p# S '43
  My faith.    Photop 24:49 My '44
  McDowall, R.    People I have met.    Lions R 3-4:no p# Jl '44
  My favorite possession.    Photop 26:57 My '45
  Bruce, J.    Mister McDowall.    Silver S 16-4:27 F '46
  McDowall, R.    Buttons and dials.    Life with Music 2:20 D '49
  Minoff, P.    Roddy, willing and able.    Cue 21-3:13 Ja 19 '52
  Bringing up Roddy.    Cue 27-17:10 Ap 26 '58
  Double exposure; excerpts.    McCalls 94:97 O '66
  The kids.    Screen Greats 1-2:48 Sum '71
  Opposite direction; bio note.    Films Illus 1-5:32 N '71
  Winogura, D.    Dialogues on apes, apes and more apes.    Cine-
    fantastique 2-2:34 Sum '72
  Haunted happening in hell house.    Films Illus 2-19:20 Ja '73
  Schuster, M.    Roddy McDowall; filmog.    Film Fan Mo 155:3 My
    '74
  (Roddy McDowall's photographs have appeared frequently in such
    major magazines as Harper's Bazaar, Life, Look, Vogue,
    Ladies Home Journal, etc.)

McDOWELL, CLAIRE
  Autobiographical.    Motion Pic Classic 2:55 Jl '16
  Obit.    Screen World 18:238 '67
  Lee, R.    The magic that was Hollywood.    Classic Film Collect
    26:43 Win '70

McDOWELL, MALCOLM
  Miller, E.    Mark this man.    Seventeen 28:89 Jl '69
  Running figure in a landscape.    Show 1-1:61 Ja '70
  Goldsmith, B.    New stars.    Harp Baz 105:70 D '71
  Burke, T.    About Malcolm McDowell.    N.Y. Times Bio Ed Ja
    30 '72
  MacDonough, S.    England's actor of the 70s.    Show 2-11:37 Ja
    '72
  From the gut.    Newsweek 79:89 F 14 '72
  Jade, J.    Interview.    Interview 20:14 Mr '72
  Ronan, M.    Interview.    Sr Schol 100:26 Ap 24 '72
  Interview.    Photop 81-5:16 My '72
  Wolf, W.    The performer may be great, but will he last?    Cue
    42-21:2 My 26 '73
  Williams, J.    Lucky, lucky man; filmog.    Films Illus 2-23:18
    My '73

Jade, J.  Interview.  Interview 34:6 Jl '73
Stoop, N. M.  O lucky man.  After Dark 6-3:20 Jl '73
Turner, A.  In search of Mick Travis.  Films Illus 3-30:235
   D '73
Filmog.  Films & Filming 20-4:58 Ja '74

McENERY, JOHN
   Bio note; filmog.  Films & Filming 21-2:56 N '74

McENERY, PETER
   McEnery, P.  The harmful formula.  Films & Filming 10-10:15
      Jl '64
   Bean, R.  Will there be film stars in 1974?  Films & Filming
      10-10:9 Jl '64
   A pride of Hamlets.  Plays & Players 18-5:19 F '71

McGARITY, BLANCHE
   Reid, J.  Interview.  Motion Pic 19:64 Jl '20

McGAVIN, DARREN
   Mirror theater.  TV Guide 1-23:13 S 4 '53
   Fremont, V.  Interview.  Interview 3-9:38 S '73
   Stump, A.  Orchestrated by hoot owls and funnier than a hyena's
      laugh.  TV Guide 21-50:18 D 15 '73
   Gardella, K.  TV survivalist accepts image of tough guy.  N. Y.
      Sunday News TVp1 D 1 '74

McGOOHAN, PATRICK
   Filmog.  Films & Filming 18-10:64 Jl '72

McGOWAN, OLIVER F.
   Obit.  Screen World 23:238 '72

McGRAIL, WALTER
   Naylor, H. S.  Interview.  Motion Pic 22:24 D '21
   Obit.  Classic Film Collect 27:60 Spg/Sum '70
      Screen World 22:238 '71

McGRATH, FRANK
   Obit.  Screen World 19:236 '68

McGREGOR, MALCOLM
   Goldbeck, W.  Sketch.  Motion Pic 23:45 Jl '22

McGUINN, JOSEPH FORD
   Obit.  Screen World 23:238 '72

McGUIRE, DOROTHY
   Air break.  Cue 6-17:10 F 19 '38
   Tucker, I. A.  Sketch.  Vogue 97:91 My 1 '41
   Sketch.  Photop 24:38 D '43
   Bangs, B.  Soft pedal on glamour.  Silver S 15-6:42 Ap '45
   Dudley, F.  Perplexing pixie.  Silver S 16-12:35 O '46

Graham, S.  Story of.  Photop 36:39 Ag '49
Keating, J.  I never left the stage.  Cue 20-50:20 D 15 '51

McGUIRE, KATHRYN
 Standish, B.  Sketch.  Motion Pic Classic 28:58 O '28
 Uselton, R. A.  The Wampus baby stars.  Films In R 21-2:73
   F '70

McGUIRE, MARCY
 Vallee, W. L.  That McGuire girl.  Silver S 13-4:44 F '43

McGUIRE, PAT
 Miss soft sell.  Show 1-4:28 Ap '70

McHUGH, FRANK
 Hartley, K.  The unholy three.  Motion Pic 50:49 O '35
 McHugh the merrier.  Lions R 1-10:no p# Je '42

McHUGH, GRACE
 Thayer, J. E.  Movie's first...and second.  Classic Film Collect 38:11 Spg '73

McHUGH, MATT
 Obit.  N. Y. Times p44 F 24 '71
 Screen World 23:258 '72

McINTYRE, FRANK
 Bartlett, R.  A lot to laugh at.  Photop 15-4:74 Mr '19

McKAY, GARDNER
 Alexander, S.  New Apollo for the ladies.  Life 47:88 Jl 6 '59
 Can he weather the storm?  TV Guide 8-25:18 Je 18 '60
 It hasn't been smooth sailing.  TV Guide 9-28:27 Jl 15 '61
 Sorensen, E.  Hear your heroes.  Seventeen 21:77 Ja '62
 Sherlock, J.  Skipper without a ship.  TV Guide 10-30:21 Jl 28
   '62
 Denton, C.  The slings and arrows of outraged critics.  TV
   Guide 10-33:6 Ag 18 '62
 How to eat a piranha before it eats you.  Sports Illus 18:48 Mr
   11 '63
 Lippert, J.  After the last adventure was filmed, McKay found
   his own paradise.  TV Guide 13-23:24 Je 5 '65
 The dangers of galloping inflation.  TV Guide 16-14:14 Ap 6 '68
 Now you see 'em, now you don't.  Look 35-18:70 S 7 '71

McKEE, DONALD MITCHELL
 Obit.  N. Y. Times p38 Je 28 '68

McKEE, RAYMOND
 Sewall, J.  Interview.  Motion Pic Classic 14:31 Je '22

McKELLEN, IAN
 Double crown.  Time 94:71 S 19 '69
 Gow, G.  Interview.  Plays & Players 22-1:15 O '74

McKENNA, SIOBHAN
  Richards, S.  A visit with Siobhan McKenna.  Theatre 2-2:22 F
    '60
  Oliver, E.  Here are ladies.  New Yorker 47:68 Mr 6 '71
  Kalem, T. E.  Saints of the world.  Time 97:48 Mr 8 '71
  Salute of the week.  Cue 40-11:1 Mr 13 '71
  Loney, G.  Nature makes you laugh--to survive.  After Dark 4-
    9:54 Ja '72

McKENZIE, EVA B.
  Obit.  Screen World 19:236 '68

McKENZIE, IDA
  Squier, E. L.  Interview.  Motion Pic Classic 11:36 Ja '21

McKIM, ROBERT
  McGaffey, K.  Sketch.  Motion Pic 17:52 Mr '19
  Gateson, E.  Interview.  Motion Pic Classic 9:43 N '19

McKNIGHT, MARIAN
  Kasindorf, J.  Once the new one is crowned, you're nothing.
    TV Guide 22-35:14 Ag 31 '74

McLAGLEN, VICTOR
  Hagen, L.  Sketch.  Motion Pic Classic 22:53 O '25
  Mattern, J.  Sketch.  Motion Pic Classic 24:48 O '26
  Spensley, D.  Sketch.  Motion Pic Classic 28:43 D '28
  Rentner, J.  Appreciation.  Movie Classic 10:48 Je '36
  Lieber, E.  Best actor of 1935.  Motion Pic 51:37 Je '36
  Home of.  Photop 53:42 Mr '39
  Bio note; filmog.  Movies & People 2:26 '40
  Benedict, P.  Virility plus.  Silver S 11-11:46 S '41
  My luckiest day.  Cosmop 123:112 S '47
  Obit.  Film R p10 '60/61
    Screen World 11:223 '60
  Corneau, E.  The Victor McLaglen story.  Classic Film Collect
    34:36 Spg '72

McLAUGHLIN, ROBERT "FROGGY"
  The kid with the gravel voice.  Lions R 1-5:no p# Ja '42
  Maltin, L.  Our Gang; Our gang filmog.  Film Fan Mo 66:3 D
    '66

McLEOD, CATHERINE
  Wilson, E.  Pride of Alhambra.  Silver S 17-1:50 N '46
  Druxman, M. B.  Letter.  Films In R 22-2:112 F '71

McLEOD, MURRAY
  Debut.  Show 1-7:56 Je 25 '70

McMAHON, HORACE
  Obit.  Classic Film Collect 32:62 Fall '71
    N. Y. Times p41 Ag 18 '71

Same.  N. Y. Times Bio Ed Ag 18 '71
Newsweek 78:55 Ag 30 '71
Screen World 23:239 '72
Time 98:50 Ag 30 '71

McMASTER, ANDREW
Pinter, H.  Mac.  Harp Baz 102:234 N '68

McMILLAN, GLORIA
The girl with no birthdays.  TV Guide 2-38:8 S 18 '54

McNAIR, BARBARA
The reel McNair.  Playboy 15-10:143 O '68
Photoplay forum.  Photop 80-6:16 D '71
Bio.  Cur Bio 32:21 N '71
Same.  Cur Bio Yrbk 1971:256 '72
A star-spangled beauty.  Show 2-5:42 Jl '72

McNALLY, HORACE
(See: McNALLY, STEPHEN)

McNALLY, MARGE
It happens every Friday.  TV Guide 11-7:28 F 16 '63

McNALLY, STEPHEN
(Also known as Horace McNally)
Acting--by a knockout.  Lions R 2-4:no p# Ap '43

McNEAR, HOWARD
Obit.  Screen World 21:239 '70

McNEIL, CLAUDIA
Blessed.  New Yorker 35:36 Ap 11 '59
Hammell, F.  A woman at work.  Cue 31-51:15 D 22 '62

McPHAIL, DOUGLAS
Young man with a voice.  Lions R 1-6:no p# F '42

McQUEEN, BUTTERFLY
Hunter, C.  Butterfly McQueen has a family now.  N. Y. Times
Bio Ed Jl 28 '70
Griffo, D.  Receives the "rosemary" award.  Classic Film Col-
lect 38:4 Spg '73
Summers, M.  Interview.  Filmograph 3-4:7 '73
Letter from Butterfly McQueen.  Filmograph 4-1:37 '73
Interview.  Interview 4-11:18 N '74

McQUEEN, STEVE
Rising star.  Film R p34 '62/63
Sanders, B.  Interview.  Motor Trend 21:88 N '69
Rollin, B.  Mr. Mansmanship.  Look 34:48 Ja 27 '70
Shuman, A. B.  Bullitt in the boondocks.  Motor Trend 22:70 Jl
'70

Speed kills.   Photop 78-4:68 O '70
Knight, A. & Alpert, H.   Sex stars of 1970.   Playboy 17-12:220
    D '70
If you can't leave him, love him.   Photop 79-2:66 F '71
Skow, J.   The 24 hours of Steve McQueen.   Playboy 18-6:114 Je
    '71
Seidler, E.   Le Mans.   Motor Trend 23:94 Je '71
Jones, R. F.   Harvey on the lam.   Sports Illus 35:55 Ag 23 '71
How he ended Natalie Wood's heartache.   Photop 81-2:51 F '72
Gregory, J.   Superstud.   Movie Dig 1-2:129 Mr '72
Why Ali turned to Steve.   Photop 82-5:64 N '72
I'm taking Ali, you can't stop me.   Mod Screen 66-12:48 D '72
Smith, L.   An embarrassment of paradoxes; interview.   Cosmop
    173-6:184 D '72
Lovers on fire.   Mod Screen 67-4:42 Ap '73
We catch Ali, Steve and the kids...   Photop 83-6:34 Je '73
Yates, P.   Bullitt.   TV Guide 21-43:16 O 27 '73
We go to Steve and Ali's wedding.   Photop 84-4:48 O '73
Bacon, J.   Hollywood's most miserable movie star.   Coronet
    12-2:14 F '74
Steve McQueen.   Photop 86-2:19 Ag '74

McREADY, PETER
    Macdonough, S.   They started in skin flicks.   Show 2-10:46 D
        '71

McSHANE, IAN
    Filmog.   Films & Filming 19-3:62 D '72

MEADE, KENT
    Gibbs, W. K.   Sketch.   Motion Pic 32:29 S '26

MEADE, SARAH
    Television's own promising starlets.   TV Guide 3-37:10 S 10 '55

MEADOWS, AUDREY
    Meadows, J.   My sister Audrey.   TV Guide 1-22:10 Ag 28 '53
    Minoff, P.   Ralph Kramden's better half.   Cue 24-4:12 Ja 29
        '55
    Just as cuckoo as the rest.   TV Guide 8-24:20 Je 11 '60

MEADOWS, JAYNE
    Parsons, L. O.   Cosmop's citation for best supporting perform-
        ance of month.   Cosmop 126:12 Ja '49
    Meadows, A.   My sister Jayne.   TV Guide 1-22:10 Ag 28 '53
    Two heads are better than one.   TV Guide 2-34:15 Ag 21 '54
    Allen, S.   My wife Jayne.   TV Guide 4-48:28 D 1 '56
    McClelland, D.   Jayne Meadows; filmog.   Film Fan Mo 154:21
        Ap '74

MEARA, ANNE
    Drake, R.   Somewhere between lobster and dessert.   TV Guide
        19-21:14 My 22 '71

Burke, T.  Ask Anne Meara about her TV series.  TV Guide
   21-32:26 Ag 11 '73

MEEK, DONALD
   Straight man.  Lions R 3-3:no p# Ap '44

MEEKER, RALPH
   Rising star.  Film R p107 '52/53
   Frazer, M.  Let's cut out the 'Brando' stuff.  Silver S 24-5:40
   Mr '54
   Eyles, A.  Ralph Meeker.  Focus On F 7:7 n. d.

MEHAFFEY, BLANCHE
   Uselton, R. A.  The Wampus baby stars.  Films In R 21-2:73
   F '70

MEIGHAN, JAMES E.
   Obit.  N. Y. Times p76 Je 21 '70

MEIGHAN, THOMAS
   Wilde, W.  Sketch.  Motion Pic 13:111 F '17
   Meighan, T.  Famous women who have cooked for me.  Photop
   14-6:48 N '18
   Delvigne, D.  Sketch.  Motion Pic 18:41 N '19
   Service, F.  Interview.  Motion Pic Classic 10:18 Mr '20
   Hall, G.  Interview.  Motion Pic 20:30 Ag '20
   McGaffey, K.  Sketch.  Motion Pic Classic 14:58 Mr '22
   Oettinger, M. H.  Interview.  Motion Pic 23:40 Ap '22
   Goldbeck, W.  Sketch.  Motion Pic 24:24 N '22
   Carr, H.  Interview.  Motion Pic 25:39 Ja '24
   Sketch of his career.  Motion Pic Classic 21:36 My '25
   Hall, G.  Sketch.  Motion Pic Classic 24:53 D '26
   de Revere, F. V.  Analysis of his face.  Motion Pic 28:42 Ja
   '25
   Obit.  Photop 50:111 S '36
   Bodeen, D.  Thomas Meighan; filmog.  Films In R 25-4:193 Ap
   '74

MELANCON, ANDRE
   McLarty, J.  Andre Melancon.  Motion p22 Mr/Je '74

MELCHOIR, LAURITZ
   Heylbut, R.  Heldentenor.  Etude 55:429 Jl '37
   Hoffman, C.  Incredible Dane.  Cue 6-5:8 N 27 '37
   Hoffman, C.  Siegfried as a family man.  Arts & Dec 47:14 N
   '37
   Expression.  Am Mag 126:156 S '38
   Great Dane.  Time 35:51 Ja 22 '40
   Bio.  Cur Bio '41
   Heroic tenor lives in a heroic house.  House B 84:32 Ap 1 '42
   Magnificent Melchoir.  Cue 12-49:11 D 4 '43
   Melchoir's Tristan.  Life 17:29 D 25 '44
   Gardner, M.  Big noise.  Sat Eve Post 217:26 F 24 '45

Tristan in Thrill of a romance.   Cue 14-14:10 Ap 7 '45
Woolf, S. J.   Portrait of the Wagnerian Mr. Melchoir.   N. Y.
  Times Mag p22 F 17 '46
Deep breath.   Time 47:65 F 25 '46
Great Dane.   Newsweek 27:84 F 25 '46
Askland, G.   Little touch of God's finger.   Etude 64:185 Ap '46
Maybe yes.   Time 52:50 Ag 23 '48
My current reading.   Sat R 31:12 O 23 '48
Nichols, W.   Words to live by.   Read Dig 53:80 N '48
What is your vocal problem? with bio note.   Etude 67:11 N '49
Hamburger, P.   Musical events.   New Yorker 25:74 F 11 '50
Marek, G.   Sweet are the uses of publicity.   Good House 130:4
  Mr '50
Alvin, J.   Can your child sing?   Parents 25:38 N '50
Danish suntan.   Mus Am 75:11 Ag '55
How I met my wife.   McCalls 84:106 Ap '57
My favorite Christmas present.   McCalls 85:8 D '57
Osborne, C. L.   Great tenor's memory kept fresh.   Hi Fi 11:76
  F '61
Ardoin, J.   Interview.   Mus Am 83:17 Je '63
Miller, P. J.   His fifty years in music.   Am Rec G 30:110 O
  '63
Loveday, L. F.   Interview.   Opera N 28:26 F 1 '64
Mephisto's musings.   Hi Fi 16:119 Mr '66
Fitzgerald, G.   Interview.   Opera N 34:6 Mr 28 '70
Zakariasen, W.   Duet of the century.   Hi Fi 20:sec I p52 Jl '70
Obit.   Classic Film Collect 39:extra 1 Sum '73
  N. Y. Times Bio Ed p465 Mr '73
  Screen World p237 '74
Schonberg, H.   The Heldentenor species dies with him.   N. Y.
  Times Bio Ed p467 Mr '73

MELIA, JOE
  Tierney, M.   Interview.   Plays & Players 20-11:32 Ag '73

MELIER, ODETTE
  Newsmakers.   Newsweek 79:18 Ja 24 '72
  People.   Time 99:31 Ja 24 '72

MELL, MARISA
  Hamilton, J.   The beauty Broadway won't see.   Look 32:82 F
  6 '68

MELLER, RAQUEL
  Discovery of a new dramatic genius in London and Paris music
    halls.   Cur Opin 69:61 Jl '20
  Wilson, B. F.   A new stage personality.   Theatre 38:24 N '23
  Roeder, R.   Raquel Meller.   Theatre Arts 8:652a O '24
  Douglas, C.   Sketch.   Motion Pic Classic 20:39 Ja '25
  Wollcott, A.   Her amazing career.   Vanity Fair 25:36 Ja '26
  Raquel Meller.   Lit Dig 89:29 My 1 '26
  Krutch, J. W.   Raquel Meller.   Nation 122:510 My 5 '26
  Young, S.   Raquel Meller.   New Rep 46:330 My 5 '26

Benchley, R.  That certain something.  Life 87:27 My 6 '26
Stage mystery.  Lit Dig 89:29 My 29 '26
Watkins, M. F.  Genius and mystic.  Pic R 27:4 My '26
Raquel Meller.  Ind 116:675 Je 12 '26
Adams, M.  Raquel Meller of Spain.  Woman Cit 11:9 Je '26
Criticism.  Theatre 43:18 Je '26
Freeman, D.  Her tour of America.  Vanity Fair 26:45 Je '26
Kalonyme, L.  Ladies' day on Broadway.  Arts & Dec 25:37 Je
    '26
Howe, M.  To enter the movies.  Motion Pic 32:64 S '26
Little street singer.  R of Rs 75:427 Ap '27

MELTON, JAMES
    Minoff, P.  Melton 'festival' has more talent than punch.  Cue
        20-22:6 Je 2 '51
    Obit.  Screen World 13:225 '62

MELTON, SID
    The worrying kind.  TV Guide 11-30:20 Jl 27 '63

MELVIN, MURRAY
    Rising star.  Film R p32 '62/63

MENJOU, ADOLPHE
    Carlisle, H.  Interview.  Motion Pic 27:46 Mr '24
    Winship, M.  Sketch.  Photop 25:74 My '24
    Service, F.  Interview.  Classic 19:41 Je '24
    Home of.  Motion Pic Classic 20:36 F '25
    de Revere, F. V.  Analysis of his face.  Motion Pic 29:54 Mr
        '25
    Autobiographical.  Motion Pic 29:39 Jl '25
    Roberts, W. A.  Sketch.  Motion Pic 30:55 D '25
    Redway, S.  Interview.  Motion Pic Classic 23:18 Mr '26
    Hall, G.  Sketch.  Motion Pic Classic 24:53 S '26
    What to wear.  Motion Pic 31:44 Je '26
    Sketch.  National 55:219 Ja '27
    Carlisle, H.  Sketch.  Motion Pic 35:34 F '28
    Tully, J.  Sketch.  Vanity Fair 30:66 Mr '28
    Goldbeck, E.  Sketch.  Motion Pic 40:66 Ja '31
    Walker, H. L.  Sketch.  Motion Pic Classic 33:52 Je '31
    Orme, M.  Criticism.  Ill Lon N 180:486 Mr 26 '32
    Tennant, M.  Divorce rumors.  Movie Classic 3:27 Ja '33
    Hall, G.  Interview.  Movie Classic 5:34 O '33
    Baskette, K.  Ladies as he likes them.  Photop 45:36 Ap '34
    Lang, H.  Story of.  Motion Pic 54:29 S '37
    Taviner, R.  That man's here again.  Screen Book 19-2:36 S '37
    Sullivan, E.  It certainly pays to be different.  Silver S 10-4:36
        F '40
    Bio note; filmog.  Movies & People 2:26 '40
    Benedict, P.  His greatest role.  Silver S 13-5:38 Mr '43
    Obit.  Film R p43 '64/65
    Corneau, E.  Hollywood's Beau Brummell.  Classic Film Collect
        32:19 Fall; 33:57 Win '71
    Leon, S.  Adolphe Menjou.  Films In R 22-10:647 D '71

MENKEN, HELEN
   Fields, W.  Miss Anderson and Miss Menken...  Cue 3-41:3 Ag
      10 '35
   Menken acts.  Cue 12-33:12 Ag 14 '43
   Your speech is you.  Am Mer 80:67 Je '55

MENKEN, MARIE
   Listing of films.  Film Culture 37:7 Sum '65
   Myers, L. B.  Marie Menken herself.  Film Culture 45:37 Sum
      '67
   Weiner, P.  New American cinema; filmog.  Film 58:22 Spg '70
   Obit.  N. Y. Times p26 D 31 '70
   Women directors; filmog.  Film Comment 8-4:42 N '72

MENZIES, HEATHER
   Tender Trapp.  Playboy 20-8:81 Ag '73

MERANDE, DORO
   A new sister act.  TV Guide 9-2:12 Ja 14 '61
   McClelland, D.  Merande of the movies... reluctantly.  After
      Dark 6-7:40 N '73

MERCER, BERYL
   Sketch.  Theatre 25:148 Mr '17
   Hall, G.  Interview.  Motion Pic 40:82 Ag '30
   Miller, L.  Fifty years of acting.  Motion Pic 46:54 O '33

MERCER, MARIAN
   Schau, M.  It just takes one "real" part.  After Dark 11-9:44
      Ja '70

MERCOURI, MELINA
   Zunser, J.  Greece's golden girl.  Cue 29-44:11 O 29 '60
   Mercouri, M.  I was born Greek; I will die Greek.  Look 31:73
      S 5 '67
   Wolf, W.  Durably demonstrating the art of entwining careers.
      Cue 39-9:9 F 28 '70
   Eyles, A.  Melina Mercouri; filmog.  Focus On F 1:15 Mr/Ap
      '70
   Salute of the week.  Cue 40-6:1 F 6 '71
   Klemesrud, J.  She can't get Greece out of her mind.  N. Y.
      Times Bio Ed F 28 '71
   First man I ever loved; excerpt from I was born Greek.  Mc-
      Calls 98:86 Ag '71
   Interview.  Ramp 10:48 Ja '72
   Rehearsal of Lysistrata.  New Yorker 48:30 S 23 '72
   Hess, J. L.  Melina Mercouri.  N. Y. Times Bio Ed p1826 O
      '72
   After 7 years, (she) comes home to Athens.  People 2-7:14 Ag
      12 '74

MEREDITH, BURGESS
   On the set of Winterset.  Stage 14:46 D '36

Carr, E. L.  Meredith then, and Meredith now.  Cue 5-49:10 O
2 '37
Elected 1st vice president of Actors' Equity.  Time 31:22 Ja 3
'38
Recollections of summer theatre.  Stage 15:4 Jl '38
Hamilton, S. & Morse, W. Jr.  Sketch.  Photop 54:20 Mr '40
Bio note; filmog.  Movies & People 2:26 '40
Franchey, J. R.  Anything can happen to Burgess.  Silver S 11-
5:46 Mr '41
Salute.  Cue 10-43:3 O 25 '41
Franchey, J. R.  A changed man.  Silver S 15-7:24 My '45
Parsons, L. O.  Cosmop's citation for best supporting role of
the month.  Cosmop 121:64 D '46
Minoff, P.  Meredith merry-go-round.  Cue 23-11:12 Mr 13 '54
Whitney, D.  Adding curry to the curriculum.  TV Guide 13-8:21
F 20 '65

MEREDITH, CHARLES
Shaw, O.  Interview.  Motion Pic Classic 11:36 O '20
Obit.  Screen World 16:224 '65

MEREDITH, JOAN
Uselton, R. A.  The Wampus baby stars.  Films In R 21-2:73
F '70

MEREDITH, JUDI
Europe can wait.  TV Guide 6-34:28 Ag 23 '58

MEREDITH, LU ANNE
Uselton, R. A.  The Wampus baby stars.  Films In R 21-2:73
F '70

MERIWETHER, LEE
Minoff, P.  Poor little rich girl.  Cue 25-16:14 Ap 21 '56
Barber, R.  Miss America... some years later.  TV Guide 19-
14:29 Ap 3 '71
Kasindorf, J.  Once the new one is crowned, you're nothing.
TV Guide 22-35:14 Ag 31 '74
The natural way to beauty.  Photop 86-3:27 S '74

MERKEL, UNA
Cohen, H.  Praising players of minor importance.  Cinema Dig
3-6:12 Ap 24 '33
Hall, G.  Men she has played with.  Motion Pic 46:35 N '33
Keats, P.  Una.  Silver S 4-6:29 Ap '34
Fender, R.  Interview.  Movie Classic 8:16 My '35
Sketch.  Photop 49:82 Ja '36
Advice to Miss Average Girl.  Movie Classic 11:44 O '36
Hamilton, S.  Her comeback.  Photop 30:135 Ap '40
Autobiographical.  Cosmop 112:28 Je '42
Maltin, L.  Interview; filmog.  Film Fan Mo 115:3 Ja '71

MERLIN, FRANK
    Obit.  N. Y. Times p37 Mr 4 '68

MERMAN, ETHEL
    Key moments in her singing Rise 'n shine.  Stage 10:34 My '33
    Sketch.  Photop 46:79 Jl '34
    Gwin, J.  Merman of Mazda Lane.  Silver S 5-5:54 Mr '35
    Work of.  Newsweek 21:60 Ja 18 '43
    Sketch.  Vogue 108:141 Ag 1 '46
    Call me madam.  Cue 19-39:17 S 30 '50
    Zunser, J.  Hollywood's calling her madam.  Cue 22-8:12 F 21
        '53
    Two girls four notes make record history.  TV Guide 1-33:11 N
        13 '53
    Gibson, M.  Bye-bye Broadway.  Cue 23-50:16 D 11 '54
    Tozzi, R. V.  Ethel Merman; letter.  Films In R 6-9:477 N '55
    Prince, H.  Cue salutes.  Cue 39-13:26 Mr 28 '70
    Salute of the week.  Cue 39-16:1 Ap 18 '70
    Dennis, L.  Ethel Merman: queen of Broadway.  Read Dig 98:
        112 Je '71

MERRILL, DINA
    Portrait, E.  The world of beauty welcomes Hollywood's beautiful
        women.  Cue 38-46:11 N 15 '69
    Hair-raising stories from the stars.  Photop 78-2:50 Ag '70
    Gittelson, N.  How Dina does it.  Harp Baz 104:46 S '71
    Lives of a blonde.  Vogue 160:122 O 1 '72
    Lord, S.  Makeup.  Harp Baz 106:52 Ja '73
    Her 24-hour beauty care.  Photop 85-3:20 Mr '74
    Interview.  Interview 4-11:37 N '74

MERRILL, GARY
    Hay, R. C.  Maine man.  Interview p20 N '73

MERSEREAU, VIOLET
    Sketch.  Motion Pic Sup 1:53 S '15
    Brodie, A. D.  Interview.  Motion Pic 10:101 N '15
    Lee, C.  Sketch.  Motion Pic 13:123 Mr '17
    Dolber, J.  Claire fixes it for Violet.  Photop 13-1:39 D '17
    Monde, N.  Interview.  Motion Pic 17:68 F '19

MESSEMER, HANNES
    Bean, R.  The face of '63--Germany.  Films & Filming 9-9:41
        Je '63

MESTAYER, HENRY (HARRY)
    Actor of a thousand roles.  Photop 7-5:98 Ap '15
    Hill, G.  Interview.  Motion Pic Classic 8:43 Jl '19

METCALFE, EARL
    How he became a photoplayer.  Motion Pic 9:117 Mr '15
    Sketch.  Motion Pic Sup 1:62 O '15
    Courtlandt, R.  Interview.  Motion Pic 10:95 N '15
    Sketch.  Photop 18:81 S '20

METHOT,* MAYO
    Bogart, M. M.   Ten weeks entertaining service men.   Photop
      24:28 My '44
    Obit.   Screen World 3:177 '53
    (*Incorrectly spelled METHOD in 1st volume.)

METRANO, ART
    Da-da da da man; interview.   New Yorker 47:26 Jl 31 '71
    Lochte, D.   Everything really was fine and dandy.   TV Guide
      20-1:21 Ja 1 '72

MEURISSE, PAUL
    Actor.   Unifrance 33:8 D '54/ Ja '55

MEYER, HANS
    Filmog.   Films & Filming 20-10:64 Jl '74

MICHAEL, GERTRUDE
    Sketch.   Photop 46:77 S '34
    Sketch.   Time 27:59 My 11 '36
    Surmelian, L.   Interview.   Motion Pic 52:54 N '36
    Obit.   Screen World 16:224 '65

MICHELENA, BEATRIZ
    Interview.   N. Y. Drama 72:25 Jl 1 '14
    Sketch.   Motion Pic 9:88 Jl '15
    How she became a photoplayer.   Motion Pic Classic 1:39  F '16
    Courtlandt, R.   Sketch.   Motion Pic Classic 4:59 Ag '17

MICHELL, KEITH
    Person of promise.   Films & Filming 3-9:6 Je '57
    Sweigart, W. R.   Letter.   Films In R 15-10:645 D '64

MICHON, PAT
    I always thought a cue was something you shot pool with.   TV
      Guide 9-29:28 Jl 22 '61

MIDDLETON, GUY
    Obit.   Screen World p238 '74

MIDDLETON, RAY
    Hamilton, S.   Sketch.   Photop 19:63 O '41
    Watkins, W.   Putting the X-Ray on Ray.   Silver S 12-6:24 Ap
      '42
    Enter Daniel.   Time 55:57 Je 12 '50
    Singing voice, speaking voice.   Etude 69:13 N '51

MIFUNE, TOSHIRO
    Richie, D.   The face of '63--Japan.   Films & Filming 9-10:15
      Jl '63
    Milius, J.   An appreciation.   Cinema (BH) 3-6:26 Win '67
    Interview.   Cinema (BH) 3-6:27 Win '67
    Interview.   Cinema (BH) 5-1:28 Spg '69

MILES, BERNARD
    Miles, B.  The minority audience.  Film 9:16 S/O '56
    Filmog.  Film 14:8 N/D '57
    Lampe, D.  Mermaid at Puddle dock.  Reporter 23:48 Jl 7 '60
    Fay, G.  London panorama.  Theatre Arts 46:68 Ja '62

MILES, SARAH
    Cowie, P.  The face of '63--Great Britain.  Films & Filming
        9-5:19 F '63
    Rising star.  Film R p42 '63/64
    Andrews, E.  I don't mind losing if I've played well.  Films
        Illus 2-17:14 N '72
    Castell, D.  A genteel state of shock.  Films Illus 3-26:54 Ag
        '73
    Friedman, B. J.  Burt Reynolds puts his pants on.  Playboy
        20-10:131 O '73

MILES, SHERRY
    Raddatz, L.  On the face of it, she's pretty pushy.  TV Guide
        20-32:32 Ag 5 '72

MILES, SYLVIA
    Zadan, C.  Doing it Miles' way.  After Dark 12-6:16 O '70
    Chase, C.  Who is Sylvia?  I'm a big star.  N. Y. Times Bio
        Ed O 31 '71
    Sylvia Miles in Hollywood.  Interview 27:16 N '72

MILES, VERA
    Failure makes good.  TV Guide 4-38:25 S 22 '56
    Hair-raising stories from the stars.  Photop 78-2:50 Ag '70
    Films on TV; partial list of TV appearances.  Films In R 22-8:
        498 O '71
    Hobson, D.  The movies' perfect wife.  TV Guide 20-10:24 Mr
        4 '72
    The most fateful decision I ever made.  Mod Screen 66-3:47 Mr
        '72
    Favorite animal stories.  Mod Screen 66-11:34 N '72
    Nolan, J. E.  Vera Miles; filmog.  Films In R 24-5:281 My '73
    Letters.  Films In R 25-5:316 My '74

MILFORD, BLISS
    Donnell, D.  Interview.  Motion Pic 9:98 Ap '15

MILIAN, THOMAS
    Lane, J. F.  The face of '63--Italy.  Films & Filming 9-7:11
        Ap '63
    Mead, T.  Interview.  Interview 2-3:12 n. d.

MILINAIRE, CATERINE
    Strick, P.  Caterine Milinaire.  Film 36:14 Sum '63

MILJAN, JOHN
    Hall, G.  Sketch.  Motion Pic 44:60 Ag '32
    Obit.  Screen World 12:222 '61

MILLAND, RAY
  Williams, W.   Royal horseguard.   Silver S 7-7:28 My '37
  Zeitlin, I.   Story of.   Motion Pic 54:50 D '37
  Maddix, B.   Ray goes into high.   Screen Book 20-3:29 Ap '38
  McFee, F.   Diplomat.   Screen Book 22-4:58 N '39
  Bio note; filmog.   Movies & People 2:26 '40
  Benedict, P.   Unmasking Milland.   Silver S 11-12:36 O '41
  Rabid Welshman.   Cue 12-18:15 My 1 '43
  Vallee, W. L.   Making a movie with Ray.   Silver S 13-10:38
    Ag '43
  Asher, J.   Conquer your complex.   Silver S 15-3:24 Ja '45
  Wins New York film critics award.   Harp Baz 80:175 F '46
  Wilson, E.   On "California" location with Ray.   Silver S 16-8:30
    Je '46
  Parsons, L. O.   Cosmop's citation for best performance of
    month.   Cosmop 124:13 Ap '48
  Hurst, T.   The Academy Award jinx.   Silver S 18-10:24 Ag '48
  Milland, R.   My regrettable past.   Silver S 21-1:24 N '50
  Barnes, H.   What's become of the weaker sex?   Silver S 21-10:
    24 Ag '51
  Minoff, P.   Notes on TV.   Cue 23-40:35 O 2 '54
  It's the sponsor who pays.   TV Guide 4-37:24 S 15 '56
  Rock, G.   Milland is back and Frog's got him.   N. Y. Times
    Bio Ed Je 25 '72
  Nolan, J. E.   Films on TV.   Films In R 23-7:420 Ag/S '70

MILLAR, MARJIE
  The case of the wayward petticoat.   TV Guide 2-43:20 O 23 '54
  Friday's date.   TV Guide 4-2:10 Ja 14 '56

MILLARDE, HARRY WILLIAMS
  Sketch.   Motion Pic 9:94 Jl '15
  Obit.   N. Y. Times p37 S 5 '69
    Screen World 21:239 '70

MILLAY, DIANA
  Her stock is high.   TV Guide 10-24:26 Je 16 '62

MILLER, ANN
  Hollywood salutes a newcomer.   Screen Book 19-5:30 D '37
  Hamilton, S.   Sketch.   Photop 18:58 Ja '41
  Gotta sing.   Gotta dance.   Film 40:9 Sum '64
  Newsmakers.   Newsweek 73:67 Je 9 '69
  Oderman, S.   Backstage with Ann Miller.   Film Fan Mo 104:16
    F '70
  Freberg, S.   All to sell a can of soup.   TV Guide 19-7:14 F 13
    '71
  Photoplay forum.   Photop 81-6:42 Je '72
  Shipley, G.   Some notes on some of film's dancers.   Filmograph
    3-1:15 '72
  Catching up with Ann Miller.   Mod Screen 67-4:20 Ap '73

MILLER, CHARLES
Mastering motion pictures.    Forum 61:611 My '19
Montanye, L.   Interview.   Motion Pic Classic 10:84 Jl '20

MILLER, CHERYL
Whitney, D.   The lady and the tiger.   TV Guide 15-13:21 Ap 1
'67

MILLER, FLOURNOY
Obit.   N. Y. Times p36 Je 7 '71

MILLER, JASON
(Citations to Acting Career only)
On the set.   New Yorker 48:32 My 20 '72
Michener, C.   Double champ.   Newsweek 80:124 S 25 '72
Wilkins, B.   "Exorcist" priest who quit the church.   People 1-5:
45 Ap 1 '74
Yes, the devil is real.   Photop 85-4:58 Ap '74
Winogura, D.   Interview.   Cinefantastique 3-4:13 '74

MILLER, MANDY
Rising star.   Film R p106 '53/54

MILLER, MARILYN
Interview.   Cosmop 57:806 N '14
Autobiographical.   Green Book 13:459 Mr '15
Work of.   Strand (NY) 50:61 Ag '15
Sketch.   Cosmop 59:506 S '15
Mullett, M. B.   Life and work.   Am Mag 91:19 My '21
Carr, H.   The new house of Pickford.   Motion Pic 25:26 O '23
Bio sketch.   National 53:195 D '24
Nathan, G. J.   As Peter Pan.   Am Mer 4:118 Ja '25
Hall, G.   Sketch.   Motion Pic 38:58 O '29
Woodward, N.   Sketch.   Photop 38:32 S '30
Hall, G.   Interview.   Motion Pic 40:42 O '30
Hall, G.   Interview.   Motion Pic 42:46 S '31
Obit.   Newsweek 7:29 Ap 18 '36
Perkins, J.   Forthcoming screen tribute.   Life 15:101 D 27 '43
The original Marilyn.   Cue 18-25:18 Je 18 '49

MILLER, PATSY RUTH
Goldbeck, W.   Interview.   Motion Pic Classic 13:34 F '22
Miller, W.   Sketch.   Classic 16:41 Ag '23
Carr, H.   Sketch.   Motion Pic 27:21 F '24
Miller, S. L.   How she entered the movies.   Motion Pic 32:46
N '26
Spensley, D.   Interview.   Photop 31:62 D '26
Johnston, C.   Sketch.   Motion Pic Classic 27:51 Je '28
Sketch.   Vanity Fair 42:17 My '34
Uselton, R. A.   The Wampus baby stars.   Films In R 21-2:73
F '70
Summers, M.   The film career of Patsy Ruth Miller.   Filmo-
graph 2-1:3 '71

Summers, M.  The film career of Patsy Ruth Miller, with re-
marks by Miss Miller; filmog.  Filmograph 2-2:2 '71
Lewis, G.  Letter.  Films In R 23-4:254 Ap '72
Summers, M.  Letter.  Filmograph 2-4:42 '72
Rubin, J.  Interview.  Classic Film Collect 41:12 Win '73

MILLS, DONNA
Whatever her name, it's a good life.  TV Guide 19-49:49 D 4
'71

MILLS, HAYLEY
Rising star.  Film R p21 '60/61
Hayley at 21.  Time 90:51 Jl 28 '67
Hamilton, J.  Hayley Mills.  Look 32:101 My 28 '68
Sketch.  Films Illus 1-16:26 O '72

MILLS, JOHN
Woollcott, A.  Story of.  Good House 116:47 F '43
Hall, G.  He's really a pip.  Silver S 18-1:43 N '47
My favorite role.  Film R p45 '56/57
Williams, J.  Oscar, oscar; filmog.  Films Illus 1-1:19 Jl '71
How to get and keep a close family.  Photop 80-2:54 Ag '71
Marill, A. H.  John Mills; filmog.  Films In R 22-7:385 Ag/S
'71
Everson, W. K.  Letter.  Films In R 22-9:581 N '71
Bio note.  Films Illus 1-5:32 N '71

MILLS, JULIET
Rising star.  Film R p34 '62/63
Lewis, R. W.  The poor relation.  TV Guide 18-13:1 Mr 28 '70
Opinions on liberation.  Photop 78-3:78 S '70
Eyles, A.  Juliet Mills; filmog.  Focus On F 15:16 Sum '73

MILNER, MARTIN
Hiding away with...  Photop 83-2:32 F '73
Davidson, B.  Law and order's Peter Pan.  TV Guide 21-31:21
Ag 4 '73

MILO, SANDRA
Lane, J. F.  The face of '63--Italy.  Films & Filming 9-7:11
Ap '63

MIMIEUX, YVETTE
Rising star.  Film R p32 '61/62
Ehrlich, H.  Yvette Mimieux.  Look 34:49 N 17 '70
Davidson, B.  She kissed her jaguar, great dane, cat, two mon-
keys and a mongrel and went to work.  TV Guide 18-48:28 N
28 '70
Brown, R.  Interview.  Interview 4-11:32 N '74

MINEO, SAL
Cook, G.  Three days to grow up.  Photop 60-1:48 Jl '61

MINNELLI, LIZA
Davidson, M.   My mom and I; interview.   Good House 167:72 Jl
  '68
Thompson, T.   Judy's daughter wants to be Liza.   Life 67:51 O
  17 '69
Salute of the week.   Cue 38-45:1 N 8 '69
Keaneas, A.   Liza.   Newsweek 74:122C N 17 '69
Blum, S.   Liza.   Redbook 134:66 F '70
Kelly, K.   Gasping for breath.   Time 95:43 Mr 9 '70
Zadan, C.   Just having a good time.   After Dark 11-12:22 Ap
  '70
Raddatz, L.   Liza arrived at the L. A. International Airport
  from New York at 11 o'clock on a recent Monday morning.
  TV Guide 18-26:22 Je 27 '70
Two young successes.   Vogue 155:106 Je '70
Clein, H.   The long wait.   Show 1-9:48 Jl 23 '70
Vallance, T.   The other Minnelli.   Film 62:35 Sum '71
Watters, J.   Liza.   Life 72:36 F 4 '72
Flatley, G.   But Liza refuses to be shocking.   N. Y. Times Bio
  Ed F 20 '72
Oberbeck, S. K.   A star is born.   Newsweek 79:82 F 28 '72
Fire, ice and a touch of anguish.   Time 99:64 F 28 '72
How Desi's kisses made a love slave of her.   Mod Screen 66-3:
  38 Mr '72
Ball, L.   My son has finally found the right girl.   Photop 81-3:
  69 Mr '72
Robbins, F.   The definitive Sally Bowles.   Show 2-1:24 Mr '72
I want to marry Liza.   Photop 81-4:54 Ap '72
Second generation.   Films Illus 1-10:13 Ap '72
Mazer, G.   Life style.   Harp Baz 105:96 My '72
Go back to your husband.   Photop 81-5:38 My '72
Peterson, M.   At the deli with Liza Minnelli.   Interview 21:17
  My '72
Desi gives her a wedding ring.   Photop 81-6:45 Je '72
Liza.   Mod Screen 66-6:26 Je '72
Desi's confession to his dad.   Photop 82-1:52 Jl '72
Vallance, T.   Bio note; filmog.   Focus On F 10:7 Sum '72
Liza and Cher.   Mod Screen 66-8:20 Ag '72
Drake, R.   She stands there limply at center stage...   TV
  Guide 20-36:24 S 2 '72
Desi's and Liza's wedding day.   Photop 82-3:60 S '72
Will Desi and Liza take Patty Duke's son?   Mod Screen 66-9:52
  S '72
Goldsmith, B.   Brilliant television concert.   Harp Baz 105:163
  S '72
In Tokyo with Desi and Liza.   Photop 82-4:62 O '72
Cooking with a star.   Mod Screen 66-10:43 O '72
Don't marry Desi.   Mod Screen 66-11:44 N '72
Liz and Liza.   Life 73:34 D 29 '72
Her first interview about Lucille Ball.   Mod Screen 67-4:26 Ap
  '73
Skurka, N.   Liza's place.   N. Y. Times Mag p27 Jl 1 '73
Desi answers...   Photop 84-1:48 Jl '73

Has Liza found out living with Sellers is impossible?  Photop
   84-3:60 S '73
Liza and Desi's new love arrangement.   Photop 84-5:40 N '73
Buckley, T.   To Liza (with a Z) New York is still the big apple.
   N. Y.  Times p54 Ja 6 '74
   Same.  N. Y.  Times Bio Ed p100 Ja '74
Mesinger, M.   Judy Garland's kids.   Coronet 12-2:156 F '74
Klemesrud, J.   Come to the nightclub old chum.  N. Y.  Times
   sec 2:15 Ap 7 '74
To marry Jack Haley Jr.   Photop 86-3:30 S '74
Andrews, E.   Liza Minnelli, singer.   Films Illus 4-39:101 N '74
Marriage to Jack Haley, jr.   Photop 86-6:58 D '74

MINNER, KATHRYN
   Obit.  Screen World 21:239 '70

MINTER, MARY MILES
   Sketch.  Green Book 15:328 F '16
   Drake, A. G.  Sketch.  Motion Pic 11:140 My '16
   Sketch.  Motion Pic 13:75 My '17
   How she got in moving pictures.   Motion Pic 14:60 Ja '18
   Brewster, E.  Influence of dress.   Motion Pic 15:72 Mr '18
   Chapman, E. M.  Interview.   Motion Pic Classic 6:33 Ag '18
   Remont, F.  Sketch.   Motion Pic Classic 8:34 Je '19
   Naylor, H. S.  Interview.   Motion Pic 19:30 Mr '20
   Wilson, B. F.  Her literary ability.   Motion Pic Classic 10:16
      Ag '20
   Fletcher, A. W.  Interview.   Motion Pic 21:44 My '21
   Astor, T.  Interview.   Motion Pic Classic 12:20 Ag '21
   Home of.  Photop 23:46 F '23
   District attorney exonerates her of Taylor death.   Lit Dig 123:10
      F 13 '37
   Mundy, R.  Some Hollywood scandals of the twenties.   After
      Dark 7-7:32 N '74

MIRANDA, CARMEN
   Sketch.  Vogue 94:50 Ag 1 '39
   Sketch.  Time 40:96 N 9 '42
   Palmer, C.  Not half as wild as you think.   Silver S 17-7:50
      My '47
   Pinup of the past.   Films & Filming 18-8:72 My '72

MIRANDA, ISA
   Smithson, E. J.  Italy's it girl.   Screen Book 21-9:58 Ap '39
   Crichton, K.  Story of.   Colliers 103:18 Je 3 '39
   Hamilton, S.  Sketch.  Photop 54:25 Ap '40

MIRREN, HELEN
   Williams, J.  Not blue, just a shade of violet.   Films Illus 2-
      24:16 Je '73

MITCHELL, CAMERON
   Shellhase, G.  Cameron Mitchell; filmog.   Films In R 24-7:446
      Ag/S '73

514                                    Motion Picture Performers

MITCHELL, DON
No pictures please.  Photop 77-6:37 Je '70
They were made for each other.  Photop 81-6:31 Je '72

MITCHELL, GEORGE
Obit.  N.Y. Times p45 S 7 '67

MITCHELL, GRANT
Barry, O.  Sketch.  Green Bk Album 4:1214 D '10
Patter, A.  Work of.  Theatre 26:274 N '17
What I do with my time away from the stage.  Theatre 44:10 Ag
'26

MITCHELL, HOWARD
Sketch.  Motion Pic 10:109 Ag '15

MITCHELL, RHEA
Kingsley, G.  Rhea, the lovely riddle.  Photop 13-5:76 Ap '18

MITCHELL, THOMAS
Sketch.  Time 35:84 F 19 '40
Hamilton, S.  Sketch.  Photop 54:19 F '40
Franchey, J. R.  Mitchell the magnificent.  Silver S 10-9:34 Jl
'40
Obit.  Film R p30 '63/64
Bio.  NCAB 51:573 '69

MITCHUM, CHRIS
Klemesrud, J.  Another Mitchum.  N.Y. Times Bio Ed Je 20
'71
I'll always love my father, but I'll never like him.  Photop 80-
5:86 N '71
How Chris suffered for Dad's wild ways.  Photop 83-4:45 Ap '73

MITCHUM, JAMES
Rising stars.  Film R p52 '64/65

MITCHUM, ROBERT
Hall, G.  There aren't many like Mitchum.  Silver S 16-2:32 D
'45
Parsons, L. O.  Cosmop's citation for best performance of
month.  Cosmop 122:66 Mr '47
Maughan, R.  His mind's his very own.  Silver S 17-10:42 Ag
'47
Mitchum, D. S.  The man I married.  Silver S 18-4:36  F '48
Churchill, R. & B.  Who me?  Silver S 18-12:40 O '48
Greer, J.  It's good to have Bob back again.  Silver S 19-9:42
Jl '49
Home of.  Photop 36:46 Ag '49
Maxwell, E.  Sketch.  Photop 36:35 D '49
Phillips, D.  Are heels better lovers?  Silver S 23-12:33 O '53
Doring, R.  Letter.  Films In R 15-6:380 Je/Jl '64
Lord, J. R.  Big tame tough guy.  Screen Legend 1-3:65 O '65

Waiting for a poisoned peanut.   Time 92:54 Ag 16 '68
Ronan, M.   Put on and put down.   Sr Schol 96:22 Ap 27 '70
Bio.   Cur Bio 31:30 S '70
    Same.   Cur Bio Yrbk 1970:302 '71
My God, I'm blind.   Photop 79-3:63 Mr '71
Mitchum, C.   I'll always love my father, but I'll never like him.
    Photop 80-5:86 N '71
How Chris suffered for dad's wild ways.   Photop 83-4:45 Ap '73
Hall, W.   Poet of a 4-letter soul; interview.   Playgirl 2-6:52 N
    '74

MIX, RUTH
St. Johns, I.   Sketch.   Photop 28:32 Jl '25

MIX, TOM
Lincks, P.   Interview.   Motion Pic 17:66 F '19
Remont, F.   Interview.   Motion Pic Classic 9:56 O '19
Montanye, L.   Interview.   Motion Pic 22:57 O '21
Dean, J.   As Dick Turpin.   Motion Pic 29:102 Ap '25
Ryan, D.   The centaur of the cinema.   Motion Pic Classic 23:
    22 Jl '26
Reid, J.   Sketch.   Motion Pic 32:21 N '26
Autobiographical.   Photop 31:42 Ja '27 and following issues.
Autobiographical.   Photop 33:38 Ja '28 and following issues.
Cruikshank, H.   Interview.   Motion Pic 35:49 Jl '28
Belfrage, C.   Interview.   Motion Pic Classic 28:55 F '29
Sketch.   Photop 39:36 F '31
Carston, B.   Sketch.   Movie Classic 1:26 F '32
Chrisman, J. E.   Interview.   Motion Pic 43:48 Mr '32
Tom and Tony.   Cinema Dig 1-8:5 Ag 22 '32
Grant, J.   Interview.   Movie Classic 3:24 S '32
Obit.   Time 36:63 O 21 '40
LaBadie, D. W.   The last roundup.   Show 2-9:74 S '62
Reynolds, R.   Hollywood's silent western stars...   8mm Collect
    5:3 Ag 15 '63
Henderson, S.   Tom Mix: frontier lawman.   8mm Collect 9:6
    S '64
Lee, R.   Tom and Tony.   Classic Film Collect 20:15 Spg '68
Tom Mix museum open in Oklahoma.   (reprint from El Paso
    Sunday Times) Classic Film Collect 24:14 Sum '69
Spears, J.   Letter.   Films In R 21-1:64 Ja '70
Swetnam, G.   Will the real Tom Mix please stand up?   Classic
    Film Collect 26:35 Win '70
The 100 finest westerns; Destry rides again.   Views & Rs 3-4:
    40 '72
Harmon, J.   For the straight shooters.   Nostalgia Illus 1-1:36
    N '74

MOBLEY, MARY ANN
My child.   Photop 80-5:6 N '71
Kasindorf, J.   Once the new one is crowned, you're nothing.
    TV Guide 22-35:14 Ag 31 '74

MOCKY, JEAN-PIERRE
    Mocky, J-P.   Penetrating the commercial barrier.   Films &
        Filming 8-1:9 O '61

MOFFAT, GRAHAM
    Obit.   Film R p21 '66/68

MOHR, GERALD
    Obit.   Film R p16 '69/70
    N. Y.  Times p47 N 11 '68
    Screen World 20:237 '69

MOISSI, ALEXANDER
    Moissi.   Lit Dig 96:28 F 11 '28
    Moissi in London.   Liv Age 338:683 Ag 1 '30
    Appreciation.   Theatre Arts 19:321 My '35
    German theatre in Milwaukee.   Theatre Arts 28:470 Ag '44

MOJICA, JOSE
    Albert, K.   Interview.   Photop 37:31 Ja '30
    Laine, J.   Making the most of the practice hour.   Musician 45:
        171 O '40
    Poore, C.   Mojica retires to a monastery in Peru.   Musician
        47:59 Ap '42
    Singing soldier.   Time 54:27 D 19 '49
    Brother Mojica.   Mus Am 70:11 Mr '50
    Favia-Artsay, A.   Bio sketch.   Hobbies 59:23 My '54
    Scully, V.   Two lives of Jose Mojica.   Read Dig 74:253 My '59
    Obit.   N. Y.  Times p55 S 22 '74
        Same.   N. Y.  Times Bio Ed p1298 S '74

MOLES, MONTE
    Morison, A.   Monte: nearly a star.   (reprint from Melbourne
        Herald) Classic Film Collect 23:41 Spg '69

MOLINARO, AL
    Raddatz, L.   Get yourself a nose job.   TV Guide 21-35:17 S 1
        '73

MONDUGNO, DOMENICO
    Sing, gypsy, sing.   Newsweek 54:77 Ag 3 '59
    Lane, J. F.   Mr. Volare finds he's become an actor.   Films &
        Filming 6-4:10 Ja '60

MONKEES, The
    Romp.   Romp.   Newsweek 68:102 O 24 '66
    Rollin, B.   TV's swinging Monkees.   Look 30:93 D 27 '66
    Lewis, R. W.   When 4 nice boys go ape.   Sat Eve Post 240:74
        Ja 28 '67
    Evolution.   Time 89:70 F 17 '67
    Miller, E.   Monkee talk.   Seventeen 26:302 Ag '67
    The great revolt of '67.   TV Guide 15-38:9 S 23 '67

Now you see 'em, now you don't.   Look 35-18:70 S 7 '71
(See also: DOLENZ, MICKEY; JONES, DAVY; NESMITH, MIKE;
   TORK, PETER)

MONROE, MARILYN
   Maddox, B.   The girl all of Hollywood envies.   Silver S 21-2:44
      D '50
   Love is my problem.   Silver S 21-12:44 O '51
   I'm not afraid to say yes.   Silver S 23-2:29 D '52
   Sheridan, M.   Marilyn's love problem.   Silver S 23-5:23 Mr '53
   Russell, J.   What I think of Marilyn.   Silver S 23-10:26 Ag '53
   Lee, E.   Her greatest temptations.   Silver S 24-6:26 Ap '54
   Marilyn goes western.   Cue 23-18:13 My 1 '54
   Honeymoon of the year.   Silver S 24-7:14 My '54
   Tusher, B.   Will her marriage last?   Silver S 24-8:26 Je '54
   White, C.   Which Marilyn Monroe do you want?   Silver S 24-9:
      32 Jl '54
   Zunser, J.   The new Marilyn.   Cue 25-30:13 Jl 28 '56
   Quotes, obit, list of films and books about her.   Screen Ed 16:
      48 S/O '62
   Marilyn Monroe.   Film 34:11 Win '62
   Letters.   Films In R 13-9:565 N '62
   Letters; list of songs from films.   Films In R 13-10:631 D '62
   Chaplin, S.   Two faces of Marilyn.   Screen Ed 21:55 S/O '63
   Obit.   Film R p29 '63/64
   M. M. remembered.   Playboy 11:100 Ja '64
   Ringgold, G.   Her legend...; filmog.   Screen Legends 1-2:5 Ag
      '65
   Rosten, N.   Dear Marilyn.   McCalls 94:75 Ag '67
   Guiles, F. L.   Norma Jean.   Ladies Home J 84:171 N '67
   Keneas, A.   American dream.   Newsweek 74:87 Jl 14 '69
   Guiles, F. L.   Excerpt from bio.   Good House 159:63 Jl '69
   Haspiel, J.   An M. M. bibliography.   Films In R 20-10:640 D
      '69
   Nine minds in trouble.   Photop 78-3:56 S '70
   Burnside, W.   Young Marilyn; photos.   Life 71:6 Jl 23 '71
   Tragedy was their co-star.   Screen Greats 1-2:38 Sum '71
   Marilyn; filmog.   Screen Greats 1-4:entire issue, n. d.
   Filmog.   Interview 19:4 F '72
   Still magic.   Time 100:69 Ag 7 '72
   Rosten, R.   About Marilyn.   McCalls 99:72 Ag '72
   Greenblatt, L.   Sugar's suicidal trance 'n' dance number; poem.
      After Dark 5-4:32 Ag '72
   The real Marilyn.   MS 1-2:37 Ag '72
   Steinem, G.   Growing up with Marilyn.   MS 1-2:36 Ag '72
   A look back in adoration.   Life 73:71 S 8 '72
   Logan, J.   A memory of Marilyn.   Show 2-6:25 S '72
   Waters, H.   Taking a new look at Marilyn.   Newsweek 80:80 O
      16 '72
   Mailer celebrates Monroe.   Pub W 202:36 N 13 '72
   Churchill, A.   The untold story.   Liberty 1-10:18 Fall '73
   Trebay, G.   Interview with Don Murray.   Interview p20 O '73
   Durgnat, R.   Mth. Marilyn Monroe.   Film Comment 10-2:23

Mr/Ap '74
The unquiet ghost of Marilyn Monroe.   People 1-9:60 Ap 29 '74
Zolotow, M.   After the fall.   TV Guide 22-49:29 D 7 '74
Haspiel, J. R.   Extra appearances.   Films In R 25-10:638 D '74

MONROE, VAUGHN
Vallee, W. L.   Music master.   Silver S 13-5:46 Mr '43
Boy with a purpose.   Lions R 3-3:no p# Ap '44
Boss record man.   Newsweek 31:74 Ja 12 '48
Davidson, B.   Voice with muscles.   Colliers 124:30 Ag 20 '49
What was called for.   Time 54:54 N 28 '49
Easier for Vaughn.   Newsweek 37:49 Ja 22 '51
Long, J.   Pied Piper of West Newton.   Am Mag 151:26 Ja '51
Boal, S.   Musical moods of Monroe.   Coronet 31:85 D '51
Crazy cyclist's song.   Life 39:149 O 10 '55
Pitts, M. R.   Popular singers on the screen; filmog.   Film Fan
   Mo 114:26 D '70
Atherton, R. D.   Vaughn Monroe.   Films In R 24-9:573 N '73
Obit.   Screen World p238 '74

MONSOUR, NYRA
Names for an act of congress.   TV Guide 7-5:20 Ja 31 '59

MONTALBAN, RICARDO
Parsons, L. O.   His acting in Fiesta.   Cosmop 122:64 Je '47
What I like about American women.   Silver S 20-12:26 O '50
Hendricks, H.   He would have to be married.   Silver S 22-5:38
   Mr '52
O'Leary, D.   Warning from the land of romance.   Silver S 23-7:
   38 My '53
Start with the word Mexican.   TV Guide 18-4:10 Ja 24 '70

MONTANA, LEWIS (BULL)
Fazenda, L.   Interview.   Motion Pic Classic 12:53 Mr '21
Goldbeck, W.   Interview.   Motion Pic 23:32 Jl '22
Howe, H.   Sketch.   Photop 24:42 O '23
Autobiographical.   Motion Pic 32:35 N '26
Wooldridge, J.   Sketch.   Motion Pic Classic 27:40 Ap '28
Howe, H.   Interview.   Photop 34:39 Jl '28
Lardner, J.   How he got into the movies.   Newsweek 18:44 Jl
   7 '41
Obit.   Screen World 2:234 '51

MONTAND, YVES
New rage of Paris.   Harp Baz 80:218 D '46
Appearance at Saville Theatre.   New Statesman 38:69 Jl 16 '49
Bio note.   Unifrance 23:10 F '53
That old ooh-la-la.   Show 1-2:82 N '61
Rising star.   Film R p31 '61/62
O'Brien, G.   Interview.   Interview 1-12:18 n. d.
Nolan, J. E.   Films on TV.   Films In R 22-4:222 Ap '71
Montand on acting.   Films Illus 1-10:31 Ap '72
Conversation with Yves Montand.   Oui 2-11:71 N '73

MONTENEGRO, CONCHITA
Jordan, A.  Spanish influence.  Silver S 1-9:38 Jl '31

MONTEVECCHI, LILIANE
She hates late.  TV Guide 8-10:16 Mr 5 '60
Como, W.  Las Vegas scene.  Dance 40:20 My '66

MONTEZ, MARIA
Franchey, J. R.  Latin, lissom and lethal.  Silver S 12-5:42 Mr
  '42
My first date.  Cosmop 113:40 N '42
Manners, M. J.  Second love for Maria.  Silver S 13-9:34 Jl '43
Hendricks, H.  Should a girl propose.  Silver S 14-5:28 Mr '44
Quinn, M.  Sketch.  Photop 26:48 D '44
Hall, G.  Advice for her kid sister.  Silver S 15-4:30 F '45
My Easter prayer.  Photop 26:43 Ap '45
Should a woman tell her age?  Photop 28:53 Ap '46
Palmer, C.  The happy Aumonts.  Silver S 16-10:35 Ag '46
The siren of Atlantis.  Newsweek 33:87 F 21 '49
Obit.  Screen World 3:178 '53
Smith, J.  The perfect filmic appositeness of Maria Montez.
  Film Culture 37:28 Win '62/63
Letters.  Films In R 14-2:124 F '63
Letters.  Films In R 14-3:185 Mr '63
Smith, J.  The memoirs of Maria Montez or Wait for me at the
  bottom of the pool.  Film Culture 31:3 Win '63/64
Letter to an unknown woman namely Jack Smith.  Film Culture
  45:21 Sum '67
Pinup of the past.  Films & Filming 18-6:70 Mr '72

MONTEZ, MARIO
McColgen, G.  The superstar; interview.  Film Culture 45:17
  Sum '67

MONTGOMERY, BELINDA
Raddatz, L.  She'll cry tomorrow, and probably the day after.
  TV Guide 18-51:21 D 19 '70

MONTGOMERY, CLIFF
St. Johns, A. R.  What happens then?  Silver S 4-6:20 Ap '34

MONTGOMERY, DOUGLASS
Grayson, C.  Clicked twice.  Silver S 4-5:17 Mr '34
Hall, H.  Attempt on his life.  Movie Classic 7:42 N '34
The theatre comes first.  Theatre World 43:33 Je '47
Obit.  Film R p21 '66/68
  Screen World 18:238 '67

MONTGOMERY, ELIZABETH
Like dad, like daughter.  TV Guide 1-17:8 Jl 24 '53
Along came the untouchables.  TV Guide 9-33:9 Ag 19 '61
Girl with the necromantic nose.  Time 84:82 O 30 '64
Lewis, R. W.  Well-scrubbed witch.  TV Guide 12-48:20 N 28 '64

Rising stars. Film R p54 '64/65
Mothner, I. Home-model witch. Look 29:75 Ja 26 '65
Hyams, J. Samantha gets her way. Sat Eve Post 238:32 Mr 13
    '65
Hano, A. Rough, tough and delightful. TV Guide 15-19:19 My
    13 '67
Wilkie, J. Secret magic of Elizabeth Montgomery. Good House
    169:54 O '69
Liz Montgomery wants out? Mod Screen 66-9:42 S '72

MONTGOMERY, GEORGE
    Hamilton, S. Sketch. Photop 18:59 Ja '41
    Manners, M. J. The real lowdown on Ginger Rogers and
        George Montgomery. Silver S 12-3:22 Ja '42
    Manners, M. J. The loves he leaves behind him. Silver S 13-
        7:26 My '43
    Kilgallen, D. Sketch. Photop 23:20 Je '43
    Condemns the labor union strike. Life 21:32 O 14 '46
    The Christmas that taught me the meaning of love. Mod Screen
        66-1:46 Ja '72
    Catching up with George Montgomery. Mod Screen 66-9:29 S '72

MONTGOMERY, ROBERT
    Walker, H. L. Interview. Motion Pic 38:84 Ja '30
    Hall, G. Sketch. Motion Pic 40:50 S '30
    Woodward, M. Sketch. Photop 38:75 N '30
    Tanner, B. Interview. Silver S 1-1:27 N '30
    Grayson, C. Interview. Motion Pic Classic 32:48 F '31
    Waterbury, R. He's grand. Silver S 1-8:22 Je '31
    Manners, D. Sketch. Motion Pic Classic 32:56 Ag '31
    Busby, M. Montgomery tells his life story. Silver S 2-1:24 N;
        2-2:50 D '31; 2-3:59 Ja '32
    Service, F. Interview. Movie Classic 1:64 Ja '32
    Whiting, M. Sketch. Movie Classic 3:41 O '32
    Moffitt, C. F. Censorship for interviews Hollywood's latest wild
        idea. Cinema Dig 2-5:9 Ja 9 '33
    Maddox, B. College girl's dream. Silver S 3-6:22 Ap '33
    Samuels, L. Bob meets the customers. Silver S 4-1:24 N '33
    Hall, G. Interview. Motion Pic 47:51 My '34
    MacDonald, B. Is Hollywood killing its leading men? Silver S
        4-9:30 Jl '34
    Manners, D. Home of. Motion Pic 48:52 D '34
    Brundidge, H. T. Sketch. Motion Pic 49:29 F '35
    Chrisman, J. E. An open letter to him. Motion Pic 49:38 Jl
        '35
    Reply. Motion Pic 50:38 Ag '35
    Zeitlin, I. His story. Motion Pic 52:43 S '36
    Hamilton, S. Interview. Photop 50:24 O '36
    Bio note; filmog. Movies & People 2:27 '40
    Driscoll, J. Experiences in naval battles. Cosmop 115:8 Jl '43
    Benedict, P. A man of action. Silver S 13-9:24 Jl '43
    Experiences in naval battles. Am Mag 136:19 Ag '43
    His first directorial assignment. Newsweek 29:73 F 3 '47

Parsons, L. O.   Cosmop's citation for best Director of month.
   Cosmop 122:58 F '47
My luckiest day.   Cosmop 122:127 Mr '47
Minoff, P.   Notes on TV.   Cue 19-8:9 F 25 '50
It's the sponsor who pays.   TV Guide 4-37:24 S 15 '56
Sarris, A.   Oddities and one shots.   Film Culture 28:45 Spg '63
Where are they now.   Newsweek 71:20 My 20 '68
Pinups of the past.   Films & Filming 17-4:72 Ja '71

MONTIEL, SARITA
Zunser, J.   Sarita has "it" too.   Cue 23-45:14 N 6 '54
Cobos, J.   The face of '63--Spain.   Films & Filming 10-1:39 O
   '63
Moro, F.   Letter; filmog.   Films In R 24-5:313 My '73

MOORE, CLAYTON
Malcomson, R. M.   The sound serial.   Views & Rs 3-1:13 Sum
   '71

MOORE, CLEO
Obit.   Classic Film Collect 42:35 Spg '74

MOORE, COLLEEN
Sketch.   Photop 18:29 Je '20
Shelley, H.   Sketch.   Motion Pic Classic 11:34 Ja '21
Smith, F. J.   Interview.   Motion Pic 21:54 Je '21
Sketch.   National 50:177 Jl/Ag '21
Gassaway, G.   Interview.   Motion Pic 23:40 Je '22
Peltret, E.   Interview.   Motion Pic Classic 14:16 Jl '22
de Revere, F. V.   Analysis of her face.   Motion Pic 28:43 S '24
Autobiographical.   Motion Pic 29:34 My '25
Roberts, W. A.   Sketch.   Motion Pic 30:54 O '25
Calhoun, D.   Her doll house.   Motion Pic 30:24 D '25
Hall, G. & Fletcher, A. W.   Interview.   Motion Pic 33:30 F '27
My career and my doll's house.   Ladies Home J 44:14 Ag '27
Carlisle, H.   Her scrapbook of stars.   Motion Pic 35:68 Je '28
Hall, G.   Sketch.   Motion Pic Classic 28:40 N '28
Calhoun, D.   Interview.   Motion Pic 39:64 F '30
Home of.   Photop 37:34 Ap '30
Wilson, H. D.   McCormick-Moore romance ends.   Motion Pic
   Classic 32:27 Ag '31
Derr, E.   Her marriage.   Movie Classic 2:32 My '32
Cheatham, M.   Her return to the screen.   Motion Pic 44:58 S
   '32
Fidler, J. M.   Moore good news.   Silver S 2-12:26 O '32
Shaffer, R.   Why she has come back.   Movie Classic 5:36 S
   '33
Flint, J.   Her doll house.   Photop 47:70 My '35
McVeigh, G.   Her doll house.   Motion Pic 49:38 Je '35
Abelson, I.   Interview.   Classic Film Collect 17:2 Win/Spg '67
Colleen Moore's cinecon address.   Classic Film Collect 19:6
   Fall/Win '67
Moore, P.   The glory days of fair Colleen.   Classic Film

Collect 20:20 Spg '68
Pryor, T. M.   Colleen Moore's 'Silent Star'...   Classic Film
     Collect (reprint from Variety) 20:21 Spg '68
Uselton, R. A.   The Wampus baby stars.   Films In R 21-2:73
     F '70
Taylor, A.   This flapper altered fashion's course.   N. Y. Times
     Bio Ed O 26 '71
Higham, C.   Long live Vidor, a Hollywood king.   N. Y. Times
     sec 2:1 S 3 '72
Patterson, G. G.   At film revivals with Colleen Moore in at-
     tendance.   Filmograph 3-4:9 '73

MOORE, CONSTANCE
Franchey, J. R.   Nonchalant nightingale.   Silver S 11-9:42 Jl
     '41
Thompson, H.   Story of.   Cosmop 113:29 O '42
Wilson, E.   The Moore the merrier.   Silver S 16-12:54 O '46

MOORE, DEL
Obit.   Screen World 22:238 '71

MOORE, DICKIE
Keats, P.   Dickie Moore's women.   Silver S 3-1:24 N '32
Maltin, L.   Our gang; Our gang filmog.   Film Fan Mo 66:3 D
     '66

MOORE, GAR
Note.   Harp Baz 82:138 Ag '48

MOORE, GRACE
Busby, M.   To sing for the screen.   Photop 38:67 Ag '30
Hall, G.   Sketch.   Motion Pic Classic 32:65 O '30
Her marriage.   Mus Cour 103:25 Jl 25 '31
Sanborn, P.   Appreciation.   Vanity Fair 37:82 N '31
Interview.   Mus Cour 104:10 Ja 2 '32
Ray, M. B.   Set for the season.   Colliers 92:12 D 23 '33
Wild applause greets One night of love.   Newsweek 4:30 S 15 '34
Shawn, B.   Her success in the movies.   Photop 46:25 O '34
Hall, G.   Interview.   Motion Pic 48:32 N '34
Lathem, M.   Interview.   Movie Classic 7:5 N '34
Maddox, B.   Grand opera love.   Silver S 5-3:47 Ja '35
Ergenbright, E. L.   Her courage and determination to succeed.
     Motion Pic 48:41 Ja '35
Fithian, T. B.   Interview concerning marriage.   Motion Pic 49:
     37 Mr '35
In grand opera in London.   Time 25:24 Je 24 '35
Ferguson, O.   Love me some other time.   New Rep 83:308 Jl
     24 '35
Chrisman, J. E.   What singing does for girls.   Movie Classic
     8:30 Jl '35
Awarded Gold Medal.   Etude 53:557 S '35
Chapman, J.   Her story.   Motion Pic 50:36 O '35
When I was a girl.   St Nich 63:22 D '35

As a hostess.  Photop 49:72 Ja '36
Ergenbright, E. L.  Her secret triumph.  Movie Classic 9:31
    Ja '36
Surmelian, L.  Interview with Mr. Parera.  Motion Pic 51:37
    F '36
Work of in The king steps out.  Newsweek 7:27 My 30 '36
Spensley, D.  Everybody loves a singer.  Silver S 6-10:23 Ag
    '36
Life has been exciting; autobiography.  Womans Home C 63:8
    Jl & Ag '36
Reid, J.  Interview.  Motion Pic 52:51 D '36
Ergenbright, E.  What Christmas means to her.  Photop 50:26
    D '36
Landers, H.  Her story.  Photop 51:21 My '37
Roberts, K.  Go the limit.  Colliers 100:22 Ag 21 '37
Zeitlin, I.  Her love for her husband.  Motion Pic 54:32 O '37
Zeitlin, I.  Story of.  Photop 52:24 Ja '38
Gillespie-Hayck, A.  The singing colonel.  Silver S 8-4:34 F '38
Home of in Connecticut.  Vogue 95:68 Mr 1 '40
Bio note; filmog.  Movies & People 2:27 '40
Uproar for Moore.  Newsweek 17:68 Ap 28 '41
Stillman, B.  Moore picks up a home.  Arts & Dec 53:16 Ap
    '41
Her gaily remodeled farmhouse.  House & Gard 82:22 Ag '42
Grace Moore blue.  Newsweek 21:62 Mr 22 '43
Cerf, B.  Trade winds.  Sat R 26:12 N 13 '43
La Moore and l'amour.  Newsweek 23:84 Mr 6 '44
Exuberant Grace.  Time 43:66 Mr 13 '44
Biography.  Cur Bio Ap '44
Some of her international recipes.  Vogue 104:138 Ag 15 '44
What's wrong with today's movies?  Mus Cour 130:5 O 15 '44
Visitor.  Newsweek 27:60 My 20 '46
Grace Moore.  Time 47:41 My 20 '46
Hudson, D.  Tribute.  Sat R 30:32 Mr 1 '47
Jacquet, M.  Her career an inspiration to young singers.  Mus
    Cour 135:22 Mr 15 '47
Obit.  Cur Bio 8 '47
    Etude 65:175 Mr '47
    Life 22:28 F 10 '47
    New Republic 116:40 F 10 '47
    Newsweek 29:70 F 3 '47
    Time 49:28 F 3 '47
Coleman, E.  Deathless diva carries on.  Theatre Arts 41:87
    Ja '57
Pluck, G.  Grace Moore.  Hobbies 63:26 O '58
Favia-Artsay, A.  Historical records.  Hobbies 67:30 Ja '63
More about Grace Moore.  Hobbies 68:31 Ap '63
Sheean, V.  Toujours la Moore.  Opera N 34:14 D 20 '69

MOORE, JOANNA
An actress in spite of herself.  TV Guide 8-43:30 O 22 '60
Parental conflict.  Photop 82-6:62 D '72

MOORE, MARY TYLER
  Whitney, D.  You've come a long way, baby.  TV Guide 18-38:
    34 S 19 '70
  Leonard, J.  Woman's role on TV.  Life 69:8 D 18 '70
  Mary tyrant Moore?  Photop 79-1:50 Ja '71
  Davidson, M.  Bright new world of Mary Tyler Moore.  Good
    House 172:59 Ja '71
  Call me Sister Mary.  Photop 79-2:68 F '71
  Bio.  Cur Bio 32:28 F '71
    Same.  Cur Bio Yrbk 1971:279 '72
  The needle that keeps Mary Tyler Moore alive.  Photop 79-3:51
    Mr '71
  I let my husband make love to Mary Tyler Moore.  Photop 79-4:
    66 Ap '71
  You must not be ashamed.  Photop 80-3:93 S '71
  At home with Mary Tyler Moore.  Photop 80-5:74 N '71
  Richter, C.  Star of the month; horoscope.  Mod Screen 66-1:54
    Ja '72
  Whitney, D.  Mary, it needs one beat of wistfulness.  TV Guide
    20-9:28 F 26 '72
  Martinez, A.  What's Mary Tyler Moore really like, daddy?
    TV Guide 20-26:17 Je 24 '72
  Freeman, D.  I'm not a comedienne; I react funny.  Show 2-9:40
    D '72
  Davidson, B.  It was hard to believe...  TV Guide 21-20:32 My
    19 '73
  Look who's here.  TV Guide 21-33:5 Ag 18 '73
  Johnston, T.  Why 30 million are mad about Mary.  N.Y.
    Times Mag p30 Ap 7 '74
    Same.  N.Y. Times Bio Ed p572 Ap '74
  Goodman, M.  (She) is the queen of the living room screen.
    People 2-14:29 S 30 '74

MOORE, MATT
  Bryant, E.  The hero brothers.  Photop 8-3:78 Ag '15
  Hall, G.  Interview.  Motion Pic 17:47 Je '19
  Tully, J.  Sketch.  Photop 28:55 O '25

MOORE, MELBA
  Salute of the week.  Cue 39-17:1 Ap 25 '70
  Futures, great.  Vogue 156:90 Jl '70
  Garland, P.  Prize winners.  Ebony 25:29 Jl '70
  Zadin, C.  Shine on Melba Moore.  After Dark 12-4:44 Ag '70
  Five young beauties and how they got that way.  Mlle 72:135 N
    '70
  Saal, H.  Peach Melba.  Newsweek 77:94 Je 28 '71
  People are talking about.  Vogue 158:106 O 15 '71
  Davidson, B.  Introducing Melba Moore.  TV Guide 20-25:30 Je
    17 '72
  Talent on approval.  Time 99:97 Je 26 '72
  Cyclops.  Melba Moore-Clifton Davis show.  Life 73:17 Jl 14 '72

MOORE, OWEN
Randolph, M.  Two enthusiasts.  Photop 7-4:88 Mr '15
Wright, E.  Sketch.  Motion Pic 10:114 Ag '15
Bryant, E.  The hero brothers.  Photop 8-3:78 Ag '15
Courtlandt, R.  Marriage of.  Motion Pic 12:108 S '16
Briscoe, J.  Sketch.  Motion Pic 13:97 Jl '17
Smith, A.  Owen talks about Mary.  Photop 17-1:58 D '19
Montanye, L.  Interview.  Motion Pic Classic 13:34 D '21

MOORE, ROGER
The stars of tomorrow.  Film R p42 '55/56
Weinraub, B.  The cool and the chutzpah.  N. Y. Times Bio Ed
    Ag 23 '70
Musel, R.  The oddest couple.  TV Guide 20-15:12 Ap 8 '72
New faces of 007.  Time 101:44 Ja 8 '73
Peeples, S.  Films on TV; listing of TV films as director.
    Films In R 24-3:171 Mr '73
Bond breaks loose.  Films Illus 2-24:23 Je '73
Ballard, R.  Dining with James Bond.  Viva 1-1:118 O '73
Photoplay forum.  Photop 85-4:4 Ap '74
d'Arcy, S.  Moore the merrier.  Films Illus 4-38:60 O '74

MOORE, TERRY
Service, F.  Down-to-earth gal speaks up.  Silver S 23-5:42 Mr
    '53
Sherwood, P.  Terry the incredible.  Silver S 23-8:31 Je '53
Moore, T.  I like a man with a mind of his own.  Silver S 24-1:
    42 N '53
Hyams, J.  Hollywood hoyden.  Cue 23-22:14 My 29 '54
Dudley, F.  Is she a trouble target?  Silver S 24-7:28 My '54
Linet, B.  Bachelor girls have fun.  Silver S 24-9:21 Jl '54

MOORE, TOM
Bryant, E.  The hero brothers.  Photop 8-3:78 Ag '15

MOORE, VICTOR
Tinee, M.  Interview.  Green Book 11:309 F '14
Lincks, P.  Sketch.  Motion Pic 15:41 Ag '18
Lang, H.  Story of.  Motion Pic 53:46 Mr '37
Bio note; filmog.  Movies & People 2:27 '40
The man on the cover.  Cue 11-19:1 My 9 '42

MOOREHEAD, AGNES
A good scout at heart.  Lions R 3-5:no p# D '44
Sketch.  Time 46:57 S 10 '45
Special report--Orson Welles.  Action 4-3:23 My/Je '69
Hair-raising stories from the stars.  Photop 78-1:62 Jl '70
Photoplay forum.  Photop 80-6:16 D '71
Obit.  Classic Film Collect 43:X7 Sum '74
    N. Y. News p73 My 1 '74
    N. Y. Times Bio Ed p725 My '74
Bowers, R.  Agnes Moorehead.  Films In R 25-7:445 Ag/S '74
She bewitched us with her charm and talent.  Photop 86-2:28 Ag
    '74

MOORHEAD, NATALIE
  Goldbeck, E.   Interview.   Motion Pic 40:77 Ag '30
  Manners, D.   Interview.   Motion Pic 40:44 D '30
  Evans, W.   A nine-to-five siren.   Silver S 1-11:26 S '31

MORAN, DOLORES
  Ferth, R.   Sketch.   Photop 29:94 N '46

MORAN, LEE
  Obit.   Screen World 13:225 '62

MORAN, LOIS
  York, C.   Sketch.   Photop 30:94 Je '26
  Sketch.   Theatre 45:40 Ja '27
  Interview.   Photop 32:70 Ag '27
  Donnell, D.   Interview.   Motion Pic 34:40 N '27
  Johnston, C.   Sketch.   Motion Pic Classic 26:51 Ja '28
  Donnell, D.   Sketch.   Motion Pic Classic 29:22 Mr '29
  Donnell, D.   Interview.   Motion Pic 38:64 S '29
  Belfrage, C.   Sketch.   Motion Pic 40:50 Ag '30
  Goldbeck, E.   Sketch.   Motion Pic 41:76 Mr '31
  Costello, T.   Sketch.   Motion Pic 43:57 Mr '32
  Pringle, H. F.   She'd better be nice.   Colliers 90:13 D 24 '32
  Pringle, H. F.   Story of.   Colliers 90:13 D 24 '32

MORAN, PATSY
  Obit.   Screen World 20:237 '69

MORAN, PEGGY
  Vallee, W. L.   Progress is her passion.   Silver S 12-4:34 F
    '42

MORAN, POLLY
  Her idea of Hollywood.   Theatre 47:20 Je '28
  Manners, D.   Sketch.   Motion Pic 37:74 F '29
  Spensley, D.   Interview.   Motion Pic Classic 31:65 Ag '30
  Hall, G.   Sketch.   Motion Pic Classic 33:48 My '31
  Ludlam, H.   Be yourself.   Silver S 2-2:43 D '31

MORE, KENNETH
  Personality of the month.   Films & Filming 1-7:3 Ap '55
  Tierney, M.   Interview.   Plays & Players 19-8:18 My '72

MOREAU, JEANNE
  Blanch, L.   Love is not child's play.   Show 2-6:91 Je '62
  Duras, M.   The affairs of Jeanne Moreau.   Show 3-3:74 Mr '63
  Graham, P.   The face of '63--France.   Films & Filming 9-8:13
    My '63
  The Moreau mystique; photos.   Playboy 12-9:106 S '65
  Arkadin.   Film Clips.   Sight & Sound 36-3:155 Sum '67
  Lindsay, M.   Interview.   Cinema (BH) 5-3:14 Win '69
  Eyles, A.   Jeanne Moreau; filmog.   Focus On F 5:5 Win '70
  Vogue a la Moreau.   Time 96:23 D 28 '70

Varin, G.  More of Moreau.  Films Illus 1-6:33 D '71
Interview.  Continental F R p9 F '72
Grenier, C.  The French actress at 40 is on top of life.  Pageant 28-7:34 F '73

MORELAND, MANTAN
Obit.  Classic Film Collect 41:53 Win '73
Films & Filming 20-3:81 D '73
N. Y. Times p65 S 30 '73
Same.  N. Y. Times Bio Ed p1508 S '73
Screen World p238 '74

MORENO, ANTONIO
How to get in moving pictures.  Motion Pic 12:99 O '16
Lachmund, M. G.  Confessions of.  Motion Pic 13:118 Jl '17
Johnson, J.  Castile, Leon and Tony.  Photop 12-3:46 Ag '17
How he got in moving pictures.  Motion Pic 14:76 D '17
Mack, G. L.  His love letters.  Motion Pic Classic 6:34 Ap '18
Naylor, H. S.  Sketch.  Motion Pic Classic 7:51 O '18
Hall, G.  Interview.  Motion Pic 18:30 D '19
Sketch.  Motion Pic 21:24 F '21
Van Dyck, E.  Interview.  Motion Pic Classic 12:60 Ag '21
Howe, M.  Interview.  Motion Pic 23:39 Je '22
Moreno, A. & Swanson, G.  Do women dress to please men?  Motion Pic 24:28 N '22
His darkest hour.  Classic 15:47 N '22
Carr, H.  Sketch.  Classic 16:36 My '23
Hall, G.  Interview.  Motion Pic 25:23 Jl '23
Home of.  Photop 25:68 Mr '24
Home of.  Classic 19:39 My '24
de Revere, F. V.  Analysis of his face.  Motion Pic 28:49 N '24
Roberts, W. A.  Sketch.  Motion Pic 29:54 Ap '25
Home of.  Theatre 42:48 S '25
Home of.  Theatre 44:52 N '26
Hall, G.  Interview.  Motion Pic Classic 31:30 My '30
Obit.  Classic Film Collect (reprint L. A. Herald Examiner) 17:42 Win/Spg '67

MORENO, RITA
Hickey, N.  Whatever became of Hollywood's most famous Latin spitfire?  TV Guide 20-49:18 D 2 '72

MOREY, HARRY
Interview.  Motion Pic 9:106 Je '15
The man with the iron in his eyes.  Photop 12-5:49 O '17
Hall, G.  Interview.  Motion Pic Classic 6:43 Ag '18
Bennett, H.  Interview.  Motion Pic Classic 8:48 Mr '19

MORGAN, DENNIS
Hamilton, S. & Morse Jr. W.  Sketch.  Photop 54:21 Mr '40
Hall, G.  The wild oats of Dennis Morgan.  Silver S 10-10:24 Ag '40

Teltscher, H. O.   His handwriting and what it reveals.   Photop
     19:63 Je '41
Holland, J.   What success hasn't brought.   Silver S 12-12:26 O
     '42
Vallee, W. L.   Dennis and the Powers girls.   Silver S 13-7:34
     My '43
Embarrassing moments.   Photop 23:58 S '43
My first love.   Photop 24:54 Mr '44
Harris, E.   Home life of.   Photop 25:56 Ag '44
Pritchett, F.   A busy day with Dennis.   Silver S 17-8:37 Je '47

MORGAN, FRANK
     Why he married a non-professional.   Photop 43:53 Mr '33
     Stone, J.   His story.   Photop 45:54 Ja '34
     Aydelotte, W.   Interview.   Movie Classic 6:34 Ap '34
     Evans, W.   One of the great screen successes.   Silver S 7-1:26
          N '36
     Bio note; filmog.   Movies & People 2:27 '40
     Pirate Morgan.   Lions R 1-9:no p# My '42
     Wood, V.   Pagliacci in reverse.   Silver S 12-8:34 Je '42
     No time for comedy.   Lions R 2-2:no p# N '42
     Morgan, F.   If I were Mickey Rooney.   Lions R 2-4:no p# Ap
          '43
     Rooney, M.   If I were Frank Morgan.   Lions R 2-4:no p# Ap
          '43
     He chose the jitters.   Lions R 2-4:no p# Ap '43
     Hollywood hayseed.   Lions R 3-4:no p# Jl '44
     His first flutter.   Lions R 3-5:no p# D '44
     Obit.   Screen World 1:234 '49
     Braff, R. E.   Filmog.   Films In R 20-8:519 O '69

MORGAN, HARRY
     His wife doesn't scare him.   TV Guide 4-40:17 O 6 '56

MORGAN, HELEN
     Cruikshank, H.   In Applause.   Motion Pic Classic 30:22 O '29
     Bolitho, W.   Two stars.   Delin 118:15 Ja '31
     Sketch.   Am Mag 117:31 Ap '34
     Sketch.   Am Mag 129:75 Ap '40
     Torchbearer's end.   Time 38:79 O 20 '41
     Voice of an era.   Newsweek 18:70 O 20 '41
     Torch singers.   Newsweek 49:65 My 20 '57

MORGAN, JOAN
     Morgan, J.   The Morgans.   Silent Pic 11/12:no p# Sum/Aut '71

MORGAN, MICHELE
     Franchey, J. R.   Flight from disaster.   Silver S 12-4:42 F '42
     Sketch.   Am Mag 133:81 My '42
     Miss Michele Morgan.   Cue 13-7:6 F 12 '44
     Vallee, W. L.   A girl, a phone and a boy.   Silver S 14-6:40 Ap
          '44
     Blanch, L.   Love is not child's play.   Show 2-6:91 Je '62

MORGAN, RALPH
    Lee, S.  Interview.  Motion Pic 46:60 N '33
    Stone, J.  His story.  Photop 45:54 Ja '34
    Bio note; filmog.  Movies & People 2:27 '40

MORGAN, TRACY
    Ooh, what you said.  TV Guide 11-24:19 Je 15 '67

MORGAN, WES
    Growing pains.  TV Guide 4-52:8 D 29 '56

MORI, TOSHIA
    Uselton, R. A.  The Wampus baby stars.  Films In R 21-2:73
    F '70

MORIARTY, MICHAEL
    Flatley, G.  From baseball hero to hustler, Moriarty's a hit.
    N. Y. Times Bio Ed p101 Ja '74

MORIN, ALBERT
    Smithson, E. J.  Ribber, keep away from my door.  Screen
    Book 22-1:60 Ag '39

MORISON, PATRICIA
    Rhea, M.  Sketch.  Photop 53:66 S '39
    Vallee, W. L.  Pat Morison, ex-wallflower.  Silver S 10-12:40
    O '40
    Princess Pat.  Lions R 2-5:no p# Jl '43

MORLAY, GABY
    Gaby Morlay.  Visages 8:entire issue.  Ja '37

MORLEY, KAREN
    Pryor, N.  Interview.  Motion Pic 42:66 O '31
    Hamilton, S.  Sketch.  Photop 41:47 F '32
    Grayson, C.  Sketch.  Motion Pic 44:26 N '32
    Bannon, J.  Her marriage.  Movie Classic 3:31 F '33
    De Kolty, J.  Karen Morley a bride?  Silver S 3-4:43 F '33
    Uselton, R. A.  The Wampus baby stars.  Films In R 21-2:73
    F '70

MORLEY, KAY
    Dudley, F.  Her marriage.  Photop 26:40 Ap '45

MORLEY, ROBERT
    Krutch, J. W.  Work of, as Oscar Wilde.  Nation 147:431 O 22
    '38
    Work of as Oscar Wilde.  Time 32:53 O 24 '38
    Talmey, A.  Work of as Oscar Wilde.  Vogue 92:45 N 15 '38
    Paxton, J.  Sketch.  Stage 16:28 N '38
    Johns, E.  The Morley plan for education of the younger genera-
    tion in knowledge of the theatre.  Theatre World 41:27 D '45
    Stokes, S.  His performance in Edward my son.  Theatre Arts

31:35 O '47
The charm of his performance in Edward my son.    Nation 167:
  501 O 30 '48
Morley, R.    Farewell to America.    Cue 18-18:17 Ap 30 '49
The screen answers back.    Films & Filming 8-8:12 My '62
England's treasure.    Films & Filming 13-4:57 Ja '67
Morley, R.    Of barking dogs and caravans and TV talk shows,
  too.    TV Guide 19-36:36 S 4 '71
Morley, R.    Mr. Morley, I presume.    Playboy 21-1:121 Ja '74
Morley, R.    Oscar Wilde.    TV Guide 22-12:17 Mr 23 '74
Morley on bluffing.    TV Guide 22-21:25 My 25 '74

MORRIS, CHESTER
    Cruikshank, H.    Sketch.    Motion Pic Classic 29:43 Jl '29
    Hall, L.    Sketch.    Photop 36:63 Jl '29
    Goldbeck, E.    Sketch.    Motion Pic Classic 32:52 O '30
    Woodward, M.    Sketch.    Photop 38:74 N '30
    Albert, D.    That old inferiority complex.    Silver S 1-9:39 Jl '31
    Bio note; filmog.    Movies & People 2:28 '40
    The role I liked best.    Sat Eve Post 218:69 Ja 19 '46
    Morris, C.    Pretty tricky business.    Silver S 16-12:60 O '46
    Obit.    Film R p13 '71/72
        N.Y. Times p27 S 12 '70
        Same.    N.Y. Times Bio Ed S 12 '70
        Newsweek 76:83 S 21 '70
        Screen World 22:238 '71
        Time 96:98 S 21 '70

MORRIS, DOROTHY
    Stars of tomorrow.    Lions R 1-11/12:no p# Jl Ag '42
    Meet the cover(all) girls.    Lions R 3-2:no p# Ja '44
    Big year for Dorothy.    Lions R 3-3:no p# Ap '44
    Raker, A.    Dorothy Morris; filmog.    Film Fan Mo 152:27 F '74

MORRIS, GREG
    Durslag, M.    He sees beyond the cameras.    TV Guide 15-19:16
      My 13 '67
    Mission impossible's Greg Morris.    Ebony 23:99 D '67
    My child.    Photop 80-6:14 D '71
    My daily prayer.    Movie Dig 1-2:41 Mr '72
    Higdon, H.    Interview with Mrs. Greg Morris.    Good House 174:
      24 Je '72

MORRIS, HOWARD
    Pint-sized comic with king-sized ambitions.    TV Guide 12-30:6
      Jl 25 '64

MORRIS, MARGARET
    Uselton, R. A.    The Wampus baby stars.    Films In R 21-2:73
      F '70

MORRIS, MARY
    O come, all ye faithful.    Theatre Arts 28:389 Jl '44

This ancient and magical art.   Theatre Arts 25:478 Jl '41
Artillery lane encounter.   Theatre Arts 32:60 O '48
Approach to the teaching of drama in high schools.   Educa 71:19
   S '50
Once more unto the breach, dear friends.   Theatre Arts 38:65
   D '54
Obit.   N. Y.  Times p31 Ja 17 '70

MORRIS, WAYNE
   Dake, A.  Story of.   Motion Pic 54:39 N '37
   O'Brien, G.  The winnah and new champeen.   Screen Book 19-4:
      78 N '37
   Hamilton, S.  Sketch.   Photop 52:68 Ja '38
   Smith, M.  Fun to be with.   Silver S 8-4:55 F '38
   Morris, W.  Kid Galahad's week off.   Screen Book 20-6:43 Jl
      '38
   Bio note; filmog.   Movies & People 2:28 '40
   Bruce, J.  Hats off to Wayne.   Silver S 16-7:37 My '46
   Obit.   Screen World 11:223 '60

MORRISON, ANNA MARIE
   Obit.   Classic Film Collect (reprint from Variety) 36:extra 2
      Fall '72

MORRISON, BARBARA
   The unflappable Miss Morrison.   TV Guide 12-28:25 Jl 11 '64

MORRISON, ERNIE "SUNSHINE SAMMY"
   Maltin, L.  Our gang; Our gang filmog.   Film Fan Mo 66:3 D
      '66

MORRISON, GEORGE "PETE"
   Obit.   Screen World p238 '74

MORRISON, JAMES
   Brodie, A. D.  Sketch.   Motion Pic 10:115 O '15
   Pollock, A.  Interview.   Motion Pic 12:51 N '16
   Scott, D.  A tip for Pershing.   Photop 14-1:39 Je '18
   Hall, G.  Interview.   Motion Pic 19:35 Je '20
   Cheatham, M.  Interview.   Motion Pic Classic 14:53 Je '22

MORRISON, JOE
   Ulman, W. Jr.  His rise to success.   Photop 48:44 Je '35

MORRISON, SHELLEY
   She actually enjoys looking like this.   TV Guide 14-30:25 Jl 23
      '66

MORROW, JO
   Rarely the same person for long.   TV Guide 12-9:26 F 29 '64

MORROW, KAREN
   Whitney, D.  Success, where is thy sting?   TV Guide 19-13:20
      Mr 27 '71

MORROW, PAT
    What's orange, red and yellow with tiny blue feet?  TV Guide
      14-18:30 Ap 30 '66
    Zolotow, M.  What did I want to do with the rest of my life?
      TV Guide 19-38:49 S 18 '71
    Catching up with Pat.  Mod Screen 66-6:67 Je '72
    Pat Morrow returns to Peyton Place.  Photop 82-1:28 Jl '72
    Inge, A.  About women.  Playgirl 1-12:18 My '74

MORROW, VIC
    Johnson, A.  The dynamic gesture:  new American independents.
      Film Q 19-4:6 Sum '66

MORSE, BARRY
    Whitney, D.  He's the long arm of the law.  TV Guide 12-37:16
      S 12 '64

MORSE, BOBBY
    Berkvist, R.  Who was that lady?  N. Y. Times Bio Ed Ap 23
      '72

MORTON, CHARLES
    Drexel, J.  Interview.  Photop 32:118 N '27
    Watson, E.  Sketch.  Motion Pic 35:42 Je '28
    Belfrage, C.  Interview.  Motion Pic Classic 29:24 Je '29

MORTON, JUDEE
    It should happen to every woman.  TV Guide 11-34:26 Ag 24 '63

MOSJOUKINE, IVAN
    O'Leary, L.  The Russian years.  Silent Pic 3:12 Sum '69
    O'Leary, L.  The years of exile.  Silent Pic 5:13 Win '69/70

MOSQUINI, MARIE
    Goldbeck, W.  Interview.  Motion Pic Classic 11:60 N '20
    Goldbeck, W.  Sketch.  Motion Pic 23:44 Jl '22
    Carr, H.  Interview.  Classic 16:35 Jl '23

MOST, KARLA
    The authentic Most.  TV Guide 9-45 N 11 '61

MOSTEL, ZERO
    Man in a comic mask.  Lions R 2-4:no p# Ap '43
    Zero hour.  Cue 13-48:12 N 25 '44
    Hammel, F.  A laurel for Zero.  Cue 31-52:15 D 29 '62
    Newsmakers.  Newsweek 73:58 My 12 '69
    Katlawitz, R.  Making of The angel Levine.  Harper 239:98 Jl
      '69
    Jenkins, S.  Zero; interview.  Opera N 35:15 F 13 '71
    Arthur, R. A.  Hanging out.  Esquire 77:30 Je '72
    Williamson, B.  Fourplay; photos.  Playboy 21-4 Ap '74
    Demarest, M.  A lunatic lexicon by Mostel.  People 1-14:25 Je
      3 '74

MOUNT, PEGGY
  Coveney, M.  Interview.   Plays & Players 21-10:14 Jl '74

MOWBRAY, ALAN
  Hamilton, S.  Story of.   Photop 52:21 My '38
  Obit.   Classic Film Collect (reprint Washington Evening Star)
    23:46 Spg '69
    Film R p15 '70/71
    N. Y.  Times p34 Mr 26 '69
    Screen World 21:239 '70
    Time 93:90 Ap 4 '69

MOWER, PATRICK
  Bio note; filmog.   Films & Filming 21-2:56 N '74

MUDIE, LEONARD
  Obit.   Screen World 17:239 '66

MUIR, JEAN
  Maddox, B.  Sketch.   Movie Classic 5:52 F '34
  Walker, H. L.   New girls to satisfy Hollywood's insatiable de-
    mand.   Silver S 4-8:30 Je '34
  Sylvia's beauty helps.   Photop 46:70 Jl '34
  Asher, J.  Interview.   Motion Pic 49:38 Mr '35
  How to become a movie star.   Am Mag 119:62 My '35
  Crichton, K.  Story of.   Colliers 100:36 S 18 '37

MULDAUR, DIANA
  Whitney, D.   One who gets up and goes to work.   TV Guide 22-
    19:18 My 11 '74

MULHALL, JACK
  Sketch.   Photop 17:66 F '20
  Peltret, E.  Interview.   Motion Pic 19:32 Jl '20
  Cheatham, M.  Interview.   Motion Pic 21:45 Je '21
  Drew, R.  Interview.   Motion Pic 23:62 Ap '22
  Home of.   Motion Pic 34:22 D '27
  Home of.   Arch & B 60:199 Je '28
  Dawson, C.  Interview.   Motion Pic 36:55 Ag '28
  Larkin, M.  Sketch.   Photop 34:75 N '28
  Hall, G.  Sketch.   Motion Pic Classic 32:52 N '30

MULHARE, EDWARD
  Lewis, E.  Mulhare wins Fair lady.   Cue 26-6:14 F 9 '57
  Prelutsky, B.   The beard is a bloody bother.   TV Guide 17-20:
    14 My 17 '69

MUNDAY, MARY
  Mary, Mary quite contrary.   TV Guide 10-25:27 Je 23 '62

MUNI, PAUL
  Pryor, N.  Interview.   Motion Pic Classic 29:39 Ag '29
  Anderson, J.  Appreciation.   Theatre Arts 15:28 Ja '31

Cruikshank.  Sketch.  Movie Classic 3:52 S '32
Cohen, H. W.  Paul Muni.  Cinema Dig 2-2:9 N 28 '32
Cruikshank, H.  Champion of the underdogs.  Silver S 3-2:24 D
    '32
Service, F.  Interviews himself.  Motion Pic 46:54 D '33
Samuels, L.  That's my business.  Silver S 4-6:34 Ap '34
Dillon, F.  Interview.  Movie Classic 7:53 Ja '35
Cooley, D. G.  Sketch.  Movie Classic 8:30 Ap '35
Lang, H.  Always the character he is playing.  Movie Classic
    9:48 F '36
Zeitlin, I.  A master of makeup.  Motion Pic 52:50 Ag '36
Hall, G.  Interview.  Movie Classic 11:28 N '36
Awarded prize for best acting in 1936.  Time 29:33 Mr 15 '37
Muni the amazing.  Cue 5-45:8 S 4 '37
Hall, G.  Story of.  Motion Pic 54:31 S '37
Best, K.  Appreciation.  Stage 15:18 Je '38
Best, K.  Story of.  Stage 16:28 Ap 1 '39
Barron, E.  I discovered Paul Muni.  Screen Book 21-10:24 My
    '39
Bio note; filmog.  Movies & People 2:28 '40
Muni returns to the theatre.  Cue 18-5:14 Ja 29 '49
Mr. Paul Muni.  Newsweek 70:72 S 4 '67
Obit.  Brit Bk Yr 1968:596 '68
    Cur Bio 28:47 N '67
    Same.  Cur Bio Yrbk 1967:480 '68
    N. Y. Times p1 Ag 26 '67
When hoods were heroes.  Screen Greats 1-2:34 Sum '71


MUNRO, JANET
    Rising star.  Film R p20 '59/60


MUNSHIN, JULES
    Obit.  Classic Film Collect (reprint N. Y. Times) 27:60 Spg/Sum
        '70
    N. Y. Times p41 F 20 '70
    Same.  N. Y. Times Bio Ed F 20 '70
    Screen World 22:238 '71
    Time 95:65 Mr 2 '70


MUNSON, ONA
    Erwin, A.  Sketch.  Motion Pic 40:78 Ja '31
    Wilson, E.  The ten worst enemies of any actress.  Silver S 11-
        8:36 Je '41


MURAT, JEAN
    Obit.  N. Y. Times p29 Ja 6 '68
    Screen World 20:238 '69


MURATORE, LUCIEN
    Shorey, J.  The romance of Cavalieri and Muratore.  Photop
        15-4:32 Mr '19
    Sanborn, P.  Singing as an individual expression.  Touchstone
        8:345 F '21
    Obit.  Mus Am 74:32 Ag '54

MURDOCK, ANN
  Interview.   Cosmop 57:554 S '14
  Sketch.   Strand (NY) 48:405 O '14
  Wolf, R.   Sketch.   Green Book 12:1023 D '14
  White, M. Jr.   Sketch.   Munsey 54:547 Ap '15
  Home of.   Theatre 22:76 Ag '15
  May, L.   Interview.   Motion Pic Classic 2:27 Je '16
  Olden, J.   Interview.   Motion Pic Classic 4:22 My '17

MURDOCK, TIM
  Ex-marine.   Lions R 3-5:no p# D '44

MURPHY, AUDIE
  Parsons, L. O.   Cosmop's citation for best performance of
    month.   Cosmop 126:13 Ap '49
  Obit.   Classic Film Collect (reprint N. Y. Times) 31:62 Sum '71
    Film R p13 '71/72
    N. Y. Times p1 Je 1 '71
    Same.   N. Y. Times Bio Ed Je 1 '71
    Newsweek 77:93 Je 14 '71
    Screen World 23:239 '72
    Time 97:77 Je 14 '71
  Mauldin, B.   Lonely, angry, wary little bobcat of a man.   Life
    70:77 Je 11 '71
  To hell and not quite back.   Time 97:27 Je 14 '71
  Pinup of the past.   Films & Filming 18-5:70 F '72
  Smith, C.   Innocence preserved or Audie Murphy died for your
    sins, America.   J of Popular F 1-4:255 Fall '72
  Smith, C.   Letter.   J of Popular F 2-1:87 Win '73
  In memoriam.   Cinema Trails 2:15 n. d.

MURPHY, BEN
  Hano, A.   The world's greatest lover.   TV Guide 20-8:20 F 19
    '72
  Bess and Ben; photos.   Viva 1-2:49 N '73

MURPHY, EDNA
  Shelley, H.   Interview.   Motion Pic Classic 13:58 F '22

MURPHY, GEORGE
  Surmelian, L.   Story of.   Motion Pic 54:51 N '37
  Smithson, E.   Triple threat George.   Screen Book 19-6:30 Ja
    '38
  Asher, J.   They found it better to bend than to break.   Silver
    S 9-8:24 Je '39
  Bio note; filmog.   Movies & People 2:28 '40
  Asher, J.   Pattern for popularity.   Silver S 11-8:46 Je '41
  Let George do it.   Lions R 2-2:no p# N '42
  He's not the type.   Lions R 2-5:no p# Jl '43
  He gets the girl.   Lions R 3-3:no p# Ap '44
  Bangs, B.   Yes man Murph.   Silver S 16-9:54 Jl '46
  Sutton, H.   Politics in the Palmlands.   Sat R 50:25 S 23 '67
  Murphy's fee.   Newsweek 75:31 Mr 23 '70
  Simon says.   Newsweek 75:34 Je 1 '70

MURPHY, PAMELA
Once I cried all the time for seven days.   Show 1-9:56 Jl 23 '70

MURRAY, BRIAN
R. & G, G. & R.   New Yorker 43:52 N 4 '67

MURRAY, CHARLIE
Murray, C.   The lens squirrel.   Photop 7-3:147 F '15
Murray, C.   If I say it myself.   Photop 12-5:21 O '17
Fairfield, L.   Sketch.   Motion Pic 35:57 F '28

MURRAY, DON
Zunser, J.   Young man on the go.   Cue 30-14:10 Ap 8 '61
Trebay, G.   Interview.   Interview p20 O '73

MURRAY, JAMES
St. Johns, I.   Sketch.   Photop 31:91 Mr '27
Sketch.   Motion Pic Classic 25:58 Ap '27
Thorpe, D.   Sketch.   Motion Pic 34:44 Ja '28
Thorp, D.   Interview.   Motion Pic Classic 30:53 D '29
Hall, H.   Wins fight to come back.   Movie Classic 3:44 F '33
Schonert, V. L.   James Murray; filmog.   Films In R 19-10:618
    D '68

MURRAY, JAN
Murray, J.   I'm married but I still go out on dates.   TV Guide
    1-18:A-4 Jl 31 '53
Minoff, P.   Notes on TV.   Cue 22-52:6 D 26 '53
Minoff, P.   Comic comes through.   Cue 23-10:14 Mr 6 '54

MURRAY, KATHLEEN
Obit.   N. Y. Times p35 Ag 25 '69

MURRAY, MAE
Briscoe, J.   Sketch.   Motion Pic 13:95 Mr '17
Lee, C.   Sketch.   Motion Pic Classic 4:35 Je '17
Lee, C.   Sketch.   Motion Pic 14:87 Ag '17
Sketch.   Green Good 18:408 S '17
McLeod, D.   Sketch.   Motion Pic 14:43 Ja '18
Bennett, A.   Interview.   Motion Pic Classic 7:25 F '19
Hall, G.   Interview.   Motion Pic Classic 13:20 N '21
Hall, G.   Interview.   Motion Pic 24:28 S '22
MacGregor, D.   Interview.   Motion Pic 25:20 Jl '23
Autobiographical.   Motion Pic 28:27 O '24
Roberts, W. A.   Sketch.   Motion Pic 30:59 S '25
Currie, H.   Interview.   Motion Pic 30:32 O '25
The milky way to beauty.   Photop 28:62 N '25
Palmborg, R. P.   The true story about her son.   Motion Pic
    36:28 D '28
Aging ex-actress found wandering in St. Louis.   8mm Collect
    (reprint from St. Louis Post-Dispatch) 8:15 My '64
Obit.   8mm Collect (reprint from San Antonio Light) 12:7 Sum '65
    Film R p45 '65/66
Minton, E.   Mae Murray, star; filmog.   Filmograph 1-3:35 '70

MUSANTE, TONY
    Galanoy, T.  Till cancellation do us part.  TV Guide 22-13:16
      Mr 30 '74
    His marriage.  Photop 86-3:49 S '74

MUSE, CLARENCE
    Mason, B. J.  Grand old man of Good Hope Valley.  Ebony 27:
      50 S '72

MUSGROVE, GERTRUDE
    The girl on the cover.  Cue 11-4:1 Ja 24 '42

MUSTIN, BURT
    Sewell, J. B.  Life begins at 67; filmog.  Films In R 22-8:515
      O '71

MYERS, CARMEL
    Hall, G.  Interview.  Motion Pic Classic 7:24 O '18
    Cheatham, M.  Interview.  Motion Pic 21:46 Mr '21
    Curtis, E. L.  Interview.  Motion Pic 13:44 F '22
    Bryers, L.  Interview.  Motion Pic 27:21 Jl '24
    Roberts, W. A.  Sketch.  Motion Pic 29:45 Je '25
    Why stage actors fail in the talkies.  Theatre 49:32 F '29
    Dibble, S.  Interview.  Movie Classic 2:32 Ap '32
    You don't have to look old.  Harp Baz 104:6 Jl '71


NABORS, JIM
    The Sylacauga flash.  TV Guide 12-12:21 Mr 21 '64
    As Gomer Pyle USMC.  TV Guide 12-47:10 N 21 '64
    Gordon, S.  Country boy next door.  Look 29:99 Je 1 '65
    Clepper, P. M.  Back to the farm.  TV Guide 13-51:15 D 18 '65
    Fox, W. P. Jr.  That Jim Nabors assignment.  TV Guide 14-41:
      20 O 8 '66
    Success is a warm puppy.  Time 90:88 N 10 '67
    Whitney, D.  It's tough to remain just plain Jim.  TV Guide 17-
      38:35 S 20 '69
    Bio.  Cur Bio 30:30 N '69
      Same.  Cur Bio Yrbk 1969:299 '70
    Hudson, R.  I did not marry Jim Nabors.  Photop 80-5:63 N '71

NADER, GEORGE
    The stars of tomorrow.  Film R p44 '55/56

NAGEL, ANN
    Palmer, G.  Her friendship for Glenda Farrell.  Photop 51:48
      Je '37

NAGEL, CONRAD
    Sherwood, C. B.  Interview.  Motion Pic Classic 8:26 Mr '19
    Lowell, A.  Interview.  Motion Pic 18:69 Ag '19
    Peltret, E.  Interview.  Motion Pic Classic 11:46 O '20

Trepel, B.  Interview.  Motion Pic 21:24 Mr '21
Goldbeck, W.  Interview.  Motion Pic Classic 13:62 N '21
Cheatham, M.  Interview.  Motion Pic 23:30 Mr '22
Howe, H.  Sketch.  Motion Pic Classic 14:36 Je '22
Nagel, R.  How it feels to be a star's wife.  Motion Pic 30:32
   Ja '26
Spensley, D.  Sketch.  Photop 31:70 F '27
Home of.  Motion Pic 33:58 Mr '27
Thorp, D.  Sketch.  Motion Pic 35:56 Mr '28
Belfrage, C.  Interview.  Motion Pic 36:42 N '28
Palmborg, R. P.  How he handles his money.  Motion Pic 39:68
   Mr '30
Walker, H. L.  Interview.  Motion Pic 39:44 Ap '30
Benham, L.  Two hicks from Hollywood.  Silver S 1-2:16 D '30
Hall, G.  Sketch.  Motion Pic 41:64 F '31
Manners, D.  Interview.  Movie Classic 1:51 F '32
Miller, R.  Greatest screen lover.  Photop 43:32 F '33
Lee, S.  Interview.  Motion Pic 45:28 Mr '33
Minoff, P.  Notes on TV.  Cue 18-28:25 Jl 9 '49
Obit.  Classic Film Collect (reprint Variety) 26:ex2 Win '70
   Film R p15 '70/71
   N. Y. Times p47 F 25 '70
   Same.  N. Y. Times Bio Ed F 25 '70
   Newsweek 75:61 Mr 9 '70
   Screen World 22:239 '71
   Time 95:70 Mr 9 '70


NAISH, J. CARROL
   Hamilton, S.  Sketch.  Photop 54:30 Jl '40
   Corneau, E. N.  I remember J. Carrol Naish.  Classic Film
      Collect 33:38 Win '71
   Obit.  Classic Film Collect 38:57 Spg '73
      Film R p13 '73/74
      N. Y. Times Bio Ed p133 Ja '73
      Screen World p238 '74


NAKAYA, NOBORU
   A conversation with two Japanese film stars.  Film Comment
      3-1:61 Win '65


NALDI, NITA
   Montanye, L.  Interview.  Motion Pic Classic 12:22 Jl '21
   Men and women in love.  Met Mag 56:40 N '22
   Cannon, R.  Interview.  Classic Ja '23
   Hall, G.  Interview.  Motion Pic 24:36 Ja '23
   de Revere, F. V.  Analysis of her face.  Motion Pic 28:45 O
      '24
   The business of being a vampire.  Motion Pic 29:42 Mr '25
   Tashman, L.  The real Nita.  Motion Pic 30:27 O '25


NAMATH, JOE
   (Citations regarding football career not documented)
   Playboy interviews.  Playboy 16-12:93 D '69

Linderman, L.   High noon for Broadway Joe.   Playboy 18-1:129
  Ja '71
Linderman, L.   I am man.   Venus 2-1:52 Ja '74

NANASI, ANNA MARIA
  Opportunity U. S. A.   TV Guide 5-14:8 Ap 6 '57

NANERIS, NIKIFOROS
  Person of promise.   Films & Filming 6-11:16 Ag '60

NAPIER, ALAN
  Tolstoy betrayed.   Film Heritage 4-3:11 Spg '69

NARDINI, TOM
  Filmog.   Films & Filming 20-10:64 Jl '74

NASH, JOHNNY
  Cutrone, R.   Interview.   Interview 3-8:36 Ag '73

NASH, MARILYN
  She planned to study medicine.   Cue 16-24:12 Je 14 '47
  Fulton, M. J.   Sketch.   Photop 31:97 S '47

NATWICK, MILDRED
  Sketch.   Life 21:9 Jl 22 '46
  Grand slam.   TV Guide 19-41:16 O 9 '71
  Cohn, E.   Thoroughly modern Millie.   TV Guide 22-20:14 My 18
    '74

NAZIMOVA, ALLA
  Becomes an American star.   Theatre 7:12 Ja '07
  As Nora in A doll's house.   Theatre 7:72 Mr '07
  Patterson, A.   Interview.   Theatre 7:219 Ag '07
  Graham, J.   Appreciation.   Canadian Mag 32:476 Mr '09
  Her American "Doll's house."   Theatre 11:168 My '10
  Comment on her work.   Munsey 43:425 Je 10
  Bell, A.   Work of.   Green Book 7:574 Mr '12
  Metcalfe, J. S.   Mannerisms of.   Life 60:2288 N 28 '12
  Interview.   Cosmop 53:835 N '12
  Work of.   Theatre 16:186 D '12
  West, M. F.   Interview.   Green Book 9:414 Mr '13
  Work in War brides.   Theatre 21:116 Mr '15
  De Foe, L. V.   Work in War brides.   Green Book 13:905 My
    '15
  Dale, A.   Sketch.   Green Book 15:303 F '16
  In repertoire.   N. Y. Drama 76:3 O 21 '16
  An apostle of the drama.   Theatre 25:114 Mr '17
  Montanye, L.   Interview.   Motion Pic Classic 4:36 Jl '17
  In Hedda Gabler.   New Rep 14:359 Ap 20 '18
  Naylor, H. S.   Interview.   Motion Pic 15:54 Jl '18
  Interview.   Mus Cour 77:6 Ag 8 '18
  Biographical.   Dram Mir 82:588 Mr 27 '20
  Gray, F.   Interview.   Motion Pic 20:30 O '20

Hall, G. & Fletcher, A. W.  Interview.  Motion Pic 22:24 Ja '22
Her darkest hour.  Classic 15:47 S '22
Service, F.  Interview.  Classic 15:18 N '22
Brush, K.  Her career.  National 52:58 Jl '23
Home of.  Classic 18:60 N '23
St. Johns, A. R.  Her temperament.  Photop 30:32 O '26
Grein, J. T.  Discovery of.  Ill Lon N 170:762 Ap 30 '27
Autobiographical.  Theatre 49:18 Ap '29
Fergusson, F.  Work of in Mourning becomes Electra.  Bookman
    75:290 Je/Jl '32
Krutch, J. W.  In Doctor Monica.  Nation 137:606 N 22 '33
Isaacs, J. R.  Work of in Ghosts.  Theatre Arts 20:97 F '36
Krutch, J. W.  Work of in Hedda Gabler.  Nation 143:641 N 28
    '36
Obit.  Cur Bio 6 '45
Women directors; directing filmog.  Film Comment 8-4:42 N '72
Bodeen, D.  Nazimova; filmog.  Films In R 23-10:577 D '72


NEAGLE, ANNA
Landy, G.  Sketch.  Movie Classic 7:52 Ja '35
As Nurse Edith Cavell.  Ill Lon N 195:630 O 21 '39
Neagle, A.  What I found out about Hollywood.  Silver S 9-12:44
    O '39
Sketch.  Time 35:82 My 6 '40
Sketch.  Theatre World 41:19 Mr '45
My favorite role.  Film R p19 '50
Tierney, M.  Nothing like a Dame.  Plays & Players 18-8:26
    My '71


NEAL, PATRICIA
Holliday, K.  Have you met Patricia Neal?  Silver S 19-5:45 Mr
    '49
Neal, P.  The Hollywood life.  Silver S 21-3:45 Ja '51
Frank, S.  Suddenly I wanted to live.  Good House 165:70 Jl '67
Newsmakers.  Newsweek 71:57 F 12 '68
Movie star again.  Good House 167:19 Jl '68
Neal, P. & McKuen, R.  Redbook dialogue.  Redbook 132:80 N
    '68
Zimmermann, G.  Does everybody love Patricia Neal?  O, yes.
    Look 33:82 F 18 '69
Road back.  Time 94:96 N 21 '69
Adler, D.  Patricia Neal comes home.  TV Guide 19-51:12 D
    18 '71
McAsh, I.  Stroke and counterstroke.  Films Illus 1-9:33 Mr
    '72


NEAL, TOM
Obit.  Classic Film Collect (reprint Elizabeth, N. J. Daily J)
    36:extra 2 Fall '72
    Film R p11 '73/74
    N. Y. Times Bio Ed p1523 Ag '72
Brock, A.  Good guy.  Classic Film Collect 38:25 Spg '73

NEAR, HOLLY
Pearsall, A.  How some of the magic went out of Stanley Sweetheart's garden.  Show 1-3:69 Mr '70

NEFF, HILDEGARDE
(See:  KNEF, HILDEGARDE)

NEGRI, POLA
Haskins, H.  Sketch.  Motion Pic Classic 11:43 F '21
Allvine, G.  Interview.  Motion Pic 24:21 S '22
Shulsinger, R.  Sketch.  Classic 15:18 O '22
Leeds, S.  Her inspiration.  Classic 15:40 F '23
Carr, H.  Sketch.  Motion Pic 25:33 Je '23
Carr, H.  Interview.  Motion Pic 27:28 Jl '24
Carr, H.  The mystery of Pola Negri.  Motion Pic 29:34 Ap '25
Carr, H.  Compared with Gloria Swanson.  Motion Pic 30:28 S
'25
Autobiographical.  Motion Pic 30:32 D '25
Tully, J.  Interview.  Vanity Fair 26:55 Ag '26
Carlisle, H.  A new view of.  Motion Pic 33:22 Ap '27
A study in artistic temperament.  Theatre 45:46 Je '27
Bagley, J.  The truth about her prince.  Motion Pic Classic 26:
20 O '27
Mortimer, R.  The first to win Bernard Shaw's consent to film
a play of his.  Motion Pic Classic 29:53 Ap '29
Grein, J. T.  From the screen to stage.  Ill Lon N 178:288 F
21 '31
Pryor, N.  Comes back to Hollywood.  Motion Pic 42:34 Ag '31
Sharon, M.  Lovelorn.  Silver S 1-11:18 S '31
Hamilton, S.  Sketch.  Photop 41:40 Ja '32
Hall, G.  Valentino still lives for her.  Motion Pic 48:46 Ja '35
Sketch.  Time 29:20 Ap 26 '37
Manners, M. J.  The Hollywood that used to be.  Silver S 13-
12:42 O '43
Bio note.  Harp Baz 82:101 S '48
Miller, N.  Letter; partial filmog.  Films In R 13-1:57 Ja '62
Tucker, G. F.  Pola Negri leaving seclusion to receive cinema
award.  (reprint from San Antonio Light) Classic Film Col-
lect 21:59 Sum '68
Where are they now?  Newsweek 75:26 Ap 20 '70
Taylor, A.  Pola Negri's memoirs:  best roles were played in
real life.  N. Y. Times Bio Ed Ap 24 '70
St. Johns, A. R.  Hollywood's gold old days.  Classic Film
Collect 27:61 Spg/Sum '70
When silence was golden.  Screen Greats 1-2:77 Sum '71

NEIL, HILDEGARD
Williams, J.  Cleopatra the tenth.  Films Illus 1-9:9 Mr '72
Cargin, P.  The actress.  Film 65:6 Spg '72

NEILAN, MARSHALL
Cohn, A. A.  Director "Mickey."  Photop 12-4:67 S '17
Naylor, H. S.  Sketch.  Motion Pic 15:34 S '18

Peltret, E.  Interview.  Motion Pic Classic 10:20 Ap/My '20
McGaffey, K.  Interview.  Motion Pic Classic 13:50 D '21
St. Johns, A. R.  Sketch.  Photop 23:39 Mr '23
Home of.  Classic 20:32 O '24
Obit.  N. Y. Times p35 O 28 '58
   Newsweek 52:66 N 10 '58
   Time 72:88 N 10 '58
Gribbel, J.  Marshall Neilan.  Films In R 11-3:190 Mr '60

NEILL, JAMES
   Neill of the guards.  Photop 13-1:62 D '17
   Peltret, E.  Sketch.  Motion Pic Classic 11:34 N '20

NEILSEN, INGA
   Whitney, D.  I was very big in Fargo.  TV Guide 18-31:24 Ag 1
   '70

NELSON, BARRY
   He couldn't afford Broadway.  TV Guide 2-44:13 O 30 '54

NELSON, BEK
   Vroommm and off you go.  TV Guide 12-42:20 O 17 '64

NELSON, DAVID
   Bennett, J.  Hollywood's apples fall close to the tree.  Sound
   Stage 1-3:4 My '65
   (See also:  NELSON FAMILY)

NELSON, ED
   Photoplay forum.  Photop 81-3:14 Mr '72

NELSON, FRANCES
   St. Paul's half-Nelson on the movies.  Photop 11-6:35 My '17

NELSON, GENE
   Nelson, G.  The girl in row 4.  Silver S 21-4:24 F '51
   MacDonald, E.  It couldn't have worked out better.  Silver S
   22-10:42 Ag '52
   Zadan, C.  Two for the show.  Dance 45:67 O '71

NELSON, GWEN
   Tierney, M.  Interview.  Plays & Players 19-4:32 Ja '72

NELSON, HARRIET
   (also known as Harriet Hilliard)
   Sketch.  Movie Classic 10:16 Ap '36
   Reid, J.  Interview.  Motion Pic 51:43 Je '36
   A new fashion for 1,000,000 women.  TV Guide 5-5:16 F 2 '57
   (See also:  NELSON FAMILY)

NELSON, OZZIE
   (See:  NELSON FAMILY)

NELSON, RICK
   Bennett, J.   Hollywood's apples fall close to the tree.   Sound
      Stage 1-3:4 My '65
   Considine, S.   Has little Ricky changed!   N. Y.  Times Bio Ed
      Ja 23 '72
   Little brother's a family man now.   Mod Screen 66-11:40 N '72
   Feiden, R. & Warhol, A.   Interview.   Interview 34:21 Jl '73
   Snyder, C.   Only an acre, but to the Rick Nelsons it's a farm.
      N. Y.  Times Bio Ed p1341 Ag '73
   Wilkins, B.   The Rick Nelsons come of age.   People 1-13:40
      My 27 '74
   (See also: NELSON FAMILY)

NELSON FAMILY
   (David, Harriet, Ozzie, Rick)
   Minoff, P.   Doings of Nelson clan make grade-A video fun.
      Cue 21-43:7 O 25 '52
   The Nelsons and how they grew.   TV Guide 4-41:8 O 13 '56
   Davidson, S.   Happy, happy, happy Nelsons.   Esquire 75:97 Je
      '71
   Nelson, O.   Reply to Davidson.   Esquire 76:22 Ag '71

NESBIT, EVELYN
   Haskins, H.   Interview.   Motion Pic 16:38 Ja '19
   Bio note.   Harp Baz 82:192 S '48
   Lovely girl, lurid crime.   Life 39:70 S 12 '55
   Out of Collier's past.   Colliers 136:96 N 11 '55
   Tired butterfly.   Newsweek 69:30 Ja 30 '67
   Ketchum, R. M.   Faces from the past.   Am Heritage 20:64 Je
      '69

NESBITT, MIRIAM
   Adventurin' with Miriam.   Movie Pictorial 2-6:12 D '15
   How she became a photoplayer.   Motion Pic Classic 1:39 F '16

NESMITH, MIKE
   (See: MONKEES, The)

NETTLETON, LOIS
   McClelland, D.   TV: where all that old-time glamour went.
      Film Fan Mo 75:11 S '67
   The girl in Marilyn Monroe's apartment.   TV Guide 15-47:26 N
      25 '67
   McClelland, D.   Lois Nettleton; filmog.   Films In R 23-5:318
      My '72
   Considine, S.   An actress for all seasons.   After Dark 5-7:46
      N '72

NEUSS, WOLFGANG
   Bean, R.   The face of '63--Germany.   Films & Filming 9-9:41
      Je '63

NEWBERG, FRANK
    Obit.  Screen World 21:239 '70

NEWHART, BOB
    Millstein, G.  New sick and/or well comic.  N. Y. Times Mag
        p22 Ag 7 '60
    Split-personality comic.  TV Guide 8-36:9 S 3 '60
    Button-down Benchley.  Newsweek 56:96 O 10 '60
    Fletcher, F.  New-style comic.  Cue 30-5:10 F 4 '61
    Martin, P.  Backstage.  Sat Eve Post 234:118 O 14 '61
    All buttoned down.  Newsweek 59:56 Ja 15 '62
    Same to you, fella.  TV Guide 10-4:7 Ja 27 '62
    Unbuttons his mind.  TV Guide 10-23:5 Je 9 '62
    Boating instructor.  Motion B 110:30 Jl '62
    Button down mind on TV.  Hi Fi 12:122 N '62
    Whitney, D.  Still button-down, but no longer buttoned up.  TV
        Guide 21-3:20 Ja 20 '73

NEWLEY, ANTHONY
    Castell, D.  The fool who dared to dream.  Films Illus 37:16
        Sum '74

NEWMAN, BARRY
    McAsh, I.  Cult hero with motivations.  Films Illus 2-15:24 S
        '72

NEWMAN, NANETTE
    Gruen, J.  He says Yes, yes Nanette.  N. Y. Times Bio Ed O
        24 '71

NEWMAN, PAUL
    Rising star.  Film R p32 '57/58
    Fletcher, F.  A new Mr. and Mrs. team.  Cue 33-15:17 Ap 11
        '64
    Parish, J.  A great actor and an outstanding citizen; filmog.
        Screen Legends 1-2:39 Ag '65
    Barr, L.  Newman has dedicated crew to help him make film.
        Making Films 1-5:4 D '67
    Wilson, J.  What if my eyes turn brown?  Sat Eve Post 241:26
        F 24 '68
    Steinem, G.  The trouble with being too good looking.  Ladies
        Home J 85:99 Ap '68
    Interview.  Playboy 15-7:59 Jl '68
    Joanne and Paul and Rachel.  Life 65:47 O 18 '68
    Davidson, M.  Joanne Woodward tells about Paul Newman.
        Good House 168:72 F '69
    Diehl, D.  The anti-hero as director.  Action 4-3:15 My/Je '69
    New lunatics.  Newsweek 73:81 Je 23 '69
    Bondurant, B.  How we turned Newman into a winning driver.
        Pop Sci 194:51 Je '69
    Ebert, R.  Newman's complaint.  Esquire 72:111 S '69
    Wells, D.  Motor Trend interview.  Motor Trend 22:86 Ag '70
    How to set your child free.  Photop 78-3:38 S '70

Miller, E.   What's behind those beautiful blue eyes?   Seventeen
   29:124 N '70
Knight, A. & Alpert, E.   Sex stars of 1970.   Playboy 17-12:220
   D '70
What directors are saying.   Action 6-1:30 Ja/ F '71
Newman on wheels.   TV Guide 19-16:12 Ap 17 '71
Higham, C.   Newman gets high on speed.   N. Y. Times Bio Ed
   Ap 18 '71
Davidson, M.   Mr. and Mrs. Paul Newman.   Good House 173:
   85 Jl '71
Bergen, C.   Lee Marvin and Paul Newman.   Vogue 158:146 O
   1 '71
Bio note.   Films Illus 1-5:32 N '71
How they teach their children to love.   Photop 81-2:59 F '72
Brode, D.   The superstar of the 60s.   Show 12:18 F '72
Blevins, W.   Director Newman on location of his film Sometimes
   a great notion.   Show 12:24 F '72
Kramer, F.   How can you be a movie star and not be a little bit
   insane?   Movie Dig 1-2:31 Mr '72
Never give an inch.   Films Illus 1-11:12 My '72
Castell, D.   Why Paul Newman is still Hollywood's blue-eyed
   boy; filmog as actor and director.   Films Illus 2-18:16 D '72
Scoop.   Paul Newman wins Oscar.   Mod Screen 67-2:26 F '73
Gow, G.   Interview; filmog.   Films & Filming 19-6:12 Mr '73
Considine, S.   The Effect of Gamma rays  on the Newmans.
   After Dark 5-11:28 Mr '73
I'm with the sexiest guys in Hollywood.   Photop 83:50 Je '73
What directors are saying.   Action 8-5:31 S/O '73
What directors are saying.   Making Films 7-6:46 D '73
Adams, C.   Interview with Joanne Woodward.   Photop 85-4:61
   Ap '74
Goodman, M.   Newman is almost 50, and living on all cylinders.
   People 2-15:44 O 7 '74
Paul of the wild.   TV Guide 22-48:12 N 30 '74

NEWMAN, PHYLLIS
   Phyllis Newman's success sort of happened.   TV Guide 12-34:22
      Ag 22 '64
   Green, A.   How to live happily with a successful wife.   Show
      4-9:60 O '64

NEWMAR, JULIE
   Taylor, T.   Follies-type girl.   Cue 25-20:16 My 19 '56
   Everyone's living doll.   TV Guide 12-50:15 D 12 '64

NEWTON, ROBERT
   Pattinson, I.   The villain of the piece.   Films & Filming 1-4:7
      Ja '55

NEY, MARIE
   Filmog.   Films & Filming 19-3:62 D '72

NEY, RICHARD
    Stars of tomorrow.    Lions R 1-11/12:no p# Jl/Ag '42
    He's in the Navy now.    Lions R 2-1:no p# S/O '42
    Drew, J.  Just for the record.    Silver S 17-6:61 My '47

NEYELOVA, MARINA
    Note.  Int F G 10:334 '73

NICHOLAS BROTHERS (Fayard and Harold)
    Shipley, G.  Some notes on some of film's dancers.    Filmograph
    3-1:15 '72

NICHOLAS, DENISE
    Wasserman, J. L.    The girl in Room 222.    TV Guide 17-38:24
    S 20 '69

NICHOLAS, PAUL
    Nicholas, P.  Awaiting sentence.    Films & Filming 20-3:23 D
    '73

NICHOLS, BARBARA
    Minoff, P.  Caesar's present.    Cue 24-29:12 Jl 23 '55

NICHOLS, MARJORIE
    Obit.  N. Y. Times p44 S 28 '70

NICHOLS, NICHELLE
    Satirical flop brings star success.    Ebony 17:41 Ja '62
    New star in the TV heavens.    Ebony 22:70 Ja '67
    Let me off at the next planet.    TV Guide 15-28:10 Jl 15 '67

NICHOLSON, JACK
    Clein, H.  Jack Nicholson.    Entertainment World N 11 '69
    Fayard, J.  Happy Jack.    Life 68:36A Mr 27 '70
    Kaufer, S.  Super gypsy.    Time 96:89 S 14 '70
    Salute of the week.    Cue 39-40:1 O 3 '70
    Success is habit-forming.    Time 96:58 N 30 '70
    New hero.    Newsweek 76:70 D 7 '70
    On the scene.    Playboy 18-1:223 Ja '71
    Atlas, J. & Butterfield, M.  Odd man in.    Show 2-3:24 My '71
    Whitman, M.  Jack Nicholson; filmog.    Films Illus 1-4:4 O '71
    Weiner, R. & others.  Interview.    Interview 2-6:16 O '71
    Bio note.  Films Illus 1-5:32 N '71
    Interview.  Playboy 19-4:75 Ap '72
    Wade, V.  Interview.    Interview 28:31 D '72
    Interview; biblio.  Dialogue 1:1 '72
    Flatley, G.  Down to the very Last detail.    N. Y. Times sec 2:
    11 F 19 '74
        Same.  N. Y. Times Bio Ed p247 F '74
    Canby, V.  There's no doubt Jack Nicholson is a major star.
    N. Y. Times sec 2:1 F 24 '74
    Kent, R.  Jack Nicholson and Angelica Huston.    Interview 4-4:12
    Ap '74

Taylor, J. R.  Profession: actor; interview.  Sight & Sound
43-3:149 Sum '74
Eyles, A.  Bio note; filmog.  Focus On F 18:8 Sum '74
Bio note; filmog.  Films Illus 3-36:472 Ag '74

NIELSEN, ASTA
Nielsen, A.  Letter.  Films In R 7-4:188 Ap '56
Obit.  Classic Film Collect (reprint Washington Post) 35:8X Sum
'72
Allen, R. C.  The silent muse.  Sight & Sound 42-4:205 Aut '73
Gress, E.  A personal impression.  Sight & Sound 42-4:209 Aut
'73

NIELSEN, LESLIE
A new Davy Crockett?  TV Guide 8-1:8 Ja 2 '60
The most fateful decision I ever made.  Mod Screen 66-3:47 Mr
'72

NIESEN, GERTRUDE
Interview.  Movie Classic 11:56 D '36
Home of.  Life 11:82 Ag 18 '41
Man overboard.  Am Mag 139:64 Ja '45
Henderson, H. & Shaw, S.  Gertie buries the torch.  Colliers
117:44 Mr 30 '46

NIGH, JANE
In the cast.  TV Guide 1-22:15 Ag 28 '53

NILSSON, ANNA Q.
How she became a photoplayer.  Motion Pic 9:90 My '15
Brodie, A. D.  Sketch.  Motion Pic Supp 1:42 N '15
Courtlandt, R.  Interview.  Motion Pic Classic 4:40 Ap '17
Q. for Querentia.  Photop 16-3:33 Ag '19
Delvigne, D.  Interview.  Motion Pic 18:45 S '19
Handy, T. B.  Interview.  Motion Pic 19:52 Je '20
Smith, F. J.  Interview.  Motion Pic Classic 11:26 N '20
Fletcher, A. W.  Interview.  Motion Pic 22:50 Ag '21
Goldbeck, W.  Interview.  Motion Pic 24:32 O '22
Morris, B.  Interview.  Motion Pic 25:58 My '23
de Revere, F. V.  Analysis of her face.  Motion Pic 29:54 Mr
'25
Her love story.  Motion Pic 29:49 My '25
Tully, J.  Interview.  Vanity Fair 27:71 S '26
Hall, G.  Interview.  Motion Pic 32:50 Ja '27
Donnell, D.  Sketch.  Motion Pic 34:34 N '27
Hall, G.  Confessions.  Motion Pic Classic 29:16 Mr '29
Dibble, S.  Returns to screen.  Movie Classic 1:38 N '31
Obit.  Classic Film Collect 42:34 Spg '74
N. Y. Times Bio Ed p249 F '74

NIMOY, LEONARD
Raddatz, L.  Product of two worlds.  TV Guide 15-9:23 Mr 4
'67

Raddatz, L.   Star Trek wins the Ricky Schwartz award.   TV
    Guide 15-46:25 N 18 '67
Hano, A.   The great impersonator refuses to strip off the last
    disguise.   TV Guide 18-17:20 Ap 25 '70
Spock speaks.   Castle of Frankenstein 12:22 n. d.

NISSEN, GRETA
    Calhoun, D.   Sketch.   Motion Pic Classic 21:32 Jl '25
    York, C.   Sketch.   Photop 28:96 Jl '25
    Sketch.   Motion Pic Classic 23:57 Mr '26
    Moen, L.   Sketch.   Motion Pic Classic 24:40 N '26
    Reid, M.   Sketch.   Motion Pic 43:58 Je '32

NIVEN, DAVID
    Reid, J.   Interview.   Motion Pic 53:42 Jl '37
    Mook, S. R.   The sun never sets on David Niven.   Silver S 9-7:
        51 My '39
    Hamilton, S.   Life story.   Photop 53:22 S '39 & following is-
        sues.
    Waxman, P.   Story of.   Cosmop 107:11 N '39
    Bio note; filmog.   Movies & People 2:28 '40
    Cline, D.   Another new start for David.   Silver S 18-7:28 My
        '48
    Wilson, E.   David never misses.   Silver S 19-3:34 Ja '49
    The screen answers back.   Films & Filming 8-8:12 My '62
    Darrach, B.   Rakish progress.   Time 99:86 F 7 '72
    Niven, D.   Around the world in 80 days; excerpt from The
        moon's a balloon.   TV Guide 20-36:10 S 2 '72
    Graham, J.   Anglo-Saxon type No. 2008 becomes the world's
        most gorgeous grandfather.   Holiday 53-1:28 Ja/ F '73

NIXON, MARIAN
    Carlisle, H.   Sketch.   Motion Pic Classic 27:55 Mr '28
    Chandler, E.   Sketch.   Motion Pic 35:71 Ap '28
    Biery, R.   Interview.   Motion Pic Classic 30:36 F '30
    Manners, D.   Sketch.   Motion Pic 43:66 Jl '32
    Uselton, R. A.   The Wampus baby stars.   Films In R 21-2:73
        F '70
    Comment on Pilgrimage.   Filmograph 2-3:9 '71

NOEL, CHRIS
    A girl named Chris Noel.   TV Guide 11-51:10 D 21 '63

NOLAN, DORIS
    Hartley, K.   Interview.   Motion Pic 53:39 F '37
    Caine, D.   Her beauty secrets.   Motion Pic 53:51 Jl '37
    Bio note; filmog.   Movies & People 2:28 '40

NOLAN, KATHY
    The unreal McCoy.   TV Guide 10-14:9 Ap 7 '62
    Hano, A.   Kathy Nolan.   TV Guide 13-2:12 Ja 9 '65

NOLAN, LLOYD
  Sketch.  Photop 50:76 O '36
  Hamilton, S.  Sketch.  Photop 54:29 Ag '40
  That guy Nolan.  Lions R 2-1:no p# S/O '42
  Actor by choice.  Lions R 2-5:no p# Jl '43
  Palmer, C.  Sleuthing on a sleuth.  Silver S 17-1:54 N '46
  Nolan, M.  The man I married.  Silver S 19-2:33 D '48
  Minoff, P.  TV's newest private eye.  Cue 20-38:14 S 22 '51
  Lewis, E.  New laurels for Nolan.  Cue 23-8:12 F 20 '54
  To search for Shangri-La is never the answer.  Movie Dig 2-1:
    16 Ja '73

NOLAN, LOUISE
  McCaughna, D.  A terribly personal business.  Motion p16 Jl/Ag
    '74

NOLAN, MARY
  Manners, D.  Interview.  Motion Pic Classic 28:21 S '28
  Biery, R.  Interview.  Motion Pic 37:44 Ap '29
  Sketch.  Photop 37:66 F '30
  Hall, G.  Sketch.  Motion Pic 41:58 My '31
  Interview.  Motion Pic Classic 32:23 Ag '31
  Manners, D.  Her tragedy.  Motion Pic 42:34 D '31

NOLAN, TOMMY
  (Also known as Butch Bernard)
  A 10-year-old's world.  TV Guide 6-34:24 Ag 23 '58

NOLAND, VALORA
  If Valora could just live up to her name.  TV Guide 11-28:19 Jl
    13 '63

NOONAN, THOMAS
  Obit.  N. Y. Times p47 Ap 25 '68

NORDBERG, EDITHA
  (See: SCHELL, IMMY)

NORMAN, LUCILLE
  Stars of tomorrow.  Lions R 1-11/12:no p# Jl/Ag '42
  The blackout girl.  Lions R 2-2:no p# N '42

NORMAND, MABEL
  Sketch.  Blue Book 19:467 Jl '14
  Sketch.  N. Y. Dram 63:16 S 16 '16
  Sketch.  Green Book 16:981 D '16
  How to get in moving pictures.  Motion Pic Classic 3:39 D '16
  Gaddis, P.  Interview.  Motion Pic 12:83 D '16
  Her return to moving pictures.  Out West 45:106 Ap '17
  Smith, F. J.  Interview.  Motion Pic 15:31 N '18
  Biographical.  Dram Mir 82:534 Mr 20 '20
  Goldbeck, W.  Interview.  Motion Pic 22:46 S '21
  Service, F.  Interview.  Classic 15:32 Ja '23

As a shopper.  Met Mag 57:40 Ap '23
Gray, C.  Appreciation.  Motion Pic Classic 31:26 My '30
In memoriam.  Motion Pic 45:52 Je '33
Fifteen years ago.  Photop 44:110 Ag '33
Peeples, S.  Madcap; the story of Mabel Normand; filmog.
  Classic Film Collect 27:24 Spg/Sum '70; 28:21 Fall '70; 29:
  26 Win '70
Women directors; directing filmog.  Film Comment 8-4:42 N '72
Normand, S.  Mabel Normand.  Films In R 25-7:385 Ag/S '74
Mundy, R.  Some Hollywood scandals of the twenties.  After
  Dark 7-7:32 N '74

NORRIS, EDWARD
  Hamilton, S.  Sketch.  Photop 52:69 Ja '38

NORTH, JAY
  A cartoon comes to life.  TV Guide 7-43:20 O 24 '59
  Not such a menace.  TV Guide 8-10:17 Mr 5 '60
  Botto, L.  Interview.  Look 35:72 S 7 '71
  Now you see 'em, now you don't.  Look 35-18:70 S 7 '71

NORTH, MICHAEL "TED"
  Turton, T. P.  Filmog.  Films In R 22-9:579 N '71

NORTH, SHEREE
  Lewis, E.  Sheree's sensational Salome.  Cue 22-17:12 Ap 25
    '53
  Taylor, T.  She's getting to be very, very popular.  Cue 24-31:
    12 Ag 6 '55
  Rising star.  Film R p32 '57/58

NORTON, BARRY
  Spensley, D.  Interview.  Photop 31:67 F '27
  Matzen, M.  Sketch.  Motion Pic Classic 25:63 My '27
  York, C.  Sketch.  Photop 35:62 Ja '29
  Lubou, D.  Interview.  Motion Pic 37:82 My '29
  Benton, C.  Interview.  Movie Classic 2:30 Ap '32

NORTON, CLIFF
  In the cast.  TV Guide 1-30:18 O 23 '53
  Ducks, it's teatime again.  TV Guide 8-50:14 D 10 '60

NOVAK, EVA
  Handy, T. B.  Interview.  Motion Pic Classic 10:52 Jl '20

NOVAK, JANE
  McKelvie, M. G.  Sketch.  Motion Pic 16:59 O '18
  Cheatham, M.  Interview.  Motion Pic Classic 10:27 Ap/My '20
  Cheatham, M.  Interview.  Movie Classic 12:60 My '21
  Gassaway, G.  Interview.  Motion Pic 23:42 Ap '22
  Donnell, D.  Interview.  Classic 19:36 Ap '24
  Adams, E.  Her horoscope.  Photop 26:108 N '24
  Fullbright, T.  Jane Novak.  Classic Film Collect 20:4 Spg;

21:4 Sum; 22:12 Fall/Win '68
Fulbright, T.    The films of Jane Novak; filmog.    Classic Film
    Collect 23:special 6 Spg '69
Novak, J.    Some comments on the filming of Lazybones.
    Filmograph 1-4:43 '70
Slide, A.    Interview.    Silent Pic 14:9 Spg '72

NOVAK, KIM
Water, R.    To be a star.    Cue 24-9:12 Mr 5 '55
Cupcake.    Films & Filming 1-12:22 S '55
Rising star.    Film R p40 '56/57
Zunser, J.    Fallen star.    Cue 26-27:11 Jl 6 '57
At home with Kim; photos.    Playboy 12-2:66 F '65
This land is Kim Novak's.    TV Guide 18-14:12 Ap 4 '70
Calendo, J.    The legend of Kim Novak; filmog.    Interview 22:9
    Je '72
The third girl from the left turns out to be Kim Novak.    TV
    Guide 21-14:12 Ap 7 '73

NOVARRO, RAMON
Sketch.    Photop 23:77 Ja '23
Sketch.    Motion Pic 28:24 Ag '24
de Revere, F. V.    Analysis of his face.    Motion Pic 29:71 Je
    '25
Howe, H.    The mystery of Ramon Novarro.    Motion Pic Classic
    22:22 O '25
Roberts, W. A.    Sketch.    Motion Pic 30:55 O '25
Carr, H.    Sketch.    Motion Pic 31:40 Je '26
Interview.    Motion Pic 32:65 S '26
Howe, H.    His life story.    Motion Pic 33:18 F '27
Hall, G.    Sketch.    Motion Pic Classic 25:53 My '27
From screen to concert stage.    Theatre 47:26 Ja '28
Copeland, R. E.    Sketch.    Motion Pic 35:55 F '29
Mullett, M. B.    Interview.    Am Mag 105:18 Mr '28
Biery, R.    Why he remained in the movies.    Photop 34:58 O '28
Donnell, D.    Sketch.    Motion Pic 37:42 F '29
Hall, G.    Sketch.    Motion Pic 38:40 Ja '30
Spensley, D.    Interview.    Motion Pic Classic 30:26 F '30
Walker, H. L.    His requirements in a wife.    Motion Pic 39:50
    Je '30
Service, F.    Interview.    Motion Pic 40:55 Ja '31
Parsons, H.    Ramon Novarro today.    Silver S 1-8:19 Je '31
Spensley, D.    Sketch.    Motion Pic Classic 33:31 Jl '31
Orme, M.    Criticism.    Ill Lon No 179:402 S 12 '31
Rush, D.    Ramon Novarro's Christmas spirit.    Silver S 2-2:20
    D '31
Pollard, E.    Sketch.    Movie Classic 1:33 F '32
Manners, D.    Romance rumors.    Motion Pic 43:44 Mr '32
Ilma, V.    Always in love.    Silver S 2-5:43 Mr '32
Fairbanks, D. Jr.    Appreciation.    Vanity Fair 39:39 O '32
Moffitt, C. F.    Censorship for interviews, Hollywood's latest
    wild idea.    Cinema Dig 2-5:9 Ja 9 '33
Service, F.    About to leave screen for a musical career.

Motion Pic 45:50 Ap '33
Samuels, L.  Novarro.  Silver S 4-7:30 My '34
Where are they now?  Newsweek 70:16 N 6 '67
Brock, A.  My friend Ramon.  Classic Film Collect 22:58 Fall/
    Win '68
Obit.  Film R p16 '69/70
    N.Y. Times p1 N 1 '68
    Newsweek 72:97 N 11 '68
    Time 92:75 N 15 '68
Bodeen, D.  Ramon Novarro.  Silent Pic 4:3 Aut '69
Pinups of the past.  Films & Filming 16-4:78 F '70
Lee, R.  The Novarro story.  Classic Film Collect 39:30 Sum
    '73

NOVELLO, IVOR
Sketch.  Theatre World 19:38 Ja '33
Novello, I.  Personal reminiscences.  Windsor 81:108 D '34
Sketch.  Theatre World 23:276 Je '35
Roberts, F.  Novello at home.  Theatre World 24:160 O '35
Hast, N.  Appreciation.  Theatre World 25:154 Ap '36
Interview.  Theatre World 28:112 S '37
Sketch.  Theatre World 30:131 S '38
Sketch.  Theatre World 31:178 Ap '39
Keep the theatres open.  Theatre World 32:142 O '39
Hast, N.  Story of.  Theatre World 33:65 S '40
Matinee idol.  World R 7:39 S '49

NOVIS, DONALD
Obit.  Screen World 18:238 '67

NOVVA, HEDA
A refugee from Russia.  Photop 14-5:71 O '18

NOWELL, WEDGWOOD
Cheatham, M. S.  Interview.  Motion Pic 18:75 Ja '20

NUGENT, EDDIE
Kingsley, G.  Interview.  Motion Pic Classic 27:63 Ag '28

NUGENT, ELLIOTT
Gray, C.  Sketch.  Motion Pic 39:42 Mr '30
Fender, R.  Sketch.  Motion Pic Classic 32:63 D '30
The versatile Nugent.  Cue 13-16:9 Ap 15 '44
Isaacs, H. R.  Featuring the voice of the turtle.  Theatre Arts
    28:280 My '44
Bio.  Cur Bio Jl '44
Hollywood's favorite rebel.  Sat Eve Post 222:25 Jl 23 '49
    Same, abridged.  Read Dig 55:53 O '49
How to stay young.  Am Mag 154:49 O '52
Wild ride.  Newsweek 66:110 D 13 '65
Hutchens, J. K.  Days of roses followed by rain.  Sat R 49:35
    Mr 5 '66

NUYEN, FRANCE
Zunser, J.  Cinderella's back on Ninth Ave.   Cue 27-9:10 Mr 1
'58

NYE, CARRIE
Dick Cavett: the art of show and tell.   Time 97:80 Je 7 '71
Klemesrud, J.  Mrs.  Cavett comes out of the shadow.   N. Y.
Times Bio Ed My 15 '72
Johnson, D.  Hello, I'm Carrie Nye.   After Dark 5-2:44 Je '72
Nye, C.  Making it in Munich.   Time p47 Jl 2 '72

NYE, LOUIS
Minoff, P.  A new "Allen's Alley."   Cue 26-25:11 Je 22 '57
Hi hi, Steverino.   TV Guide 5-41:21 O 12 '57
Poston to Knotts to Nye.   TV Guide 6-40:17 O 4 '58

NYMAN, LENA
Holloway, R.  We are playing with reality; a conversation.   Film
J 1-1:5 Spg '71

OAKIE, JACK
Biery, R.  Sketch.  Motion Pic Classic 28:40 Ja '29
Ramsey, W.  Interview.  Motion Pic 39:55 F '30
Sketch.  Motion Pic 39:66 Je '30
Sketch.  Fortune 2:41 O '30
Goldbeck, E.  Sketch.  Motion Pic 41:76 Je '31
Hall, G.  Interview.  Movie Classic 7:63 N '34
Cheatham, M.  Oakie goes back to nature.  Silver S 5-7:26 My
'35
Lane, V.  Interview.  Movie Classic 10:47 S '36
Wood, V.  King comic.  Silver S 7-6:31 Ap '37
How life cracked down on Jack Oakie.  Screen Book 19:1 34 Ag
'37
Craig, C.  Story of.  Motion Pic 54:37 D '37
Bio note; filmog.  Movies & People 2:28 '40
Vallee, W. L.  The big noise in Tin pan alley.  Silver S 11-3:
44 Ja '41
Sketch.  Time 37:54 My 19 '41
Asher, J.  He's okay with Peggy.  Silver S 15-2:34 D '44
Schwartz, W.  Jack Oakie; filmog.  Films In R 22-7:455 Ag/S
'71
Bacon, J.  Oldtimers help Oakie celebrate 68th birthday.  Clas-
sic Film Collect 34:X-4 Spg '72

OAKLAND, VIVIEN
Maltin, L.  Vivien Oakland.  Film Fan Mo 123:20 S '71

OAKMAN, WHEELER
Berg, A. D.  Sketch.  Motion Pic Classic 6:75 Ap '18
Peltret, E.  With a big show.  Photop 13-6:83 My '18
Winship, M.  Interview.  Photop 18:46 O '20

Home of.   W. Arch 32:89 Ag '23
Home of.   Classic 19:40 Ap '24
Obit.   Screen World 1:234 '49

OATES, WARREN
   Lonely, honest and true.   TV Guide 11-19:16 My 11 '63
   On the road with the New Hollywood.   Show 2-1:16 Mr '17
   Story of Oates.   Time 98:60 S 6 '71
   Kasindorf, M.   Actor's actor.   Newsweek 78:87 S 20 '71
   Wild Oates; filmog.   Films Illus 1-6:16 D '71
   Eyles, A.   Warren Oates; filmog.   Focus On F 14:18 Spg '71
   Dillinger is alive and well.   Films Illus 3-29:173 N '73

OBERMEIER, USCHI
   Kent, R.   Uschi, who's she?   Interview 3-8(35):8 Ag '73

OBERON, MERLE
   Sketch.   Movie Classic 7:51 F '35
   Kaufman, R.   Sketch.   Photop 47:58 Mr '35
   Harrison, H.   An exotic.   Silver S 5-7:22 My '35
   Americanization of.   Harp Baz 69:53 Jl '35
   Reed, D.   Interview.   Movie Classic 8:39 Jl '35
   Lane, V.   Her clothes.   Movie Classic 8:44 Ag '35
   Caine, D.   How she makes up for Oriental roles.   Motion Pic
      50:12 D '35
   Rhea, M.   Interview.   Movie Classic 10:31 My '36
   Lee, S.   Interview.   Motion Pic 51:42 Je '36
   Lee, S.   Story of.   Motion Pic 11:30 O '36
   Work of.   Life 1:46 D 21 '36
   Cheatham, M.   If...   Silver S 7-2:53 D '36
   Harris, E.   Interview.   Motion Pic 53:34 F '37
   Grimstead, H.   Merle Oberon at home.   Windsor 87:227 Ja '38
   Woolf, J.   When she faced death.   Screen Book 21-1:28 Ag '38
   Wilson, E.   Projection.   Silver S 9-2:20 D '38
   Proctor, K.   1 bride, 2 grooms.   Screen Book 21-9:19 Ap '39
   Sketch.   Time 33:78 Je 12 '39
   Service, F.   I will be a career wife.   Silver S 10-7:40 My '40
   Bio note; filmog.   Movies & People 2:29 '40
   Sketch.   Life 15:51 O 11 '43
   Wilson, E.   She can take it.   Silver S 15-1:34 N '44
   Creelman, E.   Hail to a true princess.   Silver S 16-4:44 F '46
   Wilson, E.   If I were just starting.   Silver S 17-2:30 D '46
   Parsons, L. O.   Cosmopolitan's citation for the best femine per-
      formance of the month.   Cosmop 122:58 F '47
   Snyder, C.   Green-eyed legend returns to Hollywood.   N. Y.
      Times p82 N 19 '72
   Calendo, J.   Merle Oberon is not a Hindu.   Interview 34:30 Jl
      '73

O'BRIEN, HUGH
   An ex-marine has situation well in hand.   TV Guide 4-35:17 S 1
      '56
   Jaekle, L. V.   Analyzing his handwriting.   Sound Stage 1-3:46

My '65
The dangers of galloping inflation.  TV Guide 16-14:14 Ap 6 '68
Davidson, B.   Last of the swashbucklers.   TV Guide 20-48:25
  N 25 '72

O'BRIEN, DAVE
  Smith, P.   Laughs are my business.   Colliers 131:22 Ja 31 '53
  Victorek, D.   Dave O'Brien; letter.   Those Enduring Idols 1-3:
  33 F/Mr '70
  Victorek, D.   Dave O'Brien; filmog.   Films In R 23-8:449 O
  '72

O'BRIEN, DONNELL
  Obit.   Screen World 22:239 '71

O'BRIEN, EDMOND
  Hamilton, S.   Sketch.   Photop 54:16 Ja '40
  Randall, T. L.   Sex doesn't win a man.   Silver S 21-9:36 Jl '51
  Eyles, A.   Bio note; filmog.   Focus On F 19:17 Aut '74

O'BRIEN, ERIN
  The milkman's daughter.   TV Guide 5-6:28 F 9 '57

O'BRIEN, EUGENE
  Sketch.   Green Bk Album 3:239 F '19
  Naylor, H. S.   Sketch.   Motion Pic 12:131 N '16
  The O'Brien of movieland.   Photop 12-3:45 Ag '17
  Naylor, H. S.   Interview.   Motion Pic 15:58 N '18
  Ten Eyck, J.   An iron man in a velvet manner.   Photop 14-6:83
  N '18
  Service, F.   Interview.   Motion Pic Classic 8:24 Jl '19
  Fletcher, A. W.   Interview.   Motion Pic 21:22 Jl '21
  Doyle, P.   Interview.   Motion Pic Classic 14:62 Jl '22
  Friendship, love, marriage.   Motion Pic 29:52 Je '25

O'BRIEN, GEORGE
  Donnell, D.   Sketch.   Motion Pic Classic 21:24 Ag '25
  Pierce, S.   Sketch.   Motion Pic Classic 23:56 Ag '26
  Kelton, L.   Interview.   Motion Pic Classic 26:42 O '27
  Manners, D.   Sketch.   Motion Pic Classic 31:63 My '30
  Lee, S.   Defends movies for children.   Movie Classic 5:55 D
  '33
  Mook, S. R.   Whoa.   Silver S 4-11:29 S '34
  Bio note; filmog.   Movies & People 2:29 '40
  Maltin, L.   Interview.   Film Fan Mo 119:19 My '71
  Gordon, A.   George O'Brien at Fox.   Film Fan Mo 131:7 My
  '72

O'BRIEN, JOAN
  I grew up pretty fast.   TV Guide 9-4:28 Ja 28 '61

O'BRIEN, MARGARET
  Baby Bernhardt.   Lions R 2-3:no p# D '42

Pigs don't fly.   Lions R 2-5:no p# Jl '43
F-U-N spells work.   Lions R 3-2:no p# Ja '44
Lennart, I.   Truth, the whole truth.   Lions R 3-2:no p# Ja '44
You can't cuddle medals.   Lions R 3-4(sup):no p# Jl '44
Agee, J.   The vividness of her acting in Meet me in St. Louis.
   Nation 159:670 N 25 '44
Miss O'Brien of Hollywood.   Cue 14-4:9 Ja 27 '45
My Christmas wish.   Photop 26:47 Ja '45
...and kisses from Miss O'Brien.   Lions R 4-1:no p# F '45
Remarkable Miss O'Brien.   Lions R 4-1:no p# F '45
Hall, G.   Mrs. O'Brien's daughter.   Silver S 15-10:46 Ag '45
Notes about.   Photop 28:50 Ja '46
Wins honorary award in Companion poll of favorite stars.
   Womans Home C 73:8 Je '46
Kind of clothes she likes.   Good House 127:10 Ag '48
O'Brien, G.   I hope Margaret marries at 18.   Silver S 21-4:30
   F '51
Where are they now?   Newsweek 70:20 S 25 '67
The kids.   Screen Greats 1-2:48 Sum '71

O'BRIEN, PAT
Busby, M.   Pat of the Milwaukee O'Briens.   Silver S 1-12:41
   O '31
Service, F.   Sketch.   Motion Pic 42:70 D '31
Carter, D.   He's "Cocky O'Brien."   Silver S 3-5:26 Ap '33
Hartley, K.   The unholy three.   Motion Pic 50:49 O '35
Samuels, L.   Not so tough.   Silver S 6-4:30 F '36
Baldwin, J. R.   Interview.   Motion Pic 51:26 Mr '36
Hall, G.   Interview.   Movie Classic 11:30 D '36
Home of.   Movie Classic 11:42 Ja '37
Pine, D.   Interview.   Motion Pic 53:43 F '37
O'Brien, E.   My husband.   Screen Book 21-6:27 Ja '39
Reid, J.   The man who plays Rockne.   Silver S 10-11:38 S '40
Bio note; filmog.   Movies & People 2:29 '40
Reid, J.   Devoted husband No. 1.   Silver S 13-1:42 N '42
Hall, G.   Story of.   Photop 22:63 My '43
Walker, H. L.   Ideal family man.   Silver S 14-5:32 Mr '44
The Falkenburg-O'Brien USO tour.   Life 18:22 Ja 1 '45
My Christmas wish.   Photop 26:46 Ja '45
Vallee, W. L.   Forever O'Brien.   Silver S 15-11:44 S '45
Letter to my wife.   Silver S 17-12:29 O '47
My luckiest day.   Cosmop 123:184 N '47
When hoods were heroes.   Screen Greats 1-2:34 Sum '71
Catching up with Pat O'Brien.   Mod Screen 66-5:66 My '72
O'Brien, P.   This was my favorite role.   Movie Dig 1-4:32 Jl
   '72

O'BRIEN, SHEILA
Chierichetti, D.   Sheila O'Brien.   Film Fan Mo 148:19 O '73

O'BRIEN, VIRGINIA
Hollywood poker face.   Lions R 1-9:no p# My '42
Stars of tomorrow.   Lions R 1-11/12:no p# Jl/Ag '42

V for Virginia and for victory.    Lions R 2-4:no p# Ap '43
Gremlins in the house.    Lions R 3-3:no p# Ap '44
Charness, C.    Virginia O'Brien.    Film Fan Mo 135:19 S '72

O'BRIEN-MOORE, ERIN
Caine, D.    Her charm.    Motion Pic 53:59 My '37

O'CALLAGHAN, RICHARD
Billington, M.    Interview.    Plays & Players 17-6:48 Mr '70
Beaton, C.    In Beaton's view.    Plays & Players 19-5:32 F '72

O'CONNELL, ARTHUR
Zunser, J.    New face, age 48.    Cue 25-45:14 N 10 '56

O'CONNOR, CARROLL
Adler, D.    He's the bigot next door.    N. Y. Times Bio Ed Je 13
    '71
Hudson, P.    Interview.    Sr Schol 99:7 O 25 '71
Lear, N.    Interview.    Sr Schol 99:6 O 25 '71
Hano, A.    The man under the hard hat.    TV Guide 19-47:29 N
    20 '71
Speaking about the unspeakable.    Newsweek 78:52 N 29 '71
The real-life families of these All in the family stars.    Mod
    Screen 65-11:40 N '71
The man you love to hate.    Photop 80-5:64 N '71
Hano, A.    Can Archie Bunker give bigotry a bad name?    N. Y.
    Times Mag p32 Mr 12 '73
Raddatz, L.    It's Archie Bunker, meatheads.    TV Guide 20-23:13
    Je 3 '72
Interview.    Ebony 27:186 Je '72
Bio.    Cur Bio 33:22 Jl '72
Interview.    Playboy 20-1:61 Ja '73

O'CONNOR, DONALD
Sketch.    Newsweek 22:110 O 18 '43
Foster, F.    Watch out Mickey.    Silver S 14-2:48 D '43
Trotter, M.    Prediction for 1944.    Photop 24:26 Ja '44
Hyams, J.    Young old timer hits the jackpot.    Cue 22-10:13 Mr
    14 '53
O'Connor, D.    My pal Sidney.    Cue 23-47:16 N 20 '54
The kids.    Screen Greats 1-2:50 Sum '71
Shipley, G.    Some notes on some of film's dancers.    Filmograph
    3-1:15 '72

O'CONNOR, FRANK
Gray, B.    Character actor.    Films In R 15-4:253 Ap '64

O'CONNOR, GLYNNIS
Sketch.    Films Illus 3-29:197 N '73

O'CONNOR, HARRY M.
Obit.    Classic Film Collect 33:46 Win '71
    Screen World 23:239 '72

O'CONNOR, UNA
    Johns, E.  Story of.  Theatre World 40:24 F '44
    Obit.  Film R p10 '59/60
        Screen World 11:223 '60

O'DAY, MOLLY
    Cummings, A.  Sketch.  Motion Pic Classic 26:48 O '27
    Shirley, L.  Sketch.  Photop 34:80 Ag '28
    Uselton, R. A.  The Wampus baby stars.  Films In R 21-2:73
        F '70

O'DONNELL, CATHY
    Wilson, E.  Mr. Goldwyn presents.  Silver S 16-10:37 Ag '46
    Obit.  Film R p13 '71/72
        Screen World 22:239 '71

O'DRISCOLL, MARTHA
    Hamilton, S.  Sketch.  Photop 20:55 F '42
    Vallee, W. L.  Never act your age.  Silver S 13-11:34 S '43
    My most unforgettable moment overseas.  Photop 25:53 Je '44
    O'Driscoll, M.  Letter.  Movie Dig 1-4:4 Jl '72

OGIER, BULLE
    Bulle Ogier; filmog.  Film 2-9:10 D '73

OGILVY, IAN
    Filmog.  Films & Filming 19-3:62 D '72

O'HANLON, GEORGE
    New neighbors for Riley.  TV Guide 4-1:16 Ja 7 '56
    Maltin, L.  Interview; filmog.  Film Fan Mo 157-8:3 Jl/Ag '74

O'HARA, MAUREEN
    Hamilton, S.  Sketch.  Photop 54:16 Ja '40
    Hall, G.  All the world will be talking about her.  Silver S 10-
        5:40 Mr '40
    Maddox, B.  Redhead on her own.  Silver S 12-1:26 N '41
    The girl on the cover.  Cue 11-8:1 F 21 '42
    Walker, H. L.  Dangers of sudden popularity.  Photop 21:49 Jl
        '42
    Service, F.  The stars who kiss like gentlemen.  Silver S 12-
        12:36 O '42
    Mulvey, K.  Sketch.  Womans Home C 70:24 Mr '43
    Mann, M.  Lady in distress.  Silver S 14-3:38 Ja '44
    Service, F.  Her letter to her daughter.  Silver S 15-8:38 Je
        '45
    Notes about.  Photop 27:64 O '45
    O'Leary, D.  Magnificent marriage.  Silver S 16-6:40 Ap '47
    Maddox, B.  Story of.  Photop 29:46 Ag '46
    Holland, J.  Home girl at heart.  Silver S 17-6:58 Ap '47
    Price, M. O.  The man I married.  Silver S 17-10:32 Ag '47
    Holland, J.  Has marriage lost its significance.  Silver S 18-3:
        36 Ja '48

Churchill, R. & B.   Irish pixie.   Silver S 19-8:44 Je '49
O'Hara, M.   Keeping an eye on my brothers.   Silver S 22-9:26
   Jl '52
Fox, J.   The fighting lady; filmog.   Films & Filming 19-3:33
   D '72
Maureen O'Hara answers what makes John Wayne Hollywood's
   favorite lover?   Photop 84-4:45 O '73
Henry Fonda seminar.   Dialogue 3-2:8 N '73

O'HARA, QUINN
   Her first word was cheese.   TV Guide 14-15:20 Ap 9 '66

O'HERLIHY, DAN
   O'Herlihy returns to Hollywood.   Films Illus 3-36:476 Ag '74

O'KEEFE, DENNIS
   McFee, F.   Make way for the Irish.   Screen Book 21-4:35 N '38
   Pritchett, F.   Charming devil.   Silver S 15-1:38 N '44
   McEvoy, D.   Dennis turns it on.   Silver S 17-12:45 O '47
   Pritchett, F.   The smiling Irishman has all the answers.   Silver
   S 20-4:46 F '50
   Obit.   Film R p19 '69/70
   N.Y. Times p19 S 2 '68
   Newsweek 72:69 S 16 '68
   Time 92:66 S 13 '68
   Dennis O'Keefe: 1908-1968.   Film Fan Mo 88:22 O '68

OLAND, WARNER
   Service, J.   Sketch.   Motion Pic Classic 7:22 F '19
   Handy, T. B.   Interview.   Motion Pic Classic 10:66 Je '20
   Rankin, R.   Charlie Chan reveals.   Silver S 7-9:55 Jl '37
   Connor, E.   The 6 Charlie Chans; Charlie Chan filmog.   Films
   In R 6-1:23 Ja '55
   Charlie Chan in Egypt.   Views & Rs 3-3:48 Win '72

OLBRYCHSKI, DANIEL
   Bio note; filmog.   Focus On F 3:18 My/Ag '70

OLCOTT, CHAUNCY
   Walsh, J.   Chauncy Olcott.   Hobbies 75:37 Ag; 37 S '70

OLIVER, EDNA MAY
   Churchill, E.   Edna May Oliver.   Silver S 3-3:21 Ja '33
   Sketch.   Photop 51:80 Ja '37
   Letters; partial filmog.   Films In R 13-2:123 F '62
   Hicks, S.   A lady to remember.   Cinema (BH) 1-5:12 Ag/S '63
   Hicks, J.   Edna May Oliver; filmog.   Film Fan Mo 137:3 N '72

OLIVER, SUSAN
   The girl with the balalaika.   TV Guide 8-35:29 Ag 27 '60

OLIVETTE, NINA
   Obit.   N.Y. Times p40 F 23 '71

OLIVIER, LAURENCE
 Churchill, E.  He got the habit.  Silver S 2-5:20 Mr '32
 Schrott, G.  A new kind of lover.  Silver S 9-10:36 Ag '39
 Wallace, G.  Comedy can wait.  Screen Book 22-4:70 N '39
 Hall, G.  Those amazing Oliviers.  Silver S 16-12:30 O '46
 Herlie, E.  As I know (him).  Silver S 18-4:40 F '48
 English star makes film of Hamlet.  Cue 17-8:14 F 21 '48
 Canfield, A.  A lady in love.  Silver S 21-3:36 Ja '51
 Venezky, A.  Enter the Oliviers.  Cue 20-49:10 D 8 '51
 Brinson, P.  The real interpreter.  Films & Filming 1-7:4 Ap
   '55
 British feature directors; an index to their work.  Sight & Sound
   27-6:300 Aut '58
 Cowie, P.  The face of '63--Great Britain.  Films & Filming
   9-5:19 F '63
 Sweeney, L.  Male of the species.  TV Guide 16-52:15 D 28 '68
 Ehrlich, H.  Sir says; interview.  Look 34:22 Ja 27 '70
 Sir Laurence.  Newsweek 75:57 F 2 '70
 Michell, K.  Cue salutes.  Cue 39-13:22 Mr 28 '70
 Newsmakers.  Newsweek 75:49 Je 22 '70
 Newsmakers.  Newsweek 76:69 O 12 '70
 People.  Time 96:36 O 12 '70
 Jeremiah.  The stars' stars; astrology.  Show 1-6:15 O '70
 Coleman, T.  Olivier now.  Show 1-6:43 O '70
 Newsmakers.  Newsweek 77:49 Ap 5 '71
 Bio note.  Films Illus 1-5:32 N '71
 Long, R. E.  Olivier in repertory.  No Am R 9:5 Spg '72
 Flythe, S. Jr.  Interview.  Holiday 52:32 N '72
 Meryman, R.  First lord of the stage.  Life 73:61 D 8 '72
 Costello, A.  Lord Olivier of Brighton.  Harp Baz 106:6 D '72
 Lambert, G.  The making of Gone with the wind.  Atlantic 231-
   3:56 Mr '73
 Eyles, A.  Sir Laurence Olivier; filmog.  Focus On F 14:9 Spg
   '73
 Levin, B.  Perfectionist at work.  TV Guide 22-11:21 Mr 16
   '74

OLIVIO, ROBERT
 Koutoukas, H. M.  Papal references.  Film Cult 45:22 Sum '67

OLSON, NANCY
 Rising star.  Film R p39 '51/52

O'MALLEY, PAT
 de Ronalf, J.  O'Malley of the Edison.  Movie Pictorial 2-1:16
   Jl '15
 Sherwood, C. B.  Interview.  Motion Pic Classic 11:51 Ja '21
 Byers, L.  Interview.  Motion Pic 22:22 Ag '21
 Carr, H.  Interview.  Motion Pic 29:27 F '25
 Sutter, R.  Sketch.  Motion Pic Classic 24:58 O '26

ONDRAKOVA, ANNY
 Dewey, L.  Czechoslovakia; silence into sound.  Film 60:5 n.d.

O'NEAL, PATRICK
  It's all the rage.  TV Guide 8-35:5 Ag 27 '60
  Roman, R. C.  No starving actor is Patrick O'Neal.  After
    Dark 4-9:18 Ja '72
  Filmog.  Films & Filming 19-7:66 Ap '73

O'NEAL, RON
  Peterson, M.  Ron was too light for Shaft but...  N. Y.  Times
    sec 2:11 S 17 '72
  Same.  N. Y.  Times Bio Ed p1682 S '72
  Fremont, V.; Jade, J.; Cutrone, R.  Interview.  Interview 28:6
    D '72

O'NEAL, RYAN
  Raddatz, L.  The metamorphosis of Rodney Harrington.  TV
    Guide 14-7:21 F 12 '66
  How they all played Roman games.  Photop 77-6:64 Je '70
  Miller, E.  Interview.  Seventeen 29:111 D '70
  The winning hero who can let go.  Vogue 157:133 Mr 1 '71
  Lover.  Photop 79-3:45 Mr '71
  Murray, W.  Ryan has the whole country cryin'.  N. Y.  Times
    sec 2:11 Mr 7 '71
  Same.  N. Y.  Times Bio Ed Mr 7 '71
  I get more love from my son than my husband.  Photop 79-4:47
    Ap '71
  Very brash young man.  Life 70:69 My 21 '71
  Shadow wife.  Photop 79-5:58 My '71
  Help me get him back.  Photop 79-6:72 Je '71
  His hidden children.  Photop 80-2:70 Ag '71
  Searies, B.  The appeal of Ryan O'Neal.  After Dark 4-4:44 Ag
    '71
  He returns to Barbara Parkins.  Photop 80-3:80 S '71
  Wedding for Barbra Streisand and Ryan O'Neal.  Silver S 41-10:
    21 O '71
  Taylor-Young, L.  I want another husband.  Photop 80-6:30 D
    '71
  O'Neal dumps Streisand for black actress.  Photop 80-6:27 D '71
  Rushed to surgery.  Photop 81-3:79 Mr '72
  Pray for Ryan O'Neal.  Photop 81-4:44 Ap '72
  Leigh races to Ryan's side.  Mod Screen 66-4:46 Ap '72
  Atlas, J. & Jaffe, S.  Barbra and Ryan in Bogdanovich's salute
    to the zany comedies of the '30s.  Show 2-2:24 Ap '72
  Warhol, A.  The most revealing interview Ryan O'Neal ever
    gave.  Interview 21:3 My '72
  He chooses.  Mod Screen 66-7:22 Jl '72
  Burke, T.  Sheik of Malibu.  Esquire 78:86 S '72
  Parental conflict.  Photop 82-6:62 D '72
  Klemesrud, J.  Tatum and Ryan.  Look closely, it's the same
    jaw.  N. Y. Times sec 2:13 My 20 '73
  Interview.  Interview 34:26 Jl '73
  McGillivray, D.  Ryan O'Neal; filmog.  Focus On F 15:6 Sum
    '73
  Ryan must protect Tatum now.  Photop 84-3:51 S '73

O'NEAL, TATUM
    Klemesrud, J. Tatum and Ryan. Look closely, it's the same
        jaw. N. Y. Times sec 2:13 My 20 '73
    Interview. Interview 34:26 Jl '73
    Ryan must protect Tatum now. Photop 84-3:51 S '73
    The other side of Tatum's triumph. People 1-8:19 Ap 22 '74

O'NEIL, BARBARA
    Rhea, M. Sketch. Photop 53:30 N '39

O'NEIL, NANCE
    Sketch. Motion Pic 13:77 My '17
    The unloved woman on the stage. Theatre 31:516 Je '20
    The theatre awakening. Drama 11:72 D '20

O'NEIL, PEGGY
    Dowling, G. Colleen mavoureen. Photop 10-1:113 Je '16

O'NEILL, EILEEN
    Shure, there's not anither Irish cop in the world loike... TV
        Guide 12-11:16 Mr 14 '64

O'NEILL, JENNIFER
    Debut. Show 1-8:56 Jl 9 '70
    Corrigan, E. Making a horse-show comeback. N. Y. Times
        Bio Ed F 21 '71
    Klemesrud, J. The girl you'd most like to spend the Summer of
        '42 with. N. Y. Times Bio Ed S 5 '71
    Pretty Jenny. Life 71:72 N 19 '71
    Carragher, B. The incurable romantic. Show 2-10:23 D '71
    Faces going far. Films Illus 1-10:18 Ap '72
    Filmog. Films & Filming 18-8:62 My '72
    Cohen, E. A. Jennifer. TV New York 1-6:19 Mr '73
    No nudity. Movie Dig 2-1:8 Ja '73
    City boy meets country girl. Photop 86-3:52 S '74

O'NEILL, SALLY
    Sketch. Motion Pic Classic 22:60 S '25
    Albert, K. Interview. Motion Pic 34:28 S '27
    Manners, D. Interview. Motion Pic 38:86 O '29
    Manners, D. Sketch. Motion Pic Classic 33:51 Ap '31
    Standish, J. Interview. Motion Pic 42:70 O '31
    Albert, K. How she got a contract to play the brat. Photop
        40:58 N '31
    Obit. Film R p17 '69/70
    N. Y. Times p45 Je 20 '68
    Screen World 20:238 '69
    Uselton, R. A. The Wampus baby stars. Films In R 21-2:73
        F '70
    Davis, H. R. Sally O'Neill; filmog. Films In R 23-2:126 F '72

ONTKEAN, MICHAEL
    Davidson, B. That's the way the puck bounces. TV Guide 21-4:
        26 Ja 27 '73

ONYX, NARDA
Survival.  TV Guide 10-21:19 My 26 '62

OPERTI, LE ROI
Obit.  N. Y. Times p38 Je 25 '71

ORBACH, JERRY
Sutphen, M.  Interview.  House B 112:64 F '70
Bio.  Cur Bio 31:29 My '70
Same.  Cur Bio Yrbk 1970:328 '71
Willwerth, J.  Interview.  Time 99:22 Ap 17 '72
Williamson, B.  "Fourplay," photos.  Playboy 21-4 Ap '74

ORMSBY, ALAN
George, B.  Interview.  Black Oracle 6:6 Fall '72

OSBORNE, HELEN MARIE
Sketch.  Green Book 15:833 My '16
Corliss, A.  A bear of a baby.  Photop 11-5:86 Ap '17
Ames, H.  How she got in the movies.  Motion Pic 15:41 Je '18
Johnson, T. A.  Child stars.  Films In R 15-8:519 O '64
Brock, A.  Whatever happened to Baby Marie Osborne?  Classic
    Film Collect 44:38 Fall '74

OSCARSSON, PER
Per Oscarsson; filmog.  Film 60:13 n. d.

O'SHEA, MICHAEL
Proctor, K.  The pluck of the Irish.  Silver S 13-6:38 Ap '43
Sketch.  Photop 22:68 Ap '43
Vallee, W. L.  Paging Mr. Diogenes.  Silver S 18-1:53 N '47
Hall, G.  She wishes on a star.  Silver S 20-12:30 O '50
Obit.  Classic Film Collect 42:34 Spg '74
    N. Y. Times Bio Ed p1988 D '73
    Screen World p238 '74

OSTRICHE, MURIEL
Interview.  Cosmop 56:267 Ja '14
Naylor, H. S.  Sketch.  Motion Pic Classic 4:61 Je '17
Smith, F. J.  Interview.  Motion Pic Classic 11:16 N '20

O'SULLIVAN, MAUREEN
Sketch.  Photop 37:42 F '30
Manners, D.  Interview.  Motion Pic Classic 31:58 My '30
Dickey, J.  Sketch.  Motion Pic Classic 32:51 Ja '31
Shirley, L.  Interview.  Motion Pic 41:84 Mr '31
Manners, D.  Sketch.  Motion Pic Classic 33:50 Ap '31
Fidler, J. M.  She does a psycho-soliloquey.  Silver S 3-4:21
    F '33
Beauty Advice.  Motion Pic 49:48 Ap '35
Maddox, B.  The major's daughter.  Silver S 5-6:25 Ap '35
Hill, G.  Interview regarding clothes.  Movie Classic 8:44 Jl '35
Lee, S.  Her beauty exercises.  Movie Classic 10:36 Ap '36

Lee, S. Her marriage. Motion Pic 52:35 Ja '37
Mayer, M. O'Sullivan's destiny. Screen Book 19-2:61 S '37
Franchey, J. R. Colleen of the apes. Screen Book 22-5:80 D
    '39
Bio note; filmog. Movies & People 2:30 '40
Vallee, W. L. Jungle colleen. Silver S 12-1:36 N '41
A jungle housewife. Lions R 1-4:no p# D '41
Tarzan's mate: a normal wife. Lions R 1-10:no p# Je '42
Raddatz, L. It's lovely to be back. TV Guide 20-42:29 O 14
    '72
Piper, B. M. Filmog. Films In R 24-6:381 Je/Jl '73
Canham, K. Interview; filmog. Focus On F 18:51 Sum '74

O'SULLIVAN, MICHAEL
    Obit. N.Y. Times p28 Jl 26 '71

O'TOOLE, PETER
    Zunser, J. Desert how he hated it. Cue 32-4:20 Ja 26 '63
    Desert island films. Films & Filming 9-11:11 Ag '63
    Star of the year. Film R p19 '63/64
    Interview. Playboy 12:91 S '65
    Bio. Cur Bio 29:33 S '68
        Same. Cur Bio Yrbk 1968:295 '69
    Ronan, M. Don't let anyone else play Henry; interview. Sr
        Schol 94:30 F 28 '69
    McGillivray, D. Bio note; filmog. Focus On F 10:9 Sum '72
    Flatley, G. From Lawrence to La Mancha. N.Y. Times sec
        2:1 S 17 '72
        Same. N.Y. Times Bio Ed p1687 S '72
    Buck, J. Peter O'Toole; interview. Interview 26:6 O '72
    Stanger, I. Interview. Harp Baz 106:92 D '72
    Archibald, L. A man who dreams no impossible dreams. Show
        2-10:25 Ja '73
    Anderson, M. Way out west with Peter O'Toole. Plays & Play-
        ers 21-5:15 F '74

OUSPENSKAYA, MARIA
    Rhea, M. Sketch. Photop 53:31 Jl '39
    Mulvey, K. Sketch. Womans Home C 67:8 My '40
    Obit. Screen World 1:234 '49

OVERMAN, LYNN
    Obit. Newsweek 21:6 Mr 1 '43
        Time 41:76 Mr 1 '43

OWEN, BEVERLY
    If soap goes out of style. TV Guide 12-6:26 F 8 '64

OWEN, CATHERINE DALE
    Hall, G. Sketch. Motion Pic 38:58 N '29
    York, C. Sketch. Photop 36:69 N '29
    Cohen, H. W. Catherine Dale Owen. Cinema Dig 4-3:15 My 29
        '33
    Obit. Screen World 17:240 '66

OWEN, REGINALD
He likes his job.   Lions R 2-5:no p# Jl '43
Obit.   Film R p13 '73/74
   Classic Film Collect 38:57 Spg '73
   N. Y. Times Bio Ed p2029 N '72

OWEN, SEENA
   Service, F.   Interview.   Motion Pic Classic 10:34 Je '20
   Astor, T.   Interview.   Motion Pic Classic 12:66 Ag '21
   Reid, J.   Interview.   Motion Pic 25:26 Ag '23

OWENS, BUCK
   Whitney, D.   Still just pickin' away.   TV Guide 18-45:14 N 7
   '70

OWENS, DEIRDRE
   Television's own promising starlets.   TV Guide 3-37:10 S 10
   '55

OWENS, GARY
   Barber, R.   The case of the murrish morgul.   TV Guide 19-26:
   20 Je 26 '71

OWENS, PATRICIA
   Agenoux, S.   Interview.   Interview 1-3:10 n. d.

OWSLEY, MONROE
   Mook, S. R.   He's sore because he's a hit.   Silver S 1-12:38
   O '31


PACE, JUDY
   Robinson, L.   The thinking man's star.   Ebony 26:112 Mr '71
   They were made for each other.   Photop 81-6:31 Je '72

PACINO, AL
   Buchman, D. D.   An actor who believes in taking chances.
   Show 2-2:38 S '71
   Heir apparent to the Godfather.   Life 72:62 Mr 31 '72
   Godsons.   Time 99:70 Ap 3 '72
   Miller, E.   Interview.   Seventeen 31:122 Ap '72
   Chase, C.   Will the Godfather's son live to be a godfather?
   N. Y. Times sec 2:11 My 7 '72
   Same.   N. Y. Times Bio Ed My 7 '72
   Fiore, M.; Scott, V.   Story behind The godfather by the men
   who lived it.   Ladies Home J 89:62 Je '72
   Fanger, I. M.   The basic training of Al Pacino.   After Dark
   5-3:18 Jl '72
   Manners, D.   I nominate for stardom.   Mod Screen 66-7:16 Jl
   '72
   The offer Al Pacino couldn't refuse.   Mod Screen 67-2:56 F '73
   Serpico star.   Photop 85-4:63 Ap '74
   Flatley, G.   Interview.   Game 1-1:4 N '74

PAGE, ANITA
    Pryor, N.    Sketch.    Motion Pic Classic 27:37 My '28
    Walker, H.    Sketch.    Photop 33:41 My '28
    Hall, G.    Interview.    Motion Pic Classic 28:28 S '28
    Thorp, D.    Sketch.    Motion Pic Classic 29:39 Je '29
    Conti, M.    Shopping with Anita Page.    Motion Pic 38:68 O '29
    Goldbeck, E.    Sketch.    Motion Pic Classic 31:30 Je '30
    Lee, S.    Hollywood's favorite puzzle.    Movie Classic 3:15 S '32
    Lathem, M.    Her marriage.    Movie Classic 7:38 O '34
    Uselton, R. A.    The Wampus baby stars.    Films In R 21-2:73
      F '70

PAGE, GALE
    Hamilton, S.    Sketch.    Photop 54:19 F '40

PAGE, GERALDINE
    Lewis, E.    Debutants from downtown.    Cue 22-7:12 F 14 '53
    Baldwin, J.    Bird of light.    Show 2-2:78 F '62
    Talking about people.    Film 32:6 Sum '62
    Eyles, A.    Geraldine Page; filmog.    Focus On F 14:13 Spg '73

PAGE, JOY
    She asked for it--and got it.    Lions R 3-5:no p# D '44

PAGET, DEBRA
    Gibson, M.    I brought up Debra to be a star.    Silver S 21-11:26
      S '51
    Rising star.    Film R p105 '52/53
    Holland, J.    If Debra had you over.    Silver S 24-1:34 N '53

PAGOTT, NICOLA
    Tierney, M.    Interview.    Plays & Players 17-10:22 Jl '70

PAIGE, JANIS
    Fulton, M. J.    Sketch.    Photop 32:20 Ap '48
    I love dazzle.    House & Gard 135:106 Mr 9 '69

PAIGE, JEAN
    Forthe, W.    Of the sub-deb squad.    Photop 17-1:42 D '19
    Fletcher, A. W.    Interview.    Motion Pic 19:48 Ap/My '20
    Fletcher, A. W.    Interview.    Motion Pic 21:22 Je '21

PAIGE, MABEL
    McClelland, D.    Mabel Paige; filmog.    Film Fan Mo 129:23
      Mr '72

PAIGE, ROBERT
    Perkins, R.    Paging Robert Paige.    Silver S 14-3:46 Ja '44
    Vallee, W. L.    Modest Mr. Paige.    Silver S 15-5:52 Mr '45

PALANCE, JACK
    Vallee, W. L.    Cad with a conscience.    Silver S 24-5:35 Mr '54
    Eyles, A.    Jack Palance; filmog.    Focus On F 5:5 Win '70

A very gentle villain.  Films Illus 1-10:6 Ap '72
Symposium on fear.  Playboy 20-1:180 Ja '73
Filmog.  Films & Filming 20-5:58 F '74

PALLETTE, EUGENE
Malverne, P.  Sketch.  Motion Pic Classic 11:31 Ja '21
Fare enough.  Lions R 2-4:no p# Ap '43
Braff, R.  Partial filmog.  Films In R 18-10:652 D '67

PALMER, BETSY
Heavens to Betsy.  TV Guide 4-52:29 D 29 '56
Betsy flips her wig.  TV Guide 6-37:12 S 13 '58
The strike-out queen.  TV Guide 8-34:8 Ag 20 '60

PALMER, CORLISS
Hall, G.  Interview.  Motion Pic 21:70 Mr '21
Glendenning, B.  Sketch.  Motion Pic Classic 12:58 Je '21
Hands and harmony.  Motion Pic 22:69 Ag '21
Montanye, L.  Interview.  Motion Pic Classic 13:44 O '21
Beauty talks.  Motion Pic 22:58 Ja '22
Beauty talks.  Motion Pic 21:95 (and following issues) Ap 21 '30

PALMER, LILLI
Little, J.  Two lives of Lilli.  Silver S 17-8:57 Je '47
Parsons, L. O.  Cosmop's citation for best supporting perform-
    ance of the month.  Cosmop 123:55 O '47
Parsons, L. O.  Cosmop's citation as best female star of month.
    Cosmop 124:13 F '48
Harrison, L. P.  What about the Rex Harrisons?  Silver S 18-
    10:22 Ag '48
Keating, J.  The Harrisons observed.  Cue 21-8:10 F 23 '52
Howard, M.  Must you be rude to succeed?  Silver S 22-8:34
    Je '52
Minoff, P.  A couple of veterans score solo victories.  Cue 22-
    4:7 Ja 24 '53
Pedell, K.  Life is better after 30.  TV Guide 1-23:16 S 4 '53
Zunser, J.  A chat with Lilli.  Cue 29-15:8 Ap 9 '60
Delbos, C.  Filmog.  Films In R 18-3:190 Mr '67

PALUZZI, LUCIANA
Beauty knows no boundaries.  TV Guide 7-50:21 D 12 '59

PANGBORN, FRANKLIN
Calhoun, D. D.  Sketch.  Motion Pic 35:41 Jl '28
Maltin, L.  Our gang; inc. Our Gang filmog.  Film Fan Mo 66:
    3 D '66

PAPAS, IRENE
Robbins, F.  Director Michael Cacoyannis and his Trojan women.
    Show 2-8:31 O '71
Root, N.  A friend recounts the turbulent life and career of
    Irene Papas.  Sat R Arts 1-4:64 Ap '73

PARK, E. L.
   Connor, E.  The 6 Charlie Chans; Charlie Chan filmog.  Films
     In R 6-1:23 Ja '55

PARKER, CECIL
   Obit.  Film R p13 '71/72
   N. Y.  Times p45 Ap 22 '71
   Same.  N. Y.  Times Bio Ed Ap 22 '71
   Screen World 23:239 '72

PARKER, ELEANOR
   Bio sketch.  Vogue 105:199 Mr 15 '45
   De Rig, M.  Puzzle worth solving.  Silver S 15-12:48 O '45
   MacArthur, M.  You've got to lend fate a hand.  Silver S 21-11:
     30 S '51
   Hendricks, H.  My 3 great desires.  Silver S 23-7:40 My '53

PARKER, FLORA
   Tinee, M.  Sketch.  Green Book 11:739 My '14
   Cheatham, M.  Interview.  Motion Pic 23:76 Ap '22

PARKER, JEAN
   Sketch.  Photop 44:82 Je '33
   Lane, J.  Her story.  Motion Pic 47:39 Je '34
   Sylvia's beauty helps.  Photop 46:70 Ag '34
   Dowling, M.  Interview.  Movie Classic 7:51 O '34
   Tully, J.  Her story.  Movie Classic 8:36 Je '35
   Harrison, H.  Interview.  Movie Classic 9:35 F '36
   Hover, H.  Gingham gal goes glamorous.  Screen Book 22-1:80
     Ag '39
   Bio note; filmog.  Movies & People 2:30 '40
   Mook, D.  Jean has a complaint.  Silver S 12-2:12 D '41
   Borie, M.  We visit Jean Parker today.  Movie Dig 1-6:110 N
     '72

PARKER, MAGGIE
   She'll act anywhere--as long as it's Hawaii.  TV Guide 17-3:24
     Ja 18 '69

PARKER, MARY
   Three little girls in tune.  Lions R 4-1:no p# F '45

PARKINS, BARBARA
   Whitney, D.  You gotta have a press agent with vision.  TV
     Guide 14-45:13 N 5 '66
   Helping Barbara Parkins.  Esquire 68:104 Ag '67
   Rollins, B.  Dames in the Valley of the dolls.  Look 31:58 S 5
     '67
   Hollywood's hot new sex queens.  Mod Screen 66-1:34 Ja '72

PARKS, ALLISON
   Playmate of the year.  Playboy 13-5:136 My '66

PARKS, LARRY
    Crocker, H.  Becomes Al Jolson's pal in preparation for his
        part in The Jolson story.  Good House 123:12 D '46
    Maddox, B.  Larry's phenomenal swoop.  Silver S 18-1:46 N '47
    Poles, P.  Letter; filmog.  Films In R 21-4:254 Ap '70
    Whitney, D.  One day she met a kid from Kansas.  TV Guide
        22-17:21 Ap 27 '74

PARKS, MICHAEL
    Not-so-easy riders.  TV Guide 18-15:17 Ap 11 '70
    Why I didn't marry him.  Photop 77-6:67 Je '70
    Wittgens, C.  Then came... Motion p11 Jl/Ag '73

PARKS, TRINA
    The girl who zaps James Bond.  Ebony 27:58 Mr '72

PARRISH, GIGI
    Uselton, R. A.  The Wampus baby stars.  Films In R 21-2:73
        F '70

PARRISH, HELEN
    Vallee, W. L.  Young veteran.  Silver S 11-11:44 S '41
    Obit.  Screen World 11:224 '60

PARRISH, LESLIE
    She finally left Daisy Mae behind.  TV Guide 8-38:25 S 17 '60

PARRY, NATASHA
    Rising star.  Film R p27 '50

PARSONS, MILTON
    Schaeffer, D. L.  Letter; partial filmog.  Films In R 21-9:584
        N '70

PARSONS, WILLIAM (BILL)
    Parsons, S. B.  Scare 'em or make 'em laugh.  Photop 14-4:61
        S '18

PASCO, RICHARD
    Buck, J.  Interview.  Plays & Players 20-1:28 O '72
    Totten, E.  Interview.  Plays & Players 20-9:26 Je '73

PATCH, WALLY
    Obit.  Film R p13 '71/72

PATERSON, PAT
    Blackstock, L.  Sketch.  Motion Pic 52:19 D '36
    Spensley, D.  Interview.  Motion Pic 54:26 Ag '37
    Schallert, E.  Her home.  Photop 25:52 S '44

PATRICK, GAIL
    Biery, R.  Interview.  Motion Pic 52:44 Ag '36
    Bunch, H.  They call her menace.  Screen Book 19-4:57 N '37

Churchill, E.  Her 3 severest critics.  Silver S 8-3:30 Ja '38
Devine, J. F.  Disbarred by Hollywood.  Screen Book 21-8:16
  Mr '39
Van Wyck, C.  Story of.  Photop 53:59 Ag '39
Service, F.  You won't believe your ears.  Silver S 13-9:38 Jl
  '43
Hall, G.  Will women ever be the same again?  Silver S 14-12:
  32 O '44

PATRICK, JEROME
  Beach, B.  Interview.  Motion Pic Classic 11:22 D '20

PATRICK, JOAN
  She holds Dr. Kildare's hand.  TV Guide 10-15:21 Ap 14 '62

PATRICK, LEE
  Maltin, L.  Lee Patrick; filmog.  Film Fan Mo 144:23 Je '73

PATRICK, LORY
  Down from the West Virginia hills.  TV Guide 10-22:27 Je 2 '62

PATRICK, NIGEL
  Patrick, N.  Directing my first film.  Films & Filming 3-8:7
  My '57

PATTEN, LUANA
  Letter from Liza.  Silver S 17-5:67 Mr '47

PATTERSON, ELINOR
  Fairfield, L.  Interview.  Motion Pic 34:31 S '27

PATTERSON, ELIZABETH
  Sketch.  N. Y. Drama 76:9 N 25 '16

PATTERSON, HANK
  Raddatz, L.  The Dodge City gang.  TV Guide 20-12:14 Mr 18
  '72

PATTERSON, JAMES
  Rise of a farm boy.  Life 44:116 Mr 24 '58
  Obit.  N. Y. Times Bio Ed p1530 Ag '72

PATTERSON, MELODY
  Fessier, M. Jr.  With her homework was the hangup.  TV
  Guide 15-23:14 Je 10 '67
  Marriage on the rocks.  Photop 78-4:45 O '70

PATTERSON, NEVA
  Hobson, D.  The revolt of Maggie Method.  TV Guide 19-43:47
  O 23 '71

PAUL, EUGENIA
  What makes Eugenia run?  TV Guide 6-21:20 My 24 '58

PAUL, STEVEN
  Interview.  New Yorker 46:28 F 13 '71

PAULSEN, PAT
  Fantastic face.  Newsweek 69:84 Je 12 '67
  Hobson, D.  Happiness is a pledganeous glog.  TV Guide 15-50:
    32 D 16 '67
  Conaway, J.  Paulsen for president.  N. Y.  Times Mag p58 Mr
    5 '72
  Williamson, B.  "Fourplay"; photos.  Playboy 21-4 Ap '74

PAVAN, MARISA
  Rising star.  Film R p36 '56/57

PAWN, DORIS
  Remont, F.  Interview.  Motion Pic Classic 12:58 Mr '21

PAXINOU, KATINA
  The Greeks will come down to the cities.  Cue 12-34:8 Ag 21
    '43
  Berch, B.  Story of.  Photop 23:60 N '43
  Hall, E.  Bio sketch.  Vogue 110:212 D '47
  Obit.  Classic Film Collect 39:extra 1 Sum '73
    Film R p16 '73/74
    N. Y. Times Bio Ed p287 F '73
    Screen World p238 '74

PAYNE, FREDA
  Just stunning.  Photop 85-2:18 F '74

PAYNE, JOHN
  Fraser, P.  Friendship, courtship, marriage.  Screen Book 19-
    4:44 N '37
  O'Neill, J. J.  A Payne in the right place.  Screen Book 21-3:
    43 O '38
  Gwin, J.  Living up to his name.  Silver S 9-3:47 Ja '39
  Rhea, M.  Sketch.  Photop 53:31 Ap '31
  Maddox, B.  Johnny checks out.  Silver S 13-4:30 F '43
  Watters, J.  On stage.  People 1-7:29 Ap 15 '74

PAYNE, JULIE
  She's just a typical Hollywood kid.  TV Guide 14-32:27 Ag 6 '66

PEARL, JACK
  Lane, J.  In the movies.  Movie Classic 5:27 O '33
  Hamilton, S.  Sketch.  Photop 44:69 N '33

PEARSON, VIRGINIA
  Courtlandt, R.  Interview.  Motion Pic Classic 5:28 D '17
  Hall, G.  Interview.  Motion Pic 15:79 N '18

PEARY, HAROLD
  Stooges cash in.  Newsweek 18:72 S 8 '41

Throckmorton, P. Gildersleeve. Newsweek 22:84 D 13 '43
Peary vs. Gildersleeve. Cue 13-37:15 S 9 '44
Throckmorton's giant. Time 47:64 Ap 22 '46

PECHEUR, BRUCE
Stoop, N. M. If I stop swimming, I'll drown. After Dark 6-4:
26 Ag '73

PECK, GREGORY
Bangs, B. He took Hollywood by storm. Silver S 15-2:26 D '44
Sketch. Time 45:40 Ja 1 '45
My biggest lie. Photop 26:57 Mr '45
What he and his wife argue about. Photop 27:60 Jl '45
Gallup, G. Awarded the Photoplay gold medal award for 1945.
Photop 28:28 F '46
Fourth place in Companion poll of favorite stars. Womans Home
C 73:8 Je '46
Aumont, J. P. Sketch. Photop 29:27 Jl '46
Pritchett, F. Pecking away at Gregory. Silver S 17-1:30 N '46
Parsons, L. O. Cosmop's citation for one of the best perform-
ances of the month. Cosmop 122:67 Ja '47
An open letter to Gregory Peck. Cosmop 122:126 Mr '47
Peck, Mrs. G. The man I married. Silver S 17-8:40 Je '47
Work of. Newsweek 30:97 N 17 '47
Kilgallen, D. Sketch. Photop 34:28 Ja '49
Holland, J. How to be normal in Hollywood. Silver S 20-4:36
F '50
Holland, J. Actors and their privacy. Silver S 21-8:33 Je '51
Shane, D. A peek at Peck. Silver S 22-12:37 O '52
My favorite role. Film R p17 '52/53
Reid, L. Country gentleman. Silver S 24-9:30 Jl '54
The new Captain Ahab. Films & Filming 1-5:4 F '55
Peck, G. The American Film Institute: in answer to public
demand. Action 3-1:11 Ja/F '68
Quiet acts of courage. Films Illus 2-14:18 Ag '72
Castell, D. Wearing two hats. Films Illus 3-32:310 Ap '74
Interview. Am Cinematog 55-2:172 F '74
Gow, G. Interview; filmog. Films & Filming 20-12:29 S '74
Wolf, W. No producer picks Peck, so Peck picks producing.
Cue 43-36:2 S 23 '74

PEEL, HARRY
Junale, E. Fabulous Peel; king of sensation. Classic Film
Collect 30:10 Spg '71

PELLEGRIN, RAYMOND
Bio note. Unifrance 23:10 F '53

PENDLETON, NAT
Sketch. Photop 45:47 Ap '34
Hamilton, S. Sketch. Photop 54:46 D '40
Obit. N.Y. Times p39 O 13 '67
Maltin, L. The unsung heroes. Film Fan Mo 77:13 N '67

PENHALIGION, SUSAN
  McAsh, I. F.  Penhaligion's progress.  Films Illus 4-40:136 D
    '74

PENN, LEO
  Rising star.  Film R p31 '50

PENNER, JOE
  Sketch.  Time 24:46 D 3 '34
  Ulman, W. Jr.  Now you will see Joe Penner.  Silver S 5-2:47
    D '34
  Sargent, T.  Enters the movies.  Movie Classic 7:52 D '34
  Bio note; filmog.  Movies & People 2:30 '40
  Obit.  Newsweek 17:8 Ja 20 '41

PENNICK, JACK
  Gray, J.  Jack Pennick; filmog.  Films In R 16-1:60 Ja '65

PENNINGTON, ANN
  Bartlett, R.  Only bad pennies return.  Photop 10-5:52 O '16
  Lee, C.  Sketch.  Motion Pic 14:87 Ag '17
  Seitz, C. W.  Interview.  Motion Pic 14:132 Ja '18
  Lamb, G.  Interview.  Motion Pic Classic 6:45 Ag '18
  Interview.  Dram Mir 466 S 11 '20
  Obit.  Classic Film Collect (reprint N. Y. Times) 33:53 Win '71
    N. Y. Times p46 N 5 '71
    Same.  N. Y. Times Bio Ed N 5 '71
    Newsweek 78:129 N 15 '71
    Time 98:53 N 15 '71
  Lewis, G.  Letter; filmog.  Films In R 23-2:123 F '72

PENNINGTON, JANICE
  Paging Miss Pennington.  Playboy 18-5:124 My '71

PEPPARD, GEORGE
  Rising star.  Film R p32 '61/62
  I did not attack that girl.  Photop 81-5:34 My '72
  Cleared of lurid charges.  Mod Screen 66-5:46 My '72
  Hano, A.  Private eye, Polish style.  TV Guide 20-39:26 S 23
    '72
  The haunted life of Peppard.  Photop 83-2:40 F '73

PEPPER, CYNTHIA
  A vaudevillian's revenge.  TV Guide 9-52:3 D 30 '61

PERCY, EILEEN
  Sheridan, M.  Sketch.  Motion Pic Classic 6:27 Ap '18
  Cheatham, M.  Interview.  Motion Pic Classic 11:48 D '20
  Obit.  Classic Film Collect 40:59 Fall '73
    Screen World p238 '74

PERCY, THELMA
  Remont, F.  Interview.  Motion Pic Classic 10:78 Jl '20

PERDUE, DERELYS
   Uselton, R. A.   The Wampus baby stars.   Films In R 21-2:73
      F '70

PERIER, FRANCOIS
   A panoramic shot of Perier.   Unifrance 39:no p# Mr/Ap '56
   Gray, M.   Seeing himself as others see him.   Films & Filming
      3-3:15 D '56

PERIOLAT, GEORGE EDWIN
   Remont, F.   Makeup wizzard.   Motion Pic Classic 5:39 N '17

PERKINS, ANTHONY
   (See:  PERKINS, TONY)

PERKINS, MILLIE
   Zunser, J.   Meet Millie from Passaic.   Cue 27-46:13 N 15 '58

PERKINS, OSGOOD
   They stand out from the crowd.   Lit Dig 116:11 N 11 '33
   The timing of Osgood Perkins.   Cue 3-14:13 F 2 '35

PERKINS, TONY
   Zunser, J.   Young star, annoyed.   Cue 25-46:14 N 17 '56
   Zunser, J.   Tony comes home.   Cue 26-48:10 N 30 '57
   Rising star.   Film R p28 '58/59
   Miller, E.   Hollywood scene.   Seventeen 20:16 My '61
   Ross, L.   Profile.   New Yorker 37:83 N 4 '61
   Interview.   Cinema (BH) 2-5:17 Mr/Ap '65
   Reed, R.   All steamed up about directing.   N. Y. Times Bio Ed
      Jl 26 '70
   40 not such a dangerous age after all.   Films Illus 1-16:14 O
      '72
   Carragher, B.   I had a fine childhood, how about you?   N. Y.
      Times sec 2:11 N 19 '72
      Same.   N. Y. Times Bio Ed p2033 N '72
   Berenson, B.   What's Tony Perkins really really like?   Inter-
      view 27:26 N '72
   A love story.   Interview p22 Ja '74
   Rayns, T.   Across the board.   Sight & Sound 43-3:147 Sum '74

PERREAU, GIGI
   Talent runs in the family.   Colliers 124:6 O 22 '49

PERRIN, JACK
   Naylor, H. S.   Interview.   Motion Pic Classic 13:72 S '21
   Couto, C.   Jack Perrin and 'The lion man. '   Classic Film Col-
      lect 42:11 Win '73

PERRIN, JACQUES
   Bean, R.   Will there be film stars in 1974?   Films & Filming
      10-10:9 Jl '64

PERRINE, VALERIE
Valerie.  Playboy 19-5:103 My '72
Sketch.  Movie Dig 1-6:23 N '72
Sketch.  Films Illus 3-28:154 O '73
Klemesrud, J.  The return of the Hollywood sex kitten.  N. Y.
    Times sec 2:1 D 1 '74
Sex goddess of the '70s.  People 2-23:22 D 2 '74

PERRON, SADI
Leonard Sillman's New faces of 1971.  Cue 40-8:8 F 20 '71

PERRY, JOAN
Whitehead, H.  Sketch.  Motion Pic 52:17 Ja '37

PERRY, KATHERINE
Montanye, L.  Interview.  Motion Pic Classic 13:34 D '21

PERRY, LINCOLN
(See:  FETCHIT, STEPIN)

PERRY, MARGARET
Donnell, D.  Gives up screen career.  Movie Classic 2:26 Ag
    '32

PERRY, MARY
Obit.  N. Y. Times p41 Mr 9 '71

PERRY, WANDA
Crivello, K.  Wanda Perry.  Film Fan Mo 162:3 D '74

PETERS, BERNADETTE
Stasio, M.  The stars of tomorrow on stage today.  Cue 38-9:9
    Mr 1 '69
Finstrom, A.  The song (and dance) of Bernadette Peters.  After
    Dark 7-7:40 N '74

PETERS, HOUSE
The wandering House.  Photop 12-2:24 Jl '17

PETERS, JEAN
Churchill, R. & B.  Better than red apples.  Silver S 18-2:56
    D '47
Rising stars.  Film R p105 '52/53
Lyons, D. L.  Liberation of Mrs. Howard Hughes.  Ladies Home
    J 88:112 Mr '71
Change of address.  TV Guide 21-9:25 Mr 3 '73

PETERS, SUSAN
Sketch.  Photop 20:50 Mr '42
Stars of tomorrow.  Lions R 1-11/12:no p# Jl/Ag '42
Grey-eyed Susan.  Lions R 2-1:no p# S/O '42
Now she is a lady.  Lions R 2-3:no p# D '42
The girl they picked for Random harvest.  Lions R 2-3:no p#

D '42
Hamilton, S.  Sketch.  Photop 22:44 Mr '43
Holland, J.  "Wonts" for Susan.  Silver S 13-6:42 Ap '43
Susan stays herself.  Lions R 2-4:no p# Ap '43
Susan and her 3-year plan.  Lions R 3-1:no p# S '43
Service, F.  Can an average girl succeed in the movies?  Silver
    S 14-1:24 N '43
Mother doesn't know best.  Lions R 3-2:no p# Ja '44
Turner, L.  Story of.  Photop 30:12 D '46
Christmas with the Hollywood stars.  Photop 34:42 D '48
Obit.  Screen World 4:117 '53

PETERSON, DOROTHY
    Hall, G.  Sketch.  Motion Pic Classic 33:63 My '31

PETERSON, PAUL
    Man is he far out.  TV Guide 9-29:20 Jl 22 '61

PETRIE, DORIS
    Three years ago.  Motion p35 Ja/F '73

PETRIE, HOWARD
    Obit.  Screen World 20:239 '69

PETRIE, SUSAN
    McCaughna, D.  A terribly personal business.  Motion p16 Jl/Ag
    '74

PETROVA, OLGA
    Experiences in New York.  Green Book 8:284 Ag '12
    Interview.  Cosmop 57:413 Ag '14
    Dale, A.  Interview.  Green Book 15:716 Ap '16
    Russell, L. C.  Work of.  Motion Pic Classic 3:54 F '17
    How she got in moving pictures.  Motion Pic 14:106 O '17
    Bartlett, R.  Petrova--prophetess.  Photop 13-1:24 D '17
    Seitz, C. W.  Interview.  Motion Pic Classic 5:32 F '18
    Smith, F. J.  Interview.  Motion Pic Classic 7:18 S '18
    Hall, G.  Interview.  Motion Pic 17:70 Mr '19
    Sketch.  Photop 18:49 N '20
    Autobiographical.  Photop 19:33 Mr '21
    Sketch.  Photop 21:50 My '22
    Fulbright, T.  Panther woman.  Classic Film Collect 16:28 Fall
    '66; 17:30 Win/Spg '67
    James, N.  Olga Petrova.  Silent Pic 18:5 Sum '73

PETROVITCH, MICHAEL
    Faces going far.  Films Illus 1-10:20 Ap '72

PETTIT, WANDA
    Owen, K.  Heavens, what a wonderful blonde.  Photop 13-3:101
    F '18

PFLUG, JOANN
  Photop forum.   Photop 82-3:8 S '72

PHILBIN, MARY
  Carr, H.  Sketch.  Motion Pic 25:20 F '23
  Carr, H.  Sketch.  Motion Pic 20:40 F '25
  Donnell, D.  Sketch.  Motion Pic Classic 22:40 O '25
  Interview.  Theatre 44:39 O '26
  Robinson, S.  Sketch.  Motion Pic Classic 24:54 D '26
  Gilmore, F.  Sketch.  Motion Pic Classic 27:42 Ap '28
  Uselton, R. A.  The Wampus baby stars.  Films In R 21-2:73
    F '70
  Davis, F.  Letter.  Films In R 21-6:392 Je/Jl '70

PHILIPE, GERARD
  Billard, G.  May end his career.  Films & Filming 2-1:10 O
    '55
  Duncan, C.  The magic of two heroes; filmog.  Film J (Aus)
    15:57 Mr '60
  Additional filmog.  Film J (Aus) 16:95 Ag '60; 17:124 Ap '61
  Obit.  Film R p10 '60/61
    Screen World 11:224 '60

PHILIPP, KAREN
  Adler, D.  Exquisitely played by Karen Philipp.  TV Guide 21-
    24:17 Je 16 '73

PHILLIPS, DOROTHY
  Sketch.  Photop 11-6:36 My '17
  Peltret, E.  Interview.  Motion Pic 17:38 F '19
  What the neighbors know.  Photop 15-3:53 F '19
  Remont, F.  Sketch.  Motion Pic Classic 8:34 Ap '19
  Not a single double.  Photop 16-2:86 Jl '19
  Peltret, E.  Interview.  Motion Pic 20:28 Ja '21
  Fletcher, A. W.  Interview.  Motion Pic Classic 12:18 My '21
  Gassaway, G.  Interview.  Motion Pic Classic 14:34 Mr '22
  Gassaway, G.  Interview.  Motion Pic 24:74 O '22
  Lipman, J. H.  Interview.  Classic 18:40 Ja '24
  Her return to the screen.  Photop 28:33 S '25
  Return to pictures.  Motion Pic Classic 24:48 D '26
  Leslie, A.  Sketch.  Motion Pic 31:37 Mr '27

PHILLIPS, EDDIE
  St. Johns, I.  Sketch.  Photop 26:84 Jl '24

PHILLIPS, JEAN
  Crivello, K.  She was epitome of 40's "b" feature star.  Classic
    F Collect 31:39 Sum '71

PHILLIPS, MACKENZIE
  Stephenson, R.  Introducing.  Interview p10 F '74

PHILLIPS, MICHELLE
    Headliners.   Photop 85-1:8 Ja '74

PHILLIPS, NORMA
    Rodgers, J. J.   Interview.   Green Book 13:83 Ja '15

PHILLIPS, ROBIN
    Waterhouse, R.   Interview.   Plays & Players 19-3:16 D '71
    Leech, M.   The company he keeps.   Plays & Players 20-5:16 F
      '73

PHIPPS, SALLY
    Sketch.   Photop 33:67 Ap '28
    Manners, D.   Sketch.   Motion Pic Classic 28:42 O '28
    Uselton, R. A.   The Wampus baby stars.   Films In R 21-2:73
      F '70

PIA, ISABELLE
    Do you know Isabelle Pia?   Unifrance 32:15 O/N '54

PICCOLI, MICHAEL
    Michael Piccoli; interview; filmog.   Films 60:10 n. d.
    A star of character.   Film 2-6:12 S '73

PICKFORD, JACK
    Wright, E.   Interview.   Motion Pic Sup 1:55 N '15
    McGaffey, K.   Mary's brother Jack.   Photop 12-5:74 O '17
    Kingston, R.   Interview.   Motion Pic 17:66 Ap '19
    Cheatham, M. S.   Interview.   Motion Pic Classic 11:22 S '20
    Bruce, B.   Interview.   Motion Pic 23:66 Jl '22
    The new house of Pickford.   Motion Pic 25:26 O '23
    Halton, G.   Appreciation.   Motion Pic 28:34 O '24
    de Revere, F. V.   Analysis of his face.   Motion Pic 29:43 Ap
      '25
    Calhoun, D.   His divorce.   Movie Classic 2:33 My '32
    Sketch.   Photop 43:90 Mr '33

PICKFORD, LOTTIE
    Owen, K.   Pickford the second.   Photop 8-1:27 Je '15

PICKFORD, MARY
    Sketch.   N. Y. Dram 69:10 Ja 29 '13
    White, M. Jr.   Interview.   Munsey 49:290 My '13
    Dodge, W. P.   Work of in moving pictures.   Theatre 17:176 Je
      '13
    Autobiographical.   Green Book 10:43 Jl '13
    Sketch.   Blue Book 19:700 Ag '14
    Sketch.   Motion Pic 8:116 Ja '15
    Sketch.   Motion Pic 9:92 F '15
    Sketch.   Nash's & Pall Mall 55:195 Ap '15
    Work of in moving pictures.   Everybody's 32:680 Je '15
    Dunne, H.   Sketch.   Motion Pic 10:91 Ja '16
    Courtlandt, R.   Sketch.   Motion Pic 11:111 Mr '16

Wallace, F.   Appreciation.   Motion Pic 11:82 Jl '16
Courtlandt, R.   Marriage of.   Motion Pic 12:108 S '16
Bastedo, G.   Sketch.   Motion Pic 12:131 O '16
Briscoe, J.   Sketch.   Motion Pic 12:55 N '16
Wright, E.   Sketch.   Motion Pic Classic 4:19 Mr '17
Autobiographical.   Harp Baz 52:54 Ap '17
Moore, R. F.   Interview.   Motion Pic 14:69 Ag '17
Smith, F. J.   Interview.   Motion Pic Classic 5:35 S '17
Schmid, P. G.   Sketch.   Motion Pic 14:103 N '17
McKelvie, M. G.   Interview.   Motion Pic Classic 6:37 Jl '18
Cheatham, M. S.   Interview.   Motion Pic 17:58 Je '19
Too much Mary?   Womans Home C 46:45 Ag '19
Larkin, M.   Her mother.   Motion Pic 18:35 S '19
The care of her hair.   Ladies Home J 36:222 O '19
Sketch.   National 48:400 O '19
Smith, A.   Owen talks about Mary.   Photop 17-1:58 D '19
Hall, G.   Sketch.   Motion Pic 19:52 Mr '20
Bates, B.   The Pickford-Fairbanks wooing.   Photop 18:70 Je '20
Interview.   Motion Pic 20:30 N '20
Ashworth, C. W.   Interview.   Motion Pic Classic 13:44 Ja '22
Fletcher, A. W.   Interview.   Motion Pic 23:22 Je '22
Cheatham, M.   Her darkest hour.   Motion Pic Classic 14:49 Ag
   '22
Carr, H.   Her problem.   Motion Pic 24:21 D '22
Ramsaye, T.   Her beginning in moving pictures.   Photop 24:40
   Jl '23
Wilson, B. F.   The part her hair has played in her career.
   Classic 16:18 Ag '23
Interview.   National 53:23 Jl '24
Hall, G. & Fletcher, A. W.   Interview.   Motion Pic 28:20 Ag
   '24
Adams, E.   Her horoscope.   Photop 26:35 N '24
de Revere, F. V.   Analysis of her face.   Motion Pic 28:43 Ja
   '25
Carr, H.   Interview.   Motion Pic Classic 21:16 Jl '25
Farnsworth, A.   How she stays young.   Everybodys 54:36 My
   '26
Fletcher, A. W.   A Hollywood idyl.   Motion Pic 32:20 Ag '26
St. Johns, A. R.   The married life of Doug and Mary.   Photop
   31:34 F '27
Whitaker, A.   Interview.   Photop 33:30 Mr '28
Wooldridge, D.   Her plans for the future.   Motion Pic 35:34 Je
   '28
Calhoun, D.   She bobs her hair.   Motion Pic 36:58 O '28
Woods, K.   Mary and Doug.   World Today 53:69 D '28
Interview.   National 57:268 Mr '29
Spensley, D.   Sketch.   Motion Pic 37:48 Jl '29
Goldbeck, E.   Interview.   Motion Pic 38:48 S '29
Hall, G.   Interview.   Motion Pic 39:58 My '30
Fairbanks, D. Jr.   Appreciation.   Vanity Fair 34:53 Je '30
MacCulloch, C.   Problems of the motion picture relief fund.
   Motion Pic 40:30 S '30
Fletcher, A. W.   The real Mary Pickford.   Motion Pic 40:42 D

'30
Matthews, P. Home of. Motion Pic Classic 33:36 Mr '31
Walker, H. L. Interview. Motion Pic 41:55 Mr '31
To destroy all her old films. Outlook 158:38 My 13 '31
Orme, M. Criticism. Ill Lon N 178:975 Je 6 '31
Lane, V. T. As a faith healer. Motion Pic Classic 32:22 Ag
    '31
Hall, G. The haunted house of Pickfair. Motion Pic 43:28 Ap
    '32
Home of. Photop 41:32 Ap '32
The romance that Hollywood couldn't destroy. Motion Pic 43:28
    My '32
Le Berthon, T. Interview. Motion Pic 43:56 Jl '32
Brokaw, C. B. The end of an era. Vanity Fair 38:18 Ag '32
Keen, J. H. Mary Pickford. Cinema Dig 2-1:11 N 14 '32
Welsh, W. Her ideal of a living Christmas tree for every child.
    Am For 38:636 D '32
Service, F. Interview. Motion Pic 45:60 F '33
Babcock, M. Her headline career from 1927-33. Movie Classic
    4:48 Mr '33
Melcher, E. Mary Pickford and Peter Pan. Cinema Dig 3-6:10
    Ap 24 '33
Keen, E. Pickford to make Peter Pan. Silver S 3-7:44 My '33
Schallert, E. The breaking up of Pickfair. Movie Classic 5:22
    S '33
Manners, D. Does not want sex appeal. Movie Classic 5:26
    S '33
Lee, S. Immortals of the screen. Motion Pic 46:32 O '33
Babcock, M. Who will be the queen of Hollywood? Silver S 4-
    1:21 N '33
St. Johns, A. R. The girl who was the first movie star. Silver
    S 4-4:16 F '34
Hall, G. Her own story. Motion Pic 47:30 Mr '34
Are she and Fairbanks reconciled? Movie Classic 7:38 N '34
Hartley, K. Becomes a radio entertainer. Movie Classic 7:33
    D '34
Chrisman, J. E. Interview. Movie Classic 9:34 N '35
Donnell, D. Interview. Motion Pic 51:38 F '36
Sketch. Newsweek 7:42 My 16 '36
As a hostess. Photop 49:76 My '36
Gilmore, E. Mary hunts for her old movies (reprint Pittsburgh
    Post Gazette). 8mm Collect 8:15 My '64
Brook, M. Sweetheart at 72. 8mm Collect 13:15 Fall/Win '65
McWilliams, W. A. The films of Mary Picford in the Eastman
    Kodak collection; filmog. 8mm Collect 12:34 Sum '65
Mary changes mind on old films. (reprint from Pittsburgh
    Press). 8mm Collect 13:10 Fall/Win '65
Pickford recants on having her films burned. Classic Film Col-
    lect (reprint from Tampa Tribune) 16:22 Fall '66
Brock, A. The magic of Mary Pickford conjures a little bit of
    eternity. Classic Film Collect 19:22 Fall/Win '67
Where are they now? Newsweek 70:16 N 6 '67
Weiler, A. H. Pickford gives 50 films to U. S. Film Institute.

(reprint from N.Y. Times) Classic F Collect 28:9 Fall '70
Reed, R. Sunnybrook farm in nude? Mary Pickford fears so.
Classic Film Collect 29:16 Win '70
Donnelly, T. Pickford's life was her best plot (reprint Washington Post). Classic Film Collect 29:51 Win '70
Hamilton, J. Where, oh where are the beautiful girls? Look
34-22:62 N 3 '70
Scaramazza, P. A. Rediscovering Mary Pickford. Film Fan
Mo 114:3 D '70
Patterson, G. G. Eloquent though silent. Filmograph 1-4:31 '70
Harmetz, A. America's sweetheart lives. N.Y. Times sec 2:
15 Mr 28 '71
Same. N.Y. Times Bio Ed Mr 28 '71
Slide, A. America's little sweetheart. Film 61:35 Spg '71
Bergsten, B. Mary Pickford--Comedienne. Silent Pic 10:no p#
Spg '71
Harmetz, A. Now just a voice behind a door. Classic Film
Collect 31:61 Sum '71
When silence was golden. Screen Greats 1-2:74 Sum '71
America's sweetheart is alive and well. Photop 80-3:48 S '71
Devensky, D. Mary, the golden girl. Classic Film Collect 33:
27 Win '71
Schickel, R. Doug Fairbanks: superstar of the silents. Am
Her 23:4 D '71
The inside of the bowl. Liberty 1-4:76 Spg '72
Gow, G. Mary. Films & Filming 20-3:59 D '73

PICON, MOLLY
Claxton, O. Sweetheart of Second Avenue. Cue 9-17:20 Ap 20
'40
Bio. Cur Bio Je '51

PIDGEON, WALTER
Manners, D. His sob-story. Motion Pic Classic 31:29 Ag '30
Sketch. Photop 53:69 Mr '39
Mann, M. Bank on Pidgeon. Screen Book 21-9:36 Ap '39
Smith, F. J. I'm a harmless vegetarian. Silver S 10-8:24 Je
'40
Pidgeon, W. Trust to luck. Lion R 1-4:no p# D '41
Pidgeon's rise. Lions R 1-9:no p# My '42
Pigeon-holing Pidgeon. Lions R 2-2:no p# N '42
Hopper, H. His married life. Photop 22:26 My '43
Pidgeon's 18 weeks. Lions R 3-2:no p# Ja '44
Easy does it. Lions R 3-5:no p# D '44
Second place in Companion poll of favorite stars. Womans Home
C 73:8 Je '46
Pritchett, F. Cooing over Pidgeon. Silver S 18-2:36 D '47
Pidgeon, W. Naive is the word. Silver S 18-7:36 My '48
Davis, H. B. Letter. Films In R 21-1:60 Ja '70
The love teams. Screen Greats 1-2:10 Sum '71
Nolan, J. E. Films on TV; partial TV credits. Films In R 25-
3:179 Mr '74

PIERCE, EVELYN
    Uselton, R. A.   The Wampus baby stars.   Films In R 21-2:73
    F '70

PIERCE, JIM
    Graves, H.   All American boy.   Classic Film Collect 21:58 Sum
    '68
    Ives, A.   The perfect Tarzan.   Classic Film Collect 24:17 Sum
    '69

PILON, DANIEL
    McLarty, J.   The Pilons--Canada's answer to matinee idols.
    Motion p18 Je/ F '74
    McLarty, J.   Daniel Pilon.   Motion p39 My/ Je '74

PILON, DONALD
    McLarty, J.   The Pilons--Canada's answer to matinee idols.
    Motion p18 Ja/ F '74
    McLarty, J.   Donald Pilon.   Motion p40 My/ Je '74

PINCHOT, ROSAMOND
    Mullet, M. B.   Interview.   American 105:46 Je '28
    Holey-bogey is my game.   Arts & Dec 38:40 D '32
    Ray, M. B.   Interview.   Colliers 91:26 Je 24 '33
    They stand out from the crowd.   Lit Dig 117:11 Je 30 '34

PINSENT, GORDON
    Wittgens, C.   Interview.   Motion p23 Jl/ Ag '74

PINZA, EZIO
    Opera pin up boy.   Cue 13-32:11 Ag 5 '44
    Clark, K.   Pinza crosses the Rubicon.   Cue 18-11:10 Mr 12 '49
    Pinza goes to Broadway.   Newsweek 33:85 Ap 11 '49
    Emile de Becque.   New Yorker 25:26 My 7 '49
    Why I went to South Pacific.   Etude 67:3 S '49
    Living today and living it well.   Am Mag 148:21 O '49
    Older young men.   Good House 129:10 N '49
    Life visits Pinza.   Life 27:94 D 19 '49
    Frank, S.   That wonderful guy.   Colliers 124:16 D 31 '49
    Morse, A. D.   My career as a father.   Parents 25:22 Ja '50
    Bio note.   Etude 68:11 Ja '50
    Frank, S.   That wonderful guy (abridged).   Read Dig 56:23 Mr
    '50
    Heylbut, C.   Operatic daughter.   Etude 68:21 My '50
    Enchanted evenings.   Theatre Arts 34:42 Je '50
    Pinza in Hollywood.   Life 29:159 S 18 '50
    Balling, F. D.   Why romance is ageless.   Silver S 21-2:22 D
    '50
    Pinza's picture.   Cue 20-4:15 Ja 27 '51
    West, S.   Ability and training.   Etude 71:9 F '53
    Shayon, R. L.   Bonino, starring Pinza.   Sat R 36:54 N 25 '53
    Singer as actor.   Theatre Arts 38:72 Ja '54
    Dites-moi pourquoi my child won't practice.   House & Gard

106:118 D '54
Lee, L. What the Pinzas want for their children.   Bet Home &
   Gard 34:146 Ap '56
Great basso.   Time 69:82 My 20 '57
That wonderful guy.   Newsweek 49:104 My 20 '57
Obit.   Mus Am 77:37 My '57
   Screen World 9:225 '58
Enkindling spirit.   Mus Am 77:4 Je '57
Favia-Artsay, A.   Ezio Pinza.   Hobbies 62:26 O '57
Favia-Artsay, A.   Pinza on RCA-Camden.   Hobbies 63:26 My '58
Sheean, V.   Enchanted lifetime.   Sat R 41:25 O 11 '58
Favia-Artsay, A.   Pinza in art songs.   Hobbies 65:30 Mr '60
Records.   Opera N 34:34 Ja 31 '70

PITTS, ZASU
Peltret, E.   Sketch.   Motion Pic Classic 8:38 Jl '19
Handy, T. B.   Interview.   Motion Pic 19:36 Jl '20
Gassaway, G.   Interview.   Motion Pic 24:28 Ja '23
Hall, G.   Interview.   Motion Pic 27:22 My '24
Tully, J.   Sketch.   Vanity Fair 30:62 Ag '28
Hall, G.   Sketch.   Motion Pic Classic 31:30 Ag '30
Sketch.   Photop 39:146 Ap '31
Cheatham, M.   Her divorce.   Movie Classic 2:44 Jl '32
How Sylvia renewed her beauty.   Photop 45:40 D '33
Feldkamp, F.   Zasu says it isn't so.   Screen Book 22-6:58 Ja
   '40
Charting a new course.   TV Guide 4-40:8 O 6 '56
Braff, R. E.   Letter.   Films In R 14-8:504 O '63
Obit.   Film R p30 '63/64

PLATT, ED
Obit.   N. Y. Times Bio Ed p416 Mr '74

PLATT, LOUISE
Bio note; filmog.   Movies & People 2:30 '40

PLAYTEN, ALICE
Berkvist, R.   Alice doesn't poach oysters.   N. Y. Times Bio Ed
   Je 28 '70
Awake and sing.   Time 96:41 Jl 27 '70
Kronenberger, J.   What does Alice Playten do now?   Look 34:M+
   Ag 25 '70
Commercial successes.   Newsweek 76:100 O 19 '70
Bio note.   Show 2-9:16 D '72

PLEASENCE, DONALD
Prideaux, T.   One of the ten best ever.   Life 65:77 N 1 '68
Platt, D.   Very, very Pleasence.   Harp Baz 102:126 Ap '69
Bio.   Cur Bio 30:36 Je '69
   Same.   Cur Bio Yrbk 1969:339 '70

PLESHETTE, SUZANNE
McVay, D.   The lady has talent; filmog.   Focus On F 3:53

My/Ag '70
Suzanne Pleshette.   Focus On F 4:16 S/O '70
List for a happy marriage.   Photop 82-3:62 S '72
Davidson, B.   The Suzanne Pleshette show.   TV Guide 20-51:16
   D 16 '72

PLIMPTON, SHELLEY
   Richman, R.   A girl for this season.   Show 1-1:69 Ja '70
   Actresses who are real people.   Life 68:41 My 29 '70
   Klemesrud, J.   From Hair to maturity.   N. Y. Times Bio Ed S
      13 '70
   O'Brien, G.   Interview.   Interview 2-6:24 O '71

PLUMMER, CHRISTOPHER
   McLarty, J.   Christopher Plummer.   Motion p40 My/Je '74

PODESTA, ROSSANA
   Matson, J. J.   American filmog.   Films In R 25-9:576 N '74

POITIER, SIDNEY
   Fenin, G.   The face of '63--United States.   Films & Filming 9-
      6:55 Mr '63
   Newsmakers.   Newsweek 70:46 Jl 2 '67
   Alpert, H.   Admirable Sidney.   Sat R 50:39 Jl 8 '67
   Sanders, C. L.   The man behind the superstar.   Ebony 23:173
      Ap '68
   Greenfield, J.   What's the secret of Poitier's zooming appeal?
      Good House 166:92 My '68
   Baldwin, J.   Sidney Poitier.   Look 32:50 Jl 23 '68
   New lunatics.   Newsweek 73:81 Je 23 '69
   Tornabene, L.   Walking with Poitier.   McCalls 96:52 Jl '69
   Elliston, M. H.   Bio note.   Film Comment 5-4:27 Win '69
   Sidney Poitier on Carter G. Woodson.   Negro Hist Bul 33:158 N
      '70
   Knight, A. & Alpert, H.   Sex stars of 1970.   Playboy 17-12:220
      D '70
   Goodman, G.   Poitier meets Belafonte.   Look 35:56 Ag 24 '71
   Robinson, L.   Expanding world of Poitier.   Ebony 27:101 N '71
   Hall, D. J.   Pride without prejudice; filmog.   Films & Filming
      18-3:40 D '71; 18-4:41 Ja '72
   Authur, R. A.   52 plays a year, all original, all live.   TV
      Guide 21-11:6 Mr 17 '73
   Guess who's moving on.   Films Illus 34:388 Je '74

POLACCO, MICHAEL
   Leonard Sillman's "New faces of 1971."   Cue 40-8:9 F 20 '71

POLLARD, DAPHNE
   Rodgers, J. J.   Sketch.   Green Book 14:553 S '15
   Rehearsing the audience.   Green Book 16:737 O '16

POLLARD, HARRY
   How he became a photoplayer.   Motion Pic 9:111 F '15

POLLARD, HERBERT
  McIntyre, O. O.  The man with a thousand faces.  Photop 6-1:
    103 Je '14

POLLARD, MICHAEL J.
  Miller, E.  Hail the underground hero.  Seventeen 27:151 S '68
  (He) talks about the sexy flying machine that burst from a cloud
    and other movies.  Films & Filming 15-2:10 N '68

POLLARD, SNUB
  Obit.  Screen World 14:226 '63

POLO, EDDY
  Couto, C.  Serial king; filmog.  Classic Film Collect 40:31 Fall
    '73

PONS, MARIA ANTONIETA
  Hilliard-Hughes, A.  Filmog.  Films In R 18-8:519 O '67

PORTEN, HENRY
  Obit.  Screen World 12:225 '61

PORTER, JEAN
  Spunk.  Lions R 2-4:no p# Ap '43

PORTER, ZONA
  From extra to stardom.  Motion Pic Classic 5:39 S '17

PORTMAN, ERIC
  Johns, E.  Story of.  Theatre World 44:11 N '49
  Forbes, A.  A tribute.  Plays & Players 17-5:23 F '69
  Obit.  Brit Bk Yr 1970:587 '70
    Cur Bio 31:42 F '70
    Cur Bio Yrbk 1970:468 '71
    Film R p15 '70/71
    N. Y. Times 74:92 D 22 '69
    Screen World 21:239 '70
    Time 94:65 D 19 '69

POST, GUY BATES
  Wanted: constructive criticism.  Green Book 11:616 Ap '14
  Patterson, A.  Player who can act anything.  Theatre 27:80 F
    '18
  Our national threatre audiences.  Forum 63:440 Ap '20
  Dear old university of hard knocks.  Am Mag 89:36 Je '20
  Gassaway, G.  Interview.  Motion Pic 23:74 My '22
  Carr, H.  Interview.  Classic 15:40 D '22
  Obit.  N. Y. Times p39 Ja 18 '68

POST, WILLIAM JR.
  "H" for heartbreak.  Lions R 1-5:no p# Ja '42

POSTON, TOM
  Minoff, P.  A new "Allen's alley."  Cue 26-25:11 Je 22 '57
  Poston to Knotts to Nye.  TV Guide 6-40:17 O 4 '58
  A comic goes straight.  TV Guide 8-37:17 S 10 '60

POTEL, VICTOR ALFRED
  The wooing and wedding of Slippery Sam.  Photop 7-3:127 F '15

POWELL, DAVID
  Johnson, J.  Powell, the military heart-burglar.  Photop 12-1:
    78 Je '17
  Naylor, H. S.  Interview.  Motion Pic 16:54 D '18
  Laurel, M.  Interview.  Motion Pic Classic 9:56 N '19
  Denton, F.  Powell: Chapter II.  Photop 17-1:47 D '19
  Oettinger, M. H.  Interview.  Motion Pic Classic 13:60 F '22
  Drew, L.  Interview.  Motion Pic 24:56 O '22

POWELL, DICK
  Gwin, J.  All good but the feet.  Silver S 3-12:29 O '33
  Liza.  The eligible heart-breakers.  Silver S 6-9:51 Jl '36
  Darnton, C.  In search of his age.  Silver S 7-7:32 My '37
  Mook, D.  I have no regrets.  Screen Book 20-6:32 Jl '38
  Wilson, E.  Don't get those Powells wrong.  Silver S 10-10:26
    Ag '40
  Bio note; filmog.  Movies & People 2:30 '40
  This is Dick Powell.  Lions R 3-3:no p# Ap '44
  Exit "Dimples Dick"--enter "Gumshoe Powell."  Cue 14-9:10 Mr
    3 '45
  Mook, D.  A star is reborn.  Silver S 15-7:50 My '45
  Marsh, P.  Still newlyweds.  Silver S 16-8:37 Je '46
  Powell, D.  I never had so much fun.  Silver S 20-8:30 Je '50
  Powell, D. as told to J. Hyams.  Me and the mutiny.  Cue 23-
    3:14 Ja 16 '54
  Sun, sand and history.  Films & Filming 1-6:7 Mr '55
  Here come the heroes.  TV Guide 4-37:28 S 15 '56
  Obit.  Film R p33 '63/64
  The love teams.  Screen Greats 1-2:10 Sum '71
  Corneau, E.  The crooner who turned tough guy.  Classic Film
    Collect 36:41 Fall '72

POWELL, ELEANOR
  Sketch.  Vanity Fair 45:23 O '35
  Reeves, M. W.  Her transformation.  Photop 48:70 D '35
  Baldwin, J. R.  Interview.  Motion Pic 50:34 Ja '36
  Craig, C.  Interview.  Movie Classic 9:40 Ja '36
  Surmelian, L.  Story of.  Motion Pic 52:30 O '36
  The essential qualifications for dancing.  Movie Classic 11:36 D
    '36
  Russell, B.  Her opinion of Robert Taylor.  Motion Pic 53:40
    Mr '37
  Williams, W.  How it's done.  Silver S 7-9:24 Jl '37
  Shaffer, R.  Looking down from "Heaven."  Screen Book 19-2:
    32 S '37

Hilliard, M.   The life story of Eleanor Powell.   Screen Book
   19-3:78 O '37
Tearle, D.   No wonder she's happy.   Silver S 9-10:26 Ag '39
Jacobs, M.   Will Powell and Astaire click?   Screen Book 22-5:
   87 D '39
Bio note; filmog.   Movies & People 2:31 '40
Powell, E.   Dancing's my job.   Lions R 1-1:no p# S '41
The girl on the cover.   Cue 11-20:1 My 16 '42
Eleanor Powell, choreographer.   Lions R 1-9:no p# My '42
The type of man she likes.   Photop 22:51 Ap '43
Traditional trouper.   Lions R 3-1:no p# S '43
Christening of her baby.   Photop 27:66 Jl '45
Holland, J.   He drives his wife crazy.   Silver S 21-5:42 Mr '51
Bruce, J.   The truth about the Glenn Fords.   Silver S 23-4:36
   F '53
Glenn Ford's son gets married.   Photop 79-3:48 Mr '71
Summers, M.   Interview; filmog.   Filmograph 3-1:22 '72
Shipley, G.   Some notes on some of film's dancers.   Filmograph
   3-1:15 '72
Our cover girl.   Liberty 1-14:64 Fall '74
Eleanor Powell talking to John Kobal.   Focus On F 19:23 Aut '74

POWELL, JANE
Cosmop's citation for the best supporting role of the month.
   Cosmop 121:66 S '46
Pasternak, J.   A girl just like you.   Silver S 18-5:36 Mr '48
Arnold, M.   Story of.   Photop 34:60 D '48
Hall, G.   Born so-o-o lucky.   Silver S 19-7:29 My '49
Sketch.   Photop 36:11 Jl '49
Powell, J.   Meet Liz--the bride.   Silver S 20-8:24 Je '50
Marsh, P.   Now I've got it.   Silver S 22-7:22 My '52
Holland, J.   Has Hollywood really thrown Jane?   Silver S 23-9:
   30 Jl '53
Bruce, J.   No looking back for Janie.   Silver S 24-9:26 Jl '54

POWELL, ROBERT
McAsh, I.   Wanted: dead or alive.   Films Illus 2-13:30 Jl '72
Castell, D.   Interview.   Films Illus 3-32:308 Ap '74

POWELL, WILLIAM
Hall, G.   Interview.   Motion Pic Classic 28:37 O '28
Walker, H. L.   Interview.   Motion Pic 39:55 Ap '30
Ramsey, W.   Interview.   Motion Pic Classic 31:38 Ag '30
His work in talking pictures.   Ill Lon N 177:452 S 13 '30
Biery, R.   Sketch.   Photop 40:49 Je '31
Hall, G.   Sketch.   Motion Pic Classic 33:54 Jl '31
Standish, J.   His marriage to Carole Lombard.   Movie Classic
   1:37 S '31
Moffitt, C. F.   Censorship for interviews Hollywood's latest wild
   idea...   Cinema Dig 2-5:9 Ja 9 '33
Wilson, E.   That funny divorce.   Silver S 4-6:18 Ap '34
Rankin, R.   Interview.   Photop 46:54 S '34
Lee, S.   Interview.   Motion Pic 49:30 Je '35

Lee, S.  Interview.  Motion Pic 50:32 S '35
Tully, J.  His popularity explained.  Movie Classic 9:26 N '35
Zeitlin, I.  Interview.  Motion Pic 50:28 Ja '36
Ulman, W. A. Jr.  Success of pictures with Myrna Loy.  Movie
    Classic 10:40 Mr '36
Lang, H.  Sketch.  Motion Pic 52:33 N '36
Hartley, K.  His friendly help to actresses.  Movie Classic 11:
    24 Ja '37
Craig, C.  Work of.  Motion Pic 53:44 F '37
Surmelian, L.  Interview.  Motion Pic 54:28 Ag '37
Hartley, K.  His appreciation of beautiful women.  Motion Pic
    51:30 Ap '36
Myrna Loy and William Powell.  Visages 26:entire issue Ag '38
His third marriage.  Time 35:59 Ja 15 '40
Mulvey, K.  Sketch.  Womans Home C 67:5 Ja '40
Bio note; filmog.  Movies & People 2:31 '40
Powell, W.  It isn't funny to me.  Lions R 1-3:no p# N '41
Hall, G.  I'll tell you why I'm happy.  Silver S 12-3:26 Ja '42
I, William Powell, deny...  Lions R 1-11/ 12:no p# Jl/ Ag '42
But never dull.  Lions R 3-2:no p# Ja '44
The people's choice.  Lions R 4-1:no p# F '45
Letter from Liza.  Silver S 18-2:27 D '47
Powell hooks on to underwater Lorelei.  Cue 17-29:10 Jl 17 '48
Parsons, L. O.  Cosmop's citation for the best performance of
    month.  Cosmop 125:12 S '48
Doing it.  Newsweek 77:98 Ap 12 '71
The love teams.  Screen Greats 1-2:10 Sum '71
Corneau, E. A.  Hollywood's polish gentleman.  Classic Film
    Collect 44:31 Fall '74

POWER, TYRONE SR.
    Acting on the sidewalk; interview.  Photop 7-5:87 Ap '15

POWER, TYRONE
    Lane, V. T.  Story of.  Motion Pic 52:44 Ja '37
    Walsh, W. C.  Story of.  Movie Classic 11:50 Ja '37
    Sketch.  Photop 51:78 Ap '37
    Lang, H.  Story of.  Motion Pic 53:34 My '37
    Ludlam, H. F.  A chip off the old block.  Silver S 7-8:24 Je
        '37
    Camp, D.  Story of.  Motion Pic 54:34 O '37
    Wilson, E.  Projections.  Silver S 8-3:18 Ja '38
    Lee, S.  The first 24 years are the hardest.  Screen Book 20-
        2:40 Mr '38; 20-3:33 Ap '38
    Evans, E.  His Manhattan hideout.  Screen Book 21-5:20 D '38
    Maddox, B.  His escapes from Hollywood.  Screen Book 21-7:38
        F '39
    McFee, F.  A "right" guy in wrong roles.  Screen Book 21-10:
        22 My '39
    Crulman, E.  Balancing the books on him.  Screen Book 22-1:56
        Ag '39
    Wilson, E.  Family secrets about him.  Silver S 10-1:22 N '39
    Bio note; filmog.  Movies & People 2:31 '40

Wilson, E.  They knew him when--and still do.  Silver S 11-5:
   34 Mr '41
Mook, D.  I'm through being a sucker.  Silver S 12-3:38 Ja '42
Maddox, B.  A new Ty for old.  Silver S 16-9:40 Jl '46
My luckiest day.  Cosmop 121:100 S '46
Movie star on location in Italy.  Cue 17-50:19 D 11 '48
MacDonald, E.  Truly a love story.  Silver S 19-7:30 My '49
Hendrix, W.  A man called Power.  Silver S 19-9:24 Jl '49
Pritchett, F.  Love story of the stars.  Silver S 20-5:26 Mr '50
Power, Mrs. T.  So it is with Ty and me.  Silver S 21-1:22 N
   '50
Balling, F. D.  Happy parents at last.  Silver S 22-7:42 My '52
MacDonald, E.  Exploded those Ty-Linda rumors.  Silver S 23-
   10:40 Ag '53
Gibson, M.  Power's progress.  Cue 24-4:13 Ja 29 '55
Obit.  Film R p10 '59/60
Tall, dark and handsome.  Screen Greats 1-2:24 Sum '71
McElwee, J.  The delightful duo: Darnell and Power.  Classic
   Film Collect 41:32 Win '73
Price, B.  The greatness of Tyrone Power.  Classic F Collect
   42:29 Spg '74

POWERS, LEONA
   Obit.  N. Y. Times p31 Ja 10 '70

POWERS, STEPHANIE
   Lewis, R. W.  The true-life adventures of...  TV Guide 14-58:
      22 D 31 '66

POWERS, TOM
   Obit.  Screen World 7:226 '56

PRANGE, LAURIE
   Finnigan, J.  So there was Laurie Prange sitting in the audience.
      TV Guide 18-38:43 S 19 '70

PREISSER, JUNE
   Hamilton, S.  Sketch.  Photop 18:59 Ja '41
   Where is June Preisser?  Movie Dig 2-1:66 Ja '73

PREMINGER, MARION MILL
   When you are doing good you are not making a sacrifice.  Seven-
      teen 21:98 D '62
   Obit.  N. Y. Times p50 Ap 19 '72
      Newsweek 79:85 My 1 '72

PRENTISS, ANN
   I'm the beady-eyed sister.  TV Guide 15-24:26 Je 17 '67

PRENTISS, PAULA
   Schickel, R.  1962: the year of Paula Prentiss.  Show 2-1:52
      Ja '62
   Person of promise.  Films & Filming 8-10:54 Jl '62

Rising stars.  Film R p32 '62/63
Higgins, R.  The great crazy love affair of him and her.  TV
    Guide 15-40:21 O 7 '67
Amory, C.  Trade winds.  Sat R 52:8 Jl 26 '69
Lear, M. W.  Dick Benjamin and Paula Prentiss:  to love, honor
    and analyze.  Redbook 134:55 Ja '70
Robbins, F.  Tape to type; interview.  Photop 78-4:23 O '70
MacDonough, S.  The coming of age of Paula and Richard.
    Show 24:18 Je '71
Burke, T.  Alexander Portnoy--this is your wife.  N. Y. Times
    Bio Ed D 5 '71
How I find peace of mind.  Mod Screen 66-9:62 S '72
Photoplay forum.  Photop 86-1:34 Jl '74

PRESCOTT, VIVIAN
    Smith, R. E.  Vivacious Vivian.  Photop 4-4:37 S '13

PRESLE, MICHELINE
    Bio note.  Unifrance 23:10 F '53

PRESLEY, ELVIS
    Elvis Presley.  TV Guide 4-36:5 S 8; 4-38:17 S 22; 4-39:21 S
        29 '56
    Rising stars.  Film R p28 '58/59
    Lyons, D.  Elvis Presley (special Presley issue).  Interview 1-
        12:3 n. d.
    Ames, M.  The product is sex.  Hi Fi 19:104 Ap '69
    Return of the pelvis.  Newsweek 74:83 Ag 11 '69
    Willis, E.  Rock, etc.  New Yorker 45:76 Ag 30 '69
    Hentoff, M.  Absolutely free.  Harper 239:28 N '69
    Goldman, A.  Elvis at Las Vegas.  Life 68:17 Mr 20 '70
    Kaiser, R. B.  The rediscovery of Elvis.  N. Y. Times Mag
        p28 O 11 '70
    Same.  N. Y. Times Bio Ed O 11 '70
    Sonderling, E.  Reply to above with rejoinder.  N. Y. Times
        Mag p111 N 1 '70
    Elvis and Priscilla flee to new home.  Photop 79-3:76 Mr '71
    Hopkins, J.  The hidden life of Elvis Presley.  Look 35-9:33
        My 4 '71
    Hopkins, J.  The five-million dollar years.  Look 35-10:41 My
        18 '71
    I never went to bed with that girl.  Photop 79-5:90 My '71
    Filmog.  Films Illus 1-2:38 Ag '71
    How Elvis' child brought God back into his home.  Photop 80-3:
        31 S '71
    Presleys answer the Elvis rumors.  Photop 81-3:53 Mr '72
    Why I became a narcotics agent.  Photop 81-5:71 My '72
    Elvis aeternus.  Time 99:49 Je 19 '72
    Elvis!  David!  New Yorker 48:28 Je 24 '72
    Why I lost him to Priscilla.  Photop 81-6:55 Je '72
    Willis, E.  Rock, etc.  New Yorker 48:66 Jl 1 '72
    People are talking about.  Vogue 160:70 Ag 1 '72
    Elvis' love for a dying child.  Photop 82-2:76 Ag '72

Scoppa, B. Elvis is back. Sr Schol 101:27 S 25 '72
Is it too late for Elvis to win Pris back. Mod Screen 66-10:45
  O '72
How do you divide a little girl in half? Mod Screen 66-11:58 N
  '72
Ross, M. T. Elvis soars Firebird. Movie Dig 1-6:12 N '72
Why I had to divorce. Photop 82-5:72 N '72
Edwards, H. Merchandising of Elvis. Hi Fi 22:74 N '72
Meltzer, R. The films of Elvis Presley. Take One 4-2:15 N/D
  '72
Home town girl. Photop 82-6:50 D '72
Love gift. Photop 83-1:22 Ja '73
Elvis never made me feel like a woman. Mod Screen 67-2:46 F
  '73
Elvis cries in public. Photop 83-5:30 My '73
Elvis robbed and cheated me. Photop 84-3:56 S '73
Priscilla asked. I refused to take her back. Photop 84-4:36 O
  '73
I can't breathe. Photop 85-1:10 Ja '74
Elvis' illness. Photop 85-2:47 F '74
Interview. Photop 85-5:38 My '74
Elvis and Priscilla. Photop 86-1:48 Jl '74
Happy 20th anniversary. Photop 86-5:32 N '74
York, C. Gives ring to new girl. Photop 86-6:4 D '74

PRESNELL, HARVE
Rising stars. Film R p53 '65/66

PRESTON, ROBERT
Rhea, M. Sketch. Photop 53:67 S '39
Mook, D. Typhoon is something to blow about. Silver S 10-7:
  42 My '40
Wood, V. I was an awful fool. Silver S 12-6:36 Ap '42
Letter to his wife. Photop 27:58 O '45
Parsons, L. O. Cosmop's citation for best performance of
  month. Cosmop 122:59 F '47
Preston, C. C. The man I married. Silver S 18-8:40 Je '48
Preston, C. C. The movies and I. Films In R 8-7:334 Ag/S
  '57

PRESTON, WAYDE
This time the cowboy bit the dust. TV Guide 6-26:26 Je 28 '58

PRETTY, ARLINE
Arline Pretty was born that way. Photop 12-1:74 Je '17
Montanye, L. Sketch. Motion Pic Classic 9:60 N '19

PREVOST, MARIE
Carr, H. Sketch. Motion Pic 17:49 My '19
Hall, G. Interview. Motion Pic 22:68 D '21
Goldbeck, W. Interview. Motion Pic Classic 14:16 Mr '22
Tully, J. Sketch. Motion Pic Classic 21:22 Mr '25
Wooldridge, D. Sketch. Motion Pic Classic 26:38 N '27

Donnell, D.   Marie and Ken.   Motion Pic Classic 28:26 O '28
Biery, R.   Interview.   Motion Pic 37:44 F '29
Manners, D.   Sketch.   Motion Pic 41:58 Mr '31
Bodeen, D.   Marie Prevost; filmog.   Focus On F 19:35 Aut '74

PRICE, ALAN
   d'Arcy, S.   Price treads new ground.   Films Illus 4-38:54 O '74
   Rensin, D.   Alan Price.   Viva 2-2:38 N '74

PRICE, DENNIS
   Cowie, P.   The face of '63--Great Britain.   Films & Filming 9-
      5:19 F '63
   Obit.   Films & Filming 20-3:81 D '73
      N. Y.   Times Bio Ed p1707 O '73
      Screen World p238 '74
   Partial filmog.   Films & Filming 21-2:56 N '74

PRICE, VINCENT
   Hamilton, S.   Sketch.   Photop 54:16 Ja '40
   Parsons, L. O.   Cosmop's citation for the best performance of
      month.   Cosmop 120:70 My '46
   Pritchett, F.   You never can tell.   Silver S 17-6:55 Ap '47
   In TV or art, this Price is right.   TV Guide 5-28:17 Jl 13 '57
   Zunser, J.   The "complete man."   Cue 29-34:10 Ag 20 '60
   Nolan, J. E.   The Price is right.   Films In R 15-3:189 Mr '64
   Letters.   Films In R 20-6:384 Je/Jl '69
   Austen, D.   Black cats and cobwebs; interview.   Films & Film-
      ing 15-11:52 Ag '69
   Last of the ghouls.   Newsweek 77:105 Je 14 '71
   Price, V.   The lure and lore of Indian Art.   American Way 4-6:
      12 Je '71
   McAsh, I.   The merchant of menace; filmog.   Films Illus 1-8:7
      F '72
   Prive, V.   The movie performance I will always remember.
      Movie Dig 1-2:100 Mr '72
   Partial filmog.   Films Illus 2-13:10 Jl '72
   Knight, C. & Nicholson, P.   On the set of Phibes II.   Cine-
      fantastique 2-2:38 Sum '72
   Cornea, E. N.   Menace to madcap.   Classic Film Collect 39:20
      Sum '73
   Gearhart, B.   A chat with Vincent Price.   Black Oracle 7:20
      Fall '73
   McAsh, I.   Cooking the books.   Films Illus 3-28:134 O '73

PRIEST, PAT
   Mother has long green calling cards.   TV Guide 13-13:35 Mr 27
      '65
   Laurence, M.   Premiere.   US Camera 30:56 O '67

PRIMUS, BARRY
   Stasio, M.   The stars of tomorrow on stage today.   Cue 38-9:9
      Mr 1 '69

PRINCE, WILLIAM
Cue says watch.  Cue 10-42:3 O 18 '41

PRINCIPAL, VICTORIA
Meet Desi's new girl.  Photop 84-3:49 S '73

PRINE, ANDREW
Andrew Prine; photos.  Viva 1-8:68 My '74

PRINGLE, AILEEN
Home of.  Classic 19:36 Ag '24
de Revere, F. V.  Analysis of her face.  Motion Pic 29:71 Je
'25
Dugan, P. C.  Sketch.  Motion Pic Classic 21:38 Je '25
York, C.  Sketch.  Photop 28:74 N '25
Tildesley, A. L.  Sketch.  Motion Pic Classic 22:32 Ja '26
Robinson, S.  Interview.  Motion Pic 31:31 My '26
York, C.  Sketch.  Photop 31:88 D '26
Goldbeck, E.  Sketch.  Motion Pic 28:43 N '28
Hall, G.  Confessions.  Motion Pic Classic 28:16 F '29
Donnell, D.  Her divorce.  Movie Classic 2:30 Je '32
Hoaglin, J. L.  Down memory lane.  Hollywood Stu 6-8:30 D
'71

PRINZ, FREDDIE
Diamond, S. J.  NBC's 'Chico' is a Prinz charming.  People 2-
12:36 S 16 '74

PRINZ, ROSEMARY
Can she break one of the soap bubbles?  TV Guide 11-25:14 Je
22 '63

PRIOR, HERBERT
Gaddis, P.  Her hero--and his heroine.  Photop 6-1:58 Je '14
How he became a photoplayer.  Motion Pic 9:116 Mr '15
Gaddis, P.  Interview.  Motion Pic 9:97 Ap '15

PRITCHETT, JAMES
Efron, E.  Dr. Matt is a stuffed shirt.  TV Guide 15-42:30 O
21 '67

PRITCHETT, PAULA
New-model model.  Playboy 17-12:135 D '70
The nymph from Kadar's "Adrift".  Show 2-8:51 O '71
Paula Pritchett.  Playboy 19-7:143 Jl '72

PRIVAL, LUCIEN
Irwin, M.  Sketch.  Motion Pic Classic 28:55 S '28

PROVINE, DOROTHY
Go north young lady.  TV Guide 7-39:25 S 26 '59
TV's newest tiger.  TV Guide 8-53:18 D 31 '60
Botto, L.  Interview.  Look 35:70 S 7 '71

PROVOST, JON
    A new lad for Lassie.  TV Guide 5-30:8 Jl 27 '57

PROWSE, JULIET
    Rising stars.  Film R p32 '61/62
    Veljkovic, M.  South Africa's diamond.  Dance 45:24 O '71

PRUD'HOMME, CAMERON
    Obit.  N. Y.  Times p40 N 29 '67

PRYOR, RICHARD
    Beyond laughter.  Ebony 22:87 S '67

PRYOR, ROGER
    Goldbeck, E.  Sketch.  Motion Pic 48:39 D '34

PUCCIO, MAE
    Obit.  N. Y.  Times p47 Ap 17 '69

PUGLIA, FRANK
    McClure, A.  The unsung heroes.  Film Fan Mo 87:10 S '68

PULLY, B. S.
    Obit.  N. Y.  Times p32 Ja 8 '72
        Same.  N. Y.  Times Bio Ed Ja 8 '72
        Newsweek 79:51 Ja 17 '72

PUNSLEY, BERNARD
    How tough are the Dead End Kids?  Screen Book 21-6:28 Ja '39

PURCELL, DICK
    Whitehead, H.  Sketch.  Motion Pic 54:17 S '37

PURCELL, IRENE
    Screen stars or just girls.  Silver S 1-12:24 O '31
    Obit.  Classic Film Collect 37:59 Win '72

PURCELL, LEE
    Debut.  Show 1-13:56 S 17 '70

PURDOM, EDMUND
    Silver lining star.  Cue 23-20:13 My 15 '54

PURNELL, LOUISE
    Cox, F.  Only when they larf.  Plays & Players 16-6:54 Mr '69

PURVIANCE, EDNA
    Naylor, H. S.  Interview.  Motion Pic 15:75 Ap '18
    Cheatham, M.  Interview.  Motion Pic Classic 9:54 N '19
    Stuart, C.  Interview.  Motion Pic 23:28 F '22
    Cheatham, M.  Sketch.  Motion Pic Classic 14:20 Ag '22

PUTHLI, ASHA
  Colaciello, R.  Asha Puthli; Bombay bombshell.  Interview 22:17
    Je '72
  Tru, P.  Interview.  Interview 4-7:14 Jl '74

PUTTNAM, DAVID
  Castell, D.  David and Goliath.  Films Illus 4-40:146 D '74

PYLE, DENVER
  The man who gunned down Bonnie and Clyde.  TV Guide 17-18:11
    F 22 '69

PYNE, NATASHA
  Actress or athlete?  Films Illus 3-29:196 N '73

QUAID, RANDY
  McLarty, J.  A view of us.  Motion p58 Jl/Ag '74

QUALEN, JOHN
  Peacock, T.  Partial filmog.  Films In R 19-6:387 Je/Jl '68

QUARRY, ROBERT
  The other vampires and the most promising newcomer:  Count
    Yorga.  Films Illus 1-9:21 Mr '72
  Filmog.  Films & Filming 18-9:16 Je '72
  Polwort, S.  Robert Quarry.  Cinefantastique 2-1:5 Spg '72
  Knight, C. & Nicholson, P.  On the set of Phibes II.  Cine-
    fantastique 2-2:38 Sum '72

QUARTARO, NENA
  Gilmore, F.  Sketch.  Motion Pic Classic 26:23 F '28
  Biery, R.  Sketch.  Photop 33:71 F '28

QUARTERMAINE, LEON
  Obit.  Brit Bk Yr 1968:597 '68

QUAYLE,* ANNA
  Hammel, F.  The lady is a clown.  Cue 31-42:10 O 20 '62
  *Incorrectly spelled Quale in 1st volume.

QUAYLE,* ANTHONY
  Director at Stratford.  Ill Lon N 212:688 Je 12 '48
  Director at Stratford.  World R Ag '48
  His production of Macbeth.  World R 5:61 Jl '49
  Lewis, E.  Virtuoso from England.  Cue 25-5:14 F 4 '56
  In the words of Anthony Quayle.  Cue 39-51:21 D 19 '70
  Berkvist, R.  Detective stories? Never read 'em.  N.Y. Times
    sec 2:15 Mr 14 '71
  Same.  N.Y. Times Bio Ed Mr 14 '71
  Drake, R.  Finally I had become a man.  TV Guide 19-14:20 Ap
    3 '71

Bio.   Cur Bio 32:27 D '71
   Same.   Cur Bio Yrbk 1971:333 '72
*Incorrectly spelled Quale in 1st volume.

QUIGLEY, JUANITA
   Sketch.   Photop 47:92 Mr '35

QUILLEY, DENIS
   Tierney, M.   Interview.   Plays & Players 19-8:18 My '72

QUINE, DON
   Whitney, D.   You've got to play the game.   TV Guide 15-42:19
   O 21 '67

QUINE, RICHARD
   Two babes from Broadway.   Lions R 1-5:no p# Ja '42
   Stars of tomorrow.   Lions R 1-11/12:no p# Jl/Ag '42

QUINLAN, EDDIE
   Manners, D.   Sketch.   Motion Pic 37:74 Mr '29

QUINN, ANTHONY
   Hamilton, S.   Sketch.   Photop 18:58 Ja '41
   O'Leary, D.   Quixotic Mr. Quinn.   Silver S 16-12:42 O '46
   Zunser, J.   I compete with myself.   Cue 26-41:13 O 12 '57
   Personality of the month.   Films & Filming 4-10:5 Jl '58
   Fenin, G.   The face of '63--United States.   Films & Filming
   9-6:55 Mr '63
   Tornabene, L.   Walking with Quinn; interview.   McCalls 96:60
   Mr '69
   Simons, M.   Loving world of Anthony Quinn.   Look 33:48 Ap 1
   '69
   Mexican-Americans:  the nation's best kept secret?   Sr Schol
   94:12 Ap 18 '69
   Bean, R.   Competing with myself; interview.   Films & Filming
   16-4:6 F '70
   Klemesrud, J.   From Zapata to Zorba to the Pope to...?   N.Y.
   Times Bio Ed S 20 '70
   Itria, H.   The real Anthony Quinn.   Girl Talk 2-3:31 Ap '71
   My wife practices witchcraft.   Photop 80-4:74 O '71
   Tony Quinn talks about the divorce.   Mod Screen 66-3:22 Mr '72
   Quinn on Quinn.   TV New York 1-2:7 N '72
   Madness is a must.   Films Illus 2-24:18 Je '73
   Castell, D.   The mighty Quinn.   Films Illus 3-33:345 My '74
   Elley, D.   Bio sketch; filmog.   Focus On F 8:13 n. d.

QUINN, CARMEL
   'Tis an actress she'll be.   TV Guide 8-22:20 My 28 '60

QUINN, LOUIS
   From gags to rags.   TV Guide 8-33:17 Ag 13 '60

QUO, BEULAH
    Raddatz, L.    No. 1 son is now Master Po.    TV Guide 21-25:27
        Je 23 '73


RABAL, FRANCISCO
    Cobos, J.    The face of '63--Spain.    Films & Filming 10-1:39 O
        '63

RACIMO, VICKI
    Pearsall, A.    How some of the magic went out of Stanley Sweet-
        heart's garden.    Show 1-3:69 Mr '70

RAE, ISABEL
    Sketch.    Motion Pic 9:93 Jl '15

RAE, MELBA
    Obit.    N. Y. Times p22 Ja 1 '72

RAFFERTY, CHIPS
    Collier, C.    Chips Rafferty.    Films In R 22-9:584 N '71
    Obit.    Film R p13 '71/72
        N. Y. Times Bio Ed My 29 '71
        Screen World 23:239 '72

RAFFERTY, FRANCES
    Stars of tomorrow.    Lions R 1-11/12:no p# Jl/Ag '42
    Look out--here comes Rafferty.    Lions R 3-1:no p# S '43
    Chopsticks Rafferty.    Lions R 3-4:no p# Jl '44
    Pity poor granny.    Lions R 3-4(sup):no p# Jl '44
    Franchey, J. R.    Orchids to orchids.    Silver S 14-10:24 Ag '44
    Ambition plus.    Lions R 3-5:no p# D '44

RAFFERTY, JOHN GOFFAGE
    Obit.    N. Y. Times p36 My 29 '71

RAFT, GEORGE
    Donaldson, R.    Interview.    Movie Classic 2:41 Je '32
    March, G.    George Raft.    Silver S 2-10:26 Ag '32
    Sketch.    Motion Pic 44:42 S '32
    Manners, D.    Sketch.    Motion Pic 44:47 O '32
    Walker, H. L.    Sketch.    Movie Classic 3:44 N '32
    Lieber, E.    Sketch.    Photop 43:40 D '32
    Cheasley, C. W.    His numberscope.    Movie Classic 3:51 D '32
    Manners, D.    Hollywood's opinion of him.    Movie Classic 3:37
        Ja '33
    Keats, P.    Kings in Hollywood.    Silver S 3-4:22 F '33
    Clemens, J.    Greatest idol since Valentino.    Movie Classic 4:18
        Ap '33
    Fidler, J.    Answers twenty questions.    Movie Classic 4:22 My
        '33
    Mosley, L. O.    Interview.    Motion Pic 45:49 My '33

Pryor, N.   How he rates with men.   Movie Classic 4:30 Jl '33
Hall, H.   The mystery of his "bodyguard."   Movie Classic 4:44
   Jl '33
Lynn, H.   How he makes love.   Photop 44:31 Ag '33
Lee, S.   Interview.   Motion Pic 46:49 O '33
Biery, R.   Interview.   Movie Classic 5:23 D '33
Lee, S.   Interview.   Motion Pic 47:54 F '34
Goldbeck, E.   Interview.   Movie Classic 6:28 Ap '34
Cheatham, R.   Raft.   Silver S 4-8:28 Je '34
Lee, S.   His story of his marriage.   Movie Classic 6:34 Je '34
Fletcher, J.   Interview.   Movie Classic 10:41 Ap '36
Lang, H.   Story of.   Motion Pic 53:29 Jl '37
Churchill, E.   His life story.   Photop 52:20 Ja '38 & following
   issue.
Ormiston, R.   Story of.   Photop 54:12 Ja '40
McIllwain, R.   George gives his side of it--and how.   Silver S
   10-4:48 F '40
Wilson, E.   Will Norma marry George?   Silver S 10-5:38 Mr
   '40
Bio note; filmog.   Movies & People 2:31 '40
His quarrel with E. G. Robinson.   Life 10:40 My 12 '41
Kilgallen, D.   Sketch.   Photop 23:21 Je '43
Hendricks, H.   George's side of it.   Silver S 13-9:26 Jl '43
Minoff, P.   Another crime series, another Hollywood lead.   Cue
   22-12:7 Mr 21 '53
Raft, G.   You've got to be tough in Hollywood.   Films & Filming
   8-10:15 Jl '62
When hoods were heroes.   Screen Greats 1-2:34 Sum '71
Even the cops believed he was a gangster.   Photop 85-1:42 Ja
   '74
Raft, G.   Romantic memories.   Viva 1-10:6 Jl '74

RAGLAND, "RAGS"
   A "confounded guy."   Lions R 2-4:no p# Ap '43
   Born to be funny.   Lions R 3-1:no p# S '43

RAIMU
   Raimu.   Visages 30:entire issue D '38

RAIN, JEREMY
   Fremont, V. & O'Brien, G.   Interview.   Interview 30:12 Mr '73

RAINBEAUX
   Rainbeaux.   Show 3-9:43 D '73

RAINER, LUISE
   Appreciation of acting in Escapade.   Lit Dig 120:24 Jl 20 '35
   Norden, H. B.   Sketch.   Vanity Fair 45:43 S '35
   Ergenbright, E. L.   Sketch.   Movie Classic 9:33 N '35
   Lanier, J.   Her rise to fame.   Motion Pic 51:46 My '36
   Samuels, L.   The sparkling Viennese.   Silver S 6-8:51 Je '36
   Crowley, G.   A fine emotional actress.   Motion Pic 52:37 S '36
   Awarded prize for best acting.   Time 29:33 Mr 15 '37

Hartley, K.   Her quest for knowledge.   Motion Pic 53:40 My '37
Service, F.   Story of.   Motion Pic 54:32 D '37
Hilliard, M.   The truth about Luise Rainer.   Screen Book 19-6:
  31 Ja '38
Winner of 1937 acting award.   Newsweek 11:20 Mr 21 '38
Vandour, C.   No glamour, please.   Silver S 8-9:23 Jl '38
Deane, C.   Why she made peace with Hollywood.   Screen Book
  21:42 Ag '38
Bio note; filmog.   Movies & People 2:32 '40
Der Krauts.   Screen Greats 1-2:58 Sum '71

RAINES, ELLA
Meet the cover(all) girls.   Lions R 3-2:no p# Ja '44
Franchey, J. R.   R. is for Raines--also remarkable.   Silver S
  15-3:46 Ja '45
Wilson, E.   I say what I think.   Silver S 15-11:46 S '45
If I had one wish.   Photop 29:60 O '46
Vallee, W. L.   New era for Ella.   Silver S 17-4:35 F '47
Sketch.   Life 23:22 Ag 11 '47

RAINS, CLAUDE
Who is Claude Rains?   Stage 9-8:30 My '32
Work of in The man who reclaimed his head.   Stage 10:6 O '32
Williams, W.   Sketch.   Movie Classic 5:60 D '33
Sketch.   Photop 45:77 Ap '34
Hall, H.   Interview.   Motion Pic 49:26 Mr '35
Williams, W.   But not so wicked.   Silver S 7-12:28 D '37
Roberts, K.   Story of.   Colliers 102:13 N 19 '38
Hamilton, S.   Sketch.   Photop 54:30 Jl '40
Service, F.   A villain's love story.   Silver S 11-2:42 D '40
Bio note; filmog.   Movies & People 2:32 '40
Hall, G.   He is frightened.   Silver S 18-2:44 D '47
Parsons, L. O.   Cosmop's citation for best supporting perform-
  ance of month.   Cosmop 127:13 S '49
Claude Rains cops a Tony.   Cue 20-13:13 Mr 31 '51
Obit.   Brit Bk Yr 1968:597 '68
  Cur Bio Yrbk 1967:481 '68
Note; partial filmog.   Films & Filming 19-9:66 Je '73

RAISCH, BILL
Catching up with the one-armed man.   TV Guide 13-15:10 Ap 10
  '65

RAITT, JOHN
Whitcomb, J.   Man with a big voice.   Cosmop 143:16 S '57
He wants to get out of his white tie.   TV Guide 6-28:17 Jl 12
  '58
RALL, TOMMY
Fletcher, F.   Triple-threat man.   Cue 30-43:8 O 28 '61
Filmog.   Films & Filming 19-18:56 S '73

RALSTON, ESTHER
St. Johns, I.   Sketch.   Photop 27:62 Ap '25

Brian, M.  Sketch.  Motion Pic 29:37 Jl '25
Sketch.  Photop 28:76 O '25
White, C.  Sketch.  Motion Pic Classic 22:24 D '25
Waterbury, R.  Her love story.  Photop 30:62 O '26
Pryor, N.  Sketch.  Motion Pic 35:58 Ap '28
Hall, G.  Sketch.  Motion Pic 38:58 S '29
Service, F.  Sketch.  Motion Pic 41:55 Ap '31
Service, F.  What it cost to have her baby.  Movie Classic 1:35
   D '31
Dowling, M.  Her comeback.  Movie Classic 6:59 Je '34
Schwartz, W.  Esther Ralston; filmog.  Films In R 20-10:647 D
   '69
Pack, A. C.  Partial filmog.  Films In R 21-2:124 F '70
Here is Esther Ralston.  Movie Dig 2-1:67 Ja '73
Rubin, J.  Interview.  Classic Film Collect 42:10 Win '73

RALSTON, JOBYNA
Howe, H.  Interview.  Photop 26:52 Ag '24
Tildesley, A. L.  Sketch.  Motion Pic Classic 23:38 My '26
Fidler, J. M.  Interview.  Motion Pic Classic 25:54 Ap '27
Manners, D.  Interview.  Motion Pic 34:25 Ag '27
Prosser, C. S.  Sketch.  Photop 33:58 Ap '28
Manners, D.  Interview.  Motion Pic Classic 28:42 S '28
Albert, K.  One star is enough.  Photop 35-5:72 Ap '29
Whitaker, A.  Home of.  Photop 36:62 O '29
Manners, D.  Interview.  Motion Pic 41:66 My '31
Her married life.  Movie Classic 4:52 Ap '33
Uselton, R. A.  The Wampus baby stars.  Films In R 21-2:73
   F '70

RALSTON, VERA HRUBA
Burt, T.  Skater and actress.  Silver S 14-6:26 Ap '44

RAMATI, DIDI
Global girl.  TV Guide 6-16:20 Ap 19 '58

RAMBEAU, MARJORIE
Sketch.  N. Y. Dram Ja 29 '16
Gordon, K.  Home life of.  Motion Pic Classic 4:39 Ap '17
Sherwood, C. B.  Interview.  Motion Pic Classic 7:20 F '19
Sketch.  Theatre 43:32 Je '26
Krutch, J. W.  Her acting.  Nation 123:302 S 29 '26
Manners, D.  Sketch.  Motion Pic Classic 33:58 Mr '31
Jordan, A.  She conquered defeat.  Silver S 1-7:50 My '31
Service, F.  Sketch.  Motion Pic Classic 32:63 Ag '31
Spensley, D.  Sketch.  Movie Classic 1:32 F '32
Hamilton, S.  Sketch.  Photop 54:46 D '40
Obit.  Classic Film Collect (reprint N. Y. Times) 28:ex p3 Fall
   '70
   Film R p13 '71/72
   N. Y. Times p43 Jl 8 '70
   Same.  N. Y. Times Bio Ed Jl 8 '70
   Screen World 22:239 '71
   Time 96:43 Jl 20 '70

RAMBO, DACK
  Raddatz, L.  Dack.  TV Guide 16-21:43 My 25 '68
  Clein, H.  Two stars on the horizon.  After Dark 5-11:34 Mr
    '73

RAMBOVA, NATACHA
  Waterbury, R.  Interview.  Photop 23:117 D '22
  Biery, R.  Spirit messages from Valentino.  Motion Pic 36:28
    Ja '29

RAMIREZ, CARLOS
  Colombian discovers America.  Lions R 3-4:no p# Jl '44

RAMPLING, CHARLOTTE
  Chase, D.  Interview.  Interview 29:29 Ja '73
  Note; filmog.  Films Illus 4-39:84 N '74

RAMSDEN, FRANCES
  Sketch.  Life 20:54 My 13 '46

RAND, SALLY
  Calhoun, D.  Interview.  Motion Pic 47:56 F '34
  As Sadie Thompson in Rain.  Newsweek 5:34 F 23 '35
  Bubbles become big business.  R of Rs 91:40 Ap '35
  Carskadon, T. R.  She dances to the rescue.  Am Mer 35:355
    Jl '35
  Sally's Sadie proves the fans concealed an actress.  Newsweek
    6:23 S 7 '35
  Reynolds, Q.  Business women.  Colliers 104:23 Ag 26 '39
  Sally Rand, rancher.  Cue 12-44:9 O 30 '43
  Sally's new step.  Newsweek 44:77 Ag 16 '54
  Uselton, R. A.  The Wampus baby stars.  Films In R 21-2:73
    F '70
  Fulbright, T.  Sally Rand searching for stills.  Classic Film
    Collect 28:58 Fall '70

RANDALL, SUE
  Another Philadelphia story.  TV Guide 4-20:20 My 19 '56

RANDALL, TONY
  Rising stars.  Film R p30 '58/59
  The odd couple drops in.  TV Guide 18-31:12 Ag 1 '70
  Barber, R.  Danger-mind at work.  TV Guide 19-1:15 Ja 2
    '71
  Stevenson, F.  Interview.  Opera N 36:6 F 5 '72
  Whitney, D.  Off-camera too, they are an odd couple.  TV
    Guide 20-36:14 S 2 '72
  Johnson, D.  Evening out.  After Dark 5-5:22 S '72
  Durslag, M.  Lights, camera, place your bets.  TV Guide 22-
    15:27 Ap 13 '74
  Randall, T.  The first word: perspectives on the seventies.
    Viva 1-9:6 Je '74

RANDELL, RON
   The not-so-secret life of Ron Randell.   TV Guide 6-11:20 Mr 15
      '58
   Hot pants.   TV Guide 20-6:10 F 5 '72

RANDOLPH, ISABEL
   Obit.   Screen World p239 '74

RANDOLPH, JOHN
   Frey, R.   John Randolph continues.   Sight & Sound 40-3:135 Sum
      '71

RANDOLPH, JOYCE
   Fourth banana.   TV Guide 2-51:12 D 18 '54
   Minoff, P.   That 'other woman' on Gleason's show.   Cue 25-5:
      12 F 4 '56

RANSON, HERBERT W.
   Leading to a vital, healthy theatre.   Lit Dig 119:17 Mr 16 '35
   Restoring the theatre's vigor.   Lit Dig 119:20 Mr 23 '35
   Obit.   N. Y. Times p32 N 14 '70

RAPPE, VIRGINIA
   Mundy, R.   Some Hollywood scandals of the 20s.   After Dark
      7-7:32 N '74

RASP, FRITZ
   Harmssen, H.   A tribute to Fritz Rasp; filmog.   Focus On F
      8:47 n. d.

RATHBONE, BASIL
   Home of.   Theatre 47:49 Je '28
   Goldbeck, E.   Sketch.   Motion Pic Classic 29:28 Ag '29
   Harrison, P.   Appreciation.   Motion Pic 50:32 Ag '35
   Cheatham, M.   He resents being typed.   Silver S 6-9:54 Jl '36
   Soule, L.   Interview.   Motion Pic 51:37 Jl '36
   Baird, F.   Interview.   Photop 50:55 Ag '36
   Sketch.   Photop 50:74 S '36
   Williams, W.   But not so wicked.   Silver S 7-12:28 D '37
   Cheatham, M.   Peer of the costume drama.   Screen Book 20-4:
      33 My '38
   Underhill, D.   Fans aren't fools.   Screen Book 21-7:48 F '39
   Pine, D.   At home with Basil Rathbone.   Screen Book 21-12:34
      Jl '39
   Surmelian, L.   Secrets of the Hollywood hostess.   Silver S 9-10:
      24 Ag '39
   Bio note; filmog.   Movies & People 2:32 '40
   An actor on acting.   Lions R 1-9:no p# My '42
   Born to adventure.   Lions R 1-11/12:no p# Jl/Ag '42
   Brushing shoulders with Mars.   Lions R 2-5:no p# Jl '43
   Menace man no more.   Lions R 3-4:no p# Jl '44
   Palmer, C.   The strange case of Basil Rathbone.   Silver S
      16-3:42 Ja '46

Minoff, P.  Mr. and Mrs. Basil Rathbone.  Cue 18-34:14 Ag 20
    '49
Minoff, P.  Notes on TV.  Cue 21-36:6 S 6 '52
Cabana, R. Jr.  Always Holmes.  Views & Rs 4-3:5 Spg '63
Obit.  Brit Bk Yr 1968:597 '68
    Cur Bio 28:45 O '67
    Same.  Cur Bio Yrbk 1967:482 '68
    N. Y. Times p1 Jl 22 '67
    Newsweek 70:49 Jl 31 '67
    Time 90:67 Jl 28 '67
Maltin, L.  Basil Rathbone:  1892-1967.  Film Fan Mo 75:3 S
    '67
Cutts, J.  Superswine.  Films & Filming 15-6:65 Mr '69
His last bow; interview.  Castle of Frankenstein p29 Spg '69
Farewell Basil Rathbone.  Castle of Frankenstein 12:39 n. d.

RATOFF, GREGORY
Obit.  Film R p17 '61/62

RAVEN, MARK
Knight, C.  Interview.  Cinefantastique 3-1:44 Fall '73

RAWLINSON, HERBERT
Kingsley, G.  Ragout of Rawlinson.  Photop 11-6:41 My '17
May, L.  Sketch.  Motion Pic 15:43 Je '18
Smith, A.  Cramping his style.  Photop 14-3:83 Ag '18
Naylor, H. S.  Sketch.  Motion Pic Classic 7:18 N '18
Sketch.  Photop 17:55 My '20
Sherwood, C. B.  Interview.  Motion Pic Classic 11:28 S '20
Gassaway, G.  Interview.  Motion Pic 22:68 Ja '22
Leon, S.  Herbert Rawlinson; letter.  Films In R 23-4:250 Ap
    '72

RAY, ALBERT
Delvigne, D.  Sketch.  Motion Pic 18:80 O '19

RAY, ALDO
Balling, F. D.  The sky and blushing brite.  Silver S 24-6:33
    Ap '54

RAY, ALLENE
Montanye, L.  Sketch.  Motion Pic Classic 12:26 Ap '21

RAY, CHARLES
How he became a photoplayer.  Motion Pic 9:116 Ap '15
Gaddis, P.  Sketch.  Motion Pic 14:33 S '17
Remont, F.  Sketch.  Motion Pic 15:55 S '18
Brewster, E.  Interview.  Motion Pic 17:38 Ap '19
Charlie Ray's $8,000 ball game.  Photop 15-6:72 My '19
St. Johns, A. R.  Don't cheat your sweetheart.  Photop 17-1:48
    D '19
Naylor, H. S.  Interview.  Motion Pic 18:44 Ja '20
Biographical.  Dram Mir 82:480 Mr 13 '20

Interview.   Dram Mir 183 Jl 31 '20
Porter, K. A.   Interview.   Motion Pic 20:36 O '20
Cheatham, M.   Interview.   Motion Pic Classic 12:18 Jl '21
Home of.   Photop 22:34 Je '22
Howe, H.   Interview.   Motion Pic Classic 14:18 Mr '22
Hall, G. & Fletcher, A. W.   Interview.   Motion Pic 23:22 Mr
   '22
Carr, H.   Sketch.   Motion Pic 25:21 Ap '23
Douglas, C.   Interview.   Classic 19:20 Je '24
Autobiographical.   Motion Pic 28:32 N '24
Confessions of a star-producer.   Photop 26:56 N '24
Perrin, H.   Sketch.   Motion Pic Classic 22:49 O '25
Home of.   Theatre 43:48 My '26
Tildesley, A.   Interview.   Motion Pic 31:20 My '26
Autobiographical.   Photop 32:47 S '27
Bodeen, D.   Charles Ray; filmog.   Films In R 19-9:548 N '68
Kornik, M.   Hayseed.   Classic Film Collect 23:14 Spg '69
Kornik, M.   Filmog.   Classic Film Collect 25:36 Fall '69
Bio note.   Silent Pic 14:21 Spg '72
Braff, R. E.   Partial filmog.   Films In R 24-4:247 Ap '73

RAY, HELEN
   Sketch.   Photop 20:24 O '21

RAY, JOHNNIE
   Like Mossadegh.   Time 59:42 Ja 21 '52
   Mr. Emotion.   Newsweek 39:56 Ja 21 '52
   Again, shrieks and swoons.   Life 32:99 Mr 24 '52
   Lewis, E.   Why I cry.   Cue 21-15:15 Ap 12 '52
   Et tu, Tallulah?   Life 32:101 My 12 '52
   Friends of the weeper.   New Yorker 28:20 Je 7 '52
   Sylvester, R.   Million-dollar teardrop.   Sat Eve Post 225:30 Jl
      26 '52
   Beatty, J.   Who's crying now?   Am Mag 154:28 Ag '52
   Life goes to a big Marion Davies party.   Life 33:132 O 20 '52
   Herndon, B.   Why (he) cries.   Coronet 33:60 D '52
   Humility at the hip.   Time 66:39 N 14 '55
   Pitts, M. R.   Popular singers on the screen; filmog.   Film Fan
      Mo 114:26 D '70

RAYE, MARTHA
   Smith, F.   Story of.   Movie Classic 11:47 Ja '37
   Osborn, K.   Story of.   Motion Pic 53:35 My '37
   Hunt, M.   Hoo-Raye-Martha's in pictures.   Silver S 7-7:62 My
      '37
   McFee, F.   Love's legacy to Martha.   Screen Book 20-3:35 Ap
      '38
   Bio note; filmog.   Movies & People 2:33 '40
   Minoff, P.   Tornado on TV.   Cue 22-47:14 N 21 '53
   Whitney, D.   Maggie of the boondocks.   TV Guide 18-47:16 N 21
      '70
   Corneau, E. N.   Queen of the buffoons.   Film Collectors Regis-
      try 4-3:6 My/Je '72

Kent, L.  A mouthful from Martha.  N. Y.  Times sec 2:5 O 29
   '72
   Same.  N. Y.  Times Bio Ed p1843 O '72
Byers, M.  New old face in No no Nanette.   Life 73:77 N 10 '72

RAYE, THELMA
   Shaffer, R.  Her story.   Motion Pic 41:50 F '31

RAYMOND, GENE
   Careers for four, please.   Silver S 2-1:42 N '31
   Sketch.   Photop 41:61 Ap '32
   Grayson, C.  Sketch.   Motion Pic 44:64 N '32
   Maddox, B.  All figured out.   Silver S 4-6:56 Ap '34
   Slater, C.  His complaint about Hollywood.   Movie Classic 8:56
      My '35
   Harrison, H.  Wanted.   Silver S 5-10:30 Ag '35
   Ryan, D.  Secret of his success.   Motion Pic 50:32 Ja '36
   Samuels, L.  Gene takes a "termer."   Silver S 6-7:29 My '36
   Vandour, C.  Story of.   Motion Pic 52:27 Ja '37
   Hall, G.  Most in love couple in Hollywood.   Silver S 11-12:22
      O '41
   Romantic.   Lions R 1-2:no p# O '41
   Sketch.   Womans Home C 68:15 D '41
   Pinups of the past.   Films & Filming 19-3:63 D '72

RAZETTO, STELLA
   How she became a photoplayer.   Motion Pic 9:97 Je '15

READICK, ROBERT
   Triple-threat man--at 17.   Lions R 2-4:no p# Ap '43

REAGAN, MAUREEN
   Raddatz, L.  The vote is no on politics.   TV Guide 22-35:30 Ag
      31 '74

REAGAN, RONALD
   Hamilton, S.  Sketch.   Photop 54:24 Ap '40
   Manners, M. J.  Making a double go of it.   Silver S 11-10:38
      Ag '41
   Hall, G.  Interview.   Photop 21:44 Ag '42
   Howard, M.  The typical young American.   Silver S 17-8:54 Je
      '47
   Home of.   Life 23:25 O 6 '47
   Reagan, R.  I'd love to be a louse.   Silver S 21-1:46 N '50
   Baer, M. M.  Mr. Reagan gives in.   Silver S 22-10:44 Ag '52
   Fleming, K. & Goldman, P.  Ronald Reagan story; scenario for
      a star.   Newsweek 76:28 N 2 '70
   Ronnie and Nancy: stepping down, but not out.   People 2-12:64
      S 16 '74
   (Citations to his political career are not herein noted. )

REARDON, MILDRED
   Remont, F.  Interview.   Classic 9:46 N '19
   Montanye, L.  Interview.   Motion Pic 20:56 D '20

REASON, REX
   The stars of tomorrow.   Film R p44 '55/56

REDFORD, ROBERT
   Jenkins, D.   How to succeed at racing without really racing.
      Sports Illus 31:66 N 24 '69
   Salute of the week.   Cue 38-49:1 D 6 '69
   When things come together.   Time 94:75 D 12 '69
   Schickel, R.   Redford riding high.   Life 68:38 F 6 '70
   Luckinbill, L.   Oh, you Sundance Kid.   Esquire 74:160 O '70
   Knight, A. & Alpert, H.   Sex stars of 1970.   Playboy 17-12:220
      D '70
   Bio.   Cur Bio 32:31 Ap '71
   Davidson, S.   Husband, father and sex symbol.   Redbook 137:81
      My '71
   Skiing the American West.   Harp Baz 105:38 D '71
   Robert Redford rides again.   Films Illus 1-8:13 F '72
   Miller, E.   Interview.   Seventeen 31:116 Je '72
   Stewart, J.   Nice, normal, married sex symbol.   McCalls 99:88
      Je '72
   Fayard, J.   Redford found politics a charade.   Life 73:50 Jl 28
      '72
   Filmog.   Films & Filming 18-10:64 Jl '72
   Stoop, N. M.   She just felt like feeling my hair.   After Dark
      5-4:24 Ag '72
   Mori, S. Y.   The making of The candidate.   Today's Filmmaker
      2-1:44 Ag '72
   Archibald, L.   (He) still prefers his privacy.   Show 2-6:18 S
      '72
   Winning is what counts no matter how.   Mod Screen 66-10:34 O
      '72
   Krims, M.   Jeremiah Johnson: mountain man.   Sat Eve Post
      244:78 Win '72
   Eyles, A.   Bio note; filmog.   Focus On F 12:8 Win '72
   Bio.   Cur Bio Yrbk 1971:336 '72
   I'm with the sexiest guys in Hollywood.   Photop 83-6:50 Je '73
   Bakewell, J.   Redford on privacy in public life.   Films Illus
      3-30:213 D '73
   Mind your own business.   Photop 85-3:62 Mr '74
   The year of Redford.   Films Illus 3-32:293 Ap '74
   Sketch.   Photop 85-6:44 Je '74
   Lear, M. W.   Anatomy of a sex symbol.   N. Y. Times Bio Ed
      p1023 Jl '74
   His family.   Photop 86-3:47 S '74
   Everything a bride desires.   Photop 85-5:56 My '74
   Interview.   Playboy 21-12:83 D '74

REDGRAVE, LYNN
   Wolf, W.   Meet Lynn.   Cue 36-5:8 F 8 '67
   Bio.   Cur Bio 30:33 S '69
      Same.   Cur Bio Yrbk 1969:358 '70
   Miller, E.   Beaut of a British bird.   Seventeen 26:99 D '67
   Williams, J.   Look what they've done to Lynn.   Films Illus

2-15:10 S '72
Fields, S.   Keeps her mouth shut.   N. Y.   Daily News p107 Mr
    28 '74
Klemesrud, J.   Fat? Only with pads now.   N. Y.   Times Bio Ed
    p593 Ap '74
(See also: REDGRAVE FAMILY)

REDGRAVE, MICHAEL
Sketch.   Play Pict F '37
Sketch.   Theatre World 31:34 Ja '39
Bowers, L.   Tale of a frustrated tourist.   Silver S 17-12:53 O
    '47
Comments on Strindberg's The father.   World R 1:18 Mr '49
Lewis, E.   "Egghead" actor.   Cue 24-41:16 O 15 '55
de la Roche, C.   Master of his destiny.   Films & Filming 2-3:
    11 D '55
Tierney, M.   Knights at work.   Plays & Players 18-12:19 S '71
Andrews, N.   Takeover.   Plays & Players 19-8:28 My '72
(See also: REDGRAVE FAMILY)

REDGRAVE, VANESSA
Ronan, M.   Vanessa, the innest Redgrave; interview.   Sr Schol
    91:17 O 19 '67
Maclain, J. & Sylvia, K.   Isadora; a remarkable film reincarna-
    tion.   Dance 42:43 F '68
Meehan, T.   Super girl.   Sat Eve Post 241:25 Mr 9 '68
Volatile Vanessa; photos.   Playboy 16-4:101 Ap '69
Knight, A. & Alpert, H.   Sex stars of 1970.   Playboy 17-12:220
    D '70
Robbins, F.   Director Cocoyannis and his Trojan women.   Show
    2-8:28 O '71
People are talking about.   Vogue 158:120 N 1 '71
(See also: REDGRAVE FAMILY)

REDGRAVE FAMILY
Eckman, F. M.   Redgraves talk about their children.   McCalls
    94:87 S '67
Graham, J.   Redgraves.   Good House 166:16 Ja '68

REDMOND, MARGE
Raddatz, L.   She was only a fireman's daughter.   TV Guide 16-
    28:24 Jl 13 '68

REDWING, RODD
Have guns, will teach.   Newsweek 51:64 Ja 27 '58
Bio note.   Cinema Trails 2:21 n. d.
Obit.   Screen World 23:239 '72

REED, DONALD
York, C.   Sketch.   Photop 33:74 D '27
Manners, D.   Interview.   Motion Pic 36:42 O '28

REED, DONNA
Campus queen comes to Hollywood.   Lions R 1-5:no p# Ja '42
On the star trail.   Lions R 1-7:no p# Mr '42
Corn-fed beauty.   Lions R 1-8:no p# Ap '42
Stars of tomorrow.   Lions R 1-11/12:no p# Jl/Ag '42
Wilson, C.   Cinderella--believe it or not.   Lions R 1-11/12:no
    p# Jl/Ag '42
Her first year.   Lions R 2-1:no p# S/O '42
Hamilton, S.   Sketch.   Photop 21:51 O '42
Design for stardom.   Lions R 2-5:no p# Jl '43
Cinderella has no cinch.   Lions R 3-1:no p# S '43
Service, F.   Can an average girl succeed in the movies?   Silver
    S 14-1:24 N '43
Sweetheart of the army.   Lions R 3-3:no p# Ap '44
Bangs, B.   There are no rules.   Silver S 16-7:48 My '46
Parsons, L. O.   Cosmop's citation for best performance of
    month.   Cosmop 122:66 Ja '47
Service, F.   What's happened to Donna?   Silver S 18-2:43 D '47
Tildesley, A. L.   Tips from a shady lady.   Silver S 24-2:38 D
    '53
Hamilton, J.   Where oh where are the beautiful girls.   Look 34:
    67 N 3 '70

REED, FLORENCE
West, M. F.   Work of.   Green Book 8:25 Jl '12
Sketch.   Met Mag 37:32 Ap '13
Roland Reed's daughter.   Photop 12-2:93 Jl '17
Naylor, H. S.   Interview.   Motion Pic 15:29 F '18
The sex appeal.   Theatre 27:94 Mr '18
Brennon, A.   Interview.   Motion Pic Classic 7:20 Ja '19
Wicked women on the stage.   Theatre 29:146 Mr '19
Autobiographical.   Photop 19:16 F '21
Sketch.   Theatre 38:12 Ag '23
Why I prefer to play the scarlet woman.   Theatre 44:22 Jl '26
Sketch.   Mus Court 124:35 D 1 '41
Obit.   N. Y. Times p47 N 22 '67

REED, OLIVER
Cowie, P.   The face of '63--Great Britain.   Films & Filming
    9-5:19 F '63
Bean, R.   All wound up and ready to go.   Films & Filming 13-
    9:4 Je '67
Miller, E.   Real modern artist of our time.   Seventeen 27:98
    D '68
Knight, A. & Alpert, H.   Sex stars of 1970.   Playboy 17-12:220
    D '70
McAsh, I.   Goes Up the junction in search of a Sitting target.
    Films Illus 1-7:21 Ja '72
MacDonough, S.   Britain's volatile Reed: I only bully bigger
    bullies.   Show 2-2:32 Ap '72
Interview.   Photop 82-1:24 Jl '72
d'Arcy, S.   Interview.   Films Illus 3-36:482 Ag '74
Eyles, A.   Oliver Reed; filmog.   Focus On F 7:6 n. d.

REED, PHILIP
  Goldbeck, E.   Interview.   Motion Pic 49:61 F '35
  Hamilton, S.   Sketch.   Photop 20:55 F '42

REED, ROBERT
  Gill, A.   How much influence does he have with the jury?   TV
    Guide 11-20:22 My 18 '63
  Raddatz, L.   Don't tell his Pasadena neighbors, but Robert Reed
    is an actor.   TV Guide 18-14:21 Ap 4 '70

REED, TRACY
  Stone, J.   'Barefoot' stubs a toe.   TV Guide 18-41:30 O 10 '70

REED, VIVIAN
  The girl on the calendar.   Photop 11-3:33 F '17

REEMS, HARRY
  Deacy, J.   Harry Reems comes clean.   Gallery 2-5 Ap '74
  Hard Harry and sweet Susan.   Gallery 2-12 D '74

REES, ANGHARAD
  McAsh, I.   Angharad Rees.   Films Illus 1-5:10 N '71

REESE, MASON
  Curtis, C.   What's round, wordy and freckled all over?   N.Y.
    Times Bio Ed p1528 S '73
  Schoenstein, R.   The borgasmord kid grants an audience.   TV
    Guide 21-52:16 D 29 '73

REEVES, BILLIE
  Courtlandt, R.   Interview.   Motion Pic Classic 2:27 My '16

REEVES, GEORGE
  How they make Superman fly.   TV Guide 1-26:5 S 25 '53
  Obit.   Screen World 11:224 '60
  Beaver, J. N. Jr.   Filmog.   Films In R 18-9:586 N '67
  De Carl, L.   Additional filmog.   Films In R 19-1:60 Ja '68

REGAN, PHIL
  Williams, W.   All a gamble.   Screen Book 20-1:46 F '38

REICHER, FRANK
  Obit.   Screen World 17:240 '66

REICHERT, KITTENS
  Six years old and in the phone book.   Photop 12-3:27 Ag '17

REID, BERYL
  Braun, E.   If the shoe fits.   Films & Filming 20-7:18 Ap '74

REID, CARL BENTON
  Obit.   Classic Film Collect 40:59 Fall '73
    N.Y. Times Bio Ed p489 Mr '73
    Screen World p239 '74

REID, FRANCES
    Frances faces life.  TV Guide 2-33:23 Ag 14 '54

REID, KATE
    McLarty, J.  Kate Reid.  Motion p41 My/Je '74

REID, LESLIE
    Peltret, E.  Coincidence or fate?  Photop 12-4:130 S '17

REID, WALLACE
    How he became a photoplayer.  Motion Pic 8:76 Ja '15
    Courtlandt, R.  Interview.  Motion Pic 9:109 My '15
    Courtlandt, R.  Interview.  Motion Pic Classic 2:30 Jl '16
    Briscoe, J.  Sketch.  Motion Pic 12:123 S '16
    How to get into motion pictures.  Motion Pic 12:64 N '16
    Wardell, E.  Home life of.  Motion Pic 13:65 F '17
    How he got in moving pictures.  Motion Pic 14:59 Ja '18
    Naylor, H. S.  Interview.  Motion Pic Classic 6:29 Ap '18
    Peltret, E.  Interview.  Motion Pic 18:32 S '19
    Interview.  Dram Mir 545 S 25 '20
    Cheatham, M. S.  Interview.  Motion Pic 20:32 O '20
    Shelley, H.  Interview.  Motion Pic Classic 12:22 Mr '21
    Hall, G. & Fletcher, A. W.  Interview.  Motion Pic 22:22 S '21
    Howe, H.  Interview with his sons.  Motion Pic Classic 13:18
      F '22
    Cheatham, M.  Interview.  Motion Pic Classic 14:16 My '22
    Handy, T. B.  Interview.  Motion Pic 24:48 Ag '22
    A star in the making.  Motion Pic Classic 14:18 Ag '22
    Obit.  N. Y. Clipper 70:34 Ja 24 '23
    Post, C. A.  Appreciation.  Motion Pic 25:20 Ja '24
    The Wallace Reid Foundation sanitarium.  Photop 26:74 S '24
    Hall, G.  Will his son succeed him.  Motion Pic 36:50 Ja '29
    Calhoun, D.  What if he had lived?  Motion Pic 40:28 D '30
    In memoriam.  Motion Pic 45:53 Je '33
    Letters.  Films In R 17-7:458 Ag/S '66
    Peeples, S.  The forgotten idol, the story of Wallace Reid.
      Classic Film Collect 25:6 Fall '69
    Peeples, S.  Filmog.  Classic Film Collect 26:12 Win '70

REILLY, CHARLES NELSON
    Clein, H.  I was a Mike Douglas reject.  TV Guide 18-19:18
      My 9 '70

REINER, CARL
    Second bananas.  Look 17:17 My 5 '53
    In the cast.  TV Guide 1-33:21 N 13 '53
    Wood, C.  TV personalities bio sketch book.  TV Personalities
      p83 '56
    New creative writers.  Lib J 83:489 F 1 '58
    Delbier, M.  Two TV stars on the printed page.  N. Y. Herald
      Trib Bk R p2 My 4 '58
    He puts words in his own mouth.  TV Guide 8-20:17 My 14 '60
    Bio.  Cur Bio 22:34 Ap '61

Same.  Cur Bio Yrbk 1961:386 '62
View from the lively minority.  Life 53:74 O 19 '62
Lewis, J. D.  Laughs for stage, screen & Dick Van Dyke.  TV
    Guide 12-1:6 Ja 4 '64
Kael, P.  Current cinema.  New Yorker 45:190 D 6 '69
Homecoming; interview.  New Yorker 45:47 D 13 '69
The director-actor; a conversation.  Action 5-1:21 Ja/ F '70
Rob Reiner:  I was 21 and ready for the rubber-padded room.
    TV Guide 20-16:18 Ap 15 '72
Eyles, A. & Billings, P.  Bio sketch; filmog.  Focus On F 8:6
    n. d.
Interview.  AFI Report 5-1:35 Spg '74

REINER, ROB
Speaking about the unspeakable.  Newsweek 78:52 N 29 '71
The real-life families of those All in the family stars.  Mod
    Screen 65-11:42 N '71
I was 21 and ready for the rubber-padded room.  TV Guide 20-
    16:18 Ap 15 '72

REJAUNIER, JEANNE
Beauty Trap; photos.  Playboy 17-1:165 Ja '70

REMICK, LEE
Person of promise.  Films & Filming 4-11:12 Ag '58
Rising star.  Film R p21 '60/ 61
LaBadie, D. W.  What makes Remick walk?  Show 3-2:80 F '63
Gow, G.  Cool it; interview; filmog.  Films & Filming 17-5:18
    F '71

REMINGTON, NANCY
In the cast.  TV Guide 1-11:17 Je 12 '53

REMY, ALBERT
Obit.  Screen World 19:238 '68

RENALDO, DUNCAN
Interview.  Motion Pic 37:78 Jl '29
Calhoun, D.  Sketch.  Motion Pic 40:8 Ja '31
Fairfield, L.  Renews citizenship fight.  Movie Classic 4:29 Mr
    '33
Hall, H.  Without a country.  Motion Pic 45:60 Ap '33
Riggan, B.  Interview.  Am Heritage Je '68
Marsano, W.  Where are they now?  TV Guide 18-47:48 N 21 '70
Williams, N.  All the Cisco Kids; Cisco Kid filmog.  Filmograph
    1-2:38 '70
Cabana, R. Jr.  Concerning Trader Horn.  Views & Rs 3-1:35
    Sum '71
Tuska, J.  Trader Horn.  Views & Rs 3-1:51 Sum '71
Hoaglin, J. L.  Down memory lane.  Hollywood Stu 6-8:31 D
    '71
Duncan Renaldo; filmog.  Cinema Trails 2:12 n. d.

RENAUD, MADELEINE
  Feinstein, M.   Avant-garde theatre that won an audience.
    Theatre Arts 36:21 N '52
  Hewes, H.   Se Moquer ou ne pas se Moquer.   Sat R 36:25 Ja
    24 '53
  Bio.   Cur Bio Mr '53
  Great audience.   New Yorker 33:27 F 23 '57
  Bentley, E.   One-man dialogue on the Barrault-repertory.   New
    Rep 136:21 Mr 18 '57
  Genet.   Letter from Paris.   New Yorker 40:102 F 22 '64
  Genet.   Letter from Paris.   New Yorker 47:91 F 21 '71
  Salute of the week.   Cue 40-16:1 Ap 17 '71

RENEVANT, GEORGES
  Obit.   Screen World 21:240 '70

RENNIE, JAMES
  Bruce, B.   Interview.   Motion Pic 21:48 Mr '21
  Gish, D.   Story of his marriage.   Photop 21:36 Mr '22
  Obit.   Screen World 17:240 '66

RENNIE, MICHAEL
  Zunser, J.   Rennie hits Broadway.   Cue 30-9:11 Mr 4 '61
  Obit.   Classic Film Collect 31:62 Sum '71
    Film R p12 '72/73
    N. Y. Times p38 Je 11 '71
    Same.   N. Y. Times Bio Ed Je 11 '71
    Newsweek 77:55 Je 21 '71
    Screen World 23:239 '72

RETTIG, TOMMY
  The boy grew up.   TV Guide 5-23:17 Je 8 '57
  Big changeover for Lassie.   Life 43:76 N 25 '57

REVERE, ANNE
  Hamilton, S.   Story of.   Photop 27:74 Jl '45
  Lane, L.   A rebel at heart.   Silver S 16-8:35 Je '46
  Frey, R.   Anne Revere begins again.   After Dark 13-8:28 D '70

REVIER, DOROTHY
  Hall, G.   Sketch.   Motion Pic 27:42 My '28
  Uselton, R. A.   The Wampus baby stars.   Films In R 21-2:73
    F '70

REVILL, CLIVE
  Will the real Mr. Revill stand up, please; filmog.   Films Illus
    4-40:156 D '74

REYNOLDS, ADELINE deWALT
  96 and still acting up.   TV Guide 6-35:16 Ag 30 '58

REYNOLDS, BILL
  Hano, A.   Unwrinkled, unscarred, unnoticed.   TV Guide 16-7:20
    F 17 '68

REYNOLDS, BURT
  Goodwin, F.  What makes Burt brood?  TV Guide 18-42:32 O
    17 '70
  Ebert, R.  What kind of playmate is Burt?  N. Y. Times Bio Ed
    Mr 26 '72
  Playmate of the month.  Newsweek 79:57 Ap 10 '72
  Creaturo, B.  Cosmop's playboy of the year; photos.  Cosmop
    172:185 Ap '72
  Kenedy, A.  Interview.  Vogue 160:86 Jl '72
  It's being number one that counts.  Mod Screen 66-7:48 Jl '72
  Frog prince.  Time 100:43 Ag 21 '72
  Love after 30.  Photop 82-2:28 Ag '72
  Stoop, N. M.  A hidden iceberg that broke out like gangbusters.
    After Dark 5-4:47 Ag '72
  But I can never forget her.  Mod Screen 66-8:24 Ag '72
  A good marriage almost destroyed us.  Photop 82-2:33 Ag '72
  Suddenly it's Burt Reynolds.  Films Illus 2-15:12 S '72
  Photoplay forum.  Photop 82-3:8 S '72
  McGillivray, D.  Bio note; filmog.  Focus On F 11:13 Aut '72
  Miron, C.  Actor or personality?  Show 2-7:34 O '72
  His needs for a younger woman.  Mod Screen 66-10:56 O '72
  Robbins, F.  Super stud.  Penthouse 4-3:68 N '72
  How he fought for Dinah.  Photop 82-6:57 D '72
  Secret love hideout discovered.  Mod Screen 67-3:39 Mr '73
  Our love is here to stay.  Photop 83-6:56 Je '73
  Burt rushed to hospital.  Photop 84-1:58 Jl '73
  Barber, R.  It was the turning point in the lives of 34 men.
    TV Guide 21-41:19 O 13 '73
  Friedman, B. J.  Burt Reynolds puts his pants on.  Playboy
    20-10:131 O '73
  Burt and Dinah's love letters.  Photop 84-5:30 N '73
  Up with careers, nix on marriage.  People 2-18:56 O 28 '74
  Kaiser, R. B.  Interview.  Playgirl 2-7:60 D '74
  Reynolds' longest yard.  Films Illus 4-40:143 D '74
  Bio note; partial filmog.  Films Illus 4-40:126 D '74

REYNOLDS, CRAIG
  Whitehead, H.  Sketch.  Motion Pic 52:15 D '36
  Butler, J.  Sketch.  Movie Classic 11:57 F '37
  Sketch.  Motion Pic 53:97 Mr '37
  My faith.  Photop 24:48 My '44
  Obit.  Screen World 1:234 '49

REYNOLDS, DEBBIE
  Peer, R. & R.  There's a bubble.  Silver S 21-8:30 Je '51
  Reynolds, D.  Deep in my heart.  Silver S 22-12:32 O '52
  Wilson, E.  The "take 'em off" gal.  Silver S 23-10:22 Ag '53
  Lee, L.  How to be really happy.  Silver S 23-12:31 O '53
  Rising stars.  Film R p109 '53/54
  O'Leary, D.  Don't put me on the spot.  Silver S 24-5:33 Mr '54
  Rogers, M.  Enjoy living your teens.  Silver S 24-8:35 Je '54
  Gordon, S.  Can we love Debbie too?  Look 33:90 N 18 '69
  Hano, A.  Debbie said yes.  TV Guide 18-5:16 Ja 31 '70

Debbie is really a very sick girl.   Photop 77-6:49 Je '70
Debbie as a mother.   Photop 78-1:54 Jl '70
Troubles of a teenage daughter.   Photop 78-3:77 S '70
My husband's children hated him.   Photop 79-1:40 Ja '71
Debbie Reynolds reports from Hollywood.   Silver S 41-10:4 O '71
What Debbie teaches her daughter.   Photop 80-6:78 D '71
Let's make magic.   Photop 81-2:78 F '72
Flatley, G.   Forget your troubles, come on, get Debbie.   N. Y.
    Times sec 2:1 F 25 '73
    Same.   N. Y. Times Bio Ed p293 F '73
Considine, S.   Gives her regards to Broadway.   After Dark 6-2:
    34 Je '73
Debbie arrested after her son shoots himself.   Photop 84-1:24
    Jl '73
Debbie's shocking past.   Photop 84-3:64 S '73
Entertainer of the year.   Cue 43-2:5 Ja 14 '74
Bowers, R.   An evening with...   Films In R 25-5:314 My '74
Watters, J.   Unsinkable Debbie:  at 42 she salvages her career.
    People 2-22:54 N 25 '74

REYNOLDS, JOYCE
    Sketch.   Photop 24:39 D '43
    Vallee, W. L.   Beautiful but smart.   Silver S 15-1:48 N '44

REYNOLDS, MARJORIE
    Vallee, W. L.   Super Cinderella.   Silver S 13-1:48 N '42
    Hamilton, S.   Sketch.   Photop 23:34 Je '43

REYNOLDS, PETER
    Rising stars.   Films R p31 '50

REYNOLDS, VERA
    Sketch.   Photop 23:81 Ap '23
    Uselton, R. A.   The Wampus baby stars.   Films In R 21-2:73
        F '70

RHODES, BILLIE
    Shannon, B.   The devil's little daughter.   Photop 12-2:97 Jl '17
    Peltret, E.   Sketch.   Motion Pic Classic 7:26 Ja '19

RHODES, [LITTLE] BILLY
    Obit.   Screen World 19:238 '68

RHODES, ERIK
    Penny, R.   Sketch.   Movie Classic 11:14 N '36

RHODES, HARI
    Hobson, D.   On maneuvers with Hari Rhodes.   TV Guide 16-16:
        18 Ap 20 '68

RIANO, RENIE
    Obit.   Screen World 23:239 '72

RICCARDO, CARONA
   Obit.  Dram Mir 77:28 N 10 '17
   Patterson, A.  Bill Hart's love story.  Photop 19:36 Ja '21

RICE, FLORENCE
   Her stage debut.  National 58:244 Mr '30
   Bio sketch.  Delin 130:11 Ja '37
   Condon, F.  Story of.  Colliers 103:19 Mr 11 '39
   Obit.  N. Y. Times p33 F 26 '74

RICE, JOAN
   Rising stars.  Film R p41 '51/52

RICH, IRENE
   Keane, M.  Interview.  Motion Pic Classic 10:36 Ag '20
   Squier, E. L.  Interview.  Motion Pic 20:66 Ja '21
   Shelley, H.  Sketch.  Motion Pic Classic 13:58 Ja '22
   Home of.  Classic 19:26 Mr '24
   Donnell, D.  Sketch.  Motion Pic Classic 22:38 S '25
   Johnston, C.  Sketch.  Motion Pic Classic 27:51 Ap '28
   Companionate marriage in its real sense.  Theatre 48:22 Ag '28
   Service, F.  Interview.  Motion Pic 40:50 O '30

RICH, LILLIAN
   How she got into pictures.  Photop 26:58 N '24

RICH, VIVIAN
   Courtlandt, R.  Interview.  Motion Pic 11:94 Jl '16
   The poor little rich girl.  Photop 11-1:133 D '16

RICHARD, CLIFF
   More happy than Elvis.  Newsweek 61:63 F 25 '63
   Comeback with a conscience.  Films Illus 3-28:149 O '73

RICHARD, JEAN
   A new French comedian.  Unifrance 23:21 F '53

RICHARD, PIERRE
   Milinaire, C.  The tall blond man; interview.  Interview p32 D
      '73

RICHARDS, ANN
   Stars of tomorrow.  Lions R 1-11/12:no p# Jl/Ag '42
   Ann Richards in wonderland.  Lions R 3-4:no p# Jl '44

RICHARDS, JEFF
   The stars of tomorrow.  Film R p47 '55/56

RICHARDS, PAUL
   Richards keeps an escape hatch open.  TV Guide 11-43:6 O 26
      '63

RICHARDSON, IAN
    In the words of Ian Richardson.    Cue 38-49:24 D 6 '69
    Totten, E.    Interview.    Plays & Players 20-9:26 Je '73

RICHARDSON, RALPH
    Sketch.    Theatre World 20:140 S '33
    Sketch.    Theatre World 25:61 F '36
    Sketch.    Theatre World 30:179 Ap '39
    Hast, N.    Sketch.    Theatre World 27:132 Mr '37
    Richardson, R.    Sir Alexander Korda.    Sight & Sound 25-4:214
        Spg '56
    Salute of the week.    Cue 40-3:1 Ja 16 '71
    Tierney, M.    Knights at work.    Plays & Players 18-12:19 S '71
    Gruen, J.    Interview.    Vogue 158:87 N 15 '71

RICHARDSON, WALTER P.
    Sketch.    N. Y. Dram 75:20 Ja 29 '16

RICHARD-WILLM, PIERRE
    Pierre Richard-Willm.    Visages 18:entire issue N '37

RICHMAN, HARRY
    Transatlantic types.    Time 28:54 S 14 '36
    Lawrenson, H.    The Richman era.    Show 2-6:75 Je '62
    Obit.    Classic Film Collect 38:57 Spg '73
        Film R p13 '73/74
        N. Y. Times Bio Ed p2048 N '72

RICHMAN, PETER MARK
    My child.    Photop 81-5:52 My '72

RICHMOND, KANE
    Malcomson, R. M.    The sound serial.    Views & Rs 3-1:13 Sum
        '71

RICHTER, PAUL
    Obit.    Screen World 14:226 '63

RICKERT, SHIRLEY JEAN
    Maltin, L.    Our gang; Our gang filmog.    Film Fan Mo 66:3 D
        '66

RICKLES, DON
    Merchant of venom.    Newsweek 70:118 S 25 '67
    Mr. warmth.    Time 90:35 D 29 '67
    Efron, E.    Guess who's shy, retiring...    TV Guide 16-11:14
        Mr 16 '68
    Interview.    Playboy 15-11:75 N '68
    Hudson, P.    Looking and listening.    Sr Schol 93:27 Ja 10 '69
    Davidson, B.    Mister warmth spreads a little joy around.    TV
        Guide 20-17:28 Ap 22 '72

RICKSEN, LUCILLE
  Obit.  Photop 27:90 My '25
  Uselton, R. A.   The Wampus baby stars.   Films In R 21-2:73
    F '70

RICO, MONA
  Uselton, R. A.   The Wampus baby stars.   Films In R 21-2:73
    F '70

RIDGELY, CLEO
  Henry, W. M.   The crimes of Cleo.   Photop 8-6:29 N '15
  Gaddis, P.  Sketch.   Motion Pic Classic 2:33 Ag '16
  Obit.  Screen World 14:226 '63
  Bodeen, D.  Remembrances of Cleo Ridgely; letter.   Filmograph
    1-1:42 '70

RIDGWELL, AUDREY
  Obit.  N. Y.  Times p47 O 30 '68

RIGA, NADINE
  Obit.  Screen World 20:239 '69

RIGG, DIANA
  On the scene.   Playboy 14-3:143 Mr '67
  Brown, R.  Dialogue with Diana.   Todays Filmmaker 1-4:21 My
    '72
  Who is that lady?   Time 100:62 D 18 '72
  The avenger tries on a TV role.   TV Guide 21-7:12 F 17 '73
  Brustein, R.  And where are our own Diana Riggs?   N. Y.
    Times sec 2:1 My 13 '73
  Gow, G.  Shakespeare lib.   Plays & Players 20-9:18 Je '73
  Conversation with Diana Rigg.   Oui 2-8:63 Ag '73
  Hano, A.  Tall redheads always get caught.   TV Guide 21-40:30
    O 6 '73
  Leider, R. A.  TV's new Diana is rigged for laughs.   Show 3-7:
    28 O '73
  Faces a special crisis.   Photop 85-2:41 F '74
  Diana Rigg.  Black Oracle 1:12 n. d.
  The Avengers.   Castle of Frankenstein 12:24 n. d.
  Hauptfuhrer, F.  Being Mr. Diana Rigg was too much for Guef-
    fen.  People 2-3:59 Jl 15 '74

RILEY, JEANNINE
  Raddatz, L.  Who needs Petticoat Junction?   TV Guide 17-28:14
    Jl 12 '69

RILLA, WALTER
  Under sentence of death.   Lions R 3-1:no p# S '43

RING, CYRIL
  Obit.  Screen World 19:238 '68

RIPPER, MICHAEL
    Knight, A. , Nicholson, P. , Stockbridge, R.   Interview.   Photop
        22:42 '72

RISDON, ELIZABETH
    The future of the film.   Nash & Pall Mall 55:579 Jl '15
    Mantle, B.   Sketch.   Green Book 18:992 D '17

RISSO, ATTILIO
    Obit.   N. Y. Times p45 O 16 '67

RITCHARD, CYRIL
    Ritchard's restoration.   N. Y. Times Mag p54 F 6 '55
    Cyril Ritchard.   Vogue 128:152 N 1 '56
    At the opera with Cyril Ritchard.   Dance 31:38 Ja '57
    Bio.   Cur Bio 18:44 Ja '57
        Same.   Cur Bio Yrbk 1957:465 '58
    Romp at the Met.   Time 69:58 Ja 7 '57
    Versatile Mr. Ritchard.   Life 42:90 Mr 4 '57
    Man on a small planet.   Life 42:90 Mr 4 '57
    Blackmon, R.   How to keep your audience.   Vogue 129:86 Ap 15
        '57
    Carrol, J.   Visit with a large meteor.   Theatre Arts 41:28 Jl
        '57
    Flotsam & jetsam.   Time 70:34 Ag 19 '57
    Minoff, P.   Villainy with venum.   Cue 27-7:12 F 15 '58
    Who's who cooks.   Good House 146:10 Mr '58
    The kids know he's kidding.   TV Guide 6-19:17 My 10 '58
    Couple of swell skates.   Life 45:193 D 22 '58
    Well dressed world of Cyril Ritchard.   Look 23:62 Mr 3 '59
    Morton, F.   Ritchard the great.   Holiday 28:91 S '60

RITTER, JOHN
    Cooper, T. J.   John Ritter.   Films In R 25-4:251 Ap '74

RITTER, TEX
    Cooper, T. J.   Tex Ritter; filmog.   Films In R 21-4:204 Ap '70
    Cleghorn, R.   High noon for Tex Ritter.   N. Y. Times Mag p10
        Jl 12 '70
        Same.   N. Y. Times Bio Ed Jl 12 '70
    Hedgepeth, W.   Superstars, posts, pickers, prophets.   Look 35:
        28 Jl 13 '71
    Obit.   N. Y. Times Bio Ed p113 Ja '74

RITTER, THELMA
    Brooklyn girl makes good.   Cue 20-5:12 F 3 '51
    Obit.   Classic Film Collect (reprint Washington Evening Star)
        23:46 Spg '69
        Film R p13 '69/70
        N. Y. Times p45 F 5 '69
        Newsweek 73:93 F 17 '69
        Screen World 21:240 '70
        Time 93:80 F 14 '69
    Letters.   Films In R 20-10:641 D '69

RITZ BROTHERS
(Al, Harry, Jimmie)
Lang, H.   Interview.   Movie Classic 11:46 F '37
Barrington, G.   Trailing the nit-Ritz.   Screen Book 21-12:22 Jl
'39
Bio note; filmog.   Movies & People 2:33 '40

RIVA, EMMANUELE
Flash on Emmanuele Riva.   Unifrance 51:6 O/D '59
Emmanuele Riva.   Film 33:11 Aut '62
Graham, P.   The face of '63--France.   Films & Filming 9-8:13
My '63

RIVA, MARIA
Minoff, P.   Girl with a goal.   Cue 20-24:12 Je 16 '51
Robinson, S.   I couldn't compete with my mother.   Ladies Home
J 68:54 O '51
Lyons, S. R.   Her mother's daughter.   Good House 137:57 O
'53

RIVERO, JULIAN
Gauguin, L.   Interview.   Views & Rs 4-3:17 Spg '73

RIVERS, JOAN
Funny girl.   Newsweek 65:96 Mr 22 '65
Mee, C. L. Jr.   For Joan the woe must go.   N. Y. Times Mag
p137 O 31 '65
What she went thru.   TV Guide 14-10:7 Mr 5 '66
Hot potato.   Time 88:61 O 21 '66
Jobin, J.   The last girl in Larchmont to get married.   TV Guide
16-32:18 Ag 10 '68
Rampaging Rivers.   Newsweek 73:72 Ap 28 '69
Robin, S.   Joan Rivers attacks America.   After Dark 11-12:40
Ap '70
Thompson, T.   What's so funny?   Life 70:69 Ja 8 '71
I'm glad I'm a middle-aged sex object.   McCalls 99:78 O '71
Bio.   Cur Bio Yrbk 1970:352 '71
Bigwood, C.   Joan and Edgar.   Harp Baz 105:65 Ja '72
Sage, M.   Funny sob story--or from office temp to permanent
star.   Show 3-3:44 My '73

RIX, BRIAN
Tierney, M.   Bums, bottoms and bosoms.   Plays & Players 20-
5:26 F '73

ROBARDS, JASON SR.
Biery, R.   Interview.   Motion Pic Classic 26:63 D '27

ROBARDS, JASON
Lewis, E.   New star off-Broadway.   Cue 25-30:14 Jl 28 '56
Bryson, J.   Jason Robards' long journey home.   New York 6-52:
34 D 24 '73
Gelb, B.   Jason Jamie Robards Tyrone.   N. Y. Times Mag p14

Ja 20 '74
Same.  N. Y.  Times Bio Ed p114 Ja '74
Levin, E.  Of 'Billy Big Boy,' 'The old man' and 'Ooops, bad-
hopped it.'  TV Guide 22-5:10 F 2 '74
Long voyage home.  People 1-10:48 My 6 '74

ROBB, LOTUS
Obit.  N. Y.  Times p47 S 29 '69

ROBERTI, LYDA
Vandamm.  Amazing Roberti.  Theatre 53:20 Ap '31
Sketch.  Motion Pic 44:42 Ag '32
Smalley, J.  Bio sketch.  Movie Classic 8:32 Ap '35
Her gowns in Pardon my English.  Stage 10:27 Mr '38

ROBERTO, RISSO
Person of promise.  Films & Filming 1-12:19 S '55

ROBERTS, ALLENE
Parsons, L. O.  Cosmop's citation for best supporting performance of month.  Cosmop 122:66 Mr '47

ROBERTS, BARBARA
Schwarzkopf, J.  Sketch.  Motion Pic 54:55 D '37

ROBERTS, BEVERLY
Sketch.  Motion Pic 52:17 O '36
Sketch.  Photop 50:76 D '36
Bio note; filmog.  Movies & People 2:33 '40

ROBERTS, EDITH
Sketch.  Green Book 16:336 Ag '16
Sketch.  Photop 18:28 Je '20
Reid, J.  Interview.  Motion Pic 20:59 Ja '21
Goldbeck, W.  Interview.  Motion Pic Classic 13:22 D '21
Handy, T. B.  Interview.  Motion Pic 23:32 Ap '22
Fink, L.  Interview.  Classic 15:48 N '22

ROBERTS, LOUANNE
New Zealand beauty, a fast-rising new star.  Show 2-2:42 Ap '72

ROBERTS, PERNELL
A hard man to convince.  TV Guide 8-38:15 S 17 '60
Kobrin, J.  Fugitive from the Ponderosa.  TV Guide 14-32:6 Ag
6 '66

ROBERTS, RACHEL
Klemesrud, J.  How to vex the ex. Mrs. Rex.  N. Y.  Times
Bio Ed p1999 D '73

ROBERTS, ROY
Raddatz, L.  The Dodge City gang.  TV Guide 20-12:14 Mr 18
'72

ROBERTS, SARA JANE
  Obit.  Screen World 20:239 '69

ROBERTS, THEODORE
  Versatile character actor.  Theatre 8:57 F '08
  Interview.  N. Y. Dram 65:6 Ja 11 '11
  MacGaffey, K.  Busting the hair trust.  Photop 12-2:35 Jl '17
  Remont, F.  Interview.  Motion Pic 15:64 N '18
  Squier, E. L.  Interview.  Motion Pic Classic 9:44 F '20
  Roberts, S.  Interview.  Motion Pic 21:57 F '21
  Naylor, H. S.  Interview.  Motion Pic Classic 13:48 D '21
  His darkest hour.  Classic 15:43 D '22
  Home of.  Classic 15:40 Ja '23
  Calhoun, D.  Sketch.  Motion Pic Classic 28:22 O '28
  In memoriam.  Motion Pic 45:53 Je '33
  Case, D. E.  Theodore Roberts; filmog.  Films In R 23-4:213
    Ap '72

ROBERTSON, CLIFF
  Letters.  Films In R 20-5:323 My '69
  Bio.  Cur Bio 30:35 D '69
  Same.  Cur Bio Yrbk 1969:368 '70
  Hair-raising stories from the stars.  Photop 78-2:50 Ag '70
  The most fateful decision I ever made.  Mod Screen 66-3:45 Mr
    '72
  Knight, A.  One man's movie.  Sat R 55:14 My 6 '72
  Peterson, M.  Producer, director, writer and star of J. W.
    Coop.  Show 2-4:38 Je '72
  Harmetz, A.  Cliff Robertson flies the 'Coop' to glory.  N. Y.
    Times Bio Ed p1387 Jl '72
  Castell, D.  Going to the mountain; interview; filmog.  Films
    Illus 2-20:14 F '73

ROBERTSON, DALE
  Balling, F. D.  Fan-made star.  Silver S 22-3:42 Ja '52
  Robertson, D.  Why I love Hollywood.  Silver S 23-2:46 D '52
  Rising stars.  Film R p106 '52/53

ROBERTSON, JOHN S.
  Sketch.  Photop 20:25 O '21
  Obit.  N. Y. Times p88 N 8 '64
  Screen World 16:225 '65

ROBERTSON, WILLARD
  Stewart, W. T.  Letter.  Films In R 14-8:507 O '63

ROBESON, PAUL
  Van Vechton, C.  Sketch.  Theatre 42:24 Ag '25
  Sargeant, E. S.  Man with his home in a rock.  New Rep 46:40
    Mr 3 '26
  Negroes on the stage.  Outlook 155:175 Je 4 '30
  Robeson as Othello.  Liv Age 338:563 Jl 1 '30
  Black Othello.  Lit Dig 106:16 Jl 5 '30

Robeson in London; interview.  Liv Age 341:85 S '31
Woollcott, A.  Appreciation.  Cosmop 95:54 Jl '33
Bravos.  Time 34:58 N 20 '39
Bradford, R.  Paul Robeson is John Henry.  Colliers 105:15 Ja
    13 '40
Bio.  Cur Bio '41
First U. S. appearance in Othello.  Time 40:66 Ag 24 '42
Story of.  Newsweek 22:90 N 1 '43
Bio sketch.  Time 42:70 N 1 '43
A magnificent performance as the Moor of Venice.  Life 15:87
    N 22 '43
Beatty, J.  America's No. 1 Negro.  Am Mag 137:28 My '44
Baker, G.  Interview.  Scholastic 44:19 My 22 '44
Hutchens, J. K.  Appreciation.  Theatre Arts 28:579 O '44
Some reflections on Othello.  Am Scholar 14-4:391 O '45
Pioneers in the struggle against segregation.  Survey G 36:91
    Ja '47
Art for politics sake.  Time 49:24 My 19 '47
O'Neill.  Concert in Albany.  Commonweal 46:141 My 23 '47
Let him sing it.  Canad Forum 27:53 Je '47
Either way you win.  Time 51:18 Je 14 '48
Burden of proof.  Time 53:36 Je 27 '49
Picnic at Peekskill.  Time 54:15 S 5 '49
Mr. Robeson and democracy.  Commonweal 50:524 S 9 '49
Peekskill and Germany.  Nation 169:259 S 10 '49
Robeson ruckus.  Newsweek 34:23 S 12 '49
Peekskill shadow.  Christian Cent 66:1095 S 21 '49
Notes and comment.  New Yorker 25:23 S 24 '49
Miers, E. S.  Made in America.  Nation 170:523 My 27 '50
Journey's end.  Time 56:12 Ag 14 '50
They didn't rally round.  Colliers 126:86 O 28 '50
Hamburg, A. S.  Concert.  Nation 174:536 Je 7 '52
Chaplin to Robeson to Malenkov.  Sat Eve Post 227:10 S 4 '54
Case of Paul Robeson.  U. S. News 39:79 Ag 26 '55
Reply.  Am Mag 98:128 N 2 '57
Hentoff, N.  Makes a new album.  Reporter 18:34 Ap 17 '58
In Carnegie Hall.  Sat R 41:35 My 24 '58
Eccles, P.  Afternoon in Kiev.  New Rep 140:12 Ap 6 '59
McBrown, G. P.  World renowned actor, singer and scholar.
    Negro Hist B. 33:128 My '70
Receives Ira Aldridge award.  Negro Hist B. 33:128 My '70
Cripps, T.  Black identity in American movies.  Mass R 11:468
    Sum '70
Young, N.  A tribute to Paul Robeson.  Film Comment 50/51
    12 Fall/Win '70
Scheratsky, R. E.  The films of Paul Robeson.  Sightlines 4-5:
    4 My/Je '71
Bloustein, E.  Robeson dedication speech.  Negro Hist B 35:141
    O '72
Bogle, D.  The first black movie stars.  Sat R Arts 1-2:25 F
    '73

ROBINSON, AMY
  Once they were in love with Amy, but... N. Y. Times sec 2:8
    Mr 24 '74
    Same. N. Y. Times Bio Ed p422 Mr '74

ROBINSON, ANDY
  Filmog. Films & Filming 20-12:57 S '74

ROBINSON, BILL "BOJANGLES"
  Austin, M. Buck & wing and Bill Robinson. Nation 122:476 Ap
    28 '26
  Barnum, B. Bojangles. Cue 5-42:6 Ag 14 '37
  Bio. Cur Bio '41
  Bojangles. Newsweek 25:92 Je 4 '45
  How to keep happy. Am Mag 142:48 O '46
  Strouse, R. At 70, still head hoofer. N. Y. Times Mag p17 My
    23 '48
  Obit. Newsweek 34:61 D 5 '49
    Screen World 1:235 '49
    Time 54:98 D 5 '49
  Goodbye to Bojangles. Life 27:56 D 12 '49
  Shipley, G. Some notes on some film dancers. Filmograph 3-
    1:15 '72
  Bogle, D. The first black movie stars. Sat R Arts 1-2:25 F
    '73

ROBINSON, CHRIS
  Robinson, C. The production of Catch the black sunshine. Am
    Cinematog 54-6:686 Je '73

ROBINSON, EDWARD G.
  Erwin, A. Sketch. Motion Pic Classic 32:58 N '30
  Collins, F. L. Sketch. Good House 94:45 Je '32
  Morgan-Powell, S. Credit Edward G. Robinson. Cinema Dig
    2-2:10 N 28 '32
  Hall, G. Interview. Movie Classic 3:41 N '32
  Moffitt, C. F. Censorship for interviews Hollywood's latest
    wild idea. Cinema Dig 2-5:9 Ja 9 '33
  Edward G. Robinson. Cinema Dig 4-5:12 Je 12 '33
  Orme, M. Appreciation. Ill Lon N 182:876 Je 17 '33
  Cruikshank. He's romantic too. Silver S 3-8:56 Je '33
  Hall, G. Interview. Movie Classic 5:38 N '33
  Home of. Photop 45:42 My '34
  Service, F. Interview. Motion Pic 47:45 Je '34
  Harrison, P. His home life. Motion Pic 49:34 Je '35
  Cruikshank, H. Interview. Motion Pic 53:44 Ap '37
  Kullen, G. S. Little Caesar joins the G-men. Screen Book 21-
    11:36 Je '39
  Seton, M. His collection of paintings. Studio 118:236 D '39
  His collection of paintings. Vogue 96:62 O 1 '40
  Bio note; filmog. Movies & People 2:33 '40
  Franchey, J. R. Another Dr. Jekyll & Mr. Hyde. Silver S
    11-3:38 Ja '41

His quarrel with George Raft.  Life 10:40 My 12 '41
Extra.  Read all about it.  Lions R 1-3:no p# N '41
Millier, A.  His art collection.  Art in Am 32:224 O '44
His art collection.  Life 24:64 Mr 1 '48
Parsons, L. O.  Cosmop's citation for best star of month.
    Cosmop 124:13 My '48
Personality of the month.  Films & Filming 2-6:3 Mr '56
Ellison, H.  Robinson in The Cincinnati kid.  Cinema (BH) 2-6:
    12 Jl/Ag '65
When hoods were heroes.  Screen Greats 1-2:34 Sum '71
Higham, C.  Little Caesar is still punching.  N. Y. Times Bio
    Ed p2049 N '72
Obit.  Classic Film Collect 38:57 Spg '73
    Film R p14 '73/74
    Films & Filming 19-8:79 My '73
    N. Y. Post p4 Ja 27 '73
    N. Y. Times p51 Ja 28 '73
    Same.  N. Y. Times Bio Ed p154 Ja '73
    Screen World p239 '74
Everson, W. K.  Edward G. Robinson.  Show 3-2:37 Ap '73
Cleave, A.  Goodbye to a great professional.  Movie Maker 7-4:
    238 Ap '73
Broffenbrenner, B.  This old hobo myself; filmog.  Films Illus
    2-23:30 My '73
Little Caesar was a big man.  Photop 83-5:68 My '73
Peary, G.  Edward G. Robinson: 1893-1973.  Velvet Light 8:47
    '73

ROBINSON, FRANCES
    Puzo, L.  Frances Robinson; filmog.  Films In R 22-10:647 D
        '71

ROBINSON, GERTRUDE
    Sketch.  Motion Pic Classic 2:43 My '16

ROBSON, FLORA
    What is acting?  Theatre World 20:61 Ag '33
    Sketch.  Theatre World 22:10 Jl '34
    Hast, N.  Sketch.  Theatre World 25:79 F '36
    Sketch.  Theatre World 26:34 Jl '36
    Roberts, F.  Interview.  Theatre World 28:288 D '37
    Interview.  Theatre World 32:36 Jl '39
    Sketch.  Harp Baz 76:71 D '42
    Sketch.  Theatre World 37:33 D '42
    A believer in realism on the stage.  Theatre World 43:30 Ja '47
    Johns, E.  Don't write a part for Flora.  Theatre World 45:31
        Ag '49
    Tierney, M.  Nothing like a Dame; interview.  Plays & Players
        18-9:18 Je '71

ROBSON, MAY
    My beginnings.  Theatre 7:305 N '07
    Dolliver, A.  First appearances of.  Green Bk Album 1:396 F

'09
Interview.   N. Y.   Dram 68:5 Jl 24 '12
Miller, L.   Fifty years of acting.   Motion Pic 46:54 O '33
Service, F.   Interview.   Motion Pic 47:68 Je '34
Leighton, J.   Interview.   Photop 18:35 Ja '41
Obit.   Newsweek 20:6 N 2 '42

ROCCA, DANIELLA
Lane, J. F.   The face of '63--Italy.   Films & Filming 9-7:11
Ap '63

ROCHE, JOHN F.
Redway, S.   Sketch.   Motion Pic 31:58 Mr '26

ROCKWELL, ROBERT
From mouse to muscles.   TV Guide 8-5:21 Ja 30 '60

RODD, MARCIA
Flatley, G.   Nobody sees me as fragile.   N. Y.   Times sec 2:11
Mr 14 '71
Same.   N. Y.   Times Bio Ed Mr 14 '71

RODGERS, PAMELA
She applied for a job and got a husband.   TV Guide 15-22:32 Je
3 '67

RODRIGUEZ, ESTELITA
(See: ESTELITA)

RODWAY, NORMAN
Tierney, M.   Of saints and sinners; interview.   Plays & Players
17-11:22 Ag '70

ROGERS, CHARLES "BUDDY"
Shinn, G.   Sketch.   Motion Pic 31:78 My '26
West, J. S.   Sketch.   Motion Pic 34:46 Ag '27
St. Johns, I.   Sketch.   Photop 32:98 O '27
Johnston, C.   Sketch.   Motion Pic Classic 27:51 Ag '28
Biery, R.   Sketch.   Motion Pic Classic 28:37 N '28
Biery, R.   Compared to Charles Farrell.   Motion Pic 36:55 D
'28
Diary of trip on cattle ship.   Motion Pic 37:70 My '29
Donnell, D.   Interview.   Motion Pic Classic 29:36 Je '29
Rogers, B. H.   Story of.   Photop 36:34 Jl '29
Goldbeck, E.   Sketch.   Motion Pic 40:55 S '30
Talley, A.   Buddy's feminine fancy.   Silver S 1-1:15 N '30
Hall, G.   Sketch.   Motion Pic Classic 33:58 Ap '31
York, C.   Sketch.   Photop 40:65 Je '31
Walker, H. L.   Will he rival Rudy Vallee?   Movie Classic 1:16
O '31
Fender, R.   Sketch.   Motion Pic 45:64 Mr '33
Watkins, F.   Interview.   Film Fan Mo 114:8 D '70
Tillmany, J. E.   Filmog.   Film Fan Mo 114:13 D '70
Slide, A.   Interview.   Silent Pic 11/12:no p# Sum/Aut '71

ROGERS, CECILE
  Girl of infinite variety.   TV Guide 7-45:20 N 7 '59

ROGERS, GINGER
  Cruikshank, H.   Sketch.   Motion Pic 40:74 D '30
  Dust off 4 pedestals in the hall of fame.   Silver S 2-3:36 Ja '32
  Service, F.   Interview.   Motion Pic 46:58 S '33
  Price, B.   Ginger.   Silver S 3-12:23 O '33
  French, W. F.   Sketch.   Movie Classic 7:23 S '34
  Palmborg, R. P.   Her marriage.   Movie Classic 7:32 Ja '35
  D'Arcy, R. J.   Interview.   Motion Pic 49:48 F '35
  Keats, P.   She's Ginger.   Silver S 5-4:14 F '35
  Osborne, K.   Her beauty receives new emphasis in Roberta.
    Motion Pic 47:43 My '35
  Wilson, E.   7 reasons who (she) is tops.   Silver S 5-9:18 Jl '35
  Easton, F.   How she made good.   Motion Pic 50:37 Ag '35
  Sheldon, D.   Sketch.   Movie Classic 9:38 S '35
  Tully, J.   The real Ginger.   Motion Pic 50:28 O '35
  Graham, R.   Story of.   Movie Classic 9:28 Ja '36
  Advice to girls.   Motion Pic 50:24 Ja '36
  Standish, M.   Why she is attractive and popular.   Movie Classic
    9:52 F '36
  Hartley, K.   What love has done for her.   Movie Classic 10:32
    Ap '36
  Calhoun, D.   Her plans for the future.   Motion Pic 51:30 My '36
  Alden, A.   Her beautiful hair.   Movie Classic 10:16 S '36
  Her shoes.   Photop 50:56 N '36
  Reid, J.   Her popularity.   Motion Pic 53:30 F '37
  Wilson, E.   Projections.   Silver S 7-8:32 Je '37
  Camp, D.   Story of.   Motion Pic 54:22 Ag '37
  Home of.   Photop 51:38 O '37
  Henderson, J.   What it costs to be a star.   Screen Book 19-3:
    68 O '37
  Lane, V.   Having Wonderful time.   Screen Book 20-1:44 F '38
  Story of.   Life 4:44 My 9 '38
  Sullivan, E.   Agility, joy and Ginger.   Silver S 8-7:32 My '38
  Frazer, P.   Ginger writes her mother.   Screen Book 21-3:26
    O '38
  Fred Astaire and Ginger Rogers.   Visages 31:entire issue Ja '39
  Barron, E.   Rogers & Rogers, Inc.   Screen Book 21-8:36 Mr
    '39
  Wilson, E.   She's like sparkling champagne.   Silver S 9-8:22 Je
    '39
  Steps in her career.   Photop 53:38 Je '39
  Mulvey, K.   Sketch.   Womans Home C 67:7 F '40
  Hall, G.   You never can tell about Ginger.   Silver S 10-7:24 My
    '40
  Sketch.   Photop 54:32 Jl '40
  Bio note; filmog.   Movies & People 2:33 '40
  Trotter, M.   Astrological forecast.   Photop 18:73 F '41
  Manners, M. J.   The real lowdown on Ginger and George Mont-
    gomery.   Silver S 12-3:22 Ja '42
  French, W. F.   Interview.   Photop 21:54 N '42

Trotter, M.  Her horoscope.  Photop 22:30 F '43
Bangs, B.  The "do-it-now" girl.  Silver S 15-7:38 My '45
Dudley, F.  Recipe for happiness.  Silver S 17-12:22 O '47
Astaire and Rogers reunited in new film.  Cue 18-9:12 F 26 '49
Bowers, L.  Too tempting for Ginger.  Silver S 19-6:36 Ap '49
Ginger asks the press to a party.  Cue 18-19:17 My 7 '49
Keating, J.  Snap for Ginger.  Cue 20-38:10 S 22 '51
Shane, D.  Inside story of Ginger's fourth marriage.  Silver S
    23-8:32 Je '53
Letters.  Films In R 17-4:255 Ap '66
Ginger Rogers tribute.  Film Fan Mo 69:7 Mr '67
Bio.  Cur Bio 28:38 D '67
    Same.  Cur Bio Yrbk 1967:345 '68
Uselton, R. A.  The Wampus baby stars.  Films In R 21-2:73
    F '70
The love teams.  Screen Greats 1-2:10 Sum '71
Astaire & Rogers; filmog.  Screen Greats 1-7:entire issue n. d.
Taylor, A.  A job in fashion.  N. Y. Times Bio Ed Ap 25 '72
Suardi, V.  How the voice of Ginger Rogers helped turn back
    Mussolini's black shirts in Spain.  Liberty 1-4:46 Spg '72
Photoplay forum.  Photop 82-2:10 Ag '72
Hay, R. C.  Doctor Ginger Rogers; interview.  Interview 26:22
    O '72
Shipley, G.  Some notes on some of film's dancers.  Filmograph
    3-1:15 '72
Spiegel, E.  Fred and Ginger meet Van Nest Polglase.  Velvet
    Light 10:17 Fall '73

ROGERS, JEAN
    Caine, D.  Interview.  Motion Pic 53:59 Je '37
    All this and Dostoievsky too.  Lions R 1-9:no p# My '42
    Stars of tomorrow.  Lions R 1-11/12:no p# Jl/Ag '42
    My first star.  Cosmop 113:41 N '42
    Worry pays dividends.  Lions R 2-4:no p# Ap '43
    Hollywood has everything.  Lions R 2-5:no p# Jl '43
    Glamor girl in reverse.  Lions R 3-1:no p# S '43
    Malcomson, R. M.  The sound serial.  Views & Rs 3-1:13 Sum
        '71

ROGERS, KASEY
    What is this girl's secret?  TV Guide 6-22:26 My 31 '58

ROGERS, KENNY
    Stoop, N. M.  Two different ladders to success.  After Dark 5-
        7:30 N '72

ROGERS, ROY
    Wild west hero.  Cue 12-42:13 O 16 '43
    Roy rides to fame with his guitar.  Music 27:35 Mr/Ap '49
    LaBadie, D. W.  The last roundup.  Show 2-9:74 S '62
    How I faced my drinking problem.  Photop 78-4:60 O '70

ROGERS, WAYNE
The day he almost lost his wife.     Photop 85-2:57 F '74
Davidson, B.     Vintage year for Wayne.     TV Guide 22-44:29 N
   2 '74

ROGERS, WILL
White, M. Jr.     Work of In The Wall street girl.     Munsey 47:
   468 Je '12
Smith, F. J.     Interview.     Motion Pic Classic 7:56 N '18
Biographical.     Dram Mir 82:1159 My 22 '20
Shelley, H.     Interview.     Motion Pic Classic 11:49 Ja '21
Cheatham, M.     Interview.     Motion Pic 21:28 Ap '21
Interview.     Photop 20:36 Jl '21
Patterson, A.     Interview.     Photop 21:35 D '21
Evans, D.     Sketch.     Photop 22:36 O '22
Gardner, K.     Interview.     Classic 15:36 F '23
Interview.     National 52:357 Ja/ F '24
Sketch.     Cur Opin 78:39 Ja '25
Self-made diplomat.     National 55:210 Ja '27
Golden, S. B.     Interview.     Theatre 46:9 N '27
Interview.     National 56:314 Mr '28
Donnell, D.     Sketch.     Motion Pic Classic 27:21 Ap '28
Lang, H.     Sketch.     Photop 39:54 Ap '31
Orme, M.     Criticism.     Ill Lon N 178:1052 Je 29 '31
Morse, W. Jr.     Sketch.     Motion Pic 41:30 Je '31 and following
   issues.
McIntyre, O. O.     Biographical.     Cosmop 91:82 O '31
Collins, F. L.     Sketch.     Good House 94:45 Je '32
Moffitt, C. F.     Censorship for interviews Hollywood's latest wild
   idea.     Cinema Dig 2-5:9 Ja 9 '33
Schallert, E.     Interview.     Movie Classic 4:40 Mr '33
Grant, J.     His humorous description of the winners of 1933.
   Motion Pic 47:60 Je '34
Sargent, T.     His popularity.     Photop 46:34 S '34
Chapman, J. R.     His work in Life begins at 40.     Motion Pic 47:
   35 My '35
Obit.     Newsweek 6:18 Ag 17 '35
Lyttleton, E.     Appreciation.     Spectator 155:293 Ag 23 '35
Ratcliffe, S. K.     Sketch.     Spectator 155:287 Ag 23 '35
Reid, J. E.     Appreciation.     Movie Classic 9:6 N '35
Love, P. M.     Statue of Will Rogers unveiled.     Okla Chronicles
   17:336 S '39
Keith, H.     Boys life of Will Rogers.     Okla. Chronicles 19:420
   D '41
Love, P. M.     The Will Rogers memorial erected by state of
   Oklahoma.     Okla. Chronicles 20:404 D '42
MacNeil, N.     Old cowhand.     Time 96:76 S 28 '70
Hout, A. P.     Little human happiness.     Read Dig 99:121 O '71
All I know is what I read in the papers.     Read Dig 100:131 Je
   '72
Maltin, L.     Will Rogers on the screen.     Film Fan Mo 132:3 Je
   '72
American Heritage to publish first authorized biography.     Pub W

202:57 Jl 31 '72
Lobdell, C. W.  The world laughs with him.  Liberty 1-7:50
    Win '72
Rollins, P. C.  Symbolic man and film image.  J of Pop F 2-4:
    323 Fall '73
Rubin, M.  Mr. Ford and Mr. Rogers.  Film Comment 10-1:54
    Ja/F '74

ROGERS, WILL JR.
Weekly may become a daily under Bill.  Newsweek 6:20 N 30
    '35
Will Rogers, Jr. , editor.  Lit Dig 121:17 F 22 '36
Will's boy Bill.  Time 39:14 Je 15 '42
Rovere, R. H.  Eight hopeful congressmen.  Nation 156:296 F
    27 '43
Bill Rogers.  Am Mag 135:130 My '43
Let's make this the last war.  Nat Educ Assn N 32:129 My '43
To run for U. S. senate.  Time 47:45 Ap 15 '46
Will Rogers' boy.  Life 20:142 My 27 '46
Like father, like son.  Coronet 29:117 F '51
Wood, T.  Double for dad.  Colliers 129:21 Je 7 '52
Will Rogers lives again.  Am Mag 153:60 Je '52
Bio note.  Newsweek 40:80 Jl 28 '52
Chip and block.  Time 61:68 Mr 2 '53
Bio.  Cur Bio 14:27 D '53
    Same.  Cur Bio Yrbk 1953:540 '53
Alvin, J.  Adventures in parenthood.  Parents 29:42 Ja '54
Bester, A.  Plain old Will Rogers Jr.  Holiday 20:143 D '56
Wood, C.  TV personalities biographical sketchbook.  TV Per-
    sonalities p104 '56

ROLAND, GILBERT
St. Johns, I.  Sketch.  Photop 32:71 S '27
Thorp, D.  Sketch.  Motion Pic Classic 26:36 N '27
Albert, K.  Sketch.  Photop 35:31 My '29
Hamilton, S.  Sketch.  Photop 54:33 N '40
Phillips, D.  Your mother adored him too.  Silver S 24-5:42
    Mr '54
Williams, N.  All the Cisco Kids; Cisco Kid filmog.  Filmo-
    graph 1-2:33 '70
Whitney, D.  He made your grandmother swoon.  TV Guide 19-
    19:24 My 8 '71
Pitts, M. R.  The most virile actor in the movies; filmog.
    Classic Film Collect 32:4 Fall; 33:56 Win '71; 36:13 Fall '72

ROLAND, RUTH
Sketch.  Cosmop 58:202 Ja '15
How she became a photoplayer.  Motion Pic 9:117 Ap '15
Sketch.  Green Bk 15:737 Ap '16
How she works up interest in her parts.  Motion Pic 11:48 My
    '16
Briscoe, J.  Sketch.  Motion Pic 12:121 S '16
How to get in moving pictures.  Motion Pic Classic 3:59 S '16

Petersen, E.   Sketch.   Motion Pic Classic 4:46 Ap '17
Bassett, F.   Sketch.   Motion Pic Classic 6:52 Ag '18
Bruner, F. V.   Sketch.   Motion Pic Classic 8:34 Jl '19
Peltret, E.   Interview.   Motion Pic Classic 13:22 N '21
Goldbeck, W.   Interview.   Motion Pic 22:46 D '21
Autobiographical.   Motion Pic 29:52 F '25
Service, F.   Leaves from her diary.   Motion Pic 36:68 O '28
Conti, M.   Shopping with Ruth Roland.   Motion Pic 37:68 Je '29
Everett, E. K.   Queen of the cliffhangers.   Classic Film Collect
    42:54 Spg '74

ROLLE, ESTHER
    Klemesrud, J.   Florida finds good times in Chicago.   N. Y.
        Times sec 2:17 My 5 '74
        Same.   N. Y. Times Bio Ed p750 My '74
    Riley, J.   The fishin' pole.   TV Guide 22-26:16 Je 29 '74

ROLLINS, DAVID
    Brock, A.   Salute to a friend.   Classic Film Collect 37:41 Win
        '72

ROMAN, RUTH
    O'Leary, D.   "Sleeper" gal.   Silver S 20-4:42 F '50
    Cochran, S.   I knew Ruth Roman when.   Silver S 21-8:40 Je '51
    Roman, R.   It's my life--or isn't it.   Silver S 22-4:38 F '52
    Asher, J.   Until it happens to you.   Silver S 24-4:35 F '54
    Parish, J. R.   Letter; partial filmog.   Films In R 20-8:520 O
        '69
    Stanke, D.   Ruth Roman; filmog.   Film Fan Mo 142:11 Ap '73

ROMANCE, VIVIANE
    Viviane Romance.   Visages 33:entire issue Ap '39

ROME, STEWART
    Star of the past.   Film R p22 '62/63
    Obit.   Film R p45 '65/66

ROMERO, CESAR
    Reed, D.   Romero.   Silver S 5-9:53 Jl '35
    Morton, R.   Sketch.   Motion Pic 50:56 S '35
    De Kolty, J.   Conquering Cesar.   Silver S 7-7:40 My '37
    McFee, F.   How one star sidesteps scandal.   Screen Book 21-
        9:28 Ap '39
    Cheatham, M.   Cesar talks about his girl friends.   Silver S 10-
        2:46 D '39
    Lindsay, M.   Sketch.   Photop 18:30 Ja '41
    Asher, J.   Bachelor behavior in Hollywood.   Silver S 11-6:36
        Ap '41
    Holliday, K.   Ex-man about town.   Silver S 17-11:29 S '47
    Williams, N.   All the Cisco Kids; Cisco Kid filmog.   Filmograph
        1-2:37 '70

ROONEY, MICKEY
Harrison, P. Work of as Puck. Motion Pic 50:24 N '35
Foye, T. Pals. Silver S 7-5:40 Mr '37
Johnston, J. The midget grows up. Screen Book 19-2:86 S '37
Reid, J. Mickey the menace. Screen Book 21-5:42 D '38
Reid, J. I'm not girl crazy. Screen Book 21-9:22 Ap '39
Isbell, J. I love Mickey Rooney. Screen Book 21-9:23 Ap '39
Mulvey, K. Sketch. Womans Home C 67:38 Je '40
Bio note; filmog. Movies & People 2:33 '40
Benedict, P. When tomorrow comes for Mickey. Silver S 11-3:
    24 Ja '41
Master mimic. Lions R 1-5:no p# Ja '42
Twenty years in show business. Lions R 1-5:no p# Ja '42
The Andy kid. Lions R 1-7:no p# Mr '42
Bartholomew, F. I knew Mickey Rooney when... Lions R 2-1:
    no p# S/O '42
Rooney, M. I knew Freddie Bartholomew when... Lions R 2-
    1:no p# S/O '42
Trotter, M. His horoscope. Photop 22:32 F '43
Morgan, F. If I were Mickey Rooney. Lions R 2-4:no p# Ap
    '43
Rooney, M. If I were Frank Morgan. Lions R 2-4:no p# Ap
    '43
Kilgallen, D. Sketch. Photop 23:20 Je '43
Garland, J. He's terrific. Lions R 3-1:no p# S '43
Rooney, M. Dear Jootes. Lions R 3-1:no p# S '43
Sketch. Photop 24:48 D '43
College daze. Lions R 3-3:no p# Ap '44
St. Johns, A. R. Story of. Photop 25:31 Ag '44
Agee, J. Work of in National velvet. Nation 159:783 D 23 '44
Letter to his mother. Photop 27:58 O '45
Lane, F. Martha's true love. Silver S 19-9:35 Jl '49
Baer, M. M. I'm my own worst enemy. Silver S 22-8:24 Je
    '52
Minoff, P. There was a time and place for Andy Hardy. Cue
    23-38:39 S 18 '54
Readin' ritin' and rehearsal. TV Guide 4-38:20 S 22 '56
Back to burlesque for the third time. TV Guide 14-50:12 D 10
    '66
The love teams. Screen Greats 1-2:10 Sum '71
McAsh, I. F. The child star who grew up; interview. Films
    Illus 4-38:63 O '74
The marital misadventures of Mickey Rooney: Chapter 7. Peo-
    ple 2-20:56 N 11 '74
Judy and Mickey; filmog. Screen Greats 8:entire issue n. d.

ROONEY, PAT
Kennedy, J. B. Interview. Colliers 83:39 My 11 '29
Keating, J. Ol' man Rooney...he just keeps rolling along. Cue
    20-28:15 Jl 15 '51

ROONEY, TEDDY
Harbert, R. Entertainment roundup for October. Good House

147:24 O '58
Mugger, but so's your old man.   Life 46:123 My 18 '59
Second generation.   TV Guide 7-33:5 Ag 15 '59
Andy Hardy Jr.   Newsweek 54:65 Ag 17 '59

RORK, ANN
    Spensley, D.   Sketch.   Photop 31:63 My '27

ROSAY, FRANCOISE
    Francoise Rosay.   Visages 27:entire issue S '38
    Problems of playing in a foreign language.   Theatre World 43:28
        S '47
    Obit.   N. Y. Times Bio Ed p424 Mr '74

ROSE, ALISON
    Raddatz, L.   You don't have to be a psychiatrist's daughter to
        be an actress--but it helps.   TV Guide 19-22:36 My 29 '71

ROSE-MARIE
    Now a grown-up, sophisticated actress.   Newsweek 26:89 Jl 16
        '45

ROSENBLOOM, MAXIE
    Underhill, D.   "Shulberg" picks a winner.   Screen Book 22-3:76
        O '39
    Slapsie vs. Maxie at Club 18.   Cue 15-13:11 Mr 30 '46

ROSING, BODIL
    Biery, R.   Sketch.   Photop 32:72 N '27

ROSS, BETSY KING
    Fernett, G.   The several careers of Betsy King Ross.   Film
        Fan Mo 90:16 D '68

ROSS, DIANA
    Miller, E.   Off the record with the Supremes.   Seventeen 25:
        280 Ag '66
    Diehl, D.   Diana.   TV Guide 16-49:14 D 7 '68
    Hamilton, J.   Supreme Supreme.   Look 33:68 S 23 '69
    Farrell, B.   Farewell, more or less, to the Supremes.   Life
        68:18B F 13 '70
    Robinson, L.   Why (she) left the Supremes.   Ebony 25:120 F '70
    Baby, baby, where did Diana go?   Time 96:30 Ag 17 '70
    Ross rage.   Harp Baz 104:84 Ap '71
    Miller, E.   Interview.   Seventeen 31:82 S '72
    Robinson, L.   Lady sings the blues.   Ebony 28:37 N '72
    New day for Diana.   Life 73:42 D 8 '72
    Harmetz, A.   Lady doesn't sing the blues.   N. Y. Times sec 2:
        3 D 24 '72
    Same.   N. Y. Times Bio Ed p224 8 D '72
    Entertainer of the year.   Cue 42-2:11 Ja 13 '73
    We salute a new star.   Mod Screen 67-2:14 F '73
    I may be married, but I'm still free.   Photop 83-4:52 Ap '73

All they saw was sequins.  Films Illus 2-23:14 My '73
How they suffer for their white men.  Photop 84-6:54 D '73

ROSS, JOE E.
An offbeat pair on the beat.  TV Guide 9-42:13 O 21 '61
The bluecoat blues.  TV Guide 11-3:6 Ja 19 '63

ROSS, KATHARINE
Knight, A. & Alpert, H.  Sex stars of 1970.  Playboy 17-12:220
D '70

ROSS, LANNY
Sketch.  Photop 45:38 My '34
You can't ever go back.  Am Mag 142:64 D '46

ROSS, SHIRLEY
Whitehead, H.  Sketch.  Motion Pic 53:25 Ap '37
Churchill, E.  Don't try too hard.  Screen Book 19-6:36 Ja '38
Smithson, E. J.  Salute to Shirley.  Screen Book 21-8:11 Mr
'39
Gwin, J.  Having pleasant dreams.  Silver S 9-6:51 Ap '39
Bio note; filmog.  Movies & People 2:33 '40

ROSS, THOMAS W.
Obit.  Screen World 11:224 '60

ROSSI, TINO
Tino Rossi.  Visages 14:entire issue Jl '37

ROSSI-DRAGO, ELEANORA
These faces will win top places during 1959.  Films & Filming
5-7:18 Ap '59

ROSSITER, LEONARD
Morley, S.  Two actors.  Plays & Players 16-12:50 S '69

ROTH, LILLIAN
Albert, K.  Sketch.  Photop 37:31 My '30
Goldbeck, E.  Interview.  Motion Pic 39:55 Jl '30
Roth, L.  I gave up my career for love.  Silver S 9-10:46 Ag
'39
Cogley, J.  Star reborn.  Commonweal 60:375 Jl 16 '54
I can prove there is a God.  Coronet 38:55 Ag '55
Sixteen-year-long lost weekend.  Life 40:117 Ja 9 '56
Goldsmith, B.  Women can come back.  Womans Home C 83:14
Ja '56
Debus, A. G.  Current collectors' recordings.  Hobbies 61:32
Ap '56
Watt, D.  Tables for two.  New Yorker 32:95 F 2 '57
Unsure convert.  Newsweek 51:72 Ap 14 '58

ROTHMAN, STEPHANIE
Fox, T. C.  Unearthed directors.  Focus 8:24 Aut '72

ROUNDS, DAVID
    Considine, S.   Rounds and about.   After Dark 6-4:56 Ag '73

ROUNDTREE, RICHARD
    From model to movie star.   Ebony 26:128 Je '71
    Klemesrud, J.   Shaft--a black man who is for once a winner.
        N. Y. Times Bio Ed Mr 12 '72
    The preacher's son is just a little wicked.   Photop 81-5:78 My
        '72
    Chelminski, R.   (his) big score.   Life 73:51 S 1 '72
    Strout, D.   Interview.   Mod Screen 66-10:20 O '72
    Lucas, B.   Dramatic real-life story.   Movie Dig 1-6:99 N '72
    Adler, D.   You can't put that John Shaft on TV.   TV Guide 22-
        16:26 Ap 20 '74

ROUX, MICHEL
    Bio note.   Unifrance 23:10 F '53

ROWLAND, ADELE
    Tinee, M.   Interview.   Green Book 9:235 F '13
    Sketch.   Green Book 16:42 Jl '16
    Patterson, A.   Interview.   Photop 20:68 Ag '21

ROWLAND, JADA
    Jobin, J.   Amy of Secret Storm.   TV Guide 18-39:14 S 26 '70

ROWLANDS, GENA
    Zunser, J.   His'n and Her'n.   Cue 27-23:11 Je 7 '58
    Harmetz, A.   Dear boss: I'm sorry I couldn't interview Gena...
        but John Cassavetes could.   N. Y. Times sec 2:11 F 13 '72
    Butterfield, M.   Portrait of a happy actress.   Show 12:49 F '72
    Interview: on movies, madness and myth.   Viva 2-3:61 D '74

ROWLES, POLLY
    Bonnie Auntie Laurie.   TV Guide 2-12:21 Mr 19 '54

ROYLE, SELENA
    Sketch.   Theatre 39:22 My '24
    Veteran newcomer.   Lions R 3-5:no p# D '44
    A Royle lady.   Lions R 4-1:no p# F '45

RUBENS, ALMA
    Of the "younger set."   Photop 11-5:41 Ap '17
    Peltret, E.   Sketch.   Motion Pic Classic 6:53 Ag '18
    Jameson, C.   Interview.   Motion Pic Classic 8:56 Jl '19
    Montanye, L.   Interview.   Motion Pic 19:36 Mr '20
    Lamb, G.   Interview.   Motion Pic 20:61 Ag '20
    Service, F.   Interview.   Classic 18:22 O '23
    Driver, M. W.   Interview.   Motion Pic 30:34 S '25
    Calhoun, D.   Sketch.   Motion Pic 41:32 My '31
    In memoriam.   Motion Pic 45:53 Je '33
    Lee, R.   The smile.   Classic Film Collect 20:14 Spg '68
    Peeples, S.   The girl with the beautiful eyes.   Classic Film Col-
        lect 37:16 Win '72

RUGGLES, CHARLES
  Sketch.  Green Book 14:902 N '15
  Sketch.  Theatre 22:302 D '15
  Busby, M.  The highball Hamlet.  Silver S 1-3:16 Ja '31
  Cheatham, M.  Ruggles the rugged rancher.  Silver S 5-9:21 Jl
    '35
  Cracker barrel sage.  TV Guide 2-50:18 D 11 '54
  Obit.  Classic Film Collect 30:extra 4 Spg '71
    Film R p13 '71/72
    N. Y. Times p24 D 24 '70
    Newsweek 77:49 Ja 4 '71
    Screen World 22:239 '71
    Time 97:65 Ja 4 '71
  Jacobs, J.  Thank you, Charlie Ruggles, 1892-1970; filmog.
    Focus On F 9:35 Spg '72

RULE, JANICE
  O'Leary, D.  Contradictory young miss.  Silver S 22-4:44 F '52

RUMAN, SIG
  Heffer, B. J.  Filmog.  Films In R 20-6:388 Je/Jl '69

RUSSELL, ELIZABETH
  Bodeen, D.  Letter.  Films In R 22-1:50 Ja '71

RUSSELL, GAIL
  Sketch.  Photop 25:52 N '44
  Colby, A.  Her beauty program.  Photop 30:66 My '47
  Dreier, H.  Home of.  Photop 36:64 N '49
  Russell, G.  Why I waited 4 years to marry Guy.  Silver S 20-
    4:22 F '50
  Meyer, J.  Gail Russell; filmog.  Film Fan Mo 119:3 My '71
  Crivello, K.  Gail Russell.  Classic Film Collect 33:37 Win '71
  Filmog.  Films & Filming 20-6:52 Mr '74

RUSSELL, HAROLD
  Frizell, B.  Story of.  Life 21:74 D 16 '46
  Parsons, L. O.  Cosmop's citation for best performance of
    month.  Cosmop 122:99 Ja '47
  Autobiographical sketch.  Photop 30:54 Mr '47
  Fields, A. C.  Hooked grip on life.  Sat R 32:11 Ap 2 '49
  Autographing parties.  Pub W 155:1752 Ap 23 '49
  Bio.  Cur Bio Ja '50
  Tanner, L.  Best years of their lives.  Coronet 47:88 Mr '60

RUSSELL, JANE
  Poses for pin-up photos.  Life 18:94 Ja 29 '45
  Vallee, W. L.  Girl behind the pin-up.  Silver S 16-4:50 F '46
  The song I remember.  Photop 29:59 Je '46
  Jenkins, D.  So you think you know Jane Russell?  Silver S 19-
    10:22 Ag '49
  Jane Russell is outstanding.  Mel Maker 25:2 O 1 '49
  Churchill, R. & B.  No plain Jane.  Silver S 20-9:33 Jl '50

MacDonald, E.  Letter to a star.  Silver S 22-3:30 Ja '52
Zunser, J.  When he says sizzle, I sizzle.  Cue 21-35:15 Ag 30
    '52
Sheridan, M.  Saintly siren?  Silver S 23-9:24 Jl '53
What I think of Marilyn.  Silver S 23-10:26 Ag '53
Hyams, J.  Sex and salvation.  Cue 23-26:12 Je 26 '54
Henaghan, J.  Is Jane Russell a Hollywood hoax?  Silver S 24-9:
    46 Jl '54
Where are they now?  Newsweek 70:22 N 13 '67
Hamilton, J.  Where oh where are the beautiful girls?  Look 34-
    22:64 N 3 '70
Bell, A.  Lana and Jane, they're still stars.  N. Y. Times Bio
    Ed Je 27 '71
Thompson, T.  The Outlaw girl, Broadway's newest star.  Life
    71:68 Jl 2 '71
Fry, R.  The outlaw.  Nostalgia Illus 1-2:39 D '74


RUSSELL, LILLIAN
    And now Lillian Russell becomes a movie actress.  Photop 7-3:
    111 F '15


RUSSELL, REB
    Rainey, B. G.  His interlude as western star.  Filmograph 3-3:
    32 '73
    A (provisional) filmog of Reb Russell.  Filmograph 3-4:42 '73


RUSSELL, ROSALIND
    Anderson, M.  Story of.  Movie Classic 9:34 Ja '36
    Lee, S.  Interview.  Motion Pic 52:43 N '36
    Her clothes.  Womans Home C 64:55 Jl '37
    Lee, S.  Her night of terror.  Screen Book 20-6:30 Jl '38
    Danger.  High explosives.  Screen Book 22-2:58 S '39
    Sullivan, E.  Meet Miss Connecticut Yankee.  Silver S 10-1:40
        N '39
    Bio note; filmog.  Movies & People 2:34 '40
    That Russell girl.  Lions R 1-2:no p# O '41
    Me and my shadow.  Lions R 1-4:no p# D '41
    York, C.  Her marriage.  Photop 20:12 Ja '42
    Hall, G.  Her treasure hunt marriage.  Silver S 12-5:22 Mr '42
    Walker, H.  Sketch.  Photop 21:42 N '42
    Walker, H. L.  That's the way I feel about it.  Silver S 15-1:42
        N '44
    Parsons, L. O.  Cosmop's citation for best performance of
        month.  Cosmop 121:72 O '46
    Bangs, B.  Just try a little tenderness.  Silver S 16-12:50 O '46
    My luckiest day.  Cosmop 122:86 My '47
    Wilson, E.  A very determined lady is Roz.  Silver S 18-1:44
        N '47
    Russell, R.  Women's most common mistakes.  Silver S 18-9:22
        Jl '48
    Parsons, L. O.  Cosmop citation for best performance of month.
        Cosmop 126:13 Ag '48
    Roz and The girl rish.  Cue 24-33:12 Ag 20 '55

Life is a banquet.  Cue 25-52:10 D 29 '56
Ringgold, G.  Rosalind Russell; filmog.  Films In R 21-10:585
    D '70
Peck, T.  Letter concerning her appearance at San Francisco
    Film Festival.  Films In R 22-2:110 F '71
Morris, B.  Heaven in the 40s: a man-tailored suit.  N. Y.
    Times Bio Ed Mr 26 '71
Still going great.  Screen Greats 1-2:78 Sum '71
Raddatz, L.  It's lovely to be back.  TV Guide 20-42:29 O 14
    '72
Note.  Filmograph 3-3:44 '73
Fletcher, F.  Big-biz Roz did it for laughs--not lib.  Cue 43-
    35:1 S 16 '74
Bowers, R.  New York's Rosalind Russell festival.  Films In R
    25-9:572 N '74

RUSSELL, WILLIAM
    Bill, a violet.  Photop 11-5:139 Ap '17
    Being a hero.  Motion Pic 13:111 My '17
    Malvern, P.  Interview.  Motion Pic Classic 9:59 Ja '20
    Shelley, H.  Interview.  Motion Pic Classic 9:59 Ja '20

RUSSELL, WILLIAM
    Here come the heroes.  TV Guide 4-37:28 S 15 '56
    Medieval roverboy.  TV Guide 5-9:24 Mr 2 '57

RUTHERFORD, ANGELA
    Crail, T.  Angela Rutherford's a reel ding-dong.  TV Guide 17-
        17:24 Ap 26 '69

RUTHERFORD, ANN
    Hamilton, S.  Sketch.  Photop 54:19 F '40
    Haas, D.  Andy Hardy's girl grows up.  Silver S 11-7:38 My
        '41
    Soldier's sweetheart now.  Lions R 1-7:no p# Mr '42
    Vallee, W. L.  If she hollers let her grow up.  Silver S 13-3:
        32 Ja '43
    A tale of two series.  Lions R 3-1:no p# S '43
    Russell, J.  I won't talk.  Silver S 14-3:48 Ja '44
    My favorite possession.  Photop 26:56 My '45
    Bawden, J. E. A.  Interview; filmog.  Filmograph 4-1:12 '73
    Crivello, K. & McKay, A. C.  Addenda to Bawden.  Filmograph
        4-2:47 '74

RUTHERFORD, MARGARET
    Johns, E.  Life begins at 40.  Theatre World 44:11 D '48
    Fletcher, F.  Lady from London.  Cue 29-38:12 S 17 '60
    Tierney, M.  Nothing like a Dame; interview.  Plays & Players
        18-11:18 Ag '71
    Obit.  Classic Film Collect (reprint N. Y. Times) 35:8X Sum '72
        Film R p17 '72/73
    N. Y. Times Bio Ed My 23 '72

RYAN, CHARLENE
  Kroll, J.  Girls.  Girls.  Newsweek 79:105 My 22 '72

RYAN, DICK
  Obit.  Screen World 21:240 '70

RYAN, EDDIE
  Why I'm still single.  Photop 25:57 N '44

RYAN, IRENE
  Davidson, M.  Fame arrived in a gray wig, glasses and army
    boots.  TV Guide 11-36:5 S 7 '63
  They're still single.  TV Guide 13-9:22 F 27 '65
  Raddatz, L.  When Granny was a girl.  TV Guide 15-15:28 Ap
    15 '67
  Efron, E.  American gothic on television and off.  TV Guide 16-
    16:32 Ap 20 '68
  Obit.  Classic Film Collect 39:extra 1 Sum '73
    N. Y. Times Bio Ed p711 Ap '73
    Screen World p239 '74
  Fosse, B.  Irene Ryan: 1902-1973.  N. Y. Times sec 2:3 My 6
    '73

RYAN, MITCHELL
  Gardella, K.  Webb-produced chase to star Mitchell Ryan.  N. Y.
    Daily News Ag 4 '73 p9
  Raddatz, L.  Three heroes have disappeared.  TV Guide 22-22:
    14 Je 1 '74

RYAN, PEGGY
  My teenage mistake.  Photop 25:59 Jl '44
  Asher, J.  He's okay with Peggy.  Silver S 15-2:34 D '44
  Shipley, G.  Some notes on some of film's dancers.  Filmograph
    3-1:15 '72

RYAN, ROBERT
  What I've learned from my wife.  Silver S 20-5:44 Mr '50
  Zunser, J.  Stratford: Ryan, Hepburn et al.  Cue 29-31:8 Jl 30
    '60
  Salute of the week.  Cue 38-19:1 My 10 '69
  Ryan, R.  Cue salutes Marian Anderson.  Cue 39-13:37 Mr 28
    '70
  In the words of Robert Ryan.  Cue 39-28:11 Jl 11 '70
  Acts of birth; interview; filmog.  Films & Filming 17-6:26 Mr
    '71
  Obit.  Classic Film Collect (reprint Los Angeles Herald-Examin-
    er) 40:58 Fall '73
    Film 2-7:15 O '73
    Films & Filming 20-2:80 N '73
    N. Y. Times Bio Ed p1228 Jl '73
    N. Y. Post Jl 11 '73
    Screen World p239 '74
  Kennedy, H. J.  Robert Ryan 1909-1973.  N. Y. Times sec 2:3

Jl 22 '73
Same.   N. Y.   Times Bio Ed p1230 Jl '73
Paskin, B.   Ryan, a final farewell.   Films Illus 3-29:174 N '73

RYU, CHISU
Ryu, C.   Ozu and I; reflections on my mentor.   Cinema (BH)
6-1:6 '70


SABU
Sketch.   Newsweek 12:22 S 19 '38
Sketch.   Vogue 92:54 N 15 '38
Mulvey, H.   Sketch.   Womans Home C 67:15 N '40
French, W. F.   Modern Moslem.   Silver S 12-3:36 Ja '42
The boy on the cover.   Cue 11-16:1 Ap 18 '42
Fisher, G.   The elephant boy grows up.   Silver S 17-4:55 F '47
Obit.   Film R p44 '64/65

SACHS, DAVID
Raddatz, L.   Have you heard about the actor who performs heart
surgery?   TV Guide 18-30:12 Jl 25 '70

SACKS, MICHAEL
Michael Sacks.   Photop 85-6:36 Je '74

SAINT, EVA MARIE
People of promise.   Films & Filming 1-3:12 D '54

ST. CLAIR, YVONNE
Obit.   Screen World 23:240 '72

ST. JACQUES, RAYMOND
Sanders, C. L.   Raymond the magnificent.   Ebony 25:175 N '69
Knight, A. & Alpert, H.   Sex stars of 1970.   Playboy 17-12:220
D '70
Peterson, M.   He's making a big 'numbers' racket.   N. Y. Times
sec 2:13 My 13 '73
"I destroyed my father's love for me."   Photop 84-4:39 O '73
Stoop, N. M.   "If I had been white."   After Dark 6-9:47 Ja '74

SAINT JAMES, SUSAN
Raddatz, L.   There was this girl.   TV Guide 16-46:24 N 16 '68
The girl-next-door is a mystery.   Photop 81-2:64 F '72
A show trio.   Show 2-1:34 Mr '72
Susan Saint James.   Mod Screen 66-3:27 Mr '72
Tracking down the real Susan Saint James.   Photop 82-5:36 N
'72
Hano, A.   Lunch ended up a smashing success.   TV Guide 21-7:
30 F 17 '73

ST. JOHN, BETTA
O'Leary, D.   A puzzle to solve.   Silver S 23-10:33 Ag '53

ST. JOHN, CHRISTOPHER
    St. John, C.   Top of the heap.   Action 8-4:30 Jl/Ag '73

ST. JOHN, HOWARD
    Obit.   N. Y. Times p53 Mr 17 '74

ST. JOHN, JILL
    The Hollywood swingers.   Show 3-11:88 N '63
    Interview.   Photop 81-4:30 Ap '72
    Photoplay forum.   Photop 82-1:10 Jl '72

ST. JOHN, MARCO
    Stasio, M.   The stars of tomorrow on stage today.   Cue 38-9:9
        Mr 1 '69

SAIS, MARIN
    How to get into moving pictures.   Motion Pic 12:102 S '16
    Mount, C.   Sketch.   Motion Pic Classic 3:55 S '16
    A little lesson in Spanish.   Photop 11-4:81 Mr '17
    Ames, H.   Sketch.   Motion Pic Classic 4:37 Je '17

SAKATA, HAROLD
    Hudson, P.   Odd job gets a new job.   Sr Schol 99:44 S 27 '71

SALE, CHIC
    Sketch.   Green Book 15:517 Mr '16
    Sketch.   Green Book 18:603 O '17
    Smith, F. J.   Interview.   Motion Pic Classic 14:25 Mr '22
    Bio sketch.   National 51:361 Ja '23
    Sketch.   National 58:197 F '30
    Costello, T.   Sketch.   Motion Pic 42:42 D '31

SALES, SOUPY
    19,147 pies later.   TV Guide 13-41:30 O 9 '65

SALISBURY, MONROE
    Andres, R.   Sketch.   Motion Pic 15:104 Mr '18
    McKelvie, G.   Staging a snow storm in summertime.   Motion
        Pic 15:61 S '18
    Peltret, E.   Interview.   Motion Pic 20:48 Ag '20
    Peltret, E.   Interview.   Motion Pic Classic 11:32 D '20

SALMI, ALBERT
    Lewis, E.   Bay Ridge to Broadway.   Cue 24-13:13 Ap 2 '55

SAMPSON, TEDDY
    Peltret, E.   Interview.   Motion Pic Classic 10:20 Ag '20

SAND, PAUL
    Rosen, D.   How does (his) garden grow?   N. Y. Times Bio Ed
        N 28 '71
    Barber, R.   (He) took the long route to a new series.   TV
        Guide 22-39:26 S 28 '74

SANDA, DOMINIQUE
  Ehrlich, H.   The mad and the beautiful.   Look 35:66 O 5 '71
  Saler, S.   Mystery girl.   Newsweek 79:93 Mr 13 '72
  Magnifique Dominique.   Playboy 19-3:87 Mr '72
  de Vilallonga, J. L.   Interview.   Vogue 159:148 Ap 1 '72
  Bella bambina.   Time 100:91 Jl 10 '72
  Chelminski, R.   Dominique mystique.   Life 73:66 S 29 '72

SANDE, WALTER
  Obit.   Screen World 23:240 '72

SANDERS, GEORGE
  Hamilton, S.   Sketch.   Photop 54:19 F '40
  Wilson, E.   Do ordinary girls have the deepest passion?   Silver
    S 11-2:24 D '40
  Actor-inventor.   Lions R 1-10:no p# Je '42
  Manners, M. J.   Love is a disease.   Silver S 12-10:36 Ag '42
  Hall, G.   I can't make anyone understand me.   Silver S 13-3:30
    Ja '43
  Kilgallen, D.   Sketch.   Photop 23:20 Je '43
  Should a girl propose?   Photop 24:42 F '44
  Hall, G.   Things that keep him awake.   Silver S 14-9:30 Jl '44
  Cook, A.   A spade's a spade.   Silver S 15-4:46 F '45
  Parsons, L. O.   Cosmop's citation for the best starring role of
    the month.   Cosmop 120:68 Je '46
  The song I remember.   Photop 29:59 Je '46
  Shane, D.   Learn to sing a love song.   Silver S 22-4:36 F '52
  Obit.   Classic Film Collect (reprint N. Y. Times) 35:8X Sum '72
    Cur Bio 33:45 Je '72
    Film R p16 '72/73
    Mod Screen 66-7:13 Jl '72
    N. Y. Times p48 Ap 26 '72
    Same.   N. Y. Times Bio Ed Ap 26 '72
    Newsweek 79:117 My 8 '72
    Time 99:96 My 8 '72
  Ace, G.   In memory.   Sat R 55:6 My 27 '72
  Guerin, A.   The end of a love affair.   Show 2-5:38 Jl '72
  Goodbye, my love.   Photop 82-2:40 Ag '72
  Thiede, K. & S.   The Falcon saga.   Views & Rs 3-4:52 '72

SANDLER, TONY
  Higgins, R.   The unlikely harmonizers.   TV Guide 17-30:10 Jl
    26 '69

SANDS, DIANA
  Wolff, A.   Passion of Diana Sands.   Look 32:71 Ja 9 '68
  Obit.   N. Y. Post S 22 '73
    N. Y. Times p65 S 23 '73
    Same.   N. Y. Times Bio Ed p1537 S '73
    Screen World p239 '74
  Davis, O.   Diana Sands 1934-1973.   N. Y. Times sec 2:3 S 30
    '73
    Same.   N. Y. Times Bio Ed p1537 S '73

SANFORD, STANLEY "TINY"
    Maltin, L.  Our gang; Our gang filmog.   Film Fan Mo 66:3 D
        '66

SANGER, MARK
    Raddatz, L.   The man behind the wheel chair.   TV Guide 16-48:
        22 N 30 '68

SAN JUAN, OLGA
    Bowers, L.  Doing it the smart way.   Silver S 19-3:44 Ja '49
    Crivello, K.  Olga San Juan; filmog.   Classic Film Collect 35:
        17 Sum '72

SANTELL, ALFRED
    Squier, E. L.  Interview.   Photop 18:76 Jl '20
    Sketch.   Photop 30:88 O '26
    Cruikshank, H.  Sketch.   Motion Pic Classic 29:35 Je '29
    Bio note; filmog.   Movies & People 2:45 '40
    Cort, R. F.  Berkeley and Santell; letter.   Films In R 8-6:30
        Je/Jl '57
    Letters.   Films In R 8-7:362 Ag/S '57
    Dyer, E. V.  Stroheim and Santell; letter.   Films In R 9-3:158
        Mr '58

SANTLEY, JOSEPH
    Obit.   N. Y. Times p34 Ag 10 '71

SANTSCHI, TOM
    Romaine, R.  Sketch.   Motion Pic 18:79 S '19
    Bio note.   Cinema Trails 2:20 n. d.

SARGENT, DICK
    See, C.  Think plastics.   TV Guide 18-6:24 F 7 '70

SARIS, MARILYN
    Just a coincidence.   TV Guide 5-41:16 O 12 '57

SARNE, MIKE
    Sarne, M.  How to handle directors.   Films & Filming 11-7:41
        Ap '65
    Sarne, M.  The other side of the camera.   Films & Filming
        12-10:36 Jl '66
    Sarne, M.  For love of Myra.   Films & Filming 17-5:26 F '71
    British cinema filmog.   Film 65:10 Spg '72
    Sarne, M.  Knight in the big apple.   Films & Filming 19-1:22
        O '72
    Sarne, M.  On the blacklist.   Films & Filming 20-1:12 O '73
    Our man in Bahia.   Films & Filming 20-6:22 Mr '74
    Pile, S.  Interview.   Interview 1-1:1 n. d.

SARRAZIN, MICHAEL
    Eyles, A.  Bio note; filmog.   Focus On F 3:5 My/Ag '70
    Klemesrud, J.  A good roommate is hard to find.   N. Y. Times

Bio Ed D 20 '70
Macdonough, S.  The public and private life of an enigma.
  Show 2-2:19 Ap '71
The Sarrazin conspiracy; filmog.   Films Illus 1-12:12 Je '72
Married in all but name.   Mod Screen 66-11:26 N '72
Bio note; filmog.   Films Illus 3-36:475 Ag '74

SAUNDERS, JACKIE
  How she became a photoplayer.   Motion Pic Classic 1:40 F '16
  Jeffrey, I.  Interview.   Green Book 16:353 Ag '16
  Courtlandt, R.  Sketch.   Motion Pic 13:103 My '17
  Lee, C.  Christmas shopping.   Motion Pic 14:99 Ja '18
  A missing madonna.   Photop 16-1:67 Je '19
  Gaddis, P.  Interview.   Motion Pic 19:35 Ap/My '20

SAVALAS, TELLY
  Berkvist, R.  The two sides of terrible Telly.   N.Y. Times sec
    2:19 O 7 '43
  Same.   N.Y. Times Bio Ed p1718 O '73
  Stump, A.  Tales of Telly.   TV Guide 21-42:31 O 20 '73
  Voltz, D.  Interview.   Playgirl 2-1:57 Je '74
  Robbins, F.  Interview.   Gallery 2-6:32 Je '74
  Wilkins, B.  Kojak is No. 1 and Telly knows why:  it's me.
    People 1-18:22 Jl 1 '74
  Levin, E.  A cop without a gun is like a &$!#!! streaker.   TV
    Guide 22-35:20 Ag 31 '74

SAVELYEVA, LUDMILLA
  People are talking about.   Vogue 151:80 Ap 15 '68
  War and Peace star with the wide-screen name.   Life 64:70 My
    31 '68
  The Russians are here.   Dance 42:44 Je '68
  Miller, E.  Budding dancer becomes the greatest heroine of all
    Russia.   Seventeen 27:270 Ag '68
  Gross, E. L.  Ludmilla.   Vogue 152:364 S 1 '68
  Note.   International F G 10:335 '73

SAVO, JIMMIE
  Russell, F.  It's Jimmie Savo.   Silver S 5-2:24 D '34
  Young, S.  Mountains Mouse.   New Rep 83:106 Je 5 '35
  Chrichton, K.  Clowning.   Colliers 95:22 Je 15 '35
  They stand out from the crowd.   Lit Dig 119:30 Je 15 '35
  Vaudevillian tries drama.   Newsweek 8:31 Ag 15 '36
  Young, S.  Savo solo.   New Rep 103:277 Ag 26 '40
  Savo, the wistful pixie.   Newsweek 21:70 My 24 '43
  Little man, big heart.   Coronet 27:16 N '49
  Rose, B.  Saga of Savo.   Read Dig 56:55 Ap '50
  Where are they now?   Newsweek 48:36 N 19 '56

SAWYER, LAURA
  Obit.   Screen World 22:239 '71

SAXON, JOHN
Larkin, L.   Diagnosing the doctor.   TV Guide 18-21:32 My 23
'70

SAYERS, JO ANN
Surmelian, L.   Screen "debs."   Silver S 9-4:25 F '39
Crichton, K.   Sister Sayers.   Colliers 107:14 My 24 '41

SCALA, GIA
Obit.   N. Y. Times p46 My 2 '72
Same.   N. Y. Times Bio Ed My 2 '72
Newsweek 79:58 My 15 '72

SCARDINO, DON
Faces going far.   Films Illus 1-10:18 Ap '72

SCHABLE, ROBERT
Malvern, P.   Interview.   Motion Pic Classic 12:87 Ag '21

SCHAEFER, ANNE
Schroeder, D.   Interview.   Motion Pic 11:68 Ap '16
First Hoppy.   Classic Film Collect 22:15 Fall/Win '68

SCHAFER, NATALIE
...and repeat performance.   Filmograph 3-4:46 '73
Stanke, D.   In person; filmog.   Filmograph 3-3:24 '73

SCHEIDER, ROY
Sketch.   Movie Dig 1-6:31 N '72

SCHEINPFLUGOVA, OLGA
Obit.   N. Y. Times p47 Ap 17 '68

SCHELL, CARL
Spelman, F.   The explosive Schell family.   Show 3-1:62 Ja '63

SCHELL, IMMY
(Also known as Editha Nordberg)
Spelman, F.   The explosive Schell family.   Show 3-1:62 Ja '63

SCHELL, MARIA
Zunser, J.   Die Schone blonde bombe-schell.   Cue 27-3:10 Ja
18 '58
Spelman, F.   The explosive Schell family.   Show 3-1:62 Ja '63
How I let the one I love get away.   Photop 82-1:72 Jl '72

SCHELL, MAXIMILIAN
Spelman, F.   The explosive Schell family.   Show 3-1:62 Ja '63
Bio note.   Films Illus 1-5:32 N '71
This film is a goldmine; filmog.   Films Illus 1-8:18 F '72
Additional filmog.   Films Illus 1-9:11 Mr '72
Baxter, B.   Schell schock.   Films Illus 3-31:271 Ja '74

SCHELL, RONNIE
    The lame-duck actor with the happy quack.   TV Guide 16-23:11
    Je 8 '68

SCHIAFFINO, ROSANNA
    These faces will win top places during 1959.   Films & Filming
    5-7:18 Ap '59
    Bean, R.  Will there be film stars in 1974?   Films & Filming
    10-10:9 Jl '64

SCHILDKRAUT, JOSEPH
    Lewisohn, L.  The two Schildkrauts.   Nation 116:250 F 28 '23
    Sketch.  Theatre 37:12 Ap '23
    Service, F.  The genius of gesture.   Classic 18:35 S '23
    Bay, D.  Sketch.  Motion Pic 37:78 Ap '29
    Belfrage, C.  Sketch.  Motion Pic 38:74 S '29
    Rhea, M.  Sketch.  Photop 53:31 N '39
    People.  Cue 11-4:11 Ja 24 '42
    Obit.  Film R p45 '64/65
    Davis, C.  Joseph Schildkraut; filmog.   Films In R 24-2:71 F
    '73
    Romer, C.  Partial filmog.   Films In R 24-4:253 Ap '73
    Ring, H.  Letter.   Films In R 24-5:314 My '73

SCHILDKRAUT, RUDOLPH
    Lewisohn, L.  The two Schildkrauts.   Nation 116:250 F 28 '23

SCHNEIDER, MARIA
    Self-portrait of an angel and monster.   Time 101:51 Ja 22 '73
    Klemesrud, J.  Maria says her 'Tango' is not blue.   N. Y.
    Times sec 2:13 F 4 '73
    Same.  N. Y.  Times Bio Ed p305 F '73

SCHNEIDER, ROMY
    McWhirter, W. A.  Well-kept secret weapon in the sexual revo-
    lution.  Life 71:69 Jl 9 '71
    Note; partial filmog.   Films & Filming 19-8:58 My '73

SCHREIBER, AVERY
    Hobson, D.  They're talking about...   TV Guide 14-15:12 Ap 9
    '66

SCHUBERT, KARIN
    Sweden's favorite hamburger.   Oui 2-2:89 F '73

SCHUCK, JOHN
    John Schuck.   Photop 86-1:50 Jl '74

SCHWEID, MARK
    Obit.  N. Y.  Times p55 D 3 '69

SCOFIELD, PAUL
    Whittaker, H.  Paul Scofield.   Show 1-2:70 N '61

Sweeney, L.   Male of the species.   TV Guide 16-52:15 D 28 '68
Bio.   Brit Bk Yr 1968:161 '68
Salute of the week.   Cue 40-50:1 O 11 '71
Beaton, C.   In Beaton's view.   Plays & Players 19-9:20 Je '72
Ansorge, P.   Interview.   Plays & Players 20-8:16 My '73
Note; filmog.   Films Illus 4-39:90 N '74

SCOTT, BRENDA
   Meet the grandniece of the ever-popular Mae Busch.   TV Guide
      10-48:13 D 1 '62
   Raddatz, L.   After the ice cream melted.   TV Guide 15-16:21
      Ap 22 '67

SCOTT, FRED
   Manners, D.   Interview.   Motion Pic Classic 32:51 S '30

SCOTT, GEORGE C.
   Risk actor cuts loose.   Life 64:37 Mr 8 '68
   Crist, J.   Great Scott.   New York 3-6:54 F 9 '70
   Salute of the week.   Cue 39-8:1 F 21 '70
   Eyles, A.   Bio note; filmog.   Focus On F 3:15 My/Ag '70
   Tempering a terrible fire.   Time 97:63 Mr 22 '71
   Scott on some aspects of acting.   Time 97:66 Mr 22 '71
   Rollin, B.   Nothing ever really helps.   Look 35-8:78 Ap 20 '71
   Braun, S.   Great Scott.   Playboy 18-4:138 Ap '71
   Bio.   Cur Bio 32:33 Ap '71
      Same.   Cur Bio Yrbk 1971:384 '72
   Irving, C.   Reluctant Oscars.   McCalls 98:12 Jl '71
   Barthel, J.   At grips with an angry vagabond.   Life 73-12:77 S
      22 '72
   Gregory, J.   A tormented journey to greatness.   Movie Dig 1-6:
      67 N '72
   Stoneman, E. D.   The making of Rage.   Show 2-10:47 Ja '73
   Interview.   Action 8-1:12 Ja/F '73
   I got him to marry me by living with him.   Mod Screen 67-4:55
      Ap '73
   Weismen, J.   Interview.   Penthouse 4-9:60 My '73
   What directors are saying.   Action 9-1:38 Ja/F '74
   McGuire, J. M.   Scott shows the people of Missouri.   People
      2-6:48 Ag 5 '74

SCOTT, GORDON
   The new Tarzan.   Films & Filming 1-1:25 O '54

SCOTT, JACQUELINE
   She may be the youngest old-timer in the business.   TV Guide
      20-44:24 O 28 '72

SCOTT, JANETTE
   Rising stars.   Film R p28 '50

SCOTT, LIZABETH
   Wilson, E.   Siren from Scranton.   Silver S 15-10:38 Ag '45

Churchill, R. & B.   Pitfalls of dating.   Silver S 21-6:44 Ap '51
Marill, A. H.   Filmog.   Films In R 18-4:253 Ap '67
Stanke, D.   Lizabeth Scott; filmog.   Film Fan Mo 125:3 N '71

SCOTT, MABEL JULIENNE
Blame Broadway and Cleopatra.   Photop 15-4:40 Mr '19
Hall, G.   Interview.   Motion Pic 17:52 Jl '19
Cheatham, M.   Interview.   Motion Pic Classic 13:18 S '21
Sketch.   Theatre World 19:39 Ja '33

SCOTT, MARTHA
Hamilton, S.   Sketch.   Photop 54:28 Ag '40
Mulvey, K.   Sketch.   Womans Home C 67:17 S '40
Reid, J.   You can't be a star over night.   Silver S 11-4:26 F
'41

SCOTT, RANDOLPH
Janeway, D.   Sketch.   Movie Classic 2:29 My '32
Sketch.   Motion Pic 43:27 Je '32
Costello, T.   Sketch.   Motion Pic 44:64 O '32
Maddox, B.   They keep "Bachelor's Hall."   Silver S 3-5:20 Mr
'33
Hall, G.   Sketch.   Movie Classic 4:24 Jl '33
Maddox, B.   I hope it lasts.   Silver S 6-1:24 N '35
Bio note; filmog.   Movies & People 2:34 '40
Franchey, J. R.   Randy the rage.   Silver S 12-11:38 S '42
Kilgallen, D.   Sketch.   Photop 23:20 Je '43
Ringgold, G.   Randolph Scott; filmog.   Films In R 23-10:605 D
'72
Pinup of the past.   Films & Filming 20-1:62 O '73
Druxman, M. B.   Yesterday at the movies.   Coronet 12-2:124
F '74
Bio note.   Cinema Trails 2:21 n. d.

SCOTT, SERET
Smothers, R.   (She) ages brilliantly in 'Sister. '   N. Y. Times
Bio Ed p1038 Jl '74

SCOTT, ZACHARY
Walker, H. L.   Downright domestic.   Silver S 16-1:48 N '45
My first kiss.   Photop 29:59 S '46
If I had one wish.   Photop 29:61 O '46
Hall, G.   Domesticated villain.   Silver S 18-7:40 My '48
Hurst, T.   Switcheroo by Zachary.   Silver S 19-9:39 Jl '49
Pitts, M. R.   A bio-filmography of...   Filmograph 3-1:26 '72
Parish, J. R.   Filmog.   Filmograph 31-1:31 '72

SCOURBY, ALEXANDER
Voice from Brooklyn.   Time 91:58 Mr 15 '68

SEAFORTH, SUSAN
Fellow Americans.   TV Guide 13-52:26 D 25 '65

SEAGULL, BARBARA
(formerly known as Barbara Hershey)
Burke, T.  David Carradine, king of kung fu.   N. Y. Times Bio
    Ed p560 Ap '73
(See also: HERSHEY, BARBARA)

SEARL, JACKIE
Sketch.   Child Life 15:309 Jl '36
Smile when you call him Curly.   TV Guide 10-32:20 Ag 11 '62

SEARLE, PAMELA
There'll always be an England.   TV Guide 8-46:28 N 12 '60

SEARS, HEATHER
Rising stars.   Films R p27 '58/59

SEASTROM, DOROTHY
Kibbe, V.   Sketch.   Motion Pic Classic 22:33 F '26

SEBASTIAN, CHARLES E.
Only in Los Angeles could this happen.   Photop 12-2:78 Jl '17

SEBASTIAN, DOROTHY
Sketch.   Motion Pic 29:34 Jl '25
At the crossroads.   Photop 28:32 S '25
Johnstone, N.   Sketch.   Motion Pic Classic 23:35 Jl '26
Watson, E.   Sketch.   Motion Pic 35:55 Je '28
French, J.   Sketch.   Photop 39:37 Mr '31
Albert, K.   Sketch.   Photop 42:31 O '32
Tully, J.   Sketch.   Photop 45:54 Mr '34

SEBERG, JEAN
Zunser, J.   Jean plays Joan.   Cue 26-22:16 Je 1 '57
Rising stars.   Film R p27 '58/59
Bean, R.   Will there be film stars in 1974?   Films & Filming
    10-10:9 Jl '64
Rising stars.   Film R p57 '64/65
Sean Connery strikes again (photos).   Playboy 13-7:75 Jl '66
Seaberg, J.   Lilith and I.   Cahiers (Eng) 7:35 Ja '67
Mills, B.   A show-biz saint grows up, or, whatever happened to
    Jean Seberg?   N. Y. Times sec 2:17 Je 16 '74
    Same.   N. Y. Times Bio Ed p885 Je '74
Gow, G.   Interview; filmog.   Films & Filming 20-9:13 Je '74
d'Arcy, S.   Adieu, tristesse.   Films Illus 3-36:490 Ag '74

SEDGWICK, EDIE
Edie and Andy.   Time 86:65 Ag 27 '65
Hood, E.   Edie Sedgwick.   Film Cult 45:34 Sum '67
Obit.   N. Y. Times p45 N 23 '71
    Same.   N. Y. Times Bio Ed N 23 '71
Newsweek 78:65 N 29 '71
Screen World 23:240 '72

SEDGWICK, EILEEN
  Shelley, H. Interview. Motion Pic Classic 13:34 Ja '22

SEDGWICK, JOSIE
  Obit. Screen World p240 '74

SEEGAR, MIRIAM
  Earle, E. Sketch. Photop 38:156 N '30

SEEL, CHARLES
  Raddatz, L. The Dodge City gang. TV Guide 20-12:14 Mr 18
  '72

SEGAL, GEORGE
  The playmate as fine art. Playboy 14:141 Ja '67
  MacDonough, S. Segal plays slapstick with style. Show 1-13:20
  S 17 '70
  Leave them laughing. Newsweek 76:104 D 14 '70
  Note; filmog. Films & Filming 20-3:78 Ja '74
  Eyles, A. & Billings, P. Bio sketch; filmog. Focus On F 8:6
  n. d.

SEGAL, VIVIENNE
  Sketch. Green Book 14:844 N '15
  Sketch. Theater 45:30 Mr '27
  York, C. Sketch. Photop 36:68 N '29
  Goldbeck, E. Sketch. Motion Pic 38:50 D '29
  Davis, L. & Cleveland, J. Story of. Colliers 107:21 Ap 26 '41
  Terry, W. Pal Joey's best friend. After Dark 5-8:40 My '72
  Slide, A. Vivienne Segal. Film Fan Mo 136:19 O '72

SEIGMAN, GEORGE
  Denbo, D. Sketch. Motion Pic Classic 24:35 Ja '27

SELLERS, PETER
  Rising stars. Film R p20 '60/61
  The screen answers back. Films & Filming 8-8:12 My '62
  Interview. Playboy 9:69 O '62
  Cowie, P. The face of '63--Great Britain. Films & Filming
  9-5:19 F '63
  Noble, P. Star of the year; filmog. Film R p23 '64/65
  Lawrenson, H. People inside Peter Sellers. Esquire 74:120 N
  '70
  Strout, D. Interview. Mod Screen 66-12:41 D '72
  Living with Sellers is impossible. Photop 84-3:60 S '73
  Mercer, J. Many of many parts. Film 11/12:20 F/Mr '74
  McAsh, I. F. The changing face of Peter Sellers. Films Illus
  3-33:335 My '74
  Bio note; filmog. Focus On F 17:15 Spg '74

SEMON, LARRY
  Peltret, E. Interview. Motion Pic 20:70 N '20
  Haskins, H. Sketch. Motion Pic Classic 11:43 D '20

Cheatham, M.  Interview.  Motion Pic Classic 14:38 Ap '22
Sketch.  Classic 18:55 F '24
Gill, S.  The funny men; filmog.  8mm Collect 10:12 Win '64

SENNETT, MACK
  Carr, H. C.  Laugh tester.  Photop 7-6:71 My '15
  Hewston, E. W.  Sketch.  Motion Pic Classic 1:47 Ja '16
  The split reel.  Film Players Herald 2-7:28 F '16
  The psychology of film comedy.  Motion Pic Classic 7:20 N '18
  Carr, H.  Interview.  Motion Pic 23:20 Je '22
  Carr, H.  Interview.  Motion Pic 28:37 Ag '24
  Tully, J.  Makers of comedies.  Vanity Fair 26:64 My '26
  Dreiser, T.  Interview.  Photop 34:32 Ag '28
  To produce talking pictures.  Photop 38:10 Ag '30
  Manners, D.  Defense of low-brow comedy.  Motion Pic Classic
    32:36 O '30
  Beatty, J.  Anything for a laugh; interview.  Am Mag 111:40 Ja
    '31
  Inside story of rise to fame.  Newsweek 4:26 O 27 '34
  Tully, J.  Sketch.  Motion Pic 49:33 Mr '35
  Mack Sennett, 1949.  Cue 18-33:10 Ag 13 '49
  Obit.  8mm Collect 15:13 Sum '66
    N. Y. Times p1 N 6 '60
  Maltin, L.  Mack Sennett.  8mm Collect 9:25 S '64
  Sennett comedies available on 8mm market.  8mm Collect 9:25
    S '64
  Kearns, M.  More Mack Sennett.  8mm Collect 10:11 Win '64
  Giroux, R.  Mack Sennett.  Films In R 19-10:593 D '68
  Hoffner, J. R. Jr.  King of Keystone.  Classic Film Collect
    31:22 Sum '71

SERNAS, JACQUES
  Rising stars.  Film R p31 '50
  Busch, S.  Jacques Sernas; filmog.  Films In R 22-6:383 Je/Jl
    '71

SESSIONS, ALMIRA
  McClelland, D.  Almira Sessions.  Film Fan Mo 131:36 My '72
  Obit.  N. Y. Times p38 Ag 7 '74
    Same.  N. Y. Times Bio Ed p1174 Ag '74

SEYMOUR, ANN
   In the family.  Cue 12-31:11 Jl 31 '43

SEYMOUR, CAROLYN
  Faces going far.  Films Illus 1-10:18 Ap '72

SEYMOUR, CLARINE
  Peltret, E.  Interview.  Motion Pic Classic 8:46 Jl '19
  Obit.  N. Y. Clipper 68:34 Ap 28 '20
  Haskins, H.  The last interview.  Motion Pic Classic 10:51 Jl
    '20

SEYMOUR, HARRY
Obit.   Screen World 19:239 '68

SEYRIG, DELPHINE
Nogueira, R.  The lily in the valley; interview.  Sight & Sound
    38-4:184 Aut '69
Drewnowski, A.  Mystery is her business.  Interview 22:20 Je
    '72
Filmog.  Films & Filming 20-6:52 Mr '74

SHANNON, ETHEL
Prewitt, A.  Sketch.  Photop 30:70 Je '26
Uselton, R. A.  The Wampus baby stars.  Films In R 21-2:73
    F '70

SHANNON, PEGGY
Goldbeck, E.  Sketch.  Movie Classic 1:50 S '31
Screen stars or just girls.  Silver S 1-12:24 O '31
Costello, T.  Sketch.  Movie Classic 1:19 Ja '32
Kish, F.  Sketch.  Photop 43:69 D '32

SHANNON, RAY
Obit.  N. Y. Times p35 Ja 4 '71

SHARIF, OMAR
Zunser, J.  Egypt's gift to movies.  Cue 33-8:11 F 22 '64
Rising stars.  Film R p56 '64/65
Casilli, M.  Omar acts up (photos).  Playboy 15-12:145 D '68
Tornabene, L.  Walking with Sharif.  McCalls 96:42 Ap '69
Scala, S.  My mother ruined me.  Photop 75-6:44 Je '69
Bio.  Cur Bio 31:39 My '70
    Same.  Cur Bio Yrbk 1970:390 '71
Omar and Julie.  Films Illus 3-35:445 Jl '74
Bio note.  Films Illus 4-38:44 O '74
d'Arcy, S.  The chic of Araby.  Films Illus 4-39:111 N '74

SHARPE, DAVID
Fernett, G.  Interview.  Classic Film Collect 41:X-7 Win '73;
    42:28 Spg '74

SHARPE, KAREN
The west is for the Indians.  TV Guide 8-27:9 Jl 2 '60

SHATNER, WILLIAM
Manski, A. B.  Letter.  Films In R 16-2:125 F '65
Raddatz, L.  Star Trek wins the Ricky Schwartz award.  TV
    Guide 15-46:25 N 18 '67
Evanchuck, P. M.  Captain Kirk doesn't live here anymore.
    Motion p28 My/Je '73

SHAW, OSCAR
Benson, S.  Interview.  Photop 26:84 Ag '24

SHAW, RETA
   Whitney, D.  The mover and shaker of the El Camino council of
   PTA.  TV Guide 17-48:39 N 29 '69

SHAW, ROBERT
   Here come the heroes.  TV Guide 4-37:28 S 15 '56
   Method writer.  Newsweek 64:94 D 7 '64
   On the scene.  Playboy 12-9:186 S '65
   Wolf, W.  Which Robert Shaw?  Cue 34-52:14 D 25 '65
   Kauffmann, S.  Like a knife.  New Rep 156:27 F 4 '67
   Thompson, T.  Highest paid, oldest unknown actor in the world.
   Life 63:35 N 3 '67
   Bio.  Cur Bio 29:22 My '68
   Same.  Cur Bio Yrbk 1968:355 '69
   Gussow, M.  Actor, novelist, playwright--singer?  N. Y. Times
   Bio Ed Ja 5 '70
   Running figure in a landscape.  Show 1-1:61 Ja '70
   Thomas, R. M. Jr.  For Mary Ure and Robert Shaw, marriage
   may not be bliss but it'll do.  N. Y. Times Bio Ed F 26 '72
   Roman, R. C.  A man's reach should exceed his grasp.  After
   Dark 5-1:18 My '72

SHAW, SANDRA
   Sinclaire, V.  Her engagement to Gary Cooper.  Motion Pic 47:
   32 F '34
   Grant, J. & Busby, M.  Her marriage.  Movie Classic 6:8 Mr
   '34

SHAW, SEBASTIAN
   Cox, F.  Life and soul of the company.  Plays & Players 17-4:
   56 Ja '69

SHAW, VICTORIA
   Collier, C.  Letter.  Films In R 22-1:52 Ja '71

SHAW, WINI
   O'Malley, Wini S.  Ruby came back.  Film Fan Mo 121/122:3
   Jl/Ag '71

SHAWLEE, JOAN
   Bob Hope made her a star.  TV Guide 2-18:8 Ap 30 '54
   McCague, B.  Letter.  Films In R 10-7:437 Ag/S '59
   Johnson, D.  Some like it hot.  After Dark 4-9:43 Ja '72

SHAWN, DICK
   Minoff, P.  Massa Richard arrives.  Cue 22-46:15 N 14 '53

SHEA, WILLIAM
   Sketch.  Motion Pic 8:118 Ja '15
   Russell, L. C.  Reminiscences.  Motion Pic 10:96 Ag '15
   Everett, E. K.  The grand old man of Vitagraph.  Classic Film
   Collect 38:23 Spg '73

SHEARER, LORETTA
Hall, G.   Interview.   Motion Pic 47:42 F '34

SHEARER, MOIRA
Sketch.   Vogue 10:50 Jl 1 '47
Congratulated by Princess Elizabeth.   Ill Lon N 214:323 Mr 12 '49
Newsmakers.   Newsweek 71:36 Ja 1 '68

SHEARER, NORMA
Roberts, W. A.   Sketch.   Motion Pic 29:36 Mr '25
de Revere, F. V.   Analysis of her face.   Motion Pic 29:42 Ap
   '25
Howe, H.   Sketch.   Photop 27:84 My '25
Curran, D.   Interview.   Motion Pic Classic 22:38 N '25
Thorp, D.   Interview.   Motion Pic 31:28 Je '26
St. Johns, A. R.   Interview.   Motion Pic Classic 26:37 D '27
Thorp, D.   Interview.   Motion Pic Classic 26:37 D '27
Thorp, D.   Sketch.   Motion Pic 36:67 O '28
Ramsey, W.   Interview.   Motion Pic 37:33 My '29
Sketch.   Photop 37:6 Ap '30
Hall, G.   Interview.   Motion Pic 39:58 Ap '30
Sketch.   Fortune 2:38 O '30
Albert, K.   Sketch.   Photop 39:50 My '31
Manners, D.   Interview.   Motion Pic 41:58 Je '31
Walker, H. L.   Compared with Crawford and Garbo.   Movie
   Classic 1:23 S '31
Long, P.   Her secret of life.   Silver S 2-6:43 Ap '32
Tells what a free soul really means.   Motion Pic 43:48 Ap '32
Calhoun, D.   Interview.   Movie Classic 2:34 Mr '32
Watson, N.   She lives her life in chapters.   Silver S 2-10:56
   Ag '32
Hall, G.   Sketch.   Motion Pic 44:26 Ja '33
Wilson, E.   She tells all.   Silver S 3-5:22 Mr '33
Hall, G.   Interview.   Movie Classic 4:17 My '33
Sylvia.   How I saved her figure.   Photop 43:70 My '33
Wilson, E.   A visit to Norma.   Silver S 4-5:14 Mr '34
Grant, J.   Interview.   Movie Classic 7:30 Ja '35
Brundidge, H. T.   How she got into the movies.   Motion Pic 49:
   35 Jl '35
Tully, J.   Her story.   Motion Pic 50:26 N '35
Lane, V. T.   Her secret of wearing clothes.   Motion Pic 51:46
   Ap '36
Revere, M.   Constance Collier coached her as Juliet.   Movie
   Classic 10:30 S '36
Zeitlin, I.   Interview.   Motion Pic 52:32 O '36
Shavelson, S.   Experience with her.   Photop 51:9 Ja '37
Barker, R.   Doomed to oblivion.   Movie Classic 11:28 F '37
Lorton, T.   Screen's "first lady."   Screen Book 20-4:24 My '38
Wilson, E.   Projection.   Silver S 8-10:19 Ag '38
Carnegie, H.   Her gowns in Marie Antoinette.   Pict R 39:21 S '38
Lee, S.   She reveals her romantic future.   Screen Book 21-2:24
   S '38
Danger.   High explosives.   Screen Book 22-2:58 S '39

Wilson, E.  Will Norma marry George?  Silver S 10-5:38 Mr
 '40
Bio note; filmog.  Movies & People 2:34 '40
Norma Shearer.  Lions R 1-6:no p# F '42
Shearer energy.  Lions R 1-10:no p# Je '42
Her romance.  Photop 21:32 S '42
Pinup of the past.  Films & Filming 17-11:70 Ag '71
Here's to the ladies.  Screen Greats 1-2:26 Sum '71
Lambert, G.  The making of Gone with the wind.  Atlantic 231:
 46 F '73

SHEEN, MARTIN
 Stoneman, E. D.  Sheen looks homeward.  After Dark 5-8:46
  My '72
 Bio note.  Films Illus 4-40:124 D '74

SHEFFIELD, JOHNNY
 Makes personal appearance at war savings tour.  Lions R 1-10:
  no p# Je '42

SHELBY, SARAH
 Raddatz, L.  The Dodge City gang.  TV Guide 20-12:14 Mr 18
  '72

SHELDON, JACK
 Sheldon hits some crazy notes.  TV Guide 13-26:15 Je 26 '65

SHELLEY, CAROLE
 Bosworth, P.  Being a funny girl wasn't enough.  N. Y. Times
  sec 2:1 Jl 15 '73
 Same.  N. Y. Times Bio Ed p1234 Jl '73

SHELTON, JOHN
 Anders, J.  His marriage.  Photop 19:68 O '41
 Ormiston, R.  Interview.  Photop 23:57 Je '43
 Hall, G.  The rumors no longer are true.  Silver S 13-9:48 Jl
  '43

SHELTON, YVONNE
 Interview.  Motion Pic Classic 8:26 Ag '19

SHENDRIKOVA, VALENTINA
 Note.  Int F G 10:336 '73

SHEPHERD, CYBILL
 Feitler, B. L.  New stars.  Harp Baz 105:70 D '71
 Klemesrud, J.  Even before her movie, face was familiar.
  N. Y. Times Bio Ed Ja 12 '72
 O'Brien, G.  Interview.  Interview 19:14 F '72
 Miller, E.  Interview.  Seventeen 31:146 F '72
 Weller, S.  Really goodbye, American pie.  Movie Dig 1-4:112
  Jl '72
 Who needs marriage?  People 1-11:19 My 13 '74

SHEPHERD, ELIZABETH
  Keil, M.  On acting.  Motion p35 S/O '74

SHERIDAN, ANN
  How the glamour girl is made.  Vogue 90:96 N 1 '37
  Asher, J.  Announcing Miss Sheridan.  Screen Book 21-3:36 O
    '38
  Shupper, A.  Ann how.  Silver S 9-1:34 N '38
  Sketch.  Photop 53:69 Mr '39
  Watson, J.  We must see Annie.  Screen Book 21-9:26 Ap '39
  Wilson, E.  The glamour girl sweepstakes.  Silver S 9-7:16 My
    '39
  Sketch.  Time 34:24 Jl 31 '39
  Busch, N. F.  Story of.  Life 7:35 Jl 24 '39
  Hall, G.  Men I can't forget.  Silver S 10-8:38 Je '40
  Bio note; filmog.  Movies & People 2:34 '40
  Trotter, M.  Astrological forecast.  Photop 18:75 F '41
  Wilson, E.  If she becomes Mrs. George Brent.  Silver S 11-7:
    22 My '41
  Reid, J.  Why Ann changed her mind.  Silver S 12-7:22 My '42
  Sheridan, A.  Brother Bogie.  Silver S 13-3:22 Ja '43
  Bogart, H.  Sister Annie.  Silver S 13-5:26 Mr '43
  Entertainment for servicemen.  Newsweek 24:35 O 23 '44; Time
    44:68 O 23 '44; Newsweek 24:8 O 30 '44
  Reid, L.  Ann's USO tour.  Silver S 15-3:22 Ja '45
  Hall, G.  If you were me.  Silver S 16-11:48 S '46
  Parsons, L. O.  Cosmop's citation for best performance of
    month.  Cosmop 123:58 Jl '47
  Sheridan, A.  What makes a "good Sam?"  Silver S 18-3:24 Ja
    '48
  Sheridan, A.  This guy Clark Gable.  Silver S 19-11:20 S '49
  Letter from Liza.  Silver S 19-12:38 O '49
  Obit.  Brit Bk Yr 1968:598 '68
    Film R p21 '66/68
  Pinup of the past.  Films & Filming 20-5:56 F '74
  Kobal, J.  Interview.  Film 2-21:21 D '74

SHERIDAN, DINAH
  My favorite role.  Film R p22 '53/54

SHERIDAN, MARGARET
  Murphy, F.  Adventurous young lady.  Silver S 21-10:48 Ag '51

SHERMAN, BOBBY
  Young, A. S.  The wheel takes another turn.  TV Guide 18-6:18
    F 7 '70
  What every woman who wants him must know.  Photop 80-2:66
    Ag '71
  The girl he hides, and why.  Mod Screen 65-11:59 N '71
  Diehl, D.  Bob-b-e-e-e-e-e.  TV Guide 19-52:16 D 25 '71
  Girl crazy.  Mod Screen 66-3:56 Mr '72

SHERMAN, FRED E.
  Obit.  N. Y.  Times p47 My 21 '69
    Screen World 21:240 '70

SHERMAN, LOWELL
  Sketch.  N. Y. Dram 69:12 My 7 '13
  Sketch.  Theatre 31:520 Je '20
  Hall, G.  Interview.  Motion Pic Classic 11:32 F '21
  Sketch.  Photop 24:52 Jl '23
  Sketch.  Theatre 45:30 Ja '27
  Belfrage, C.  Sketch.  Motion Pic 39:82 Je '30
  Service, F.  Sketch.  Motion Pic Classic 32:51 D '30
  Hamilton, S.  Sketch.  Motion Pic 43:70 F '32

SHERWOOD, MADELEINE
  (Also known as Madeleine Thornton-Sherwood)
  Hausvater, A.  Acting is my religion.  Motion p12 Jl/Ag '74

SHIELDS, ARTHUR
  Obit.  Classic Film Collect 27:60 Spg/Sum '70
    N. Y. Times p41 Ap 28 '70
    Same.  N. Y. Times Bio Ed Ap 28 '70
    Screen World 22:240 '71

SHIELDS, BROOKE
  Lang, C.  Interview.  Interview 4-12:10 D '74

SHILLING, MARION
  Uselton, R. A.  The Wampus baby stars.  Films In R 21-2:73
    F '70

SHIMKUS, JOANNA
  Miller, E.  Real like you.  Seventeen 28:157 My '69
  Nemy, E.  And, besides, she can type.  N. Y. Times Bio Ed Je
    19 '70
  Knight, A. & Alpert, H.  Sex stars of 1970.  Playboy 17-12:220
    D '70
  Robbins, F.  Tape to type; interview.  Photop 79-5:41 My '71
  Filmog.  Films & Filming 18-8:62 My '72

SHINER, RONALD
  My favorite role.  Film R p19 '53/54

SHIPMAN, NELL
  A jill of all trades.  Photop 11-5:38 Ap '17
  Shipman, N.  Me.  Photop 15-3:47 F '19
  Movie that couldn't be screened.  Atlantic 135:326 Mr; 477 Ap;
    645 My '25
  This little bear went to Hollywood.  Good House 92:30 Ja '31
  Fulbright, T.  Queen of the dog sleds.  Classic Film Collect
    25:30 Fall '69
  Still a trailblazer.  Filmograph 1-1:3 '70
  Summers, M.  Fragments from her letters.  Filmograph 4-2:18
    '74

SHIPP, MARY
Things are Shipp shape. TV Guide 2-21:12 My 21 '54

SHIRLEY, ANNE
Whitfield, H. Story of. Photop 48:42 Ag '35
Gorman, E. W. The little girl who kept on growing. Silver S
6-3:21 Ja '36
Janisch, A. Her popularity. Movie Classic 11:41 Ja '37
Mack, G. Story of. Motion Pic 54:50 O '37
Fraser, P. Friendship, courtship, marriage. Screen Book 19-
4:44 N '37
Hartley, K. Marriage a la carte. Screen Book 20-5:36 Je '38
Bio note; filmog. Movies & People 2:34 '40
Hall, G. I stand accused. Silver S 13-8:28 Je '43
Manners, M. J. The lowdown on the Vic Mature-Anne Shirley
romance. Silver S 14-4:24 F '44
Borie, M. We visit Anne Shirley today. Movie Dig 2-1:34 Ja
'73

SHOCKLEY, MARIAN
Uselton, R. A. The Wampus baby stars. Films In R 21-2:73
F '70

SHOCKLEY, SALLIE
Swisher, V. H. Hollywood's professional training ground. After
Dark 13-7:38 N '70

SHORE, DINAH
The girl on the cover. Cue 11-7:1 F 14 '42
Jefferson, S. Her romance with George Montgomery. Photop
23:38 S '43
York, C. Her marriage. Photop 24:4 Mr '44
Der Bingle and Dinah are back. Cue 13-43:11 O 21 '44
Is there anyone finer? TV Guide 1-13:8 Je 26 '53
An artist off stage. TV Guide 1-35:9 N 27 '53
Minoff, P. A doll named Dinah. Cue 24-7:12 F 19 '55
Hano, A. The new Dinah Shore. TV Guide 19-10:16 Mr 6 '71
Someone's in the kitchen with Dinah. Ladies Home J 89:100 Ja
'72
Dinah's real kitchen. House Beaut 114:126 My '72
Higham, C. Nothin' could be finah for Dinah Shore. N. Y.
Times sec 2:13 Ag 27 '72
Same. N. Y. Times Bio Ed p1547 Ag '72
Love after 30. Photop 82-2:28 Ag '72
Bell, J. N. Dinah Shore. Good House 175:62 Ag '72
How I fought for Dinah. Photop 82-6:57 D '72
Secret love hideout discovered. Mod Screen 67-3:39 Mr '73
Durslag, M. Caddie, hand me my 9-iron and a blonde wig. TV
Guide 21-15:25 Ap 14 '73
Our love is here to stay. Photop 83-6:56 Je '73
Burt rushed to hospital. Photop 84-1:58 Jl '73
Burt and Dinah's love letters. Photop 84-5:30 N '73
Up with careers, nix on marriage. People 2-18:56 O 28 '74

SHORE, ROBERTA
And I never tested anyone else.   TV Guide 10-44:26 N 3 '62

SHORT, ANTRIM
Remont, F.   Interview.   Motion Pic Classic 10:36 Jl '20

SHOSHANO, ROSE
Obit.   N. Y.   Times p89 N 3 '68

SHRINER, HERB
Cook, G.   Fine fresh corn.   Life 31:29 O 15 '51
Beatty, J.   Funny man from back home.   Am Mag 152:32 N '51
Same.   Abridged.   Read Dig 60:58 My '52
Ordway, P.   Shrewd bumpkin.   Sat Eve Post 225:25 N 29 '52
Hoosier hot rod.   TV Guide 1-1:16 Ap 3 '53
Back home in Indiana.   Coronet 35:41 Ap '54
Major, R. H.   (His) story.   Coronet 37:157 Mr '55
He branches out.   Look 19:89 N 15 '55
He wants to go back.   TV Guide 3-53:13 D 31 '55
Two general views of humor.   Life 45:45 N 10 '58
Obit.   N. Y.   Times Bio Ed Ap 25 '70

SHURANOVA, ANTONINA
Note.   Int F G 10:336 '70

SHUTTA, ETHEL
Once and future Follies.   Time 97:73 My 3 '71

SIBBALD, LAURIE
'That drip,' he said.   TV Guide 13-30:11 Jl 24 '65

SIDNEY, SYLVIA
Manners, D.   Sketch.   Motion Pic Classic 33:56 My '31
Harris, R.   Sylvia Sidney.   Silver S 1-12:20 O '31
Grayson, C.   Interview.   Motion Pic 42:58 O '31
Sketch.   Photop 41:58 D '31
Cheasley, C. W.   Her numberscope.   Motion Pic 43:42 F '32
Gallant, T.   Sketch.   Movie Classic 2:23 Je '32
Melcher, E.   Sylvia Sidney.   Cinema Dig 1-11:10 O 3 '32
Goldbeck, E.   Sketch.   Motion Pic 44:26 O '32
Service, F.   Interview.   Motion Pic 45:35 Mr '33
Grayson, C.   Little "one-take" Sidney.   Silver S 3-10:52 Ag '33
Hall, G.   Interview.   Movie Classic 5:21 S '33
Hall, G.   Interview.   Motion Pic 47:42 Ap '34
Maxwell, V.   Interview.   Photop 45:60 My '34
Reed, D.   Interview.   Movie Classic 7:61 N '34
Harris, R.   Escaping us.   Silver S 5-1:25 N '34
Grant, J.   Why she never goes to parties.   Movie Classic 7:6
   D '34
Reilly, P.   Interview.   Motion Pic 49:45 Mr '35
Brundidge, H. T.   How she got into motion pictures.   Motion
   Pic 49:35 Jl '35
Beauty hints.   Motion Pic 50:50 Ag '35

Wilson, E.   I do as I darn please.   Silver S 6-1:30 N '35
Harrison, H.   Interview.   Movie Classic 9:31 D '35
Simon, F.   Interview.   Movie Classic 10:13 Ap '36
Ellis, J.   No party gal.   Silver S 6-10:34 Ag '36
Cruikshank, H.   Experiences in England.   Motion Pic 52:42 S
   '36
Sylvia Sidney.   Visages 9:entire issue F '37
Wilson, E.   Projections.   Silver S 7-6:24 Ap '37
Caine, D.   Interview.   Motion Pic 54:51 Ag '37
Bio note; filmog.   Movies & People 2:35 '40
Wallace, D.   Make it so.   Silver S 16-10:50 Ag '46
Grandslam.   TV Guide 19-41:16 O 9 '71
Catching up with Sylvia Sidney.   Mod Screen 66-1:8 Ja '72
Bell, A.   Sylvia's souvenirs.   N.Y. Times sec 2:3 D 17 '72
   Same.   N.Y. Times Bio Ed p2260 D '72
At Town Hall.   Film Fan Mo 141:20 Mr '73

SIGEL, BARBARA
   Finnigan, J.   TV ingenue.   TV Guide 19-10:41 Mr 6 '71

SIGNORET, SIMONE
   Blanch, L.   Love is not child's play.   Show 2-6:92 Je '62
   Forgotten dance.   Atlas 11:47 Ja '66

SILLS, MILTON
   Sketch.   Theatre 9:113 Ap '09
   Sketch.   Green Bk Albm 3:174 Ja '10
   Smith, A.   A gentleman and a scholar.   Photop 14-1:87 Je '18
   Squier, E. L.   Interview.   Motion Pic Classic 12:32 Je '21
   Tully, G.   Interview.   Motion Pic 22:24 N '21
   Interview.   Classic 15:38 Ja '23
   de Revere, F. V.   Analysis of his face.   Motion Pic 29:55 Mr
      '25
   Roberts, W. A.   Sketch.   Motion Pic 29:55 Ap '25
   Home of.   Arch & B 60:165 My '28
   Tibbett, G.   Home of.   Photop 37:66 Mr '30
   Manners, D.   His sob story.   Motion Pic Classic 31:29 Je '30
   Devon, L.   Milton Sills; filmog.   Films In R 22-10:611 D '71
   Ames, A.   Partial filmog.   Films In R 23-1:57 Ja '72

SILVERA, FRANK
   Obit.   N.Y. Times p27 Je 12 '70
      Same.   N.Y. Times Bio Ed Je 12 '70
      Newsweek 75:61 Je 22 '70
      Screen World 22:240 '71
   Lambert, C. C.   Frank Silvera; filmog.   Films In R 21-7:454
      Ag/S '70

SILVERHEELS, JAY
   My child.   Photop 82-3:12 S '72

SILVERS, PHIL
   Keating, J.   Glad to see him.   Cue 20-43:15 O 27 '51

Minoff, P.   Top banana to top kick.   Cue 24-3:20 Ja 22 '55
Klemesrud, J.   A funny thing about Phil.   N. Y. Times Bio Ed
    Ap 16 '72
Silvers, P. & Saffron, R.   Bilko-rowdy child of accident and
    coincidence.   TV Guide 21-40:6 O 6 '73

SIM, ALASTAIR
    McGillivray, D.   Bio note; filmog.   Focus On F 10:9 Sum '72

SIMMONS, DICK
    Stars of tomorrow.   Lions R 1-11/12:no p# Jl/Ag '42
    $5 career.   Lions R 2-4:no p# Ap '43

SIMMONS, JEAN
    English ingenue is new star.   Cue 17-30:11 Jl 24 '48
    My favorite role.   Film R p20 '50
    Holland, J.   The man Jean Simmons married.   Silver S 21-6:36
        Ap '51
    Star of the year; filmog.   Film R p23 '61/62
    Marill, A. H.   Jean Simmons; filmog.   Films In R 23-2:71 F
        '72
    Hudson, G.   Letter.   Films In R 23-7:445 Ag/S '72

SIMMS, GINNY
    Holland, J.   Home girl.   Silver S 14-2:40 D '43
    Eyes right on Ginny.   Lions R 3-3:no p# Ap '44

SIMMS, LU ANN
    The youngest Godfrey.   TV Guide 2-22:8 My 28 '54

SIMON, SIMONE
    Sketch.   Time 28:30 Ag 24 '36
    Hartley, K.   Interview.   Motion Pic 52:43 O '36
    Magee, T.   Sketch.   Movie Classic 11:40 N '36
    Darnton, C.   Interview.   Movie Classic 11:36 Ja '37
    Reid, J.   Interview.   Motion Pic 53:42 Je '37
    Simon Simone.   Visages 19:entire issue D '37
    Sweigart, W. R.   Letter.   Films In R 15-10:645 D '64
    Bodeen, D.   Remembering Simone; letter.   Filmograph 1-1:42
        '70

SIMPSON, RUSSELL
    Cruikshank, H.   Forecasts more melodrama in the talkies.
        Motion Pic Classic 29:60 Ap '29
    Obit.   Screen World 11:224 '60

SINATRA, FRANK
    Success story.   Cue 10-22:3 My 31 '41
    Henderson, H. & Shaw, S.   Story of.   Colliers 111:69 Ap 11
        '43
    York, C.   Sketch.   Photop 24:10 Ap '44
    Semper, Sinatra.   Cue 12-24:13 Je 12 '43
    Vallee, W. L.   That old Sinatra magic.   Silver S 14-1:38 N '43

Trotter, M.  Prediction for 1944.  Photop 24:27 Ja '44
Story of.  Time 43:88 Ja 3 '44
At Democratic headquarters.  Life 17:27 N 20 '44
Sinatra and Tibbett, hail and farewell.  Cue 14-3:7 Ja 20 '45
Holland, J.  Is Frankie The voice or The head?  Silver S 15-5:
  22 Mr '45
Holland, J.  Temptations of a bachelor girl.  Silver S 15-11:24
  S '45
His campaign against race intolerance.  Time 46:61 O 1 '45
Fisher, J.  This isn't child's play.  Silver S 16-4:22 F '46
O'Leary, D.  Rudy Vallee's advice to Sinatra.  Silver S 17-5:30
  Mr '47
Pritchett, F.  Confidential memo.  Silver S 18-5:22 Mr '48
Sketch.  Cosmop 127:73 O '49
Rogers, V.  What about Ava's career?  Silver S 22-5:28 Mr '52
Balling, F. D.  Just because of Ava.  Silver S 23-10:24 Ag '53
Hyams, J.  Comments on a comeback.  Cue 23-36:12 S 4 '54
Taylor, T.  Frankie comes back.  Cue 25-32:13 Ag 11 '56
Reisner, R. G.  Sinatra.  Playboy 5:63 N '58
Barter, C.  Sinatra on discs; discography.  Cue 28-49:11 D 5
  '59
Interview.  Playboy 10:35 F '63
Krasner, L.  Mama, what's a Frank Sinatra?  Sound Stage 1-4:
  28 Je '65
Action in Las Vegas.  Time 90:101 S 22 '67
Render unto Caesars.  Newsweek 70:32 S 25 '67
Hamilton, J.  Working Sinatras.  Look 31:86 O 31 '67
TV Christmas with the Martins and the Sinatras.  Look 31:76 D
  26 '67
Newsmakers.  Newsweek 70:52 D 4 '67; 71:44 Ja 15 '68
Newquist, R.  Sinatra power.  McCalls 95:79 Jl '68
Korall, B.  Sinatra syndrome.  Sat R 52:47 F 8 '69
Lees, G.  Confessions and contradictions.  Hi Fi 19:120 Mr '69
Lees, G.  Underrated Sinatra.  Hi Fi 19:109 Je '69
Lerner, A. J.  Cue salutes.  Cue 39-13:51 Mr 28 '70
Knight, A.  Star time?  Sat R 53:56 N 21 '70
Altobell, D.  Have you heard Sinatra?  Audio 54:40 D '70
Ali-Frazier fight; photos.  Life 70:20 Mr 19 '71
Get me to the church--now.  Photop 79-3:58 Mr '71
Chairman emeritus.  Time 97:58 Ap 5 '71
Thompson, T.  Sinatra's swan song.  Life 70:70A Je 25 '71
Newsmakers.  Newsweek 77:49 Je 28 '71
Newsmakers.  Newsweek 78:52 Jl 12 '71
Sinatra to wed.  Photop 80-2:73 Ag '71
Shaw, A.  A Sinatra retrospective.  Hi Fi 21:65 Ag '71
Lees, G.  That certain magic.  Sat R 54:45 Ag 28 '71
Dean Martin fearful for Sinatra's health.  Photop 80-3:65 S '71
Hit by throat cancer?  Photop 80-4:32 O '71
What's really wrong with Sinatra?  Silver S 41-10:25 O '71
Bio note.  Films Illus 1-5:32 N '71
Davis, S. Jr.  How Sinatra taught me friendship.  Todays
  Health 49:30 N '71
Sinatra risking his life?  Mod Screen 65-12:41 D '71

Rhall, J.  Sinatra in nightclub brawl.  Mod Screen 67-1:25 Ja
'72
Sinatra answers the cancer rumors.  Photop 81-2:46 F '72
Best defense.  Newsweek 80:21 Jl 31 '72
New young love.  Mod Screen 66-7:42 Jl '72
How I let the one I love get away.  Photop 82-1:72 Jl '72
His new woman.  Photop 82-5:32 N '72
The woman Sinatra attacked fights back.  Photop 83-5:48 My '73
Wilson, E.  The voice.  Liberty 1-8:31 Spg '73
Turner, W.  Agnew host, Sinatra now G.O.P. 'insider.'  N.Y.
Times Bio Ed p1384 Ag '73
Whitney, D.  Ol' blue eyes is back.  TV Guide 21-46:30 N 17
'73
O'Connor, J. L.  Sinatra came back, and the rest was music.
N.Y. Times sec 2:19 D 2 '73
Frank the crank fights trouble down under.  People 2-5:6 Jl 29
'74
Pleasants, H.  Appoggiatura, tempo rubato, portamento--he uses
'em all.  N.Y. Times sec 2:1 O 13 '74
Lear, M. W.  The bobby sox have wilted, but the memory re-
mains fresh.  N.Y. Times sec 2:1 O 13 '74

SINATRA, NANCY
Daughter of the chairman.  Newsweek 67:100 My 16 '66
Chapman, D.  Another swinging Sinatra.  Look p58 Jl 12 '66
Scott, V.  Nancy talks about life with father.  Ladies Home J
83:82 S '66
Mini Mata Hari.  Time 89:62 My 5 '67
Markel, H. & Hershey, L.  Sinatra power.  McCalls 95:79 Jl
'68
Get me to the church--now.  Photop 79-3:58 Mr '71

SINATRA, TINA
Does Tina love Uncle Bob?  Photop 78-3:55 S '70

SINCLAIR, HUGH
Obit.  Film R p32 '63/64

SINCLAIR, MARY
Out of the past.  TV Guide 8-18:13 Ap 30 '60

SINDEN, DONALD
My favorite role.  Film R p25 '55/56

SINGLETON, CATHERINE
Obit.  Screen World 21:240 '70

SINGLETON, PENNY
Walker, H. L.  "Blondie"--our cutest star.  Silver S 9-8:28 Je
'39
McGuire, H.  Recollections of 14-year-old Dorothy McNulty.
Newsweek 24:4 Jl 31 '44
Anecdote.  Am Mag 142:92 Ag '46
Bowers, L.  Blondie isn't so dumb.  Silver S 18-10:47 Ag '48

SISSON, VERA
    Peterson, E.   Sketch.   Motion Pic Classic 3:33 S '16

SKELTON, RED
    Sketch.   Newsweek 18:57 Ag 18 '41
    Success story.   Cue 10-38:3 S 20 '41
    Discovering Red Skelton.   Lions R 1-1:no p# S '41
    Skelton, E.   It's no laughing matter.   Lions R 1-9:no p# My '42
    That's the stuff to give the troops.   Lions R 1-10:no p# Je '42
    Reid, J.   I married a screwball.   Silver S 12-8:22 Je '42
    Skelton, R.   Red's skeletons.   Lions R 2-1:no p# S/O '42
    Red in concrete.   Lions R 2-3:no p# D '42
    Simon, S. S.   He keeps 'em laughing.   Lions R 2-3:no p# D
        '42
    No playboy.   Lions R 2-4:no p# Ap '43
    A mistake I wouldn't make again.   Photop 22:47 My '43
    Busy buffoon.   Lions R 3-1:no p# S '43
    Red's serious side.   Lions R 3-1:no p# S '43
    Man in motion.   Lions R 3-4:no p# Jl '44
    O'Leary, D.   Serious side of Red.   Silver S 16-11:43 S '46
    Arnold, M.   Story of.   Photop 32:66 F '48
    Minoff, P.   Red climbs aboard.   Cue 20-43:22 O 27 '51
    Skelton, G.   Living with Red is fun.   Silver S 22-10:24 Ag '52
    Minoff, P.   Red's got it taped.   Cue 23-12:16 Mr 20 '54
    Whitney, D.   Big Red.   TV Guide 18-40:30 O 3 '70
    Williams, M.   So long, clown.   Nat R 23:823 Jl 27 '71
    Corneau, E. N.   The clown of clowns.   Classic Film Collect
        41:4 Win '73

SKIPWORTH, ALLISON
    Miller, L.   50 years of acting.   Motion Pic 46:55 O '33
    Obit.   Screen World 4:177 '53

SKULNIK, MENASHA
    Zunser, J.   Debutants from downtown.   Cue 22-7:13 F 14 '53
    Second Avenue was never like this.   Theatre Arts 37:11 S '53
    New play in Manhattan.   Time 65:34 Ja 10 '55
    Black sheep.   New Yorker 30:23 F 5 '55
    Gibbs, W.   Theatre.   New Yorker 32:52 Ja 5 '57
    Charming Menasha.   Newsweek 49:46 Ja 7 '57
    Obit.   N. Y. Times p35 Je 5 '70
        Newsweek 75:62 Je 15 '70
        Time 95:54 Je 15 '70

SLEEPER, MARTHA
    Robinson, S.   Gadget girl.   Colliers 102:20 D 17 '38
    $300,000 a year from a hobby.   Am Mag 134:96 D '42
    She went native.   McCalls 81:15 Ap '54
    Uselton, R. A.   The Wampus baby stars.   Films In R 21-2:73
        F '70

SLEZAK, WALTER
    Hamilton, S.   Sketch.   Photop 23:65 S '43
    Perkins, R.   Hayseed villain.   Silver S 13-11:38 S '43

SLOANE, EVERETT
    One of radio's best and highest-priced actors.   Newsweek 24:80
        S 4 '44
    Coulson, A.   Everett Sloane.   Film 37:13 Aut '63
    Pickard, R.   Everett Sloane; filmog.   Films In R 23-6:380 Je/
        Jl '72

SMALLEY, PHILLIPS
    Interview.   Motion Pic 9:108 My '15

SMITH, ALEXIS
    Hamilton, S.   Sketch.   Photop 20:52 D '41
    Waterbury, R.   Sketch.   Photop 20:4 F '42
    Manners, M. J.   Sketch.   Silver S 12-4:38 F '42
    Mulvey, K.   Sketch.   Womans Home C 69:34 Mr '42
    The type of man she likes.   Photop 22:50 Ap '42
    Her ideas about love.   Photop 23:40 N '43
    What she and Mr. Stevens argue about.   Photop 27:60 Jl '45
    Bangs, B.   Really the pigtail type at heart.   Silver S 15-9:46
        Jl '45
    Creelman, E.   The change in Alexis.   Silver S 16-8:52 Je '46
    Meyer, J.   Letter.   Films In R 14-3:186 Mr '63
    Decarl, L.   Alexis Smith; filmog.   Films In R 21-6:355 Je/Jl
        '70
    Once and future Follies.   Time 97:70 My 3 '71
    Flatley, G.   Three show-biz girls and how they grew.   N. Y.
        Times Bio Ed Ap 4 '71
    Mager, A. G.   Alexis Smith and Craig Smith: nostalgic?   Not
        on your life.   Harp Baz 105:107 D '71
    Zadan, C.   One last look at where it all began.   After Dark
        4-10:48 F '72

SMITH, ART
    Obit.   N. Y. Times Bio Ed p303 F '73
        Screen World p239 '74

SMITH, C. AUBREY
    Hamilton, S.   Story of.   Photop 72:20 My '38
    Hamilton, S.   Sketch.   Photop 54:29 Ag '40
    Grand old boy.   Lions R 3-4:no p# Jl '44
    Bio.   Cur Bio 5 '44

SMITH, CHARLIE MARTIN
    Bio note; filmog.   Focus On F 17:9 Spg '74

SMITH, CONSTANCE
    Rising stars.   Film R p39 '51/52

SMITH, ETHEL
    She's got rhythm.   Newsweek 21:68 Ja 29 '42
    Antrim, D. K.   Instrument of 253 million tonal quality combina-
        tions.   Etude 62:269 My '44
    Latin from Manhattan.   Lions R 3-4:no p# Jl '44

Asklund, G.  What about the electric organ? with bio note.
    Etude 65:264 My '47

SMITH, HAL
    Mayberry's bon vivant.   TV Guide 10-52:22 D 29 '62

SMITH, HONUS
    Haskins, G.   Who me?   You don't mean me?   Photop 10-1:51
    Je '16

SMITH, HOWARD
    Obit.  N. Y. Times p33 Ja 11 '68
    Screen World 20:239 '69

SMITH, LOIS
    Acting their age.   Vogue 126:154 O 1 '55
    Taylor, T.  Accent on talent.   Cue 24-43:14 O 29 '55
    Smith dazzles as a neurotic siren.   Life 39:102 N 21 '55
    Goodman, S.  Bio sketch.   Dance Mag 30:32 Ap '56

SMITH, MAGGIE
    Rising stars.   Film R p58 '64/65
    Salute of the week.   Cue 38-10:1 Mr 8 '69
    Ronau, M.  Lively art.   Sr Schol 94:18 Mr 14 '69
    In the words of Maggie Smith.   Cue 38-43:17 O 25 '69
    Lewis, A.  Even an Oscar can't help cheer up Maggie Smith.
    N. Y. Times Bio Ed Ap 17 '70
    Prime of Miss Downbeat.   Time 95:72 Ap 20 '70
    Bio.  Cur Bio 31:29 Je '70
    Same.  Cur Bio Yrbk 1970:405 '71
    People are talking about.   Vogue 156:83 Ag 15 '70
    Lurie, D.  New Lunts?  No, the original Stephenses.   Life 71:
    62 Jl 16 '71
    Bio.  Brit Bk Yr 1971:158 '71
    Goldstein, N.  Love and pain and the whole damn thing; inter-
    view.  Show 2-8:28 N '72
    Leech, M. T.  Maggie is definitely in her prime.   After Dark
    7-6:70 O '74

SMITH, REBECCA DIANA
    Clein, H.  Two stars on the horizon.   After Dark 5-11:34 Mr
    '73

SMITH, ROGER
    Ann-Margret's fears for her future...  Mod Screen 66-5:20 My
    '72
    It happened in Las Vegas.   Photop 81-6:16 Je '72
    How I told my children about my divorce.   Photop 82-4:56 O '72
    Interview.  Mod Screen 66-12:57 D '72
    Interview with Ann-Margret.   Photop 83-1:31 Ja '73

SMITH, SHEILA
    Bosworth, P.  It's my turn to be lucky.   Today's Health 49:24
    D '71

SMITH, STANLEY
   Goldbeck, E.   Sketch.   Motion Pic Classic 31:45 Photop 37:74
      Ja '30
   Wilson, K.   The singing jewel.   Silver S 1-2:37 D '30

SNODGRESS, CARRIE
   Actresses who are real people.   Life 68:42 My 29 '70
   Reed, R.   A new Bette Davis, blah, blah.   N. Y. Times Bio Ed
      S 13 '70
   Five young beauties and how they got that way.   Mlle 72:135 N
      '70
   Actresses.   Newsweek 76:73 D 7 '70
   American good looks.   Vogue 157:164 F 1 '71
   Goodman, G.   Can a nice girl with high ideals find happiness as
      a big-time Hollywood star?   Look 35:50 Ap 6 '71
   Gow, G.   A star at dawn.   Films & Filming 17-8:61 My '71
   Hollywood's hot new sex queens.   Mod Screen 66-1:34 Ja '72

SNOW, MARGUERITE
   Interview.   Blue Book 19:909 S '14
   Interview.   Cosmop 58:92 D '14
   Peterson, E.   Sketch.   Motion Pic Classic 2:36 My '16
   How to get into moving pictures.   Motion Pic Classic 3:39 D '16
   Briscoe, J.   Sketch.   Motion Pic 13:41 Ap '17
   Courtlandt, R.   Interview.   Motion Pic 14:97 Ag '17
   Kornick, M.   Marguerite Snow.   Films In R 9-6:346 Je/Jl '58

SNYDER, EARL "SPANKY"
   Obit.   Classic Film Collect 38:57 Spg '73

SNYDER, MATT B.
   Gordon, S.   A youth of promise.   Photop 11-1:105 D '16

SOFAER, ABRAHAM
   A breed apart.   TV Guide 11-26:19 Je 29 '63

SOJIN, KAMIYAMA
   Showers, P.   Bath with Sojin.   New Yorker 22:98 Ap 13 '46
   Connor, E.   The 6 Charlie Chans; Charlie Chan filmog.   Films
      In R 6-1:23 Ja '55

SOLANAS, VALERIE
   Felled by SCUM.   Time 91:25 Je 14 '68
   Sweet assassin.   Newsweek 71:86 Je 17 '68

SOLOVGEY, YELYENA
   Note.   Int F G 10:336 '70

SOMACK, JACK
   Commercial successes.   Newsweek 76:100 O 19 '70

SOMMARS, JULIE
   Who was that lady I saw last night?   TV Guide 14-19:24 My 7 '68

Opinions on liberation. Photop 78-3:78 S '70
Meryman, R.   Can two TV beauties survive TV?   Life 70:54 Ja
   22 '71

SOMMER, ELKE
   James, H.   Celluloid pagan.   Cinema (BH) 1-3:24 '63
   Rising stars.   Film R p53 '65/66
   The wicked dreams of Elke Sommer; photos.   Playboy 14-12:166
      D '67
   Hair-raising stories from the stars.   Photop 78-1:62 Jl '70
   Hyams, J.   Elke; photos.   Playboy 17-9:159 S '70

SONDERGAARD, GALE
   Shupper, A.   Viking's daughter.   Silver S 8-1:34 N '37
   Lynn, H.   Villainy pays.   Screen Book 19-4:66 N '37
   Maltin, L.   Interview; filmog.   Film Fan Mo 118:6 Ap '71

SORDI, ALBERTO
   Lane, J. F.   The face of '63--Italy.   Films & Filming 9-7:11
      Ap '63

SORRENTINA, La
   (See: FRASCA, MARY)

SORVINO, PAUL
   Bosworth, P.   Let's just say it's my inning.   N. Y. Times sec
      2:1 N 26 '72

SOTHERN, ANN
   Ettinger, M.   It's worth it.   Silver S 4-8:29 Je '34
   Donnell, D.   Interview.   Movie Classic 6:52 Ag '34
   Baskette, K.   Sketch.   Photop 46:40 Ag '34
   Service, F.   Interview.   Motion Pic 48:51 Ja '35
   Lee, S.   Romance has influenced her life.   Movie Classic 7:52
      F '35
   Madison, C.   Interview.   Movie Classic 8:24 Ag '35
   Fender, R.   Interview.   Motion Pic 50:26 O '35
   Hill, G.   Interview.   Movie Classic 9:44 O '35
   Reed, D.   It's fun to be in love.   Silver S 6-11:59 S '36
   Lane, V. T.   Interview.   Motion Pic 53:43 Jl '37
   Baldwin, F.   Her romance.   Photop 51:27 N '37
   Hall, G.   A ghost for a year.   Silver S 9-10:42 Ag '39
   Lynn, J.   Sleeply time girl.   Screen Book 22-3:72 O '39
   Asher, J.   Maisie makes good.   Screen Book 22-4:66 N '39
   Wilson, E.   Dulcy struts her stuff.   Silver S 10-12:26 O '40
   Bio note; filmog.   Movies & People 2:35 '40
   Paris with a Sothern accent.   Lions R 1-1:no p# S '41
   Fredericks, J.   Sexposure.   Silver S 12-1:34 N '41
   Sothernisms.   Lions R 1-10:no p# Je '42
   Dangers of sudden popularity.   Photop 21:48 Jl '42
   Sothern exposure.   Lions R 2-1:no p# S/O '42
   Sothern, A.   Women aren't cats.   Lions R 2-3(sup):no p# Ja '43
   American girl--1943 model.   Lions R 2-5:no p# Jl '43

War bride problems.  Lions R 3-2:no p# Ja '44
She's a card.  Lions R 3-5:no p# D '44
Dudley, F.  True Sothern hospitality.  Silver S 18-6:41 Ap '48
Sothern, A.  How to cure heartbreak.  Silver S 19-9:20 Jl '49
Briggs, C.  Filmog.  Films In R 14-7:444 Ag/S '63
Valentino, L.  Letter.  Films In R 14-8:504 O '63
Bowers, R.  Ann Sothern; filmog.  Films In R 25-1:15 Ja '74

SOUTHERN, EVE
    Sketch.  Photop 32:49 S '27
    Gilmore, F.  A study in temperaments.  Motion Pic Classic
        26:55 S '27
    Calhoun, D.  Sketch.  Motion Pic 38:40 D '29

SPACEK, SISSY
    Bio note.  Films Illus 4-40:124 D '74

SPAETH, MERRIE
    Merrie and Tippy.  New Yorker 40:35 My 23 '64
    Miller, E.  New faces in a smash new movie.  Seventeen 23:132
        Je '64
    Rising stars.  Film R p53 '65/66
    And the winner is...  TV Guide 19-42:17 O 16 '71
    Willig, J. M.  Merrie-ly she still bubbles along.  N. Y. Times
        Bio Ed Mr 19 '72

SPAIN, FAY
    Chalk one up for science.  TV Guide 5-32:16 Ag 10 '57

SPARKS, NED
    Keats, P.  Picture savers.  Silver S 5-5:32 Mr '35

SPELVIN, GEORGINA
    West, U.  Forget the devil--meet Miss Jones.  Viva 1-2:90 N
        '73

SPENSER, JEREMY
    Rising stars.  Film R p27 '50
    Rising stars.  Film R p30 '57/58

SPERLING, KAREN
    Kevles, B.  Looking for Karen Sperling.  Show 1-6:30 O '70
    Buchanan, J.  I'll keep on persisting.  After Dark 4-8:26 D '71

SPRIGGS, ELIZABETH
    Cox, F.  Only when they larf.  Plays & Players 16-6:54 Mr '69

SQUIRE, KATHERINE
    Actress discusses the theatre.  Cue 13-37:13 S 9 '44

SQUIRE, RONALD
    Obit.  Screen World 10:225 '59

## STACK, ROBERT
Hamilton, S.  Sketch.  Photop 54:15 Ja '40
Teltscher, H. O.  His handwriting.  Photop 19:62 Je '41
Hall, G.  The kind of husband I'll make.  Silver S 12-8:38 Je
'42
Canfield, A.  Romantic athlete.  Silver S 19-6:35 Ap '49
Loving one woman is the toughest game in town.  Photop 77-6:50
Je '70
Condon, C. C.  The playboy and the actor.  TV Guide 18-44:14
O 31 '70
How I tell my child the story of Christmas.  Photop 81-1:51 Ja
'72
The most fateful decision I ever made.  Mod Screen 66-3:45 Mr
'72

## STAFFORD, HANLEY
Obit.  N. Y. Times p47 S 11 '68

## STAMP, TERENCE
Cowie, P.  The face of '63--Great Britain.  Films & Filming
9-5:19 F '63
Bean, R.  Frames and feelings; interview.  Films & Filming
15-3:4 D '68
Bean, R.  Acting on instinct; interview.  Films & Filming 15-
4:4 Ja '69

## STANDER, LIONEL
Williams, W.  Laugh champ.  Silver S 6-8:52 Je '36
Reid, J.  His story.  Movie Classic 10:31 Jl '36
Reid, J.  Interview.  Motion Pic 52:36 S '36
Lawrenson, H.  Who is the world's foremost actor?  Esquire
68:180 D '68
Lion of the Via Veneto.  Life 95:76 My 4 '70
Flatley, G.  Lionel Stander.  N. Y. Times Bio Ed My 23 '71

## STANDING, GUY
Prescription for a good actor.  Theater 53:44 Ap '31
Grant, J.  Sketch.  Movie Classic 6:6 Ap '34
Ulman, W. Jr.  The only "sir" in pictures.  Silver S 5-1:22 N
'34
Schwartz, W.  Filmog.  Films In R 17-10:672 D '66

## STANDING, HERBERT
Craig, G.  Filmland's champion "daddy."  Photop 10-6:42 N '16
Handy, T. B.  Pudding and progeny.  Photop 16-6:69 N '19

## STANDING, WYNDHAM
Beach, B.  Interview.  Motion Pic Classic 8:24 Je '19
Lamb, G.  Interview.  Motion Pic 21:54 Ap '21
Brady, S. E.  Interview.  Classic 15:61 S '22

## STANG, ARNOLD
So what's to like?  Cue 17-12:15 Mr 20 '48

Stang the fang talks back.   TV Guide 2-17:8 Ap 23 '54
The near-sighted chipmunk.   TV Guide 5-23:14 Je 8 '57

STANLEY, FORREST
  Naylor, H. S.   Interview.   Motion Pic 20:36 D '20
  Peltret, E.   Interview.   Motion Pic Classic 11:26 Ja '21

STANLEY, ILSE
  Schoenberner, F.   Journeys to hell.   Sat R 40:33 My 25 '57
  Obit.   Time 96:45 Ag 3 '70

STANLEY, JOAN
  She hits homers in TV, too.   TV Guide 10-34:27 Ag 25 '62

STANLEY, KIM
  Minoff, P.   The forthright Kim Stanley.   Cue 25-6:12 F 11 '56

STANTLEY, RALPH
  Obit.   N. Y. Times p34 My 13 '72

STANWYCK, BARBARA
  Sketch.   Photop 38:74 Jl '30
  Harris, R.   This thing called love.   Silver S 1-2:27 D '30
  Morse, W. Jr.   Sketch.   Motion Pic Classic 33:72 Je '31
  York, C.   Her love story.   Photop 40:55 O '31
  Standish, J.   Her marriage to Frank Fay.   Movie Classic 1:39
    O '31
  Moak, E. R.   (Her) hot story.   Silver S 2-4:35 F '32
  Hall, L.   Her love story.   Photop 41:46 My '32
  Walker, H. L.   Interview.   Movie Classic 2:17 Je '32
  Chensley, C. W.   Her numberscope.   Motion Pic 44:32 Ag '32
  Service, F.   Interview.   Motion Pic 44:50 D '32
  Biery, R.   Sketch.   Photop 43:52 Ja '33
  Calhoun, D.   Divorce rumors.   Movie Classic 4:31 Mr '33
  Grant, J.   Divorce rumors denied.   Movie Classic 4:26 Ap '33
  Fidler, J.   Interview.   Movie Classic 4:22 Je '33
  Gwin, J.   She's a movie fan, too.   Silver S 4-3:47 Ja '34
  Lee, S.   Secret of suffering from spine injury revealed.   Movie
    Classic 5:19 F '34
  French, W. F.   Sketch.   Motion Pic 48:42 D '34
  Ergenbright, E. L.   Life forced her to be an actress.   Movie
    Classic 8:54 Ap '35
  French, W. F.   Sketch.   Motion Pic 50:34 D '35
  Harrison, H.   Secret of her success.   Movie Classic 9:39 Ja
    '36
  Ganley, H.   Interview.   Motion Pic 51:35 Mr '36
  Lane, J.   Sketch.   Motion Pic 52:31 N '36
  Wilson, E.   Projections.   Silver S 7-2:26 D '36
  Gardner, M.   Story of.   Motion Pic 53:32 My '37
  Magee, T.   The tragedy that haunts Stanwyck.   Screen Book 20-
    3:26 Ap '38
  Campbell, S.   Stanwyck speaks her mind on Taylor.   Screen
    Book 21-5:22 D '38

Tully, J.  Story of.  Photop 54:17 F '40
Asher, J.  The amazing Mrs. Taylor.  Silver S 10-5:26 Mr '40
Walker, H. L.  Sketch.  Photop 54:40 O '40
Bio note; filmog.  Movies & People 2:35 '40
Reid, J.  Why (she) keeps getting into jams.  Silver S 11-8:24
  Je '41
Mulvey, K.  Sketch.  Womans Home C 68:28 N '41
The girl on the cover.  Cue 11-2:1 Ja 10 '42
Wilson, E.  Catching up with Barbara.  Silver S 12-9:32 Jl '42
Wilson, E.  Gypsy Rose Stanwyck.  Silver S 13-7:24 My '43
Embarrassing moments.  Photop 23:58 S '43
Her ideas on love.  Photop 23:41 N '43
Manners, M. J.  Saturdays are loneliest.  Silver S 14-11:22 S
  '44
Wilson, E.  Elusive Barbara.  Silver S 16-2:30 D '45
Holland, J.  Mind your own business.  Silver S 16-9:30 Jl '46
My first kiss.  Photop 29:58 S '46
Parsons, L. O.  Cosmop's citation for best performance of
  month.  Cosmop 122:65 Je '47
My luckiest day.  Cosmop 123:112 Ag '47
Work of in Sorry wrong number.  Life 25:70 Ag 23 '48
O'Leary, D.  What's wrong with corn?  Silver S 18-12:28 O '48
Stanwyck, B.  The new Clark Gable.  Silver S 19-8:24 Je '49
Baer, M. M.  Barbara with Bob in Rome.  Silver S 21-4:38 F
  '51
Stanwyck, B.  I haven't always been right.  Silver S 22-9:30 Jl
  '52
Rattigan, R.  Bring back romance.  Silver S 24-7:44 My '54
Stanwyck plagued by peeping tom.  Photop 77-5:50 My '70
Hair-raising stories from the stars.  Photop 78-1:62 Jl '70
Interview.  Photop 79-3:79 Mr '71
Still going great.  Screen Greats 1-2:78 Sum '71
It's time we admitted we've got a lot to learn.  Photop 80-4:37
  O '71
Talks about the generation gap.  Photop 80-4:37 O '71
A miracle saves her from death.  Photop 81-3:67 Mr '72
Righter, C.  Star of the month; horoscope.  Mod Screen 66-7:18
  Jl '72


STAPLETON, JEAN
Stone, J.  What's it like being the wife of a bigot?  N. Y. Times
  Bio Ed Ag 29 '71
The real-life families of these All in the family stars.  Mod
  Screen 65-11:40 N '71
Klemesrud, J.  (She) hopes most wives aren't like Edith.  N. Y.
  Times Bio Ed My 17 '72
Whitney, D.  For the dingbat, these are the days.  TV Guide
  20-22:21 My 27 '72
Cuskelly, R.  All in the family's success proves that we've been
  underestimating the sophistication of the TV audience.  Show
  2-3:47 My '72
Ehrlich, H.  Prime of Mrs. William H. Putch.  McCalls 99:40
  S '72

Cooking with a star.  Mod Screen 66:11:28 N '72
TV's dingbat and husband.  People 2-4:43 Jl 22 '74

STAPLETON, MAUREEN
  Keating, J.  No marabou for Maureen.  Cue 20-11:12 Mr 17 '51
  Burke, T.  And a terrific tap dancer.  N. Y.  Times Bio Ed Ja
    3 '71
  Salute of the week.  Cue 40-5:1 Ja 30 '71
  People are talking about.  Vogue 157:145 F 1 '71
  Considine, S.  A terrific broad.  After Dark 4-4:44 Ag '71

STARKE, PAULINE
  From extra to stardom.  Motion Pic Classic 5:41 S '17
  Pity poor Pauline.  Photop 14-2:57 Jl '18
  Hall, G.  Interview.  Motion Pic 22:56 N '21
  Cheatham, M.  Interview.  Motion Pic Classic 13:22 Ja '22
  Gassaway, G.  Interview.  Motion Pic 25:47 O '23
  Tildesley, A.  How she won silverscreen prominence.  Motion
    Pic Classic 22:30 F '26
  Burdin, J.  Sketch.  Movie Classic 3:28 Ja '33
  Uselton, R. A.  The Wampus baby stars.  Films In R 21-2:73
    F '70

STARR, RINGO
  Hicks, J.  Is that you in there, Ringo?  Life 66:59 Je 13 '69
  Hamilton, J.  Ringo goes single.  Look 34:41 F 10 '70
  Beatle roundup.  Newsweek 76:85 S 7 '70
  Bender, W.  Y'all come hear Ringo.  Time 96:86 O 26 '70
  Watts, M.  Ringo gets it off his chest; interview.  Circus 6-2:
    8 N '71
  (See also:  BEATLES, THE)

STARR, SALLY
  Spensley, D.  Sketch.  Motion Pic Classic 30:46 N '29
  Jordan, A.  Two first-rate girls who refuse to be seconds.  Sil-
    ver S 1-2:14 D '30

STARRETT, CHARLES
  Charles Starrett; filmog.  Cinema Trails 2:1 n. d.

STAUDTE, WOLFGANG
  Bean, R.  The face of '63--Germany.  Films & Filming 9-9:41
    Je '63
  Bachmann, J.  Wolfgang Staudte; filmog.  Film 36:12 Sum '63

STEDMAN, LINCOLN
  Autobiographical.  Motion Pic 31:40 Ap '27

STEDMAN, MYRTLE
  How she became a photoplayer.  Motion Pic 9:118 Mr '15
  Powers, B.  Smiling Myrtle.  Movie Pictorial 2-3:12 S '15
  How to get into moving pictures.  Motion Pic Classic 3:40 O '16
  Courtlandt, R.  Sketch.  Motion Pic 12:97 D '16

Bastedo, J. G.   Sketch.   Motion Pic 14:39 Ag '17
Peltret, E.   Interview.   Motion Pic Classic 11:20 N '20
Sketch.   Photop 24:52 Jl '23
Secret of her youthfulness.   Motion Pic Classic 21:68 Je '25
Growing old gracefully.   Photop 29:44 Ja '26

STEEL, ANTHONY
Steel man.   Films & Filming 2-7:5 Ap '56

STEELE, BARBARA
Filmog.   Films & Filming 20-6:52 Mr '74

STEELE, KAREN
Young whip snapper.   TV Guide 4-38:8 S 22 '56

STEELE, MARJORIE
Lewis, E.   Broadway newcomer.   Cue 24-51:14 D 24 '55

STEELE, STEPHANIE
Miller, E.   Interview.   Seventeen 31:92 Ap '72

STEELE, TOM
Parkhurst, C. M.   Interview.   Those Enduring Idols 2-7:244 Je/
Jl '72

STEELE, TOMMY
Miller, E.   Tommy Steele.   Seventeen 26:78 Jl '67

STEELE, VERNON
Life of.   Motion Pic Classic 8:31 Ag '19

STEFAN, VIRGINIA
From cereal to serial.   TV Guide 4-26:25 Je 30 '56

STEHLI, EDGAR
Obit.   N. Y. Times Bio Ed p1238 Jl '73

STEIGER, ROD
Minoff, P.   It's Steiger's year.   Cue 22-30:13 Jl 25 '53
Gow, G.   The quest for realism; discussion.   Films & Filming
4-3:13 D '57
Rising stars.   Film R p32 '57/58
The year of the Steigers; interview.   Cinema (BH) 3-2:19 Mr '66
Steiger on acting.   Cinema (BH) 3-6:18 Win '67
No way to treat a lady.   Time 91:98 Mr 29 '68
Interview.   Cinema (Lon) 1:12 D '68
Evans, P.   Steiger power.   New York 2-1:48 Ja 6 '69
Interview.   Playboy 16-7:61 Jl '69
Barthel, J.   No happy ending; interview.   Redbook 133:98 Jl '69
Steiger, R.   Let us now praise famous me.   Esquire 72:160 N
'69
Steiger, R.   The director; an actor's view.   Action 5-4:27 Jl/Ag
'70

Nine minds in trouble.   Photop 78-3:56 S '70
Hall, D. J.   Method master; filmog.   Films & Filming 17-3:28
    D '70; 17-4:28 Ja '71
Steiger talks about directors.   Making Films 5-1:13 F '71
Guerin, A.   Steiger's Napoleon: a self-defeated man.   Show 2-
    3:30 My '71
Hutchinson, T.   Interview.   Films Illus 4-40:132 D '74

STEINBERG, DAVID
    Rosin, M. B.   Interview.   Harp Baz 104:138 F '71
    Davidson, S.   A funny man for this season.   N. Y. Times Mag
        p26 Ap 25 '71
    Same.   N. Y. Times Bio Ed Ap 25 '71
    Higham, C.   So here am I, David Steinberg, with my big gorilla
        foot.   N. Y. Times Bio Ed p1402 Jl '72
    Less Ed, please, and more David.   Life 73:19 Ag 4 '72
    Davidson, B.   Offbeat, racy, outrageous and establishment-bait-
        ing.   TV Guide 20-32:24 Ag 5 '72
    Star of David.   Time 100:68 Ag 7 '72

STEN, ANNA
    Cruikshank.   Sketch.   Movie Classic 2:56 Jl '32
    Sketch.   Movie Classic 3:25 D '32
    Million dollar gamble.   Lit Dig 117:47 F 17 '34
    Spensley, D.   Sketch.   Movie Classic 5:24 F '34
    Norden, H. B.   Appreciation.   Vanity Fair 42:45 Mr '34
    Calhoun, D.   Million dollar gamble.   Movie Classic 6:5 Ap '34
    Babcock, M.   The victory of beauty.   Silver S 4-8:27 Je '34
    Lee, S.   Interview.   Movie Classic 7:5 O '34
    Hall, G.   Interview.   Motion Pic 48:44 N '34
    French, W. F.   What price glamour.   Motion Pic 48:28 N '34
    Brundidge, H. T.   Life of.   Motion Pic 48:40 D '34
    Hunter, L.   Sketch.   Motion Pic 49:68 F '35
    Gersdorf, P.   Sketch.   Movie Classic 8:26 Mr '35
    Interview.   Motion Pic 49:42 Mr '35
    Walker, H. L.   A fatalistic girl in an optimistic town.   Silver
        S 5-7:20 My '35
    Cheatham, M.   Returns to American screen.   Motion Pic 54:37
        Ag '37
    Smithson, E. J.   American citizen.   Screen Book 20-1:42 F '38

STEPHENS, LARAINE
    Lewis, R. W.   In Bracken's World live beautiful people.   TV
        Guide 18-7:29 F 14 '70

STEPHENS, ROBERT
    Cowie, P.   The face of '63--Great Britain.   Films & Filming
        9-5:19 F '63
    People are talking about.   Vogue 149:180 Mr 1 '67
    Lurie, D.   Interview.   Life 71:62 Jl 16 '71

STEPHENSON, JAMES
    Hamilton, S.   Sketch.   Photop 18:36 Mr '41
    Smith, F. J.   Opportunity finally knocked.   Silver S 11-5:24 Mr '41

STEPPAT, ILSE
Obit.  Screen World 21:240 '70

STERKE, JEANETTE
People of promise.  Films & Filming 1-9:19 Je '55

STERLING, FORD
Redway, S.  Interview.  Motion Pic Classic 22:30 Ja '26

STERLING, JAN
Reid, L.  The taming of "the big brute."  Silver S 20-12:46 O
'50
Service, F.  Completely nuts about the guy.  Silver S 21-11:38
S '51

STERLING, ROBERT
Bachelor boy.  Lions R 1-7:no p# Mr '42
Stars of tomorrow.  Lions R 1-11/12:no p# Jl/Ag '42
Ringing doorbells.  Lions R 2-1:no p# S/O '42

STERLING, TISHA
An only child grows up.  TV Guide 16-25:24 Je 22 '68

STERN, WES
Clein, H.  The real people:  featuring Hollywood's new breed of
character actors.  Show 1-8:14 Jl 9 '70
The wild and wicked Wes Stern.  Photop 81-1:65 Ja '72

STEVENS, CONNIE
What makes a show successful?  TV Guide 8-22:17 My 28 '60
Musel, R.  She doesn't look like a fighter.  TV Guide 19-34:16
Ag 21 '71
I'm crazy about him.  Photop 80-2:68 Ag '71
Cooking with a star.  Mod Screen 65-12:54 D '71
Hollywood's hidden children.  Mod Screen 66-2:63 F '72
How I let the one I love get away.  Photop 82-1:72 Jl '72
Righter, C.  Star of the month; horoscope.  Mod Screen 66-8:54
Ag '72
How I told my children about my divorce.  Photop 82-4:56 O '72

STEVENS, CRAIG
Shamus to flack.  TV Guide 12-48:15 N 28 '64
Mager, A. G.  Alexis Smith and Craig Stevens nostalgic?  Not
on your life.  Harp Baz 105:107 D '71

STEVENS, EMILY
Stage history.  Pearson (NY) 23:230 F '10
Barry, O.  Sketch.  Green Bk Album 4:1215 D '10
Interview.  Cosmop 56:847 My '14
Patterson, A.  Work of.  Theater 22:292 D '15
Sketch.  Green Book 15:357 F '16
The brilliant Mrs. Fiske's brilliant niece.  Photop 12-3:31 Ag '17
Montanye, L.  Interview.  Motion Pic 15:73 Je '18

STEVENS, INGER
  The Hollywood swingers.  Show 3-11:92 N '63
  Obit.  Film R p15 '70/71
    Film R p13 '71/72
    N. Y.  Times p35 My 1 '70
    Same.  N. Y.  Times Bio Ed My 1 '70
    Newsweek 75:110 My 11 '70
    Screen World 22:240 '71
    Time 95:89 My 11 '70
    After you're dead, no one gives a damn.  Photop 78-1:38 Jl '70

STEVENS, LILA
  Your first guess is wrong.  Photop 16-2:96 Jl '19

STEVENS, MARK
  Dudley, F.  Women are wonderful.  Silver S 17-2:37 D '46
  Stevens, A. H.  The man I married.  Silver S 17-9:48 Jl '47
  Sammis, F. R.  His separation from his wife.  Photop 31:33 S
    '47
  Case history of a star.  TV Guide 4-41:17 O 13 '56

STEVENS, ONSLOW
  Churchill, E.  The name is Stevens.  Silver S 3-2:21 D '32
  Tribute to a professional.  Theatre Arts 22:527 Jl '38

STEVENS, RAY
  Hickey, N.  This stand-in doesn't stand out.  TV Guide 18-27:18
    Jl 4 '70

STEVENS, STELLA
  Centerfold.  Playboy Ja '60
  Talking about people.  Film 31:4 Spg '62
  Rising stars.  Film R p31 '62/63
  Bean, R.  Will there be film stars in 1974?  Films & Filming
    10-10:9 Jl '64
  Encore for Stella (photos).  Playboy 15-1:104 Ja '68
  Knight, A. & Alpert, H.  Sex stars of 1970.  Playboy 17-12:220
    D '70
  Johnson, D.  A combination of beauty and brains in a lady who
    knows what she wants and how to get it.  Show 2-10:31 Ja
    '73
  Harmetz, A.  Why won't they let Haskell and Stella be directors?
    N. Y.  Times sec 2:11 Ag 12 '73
    Same.  N. Y.  Times Bio Ed p1388 Ag '73
  Jenson, L.  The ever new Stella Stevens; interview.  Adam F
    World 4-7:24 Ag '73

STEVENS, WARREN
  Here comes the heroes.  TV Guide 4-37:28 S 15 '56

STEVENSON, PARKER
  Lyons, D.  Interview.  Interview 29:28 Ja '73

STEVENSON, VENETIA
The most photogenic girl in the world.  Pop Phot 41:76 S '57
Most photogenic girl seen by TV millions.   Pop Phot 41:136 N
    '57
Agree with Ed?   TV Guide 6-5:16 F 1 '58

STEWART, ANITA
Interview.  Green Book 12:630 O '14
Sketch.  Cosmop 58:461 Mr '15
Meriden, O.  A darling of filmland.  Theatre 22:16 Jl '15
Porter, V. H.  Sketch.  Green Book 15:812 My '16
Hornblow, A. Jr.  How she got in the moving pictures.  Motion
    Pic Classic 2:23 My '16
Bret, T.  Sketch.  Motion Pic Classic 2:43 Je '16
Briscoe, J.  Sketch.  Motion Pic 11:77 Jl '16
How to get in moving pictures.  Motion Pic 12:126 Ag '16
Lachmund, M. G.  Sketch.  Motion Pic 13:73 Ap '17
Sketch.  Motion Pic 14:86 O '17
How she got in moving pictures.  Motion Pic 14:117 N '17
Hall, G.  Interview.  Motion Pic 15:97 Ag '18
Sketch.  Photop 17:28 Mr '20
Handy, T. B.  Interview.  Motion Pic 19:62 Ap/My '20
Goldbeck, W.  Interview.  Motion Pic Classic 12:24 Jl '21
Martin, P.  Interview.  Motion Pic 22:30 O '21
Goldbeck, W.  Interview.  Motion Pic 23:44 Je '22
de Revere, F. V.  Analysis of her face.  Motion Pic 28:44 D
    '24
Autobiographical.  Motion Pic 29:40 Je '25
Fifteen years ago.  Photop 44:116 O '33

STEWART, DON
Levin, E.  This face stopped a thousand steam irons.  TV
    Guide 21-52:9 D 29 '73

STEWART, ELAINE
Hyams, J.  MGM's brunette bombshell.  Cue 22-41:16 O 10 '53
Lee, T.  Once is enough.  Silver S 24-1:40 N '53
Hilland, J.  Let's put sex in its place.  Silver S 24-6:35 Ap '54
Wilson, E.  How (she) handles her guys.  Silver S 24-8:39 Je
    '54

STEWART, FRED
Obit.  N. Y. Times p48 D 7 '70
    Same.  N. Y. Times Bio Ed D 7 '70
    Screen World 22:240 '71

STEWART, JAMES
Sketch.  Photop 49:74 Je '36
Liza.  The eligible heart-breakers.  Silver S 6-9:51 Jl '36
Spensley, D.  His standards of stardom.  Motion Pic 52:46 S
    '36
Cheatham, M.  Jimmy to you.  Silver S 6-12:53 O '36
Zeitlin, I.  Interview.  Movie Classic 11:50 N '36

Sharpe, H. Interview. Photop 51:46 Ja '37
Hall, G. Story of. Motion Pic 54:39 O '37
His preparation for stardom. Womans Home C 64:22 O '37
Lane, V. T. Love is a headache. Screen Book 20-6:40 Jl '38
Jim at home. Silver S 8-12:51 O '38
Jacob, M. Stewart's no sap. Screen Book 21:29 Jl '39
Morse, W. Jr. Life story. Photop 53:16 Jl '39 & following
   issues.
Tearle, D. Mr. Stewart goes to Washington. Silver S 10-1:26
   N '39
Mulvey, K. Sketch. Womans Home C 67:8 Ag '40
Bio note; filmog. Movies & People 2:35 '40
Lindsay, M. Sketch. Photop 18:30 Ja '41
Trotter, M. Astrological forecast. Photop 18:31 F '41
Hamman, M. Sketch. Good House 112:16 Ap '41
Receives the Distinguished flying cross. Time 43:34 My 15 '44
Parsons, L. O. Cosmop's citation for best performance of
   month. Cosmop 122:66 Ja '47
Palmer, G. If I were 21. Ladies Home J 64:37 Ja '47
Bangs, B. Still the same old Jimmy. Silver S 17-3:30 Ja '47
Colby, A. His preferences in feminine beauty. Photop 30:63
   Mr '47
Maugham, R. Jimmy'll always be Jimmy. Silver S 17-11:27
   S '47
Acquits himself nobly in the role of Harvey. Theatre World
   43:29 S '47
Pritchett, F. Why (he) is still a bachelor. Silver S 19-4:22
   F '49
Parsons, L. O. Cosmop's citation for the best performance of
   month. Cosmop 126:13 Je '49
Holland, J. If I had it to do over. Silver S 19-12:24 O '49
Baer, M. M. That fabulous average guy. Silver S 21-8:26 Je
   '51
Zunser, J. We need more clean films. Cue 31-16:10 Ap 21
   '62
In the words of Jimmie Stewart. Cue Mr 21 '70
Whitney, D. Conversation with a non-talker. TV Guide 18-20:
   38 My 16 '70
Innocent revisited. Time 95:54 Je 29 '70
(His) personal picture album. Good House 172:88 Ap '71
Still going great. Screen Greats 1-2:78 Sum '71
Davidson, B. 'Wal, you see, I'm an actor.' TV Guide 19-40:
   29 O 2 '71
The orangutan upstaged Jimmy Stewart. TV Guide 19-49:43 D
   4 '71
40 years a star; filmog. Films Illus 1-9:12 Mr '72
Hall, D. J. Box office drawl; filmog. Films & Filming 19-3:
   25 D '72; 19-4:36 Ja; 19-5:36 F '73
O'Connor, J. L. Aw, shucks, do we finally have a hit series
   here? N.Y. Times sec 2:23 O 14 '73
Zolotow, M. Wal, in the old days, y'see. TV Guide 22-9:21
   Mr 2 '74

STEWART, PAUL
  Special report--Orson Welles.  Action 4-3:23 My/Je '69
  Nolan, J. E.  Films on TV.  Films In R 21-7:426 Ag/S '70

STEWART, ROY
  St. Johns, A. R.  A blue-ribbon baby.  Photop 14-4:93 S '18
  Henderson, F.  A college cowboy.  Photop 17-1:94 D '19
  Kirk, L.  Interview.  Motion Pic Classic 12:26 Jl '21

STICH, PATRICIA
  Raddatz, L.  She refuses to dress like a penguin.  TV Guide
    22-30:12 Jl 27 '74

STICKNEY, DOROTHY
  Rosen, V.  Story of.  Cosmop 113:8 S '42

STILLER, JERRY
  Drake, R.  Somewhere between lobster and dessert.  TV Guide
    19-21:14 My 22 '71

STIRLING, LINDA
  Filmog.  Films & Filming 19-5:58 F '73

STOCKWELL, DEAN
  Story of.  Photop 36:50 Jl '49
  Dean Stockwell on a long day; interview.  Cinema (BH) 1-3:10
    '63
  Bean, R.  Will there be film stars in 1974?  Films & Filming
    10-10:9 Jl '64

STOLLER, SHIRLEY
  Honeymoon killer; interview.  Interview 26:25 O '72

STOLLERY, DAVID
  The boys from Triple R.  TV Guide 5-22:29 Je 1 '57

STONE, ELLY
  Alive and well.  Time 95:64 My 18 '70
  Courtney, R.  Records.  Ramp Mag 9:56 S '70
  Saal, H.  Precious Stone.  Newsweek 80:98 O 30 '72
  Bell, A.  Elly rides a crazy Carousel.  N. Y. Times Bio Ed
    p1871 O '72

STONE, EZRA
  Crichton, K.  Story of.  Colliers 105:11 Ap 27 '40
  Scheuer, P. K.  Directing radio comedy.  Action 4-6:16 N/D
    '69

STONE, FRED
  Macfarlane, P. C.  Clown and superclown:  Montgomery and
    Stone.  Everybodys 30:399 Mr '14
    Same.  Cur Opinion 56:278 Ap '14
  Tinee, M.  Interview.  Green Book 11:922 Je '14

Work in Chin-chin.   Strand (NY) 49:116 F '15
De Foe, L. V.   Work of.   Green Book 13:1003 Je '15
Master of makeup.   Theatre 21:310 Je '15
Autobiographical.   Am Mag 84:32 O '17
Harris, C. L.   In moving pictures.   Motion Pic Classic 7:52
    S '18
Merritt, P.   (His) becomingest picture.   Everybodys 39:29 D
    '18
Shirk, A. H.   Interview.   Motion Pic 16:37 D '18
Religion behind the footlights.   Lit Dig 76:34 Mr 24 '23
Eaton, W. P.   The wizards of vaudeville.   McClure 55:43 S '23
Benchley, R. C.   Acting of.   Life 82:18 N 29 '23
Sketch.   National 52:548 Je '24
His home at Lyme, Conn.   National 55:78 O '26
Mullett, M. B.   Climbing a greased pole was (his) first tri-
    umph; interview.   Am Mag 102:18 D '26
Clark, N. M.   They said he'd never dance again.   Am Mag 111:
    50 My '31
Let your costume reflect you; interview.   Womans Home C 59:82
    Mr '32
Makes talkie debut in a Rogers part.   Newsweek 6:29 Ag 24 '35
Sketch.   Photop 48:82 N '35
Baskette, K.   A new career at 62.   Photop 48:37 D '35
Morley, D.   A danged good actor.   Silver S 6-6:56 Ap '36
Stone, P.   Tribute to.   Movie Classic 10:40 Je '36
Craig, C.   Interview.   Motion Pic 52:52 N '36
People.   Lit Dig 124:12 Ag 7 '37
Stone in Florida.   Theatre Arts 23:755 O '39
Obit.   Am Ann 1960:859 '60
    Brit Bk Yr 1960:515 '60
    Newsweek 53:61 Mr 16 '59
    Screen World 11:224 '60
    Time 73:86 Mr 16 '59

STONE, GEORGE E.
    Aydelotte, W.   Story of the making of Viva Villa.   Movie Clas-
        sic 6:54 My '34
    Ergenbright, E. L.   His tragic childhood.   Motion Pic 48:40 Ja
        '35
    His makeup in Anthony Adverse.   Photop 49:86 Ap '36

STONE, HAROLD J.
    A breed apart.   TV Guide 11-26:19 Je 29 '63

STONE, HENRY L.
    Corneau, E. N.   The biggest little daredevil in the movies.
        Classic Film Collect 38:32 Spg '73

STONE, LEWIS
    Peltret, E.   Interview.   Motion Pic Classic 10:21 Jl '20
    Beach, B.   Interview.   Motion Pic 22:38 N '21
    Goldbeck, W.   Sketch.   Motion Pic Classic 14:66 Ap '22
    Winship, M.   Interview.   Photop 22:49 Je '22

The cosmic urge.   Classic 19:24 My '24
St. Johns, I.   Sketch.   Photop 27:63 My '25
Perrin, H.   Sketch.   Motion Pic Classic 22:40 D '25
Steele, J. H.   Sketch.   Motion Pic Classic 27:23 Ap '28
Manners, D.   Sketch.   Motion Pic Classic 29:39 Ap '29
Walker, H. L.   Interview.   Motion Pic 39:42 Je '30
Hall, G.   Sketch.   Motion Pic Classic 33:52 Ap '31
Jamison, J.   Everybody's father confessor.   Silver S 1-7:25 My
   '31
Baskette, K.   Sketch.   Photop 45:62 D '33
Sketch.   Photop 54:40 F '40
Officer and gentleman.   Lions R 1-5:no p# Ja '42
Colonel Lewis Stone.   Lions R 1-7:no p# Mr '42
Since the turn of the century.   Lions R 3-3:no p# Ap '44

STONE, MILBURN
   Back from the dead.   Mod Screen 66-1:41 Ja '72
   Tusher, W.   Please tell them to let me die.   Movie Dig 1-2:91
   Mr '72

STONE, PAULA
   Hostess at annual movieland tour.   Motion Pic 51:20 Ap '36
   Lansdale, N.   Showbusiness women.   Theatre Arts 36:45 Ag '52

STONEHOUSE, RUTH
   Synon, K.   Ruth entertains.   Photop 7-3:98 F '15
   How she became a photoplayer.   Motion Pic 11:86 Ap '16
   Hall, R. E.   Sketch.   Motion Pic Classic 2:48 Ap '16
   Ruth and her house; interview.   Photop 12-4:140 S '17
   Lamb, G.   Interview.   Motion Pic 17:54 F '19
   Bruce, B.   Interview.   Motion Pic 19:36 F '20

STOPPELMOOR, CHERYL JEAN
   Raddatz, L.   Once people know my name, they don't forget it.
   TV Guide 21-3:27 Ja 20 '73

STORCH, LARRY
   Minoff, P.   Cavalcade gets a new star.   Cue 21-28:16 Jl 12 '52
   Fessier, M. Jr.   The world of Larry Storch.   TV Guide 14-33:
   15 Ag 13 '66

STOREY, EDITH
   Smith, F. J.   Sketch.   N.Y. Dram 69:25 My 28 '13
   Sketch.   Blue Book 19:14 My '14
   Dickinson, J.   Interview.   Green Book 12:1013 D '14
   Brodie, A. D.   Sketch.   Motion Pic 9:91 Ap '15
   How to get into moving pictures.   Motion Pic Classic 2:47 Ag '16
   Putting it over.   Motion Pic 12:121 Ja '17
   Fletcher, A. W.   Interview.   Motion Pic 15:83 My '18
   Johnsons, J.   The story of Storey.   Photop 14-6:28 N '18
   Haskins, H.   Sketch.   Motion Pic Classic 8:26 Je '19
   Edith Storey is still at war.   Photop 16-2:66 Jl '19
   Peltret, E.   Interview.   Motion Pic Classic 9:46 Ja '20

STORM, GALE
    Hamilton, S.   Story of.    Photop 31:28 S '47
    Charting a new course.   TV Guide 4-40:8 O 6 '56
    Catching up with Gale Storm.   Mod Screen 66-10:22 O '72
    Raddatz, L.   Where are they now?   TV Guide 21-4:32 Ja 27 '73

STOSSEL, LUDWIG
    Obit.   Screen World p239 '74

STOWELL, WILLIAM
    Matinee idol.   Photop 16-1:47 Je '19

STRADNER, ROSE
    Obit.   Screen World 10:225 '59

STRANGE, GLENN
    Bio note.   Cinema Trails 2:20 n. d.
    Raddatz, L.   The Dodge City gang.   TV Guide 20-12:14 Mr 18
       '72
    Obit.   Classic Film Collect 41:53 Win '73
       Screen World p239 '74

STRANGIS, JUDY
    Raddatz, L.   A prize pupil hands in her report card.   TV Guide
       20-27:28 Jl 1 '72

STRASBERG, SUSAN
    Taylor, T.   Accent on talent.   Cue 24-43:14 O 29 '55
    Vigil, C.   The season for Susan.   Cue 26-36:11 S 7 '57
    Lawrenson, H.   The route from Anne Frank to Camille is
       straight down the Appian Way.   Show 2-7:69 Jl '62
    Kiester, E. Jr.   Dying all the time does get tiresome.   TV
       Guide 21-51:26 D 22 '73

STRASSER, ROBIN
    Efron, E.   Living in two worlds.   TV Guide 19-45:48 N 6 '71

STRATTON, CHESTER
    Obit.   N. Y. Times p37 Jl 9 '70
       Same.   N. Y. Times Bio Ed Jl 9 '70
       Screen World 22:240 '71

STRAUSS, PETER
    Miller, E.   Interview.   Seventeen 29:140 My '70

STREISAND, BARBRA
    Lewis, E.   Bravos for Barbra.   Cue 32-52:11 D 28 '63
    Mothner, L.   Mamma Barbra.   Look 31:75 Jl 25 '67
    Hallowell, J.   Funny girl goes West.   Life 63:139 S 22 '67
    Lear, M. W.   Her name is Barbra.   Redbook 130:54 Ja '68
    People are talking about.   Vogue 151:154 Mr 1 '68
    Symbiosis continued.   Action 3-2:17 Mr/Ap '68
    Hallowell, J.   The truth game.   New York 1-23:40 S 9 '68

Crist, J. The bagel as superstar. New York 1-27:56 O 7 '68
Korall, B. Her name is Barbra. Sat R 52:108 Ja 11 '69
Ephron, N. Private world of Barbra. Good House 168:93 Ap
  '69
Salute of the week. Cue 38-50:1 D 13 '69
Hamilton, J. On a clear day you can see Dolly. Look 33:58
  D 16 '69
Morgenstern, J. Superstar. Newsweek 75:36 Ja 5 '70
Schiller, L. Who am I anyway? Interview. Life 68:91 Ja 9
  '70
The Streisand year. Cue 39-2:12 Ja 10 '70
Barbra Streisand. Vogue 155:104 Je '70
Live together? No. Love together? Yes. Photop 78-4:48 O
  '70
Robbins, F. Interview. Photop 79-1:80 Ja '71
Wedding for Barbra and Ryan? Silver S 41-10:21 O '71
Ryan dumps Barbra for black actress. Photop 80-6:27 D '71
Threatened by kidnapper. Mod Screen 66-1:41 Ja '72
Atlas, J. & Jaffe, S. Bogdanovich's salute to the zany comedies
  of the 30s. Show 2-2:24 Ap '72
Pray for Ryan O'Neal. Photop 81-4:44 Ap '72
An open letter to Barbra. Mod Screen 66-5:37 My '72
Superdrive. Films & Filming 18-9:13 Je '72
Weller, S. Hollywood's unhappy queen. Movie Dig 1-4:67 Jl
  '72
Thanks to Natalie he's got Streisand. Photop 82-2:32 Ag '72
Chutzpah power funny girl, cover girl, gall into glamour. Harp
  Baz 106:98 N '72
Flatley, G. Bewitched, Barbra'd and bewildered. N. Y. Times
  sec 2:1 Ja 21 '73
  Same. N. Y. Times Bio Ed p170 Ja '73
Success is empty. Mod Screen 67-4:52 Ap '73
And I picked this one up at the thrift shop. TV Guide 21-43:12
  O 27 '73
Barbra Streisand today. Photop 85-5:54 My '74
Everything but married. Photop 85-6:50 Je '74
Canby, V. Two formidable female stars. N. Y. Times sec 2:1
  Jl 21 '74
Bio note; filmog. Films Illus 3-36:475 Ag '74
Her romance with Jon Peters. Photop 86-3:42 S '74

STRICKLYN, RAY
  Alderson, K. Ray Stricklyn; filmog. Films In R 15-1:54 Ja '64

STRIMPELL, STEPHEN
  Whitney, D. What's a nice kid like you doing in a place like
    this? TV Guide 15-21:29 My 27 '67

STRITCH, ELAINE
  She can play it without stritching. TV Guide 9-14:29 Ap 8 '61
  Wilson, J. S. Elaine Stritch. N. Y. Times Bio Ed O 25 '70
  Gow, G. Coming on strongly. Plays & Players 20-5:24 F '73

STRODE, WOODY
    Hunter, C.  He wasn't the star but he stole the movie.  N. Y.
        Times Bio Ed S 19 '71

STROMSTEDT, ULLA
    Crail, T.  I have never been a field idiot.  TV Guide 14-13:22
        Mr 26 '66

STROUD, DON
    I really dig my life; centerfold.  Playgirl 1-6:72 N '73

STROUD, PAULINE
    Rising stars.  Film R p106 '52/53

STRUTHERS, SALLY
    Hobson, D.  Have you heard the one about the Warsaw Hilton?
        TV Guide 19-28:31 Jl 10 '71
    The real-life families of these All in the family stars.  Mod
        Screen 65-11:42 N '71
    How we will live happily ever after.  Mod Screen 66-4:62 Ap '72
    Bell, A.  What would Archie Bunker say?  N. Y. Times sec 2:15
        O 29 '72
        Same.  N. Y. Times Bio Ed p1873 O '72
    I go home at night and cry myself to sleep.  Mod Screen 67-2:50
        F '73
    Leider, R. A.  Memoirs of a dancing hamburger.  Show 3-4:40
        Je '73
    Sally struts her stuff.  People 1-9:41 Ap 29 '74

STUART, ALEXANDRA
    The night Jane Fonda's husband flew off with another woman.
        Photop 77-5:38 My '70

STUART, GLORIA
    Sketch.  Motion Pic 44:42 S '32
    Dillon, F.  Sketch.  Motion Pic 44:60 O '32
    Churchill, E.  Ambition's daughter.  Silver S 3-5:29 Mr '33
    Jamison, J.  Gloria Stuart.  Silver S 4-4:19 F '34
    Dillon, F.  Interview.  Motion Pic 47:32 My '34
    Ergenbright, E. L.  Interview.  Movie Classic 7:39 O '34
    Calhoun, D.  What love has done for her.  Movie Classic 8:27
        Ap '35
    Haddon, J. L.  Her philosophy.  Movie Classic 11:32 O '36
    Alden, A.  Interview.  Movie Classic 11:20 N '36
    Uselton, R. A.  The Wampus baby stars.  Films In R 21-2:73
        F '70

STUART, IRIS
    Uselton, R. A.  The Wampus baby stars.  Films In R 21-2:73
        F '70

STUART, JOHN
    Dilys Powell on John Stuart.  Silent Pic 14:23 Spg '72

STUART, MARY
Life in the problem factory.   TV Guide 8-47:18 N 19 '60
Moore, S.   Queen of the soaps.   People 1-13:63 My 27 '74

STUART, NICK
Wooldridge, A.   Sketch.   Motion Pic Classic 27:26 Mr '28
Manners, D.   Sketch.   Motion Pic 36:50 S '28
Shirley, L.   Interview.   Photop 34:63 O '28
Biery, R.   His secret marriage.   Motion Pic 39:8 F '30
Obit.   N. Y. Times p81 Ap 8 '73
Same.   N. Y. Times Bio Ed p720 Ap '73
Screen World p240 '74

STUBBS, UNA
Nicky and Una together again for the first time; filmog.   Films
Illus 2-22:24 Ap '73

STYMIE
(See:   BEARD, MATTHEW JR.)

STYPULKOWSKA, KRYSTYNA
The Polish cinema.   Film 31:25 Spg '62

SUDLOW, JOAN
Obit.   Screen World 22:240 '71

SUES, ALAN
Inflation hits the greeting-card business.   TV Guide 18-24:14 Je
13 '70
Raddatz, L.   Six who bowed out.   TV Guide 20-38:23 S 16 '72

SULLAVAN, MARGARET
Ferguson, F.   Work of.   Bookman 73:524 Jl '31
Nicholai, B.   Why she hasn't been interested in men.   Movie
Classic 5:34 F '34
Sketch.   Motion Pic 47:49 F '34
Hall, H.   Interview.   Movie Classic 6:35 Ap '34
Bio sketch.   Time 23:48 Je 11 '34
Keats, P.   Can she repeat?   Silver S 4-8:22 Je '34
Schellert, E.   Interview.   Motion Pic 47:44 Jl '34
French, W. F.   Sketch.   Movie Classic 6:32 Jl '34
Hall, H.   Most misunderstood star in Hollywood.   Movie Classic
7:27 Ja '35
Hogarth, D.   Her marriage.   Motion Pic 49:27 F '35
Lane, V.   Interview.   Movie Classic 9:26 O '35
Blythe, A.   Sketch.   Motion Pic 51:51 Ap '36
McHenry, M.   Her love tangle.   Movie Classic 10:36 Je '36
Hartley, K.   Work of in The moon's our home.   Movie Classic
10:38 My '36
Sketch.   Life 1:61 N 30 '36
Karel, P.   Three chances for happiness.   Silver S 8-11:24 S '38
Home life of.   Vogue 95:58 My 15 '40
Story of.   Life 8:42 Je 17 '40

Bio note; filmog.   Movies & People 2:35 '40
Sullavan's return.   Lions R 3-2:no p# Ja '44
Gardner, M.   Story of.   Cosmop 116:8 Ap '44
Obit.   Film R p10 '60/61

SULLIVAN, BARRY
    Parsons, L. O.   Cosmop's citation for the best supporting per-
        formance of month.   Cosmop 120:68 Je '46
    Hall, G.   All things to all women.   Silver S 21-11:42 S '51

SULLIVAN, ELLIOTT
    Obit.   N. Y. Times Bio Ed p894 Je '74

SULLIVAN, FRANCIS L.
    Sketch.   Theatre World 23:107 Mr '35

SULLIVAN, PAMELA
    N. Y. Times p39 F 10 '69

SUL-TE-WAN, MADAME
    Lee, R.   Night watch.   Classic Film Collect 18:39 Sum '67
        (reprint from The Villager N '53)

SUMMERS, HOPE
    Chierichetti, D.   The unsung heroes.   Film Fan Mo 89:21 N '68

SUMMERS, WALTER
    Pedler, G.   Walter Summers.   Silent Pic 16:31 Aut '72

SUMMERVILLE, SLIM
    Walker, H. L.   Sketch.   Motion Pic Classic 32:70 D '30
    Hill, J.   Interview.   Photop 43:53 Ja '33

SUNDSTROM, FLORENCE
    New neighbors for Riley.   TV Guide 4-1:16 Ja 7 '56

SUTHERLAND, DONALD
    Who was that guy?   Time 95:41 F 2 '70
    Flatley, G.   The name is S*U*T*H*E*R*L*A*N*D.   N. Y. Times
        Bio Ed F 15 '70
    On the scene.   Playboy 17-8:149 Ag '70
    Mothner, I.   New faces.   Look 34:75 N 3 '70
    Knight, A. & Alpert, H.   Sex stars of 1970.   Playboy 17-12:220
        D '70
    Atlas, J.   Canada's gift to Hollywood.   Show 2-2:40 Ap '71
    Robbins, F.   Interview.   Photop 79-6:32 Je '71
    Mills, B.   A new M*A*S*H-terpiece for Elliot and Don?   N. Y.
        Times sec 2:13 S 16 '73
    Eyles, A.   Bio note; filmog.   Focus On Film 16:10 Aut '73
    McAsh, I.   As good as Gould.   Films Illus 3-31:273 Ja '74

SUTTON, FRANK
    The sound and the fury boys.   TV Guide 13-26:6 Je 26 '65

Behind the blustry bombast.  TV Guide 15-49:10 D 9 '67
Obit.  N. Y. Times p37 Je 30 '74
    Same.  N. Y. Times Bio Ed p892 Je '74

SUTTON, JOHN
    Hamilton, S.  Sketch.  Photop 54:14 Ja '40

SUZMAN, JANET
    Popkin, H.  New stars.  Harp Baz 105:71 D '71
    Suzman on Alexandra.  Show 2-11:35 Ja '72
    Feiden, R.  Interview with Nicholas and Alexandra.  Interview
        20:31 Mr '72
    Archibald, L.  An actress who does not talk, she orchestrates.
        Show 2-3:44 My '72
    Andrews, E.  A chapter in the life of Janet Suzman.  Films Il-
        lus 1-12:24 Je '72
    Gow, G.  Shakespeare lib.  Plays & Players 20-9:18 Je '73
    Bio note; filmog.  Films Illus 3-36:470 Ag '74

SUZUKI, PAT
    Little girl, big voice.  Time 70:45 Jl 22 '57
    Other touches of the Far East.  Life 43:178 O 7 '57
    Girls on Grant Avenue.  Time 72:42 D 22 '58
    Brown, C.  Many sides of Pat Suzuki.  Redbook 116:20 Ja '61
    Groovy scene.  Michael's Thing 1-33:3 Ag 23 '71

SVERDLIN, LEV N.
    Obit.  N. Y. Times p37 S 5 '69

SWAIN, MACK
    Gill, S.  The funny men.  8mm Collect 13:32 Fall/Win '65

SWANSON, GLORIA
    Remont, F.  Interview.  Motion Pic 16:102 D '18
    Remont, F.  Interview.  Motion Pic Classic 8:22 Jl '19
    Peltret, E.  Interview.  Motion Pic 18:33 D '19
    Smith, F. J.  Interview.  Motion Pic Classic 9:16 F '20
    Naylor, H. S.  Sketch.  Motion Pic 21:24 Ap '21
    Goldbeck, W.  Interview.  Motion Pic Classic 13:24 O '21
    Fletcher, A. W.  Interview.  Motion Pic 22:28 D '21
    A star in the making.  Motion Pic Classic 14:18 Ag '22
    Cheatham, M.  Her darkest hour.  Classic 15:52 O '22
    Moreno, A. & Swanson, G.  Do women dress to please men.
        Motion Pic 24:28 N '22
    Home of.  Photop 23:64 Mr '23
    Carter, J.  Interview.  Classic 16:32 Je '23
    Carr, H.  Still a star.  Motion Pic 25:36 O '23
    Adams, E.  Her horoscope.  Photop 26:106 N '24
    de Revere, F. V.  Analysis of her face.  Motion Pic 28:45 D
    Wilson, B.  Interview.  Classic 20:38 D '24
    Douglas, C.  Sketch.  Motion Pic Classic 21:50 My '25
    Quirk, J. R.  Her husband.  Photop 28:34 Je '25
    Carr, H.  Sketch.  Motion Pic 29:34 Je '25

Bromfield, L.  In Madame Sans-Gene.  Bookman 61:579 Jl '25
Carr, H.  Compared with Pola Negri.  Motion Pic 30:28 S '25
Ashley, R.  An exciting location trip to Martinsville, W. Va.
     Photop 28:32 N '25
Sketch.  Motion Pic Classic 22:25 N '25
Roberts, W. A.  Sketch.  Motion Pic 30:54 D '25
White, C.  Interview.  Motion Pic Classic 22:52 F '26
Autobiographical.  Motion Pic Classic 23:18 Jl '26
Hall, G. & Fletcher, A. W.  Interview.  Motion Pic 32:28 O
     '26
Gloria Swanson and her crew.  Theatre 44:38 N '26
Thorp, D.  Interview.  Motion Pic Classic 24:26 Ja '27
Service, F.  Interview.  Motion Pic 33:30 Ap '27
Robinson, S.  Interview.  Motion Pic 31:31 Ap '27
Brenon, A.  Sketch.  Motion Pic 35:31 Jl '28
Hall, G.  Her hoax as Rosalie Grey.  Motion Pic 36:28 N '28
Orme, M.  Criticism.  Ill Lon N 175:546 S 28 '29
Manners, D.  Interview.  Motion Pic 39:48 Mr '30
Hall, G.  Interview.  Motion Pic 40:50 N '30
Calhoun, D.  Sketch.  Motion Pic 41:8 F '31
Walker, H. L.  Sketch.  Motion Pic Classic 33:65 My '31
Biery, R.  Sketch.  Photop 40:44 Je '31
Shirley, L.  Interview about clothes.  Photop 40:32 Jl '31
Hall, G.  Will she marry again?  Movie Classic 1:50 N '31
Dibble, S.  Sketch.  Movie Classic 1:43 Ja '32
Wilson, E.  Sketch.  Photop 41:28 F '32
Babcock, M.  Her career during 1916-1931.  Movie Classic 1:
     22 F '32
Cheatham, M.  Sketch.  Movie Classic 2:44 Je '32
Gloria Swanson's progeny.  Cinema Dig 1-11:11 O 3 '32
Luxuries are necessary.  Movie Classic 3:30 N '32
Hall, H.  Swanson's swan song?  Cinema Dig 3-3:3 Ap 3 '33
Cruikshank.  Will continue her work in pictures.  Motion Pic
     45:57 Je '33
How Sylvia tamed her jumpy nerves.  Photop 44:54 O '33
Hall, G.  Interview.  Movie Classic 6:5 My '34
Reed, D.  Never a dull moment.  Silver S 4-11:28 S '34
Her perfect foot.  Photop 47:56 F '35
Lane, V. T.  Story of.  Motion Pic 54:45 O '37
Talmey, A.  Story of.  Vogue 98:78 Ag 15 '41
Hall, G.  Return to glory.  Silver S 11-10:24 Ag '41
It's a new kind of screen for La Swanson.  Cue 17-28:16 Jl 10
     '48
Swanson stars in film about a screen star.  Cue 18-43:16 O 22
     '49
Has Hollywood changed?  Silver S 20-1:36 N '49
Keating, J.  La Swanson tours America.  Cue 19-31:15 Ag 5 '50
Leslie, A.  You don't forget a name like Swanson.  8mm Collect
     9:12 S '64
Brownlow, K.  Gloria Swanson.  Film 41:7 Aut '64
Whatever happened to the girl who drove men mad.  8mm Collect
     14:35 Spg '66
Brownlow, K.  The Countess set.  Film 46:4 Sum '66

Silver, C.  17 years down the boulevard.  Classic Film Collect
19:3 Fall/Win '67
Nogueira, R.  I am not going to write my memoirs; interviews.
Sight & Sound 38-2:58 Spg '69
When silence was golden.  Screen Greats 1-2:74 Sum '71
Markham, J. M.  Gloria Swanson is returning to Broadway.
N. Y. Times Bio Ed Ag 20 '71
Paley, M.  Gloria is back, full of organic beans.  Life 71:77 S
17 '71
Klemesrud, J.  Name, nose, teeth, bosom, hair, kidneys--
everything but eyelashes--is real.  N. Y. Times Bio Ed O
10 '71
Leech, M. T.  The high point of her career is now.  Show 2-9:
44 N '71
Shepard, R. F.  Stars as a visitor.  N. Y. Times Bio Ed Ja 19
'72
Boe, E.  I want to come back as a new woman.  New Woman
1-8:68 F '72
Miss Swanson in excelsis.  Interview 25:23 S '72
MacKenzie, B.  Queen bee.  TV Guide 22-8:12 F 23 '74
d'Arcy, S.  Still ready for that close-up, Mr. DeMille.  Films
Illus 4-40:138 D '74

SWANSON, MAUREEN
Rising stars.  Film R p31 '57/58

SWARTHOUT, GLADYS
Bio note; filmog.  Movies & People 2:36 '40
Edwards, B.  Gladys Swarthout.  Films In R 9-2:111 F '58
Obit.  Screen World 21:240 '70
(Citations to Film Career only)

SWEENEY, BOB
In the cast.  TV Guide 1-39:18 D 25 '53

SWEET, BLANCHE
Interview.  Cosmop 58:330 F '15
Sketch.  Motion Pic 10:110 Ag '15
Willis, R.  Idealist.  Movie Pictorial 2-2:7 Ag '15
Courtlandt, R.  Sketch.  Motion Pic 11:143 Ap '16
How to get in moving pictures.  Motion Pic 12:65 N '16
Smith, F. J.  Interview.  Motion Pic Classic 7:16 N '18
Sherwood, C. B.  Interview.  Motion Pic 20:30 D '20
Carr, H.  Her return to the screen.  Motion Pic 25:21 Ag '23
Le Berthon, T.  Interview.  Motion Pic 25:24 N '23
Carr, H.  Interview.  Classic 18:18 F '24
Carr, H.  Sketch.  Motion Pic 28:27 Ja '25
Roberts, W. A.  Sketch.  Motion Pic 30:52 N '25
Sketch.  Motion Pic 30:52 D '25
Hall, G.  Her life story.  Motion Pic Classic 28:16 O '28
Hall, G.  Interview.  Motion Pic 39:58 F '30
Endearing young charm.  Cue 12-28:9 Jl 10 '43
Bodeen, D.  Letter.  Films In R 18-9:581 N '67
Slide, A.  Interview.  Silent Pic 14:12 Spg '72

SWIT, LORETTA
   McCoy, K.  Auggghh!  TV Guide 19-5:15 Ja 30 '71
   Strout, D.  Interview.  Mod Screen 67-4:64 Ap '73
   M*A*S*H's Loretta Swit.  Show 3-6:50 S '73
   Kiester, E. Jr.  She's what a woman should be.  TV Guide 22-
     6:21 F 9 '74

SWITZER, CARL "ALFALFA"
   Obit.  Film R p10 '59/60
   Screen World 11:225 '60
   Maltin, L.  Our gang; Our gang filmog.  Film Fan Mo 66:3 D
    '66

SWOPE, TOPO
   Second generation.  Films Illus 1-10:12 Ap '72

SYDNEY, BASIL
   Obit.  Brit Bk Yr 1969:580 '69
   N. Y. Times p33 Ja 11 '68

SYKES, BRENDA
   99 pounds of surprises.  TV Guide 19-15:20 Ap 10 '71

SYLVESTER, WILLIAM
   Rising stars.  Film R p106 '53/54

SYMS, SYLVIA
   Rising stars.  Film R p40 '56/57
   Rising stars.  Film R p29 '58/59


TABORI, KRISTOFFER
   Zadan, C.  Penny wars.  After Dark 4-8:26 D '71
   Kids want to see movies about people the way they are.  Seven-
    teen 31:96 Ja '72
   Second generation.  Films Illus 1-10:12 Ap '72
   Sketch.  Movie Dig 1-6:31 N '72

TADEUSZ, LOMNICKI
   The Polish cinema.  Film 31:25 Spg '62

TAEGER, RALPH
   When ignorance is really bliss.  TV Guide 8-52:21 D 24 '60
   Prelutsky, B.  He can always go back to polishing floors.  TV
    Guide 15-48:32 D 2 '67

TAKA, MIIKO
   Zunser, J.  Miiko from Seattle.  Cue 26-47:16 N 23 '57

TALBOT, LYLE
   Sketch.  Motion Pic 44:42 D '32
   Gwin, J.  Off the reservation.  Silver S 5-11:51 S '35

TALBOT, NITA
A 'Brooklyn-type' doll--with a Charles Laughton education.    TV
    Guide 4-15:12 Ap 14 '56

TALBOTT, GLORIA
She did something about it.    TV Guide 5-41:28 O 12 '57

TALIAFERRO, MABEL
    Hirsh, S. M.    Evolution of a child of the stage.    Theater 8:158
        Je '08
    She's an actress.    Success 12:494 Ag '09
    Her reminiscenses of girlhood.    Green Bk Albm 2:232 Ag '09
    Taliaferro sisters as joint stars.    Munsey 50:464 D '13
    Patterson, A.    The Taliaferros, sisters and co-stars.    Theater
        19:70 F '14
    How the small woman should dress.    Green Book 11:914 Je '14

TALLICHET, MARGARET
    Schwarzkoff, J.    Sketch.    Motion Pic 53:21 My '37

TALMADGE, CONSTANCE
    Sketch.    Motion Pic 9:117 My '15
    Lachmund, M. G.    Sketch.    Motion Pic 12:110 Ja '17
    Courtland, R.    Interview.    Motion Pic Classic 6:49 Jl '18
    Naylor, H. S.    Sketch.    Motion Pic 16:100 O '18
    McGaffey, K.    Sketch.    Motion Pic 17:50 Ap '19
    Smith, F. J.    Interview.    Motion Pic Classic 8:16 Jl '19
    Miriam, G.    Interview.    National 49:165 Jl '20
    O'Reilly, E. S.    Interview.    Photop 18:54 S '20
    Hall, G.    Interview.    Motion Pic Classic 13:16 F '22
    Goldbeck, W.    Interview.    Motion Pic 23:24 My '22
    Carr, H.    Interview.    Classic 15:52 S '22
    Carr, H.    Sketch.    Classic 15:32 D '22
    The kind of man she would like to marry.    Photop 24:36 O '23
    de Revere, F. V.    Analysis of her face.    Motion Pic 28:42 S
        '24
    Why men fall in love with actresses.    Photop 27:32 F '25
    My pep, and how I keep it.    Motion Pic Classic 21:24 Ap '25
    Roberts, W. A.    Sketch.    Motion Pic 29:54 Ap '25
    Carr, H.    The millionaire actress.    Motion Pic Classic 21:42
        Jl '25
    The most dramatic moments of my life.    Motion Pic 30:48 N
        '25
    Hall, G.    Sketch.    Motion Pic 32:29 D '26
    Interview.    Theatre 44:38 D '26
    The tragedy of being funny.    Motion Pic 34:54 Ag '27
    Hall, G.    Life story.    Motion Pic Classic 28:18 N '28
    Hall, G.    Peg Talmadge, the mother of 3 famous daughters.
        Motion Pic Classic 28:26 D '28
    Babcock, M.    The Talmadge sisters still in the headlines.
        Movie Classic 3:18 D '32
    Braff, R. E.    Letter.    Films In R 23-7:444 Ag/S '72
    Obit.    Classic Film Collect 42:34 Spg '74

N. Y. Times Bio Ed p1875 N '73
Screen World p240 '74

TALMADGE, NATALIE
  Hall, G.   Peg Talmadge, the mother of 3 famous daughters.
    Motion Pic Classic 28:26 D '28
  Babcock, M.   The Talmadge sisters still in the headlines.
    Movie Classic 3:18 D '32
  Obit.   Classic Film Collect 24:14 Sum '69
    N. Y. Times p27 Je 21 '69
    Screen World 21:240 '70

TALMADGE, NORMA
  How to get in moving pictures.   Motion Pic Classic 3:58 S '16
  How she got in moving pictures.   Motion Pic 14:109 O '17
  Field, G. H.   Her vogue.   Motion Pic 15:71 Ap '18
  Service, F.   Interview.   Motion Pic Classic 9:22 Ja '20
  Biographical.   Dram Mir 82:744 Ap 17 '20
  Miriam, G.   Interview.   National 49:253 S '20
  Smith, F. J.   Interview.   Motion Pic Classic 11:25 D '20
  Good and bad taste in clothes.   Photop 19:47 F '21
  Fletcher, A. W.   Interview.   Motion Pic 21:22 Mr '21
  Fletcher, A. W.   Interview.   Motion Pic Classic 13:20 D '21
  Home of.   Photop 23:38 My '23
  Home of.   Classic 16:40 Jl '23
  Is woman's love greater than man's?   Motion Pic 25:59 Ag '23
  Carr, H.   About Mrs. Joseph Schenck.   Motion Pic 25:27 N
    '23
  de Revere, F. V.   Analysis of her face.   Motion Pic 28:43 S
    '24
  Alexander, K.   As she appears to her photographer.   Motion
    Pic 29:88 Mr '25
  Rittenhouse, M.   Interview.   Motion Pic 31:39 Jl '26
  Service, F.   Normaisms.   Motion Pic 32:40 N '26
  Interview.   Theatre 44:28 D '26
  Donnell, D.   Paris as it seems to her.   Motion Pic 34:38 Ja
    '28
  Hall, G.   Her philosophy of life.   Motion Pic 35:33 My '28
  Hall, G.   Peg Talmadge, the mother of 3 famous daughters.
    Motion Pic Classic 28:26 D '28
  Hall, G.   Interview.   Motion Pic Classic 32:38 F '31
  Schallert, E.   Is her marriage to end in unusual divorce?
    Motion Pic 43:40 My '32
  Cruikshank.   Her love affairs.   Motion Pic 44:62 D '32
  Babcock, M.   The Talmadge sisters still in the headlines.
    Movie Classic 3:18 D '32
  Melcher, E.   Norma Talmadge.   Cinema Dig 4-3:14 My 29 '33
  Braff, R. E.   More films of Norma Talmadge; partial filmog.
    Films In R 23-2:118 F '72

TALMAN, BILL
  Gehman, R.   He never comes in first.   TV Guide 11-17:22 Ap
    27 '63

**TALTON, ALIX**
Georgia peach on TV.   TV Guide 2-26:12 Je 25 '54

**TAMBLYN, RUSS**
People of promise.   Films & Filming 1-4:23 Ja '55

**TAMIROFF, AKIM**
Zeitlin, I.   Sketch.   Motion Pic 54:49 S '37
Surmelian, L.   He'd rather act than eat.   Screen Book 19-6:40
  Ja '38
Tireless Tamiroff.   Lions R 1-9:no p# My '42
Happy Tamiroff.   Cue 12-23:13 Je 5 '43
Cosby, V.   How he helps nervously exhausted service men.
  Photop 25:18 Je '44
Tamiroff, perfectionist.   Lions R 3-4:no p# Jl '44
Good actor Tamiroff.   Cue 13-30:10 Jl 22 '44
Obit.   Classic Film Collect 37:59 Win '72
N. Y.   Times Bio Ed p1709 S '72
Film R p12 '73/74

**TAMM, MARY**
Tomorrow people.   Films Illus 3-35:443 Jl '74

**TANDY, JESSICA**
Mr. and Mrs. 24 hours a day.   Lions R 3-4(sup):no p# Jl '44
It's the sponsor who pays.   TV Guide 4-37:24 S 15 '56
Chase, C.   Tandy and Cronyn are wed to the theater, too.   N. Y.
  Times sec 2:1 Mr 24 '74
Same.   N. Y.   Times Bio Ed p443 Mr '74

**TASHMAN, LILYAN**
Pryor, N.   Sketch.   Motion Pic 35:72 F '28
Conti, M.   Shopping with Tashman.   Motion Pic 37:78 Mr '29
Larkin, M.   How to hold a husband in Hollywood.   Photop 36:64
  Je '29
Manners, D.   Sketch.   Motion Pic Classic 30:23 D '29
Biery, R.   Interview.   Motion Pic 39:66 Mr '30
Manners, D.   Interview.   Motion Pic 40:44 N '30
Churchill, E.   She uses her head.   Silver S 1-3:17 Ja '31
Busby, M.   Sketch.   Motion Pic 41:44 Mr '31
Service, F.   Interview.   Movie Classic 1:23 N '31
Marion, J.   Just a home girl.   Silver S 2-2:44 D '31
Peabody, A.   Tashman looks at tomorrow.   Silver S 2-11:26 S
  '32
Stuart, B. T.   Whose clothes are you wearing?   Colliers 90:17
  N 19 '32
As a hostess.   Vogue 81:31 Ja 1 '33
Taviner, R.   Her married life.   Photop 43:52 Mr '33
Haddon, J. L.   The Tashman-Hopper feud.   Motion Pic 45:58
  Jl '33
Appreciation.   Motion Pic 47:8 Je '34
Hall, G.   Tribute.   Movie Classic 6:34 Jl '34
Pinups of the past.   Films & Filming 17-2:70 N '70

TATE, SHARON
  Malanga, G.  Interview.  Interview 1-1:27 n. d.
  The Tate gallery; photos by Roman Polanski.  Playboy 14-3:70
    Mr '67
  Rollins, B.  Dames in the Valley of the dolls.  Look 31:54 S 5
    '67
  Obit.  Film R p15 '70/71
    N. Y. Times p1 Ag 10 '69
    Screen World 21:241 '70
  Nothing but bodies.  Time 94:24 Ag 15 '69
  Hollywood murders.  Newsweek 74:28 Ag 18 '69
  Night of horror.  Time 94:16 Ag 22 '69
  Tate set.  Newsweek 74:24 Ag 25 '69
  Thompson, T.  Tragic house on the hill.  Life 67:42 Ag 29 '69
  Ghoulish moguls.  Christian Cent 86:1186 S 17 '69
  Farrell, B.  In Hollywood, the dead keep right on dying.  Life
    67:4 N 7 '69
  Demon of death valley.  Time 94:22 D 12 '69
  Maas, P.  Sharon Tate murders.  Ladies Home J 87:52 Ap '70
  Hair-raising stories from the stars.  Photop 78-1:62 Jl '70

TATI, JACQUES
  Jacques Tati.  Film 17:10 S/O '58
  The French film; discussion.  Film 26:10 N/D '60
  Lachize, S.  Close to a masterpiece.  Atlas 15:55 Mr '68
  Chapier, H.  Gauche and ridiculous.  Atlas 15:56 Mr '68
  Maelstaf, R.  Interview.  CTVD 5-4:8 Sum '68
  Director of the year; filmog.  Int F G 6:25 '69
  Armes, R.  The comic art of Tati.  Screen 11-1:68 F '70
  What directors are saying.  Action 5-6:22 N/D '70
  Gilliatt, P.  Current cinema.  New Yorker 47:58 Ag 28 '71
  What directors are saying.  Action 8-1:32 Ja/F '73
  Rosenbaum, J.  Interview; filmog.  Film Comment 9-3:36 My/Je
    '73
  Canby, V.  Bravo Chaplin.  Bravo Tati.  N. Y. Times sec 2:1 Jl
    8 '73
  Eyles, A.  Bio sketch; filmog.  Focus On F 8:8 n. d.

TAYLOR, BUCK
  Raddatz, L.  Gunsmoke's designated hitter.  TV Guide 21-49:17
    D 8 '73

TAYLOR, DON
  Winogura, D.  Dialogues on apes, apes and more apes; inter-
    view.  Cinefantastique 2-2:22 Sum '72

TAYLOR, ELIZABETH
  Her role in National Velvet.  Newsweek 24:80 D 18 '44
  Agee, J.  Appreciation.  Nation 159:781 D 25 '44
  Carling, J.  Wise little owl.  Silver S 18-8:36 Je '48
  Her first formal party.  Photop 33:56 O '48
  Graham, S.  Sketch.  Photop 33:41 N '48
  Greets Glenn Davis on his return from Korea.  Life 26:49 Mr

21 '49
Visits her old home in London.  Photop 34:42 Mr '49
Parrish, C.  Memories she won't forget.  Silver S 19-8:36 Je
   '49
Norman, D. C.  Sketch.  Ladies Home J 66:64 S '49
Taylor, E.  Wardrobe for Florida.  Silver S 19-12:46 O '49
Morris, T. & J.  Seventeen is a wonderful age.  Silver S 20-1:
   42 N '49
Howard, M.  (Her) love story.  Silver S 20-8:22 Je '50
Powell, J.  Meet Liz--the bride.  Silver S 20-8:24 Je '50
Taylor, E.  My day as an extra in Quo Vadis.  Silver S 21-2:
   24 D '50
Balling, F. D.  Elizabeth's most exciting party.  Silver S 21-4:
   22 F '51
Baer, M. M.  Heart to heart talk with Liz.  Silver S 22-7:26
   My '52
Rogers, V.  The Liz Taylor-Michael Wilding rumors.  Silver S
   24-5:31 Mr '54
Lawrenson, H.  The nightmare of the iguana.  Show 4-1:46 Ja
   '64
Glenville, P.  Glenville talks about the Burtons.  Vogue 150:282
   S 1 '67
Pepper, C. G.  Voyage with the Burtons.  McCalls 95:56 Ja '68
Sheed, W.  Burton and Taylor must go.  Esquire 70:173 O '68
Thompson, T.  While Burton romances Rex, Liz weighs her
   power and her future.  Life 66:65 Ja 17 '69
Birstein, A.  What it's like to be walking investments.  Vogue
   153:100 F 15 '69
Lurie, D.  Taylor talks about being a mother.  Ladies Home J
   86:83 Mr '69
Liz's million dollar rock.  Life 67:65 N 14 '69
Smith, L.  $10,000,000 jewels of Taylor and Jackie Onassis.
   Ladies Home J 86:64 D '69
Love is losing 40 pounds and giving it to your husband.  Photop
   77-5:36 My '70
Roddy, J.  How do I love thee?  Look 34:28 Je 16 '70
Why do they call my son girlie?  Photop 78-1:68 Jl '70
Liz and Burton attacked for the nude beach party.  Photop 78-2:
   56 Ag '70
Essoe, G.  Taylor still has a chance to escape from the obvi-
   ous.  Films In R 21-393 Ag '70
Bacon, J.  All I could see was Elizabeth and that rock.  TV
   Guide 18-36:16 S 5 '70
Liz has operation no woman wants to talk about.  Photop 78-3:
   47 S '70
A look at two lost virgins.  Photop 78-4:54 O '70
Mertes, J.  Letter.  Films In R 21-9:582 N '70
What it's like to be in bed with Burton.  Photop 79-1:45 Ja '71
Liz's 17 year old hippie, hairy son weds.  Photop 79-1:47 Ja
   '71
Liz gets advice from a 74-year-old grandmother.  Photop 79-2:
   49 F '71
Bain, R.  Our marriage after 7 years.  Ladies Home J 88:88

Ap '71

Taylor weeps at death of friend.   Photop 79-4:63 Ap '71

Burton, R.  Travelling with Elizabeth.   Vogue 157:68 Ap 15
   '71

The mystery man who wants to destroy them.   Photop 79-5:85
   My '71

The kids.   Screen Greats 1-2:50 Sum '71

Liz walks out on Burton.   Photop 80-2:64 Ag '71

Knapp, D.  On location in Mexico.   Show 2-7:18 S '71

Burton, R.  Dauntless travelers.   Vogue 158:130 O 15 '71

Will Burton want a younger woman now?   Mod Screen 65-11:27
   N '71

I won't let my son raise my grandchild like a gypsy.   Photop
   80-5:61 N '71

Liz saves Burton's life.   Photop 80-6:66 D '71

Mad killer hunts down Taylor.   Photop 81-1:68 Ja '72

Liz is told: I want a divorce.   Mod Screen 67-1:35 Ja '72

Thompson, T.  Happy 40th, dear Liz.   Life 72-7:57 F 25
   '72

Liz and Dick scandalize guests at decadent French party.   Mod
   Screen 66-3:34 Mr '72

Bain, R.  Ten years since scandal time.   Harp Baz 105:126 Ap
   '72

Happiest role.   Ladies Home J 89:115 Ap '72

How they abuse their bodies to please their men.   Photop 81-4:
   36 Ap '72

How you can be your husband's mistress.   Mod Screen 66-4:21
   Ap '72

Life may not begin at 40.   Mod Screen 66-5:43 My '72

Her million dollar birthday bash.   Mod Screen 66-6:38 Je
   '72

Nye, C.  Making it in Munich.   Time p47 Jl 2 '72

Why we want to adopt another baby.   Photop 82-2:48 Jl '72

Public passion.   Mod Screen 66-9:33 S '72

Burton & Taylor; filmog.   Films Illus 1-16:19 O '72

Cameron, G.  Search for (her) son.   McCalls 100:104 N
   '72

Liz and Liza, still blooming.   Life 73:35 D 29 '72

Plot to kidnap.   Photop 83-1:48 Ja '73

Musel, R.  Not bad for 40 years old, eh?   TV Guide 21-5:16
   F 3 '73

Botsford, K.  The white Rolls-Royce.   N.Y. Times Mag p56
   Mr 25 '73

The right and wrong way to love.   Photop 83-5:54 My '73

Edwards, J. P.  Her story.   Liberty 1-10:53 Fall '73

Liz today.   Photop 84-3:44 S '73

Liz tells all.   Photop 84-4:56 O '73

After the divorce.   Photop 84-5:26 N '73

Liz needs me.   Photop 84-6:24 D '73

Liz to marry.   Photop 85-1:30 Ja '74

Why (she) took Burton back.   Photop 85-3:34 Mr '74

Elizabeth Taylor.  Photop 85-4:56 Ap '74
Ian Bannen talks about Taylor.  Photop 85-6:41 Je '74
New scandal.  Photop 86-1:17 Jl '74
Elizabeth Taylor gave me courage.  Photop 86-1:42 Jl '74
Passions aroused again.  Photop 86-2:44 Ag '74
No more men, no more marriages.  Photop 86-3:60 S '74
I'm not going to rush into marriage.  Photop 86-6:35 D '74

TAYLOR, ESTELLE
Rosemon, E.  Interview.  Motion Pic Classic 10:60 Ag '20
Boone, A.  Sketch.  Photop 19:49 Ja '21
Cheatham, M.  Interview.  Motion Pic Classic 14:32 Je '22
Handy, T. B.  Interview.  Motion Pic 25:38 Mr '23
Smith, P.  A day with a movie star.  Photop 27:30 Ap '25
Sketch.  Motion Pic 32:55 Ja '27
Spensley, D.  Interview.  Photop 31:62 Mr '27
Carlisle, H.  Sketch.  Motion Pic 33:74 Jl '27
Wilson, E.  Sketch.  Motion Pic Classic 26:40 O '27
Fields, J.  Sketch.  Motion Pic Classic 26:37 F '28
Johnston, C.  Impressions of "Mr. Ginsberg" and his wife.
   Motion Pic Classic 28:51 S '28
Hall, G.  Interview.  Motion Pic 37:50 Mr '29
Pryor, N.  Interview.  Motion Pic 39:45 Jl '30
Calhoun, D.  Sketch.  Motion Pic Classic 33:30 Je '31
Hall, G.  Sketch.  Motion Pic 41:8 Jl '31
Standish, J.  Her divorce from Jack Dempsey.  Movie Classic
   1:43 N '31
Calhoun, D.  Sketch.  Movie Classic 2:28 Ap '32
Derr, E.  Interview.  Movie Classic 2:27 Jl '32

TAYLOR, JEANETTE
Taylor, J.  And then the roof fell in.  TV Guide 6-49:18 D 6
   '58
Sometimes the dream comes true.  Seventeen 23:66 Mr '64

TAYLOR, JOAN
She stops behind the counter.  TV Guide 10-16:28 Ap 21 '62

TAYLOR, JOYCE
Miss Taylor from Taylorville.  TV Guide 8-37:29 S 10 '60

TAYLOR, KENT
Williams, W.  Signed by mistake.  Screen Book 19-1:89 Ag '37

TAYLOR, RENEE
Adler, D.  Coming this week: Joe and Renee.  New York 4-50:
   35 D 13 '71
Johnson, D.  Taylor-made for each other.  After Dark 4-11:44
   Mr '72
MacDonough, S.  Made for each other.  Show 2-1:20 Mr '72
Bailey, P. J.  Interview.  Playgirl 2-5:14 O '74

## TAYLOR, ROBERT
Surmelian, L.   24 and very fickle.   Silver S 6-5:29 Mr '36
Langford, H.   Interview.   Motion Pic 51:37 Ap '36
Hill, M.   Interview.   Movie Classic 10:39 My '36
Liza.   The eligible heart-breakers.   Silver S 6-9:51 Jl '36
Samuels, L.   A very modest gentleman.   Silver S 6-10:24 Ag
   '36
Mack, G.   His popularity.   Motion Pic 52:30 Ag '36
Brugh, R.   His life story.   Movie Classic 10:28 S '36 & follow-
   ing issues.
Answers questions.   Movie Classic 10:22 S '36
Taylor wins the Silver Screen gold medal.   Silver S 7-1:10 N
   '36
Surmelian, L.   Interview.   Motion Pic 52:28 Ja '37
Babcock, M.   Is he a stuffed shirt?   Silver S 7-4:16 F '37
Fairweather, D.   Appreciation.   Theatre World 28:138 S '37
Shaffer, R.   Looking down from "Heaven."   Screen Book 19-2:
   32 S '37
Wilson, E.   Projections.   Silver S 8-2:26 D '37
Robert Taylor.   Visages 20:entire issue Ja '38
Maddox, B.   Taylor's greatest thrills.   Silver S 8-8:22 Je '38
Hill, M.   Behind the scenes with Taylor.   Screen Book 20-5:26
   Je '38
Asher, J.   The Taylor Hollywood doesn't know.   Screen Book
   21-2:32 S '38
Campbell, S.   Stanwyck speaks her mind on Taylor.   Screen
   Book 21-5:22 D '38
Mr. & Mrs. R. Taylor visit the races.   Life 7:32 Jl 10 '39
McFee, F.   Hedy Lamarr and Taylor--lovers.   Screen Book
   22-1:58 Ag '39
Bio note; filmog.   Movies & People 2:36 '40
Autobiographical.   Cosmop 111:36 S '41
Actor-flyer.   Lions R 1-5:no p# Jl '43
A valuable rage.   Lions R 1-10:no p# Je '42
Taylor's contradictions.   Lions R 2-3:no p# D '42
Star in the sky.   Lions R 2-5:no p# Jl '43
Wilson, E.   Taylor bids adieu.   Silver S 13-11:24 S '43
Salute to a lieutenant.   Lions R 3-2:no p# Ja '44
Taylor in Carnegie Hall?   Lions R 3-2:no p# Ja '44
You can't take luck for granted.   Lions R 3-5:no p# D '44
Actor Taylor vs. Lieut. Taylor.   USNR.   Cue 14-4:8 Ja 27 '45
Pritchett, F.   Surprise story.   Silver S 18-1:28 N '47
Bruce, J.   Must you be pretty?   Silver S 19-11:42 S '49
Baer, M. M.   Handsome men can be noble men.   Silver S 21-3:
   30 Ja '51
Baer, M. M.   Barbara with Bob in Rome.   Silver S 21-4:38 F
   '51
Swisher, V.   Darn that dignity.   Silver S 21-12:36 O '51
Baer, M. M.   Personal report on Bob.   Silver S 22-6:26 Ap '52
Obit.   Brit Bk Yr 1970:590 '70
   Classic Film Collect 24:14 Sum '69
   Cur Bio 30:46 Jl '69
   Same.   Cur Bio Yrbk 1969:474 '70

Film R p15 '70/71
N.Y. Times p1 Je 9 '69
Newsweek 73:71 Je 16 '69
Screen World 21:241 '70
Time 93:72 Je 20 '69
Tall, dark and handsome.    Screen Greats 1-2:24 Sum '71

TAYLOR, ROD
Davidson, B.    Why can't Taylor be a pussycat?    TV Guide 19-
43:16 O 23 '71

TAYLOR, RUTH
Waterbury, R.    To play Lorelei Lee.    Photop 32:62 N '27
Johnston, C.    Sketch.    Motion Pic 35:49 My '28
Uselton, R. A.    The Wampus baby stars.    Films In R 21-2:73
F '70

TAYLOR, VAUGHN
Taylor-made for TV.    TV Guide 2-31:5 Jl 31 '54

TAYLOR-YOUNG, LEIGH
Lewis, R. W.    New girl in town.    TV Guide 14-49:24 D 3 '66
Year of the anatomy.    Vogue 153:80 Ja 1 '69
Leigh Taylor-Young.    Vogue 153:205 My '69
Simons, M.    Where do you go from Peyton Place?    Look 33:M
D 2 '69
How they all played Roman games.    Photop 77-6:64 Je '70
Knight, A. & Alpert, H.    Sex stars of 1970.    Playboy 17-12:220
D '70
I want another husband.    Photop 80-6:30 D '71
Hollywood's hot new sex queens.    Mod Screen 66-1:34 Ja '72
Leigh races to Ryan's side.    Mod Screen 66-4:46 Ap '72

TEAL, RAY
Ray Teal; filmog.    Cinema Trails 2:10 n.d.

TEARE, ETHEL
Mount, C.    Sketch.    Motion Pic Classic 2:25 Je '16

TEARLE, CONWAY
Naylor, H. S.    Sketch.    Motion Pic Classic 8:20 My '19
Confessions as a love maker.    Motion Pic 18:39 Ja '20
Malvern, P.    Interview.    Motion Pic Classic 11:32 O '20
Carr, H.    Interview.    Classic 16:26 Ap '23
Home of.    Photop 26:73 Ag '24
de Revere, F. V.    Analysis of his face.    Motion Pic 28:42 S '24

TEARLE, GODFREY
Experiences in moving pictures.    Strand (NY) 50:829 Ja '16
Gardner, K.    Interview.    Motion Pic 23:46 Ap '22
Sketch.    Theatre World 20:140 S '33
Gibbs, P.    Our first Shakespearean actor.    World R p44 S '47
Obit.    Newsweek 41:62 Je 22 '53
Time 61:75 Je 22 '53

TELICHKINA, VALENTINA
    Note.  Int F G 10:335 '73

TELL, OLIVE
    Interview.  N. Y.  Dram 76:5 O 14 '16
    Sketch.  Dram Mir 77:13 Je 23 '17
    Underhill, H.  Olive tells her secrets.  Photop 13-3:43 F '18
    Hall, G.  Interview.  Motion Pic Classic 7:24 N '18

TELLEGEN, LOU
    Sketch.  Theatre 18:xv Ag '13
    Life of.  Strand (NY) 49:794 Jl '15
    Interview.  Theatre 22:132 S '15
    Interview.  Dram Mir 82:793 Ap 24 '20

TEMPLE, SHIRLEY
    Bio sketch.  Time 24:24 Jl 23 '34
    Shawn, B.  Sketch.  Photop 46:68 Ag '34
    Keats, P.  Little Shirley.  Silver S 4-11:26 S '34
    Morgan, F.  Is Hollywood overworking her?  Movie Classic 7:32
      O '34
    Sketch.  Time 24:14 D 31 '34
    Hartley, K.  One of the biggest influences in J. Dunn's life.
      Movie Classic 7:32 F '35
    Sharon, M.  How I raised Shirley Temple.  Silver S 5-5:22 Mr
      '35
    Williams, W.  Her first year in the movies.  Movie Classic 8:
      52 Mr '35
    Harris, G.  Story of.  Child Life 14:162 Ap '35
    Wilson, E.  Her education.  Silver S 5-8:51 Je '35
    Calhoun, D.  What fame has done for her.  Movie Classic 8:36
      Jl '35
    Baldwin, J. R.  How long will she last?  Motion Pic 50:42 S '35
    Meyers, A. E.  Story of.  Movie Classic 9:32 O '35
    Lang, H.  Her mother refuses fortune for her.  Movie Classic
      9:24 D '35
    Wilson, E.  Give your children a Shirley Temple Christmas
      party.  Silver S 6-2:30 D '35
    Rhea, M.  Interview.  Motion Pic 50:26 Ja '36
    Rhea, M.  Her future predicted.  Movie Classic 9:43 F '36
    Award of the Silver Screen gold medal.  Silver S 6-4:25 F '36
    Lee, S.  Plans for her next ten years.  Motion Pic 51:33 Mr
      '36
    Rhea, M.  Sketch.  Movie Classic 10:31 Ap '36
    Dances the hula-hula.  Movie Classic 10:42 My '36
    Spensley, D.  Her popularity.  Motion Pic 51:34 Jl '36
    Her seventh-birthday.  Photop 50:76 Ag '36
    Her rooms in her home.  Child Life 15:447 O '36
    Her bungalow on the Fox lot.  Photop 50:8 O '36
    Shirley Temple.  Visages 6:entire issue N '36
    Lang, H.  Stories of.  Motion Pic 52:46 Ja '37
    Hollywood's queen.  Life 2:32 My 3 '37
    Hall, G.  A day with Shirley.  Child Life 16:263 Je '37

Lee, S.  In Wee Willie Winkie.  Motion Pic 53:48 Jl '37
Blackford, M.  The house that Shirley's "jack" built.  Screen
    Book 19-1:32 Ag '37
Her trip across country.  Life 5:58 Jl 11 '38
McGinnis, E. W.  Story of.  St. Nich 65:40 Jl '38
Barrington, G.  Making valentines with Shirley.  Screen Book
    21-7:36 F '39
Herendeen, A.  Pioneer.  Screen Book 22-1:64 Ag '39
Darnton, C.  My, how Shirley's growing up.  Silver S 9-10:44
    Ag '39
Waterbury, R.  Story of.  Photop 54:13 Ag '40
Bio note; filmog.  Movies & People 2:37 '40
Trotter, M.  Astrological forecast.  Photop 18:31 F '41
Miss Temple resumes.  Lions R 1-4:no p# D '41
Exacting adventurer.  Lions R 1-4:no p# D '41
Hall, G.  Nearing sweet sixteen.  Silver S 14-3:32 Ja '44
Mulvey, K.  Sketch.  Womans Home C 71:12 Ap '44
On bond-selling tour.  Time 44:46 S 11 '44
My Christmas wish.  Photop 26:47 Ja '45
Sketch.  Life 21:140 S 16 '40
Colby, A.  Story of.  Photop 29:48 O '46
Maddox, B.  That surprising Shirley Temple.  Silver S 17-3:35
    Ja '47
Dream tour of Hollywood with the Agars.  Photop 31:46 S '47
End of an era, Shirley is 21.  Cue 18-14:14 Ap 2 '49
Holliday, K.  Seventeen is a difficult age.  Silver S 19-12:26 O
    '49
Temple, S.  Why I'd love my daughter to be in pictures.  Silver
    S 20-3:22 Ja '50
Benedict, P.  Why Deanna and Shirley won't return.  Silver S
    23-10:42 Ag '53
Readin' ritin' and rehearsal.  TV Guide 4-38:20 S 22 '56
Mrs. Black for Congress.  Time 90:16 S 8 '67
People of the week.  U. S. News 63:20 S 11 '67
Baby take a bow.  Newsweek 70:21 S 11 '67
Duscha, J.  How do you fight Shirley Temple?  Reporter 37:21
    N 2 '67
Moms and pops, arise.  Newsweek 70:35 N 6 '67
Williams, L.  Little Miss Candidate.  Look 31:86 N 14 '67
Lolliplop.  Newsweek 70:35 N 27 '67
Prague diary.  McCalls 96:74 Ja '69
Leading lady.  Newsweek 74:62 S 29 '69
Youth related activities of the UN; statement.  Dept State Bull
    61:380 N 3 '69
Flagler, J. M.  Shirley Temple at the UN.  Look 33:M D 16
    '69
U. S. comments on work of UNICEF.  Dept State Bull 61:642 D
    29 '69
UN conference on the human environment.  Dept State Bull 62:99
    Ja 26 '70
Bio.  Cur Bio 31:3 Ap '70
    Same.  Cur Bio Yrbk 1970:36 '71
The kids.  Screen Greats 1-2:48 Sum '71

Kevles, B.  When I was seventeen.  Seventeen 30:131 O '71
U. S. discusses priorities for the 1972 UN.  Dept State Bull 65:
    531 N 8 '71
Kevles, B.  A U. S. diplomat at the UN.  Sat Eve Post 244:32
    Sum '72
Interview.  Photop 83-2:30 F '73
Pinup of the past.  Films & Filming 20-4:65 Ja '74
Windeler, R.  (Her) new line: call me Madame.  People 2-11:
    21 S 9 '74
Is Ghana ready for Shirley?  New York 7-44:86 N 4 '74

TENNANT, VICTORIA
New faces.  Films Illus 1-7:8 Ja '72

TEPPER, BILL
Jack Nicholson comments on Bill Tepper.  Dialogue 1:21 '72

TEREKHOVA, MARGARITA
Batashov, A.  Margarita Terekhova.  Soviet Film 5(192):29 '73

TERHUNE, MAX
Williams, N.  Three comedians of the horse opera; partial fil-
    mog.  Filmograph 1-4:19 '70
Corneau, E. N.  The Max (Alibi) Terhune story.  Classic Film
    Collect 40:38 Fall '73
Obit.  Screen World p240 '74

TERNBERG, JEAN-MARC
Bio note.  Unifrance 19:7 Jl/Ag '52
Bio note.  Unifrance 23:10 F '53

TERRANOVA, DINO
Obit.  Screen World 21:241 '70

TERRIS, NORMA
York, C.  Sketch.  Photop 37:41 D '29

TERRISS, ELLALINE
Obit.  N. Y. Times p44 Je 17 '71

TERRY, ALICE
Cheatham, M.  Interview.  Motion Pic Classic 12:32 Jl '21
Beach, B.  Interview.  Motion Pic 22:22 Ja '22
Goldbeck, W.  Interview.  Motion Pic Classic 14:20 Mr '22
Her darkest hour.  Classic 15:47 N '22
Robinson, S.  Word-portrait of.  Motion Pic 28:24 N '24
Sebastain, D.  Sketch.  Motion Pic 31:58 F '26
Benthall, D.  Interview.  Motion Pic 32:36 Ja '27

TERRY, DON
Bailey, V.  Sketch.  Photop 35:74 Ja '29

TERRY, ETHEL GREY
  Sketch.  N.Y.  Dram 70:17 Ag 20 '13
  Sketch.  N.Y.  Dram 72:11 Jl 1 '14
  Goldbeck, W.  Interview.  Motion Pic Classic 13:44 N '21
  Handy, T. B.  Interview.  Motion Pic 24:72 D '22

TERRY, PHILIP
  Hamilton, S.  Sketch.  Photop 20:52 D '41

TERRY-THOMAS
  A sour note?  Heaven forbid.  TV Guide 18-17:40 Ap 25 '70
  Terry-Thomas tailpiece.  Films Illus 3-26:77 Ag '73

THAXTER, PHYLLIS
  Meet Phyllis Thaxter.  Lions R 3-5:no p# D '44

THAYER, TINA
  Mickey's new gal.  Lions R 2-1:no p# S/O '42

THEBY, ROSEMARY
  Interview.  Motion Pic 9:100 Ap '15
  May, L.  Interview.  Motion Pic Classic 2:34 My '16
  How to get into motion pictures.  Motion Pic Classic 3:24 N '16
  Delvigne, D.  Interview.  Motion Pic 18:52 N '19
  Montanye, L.  Interview.  Motion Pic 20:38 O '20
  Peltret, E.  Interview.  Motion Pic Classic 12:89 Ag '21
  Dryden, P.  Interview.  Motion Pic 23:54 F '22

THIBAULT, OLIVETTE
  McLarty, J.  C'est ma vie.  Motion p13 Jl/Ag '73

THIMIG, HELENE
  Rode, D.  Helene Thimig; filmog.  Film Fan Mo 153:27 Mr '74

THINNIS, ROY
  Wow.  TV Guide 14-15:15 Ap 9 '66

THOMAS, BILLY "BUCKWHEAT"
  Maltin, L.  Our gang; Our gang filmog.  Film Fan Mo 66:3 D
  '66

THOMAS, DANNY
  One man musical.  Cue 12-51:11 D 18 '43
  Zunser, J.  "The jazz singer" is back.  Cue 21-50:14 D 13 '52
  Thomas, R.  This is my Danny.  Silver S 23-4:42 F '53
  Father's hour.  TV Guide 3-25:8 Je 18 '55
  Readin' ritin' and rehearsal.  TV Guide 4-38:20 S 22 '56
  The wailing comedian.  TV Guide 6-50:17 D 13 '58
  The toothless lion.  TV Guide 7-50:17 D 12 '59
  Davidson, B.  Toothless tiger.  TV Guide 10-7:4 F 17; 10-8:19
  F 24; 10-9:15 Mr 3 '62
  Whitney, D.  So who needs wall street.  TV Guide 12-17:21 Ap
  25 '64

Back to burlesque for the third time.   TV Guide 14-50:12 D 10
    '66
Raddatz, L.   Mother, Miss Independence has ants.   TV Guide
    15-48:20 D 2 '67
Thomas in the role of executive producer.   Broadcasting 79:69
    O 26 '70
Eisenberg, A. H.   Thanksgiving with a Lebanese flavor.   Good
    House 173:84 N '71

THOMAS, MARLO
She wasn't raised to be an actress.   TV Guide 10-20:11 My 19
    '62
Hano, A.   The velvet steam roller.   TV Guide 14-46:24 N 12
    '66
McCormick, B.   I know her--that's what's his name's daughter.
    TV Guide 15-40:8 O 7 '67
Rollin, B.   That girl is some girl.   Look 31:124 O 17 '67
Raddatz, L.   Mother, Miss Independence has ants.   TV Guide
    15-48:20 D 2 '67
The dangers of galloping inflation.   TV Guide 16-14:14 Ap 6 '68
Efron, E.   I can.   TV Guide 17-20:30 My 17 '69
Interview.   Cinema (BH) 5-4:8 Win '69
That tough girl.   Photop 77-6:60 Je '70
Raddatz, L.   In search of Marlo.   TV Guide 18-32:18 Ag 8 '70
Roberts, M.   Young world of Marlo.   Good House 171:20 Ag '70
Mysterious Marlo.   Photop 78-4:53 O '70
My sister runs my love life.   Photop 79-1:35 Ja '71
Marlo, the movie star.   Photop 79-4:76 Ap '71
The most fateful decision I ever made.   Mod Screen 66-3:45 Mr
    '72
Viorst, J.   My father wouldn't marry someone like me.   Red-
    book 140:92 N '72
Flatley, G.   What happened after the 'Princess of Sitcom' left
    her cotton-candy kingdom.   TV Guide 21-10:24 Mr 10 '73
Kelly, K.   My whole life I've had my dukes up.   N. Y. Times
    sec 2:17 Mr 11 '73
    Same.   N. Y. Times Bio Ed p517 Mr '73
Cyclops.   Free to be Marlo, and hooray.   N. Y. Times sec 2:15
    Mr 10 '74
Marlo Thomas sings out against sexism.   People 1-2:30 Mr 11
    '74

THOMAS, OLIVE
Howe, H.   Sketch.   Motion Pic Classic 5:36 F '18
Roberts, S.   Interview.   Motion Pic Classic 8:37 Ap '19
Peltret, E.   Interview.   Motion Pic 17:38 Je '19
Is beauty essential to success.   Photop 17:29 F '20
Service, F.   Interview.   Motion Pic Classic 10:24 Mr '20
Obit.   N. Y. Clipper 68:13 S 15 '20
Collins, F. L.   Story of.   Good House 94:40 Jl '32

THOMAS, RICHARD
Johnson, D.   I change every five seconds.   After Dark 4-4:16

Ag '71

(He) is so easy to love.  Photop 83-6:72 Je '72

He's more man than boy.  Photop 82-6:52 D '72

Graustark, B.  Merlin the magician meets The Waltons.  Circus
7-5:41 F '73

Filmog.  Films & Filming 19-6:59 Mr '73

Maynard, J.  John-Boy comes home--to Manhattan.  N. Y. Times
sec 2:11 Jl 22 '73

Same.  N. Y. Times Bio Ed p1245 Jl '73

Davidson, B.  John-Boy can order grits in French.  TV Guide
21-39:31 S 29 '73

Sex, drugs and God in our lives.  Photop 84-5:51 N '73

(His) Puerto Rican brother.  Photop 85-3:50 Mr '74

Stoneman, D.  Off set with Richard Thomas.  Interview p24 Mr
'74

Watters, J.  Even the Waltons get a vacation.  People 1-11:52
My 13 '74

THOMPSON, DUANE
Uselton, R. A.  The Wampus baby stars.  Films In R 21-2:73
F '70

THOMPSON, KAY
Zany satire sensation.  Cue 17-13:14 Mr 27 '48

Taylor, T.  After dark.  Cue 23-4:35 Ja 23 '54

Reed, R.  You've never seen anything like her.  Harp Baz 106:
114 N '72

THOMPSON, MARSHALL
Tall, blond and boyish.  Lions R 4-1:no p# F '45

THOMPSON, SADA
Salute of the week.  Cue 39-19:1 My 16 '70

Weales, G.  Stage.  Commonweal 93:48 O 9 '70

Shepard, R. F.  A theatrical quartet.  N. Y. Times Bio Ed N 17
'71

Kalem, T. E.  From the coloring book.  Time 98:70 N 29 '71

Kroll, J.  Four faces of Sada.  Newsweek 78:109 N 29 '71

Burke, T.  Twigs and tree are Sada.  N. Y. Times Bio Ed D
19 '71

Prideaux, T.  Sada times four.  Life 72:70A Ja 28 '72

THOMPSON, WILLIAM
Obit.  N. Y. Times p49 Jl 18 '71

THOMSON, FRED
LaBadie, D. W.  The last roundup.  Show 2-9:75 S '62

Peeples, S. A.  Films on 8 & 16.  Films In R 17-1:41 Ja '66

Pucci, J.  Letter.  Films In R 17-2:125 F '66

Barton, W.  Fred Thomson rides again.  Classic Film Collect
29:12 Win '70

Brennen, T.  I can't forget.  Classic Film Collect 30:44 Spg '71

THORNDIKE, SYBIL
    Swaffer, H.  The tragedienne.  Graphic 106:810 D 2 '22
    Her recent plays.  Graphic 124:487 Je 8 '29
    Sketch.  Theatre World 21:192 Ap '34
    Her horoscope.  Theatre World 37:80 O '42
    Discusses Greek tragedy.  Theatre World 41:25 N '45
    Thoughts on working with her husband.  Theatre World 43:11 N
        '47
    In the words of Dame Sybil.  Cue 38-45:15 N 8 '69
    Tierney, M.  Nothing like a Dame; interview.  Plays & Players
        18-10:14 Jl '71

THORNTON-SHERWOOD, MADELEINE
    (See: SHERWOOD, MADELEINE)

THORSON, LINDA
    Can she make them forget Mrs. Peele?  TV Guide 16-9:12 Mr 2
        '68

THREATT, ELIZABETH
    Rising stars.  Film R p109 '53/54

THREE STOOGES
    (Joe de Rita, Larry Fine, Moe Howard)
    Thomson, B.  Three left-overs from the fun factory.  8mm Col-
        lect 13:35 Fall/Win '65

THULIN, INGRID
    Cowie, P.  Ingrid Thulin; filmog.  Focus On Film 5:12 Win '70
    Women directors; dir. filmog.  Film Comment 8-4:45 N '72
    Interview.  Dialogue 3:15 '72

THUNDER CLOUD, CHIEF
    (See: WILLIAMS, SCOTT T.)

THURMAN, MARY
    Naylor, H. S.  Interview.  Motion Pic 20:62 O '20
    Cheatham, M.  Interview.  Motion Pic Classic 13:44 S '21

THURSTON, CAROL
    De Mille discovery.  Cue 13-25:12 Je 17 '44
    Crivello, K.  She couldn't live down "three martini."  Classic
        Film Collect 28:ex p2 Fall '70
    Crivello, K.  Letter; filmog.  Films In R 22-5:320 My '71

TIBBETT, LAWRENCE
    New American star at the opera.  Lit Dig 84:26 F 7 '25
    Young baritone leaps to fame.  Cur Op 78:331 Mr '25
    Gabriel, G. W.  Baritone from Bakersfield.  Worlds Work 50:
        282 Jl '25
    Everything counts in your musical success.  Etude 44:411 Je '26
    Kennedy, J. B.  Interview.  Colliers 80:27 D 31 '27
    Operetta on the sound film.  Lit Dig 104:32 F 22 '30

Hughes, R.  Getting paid for having a good time.  Am Mag 110:
    42 Ag '30
Preston, J. H.  Youth at the top.  Worlds Work 59:36 S '30
Wollstein, R. H.  Talk on the talkies.  Etude 49:539 Ag '31
Melcher, E. S.  Lawrence Tibbett.  Cinema Dig 2-2:11 N 28
    '32
Moffitt, C. F.  Censorship for interviews Hollywood's latest wild
    idea.  Cinema Dig 2-5:9 Ja 9 '33
Taubman, H. H.  Opera can be saved by the movies.  Pict R
    34:8 F '33
Along the glory road.  Am Mag 116:11 Ag; 32 S; 26 O; 56 N '33
Thomajan, P. K.  A temperament-silhouette.  Musician 39:3 Ja
    '34
Eaton, Q.  (He) talks about lullabies.  Bet Home & Gard 13:36
    O '34
Laine, J.  Should I change teachers?  Etude 53:458 Ag '35
Reed, D.  The troubadour.  Silver S 6-2:24 O '35
Goossens gives Tibbett an ideal role.  Newsweek 10:26 Jl 3 '37
Tibbett as Falstaff.  Newsweek 12:24 D 26 '38
Opera in English?  Rotarian 53:12 D '38
Heylbut, R.  There is no open-sesame.  Etude 58:820 D '40
What the little mother did.  Etude 59:370 Je '41
Heylbut, R.  My most momentous musical moment.  Etude 59:
    670 O '41
Simms, M.  Boyhood of a flier.  N. Y. Times Mag p33 O 25 '42
    Same.  Scholastic 41:21 Ja 4 '43
Voice, sr.  Newsweek 25:83 Ja 15 '45
Sinatra and Tibbett, hail and farewell.  Cue 14-3:7 Ja 20 '45
Bio.  Cur Bio F '45
Tibbett tribute.  Newsweek 33:68 Ja 24 '49
Smith, C.  Tibbett's anniversary.  New Rep 120:27 F 14 '49
Smith, C.  American pioneer at the Met.  Mus Am 69:8 F '49
Feted at dinner.  Mus Am 74:6 Mr '54
Opera's grand trouper.  Time 76:51 Jl 25 '60
Voice we knew.  Newsweek 56:98 Jl 25 '60
Sabin, R.  Lawrence Tibbett.  Mus Am 80:24 Ag '60
Obit.  Screen World 12:226 '61
Merkling, F.  Tibbett on tape.  Opera N 28:6 D 21 '63
Miller, P. L.  Artistry of.  Am Rec G 35:385 Ja '69

TIERNEY, GENE
    Mulvey, K.  Sketch.  Womans Home C 67:23 O '40
    Benedict, P.  Gene with a capital G.  Silver S 11-4:38 F '41
    Hamman, M.  Sketch.  Good House 114:8 F '42
    Manners, M. J.  Love in a cottage.  Silver S 12-36:5 Mr '42
    Reid, J.  "Mister" Cassini's war bride.  Silver S 12-11:42 S
        '42
    If I could have one perfect day.  Cosmop 114:54 Ap '43
    Wilson, E.  Gene takes a tip from the soldiers.  Silver S 13-8:
        26 Je '43
    Wilson, E.  Cause for complaint.  Silver S 15-6:32 Ap '45
    Hall, G.  Practical but provocative.  Silver S 16-4:32 F '46
    Notes about.  Photop 28:54 Mr '46

Howe, H.  Story of.  Photop 30:44 D '46
Hall, G.  My Gene Tierney.  Silver S 17-2:35 D '46
My luckiest day.  Cosmop 122:108 F '47
Dudley, F.  Laugh or go mad.  Silver S 19-1:28 N '48
Perkins, R.  Repeat performance.  Silver S 20-1:30 N '49
Holland, J.  Must you step on people's toes?  Silver S 21-6:38
     Ap '51
Tierney, G.  You're never too young to be glamorous.  Silver S
     21-6:38 Ap '51
Balling, F. D.  It's fun to be fancy free.  Silver S 22-12:39 O
     '52
Wilson, E.  Tips about Aly for Gene.  Silver S 24-1:22 N '53
Where are they now?  Newsweek 71:8 Ja 29 '68
Nine minds in trouble.  Photop 78-3:56 S '70
Here's to the ladies.  Screen Greats 1-2:28 Sum '71
Whatever happened to Gene Tierney?  Silver S 41-10:50 O '71
Shields, J.  Gene Tierney; filmog.  Films In R 22-9:541 N '71
Letters.  Films In R 23-1:60 Ja '72
Keith, D. L.  Because she's Laura...  After Dark 5-3:54 Jl '72

TIFFIN, PAMELA
     A toast to Tiffin; photos.  Playboy 16-2:132 F '69

TIGHE, KEVIN
     Lewis, R. W.  Saturday night celebrity.  TV Guide 22-31:20 Ag
     3 '74

TINCHER, FAY
     Denny, M.  Interview.  Motion Pic 12:76 Ag '16
     How to get into moving pictures.  Motion Pic Classic 3:41 O '16
     Sketch.  Motion Pic 14:65 N '17
     Remont, F.  Interview.  Motion Pic 15:29 Ag '18
     Is polite comedy polite?  Photop 16-3:94 Ag '19

TINDALL, LOREN
     Obit.  Screen World p240 '74

TINGWELL, CHARLES
     Manski, A. B.  Letter.  Films In R 24-5:315 My '73

TINY TIM (Herbert B. Khoury)
     Newman, D. & Benton, R.  Why the truth about Tiny Tim has
        never before appeared on these pages.  New York 1-10:48
        Je 10 '68
     Hobson, D.  Clark Kent, after all, can turn into Superman.  TV
        Guide 16-41:44 O 12 '68
     The great crooners.  Playboy 16:195 D '69
     Interview.  Playboy 17-6:65 Je '70
     Campbell, J.  My mother, right or wrong.  McCalls 98:110 My
        '71

TISSOT, ALICE
     Obit.  N. Y. Times p44 My 7 '71
     Screen World 23:240 '72

TOBEY, KENNETH
    Frank, M.   Interview.   Photon 22:11 '72
    The fantasy films of Kenneth Tobey.   Photon 22:24 '72

TOBIN, GENEVIEVE
    Horton, H.   Sketch.   Motion Pic 41:84 Jl '31
    Hall, G.   Her ideal of a husband.   Movie Classic 2:56 Ag '32

TODD, ANN
    Dundass, L.   Sketch.   Theatre World 39:30 D '43
    Zunser, J.   Meet London's Ann Todd.   Cue 26-37:12 S 14 '57

TODD, BEVERLY
    Actresses who are real people.   Life 68:46 My 29 '70

TODD, LISA
    The power of positive chanting.   TV Guide 19-16:20 Ap 17 '71

TODD, LOLA
    Uselton, R. A.   The Wampus baby stars.   Films In R 21-2:73
        F '70

TODD, RICHARD
    Rising stars.   Film R p30 '50
    Billard, G.   Todd tells why Britain should film in France.
        Films & Filming 2-5:7 F '56

TODD, THELMA
    Graves, M.   Sketch.   Motion Pic Classic 26:49 F '28
    Lubou, D.   Interview.   Motion Pic 37:78 Je '29
    Jones, C. P.   Thelma Todd.   Cinema Dig 1-10:9 S 19 '32
    Lawlor, D.   Sketch.   Photop 49:56 F '36
    Parks, J.   The Thelma Todd death riddle.   Screen Book 19-1:62
        Ag '37
    Berkow, G.   Letter.   Films In R 20-3:189 Mr '69

TOLER, SIDNEY
    Sullivan, E.   Damned clever, these Missourians.   Silver S 10-12:
        34 O '40
    Connor, E.   The 6 Charlie Chans; Charlie Chan filmog.   Films
        In R 6-1:23 Ja '55

TOLL, PAMELA
    Higgins, R.   Exciting as an unbaked taco.   TV Guide 18-18:24
        My 2 '70

TOLSKY, SUSAN
    Wasserman, J.   She took off her glasses and nothing happened.
        TV Guide 17-25:10 Je 21 '69

TOMLIN, LILY
    Bell, J. N.   How Lily helps keep 'em laughin'.   N.Y. Times
        Bio Ed N 8 '70

710                                    Motion Picture Performers

Hobson, D.  It figures.  TV Guide 18-46:36 N 14 '70
Lily Tomlin at the circus.  New Yorker 47:33 Ap 10 '71
Kent, L.  Most wanted 1971; funny Lily; interview.  Vogue 157:
    102 Je '71
Michener, C.  Lily's world.  Newsweek 79:91 Ap 17 '72
Guerin, A.  Works from the truth.  Show 2-4:28 Je '72
Stoop, N. M.  This story doesn't have an ending.  After Dark
    5-2:18 Je '72
Kent, L.  They'll leave you laughing--and thinking.  N. Y. Times
    sec 2:17 Mr 11 '73
    Same.  N. Y. Times Bio Ed p519 Mr '73
Goodbye to duddiness.  MS 2-7:46 Ja '74

TOMLIN, PINKY
    Williams, W.  Introducing Pinky Tomlin.  Silver S 5-7:30 My
        '35
    Magee, T.  Tales of a love bug bearer.  Screen Book 19-3:75
        O '37
    Fernett, G.  Do you remember Pinky Tomlin?  Classic Film
        Collect 35:31 Sum '72

THOMPKINS, ANGEL
    Clein, H.  Debut.  Show 1-11:56 Ag 20 '70
    Raddatz, L.  She lives on Bob Hope's street.  TV Guide 19-2:15
        Ja 9 '71
    Angel.  Playboy 19-2:87 F '72

TONE, FRANCHOT
    Hall, G.  Sketch.  Motion Pic 45:48 Je '33
    Keats, P.  Giving Tone to Hollywood.  Silver S 3-8:44 Je '33
    Sketch.  Photop 44:71 Jl '33
    Grant, J.  His romance.  Movie Classic 5:26 F '34
    Dowling, M.  Sketch.  Movie Classic 6:16 Mr '34
    Asher, J.  Interview.  Motion Pic 49:39 F '35
    Douglas, E.  The winning Mr. Tone.  Silver S 5-7:23 My '35
    Parker, K.  Interview.  Motion Pic 50:36 S '35
    Gwin, J.  Sketch.  Silver S 6-3:20 Ja '36
    Langford, H.  Ideal husband.  Motion Pic 52:46 O '36
    Asher, J.  Distinctive.  Silver S 7-2:52 D '36
    Asher, J.  His friendship with Katharine Hepburn.  Motion Pic
        53:26 Jl '37
    McFee, F.  I like Broadway.  Screen Book 21-7:30 F '39
    Bio note; filmog.  Movies & People 2:36 '40
    Manners, M. J.  Is it true what they say about Franchot.  Silver
        S 11-4:34 F '41
    Franchot Tone.  Lions R 2-5:no p# Jl '43
    Tone comes back to Broadway.  Cue 14-5:9 F 3 '45
    Cook, A.  Young man with a message.  Silver S 15-9:42 Jl '45
    Sketch.  Photop 32:127 Mr '48
    Obit.  Cur Bio 29:43 N '68
        Same.  Cur Bio Yrbk 1968:463 '69
        Film R p17 '69/70
        N. Y. Times p58 S 19 '68

Newsweek 72:115 S 30 '68
Time 92:92 S 27 '68
Franchot Tone: 1905-1968.  Film Fan Mo 89:7 N '68

TONG, KAM
Obit.  Screen World 21:241 '70

TOOMEY, REGIS
Cruikshank, H.  Sketch.  Motion Pic Classic 30:24 N '29
Albert, K.  Sketch.  Photop 36:45 N '29
Mook, S. R.  Regis--he's regular.  Silver S 2-2:26 D '31

TOPOL, CHAIM
Moskin, J. R.  Topol, Israel's star joker.  Look 32:M20 N 12
'68
Sleight of tongue artist.  Time 93:E16 Ap 18 '69
Hemming, R.  Lively arts; interview.  Sr Schol 94:32 Ap 25 '69
Phillips, M.  Topol, film Tevye, looks back at role.  N. Y.
Times Bio Ed N 3 '71
Bonfante, J.  Dayan's advice he didn't take.  Life 71:87 D 3 '71
Lawes, D. N.  A conversation with Topol.  Show 3-2:20 Ap '73
Guerin, A.  Topol on Brando.  Shoe 3-2:23 Ap '73

TOREN, MARTA
I'm not a cold Swede.  Silver S 22-10:26 Ag '52

TORK, PETER
(See: MONKEES, THE)

TORME, MEL
Successor to The voice?  Newsweek 29:80 Je 23 '47
Sketch.  Time 50:83 S 15 '47
Dugan, J.  Little Mel.  Colliers 120:16 O 11 '47
Out of the fog.  Time 81:68 Mr 1 '63
Fog lifts.  Newsweek 63:47 Ja 6 '64
Lees, G.  Melvin and the little people.  Hi Fi 16:120 D '66
The velvet fog has lifted.  TV Guide 19-28:14 Jl 10 '71
Nolan, J. E.  Films on TV; partial TV filmog.  Films In R 25-
1:39 Ja '74
Henry, M.  Mel Torme; filmog.  Film Fan Mo 160:25 O '74
Behlmer, R.  Letter.  Films In R 25-8:511 O '74

TORN, RIP
Jeremiah, the stars' stars; astrology.  Show 1-4:25 Ap '70
Eliscu, L.  Rip Torn is just the name.  Show 1-4:74 Ap '70
Pyes, C.  Rip Torn.  Ramp Mag 9:41 Mr '71
Southern, T.  One of the real...ah...originals.  Sat R Arts 1-4:
36 Ap '73
Headliners.  Photop 83-6:26 Je '73
Rivers, S.  I am an actor.  Interview 4-7:33 Ag '74

TORRENCE, ERNEST
Lipman, J. H.  Interview.  Classic 16:36 Je '23

Sketch.   Photop 24:58 Je '23
Halton, G.   Interview.   Motion Pic 27:33 Je '24
Home of.   Classic 19:40 Jl '24
As Capt. Hook in Peter Pan.   Motion Pic 29:96 Mr '25
Sketch.   National 54:242 Ja '26
Donaldson, R.   Interview.   Motion Pic Classic 25:42 Je '27
Home of.   Motion Pic 34:22 N '27
Obit.   Mus Cour 106:18 My 27 '33

TORRES, RAQUEL
Thorp, D.   Sketch.   Motion Pic Classic 28:63 Ja '29
Manners, D.   Interview.   Motion Pic Classic 32:65 D '30
Manners, D.   Sketch.   Motion Pic Classic 33:50 Ap '31
Woods, M. L.   Sketch.   Movie Classic 1:36 Ja '32
Madden, M.   Her marriage.   Movie Classic 6:41 Jl '34

TOTO
Lane, J. F.   The face of '63--Italy.   Films & Filming 9-7:11
Ap '63

TOTTER, AUDREY
Hall, G.   Leo the lion's new love.   Silver S 17-4:50 F '47
Hamilton, S.   Story of.   Photop 30:110 Ap '47
Bruce, J.   Should a girl pursue a man?   Silver S 20-9:36 Jl '50
Totter, A.   I laugh at wolves and it works.   Silver S 22-12:26
O '52
Tildesley, A. L.   How marriage looks from here.   Silver S 23-
10:44 Ag '53
Martinez, A.   It pays to marry a doctor; interview.   TV Guide
22-39:18 S 28 '74

TOUMANOVA, TAMARA
Cover girl.   Colliers 113:32 My 6 '44
Vallee, W. L.   Ballerina on leave.   Silver S 14-12:46 O '44
Swisher, V. H.   Toumanova in Hollywood.   Dance 40:26 Mr '66
Swisher, V. H.   And now, says Toumanova, Billy Wilder.   After
Dark 11-11:22 Mr '70
Swisher, V. H.   A unique career.   Dance 44:44 S '70

TOWNES, HARRY
A breed apart.   TV Guide 11-26:19 Je 29 '63

TOWNSEND, COLLEEN
Big build-up.   Life 25:77 Ag 30 '48
Levin, R. J.   They live with love.   Good House 149:80 D '59

TOZERE, FREDERIC
Obit.   N.Y. Times Bio Ed p1562 Ag '72

TRACEY, EMERSON
Maltin, L.   Our gang; Our gang filmog.   Film Fan Mo 66:3 D
'66

TRACY, LEE
  Goldbeck, E.  Sketch.  Motion Pic 38:66 D '29
  Winters, D.  Sketch.  Movie Classic 3:26 O '32
  Cheatham, M.  That hard-boiled Tracy.  Silver S 3-1:23 N '32
  Hall, G.  Interview.  Motion Pic 45:49 Ap '33
  Ergenbright, E. L.  Interview.  Movie Classic 4:22 Jl '33
  Jamison, J.  Tracing the travels of Tracy.  Silver S 4-1:29 N
    '33
  Biery, R.  Interview.  Movie Classic 5:30 D '33
  Donnell, D.  How he "insulted" Mexico.  Motion Pic 47:51 F '34
  The Mexican mixup.  Movie Classic 6:42 My '34
  Tracy, L.  Actors are younger than other people.  Motion Pic
    48:60 Ja '35
  Obit.  Film R p16 '69/70
    N. Y.  Times p37 O 19 '68
    Newsweek 72:72 O 28 '68
    Time 92:98 O 25 '68
  Marlowe, D.  Lee Tracy.  Classic Film Collect 31:15 Sum '71

TRACY, SPENCER
  Sketch.  Movie Classic 3:22 N '32
  Mook, S. R.  Everyday Tracy.  Silver S 3-3:20 Ja '33
  Service, F.  How his son made him what he is today.  Movie
    Classic 4:34 Ag '33
  Hall, G.  Interview.  Movie Classic 10:31 S '36
  Sullivan, E.  The best bet of the year.  Silver S 6-11:32 S '36
  Lang, H.  Story of.  Motion Pic 52:32 D '36
  Hall, G.  Story of.  Motion Pic 54:30 N '37
  Winner of 1937 acting award.  Newsweek 11:20 Mr 21 '38
  Mook, S. R.  Tracy as I know him.  Screen Book 20-2:33 Mr
    '38
  Mook, S. R.  My pal, Tracy.  Screen Book 21-8:20 Mr '39
  Wins Academy award second time.  Stage 16:29 Je '39
  Walsh, L.  Virtue's victim.  Screen Book 22-3:54 O '39
  Sullivan, E.  A prediction that came doubly true.  Silver S 10-6:
    24 Ap '40
  Bio note; filmog.  Movies & People 2:37 '40
  Spencer Tracy presents Spencer Tracy.  Lions R 1-1:no p# S
    '41
  Tracy plays straight.  Lions R 1-6:no p# F '42
  Tracy, realist.  Lions R 1-9:no p# My '42
  Sketch.  Harp Baz 76:23 Jl '42
  Tracy.  Lions R 2-3:no p# D '42
  A guy named Tracy.  Lions R 3-2:no p# Ja '44
  Pistol-packin' Tracy.  Lions R 34(sup):no p# Jl '44
  Tracy salutes Doolittle.  Lions R 3-5:no p# D '44
  St. Johns, A. R.  Story of.  Photop 25:31 Ag '44
  O'Leary, D.  T. N. T. means Tracy 'n' Turner.  Silver S 18-2:
    24 D '47
  Hill, D.  Sixty round the bend.  Films & Filming 1-8:5 My '55
  Zunser, J.  Tracy: the great stone face.  Cue 27-28:11 Jl 12
    '58
  Hamilton, J.  Last visit with two undimmed stars.  Look 31:26

Jl 11 '67
Obit.  Brit Bk Yr 1968:599 '68
    Cur Bio 28:46 O '67
    Same.  Cur Bio Yrbk 1967:484 '68
Spencer and Katharine.  Ladies Home J 85:94 D '68
Keneas, A.  Spencer.  Newsweek 73:116 Je 9 '69
The love teams.  Screen Greats 1-2:10 Sum '71
Kanin, G.  Excerpt from Tracy & Hepburn.  Vogue 158:142 N 1
    '71
Kanin, G.  Excerpt from Tracy & Hepburn.  Read Dig 100:213
    F '72
Katharine Hepburn and Spencer Tracy.  Mod Screen 66-3:48 Mr
    '72
Reingold, C. B.  A very special love.  Movie Dig 1-2:16 Mr '72
Canby, V.  Tracy and Hepburn--the potato and the dessert.  N. Y.
    Times sec 2:1 S 17 '72
Gilliatt, P.  Current cinema.  New Yorker 48:64 S 23 '72
Ardmore, J.  Interview with Mrs. Tracy.  Ladies Home J 89:90
    D '72
Tracy & Hepburn; filmog.  Screen Greats 1-5:entire issue n. d.

TRASK, DIANA
    Sweet Australian singer.  Life 48:49 Je 27 '60
    She wants to be good.  TV Guide 9-30:25 Jl 29 '61
    Huizenga, C.  Miss country soul makes it happen.  After Dark
        7-1:46 My '74

TRAVERS, HENRY
    Brown, B.  Henry Travers; filmog.  Films In R 25-6:337 Je/Jl
        '74

TRAVERS, RICHARD
    How he became a photoplayer.  Motion Pic 9:113 F '15
    McKelvie, M. G.  Interview.  Motion Pic 13:98 Je '17
    McKelvie, M. G.  Interview.  Motion Pic Classic 6:33 Je '18

TRAVIS, JUNE
    Schwarzkopf, J.  Sketch.  Motion Pic 51:57 My '36

TREACHER, ARTHUR
    Sketch.  Movie Classic 10:50 Jl '36
    Hamilton, S.  Story of.  Photop 52:20 My '38
    Permanent second fiddles.  Newsweek 74:45 S 1 '69
    Peck, I.  Arthur Treacher--76 and all that.  N. Y. Times Bio
        Ed Jl 19 '70

TRESSLER, GEORG
    Bean, R.  The face of '63--Germany.  Films & Filming 9-9:41
        Je '63
    Streibig, D.  Children's game.  Pop Phot 54:141 Ja '64

TREVELYN, UNA
    Cheatham, M. S.  Interview.  Motion Pic Classic 11:58 S '20

TREVOR, CLAIRE
  Sketch.   Photop 45:77 Ap '34
  French, W.   Her rise to fame.   Movie Classic 10:24 Jl '36
  Lorton, T.   No lull in her life.   Screen Book 21-2:35 S '38
  Maddox, B.   Love is first with me.   Silver S 9-7:34 My '39
  Bio note; filmog.   Movies & People 2:37 '40
  Wilson, E.   It's more fun to be bad.   Silver S 11-11:24 S '41
  Holland, J.   What a wife can learn from "other woman."   Silver
    S 15-8:30 Je '45
  Service, F.   My black lace moments.   Silver S 17-5:58 Mr '47
  Parsons, L. O.   Cosmop's citation for the best supporting per-
    formance of month.   Cosmop 125:12 Ag '48
  Sketch.   Photop 34:100 Ap '49
  Holland, J.   What can a man teach a woman?   Silver S 19-11:36
    S '49
  Trevor, C.   The company remembers Stagecoach.   Action 6-5:
    26 S/O '71

TRINTIGNANT, JEAN-LOUIS
  Two actors; interview.   Films & Filming 7-1:13 O '60
  Cowie, P.   Jean-Louis Trintignant; filmog.   Focus On F 1:14
    Ja/F '70
  Haskell, M.   The life and times of a superstar.   Show 1-11:35
    Ag 20 '70
  Knight, A. & Alpert, H.   Sex stars of 1970.   Playboy 17-12:220
    D '70
  Grumback, P.   Interview.   Sat R 55:34 F 26 '72
  Man with a valise.   Time 99:97 Je 26 '72
  Elkin, S.   Inside Jean-Louis Trintignant.   Oui 2-1:85 Ja '73
  Swisher, V. H.   The French line.   After Dark 6-7:48 N '73
  Jean-Louis Trintignant; filmog.   Film 60:13 n. d.

TRISTAN, DOROTHY
  A woman's power is in reacting to a man.   Life 67:66 N 7 '69
  Actresses.   Newsweek 76:74 D 7 '70

TROWBRIDGE, CHARLES
  Stewart, W. T.   Letter; partial filmog.   Films In R 19-4:249
    Ap '68

TRUEX, ERNEST
  Sketch.   Strand (NY) 48:113 Ag '14
  Mantle, B.   Sketch.   Green Book 18:988 D '17
  Lincks, P.   Sketch.   Motion Pic 17:37 Mr '19
  Elvidge, E.   Sketch.   Motion Pic Classic 8:32 Je '19
  In the cast.   TV Guide 2-9:18 F 26 '54
  Obit.   Classic Film Collect (reprint N. Y. Times) 40:58 Fall '73
    N. Y. Times Bio Ed p1059 Mr '72
    Screen World p240 '74
  Gordon, R.   Ernest Truex.   N. Y. Times sec 2:3 Jl 15 '73
    Same.   N. Y. Times Bio Ed p1248 Jl '73
  In memory.   Show 3-6:74 S '73

TRUNDY, NATALIE
    A freckle-faced girl of 19.    TV Guide 9-25:29 Je 24 '61

TRUNNELLE, MABELLE
    Gaddis, P.   Her hero, and his heroine.   Photop 6-1:58 Je '14
    Courtlandt, R.   Interview.   Motion Pic 10:102 D '15

TRYON, TOM
    Davy Crockett, move over.   TV Guide 6-46:22 N 15 '58
    Murals while you wait.   TV Guide 7-50:29 D 12 '59
    The Hollywood swingers.   Show 3-11:89 N '63
    Eyles, A.   Bio note; filmog.   Focus On F 11:66 Aut '72
    Wilkie, J.   Interview.   Playgirl 1-3:52 Ag '73

TSIANG, H. T.
    Obit.   Screen World 23:240 '72

TSU, IRENE
    Hobson, D.   This cool Oriental is hot on TV.   TV Guide 16-51:
        13 D 21 '68

TUCKER, FORREST
    Aguino, D. & Stover, G.   A chat with Forrest Tucker.   Black
        Oracle 8:16 Fall '74

TUCKER, GEORGE LOANE
    Macgowan, K.   Sketch.   Motion Pic Classic 9:37 D '19
    St. Johns, A. R.   Interview.   Photop 17:80 Ja '20
    Obit.   Dram Mir 83:1087 Je 25 '21
        Motion Pic 22:62 S '21
        N. Y. Clipper 69:30 Je 29 '21
    Appreciation.   Photop 20:55 S '21

TUCKER, SOPHIE
    Interview.   N. Y. Dram 72:18 Ag 26 '14
    Ennis, B.   Interview.   Motion Pic Classic 29:43 My '29
    Wows Britain's royal family.   Newsweek 3:33 My 19 '34
    Pine, D.   Story of.   Motion Pic 54:50 S '37
    Zeitlin, I.   Sketch.   Photop 51:67 O '37
    Roberts, K.   Your gal Sophie.   Colliers 101:26 F 19 '38
    Red hot Sophie.   Newsweek 25:106 Mr 26 '45
    Bio.   Cur Bio Ap '45
    Cartmell, V. H.   Trade winds.   Sat R 29:19 S 14 '46
    Miss Show Business.   Coronet 29:6 Mr '51
    Minoff, P.   Tribute to Tucker.   Cue 22-40:14 O 3 '53
    50 years of Sophie.   Newsweek 42:80 O 5 '53
    Milestone for a red hot mama.   Theatre Arts 37:12 O '53
    Millstein, G.   First of the red hot mammas.   N. Y. Times Mag
        p19 S 27 '53
    Obit.   Newsweek 67:91B F 21 '66
        Screen World 18:240 '67

TUFTS, SONNY
   Heart-throb "Kansas." Cue 12-40:11 O 2 '43
   Story of. Time 42:54 D 6 '43
   Sketch. Photop 24:39 D '43
   Hall, G. You diagnose Sonny. Silver S 15-6:46 Ap '45
   Holliday, K. Sonny and the quiet life. Silver S 17-5:44 Mr '47
   Parsons, L. O. Cosmops citation for best supporting perform-
     ance of month. Cosmop 126:13 Je '49
   Marill, A. H. Filmog. Films In R 18-4:253 Ap '67
   Obit. Classic Film Collect (reprint N. Y. Times) 27:60 Spg/Sum
     '70
   Film R p13 '71/72
   N. Y. Times p31 Je 6; p84 Je 7 '70
   Same. N. Y. Times Bio Ed Je 6 '70
   Newsweek 75:62 Je 15 '70
   Screen World 22:240 '71

TULLY, TOM
   Inspector Damon and Lieutenant Pythias. TV Guide 6-46:20 N
     15 '58

TUNE, TOMMY
   Koch, M. Interview. Interview 20:16 Mr '72
   Filmog. Films & Filming 19-7:66 Ap '73
   Ast, P. Interview. Interview 33:26 Je '73

TURNER, F. A.
   Willis, R. Three rough-necks from The escape. Photop 7-3:
     136 F '15

TURNER, FLORENCE
   Peltret, E. Interview. Motion Pic Classic 7:28 F '19
   Bahn, C. B. Personalities prominent in the press. Cinema Dig
     1-3:7 Je 13 '32

TURNER, LANA
   Gillespie-Hayck, A. Lana. Silver S 9-6:34 Ap '39
   Hall, G. Her advice to all the school girls. Silver S 10-3:22
     Ja '40
   Guest of honor at party on U. S. S. Idaho. Life 9:122 O 28 '40
   Her friendship with Tony Martin. Photop 18:30 Mr '41
   Franchey, J. R. Invitation to insomnia. Silver S 11-6:34 Ap
     '41
   Miss Turner. Lions R 1-1:no p# S '41
   Clark Gable meets Lana Turner. Lions R 1-2:no p# O '41
   Drama vs. glamour. Lions R 1-2:no p# O '41
   What price romance. Lions R 1-5:no p# Ja '42
   We nominate... Lions R 2-1:no p# S/O '42
   Walker, H. L. Sketch. Photop 21:43 N '42
   Manners, M. J. Lana faces her future. Silver S 13-6:24 Ap
     '43
   If you knew Lana. Lions R 2-4:no p# Ap '43
   Cheryl Christina Crane, newest pin-up girl. Photop 24:32 D '43

Trotter, M.   Prediction for 1944.   Photop 24:27 Ja '44
Mulvey, K.   Sketch.   Womans Home C 71:10 Mr '44
Marrin, K.   Can Lana make love last?   Silver S 14-5:40 Mr '44
Notes on.   Photop 25:52 O '44
L-A-N-A spells glamor.   Lions R 3-5:no p# D '44
Haas, D. B.   Lana gets serious.   Silver S 16-5:30 Mr '46
Pritchett, F.   Sketch.   Photop 29:42 S '46
Palmer, C.   Lana sure loves those Latins.   Silver S 17-3:40 Ja
    '47
O'Leary, D.   TNT means Tracy 'n' Turner.   Silver S 18-2:24
    D '47
Actress of the year.   Cosmop 123:12 D '47
Parsons, L. O.   Cosmop's citation for best performance of
    month.   Cosmop 123:13 D '47
Her love affairs.   Time 51:18 Ja 12 '48
Fletcher, A. W.   Story of her loves.   Photop 32:38 My '48
Graham, S.   Sketch.   Photop 33:40 N '48
As a good sport.   Photop 36:60 S '49
MacDonald, E.   Letter to a star.   Silver S 22-4:30 F '52
Sheridan, M.   Lana's tragic love life.   Silver S 23-4:28 F '53
Wilson, E.   I love Lana.   Silver S 23-9:22 Jl '53
Reid, L.   Lana tries marriage again.   Silver S 24-2:35 D '53
Barthel, J.   Survivor on TV.   Life 67:79 S 26 '69
Valentino, L.   For love of Lana.   Show 1-1:72 Ja '70
Bell, A.   Lana and Jane--they're still stars.   N. Y. Times Bio
    Ed Je 27 '71
The pinup girls.   Screen Greats 1-2:20 Sum '71
Considine, S.   What becomes a legend most?   After Dark 4-9:
    38 Ja '72
Wallace, I.   The loves of Lana Turner.   Liberty 1-4:36 Spg '72
Raborn, G.   Lana Turner; filmog.   Films In R 23-8:465 O '72
Osborne, R.   Lana Turner.   Films In R 24-4:246 Ap '73

TURPIN, BEN
    Sketch.   Motion Pic Classic 6:55 Mr '18
    McGaffey, K.   Interview.   Motion Pic 22:59 N '21
    Hall, G.   Interview.   Motion Pic Classic 13:26 F '22
    Sketch.   Photop 26:74 Ag '24
    Donnell, D.   His love story.   Motion Pic Classic 21:24 Jl '25
    Ten years ago.   Photop 44:84 N '33
    Agee, J.   Story of.   Life 27:15 S 5 '49
    LaHue, K. C.   Turpin.   8mm Collect 9:3 S '64

TUSHINGHAM, RITA
    Rising stars.   Film R p31 '62/63

TUTIN, DOROTHY
    Queens.   New Yorker 39:33 Mr 33 '63
    Morley, S.   Ladies only; interview.   Plays & Players 17-5:24 F
        '69

TWEDDELL, FRANK
    Obit.   N. Y. Times p40 D 21 '71

TWELVETREES, HELEN
Ramsey, W.   Sketch.   Motion Pic Classic 29:40 My '29
Hall, G.   Sketch.   Motion Pic Classic 31:48 Je '30
Sketch.   Motion Pic Classic 33:48 Mr '31
Benham, L.   Sorrow was her teacher.   Silver S 2-5:44 Mr '32
How traces of melancholy were taken out of her face.   Photop
   44:54 Je '33
Manners, D.   Does not want sex appeal.   Movie Classic 5:26
   S '33
Fidler, J.   Interview.   Motion Pic 46:49 N '33
Uselton, R. A.   The Wampus baby stars.   Films In R 21-2:73
   F '70
McGregor, D.   Helen Twelvetrees; filmog.   Film Fan Mo 127:3
   Ja '72

TWIGGY (Leslie Hornby)
Cockney kid.   Time 88:49 N 11 '66
Arrival of Twiggy.   Life 62:33 F 3 '67
Devlin, P.   Twiggy haute couture.   Vogue 149:64 Mr 15 '67
Twiggy.   Seventeen 26:116 Mr '67
Twig.   Newsweek 69:62 Ap 3 '67
Is it a girl? is it a boy? no, it's Twiggy.   Look 31:84 Ap 4 '67
Twiggy, click, click.   Newsweek 69:62 Ap 10 '67
Twiggy makes U. S. styles swing too.   Life 62:99 Ap 14 '67
Crist, J.   What Twiggy's got.   Ladies Home J 84:60 Je '67
Twiggy talks about the Twiggy look.   Ladies Home J 84:62 Je
   '67
Hornby, Mrs. N.   My girl Twiggy.   Mlle 65:122 Je '67
Kerr, J.   Twiggy who?   McCalls 94:62 Jl '67
Davies, N.   Justin looks at Twiggy.   Mlle 65:76 Jl '67
Fallaci, O.   My name is Twiggy.   Sat Eve Post 240:60 Ag 12
   '67
Twiggy.   U. S. Camera 30:34 Ag '67
Whiteside, T.   Reporter at large.   New Yorker 43:64 N 4 '67
Whatever happened to Twiggy?   Look 32:78 Ag 6 '68
Avedon, R.   The four seasons of a woman's life.   McCalls 96:86
   Mr '69
Ehrlich, H.   Now blooming Twiggy.   Look 35:58 My 4 '71
Appelbaum, N.   The model and The boyfriend.   After Dark 4-7:
   50 N '71
Model into movie star.   Mlle 74:138 N '71
Taylor, A.   Twiggy is back.   N. Y. Times Bio Ed D 1 '71
Interview.   New Yorker 47:30 D 18 '71
Now it's Twiggy's turn.   Harp Baz 105:112 D '71
Chase, C.   Twiggy and her boy friend.   N. Y. Times Bio Ed Ja
   2 '72
Flack, S.   The grooming of a star.   Show 2-11:27 Ja '72
English dream.   Time 99:56 F 7 '72
Twiggy talks about her only love.   Mod Screen 66-4:24 Ap '72

TYLER, BEVERLY
Hamilton, S.   Story of.   Photop 29:24 O '46
Sketch.   Am Mag 143:121 Ja '47

TYLER, JUDY
    In the cast.  TV Guide 1-4:12 Ap 24 '53
    Young hopefuls do bit parts now.  TV Guide 1-7:20 My 15 '53
    Television's own promising starlets.  TV Guide 3-37:10 S 10 '55
    Jester, L.   Pipe dream for Judy.  Cue 24-47:13 N 26 '55

TYLER, TOM
    Calhoun, D.   Sketch.   Motion Pic Classic 27:40 Jl '28
    Connor, E.   Letter.   Films In R 5-6:316 Je/Jl '54
    Kinkade, H. Jr.   Retracing Tom Tyler's career; filmog.   Filmo-
        graph 1-1:17 '70
    Smith, R.   Additional filmog.   Filmograph 1-2:44 '70
    Malcomson, R. M.   The sound serial.   Views & Rs 3-1:13 Sum
        '71
    Harris, G. Jr.   Tom Tyler's filmog; letter.   Filmograph 2-1:
        50 '71
    Billings, E. R.   Additional filmog.   Filmograph 2-2:48 '71

TYRRELL, SUSAN
    Klemesrud, J.   Fat city's Susie.  N.Y. Times Bio Ed p1564 Ag
        '72
    Kirkland, S.   The lady from Fat city.   Interview 26:18 O '72

TYSKIEWICZ, BEATA (Also Tyszkiewicz)
    Beata Tyskiewicz; filmog.   Film 60:15 n. d.
    Elley, D.   Bio note; filmog.   Focus On F 16:13 Aut '73

TYSON, CICELY
    Klemesrud, J.   The looker from Sounder.   N.Y. Times sec 2:
        13 O 1 '72
    Same.   N.Y. Times Bio Ed p1879 O '72
    First step.   Time 100:58 O 9 '72
    Manners, D.   I nominate for stardom.   Mod Screen 67-3:18 Mr
        '73
    Gardella, K.   Actress by accident, star by design.   N.Y. Sun
        News p12 Ja 6 '74
    Davidson, M.   What makes Miss Tyson run.   TV Guide 22-4:14
        Ja 26 '74
    Windeler, R.   From the typing pool to an Emmy.   People 1-14:
        36 Je 3 '74
    Interview.   Photop 85-6:55 Je '74
    The importance of Cicely Tyson.   MS 3-2:45 Ag '74

TYSZKIEWICZ, BEATA
    (See:  TYSKIEWICZ, BEATA)


UGGAMS, LESLIE
    Things slowed down a bit at 12.   TV Guide 10-3:27 Ja 20 '62
    She sings along with Mitch.   Ebony 17:40 Mr '62
    Lacely ugigimous.   Time 80:66 D 7 '62
    Growing up.   Newsweek 62:59 D 30 '63

Astor, G.  Little girl grows up.  Look 28:42 Je 30 '64
Curnow, H.  Why I married an Australian.  Ebony 22:140 My
  '67
Prideaux, T.  A cool bombshell.  Life 62:88 Je 23 '67
Star in a new galaxy.  Newsweek 70:63 Jl 17 '67
People are talking about.  Vogue 150:78 Jl '67
Reed, R.  (She) polishes up her new image.  Good House 166:50
  Ap '68
Watt, D.  Popular records.  New Yorker 44:186 D 14 '68
Her secret.  Harp Baz 102:150 F '69
Sohigian, K.  Interview.  House Beaut 112:68 F '70
How they suffer for their white men.  Photop 84-6:54 D '73

ULLMAN, LIV
  Heroic despair.  Time 93:71 Ja 10 '69
  Flatley, G.  Liv and Bergman remain...such good friends.
    N. Y. Times Bio Ed Ap 9 '72
  Peterson, M.  Liv from Bergman to Hollywood Blvd Ullman.
    Interview 25:46 S '72
  Whitman, M.  A special kind of superstar.  Films Illus 2-22:29
    Ap '73
  Rosenthal, S.  Liv Ullman; filmog.  Focus On F 14:6 Spg '73
  Partial filmog.  Focus On F 15:17 Sum '73

ULRIC, LENORE
  Modern Red-Riding Hood.  Movie Pictorial 2-4:8 O '15
  How to get into moving pictures.  Motion Pic Classic 2:23 Jl '16
  Schmid, P. G.  Sketch.  Motion Pic 12:73 Ja '17
  Interview.  Mus Cour 77:7 Ag 8 '18
  Carr, H.  Sketch.  Classic 18:19 Ja '24
  Bio sketch.  National 53:123 S '24
  Where I get my "pep."  Theatre 44:9 S '26
  Manners, D.  Interview.  Motion Pic 38:35 O '29
  Obit.  Classic Film Collect 30:extra 4 Spg '71
    N. Y. Times p26 D 31 '70
    Same.  N. Y. Times Bio Ed D 31 '70
    Newsweek 77:80 Ja 11 '71
    Screen World 22:241 '71
  Brooks, D. E.  The mistress of a thousand emotions.  Classic
    Film Collect 37:27 Win '72

ULTRA-VIOLET
  He lit the way for Ultra-Violet.  Life 64:61 O 4 '68
  Colaciello, R.  At home with Ultra.  Interview 23:17 Jl '72

UNDERDOWN, EDWARD
  Rising stars.  Film R p40 '51/52

URE, MARY
  Thomas, R. M. Jr.  For Mary Ure and Robert Shaw, marriage
    may not be bliss but it'll do.  N. Y. Times Bio Ed F 26 '72

USTINOV, PETER
  Ustinov, P.   Max Ophuls.   Sight & Sound 27-1:49 Sum '57
  Directing filmog.   Film 14:8 N/D '57
  Tiring, wearing, infuriating...but great fun.   Int F A 1:66 '57
  Cowie, P.   The face of '63--Great Britain.   Films & Filming
    9-5:19 F '63
  Ustinov on tennis.   Sports Illus 30:40 Je 23 '69
  Interview.   Motor Trend 22:98 My '70
  Levy, A.   Plays Santa to the children of many nations.   Good
    House 171:38 D '70
  Musel, R.   One man show.   TV Guide 19-11:20 Mr 13 '71
  Knapp, D.   On location in Mexico.   Show 2-7:18 S '71
  Mount, D. N.   Interview.   Pub W 200:15 O 25 '71
  What directors are saying.   Action 7-1:36 Ja/F '72


VACCARO, BRENDA
  Actresses who are real people.   Life 68:42 My 29 '70
  Clein, H.   The real people: featuring Hollywood's new breed of
    character actors.   Show 1-8:14 Jl 9 '70
  Zadan, C.   Grabbing it by the old checungas.   After Dark 4-6:
    30 O '71
  Whitney, D.   You were born too late, darling.   TV Guide 20-21:
    20 My 20 '72
  Note; filmog.   Films & Filming 18-11:60 Ag '72
  Is out-of-wedlock no longer in?   People 2-10:50 S 2 '74

VAGUE, VERA
  (Also known as Barbara Jo Allen)
  Vera Vague vs. Barbara Jo Allen.   Lions R 1-4:no p# D '41
  The trouble with men.   Cosmop 115:63 O '43
  Obit.   N. Y. Times Bio Ed p1349 S '74

VAIL, LESTER
  Ogden, E.   Sketch.   Photop 39:40 Mr '31
  Obit.   Screen World 11:226 '60

VALDIS, SIGRID
  Hunting for the brass ring.   TV Guide 15-31:24 Ag 5 '67

VALE, VOLA
  Rogers, A.   Interview.   Motion Pic 17:64 Ap '19

VALENTINE, GRACE
  Sketch.   Motion Pic 14:82 O '17

VALENTINE, KAREN
  Raddatz, L.   Listening to the sound of success.   TV Guide 18-
    25:14 Je 20 '70
  Student wife.   Photop 78-2:72 Ag '70
  Opinions on liberation: my man and me.   Photop 78-3:78 S '70
  Mangel, C.   There's a mad, funny girl in Room 222.   Look

35-13:M66 Je 29 '71
Cooking with a star.  Mod Screen 66-2:54 F '72

VALENTINO, ALBERTO
The tragedy of his nose.  Lit Dig 102:43 S 21 '29

VALENTINO, RUDOLPH
Sherwood, C. B.  Sketch.  Motion Pic Classic 11:18 N '20
As Julio in The four horsemen of the Apocalypse.  Lit Dig 68:29
    Mr 26 '21
Gassaway, G.  Sketch.  Motion Pic 21:40 Jl '21
Howe, H.  Interview.  Motion Pic Classic 13:18 D '21
Goldbeck, W.  Interview.  Motion Pic 23:40 My '22
Winship, M.  How to dance.  Photop 21:45 My '22
Cheatham, M.  His darkest hour.  Classic 15:52 O '22
Is the American girl playing a losing game?  Met Mag 56:40 Ja
    '23
An open letter from Valentino.  Photop 23:34 Ja '23
The vogue of Valentino.  Motion Pic 25:27 F '23
Fletcher, A. W. & Hall, G.  Interview.  Motion Pic 25:20 Je '23
Interview.  Classic 18:22 D '23
de Revere, F. V.  What I read in his face.  Motion Pic 28:45
    O '24
Adams, E.  His horoscope.  Photop 26:107 N '24
Tully, J.  His popularity.  Motion Pic Classic 21:16 Je '25
Carr, H.  Home life of.  Motion Pic 30:32 Ag '25
Sheldon, J.  Interview.  Motion Pic 30:24 N '25
Ryan, D.  Has the great lover become just a celebrity?  Motion
    Pic Classic 23:20 My '26
Valentino and yellow journalism.  Nation 123:207 S 8 '26
Sangster, M.  In memoriam.  Photop 30:39 O '26
Interview.  Theatre 44:39 O '26
Tully, J.  His career.  Vanity Fair 27:86 O '26
Smith, F. J.  Does he send spirit messages?  Photop 31:38 F
    '27
The real Valentino.  Photop 31:76 F '27
Madden, E.  Eulogies still being paid to his memory.  Motion
    Pic 35:31 F '28
Biery, R.  His haunted house.  Motion Pic 36:34 N '28
Biery, R.  Spirit messages to Natacha Rambova.  Motion Pic
    36:28 Ja '29
His unknown love.  Motion Pic 38:58 Ja '30
Calhoun, D.  What if he had lived?  Motion Pic 40:29 D '30
Walker, H. L.  His death a valuable publicity stunt for those
    who profited from his last production.  Motion Pic 41:32 Mr
    '31
Taviner, R.  Story of his marriages.  Motion Pic 41:34 Jl '31
Grant, J.  Has no permanent tomb.  Motion Pic 44:30 S '32
Moffitt, C. F.  Censorship for interviews Hollywood's latest wild
    idea.  Cinema Dig 2-5:9 Ja 9 '33
In memoriam.  Motion Pic 45:52 Je '33
Lee, S.  Immortals of the screen.  Motion Pic 46:32 O '33
Grant, J.  Long-missing Valentino film found.  Movie Classic

7:30 S '34

Hall, G.  He still lives for Pola Negri.  Motion Pic 48:46 Ja '35

16 years later the sheik rides on.  Cue 6-34:9 Je 18 '39

Revival of The son of the sheik.  Life 4:54 Je 20 '38

Revival of The son of the sheik.  Photop 52:46 S '38

Return of the Sheik?  Time 54:64 Ag 1 '49

Crane, E.  Legend with feet of clay? filmog.  Screen Legend 1-3:4 O '65

Peeples, S. A.  Out, brief candle.  The story of Valentino; filmog.  8mm Collect 14:6 Spg '66

Rambova death calls back interview with Valentino.  Classic Film Collect 15:38 Sum '66

Mencken, H. L.  On Hollywood--and Valentino.  Cinema J 9-2: 13 Spg '70

Mank, C.  Valentino still lives.  Classic Film Collect 27:35 Spg/Sum '70

When silence was golden.  Screen Greats 1-2:77 Sum '71

St. Johns, A. R.  The life story of The sheik.  Liberty 1-10:26 Fall '73

VALERIE, JEANNE

Flash on Jeanne Valerie.  Unifrance 50:9 Jl/S '59

VALKYRIEN

A Brunhilde from Denmark.  Photop 10-4:50 S '16

VALLEE, RUDY

Claxton, O.  Sketch.  Motion Pic Classic 30:37 S '29

Belfrage, C.  Interview with his parents.  Motion Pic 38:35 Ja '30

Sketch.  Photop 37:36 Ap '30

Scott, H.  Sketch.  Movie Classic 2:30 My '32

Walker, H. L.  The untold story of his last interview.  Motion Pic 46:30 S '33

Ten years ago.  Photop 45:108 D '33

Roberts, D.  Interview.  Movie Classic 6:27 Mr '34

English, R.  Big business man.  Movie Classic 8:27 Mr '35

Manners, M. J.  To be or not to be--a bachelor.  Silver S 11-8:26 Je '41

O'Leary, D.  His advice to Frank Sinatra.  Silver S 17-5:30 Mr '47

Dudley, F.  The gentleman from Maine.  Silver S 19-4:42 F '49

How to succeed in How to succeed.  Playboy 9:87 D '62

Pitts, M. E.  Filmog.  Films In R 18-5:318 My '67

Presentation:  Record album called MacArthur's legacy presented to Mrs. MacArthur.  New Yorker 47:24 Jl 17 '71

VALLI, ALIDA

Pritchett, F.  Early morning tete-a-tete.  Silver S 18-7:24 My '48

Lane, J. F.  The face of '63--Italy.  Films & Filming 9-7:11 Ap '63

VALLI, VIRGINIA
  Peltret, E.  Interview.  Motion Pic Classic 13:32 N '21
  Gassaway, G.  Interview.  Motion Pic 24:70 Ag '22
  The men with whom she has played.  Motion Pic Classic 21:32
    My '25
  Tully, J.  Interview.  Vanity Fair 28:70 Mr '29
  Spensley, D.  Interview.  Photop 31:73 My '27
  Johnston, C.  Sketch.  Motion Pic Classic 26:51 F '28
  Wooldridge, D.  Interview.  Motion Pic 35:55 Jl '28
  Sketch.  Motion Pic Classic 33:26 My '31
  Manners, D.  Interview.  Motion Pic 42:39 S '31
  Obit.  N. Y. Times p47 S 26 '68

VAN, GUS
  Obit.  N. Y. Times p47 Mr 13 '68
    Newsweek 71:65 Mr 25 '68
    Time 91:80 Mr 22 '68

VAN, WALLY
  Sketch.  Motion Pic 10:110 Ag '15

VAN ARK, JOAN
  Lochte, D.  What do nurses do anyway?  TV Guide 21-4:16 Ja
    27 '73

VANCE, VIVIAN
  She can now laugh off-camera, too.  TV Guide 11-6:15 F 9 '63

VAN CLEEF, LEE
  Letters; partial filmog.  Films In R 19-5:316 My '68
  Letters.  Films In R 19-7:464 Ag/S '68

VANDEL, MAGALI
  Bio note.  Unifrance 19:7 Jl/Ag '52

VAN DER VLIS, DIANA
  She's just like...  TV Guide 6-47:24 N 22 '58

VAN DEVERE, TRISH
  Miller, E.  Interview.  Seventeen 30:64 Je '71
  Richards, J.  A deluctable dream come true.  Show 2-2:48 S
    '71
  Sketch.  Movie Dig 1-6:24 N '72
  Klemesrud, J.  Trish? Mrs. Scott? Both?  N. Y. Times sec
    2:9 D 31 '72
  Same.  N. Y. Times Bio Ed p2297 D '72

VAN DYKE, DICK
  Faith, hope and hilarity; excerpts.  Read Dig 98:231 F '71
  New Van Dyke family blooms in the desert.  Life 71:39 S 17 '71
  Whitney, D.  Squire of Cave Creek.  TV Guide 19-41:32 O 9
    '71
  Richter, C.  Star of the month; horoscope.  Mod Screen 65-12:52

D '71
Finnigan, J. & Raddatz, L.   The morning after.   TV Guide 22-
6:13 F 9 '74

VANEL, CHARLES
Bio note.   Unifrance 23:10 F '53

VAN EYCK, PETER
Hamilton, S.   Sketch.   Photop 23:64 S '43
Letters; filmog.   Films In R 21-6:390 Je/Jl '70
Letters.   Films In R 21-7:450 Ag/S '70
Obit.   Film R p15 '70/71
    N.Y. Times p27 Jl 17 '69
    Screen World 21:241 '70

VAN PALLANDT, NINA
Manners, D.   I nominate for stardom.   Mod Screen 66-11:16 N
'72

VAN PATTEN, JOYCE
Raddatz, L.   Breathe deeply before reading.   TV Guide 17-26:
23 Je 28 '69

VAN ROOTEN, LUIS
Obit.   N.Y. Times p44 Je 20 '73
    Same.   N.Y. Times Bio Ed p1061 Je '73

VAN SLOAN, EDWARD
Stewart, W.F.   Filmog.   Films In R 16-6:396 Je/Jl '65

VAN VLEET, RICHARD
Swisher, V.H.   Hollywood's professional training ground.   After
Dark 13-7:40 N '70

VAN VOOREN, MONIQUE
Colaciello, R.   At home with Monique.   Interview 21:42 My '72

VARCONI, VICTOR
Sketch.   Photop 32:34 Jl '27
Watkins, F.   Victor Varconi; interview; filmog.   Film Fan Mo
139:9 Ja '73

VARDEN, EVELYN
Sketch.   Dram Mir 77:27 Ag 11 '17

VARLEY, NATALYA
Note.   Int F G 10:334 '73

VARNEY, REG
Why (he) got off the busses and into drag.   Films Illus 2-21:24
Mr '73

VARSI, DIANE
  Rising stars.   Film R p21 '59/60
  Where are they now?   Newsweek 77:10 My 31 '71
  Stone, J.   Diane Varsi drops back in.   N. Y. Times Bio Ed Ja
    9 '72

VAUGHN, ADAMAE
  Uselton, R. A.   The Wampus baby stars.   Films In R 21-2:73
    F '70

VAUGHN, ALBERTA
  Carr, H.   Interview.   Classic 20:34 D '24
  Leslie, A.   Interview.   Motion Pic 31:67 My '26
  Matzen, M.   Sketch.   Motion Pic Classic 25:32 Ap '27
  Uselton, R. A.   The Wampus baby stars.   Films In R 21-2:73
    F '70

VAUGHN, ROBERT
  Bio.   Cur Bio 28:41 S '67
    Same.   Cur Bio Yrbk 1967:434 '68
  How I faced my drinking problem.   Photop 78-4:60 O '70
  Robert Vaughn's love baby.   Mod Screen 66-9:44 S '72
  Peck, I.   That man from U. N. C. L. E. gets his Ph. D.   N. Y.
    Times sec 2:17 S 17 '72
    Same.   N. Y. Times Bio Ed p1713 S '72
  Musel, R.   The backsliding of Robert Vaughn.   TV Guide 21-2:
    22 Ja 13 '73
  Bachelor Vaughn has a last fling.   People 2-3:52 Jl 15 '74

VEE, BOBBY
  Edwards, H.   Taking care of Bobby.   After Dark 5-11:19 Mr '73

VEIDT, CONRAD
  Interview.   Theatre 45:38 Ap '27
  Paton, C.   Interview.   Motion Pic Classic 25:49 Jl '27
  Bay, D.   Sketch.   Motion Pic 34:44 D '27
  Hall, G.   Veidt looks in the mirror.   Silver S 11-11:38 S '41
  Double life.   Lions R 1-7:no p# Mr '42
  Obit.   Ill Lon N 202:400 Ap 10 '43
    Newsweek 21:6 Ap 12 '43
  Sketch.   Time 42:94 Ag 23 '43
  Clarke, F. S.   Rasputin on film.   Cinefantastique 1-1:6 Fall '70

VELEZ, LUPE
  Sketch.   Photop 32:48 S '27
  Gilmore, F.   Study in temperaments.   Motion Pic Classic 26:55
    S '27
  Hall, G.   Interview.   Motion Pic 35:58 Jl '28
  Reid, M.   Her quarrel with Jetta Goudal.   Motion Pic Classic
    28:58 D '28
  Biery, R.   Interview.   Motion Pic 36:44 Ja '29
  Biery, R.   Sketch.   Motion Pic Classic 29:22 Jl '29
  Belfrage, C.   Interview.   Motion Pic 39:50 Ap '30

Horton, H.  Sketch.  Motion Pic Classic 32:63 Ja '31
Manners, D.  Sketch.  Motion Pic 41:54 Je '31
Rivers, A.  Marriage rumors.  Motion Pic Classic 32:26 Ag '31
Hall, L.  Her love story.  Photop 40:51 S '31
Pryor, N.  Her romance with Gary Cooper.  Movie Classic 1:
    60 N '31
DeKolty, J.  Hot Lupe.  Silver S 2-3:40 Ja '32
Reid, M.  Interview.  Movie Classic 2:26 Ap '32
Janeway, D.  Her romance with Randolph Scott.  Movie Classic
    2:29 My '32
Hall, G.  Interview.  Motion Pic 44:40 N '32
Biery, R.  Her friendship with Walter Huston.  Photop 42:46 N
    '32
Manners, D.  Adopts a daughter.  Movie Classic 3:30 D '32
Williams, W.  Interview.  Motion Pic 46:42 N '33
Ergenbright, E. L.  Interview.  Movie Classic 5:27 D '33
Calhoun, D.  Home of.  Motion Pic 47:50 Jl '34
Slater, A.  Sketch.  Movie Classic 7:37 O '34
Talmey, A.  Sketch.  Vogue 92:74 O 1 '38
Vallee, W. L.  She heet de bool's eye.  Silver S 10-9:42 Jl '40
MacDonald, J.  Farewell to Lupe.  Silver S 15-6:24 Ap '45
Obit.  Cur Bio 6 '45
Uselton, R. A.  The Wampus baby stars.  Films In R 21-2:73
    F '70
Pinups of the past.  Films & Filming 19-6:66 Mr '73

VELOZ, YOLANDA
    Raddatz, L.  Now you see her, but generally you don't.  TV
        Guide 19-33:30 Ag 14 '71

VENABLE, EVELYN
    Walker, H. L.  New girls to satisfy Hollywood's insatiable de-
        mand.  Silver S 4-8:30 Je '34
    Sylvia's beauty helps.  Photop 46:56 S '34
    What they are doing now.  Show 2-8:106 Ag '62
    Schwartz, W.  Partial filmog.  Films In R 17-3:194 Mr '66

VENTURA, LINO
    Nolan, J. E.  Films on TV.  Films In R 23-4:233 Ap '72

VERA-ELLEN
    York, C.  Sketch.  Photop 28:19 My '46
    Marsh, P.  Dancer with a message.  Silver S 17-1:44 N '46
    Peer, R. & R.  Romance must wait.  Silver S 22-1:45 N '51
    Maddox, B.  Smart girl, that Vera.  Silver S 22-11:41 S '52
    Corpening, S.  I'm no gay butterfly.  Silver S 23-8:42 Je '53
    Oderman, S.  Vera-Ellen; filmog.  Film Fan Mo 120:3 Je '71

VERDON, GWEN
    Wilson, E.  The girl who showed 'em how.  Silver S 24-4:24 F
        '54
    Rising stars.  Film R p21 '59/60
    How she suffered for success.  Mod Screen 66-7:52 Jl '72
    Verdon with washed face.  Cue 43-38:4 O 7 '74

VERDUGO, ELENA
  Meet Millie.   TV Guide 2-25:13 Je 18 '54
  Jenkins, D.   Meet Millie--today.   TV Guide 11-49:27 D 7 '63
  Davidson, B.   Another illness, another show.   TV Guide 19-17:
    25 Ap 24 '71
  Wedding.   Photop 82-1:54 Jl '72
  Her bridal shower.   Mod Screen 66-7:26 Jl '72
  Verdugo, E.   The movie performance I will always remember.
    Movie Dig 1-6:141 N '72

VEREEN, BEN
  Guided missile.   Time 100:57 N 27 '72
  Flatley, G.   To be young, gifted and Ben Vereen.   N. Y. Times
    Bio Ed p2075 N '72
  Stoop, N. M.   Moving on the next beat; interview.   After Dark
    5-5:18 D '72
  Purvis, C.   Ben Vereen.   Interview 4-3:18 Mr '74

VERLEY, BERNARD
  Verley, B.   Bunuel's Christ.   Film 56:23 Aut '69

VERNE, KAREN
  Refugee.   Am Mag 133:71 Ja '42
  Obit.   Screen World 19:240 '68

VERNON, ANNE
  Bio note.   Unifrance 10:6 Je '51
  Our stars at home.   Unifrance 33:11 D '54/Ja '55

VERNON, BOBBY
  Lubou, D.   Sketch.   Motion Pic Classic 29:65 My '29

VERNON, JOHN
  Interview.   Motion p4 My/Je '73

VERNON, WALLY
  Obit.   N. Y. Times p88 Mr 8 '70
    Screen World 22:241 '71

VERSOIS, ODILE
  Rising stars.   Film R p41 '51/52

VERTINSKAYA, ANASTASIA (Anastasiya)
  Orlova, G.   Two actresses.   CTVD 9-3:23 Spg '73
  Note.   Int F G 10:334 '73

VERUSHKA
  Stalking the wild Verushka.   Playboy 18-1:96 Ja '71
  Avedon, R.   Verushka is the most beautiful woman in the world.
    Vogue 159:140 My '72

VICKERS, MARTHA
  Fulton, M. J.   Sketch.   Photop 31:102 Je '47

Westmore, P.  You can be 5 persons.  Am Mag 144:140 D '47
Lane, F.  Martha's true love.  Silver S 19-9:35 Jl '49
Obit.  Classic Film Collect (reprint Los Angeles Times) 33:53
  Win '71
  N. Y. Times p46 N 5 '71
  Screen World 23:240 '72

VICKERS, YVETTE
  Everyday is a sundae for Yvette.  TV Guide 6-14:24 Ap 5 '58

VICTOR, INA
  She acts too.  TV Guide 12-14:13 Ap 4 '64

VIDAL, HENRI
  Bio note.  Unifrance 45:9 D '57
  Obit.  Film R p10 '60/61
    Screen World 11:225 '60
  Pinup of the past.  Films & Filming 20-3:72 D '73

VIDOR, FLORENCE
  Carew, O.  Sketch.  Motion Pic Classic 7:41 F '19
  Cheatham, M.  Interview.  Motion Pic Classic 12:18 Ap '21
  Stacey, M.  Interview.  Motion Pic Classic 13:34 S '21
  Handy, T. B.  Interview.  Motion Pic 23:38 Mr '22
  Cheatham, M.  Interview.  Classic 16:22 Ap '23
  Carr, H.  Sketch.  Motion Pic 30:27 Ja '26
  Tildesley, A. L.  Sketch.  Motion Pic Classic 23:32 Jl '26
  Hall, G. & Fletcher, A. W.  Interview.  Motion Pic 32:30 Ja
    '27
  Hall, G.  Sketch.  Motion Pic 36:58 Ag '28
  Calhoun, D.  Sketch.  Motion Pic Classic 28:26 N '28
  Dunham, H.  Florence Vidor; filmog.  Films In R 21-4:21 Ja
    '70
  Case, D. E.  Letter.  Films In R 21-8:518 O '70

VIGNOLA, ROBERT G.
  Poland, J. F.  Sketch.  Motion Pic 15:86 Jl '18
  May, L.  Interview.  Motion Pic Classic 12:43 Ap '21
  Evans, D.  Sketch.  Photop 23:74 Ja '23
  St. Johns, I.  Interview.  Photop 30:58 O '26
  Obit.  Screen World 5:209 '54

VIGNON, JEAN-PAUL
  Holt, T.  Chevalier continued; centerfold.  Playgirl 1-7:64 D '73

VILA, ALBERTO
  Stars of tomorrow.  Lions R 1-11/12:no p# Jl/Ag '42

VILAR, JEAN
  Klein, L. & A.  France's new popular theatre.  Theatre Arts
    36:25 My '52
  Hewes, H.  Sketch.  Sat R 36:24 Ag 22 '53
  Dumur, G.  The theatre of Jean Vilar.  Reporter 13:44 N 3 '55

Gilder, R.  T. N. P. for the U. S. A.  Theatre Arts 42:9 S '58
Hewes, H.  Genius of Chaillot.  Sat R 41:30 O 11 '58
Lenoir, J. P.  Openings.  Theatre Arts 47:62 Ja '63
Maguire, J.  Out of decay, an operatic prophet.  Hi Fi 17:Ma28
    Mr '67
Obit.  Cur Bio 32:45 S '71
    Same.  Cur Bio Yrbk 1971:472 '72
    N. Y. Times p26 My 29 '71
    Same.  N. Y. Times Bio Ed My 29 '71
Opera N 36:31 O '71

VILLEGAS, LUCIO
    Stewart, W. T.  Filmog.  Films In R 20-6:386 Je/Jl '69

VINCENT, ALLEN
    Careers for four, please.  Silver S 2-1:43 N '31

VINCENT, JAN-MICHAEL
    Sketch.  Films Illus 2-17:8 N '72
    Faces going far.  Films Illus 1-10:19 Ap '72
    He's a guy you can't push around.  Photop 81-4:43 Ap '72
    Love means telling the world he's married.  Mod Screen 67-3:24
        Mr '73
    The future starts today for the world's greatest athlete.  Films
        Illus 3-25:14 Jl '73
    Bio note; filmog.  Films Illus 3-36:468 Ag '74
    Blond, S.  Interview.  Interview 4-8:13 S '74
    His marriage.  Photop 86-6:54 D '74

VINCENT, JUNE
    The other woman.  TV Guide 5-1:16 Ja 5 '57

VINSON, HELEN
    DeVane, T.  Sketch.  Movie Classic 5:47 N '33
    Gay, V.  Story of.  Movie Classic 9:39 O '35
    Samuels, L.  Our good-will star.  Silver S 6-1:51 N '35
    Biery, R.  Interview.  Motion Pic 50:29 Ja '36
    Crichton, K.  Story of.  Colliers 100:40 Ag 14 '37

VITEZ, ANTOINE
    Cowie, P.  Antoine Vitez.  Focus On F 1:14 Ja/F '70

VITTI, MONICA
    Lucas, C.  In life, on film--an adventure.  Show 1-1:103 O '61
    Interesting woman.  McCalls 96:99 Mr '69
    Robinson, W. R.  The movies as a revolutionary moral force.
        Contempora 2-1:26 S/F '72
    Cowie, P.  A zest for clowning; filmog.  Focus On F 8:38 n. d.

VIVA
    Goldsmith, B. L.  La dolce Viva.  New York 1-4:36 Ap 29 '68
    Viva's diary.  MS 1-11:52 My '73
    Wicked women on the moon.  Interview 1-4:20 n. d.

VIVIAN
  Sonbert, W.  Vivian.  Film Cult 45:33 Sum '67

VLADY, MARINA
  Talks to Marina Vlady.  Continental F R p9 F '72

VOGEL, MITCH
  Durslag, M.  How he joined a show older than his pigeons, rab-
    bit and chameleon combined.  TV Guide 19-13:28 Mr 27 '71

VOHS, JOAN
  Rude awakening.  TV Guide 5-4:16 Ja 26 '57

VOIGHT, JON
  Pleshette, M.  Westchester cowboy.  Newsweek 74:85 Jl 28 '69
  Miller, E.  V for Voight.  Seventeen 28:149 S '69
  On the scene.  Playboy 17-6:156 Je '70
  Gordon, S.  Voight: fresh eye on Hollywood.  Look 34-22:78 N
    3 '70
  Knight, A. & Alpert, H.  Sex stars of 1970.  Playboy 17-12:220
    D '70
  McGillivray, D.  Bio note; filmog.  Focus On F 11:13 Aut '72
  Brisken, S.  Jon Voight knockout.  Movie Dig 2-1:27 Ja '73
  Interview.  Dialogue 2-8:entire issue Je '73
  Castell, D.  High noon for the midnight cowboy.  Films Illus 3-
    36:486 Ag '74
  McLarty, J.  A view of us.  Motion p41 S/O '74
  Miles, S.  Interview.  Interview 4-10:21 O '74

VOLONTE, GIANMARIA
  Lane, J. F.  The face of '63--Italy.  Films & Filming 9-7:11
    Ap '63

von BERNE, EVA
  Willis, M.  Sketch.  Motion Pic Classic 28:63 S '28
  Alpert, K.  Story of.  Photop 34:45 N '28

von FURSTENBERG, BETSY
  Roman, R. C.  Better late than never.  After Dark 4-3:21 Jl
    '71
  Actors are not the only ones who act.  N. Y. Times sec 2:1 S
    24 '72

VON SCHERIER, SASHA
  Johnson, D.  From Strindberg to soap.  After Dark 4-5:20 S '71

von STROHEIM, ERICH
  Yost, R. M. Jr.  Gosh, how they hate him.  Photop 17-1:80 D
    '19
  Cheatham, M.  Interview.  Motion Pic Classic 9:34 Ja '20
  Fredericks, J.  Interview.  Motion Pic 20:73 Ag '20
  Gassaway, G.  Interview.  Motion Pic 22:40 O '21
  Fletcher, A. W.  Interview.  Classic 15:18 S '22

Gassaway, G. Interview. Motion Pic 25:36 S '23
Carr, H. As a director. Classic 18:24 N '23
Tully, J. Interview. Classic 19:20 My '24
Quirk, J. R. Estimate. Photop 27:27 Ja '25
Tully, J. Sketch. Vanity Fair 26:50 Mr '26
Ryan, D. The Don Quixote of pictures. Motion Pic Classic 23: 22 My '26
Leslie, A. Interview. Motion Pic 31:39 Ap '27
Sorensen, B. A close-up of Von. Motion Pic 33:39 Jl '27
The seamy side of directing. Theatre 46:18 N '27
Bay, D. Sketch. Motion Pic Classic 26:23 D '27
Carr, H. Sketch. Photop 33:38 My '28
Welch, T. Sketch. Motion Pic 37:42 My '29
Gray, C. W. Sketch. Motion Pic Classic 30:21 S '29
Calhoun, D. Interview. Motion Pic Classic 31:30 Ap '30
Belfrage, C. Charges against him and his reply. Motion Pic Classic 31:36 Je '30
Erich von Stroheim. Visages 24:entire issue Je '38
Hamilton, S. Sketch. Photop 54:72 Je '40
Work of. Newsweek 21:87 My 31 '43
Weinberg, H. G. An index to the creative work of Erich von Stroheim. Sight & Sound (special sup) Index Series #1 Je '43
Anstey, E. Work of. Spectator 171:59 Jl 16 '43
Lambert, G. Stroheim revisited. Sight & Sound 22-4:165 Ap/Je '53
Curtiss, T. Q. The last years of von Stroheim. Film Cult 4-18:3 '58
Watts, R. Jr. A few reminiscences. Film Cult 4-18:5 '58
Eisner, L. H. Homage to an artist. Film Cult 4-18:7 '58
Arnheim, R. Portrait of an artist. Film Cult 4-18:11 '58
Eisner, L. H. Notes on the style of Stroheim. Film Cult 4-18: 13 '58
Sarris, A. Pantheon directors; filmog. Film Cult 28:2 Spg '63
Estes, O. Jr. The compromised maestro of Foolish wives. 8mm Collect 8:14 My '64
Weinberg, H. G. Sternberg and Stroheim. Sight & Sound 35-1: 50 Win '65/66
Dulaney, J. Art and the business of art. Classic Film Collect 18:13 Sum '67
Letters. Films In R 18-7:449 Ag/S '67
Lee, R. Count von realism. Classic Film Collect 23:43 Spg '69
Blakeston, O. The star I'll never forget. Film R p196 '69/70
Finler, J. Stroheim's Walking down Broadway. Screen 11-4/5: 89 N '70
Bio note. Films Illus 1-5:33 N '71
Weinberg, H. G. A note on... Am Film I Report p8 #1 '72
Rosenbaum, J. Second thoughts on Stroheim. Film Comment 10-3:6 My/Je '74

VON SYDOW, MAX
Gauguin, L. The man who plays Christ. Sound Stage 1-2:25 F '65
Bio. Cur Bio Yrbk 1967:408 '68

Photoplay forum.    Photop 85-5:34 My '74
Bio note; filmog.    Films & Filming 21-3:58 D '74

VORONINA, VERA
    Fairfield, L.    Interview.    Motion Pic 34:34 S '27

VOSS, PETER
    Busch, S.    Peter Voss; partial filmog.    Films In R 23-1:63 Ja
        '72


WAGENHEIM, CHARLES
    Raddatz, L.    The Dodge City gang.    TV Guide 20-12:14 Mr 18
        '72

WAGGONER, LYLE
    Hobson, D.    The door-to-door actor.    TV Guide 19-7:18 F 13
        '71
    Holt, T.    Playgirl's man for June; centerfold.    Playgirl 1-1:59
        Je '73
    My child.    Photop 84-5:15 N '73

WAGNER, JACK
    Obit.    Screen World 17:241 '66

WAGNER, ROBERT
    Lescott, L.    I've learned about women.    Silver S 24-9:28 Jl '54
    Does Tina Sinatra love Uncle Bob?    Photop 78-3:55 S '70
    Natalie Wood and Bob Wagner to marry again.    Mod Screen 66-
        6:35 Je '72
    Natalie Wood and Bob Wagner in love again.    Photop 81-6:38 Je
        '72
    Love after 30.    Photop 82-2:31 Ag '72
    Public passion.    Mod Screen 66-9:30 S '72
    Their wedding.    Mod Screen 66-10:49 O '72
    Their wedding.    Photop 82-4:35 O '72
    Like a bride every night.    Photop 82-5:47 N '72
    Every night is like our first.    Mod Screen 66-12:46 D '72
    Two days without him.    Photop 83-1:32 Ja '73
    We made a terrible mistake.    Mod Screen 67-2:42 F '73
    Why they had to marry.    Photop 84-1:32 Jl '73
    Bob and I waited 15 years for our love child.    Photop 84-5:36
        N '73
    Paskin, B.    Success and Robert Wagner.    Films Illus 3-31:256
        Ja '74
    We almost died together.    Photop 85-1:50 Ja '74
    She wants a baby.    Photop 83-4:56 Ap '74
    The couple most likely.    Films Illus 3-33:331 My '74
    Baby girl.    Photop 85-6:63 Je '74
    Rules for their second marriage.    Photop 86-5:50 N '74

WAINWRIGHT, GREG
Moving on.   Playgirl 1-6:88 N '73

WAINWRIGHT, JAMES
Manners, D.   I nominate for stardom.   Mod Screen 66-10:18 O
    '72
Three inches is a long way.   TV Guide 20-53:14 D 30 '72

WAITE, GENEVIEVE
Wolf, W.   The London look in films.   Cue 37-11:10 Mr 16 '68
Evans, P.   Aren't I a lucky girl?   New York 1-35:41 D 2 '68
Gross, E. L.   Oh, Genevieve.   Vogue 155:183 Ap 1 '70
Warhol, A.   Interview.   Interview 4-8:23 S '74
Interview.   Viva 2-2:25 N '74

WAITE, RALPH
Once a preacher.   Photop 86-5:40 N '74

WAKAO, AYAKO
Richie, D.   The face of '63--Japan.   Films & Filming 9-10:15
    Jl '63

WALBROOK, ANTON
Obit.   N. Y. Times p37 Ag 10 '67
    Newsweek 70:46 Ag 21 '67
Miller, N.   Partial filmog.   Films In R 19-1:61 Ja '68

WALBURN, RAYMOND
Conlon, S.   That lovable rascal.   Screen Book 20-6:48 Jl '38
Obit.   Film R p15 '70/71
    N. Y. Times p31 Jl 28 '69
    Screen World 21:241 '70
Corneau, E.   The lovable rascal.   Classic Film Collect 43:41
    Sum '73

WALCAMP, MARIE
Marple, A.   Sketch.   Motion Pic 9:105 Jl '15
Cheating the animals.   Photop 14-5:61 O '18
Peterson, E.   Sketch.   Motion Pic 18:82 S '19
Remont, F.   Interview.   Motion Pic Classic 9:48 Ja '20

WALCOTT, GREGORY
The workaday cop.   TV Guide 10-17:7 Ap 28 '62

WALDRON, JACK
Obit.   N. Y. Times p87 N 23 '69

WALKEN, CHRISTOPHER
Stoop, N. M.   All I want to do is feel the warmth.   After Dark
    6-1:44 My '73

WALKER, CHERYL
Wilson, E.   Claudette's advice to Cheryl.   Silver S 13-10:34 Ag
    '43

WALKER, HELEN
    Obit.  N. Y. Times p43 Mr 12 '68
    Vilanova, P.  Filmog.  Films In R 21-5:319 My '70

WALKER, JIMMIE
    Barber, R.  No time for jivin'.  TV Guide 22-50:28 D 14 '74

WALKER, JOHNNY
    Obit.  Screen World 1:235 '49

WALKER, JUNE
    Obit.  Screen World 18:240 '67

WALKER, LILLIAN
    Sketch.  Blue Book 19:18 My '14
    Sketch.  Nash's 54:468 Ja '15
    How she became a photoplayer.  Motion Pic Classic 1:41 F '16
    Sketch.  Motion Pic Classic 2:29 Je '16
    How to get into moving pictures.  Motion Pic Classic 2:22 Jl '16
    Fletcher, A.  Her gowns.  Motion Pic 12:106 O '16
    Reid, J.  Interview.  Motion Pic Classic 7:37 N '18

WALKER, NANCY
    Success story.  Cue 10-46:3 N 15 '41
    Stars of tomorrow.  Lions R 1-11/12:no p# Jl/Ag '42
    Barry, I.  Nancy sports a badge.  Cue 26-41:12 O 12 '57
    Gruen, J.  Her face is her fortune.  N. Y. Times sec 2:1 O 14
        '73
        Same.  N. Y. Times Bio Ed p1731 O '73
    Raddatz, L.  She cried when they laughed.  TV Guide 22-25:17
        Je 22 '74

WALKER, ROBERT SR.
    Meet Bob Walker, Horatio Alger hero.  Lions R 2-5:no p# Jl
        '43
    Lucky Bob.  Lions R 3-2:no p# Ja '44
    See here, "Sergeant" Hargrove.  Lions R 3-3:no p# Ap '44
    You're a better me than I am.  Lions R 3-5:no p# D '44
    Pritchett, F.  Please get me straight.  Silver S 15-9:22 Jl '45
    Obit.  Screen World 3:178 '53
    Zucker, P.  Robert Walker; filmog.  Films In R 21-3:136 Mr
        '70
    Pinup of the past.  Films & Filming 19-11:62 Ag '73
    Newman, D.  People we like.  Film Comment 10-3:36 My/Je
        '74

WALKER, TIPPY
    Merrie and Tippy.  New Yorker 40:35 My 23 '64
    Miller, E.  New faces in a smash movie.  Seventeen 23:132 Je
        '64
    Rising stars.  Film R p53 '65/66

WALL, GERALDINE
  Obit.  Screen World 22:241 '71

WALLACE, BERYL
  Crivello, K.  Whatever happened to the most beautiful girls in
    the world?  Film Fan Mo 109/110:38 Jl/Ag '70

WALLACE, IRENE
  Trials of a moving picture actress.  Green Book 12:981 D '14
  Squier, E. L.  Interview.  Motion Pic Classic 13:36 D '21

WALLACE, JEAN
  Crivello, K.  Whatever happened to the most beautiful girls in
    the world?  Film Fan Mo 109/110:38 Jl/Ag '70

WALLACE, MARCIA
  Raddatz, L.  There's no such thing as a really funny fat girl.
    TV Guide 21-23:23 Je 9 '73

WALLACH, ELI
  Wallach on The misfits.  Film 29:13 Sum '61
  Hammel, F.  The Wallachs at home.  Cue 32-21:10 My 25 '63
  Robinson, D.  The day I was proudest of my wife; interview.
    Good House 167:77 Ag '68

WALLS, TOM
  Obit.  Ill Lon N 215:851 D 3 '49

WALSH, GEORGE
  Naylor, H. S.  Bio sketch.  Motion Pic 16:32 O '18
  Black, B.  Early life of.  Motion Pic Classic 8:18 Ag '19
  Bruce, B.  Interview.  Motion Pic 20:36 Ja '21
  Handy, T. B.  Interview.  Motion Pic Classic 14:36 My '22
  Carr, H.  Sketch.  Motion Pic 25:25 D '23
  Keel, A. C.  The fiasco of Ben Hur.  Photop 26:32 N '24
  Human nature the keynote of screen art.  Theatre 47:42 Ap '28
  Conley, W.  George Walsh.  Films In R 21-3:183 Mr '70
  Conley, W.  George Walsh.  Silent Pic 11/12:no p# Sum/Aut
    '71
  Slide, A.  Interview.  Silent Pic 16:12 Aut '72

WALSH, MIRIAM COOPER
  Wood, B.  Miriam Cooper Walsh.  Films In R 21-4:246 Ap '70

WALTHALL, HENRY B.
  Master emotionalist.  Movie Pictorial 2-3:14 S '15
  Sketch.  Motion Pic 10:113 O '15
  Ames, H.  Sketch.  Motion Pic 11:138 Ap '16
  Willis, R.  Sketch.  Motion Pic Classic 2:55 Je '16
  Peltret, E.  Interview.  Motion Pic Classic 7:49 N '18
  McGaffey, K.  Sketch.  Motion Pic 17:32 My '19
  Wright, J. C.  Interview.  Classic 15:66 N '22
  Donnell, D.  Interview.  Motion Pic Classic 22:40 N '25

Hill, G.  A gentleman of Hollywood.  Silver S 4-12:26 O '34
Stern, S.  Henry B. Walthall.  Film Cult 36:43 Spg/Sum '65

WALTON, DOUGLAS
   Obit.  Screen World 13:226 '62

WALTON, GLADYS
   Beach, B.  Interview.  Motion Pic Classic 12:64 Je '21
   Schallert, E.  Interview.  Motion Pic 22:72 Ag '21

WANAMAKER, SAM
   Nolan, J. E.  Films on TV.  Films In R 21-3:164 Mr '70

WARBURTON, JOHN
   Nominated for stardom.  Motion Pic 45:42 Mr '33

WARD, BURT
   Botto, L.  Interview.  Look 35:71 S 7 '71
   Raddatz, L.  Where are they now?  TV Guide 21-4:33 Ja 27 '73

WARD, DOUGLAS TURNER
   Salute of the week.  Cue 38-36:1 S 6 '69

WARD, FANNIE
   Overholt, M.  Sketch.  Green Book 16:550 S '16
   Interview.  Motion Pic Classic 4:24 Ag '17
   Courtland, R.  Interview.  Motion Pic Classic 6:35 Je '18
   Hall, G.  Interview.  Motion Pic 17:38 My '19
   Mason, L. K.  Interview.  Motion Pic 33:52 My '27
   How to be young at 60.  Graphic 121:62 Jl 14 '28
   Bio note.  Harp Baz 82:192 S '48
   Obit.  Screen World 4:178 '53

WARD, SIMON
   People are talking about.  Vogue 151:65 Ja 15 '68
   Young Winston.  Films Illus 2-13:12 Jl '72

WARDE, FREDERICK
   Beatty, J.  Perpetuate my art?  Never.  Photop 11-2:31 Ja '17

WARE, HELEN
   The Split reel.  Film Players Herald 2-7:28 F '16

WARFIELD, IRENE
   Obit.  Screen World 13:226 '62

WARNER, DAVID
   People are talking about.  Vogue 145:80 Ap 15 '65
   Edwards, S.  David Warner--after the fall.  N. Y. Times Bio
      Ed D 19 '71
   Tierney, M.  Interview.  Plays & Players 19-8:18 My '72
   Johns, L.  Talking about I Claudius.  Plays & Players 19-11:20
      Ag '72

WARNER, H. B.
His impressions of America. Green Bk Alb 3:1066 My '10
Sketch. N. Y. Dram 69:13 Ap 2 '13
Beach, B. Interview. Motion Pic Classic 8:22 Ap '19
Peltret, E. Interview. Motion Pic 18:30 N '19
If I were a manager. Theatre 38:22 Ag '23
One lives as one must. Theatre 47:14 F '28
Hall, G. Sketch. Motion Pic 37:42 Ap '29
Obit. Film R p10 '59/60

WARNER, JACK
My favorite role. Film R p20 '53/54

WARNER, JODY
The girl from Squaresville. TV Guide 9-21:29 My 27 '61

WARNER, SANDRA
Sandra's really a bookish girl. TV Guide 11-4:27 Ja 26 '63

WARREN, JAMES
Stars of tomorrow. Lions R 1-11/12:no p# Jl/Ag '42

WARREN, LESLEY (ANN)
Hobson, D. That glass slipper really pinched. TV Guide 18-40:
14 O 3 '70
Lesley Warren lives. Harp Baz 105:84 Ap '72

WARREN, MARY
Stifling the tears. Photop 14-4:39 S '18

WARRICK, RUTH
Efron, E. Establishment? Bah. TV Guide 20-3:14 Ja 15 '72

WARWICK, ROBERT
Peterson, E. Sketch. Motion Pic 12:43 Ja '17
A western Warwick. Photop 11-4:35 Mr '17
The new American face. Photop 14-5:29 O '18
Service, F. Interview. Motion Pic Classic 8:24 My '19
Gray, J. A. Experiences in the war. Photop 17:110 Ja '20
Bio. NCAB 52:190 '70

WARWICK, VIRGINIA
Goldbeck, W. Interview. Motion Pic Classic 11:63 Ja '21

WASHBOURNE, MONA
Tierney, M. Interview. Plays & Players 19-4:32 Ja '72

WASHBROOK, JOHNNY
Readin' ritin' and rehearsal. TV Guide 4-38:20 S 22 '56

WASHBURN, BEVERLY
For crying out loud. TV Guide 5-15:20 Ap 13 '57

WASHBURN, BRYANT
    How he became a photoplayer.    Motion Pic 9:115 Mr '15
    The devil a saint will be.    Photop 7-6:92 My '15
    Sketch.    Motion Pic 9:118 My '15
    Hobart, P. G.    Interview.    Motion Pic 10:105 D '15
    Courtlandt, R.    Home life of.    Motion Pic Classic 3:31 S '16
    How to get into motion pictures.    Motion Pic 12:100 S '16
    Jacobs, F. S.    On the job with Bryant Washburn.    Photop 12-3:
        23 Ag '17
    How he got into motion pictures.    Motion Pic 14:93 S '17
    McKelvie, M. G.    Interview.    Motion Pic Classic 5:36 Ja '18
    Peltret, E.    Interview.    Motion Pic Classic 7:20 D '18
    Cheatham, M.    Interview.    Motion Pic Classic 10:34 Ag '20
    Bruce, B.    Interview.    Motion Pic 20:64 N '20
    Peltret, E.    Interview.    Motion Pic Classic 14:60 My '22
    Bishop, R.    Interview.    Motion Pic 23:46 Jl '22

WASHINGTON, LAMONT
    Obit.    N. Y. Times p39 Ag 26 '68

WATERBURY, RUTH
    Slide, A.    Interview.    Film Fan Mo 141:21 Mr '73

WATERS, ETHEL
    Rhapsodies in brown.    Cue 7-4:8 N 19 '38
    Sketch.    Life 6:49 Ja 23 '39
    Green, E. M.    Work of.    Theatre World 31:84 F '39
    Green, E. M.    Her success.    Theatre World 33:139 D '40
    Sepia rhapsody.    Lions R 2-1:no p# S/O '42
    Better than a rabbit's foot.    Lions R 2-4:no p# Ap '43
    Where are they now?    Newsweek 70:14 Jl 17 '67
    Kucharsky, D.    Study in inspiration.    Chr. Today 14:44 Mr 13
        '70
    Erwin, F.    A special tribute to.    Hollywood Stu 7-7:39 N '72
    Rankin, A.    Three lives of Ethel Waters.    Read Dig 101:81 D
        '72
    Carley, C. E.    Ethel Waters.    Classic Film Collect 42:26 Win
        '73

WATERSTON, SAM
    Chase, C.    Much ado about Waterston.    N. Y. Times sec 2:1 D
        3 '72
    Same.    N. Y. Times Bio Ed p2308 D '72

WATKINS, LINDA
    Screen stars are just girls.    Silver S 1-12:24 O '31
    Sketch.    Photop 41:59 D '31
    Costello, T.    Sketch.    Motion Pic 42:70 Ja '32

WATLING, DEBBIE
    McAsh, I.    Debbie's good news.    Films Illus 3-30:232 D '73

WATSON, BOBBY
Obit.  Screen World 17:241 '66

WATSON, DEBBIE
Suddenly a star.  TV Guide 13-3:22 Ja 16 '65
Wilkie, J.  Daughter is a TV star.  TV Guide 14-7:12 F 12 '66

WATSON, LUCILE
Sketch.  N. Y. Dram 69:9 Mr 5 '13
Sketch.  Theatre Arts 25:440 Je '41
I live in the future.  Lions R 4-1:no p# F '45

WATSON, MINOR
Wood, P.  Sketch.  Theatre 50:23 N '29

WATTS, CHARLES
Obit.  Screen World 18:241 '67

WAYNE, DAVID
Asher, J.  You don't have to be handsome.  Silver S 22-6:44
   Ap '52
Lewis, E.  David Wayne of Hollywood and Okinawa.  Cue 22-47:
   17 N 21 '53
Minoff, P.  TV's newest family man.  Cue 24-1:13 Ja 8 '55

WAYNE, GARRISON
Tucker, R.  Playgirl's man for May.  Playgirl 1-12:68 My '74

WAYNE, JOHN
Goldbeck, E.  Sketch.  Motion Pic 41:76 F '31
Whitehead, H.  Sketch.  Motion Pic 53:15 Jl '37
Reid, J.  From mustangs to...  Silver S 11-1:26 N '40
Manners, M. J.  Fool-proof marriage insurance.  Silver S 12-
   11:26 S '42
Duke of Glendale.  Lions R 2-3(sup):no p# Ja '43
Wilson, E.  He's the hottest thing in pictures today.  Silver S
   14-2:26 D '43
Bangs, B.  They grew up together.  Silver S 15-12:42 O '45
Palmer, C.  Big business is his hobby.  Silver S 17-9:45 Jl '47
Parsons, L. O.  Cosmop's citation for the best performance of
   the month.  Cosmop 127:12 S '49
Barnett, B.  No overnight sensation.  Silver S 21-10:42 Ag '51
My favorite role.  Film R p30 '51/52
Cox, S. B.  The male point of view.  Silver S 23-8:29 Je '53
Zunser, J.  Conqueror at the box-office.  Cue 25-12:13 Mr 24
   '56
Failure makes good.  TV Guide 4-38:25 S 22 '56
Sarris, A.  Oddities and one shots.  Film Cult 28:45 Spg '63
Braff, R.  John Wayne; filmog.  Sound Stage 1-1:34 D '64
Barthel, J.  John Wayne, superhawk.  N. Y. Times Mag p4 D
   24 '67
Dusty and the Duke.  Life 67:36 Jl 11 '69
John Wayne as the last hero.  Time 94:53 Ag 8 '69

Thiede, K.   John Wayne; filmog.   Views & Rs 1-2:36 Fall '69
Hall, D. J.   Tall in the saddle.   Films & Filming 16-1:12 O '69
Eyles, A.   John Wayne; filmog.   Focus On F 1:8 Ja/F '70
Super father of the year.   Photop 77-5:49 My '70
Bernstein, B.   Not likely; John Wayne and True grit.   Focus
      6:3 Spg '70
I have to make an appointment to kiss him.   Photop 78-3:53 S
      '70
Reddy, J.   John Wayne rides again and again and again.   Read
      Dig 97:138 S '70
Finnigan, J.   America--a Wayne's eye view.   TV Guide 18-48:
      20 N 28 '70
John Wayne: a symposium.   Views & Rs 1-3:6 Win '70
Fernett, G.   A "Duke" with spurs on.   Views & Rs 1-3:14 Win
      '70
From the 100 finest westerns: Dark Command.   Views & Rs
      1-3:48 Win '70
Shapon, R. L.   United we fall; divided we stand.   Sat R 54:59
      Ja 2 '71
His screaming battle with his wife.   Photop 79-2:53 F '71
Playboy interviews.   Playboy 18-5:75 My '71
Still going great.   Screen Greats 1-2:78 Sum '71
Newsmakers.   Newsweek 78:39 Ag 23 '71
Wayne, J.   The company remembers Stagecoach.   Action 6-5:24
      S/O '71
Miller, E.   Do you ever think of Duke as big daddy?   Seventeen
      30:122 O '71
Wayne, P.   Wife explains the man behind the legend.   Ladies
      Home J 88:72 N '71
Wayne, P.   I never knew my father until I was man enough to
      fight him.   Photop 80-5:83 N '71
Bio note.   Films Illus 1-5:32 N '71
Two screen cowboys talk about the reel west, and the real west.
      Sr. Schol 99:10 D 6 '71
Viet Cong flag waver tries to jail John Wayne.   Mod Screen 65-
      12:48 D '71
Bio.   Brit Bk Yr 1971:161 '71
Kluge, P. F.   First and last cowboy.   Life 72:42 Ja 28 '72
How I tell my child the story of Christmas.   Photop 81-1:51 Ja
      '72
The calm years are wild.   Photop 81-3:45 Mr '72
Ditlea, S.   The giant of the west.   Show 2-1:28 Mr '72
Bentley, E.   The political theatre of John Wayne.   Film Soc R
      7-7/8/9:51 Mr/Ap/My '72
Big John meets his match.   Films Illus 1-10:30 Ap '72
Generation gap? Nuts.   Mod Screen 66-5:34 My '72
Bogdanovich, P.   Hollywood.   Esquire 77:66 My '72
Hendrickson, P. J.   The iron duke.   Sat Eve Post 244:84 Spg
      '72
Bio.   Cur Bio 33:39 Jl '72
Photoplay on location.   Photop 82-2:34 Ag '72
Ford, G.   Mostly on Rio Lobo.   Film Heritage 7-1:2 Fall '72
Riley, C.   John Wayne dethroned.   Ebony 27:127 S '72

McInerney, J.   John Wayne talks tough; interview.   Film Com-
    ment 8-3:52 S/O '72
Belton, J.   As sure as the turning o' the earth.   Velvet Light
    7:25 Win '72/73
Boyhood memories.   Photop 82-5:38 N '72
Zolotow, M.   How John Wayne learned to love TV.   TV Guide
    20-45:28 N 4 '72
Zolotow, M.   Well, there were these two fellers...   TV Guide
    20-46:34 N 11 '72
The right and the wrong way to love.   Photop 83-5:54 My '73
Rushes wife to hospital.   Photop 83-5:60 My '73
Mace, J. W.   John Wayne rareties.   Classic Film Collect 38:30
    Spg '73
Ann-Margret:   John Wayne made me more of a woman.   Photop
    83-6:60 Je '73
Gauguin, L.   With Duke down Mexico way.   Views & Rs 5-1:4
    S '73
Maureen O'Hara answers what makes John Wayne Hollywood's
    favorite lover?   Photop 84-4:45 O '73
Leider, R. A.   John Wayne supercop.   Show 3-8:46 N '73
The day the cops arrested me.   Photop 84-5:55 N '73
I won't divorce Duke.   Photop 84-6:12 D '73
Flatley, G.   Wayne never wanes.   N. Y. Times Bio Ed p2026 D
    '73
My dad.   Photop 85-2:51 F '74
Why they've split.   Photop 85-2:53 F '74
Marriage reconciliation.   Photop 85-4:32 Ap '74
Zmijewsky, S.   Greatest cowboy of them all.   Liberty 1-12:22
    Spg '74
Illness.   Photop 86-2:47 Ag '74
Waxen Wayne.   Films Illus 3-36:476 Ag '74
Marital problems.   Photop 86-5:46 N '74
Kate and Duke team up to make Hollywood history.   People 2-21:
    8 N 18 '74

WAYNE, NAUNTON
    Obit.   Film R p13 '71/72
        N. Y. Times p50 N 19 '70
        Screen World 22:241 '71

WAYNE, NINA
    Caprice Yeudleman.   TV Guide 14-11:25 Mr 12 '66

WAYNE, PATRICK
    Rising stars.   Film R p53 '64/65
    Bennett, J.   Hollywood's apples fall close to the tree.   Sound
        Stage 1-3:4 My '65
    Klemesrud, J.   Another Wayne.   N. Y. Times Bio Ed Ja 20 '71
    I never knew my father until I was man enough to fight him.
        Photop 80-5:83 N '71

WEAVER, CHARLIE
    (See:  ARQUETTE, CLIFF)

WEAVER, DENNIS
  Durslag, M.   Vegetarian on horseback.   TV Guide 18-50:32 D
    12 '70
  Eyles, A.   Bio note; filmog.   Focus On F 12:14 Win '72
  Burke, T.   Include me out.   TV Guide 21-26:34 Je 30 '73

WEAVER, MARJORIE
  Magee, T.   Sketch.   Screen Book 20-1:34 F '38
  Bio note; filmog.   Movies & People 2:37 '40

WEBB, ALAN
  Beaton, C.   In Beaton's view.   Plays & Players 19-8:36 My '72

WEBB, CLIFTON
  His makeup in As thousands cheer.   Vanity Fair 42:47 Ag '34
  Sketch.   Photop 33:30 S '48
  Maddox, B.   Smartest bachelor.   Silver S 19-8:29 Je '49
  Note.   Vogue 114:126 D '49
  Letters.   Films In R 21-3:186 Mr '70
  Note; partial filmog.   Films & Filming 19-9:66 Je '73

WEBB, FAY
  Tennant, M.   Changes her mind about getting a divorce.   Movie
    Classic 3:33 N '32

WEBB, JACK
  Dragnet catches 38 million viewers.   TV Guide 1-2:5 Ap 10 '53
  Who's doing it in the whodunits.   TV Guide 1-25:16 S 18 '53
  Why (he) wants to give up Dragnet.   TV Guide 1-37:5 D 11 '53
  Phipps, C.   Webb's electricality.   Films In R 6-10:539 D '55
  The stars of tomorrow.   Film R p43 '55/56
  The house that Jack built.   TV Guide 5-5:20 F 2 '57
  Jorgensen, P. A.   The permanence of Dragnet.   Film Q 12-1:
    35 Fall '58
  Adler, D.   I've always felt that policemen have been the under-
    dogs.   TV Guide 20-30:24 Jl 22 '72

WEBB, MILLARD
  Cruikshank, H.   Sketch.   Motion Pic Classic 29:35 Ag '29

WEDGEWORTH, ANN
  Headliners.   Photop 84-6:30 D '73

WEEKS, BARBARA
  Will they become famous stars or forgotten faces?   Silver S 2-
    2:36 D '31
  Uselton, R. A.   The Wampus baby stars.   Films In R 21-2:73
    F '70

WEEKS, MARION
  Obit.   N. Y. Times p47 Ap 22 '68
    Screen World 20:241 '69

WEHLEN, EMMY
  Sketch.  Cosmop 53:410 Ag '12
  Rise of.  Pall Mall 51:832 Je '13
  Interview.  Cosmop 58:679 My '15
  Montanye, L.  Interview.  Motion Pic 17:61 Mr '19

WEIDLER, VIRGINIA
  Rhea, M.  Interview.  Movie Classic 10:34 S '36
  Hamilton, S.  Sketch.  Photop 52:30 S '38
  Rhea, M.  Sketch.  Photop 53:31 Ap '39
  Mulvey, K.  Sketch.  Womans Home C 67:7 Ap '40
  Bio note; filmog.  Movies & People 2:37 '40
  Miss Pigtails.  Lions R 1-6:no p# F '42
  Young veteran.  Lions R 1-7:no p# Mr '42
  Franchey, J. R.  Bantam Bernhardt.  Silver S 12-7:44 My '42
  Stars of tomorrow.  Lions R 1-11/12:no p# Jl/Ag '42
  Stars for Virginia.  Lions R 2-4:no p# Ap '43
  Weidler, Mrs. M.  Life with daughter.  Lions R 3-1:no p# S
    '43
  My teenage mistakes.  Photop 25:58 Jl '44

WEISSMULLER, JOHNNY
  Benton, C.  Sketch.  Movie Classic 1:39 Ja '32
  Benton, C.  Interview.  Motion Pic 43:60 Mr '32
  Sharon, M.  Tarzan.  Silver S 2-5:18 Mr '32
  Cheasley, C. W.  His numberscope.  Motion Pic 44:33 S '32
  Janeway, D.  Divorce gossip.  Movie Classic 3:33 O '32
  Miller, M.  As a swimmer.  Photop 44:38 Jl '33
  Manners, D.  Interview.  Motion Pic 45:40 Jl '33
  Brundidge, H. T.  Sketch.  Motion Pic 49:29 F '35
  The Weissmuller way.  Lions R 1-4:no p# D '41
  Tarzan: a profession.  Lions R 1-10:no p# Je '42
  Big jocks.  Esquire 73:125 Ap '70
  Weissmuller enters franchise jungle.  Classic Film Collect 27:46
    Spg/Sum '70
  Begley, M.  Tarzan quits swinging (reprint Los Angeles Times)
    Classic Film Collect 27:46 Spg/Sum '70
  Kirshenbaum, J.  ...Umgawa.  Sports Illus 33:58 Ag 17 '70
  They made a splash.  Screen Greats 1-2:61 Sum '71
  Durslag, M.  Now he's swimming in money (mostly about Mark
    Spitz).  TV Guide 21-22:45 Je 2 '73

WELCH, NILES
  A lover--off and on.  Photop 15-2:39 Ja '19
  Cheatham, M.  Interview.  Motion Pic 29:54 D '20

WELCH, RAQUEL
  Hamilton, J.  Raquel.  Look 31:M8 Ag 8 '67
  Lewis, R. W.  Sudden stardom of Raquel Welch.  Sat Eve Post
    240:33 N 18 '67
  Larson, J.  Sea of cups.  Time 93:92 Ap 4 '69
  Hamilton, J.  Interview.  Look 33:78 Ap 15 '69
  Myra/Raquel: the predator of Hollywood.  Time 94:85 N 28 '69

Interview.   Playboy 17-1:75 Ja '70
Hamilton, J.   Raquel Welch and Mae West talks about men,
   morals and Myra Breckenridge.   Look 34:44 Mr 24 '70
The dream life of Raquel Welch.   TV Guide 18-17:14 Ap 25 '70
Making of Raquel.   Newsweek 75:91 Ap 27 '70
Ferrell, T.   Raquel Welch retrospective exhibition 1964-1970.
   Esquire 73:123 My '70
Robbins, F.   Tape to type; interview.   Photop 78-1:36 Jl '70
Knapp, D.   Through a lens darkly.   Show 1-6:63 O '70
Knight, A. & Alpert, H.   Sex stars of 1970.   Playboy 17-12:220
   D '70
Bio.   Cur Bio 32:41 My '71
   Same.   Cur Bio Yrbk 1971:436 '72
Looking for a man; filmog.   Films Illus 1-5:15 N '71
Hottest thing on wheels.   Life 72:48 Je 2 '72
A batchy, sweaty, funky life.   N. Y. Times Bio Ed p1421 Jl '72
The Kansas City bomber.   Films Illus 2-15:4 S '72
The actress is also a sex symbol.   Show 2-7:40 O '72
Hamilton, J.   Interview.   Penthouse 4-4:100 D '72
Gardella, K.   Raquel tosses us a few curves in a CBS special.
   N. Y. Daily News p75 Mr 1 '74
Watters, J.   What does an aging sex symbol do?   People 1-4:55
   Mr 25 '74
Behind the scenes with Raquel.   Photop 85-5:63 My '74
Photoplay forum.   Photop 85-6:8 Je '74

WELD, TUESDAY
Rising stars.   Film R p31 '61/62
Milne, T.   On the way up; filmog.   Focus On F 1:50 Ja/F '70
Flatley, G.   Most of all, Tuesday remembers mama.   N. Y.
   Times Bio Ed N 7 '71
Ronea, M.   If it's Monday, it must be Tuesday.   Sr Schol 99:24
   D 13 '71
MacDonough, S.   The high voltage star of A safe place.   Show
   2-11:20 Ja '72
Survival of Tuesday.   Time 99:70 My 15 '72
Hirsch, F.   Dear Tuesday, this hurts me more than it hurts you;
   letter.   N. Y. Times sec 2:9 N 26 '72
With him for a fan, does Tuesday need an enemy?   Letters.
   N. Y. Times sec 2:16 D 10 '72

WELLES, ORSON
Work of.   Newsweek 9:31 Ja 23 '37
Sedgwick, R. W.   Story of the Mercury theatre.   Stage 15:6 My
   '38
Sedgwick, R. W.   Appreciation.   Stage 15:5 Je '38
Work of.   Stage 15:30 S '38
Work of.   Life 5:58 N 14 '38
Franchey, J.   That man from Mars.   Screen Book 22-4:76 N '39
About the moving picture industry.   Stage 1:34 F '41
McEvoy, J. P.   Story of.   Vogue 98:66 O 15 '41
Welles labors over The magnificent Ambersons and emerges with
   good film but minus RKO job.   Newsweek 20:56 Jl 20 '42

Controversy with RKO. Time 40:44 Jl 20 '42
Denton, J. F. & Crichton, K. Welles' wonderland. Colliers
  112:14 S 4 '43
Talmey, A. His magic show for servicemen. Vogue 102:103
  O 1 '43
Hopper, H. Story of. Photop 24:30 D '43
Hendricks, H. Why Rita Hayworth really married Orson Welles.
  Silver S 14-2:24 D '43
Trotter, M. Prediction for 1944. Photop 24-27 Ja '44
At democratic headquarters. Life 17:27 N 20 '44
Pritchett, F. The odd Mr. Welles. Silver S 15-6:38 Ap '45
Welles, young man of 1,000 faces. Cue 15-26:9 Je 29 '46
Russell, R. Orson. Playboy 1:15 Je '54
Lewis, E. Return of the prodigy. Cue 25-2:15 Ja 14 '56
Welles, O. The scenario crisis. Int F A 1:119 '57
Welles, O. Ribbon of dreams. Int F A 2:163 '58
Stanbrook, A. The heroes of Welles. Film 28:12 Mr/Ap '61
Cowie, P. Gallery of great artists. Films & Filming 7-7:10
  Ap '61
Tynan, K. Orson Welles. Show 1-1:65 O '61; 1-2:60 N '61
Orson Welles. Film 33:12 Aut '62
The day Orson Welles frightened the world. Film Cult 27:49 Win
  '62/63
Sarris, A. Pantheon directors; filmog. Film Cult 28:2 Spg '63
Tyler, P. Orson Welles and the big experimental film cult.
  Film Cult 29:30 Sum '63
Director of the year; filmog. Int F G p15 '64
Cobos, J.; Rubio, M.; Pruneda, J. A. A trip to Don Quixote-
  land. Cahiers (Eng) 5:35 '66
Interview. Playboy 14-3:53 Mr '67
Welles on Falstaff; interview. Cahiers (Eng) 11:5 S '67
Daney, S. Welles in power. Cahiers (Eng) 11:17 S '67
Duboeuf, P. The other side. Cahiers (Eng) 11:18 S '67
Comolli, J-L. Jack le fataliste. Cahiers (Eng) 11:21 S '67
Narboni, J. Sacher & Masoch. Cahiers (Eng) 11:23 S '67
Roud, R. Memories of Resnais. Sight & Sound 38-3:124 Sum
  '69
McBride, J. Welles' Chimes at midnight. Film Q 23:11 Fall '69
Higham, C. It's all true. Sight & Sound 39-2:93 Spg '70
McBride, J. Welles before Kane. Film Q 23-3:19 Spg '70
What directors are saying. Action 5-4:30 Jl/Ag '70
Sokolov, R. A. Orsonology. Newsweek 76:64 Ag 3 '70
Beamgold, J. I never promised you a rosebud. New York 3-
  35:42 Ag 31 '70
McBride, J. Welles' immortal story. Sight & Sound 39-4:194
  Aut '70
Wilson, R. It's not quite all true. Sight & Sound 39-4:188 Aut
  '70
By Orson Welles, but where are we going? Look 34-22:34 N 3
  '70
Higham, C. It's all true. Sight & Sound 40-1:55 Win '70/71
Wilson, R. Reply to Higham's It's all true. Sight & Sound 40-
  1:55 Win '70/71

The night the Martians didn't land.   Life 70:56 B F 19 '71
Kael, P.   Onward and upward with the arts.   New Yorker 47:43
    F 20; 44 F 27 '41
Love is the word.   Making Films 5-2:5 Ap '71
Westerbeck, C. L. Jr.   All's Welles.   Commonweal 94:286 My
    28 '71
Henderson, B.   The long take.   Film Comment 7-2:6 Sum '71
Prokosch, M.   Orson Welles; filmog.   Film Comment 7-2:29
    Sum '71
Delson, J.   Heston on Welles; interview with Charlton Heston.
    Take One 3-6:7 Jl/Ag '71
What directors are saying.   Action 6-4:20 Jl/Ag '71
Goldfarb, P.   Orson Welles's use of sound.   Take One 3-6:10
    Jl/Ag '71
The professional director speaks.   Making Films 5-4:40 Ag '71
Bucher, F. & Cowie, P.   Welles and Chabrol.   Sight & Sound
    40-4:188 Aut '71
McBride, J.   First person singular.   Sight & Sound 41-4:40 Win
    '71/72
Rossell, D.   The Orson Welles complex.   AFI Report p4 O '71
Bio note.   Films Illus 1-5:33 N '71
What directors are saying.   Action 7-1:36 Ja/F '72
Ingrid Thulin comments on Welles.   Dialogue 1:2 '72
Ken Russell writes on Raising Kane.   Films & Filming 18-8:16
    My '72
Gilling, T.   The Citizen Kane book; interview with George
    Coulouris and Bernard Herrman.   Sight & Sound 41-2:71 Spg
    '72
Rubin, B.   Orson Welles and I.   J Pop F 1-2:109 Spg '72
Bogdanovich, P.   Kane meeting.   Esquire 78:99 O '72
Musel, R.   Who needed success?   TV Guide 20-48:10 N 25 '72
Shivas, M.   Guess who's coming to dinner now?   N. Y. Times
    sec 2:13 N 26 '72
    Same.   N. Y. Times Bio Ed p2083 N '72
Introductory sequence to the unproduced Heart of darkness, with
    commentary by J. Rosenbaum.   Film Comment 8-4:24 N/D
    '72
Mark Robson remembers RKO, Welles and Lewton.   Velvet Light
    10:32 Fall '73
Harding, L. S.   The night the Martians landed.   Touch 1-2:51 Jl
    '74
Hale, N.   Welles and the logic of death.   Film Heritage 10-1:31
    Fall '74
Gow, G.   A touch of Orson.   Films & Filming 21-3:23 D '74
Mills, W. E.   Orson Wells and Othello.   F Journal (Aus) 5:1
    n. d.

WELLES, REBECCA
    Picture of an actress beside herself.   TV Guide 5-31:4 Ag 3 '57
    She's a treasury of unexpected talents.   TV Guide 12-22:8 My
        30 '64

WELLMAN, WILLIAM JR.
  Wellman, W. Jr. William Wellman, director rebel.  Action 5-
    2:13 Mr/Ap '70
  Wellman, W. Jr.  Howard Hawks, the distance runner.  Action
    5-6:8 N/D '70

WELLS, CAROLE
  The horse is not the only one in clover.  TV Guide 9-48:27 D 2
    '61
  She's Mrs. Doheny.  TV Guide 15-12:11 Mr 25 '67

WELLS, JACQUELINE
  (See: BISHOP, JULIE)

WERNER, OSKAR
  Wolf, W.  New movie idol coming up.  Cue 34-30:12 Jl 24 '65
  On the scene.  Playboy 12-12:219 D '65
  Note; partial filmog.  Films & Filming 19-18:56 S '73
  Elley, D.  Bio sketch; filmog.  Focus On F 8:14 n. d.

WESSEL, RICHARD
  Obit.  Screen World 17:241 '66

WEST, ADAM
  Skow, J.  Has TV gasp! gone Batty!  Sat Eve Post 239:93 My 7
    '66
  Whitney, D.  How does one get rid of an anchor?  TV Guide 15-
    6:14 F 11 '67
  Botto, L.  Interview.  Look 35:71 S 7 '71
  Now you see 'em, now you don't.  Look 35-18:70 S 7 '71
  Catching up with Adam West.  Mod Screen 67-2:20 F '73

WEST, CHRISTOPHER
  How not to get a TV role.  TV Guide 14-31:26 Jl 30 '66

WEST, MAE
  Miss Mae West in Diamond Lil.  Dial 84-531 Je '28
  Melcher, E.  Personalities prominent in the press.  Cinema Dig
    1-6:4 Jl 25 '32
  Tennant, M.  Enters the movies.  Movie Classic 3:32 S '32
  Bell, N. B.  Mae West.  Cinema Dig 2-6:9 Ja 16 '33
  Donnell, D.  Is robbed of famous diamonds.  Movie Classic 3:25
    Ja '33
  Mae West.  Cinema Dig 2-10:11 F 20 '33
  Samuels, L.  Back to the Gay 90's.  Silver S 3-7:26 My '33
  Schallert, E.  Interview.  Motion Pic 45:32 My '33
  Chapman, J. B.  Garbo's rival.  Motion Pic 44:28 Jl '33
  Lynn, H.  How she makes love.  Photop 44:30 Ag '33
  Hall, G.  Advice to young girls in love.  Movie Classic 4:17 Ag
    '33
  Ergenbright, E. L.  Answers questions.  Motion Pic 46:54 Ag
    '33
  Ager, C.  The foundation of the 1900 mode.  Vogue 82:67 S 1 '33

Answers questions.  Movie Classic 5:28 S '33
Ray, M. B.  Sets the fashion in curves.  Colliers 92:24 O 7 '33
Sketch.  Time 22:34 O 16 '33
Troy, W.  West and the classic tradition.  Nation 137:547 N 8
    '33
Sketch.  Motion Pic N '33
Keats, P.  Sex is beautiful.  Silver S 4-1:20 N '33
Orme, M.  A sensational star.  Ill Lon N 183:978 D 16 '33
Sargent, T.  Her advice to the lovelorn.  Movie Classic 7:28
    Ja '35
Biery, R.  Her private life.  Movie Classic 5:20 Ja '34 & fol-
    lowing issues.
Hall, G.  Sketch.  Motion Pic 46:28 Ja '34
Hall, G.  What are they trying to make of her?  Motion Pic 46:
    29 Ja '34
Rush, D.  Anecdotes of bygone days.  Photop 45:60 F '34
Champion, C.  Katharine Hepburn, Mae West and sex appeal.
    Motion Pic 47:28 Mr '34
Lathem, M.  Interview.  Motion Pic 47:28 My '34
Davis, G.  Is she declining?  Vanity Fair 42:46 My '34
Mead, E.  Interview.  Movie Classic 6:28 Ag '34
French, W. F.  What price glamour?  Motion Pic 48:29 N '34
Dowling, M.  Her private life.  Motion Pic 48:32 D '34
French, W. F.  Interview.  Movie Classic 7:27 D '34
Fidler, J.  An interview.  Silver S 5-4:19 F '35
Her selection of the six most romantic men.  Movie Classic 8:
    32 Je '35
Churchill, E.  Story of.  Motion Pic 49:49 Jl '35
Chrisman, J. E.  An open letter to.  Motion Pic 50:38 Ag '35
Reply to Chrisman.  Motion Pic 50:38 S '35
Calhoun, D.  And other Mae Wests.  Motion Pic 50:39 N '35
Rhea, M.  Interview.  Motion Pic 51:50 Mr '36
Fisher, B.  Interview.  Movie Classic 10:44 Ap '36
Calhoun, D.  Interview.  Motion Pic 52:47 S '36
Criticism of acting in Go west young man.  Lit Dig 122:26 N 21
    '36
Answers questions.  Movie Classic 11:36 F '37
Her marriage.  Time 30:62 Jl 19 '37
Her radio broadcast objected to.  Time 30:30 D 27 '37
Sketch.  Life 8:63 F 19 '40
Reid, J.  She still has too much sex appeal.  Silver S 10-4:38
    F '40
Sketch.  Time 43:94 D 13 '43
Mae does right by Catherine.  Cue 13-31:8 Jl 29 '44
Story of.  Theatre World 44:11 Mr '48
The lady known as Lil.  Cue 18-6:14 F 5 '49
Fox, C.  Mae West.  Film 8:19 Mr/Ap '56
Lawrenson, H.  Mirror, mirror, on the ceiling:  how'm I doin'?
    Esquire 68:72 Jl '67
Bio.  Cur Bio 28:40 N '67
    Same.  Cur Bio Yrbk 1967:455 '68
Meryman, R.  Interview.  Life 66:60 Ap 18 '69
Roberts, S. V.  76--and still Diamond Lil.  N. Y. Times Mag

p64 N 2 '69
On the set: Mae and Myra.    Films & Filming 16-5:69 F '70
Lewis, S.   Still knocking them dead.    After Dark 11-10:16 F '70
Mae makes Myra.    Show 1-3:61 Mr '70
Hamilton, J.    Raquel Welch and Mae West talk about men,
   morals and Myra.    Look 34:44 Mr 24 '70
Beaton, C.   Unconquerable Mae.    Vogue 155:130 Je 1 '70
Hair-raising stories from the stars.    Photop 78-2:50 Ag '70
Efron, E.    Television should be censored.    TV Guide 18-34:16
   Ag 22 '70
I'm no angel.    Views & Rs 2-1:3 Sum '70
She done him wrong.    Views & Rs 2-2:5 Fall '70
Braun, E.    Doing what comes naturally.    Films & Filming 17-1:
   27 O '70
Braun, E.    One for the boys; filmog.    Films & Filming 17-2:
   38 N '70
Summers, M.    Mae West's back.    Filmograph 1-3:29 '70
Interview.    Playboy 18-1:73 Ja '71
Goin' to town.    Views & Rs 2-4:4 Spg '71
Klondike Annie.    Views & Rs 3-1:5 Sum '71
Good girl, bad girl.    Screen Greats 1-2:65 Sum '71
Night after night.    Views & Rs 3-2:5 Fall '71
Belle of the nineties.    Views & Rs 2-3:14 Win '71
Filmog.    Films & Filming 18-9:16 Je '72
Eyman, W. S.    Hollywood isn't dead...it's just taking a siesta.
   Take One 4-1:19 S/O '72
Mellen, J. What Mae West really meant was...    MS 1-5:46 N
   '72
Tuska, J.    Interlude: Mae West on radio.    Views & Rs 4-2:4
   Win '72
W. C. Fields and Mae West.    Nostalgia Illus 1-1:40 N '74
Huston, A. & Lester, P.    Interview.    Interview 4-12:12 D '74

WESTERFIELD, JAMES
   Obit.    N.Y. Times p38 S 23 '71
      Same.    N.Y. Times Bio Ed S 23 '71
      Screen World 23:240 '72

WESTLEY, HELEN
   Bird, C.    An actress who plays unusual women.    Theatre 36:72
      Ag '22
   Sketch.    Theatre 42:18 O '25
   Obit.    Cur Bio '43
      Newsweek 20:4 D 21 '42
      Time 40:80 D 21 '42

WESTMAN, NYDIA
   Obit.    Classic Film Collect (reprint Los Angeles Herald-Examin-
      er) 27:60 Spg/Sum '70
      Screen World 22:241 '71

WESTON, JACK
   Him an actor?    TV Guide 10-28:10 Jl 14 '62

Clein, H.   The real people:  featuring Hollywood's new breed of
character actors.   Show 1-8:14 Jl 9 '70

WESTOVER, WINIFRED
Lamb, G.   Interview.   Motion Pic 20:68 D '20
Hall, G.   Interview.   Motion Pic Classic 13:48 S '21
St. Johns, A. R.   Bill Hart's bride.   Photop 21:46 Ap '22
Cheatham, M.   Interview.   Motion Pic 23:36 Je '22
Kingsley, G.   Sketch.   Motion Pic 35:31 Mr '28

WEXLER, JODI
English, M.   That magnificent girl in The love machine.   Look
35:31 Ag 10 '71

WHALEN, ARLEEN
Smithson, E. J.   Cinderella girl--1938 style.   Screen Book 20-
5:39 Je '38

WHALEN, MICHAEL
Liza.   The eligible heart-breakers.   Silver S 6-9:51 Jl '36
Sketch.   Photop 50:78 Ag '36
Lieber, E.   Story of.   Motion Pic 52:42 N '36
Walker, W. G.   Lady luck smiles. Silver S 7-5:30 Mr '37
Smithson, E. J.   Luck of the Irish.   Screen Book 20-4:44 My '38

WHEELER, BERT
Manners, D.   His sob story.   Motion Pic Classic 31:29 Ap '30
Grant, J.   Partnership with R. Woolsey broken.   Movie Classic
2:34 Ag '32
Obit.   N. Y. Times p44 Ja 19 '68
Newsweek 71:75 Ja 29 '68
Screen World 20:241 '69
Time 91:63 Ja 26 '68

WHELAN, TIM
Funny business.   Lions R 3-2:no p# Ja '44
Obit.   Screen World 9:226 '58

WHITAKER, JOHNNY
See, C.   A family is a family is a family.   TV Guide 17-22:18
My 31 '69
Fitzgerald, R.   For Buffy and Jody two very special rooms.
House B 112:37 D '70

WHITE, ALICE
Harper, G.   Sketch.   Motion Pic Classic 25:54 My '27
Cummings, A.   Interview.   Motion Pic 35:41 F '28
Biery, R.   Interview.   Motion Pic 36:44 D '28
Belfrage, C.   Interview.   Motion Pic 37:48 Je '29
Manners, D.   Interview.   Motion Pic Classic 29:27 Ag '29
Manners, D.   Interview.   Motion Pic Classic 31:38 Mr '30
Ramsey, W.   Interview.   Motion Pic Classic 31:24 My '30
Fender, R.   Sketch.   Photop 39:54 Ja '31

Hall, G.  Interview.  Motion Pic 45:60 Mr '33
Miller, L.  Sketch.  Movie Classic 4:44 Ag '33
Lee, S.  Interview.  Motion Pic 47:60 Mr '34
Minton, E.  Considering some surviving films of two 'lost' stars.
 Filmograph 1-2:21 '70

WHITE, BETTY
 Watch those scales.  TV Guide 6-7:24 F 15 '58
 The orangutan upstaged Jimmy Stewart.  TV Guide 19-49:43 D 4
 '71
 Back in the club.  TV Guide 22-29:10 Jl 20 '74

WHITE, CAROL
 People are talking about.  Vogue 151:84 Mr 15 '68
 Wolf, W.  The London look in films.  Cue 37-11:10 Mr 16 '68

WHITE, JACQUELINE
 Stars of tomorrow.  Lions R 1-11/12:no p# Jl/Ag '42
 From college to comedy.  Lions R 2-4:no p# Ap '43

WHITE, JESSE
 He's the champion 10-percenter.  TV Guide 4-42:28 O 20 '56

WHITE, MARJORIE
 Manners, D.  Interview.  Motion Pic Classic 31:48 Jl '30

WHITE, PAT
 Who needs Hollywood?  TV Guide 4-25:16 Je 23 '56

WHITE, PAULINE
 Reynolds, R.  When Pauline had her perils.  8mm Collect 2:3
 S 24 '62

WHITE, PEARL
 Interview.  Cosmop 57:262 Jl '14
 Work of in photoplays.  Nash & Pall Mall 55:74 Mr '15
 Sketch.  Motion Pic 11:132 F '16
 Ames, H.  Sketch.  Motion Pic Classic 2:50 Je '16
 Meriden, O.  Work of.  Theatre 24:35 Jl '16
 Wade, P.  Sketch.  Motion Pic Classic 3:65 Ja '17
 Putting it over.  Motion Pic 13:61 F '17
 Naylor, H. S.  Filming The house of hate.  Motion Pic 15:45
 My '18
 Smith, F. J.  Interview.  Motion Pic Classic 7:16 Ja '19
 Bruner, F. V.  Sketch.  Motion Pic 17:32 Jl '19
 Fletcher, A. W.  Interview.  Motion Pic 21:28 F '21
 Montanye, L.  Interview.  Motion Pic Classic 13:16 Ja '22
 Sketch.  Photop 27:76 Mr '25
 The Pearl White of 1926.  Motion Pic Classic 22:57 F '26
 Sketch.  Photop 27:76 Mr '25
 Story of the original star of The perils of Pauline.  Life 21:75
 Jl 1 '46
 Modern Perils of Pauline dramatizes life story of Pearl White.

Cue 16-23:14 Je 7 '47
Dino, T.   The heroine of the cliffs.   8mm Collect 14:13 Spg '66
Mackenzie, D.   Pearl White.   Classic Film Collect 26:6 Win '70
Lochbiler, D.   Hiss the villain, cheer pearl (reprint Detroit
News)   Classic Film Collect 26:ex 4 Win '70

WHITE, RUTH
    Obit.   Brit Bk Yr 1970:591 '70
    N. Y. Times p53 D 4 '69
    Newsweek 74:118 D 15 '69
    Screen World 21:241 '70

WHITE, SHEILA
    Morley, S.   A dame at the Duchess; interview.   Plays & Players
        17-1:41 O '69

WHITE, THELMA
    Preston, H.   Thelma White.   Films In R 16-9:589 N '65

WHITELEY, JON
    Rising star.   Film R p106 '52/53

WHITFIELD, ANNE
    Penelope is now growing up--and how.   TV Guide 17-21:40 My
        24 '69

WHITFIELD, JORDAN
    Obit.   Screen World 19:241 '68

WHITING, BARBARA
    Jensen, M. S.   Letter; filmog.   Films In R 22-5:320 My '71

WHITING, JACK
    Goldbeck, E.   Sketch.   Motion Pic 41:84 F '31
    Sketch.   Theatre World 24:84 Ag '35
    Obit.   Screen World 13:226 '62

WHITING, LEONARD
    People are talking about.   Vogue 150:88 Ag 1 '67
    Miller, E.   Love is the sweetest thing.   Seventeen 27:83 Ja '68
    Whiting, it's your A levels or this acting.   Films Illus 4-39:112
        N '74

WHITMORE, JAMES
    MacNeil, N.   Old cowhand, Will Rogers USA, at Washington's
        Ford's Theater.   Time 96:76 S 28 '70
    Shayon, R. L.   Resurrection of a poet lariat.   Sat R 55:22 Ap
        1 '72

WHITNEY, CLAIRE
    Sketch.   Motion Pic Classic 5:43 N '17
    Fletcher, A. W.   Interview.   Motion Pic 19:54 Mr '20
    Obit.   Screen World 21:241 '70
    Briggs, R.   Partial filmog.   Films In R 22-4:248 Ap '71

WHITNEY, ELEANORE
  Sketch.  Movie Classic 10:7 Je '36
  Schwarzkopf, J.  Sketch.  Motion Pic 51:17 Jl '36

WHITTY, MAY
  Great Dame.  Lions R 1-9:no p# My '42
  Golden romance.  Lions R 3-1:no p# S '43
  Pinup Dame.  Lions R 3-3(sup):no p# Ap '44
  Bio sketch.  Harper 79:128 O '45
  Obit.  Ill Lon N 212:641 Je 5 '48

WHORF, RICHARD
  Success story.  Cue 10-44:33 N 1 '41
  The persistent Mr. Whorf.  Lions R 2-4:no p# Ap '43
  Hamilton, S.  Sketch.  Photop 23:35 Je '43
  Whorf, R.  As I see them.  Lions R 3-2:no p# Ja '44
  Richard Whorf of the movies.  Cue 13-50:13 D 9 '44
  Versatile guy.  Lions R 4-1:no p# F '45
  Whorf, R.  Cronyn's a character.  Lions R 4-1:no p# F '45
  The Beverly what?  TV Guide 12-3:12 Ja 18 '64

WHYTE, DONN
  Stoop, N. M.  Two for the show.  After Dark 5-9:24 Ja '73

WICKES, MARY
  Stanke, D.  Mary Wickes; filmog.  Film Fan Mo 147:3 S '73

WICKI, BERNHARD
  Zurback, W.  From actor to director.  Film J (Aus) 15:60 Mr
    '60
  Wicki, B.  Lesson of the hate makers.  Films & Filming 8-7:11
    Ap '62
  Bean, R.  The face of '63--Germany.  Films & Filming 9-9:41
    Je '63
  Three enterprising filmmakers.  Int F G 1:96 '64

WIDDECOMBE, WALLACE
  Obit.  N. Y. Times p45 Jl 16 '69

WIDDOES, KATHLEEN
  Berkvist, R.  She'll do Much ado on TV.  N. Y. Times sec 2:19
    Ja 28 '73
  Same.  N. Y. Times Bio Ed p191 Ja '73

WIDMARK, RICHARD
  Kilgallen, D.  Sketch.  Photop 34:28 Ja '49
  Widmark, J.  The man I married.  Silver S 19-3:28 Ja '49
  Graham, S.  Sketch.  Photop 35:64 My '49
  Note.  Harp Baz 83:81 Je '49
  Maddox, B.  Not quite the same fellow.  Silver S 21-5:46 Mr
    '51
  Maddox, B.  The way to understand men.  Silver S 24-4:52 F
    '54

Interview.   Cinema (BH) 2-5:21 Mr/Ap '65
Simon, J. S.   Richard Widmark; filmog.   Films In R 22-1:1 Ja
    '71
Letters in response to Simon.   Films In R 22-2:117 F '71
Adler, D.   The private life of Richard Widmark is private.
    N. Y. Times sec 2:17 Mr 7 '71
    Same.   N. Y. Times Bio Ed Mr 7 '71
  Adler, D.   He lives by Bogart's law.   TV Guide 21-23:28 Je 9
    '73
A guy who survives the hard way.   Photop 84-4:55 O '73

WIECK, DOROTHEA
    Spensley, D.   Sketch.   Motion Pic 45:53 Jl '33
    Parsons, H.   There is only one Dorothea.   Silver S 4-5:47 Mr
        '34
    Sketch.   Movie Classic 6:6 Mr '34
    Goldbeck, E.   Denies rumors of Nazi ties.   Movie Classic 6:41
        Je '34

WILBUR, CRANE
    Autobiographical.   Motion Pic 10:97 O '15
    How to get into moving pictures.   Motion Pic Classic 3:57 S '16
    Poppe, H.   Sketch.   Motion Pic 13:41 My '17
    How to get into moving pictures.   Motion Pic 14:75 D '17
    Poppe, H.   Sketch.   Motion Pic 14:38 D '17
    Smith, F. J.   Interview.   Motion Pic Classic 9:25 D '19
    Leon, S.   Crane Wilbur.   Films In R 23-1:64 Ja '72
    Obit.   Classic Film Collect 41:53 Win '73

WILCOXON, HENRY
    Ergenbright, E. L.   Appreciation.   Motion Pic 48:58 N '34
    Samuels, L.   An artist in armor.   Silver S 5-12:51 O '35
    Sherwin, T.   Interview.   Motion Pic 50:42 Ja '36
    Sketch.   Photop 49:84 Ap '36
    Maltin, L.   Henry Wilcoxon interview; filmog.   Film Fan Mo
        104:3 F '70
    Pinup of the past.   Films & Filming 17-10:70 Jl '71

WILD, JACK
    The 14.   Films Illus 1-16:17 O '72

WILDE, CORNEL
    Ames, A.   A name to remember.   Silver S 15-3:32 Ja '45
    Should a woman tell her age?   Photop 28:52 Ap '46
    Maddox, B.   Success is no cinch.   Silver S 17-7:35 My '47
    Pritchett, F.   Cornel speaks out.   Silver S 18-8:24 Je '48
    Asher, J.   At last I've stopped simmering.   Silver S 22-2:24 D
        '51
    Asher, J.   I wanted revenge.   Silver S 23-2:26 D '52
    Guy, R.   Africa goes Wilde; interview.   Cinema (BH) 3-1:44 D
        '65
    Coen, J.   Producer/director; filmog.   Film Comment 6-1:52
        Spg '70

Gow, G.  Survival; interview; filmog.  Films & Filming 17-1:4
O '70
What directors are saying.  Action 6-3:28 My/Je '71
The professional director speaks.  Making Films 5-4:40 Ag '71
Directing filmog.  Films & Filming 18-11:60 Ag '72

WILDE, LEE and LYN
Double trouble.  Lions R 3-3:no p# Ap '44
Where are Lee and Lyn Wilde?  Movie Dig 1-4:17 Jl '72

WILDER, GENE
Happy peasant.  Time 96:44 Jl 20 '70
Eyles, A.  Bio sketch; filmog.  Focus On F 8:9 n. d.

WILDING, MICHAEL
My favorite role.  Film R p19 '50
Parsons, L. O.  Cosmop's citation for the best supporting per-
formance of month.  Cosmop 127:13 O '49
Balling, F. D.  Overseas charmer.  Silver S 21-11:36 S '51
Baer, M. M.  Heart to heart talk with Liz.  Silver S 22-7:26
My '52
Rogers, V.  The Liz Taylor-Michael Wilding rumors.  Silver S
24-5:31 Mr '54

WILKERSON, GUY
Bio note.  Cinema Trails 2:21 n. d.
Obit.  Screen World 23:240 '72

WILKINSON, LESLIE
Obit.  N. Y. Times p34 D 29 '71

WILLIAM, WARREN
Willis, B.  The newest screen lover.  Movie Classic 1:59 S '31
Keen, J. H.  Personalities prominent in the press.  Cinema
Dig 1-2:4 My 30 '32
Hall, G.  Sketch.  Movie Classic 2:52 My '32
Jones, C. B.  Warren William.  Cinema Dig 2-11:11 F 27 '33
Donnell, D.  How he escapes from the make-believe of acting.
Motion Pic 47:74 My '34
Home of.  Movie Classic 11:38 D '36

WILLIAMS, BILL
Parsons, L. O.  Cosmop's citation for the best supporting role
of the month.  Cosmop 120:71 Mr '46
Palmer, C.  When dreams come true.  Silver S 16-11:60 S '46

WILLIAMS, BILLY DEE
My son and I have no secrets from each other.  Mod Screen 67-
1:53 Ja '72
Pile, S., Walsh, E. & Moran, J.  Interview.  Interview 32:8
My '73

WILLIAMS, BUD
    Thomson, B.  Interview.  Classic Film Collect 16:45 Fall '66

WILLIAMS, CINDY
    Bio note; filmog.   Focus On F 17:9 Spg '74

WILLIAMS, CLARA
    Bio note.  Silent Pic 14:21 Spg '72

WILLIAMS, CLARENCE III
    Riley, J.  How I feel about being black and playing a cop and
       blah, blah, blah.  TV Guide 18-9:20 F 28 '70
    Robinson, L.  Star couple.  Ebony 25:142 Mr '70
    Robbins, F.  Tape to type; interview.  Photop 77-2:22 Ag '70

WILLIAMS, EARLE
    Williams, E.  Sweethearts.   Photop 7-6:44 My '15
    Brodie, A. D.  Interview.  Motion Pic 10:97 N '15
    Owens, H.  Sketch.  Green Book 16:372 Ag '16
    Briscoe, J.  Sketch.  Motion Pic 12:57 N '16
    Dickinson, D.  Sketch.  Motion Pic 4:28 Ag '17
    Sketch.  Motion Pic 14:84 O '17
    How he got in moving pictures.  Motion Pic 14:107 O '17
    Pike, C.  Getting down to brass tacks.  Photop 13-2:61 Ja '18
    Autobiography.  Motion Pic 15:55 Je '18
    Norton, H.  Sketch.  Motion Pic 16:91 Ja '19
    Remont, F.  Interview.  Motion Pic Classic 8:36 My '19
    Hall, G.  Interview.  Motion Pic 19:48 Mr '20
    Cheatham, M.  Interview.  Motion Pic 23:68 Je '22

WILLIAMS, EDY
    Koch, M.  Interview.  Interview 19:22 F '72
    A show trio.  Show 2-1:34 Mr '72
    Williams, E.  Letter.  Show 2-7:4 O '72
    Pile, S., Moran, J. & Close, P. T.  Interview.  Interview 34:
       16 Jl '73

WILLIAMS, EMLYN
    Sketch.  Theatre World 19:218 My '33
    Sketch.  Theatre World 24:34 Jl '35
    Hast, N.  Sketch.  Theatre World 24:125 S '35
    Sketch.  Theatre World 24:34 Ja '37
    Sketch.  Theatre World 30:179 O '38
    Appreciation.  Theatre World 34:80 Ap '41
    Johns, E.  Sketch.  Theatre World 35:55 S '41
    Johns, E.  Playwright par excellence.  Theatre World 39:7 S '43
    Jacobson, R.  Williams as Thomas.  Sat R 53:74 Ap 25 '70

WILLIAMS, ESTHER
    Stars of tomorrow.  Lions R 1-11/12:no p# Jl/Ag '42
    She's in the swim, now.  Lions R 2-3:no p# D '42
    Sketch.  Life 16:62 Ap 17 '44
    Franchey, J. R.  She wouldn't say yes.  Silver S 14-8:44 Je '44

Splashing to stardom.  Lions R 3-4:no p# Jl '44
Sketch.  Photop 25:52 N '44
Holliday, K.  Story of.  Photop 26:40 Ja '45
Story of.  Photop 28:34 D '45
York, C.  Her marriage.  Photop 28:6 F '46
What changed my life.  Photop 28:61 My '46
Pritchett, F.  Sketch.  Photop 29:42 S '46
If I had one wish.  Photop 29:61 O '46
Gage, E. W.  The man I married.  Silver S 17-11:34 S '47
Mulvey, K.  Her living room barbecue.  Photop 33:64 O '48
Gwynn, E.  Models a new style of hat.  Photop 34:64 D '48
Bruce, J.  The beliefs I really live by.  Silver S 19-5:34 Mr
    '49
Lane, F.  Nothing's impossible to Esther.  Silver S 22-11:24 S
    '52
Tildesley, A. L.  Another woman in the house.  Silver S 24-6:
    29 Ap '54
Pratt, W. J.  Esther Williams; filmog.  Screen Facts 21:5 n. d.
They made a splash.  Screen Greats 1-2:61 Sum '71

WILLIAMS, GRANT
    Private eye with the nimble tongue.  TV Guide 10-6:15 F 10 '62

WILLIAMS, GUINN "BIG BOY"
    Cruikshank, H.  Sketch.  Motion Pic Classic 29:63 My '29
    Comeback for Big Boy.  TV Guide 4-36:16 S 8 '56

WILLIAMS, GUY
    Zorro foiled his rivals.  TV Guide 6-17:24 Ap 26 '58
    Fessier, M. Jr.  When Guy hisses the villain--he means it.
    TV Guide 14-39:24 S 24 '66

WILLIAMS, HUGH
    Obit.  Brit Bk Yr 1970:591 '70
        Film R p15 '70/71
        N. Y. Times p47 D 8 '69
        Screen World 21:241 '70
    Partial filmog.  Films & Filming 19-4:58 Ja '73

WILLIAMS, JOYCE
    Ryan O'Neil dumps Streisand for black actress.  Photop 80-6:27
        D '71

WILLIAMS, KATHERINE
    Uselton, R. A.  The Wampus baby stars.  Films In R 21-2:73
        F '70

WILLIAMS, KATHLYN
    Sketch.  Blue Book 19:13 My '14
    Edwards, G.  Kathlyn unafraid.  Movie Pictorial 2-3:8 S '15
    Sketch.  Motion Pic Classic 2:34 Mr '16
    Ames, H.  Home of.  Motion Pic 11:89 Jl '16
    How to get in moving pictures.  Motion Pic 12:61 N '16

Burgess, B.   The lady of lions reconsiders.   Photop 11-2:138
   Ja '17
Schmid, P. G.   Interview.   Motion Pic Classic 3:32 Ja '17
Delvigne, D.   Interview.   Motion Pic 19:58 F '20
Carter, A.   Interview.   Motion Pic 22:53 Ag '21
Lake, M.   Interview.   Motion Pic Classic 13:51 N '21
Home of.   Classic 16:34 My '23
Bio note.   8mm Collect 10:6 Win '64

WILLIAMS, RHYS
   Obit.   N. Y. Times p39 My 29 '69
      Screen World 21:241 '70

WILLIAMS, SCOTT T.
   (Also known as Chief Thunder Cloud)
   Obit.   Screen World 19:241 '68

WILLIAMS, VAN
   Raddatz, L.   Banker with a sting.   TV Guide 14-44:20 O 29 '66

WILLIAMSON, FRED
   Durslag, M.   Williamson may have a big head, but it isn't
      empty.   TV Guide 18-52:15 D 26 '70
   Klemesrud, J.   Don't compare me with Sidney.   N. Y. Times
      Bio Ed p527 Mr '73
   Sabio, L.   The hammer; interview.   Adam F World 4-7:33 Ag
      '73
   The hammer hits; centerfold.   Playgirl 1-5:74 O '73
   Hoffman, L.   Super Fred T. N. T.   Show 3-7:52 O '73
   Fred the hammer makes a deal with ABC and a girl.   People
      2-5:46 Jl 29 '74

WILLIAMSON, NICOL
   Drinking man's actor.   Time 86:53 D 17 '65
   Where violence happens.   Newsweek 66:69 D 27 '65
   Member of the company.   Time 93:74 F 28 '69
   Hewes, H.   Fresh Hamlet.   Sat R 52:58 Ap 12 '69
   Sokolov, R. A.   Angry young Hamlet.   Newsweek 73:119 My 12
      '69
   Salute of the week.   Cue 38-20:1 My 17 '69
   Clurman, H.   Theatre.   Nation 208:643 My 19 '69
   People are talking about.   Vogue 154:102 Jl '69
   Maddocks, M.   Mod Hamlet.   Atlantic 224:132 O '69
   Bio.   Cur Bio 31:45 Ja '70
      Same.   Cur Bio Yrbk 1970:449 '71
   Enlivening the gray.   Time 95:20 Mr 30 '70
   Bio.   Brit Bk Yr 1970:166 '70
   Tynan, K.   Are you the entertainment?   New Yorker 47:35 Ja
      15 '72
   Gow, G.   Interview.   Plays & Players 21-1:20 O '73
   Berkvist, R.   The new Nicol, or the tiger tamed.   N. Y. Times
      sec 2:1 Je 24 '73
      Same.   N. Y. Times Bio Ed p1066 Je '73

WILLIS, PAUL
   Paul is quite some actor.   Photop 12-3:113 Ag '17

WILLS, CHILL
   Sergeant softie.   Lions R 3-3:no p# Ap '44
   Chill gets hot.   Lions R 3-4(sup):no p# Jl '44
   Amata, C.   Interview.   Classic Film Collect 43:32 Sum '74

WILSON, ALEX
   Stoop, N. M.   The God next door.   After Dark 5-10:32 F '73

WILSON, BILLY
   Hasty pudding a la Broadway.   Ebony 24:134 Mr '69

WILSON, CAREY
   He's Nostradamus.   Lions R 1-8:no p# Ap '42

WILSON, CLARENCE
   Maltin, L.   Our gang; Our gang filmog.   Film Fan Mo 66:3 D
      '66

WILSON, DEMOND
   Adler, D.   Look what they found in a junkyard.   TV Guide 20-
      20:28 My 13 '72
   Robinson, L.   Sanford and son.   Ebony 27:52 Jl '72
   Young, J. R.   Include him out.   TV Guide 22-40:21 O 5 '74

WILSON, DENNIS
   On the road with the new Hollywood.   Show 2-1:16 Mr '71

WILSON, DOROTHY
   Sketch.   Motion Pic 44:42 O '32
   Sharon, M.   Lucky Wilson.   Silver S 2-12:20 O '32
   Dowling, M.   Sketch.   Movie Classic 6:16 Mr '34
   Uselton, R. A.   The Wampus baby stars.   Films In R 21-2:73
      F '70

WILSON, FLIP
   Boe, E.   The making of a comic.   Cue 36-48:18 D 2 '67
   Pierce, P.   All flip over Flip.   Ebony 23:64 Ap '68
   Flipping it.   Newsweek 72:85 Ag 12 '68
   Bio.   Cur Bio 30:41 N '69
      Same.   Cur Bio Yrbk 1969:454 '70
   Higgins, R.   Black can be beautifully funny.   TV Guide 18-3:36
      Ja 17 '70
   I don't care if you laugh.   Time 96:71 O 19 '70
   Robinson, L.   Evolution of Geraldine.   Ebony 26:176 D '70
   Davidson, B.   Likability.   TV Guide 19-4:20 Ja 23 '71
   Davidson, B.   Many faces of Flip Wilson.   Good House 172:15
      Ap '71
   Flip!   Photop 79-4:73 Ap '71
   A woman has to love him.   Photop 80-3:60 S '71
   Greenfield, J.   My life is my own.   N. Y. Times Bio Ed N 14

762 Motion Picture Performers

'71
Whitney, D. I'm on the case. TV Guide 20-2:20 Ja 8 '72
When you're hot, you're hot. Time 99:56 Ja 31 '72
Hitchhikers. Be on the lookout for this man. Photop 81-1:72
Ja '72
Feather, L. Interview. Penthouse 3-5:36 Ja '72
How Geraldine taught Flip to respect women. Mod Screen 66-2:
26 F '72
What Flip wants his fans to know. Mod Screen 66-7:31 Jl '72
Brome, G. O. Geraldine? She isn't so flip. N.Y. Times sec
2:11 S 3 '72
Graustark, B. Funny has no color. Show 2-6:44 S '72
Righter, C. Star of the month; horoscope. Mod Screen 66-12:
62 D '72
The best Christmas of my life. Photop 83-1:27 Ja '73
You fathered my baby. Mod Screen 67-2:55 F '73
Paternal charge. Photop 83-2:30 F '73

WILSON, LILLIAN BROWN
Obit. N.Y. Times p47 Je 11 '69

WILSON, LOIS
Gaddis, P. Sketch. Motion Pic 13:96 My '17
Delvigne, D. Interview. Motion Pic 18:58 Ag '19
Goldbeck, E. Interview. Motion Pic 21:70 F '21
Shelley, H. Interview. Motion Pic Classic 13:32 S '21
Cheatham, M. Interview. Motion Pic 22:22 D '21
Gassaway, G. Interview. Classic 15:38 S '22
Sketch. Photop 24:53 Jl '23
Autobiographical. Motion Pic 29:26 Ap '25
Autobiographical. Motion Pic Classic 21:20 My '25
Peterson, E. Interview. Motion Pic 31:34 Jl '26
Waterbury, R. Interview. Photop 31:39 Mr '27
Hall, G. Confessions. Motion Pic Classic 29:20 Ap '29
Service, F. Sketch. Motion Pic 42:80 S '31
Bailey, K. Story of. Photop 52:25 F '38
Sketch. Photop 54:40 F '40
Uselton, R. A. The Wampus baby stars. Films In R 21-2:73
F '70
Brock, A. In appreciation of Lois Wilson. Classic Film Col-
lect 29:10 Win '70
Summers, M. Interview. Filmograph 1-4:3 '70
Lois Wilson donates material to Kent. Classic Film Collect 33:3
Win '71
Collins, W. S. Lois Wilson; filmog. Films In R 24-1:18 Ja '73
Braff, R. Partial filmog. Films In R 24-4:253 Ap '73
Slide, A. Partial filmog. Films In R 24-4:254 Ap '73
Davis, H. R. Letter; partial filmog. Films In R 24-5:310 My
'73
Braff, R. E. Partial Filmog. Films In R 24-6:382 Je/Jl '73
Lane, D. Star adopts KSU. Classic Film Collect 39:13 Sum '73
Patterson, G. G. At film revivals with Lois Wilson in attend-
ance. Filmograph 3-4:9 '73

WILSON, MARGERY
    Jordan, O.  Kentucky babe.  Photop 10-5:41 O '16
    From extra to stardom.  Motion Pic Classic 5:40 S '17
    Norton, H.  Interview.  Motion Pic 17:30 Mr '19
    Slide, A.  Interview.  Silent Pic 17:17 Spg '73

WILSON, MARIE
    Quigg, M.  A peach from the orange belt.  Screen Book 19-6:48
      Ja '38
    Sketch.  Life 5:36 Ag 29 '38
    Churchill, D.  Story of.  Stage 15:12 My '38
    Bio note; filmog.  Movies & People 2:38 '40
    Dumb like a fox.  Lions R 4-1:no p# F '45
    Marshall, J.  Little Miss Innocent.  Colliers 117:16 F 23 '46
    Obit.  Classic Film Collect 38:57 Spg '73
      Film R p13 '73/74
      N. Y. Times Bio Ed p2081 N '72
      Show 2-11:66 F '73
      Washington Post pC16 N 24 '72
    Puzo, L.  Marie Wilson; filmog.  Films In R 24-2:125 F '73

WILSON, WHIP
    Obit.  Screen World 16:226 '65

WINDOM, WILLIAM
    Raddatz, L.  The world of William Windom.  TV Guide 12-18:15
      My 2 '64
    See, C.  Windom's world.  TV Guide 17-43:30 O 25 '69

WINDSOR, BARBARA
    Coveney, M.  Playing it all up.  Plays & Players 21-1:28 O '73

WINDSOR, CLAIRE
    Goldbeck, W.  Interview.  Motion Pic Classic 12:22 Ap '21
    Gassaway, G.  Interview.  Motion Pic 22:24 S '21
    Cheatham, M.  Interview.  Motion Pic Classic 14:20 Ap '22
    Adams, E.  Her horoscope.  Photop 26:108 N '24
    Dickey, J.  Sketch.  Movie Classic 2:34 Je '32
    Uselton, R. A.  The Wampus baby stars.  Films In R 21-2:73
      F '70
    Lewis, G.  Letter.  Films In R 23-4:254 Ap '72
    Obit.  Classic Film Collect 37:59 Win '72
      N. Y. Times Bio Ed p1895 O '72
    Claire Windsor, 1897-1972.  Filmograph 3-2:47 '72

WINDSOR, MARIE
    Meyer, J.  Marie Windsor talks about some of her films.
      Filmograph 2-2:25 '71
    Meyer, J.  Marie Windsor invites me to her house.  Filmograph
      3-2:15 '72

WING, TOBY
    Sketch.  Photop 46:45 Je '34
    Schwartz, W.  Filmog.  Films In R 17-8:535 O '66

WINN, KITTY
    Klemesrud, J.  Her name is Kitty Winn, as in winner.  N. Y.
        Times Bio Ed Jl 11 '71

WINNICKA, LUCYNA
    The Polish cinema.  Film 31:25 Spg '62
    Lucyna Winnicka; filmog.  Film 60:15 n. d.

WINNINGER, CHARLES
    His career.  National 57:173 Ja '29
    His views on stage, movies and radio.  Stage 12:47 D '34
    Surmelian, L.  Stage struck.  Silver S 7-11:26 S '37
    Accent on accident.  Lions R 3-3:no p# Ap '44
    Obit.  Classic Film Collect 23:46 (reprint Washington Evening
        Star) Spg '69
        Film R p13 '69/70
        N. Y. Times p41 Ja 29 '69
        Newsweek 73:91 F 10 '69
        Screen World 21:241 '70
        Time 93:70 F 7 '69

WINONA, KIM
    Honest Injun.  TV Guide 4-12:12 Mr 24 '56

WINTER, DAVID
    Cheatham, M.  Interview.  Motion Pic Classic 12:58 Ap '21

WINTERS, DEBORAH
    Eyles, A.  Bio note; filmog.  Focus On F 9:7 Spg '72

WINTERS, GLORIA
    Love at first sight.  TV Guide 6-27:28 Jl 5 '58

WINTERS, JONATHAN
    Lownes, V.  Jonathan Winters and his purple owl.  Playboy 2:13
        N '55
    Quick, Jonathan, the flit.  TV Guide 5-13:22 Mr 30 '57
    Hip comics and the new humor; discussion.  Playboy 8:35 Mr '61
    Gill, A.  The joyous world of Jonathan Winters.  TV Guide 12-
        6:8 F 8 '64
    Frank, S.  Winters wings it.  TV Guide 13-1:8 Ja 2 '65
    Interview.  Cinema (BH) 2-6:9 Jl/Ag '65
    Efron, E.  Winters comes out of hiding.  TV Guide 17-10:16 Mr
        8 '69
    Ballard, R.  Interview.  Penthouse 5-8:89 Ap '74

WINTERS, KAY and LINDA
    (See:  COMINGORE, DOROTHY)

WINTERS, ROLAND
    Connor, E.  The 6 Charlie Chans; Charlie Chan filmog.  Films
        In R 6-1:23 Ja '55

WINTERS, SHELLEY
  Sketch.   Photop 36:18 N '49
  Holland, J.   What's good about being a bachelor girl?   Silver S
    20-1:24 N '49
  Winters steps into Harlow's shoes.   Cue 19-24:14 Je 17 '50
  Winters, S.   Next time I want to be a man.   Silver S 20-10:24
    Ag '50
  Churchill, R. & B.   Is it important to be the first girl in a
    man's life?   Silver S 22-2:22 D '51
  Maddox, B.   Gloriously in love.   Silver S 22-6:36 Ap '52
  Gassman, V.   Let me tell you about my Shelley.   Silver S 24-4:
    36 F '54
  Benedict, P.   To be or not to be.   Silver S 24-7:40 My '54
  Taylor, T.   A hatful of confidence.   Cue 25-1:14 Ja 7 '56
  Interview re The balcony.   Cinema (BH) 1-4:7 Je/Jl '63
  Noble, P.   Star of the year; filmog.   Film R p18 '64/65
  Buckley, M.   Shelley Winters; filmog.   Films In R 21-3:146 Mr
    '70
  Flatley, G.   I'm bloody but unbowed.   N.Y. Times Bio Ed Ja
    19 '71
  Davidson, B.   To find Shelley Winters, even at several hundred
    paces, you don't need radar.   TV Guide 21-1:24 Ja 6 '73
  Winters, S.   A feeling of deja vu (comment on obscenity ruling).
    N.Y. Times sec 2:11 Ag 5 '73

WINTON, JANE
  Johnstone, N.   Sketch.   Motion Pic Classic 23:43 Je '26
  Pryor, N.   Interview.   Motion Pic 36:67 Ag '28
  Cruikshank, H.   Interview.   Motion Pic 37:40 Mr '29
  Obit.   Screen World 11:225 '60

WINWOOD, ESTELLE
  Heinemann, E.   Interview.   Motion Pic 15:54 F '18
  Johaneson, B.   Interview.   Theatre 36:316 N '22
  Sketch.   Theatre 43:523 Ap '26
  Sketch.   Theatre 44:36 Jl '26

WISDOM, NORMAN
  Robinson, D.   A new clown.   Sight & Sound 23-4:213 Ap/Je '54
  Marks, L.   Top billing.   Films & Filming 1-3:11 D '54
  The screen answers back.   Films & Filming 8-8:12 My '62
  Interview.   New Yorker 42:44 D 17 '66

WITHERS, GRANT
  (Incorrectly listed as Grant WINTERS in first Volume of this
    work)
  Calhoun, D.   Interview.   Motion Pic 38:64 O '29
  Belfrage, C.   Interview.   Motion Pic 39:48 F '30
  Obit.   Screen World 11:225 '60

WITHERS, JANE
  Williams, W.   Fun for Jane.   Silver S 5-11:23 S '35
  Appreciation of her acting in Pepper.   Lit Dig 122:18 Jl 25 '36

Sheldon, D. P.    Story of.    Movie Classic 10:42 Ag '36
Sketch.    Photop 50:76 S '36
Hall, G.    Sketch.    Child Life 15:567 D '36
A letter from Jane Withers.    Child Life 16:70 F '37
Wilson, E.    Projection.    Silver S 8-8:30 Je '38
Simpson, G.    Jane raises the devil.    Screen Book 21-3:33 O '38
Her birthday party.    Life 6:82 My 8 '39
Maddox, B.    Mother confides about Jane.    Silver S 10-3:44 Ja
    '40
Bio note; filmog.    Movies & People 2:38 '40
Vallee, W. L.    Exit Miss Fixit.    Silver S 12-12:44 O '42
My teenage mistake.    Photop 25:58 Jl '44
Sable, M.    Janie gets married.    Silver S 18-3:40 Ja '48
Where are they now?    Newsweek 70:20 S 25 '67
The kids.    Screen Greats 1-2:48 Sum '71
Andrews, P.    Her career has gone down the drain and Jane
    Withers is delighted.    TV Guide 19-47:23 N 20 '71
Catchup with Jane Withers.    Mod Screen 67-1:22 Ja '72
Windeler, R.    Jane Withers is cleaning up.    People 1-15:19 Je
    10 '74


WOLFF, FRANK
    Obit.    Screen World 23:240 '72


WOLFIT, DONALD
    His achievement for the theatre in war time.    Theatre World
        34:9 Ja '41
    Williamson, A.    Tribute to.    Theatre World 37:29 Mr '42
    His production of Ben Jonson's plays.    Spectator 172:267 Mr 24
        '44
    Worsley, T. C.    Mr. Donald Wolfit.    New States 38:354 O 1 '49
    The screen answers back.    Films & Filming 8-8:12 My '62
    Obit.    Cur Bio 29:45 Ap '68
        Cur Bio Yrbk 1968:464 '69
        N. Y. Times p80 F 18 '68


WOLFSON, MARTIN
    Types and makeup in Russian theatre.    Theatre Arts 15:337 Ap
        '31
    Leningrad Theatre for the young spectator.    Theatre Arts 15:420
        My '31
    Obit.    N. Y. Times Bio Ed p1571 S '73


WOLHEIM, LOUIS
    Bird, C.    Enter the monkey man.    Theatre 36:102 Ag '22
    I prefer the movies to the stage.    Theatre 46:41 S '27
    Gilmore, F.    Interview.    Motion Pic Classic 26:25 D '27
    Gray, C.    Sketch.    Motion Pic Classic 31:70 My '30
    Horton, H.    Interview.    Motion Pic 40:77 Ja '31
    Donnell, D.    Appreciation.    Motion Pic Classic 33:36 My '31
    Collins, F. L.    Appreciation.    Good House 94:63 Ag '32
    In memoriam.    Motion Pic 45:53 Je '33
    Spears, J.    Louis Wolheim; filmog.    Films In R 23-3:158 Mr '72

WONG, ANNA MAY
Carlisle, H.   Sketch.   Motion Pic 35:41 Mr '28
Willis, B.   Returns to the screen.   Motion Pic 42:43 O '31
Rivers, A.   Fated to tragic screen life.   Movie Classic 1:39 N
'31
Teague, R. M.   Menu for Chinese dinner, American style.
Ladies Home J 65:242 O '48
Pinup of the past.   Films & Filming 17-9:98 Je '71

WOOD, EUGENE R.
Gown comes to town.   Theatre Arts 41:12 Ag '57
Obit.   N. Y. Times p32 Ja 23 '71

WOOD, JOHN
Interview.   New Yorker 43:52 N 4 '67
Ansorge, P.   Interview.   Plays & Players 20-11:26 Ag '73

WOOD, JUDITH
Screen stars or just girls.   Silver S 1-12:24 O '31
Horton, H.   Sketch.   Motion Pic 43:70 Ap '32
Sketch.   Photop 45:69 My '34
Uselton, R. A.   The Wampus baby stars.   Films In R 21-2:73
F '70

WOOD, LANA
Prevetti, F.   Problems?   I have none.   TV Guide 15-7:24 F 18
'67

WOOD, NATALIE
Chosen child of the year.   Newsweek 34:51 O 10 '49
Taylor, T.   Talented teenager.   Cue 25-36:12 S 8 '56
Rising star.   Film R p34 '57/58
Kempton, M.   Mother, men and the muse (the dilemma of the
girl next door).   Show 2-3:50 Mr '62
Nine minds in trouble.   Photop 78-3:56 S '70
I waited to have my love baby.   Photop 80-4:45 O '71
Guarded to keep husband from molesting her.   Photop 80-5:81
N '71
How Steve McQueen ended Natalie's heartache.   Photop 81-2:51
F '72
I'll never marry again.   Photop 81-4:74 Ap '72
Natalie Wood and Bob Wagner to marry again.   Mod Screen 66-
6:35 Je '72
Natalie Wood and Bob Wagner in love again.   Photop 81-6:38 Je
'72
Thanks to Natalie he's got Streisand.   Photop 82-2:32 Ag '72
Love after 30.   Photop 82-2:31 Ag '72
Public passion.   Mod Screen 66-9:30 S '72
Their wedding.   Mod Screen 66-10:49 O '72
Their wedding.   Photop 82-4:35 O '72
Like a bride every night.   Photop 82-5:47 N '72
Every night is like our first.   Mod Screen 66-12:46 D '72
Two days without him.   Photop 83-1:32 Ja '73

We made a terrible mistake.   Mod Screen 67-2:42  F '73
Why they had to marry.   Photop 84-1:32  Jl '73
Durslag, M.   Look what's happening on Stage 5.   TV Guide 21-
   46:23  N 17 '73
Bob and I waited 15 years for our love child.   Photop 84-5:36  N
   '73
We almost died together.   Photop 85-1:50  Ja '74
She wants a baby.   Photop 83-4:56  Ap '74
The couple most likely.   Films Illus 3-33:331  My '74
Baby girl.   Photop 85-6:63  Je '74
Rules for their second marriage.   Photop 86-5:50  N '74

WOOD, PEGGY
   Stage entrances.   Green Book 75:522  Mr '16
   The art of makeup.   Green Book 16:615  O '16
   Cheatham, M.   Interview.   Motion Pic Classic 9:22  O '19
   Sketch.   Photop 17:84  Ja '20
   Weaver, J. V. A.   My wife cured me.   Cosmop 77:48  N '24
   Cruikshank, H.   Sketch.   Motion Pic 38:82  N '29
   Hark, A.   Side by side with their husbands.   Ladies Home J 47:
      14  F '30
   Sketch.   Vogue 97:78  Mr 15 '41
   I remember Emma.   Opera N 35:26  F 6 '71

WOODLAWN, HOLLY
   Flatley, G.   He enjoys being a girl.   N. Y. Times Bio Ed N 15
      '70
   The Holly Woodlawn story.   Viva 1-6:25  Mr '74

WOODRUFF, ELEANOR
   Requirements for becoming a picture actress.   Blue Book 19:251
      Je '14
   Interview.   Cosmop 57:415  Ag '14

WOODS, DONALD
   Sketch.   Photop 46:72  Jl '34
   Woods, J.   Sketch.   Movie Classic 11:47  D '36
   Holland, J.   A short-short visit with Donald Woods.   Silver S
      7-9:51  Jl '37

WOODS, ELEANOR
   Manners, D.   Interview.   Motion Pic Classic 33:74  Je '31
   Parsons, H.   Interview.   Motion Pic 41:72  Jl '31

WOODS, HARRY
   Brion, P.   Filmog.   Films In R 17-6:388  Je/Jl '66

WOODVILLE, KATE
   Mrs. Macnee goes it alone.   TV Guide 16-8:38  My 4 '68

WOODWARD, JOANNE
   Zunser, J.   New star traveling fast.   Cue 26-31:11  Ag 3 '57
   Rising star.   Film R p30 '58/59

Fletcher, F.   A new Mr. and Mrs. team.   Cue 33-15:17 Ap 11
 '64
Crist, J.   The real Joanne Woodward stands up.   New York 1-
 25:54 S 23 '68
Joanne and Paul and Rachel.   Life 65:47 O 18 '68
Davidson, M.   Joanne talks about Paul; interview.   Good House
 168:72 F '69
How to set your child free.   Photop 78-3:38 S '70
Davidson, M.   Mr. and Mrs. Paul Newman.   Good House 173:85
 Jl '71
Efron, E.   The star in search of an identity.   TV Guide 19-48:
 21 N 27 '71
How they teach their children to love.   Photop 81-2:59 F '72
MacDonough, S.   The 23 faces of Eve.   Show 2-11:21 F '73
Considine, S.   The effect of Gamma rays on the Newmans.   Af-
 ter Dark 5-11:28 Mr '73
Cincinelli, R.   Tribute to Joanne Woodward at San Francisco
 Film Festival; letter.   Films In R 25-2:125 F '74
Adams, C.   Interview.   Photop 85-4:61 Ap '74
Bowers, R.   An evening with...   Films In R 25-5:314 My '74

WOODWORTH, MARJORIE
 Groomed to fill Harlow's shoes.   Life 10:54 Mr 31 '41

WOOLLEY, MONTY
 Berger, M.   Story of.   Vogue 101:53 Ja 15 '43
 Arrives at Harvard to play The man who came to dinner.   Life
 26:45 Ap 18 '49
 Obit.   Film R p32 '63/64

WOOLSEY, ROBERT
 Grant, J.   Partnership with Bert Wheeler broken.   Movie Clas-
 sic 2:34 Ap '32
 Lynn, H.   Interview.   Photop 44:45 O '33

WORLEY, JO ANNE
 Raddatz, L.   Six who bowed out.   TV Guide 20-38:23 S 16 '72

WORONOV, MARY
 Lyons, D.   Interview.   Interview 32:31 My '73

WORTH, BARBARA
 Pryor, N.   Interview.   Motion Pic 36:67 S '28

WORTH, CONSTANCE
 Proctor, K.   Sketch.   Photop 51:22 Ag '37

WORTH, IRENE
 Bio.   Cur Bio 29:35 My '68
  Same.   Cur Bio Yrbk 1968:437 '69
 Private masterpiece.   Time 95:70 Je 22 '70
 Beaton, C.   In Beaton's view.   Plays & Players 19-4:30 Ja '72

WRAY, FAY
  Spensley, D.   Interview.   Photop 31:58 Ja '27
  Carr, H.   Sketch.   Motion Pic 33:37 F '27
  Calhoun, D.   Sketch.   Motion Pic 36:58 Ja '29
  Shirley, L.   Home of.   Photop 35:64 Mr '29
  Mason, L.   No more "horror" pictures for her.   Movie Classic
    4:19 Ag '33
  Five years ago.   Photop 44:84 N '33
  Taviner, R.   Interview.   Photop 44:52 N '33
  Maddox, B.   I'm happily married.   Silver S 4-1:47 N '33
  Manners, D.   Sketch.   Movie Classic 6:33 Je '34
  Samuels, L.   A Wray of sunshine.   Silver S 4-11:23 S '34
  Secrets of the dressing table.   Motion Pic 48:60 D '34
  Craig, C.   Interview.   Movie Classic 8:36 Ag '35
  Smith, H.   Fay Wraydiant.   Silver S 5-12:32 O '35
  Walkley, J.   Traveling lady.   Silver S 6-9:34 Jl '36
  Spensley, D.   Her design for marriage.   Motion Pic 52:45 Ag
    '36
  Bio note; filmog.   Movies & People 2:38 '40
  How Fay met Kong, or the screen that shook the world.   (re-
    print from N. Y. Times) Classic Film Collect 25:22 Fall '69
  Uselton, R. A.   The Wampus baby stars.   Films In R 21-2:73
    F '70
  Pinups of the past.   Films & Filming 19-4:64 Ja '73
  Bawden, J.   The Fay Wray story; filmog.   Film Fan Mo 161:3
    N '74

WRIGHT, TERESA
  Cue says watch.   Cue 10-36:3 S 6 '41
  Hamilton, S.   Sketch.   Photop 20:52 D '41
  What, no legs?   Lions R 1-9:no p# My '42
  Reid, J.   Surprising, what?   Silver S 12-8:42 Je '42
  Service, F.   Can an average girl succeed in the movies?   Silver
    S 14-1:24 N '43
  Wilson, E.   Teresa can do no wrong.   Silver S 17-3:55 Ja '47
  Parsons, L. O.   Cosmop's citation for the best performance of
    month.   Cosmop 122:99 Ja '47

WRIGHT, TONY
  Rising star.   Film R p34 '56/57

WYATT, JANE
  Her gowns in Evensong.   Stage 10:28 Mr '33
  Gaines, W. P.   Interview.   Motion Pic 49:24 Mr '35
  Schwarzkopf, J.   Sketch.   Motion Pic 52:13 S '36
  Zeitlin, I.   Interview.   Motion Pic 53:45 Je '37
  24 hours in tyrantland.   TV Guide 7-28:15 Jl 11 '59
  Dooley, R. B.   Jane Wyatt; filmog.   Films In R 23-1:28 Ja '72

WYCHERLY, MARGARET
  Mantle, B.   Sketch.   Green Book 17:794 My '17

## WYMAN, JANE
Williams, W.   Which will win the golden apple of success?   Silver S 8-1:24 N '37
Hamilton, S. & Morse, W. Jr.   Sketch.   Photop 54:20 Mr '40
Manners, M. J.   Making a double go of it.   Silver S 11-10:38 Ag '41
Wyman, J.   Career mother.   Silver S 17-1:40 N '46
Hall, G.   Marital troubles.   Photop 32:37 F '48
Parsons, L. O.   Cosmop's citation for best performance of month.   Cosmop 125:13 O '48
Graham, S.   Sketch.   Photop 33:41 N '48
Holland, J.   Take my word.   Silver S 19-4:32 F '49
Academy Award winner of 1948.   Life 26:58 Ap 11 '49
Clayton, C.   Why Jane won't talk.   Silver S 20-7:40 My '50
Rowland, R. C.   The two-in-one girl.   Silver S 22-9:28 Jl '52
It's the sponsor who pays.   TV Guide 4-37:24 S 15 '56
Strictly business.   TV Guide 5-5:17 F 2 '57

## WYMAN, KAREN
Jobin, J.   She's just the original Karen Wyman.   TV Guide 18-10:16 Mr 7 '70
Awake and sing.   Time 96:41 Jl 27 '70
Star is born--and starts to grow up.   Life 71:64 Jl 9 '71

## WYMARK, PATRICK
Obit.   Film R p13 '71/72
N.Y. Times p50 O 21 '70
Same.   N.Y. Times Bio Ed O 21 '70
Screen World 22:241 '71

## WYMORE, PATRICE
Wymore, P.   My life with Errol Flynn.   Silver S 21-9:24 Jl '51

## WYNN, ED
Mackall, L.   Interview.   Everybodys 53:16 Ag '25
Golden, S. B.   To enter the movies.   Theatre 45:40 F '27
Thorp, D.   Interview.   Motion Pic Classic 25:43 Ap '27
Benchley, R.   Estimate.   Life 90:19 O 27 '27
Sketch.   Theatre Guild 9:32 Ja '32
McIntyre, O. O.   Sketch.   Cosmop 94:56 Mr '33
Service, F.   Interview.   Movie Classic 5:26 O '33
Autobiographical.   Am Mag 122:28 O '36
Gilder, R.   The perfect fool.   Theatre Arts 22:639 S '38
Shoes made the man.   Cue 13-40:8 S 30 '44
Perfect fool is back.   Cue 17-4:12 Ja 24 '48

## WYNN, KEENAN
Wynn, E.   My best hobby--my son.   Am Mag 122:28 O '36
Stars of tomorrow.   Lions R 1-11/12:no p# Jl/Ag '42
So's his old man.   Lions R 3-3:no p# Ap '44
What changed my life.   Photop 28:61 My '46
Hall, G.   Comic, by Freud.   Silver S 16-10:55 Ag '46

WYNN, NAN
  Hopkins, J.   Courage vs. cancer.   Good House 156:36 Ap '63
  Obit.   N. Y. Times p39 Mr 30 '71
  N. Y. Times Bio Ed Mr 30 '71

WYNNE, BERT
  Obit.   Silent Pic 14:38 Spg '72

WYNTER, DANA
  Rising star.   Film R p40 '56/57

WYNTER, GEORGINA
  Carlisle, H.   Sketch.   Motion Pic Classic 26:27 Ja '28
  Wheaton, J.   Sketch.   Motion Pic 35:74 F '28

WYNYARD, DIANA
  Albert, K.   Sketch.   Photop 38:6 O '30
  Nominated for stardom.   Motion Pic 44:42 Ja '33
  Grayson, C.   Near to stardom.   Movie Classic 4:51 Mr '33
  Melcher, E.   Screen sensation of the year.   Cinema Dig 3-5:9
    Ap 17 '33
  Sketch.   Theatre World 19:270 Je '33
  Grein, J. T.   A rising star.   Ill Lon N 185:840 N 24 '34
  Roberts, F.   Home of.   Theatre World 26:82 Ag '36
  Her flat.   Lon Studio 12:334 D '36
  Obit.   Film R p46 '64/65


YAMADA, ISUZU
  Yamada, I.   Memories of Mizoguchi.   Cinema (BH) 6-3:19 Spg
    '71

YAMAGUCHI, SHIRLEY
  Zunser, J.   Star from the East.   Cue 24-28:11 Jl 16 '55

YAMAMOTO, FUJIKO
  Richie, D.   The face of '63--Japan.   Films & Filming 9-10:15
    Jl '63

YANNE, JEAN
  Eyles, A.   Jean Yanne; filmog.   Focus On F 4:9 S/O '70

YARNELL, BRUCE
  Obit.   N. Y. Times Bio Ed p2037 D '73

YARNALL, CELESTE
  Raddatz, L.   I'm the next big star.   TV Guide 16-23:23 Je 8 '68

YELM, SHIRLEY
  The liveliest one.   TV Guide 10-51:22 D 22 '62

YORK, FRANCINE
After all, I was a roller-skating champion of the Mesabi Iron
Range. TV Guide 11-29:11 Jl 20 '63

YORK, MICHAEL
Miller, E. I've come to conquer you. Seventeen 28:168 Ap '69
Weaver, N. Modest is the word for him; interview. After Dark
12-4:19 Ag '70
Colaciello, R. Interview. Interview 20:4 Mr '72
MacDonough, S. A quiet actor dedicated to doing "good things. "
Show 2-4:24 Je '72
Williams, J. Michael York talking; filmog. Films Illus 2-19:17
Ja '73
Filmog. Films & Filming 19-10:64 Jl '73
Stoneman, E. D. Someone for everyone. After Dark 6-10:42
F '74
d'Arcy, S. Change of image. Films Illus 3-32:296 Ap '74
Gow, G. Interview; filmog. Films & Filming 20-8:15 My '74
Efron, E. Dickens performed a function now being performed
by TV. TV Guide 22-46:17 N 16 '74

YORK, SUSANNAH
Zunser, J. Package from Britain. Cue 30-37:15 S 16 '61
Lawrenson, H. Susannah York. Show 2-1:69 Ja '62
Cowie, P. The face of '63--Great Britain. Films & Filming
9-5:19 F '63
Bean, R. Will there be film stars in 1974? Films & Filming
10-10:9 Jl '64
Rising stars. Film R p59 '64/65
Elley, D. Experiences; interview. Focus On F 9:25 Spg '72
Elley, D. Wistfulness and dry hankies; filmog. Focus On F
10:42 Sum '72
Williams, J. The house of York; interview. Films Illus 2-17:
25 N '72
Calendo, J. Interview. Interview 29:36 Ja '73

YOUNG, ALAN
Shearer, L. Beloved bumbler. Colliers 128:26 O 6 '51
Three new shows. Newsweek 41:76 Mr 2 '53
Minoff, P. Pressures of video are unfair to Mr. Young. Cue
22-11:7 Mr 14 '53
The horse gets all the laughs. TV Guide 9-18:8 My 6 '61
Mister Ed comes on like Whirlaway. TV Guide 10-13:7 Mr 31
'62
Does he or doesn't he? TV Guide 13-51:24 D 18 '65
Efron, E. He's gone from Mister Ed to Don Quixote. TV
Guide 19-31:28 Jl 31 '71

YOUNG, CARLETON
Bio note. Cinema Trails 2:21 n. d.
Obit. Screen World 23:240 '72

YOUNG, CLARA KIMBALL
  Patersen, E. A.   Interview.   Motion Pic Classic 4:24 Je '17
  Her most difficult scene.   Motion Pic 15:75 My '18
  Brewster, E.   Sketch.   Motion Pic 17:54 Mr '19
  Squier, E. L.   Interview.   Motion Pic Classic 9:20 D '19
  Fletcher, A. W.   Interview.   Motion Pic 20:24 Ja '21
  Cheatham, M.   Interview.   Classic 16:32 Mr '23
  Ulman, W. A. Jr.   Interview.   Motion Pic 50:25 S '35

YOUNG, ELIZABETH
  Samuels, L.   The first American aristocrat in pictures.   Silver
    S 3-10:21 Ag '33
  Young, H. S.   Movie mother.   Delin 124:4 F; 25 Mr '34

YOUNG, GIG
  Harmetz, A.   Gig finally made it, didn't he?   N. Y. Times Bio
    Ed Ap 26 '70
  Eyles, A.   Bio note; filmog.   Focus On F My/Ag '70
  My wife had another man's baby.   Photop 79-2:59 F '71
  Buckley, M.   Gig Young; filmog.   Films In R 22-2:66 F '71
  Ringgold, G.   Letter.   Films In R 22-3:181 Mr '71
  Letters.   Films In R 22-4:245 Ap '71

YOUNG, HEATHER
  Raddatz, L.   Who'd hire a plain girl like me?   TV Guide 17-18:
    37 My 3 '69

YOUNG, LORETTA
  Cummings, A.   Interview.   Motion Pic 35:73 My '28
  Manners, D.   Interview.   Motion Pic 39:82 Ap '30
  Sketch.   Photop 38:6 N '30
  Goldbeck, E.   Interview.   Motion Pic 40:55 D '30
  Babcock, M.   Her marital troubles.   Motion Pic 41:8 My '31
  Dibble, S.   Divorced from Grant Withers.   Motion Pic Classic
    32:28 Ag '31
  Sketch.   Photop 41:39 D '31
  Ex-wife who went back to girlhood.   Silver S 2-3:60 Ja '32
  Prior, N.   Doesn't want Hollywood romance.   Movie Classic 3:
    17 F '33
  Cheatham, M.   Loretta learned her lesson.   Silver S 3-10:27
    Ag '33
  Hall, G.   Interview.   Motion Pic 46:51 O '33
  Grant, J.   Interview.   Movie Classic 6:19 Mr '34
  Sylvia's beauty helps.   Photop 46:52 Je '34
  Maddox, B.   Sparkling Loretta.   Silver S 4-10:47 Ag '34
  Walker, H. L.   I have grown up.   Silver S 4-12:49 O '34
  Hall, G.   Interview.   Movie Classic 7:27 Ja '35
  Lane, J.   Her romantic secrets.   Movie Classic 8:26 Jl '35
  Hartley, K.   Sketch.   Motion Pic 50:36 Ag '35
  Sullivan, E.   Stepping out with Loretta Young.   Silver S 5-12:20
    O '35
  Lane, V. T.   Interview.   Motion Pic 51:39 Jl '36
  Wilson, E.   Projections.   Silver S 7-4:20 F '37

Camp, D.   Sketch.   Motion Pic 53:32 Je '37
Deane, J.   The amazing change in Loretta Young.   Screen Book 20-3:30 Ap '38
Sharpe, H.   Story of.   Photop 52:60 Ag '38
Surmelian, L.   Just what is it about Loretta?   Silver S 9-9:44 Jl '39
Waxman, P.   Story of.   Cosmop 107:11 N '39
Bio note; filmog.   Movies & People 2:38 '40
Hall, G.   Recipe for happiness.   Silver S 11-7:24 My '41
Manners, M. J.   Can exciting love survive in marriage?   Silver S 13-3:26 Ja '43
Wilson, E.   Loretta tries an experiment.   Silver S 14-3:26 Ja '44
Dudley, F.   Swell people.   Silver S 15-5:46 Mr '45
My first kiss.   Photop 29:59 S '46
Watkins, W.   Patient and self-reliant.   Silver S 17-3:46 Ja '47
Colby, A.   Her blueprint for beauty.   Photop 30:70 F '47
My luckiest day.   Cosmop 122:112 Ap '47
Parsons, L. O.   Cosmop's citation for best performance of month.   Cosmop 122:66 Ap '47
Howard, M.   Learning Loretta's formula.   Silver S 17-10:27 Ag '47
Letter from Liza.   Silver S 18-3:60 Ja '48
Winner of Academy award for 1947.   Life 24:79 Ap 26 '48
Bruce, J.   If I were a teenster today.   Silver S 19-2:28 D '48
Hendricks, H.   Will you be happy ever after?   Silver S 22-8:26 Je '52
Hull, W.   Help yourself.   Silver S 24-7:46 My '54
It's the sponsor who pays.   TV Guide 4-37:24 S 15 '56
Madden, J. C.   Letter.   Films In R 20-5:322 My '69
Uselton, R. A.   The Wampus baby stars.   Films In R 21-2:73 F '70
Here's to the ladies.   Screen Greats 1-2:26 Sum '71

YOUNG, OTIS
   Hobson, D.   The odyssey of a black man in 'white man's' television.   TV Guide 17-9:18 Mr 1 '69

YOUNG, POLLY ANN
   Branch, H.   Sketch.   Motion Pic 34:72 Ja '28

YOUNG, RALPH
   Higgins, R.   The unlikely harmonizers.   TV Guide 17-30:10 Jl 26 '69

YOUNG, ROBERT
   Sketch.   Motion Pic 44:42 Ag '32
   Goldbeck, E.   Interview.   Movie Classic 3:52 O '32
   Maddox, B.   The trick is to be together.   Silver S 4-9:26 Jl '34
   Samuels, L.   Talking it over with Bob.   Silver S 5-8:52 Je '35
   Henderson, J.   Glamour is the bunk.   Screen Book 21-2:43 S '38
   Asher, J.   Home of.   Photop 53:44 N '39
   Bio note; filmog.   Movies & People 2:38 '40

Wilson, E.  Actors can be quite normal.  Silver S 11-4:24 F '41
Young ideas.  Lions R 1-1:no p# S '41
Average man.  Lions R 1-2:no p# O '41
It paid him to wait.  Lions R 1-4:no p# D '41
Average Young.  Lions R 1-6:no p# F '42
Wilson, E.  Robert has done it again.  Silver S 12-4:22 F '42
Young, B.  My husband Bob.  Lions R 2-1:no p# S/O '42
Young, R.  Kid stuff.  Lions R 2-3:no p# D '42
Kisses for Bob.  Lions R 2-4:no p# Ap '43
Evans, E.  I was an also ran.  Silver S 13-10:26 Ag '43
Not the worrying type--any more.  Lions R 3-4(sup):no p# Jl '44
Dudley, F.  Bringing up father.  Silver S 15-12:23 O '45
Hurst, T.  How's your emotional maturity?  Silver S 18-9:36 Jl
     '48
Parsons, L. O.  Cosmop's citation for best performance of
     month.  Cosmop 126:13 F '49
Young, E.  The man I married.  Silver S 19-6:46 Ap '49
Reid, L.  Just a dairy farmer at heart.  Silver S 20-10:46 Ag
     '50
24 hours in tyrantland.  TV Guide 7-28:15 Jl 11 '59
Diehl, D.  Grandfather knows best.  TV Guide 18-23:24 Je 6 '70
We didn't believe in giving religion to our children.  Photop 77-6:
     45 Je '70
Why I gave up martinis for breakfast.  Photop 78-3:68 S '70
Four times God denied me a son.  Photop 79-1:28 Ja '71
Astor, G.  TV's Dr. Marcus Welby.  Look 35-6:56 Mr 23 '71
Young's formula for staying sexy after 60.  Photop 79-4:53 Ap
     '71
Ellison, B.  Young's toughest role.  Todays Health 49:25 My '71
For 58 years I lived in a cold sweat.  Photop 79-6:60 Je '71
Schroeder, C.  TV's Dr. Welby.  Good House 172:43 Je '71
Martin, P.  Marcus Welby, M.D.  Sat Eve Post 243:58 Fall '71
Young, Mrs. R.  Bob was the most daring lover a woman could
     have.  Photop 80-5:48 N '71
Halberstam, M. J.  An M.D. reviews Dr. Welby of T.V.  N.Y.
     Times Mag p12 Ja 16 '72
Why too much love isn't enough.  Photop 81-3:48 Mr '72
Robert Young.  Photop 82-1:64 Jl '72
Why his daughter left the convent.  Photop 82-3:68 S '72
The liberalism of Betty Young.  Photop 83-4:38 Ap '73

YOUNG, ROLAND
     Hall, G.  Cigarettes and Mr. Young.  Shadowland 6-6:21 Ag '22
     Sketch.  Theatre 44:36 Jl '26
     Horton, H.  Interview.  Movie Classic 2:56 Je '32
     Seldes, G.  Sketch.  Motion Pic 49:34 My '35
     To wit--Roland Young.  Cue 13-10:9 Mr 4 '44

YOUNG, STEPHEN
     Raddatz, L.  Nobody bought 'I married a bear.'  TV Guide 17-5:
          18 F 1 '69

YOUNGMAN, HENNY
No time for comedy.   TV Guide 2-27:18 Jl 2 '54
Henny.   New Yorker 37:36 Mr 18 '61

YULE, JOE
Mickey's old man.   Time 34:46 Ag 28 '39
Obit.   Newsweek 35:59 Ap 10 '50
Screen World 2:235 '51

YUNG, VICTOR SEN
Hobson, D.   The Cartwrights never order mandarin duck.   TV
Guide 19-41:49 O 9 '71
Raddatz, L.   No. 1 son is now Master Po.   TV Guide 21-25:27
Je 23 '73

YURKA, BLANCHE
Sketch.   N.Y. Dram 75:5 My 27 '16
Row, A. W.   Interview.   Drama 18:196 Ap '28
Advice to would be actors.   Theatre 53:50 F '31
Zachary, R.   Flower maiden; interview.   Opera N 35:12 Ap 3 '71
Obit.   N.Y. Times p38 Je 7 '74
Same.   N.Y. Times Bio Ed p901 Je '74

YVES, ROBERT
Bio note.   Unifrance 45:10 D '57

ZANIN, BRUNO
Dobrin, R.   Success Italian style.   After Dark 7-7:66 N '74

ZARZO, MANOLO
Cobos, J.   The face of '63--Spain.   Films & Filming 10-1:39
O '63

ZAWADZKA, MAGDALENA
Bio note; filmog.   Focus On F 3:18 My/Ag '70

ZETTERLING, MAI
Interview at Cannes.   Cinema (BH) 2-6:39 Jl/Ag '65
Wolf, W.   Zetterling censures the censor.   Cue 35-41:12 O 8 '66
Meeting with Zetterling.   Cahiers (Eng) 6-63 D '66
Pyros, J.   Notes on women directors.   Take One 3-2:7 N/D '70
McGregor, C.   Mai is behind the camera now.   N.Y. Times
Bio Ed Ap 30 '72
Zetterling at the Olympic Games.   Am Cinematog 53-11:1277 N
'72
Women directors; filmog.   Film Comment 8-4:45 N '72
Elley, D.   Hiding it under a bushel.   Films & Filming 20-7:29
Ap '74

ZIMBALIST, EFREM
The case of a wonderful father.   Photop 79-3:60 Mr '71

ZORINA, VERA
    Sketch.   Life 4:48 My 30 '38
    Paxton, J.   Story of.   Stage 15:28 Jl '38
    Peterson, E. B.   The gay legend of Zorina.   Silver S 12-1:44 N
        '41
    Lewis, E.   Back on her toes.   Cue 23-40:12 O 2 '54
    What they are doing now.   Show 3-2:132 F '63
    Terry, W.   Dancer's composer.   Sat R 54:43 My 29 '71

ZOUZOU
    Runaway star.   Newsweek 80:102 N 13 '72
    Guerin, A.   The latest and liveliest of director Eric Rohmer's
        leading ladies.   Show 2-11:45 F '73

ZUCCO, GEORGE
    McClelland, D.   George Zucco; filmog.   Film Fan Mo 162:3 D
        '74

APPENDIX I

## ABBREVIATIONS FREQUENTLY USED

Ap - April
Ag - August

bio - Biography

D - December

F - February
filmog - Filmography

Ja - January
Je - June
Jl - July

Mr - March
My - May

O - October
obit - Obituary

N - November
n. d. - Not Dated

P - Page
Pic - Picture

R - Review
Rs - Reviews

S - September
sec - Section
sup - Supplement

## LIST OF PUBLICATIONS
## REFERRED TO IN THIS VOLUME

Action: Director's Guild of
  America
AFI Report
After Dark; Magazine of Enter-
  tainment
Afterimage
American Cinematographer
American Forum
American Heritage
American Home
American Magazine
American Mercury
American Projectionist
American Record Guide
American Scandinavian Review
American Scholar
Americas
Architectural Record
Architecture
Architecture & Buildings
Arizona Quarterly
Art In America
Atlantic Monthly
Aviation Week & Space Tech-
  nology

Better Homes & Gardens
Black Oracle
Blue Book Magazine
Bookman, The
Brighton Film Review
British Book Year
Broadcasting
Business Week

Cahiers du Cinema (Eng.)
Canadian Bookman

Canadian Forum
Canadian Magazine
Castle of Frankenstein
Catholic World
Changes
Child Life
Christian Century
Christian Science Monitor Maga-
  zine
Christianity Today
Cineaste
Cinefantastique
Cinema (Beverly Hills)
Cinema (London)
Cinema Arts
Cinema Digest
Cinema Journal
Cinema Trails
Classic
Classic Film Collector
Colliers
Commonweal
Conservationist
Contempora
Continental Film Review
Coq
Coronet
Cosmopolitan
CTVD: Cinema-TV-Digest
Cue
Current
Current Biography
Current Biography Yearbook
Current History
Current Literature
Current Opinion

Dance
Delineator
Dial, The
Dialogue On Film
Drama Review
Dramatic Mirror
Dun's Review and Modern Industry

Ebony
Editor & Publisher
Education
Educational Theatre Journal
8mm Collector
Encounter
Esquire
Etude
Everybody's Magazine

Famous Monsters of Filmland
Film
Film Collector's Registry
Film Comment
Film Culture
Film Dope
Film Fan Monthly
Film Heritage
Film Journal, The
Film Journal (Australia)
Film Library Quarterly
Film Players Herald & Movie Pictorial
Film Quarterly
Film Review
Filmmaker's Newsletter
Filmograph
Filmplay Journal
Films and Filming
Films Illustrated
Films In Review
Flying
Focus! Chicago's Movie Journal
Focus On Film
For Monsters Only
Fortnightly Review
Fortune
Forum
Funnyworld

Game
Good Housekeeping
Gore Creatures
Graphic

Green Book Album
Green Book Magazine

Harper's Bazaar
Harper's Monthly
Harvest Years
Hearst's Magazine
High Fidelity
Hobbies
Holiday
Hollywood Quarterly
Horizon
Horticulture
House & Garden
House Beautiful

Illustrated London News
Illustrated World
Independent
Independent Woman
Inter-American
International Film Annual
International Film Guide
International Studio
Interview

John Rylands Library Bulletin
Journal of Popular Film

Kaleidoscope

Ladies Home Journal
Leisure
Liberty
Library Journal
Life
Life with Music
Lion's Roar
Literary Digest
Living Age
Look

Mademoiselle
Making Films in New York
Massachusetts Review
McCall's
Melody Maker
Metronome
Metropolitan Magazine
Mise-En-Scene
Modern Photography
Modern Screen
Monogram

Motion
Motion Pictorial
Motion Picture
Motion Picture Classic
Motion Picture Supplement
Motor Boat
Motor Trend
Movie
Movie Classic
Movie Digest
Movie Maker
Movie Pictorial
Movies and the People Who
   Make Them
MS
Munsey's Magazine
Musical America
Musical Courier

Nash's & Pall Mall
Nation, The
National Cyclopaedia of Amer-
   ican Biography
National Education Association
   News
National Magazine
National Review
Negro History Bulletin
New England Magazine
New Republic
New Statesman
New Woman
New York
New York Dramatic Mirror
New York History
New York Times
New York Times Biographical
   Edition
New York Times Magazine
New Yorker
Newsweek
19th Century
North American
Nostalgia Illustrated

Oklahoma Chronicles
Opera News
Opportunity
Oui
Out West
Outlook, The

PTA Magazine

Pageant
Parents Magazine
Parks & Recreation
Pearson (New York)
Penthouse
People
Photon
Photoplay
Pictorial Review
Play Pictorial
Players
Playboy
Playgirl
Plays and Players
Popular Mechanics
Popular Photography
Popular Science
Publishers Weekly

Ramparts Magazine
Reader's Digest
Redbook
Reporter
Review of Reviews (London)
Rotarian

St. Nicholas
Saturday Evening Post
Saturday Review
Saturday Review of Arts
Scanlans
Scholastic
Scientific America
Screen; the Journal of the Soci-
   ety for Education in Films
   and Television
Screen Book
Screen Education Studies
Screen Greats
Screen Legends
Screen World
Senior Scholastic
Sepia
Seventeen
Show
Sight & Sound
Sightlines
Silent Picture, The
Silver Screen
Sound Stage
Spectator
Stage, The
Strand (New York) Magazine

Studio
Success
Sunset
Survey Graphic

Take One
Theatre
Theatre Arts Magazine
Theatre Guild Magazine
Theatre World
Those Enduring Matinee Idols
Time
Today's Education
Today's Filmmaker
Today's Health
Trans-Action
Travel & Camera
Travel & Leisure
Tulane Drama Review
TV Guide

Unifrance
U. S. Camera
U. S. News & World Report

Vanity Fair
Velvet Light Trap, The
Venus
Views & Reviews
Visages (in French)
Vital Speeches
Viva
Vogue

Weekend Review
Western Architecture
Wilson Library Bulletin
Windsor
Woman Citizen
Womans Home Companion
Women & Film
World Review
World Today
World's Work
World's Work (London)
Writer's Digest

Yachting
Yale Review